JIM MURRAY'S
WHISKY
B I B L E
2 0 1 6

This 2016 edition is dedicated to
Jim Rutledge
a whiskey man to the core of his being.

This edition first published 2015 by Dram Good Books Ltd

10 9 8 7 6 5 4 3 2

The "Jim Murray's" logo and the "Whisky Bible" logo are trade marks of Jim Murray.

For information regarding using tasting notes from Jim Murray's Whisky Bible contact:
Dram Good Books Ltd, Unit 2, Barnstones Business Park, Litchborough, UK, NN12 8JJ
Tel: 44 (0)117 317 9777. Or contact us via www.whiskybible.com

A CIP catalogue record for this book is available from the British Library

ISBN: 978-0-9932986-0-8

Printed in Belgium by Graphius Group Eekhoutdriesstraat 67, B-9041 Gent.

Written by: Jim Murray
Edited by: David Rankin
Design: Len (Typo) Davis, Robin Pulford, Jim Murray
Maps: James Murray
Production: Len (Typo) Davis, Vincent Flint-Hill, Billy Jeffrey
Chief Researcher: Vincent Flint-Hill
Sample Research: Vincent Flint-Hill, Ally Telfer, Julia Nourney, Mick Secor
Other Research: Emma Thomson
Sales: Billy Jeffrey

Author's Note
I have used the spelling "whiskey" or "whisky" depending on how the individual distillers
prefer. All Scotch is "whisky". So is Canadian. All Irish, these days, is "whiskey", though
that was not always the case. In Kentucky, bourbon and rye are spelt "whiskey", with the
exception of the produce of the early Times/Old Forester Distillery and Maker's Mark which
they bottle as "whisky". In Tennessee, it is a 50-50 split: Dickel is "whisky", while Daniel's is
"whiskey".

JIM MURRAY'S
WHISKY
BIBLE
2016

DRAM GOOD BOOKS

Contents

Introduction

As I nosed and tasted the initial sample for the first-ever Whisky Bible – a Scotch blend called Swords – did I expect sales of this book to top half a million copies?

Maybe. But certainly not in English language alone. To hit that massive landmark, I had envisaged the Bible being available in many versions: Spanish, French, Chinese, Japanese, German among others. Which has so far not happened but will quite soon, I suspect. Had those editions been available from day one, we would have passed the million mark some while back. For that to be achieved the way the Bible is researched and written would have to be fundamentally changed. At the moment, whiskies are gathered in during the year and tasted from late April through the summer months, when the bulk of the samples arrive. Using this method to write, there is simply insufficient time to translate into another language before the Bible hits the shelves in October. However, by the time you read this I will probably already have begun work on tasting for the 2017 edition. As you can imagine, the outpouring of new whiskies from around the world is relentless. And I fully understand why whisky lovers are so daunted by the enormous number of whiskies they are able to buy online, or even might face them in their local whisky shop. It is perhaps why Jim Murray's Whisky Bible remains so popular: it helps sort out the wheat from the chaff by commenting without fear or favour.

The one advantage of my tasting all the whiskies in a single period is that it helps concentrate the mind. Disadvantages include the fact that by the end of the process I am pretty exhausted, barely able, after so many months of solid concentration to do much else for many weeks after. But spreading the tasting of these whiskies evenly through the year, so reducing the exhaustion factor, will not mean I will be less able to judge the greatest of the whiskies on offer. Because they will still, as is the practice now, be thrown back together for a few weeks if scoring 95 and above, so I can revisit and forensically dissect again and choose from among them the champions of their type.

Going back to that first-ever Bible, did I expect a scotch to win World Whisky of the Year only once in four annual editions? Probably not. Now after last year's phenomenal success by Yamazaki in Japan - covered in far greater detail in Bible Thumping – we now have another new nation triumphant with Canadian picking up the top award. And here we do have something of a turn up for the book. At the beginning of planning this edition, we discussed the possibility of taking from Canada the right of it boasting its own section as the quality of Canadian whisky has nose-dived so badly in recent years. When the right was granted for Canadian to be allowed 9.09% of the product not to contain Canadian whisky, the argument was for it to include principally rye from the USA as a flavouring agent. Instead, that loophole has been abused by putting in other agents which are not spirits at all in an effort to change the flavour and texture of the whisky, and mainly towards giving it a sweeter persona and softer, more lush mouth feel. The results in recent years have been a succession of genuinely unimpressive bottlings that are so far removed from what Canadian whisky used to be about that they are close to being an insult to the great Canadian blenders and traditions of the past. Then along came the Crown Royal.... Showing just what Canadian whisky should taste like and that it can trump any other whisky in the world.

If asked my favourite group of whiskies encountered in the 15,000 plus samples I have tasted for this book, it would have to be the epic outpouring from Buffalo Trace: their Single Oak project. That began in 2011 when I included in the Whisky Bible 2012 the first 24 different bottlings. And this year they concluded their extraordinary experiment, by far the most important ever commercially undertaken in whisk(e)y history. Here, bourbon was produced 192 varying ways simply by adjusting which part of the tree the oak came from, warehouse type, degree of char, mashbill and so on, and in the last year came the final issue of two dozen releases. Picking out the differences was almost certainly the most fascinating project of a career covering a quarter of a century. So I am immensely proud that the Whisky Bible contains in this edition my scores and tasting summaries of each and every one of the 192 different bottles produced. That I was able to do this and to savour and cherish the most intensely beautiful moments of exploration in my whisky writing life, was due to one person only. So my heartfelt thanks to Amy Preske at BT for cheerfully and so warmly attending to my many time-stricken demands over the years and ensuring something truly unique, fabulously special and never-to-be-forgotten, nor most probably repeated, was possible.

Jim Murray
Willow Cottage
Somewhere in rural Northamptonshire.
Sept 2015

How to Read The Bible

The whole point of this book is for the whisky lover – be he or she an experienced connoisseur or, better fun still, simply starting out on the long and joyous path of discovery – to have ready access to easy-to-understand information about as many whiskies as possible. And I mean a lot. Thousands.

This book does not quite include every whisky on the market... just by far and away the vast majority. And those that have been missed this time round – either through accident, logistics or design – will appear in later editions once we can source a sample.

WHISKY SCORING

The marking for this book is tailored to the consumer and scores run out just a little higher than I use for my own personal references. But such is the way it has been devised that it has not affected my order of preference.

Each whisky is given a rating out of 100. Twenty-five marks are given to each of four factors: nose (n), taste (t), finish (f), balance and overall complexity (b). That means that 50% of the marks are given for flavour alone and 25% for the nose, often an overlooked part of the whisky equation. The area of balance and complexity covers all three previous factors and a usually hidden one besides:

Nose: this is simply the aroma. Often requires more than one inspection as hidden aromas can sometimes reveal themselves after time in the glass, increased contact with air and changes in temperature. The nose very often tells much about a whisky, but – as we shall see – equally can be quite misleading.

Taste: this is the immediate arrival on the palate and involves the flavour profile up to, and including, the time it reaches maximum intensity and complexity.

Finish: often the least understood part of a tasting. This is the tail and flourish of the whisky's signature, often revealing the effects of ageing. The better whiskies tend to finish well and linger without too much oak excess. It is on the finish, also, that certain notes which are detrimental to the whisky may be observed. For instance, a sulphur-tarnished cask may be fully revealed for what it is by a dry, bitter residue on the palate which is hard to shake off. It is often worth waiting a few minutes to get the full picture of the finish before having a second taste of a whisky.

Balance: This is the part it takes a little experience to appreciate but it can be mastered by anyone. For a whisky to work well on the nose and palate, it should not be too one-sided in its character. If you are looking for an older whisky, it should have evidence of oak, but not so much that all other flavours and aromas are drowned out. Likewise, a whisky matured or finished in a sherry butt must offer a lot more than just wine alone and the greatest Islay malts, for instance, revel in depth and complexity beyond the smoky effects of peat.

Each whisky has been analysed by me without adding water or ice. I have taken each whisky as it was poured from the bottle and used no more than warming in an identical glass to extract and discover the character of the whisky. To have added water would have been pointless: it would have been an inconsistent factor as people, when pouring water, add different amounts at varying temperatures. The only constant with the whisky you and I taste will be when it has been poured directly from the bottle.

Even if you and I taste the same whiskies at the same temperature and from identical glasses – and even share the same values in whisky – our scores may still be different. Because a factor that is built into my evaluation is drawn from expectation and experience. When I sample a whisky from a certain distillery at such-and-such an age or from this type of barrel or that, I would expect it to offer me certain qualities. It has taken me 30 years to acquire this knowledge (which I try to add to day by day!) and an enthusiast cannot be expected to learn it overnight. But, hopefully, Jim Murray's Whisky Bible will help...!

SCORE CHART

Within the parentheses () is the overall score out of 100.

0–50.5 Nothing short of absolutely diabolical.
51–64.5 Nasty and well worth avoiding.
65–69.5 Very unimpressive indeed.
70–74.5 Usually drinkable but don't expect the earth to move.
75–79.5 Average and usually pleasant though sometimes flawed.
80–84.5 Good whisky worth trying.
85–89.5 Very good to excellent whiskies definitely worth buying.
90–93.5 Brilliant.
94–97.5 Superstar whiskies that give us all a reason to live.
98–100 Better than anything I've ever tasted!

KEY TO ABBREVIATIONS & SYMBOLS

% Percentage strength of whisky measured as alcohol by volume. **b** Overall balance and complexity. **bott** Date of bottling. **db** Distillery bottling. In other words, an expression brought out by the owners of the distillery. **dist** Date of distillation or spirit first put into cask. **f** Finish. **n** Nose. **nc** Non-coloured. **ncf** Non-chill-filtered. **sc** Single cask. **t** Taste. ⁂ New entry for 2016. ⊙ Retasted – no change. ⊙ ⊙ Retasted and re-evaluated. **v** Variant WB16-001 Code for Whisky Club bottling.

Finding Your Whisky

Worldwide Malts: Whiskies are listed alphabetically throughout the book. In the case of single malts, the distilleries run A–Z style with distillery bottlings appearing at the top of the list in order of age, starting with youngest first. After age comes vintage. After all the "official" distillery bottlings are listed, next come other bottlings, again in alphabetical order. Single malts without a distillery named (or perhaps named after a dead one) are given their own section, as are vatted malts.

Worldwide Blends: These are simply listed alphabetically, irrespective of which company produce them. So "Black Bottle" appears ahead of "White Horse" and Japanese blends begin with "Ajiwai Kakubin" and end with "Za". In the case of brands being named after companies or individuals the first letter of the brand will dictate where it is listed. So William Grant, for instance, will be found under "W" for William rather "G" for Grant.

Bourbon/Rye: One of the most confusing types of whiskey to list because often the name of the brand bears no relation to the name of the distillery that made it. Also, brands may be sold from one company to another, or shortfalls in stock may see companies buying bourbons from another. For that reason all the brands have been listed alphabetically with the name of the bottling distiller being added at the end.

Irish Whiskey: There are four types of Irish whiskey: (i) pure pot still; (ii) single malt, (iii) single grain and (iv) blended. Some whiskies may have "pure pot still" on the label, but are actually single malts. So check both sections.

Bottle Information

As no labels are included in this book I have tried to include all the relevant information you will find on the label to make identification of the brand straightforward. Where known I have included date of distillation and bottling. Also the cask number for further recognition. At the end of the tasting notes I have included the strength and, if known, number of bottles (sometimes abbreviated to btls) released and in which markets.

PRICE OF WHISKY

You will notice that Jim Murray's Whisky Bible very rarely refers to the cost of a whisky. This is because the book is a guide to quality and character rather than the price tag attached. Also, the same whiskies are sold in different countries at varying prices due to market forces and variations of tax, so there is a relevance factor to be considered. Equally, much depends on the size of an individual's pocket. What may appear a cheap whisky to one could be an expensive outlay to another. With this in mind prices are rarely given in the Whisky Bible.

How to Taste Whisky

It is of little use buying a great whisky, spending a comparative fortune in doing so, if you don't get the most out of it.

So when giving whisky tastings, no matter how knowledgable the audience may be I take them through a brief training schedule in how to nose and taste as I do for each sample included in the Whisky Bible.

I am aware that many aspects are contrary to what is being taught by distilleries' whisky ambassadors. And for that we should be truly thankful. However, at the end of the day we all find our own way of doing things. If your old tried and trusted technique suits you best, that's fine by me. But I do ask you try out the instructions below at least once to see if you find your whisky is talking to you with a far broader vocabulary and clearer voice than it once did. I strongly suspect you will be pleasantly surprised – amazed, even - by the results.

Amusingly, someone tried to teach me my own tasting technique some years back in an hotel bar. He was not aware who I was and I didn't let on. It transpired that a friend of his had been to one of my tastings a few years earlier and had passed on my words of "wisdom". I'd be lying if I said I didn't smile when he informed me it was called "The Murray Method." It was the first time I had heard the phrase... though certainly not the last!

"THE MURRAY METHOD"

1. Drink a black, unsweetened, coffee or chew on 90% minimum cocoa chocolate to cleanse the palate, especially of sugars.

2. Find a room free from distracting noises as well as the aromas of cooking, polish, flowers and other things which will affect your understanding and appreciation of the whisky.

3. Make sure you have not recently washed your hands using heavily scented soap or are wearing a strong aftershave or perfume.

4. Use a tulip shaped glass with a stem. This helps contain the alcohols at the bottom yet allows the more delicate whisky aromas you are searching for to escape.

5. Never add ice. This tightens the molecules and prevents flavours and aromas from being released. It also makes your whisky taste bitter. There is no better way to get the least from your whisky than by freezing it.

6. Likewise, ignore any advice given to put the bottle in the fridge before drinking.

7. Don't add water! Whatever anyone tells you. It releases aromas but can mean the whisky falls below 40%...so it is no longer whisky. Also, its ability to release flavours and aromas diminish quite quickly. Never add ridiculous "whisky rocks" or other supposed tasting aids.

8. Warm the undiluted whisky in the glass to body temperature before nosing or tasting. Hence the stem, so you can cradle in your hand the curve of the thin base. This excites the molecules and unravels the whisky in your glass, maximising its sweetness and complexity.

9. Keep an un-perfumed hand over the glass to keep the aromas in while you warm. Only a minute or two after condensation appears at the top of your glass should you extend your arms, lift your covering hand and slowly bring the glass to your nose, so the alcoholic vapours have been released before the glass reaches your face.

10. Never stick your nose in the glass. Or breathe in deeply. Allow glass to gently touch your top lip, leaving a small space below the nose. Move from nostril to nostril, breathing normally. This allows the aromas to break up in the air, helping you find the more complex notes.

11. Take no notice of your first mouthful. This is a marker for your palate.

12. On second, bigger mouthful, close your eyes to concentrate on the flavour and chew the whisky - moving it continuously around the palate. Keep your mouth slightly open to let air in and alcohol out. It helps if your head is tilted back very slightly.

13. Occasionally spit – if you have the willpower! This helps your senses to remain sharp for the longest period of time.

14. Look for the balance of the whisky. That is, which flavours counter others so none is too dominant. Also, watch carefully how the flavours and aromas change in the glass over time.

15. Assess the "shape" and mouth feel of the whisky, its weight and how long its finish. And don't forget to concentrate on the first flavours as intensely as you do the last. Look out for the way the sugars, spices and other characteristics form.

16. Never make your final assessment until you have tasted it a third or fourth time.

17. Be honest with your assessment: don't like a whisky because someone (yes, even me!), or the label, has tried to convince you how good it is.

18. When you cannot discriminate between one whisky and another, stop immediately.

Immortal Drams:
The Whisky Bible
Winners 2004-2015

	World Whisky of the Year	Second Finest Whisky of the Year	Third Finest Whisky of the Year
2004	George T Stagg	N/A	N/A
2005	George T Stagg	N/A	N/A
2006	George T Stagg	Glen Moray 1986 Cask 4696 distillery bottling	N/A
2007	Old Parr Superior 18 Years Old	Buffalo Trace Experimental Collection Twice Barreled	N/A
2008	Ardbeg 10 Years Old	The Ileach Single Islay Malt Cask Strength	N/A
2009	Ardbeg Uigedail	Nikka Whisky Single Coffey Malt 12 Years	N/A
2010	Sazerac Rye 18 Years Old (bottled Fall 2008)	Ardbeg Supernova	Amrut Fusion
2011	Ballantine's 17 Years Old	Thomas H Handy Sazerac Rye (129 proof)	Wiliam Larue Weller (134.8 proof)
2012	Old Pulteney Aged 21 Years	George T Stagg	Parker's Heritage Collection Wheated Mash Bill Bourbon Aged 10 Years
2013	Thomas H Handy Sazerac Rye (128.6 proof)	William Larue Weller (133.5 proof)	Ballantine's 17 Years Old
2014	Glenmorangie Ealanta 1993	William Larue Weller (123.4 proof)	Thomas Handy Sazerac Rye (132.4 proof)
2015	Yamazaki Single Malt Sherry 2013	William Larue Weller (68.1 abv)	Sazerac Rye 18 Years Old (bottled Fall 2013)

Who has won it this year?
Go to page 14

Bible Thumping
Give Light to Them Who Sit in Darkness

First came the light breaking through previously closed curtains, seeping past ancient, irremovable shutters; a single radiant finger reaching into the dungeons of denial and pointing towards the hidden door from which to escape.

Just a chink at first, vulgar and annoying; an insult to the perfect blackness that engulfed the stuffy room. Then, overnight it seemed, that single, mocking, querying, penetrating shaft became a blaze, one bright enough to banish the morbid dusty dullness once and for all. And, finally, unseeing eyes were opened, adjusting and blinking at the dazzling truth; then ears uncovered and voices, long ignored, heard.

Which leaves the question: did the earth move for you last Spring? Did you feel the sudden impact that knocked the Whisky World slightly off its axis? And see the light which surged into previously impenetrable depths? If you didn't, then you may well be in the minority, for, so I have been led to believe, a great many did. To the extent that no matter where I went on this planet in the last dozen months it has been, without exception, the main topic of conversation: sometimes the only topic.

Even in the last couple of weeks, nearly a year on, I have been told by friends that it is still a subject randomly discussed on radio stations the world over; even a few days ago a question on one of the BBC's most popular television quizzes. Still, every week, a journalist, somewhere, contacts me requesting an interview with this, invariably, as the central theme.

And though it was a subject rarely, if ever, raised by me, it is what I have been thanked for most, touchingly, often wholeheartedly; always with profound sincerity. As though burdens had been lifted and horizons, once too near to justify the name, had been pushed back to the far distance, offering an entirely new landscape to marvel at and explore.

To help make this happen I have needed to sell half a million copies of this book, to appear on countless television and radio programmes in dozens of countries over the last decade or more, to make personal appeals at scores, probably hundreds, of shows. But at last the message has been heard. Word has got through. Worlds have collided.

So, what was this seismic event, this happening, which so violently shook the whisky world?

It was, of course, the naming of a Japanese single malt, the Yamazaki Sherry Casks, as the Whisky Bible 2015's World Whisky of the Year. The reaction to how this news was absorbed globally surprised even me. After all, it was hardly the first time I had given World Whisky of the Year to liquid gold distilled and matured outside Scotland. Indeed, it has been a regular occurrence in the book's long history. For the good reason that I treat all whiskies as equal and mark entirely on merit and nothing more. For me, reputation is an irrelevance the moment you break the seal of the cap, or withdraw the cork from the bottle. It is the tale that the whisky tells in the glass which counts. For every atom of aroma, every molecule of mouth feel tells us something about how the whisky was made and matured. It is the story which unfolds and is carefully listened to. And it is the tale which moves me most; offers myriad deliciously spellbinding twists and turns yet is unfailingly true to its narrative and type and steers clear of an oaky faux pas. Those are the whiskies which score the highest, no matter who makes the whisky. Or where. Scotch - malt, blend or grain – Irish, Bourbon, Rye, Canadian, Japanese, English, Swedish, Indian, Australian....it makes no difference when the book starts being written: they begin all as equals. It is the whisky alone that counts.

But this was different. For the first time people across all spectrums were curious enough to actually go out and really see what the fuss was about. It is now a well-known fact that a whisky given the top accolade in this Bible sells out within days. And it may spread to further investigation of that distillery or brand at other ages.

Here, though, we had a world now wanting genuinely to discover an entire nation's output, not just a single distillery's. To test it against what they had previously believed to be an invincible foe: Scotch. Most people had heard that the Japanese made malt and whisky. But for the first time they were given the confidence to buy it and discover its personality with a positive mind-set. To enjoy it without any feeling of guilt or foolishness, or that maybe they were doing the wrong thing, wasting their money on make-believe malt. From countless conversations over the years I knew people, especially those who had never got round to trying it, regarded Japanese as an inferior imitation – a wannabe Scotch. Sometimes only subconsciously. But the doubt was always there. Then overnight it seemed, with the announcement of the Yamazaki Sherry Casks as the world's top whisky, those fears, those previous misgivings were blown straight out of the water. The theory that Japanese should kow-tow to Scotch has of late been conspicuous by its absence. Face-to-face, no one in the last year has said it to me at all.

Of course the announcement raised hackles, especially from those with vested interests. It brought forth the predictable outpouring of rage and scorn from the Establishment. Having seen close up how this industry has developed in the last 25 years I would have been amazed if it hadn't. Memorably, a day or two after the announcement I found myself discussing the Award on the BBC's World Service. Brought in to offer a countering point of view was someone from some Edinburgh whisky shop or other – the name of which escapes me - though I do remember they refused to stock the Whisky Bible years ago because we would not give them a discount greater than even those who buy in their thousands and would, if it were to be applied it across the board, have put us swiftly out of business.

Anyway, off trills this individual about me being wrong. Of course everyone is entitled to his or her view and I was looking forward to a sensible, lively, stimulating and knowledgeable debate with rapier thrust and parry points to test me. But from his first sentence or two it became pretty clear that this was far more a question of protecting his Scotch whisky sales rather than entering into a proper, professional, enlightened discussion into the merits – or otherwise - of a Japanese malt. In a nutshell, his argument was that Scotch was superior to Japanese...errr...end of. Rather than cut and thrust, with the odd dramatic "touché!" thrown in now and again by both sides as one got the better of the other, it was as though I was being intellectually assaulted by a five-year-old with a pop-gun, or having my cutlass charged by someone waving a tin tack. And even the presenter laughed in incredulity when Scotch Vested Interest Bloke admitted that he had never even tasted the whisky I had given the Award to, rendering his entire argument – such as it was - null and void.

At the end of this embarrassingly uneven contest, rather than savouring victory one was left with the unpleasant taste in the mouth that it was all about money. From one side there was no celebration that whisky lovers were at last able to discover a bottling which gave a master class in what Scotch single malt matured in sherry used to taste like a generation or two back, but now hardly ever does. And if this was a true representation of the calibre of impartial knowledge and open-mindedness that was being used to supposedly help whisky devotees when entering a shop, then it is not hard to see why it has taken so long for people to discover the great whiskies from outside Scotland; why for so long I have felt I have been banging my head against a granite wall. That said, I'm pleased to say for every throwback such as the one I encountered on the radio debate I know of an outstanding whisky shop owner or manager determined to be at the vanguard of the movement forward into discovering great whisky, wherever it hails from. But we need so many more...

Much more sinister were certain Internet articles and broadcast blogs which implied I took money from the Japanese to give them the award. Again, some of these people appeared to have vested interests in selling whisky. Or just massive egos unable to cope with having their Scotch rules mantra undermined. And here they proved they knew about as much about how Jim Murray's Whisky Bible and publishing in general operates as they do about whisky.

For a start, my giving this award to a Japanese distillery was probably a sure-fire way of damaging Whisky Bible sales, not increasing them. As we knew would be the case, a number of distilleries and whisky shops failed to order when the announcement was made. And as we don't have a Japanese language edition we couldn't sell copies in their tens of thousands to compensate. Also, Suntory didn't even know we had the whisky in the first place as it was a bottle my chief researcher, Vincent Flint-Hill, randomly tracked down and bought with hundreds of others from various online and bricks and mortar shops. (Oh, and how's this for delicious irony: the whisky shop which would not sell The Whisky Bible unless we gave them a suicidal 65% discount said they could afford to give us only a 5% reduction on any whisky we bought from them!) And, lastly, we told the victorious Japanese company as late as possible before publication that they had won the Award so there was little or no chance of word accidentally getting out and the price being raised prior to the Bible's publication or someone buying up stocks. We didn't even buy bottles of it ourselves to profiteer from our own inside knowledge.

I do believe these selfless bloggers whose rare insight serves such great purpose to the whisky world, already have sitting on their desks letters baring my lawyer's signature reminding them that we do not and have never taken a single penny to add - or subtract - as much as a single half mark to a Whisky Bible score. This book is fiercely independent and honest. I do not possess as much as a single cask, let single share in a whisky company; or even Volkswagen. If I am accused of talking rubbish, giving scores that people disagree with and hold views contrary to others', that's fine by me. I don't mind in the least being criticised for my take on all things whisky, and as a professional writer of over 42 years standing I would defend that person's right to criticise me with my dying breath. But the one thing that can never be levelled at me is being corrupt. So, as you can see, for helping bring some light to the whisky world, I have had to deal with some of the darker arts. We have upset people by naming Yamazaki as World's Number 1. Actually, it surprised me, too: I had always regarded Hakushu the superior of Suntory's malt distilleries. But it is what has happened with the public that has really made the difference. And it is the public, above all, which counts.

For instance, a week or two back I was flying from Shanghai to Hong Kong when, in that vacant 20 minutes before we were about to land, my neighbour, an American, and I struck up a conversation for the first time. He asked what I did, and I told him I was involved in whisky. He then said that cost him a lot of money, explaining that he had bought a couple of bottles of the Yamazaki Sherry Casks after it had been given the Bible's title of World Whisky of the Year. Only after I apologised for his outlay did the penny drop for him who I was. So I asked him: "Are you going to keep them as an investment? Or drink them?"

"Drink them," he said without even pausing to consider. "I opened one and it really is the best whisky I've ever tasted. So I will savour the experience."

It was not the first time I had received this very same reply. After nearly a quarter of a century of battling to get the world's whisky lovers to drink with both an open palate and mind, this has been a very special year for me: one of validation. Perhaps for Japanese distillers, also. And, oh! The joy to see the whisky-adoring public take the lead, to pick up the torch and show the way to so many self-appointed whisky "specialists" who worship blindly but so noisily at the altar of Scotch.

For the message has been heard. Word has got through. Worlds have collided. There is no dark side now...

Join our Tasting Club

How would you like to compare your own tasting notes from the very same bottle I have used for each whisky? Set your nose and taste buds against mine.

That is the concept we are now going to make happen. Since the very first edition was launched way back in 2003 readers have asked if we could sell samples of the whiskies I have tasted. I have also had numerous approaches by business types over the years asking me to sell whisky off the back of the Bible...and been offered vast sums to do so.

In order to underline this book's impartiality, the very bedrock of its existence, I declined those offers. I did not want to be incorrectly perceived favouring a whisky; people thinking I was feathering my own nest by making a profit from increased sales of whiskies I had given high scores or even awards to...which would be entirely opposite to absolutely everything I believe in and stand for. So, just like advertising, I turned my back on that potential source of revenue. But for simple health reasons I have had to drastically rethink how to make the Bible happen. Because during the writing of the 2014 edition I developed two blood clots which could easily have had fatal consequences. They came about because samples were, as usual, sent to me by some distillers and bottlers so late in the day I had to spend almost six weeks tied to a desk. Tasting twelve to fourteen hours a day, seven days a week in order to somehow hit the publishing deadline. Deep vein thrombosis was, not surprisingly, the result.

So we will, whenever possible, be buying the whiskies as they are launched and I will be tasting them throughout the year to even the burden, rather than just in the summer months prior to publication. The whiskies we bought in over the last two editions have been split into seven sealed 10cl bottles: one for me to work from, the others to be made available to Whisky Club members on a first-come, first-served basis. We are still in the development phase of making this happen and investigating the final mechanics of how. Because of the enormous pressure on time to hit the deadline for this edition we have yet to fully determine just how the samples will be made available. But they will be and we ask you keep a close eye on **Whiskybible.com** to monitor developments and instructions how to join the Whisky Bible Club. The money we raise from this means we then have the funds to buy more whiskies as they become available. Not just the whiskies the distillers and bottlers want us to have. But the ones my researchers find out there. You will know my score for the samples available for the 2015 and 2016 Bibles. For the 2017 edition onwards you will not. You will have to use your judgement to guess which will be the high flyers because scores will still not be given until the Whisky Bible is launched each October. And the chance to build your own whisky library.

I will look forward to welcoming you to the Jim Murray Whisky Bible Tasting Club very soon.

Jim Murray's Whisky Bible Awards 2016

It is hard to know which is the more difficult.

Nosing and tasting over 1,000 different whiskies of every conceivable hue and variety in just a matter of a few months? Or working your way through the absolute top scorers, in the painstaking way a forensic scientist might inspect complex evidence, to decide which is the champion whisky of its type in just a couple of weeks? Probably the latter.

Certainly this year demanded my senses be on full alert and working to the very limits of their capabilities to choose not just the sectional awards, but the World Whisky of the Year in particular. This was because this year was different from any other from the point of view that I had in the glasses before me a series of absolutely near faultless examples of their whisky type. It was as if they sat in front of me and asked: "Did you hear the one about the Canadian, the American and Irishman?"

What the three had in common was that the moment you nosed each of these whisk(e)ys you simply knew you were about to embark on a classic journey around exactly how a particular whisky should taste, with its grain style or barrel style shimmering with faultless intensity. And that was exactly what happened. During the course of writing the Bible, I had tasted the Pikesville Rye first. And that set the benchmark which, I admit, I did not expect to see bettered. But then the Crown Royal Northern Harvest from Canada popped up some weeks later and I knew a battle of some magnitude had commenced. For both of these, plus the Midleton showing all its classic Pot Still finery and even Irish oak, to dazzle to the extent that even the Classics of Buffalo Trace had to take an unaccustomed step backwards showed just how breathtakingly magnificent the truly great whiskies were this year. In the end the Crown Royal edged it, on the grounds that there was a certain level of satisfaction and brilliance which perhaps on the fifth or sixth taste I realised the Pikesville, for all its near perfection, did not quite match. So when the decision was made you thought, despite the tasting and re-tasting: "Yep. That really is the one."

Again, as was the case last year, a Scotch standard brand didn't make the top five in the taste offs, though the Glenfarclas 1957 deservedly won World Single Cask of the Year, narrowly edging out its sister cask from 1966. And as for the Japanese, who sensationally scooped top prize last year? Well, an honourable 5th place this year and, true to form, it did so by pitching in with a uniquely Japanese style with the flavour shaped by native oak.

It was as though the distilleries this year went out of their way to show the most elegant display of their traditional national dress they possibly could. And you won't hear me complaining for a single second if the same happens next year as well. I hope so.

2016 World Whisky of the Year
Crown Royal Northern Harvest Rye

Second Finest Whisky in the World
Pikesville 110 Proof Straight Rye

Third Finest Whisky in the World
Midleton Dair Ghaelach

Fourth Finest Whisky in the World
William Larue Weller

Fifth Finest Whisky in the World
Yamazaki Mizunara 2014

Single Cask of the Year
Glenfarclas Family Cask 1957

SCOTCH

Scotch Whisky of the Year
Glenfarclas Family Cask 1957
Single Malt of the Year (Multiple Casks)
Glen Grant 10
Single Malt of the Year (Single Cask)
Glenfarclas Family Cask 1957
Scotch Blend of the Year
The Last Drop 50 Years Old
Scotch Grain of the Year
Clan Deny Cambus 25 Years Old
Scotch Vatted Malt of the Year
Compass Box The Lost Blend

Single Malt Scotch

No Age Statement (Multiple Casks)
Ardberg Supernova
No Age Statement (Runner Up)
Laphroaig An Cuan Mor
10 Years & Under (Multiple Casks)
Glen Grant 10
10 Years & Under (Single Cask)
Saar Gruwehewwel
11-15 Years (Multiple Casks)
Gordon and MacPhail CC Strathmill 2002
11-15 Years (Single Cask)
SMWS 4.199 (Highland Park 1999)
16-21 Years (Multiple Casks)
Old Pulteney 21
16-21 Years (Single Cask)
Old Malt Cask Highland Park 1998
22-27 Years (Multiple Casks)
Glen Moray Port Cask Finish
22-27 Years (Single Cask)
Wemyss Bunnahabhain 1988
28-34 Years (Multiple Casks)
Tomatin 1988
28-34 Years (Single Cask)
Glenfarclas Family Cask 1985
35-40 Years (Multiple Casks)
Tomatin 36 Years Old
35-40 Years (Single Cask)
BenRiach 1977 Batch 11
41 Years & Over (Multiple Casks)
Ledaig 42 Years Old
41 Years & Over (Single Cask)
Glenfarclas Family Cask 1957

BLENDED SCOTCH

No Age Statement (Standard)
Ballantine's Finest
No Age Statement (Premium)
Ballantine's Limited
5-12 Years
Johnie Walker Black Label
13-18 Years
Ballantine's 17
19 - 25 Years
Royal Salute 21
26 - 50 Years
The Last Drop 50 Years Old Sherry Wood

IRISH WHISKEY

Irish Whiskey of the Year
Midleton Dair Ghaelach

Irish Pot Still Whiskey of the Year
Midleton Dair Ghaelach
Irish Single Malt of the Year
SMWS 118.3 (Cooley) 1991
Irish Blend of the Year
Powers Gold Label

AMERICAN WHISKEY

Bourbon of the Year
William Larue Weller
Rye of the Year
Pikesville Straigh Rye 110 Proof
US Micro Whisky of the Year
Notch 12
US Micro Whisky of the Year (Runner Up)
McCarthy's Batch U14-01

BOURBON

No Age Statement (Multiple Barrels)
William Larue Weller
No Age Statement (Single Barrel)
Buffalo Trace Single Oak Project Barrel 20
9 Years & Under
Booker's 7 Years 5 Months 63.95
10-17 Years (Multiple Barrels)
Eagle Rare

RYE

No Age Statement
Thomas Handy
Up to 10 Years
Pikesville Straight Rye 110 Proof
11 Years & Over
Sazerac 18

WHEAT

Wheat Whiskey of the Year
Parker 13

CANADIAN WHISKY

Canadian Whisky of the Year
Crown Royal Northern Harvest Rye

JAPANESE WHISKY

Japanese Whisky of the Year
Yamazaki Mizunara
Single Malt of the Year (Multiple Barrels)
Yamazaki Mizunara
Single Malt of the Year (Single Barrel)
SMWS 119.14 (Yamazaki) 2003

EUROPEAN WHISKY

European Whisky of the Year (Multiple)
English Whisky Co. Chapter 16
European Whisky of the Year (Single)
Kornog Chwee'hved 14 BC

WORLD WHISKIES

Asian Whisky of the Year
Amrut Greedy Angels 46%
Southern Hemisphere Whisky of the Year
Heartwood Port 71.3%
*Overall age category winners are presented
in **bold**.*

The Whisky Bible Liquid Gold Awards (97.5-94)

Jim Murray's Whisky Bible is delighted to again make a point of celebrating the very finest whiskies you can find in the world. So we salute the distillers who have maintained or even furthered the finest traditions of whisky making and taken their craft to the very highest levels. And the bottlers who have brought some of them to us.

After all, there are over 4,700 different brands and expressions listed in this guide and from every corner of the planet. Those which score 94 and upwards represents only a very small fraction of them. These whiskies are, in my view, the élite: the finest you can currently find on the whisky shelves of the world. Rare and precious, they are Liquid Gold.

So it is our pleasure to announce that all those scoring 94 and upwards automatically qualify for the Jim Murray's Whisky Bible Liquid Gold Award. Congratulations!

97.5

Scottish Single Malt
Ardbeg Uigeadail
Glenmorangie Ealanta 1993 Vintage
Gordon & MacPhail Linkwood
Old Pulteney Aged 21 Years

Scottish Blends
Ballantine's 17 Years Old

Bourbon
George T Stagg
William Larue Weller
William Larue Weller bott Spring 2001

American Straight Rye
Pikesville Straight Rye Whiskey aged at least 6 years
Thomas H Handy Sazerac Straight Rye

Canadian Blended Malt
Crown Royal Northern Harvest Rye

Japanese Single Malt
Yamazaki Single Malt Whisky Sherry Cask

97

Scottish Single Malt
Aberfeldy Single Cask Aged 21 Years
Ardbeg 10 Years Old
Ardbeg Day Bottling
Ardbeg Supernova
Ardbeg Supernova 2015
Brora 30 Years Old
Glenfarclas The Family Casks 1966
Glenfarclas The Family Casks 1985
Glenfiddich 50 Years Old

Scottish Grain
Clan Denny Cambus 47 Years Old

Scottish Blends
Johnnie Walker Blue The Casks Edition
The Last Drop 50 Year Old
Old Parr Superior 18 Years Old

Irish Pure Pot Still
Redbreast Aged 12 Years Cask Strength

Irish Blend
Midleton Dair Ghaelach

Bourbon
Four Roses 2013 Single Barrel #3-4P
Parker's Wheated Mash Bill Aged 10 Years
William Larue Weller

American Straight Rye
Thomas H. Handy Sazerac Straight Rye

Colonel E.H. Taylor Straight Rye
Sazerac 18 Years Old

Japanese Single Malt
Nikka Whisky Single Coffey Malt 12 Years
The Yamazaki Single Malt Whisky Mizunara

Czech Rebublic Single Malt
Gold Cock Single Malt Whisky Festival

French Single Malt
Kornog Taouarc'h Chwec'hved 14

German Single Malt
Spinnaker Single Cask Fassstärke

Indian Single Malt
Amrut Fusion

Taiwanese Single Malt
Kavalan Solist Fino Sherry Cask
Kavalan Single Malt Amontillado Sherry

96.5

Scottish Single Malt
Ardbeg Corryvreckan
Ardbeg Supernova
Balblair 1965
Balblair 1983 Vintage 1st Release
The Balvenie Single Barrel Aged 12 Years
BenRiach Batch 11 1977 37 Years Old
Bruichladdich 1991 Valinch Anaerobic Digestion 19 Years Old
Octomore Orpheus 5 Yrs Ed 02.2 PPM 140
Octomore Edition 7.1 Aged 5 years
Port Charlotte PC6
Berry's Own Bunnahabhain Aged 26 Years
Old Particular Islay Bunnahabhain 17 YO
Romantic Rhine Collection Bunnahabhain
Wemyss Malts 1988 Single Islay Bunnahabhain "Kirsch Gateau"
Old Malt Cask Caol Ila Aged 29 Years
The Maltman Clynelish Aged 15 Years
First Editions Clynelish 1996 Aged 17 Yrs
Signatory Glenburgie 1983 Aged 29 Years
The GlenDronach 18 Years Old
GlenDronach Batch 10 1993 21 Years Old
Abbey Whisky GlenDronach Aged 20 Years
Glenfarclas The Family Casks 1957
Glenfarclas The Family Casks 1967
Riegger's Selection Eagle of Spey Glenfarclas 1993

Glen Grant 50 Year Old
Gordon & MacPhail Glen Grant 50 Year Old
The Glenlivet Single Cask Inveravon 21 Yrs
Glenmorangie Sonnalta PX
Cadenhead Glenrothes-Glenlivet 24 Years
Highland Park 50 Years Old
SMWS Cask 4.186 Aged 22 Years
AnCnoc Cutter 20.5 ppm
AnCnoc Rutter 11 ppm
Lagavulin 12 YO Special Release 2011
Laphroaig Aged 25 Years Cask Strength 2011
Aflodal's Whisky The Famous Leapfrog
Cadenhead's Authentic Collection Laphroaig Aged 16 Years
Signatory Laphroaig 1998 Aged 15 Years
Berry's Own Linkwood 1987 Aged 26 Years
The Cooper's Choice Lochside 1967 Aged 44 Years
Tomatin 36 Year Old
Master Of Malt Speyside 50 Yrs 3rd Edition
Saar Whisky Gruwehewwel

Scottish Grain
Clan Denny Cambus Vintage Aged 25 Years Old
Clan Denny Dumbarton Aged 48 Years Old
The Sovereign Dumbarton Aged 50 Years Old
Sovereign Single Cask Port Dundas 1978

Scottish Vatted Malt
The Last Vatted Malt

Scottish Blends
Ballantine's Limited Release no. L40055
The Last Drop 1965
Teacher's Aged 25 Years

Irish Pure Pot Still
Midleton Single Pot Still Single Cask 1991
Powers John's Lane Release Aged 12 Years

Bourbon
Blanton's Gold Original Single Barrel
Blanton's Uncut/Unfiltered
Elmer T. Lee Bourbon 1919 - 2013
Four Roses 125th Anniversary Bourbon
George T. Stagg Limited Edition
George T Stagg
Virgin Bourbon 7 Years Old

American Straight Rye
Sazerac Rye 18 Year Old

American Microdistilleries
Arkansas Single Barrel Reserve Bourbon
The Notch Aged 12 Years

Canadian Blended
Masterson's 10 Year Old Straight Rye

Japanese Single Malt
Chichibu 'The Peated' 2013
The Hakushu Sherry Cask
Scotch Malt Whisky Society 132.1 28 Years
Scotch Malt Whisky Society Cask 119.14 Aged 11 Years

Swedish Single Malt
Mackmyra Moment "Glod" (Glow)

Swiss Single Malt
Langatun 10 Years

Welsh Single Malt
Penderyn Portwood
Penderyn Portwood Swansea City Special

Indian Single Malt
Amrut Greedy Angels 10 Years Old
Paul John Edited

New Zealand Single Malt
The New Zealand Whisky Collection Willowbank 1988 25 Years Old

96

Scottish Single Malt
Aberfeldy Single Cask Unravel
Ardbeg 1977
Ardbeg Kildalton 1980
Ardbeg Provenance 1974
Dun Bheagan Ardberg 15 Year Old
Wemyss Malts 1998 Single Lowland "Tarte Au Citron"
Cadenhead Banff 34 Years Old
Anam na h-Alba The Soul of Scotland BenRiach 1998
Glen Farhn BenRiach Single Cask 1996 Aged 18
Brora 25 Year Old 7th Release
Octomore 5 Years Old
Port Charlotte PC10
Whisky-Fässle Bunnahabhain 23 Year Old
Hunter Laing's Old & Rare Caol Ila Aged 30 Years
The Dalmore Candela Aged 50 Years
Gordon & MacPhail Glen Albyn 1976
Glencadam 30 Years Old Single Cask 1982
Gordon & MacPhail Connoisseurs Choice Glencadam 1993
The GlenDronach Single Cask 1992 21 Years
The GlenDronach Single Cask 1994 19 Years
The Last Drop Glen Garioch 47 Years Old
Glenglassaugh Batch 1 1968 45 Years Old
Glen Grant Aged 10 Years
Gordon & Macphail Glen Grant 1948
Gordon & MacPhail Con. Choice Glenlossie
Romantic Rhine Collection Glenlossie
Glen Scotia 1989 23 Years Old
Master of Malt Glentauchers 15 Year Old
Highland Park Sigurd
Highland Park Loki Aged 15 Years
Highland Park Aged 25 Years
Highland Park 1973
Old Malt Cask Highland Park 18 Years Old
Kilchoman Port Cask Matured
Master of Malt Kilchoman 5 Year Old
Laphroaig PX Cask
Laphroaig Quarter Cask
Glen Fahrn Airline Nr 10 Laphroaig 1998 Aged 14 Years

Rosebank 25 Years Old
SMWS Cask 25.66 Aged 23 Years
Single Cask Collection 23 Yr Old Strathmill
World of Orchids Teaninich 2007 7 Year Old
Ledaig Dùsgadh 42 Aged 42 Years
Elements of Islay BR5
Old Malt Cask Probably Speyside's Finest 28 Years Old
Whisky-Fässle Speyside Malt 20 Year Old

Scottish Grain
Clan Denny Caledonian 45 Years Old
The Clan Denny Cambus Aged 25 Years
The Last Drop Dumbarton 54 Year Old
The Pearls of Scotland Invergordon 1972
Cadenhead's Port Dundas Aged 25 Years

Scottish Blends
Ballantine's Finest

Irish Pure Pot Still
Redbreast Aged 12 Years Cask Strength
Redbreast Aged 21 Years

Irish Single Malt
Scotch Malt Whisky Society Cask 118.3 Aged 22 Years

Irish Single Blends
Powers Gold label

Bourbon
Ancient Ancient Age 10 Years Old
Buffalo Trace Single Oak Project Barrel #101
Old Weller Antique 107
Pappy Van Winkle's Family Reserve 15 YO

American Straight Rye
Bulleit 95 Rye
Rittenhouse Very Rare 21 YO Barrel 28
Rittenhouse Rye Single Barrel Aged 25 Years Barrel 19
Rittenhouse Rye Aged 25 Years Barrel 19

American Small Batch
Balcones Crooked Texas Bourbon Barrel
McCarthy's Oregon Single Malt Aged 3 Years
Cowboy Bourbon Texas Aged Three Years

Canadian Blended
Crown Royal Special Reserve

Japanese Single Malt
Scotch Malt Whisky Society Cask 124.5
The Yamazaki Single Malt Aged 18 Years
SMWS Cask 116.17 Aged 25 Years (Yoichi)

Japanese Blended
Hibiki Aged 21 Years

Belgian Single Malt
The Belgian Owl Single Malt '64 Months'
Gouldys 12 Years Old Distillers Range

English Single Malt
Hicks & Healey Cornish Whiskey 2004
The English Whisky Co. Ch. 6 Not Peated
The English Whisky Co. Chapter 14

Swedish Single Malt
Mackmyra Moment "Malström"

Swiss Single Malt
Langatun Old Bear Châteauneuf-du-Pape

Welsh Single Malt
Penderyn Bourbon Matured Single Cask

Australian Single Malt
The Good Convict Port Cask
Southern Coast Single Malt Batch 002
Timboon Single Malt Whisky

Indian Single Malt
Amrut Greedy Angels 10 Years Old
Amrut Greedy Angels
Select Cask Peated
Paul John Single Malt Single Cask No 164
Paul John Single Malt Cask No 780
Paul John Single Malt Cask No 1846

Taiwanese Single Malt
Kavalan Single Malt Whisky
Kavalan Single Malt Pedro Ximenez

95.5

Scottish Single Malt
Aberlour A'bunadh Batch No. 50
Scotch Malt Whisky Society Cask 66.60 Aged 12 Years
AnCnoc 1999
World of Orchids Ardmore 2000 13 Year Old
Cadenhead's Ardbeg Aged 20 Years
Pearls of Scotland Ardmore 1988 25 YO
Cadenhead's Balblair Aged 23 Years
Gordon & MacPhail Rare Old Banff 1966
The BenRiach Aged 12 Years Sherry Wood
Benromach 30 Years Old
Cadenhead's Single Cask Bowmore 2001
Gleann Mór Bowmore 30 Year Old
Bruichladdich Redder Still 1984
The Single Malts of Scotland Bunnahabhain 25 Years Old
Whisky-Fässle Bunnahabhain 22 Year Old
Caol Ila 33 Years
Caol Ila 14 Years Old Unpeated Style
Old Malt Cask Caol Ila Aged 17 Years
Old Malt Cask Caol Ila 18 Years Old
Whisky-Fässle Clynelish 16 Year Old
The Dalmore Visitor Centre Exclusive
Glenfarclas The Family Casks 1955
Glenfarclas The Family Casks 1956
Glenfarclas The Family Casks 1963
Glenfarclass 1994
Glengoyne 25 Year Old
Scotch Malt Whisky Society Cask 123.11
The Glenlivet Nàdurra First Fill Selection
Cadenhead's Small Batch Speyside-Glenlivet Aged 18 Years
The Pearls of Scotland Golden Pearl Collection Glenrothes 1988
Cadenhead's Authentic Collection Glentauchers Aged 38 Years
Gordon & MacPhail Cask Highland Park
Old Particular Highland Park 18 Years
Scotch Malt Whisky Society Cask 4.199
First Editions Glen Garioch 1993
Glenfarclas 105

Glen Grant Distillery Edition Cask 20 Years Old

Glenglassaugh Batch 1 1978 35 Years Old

The Glenlivet Archive 21 Years of Age

The Glenlivet Nadurra Aged 16 Years

Glenmorangie 25 Years Old

Glen Moray 1995 Port Wood Finish

Hazelburn Rundlets & Kilderkins 10 Years

Hazelburn Rundlets & Kilderkins Aged 11 Years

Highland Park Aged 18 Years

Highland Park Vintage 1978

Adelphi Selection Highland Park 26 YO

Glen Fahrn Airline Nr 06 Arran 1996 Aged 15 Years

Kilchoman 2007 Vintage

Kilchoman 100% Islay The 5th Edition

Kilchoman Single Cask Release

Old Particular Highland Leidaig Aged 21 Yrs

Cadenhead's Small Batch Linkwood-Glenlivet Aged 26 Years

Signatory Vintage Linkwood 1995

The Peated Arran "Machrie Moor" 4th Ed.

The First Editions Author's Series No. 1 Macallan Aged 21 Years

Hunter Laing's Old & Rare Macallan Aged 21 Years

SMWS Cask 53.205 Aged 22 Years

SMWS Cask 73.61 Aged 24 Years

The Macallan Fine Oak 12 Years Old

The Macallan Oscuro

Gordon & MacPhail Connoisseurs Choice Macduff 2000

Gordon & MacPhail Connoisseurs Choice Mannochmore 1994

Port Charlotte The Peat Project

That Boutique-y Whisky Company Port Ellen

Alexander Weine & Destillate Port Charlotte 10 Year Old

Cadenhead's Tamdhu-Glenlivet Port Cask Aged 22 Years

Old Particular Highland Teaninich 30 Years

Tomatin Cù Bòcan Highland 1989 Vintage

Tomatin 1988

Tomintoul Aged 33 Years

Glen Fahrn Airline Nr 05 Tomintoul 1968 Aged 43 Years

Old Malt Cask Tormore 26 Years Old

Celtique Connexion Origine Islay Affine Sauternes cask

Wemyss 30 Years Islay "Heathery Smoke"

Scottish Grain

The Coopers Choice Lochside 1964 47 YO

A.D. Rattray Girvan Grain

The Pearls of Scotland North of Scotland 1971

The Sovereign Port Dundas Aged 36 Years

The Pearls of Scotland Strathclyde 1988

Scottish Vatted Malt

Compass Box Flaming Heart

Compass Box The Lost Blend

Compass Box The Spice Tree

Scottish Blends

Ballantine's Limited Release no. J13295

Johnnie Walker Black Label 12 Years Old

Royal Salute "62 Gun Salute"

William Grant's 25 Years Old

Irish Pure Pot Still

Irish Single Malt

The Tyrconnell Single Cask 11 Year Old

Bushmills Aged 21 Years

Bourbon

Buffalo Trace Single Oak Project Barrel #27

Buffalo Trace Single Oak Project Barrel #30

Buffalo Trace Single Oak Project Barrel #63

Buffalo Trace Single Oak Project Barrel #183

Buffalo Trace Experimental Collection Entry Proof 125 Floor 9

Charter 101

Elijah Craig Barrel Proof Bourbon 12 Years

Elijah Craig 21 Year Old Single Barrel

Smooth Ambler Old Scout Straight Bourbon 10 Years Old

Willett Pot Still Reserve

American Straight Rye

Michter's No. 1 Straight Rye

Sazerac Kentucky Straight Rye 18 Years Old

Thomas H. Handy Sazerac Straight Rye

American Straight Wheat

Parker's Heritage Collection Original Batch Kentucky Straight Wheat Whiskey Aged 13 Years

American Microdistilleries

Bad Guy Bourbon

Stranahan's Snowflake Cab Franc

The Notch Aged 8 Years

Westland American Single Malt Whiskey Single Cask 115

The Notch Aged 10 Years

Canadian Blended

Alberta Premium

Forty Creek Port Wood Reserve

Gibson's Finest Rare Aged 18 Years

Japanes Single Malt

Golden Horse Chichibu Aged 12 Years

SMWS Cask 120.7 Aged 14 Years

Ichiro's Malt Aged 20 Years

Japanes Single Grain

Kawasaki Single Grain

Austrian Single Malt

Pure Rye Malt J.H. bott code LPR 07

English Single Malt

Stephen Notman Whisky Live Taipei 2013

French Single Malt

Kornog Saint Ivy 2015

German Single Malt

Valerie Amarone Single Malt Whisky 4 Years Old

Swiss Single Malt

Langatun Old Mustang Bourbon 4 Year Old recipe

The Swiss Malt

Swedish Single Malt

Mackmyra Moment "Rimfrost"

Welsh Single Malt
Penderyn Portwood
Australian Single Malt
Heartwood The Beagle 3 Tasmania Vatted Malt Whisky
Heartwood Devil in the Detail
The Nant 3 Years Old Cask Strength
Sullivan's Cove American Oak Single Cask
Timboon Single Malt Port Expression
Indian Single Malt
Paul John Indian Single Malt Bold
Paul John Single Malt Cask No 692
Paul John Single Malt Cask No 784
Paul John Single Malt Cask No 1444
Indian Blends
Rendezvous
Taiwanese Single malt
Kavalan Single Malt Manzanilla Sherry Cask
Kavalan Solist Brandy Cask

95
Scottish Single Malt (New Entries Only)
Balblair 1983 Vintage 1st Release
Old Malt Cask Bowmore 16 Years Old
Dun Bheagan Clynelish 16 Year Old
Glenfarclas The Family Casks 1994
That Boutique-y Whisky Company Glen Keith
Glen Moray 25 Year Old Port Cask Finish
Old Malt Cask Glen Spey 18 Years Old
Cadenhead's Authentic Collection Isle of Arran Aged 16 Years
Laphroaig Au Cuan Mòr
Whisky-Fässle Longmorn 21 Year Old
Svenska Eldvatten Speyside 1994
Gordon & MacPhail Connoisseurs Choice Strathmill 2002
Old Malt Cask Strathmill 25 Years Old
Tomintoul Aged 25 Years
Tormore Aged 16 Years
Spirit & Cask Maximum Peat
Scottish Vatted Malt
Douglas Laing's Double Barrel Ardbeg & Craigellachie
Scottish Grain
The Sovereign Cambus Aged 40 Years
The Pearls of Scotland Invergordon 1997
Bourbon
Booker's 7 Years 5 Months
Buffalo Trace Single Oak Project Barrel #20
Eagle Rare 17 Year Old
Woodford Reserve Double Oaked
American Straight Rye
Jim Beam Pre-Prohibition Style Rye
Belgium Single Malt
The Belgian Owl Single Malt 40 Months
Dutch Single Malt
Millstone Aged 12 Years Sherry Cask
English Single Malt
The English Whisky Co. Chapter 16 Single Malt Peated, Sherry Cask

HRH Princess Charlotte of Cambridge
French Single Malt
Kornog Taouarc'h Seizued 14
German Single Malt
Spinnaker Single Cask Malt Whisky Fasssstärke
Swedish Single Malt
Smögen Svensk Single Malt Whisky Single Cask
Spirit of Hven Urania
Welsh Single Malt
Penderyn Madeira
Australian Single Malt
The Beagle Tasmanian Vatted Malt Whisky
The Lark Distillery Single Malt Whisky Limited Release
Taiwanes Single Malt
Kavalan Distillery Reserve

94.5 (New Entries Only)
Scottish Single Malt
Ardbeg Perpetuum
Master of Malt Single Cask Ardbeg 23 Year Old
Old Particular Highland Ardmore 14 Years Old
Auchentoshan 1988 25 Year Old Wine Cask Finish
Whisky-Fässle Auchroisk 22 Year Old
Scotch Malt Whisky Society Cask 50.54 Aged 23 Years
World of Orchids Caol Ila 1983 30 Year Old
Old Particular Highland Clynelish 18 YO
The Glendronach 2003 11 YO
Glenfarclas The Family Casks 1980
Cadenhead's Small Batch Glen Grant Aged 24 Years
Kilchoman Machir Bay
Douglas of Drumlanrig Laphroaig 13 YO
Old Malt Cask Laphroaig Aged 14 Years
Provenance Laphroaig Over 8 Years
Scotch Malt Whisky Society Cask 7.111 Aged 11 Years
Whiskyjace Miltonduff 21 Year Old
Provenance Talisker Over 6 Years
Whiskyjace Tamdhu 20 Year Old
First Edition The Freedom of 811 Ledaig 2004 10 Years Old
Cù Bòcan The Virgin Oak Edition
Tomatin Contrast
Tomintoul 1976 Vintage
Chapter 7 Tormore 1995 19 Year Old
Smokey Joe Islay Malt
Scottish Vatted Malt
Highland Journey Blended Malt
The Loch Fyne The Living Cask 1745
Irish Pure Pot Still
Scotch Malt Whisky Society Cask 11.74 Aged 22 Years
Bourbon
1792 Sweet Wheat Kentucky Straight Bourbon

Buffalo Trace Single Oak Project Barrel #181

I.W. Harper Kentucky Straight Bourbon 15 Year Old

Orphan Barrel Rhetoric 21 Year Old

American Micro Distilleries

Westland American Single Malt Whiskey Single Cask 177

English Single Malt

The English Whisky Co. Chapter 12 Single Malt Sherry Cask

The English Whisky Co. Chapter 15 Single Malt Heavily Peated

Finland Single Malt

Teerenpeli Single Malt Distiller's Choice HOSA 10 Year Old

French Single Malt

Kornog Taouarh'h Kentan 15

German Single Malt

Tronje Von Hagen Single Malt Höhlenwhisky

Swiss Single Malt

Langatun Winter Wedding Single Malt Whisky

Australian Single Malt

Belgrove Distillery Rye Whisky 100% Rye Aged 3 Years

Overeem Port Cask Matured

New Zealand Single Malt

The New Zealand Whisky Collection 25 YO

94 (New Entries Only)

Scottish Single Malt

Hunter Laing's Old & Rare Ardbeg Aged 21 Years

Kingsbury Gold Auchentoshan 16 Year Old 1997

The Balvenie TUN 1509

Wilson & Morgan Barrel Selection Ben Nevis 18 Year Old

Benromach 100° Proof

Old Particular Islay Bowmore 15 Years Old

Scotch Malt Whisky Society Cask 127.43 Aged 12 Years

Hepburn's Choice Caol Ila Aged 5 Years

Gordon & MacPhail Rare Old Convalmore 1975

Old Particular Speyside Glenburgie 25 Years Old

Abbey Whisky GlenDronach Aged 20 Years

Glenfarclas The Family Casks 1962

Glenfarclas The Family Casks 1996

Old Particular Speyside Glen Grant 20 Years Old

Glenmorangie Milsean

Scotch Malt Whisky Society Cask 35.131 Aged 19 Years

Anam na h-Alba The Soul of Scotland Glenrothes 1988

Gordon & MacPhail The Macphails Collection Glenrothes 1971

Glen Scotia Single Cask Distillery Edition 001

Endangered Drams Glentauchers 16 Year Old

AnCnoc 24 Years Old

Gleann Mór Lagavulin 10 Year Old

Old Malt Cask Longmorn Aged 19 Years

Scotch Malt Whisky Society Cask 25.66 Aged 23 Years

Scotch Malt Whisky Society Cask 55.24 Aged 20 Years

Gordon & MacPhail Connoisseurs Choice Speyburn 1991

Old Particular Highland Speyside 18 Years Old

Scottish Vatted Malt

Deerstalker Blended Malt Highland Edition

Spirit of Caledonia Flaitheanas 18 Years Old

Wilson & Morgan Barrel Selection Speybridge

Irish Pure Pot Still

Scotch Malt Whisky Society Cask 117.5 Aged 22 Years

Teeling Single Grain Irish Whiskey

Bourbon

Buffalo Trace Single Oak Project Barrel #84

Buffalo Trace Single Oak Project Barrel #148

Four Roses Limited Edition 2014 Small Batch

Japanese Single Malt

Scotch Malt Whisky Society Cask 124.4 Aged 17 Years

Scotch Malt Whisky Society Cask 119.13 Aged 10 Years

Japanese Single Grain

Scotch Malt Whisky Society Cask G11.1 Aged 14 Years

Czech Republic Single Malt

Gold Cock Single Malt Whisky Small Batch 1992

English Single Malt

Cotswolds Distillery New Make

German Single Malt

Finch Schwäbischer Highland Whisky Barrel Proof

Derrina Hafer Schwarzwälder Single Grain

Blaue Maus Single Cask Malt Whisky Fassstärke

Swedish Single Malt

Mackmyra Reserve "Queen of Fucking Everything"

Smögen Svensk Single Malt Whisky Sherry Project 1:2

Australian Single Malt

Sullivans Cove French Oak Cask

Iniquity Single Malt

Indian Single Malt

Amrut Naarangi

New Zealand Single Malt

The New Zealand Whisky Collection Willowbank 1988 25 Years Old

Scottish Malts

For those of you deciding to take the plunge and head off into the labyrinthine world of Scotch malt whisky, a piece of advice. And that is, be careful who you take your advice from. Because, too often, I hear that you should leave the Islays until you have tackled the featherlight Speysiders and the bolder, weightier Highlanders. This is just complete, patronising nonsense. The only time that rings true is if you are tasting a number of whiskies in one day. Then leave the smoky ones till last, so the lighter chaps get a fair hearing.

I know many people who didn't like whisky until they got a Talisker from Skye inside them, or a Lagavulin to swamp their tastebuds with oily iodine. The fact is, you can take your map of malt whisky, start at any point and head in whichever direction you feel. There are no hard and fast rules. Certainly with nearly 3,000 tasting notes for Scottish malts here you should have some help in picking where this journey of a lifetime begins.

It is also worth remembering not always to be seduced by age. It is true that many of the highest scores are given to big-aged whiskies. The truth is that the majority of malts, once they have lived beyond 25 years or so, suffer from oak influence rather than benefit. Part of the fun of discovering whiskies is to see how malts from different distilleries perform to age and type of cask. Happy discovering.

Abhainn Dearg
LEWIS

SKYE
Talisker

Ardna
Tobermory
MULL
Oba

Isle o
ISLAY
Isle o

Springbank
Glen Scotia
Glengyle

Islay

Bunnahabhain

Caol Ila

Kilchoman
Bruichladdich

Bowmore

Port Ellen
Laphroaig
Ardbeg
Lagavulin

ORKNEY ISLANDS
Highland Park
Scapa

Wolfburn

Pultney

Clynelish
✝ Brora

Balblair
Glenmorangie
Dalmore
Invergordon
Teaninich

Glen Ord
Royal Brackla

Inverness
Glen Albyn ✝
Glen Mhor ✝
Millburn ✝
Tomatin

The Speyside Distillery
Royal Lochnagar

Speyside see page 24
Glenglassaugh
Knockdhu
Glendronach
Ardmore

Banff ✝
Macduff

Glenugie

Glen Garioch

Aberdeen

Dalwhinnie

✝ Glenury Royal
Fettercairn

Fort William
Ben Nevis
Glenlochy ✝

Blair Athol
Edradour
Aberfeldy

Glencadam
✝ North Port
✝ Lochside

Glenesk ✝

Strathearn
Glenturret
Perth
Daftmill

Tullibardine

Deanston

Cameronbridge

Glengoyne
Rosebank
St. Magdelene

Glenkinchie

Edinburgh
North British

Loch Lomond
✝ *Dumbarton*
✝ Interleven
✝ Littlemill
Auchentoshan

Glasgow
Strathclyde
Port Dundas
Kinclaith ✝

Girvan
Ailsa Bay
Ladyburn ✝

Bladnoch

Dundee

Key

● **Major Town or City**
▲ Single Malt Distillery
▲ (*Italics*) Grain Distillery
✝ Dead Distillery

Speyside

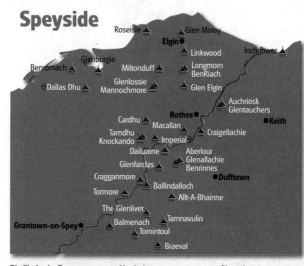

Distilleries by Town	Mortlach	Glenrothes
Dufftown	Dufftown	Glenspey
Glenfiddich	Pittyvaich	**Keith**
Convalmore	**Rothes**	Aultmore
Balvenie	Speyburn	Strathmill
Kininvie	Glen Grant	Glen Keith
Glendullan	Caperdonich	Strathisla

SINGLE MALTS
ABERFELDY

Highlands (Perthshire), 1898. John Dewar & Sons. Working.

◈ **Aberfeldy 12 Year Old** db (81) n21 t21 f19 b20. A puzzling malt. Aberfeldy makes and matures some of the greatest whisky on this planet, make no mistake. So why this conservative, ultra safe toffee-sultana-fudge offering when their warehouses are crammed with casks which could blow the world away? Pleasant. But so relentlessly dull and disappointing. And 40% abv...? Really...? 40% WB16/031

Aberfeldy Bits of Strange 16 Year Old db (94.5) n24 that just about unique aroma of a freshly-breeched cask: all dank oak, fruit and barley. Timeless and flawless...; t23.5 magnificent delivery with the sherry ringing loud and clear...and I mean clear...!!! Fabulous spices pepper the palate with oaky splinters; f23 long, forever drying with the oak, but enough voluptuous esters to make a big difference and balance out the finale; b24 one of those lovely casks which combines oaky and sugary bits in just the right proportions. A cracker of a cask – and sublime by present day sherry standards. The perfect way to start or end a day... 55.1%. sc.

Aberfeldy 16 Year Old Ramble db (93.5) n23.5 even nuttier than usual, the spices positively pulse. Loads of sharp marmalade and walnut oil combine with stand-your-spoon-in oloroso; t24 heavy molasses notes arrive early and keep their foot in the door. Elsewhere the juiciest of Demerara sugars melt on the palate and begin to form a fabulous Melton Mowbray Hunt Cake richness. Again, walnuts are present and mix perfectly with the syrupy dates; f22 a slight buzz at the death tells its own tale, but before then enjoy the fade to the richest of all fruits cakes with the raisins now at their toastiest; b24 an almost flawless cask good enough for a big, robust, grape-exploding treat. 56%. 643 bottles. Whisky Shop Exclusive.

Aberfeldy Aged 18 Years "Chris Anderson's Cask" db (90) n24 plays the range from bourbon-rich red liquorice right down to diced kumquat; sharp, angular, bold, salty and very enticing; not a single blemish in distillate or wood; t23.5 sharp delivery with a mouth watering malty juiciness, but also weighty, too, with heavy oaks immediately apparent. Any threatening bitterness is seen off by a light dusting of muscovado and dried dates; f21.5 bites deep and caramels out; b22 had the natural caramels just not ticked over a little too exuberantly, this would have headed for a very high score. Aberfeldy in a very unusual light... 54.9%. 248 bottles.

Aberfeldy 21 Year Old db (88) n22 not exactly faultless, but there is at least an attractive degree of landscaping to this fruity aroma; t22.5 exactly the silky toffee-laden delivery one might expect from the nose. But some charming spices burst through, and even some voluptuous and juicy malts; f21.5 coffee cake with an irritating injection of light sulphur; b22 the kind of malt I wish I could be let loose on...this really could be world class. But... 40% WB16/032

Aberfeldy Aged 25 Years db (85) n24 t21 f19 b21. Just doesn't live up to the nose. When Tommy Dewar wrote, "We have a great regard for old age when it is bottled," as quoted on the label, I'm not sure he had as many as 25 years in mind. 40%.

Aberfeldy Single Cask Aged 21 Years bott 10 Oct 12 db (97) n24 what can you say: the colour of clear honey and with a nose to match...except the salty oakiness adds intriguing depth of fine whisky proportions; t24.5 near enough perfect mouth feel with the kind of punchy bite that every cask strength whisky should have. Actually, make that EVERY whisky. The oak skips around offering a chewy custard tart richness. But that clear honey (perfectly depicted by the bees on the label) is always there or thereabouts; f24 fantastic butterscotch layering, though with delicate marzipan and honey sub layers. The oak is profound but of the highest possible quality, injecting a fabulous drier balance, bordering on cocoa dusting; b24.5 if I find a better single cask this year, it might well be World Whisky of the Year. Just buzzes with magnificence... I have long regarded this not just one of the great distilleries of Scotland, but, even from its Diageo days, one of the true underachievers of world whisky. Not anymore. Someone who knows exactly what they are doing has invaded the Aberfeldy warehouses and made a beeline for the honey casks. This is exactly how malt whisky should bee.... 55.3%. sc.

Aberfeldy Single Cask 1996 Vintage bott 2013 db (94.5) n23 adorable sharp, nutty, honey-tinged malt: like a breakfast cereal with attitude; t24 surprising oaky countenance; definitely on the warm to hostile side but there is something so seductive about the sweet, rambling malt; the bite is from the old school and simply sublime; f23.5 goes into full dry cocoa mode; b24 so rare to fine Feldy this full on and aggressive. But, as usual with this distillery, all the parts feel right and fall into place with majestic ease. Just so my kind of whisky. Brilliant! 61.5%. Exclusive to The Whisky Shop.

Aberfeldy Single Cask Unravel db (96) n24 a beautiful amalgam of dank oak casks (even from the outside) and freshly grated, juicy ginger. The soft distant oak-induced creamed rice and honey, topped with light molasses is superb; some major bourbon traits suggest a pretty virgin type of cask in play here; t24 intense oak but with all the bourbony sugars forming an unforgettable alliance with the black peppers which scorch into the roof of the mouth; like the other two Aberfeldys, the mouth feel is just about perfect...; f24 long, with that formidable coppery flourish sitting happily with the brown sugar and spices; so many layers, you almost give up counting... b24 this completes the best set of single cask malts I have tasted from any Scottish distillery for the last four or five years. Restores one's faith, it does... Oh, and this is supposed to be savoured while listening to some music. Don't bother; it conjures a major symphony of its own...56.5%. sc. John Dewar & Sons.

Gordon & Macphail Cask Strength Aberfeldy refill sherry hogsheads, cask no. 2488, 2489 & 2491, dist 07 Apr 1995, bott 29 Jan 2014 (93) n22 that vague nuttiness...can be from only one distillery. Ultra deft fruit..; t23.5 a perfectly sharp delivery with the alcohohol doing no more than ensuring the intense barley lands with a thump; superb spices and a growing intensity of moist fruitcake; f24 a finish to die for: so busy yet brilliantly structured with the slow build of Venezualan cocoa finding just the right weight to accompany the persistent malt. Really top quality butterscotch, too; b23.5 a fabulous meal of a malt. What a wonderful distillery this is. 55.8%. WB15/113

Provenance Aberlour Over 7 Years refill barrel, cask no. 10766, dist Summer 08, bott Summer 15 (89) n22 youthful, effervescent barley; t23 young, brimming with fresh, malty sugars; f22 citrussy, grassy and, latterly, spicy; b22 tasted on the hottest July day on record in Britain, this refreshing youngster could not have come along at a better time. 46%. nc ncf sc.

Wemyss Malts Aberfeldy 1994 Single Highland "Melon Vine" hogshead, dist 94, bott 14 (91) n23.5 milk chocolate Jaffa cake; t23 brilliant delivery: the oak pounds hard, but soft oils, manuka honey and malt keeps it in check; f22 long, with some tangy old tannins but the sugars hold firm; b22.5 sound and lazily complex malt from an effortlessly good distillery. 46%. sc. 242 bottles.

Wemyss Malts 1999 Single Highland Aberfeldy "Snuffed Candle" hogshead, bott 2014 (88) n23.5 a freshly blasted shotgun offers the earthier tones to this where elsewhere glazed fruit abounds; t23 voluptuous mouth-feel. There is an immediate impact of spice, half-hearted at first but grows – and glows – quickly. After an initial malty spurt, the fruit holds ground; f20 curiously bitter and rigid; b21.5 some disappointing oak at the death puts the dampeners on an otherwise full blood malt. 46%. sc. 379 bottles.

ABERLOUR

Speyside, 1826. Chivas Brothers. Working.

Aberlour 10 Years Old db **(87.5) n22.5 t22 f21 b22.** Remains a lusty fellow though here nothing like as sherry-cask faultless as before, nor displaying its usual honeyed twinkle. 43%

Aberlour 10 Years Old Sherry Cask Finish db **(85) n21 t21 f21 b22.** Bipolar and bitter-sweet with the firmness of the grain in vivid contrast to the gentle grape. 43%

Aberlour 12 Years Old Double Cask Matured db **(88.5) n22 t22.5 f22 b22.** Voluptuous and mouth-watering in some areas, firmer and less expansive in others. Pretty tasty in all of them. 43%

Aberlour 12 Years Old Non Chill-Filtered db **(87) n22.5 t22 f21 b21.5.** There are many excellent facets to this malt, not least the balance between barley and grape and the politeness of the gristy sugars. But a sulphured butt has crept into this one, taking the edge off the excellence and bringing down the score like a cold front drags down the thermometer. 48%. ncf.

Aberlour 12 Years Old Sherry Cask Matured db **(88) n23 t22 f21 b22.** Could do with some delicate extra sweetness to take it to the next level. Sophisticated nonetheless. 40%

Aberlour 13 Years Old sherry cask, hand fill db **(84) n21 t22 f20 b21.** Skimps on the complexity. 58.8%

Aberlour 15 Year Old Double Cask Matured db **(84) n23 t22 f19 b20.** Brilliant nose full of vibrant apples and spiced sultana, but then, after a complex, chewy, malt-enriched kick-off, falls surprisingly flat on its face. 40%

Aberlour 15 Years Cuvee Marie d'Ecosse db **(91) n22 t24 f22 b23.** This always was a deceptive lightweight, and it's got lighter still. It is sold primarily in France, and one can assume only that this is God's way of making amends for that pretentious, over-rated, caramel-ridden rubbish called Cognac they've had to endure. 43%

Aberlour 15 Year Old Sherry Finish db **(91) n24** exceptionally clever use of oak to add a drier element to the sharper boiled cooking apple. And a whiff of the fermenting vessel, too; **t22** the sharp rigor of the nose is magnified ten times; **f23** wave upon wave of malt concentrate; **b22** quite unique: freaky, even. Really a whisky to be discovered and ridden. Once you acclimatize, you'll adore it. 43%

Aberlour Aged 16 Years Double Cask Matured bott 23 Feb 10 db **(94.5) n24** a magnificent marriage between sweet, juicy fruit and lively spice; sturdy-framed but giving grape, too; **t24** the softest delivery of lightly sugared grape, salivating and sensuous; light spices struggle to free themselves from the gentle oils; **f23** pithy with the vanilla determined to ensure a drier finale; **b23.5** a joyous malt reminding us of just what clean, fresh sherry butts are capable of. A malt of unbridled magnificence. 43%

Aberlour 18 Years Old db **(91) n22** thick milkshake with various fruits and vanilla; **t22** immediate fresh juice which curdles beautifully as the vanilla is added; **f24** wonderful fruit-chocolate fudge development: long, and guided by a gentle oiliness; **b23** another high performance distillery age-stated bottling. 43%

Aberlour 100 Proof db **(91) n23 t23 f22 b23.** Stunning, sensational whisky, the most extraordinary Speysider of them all...which it was when I wrote those official notes for the bottling back in '97, I think. Other malts have superseded it now, but on re-tasting I stand by those original notes, though I disassociate myself entirely with the rubbish: "In order to savour Aberlour 100 at its best add 1/3 to 1/2 pure water. 571%

Aberlour a'Bunadh Batch No. 40 db **(93.5) n24** one of the freshest fruit noses you could hope for, with a barrow-full of greengages so ripe they are fit to explode...; **t23.5** silky and succulent, the barley and spice make a big impact after the grape skin introduction; inevitable spices lead to a drier butterscotch tart middle; **f22.5** relatively lightweight for an a'Bunadh with the accent firmly on the barley; **b23.5** a shapely malt with no little barley. 61%. nc ncf.

Aberlour a'Bunadh Batch No. 41 db **(83) n21 t22 f20 b20.** By normal standards, not too bad a malt, and another with the emphasis on the barley. But as an a'Bunadh, rather lacking... with one or two unattractive tangs too many. 59.7%. nc ncf.

Aberlour A'Bunadh Batch No. 45 Spanish oloroso sherry butts db **(95) n24** Demerara rum meets Java coffee...and dripping grape juice; **t24** fabulous spices give an extra lift to an already full on delivery. Full salivation by about the fifth flavour wave and mocha joins soon after. The fruit is piled high, the sugars higher still; **f23** settles for a more sedate, drier finale, though the dried date and manuka honey tries to have a say about that; late chocolate Swiss roll; **b24** faultless sherry of the old school. 60.2%. sc nc ncf. WB15/332

Aberlour A'Bunadh Batch No. 47 db **(88.5) n22** for oloroso the grape is a little too firm, giving suspicion of perhaps a weakness. And there is nip, too, which bares no relation to the alcohol. But there is a sherry trifle edge to this and black cherry...! **t24** that is one very serious delivery... a warming degree of plum pudding, followed by Melton Hunt Cake doused in brandy; the sugars are gritty and dark, a little treacle and then a return to fruitcake...the burned outside bits; **f20.5** calms as a few caramels appear. But there is grape, too. And now confirmation of only the most distant rumble of sulphur, not easily spotted at first but acting like a slow puncture with the bitterness taking a full five minutes to make its effects felt; **b22** a valued friend of mine, Byron Rodgers, one of Britain's greatest living essayists, asked me over a pint the other night what I thought of the A'Bunadh batch 47 they were selling at our nearest Waitrose. You see, I had recently brought him, wide eyed and innocent, into a world of cask strength whisky; and being a man of infinite curiosity he was determined to learn more very much in the manner of an astronaut having landed on an alien and wondrous landscape. I couldn't tell him, as I had not yet tasted it. Well, I have now. And tomorrow I will advise him to go forth and invest in a bottle, though with a warning. Because as learning curves go, by and large this is a pretty delicious one. Yet perhaps better still for the explorer, it contains a fault from which much can be learned. Like what happens when you pit one bad butt against many good ones. *60.7%.*

Aberlour A'Bunadh Batch No. 48 Spanish oloroso sherry butts db **(92) n24** grape must and nippy mixed spice; **t22** for once, the barley is heard early. But not for long, as lots of natural caramels mix with the grape to make for a thick mouth feel. Elsewhere the spices kick in with a degree of venom; **f23** still nips and tingles, though Demerara sugar tries to heal the wounds; **b23** delicious. But surprisingly aggressive for an a'bunadh. *59.7%. sc nc ncf. WB15/333*

◇ **Aberlour A'Bunadh Batch No. 50** db **(95.5) n23.5** the vaguest blip is easily overcome here by the mesmerising depth of the lightly spiced sultana; **t24.5** wow! Even by this great brand's very high standards, that is one enormous entry on the palate with the fruit truly radiating into every crevice, helped along the way by lively, warming spice: a kind of hot cross bun on steroids; **f24** long, with a slight crack in its voice. But the slow movement towards a praline finale is deft, though the juicy dates stay to the very end; **b23.5** it seems a long time ago now. But I can remember sitting with the good people of Aberlour when they showed me what they had planned for batch 1 of a new brand called a'bunadh. I was thrilled that they were going for it with a no-holds barred malt...but nervous they were using sherry butts. That was some time ago...and now they have reached 50 not out. Miraculously, they have managed, usually, to avoid the worst excesses of present day sherry butts. And they have done so again here to bring their half century up in style. Ladies and gentlemen of Aberlour: I raise a glass to you in celebration. *59.6% WB16/027*

Cadenhead's Small Batch Aberlour-Glenlivet Aged 23 Years bourbon hogsheads, dist 1989, bott 2013 **(93.5) n23** thin-ish and warming...the spirit safe was taking a bit of a pounding. But the cut was true, leaving the malt to show a rare, warming clarity. The cask is in perfect sync, offering just a light banana and custard accompaniment; **t24.5** astonishingly clean and salivating. The grist appears to have been set in icing sugar; the warm buzz does not appear to be oak-induced spice...; some gorgeous heather-honey adds perfect weight; **f23** more of the same...forever, it seems; and still warms...; **b23** one of the cleanest, sweetest 23 year olds you'll ever encounter. But I suspect the distiller manager of the time, Puss Mitchell, had the stills at full revs when this was made. A hottie! *54.9%. 522 bottles. WB15/069*

Darkness! Aberlour Aged 20 Years Oloroso Cask Finish (95) n23.5 rich fruitcake but with demonic amounts of extra spice; **t24** quite brilliant! In true and very old Aberlour style, this not only bristles with spiced sultanas and Demerara sugar but finds the grace to allow in the malt to ensure balance; **f23.5** long, malty but with a lovely fruitcake backing. Delicate for its enormity. And, above all...clean! **b24** "Subtlety, poise and elegance have no place here" claims the back label. Now, I wonder where they get that phrase from...? But, as it happens, this is exactly what the whisky has, helped enormously by the fact that sulphur is wonderfully conspicuous by its absence... *53.4%. 96 bottles. WB15/199*

Darkness! Aberlour Aged 20 Years Pedro Ximenez Cask Finish (94) n24 subtle; **t23.5** poised; **f24** elegant; **b23** Thank you for using a PX cask on something that is not a heavily peated monster. Here we can see the sweet sherry at work and play, working alongside the striking intensity of the outstanding barley. In many ways, big, blustery and heavy on the molasses, but beneath the surface a fabulous charm offensive is going on where elegance really is the key. Oh, and for the sheer delight of NOT being assaulted by sulphur...thank you, chaps! *53.7%. WB15/236*

The Maltman Aberlour Aged 19 Years bourbon cask **(94.5) n23** wonderful weight to both the barley and the heather honey which also draws in a light mintiness; **t23.5** follows through with an almost identical trick: big malty blast, then heather-honey until the oak makes an impressive incursion without denting the solidity of the bedrock malt; **f24** enriched by copper, almost certainly one of the stills or condensers was replaced/repaired just prior to this malt being made. A real tanginess for the intense malt to grip onto; **b24** absolutely brilliant to see Aberlour naked and not hiding behind sherry: there is rare beauty to behold... *46%*

◈ **Old Particular Speyside Aberlour 21 Years Old** refill hogshead, cask no. 10436, dist Sep 92, bott Aug 14 (**88**) **n22** apples....!!! This is principally the nose of cider brandy; **t22** again, the malt has been lost under an entire windfall of bramley; **f22** the vanilla of the oak works well with the spices and softening sugars; **b22** you will be hard pressed to find a lighter Aberlour this year..and probably next. *51.5%. nc ncf sc. 331 bottles.*

◈ **That Boutique-y Whisky Company Aberlour** batch 3 (**90.5**) **n23.5** superb Speyside-style nose; clean malt showing both confidence and a shrill austerity; **t23** superb delivery: a bunch of sugars – mainly from the maple syrup family – cling to the malty coattails; **f21.5** bitters slightly, but that malt carries on undeterred; **b22.5** some 30 years ago Aberlour had very little body and would not have impressed in this form. Certainly not the case today: though a light whisky, enough oils cling to the frame to make for something substantial. *49.2%.*

ABHAINN DEARG
Highlands (Outer Hebrides), 2008. Marko Tayburn. Working.

Abhainn Dearg db (**91**) **n22** the odd feint when pouring, but let the glass warm for a few minutes and the stronger elements soon burn off. What is left is a soft, pulpy gooseberry note as well as barley sugar and vague spice; **t22.5** intense and chewy, the delivery confirms the wide cut and for a while the flavours are in suspension. Slowly, a meaningful dialogue with the palate begins and it's those gorgeous barley notes which are first to speak up, soon joined by maple syrup and butterscotch tart; the tongue nearly wipes a hole in the roof of your mouth as it tackles the flavour orgy; **f23.5** a wonderful finish, not least because the malt appears to have relaxed into a sugary barleyfest with only a light coppery tang reminding us this is all from a brand new distillery forging its place in island folk lore; **b23** so here we go: the 1,000th new whisky of the 2013 Jim Murray Whisky Bible. And this year I give the honour of that landmark to Abhainn Dearg: the first bottling of a brand new Scotch single malt distillery is that very rarest of species. The fact it comes from Lewis really puts the icing on the cake. Some may remember that a couple of years back I made their new make the 1,001st new whisky for the 2011 edition: I have been keeping a close eye on this, now the most western scotch distillery. And it is strange to think that this is the first malt whisky to come from the Outer Hebrides with a licence attached... My word, it was worth the wait. For after an unsteady start the quality becomes so clearly touched by angels. I can see everyone on the island having no qualms in tucking into this, even on the Sabbath. Well, maybe not... *46%. nc ncf sc.*

Abhainn Dearg New Make db (**92.5**) **n23 t23 f23.5 b23**. Exceptionally well made with no feints and no waste, either. Oddly salty – possibly the saltiest new make I have encountered, and can think of no reason why it should be – with excellent weight as some extra copper from the new still takes hold. Given a good cask, no reason this impressive new born son of the Outer Hebrides won't go on to become something significant. *67%*

Abhainn Dearg New Make db (**88**) **n21.5 t23 f21.5 b22**. OK. I admit that the 1,001st new whisky for the 2011 Bible wasn't whisky at all, but new make. But, as the Isle of Lewis has made it impossible for me not to visit there by now being an official whisky-making island, I thought it was worth celebrating. The new make in this form is rich, clean and malty but with a much heightened metallic feel to it, both on nose and taste, by comparison to other recently-opened distilleries. This is likely to change markedly over time as the stills settle in. So I had better start looking at the Cal-Mac Ferry timetables to go and find out for myself if it does...

ALLT-Á-BHAINNE
Speyside, 1975. Chivas Brothers. Working.

◈ **Chapter 7 Allt-A-Bhainne 1995 18 Year Old** bourbon hogshead, cask no. 166300 (**91.5**) **n22.5** what an enticing mix of clean oak and even cleaner barley; **t24** concentrated barley....in concentrate. A magnificent delivery, about as good as anything from Speyside this year, with the sugars sympathetic to the gristiness already on show; intense but never overpowering – a blender's dream if he is looking to create a malty impact..!! **f21.5** by contrast, the finish is reached quickly, as the malt fades fast leaving half-hearted vanilla; **b23.5** have been disappointed with the quality of the offering of this distillery in recent times, knowing that it is capable of something much better. This is a much better representation of the distillery in form, though the finish is thin. *59.2%. sc. 264 bottles.*

◈ **Deerstalker Allt-á-Bhainne Limited Release 1995 aged 18 years, 9 months** (**86.5**) **n22 t22 f21 b21.5** An easy going malt which tries to concentrate on its fresh, juicy charm as much as is possible. A little oak-induced bitterness creeps in towards the end, but the barley plows on regardless. *48%. nc ncf.*

◈ **Master of Malt Single Cask Allt-a-Bhainne 18 Year Old** sherry hogshead, dist 25 Sept 92, bott 24 Mar 15 (**86**) **n21.5 t22 f21 b21.5**. Warming, spicy and thinly malty, the cask intervention may be what you expect of a 22-year-old. *55.2%. sc. 166 bottles.*

Master of Malt Single Cask Allt-A-Bhainne 20 Year Old (92) n22 gooseberry jam; t24 salivating barley: grassy, fresh and intense but with a delicate sliver of ulmo honey to thicken things out; f22.5 long, with the oils capturing the vanilla as well as the sweet spiced barley; b23.5 seeing as this comes in a 3cl bottle, this literally is a little gem. 54.9%. sc.

⬧⬧ **Old Malt Cask Allt-A-Bhainne Aged 18 Years** refill hogshead, cask no. 10825, dist Jun 96, bott Aug 14 (85.5) n21.5 t22 f20.5 b21.5 A slightly lazy cask has subtracted slightly from what might otherwise been a stunner. Really well constructed at the still: the malt and oils are in harmony with no apparent power struggle. The sugars are also clean and striking, at times heading into acacia honey territory but for its age, undercooked with not quite enough oak added to the recipe. 50%. nc ncf sc. 337 bottles. OMC2407

Old Particular Speyside Allt-A-Bhainne 18 Years Old refill hogshead, cask no. 10370, dist Jun 96, bott Jul 14 (87.5) n22 heavy oak lightened by malt; t22.5 honeydew melon – with emphasis on the honey; f22 golden syrup with a touch of lime; b22.5 a minor if faultless little gem. 48.4%. nc ncf sc. 275 bottles.

Provenance Allt A Bhaine Over 12 Years sherry butt, cask no. 9513, bott Winter 13 (91.5) n22.5 t23.5 f22 b23.5. From the boiled gooseberry school of deliciousness. And about as clean a Speysider as you'll find this year. 46%. nc ncf sc.

Signatory Vintage Cask Strength Collection Allt-A-Bhainne 1991 Aged 22 Years hogheads, cask no. 90112+90115, dist 09 Jul 91, bott 23 Oct 13 (90.5) n22.5 the malt is so light and delicate the footprint of the tannins is easily identifiable; soft citrus; a tad earthy; t23 excellent body: a little more oily than usual but the spices erupt early; massive barley surge; f22 an impressive biscuit vanilla fade, with a sophisticated dusting of cocoa powder to remind you of its age; b23 an elegant example of a malt performing beyond the years it was designed for. 54%. nc. 444 bottles. WB15/004

Signatory Vintage Single Malt Allt-A-Bhainne 1995 Aged 18 Years, hogsheads, cask no. 147071+147072, dist 22 Sep 95, bott 07 Feb 14 (87.5) n22 t22 f21.5 b22. A kind of Chivas blending blueprint malt. Cut glass and clean barley: simple with no frills. 43%. nc. WB15/015

That Boutique-y Whisky Allt-A-Bhainne batch 1 (77) n19 t20 f19 b19. Pleasant and sweet...if you like gin! All kinds of botanicals on the nose and follow through on delivery. Maybe the bottling filters had just done a gin run... Disappointing. 49.2%. WB15/193

⬧⬧ **That Boutique-y Whisky Company Allt-a-Bhainne** batch 2 (85.5) n22 t22.5 f20 b21 A safe, juicy, perhaps too clean Speysider which runs out of steam early on. 49.9%. 40 bottles.

ARDBEG
Islay, 1815. Glenmorangie Plc. Working.

Ardbeg 10 Years Old db (97) n24 more complex, citrus-led and sophisticated than recent bottlings, though the peat is no less but now simply displayed in an even greater elegance; a beautiful sea salt strain to this; t24 gentle oils carry on them a lemon-lime edge, sweetened by barley and a weak solution of golden syrup; the peat is omnipotent, turning up in every crevice and wave, yet never one once overstepping its boundary; f24 stunningly clean, the oak offers not a bitter trace but rather a vanilla and butterscotch edge to the barley. Again the smoke wafts around in a manner unique in the world of whisky when it comes to sheer élan and adroitness; b25 like when you usually come across something that goes down so beautifully and with such a nimble touch and disarming allure, just close your eyes and enjoy... 46%

Ardbeg 10 bottling mark L10 152 db (95) n24.5 mesmerising: bigger oak kick than normal suggesting some extra age somewhere. But fits comfortably with the undulating peat and dusting of salt; captivating complexity: hard to find a ten year old offering more than this...; t23.5 a shade oilier than the norm with orange and honey mingling effortlessly with the smoke: more than a hint of icing sugar; melts in the mouth like a prawn cracker...but without the prawns...; f23.5 drying oak with cocoa powder. The oils help the sugars linger; b23.5 a bigger than normal version, but still wonderfully delicate. Fabulous and faultless. 46%. Canadian market bottling in English and French dual language label.

Ardbeg 17 Years Old earlier bottlings db (92) n23 t22 f23 b24. OK, I admit I had a big hand in this, creating it with the help of Glenmorangie Plc's John Smith. It was designed to take the weight off the better vintages of Ardbeg whilst ensuring a constant supply around the world. Certainly one of the more subtle expressions you are likely to find, though criticised by some for not being peaty enough. As the whisky's creator, all I can say is they are missing the point. 40%

Ardbeg 17 Years Old later bottlings db (90) n22 t23 f22 b23. The peat has all but vanished and cannot really be compared to the original 17-year-old: it's a bit like tasting a Macallan without the sherry: fascinating to see the naked body underneath, and certainly more of a turn on. Peat or no peat, great whisky by any standards. 40%

Ardbeg Guaranteed 30 Years Old db (91) n24 t23 f21 b23. An unsual beast, one of the last ever bottled by Allied. The charm and complexity early on is enormous, but the fade rate is surprising. That said, still a dram of considerable magnificence. 40%

Ardbeg 1977 db (96) n25 t24 f23 b24. When working through the Ardbeg stocks, I earmarked '77 a special vintage, the sweetest of them all. So it has proved. Only the '74 absorbed that extra oak that gave greater all-round complexity. Either way, the quality of the distillate is beyond measure: simply one of the greatest experiences – whisky or otherwise – of your life. 46%

Ardbeg 1978 db (91) n23 t24 f22 b22. An Ardbeg on the edge of losing it because of encroaching oak, hence the decision made by John Smith and I to bottle this vintage early alongside the 17-year-old. Nearly ten years on, still looks a pretty decent bottling, though slightly under strength! 43%

Ardbeg Alligator 1st Release db (94) n24 delicate: like a bomb aimer...steady, steady, steady...there she goes...and suddenly spices light up the nose; some coriander and cocoa, too; t22.5 surprisingly silky, soft and light; milky chocolate hides some lurking clove in the soothing smoke; f24 hits its stride for a magnificent finale: as long as you could possibly hope for and an-ever gathering intensity of busy, prickly spice. Mocha and a dab of praline see off any potential bitterness to the oaky fight back; b23.5 an alligator happy to play with you for a bit before sinking its teeth in. The spices, though big, are of the usual Ardbegian understatement. 51.2%. ncf. *Exclusive for Ardbeg Committee members.*

Ardbeg Alligator 2nd Release db (93) n24 clove and black pepper; a degree of bourbony polished leather and liquorice, too; t23 early Demerara sugars and smoke make way for that slow build up of spices again; though perhaps missing the subtlety of the first edition's quietness, it more than has its macho compensations; f23 curiously, a short finale, as though more energy was expended in the delivery. Much drier with the oak having a good deal to say, though the spices nip satisfyingly; b23 something of a different species to the Committee bottling having been matured a little longer, apparently. Well long enough for this to evolve into something just a little less subtle. The nose, though, remains something of striking beauty – even if barely recognisable from the first bottling. 51.2%. ncf.

Ardbeg Almost There 3rd release dist 1998, bott 2007 db (93) n23 t24 f23 b23. Further proof that a whisky doesn't have to reach double figures in age to enter the realms of brilliance... 54.1%

Ardbeg Aurivedes American oak casks with specially toasted cask lids. db (91.5) n22 a light Kentucky char nip to this, forming a type of phenol that has nothing to do with peat. Liquorice and butterscotch appear to outdistance the smoke...; t22.5 astonishingly light delivery: softer than any baby's bottom and maltier, too. Indeed the gristy malt is unusually powerful for an Ardbeg but only because the smoke, which is definitely there, seems preoccupied with a massive surge of vanilla; f24 way better balanced now as some milky mocha notes take control and a blend of ulmo and manuka honey props up the sugars; the peat remains surprisingly shy and elusive, though the spice tingle on the tongue tells you it is hiding there somewhere; b23 I have spoken to nobody at Ardbeg about this one but from the slight bourbon character of the nose and the heavy vanilla, this version appears to be about the casks, possibly the char of the barrels. Fascinating, enjoyable...but whatever this is, the usual complexity of the peat feels compromised in the same way a wine cask might. Except here I detect no telling fruit. A real curiosity, whatever it is... 49.9%. Moet Hennessy.

Ardbeg Blasda db (90.5) n23.5 distant kumquat and lime intertwine with gentle butterscotch tart; it's all about the multi-layered barley and the most vague smokiness imaginable which adds a kind of almost invisible weight; the overall clarity is like that found swimming off a Pacific atoll; t22.5 sharp barley hits home to almost mouth-watering effect; again there is the most pathetic hint of something smoky (like the SMWS cask, perhaps from the local water and warehouse air), but it does the trick and adds just the right ballast; f22 soft spices arrive apologetically, but here it could do with being at 46% just to give it some late lift; b22.5 a beautiful, if slightly underpowered malt, which shows Ardbeg's naked self to glowing effect. Overshadowed by some degree in its class by the SMWS bottling, but still something to genuinely make the heart flutter. 40%

Ardbeg Corryvreckan db (96.5) n23 excellent, thick, not entirely un-penetrable – but close – nascent smoke and a vignette of salty, coastal references save the day; t24.5 amazing: here we have Ardbeg nutshelled. Just so many layers of almost uncountable personalities with perhaps the citrus leading the way in both tart and sweet form and then meaningful speeches from those saline-based, malty sea-spray refreshed barley notes with the oak, in vanilla form, in close proximity. The peat, almost too dense to be seen on the nose, opens out with a fanfare of phenols. It is slumping-in-the-chair stuff, the enormity of the peat taking on the majesty of Cathedral-esque proportions, the notes reverberating around the hollows and recesses and reaching dizzying heights; such is its confidence, this is a malt which says: "I know where I'm going...!"; f24 long, outwardly laconic but on further investigation just brimming with complexity. Some brown sugary notes help the barley to come up trumps late on but it's the uniquely salty shield to the mocha which sets this apart. Simply brilliant and unique in its effortless enormity...even by Ardbeg standards; **b25** as famous writers – including the occasional genius film director (stand up wherever you are my heroes Powell and Pressburger) – appear to be attracted to Corryvreckan, the third most violent whirlpool found in the world and just off Islay, to boot, - I selected this as my 1,500th whisky tasted for the historic Jim Murray Whisky Bible 2009. I'm so glad I did because many have told me they thought Blasda ahead of this. To me, it's not even a contest. Currently I have only a sample. Soon I shall have a bottle. I doubt if even the feared whirlpool is this deep and perplexing. *57.1%. 5000 bottles.*

Ardbeg Day Bottling db **(97)** n24.5 a dry lead...seemingly. But it's the busy stuff behind the scenes which intrigues. In typical Ardbegian fashion it's what you have to take a little extra time to find which is the real turn on...apart from the rock pool salt, apart from the squeeze of slightly sugared lime, apart from the thinnest layer of honey, apart from the fracturing hickory, apart from the kelp;...; **t24.5** and while the nose at times seems hard and brittle, the delivery moulds itself into the shape of your palate. Soft oils fill the contours; dissolving sugars counter the well-mannered but advancing oak; the phenols take on an earthy form, languid spices and omnipresent smoke; **f23.5** dries again in a vanilla direction with the oak determined to have its say. But it is a gentle speech and one inclusive of the delicate phenols encouraging the growing citrus. The oils remain just higher than the norm and thicken the muscovado-sweetened mocha. The finish, one of the longest you will find this year, carries on beyond what you would normally expect of an Ardbeg. And that is saying something; **b24.5** I left this to be one of the last whiskies I tasted this year. I had an inkling that they might come up with something a little special, especially with the comparative disappointment of the fundamentally flawed Galileo. On first sweep I thought it was pretty ordinary. but I know this distillery a little too well. So I left the glass for some 20 minutes to breathe and compose itself and returned. To find a potential world whisky of the year... *56.8%. Available at distillery and Ardbeg embassies.*

Ardbeg Feis Ile 2011 db **(67)** n16 t19 f15 b17. If anyone asked me what not to do with an Ardbeg, my answer would be: don't put it into a PX cask. And if asked if anything could be worse, I'd say: yeah, a PX Cask reeking of sulphur. To be honest, I am only assuming this is PX, as there is no mention on my sample bottle and I have spoken to them about it. But for something to fail as completely as this my money is on PX. And sulphur. *55.4%*

Ardbeg Galileo 1999 db **(87.5)** n23 t23.5 f19 b22. Today, as I taste this, I am celebrating the first birthday of my grand-daughter Islay-Mae, named after the greatest whisky island in the world. And this was one of half a dozen special whiskies I set aside to mark the event. For it is not often you get the chance to celebrate the first birthday of your first grand-daughter. Nor to taste a malt specially bottled to celebrate some of its fellow Ardbeg whisky that was sent into orbit for experimentation in the Space Station...At least I know a day like this will never be repeated. *49%*

Ardbeg Kildalton db **(94)** n23.5 didn't expect that: smoke! Light, dry, ashy but also slightly undercooked in the cask; quite an oily aroma; an unusual, fuzzy aroma of fruit that, for once, isn't citrus-based; **t23** unusually thin first few moments on the palate and takes a while for the smoke, accompanied by the thin layer of plum jam, to make an impact. When it arrives; it stays...; **f23.5** now showing off... the elegance can only be admired as a little ulmo honey and lavender give a deft edge to the already gentle smoke; just a little chocolate raisin on the slightly furry finish; **b24** youthful and lightly smoked, unlike the days when I blended the first-ever Kildalton which was middle aged and, for all intents and purposes, peat free. The most subtle of Ardbegs which whispers its beauty, though quite audibly... *46%*

Ardbeg Kildalton 1980 bott 2004 db **(96)** n23 t24 f24 b25. Proof positive that Ardbeg doesn't need peat to bring complexity, balance and Scotch whisky to their highest peaks... *57.6%*

Ardbeg Lord of the Isles bott Autumn 2006 db **(85)** n20 t22 f22 b21. A version of Ardbeg I have never really come to terms with. This bottling is of very low peating levels and shows a degree of Kildalton-style fruitiness. No probs there. But some of the casks are leaching a soft soapy character noticeable on the nose. Enjoyable enough, but a bit frustrating. *46%*

Ardbeg Mor db **(95)** n24 coastal to the point of sea spray showering you, with the smell of salt all the way home until you reach the peat fire. Evocative, sharp with elements of vinegar to the iodine; **t24** one of the biggest deliveries from Ardbeg for yonks; the peat appears way above the normal 50%, thickset and gloriously bitter-sweet, the steadying vanillas carried on the soft oils; **f23** mocha enters the fray with a raspberry jam fruitiness trying to dampen the continuing smoke onslaught; **b24** quite simply... more the merrier... *57.5%*

⬩ **Ardbeg Perpetuum** db **(94.5)** n23.5 if you think dry doesn't work on a nose, then try this for size: the sugars hide in every corner while the smoke has a distinctly peatish quality; **t23.5** mouth-watering for all the nose's qualities. Unusually, the malt and peat appear to be working at different levels, so the barley, unencumbered by smoke, is clearly visible; **f23.5** that dual-planed personality continues, with the sugars showing even greater autonomy; **b24** what a beautifully structured malt. There is no escaping the youth of some of the phrases. But you can't help enjoying what it says. 47.4%. ncf.

Ardbeg Provenance 1974 bott 1999 db (**96**) **n24 t25 f23 b24**. This is an exercise in subtlety and charisma, the beauty and the beast drawn into one. Until I came across the 25-year-old OMC verson during a thunderstorm in Denmark, this was arguably the finest whisky I had ever tasted: I opened this and drank from it to see in the year 2000. When I went through the Ardbeg warehouse stocks in 1997 I earmarked the '74 and '77 vintages as something special. This bottling has done me proud. 55.6%

Ardbeg Renaissance db (**92**) **n22.5 t22.5 f23.5 b23.5**. How fitting that the 1,200th (and almost last) new-to-market whisky I had tasted for the 2009 Bible was Renaissance... because that's what I need after tasting that lot...!! This is an Ardbeg that comes on strong, is not afraid to wield a few hefty blows and yet, paradoxically, the heavier it gets the more delicate, sophisticated and better-balanced it becomes. Enigmatically Ardbegian. 55.9%

Ardbeg Rollercoaster db (**90.5**) **n23** youthful malts dominate; a patchwork of smoke on many different levels from ashy to ethereal: almost dizzying; **t23** again, it's the young Ardbeg which dominates; the delivery is almost painful as you shake your head at the shock of the spices and unfettered peat. A genuine greenness to the malts though some natural caramels do make a smoky surge; **f23** long, buttery in part, limited sweetness; almost a touch of smoked bacon about it; **b21.5** to be honest, it was the end of another long day – and book – when I tasted this and I momentarily forgot the story behind the malt. My reaction to one of my researchers who happened to be in the tasting room was: "Bloody hell! They are sending me kids. If this was any younger I'd just be getting a bag of grist!" This malt may be a fabulous concept. And Rollercoaster is a pretty apt description, as this a dram which appears to have the whisky equivalent of Asperger's. So don't expect the kind of balance that sweeps you into a world that only Ardbeg knows. This, frankly, is not for the Ardbeg purist or snob. But for those determined to bisect the malt in all its forms and guises, it is the stuff of the most rampant hard-ons. 573%

Ardbeg Still Young 2nd release dist 1998, bott 2006 db (**93**) **n24 t24 f22 b23**. A couple of generations back – maybe even less – this would not have been so much "Still Young" as "Getting on a Bit." This is a very good natural age for an Ardbeg as the oak is making a speech, but refuses to let it go on too long. Stylish – as one might expect. And, in my books, should be a regular feature. Go on. Be bold. Be proud say it: Ardbeg Aged 8 Years. Get away from the marketing straightjacket of old age... 56.2%. ncf.

Ardbeg Supernova db (**96.5**) **n24.5** rare to find an Ardbeg which positively bristles with peat. Usually it is all smoke and mirrors: here you are steamrollered by the overwhelming peatiness – acrid at its most bruising and direct, smothering once the smoke gets to work... but never less than compelling and not least because of the freshness of the grist which sparkles like the brightest star once the cosmic peat dust has settled...; **t24** for a moment, a gentle silkiness, aided by molten, citrus-molested muscovado, fools you into thinking this is going to be easy. Soon you are jolted into the reality of this dram: it is huge! There is no burn, just a massive piling up of phenols of nuclear fission strength, which erupt around the palate offering a youthful insight into the creation of this malt and a far older tannin-stained echo of passing summers; **f23.5** the finish of a reverberating echo of the explosion before: treacle of subtle finesse, peat which still appears to consist of several different layers of intensity, cocoa still powdery and dry...it just stretches and stretches and stretches...; **b24.5** a spot on bottling which upholds the brand's unique style and never compromises: shows Ardbeg at its biggest and meanest, yet still somehow charms with wondrous intensity and ease. 55%

Ardbeg Supernova db (**97**) **n24.5** moody, atmospheric; hints and threats; Lynchian in its stark black and white forms, its meandering plot, its dark and at times indecipherable message and meaning...; **t24** at first a wall of friendly phenols but only when you stand back and see the overall picture you can get an idea just how mammoth that wall is; there are intense sugary gristy notes, then this cuts away slightly towards something more mouth-fillingly smoky but now with a hickory sweetness; a light oil captures the long, rhythmic waves, a pulse almost; **f24** gentle, sweetening cocoa notes evolve while the peat pulses... again...and again... **b24.5** apparently this was called "Supernova" in tribute of how I once described a very highly peated Ardbeg. This major beast, carrying a phenol level in excess of 100ppm, isn't quite a Supernova...much more of a Black Hole. Because once you get dragged into this one, there really is no escaping... 58.9%

Ardbeg Supernova 2010 db (**93.5**) **n24** youthful, punchy and spicy; vanillas and bananas add a sweetness to the molten peat; **t23.5** an explosion of sharp citrus and grassy malt. Not quite what was expected but the smoke and spices cause mayhem as they crash around the palate: eye-watering, safety harness-wearing stuff; **f23** the oak has a bitter-ish surprise but soft sugars compensate. Elsewhere the smoke and spice continues its rampage; **b23** there are Supernovas and there are Supernovas. Some have been going on a bit and have formed a shape and indescribable beauty with the aid of time; others are just starting off and though full of unquantifiable energy and wonder have a distance to travel. By comparison to last year's blockbusting Whisky Bible award winner, this is very much in the latter category. 60.1%

 Ardbeg Supernova 2015 db **(97) n24** gosh! Few whiskies pulse so impressively, or for quite so long, with a slight mocha subplot to the ever-interchanging peat one moment smoky, the next gritty, then acidic... Not peat on steroids, as someone once described it to me...this is far too natural and beautiful..! **t24.5** a consuming delivery: frisky, smoky, sugary, ashy, playful, stern... and naturally, as Ardbeg will, amid all the enormity, comes the counterpoint of delicate citrus...; **f24** long, with the grist still leaving behind its smoky essence, like a comet might leave its lingering tail... **b24.5** in many ways an essay in balance. This is a huge beast of a malt with seemingly insurmountable peat...until it encourages, then allows you to climb upon its back. Magnificent. 54.3%

 Ardbeg Ardbog The Ultimate db ex-Manzanilla sherry cask **(78.5) n20 t22 f17.5 b19**. The best advice one can be given about bogs is to avoid them. 52.1%. Glenmorangie PLC.

 Ardbeg Uigeadail db **(97.5) n25 t24.5 f23.5 b24.5**. Massive yet tiny. Loud yet whispering. Seemingly ordinary from the bottle, yet unforgettable. It is snowing outside my hotel room in Calgary, yet the sun, in my soul at least, is shining. I came across this bottling while lecturing the Liquor Board of British Columbia in Vancouver on May 6th 2008, so one assumes it is a Canadian market bottling. It was one of those great moments in my whisky life on a par with tasting for the first time the Old Malt Cask 1975 at a tasting in Denmark. There is no masking genius.The only Scotch to come close to this one is another from Ardbeg, Corryvreckan. That has more oomph and lays the beauty and complexity on thick...it could easily have been top dog. But this particular Uigeadail (for I have tasted another bottling this year, without pen or computer to hand and therefore unofficially, which was a couple of points down) offers something far more restrained and cerebral. Believe me: this bottling will be going for thousands at auction in the very near future, I wager. 54.2%

 Ardbeg Uigeadail db **(89) n25 t22 f20 b22**. A curious Ardbeg with a nose to die for. Some tinkering - please guys, as the re-taste is not better - regarding the finish may lift this to being a true classic 54.1%

 Cadenhead's Authentic Collection Ardbeg Aged 20 Years bourbon barrel, dist 93, bott Jun 14 **(95.5) n24.5** dry peat soot; lavender and cloves assert the age; a hint of citrus tries to lighten matters but with very limited success, especially when the cow sheds kick in; the complexity levels defy belief... **t24** soft oils ensure a friendly delivery, mainly of lightly molassed smoke. Then a much more expansive development of gently peated tannins - cue spices - but the sugars dig deep and ramp up the toasty feel: how can something so enormous be quite so gentle and refined? **f23** a little old Allied barrel bitterness accompanies the slowly fading smoked grist; **b24** as this was the 666th new Scottish malt tasted for the Bible 2015, I chose an Ardbeg from one of the most consistently excellent bottlers: I just knew it would be devilishly good.... 55.9%. 186 bottles. WB15/274

 Dun Bheagan Ardberg 15 Year Old dist Jun 98 **(96) n24** classic Ardbeg ambiguity: smoky yet light, a hint of citrus yet dry, peaty yet complex; confident yet non-threatening...; **t24** a delivery every Islayphile dreams of: pounding peat, a volley of spice, a spoonful or two of Demerara, creamy and chewy without it clogging the complexity; **f24** sweetens just the right degree as an almost bourbon liquorice depth forms. The peat remains ashy and spiced...; **b24** when's the next plane to Tokyo...? 57.5%. Bottled for 3 Rivers Tokyo.

 Hunter Laing's Old & Rare Ardbeg Aged 21 Years refill hogshead, dist Oct 93, bott Jan 15 **(94) n23** all kinds of lemon and lime at play....with some soothing – yet complex - smoke, naturally...mmm! **t24** on delivery the spices mmmm...!!! Not behind the delicate peats mmmm! Mmmm mmm mmmmm mm mmmmmmmmm mmmmm mmm smoky mmm! **f23.5** mmmmm! **b23.5** aaaarrrhhh.......! 56.4%. ncf sc. 111 bottles.

 Master of Malt Single Cask Ardbeg 23 Year Old refill bourbon hogshead, dist Feb 91, bott Jan 15 **(94.5) n23** buttery phenols make for a heavy experience; allotment bonfires on a seashore prevail...; **t24** surprisingly, it's the sugar – most pretty sharp and tart and of a processed white variety – which make the early running before the gristy phenols make up ground...; **f23.5** soft oils descend to maximise the length of the smoke's stay. Butterscotch intertwangles with the fading peat; **b24** long, and of a variety of hues and humours. Ridiculously complex....and it doesn't even try! 50.6%. sc. 216 bottles.

 Scotch Malt Whisky Society Cask 33.121 Aged 8 Years 1st fill barrel, dist 1 Jul 04 **(94.5) n24** adorable gristy smoke. Hard to better the balance between salt, malt, smoke and sugar.

The phenols are probably lower than the norm, but the complexity is right up there...; **t23.5** as expected, it is sweet, juicy, gristy barley first to cross the threshold; the spices appear to radiate from the centre outwards, the sugars solidifying in their wake; the mid-ground has some fascinating coppery moments lubricated by the softest of oils; **f23** the copper theme continues, with the spices pinging off the metallic firmness; **b24** very unusual Ardbeg which appears to be showing some recent work to a still. The smoke, though constantly heard, is merely a spectator. *59%. nc ncf sc. 243 bottles.*

◇ **That Boutique-y Whisky Company Ardbeg** batch 5 **(88.5) n22** a simple array of peat tones embedded in unusual degrees of oil; **t22.5** beautiful enough, especially with the light ulmo honey and Demerara sugar arrival. But those oils....where have they come from? **f22** oily, lightly smoked and surprisingly flat; **b22** rare to find Ardbeg this oily and docile. Delicious, but lacking anything like the distillerey's normal depth and complexity. *47.5%. 23 bottles.*

ARDMORE

Speyside, 1899. Beam Inc. Working.

Ardmore 1996 db **(87) n22 t22 f21 b22.** Very curious Ardmore, showing little of its usual dexterity. Perhaps slightly more heavily peated than the norm, but there is also much more intense heavy caramel extracted from the wood. Soft, very pleasant and easy drinking it is almost obsequious. *43%.*

Ardmore 100th Anniversary 12 Years Old dist 1986, bott 1999 db **(94) n24 t23.5 f22.5 b24.** Brilliant. Absolutely stunning, with the peat almost playing games on the palate. Had they not put caramel in this bottling, it most likely would have been an award winner. So, by this time next year, I fully expect to see every last bottle accounted for... *40%*

Ardmore 25 Years Old db **(89.5) n21 t23.5 f22.5 b22.5** a 25-y-o box of chocolates: coffee creams, fudge, orange cream...they are all in there. The nose maybe ordinary: what follows is anything but. *51.4%. ncf.*

Ardmore 30 Years Old Cask Strength db **(94) n23.5** the first time I have encountered a cough-sweetish aroma on an Ardmore but, like every aspect, it is played down and delicate. Melting sugar on porridge. Citrus notes of varying intensity. Fascinating for its apparent metal hand in velvet glove approach; **t23.5** sweet, gristy delivery even after all these years. And a squeeze of share lime, too, and no shortage of spices. Does all in its power to appear half its age. This includes blocking the oaks from over development and satisfying itself with a smoky, mocha middle; the muscovado sugars are, with the smoke, spread evenly; **f23** busy spices and a lazy build up of vanillas; **b24** I remember when the present owners of Ardmore launched their first ever distillery bottling. Over a lunch with the hierarchy there I told them, with a passion, to ease off with the caramel so the world can see just how complex this whisky can be. This brilliant, technically faultless, bottling is far more eloquent and persuasive than I was that or any other day... *53.7%. nc ncf. 1428 bottles.*

Ardmore Fully Peated Quarter Casks db **(89) n21 t23 f23 b22.** This is an astonishingly brave attempt by the new owners of Ardmore who, joy of all joys, are committed to putting this distillery in the public domain. Anyone with a 2004 copy of the Whisky Bible will see that my prayers have at last been answered. However, this bottling is for Duty Free and, due to the enormous learning curve associated with this technique, a work in progress. They have used the Quarter Cask process which has been such a spectacular success at its sister distillery Laphroaig. Here I think they have had the odd slight teething problem. Firstly, Ardmore has rarely been filled in ex-bourbon and that oak type is having an effect on the balance and smoke weight; also they have unwisely added caramel, which has flattened things further. I don't expect the caramel to be in later bottlings and, likewise, I think the bourbon edge might be purposely blunted a little. But for a first attempt this is seriously big whisky that shows enormous promise. When they get this right, it could – and should – be a superstar. Now I await the more traditional vintage bottlings... *46%. ncf.*

◇ **Ardmore Legacy** db **(71.5) n17 t19 f17.5 b18.** Must win an award as the most disappointing whisky of the year. Not least because this is one of the world's great distilleries. The nose is dirty and off-key. After a too brief fight back on delivery, it soon descends on the palate to the same mess found on the nose. As this distillery's first and oldest advocate, frankly, for me, a massive shock and disappointment. *40%*

Ardmore Traditional Cask db **(88.5) n21.5 t22 f23 b22.** Not quite what I expected. "Jim. Any ideas on improving the flavour profile?" asked the nice man from Ardmore distillery when they were originally launching the thing. "Yes. Cut out the caramel." "Ah, right..." So what do I find when the next bottling comes along? More caramel. It's good to have influence... Actually, I can't quite tell if this is a result of natural caramelization from the quarter casking or just an extra dollop of the stuff in the bottling hall. The result is pretty similar: some of the finer complexity is lost. My guess, due to an extra fraction of sweetness and spice, is that it is the former. All that said, the overall experience remains quite beautiful. And this remains one of my top ten distilleries in the world. *46%. ncf.*

Teacher's Highland Single Malt quarter cask finish db **(89)** n22.5 t23 f21.5 b22. This is Ardmore at its very peatiest. And had not the colouring levels been heavily tweaked to meet the flawed perceptions of what some markets believe makes a good whisky, this malt would have been better still. As it is: superb. With the potential of achieving greatness if only they have the confidence and courage... *40%. India/Far East Travel Retail exclusive.*

⬥ **Adelphi Selection Ardmore 2000 14 Year Old** cask no. 245 **(93)** n23.5 I think they'll have to rename Arbroath Smokies Ardmore Smokies...though this one has been served up on the plate with a little treacle as a side dish; t23.5 good grief!! That hint of sugar on the nose comes at you like the Aberdeen Express....which happens not to be stopping at your station. A mighty whoosh of maple syrup, lightly doused in phenols; f22.5 a mild degree of bitterness escapes from the oak. But the spices tingle and the genteel smoke caresses; b23.5 a very good insight to a great distillery. *55.6%. 157 bottles. WB16/009*

⬥ **Anam na h-Alba The Soul of Scotland Ardmore 2000** bourbon cask, dist Jun 00, bott May 14 **(90)** n22 half-hearted smoke – even by Ardmore's gentle standards. Superb light pear, vanilla and icing sugar mix; t23.5 an elegant caress of smoke then a wonderful run through varying sugar tones, though grist leads the way. With the sap rising, these tend to get weightier and darker in style. Excellent spice, too; f22 tannin leads, the last vestiges of smoke follows; b22.5 distilled on a low peating day, the sugars have taken the opportunity to star. Elegant malt. *52.9%. 88 bottles.*

⬥ **Alexander Murray & Co Ardmore 2000 13 Years Old** **(87.5)** n22 t22.5 f21.5 b21.5. A dusty smokiness on the nose is followed by a chewy smokiness on delivery. Strangely bitter towards the end, and a general lack of sparkle for an Ardmore this age. *40%*

⬥ **Chieftain's Ardmore Aged 21 Years** barrel, dist Jun 92, bott Jun 14 **(89.5)** n22.5 a vague smokiness fails to interrupt the citrusy theme; t23.5 probably the softest delivery I've found this year: spices make a bigger impact, like stones skimming over a placid lake; f21 bitters out slightly; b22.5 some of the smoke has been replaced by pure silk... *46%. nc ncf.*

⬥ **Crom Ardmore 13 Years Old Warlords & Warriors Edition Peated** sherry hogshead, dist Apr 01, bott Aug 14 **(92.5)** n23 lightly smoked but more heavily oaked; t23.5 salivating malt with a warming, sugary second wave; the malt remains crisp throughout; f23 a light marmalade twist to the finish; the malt remains thick and chewy to the end, while the spices continue to buzz; b23 a slightly more angular and fruity Ardmore bottling than most. Delicious, though! *56.4% sc*

⬥ **Glen Fahrn Airline Nr 11 Ardmore 1992 Aged 20** Years cask no. 4957 **(87)** n22 t22 f21 b22. Sssh! Don't nose this too loudly: you might wake it up. A docile dram where the peat is on the low side and tannins dominate late on. Pleasant, oily, sweet.... and soporific. *51.4%. sc. 236 bottles.*

⬥ **Gordon & MacPhail Distillery Label Ardmore 1996 (92)** n23.5 relaxed peat works well with the minty vanilla; even a little dried date has crept in from the sugars; expect some oak further down the line as the big tannin is here to stay; t23.5 the smoke works wonderfully with the sugars to help form a cocoa-covered fudge, with a bit of molasses thrown in to add some weighty drama; f22 some serious oak bite shows that age has caught up with this a little; b23 even when the oak is beginning to get the upper hand, this distillery has the charisma to charm you into pouring another glass before you know you've done it... *43%*

Old Masters Ardmore 14 Years Old cask no. 217, dist 2000, bott 2014 **(89.5)** n23 lightly minted smoke: it really doesn't come more delicate than this...; t23.5 the peat arrives early, though plays second fiddle to the combination of mouth-watering grist and sharper crystalised sugars; f21 good spice but shame about the "Allied bitterness"...; b22 without the cask blemish – common amongst casks from its previous owners – this really would have been a gem. *58.3%.*

Old Particular Highland Ardmore 14 Years Old refill barrel, cask no. 10359, dist May 00, bott May 14 **(89)** n22 a high peat register on this; displays a Love Heart candy fizziness, with the barley showing an unsuspected fruity quality; t22 light oils travel far taking some major sugars and even a degree of delicate tannin with it. The smoke quietly celebrates its powers; f23 at first a whisper, a highly attractive touch of everything...and nothing. Even the peat has backed off, but retains an elegant presence as a charming degree of mocha grows; b22 from a barrel made from the same oak from which The Ark was probably built from, this near colourless Ardmore shows certain properties at this age perhaps never before commercially seen... *48.4%. nc ncf sc. 176 bottles.*

⬥ **Old Particular Highland Ardmore 14 Years Old** refill barrel, cask no. 10593, dist May 00, bott Dec 14 **(94.5)** n23.5 busy: playful smoke initially lightened by citrus, but the peat increases its depth; t24 now when you picture Ardmore at this age in your mind's eye, you get something like this: teasing smoke, vaguely gristy sugar and outstanding layering. You don't picture the big spice explosion, though! **f23.5** fabulous finale: the Venezuelan cocoa is topped up with more of the same; **b23.5** does its best to impersonate Talisker – complete with insane spices. Superb. 48.4%. nc ncf sc. 195 bottles.

Provenance Ardmore 'Young & Feisty' cask no. 9879, bott summer 2013 **(84) n22 t20 f21.5 b20.5** Anyone who knows this distillery will half expect what they get here from a spirit so young it is virtually unborn. Rock hard on the palate and no shortage of dry, sooty smoke on the finale. 46%. nc ncf sc. Douglas Laing & Co.

Scotch Malt Whisky Society Cask 66.46 Aged 11 Years refill butt, dist 17 Jul 02 **(72.5) n21 t22 f12.5 b17.** In my mind Ardmore is one of the best distilleries in Scotland, and probably the most unsung. And I adore non-sulphured sherry. So why doesn't this work, then? Well, apart from the fact it is not entirely free of the venomous S word (the fuzzy finale confirms that), this is just too gloopy and gungy, meaning the sugars really are sickly and over the top. An intermittently pleasant exp/erience. But a poor substitute for the old butts of a generation back. 56.7%. nc ncf sc. 440 bottles.

◇ **Scotch Malt Whisky Society Cask 66.60 Aged 12 Years** refill barrel, dist 26 Nov 01 **(95.5) n24** not sure how a peated malt can come any more subtle than this. Takes a few moments for the smoke to actually register, but once it does it begins to build in weight... though never anything more than a tease. A gentle lemon and lime sub strata bolsters the barley thread. But it is pastel shading and whispers all the way...; **t23.5** the palate is massaged by a gently oily, vaguely lush, smoked gristiness, though the sugars are already being dulled by early arriving oak; **f24** soft Columbian cocoa and softer Columbian coffee, all very lightly smoked and spiced; **b24** ridiculously sexy malt. 56.5%. sc. 228 bottles.

The Pearls of Scotland Ardmore 1988 25 Year Old cask no. 2455, dist Apr 88, bott Feb 14 **(95.5) n23.5** they were running low on peat the day this was made...some beautiful floral, citrus and earthy notes nonetheless; **t24.5** ah-ha! The delivery, at first swirling in a rich whirlpool of salty barley, reveals its truer, smokier self. It remains a gentle phenol attack, though it intensifies to enormous satisfaction. The lighter, more lemon-clad elements, appear to have been discarded for a busier spicier sub plot. It perhaps the weight and sublime balance, though, which sets this apart as something a little special; **f23.5** long, with some buzzing, peat-stained spices homing in on the vanilla; **b24** superb, near faultless, whisky. Takes a long time before the Ardmore make up is applied. 45%.

The Whisky Cask Ardmore Aged 13 Years peated, bourbon cask, dist 2000, bott 2013 **(86.5) n22 t23 f20 b21.5** Sweet and malty, undone slightly by the not uncommon "Allied Bitterness" at the death. Most remarkable, though, is the lightness of touch of the smoke: barely discernable on the nose and though found on the finish, not in force to overcome the fault lines. 57%. nc ncf.

◇ **World of Orchids Ardmore 2000 13 Year Old** bourbon cask **(95.5) n23.5 t23.5 f24 b24.5.** An adorable Ardmore! This is from slightly above the norm peating stock. But the secret is the balance, helped along by a confident degree of oil and some dazzling peppery spices. The deft molasses also makes a massive contribution. Truly superb whisky. 57%. 119 bottles.

AUCHENTOSHAN
Lowlands, 1800. Morrison Bowmore. Working.

Auchentoshan 10 Years Old db **(81) n22 t21 f19 b19.** Much better, maltier, cleaner nose than before. But after the initial barley surge on the palate it shows a much thinner character. 40%

Auchentoshan 12 Years Old db **(91.5) n22.5** sexy fruit element – citrus and apples in particular – perfectly lightens the rich, oily barley; **t23.5** oily and buttery; intense barley carrying delicate marzipan and vanilla; **f22.5** simplistic, but the oils keep matters lush and the delicate sugars do the rest; **b23** a delicious malt very much happier with itself than it has been for a while. 40%

Auchentoshan 14 Years Old Cooper's Reserve db **(83.5) n20 t21.5 f21 b21.** Malty, a little nutty and juicy in part. 46%. ncf.

Auchentoshan 21 Years Old db **(93) n23.5** a sprig of mint buried in barely warmed peat, all with an undercoat of the most delicate honeys; **t23** velvety and waif-like, the barley-honey theme is played out is hushed tones and unspoiled elegance; **f23** the smoke deftly returns as the vanillas and citrus slowly rise but the gentle honey-barley plays to the end, despite the shy introduction of cocoa; **b23.5** one of the finest Lowland distillery bottlings of our time. A near faultless masterpiece of astonishing complexity to be cherished and discussed with deserved reverence. So delicate, you fear that sniffing too hard will break the poor thing...! 43%.

Auchentoshan 1975 db (88) n22.5 a soft, pliable nose: no bites or nibbles. Just orange and caramel...; only as the glass dries does the enormity of the oak begin to reveal itself; t22.5 takes time before the age begins to tell: after a silky, if slightly untaxing, start the tannins and spices begin to roll over the palate; sharp sugars spike here and there; f21 back to sleep with the caramel, though a little spice does pulse; b22 goes heavy on the natural caramels. Does not even remotely show its enormous age for this distillery. I detest the word "smooth". But for those who prefer that kind of malt...well, your dreams have come true...; 45.6%

Auchentoshan 1977 Sherry Cask Matured oloroso sherry cask db (89) n23 t22 f22 b22. Rich, creamy and spicy. Almost a digestive biscuit mealiness with a sharp marmalade spread. 49%. sc. Morrison Bowmore. 240 bottles.

Auchentoshan 1979 db (94) n23.5 very well aged Christmas fruit cake. With an extra thick layer of top quality marzipan; t24 sumptuous delivery with the burnt raisin biting deep; bursting with juicy barley; f23 long with the emphasis on the dryness of the sherry; b23.5 it's amazing what a near faultless sherry butt can do. 50.1%

◈ **Auchentoshan 1988 25 Year Old Wine Cask Finish** db (94.5) n23 a fresh mix of grape juice and headier dessert wine mingles with polite but drier oak; t24 gorgeous delivery with a massive crashing of almost syrupy fruit sugars and buzzing spices...a wonderful busyness. Excellent oak layering highlights the age; f23.5 much drier, almost biscuity. All kinds of caramels and cocoa at work, too; b24 the thing about a triple distilled malt is that a confident influence can have a very loud say. And the clean wine here certainly calls the shots, though some pretty high quality oak ensures the speech is balanced. A delightful malt which makes a very respectful nod to the combined skills of distiller, wood manager and blender. 48%

Auchentoshan 1998 Sherry Cask Matured fino sherry cask db (81.5) n21 t22 f18.5 b20. A genuine shame. Before these casks were treated in Jerez, I imagine they were spectacular. Even with the obvious faults apparent, the nuttiness is profound and milks every last atom of the oils at work to maximum effect. The sugars, also, are delicate and gorgeously weighted. There is still much which is excellent to concentrate on here. 54.6%. ncf. 6000 bottles.

Auchentoshan American Oak db (85.5) n21.5 t22 f20.5 b21.5. Very curious: reminds me very much of Penderyn Welsh whisky before it hits the Madeira casks. Quite creamy with some toasted honeycomb making a brief cameo appearance. 40%

Auchentoshan Classic db (80) n19 t20 f21 b20. Classic what exactly...? Some really decent barley, but goes little further. 40%

Auchentoshan Select db (85) n20 t21.5 f22 b21.5. Has changed shape of late, if not quality. Much more emphasis on the enjoyable juicy barley sharpness these days. 40%

Auchentoshan Silveroak 1990 Limited Release db (94.5) n23.5 t23 f24 b24. Okay... tasting pretty blind on this: have only the sample bottle, showing the name of the brand and the strength, but no accompanying production notes. Appears to have good age, probably above 17, and the sherry butts used here (and I don't think it is exclusively wine oak at work) are of rare high quality for these days. Appears to have the imprint of outstanding blender Rachael Barry. 50.9%. Exclusive for Global Travel Retail.

Auchentoshan Solera db (88) n23 t22 f22 b21. Enormous grape input and enjoyable for all its single mindedness. Will benefit when a better balance with the malt is struck. 48%. ncf.

Auchentoshan Three Wood db (76) n20 t18 f20 b18. Takes you directly into the rough. Refuses to harmonise, except maybe for some late molassed sugar. 43%

Auchentoshan Virgin Oak db (92) n23.5 like a busy bourbon with the accent on the buzzing small grains: all the regulation manuka honey and liquorice there in respectful amounts; t23 big, sugary delivery, but a cushion of hickory and vanilla keeps the sweetness under control; a little molasses adds extra weight to the middle; f22.5 pretty dry, with a bit of a coppery sheen, as though some work had recently been done to a still; b23 not quite how I've seen 'Toshan perform before: but would love to see it again! 46%

◈ **Anam na h-Alba The Soul of Scotland Auchentoshan 1998** sherry cask, dist Feb 98, bott May 15 (78) n18 t22 f18 b20. Big sherry signature, deliciously so on delivery. But, sadly, smudged a little by sulphur. 50.7%. 150 bottles.

Cadenhead's Authentic Collection Auchentoshan Aged 24 Years bourbon barrel, dist 90, bott Jun 14 (88) n22 t24.5 f20 b21.5. The high point is the delivery: fabulously juicy and defying the years. But here we have the unusual case of an Auchentoshan being let down by the cask, rather than the other way round as the slight milkiness on the nose develops into a minor fault on the finale as the cask tires beyond endurance. 52.3%. 150 bottles. WB15/273

Hepburn's Choice Auchentoshan 2001 Aged 12 Years refill hogshead, bott 2014 (88) n22 still some youth to be found; thin, fruity with barely an oaky breeze to be felt; t23 clean, refreshing, gorgeously salivating barley; f21 thins out to the vanilla-clad bone; b22 almost certainly a third fill cask. Yet no signs of tiredness causing damage and a lovely study of an unusual distillery virtually disrobed. 46%. nc ncf sc. 372 bottles. WB15/063

Hepburn's Choice Auchentoshan 2002 Aged 11 Years refill hogshead, dist 2002, bott 2014 **(86) n22 t22 f20.5 b21.5.** The oak has barely scratched the surface of this blond bombshell. Has the build and personality of a malt half its age so there can be no surprise that the barley dominates from beginning to end. *46%. nc ncf sc. 182 bottles.*

⟡ **Hepburn's Choice Auchentoshan Aged 12 Years** refill hogshead, dist 2002, bott 2015 **(83) n20 t21.5 f21 b20.5.** Malty but rather too light and lacking in substance: triple distilled but under matured. *46%. nc ncf sc. 378 bottles.*

⟡ **Kingsbury Gold Auchentoshan 16 Year Old 1997** hogshead, cask no. 10370 **(94) n23** beautiful gooseberry jam; **t24** one of the most heavy-bodied, intensely malty and generously spiced 'Toshan's I've ever encountered; **f23.5** the thick malt plays out with chewy panache: where did all this weight come from...? **b23.5** amazed: sampled blind, would not have recognised it as a 'Toshan in a 1,000 tastings...*53.5%. 308 bottles.*

Old Malt Cask Auchentoshan Aged 16 Years refill hogshead, cask no. 10739, dist Oct 97, bott Jul 14 **(84.5) n21 t21.5 f21 b21.** Malty to an almost ridiculous degree but a little bit thin and incendiary. *50%. nc ncf sc. 299 bottles.*

⟡ **Old Malt Cask Auchentoshan 17 Years Old** refill hogshead, cask no. 10890, dist Oct 97, bott Feb 15 **(90.5) n23** soft malt, yet beautifully textured and full. A slight herbal note to the delicate vanilla; **t23** much fuller now. The sub-current of vanilla appears to give an impression of primness. But the malt, as on the nose, has a deceptively rich texture; **f22** reverts to a more gristy feel; excellent late spice; **b22.5** so elegant. *50%. nc ncf sc. 313 bottles.*

Old Masters Auchentoshan 15 Year Old cask no. 102339, dist 1998, bott 2014 **(87.5) n21.5 t22 f21 b22.** Clean lemon-zesty but equally hot and thin. Salivation levels are raised but austere oak counters any complexity build. Pleasant enough, though. *60.5%.*

Old Particular Lowland Auhentoshan 16 Years Old refill hogshead, cask no. 10201, dist Nov 1997, bott Jan 2014 **(90.5) n22** bubbling nose, spikey and sparky with excellent malt-oak integration; **t23.5** launches on the palate with a big malty flourish; **f22.5** thins but now the lemon sherbet kicks in; **b22.5** effervescent but with a light touch *48.4%. nc ncf sc. 357 bottles.*

⟡ **Old Particular Lowland Auchentoshan 17 Years Old** refill hogshead, cask no. 10555, dist Nov 97, bott Dec 14 **(89) n23** lemon drizzle cake, with sawdust for icing sugar; **t22** lively, fizzy, juicy, but with the oak hardly wiping its feet before entering; **f22** dry and spicy; **b22** just enough malty body to carry the oak. *48.4%. nc ncf sc. 350 bottles.*

⟡ **Old Particular Auchentoshan 14 Years Old** refill hogshead, cask no. 10716, dist Sept 00, bott Feb 15 **(91) n23** gloriously intense malt – not unlike a night-time sleeping draught; **t23** thick malt, unusually creamy textured with a light citrus tint; **f22.5** a slow interplay between confident malt and gentle oak; **b22.5** a more compact and richer-bodied example from this distillery than most. *48.4%. nc ncf sc. 324 bottles.*

⟡ **The Pearls of Scotland Auchentoshan 1998** cask no. 2197, dist Sept 98, bott May 15 **(93) n23.5** you'll be taken aback by the enormity of the malt; spices and malted milk biscuits pitch in; **t24** no less intense on delivery – actually even more so with the barley coming through at its most distinguished and clean. Almost one dimensional, but what a dimension...! **f23** the concentrated grist and the surprise manuka honey make for a thumping send off; **b23** rare to find the distillery this chunky and weighty. *55.3%. sc.*

Provenance Auchentoshan Over 12 Years hoghshead, cask no. 9755, dist Autumn 00, bott Spring 13 **(87.5) n21.5 t23 f21 b22.** Clearly from the same stable as cask 9311. Except this has a little more oomph and much better use of sugars. *46%. nc ncf sc.*

⟡ **Scotch Malt Whisky Society Cask 5.42 Aged 13 Years** refill hogshead, dist 11 Oct 00 **(81.5) n20 t20 f21.5 b20.** Thin, niggardly and mean of spirit. Gives up what little malt and honey it possesses with hot, ungracious parsimony. *59.5%. sc. 274 bottles.*

Single Cask Collection 1995 Auchentoshan 17 Year Old sherry butt, dist 1995 **(91) n22.5** heady grape outweighs the half-hearted malt; **t23** a chewy delivery- not the norm for this distillery! The spices attached to the sultana is some treat; **f22.5** dries towards fruit and custard; **b23** that rarest of beasts in Scotland: the sherry butt entirely free of sulphur. Congratulations on producing a real whisky... *53.5%. sc. Single Cask Collection.*

Signatory Vintage Un-Chillfiltered Collection Auchentoshan 1997 Aged 15 Years bourbon barrels, cask no. 101832+101833, dist 17 Dec 97, bott 26 Feb 13 **(91.5) n22.5** a little celery and vanilla combine well; **t23** unusually oily for a 'Toshan: fat malt carries the muscovado easily; **f22.5** traces of citrus on the broad vanilla; dries, but with aplomb; **b23.5** a quite lovely pairing of barrels gives a rarely-found sheen to this Lowlander. Almost perfect spice involvement. Quality. *46%. nc ncf. 654 bottles. WB15/028*

Wemyss Malts 1998 Single Lowland Auchentoshan "Lemon Zest" bott 2013 **(78.5) n19 t20 f19 b19.5.** I for one very much enjoy Wemyss' contribution to the whisky world. But am left more than confused by many of their bizarre descriptors of their whisky. This, with their "Lemon Zest" is like so many others in being not even close to the actual character of the malt they have bottled. Not a single atom of citrus to be found anywhere and the unwelcome earthiness of the cask is countered only by some thin sugars. *46%. sc. 342 bottles.*

Wemyss Malts 1998 Single Lowland Auchentoshan "Summer Fruit Cup" barrel, dist 98, bott 14 **(88) n22** a tube of fruit pastilles; **t22.5** salivating, deliciously malty but a little fiery nip; **f21.5** thins out as vanilla moves in; **b22** a bottling where the triple distillation is very apparent. *46%. sc. 295 bottles.*

Wemyss Malts 1998 Single Lowland Auchentoshan "Tarte Au Citron" dist 1998 bott 2013 **(96) n23.5** delicate and multi complex with clever layering of vanilla – almost to ice cream proportions – complete with the drier wafer cone; **t24** stunning texture and weight. Oiler than to be expected with some tangerine cutting through the gristy butterscotch; **f24** a marvellous display of controlled oak, at times almost on a bourbon liquorice level; **b24.5** a distillery classic with neither a false step nor the vaguest hint of a weakness: simply a complex delight...! *46%. Sc. 342 bottles.*

◈ **Whisky Fair Auchentoshan 23 Year Old** bourbon barrel, dist 1992, bott 2015 **(88.5) n23** beautifully demure and complex: confident, dry oak which offsets the clementine and honeyed barley; **t22.5** early juicy barley is soon extinguished by marauding oak. Good spice; **f21** heavy tannin; **b22** with such a light body, oak encircles the malt threateningly. But just enough sugar to do the job. *46.3%. 69 bottles.*

◈ **Whisky-Fässle Auchentoshan 21 Year Old** sherry hogshead, dist 1992, bott 2014 **(88) n23** a dessert wine sweetness and passion fruit and mango sharpness; **t23** a thin body and some weird, chalky tones. But bailed out by the integrity of the grape; **f20** just a little sulphur buzz on the finale; **b22** good, clean grape until it falls at the very last hurdle. *52.1%. nc ncf.*

◈ **Whisky-Fässle Auchentoshan 23 Year Old** hogshead, dist 1990, bott 2014 **(92) n22** malty, hazelnut and milky chocolate; **t23** gorgeous delivery: flinty barley sugar and superb spice; **f23.5** a long tail of intense barley. Late and delicious coffee cake; outstanding malts to the very end; **b23.5** neat, tidy, beautifully clean and nutty. A must experience charmer. *47.7%. nc ncf.*

◈ **Whisky Tales Auchentoshan Aged 19 Years** sherry cask, dist 1995, bott 2015 **(90) n22** wonderful, lively nip to the spice as it bursts through the toffee; **t23** beautifully intense: a real chewy bit of spiced fruit fudge; **f22.5** long, with the oak radiating some decent late honey... and spice, of course; **b22.5** 'Toshan showing a little muscle and grace. Delicious. *48%. nc ncf sc. 110 bottles.*

AUCHROISK
Speyside, 1974. Diageo. Working.

Auchroisk Aged 10 Years db **(84) n20 t22 f21 b21.** Tangy orange on the nose, the malt amplified by a curious saltiness on the palate. *43%. Flora and Fauna.*

Auchroisk 30 Years Old Special Release 2012 American and European Oak refill casks, dist 1982, bott 2012 db **(91.5) n22** borderline bourbon with a wonderful hickory and liquorice edge to the duller fruit; **t23** outstanding delivery with a mouth feel to die for; the spices buzz busily and with intent, but can never get the better of the soft oils, layered hickory and dried molasses; **f23** the oils intensify, even with a degree of rum-like esters allowing the oak to surge without causing damage; **b23.5** a hugely – and surprisingly - impressive singleton of tannins. *54.7%. nc ncf. Diageo.*

Auchroisk Special Release 2010 20 Years Old American and European oak db **(89) n22.5 t22 f22.5 b22.** Can't say I have ever seen Auchroisk quite in this mood before. Some excellent cask selection here. *58.1%. nc ncf. Diageo. Fewer than 6000 bottles.*

Berry's Own Selection Auchroisk 1991 Aged 21 Years cask 7476, bott 2013 **(87.5) n21.5 t22.5 f21.5 b22.** A juicy, attractive and very simple ensemble of malt and toffee. *52.1%. WB15/240*

Berry's Own Selection Auchroisk 2000 Aged 14 Years cask no. 20, bott 2014 **(85.5) n21.5 t22 f21 b21.** A light, clean run of the mill Speyside-style dram with all the emphasis on the barley and, though pleasant and without fault, very timid and has little of interest to say. *46%. ncf ncf. WB15/251*

Cadenhead's Small Batch Auchroisk Aged 24 Years butts, dist 1989, bott 2014 **(71) n19 t19 f16 b17.** Spicy. Lush. And fatally furry. A crying shame as the grapey intensity of the butts is something to genuinely behold. *57.5%. 1140 bottles. WB15/086*

Càrn Mòr Strictly Limited Edition Auchroisk Aged 13 Years hogshead, dist 2000, bott 2014 **(88.5) n21** rather too light for greatness with thin Lincoln biscuit and a hint of mallow; **t23** just doesn't cleaner on delivery: crystalline barley which multiply in intensity. Something alluringly gristy about the sweetness; **f22.5** simple vanilla; **b22** blenders' delight being so clean and graceful. Stands up well as a singleton, too... *46%. nc ncf. WB15/064*

◇ **Deerstalker Auchroisk Limited Release 1997 aged 16 years, 9 months** (84.5) n20.5 t22.5 f20.5 b21. Although not a distillery that naturally lends itself to brilliance, for a few brief moments on delivery it has a fair crack at it. While the thin nose and finish are, at best, average, there is a serious yumminess to the entry of the youthful barley and accompanying sugars. The spices don't hurt, either. *48%. nc ncf.*

◇ **Drams By Dramtime Auchroisk 14 Year Old 1999** sherry hogshead, dist 3 Dec 99, bott 21 Oct 14 (93) n23 lush grape: clean, intense with an enticing salty nip; t23.5 a knife and fork might be useful to cut through the seasoned sultana. A surprising, vague phenol note followed by some zippy spices; a half-hearted juiciness adds a degree of levity; f23 long, with spices showing more of an oak bent by the minute...; b23.5 amazing the beauty that can be had from a clean, top-notch wine cask. *46%. nc ncf sc. 63 bottles.*

Hepburn's Choice Auchroisk Aged 12 Years refill hogshead, dist 01, bott 14 (87) n21.5 t22 f22 b21.5. One of the lightest of all Scotland's malts. The singular fresh barley theme is pretty attractive. *46%. 367 bottles.*

Old Malt Cask Auchroisk Aged 18 Years refill hogshead, cask no. 9877, bott Oct 94, dist Jun 13 (76) n20 t19 f18 b19. After all these years the malt has little to thank the cask for... *50%. nc ncf sc. 311 bottles.*

◇ **Old Malt Cask Auchroisk 21 Years Old** refill hogshead, cask no. 11238, dist Jan 94, bott Feb 15 (90) n22 beautiful vanilla fully underlines the age. The malt is clean, confident and true..; t23 wow! Didn't expect that! The malt is full-bodied and lush and copes with the oak and spice with consummate ease; f22.5 long, with the malt and vanilla happily taking turns to lead the way; b22.5 a beautiful – and unusual - example of this distillery going into well weighted malty overdrive. Simple, but wonderfully effective. *50%. nc ncf sc. 264 bottles.*

◇ **Old Particular Speyside Auchroisk 16 Years Old** refill hogshead, cask no. 10572, dist May 98, bott Dec 14 (87.5) n20 t22.5 f22.5 b22.5. From the lackadaisical nose, and knowing the distillery as well I do, I expected very little. But ended up with so much more! One of the maltiest and juiciest Speysiders you will find this year which makes up for its lack of complexity with a barley-rich charm offensive. Clean and rather lovely. *48.4%. nc ncf sc. 273 bottles.*

Old Particular Speyside Auchroisk 18 Years Old refill hogshead, cask no. 9899, dist Oct 94 bott Aug 13 (85.5) n22.5 t22 f20 b21. Makes little effort other than to maximise the maltiness on the nose and delivery. Thins rather a little too quickly, as is this distillery's wont. But the citrusy elegance of the nose is some compensation. *48.4%. nc ncf sc. 335 bottles. Douglas Laing & Co.*

Old Particular Speyside Auchroisk 20 Years Old refill hogshead, cask no. 10341, dist Apr 94, bott May 14 (84) n21.5 t21 f20.5 b21. A malt which struggles to handle the tannins... *50.1%. nc ncf sc. 312 bottles.*

Robert Graham 17 Year Old Speyside Malts cask no. 1977, bott Nov 2013 (83) n19 t22 f21 b21. Possibly a third fill cask containing one of Speyside's thinnest whiskies. And though there is a genuine sense of a malt undercooked, you cannot but enjoy the freshness of the barley. *49.8%. ncf sc. Cask strength, 252 bottles.*

◇ **Scotch Malt Whisky Society Cask 95.17 Aged 23 Years** refill barrel, dist 25 Jun 90 (88.5) n23 a subtle fruitiness, even with a few strawberries in the offing. Creamy Swiss roll, too; t21.5 a nod towards the trademark house austerity but a big malty blast lifts it; f22 good malt/oak interplay; b22 an unspectacular but often pleasing Speysider. *49.5%. sc. 66 bottles.*

◇ **Whisky-Fässle Auchroisk 22 Year Old** sherry cask, dist 1990, bott 2013 (94.5) n23.5 t23.5 f24 b23.5. If you can track this bottle down, get it! This is one of the last true sherry butts to be brought to Scotland before sulphur treatment became standard practice and ruined an entire generation of sherry butts. The spirit is so insignificant, it barely counts, other than to add just enough background texture as to ensure balance. No, this is all about the sherry butt, showing a depth of intensity and clarity which became lost for over 20 years... *49.8%. nc ncf.*

AULTMORE
Speyside, 1896. John Dewar & Sons. Working.

Aultmore 12 Years Old db (86) n22 t22 f20 b22. Do any of you remember the old DCL distillery bottling of this from, what, 25 years ago? Well, this is nothing like it. *40%*

◇ **Aultmore 12 Year Old** db (85.5) n22 t22 f20 b21.5. Not quite firing on all cylinders due to the uncomfortably tangy oak. But relish the creamy malt for the barley is the theme of choice and for its sheer intensity alone, it doesn't disappoint; a little ulmo honey and marzipan doff their cap to the kinder vanillas. *46% WB16/028*

◇ **Aultmore 25 Year Old** db (92.5) n23 intense aroma, full of buttery sugars and fruity fudge; t23.5 those toasted sugars get off to a flyer. The malt won't be outdone and injects a stunning degree of salivation. Gorgeously roasty, or maybe like a cake with a high molasses content; **f23** runs long, runs deep....the tannins show not a hint of aggression or discomfort; **b23** now here's a curiosity: this is the first brand I have ever encountered which on the label lists the seasons the distillery was silent (1917-19, 1943-45, 1970-71) like a football club would once list on the front page of their official programme the years they won the FA Cup! Strange, but rather charming. And as for the whisky: succulent stuff!! 46% WB16/029

Cadenhead's Small Batch Aultmore-Glenlivet Aged 17 Years bourbon hogsheads, dist 97, bott 14 **(88) n22** lemon sherbet...and hints of coal; **t22.5** lively delivery: eye-watering barley with an off-centre bitter note from the oak; **f21** a little too bitter but the toffee-vanilla works well; **b22.5** most whiskies would succumb to the tightness of the bitter oak. But this is so well endowed with explosive barley and lightly sugared citrus, it gets away with it. Some great moments. 54.9%. 450 bottles. WB15/261

Darkness! Aultmore Aged 16 Years Oloroso Cask Finish (94) n23 a nose from the old school of faultless oloroso: spiced, dripping in molasses yet a malty sub strata is there for enjoyment; **t24** truly magnificent delivery: over ripe plums, thinned a little by greengages. Juicy dates and scorched raisins abound. Meanwhile spices buzz, while a little sherry trifle hits the mark; **f23.5** malty, a tad salty and now vanilla joins the fruity fray; **b23.5** once I might have called this top heavy with sherry. But after the nightmare of the last decade it would be churlish to find too much fault with this new cask from the past.... 53.6%. 81 bottles. WB15/203

Gordon & MacPhail Connoisseurs Choice Aultmore dist 2000, bott 2013 **(91) n22** gooseberries and grass; **t24** fabulous weight: juicy fresh barley in golden syrup. Back to gooseberries again – uncooked and bursting at the seams; **f22** just bitters a little at the fade as some unfriendly oak gets a small foothold; **b23** the kind of malt I can drink all day and every day. Just so wonderfully refreshing and alive. 46%. nc ncf. WB15/145

◈ **Master of Malt Single Cask Aultmore 5 Year Old** sherry hogshead, dist May 06, bott Apr 15 **(81.5) n19 t22 f20 b20.5**. Young, malty and underdeveloped, though has matured long enough to pick up some late bitterness. 65.4%. sc. 122 bottles.

Master of Malt Single Cask Aultmore 20 Years Old refill, dist 10 Oct 91, bott 1 Jun 12 **(92) n21.5** sawdust-dry oak; sharp malt; **t24** massively pleasing delivery with the palate being washed by magnificently intense barley, some of it salivating. Pepped by spice and oak. Simple, but gloriously effective; **f23** an elegant and now intrinsically complex fade, long and with the malt and vanilla on equal terms; **b23.5** only 20 bottles of this stuff, so hardly surprising it took us two years to track one down. Worth the search. 54.4%. sc. WB15/211

Old Malt Cask Aultmore Aged 21 Years refill hogshead, cask no. 9869, dist Sept 91, bott Jul 13 **(81) n19 t22 f19 b20**. 50% A bit of a shame: the delivery shows just how up for it the barley is, so fresh, clean and salivating is is. However, the nose and finish are clear indicators of a cask with just a little too much extracted in previous lives. 50%. nc ncf sc.

Provenance Aultmore 'Commemorative 1,000 Bottlings' Over 5 Years dark sherry casks **(77) n19 t21 f18 b19** A young sherry cask, presumably. A good try, but hmmm... 50%. nc ncf sc. Douglas Laing & Co.

Scotch Malt Whisky Society Cask 73.61 Aged 24 Years refill butt, dist 31 May 89 **(95.5) n23.5** both rugged and relaxing within the same sniff: the light fruits mingle with ease in the company of a craftman's sawdust and a batsman's linseed; the toasted hazelnuts tops off the experience; **t24.5** truly masterful delivery. The barley is in its most concentrated form, yet softened and encrusted in a toasted raisin case....almost a hint of Eccles cake about this. Crisp, chunky, mind-blowingly intense..yet with an elegant softness; **f23.5** long, spiced and immensely satisfying; **b24** the kind of malt which makes you purr... Truly superb. 57.1%. nc ncf sc. 521 bottles.

Scotch Malt Whisky Society Cask 73.62 Aged 24 Years dist 31 May 89 **(83.5) n21 t22 f19 b21.5**. Superficially very similar to 73.61. But look closely and the cracks appear, especially with the light yet tight, furry, finale. Excellent spice, though. 57.8%. nc ncf sc. 386 bottles.

That Boutique-y Whisky Aultmore batch 3 **(88) n21.5** dry: sandalwood and malt; **t23** resounding barley with a Malteser candy feel; **f21.5** reverts to the nose in style; **b22** understated and malty. 53.2%. 175 bottles. WB15/194

That Boutique-y Whisky Aultmore batch 4 **(89) n21.5 t23 f22.5 b22.5**. Very similar in style to Batch 4 but with a little extra spice and mid-ground gristy sugar. 47.3%. WB15/232

◈ **That Boutique-y Whisky Company Aultmore** batch 5 **(79.5) n20 t20.5 f19 b20**. Aggressive: lacking depth, charm and quality. 48.8%. 216 bottles.

The Single Malts of Scotland Aultmore 15 Years Old hogshead, cask no. 2619, dist 19 Mar 98, bott 29 Oct 13 **(87.5) n21 t22 f22.5 b22**. Huge natural caramels fill in the gaps where the complexity should be. Salivating and excellently chewy. 51.3%. 220 bottles. WB15/317

Wemyss Malts 1991 Single Speyside Aultmore "Sweet Mint Infusion" dist 1991 bott 2013 **(90) n22** delicately floral and earthy; something of dank Spring forest floors;

t23 gorgeous firmness to the malt- almost Glen Grant in style. The barley sings proudly and with the cleanest of voices; a gentle sugary breeze while a soft smoke strums almost imperceptibly at the rear; f22.5 back to the earthiness, now intermingling with toasty ice cream cones; b22.5 solid and quite beautifully constructed; makes outstanding use of the small degree of smoke at its disposal. 46%. sc. 354 bottles.

⬧ **Whic.de Aultmore 8 Year Old** sherry butt, cask no. 900016, dist 12 Mar 07, bott 12 Mar 15 (88.5) n22 although there is a crystal clarity to certain aspects of the fruits, something duller lingers a little deeper; t23.5 a lovely age for Aultmore as the crispness of the grain breaks through the big fruit statement; f21 spices, and a dull nagging ache of sulphur; b22 a lovely, fresh malt let down slightly in the latter stages. 53.9%. sc. 60 bottles.

⬧ **Whiskybroker Aultmore 8 Years** sherry butt, cask no. 900016, dist 12 Mar 07 (92) n23 t24 f22 b23. From the same sherry butt as Whic.de at identical strength. Yet this one can claim a more concentrated fruit factor on the nose and a massively more confident – borderline aggressive – taste on delivery with the grape coming out with rare richness and bravado. And acting more like an 8-year-old. Also, there is cocoa on the finish which doesn't appear on its twin bottling. A sulphur bite does hit a little later, though. Two identical whiskies from the same cask...yet one very different from the other. Go figure... 53.9%. sc.

BALBLAIR
Highlands (Northern), 1872. Inver House Distillers. Working.

Balblair 10 Years Old db (86) n21 t22 f22 b21. Such an improved dram away from the clutches of caramel. 40%

Balblair Aged 16 Years db (84) n22 t22 f20 b20. Definitely gone up a notch in the last year. The lime on the nose has been replaced by dim Seville oranges; the once boring finish reveals elements of fruit and spice. It's the barley- rich middle that shines, though, and some more work will belt this up into the high 90s where this great distillery belongs. 40%

Balblair 1965 db (96.5) n23 any more Kentuckian and I do declare that I'd swear this'd been matured in a log cabin with racoons for guards...; a lovely procession of manicured bourbon notes, with semi-peeled kumquats at the van; t24.5 you will not find a more superbly complex delivery, with this seemingly possessing two bodies in one: the first is a little oily and soft but carrying the darker oaky notes, while simultaneously the mouth fills with juices from both barley and fruit; f24.5 a mix of peach and melon yogurt mixed in with chocolate mousse, a rare but delightful concoction; light liquorice and hickory dusted with muscovado sugars reminds one of Kentucky again; b24.5 many malts of this age have the spirit hanging on in there for grim life. This is an exception: the malt is in joint control and never for a moment allows the oak to dominate. It is almost too beautiful for words. 52.3%

Balblair 1969 db (94.5) n22.5 t23.5 f24 b24.5. A charmer. Don't even think about touching this until it has stood in the glass for ten minutes. And if you are not prepared to give each glass a minimum half hour of your time (and absolutely no water), then don't bother getting it for, to be honest, you don't deserve it... 41.4%

Balblair 1975 db (94.5) n24.5 t23.5 f23 b23.5. Essential Balblair. 46%

Balblair 1978 db (94) n24 t24 f23 b23. Just one of those drams that exudes greatness and charm in equal measures. Some malts fall apart when hitting thirty: this one is totally intact and in command. A glorious malt underlining the greatness of this mostly under-appreciated distillery. 46%

Balblair 1983 Vintage 1st Release dist 1983 bott 2013. db (96.5) n24.5 the weight has been touched by a wand: Demerara enriched Dundee cake without a trace of dissention in the ranks. The gentle grapey, sultana notes are almost ghostlike and are happy to enjoy top billing with the candy store barley sugar and chocolate coconut. Almost impossible to describe the full story, as the changes with the temperature can be as startling as they beautiful. Touches greatness...; t24 an almost exact carbon copy of the nose on the palate, except here the mouth feel tallies exactly with the weight. The sugars dissolve disarmingly and the fruitiness is little more than the odd breeze. A little more spice, though, than can be detected nasally though this reveals a nimbleness of Ali in his pomp. f23.5 like lengthening shadows on a summer's evening, the oak begins to make itself slightly better known. The barley recedes, though leaving behind a gristiness enhanced by syrup-dank coconut flakes; meanwhile, like bees going about their daily chores, the spices buzz and hum; b24.5 very few malts are this comfortable, or vibrant, by the time they reach their third decade in the cask. A Highland gathering of sensational casks resulting in a celebration of what great Scotch whisky is really all about. Magnificent. 46%. nc ncf. Inverhouse Distilleries.

⬧ **Balblair 1983 Vintage 1st Release** dist 1983, bott 2014 db (95) n23.5 hmmm: that oak has much to say for itself. Orange blossom honey at its softest and drier hickory/cocoa and spice when it growls; **t23** not surprisingly, a tad aggressive on delivery. The drier spices bite hard but there is a superb oiliness (weirdly, very similar to corn oil in bourbon) which soothes and dresses the oak burn, all framed by excellent sugars; **f24.5** now at its very best, as the spiced oak has calmed allowing a clearer view of the still intact barley notes and the wide range of cocoa (including Nutella) and honey notes, manuka at the fore...; **b24** the last Balblair 83 I tasted fair won my heart and undying devotion with its beauty and complexity. This may also be a beautiful and shapely morsel, but the over exuberance of the oak means this is more of a spicy, pleasure-indulging, hedonistic one night-stand than lasting, tender love. Mind you... 46%. nc ncf.

Balblair 1989 db **(91) n23 t23 f22.5 b22.5.** Don't expect gymnastics on the palate or the pyrotechnics of the Cadenhead 18: in many ways a simple malt, but one beautifully told. Almost Cardhu-esque in the barley department. 43%

Balblair 1989 db **(88) n21.5 t22 f22.5 b22.** A clean, pleasing malt, though hardly one that will induce anyone to plan a night raid on any shop stocking it... 46%

Balblair 1990 db **(92.5) n24 t23.5 f22 b23.** Tangy in the great Balblair tradition. Except here this is warts and all with the complexity and greatness of the distillery left in no doubt. 46%

Balblair 1990 Vintage 2nd Release dist 1990 bott 2013. db **(83.5) n22 t21 f20 b20.5.** Full bodied yet tight and tangy. 46%. nc ncf. Inverhouse Distilleries.

Balblair 1997 2nd Release db **(94) n23.5** gooseberry tart with a curious salt and sugar seasoning; a shaving of ginger and a little physalis adds no end of complexity; **t23.5** sharp, tangy, pulsing barley both salivating and showing verve and a complex drier side: quintessential Balblair...; **f23** the vanillas walk hand-in-hand with the barley towards a cocoa-rich, late-spiced finale; **b24** a very relaxed well-made and matured malt, comfortable in its own skin, bursting with complexity and showing an exemplary barley-oak ratio. A minor classic. 46%. nc ncf.

Balblair 1999 Vintage 1st Release dist 1999 bott 2014. db **(92.5) n23** an apparent diaspora of mixed casks at times singing together; at others happy to knock each other about. Weighty, fruity but with a sharp malt theme, too; **t23.5** fabulous mouth feel: lush without cloying and despite the apparent grape, more than happy for the barley to weild its full juicy might; **f23** a little tangy, perhaps, but nothing too serious. Some lovely marmalade to enrich the toast; **b23** the same colour as the cockerel which wakes me each morning...and crows as loudly. Gorgeous. 46%. nc ncf. Inverhouse Distilleries.

⬩⬩⬩ **Balblair 1999 Vintage 2nd Release** dist 1999, bott 2014 db **(83.5) n22 t22.5 f19 b20.** You know one of those old vintage sports cars which looks amazing, sounds just the thing but when you get inside and put your foot down nothing happens...? Well this is a bit like that. The dried dates have flattened all the higher notes so everything is a bit nondescript and shapeless. There are, of course, some attractive toffee-fruit moments. But a certain furriness on the finish negates the good. 46%. nc ncf.

Balblair 2000 db **(87.5) n21.5 t22.5 f21.5 b22.** No toffee yet still a clever degree of chewy weight for all the apparent lightness. 43%

Balblair 2001 db **(90.5) n23.5** gooseberries at varying stages of ripeness; barley so clean it must be freshly scrubbed; the kind of delicate spice prickle that is a must; **t23.5** majestic delivery: hard to imagine barley making a more clean, intense and profound entrance than that. The malt forms many layers, each one sugar accompanied but taking on a little more oak; **f21.5** dries, spices up but bitters a little; **b22.5** a typically high quality whisky from this outrageously underestimated distillery. 46%

Balblair 2002 1st release bott 2012 db **(90.5) n22 t23 f22.5 b23.** A malt which reminds you how cold it is during Scottish winters...there is a lot of fresh-faced youth to this. But just so beautiful thanks to its understated complexity and honesty. 46%. nc ncf.

Balblair 2003 Vintage 1st Release dist 2003 bott 2013. db **(88.5) n20** strangely tart, at times off key. Not Balblair's nose showing by any means its greatest profile...; **t23.5** ...yet the delivery is an absolute treat, churning out a succession of confident barley themes in classic Balblair style, from eyewateringly salivating and rich to crisp and precise. The sugars are crunchy and follow a gristy route; **f22** a rather lovely succession of vanilla and butterscotch notes, always with a barley theme; **b23** the nose maybe a bit odd, even unattractively flawed. But this a tale with a happy ending. 46%. nc ncf. Inverhouse Distilleries.

⬩⬩⬩ **Balblair 2003 Vintage 1st Release** dist 2003, bott 2015 db **(89) n21** a fidgety, ill-at-ease aroma where the oak tentatively dominates but without establishing a character; **t23** mainly citrus flavours at work, though the barley is clean and bright. Excellent, delicate oak sub-text, leading into light mocha; **f22.5** a bit of spice buzz and praline; **b22.5** just like their 2013 bottling, gets off to an uncertain start on the nose but makes its mark on delivery. 46%. nc ncf.

Balblair 2004 Vintage 1st Release bourbon Matured, dist 2004, bott 2014. db **(88) n22** a busy chap full of ginger and liquorice; **t22.5** stoked-up sugars find an early release and show a maple syrup edge. The oak is pretty well charged too and reveals a bitter marmalade counter; **f21.5** after the punchy delivery a more pithy finale, again with the oak holding sway; **b22** maybe could have done with a higher percentage of 2nd fill casks to soften the experience and magnify the complexity. *46%. nc ncf. Inverhouse Distilleries.*

Balblair 2004 Vintage 1st Release Sherry Matured dist 2004 bott 2014. db **(68) n16 t19 f16 b17.** The sadness, of course, is that there are some pretty decent sherry butts amongst duds. *46%. nc ncf. Inverhouse Distillers.*

Cadenhead's Small Batch Balblair Aged 23 Years bourbon barrels, dist 1990, bott 2013 **(95.5) n23.5** tangy orange...and malt concentrate; **t24.5** tangy orange sweetened by muscovado sugar and a vanilla-butterscotch oak edge; the spices are all embracing...; **f23.5** creamy vanilla...and spiced tangy orange; **b24** the thing about Cadenhead is that they rarely get it wrong when it comes to bottling a cask: for the last 25 years they have been probably the most consistently good of all the independents. And the thing about Balblair is that the house style for those of us who blend with it also, is a sweetness suffused with a tangy orange note. So trust Cadenhead to choose a cask which nails it to perfection. *51.7%. 318 bottles. WB15/070*

⬩⬩⬩ **Gordon & MacPhail Cask Strength Balblair 1993 (87) n21.5 t23.5 f21 b21.** No damaging sulphur: hurrah! But the grape is very loose fitting, swamping the whisky like granny's oversized knitted jumper engulfs a toddler. Little shape, though the spiced juiciness is delightful. *53.4%*

⬩⬩⬩ **Kingsbury Gold Balblair 23 Year Old 1990** refill sherry cask, cask no. 10116 **(85.5) n22 t22.5 f20 b21.** Oddly enough, although the weakness of this malt is in the cask, it has nothing to do with sulphur treatment. Rather, it is in the oak itself. So that means we are treated to a superb plummy fruitiness on delivery to be savoured while you can. The spices impress, too. *52.9%. 240 bottles.*

⬩⬩⬩ **Old Malt Cask Balblair 1990 Aged 21 Years** refill hogshead, cask no. 7825 **(86) n21 t23 f21.5 b21.5.** A tangy, mouth-watering individual where the malt plays second fiddle to the oak in the opening sequences before at last finding its voice. Salty and, at times, sharp. *55.8%. sc. 253 bottles. Exclusive to Glen Farhn, Germany.*

BALMENACH
Speyside, 1824. Inver House Distillers. Working.

Balmenach Aged 25 Years Golden Jubilee db **(89) n21 t23 f22 b23.** What a glorious old charmer this is! An essay in balance despite the bludgeoning nature of the beast early on. Takes a little time to get to know and appreciate: persevere with this belter because it is classic stuff for its age. *58%. Around 800 decanters.*

Adelphi Selection Balmenach 11 Years Old dist 2001, bott 2013 **(91) n22** resounding malt. The grist is doused in citrus; **t24** the delivery fairly rockets into life with a juicy barley intro to die for; the grist, like the nose, enters a little later; **f22.5** much drier. Anyone who can remember a Micky chocolate milk that used to be delivered to the door in the early 60s will recognise this fade; **b22.5** eye-wateringly bright and lively. And lovely... *58.7%. WB15/411*

⬩⬩⬩ **Cadenhead's Single Cask Balmenach Aged 25 Years** bourbon cask **(92.5) n23.5** a nose which sings sweetly to you: though from a bourbon cask, light marmalade notes and plump, case-bursting gooseberries serenade while the light maple syrup provides the backing; **t23.5** gristy, lightly fruited malt of exceptional clarity. The barley is almost on steroids, but the gooseberry pie – upping the salivation levels further - is magnificent; **f22.5** dries and dulls as the vanilla gains a toehold; **b23** almost the perfect prandial dram. *sc. 48.6%*

⬩⬩⬩ **Liquid Treasures Balmenach 14 Year Old** dist 2001, bott 2015 **(83.5) n20 t22 f20.5 b21.** Some tangy old oak at play here, never quite allowing the sugars to settle. Attractive fresh barley on delivery, though. *51.9%. 245 bottles.*

Scotch Malt Whisky Society Cask 48.41 Aged 25 Years refill hogshead, dist 30 Mar 88 **(87) n21.5 t23 f21 b21.5** A really lovely malt full of highly revved barley but diminished slightly by an oaky charge which gets a little out of hand. *48.2%. nc ncf sc. 239 bottles.*

Signatory Cask Strength Collection Balmenach 1988 Aged 25 Years hogshead, cask no. 1132, dist 4 Apr 88, bott 23 Sep 13 **(89.5) n22** a tad OTT oak but balanced by Manor House cake sweetness and a series of vanilla notes of varying sweetness; **t23** the sugars get in before the eye-watering tannin takes too great a grip, ensuring a relatively delicate delivery. A fair amount of natural caramel is swashing about; **f22** caramel and toasty tannin all the way...and don't forget to spit out the splinters; **b22.5** a very sturdy malt which makes the most of its big oak signature. *55.6%. sc nc. Cask handpicked by The Whisky Exchange. WB15/325*

⬩⬩⬩ **Single Cask Collection Balmenach 2006 8 Year Old** rum finish **(84.5) n21 t22 f20.5 b21.** Many rum-finished malts tend to be tight, crisp and seemingly shrink-wrapped in a sugar coating. This doesn't appear to be an exception. *55%. sc.*

Speyside Single Malt Balmenach 30 Years Old refill hogshead, cask no. 10162, dist Sep 83 bott Dec 13 **(88) n22.5** borderline OTT oak but hangs on to offer just enough sugars to make for an attractive experience, though leaving the antiquity in no doubt; **t22.5** the egg custard nose shows little evidence here as the drier oak notes take an early grip. Just enough malt, some juicy, hangs on...; **f21** pretty austere toward the end; **b22** at times threatens to overload on the oak with the malt body not quite broad enough to carry the oaky burden. The whole, though, has a noble presence. *52.8%. nc ncf sc. 111 bottles.*

THE BALVENIE
Speyside, 1892. William Grant & Sons. Working.

The Balvenie Aged 10 Years Founders Reserve db **(90) n23** astonishing complexity: the fruit is relaxed, crushed sultanas and malty suet. A sliver of smoke and no more: everything is hinted and nudged at rather than stated. Superb; **t24** here we go again: threads of malt binding together barely detectable nuances. Thin liquorice here, grape there, smoke and vanilla somewhere else; **f20** Light muscovado-toffee flattens out the earlier complexity. The bitter-sweet balance remains brilliant to the end; **b23** just one of those all-time-great standard 10-year-olds from a great distillery – pity they've decided to kill it off. *40%*

The Balvenie Double Wood Aged 12 Years db **(80.5) n22 t20.5 f19 b19**. OK. So here's the score: Balvenie is one of my favourite distilleries in the world, I confess. I admit it. The original Balvenie 10 is a whisky I would go to war for. It is what Scotch malt whisky is all about. It invented complexity; or at least properly introduced me to it. But I knew that it was going to die, sacrificed on the altar of ageism. So I have tried to get to love Double Wood. And I have tasted and/or drunk it every month for the last couple of years to get to know it and, hopefully fall in love. But still I find it rather boring company. We may have kissed and canoodled. But still there is no spark. No romance whatsoever. *40%*

The Balvenie 14 Years Old Cuban Selection db **(86) n20 t22 f22.5 b21.5**. Unusual malt. No great fan of the nose but the roughness of the delivery grows on you; there is a jarring, tongue-drying quality which actually works quite well and the development of the inherent sweetness is almost in slow motion. Some sophistication here, but also the odd note which, on the nose especially, is a little out of tune. *43%*

The Balvenie 14 Years Old Golden Cask db **(91) n23.5** mildly tart: rhubarb and custard, with a vague sprinkling of brown sugar; bourbon notes, too; **t23** mouth-watering and zingy spice offer up a big delivery, but settles towards the middle towards a more metallic barley-rich sharpness; **f22** soft spices peddle towards the finish and a wave or three of gathering oak links well with the sweetened barley strands; **b22.5** a confident, elegant malt which doesn't stint one iota on complexity. Worth raiding the Duty Free shops for this little gem alone. *47.5%*

⏃ **The Balvenie 16 Year Old Triple Cask** db **(84.5) n22 t22.5 f19 b21**. Well, after their single cask and then double wood, who saw this coming...? There is nothing about this whisky you can possibly dislike: no diminishing off notes (OK, well maybe at the very death) and a decent injection of sugar, especially early on. The trouble is, when you mix together sherry butts (even mainly good ones, like here) and first fill bourbon casks, the intense toffee produced tends to make for a monosyllabic, toffeed, dullish experience. And so it proves here. *40% WB16/030*

The Balvenie Double Wood Aged 17 Years db **(84) n22 t21 f20 b21**. Balvenie does like 17 years as an age to show off its malt at its most complex, & understandably so as it is an important stage in its development before its usual premature over maturity: the last years or two when it remains full of zest and vigour. Here, though, the oak from the bourbon cask has offered a little too much of its milkier, older side while the sherry is a fraction overzealous and a shade too tangy. Enjoyable, but like a top of the range Mercedes engine which refuses to run evenly. *43%.*

The Balvenie Double Wood Aged 17 Years bott 2012 db **(91) n22.5** the sherry does a good job injecting a controlled softness to the experience, perhaps at the expense of some of the higher bourbon cask notes; **t23.5** the softness on the nose is transformed into silkiness on delivery, followed by a really outstanding layering of spice; a few apple notes thins the grape and bourbon style liquorice which piles in with early gusto; **f22** a more restrained and relaxed fade with the higher oak notes playing us out, helped by delicate muscovado sugars; **b23** a far friskier date than the 12-year-old. Here, maturity equals a degree of sophistication. Still not as outrageously sexy as a straightforward high grade bourbon cask offering from the distillery. But easily enough to get you hot under the collar. Lip smacking, high quality entertainment. *43%*

The Balvenie Roasted Malt Aged 14 Years db **(90) n21 t23 f22 b24**. Balvenie very much as you've never seen it before. An absolute, mouth-filling cracker! *47.1%*

The Balvenie Rum Wood Aged 14 Years db **(88) n22 t23 f21 b22**. Tasted blind I would never have recognized the distillery: I'm not sure if that's a good thing. *47.1%*

Balvenie 17 Years Old Rum Cask db **(88.5)** n22 t22.5 f22 b22. For all the best attentions of the rum cask at times this feels all its 17 years, and perhaps a few Summers more. Impossible not to love, however. *43%*

Balvenie New Wood Aged 17 Years db **(85)** n23 t22 f19 b21. A naturally good age for Balvenie; the nose is lucid and exciting, the early delivery is thick with rich malt. This, though, has sucked out lots of caramel from the wood to leave an annoyingly flat finish. *40%*

The Balvenie 17 Year Old Sherry Oak db **(88)** n23 t22.5 f21 b21.5. Clean as a nut. High-class sherry it may be but the price to pay is a flattening out of the astonishing complexity one normally finds from this distillery. Bitter-sweet in every respect. *43%*

The Balvenie Aged 21 Years Port Wood db **(94.5)** n24 chocolate marzipan with a soft sugar-plum centre; deft, clean and delicate; **t24** hard to imagine a delivery more perfectly weighted: a rich tapestry of fruit and nut plus malt melts on the palate with a welter of drier, pithy, grape skin balancing the vanillas and barley oils; **f23** delicately dry with the vanilla and buttered fruitcake ensuring balance; **b23.5** what a magnificently improved malt. Last time out I struggled to detect the fruit. Here, there's no escaping. *40%*

⬧ **The Balvenie Aged 50 Years** cask no. 4567 db **(74.5)** n18.5 t20 f17.5 b18.5. The milky, soapy nose gives the game away from the first minute: the spirit has gone through the cask and is now extracting some unwanted oaky residue. This re-emerges on the finale. There is, betwixt these hefty oaky footprints, a few moments of charm and cocoa-enriched enjoyment. But it is fleeting. *45.4%*

⬧ **The Balvenie Aged 50 Years** cask no. 4570 db **(84)** n21 t22 f20 b21. It's like an elegant aircraft trying to take off and barely making it because of all the timber on board. The best bits have a bourbon tendency, with a special nod towards liquorice and hickory. But the truth is: it's simply too old and lumbering for greatness. *45.9%*

The Balvenie Single Barrel Aged 12 Years 1st fill ex bourbon, cask no. 12755 db **(96.5)** n24.5 bananas to roast yam; lime marmalade to honeysuckle; golden syrup to malt grist... keep on looking. They are all there with much else besides...; **t24.5** just about perfect weight on delivery: soft without being gooey, a firm sub-strata without being aggressive. The most delicate honeys are put into play: mainly acacia, though ulmo comes through later on as the vanillas mount; **f23.5** a vague bitterness but absorbed by the welcoming sweetness of the butterscotch tart, ulmo honey and chocolate caramel; **b24** about as close to perfection as a single cask may get. David Stewart, the finest blender of the last decade, may have half retired. But a cask like this shows he has lost none of his magic touch. Sublime. *47.8%. sc ncf. WB15/283*

The Balvenie Single Barrel Aged 15 Years sherry cask, cask no. 609 db **(95)** n24 huge, faultless sherry: clean, confident and muscling in with wonderful spices and burnt raisin. Enormous...but how is the body going to cope with this little lot..? **t24** a complete sherry fest from first to last. Melton Hunt cake at its moistest, with as many burnt raisins as they could throw into the mix and a few extra dollops of molasses for good measure; **f23.5** some bitterness was bound to catch up at some stage...it cannot with this kind of cask as toastiness abounds. But long and satisfying all the way...; **b23.5** a faultless cask – not a shadow of sulphur anywhere. But a case of where the grape has overwhelmed the barley, meaning balance has been compromised: and on the palate it feels as though you have been mugged by an oloroso butt. That said, this is still a stunning experience - a silky delight to be savoured. *47.8%. sc ncf. No more than 650 bottles. WB15/334*

The Balvenie Thirty Aged 30 Years db **(92)** n24 has kept its character wonderfully, with a real mixture of varied fruits. Again the smoke is apparent, as is the panting oak. Astonishing thet the style should have been kept so similar to previous bottlings; **t23** big, full delivery first of enigmatic, thick barley, then a gentle eruption of controlled, warming spices; **f22** much more oaky involvement but such is the steadiness of the barley, its extraordinary confidence, no damage is done and the harmony remains; **b23** rarely have I come across a bottling of a whisky of these advanced years which is so true to previous ones. Amazing. *47.3%*

The Balvenie 1993 Port Wood db **(89)** n21 t23 f22 b23. Oozes class without getting too flash about it: the secret is in the balance. *40%*

The Balvenie TUN 1401 batch 1 db **(91)** n22.5 t23 f22.5 b23. I have experienced Balvenie a lot more complex than this. But there is no faulting the feel good factor... *48.3%. nc ncf.*

The Balvenie TUN 1401 batch 2 db **(89.5)** n23 t23 f21.5 b22. The odd moment here hits high notes from this distillery I only ever before experienced with the old 10-years-old some quarter of a century ago. *50.6%. nc ncf.*

The Balvenie TUN 1401 batch 3 db **(91)** n22 t23.5 f22 b23.5. One of those bottlings which again hits some magnificent heights; it is as though David Stewart is taking his beloved distillery through its repertoire. Still much prefer if he'd keep sherry off the programme, though. *50.3%.*

The Balvenie TUN 1401 batch 4 db **(80.5)** n21.5 t23 f17 b19. The finish has all the quality of an Andy Murray line call challenge. In this case it is unacceptably bitter, nowhere near matching up with the utter brilliance of the delivery. *50.4%. nc ncf.*

The Balvenie TUN 1401 batch 5 db **(87.5)** n22 t22 f21.5 b22. About as heavy duty a Balvenie as I can remember. Hardly surprising as the bourbon barrels appear to have had all their natural caramels dredged from them and this makes it a double whammy with the sherry. *50.1%. nc ncf.*

The Balvenie TUN 1401 batch 6 db **(90)** n22.5 t23 f22 b22.5. I'm amazed my stemmed nosing glass hasn't cracked under the weight of this Speyside monster of a dram. With the mix of fruit and big oak, probably distilled in lead stills... *49.8%. nc ncf.*

The Balvenie TUN 1401 batch 7 db **(87)** n22.5 t23 f20 b21.5. More juiciness to the fruit and sugar allows more clarity than the previous batch. *49.2%. William Grant & Sons.*

◇ **The Balvenie Tun 1401** Batch 9 db **(88)** n22 the malt waves a white flag as the oak threatens...; t22 some real aggression on the delivery; don't expect a soft ride here: the oak wades in with some major cocoa themes; f22.5 thinks about giving it some bourbon, but after a fleeting moment of sweetness the dry, now spicy, cocoa returns with a vengeance; b21.5 the kind of rough-house oak which grabs you when you are looking for a quiet night in and gives you a good duffing up. *49.3%*

◇ **The Balvenie Tun 1509** Batch 1 db **(89)** n23 a quite wonderful nose for its type: it's all about the oak but a few very dry dates and steamed rice as well; though slightly OTT balances out attractively; t22.5 not as basic as Tun 1401, or as aggressive...which means it lacks a little character...but the malt does have a much bigger say; f21.5 dry, shortish and oak-weighted; b22 Balvenie is a distillery which struggles with age. And this is hanging on for life by its bloodied claws... *47.1%*

◇ **The Balvenie TUN 1509** batch 2 db **(94)** n23.5 crushed roast hazelnut in a barley sugar and spiced toffee apple bed; t24 now that is a Balvenie style I recognise: the barley is huge, both juicy and lush. The oak enjoys a clever interplay, maximising the fudge and maple syrup....just so salivating and pulsating! f23 the spices pulse to their hearts' content in the long fade out; some late toasty sugars emphasise the cask involvement; b23.5 a far happier and all round better balanced bottling than Batch 1. A big whisky, though you won't at first realise it... *50.3%*

BANFF
Speyside, 1863–1983. Diageo. Demolished.

Cadenhead Banff 34 Years Old bourbon cask, dist 76, bott 10 **(96)** n23.5 some serious breakfast cereal notes here (especially those which have honey involved), mixing comfortably with salt and creamy, orangey tannin; t24.5 the delivery borders perfection: all kinds of tangerine notes here, mixing easily with fresh barley, for all its years, which meld with lime and watered-down orange blossom honey; f23.5 even the arrival of tannin and leather-style oak seems only to hit the right chord with the sugars and honey notes which linger to the end; b24.5 I wrote long ago that it is likely that during the mid '70s Banff was making some of the best malt in the world. Don't believe me? Taste this... *53.8%. sc. 232 bottles.*

◇ **Gordon & MacPhail Rare Old Banff 1966 (95.5)** n24 thick oak proudly shows the rings of each passing summer. Yet the buttery manuka honey mixes it with the mint and menthol and rounds out any rough edges which threaten; chalky, with a light citrus thread – but where you find chalk, there's flint and the flinty fruit/muscovado sugar is stunning...; t24 beautiful, two-toned delivery. Seemingly soft, with the barley linking with the gentlest vanilla. The sugars compensate the more tired oak tones: just outrageously salivating for its age; f23.5 now settles into a wonderfully delicate, pastel-shaded countdown to the end. But it is a long count, as the butterscotch even begins to show some tantalising spice; a final oaky tang bids you farewell; b24 a rare whisky on at least two major counts: one because casks of this are harder to come by than Millwall wins under Ian Holloway. And, secondly, because few casks get to this kind of age with its honey and sugars still intact. What a loss this distillery was. But what a gain it is for anyone who finds this bottle: it is a true classic. *45.2%*

BEN NEVIS
Highlands (Western), 1825. Nikka. Working.

Ben Nevis 10 Years Old db **(88)** n21 t22 f23 b22. A massive malt that has steadied itself in recent bottlings, but keep those knives and forks to hand! *46%*

Ben Nevis Synergy 13 Years Old db **(88)** n22 firm, crisp brown sugars; t22 intense: all the emphasis on broad muscavado sugars with a degree of a taste of marmalade; f21.5 long, dries, just a little fuzzy; b22.5 one of the sweetest Ben Nevis's for a long time, but as chewy as ever! A bit of a lady's dram to be honest. *46%*

◇ **Aflodal's Whisky The First Dram Ben Nevis 26 Year Old** cask no. 1868, refill bourbon barrel, dist 5 Mar 86, bott 18 Oct 12 **(92)** n22 tangy, salty bourbon – red liquorice dipped in the sea...! t23.5 lush barley: manuka honey with an injection of extra oil; still salivating and gristy; f23 cleaner, brighter now with the emphasis on rich barley; b23.5 a malt which wears

47

its age beautifully. The oak offers no degree of weary negativity and adds only weight. The dexterity of the rich barley is immense. 51.6%. 470 bottles.

◇ **Alexander Murray & Co Ben Nevis 1997 17 Years Old** (85) n21.5 t22 f20.5 b21. Briefly juicy on delivery with a big malt surge, then resumes house chewy style – though with much more toffee on display than normal. 40%

◇ **Anam na h-Alba The Soul of Scotland Ben Nevis 1998** bourbon cask, dist Dec 98, bott May 15 (89.5) n21.5 some ye olde oak tang. But an invigorating salt kick, too; t23 blistering delivery: eye-watering intensity to that saline-barley, then...wow! Citrusy sugars up the salivation factor; f22 malty, though there is that catch in the oak noticeable on the nose; b22.5 a pretty sound malt. 52.6%. 150 bottles.

Berry's Own Selection Ben Nevis 1998 Aged 15 Years cask no. 1351, bott 2014 (86) n19 t22.5 f22.5 b22. From the elephantine school of Ben Nevis. A soupy mass of melted fudge, sticky toffee and molasses with a few over-ripe plums tossed in: delicious...especially with that spice. The ugly nose, though, is less kind. 46%. ncf ncf. WB15/238

Càrn Mòr Strictly Limited Edition Ben Nevis Aged 17 Years dist 1997, bott 2014 (86.5) n20.5 t22.5 f21.5 b22 Pleasant-ish if unremarkable. Unhappy oak on the nose, but there is no denying the freshness of the grape on delivery. Some butterscotch and ulmo honey make contributions to an otherwise simplistic dram. 46%. nc ncf. 747 bottles from 1 cask. WB15/054

The Coopers Choice Ben Nevis 1996 Aged 17 Years hogshead, cask no. 1317, bott 2014 (86.5) n21 t22 f22 b21.5. A chunky, steady dram. Heavy handed on both nose and delivery it settles into an easy going, well spiced fellow content to allow the sharp, toasted barley sugar have its own way. 46%. 320 bottles. WB15/292

The Maltman Ben Nevis Aged 15 Years oloroso sherry cask (67) n16 t18 f16 b17. Would have been as sweet as a nut. But the dreaded 's' word has decreed otherwise. 49.1%

◇ **Master of Malt Single Cask Ben Nevis 17 Year Old** refill bourbon hogshead, dist Oct 96, bott Jun 14 (87.5) n21.5 t22.5 f21.5 b22. Very similar to their Batch 2 bottling: certainly enjoys, if that is the right word, a degree of muckiness to the palate. But the malt-sugar mix is certainly something you have to take note of and does a far better job for the finish in particular. Some good oak involvement, too, insuring a touch of complexity and even, for the odd moment or two, class. 51.4%. sc. 34 bottles.

Old Malt Cask Ben Nevis Aged 16 Years sherry butt, cask no. 9639, dist Nov 96, bott Mar 13 (80) n17 t22 f20 b21. Once you get past the uncomfortably tight nose things aren't as bad as might be feared. Indeed, the delivery is just dripping with fresh fruit, aided by light muscovado sugar and some compelling heather honey. Would love to have seen this guy had it not been treated in Jerez. The finish is also tight, but could be a lot worse. For those immune to relatively minor sulphurous incursions, go for it. 50%. nc ncf sc. 299 bottles. WB15/133

◇ **Old Malt Cask Ben Nevis 16 Years Old** sherry butt, cask no. 10982, dist Jun 98, bott Oct 14 (72.5) n18 t19 f17.5 b18. Ticks lots of boxes...but few of them are the right ones. Stodgy though occasionally juicy, there is a definite grubbiness to this which may appeal to some, though not the purists. 50%. nc ncf sc. 714 bottles.

Old Malt Cask Ben Nevis Aged 18 Years refill hogshead, cask no. 10503, dist May 96, bott May 14 (87) n21 t22.5 f21.5 b22. There are no claims to greatness here or pretensions regarding complexity. An old cask means an insipid colour for 18 years and a malt looking at all the barley-driven angles. Pleasant enough delivery, though, with an attractive sharpness of phrase and sugars which sit comfortably. 50%. nc ncf sc. 305 bottles.

◇ **Old Particular Highland Ben Nevis 16 Years Old** refill hogshead, cask no. 10556, dist May 98, bott Nov 14 (85.5) n21.5 t21 f22 b21. The lightest-bodied Nevis I have come across in years. The oak plays a telling role only at the end. Until then, it's clean, uncomplicated barley all the way. 48.4%. nc ncf sc. 306 bottles.

The Pearls of Scotland 1997 16 Year Old cask no. 45, dist Jan 97, bott Nov 13 (92) n22.5 huge, mountainous nose: thick with coconut and maple-syrup-lightened tannin; t23.5 spitting splinters from the off, the oils are voluptuous but again it is the sugars really pulling the string: molassed and a little crunchy they make for a stunning mouth feel; f23 spices are in full swing, with a little molassed liquorice for company; b23 a Ben Nevis living up to its name...superb! 51.8%

The Pearls of Scotland Ben Nevis 1997 cask no. 612, bott Jun 14 (93) n23.5 a trifle and blancmange dessert, though the depth of citrusy oak present suggests this will not be a malt to be trifled with... t23...sure enough the oak is out first and with a rugged, bitting early detachment; the malt catches up a few beats later, showing superb richness; myriad layers of malt and oak intertwining; f23 now moves into spicy mode, though the oak and malt throb beautifully; b23.5 a massive Ben Nevis scaling the heights... 50.6%. sc

◈ **The Pearls of Scotland Ben Nevis 1997** cask no. 614, dist May 97, bott May 15 (**87.5**) n22 t21.5 f22 b22. Tart and a little tangy, though the intense malt grist and sugars are happy to come out and play. *50.9%. sc.*

◈ **Premier Barrel Selection Ben Nevis Aged 8 Years** (83) n20 t21 f21 b21. Eye-wateringly intense barley hits the kind of high note which can shatter glass. Youthful, ultra-energetic but finesse-free. *46%. nc ncf sc. 419 bottles.*

Provenance Ben Nevis Over 8 Years refill hogshead, cask no. 10328, dist Summer 06, bott Summer 14 (**82**) n20 t21 f21 b20. Woe! Hasn't really moved in eight years...as close to new make as you can possibly get at this age. Certainly malty! *46%. nc ncf sc.*

◈ **Romantic Rhine Collection Ben Nevis** sherry hogshead, cask no. 55, dist 24 Jan 97, bott 2 Apr 13 (**87**) n21 t22.5 f21.5 b22. Not a spoiled butt. But perhaps not the greatest to have visited Jerez, either. At its best, Cadbury's Fruit and Nut at play. Love the unscheduled big spice kick. *52.8%. 120 bottles.*

Signatory Vintage Cask Strength Collection Ben Nevis 1992 Aged 20 Years sherry butt, cask no. 2310, dist 03 Jul 92, bott 02 Jul 13 (**92.5**) n22.5 steaming suet pudding with the accent on the sultanas; t24 the first note or two on delivery is wobbly and unsure. Then piles in with sumptuous grape in the grandest old fruit cake style. The fruit clarifies for a short juicy burst; f23 a fruitcake which seems to have acquired a chocolatey lid; b23 by far from textbook, but wonderfully sulphur free and somehow encapsulates the quirkiness of the distillery. *55.5%. nc sc. 623 bottles. WB15/005*

Signatory Vintage Un-chillfiltered Collection Ben Nevis 1991 Aged 22 Years sherry butt, cask no. 2910, dist 16 Aug 91, bott 10 Apr 14 (**81**) n19 t22 f20 b20. Curiously, not a great whisky...and has absolutely nothing to do with sulphur as this has none on show. Just lacks quality on the oak front in general and even after 22 years the malt has not been able to find a way to engineer a harmonious relationship. Tangy and disjointed, though the delivery does offer a few moments of juicy respite. *46%. nc ncf sc. 819 bottles. WB15/029*

◈ **Single Cask Collection Ben Nevis 1996 18 Year Old** sherry butt (**93**) n22.5 a firm outline to the fruit: some oak is threaded through the moist plum cake; t24 satisfying delivery: full bodied and mildly oily but the star attraction is the simultaneous juice and spice explosion; f23 remnants of molasses filter through to the toasty vanilla fade; b23.5 Nevis in very fine fettle from an untainted sherry butt. *53.1%. sc.*

◈ **That Boutique-y Whisky Ben Nevis** batch 1 (**89**) n22 rich, fulsome, treacly sugars and biscuity malt; t23 massively chunky delivery. All kinds of fruit in play, as well as barley sugar concentrate: chew this until your jaws ache; f22 a little honey on the fade, but plenty of copper, too; b22 a malt to match the mountain: just...big! *49.7%. 161 bottles. WB15/205*

◈ **That Boutique-y Whisky Company Ben Nevis** batch 2 (**84**) n20 t22 f20.5 b21.5. Not just a knife and fork type malt, but occasionally needs a chainsaw, too. This is dense stuff offering little finesse and could be cleaned up a bit. But the sugars and chewability are top notch! *48.7%. 52 bottles.*

◈ **Wilson & Morgan Barrel Selection Ben Nevis 18 Year Old** sherry wood, cask no. 657, dist 1995, bott 2013 (**94**) n23 dank warehouses: big, dark, salty and brooding; t24 one of the best deliveries for a Ben Nevis I have enjoyed for several years: the fruit is thick yet pristine, the sugars sharp and focused, giving way to a mix of moody Zambian forest honey and molasses. The brief spices add just the right degree of aggression...; f23.5 beautiful chocolate mousse laced with over-ripe cherries; b23.5 oh, if only all Ben Nevis was matured in butts of this high standard. *55.5%. sc 611 bottles.*

◈ **Whisky-Fässle Ben Nevis 18 Year Old** hogshead, dist 1996, bott 2014 (**85**) n21.5 t22.5 f20 b21. Despite the intense, juicy barley which socks you right between the eyes, this turns into a lumpy and bumpy experience thanks to some pretty average oak. *50.8%. nc ncf.*

◈ **World of Orchids Ben Nevis 1996 17 Year Old** bourbon cask, cask no. 315 (**88**) n21.5 t23 f21.5 b22. Prime blending malt: supremely barley-rich with excellent body. The sugars offer a crispness in contradiction to the oily background and lasts the pace beautifully. A blender worth his salt would love to get his or her hands on this stuff. *50.5%. sc. 291 bottles.*

BENRIACH
Speyside, 1898. The BenRiach Distillery Co. Working.

The BenRiach db (**86**) n21 t22 f21.5 b21.5. The kind of soft malt you could wean nippers on, as opposed to Curiositas, which would be kippers. Unusually for a BenRiach there is a distinct toffee-fudge air to this one late on, but not enough to spoil that butterscotch-malt charm. No colouring added, so a case of the oak being a bit naughty. *40%*

◈ **BenRiach 10 Year Old** db (**87.5**) n20 t23 f22.5 b22. A much fatter spirit than from any time when I worked those stills. The dry nose never quite decides where it is going. But there's no doubting the creamy yet juicy credentials on the palate. Malty, with graceful fruit sugars chipping in delightfully. *43%*

 BenRiach 35 Year Old db **(90)** n23 juicy dates and plums are tipped into a weighty fruitcake; **t24** sit right back in your armchair (no..? Then go and find one...!!) having dimmed the lights and silenced the room and just let your taste buds run amok: those plums and toasted raisins really do get you salivating, with the spices also whipping up a mid-life storm; **f21.5** angular oak dries and bitters at a rate of knots; **b22** sexy fruit, but has late oaky bite. *42.5%*

The BenRiach Curiositas Aged 10 Years Single Peated Malt db **(90.5)** n23 the thin smoke is losing out to the honey-fudge; **t23** the peat takes a little time to gather its speech, but when it comes it is fine and subtly delivered. In the meantime soft barley and that delicious but curiously dampening sweet fudge struts its stuff; **f22** chalky vanillas and a squirt of chocolate like that found on ice cream cones; **b22.5** "Hmmmm. Why have my research team marked this down as a 'new' whisky" I wondered to myself. Then immediately on nosing and tasting I discovered the reason without having to ask: the pulse was weaker, the smoke more apologetic...it had been watered down from the original 46% to 40%. This is excellent malt. But can we have our truly great whisky back, please? As lovely as it is, this is a bit of an imposter. As Emperor Hadrian might once have said: "ifus itus aintus brokus..." *40%*

The BenRiach Aged 12 Years db **(82.5)** n21 t20 f21 b20.5. More enjoyable than the 43% I last tasted. But still an entirely inoffensive malt determined to offer minimal complexity. *40%*

The BenRiach Aged 12 Years db **(78.5)** n21.5 t20 f18 b19. White peppers on the nose, then goes uncharacteristically quiet and shapeless. *43%*

The BenRiach Aged 12 Years Dark Rum Wood Finish db **(85.5)** n21 t22 f21 b21.5. More than a decade ago, long before it ever became fashionable, I carried out an extensive programme of whisky maturation in old dark rum casks. So, if someone asked me now what would happen if you rounded off a decently peated whisky in a rum cask, I'd say – depending on time given for the finish and type of rum – the smoke would be contained and there would be a ramrod straight, steel-hard sweetness ensuring the most clipped whisky you can possibly imagine. And this here is exactly what we have... *46%*

The BenRiach Aged 12 Years Matured In Sherry Wood db **(95.5)** n23.5 big, juicy, compelling grape. Absolutely clean and stupendous in its multi-layering; **t24** quite magnificent! How I pray whiskies to be on delivery, but find they so rarely are. Some caramels are caught up in the genteel squabble between the grape juice and the rich barley; **f24** long, faultless and ushering in a chocolate raisin depth; late vanilla and any amount of spice; **b24** since I last tasted this the number of instances of sampling a sherry wood whisky and not finding my taste buds caked in sulphur has nosedived dramatically. Therefore, to start my tasting day at 7am with something as honest as this propels one with myriad reasons to continue the day. A celebration of a malt whisky in more ways than you could believe. *46%. nc ncf.*

The BenRiach Aged Over 12 Years "Arumaticus Fumosus" richly peated style, ex-dark rum barrels db **(91)** n23 t23 f22 b23. Very often finishing in rum can sharpen the mouthfeel yet at the same time add a sugary sheen. This little gem is no exception. *46%*

The BenRiach Aged Over 12 Years "Heredotus Fumosus" peated PX finish db **(92.5)** n23 the peat is so thick you could grow a grape vine in it; **t23** the sweetness of the grape arrives in spicy waves, comfortably supported by the thick, oily peat; **f23** long, more sugared smoke and cocoa; **b23.5** at last a PX-peat marriage not on the rocks. What an improvement on the last bottling. Smokograpus Miraculus. *46%. nc ncf.*

The BenRiach Aged Over 12 Years "Importanticus Fumosus" richly peated style, ex-port hogshead db **(87)** n22 t22 f21 b22. Hardicus asius Nailsus. *46%*

The BenRiach Aged 12 Years "Importanticus Fumosus" Tawny port wood finish db **(91.5)** n23 no matter here had it been finished in Short-eared, Long-eared, Little, Barn or Tawny Port, the peat would have come out tops. The smoke is enormous: owl do they do it...? **t22.5** a peaty custard pie in the mush: enormous impact with more early vanilla than fruit; **f23.5** now the grape begins to get its head above the smoky parapet; a beautiful balance with the smoke, vanilla and minor spices; **b22.5** you'd be a twit not to buy two of 'em. *46%*

The BenRiach Aged 13 Years "Maderensis Fumosus" peated madeira finish db **(85.5)** n20 t23.5 f21 b21. Never a shrinking violet, this still enjoys some pretty off the wall moments. But for a brief success on delivery where the richness of the sugars and smoke work in astonishing harmony, the remainder of the journey is one of vivid disagreement. *46%. nc ncf.*

The BenRiach Aged 15 Years Dark Rum Finish db **(86)** n20 t22 f22 b22. Drier, spicier than before. Old Jamaica chocolate candy. *46%. nc ncf.*

The BenRiach Aged 15 Years Madeira Wood Finish db **(89.5)** n22.5 t21.5 f23 b22.5. Very much drier than most Madeira finishes you will find around. Once the scramble on delivery is over, this bottling simply exudes excellence. A collector's must have. *46%*

The BenRiach Aged 15 Years Pedro Ximénez Sherry Wood Finish db **(94.5)** n25 t23.5 f22.5 b23.5. Some of the strangest Scotch malts I have tasted in the last decade have been fashioned in PX casks. And few have been particularly enjoyable creations. This one, though, bucks the trend thanks principally to the most subtle of spice imprints. All the hallmarks of some kind of award-winner. *46%*

The BenRiach Aged 15 Years Tawny Port Wood Finish db (89.5) n21.5 t23 f22.5 b22.5. Now that really is the perfect late night dram. *46%*

The BenRiach Aged 16 Years db (83.5) n21.5 t21 f20 b21. Although maltily enjoyable, if over dependent on caramel flavours, you get the feeling that a full works 46% version would offer something more gripping and true to this great distillery. *40%*

The BenRiach Aged 16 Years db (83.5) n21.5 t21 f20 b21. Pleasant malt but now without the dab of peat which gave it weight; also a marked reduction of the complexity that once gave this such a commanding presence. *43%. nc ncf.*

The BenRiach Aged 16 Years Sauternes Wood Finish db (85) n19.5 t23 f21.5 b21. One of the problems with cask finishing is that there is nothing like an exact science of knowing when the matured whisky and introduced wood gel to their fullest potential. BenRiach enjoy a reputation of getting it right more often than most other distillers and bottlers. But here it hasn't come off to quite the same effect as previous, quite sensational, versions I have tasted of the 16-y-o Sauternes finish. No denying the sheer joy of the carpet bombing of the taste buds on delivery, though, so rich is the combination of fresh grape and delicate smoke. *46%*

The BenRiach Aged 17 Years "Septendecim" Peated Malt db (93.5) n24 easily one of the most complex of all the new peaty noses of the year. Both sweet and dry, with an ashy feel to the peat fire mingling with dangerous complexity. Almost perfectly weighted and balanced; t24.5 the delivery reveals a light oiliness which is entirely absent from the nose. This in turn maximises the intensity of both the sugars and smoke. When the spices arrive, the harmony is just about complete; f23 just a dash of oaky bitterness reveals a degree of discord. But the Demerara sugars are so crisp and painstaking in their efforts to ensure balance that all can be forgiven....; b24 proof, not that it is now needed, that Islay is not alone in producing phenomenal phenols... *46%. nc ncf.*

The BenRiach "Solstice" 17 Years Old 2nd Edition port finish, heavily peated db (94) n23.5 a touch of the Bowmores with this: definitely a hint of Fisherman's Friend, but also creamy celery soup; t23 big and thick, coating the palate superbly, first with peat and then with a rich molassed fruitiness, especially with juicy dates to the fore; f23.5 reverts back to a Fisherman's Friend stance with the fruit now vanished and some half-hearted spices enlivening the delicate late sugars; b24 well, it's the 21st June 2012, the summer solstice. And, naturally, pouring down with rain outside. So what better time to taste this whisky? With all that heart-warming, comforting peat as thick as a woolly jumper, this is the perfect dram for a bitterly cold winter's day the world over. Or midsummer's day in England... *50%. nc ncf.*

The BenRiach Aged 18 Years Gaja Barolo Wood Finish db (89) n22 t23 f21.5 b22.5. The delivery gives one of the most salivating experiences of the year. *46%*

The BenRiach Aged 18 Years Moscatel Wood Finish db (92.5) n23.5 one of those sublime noses where everything is understated: the fresh apples and grape, the most delicate of smoke, the jam on toast, the vanilla...; t23.5 textbook delivery: every note clean and clear, especially the juicy fruits melting into the lush barley. A buzz of distant background smoke all helped along by the most subtle of oils; f22 leans towards the vanilla; b23.5 one of those rare whiskies which renews and upholds any belief I have for cask finishing. Superb. *46%*

The BenRiach Aged 20 Years db (85.5) n21.5 t23 f19 b22. A much more attractive version than the American Release 46%. The barley offers a disarming intensity and sweetness which makes the most of the light oils. Only a bittering finish shuts the gate on excellence. *43%. nc ncf.*

The BenRiach Aged 20 Years db (78) n19 t20 f19 b20. This is big, but not necessarily for the right reasons or in the right places. A big cut of oiliness combines with some surging sugars for a most un-BenRiachy ride. *46%. US Market.*

The BenRiach Aged 21 Years "Authenticus" Peated Malt db (85.5) n22 t21.5 f21 b21. A heavy malt, though the smoke only adds a small degree to its weight. The barley is thick and chewy but the oak has a very big say. *46%*

The BenRiach 25 Years Old db (87.5) n21.5 t23 f21 b22. The tranquillity and excellent balance of the middle is the highlight by far. *50%*

The BenRiach 30 Years Old db (94.5) n24 the fruit, though very ripe and rich, remains uncluttered and clean and is helped along the way by a superb injection of sweetened cloves and Parma Violets; the oak is present and correct offering an egg custard sub-plot; t24 how ridiculously deft is that? There is total equilibrium in the barley and fruit as it massages the palate in one of the softest deliveries of a 30-y-o around; the middle ground is creamy and leans towards the vanilla; even so, there are some amazingly juicy moments to savour; f23 very lightly oiled and mixing light grist and rich vanilla; b23.5 it's spent 30 years in the cask: give one glass of this at least half an hour of your time: seal the room, no sounds, no distractions. It's worth it...for as hard as I try, I can barely find a single fault with this. *50%*

BenRiach Batch 11 1976 37 Years Old sherry cask matured, bourbon finish, cask no. 529 db **(92) n22.5** shuddering monoliths of oak. Trees, in fact. But the nipping spice, poppy seed and floor polish certainly bring the brain into focus...; **t23.5** waxy, oily and thicker than a butt of molasses. The oaks are at forest level, but somehow the barley and dates keep the game going; **f23** pulsing spices somehow overcome the excesses of the oak – and there are many. Still the barley delivers, as well as a plum pudding and custard; **b23** when tasted live, I gave this a similar knee-jerk appraisal to the 1978 version. But on analysing countless replays I found I was wrong and the goal not only good but quite spectacular. Goooooooooooalllllllllll!!!!! Bennnn-Reeeee-Ack!!!!!! Blimey. And this is even before the 2014 World Cup has started....! *44.2%. sc.*

BenRiach Batch 11 1976 37 Years Old peated, sherry cask finish, bourbon finish, cask no. 5463 db **(95) n24.5** bold and allowing the oak only limited dominance. This must have been a supreme sherry butt in its day as the spices rock, not least for their understated beauty and the lightness of touch to the honeys, despite the relative great weight of the nose; **t23** where the nose shows no age at all, the first few waves here are sent crashing onto the taste buds by the great god Quercus himself; slowly recovers as the grape establishes a foothold: a kind of toasty fruitcake at first and then a topping of Demerara; **f23.5** quite sublime with the oils gliding the spicier Genoa cake into place; **b24** with the bourbon finish on the original sherry butt, a reversal of the norm. And with so much sulphur around these days, thank heavens for that! No sulphur here. Interesting to compare the vitality on this bottling to the flagging cask 529 sister bottling. A joy of a dram. *51.9%. sc.*

BenRiach Batch 11 1977 37 Years Old hogshead, cask no. 7114 db **(92.5) n24** delicate, lime encrusted and even a touch of kiwi fruit. Indeed, that exotic fruit says all you need to know about its age...; **t23.5** just so gentle. The rich barley flavours glide onto the palate, most of them of a sugary disposition and all with an oaky fingerprint; the oils are graceful and kind; **f22** pretty oaky, but enough maple syrup for damage limitation; **b23** I was hitch-hiking through the Sahara Desert with my life before me when this was filled into cask, most likely to end up as a three year old blend somewhere. Fate decreed otherwise. Now this beautiful, graceful old dram is in a place where the oak the is now casting a long shadow in the setting sun... *48.3%. sc.*

BenRiach Batch 11 1977 37 Years Old dark rum finish, cask no. 1891 db **(96.5) n25** the gooseberry, the marzipan, the citrus-edged creamy fudge, the astonishing deftness to the maple syrup and ulmo honey, the patient restraint of the oak-laden spice: quiet, unassuming perfection. One of the great whisky noses of the year...; **t24.5** a soft delivery with the vanilla out in force but happy to take the vanilla route. Elsewhere the malt drifts in with a barley-sugar opus while the spices plant little oaky flags around the palate; **f23** dries and thins in typical rum cask style: short but with a lovely chocolate biscuit flourish; **b24** if you tip your whisky into a rum cask then you have to expect its wings to be clipped. It's what rum does to a whisky, almost without exception. Now, Benriach was not designed for long term maturation: certainly not 39 years. So although there may be a degree of frustration regarding the tightness of the mid-term and finish, there is no doubt this has improved a tiring whisky beyond measure, perhaps beyond comprehension. The nose, a beauty creature to be adored and cherished, generates the suspicion that it has. *43.2%. sc.*

BenRiach Batch 11 1978 36 Years Old sherry cask matured. bourbon finish cask no. 5469 db **(85.5) n22 t21.5 f21 b21.** I know some people will probably beat their bare chests until they bleed, declaring this the greatest thing they have ever tasted. But I have to say the oak has just marginally crossed the line here, like a football might before being centred for a headed goal. So much beauty on the grape and fruit and chocolate, not to mention stem ginger-tinged spice. But the flag is up...and, like the referee ruling out a winning gal for Rangers again Celtic, doubtless I'll take dog's abuse...*41.7%. sc.*

BenRiach Batch 11 1984 29 Years Old peated, cask no. 488 db **(77) n19 t20 f19 b19.** Sweet, massively smoked. But just doesn't do it for me at all. Too tangy, agricultural and incapable of finding a cord. *51.1%. sc.*

BenRiach Batch 11 1984 29 Years Old peated, Tawny port finish, cask no. 4051 db **(85.5) n21 t21.5 f22 b21.** A must have for the warts-and-all peatophiles. And there are some memorable moments. But too often just a little awkward and fruit pie in the face as the two main constituents haven't really found their range together. *50.3%. sc.*

BenRiach Batch 11 1994 20 Years Old Tawny port finish, cask no. 1703 db **(94) n23.5** the grape is so thick your nose has to blast a course through it to get to the underlying bourbon notes; **t23** sharp, medium sweetness but with a surprising degree of oil. Thick, chewy and wine-glazed. Some jammy, Bakewell tart notes in the mid ground; **f23.5** dries, then a steady build up of cocoa...with the a single toasted raisin tossed in for good measure; **b24** has one of the chunkiest and most overt displays of port I have seen in any Port Finish since the first was launched over 20 years ago. As ports go, about Rotterdam in size...55.6%. sc.

BenRiach Batch 11 1994 20 Years Old peated, Madeira hogshead, cask no. 5626 db **(93)** n22.5 peat. Smoke. More peat. A little more peat. Plenty more smoke. And finally a dose of peat concentrate...oh, with a raisin perched pathetically on top as an afterthought... t24 a surprisingly non-hostile beginning with molten muscovado mingling with hickory. Then the peat gains a slightly oily foothold after which all smoky hell breaks loose.... f23.5 guess.... Oh, and a tranquil squeeze of grape juice very late in the show; b23 for a whisky to show this much peat after 20 years, this must have been one of the smokiest Benriach's ever distilled. For it to be this peaty after 20 years, during which its latter ones have been spent being tamed in a Madeira cask...then it probably ranks as one the smokiest Speysiders in history. Massive is an understatement. 53.2%. sc.

BenRiach Batch 11 1996 18 Years Old Pedro Ximenez sherry puncheon finish, cask no. 7176 db **(90)** n23 the grape takes a step backwards to allow the sweet, gentle smoke centre stage; t22 soft and oily beginnings, then a plethora of crisp sugars cushioned in smoky velvet; f23 complex finale with a the spices adding a tingle to chewey procedings; the peat becomes almost sooty and dry; the fruits move towards apricot...engulfed in butterscotch; b22 OK, OK...I admit it...: I actually like this PX peat mix. Now I've said it! 52.4%. sc.

BenRiach Batch 11 1997 16 Years Old Marsala finish, cask no. 4435 db **(93)** n23 borderline shy with the clean, nut and clove-enriched fruit holding both map and the steering wheel; pretty creamy; t23.5 a finish which works brilliantly on delivery, the grape enjoying a piquancy which salivates, an intensity which ethralls; the creaminess on the nose translates perfectly while a pithy elements comes through; f23 soft with the sugars slowly panning out, perhaps aided by a smidgeon of molasses; b23.5 people say I like neither finishes nor whisky matured in wine casks, whatever they may be. Show me something a delicious as this and I'll show you its greatest supporter... 56.1%. sc.

BenRiach Batch 11 1998 16 Years Old triple distilled, Pedro Ximenez sherry finish, cask no. 5171 db **(82.5)** n19 t21.5 f21 b21. One of the most uncompromising drams of the year. I have actually spent an hour trying to fathom this one, but it sticks in the glass as an opaque mass of peat and grape. Nowhere near as unpleasant as the nose suggested it might be. It is just that it is an indecipherable wall of taste... 57.9%. sc.

BenRiach Batch 11 2000 14 Years Old bourbon barrel, cask no. 38131 db **(87)** n21.5 t23 f21 b21.5. Sugars dominate; fruit revolves around a gooseberry style, while salt intensifies.... so much is right about this. Shame that the actual cask adds only limited positivity... 59.3%. sc.

BenRiach Batch 11 2005 9 Years Old peated, virgin American oak finish, cask no. 3781 db **(94.5)** n23 a strange cross between a honeyed breakfast cereal and very smoky bacon...; t24 gosh...so sweet! Any sweeter and you'd want to kiss it and ask its father for permission to marry it rather than drink the thing! The oaky sugars have rushed headlong into the gristy sugars of the smoky malt...that is some phenolic explosion...; f23.5 long, pulsing, with the spices now at least on a par with the sugar and b24 peat, America and virgins. Oh, and Benriach distillery. What is there not to like...? Brilliant! 58.7%. sc.

The BenRiach Vintage 1999 Bottling Aged 13 Years finished in virgin American oak casks, dist 12 Aug 99 db **(91)** n24.5 like dipping into Trumper's off Jermyn Street for my three monthly supply of virtually odourless soap: an amalgamation of attractively scented notes, though here they all seem to be tannin related. Particularly love the dark cherry, the moist Lubek marzipan (perhaps over a layer of Jaffa Cake)...and then a succession of delicate bourbony toasted honey-rich tones. Wow! t22.5 all kinds of natural caramel fills in any gap on the palate from which the barley has retreated – which makes a lot of them; incredibly soft mouthfeel ... almost sticky; f22 a dry-ish though pleasant toffee and vanilla finale; b22 doesn't quite live up to the billing on the nose...but then not much would. 46%. ncf nc. WB15/330

The BenRiach "Heart of Speyside" db **(85.5)** n21.5 t22 f21 b21. A decent, non-fussy malt where the emphasis is on biscuity barley. At times juicy and sharp. Just a tease of very distant smoke here and there adds weight. 40%

The BenRiach "Horizons" db **(87)** n22 t22.5 f21 b21.5. Few mountains or even hills on this horizon. But the view is still an agreeable one. 50%. nc ncf.

The BenRiach "Solstice" db **(94)** n23.5 t24 f23 b23.5. On midsummer's day 2011, the summer solstice, I took a rare day off from writing this book. With the maximum light available in my part of the world for the day I set off at daybreak to see how many miles I could walk along remote country paths stopping, naturally, only at a few remote pubs on the way. It was a fraction under 28 miles. Had this spellbinding whisky been waiting for me just a little further down the road, I am sure, despite my troubled left knee and blistered right foot, I would have made it 30... 50%. nc ncf.

❖ **Anam na h-Alba The Soul of Scotland Benriach 1990** refill sherry cask, dist Feb 90, bott Mar 14 **(89.5) n22** busy: younger than its years and with the oak seemingly given up trying to chase the barley; a little weak lemon and orange juice thins it out further; **t23.5** salivating with ridiculously fresh barley. Almost gristy still, with butterscotch about as close to weight as it gets; some maple syrup fills the mid-ground. Superb spices throughout; **f22** fat with lingering sugar and biscuity malt linger...then a little untidy; **b22** plenty of pizzazz for its age. Just don't expect much sherry influence. *59.7%. 86 bottles.*

❖ **Anam na h-Alba The Soul of Scotland Benriach 1998** px sherry cask, dist Feb 98, bott Aug 14 **(96) n23** the vaguest hint of smoke vanishes as soon as the tight, crisp sugars get serious; at times, the tannins proffer something closer to bourbon – or even rye - than Scotch; but other layers are of the Melton Hunt Cake fraternity; **t24** sensual mouth feel: fruit and spices combine to ride the wave of thick barley. Chewy, then a slow, salivating build up of Demerara sugars, though with the big oak encroaching almost in a pot still rum style; **f24.5** a finish to make you swoon: more of those Kentucky-style notes – the fruity sweetness not unlike sugars unlocked from virgin oak and mixing with rye – with the oils now really taking over and extending the life of all the mouth-kissing protagonists; **b24.5** from someone who is not the greatest fan of PX casks, I have to say this is a bewildering and quite brilliant whisky. *53.4%. 589 bottles.*

Birnie Moss Intensely Peated db **(90) n22** youthful, full of fresh barley and lively, clean smoke; **t23.5** juicy, fabulously smoked, wet-behind the ears gristy sugars; **f22** some vanillas try to enter a degree of complexity; **b22.5** before Birnie Moss started shaving... or even possibly toddling. Young and stunning. *48%. nc ncf.*

❖ **Glen Farhn BenRiach Single Cask 1996 Aged 18 Years** virgin American oak finish, cask no. 7969 **(96) n24 t24 f23.5 b24.5.** There are a huge number of reasons why you should go to Germany. To watch Bayern Munich in their prime may be one. To witness first hand, spellbound, the exquisite beauty, finesse and skill of a baroque first violinist at the very peak of her art would be another. Or simply to go and buy a bottle of this magnificent whisky: this celebration of great maturation. The virgin oak casks have cast a spell of marzipan and honey around the malt, while the spices nip and dazzle but without overpowering the rich strands of barley. Elsewhere, marmalade notes dovetail with liquorice. The secret is timing, dedication to detail and professionalism; where natural brilliance meets artistry. Like a Lahm or Linder-Dewan, this is something to behold and cherish while we are lucky enough to be able. *54.9%. sc. 349 bottles.*

❖ **Old Masters BenRiach 22 Year Old** cask no. 110693, dist 1991, bott 2014 **(88.5) n22.5** mildly complex, thanks mainly to the composition of the oak. Showing the first signs of big age, though the tannins have a slight gooseberry jelly tinge; **t22** after a slightly unwieldy delivery, soon sets out in a more elegant oak mode; a nonspecific maltiness attaches itself to the tannin; **f22** more of the same, though, inevitably, it is the tannin which bites at the last; **b22** a steady as she goes oldie, surprisingly consistent throughout. *54.2%. sc. James MacArthur & Co Ltd*

❖ **The Single Malts of Scotland Benriach 24 Year Old** bourbon cask, cask no. 100142, dist 1990, bott Jul 14 **(91) n23** coconut and pineapple, but with an attractive sprinkling of cocoa powder; **t22.5** mild dose of exotic fruit; soft muscovado sugars see off the encroaching tannins; **f22.5** dry and a little sawdusty but brought back to life by a delightful chocolate-mint finale; **b23** pleasant, malty, confident Speysider for its age, happy to underline the passage of time and the way it has, mostly, cocked a snook at it.... *50.2%. 315 bottles. WB16/011*

BENRINNES

Speyside, 1826. Diageo. Working.

Benrinnes Aged 15 Years db **(70) n16 t19 f17 b18.** What a shame that in the year the independent bottlers at last get it right for Benrinnes, the actual owners of the distillery make such a pig's ear of it. Sulphured and sicklysweet, this bottling has little to do with the very good whisky made there day in day out by its talented team. Depressing. *43%. Flora and Fauna.*

A.D. Rattray Stronachie 10 Years Old oak **(94) n23** thin, nippy, malty but with a grainy harshness; **t24** rips into the throat, claws at the taste buds with a vicious maltiness; **f23** long, a slight malty tang, some vague fruity notes but still bites and kicks and reaches its conclusion anything but sedately...; **b24** curiously, utterly bizarrely, has the fizz and bite of an old fashioned standard thin, if decently malted, blend of three decades ago. Complex, brain-explodingly busy...and I absolutely love it...! *43% WB15/338*

A.D. Rattray Stronachie 18 Years Old oak **(88.5) n22.5** heavy duty fruit with some pretty ancient apple and pear in play; **t22.5** one of the more fuller bodied Benrinnes you are likely to find with a spiced fruitcake feel; someone forgot to say 'whoa!' When the golden syrup was being poured; **f21.5** slightly tangy, earthy, toffeed residue; **b22** not how Benrinnes normally pans out. Rather love this opulent feel: a real chewer. *46% WB15/310*

Cadenhead's Authentic Collection Benrinnes Cask Strength Aged 25 Years bourbon hogshead, bott Jul 13 **(84) n20.5 t21 f21.5 b21.** You'll do well to find a thinner 25-year-old all year. Warming, at times aggressive with crisp barley sugar. *53%. 270 bottles. WB15/095*

Darkness! Benrinnes Aged 15 Years Oloroso Cask Finish (85) n21 t21 f22 b21. Had a few reservations about this fellow even before I tasted it. If you are going to have big sherry, then fruity muscle needs a backbone. And this distillery provides little at the best of times. Pleasant, thanks to being sulphur-free, and spicy. But otherwise devoid of complexity and structure. *52.9%. 96 bottles. WB15/202*

Darkness! Benrinnes Aged 15 Years Pedro Ximenez Cask Finish (86) n21.5 t22 f21 b21.5. Very much the same can be said for this as the oloroso version. The PX does crank up the sugars as well as the spice big time, though. *53.3%. 94 bottles. WB15/235*

Hepburn's Choice Benrinnes Aged 11 Years sherry butt, dist 02, bott 14 **(87) n21 t22 f22 b22.** Thin, but makes its malty, banana and custard statement very well. Enjoyably refreshing and sales should get their just desserts... *46%. nc ncf sc. 672 bottles.*

The Maltman Benrinnes Aged 17 Years (83) n20 t21.5 f21 b20.5. Surprisingly dull and passionless. A soft caramel and milk chocolate softness engulfs frustrated flames. *43% WB15/216*

Montgomerie's Single Cask Collection Benrinnes cask no. 2835, dist 5 Oct 88, bott Mar 13 **(86.5) n21.5 t21.5 f22 b21.5.** Typically light, simplistic and warming, this has an attractive profile in which the barley is highlighted well. Is it because it is 6.30am and my first sample of the day, but is that a little sugared instant coffee I taste at the death.....? *46%. nc ncf sc. WB15/124*

⟐ **Old Malt Cask Benrinnes 15 Years Old** sherry butt, cask no. 10891, dist Jul 99, bott Oct 14 **(89.5) n22.5** soft and fruity: almost like a wine gum; **t23** a teasing delivery with oak and fruit overlapping deliciously: juicy, salivating and chewy; **f21.5** dries and thins in typical distillery style; but good oak at work; **b22.5** Benrinnes in tip-top form showing with unusual depth. *50%. nc ncf sc. 567 bottles.*

Old Malt Cask Benrinnes Aged 19 Years bourbon barrel, cask no. 10577, dist May 95, bott Jun 14 **(88) n22.5** much bigger and more to say than normal: a vague hint of (not unpleasant) boiled carrot amid the earthier oak; **t22** usually barnstorming, hot-as-hell delivery, this time a little salty but settles into an immediate chorus of cocoa; **f21.5** malt re-emerges and remains salivating until the death; **b22** a distillery not over-given to complexity or surprises, this entertains with more force and consistence than normal. *50%. nc ncf sc. 221 bottles.*

⟐ **Riegger's Selection Cask Strength Benrinnes 16 Year Old** 2nd fill sherry butt, bott 12 Mar 15 **(91) n23.5** spiced dried dates; walnuts, too. Unusually elegant for this distillery; **t23** no sweeter on delivery: the dry sherry almost makes your eyes water. But slowly a substratum of high nut content marzipan makes an entry: a bit like a low calorie, virtually sugarless fruitcake; **f22** just enough sweetness to see off the worst of the drying oak..; **b22.5** Benrinnes singing in its very finest voice. And, for once, in tune... *53.6%*

Scotch Malt Whisky Society Cask 36.74 Aged 9 Years 1st fill barrel, dist 17 Jun 04 **(81.5) n21 t21.5 f19 b20** As ever, too thin to be an effective single malt, though the barley has some attractive moments early on. From the bubble gum school of whisky. *59.9%. nc ncf sc. 235 bottles.*

Signatory Vintage Single Malt Benrinnes 1999 Aged 14 Years, bourbon barrels, cask no. 9919+9921, dist 18 Oct 99, bott 06 Feb 14 **(85) n21 t22.5 f20 b21.** Sweet and syrupy with very little structure. Not unpleasant, and quite well spiced, but you find yourself shouting at the glass to go do something else... *43%. nc. 723 bottles. WB15/017*

⟐ **Stronachie 18 Years Old (83.5) n21.5 t21 f20 b21** This is so much like the older brother of the Stronachie 12: shows the same hot temper on the palate and even sharper teeth. Also, the same slim-line body. Have to say, though, something strangely irresistible about the intensity of the crisp malt. *46%*

BENROMACH
Speyside, 1898. Gordon & MacPhail. Working.
⟐ **Benromach 100° Proof** db **(94) n23** proof positive that toasty oak, a dash of fruit and several puffs of peat can go a long, long way...; **t23.5** beautiful mouth-feel, as thick as anything I have seen from the new Benromach before. The fabulous spice really does make a name for itself, but all those notes recognised on the nose are present and correct here; **f23.5** more of the same, but a layer of Jaffa Cake towards the finish, though it is short-lived as it dries...; **b24** for any confused US readers, the strength is based on the old British

proof strength, not American! What is not confusing is the undisputed complexity and overall excellence of this malt. *57%*

Benromach 10 Years Old matured in hand selected oak casks db **(87.5) n22 t22 f21.5 b22.** For a relatively small still using peat, the experience is an unexpected and delicately light one. *43%*

⬥ **Benromach 15 Year Old** db **(78) n20 t22 f17 b19**. Some charming early moments, especially where the grape escapes its marker and reveals itself in its full juicy and sweet splendour. But it is too short lived as the sulphur, inevitably takes over. *43%*

Benromach 21 Years Old db **(91.5) n22** some exotic fruit and green banana is topped off with a splodge of maple syrup; **t23.5** excellent interplay between the sweeter, barley-rich components and the elegant, spiced oaky backbone; virtually no bite and softened further by an unfurling of vanilla on the middle; **f23** long, oak-edged with a slow, tapering dryness which does nothing to confront the sugared backnotes or even the suggesting of the most delicate smoke; **b23** an entirely different, indeed lost, style of malt from the old, now gone, big stills. The result is an airier whisky which has embraced such good age with a touch of panache and grace. *43%*

Benromach 22 Years Old Finished in Port Pipes db **(86) n22 t23 f20 b21.** Slightly Jekyll and Hyde. *45%. 3500 bottles.*

Benromach 25 Years Old db **(92) n24** seriously sexy with spices interplaying with tactile malt: the bitter-sweet balance is just so. There is even the faintest flicker of peat-smoke to underscore the pedigree; **t22** an early, surprising, delivery of caramel amongst the juicy barley; **f23** lots of gentle spices warm the enriched barley and ice-creamy vanilla; **b23** a classic old-age Speysider, showing all the quality you'd hope for. *43%*

Benromach 30 Years Old db **(95.5) n23.5** spiced sultana, walnuts and polished bookcases; **t24** no malt has the right to be anything near so silky. The sugars are a cunning mix of molasses and muscovado; the honey is thinned manuka. Still the barley gets through, though the vanilla is right behind; **f24** drier, but never fully dries and has enough spotted dog in reserve to make for a moist, lightly spiced finish. And finally a thin strata of sweet, Venezulan cocoa; **b24** you will struggle to find a 30-year-old with less wrinkles than this.. Magnificent: one of the outstanding malts of the year. *43%*

Benromach Cask Strength 1981 db **(91) n21.5 t23 f23.5 b23.** Really unusual with that seaweedy aroma awash with salt: stunningly delicious stuff. *54.2%*

Benromach Cask Strength 2001 db **(89) n21.5 t23 f22 b22.5.** Just fun whisky which has been very well made and matured with total sympathy to the style. Go get. *599%*

Benromach 2002 Cask Strength db **(88.5) n22 t22.5 f22 b22.** Most peaty malts frighten those who aren't turned on by smoky whisky. This might be an exception: they just don't come any friendlier. *60.3%*

Benromach Cask Strength 2003 db **(92) n22.5** the smoke is elusive and registers little more than the outline of your previous night's dream. Dry, with a little earthy nip and pinch; **t23.5** it takes a long time for the peat to finally arrive. But when it gets there it stays, though little more than a shadow to the rampant muscovado sugar; **f23** long, a little fizz and spice to the smoke now, but those sugars make light work of the gathering vanilla; **b23.5** hats off to the most subtle and sophisticated Benromach I have tasted in a while. *59.4%*.

Benromach 2002 Sassicaia Wood Finish db **(86) n21 t22 f21 b22.** Again this entirely idiosyncratic wood-type comes crashing head to head with the smoke to form a whisky style like nothing else. Dense, breathless and crushed, there is little room for much else to get a word in, other than some oak-extracted sugars. A must experience dram. *45%*

Benromach 2005 Sassicaia Finish db **(92.5) n22.5 t24 f23 b23.** A sassy dram in every way... *45%*

Benromach Madeira Wood db **(92) n22 t24 f23 b23.** If you want a boring, safe, timid malt, stay well away from this one. Fabulous: you are getting the feeling that the real Benromach is now beginning to stand up. *45%*

Benromach Marsala Wood db **(86.5) n21.5 t22 f22 b21.** Solid, well made, enjoyable malt, which in some ways is too solid: the imperviousness of both the peat and grape appears not to allow much else get through. Not a dram to say no to, however, and the spices in particular are a delight. *45%*

Benromach Organic db **(91) n23 t23 f22 b23.** Young and matured in possibly first fill bourbon or, more likely, European (even Scottish) oak; you cannot do other than sit up and take notice of this guns-blazing big 'un. An absolute treat! *43%. nc ncf.*

Benromach Organic Special Edition db **(85.5) n22 t21 f21.5 b21.** The smoky bacon crisp aroma underscores the obvious youth. Also, one of the driest malts of the year. Overall, pretty. But pretty pre-pubescent, too... *43%*

◇ **Benromach Organic 2008** bott 2014 db (93) n23 huge toasty oak: a degree of bourbon-style liquorice and ulmo honey, pepped up further by barley on heat...; t23.5 good grief: just didn't expect that! The sugars from the oak have linked with the sweeter bits of the barley and rocketed off, with spices forming when the energy begins to dip; f23 long, with the barley sugar refusing to allow any oaky bitterness to climb onboard at all; b23.5 for a whisky at a meagre 43%, the most astonishing explosion of intense barley and oak. More orgasmic than organic... 43%

Benromach Origins db (84.5) n20 t22 f21 b21.5. You'd think after tasting over 1,250 whiskies in the space of a few months you'd have nosed and tasted it all. But no: here is something very different. Discordant noises from nose to finish, it is saved by the extraordinary richness of the coppery input and a vague smoky richness finishing with cold latte. 50%

Benromach Origins Batch 1 "Golden Promise" dist 1999 db (69.5) n17 t17.5 f17.5 b17.5. The nose is less than promising. And with good reason. 50%

Benromach Origins Batch 2 "Port Pipe" dist 1999 db (86) n22 t20.5 f23 b20.5. Dense whisky with huge spice. But it is as if in concentrate form with little room for complexity to develop into its full potential. Some charming chocolate and toffee on the finish. 50%

Benromach Origins Batch 3 "Optic" dist 2000 db (83.5) n21 t20 f21.5 b21. Another chunky, tight malt from the new Benromach. Some serious chewing, but a few feints on which to chew... 50%

Benromach Peat Smoke Batch 3 db (90.5) n22 excellent nose: pretty decent levels of peak reek evident but dried, rather than cured...; t23 the dry peat builds in intensity, though not after the clean and powering barley makes the first speech; f22.5 dry, chalky and compact; damn it – this is very good, indeed! b23 An excellent malt that has been beautifully made. Had it been bottled at 46 we would have seen it offer an extra degree of richness. 40%

Benromach Peat Smoke 2005 67ppm db (88.5) n22 dry, peat soot; t22.5 light oils and slightly over sugared barley. The smoke, surprisingly, takes a bit of a back seat while gentle oak calm the over zealous maple syrup; a fair chunk of marmalade in there; f21.5 falls away rather too quickly with lightly smoked butterscotch; b22.5 this may be 67 parts per million phenols when it started. But size, so I have been told, is not important. Stamina and finesse both are. And while this may enjoy a degree of the latter, it has little of the former. 46%.

◇ **Benromach Peat Smoke 2006** db (90.5) n22.5 a soothing softness to the peat reveals attractive degrees of mint and vanilla; t23.5 the gristy sugars are up front and carry with them a surprisingly dense smokiness, which soon dissipates; beautifully even middle, with that weak mint humbug touch drifting in; f22 long, a little tart as a few tannins nip; b22.5 a more measured malt than the previous vintage. 46%

Benromach Traditional db (86) n22 t21 f21.5 b21.5. Deliciously clean and smoky. But very raw and simplistic, too. 40%

Benromach Wood Finish Hermitage dist 2001 db (84) n19 t23 f21 b21. A sweet, tight dram with all the shape crushed out of it. It does have its moment of greatness, though: about three or four seconds after arrival when it zooms into the stratosphere on a massively fruity, sensuously spiced rocket. Then it just fades away... 45%

Benromach Wood Finish Pedro Ximénez dist 2002 db (85.5) n21 t22.5 f21 b21. Combining PX with peated whisky is still probably the hardest ask in the maturation lexicon. Lagavulin are still to get it right. And they have not quite managed it here, either. It's a bumpy old ride, though some of the early chewing moments are fun. Not a bad attempt, at all. Just the learning curve is still on the rise... 45%

Benromach Vintage 1968 db (94.5) n23 t23 f24.5 b24. A 40 year plus whisky of astonishing quality...? A piece of cake... 45.4%

Benromach Vintage 1969 db (92) n22 t24 f23 b23. The odd branch of the old oak too many. But still has many magical mahogany moments. 42.6%

Benromach Vintage 1976 db (89.5) n23 exotic fruit is expected...and doesn't disappoint; yawns a little from tiredness here and there; t23.5 silky, mouth-watering though attractively tart. Any blender looking to ensure the malty but exotic frame to an old blend would be searching in his arsenal for a series of Speysiders just like this; f21 mainly vanilla and cocoa milkshake; bitters out slightly as the oak bites; b22 hardly complex and shows all the old age attributes to be expected. That said...a very comfortable and satisfying ride. 46%

Gordon & MacPhail Benromach Vintage 1976 db (89) n22.5 t22 f22 b22.5. For all the massive oak which shapes every inch of this dram, the degree of ulmo honey at work is extraordinary. 46%. ncf.

Gordon & MacPhail Benromach Port Wood finish 2000 db (86.5) n22 t21 f22 b21.5. A pleasant experience with a distinctive chocolate liqueur feel to it. Just a little too heavily laden with grape (though thankfully clean and entirely sulphur-free) for greatness as the malt is all but obliterated, though the spices rack up the complexity levels. 45%. ncf.

BLADNOCH

Lowlands, 1817. Armstrong Brothers. Working.

Bladnoch Aged 6 Years Bourbon Matured db (91) n21.5 young, yes. But the soft feints have nothing to do with that; t22.5 a youthful, oily delivery, not exactly a picture of harmony, gives way to a brutal coup d'etat of ultra intense prisoner-slaughtering barley; f24 intense barley-concentrate oils offer a perplexing array of sweet, grassy tones; you simply chew and chew until the jaw aches. Cocoa at last arrives, all with a spiced buzz and a smearing of vanillas. Meanwhile your tongue explores the mouth, wondering what the hell is going on; b23 the fun starts with the late middle, where those extra oils congregate and the taste buds are sent rocking. Great to see a Lowlander bottled at an age nearer its natural best and even the smaller cut, in a roundabout way, ensures a mind-blowing dram. 573%

Bladnoch Aged 6 Years Lightly Peated db (93) n23 a peat fire just bursting into life; t23 firm, bitter-sweet; the layering of the peat is awesome, with the youth of the malt adding an extra dimension; some citrus notes help lighten the load; f23.5 smoky hickory; the vanillas make a feeble entry, a gentle oiliness persists; b23.5 the peat has nothing to do with the overall score here: this is a much better-made whisky with not a single off-note and the cut is spot on. And although it claims to be lightly peated, that is not exactly true: such is the gentle nature of the distillate, the smoke comes through imperiously and on several levels. "Spirit of the Lowlands" drones the label. Since when has outstanding peated malt been associated with that part of the whisky world...?? 58.5%

Bladnoch Aged 6 Years Sherry Matured db (73.5) n18 t19 f18.5 b18. A sticky, lop-sided malt where something, or a group of somethings, conjures up a very unattractive overture. Feints on the palate but no excellent bourbon cask to the rescue here. 56.9%

Bladnoch Aged 10 Years db (94) n23 lemon and lime, marmalade on fresh-sliced flour-topped crusty bread; t24 immensely fruity and chewy, lush and mouthwatering and then the most beguiling build-up of spices: the mouthfeel is full and faultless; f23 long, remains mildly peppery and then a dryer advance of oak. The line between bitter and sweet is not once crossed; b24 this is probably the ultimate Bladnoch, certainly the best I have tasted in over 25 years. This Flora and Fauna bottling by then owners United Distillers should be regarded as the must-get-at-all-costs Bladnoch. If the new owner can create something even to hang on to this one's coat-tails then he has excelled himself. For those few of us lucky enough to experience this, this dram is nothing short of a piece of Lowland legend and folklore. 43%

Bladnoch Aged 15 Years db (91) n22.5 remnants of zest and barley sit comfortably with the gentle oaks; t22.5 excellent delivery and soon gets into classic Bladnoch citric stride; f23 wonderfully clean barley belies the age and lowers the curtain so delicately you hardly notice; b23 quite outstanding Lowland whisky which, I must admit, is far better than I would have thought possible at this age. 55%

Bladnoch Aged 16 Years "Spirit of the Lowlands" db (88) n22 t22 f22 b22. Really lovely whisky and unusual to see a Lowlander quite this comfortable at such advanced age. 46%. ncf.

Bladnoch 18 Years Old db (88.5) n21 t23.5 f22 b22. The juiciness and clarity to the barley, and especially the big gooseberry kick, early on makes this a dram well worth finding. 55%

Adelphi Selection Bladnoch 23 Years Old cask no. 30043, dist 90, bott 13 (89) n22.5 weighty and nutty: marzipan with low sugar content...slightly Aberfeldy-ish in style; t23 superb delivery: magnificent weight to the oil which carries a wonderful maple syrup and acacia honey blend; f21.5 at first profound butterscotch tart, then bitters slightly as the oak grabs hold; b22 Bladnoch at its most full bodied. Remarkably fit for its age. 49.2%. ncf ncf sc. 74 bottles. WB15/412

Cadenhead's Small Batch Bladnoch Aged 21 Years bourbon hogsheads, dist 1992, bott 2014 (92) n22 lively barley on all levels – from grassy to malty and embraces the Black Jacks easily; t24 one of the most eye-watering and stunningly clean deliveries you could imagine: like watching a five-year-old with a grey beard...; the sugars stay gristy and bounce beautifully alongside the peppers; f23 long, at last some vanilla, but that malt won't stop chasing...; b23 a fizzing little malt-concentrated beauty which defies the years! 54.9%. 510 bottles. WB15/091

Cadenhead's Authentic Collection Bladnoch Cask Strength Aged 23 Years bourbon hogshead, dist 1990, bott Jul 13 (87) n21 t22 f22 b22. A real softie of a dram which doesn't really want to cover much more than the basics. Very sweet malt is at its heart. And with the creamy Ovaltine at the finish, a good one as a night cap. 48.5%. 282 bottles. WB15/094

Old Malt Cask Bladnoch Aged 21 Years refill hogshead, cask no. 10418, dist Nov 92, bott May 14 (86) n21.5 t23 f20.5 b21. Beautifully malty on delivery. But has the sharpness of a lemon drop at times – a malt certainly not behaving its age. 50%. nc ncf sc. 322 bottles.

Signatory Vintage Single Malt Bladnoch 1993 Aged 20 Years hogsheads, cask no. 767+773, dist 08 Mar 93, bott 25 Apr 13 (88) n20 messy: the two casks have not gelled. All kinds of in-fighting going on. Off key; t23.5 makes amends on the eye-watering delivery which appears to be barley concentrate infiltrated by heather and orange blossom honey;

f22 reverts to a theme noticeable on the nose, but now enough spices and mocha to add to the complexity; **b22.5** you get the feeling you have dodged a bullet here. The nose puts you on your guard as some of the oak used isn't what it might be. But it ends up working a treat, especially on the brilliant delivery. *43%. nc. 798 bottles. WB15/016*

⟐ **Scotch Malt Whisky Society Cask 50.54 Aged 23 Years** refill barrel, dist 10 Jul 90 **(94.5) n23.5** very similar to whisky barrels I find maturing beside cider brandy casks...apples everywhere...! **t23.5** delicate, juicy malt finds itself in an early tussle with prominent liquorice and drier oak notes, yet the sugars are always where they should be; **f24** the early oils settle and allow the fabulous small grain barley notes full scope to reveal its complexity; **b23.5** a stunning marriage of Somerset cider brandy and hardcore bourbon. Superb!! *50%. sc. 104 bottles.*

⟐ **Scotch Malt Whisky Society Cask 50.55 Aged 23 Years** refill barrel, dist 10 Jul 90 **(86) n21 t21.5 f22 b21.5.** Altogether more aggressive than 50.54, though there is little respite from the apple-rich character. The oak notes are a little more austere, too, allowing the spice a louder hum. *53.9%. sc. 70 bottles.*

⟐ **Scotch Malt Whisky Society Cask 50.58 Aged 24 Years** refill barrel, dist 26 Jan 90 **(89) n22** excellent age seeps through the malt; the apple here shows a little more pip; **t21.5** a little buzz and burn early on. But the apple-malt double act plugs the aging holes; **f23.5** an outstanding finish. A little custard and banana counters the impact of the apple while bourbon-style small grains make for a busy and beautifully-balanced finale. High quality oak stands its ground without dominating. Lots of boxes ticked here; **b22** a kinder cask allows the malt to progress at full throttle. *55%. sc. 90 bottles.*

BLAIR ATHOL
Highlands (Perthshire), 1798. Diageo. Working.

Blair Athol Aged 12 Years db **(77) n18 t19 f21 b19.** Thick, fruity, syrupy and a little sulphury and heavy. The finish has some attractive complexity among the chunkyness. *43%. Flora and Fauna.*

Berry's Own Selection Blair Athol 1989 Aged 23 Years cask no. 6333, bott 2013 **(87.5) n21.5 t22 f21.5 b22.** Bold, full bodied and fat. Slightly puckering and a little greasy. *46%. ncf. WB15/243*

Cadenhead's Authentic Colleection Blair Athol Cask Strength Aged 24 Years bourbon hogsheads, dist 1989, bott Jul 13 **(92) n23** kind of similar to this year's G&M bottling, only here the buttery honey is sharper and three dimensional; **t23.5** suerb delivery with the creamy, intense malt bursting out with a wonderful gristy barley starburst; **f22.5** creamy butterscotch; **b23** great to see the distillery at full throttle taste and quality-wise. *50.8%. 186 bottles. WB15/093*

Càrn Mòr Strictly Limited Edition Blair Athol Aged 15 Years hogshead, dist 1998, bott 2013 **(67) n17 t19 f16 b17.** Furry and woefully off key. *46%. nc ncf. 736 bottles. WB15/159*

Gordon & MacPhail Connoisseurs Choice Blair Athol dist 1997, bott 2013 **(87) n22 t22 f21 b22.** How soft and friendly is the honey on this? At other times like distilled Worther's Originals candy. A little late oak bitterness. *46%. nc ncf. WB15/110*

⟐ **Gordon & MacPhail Connoisseurs Choice Blair Athol 2005 (89.5) n21.5** a bit rough and ready but the barley means well; **t23.5** big and chewy: a rough diamond of a delivery, with sparkling barley sugar cutting through the viscous body; a little earthy as well...and it works...; **f22** a little cocoa mingles with the lingering oily sugars; **b22.5** a malt with a bit of attitude and in pretty good nick. *46%*

Hepburn's Choice Blair Athol 2002 Aged 11 Years refill hogshead, dist 2002, bott 2014 **(80.5) n19.5 t22 f19 b21.** The delivery works fine and the entire piece falls within a malty framework. But the nose and finish reveals enough weaknesses to make this an uphill battle. *46%. ncf sc. 421 bottles.*

Hepburn's Choice Blair Athol 2002 Aged 11 Years refill hogsead, dist 02, bott 14 **(87.5) n21.5 t22 f22 b22.** A robust dram absolutely bursting with all kinds of malty life. Lively, fresh, clean and naughtily warming. *46%. nc ncf sc. 394 bottles.*

⟐ **Hepburn's Choice Blair Athol Aged 12 Years** refill hogshead, dist 2002, bott 2015 **(87.5) n21.5 t21.5 f22.5 b22.** Thumping liquid barley. The nose and early delivery both on the meagre side. But the maltiness, catching the sugars and drier oak notes just right, more than makes amends. *46%. nc ncf sc. 165 bottles.*

Old Malt Cask Blair Athol Aged 16 Years sherry butt, cask no. 10127, dist May 97, bott Oct 13 **(85.5) n21.5 t22 f21 b21.5.** A pretty enough picture, thanks mainly to the muscovado sugars. But a bit like a jigsaw with some of the pieces in the wrong place... *50%. sc. 545 bottles.*

⟐ **Old Particular Highland Blair Athol 18 Years Old** sherry butt, cask no. 10457, dist Sept 95, bott Aug 14 **(90) n22** clean with the accent very much on the barley and custard powder; **t22.5** cleans the palate with rare precision and efficiency! Again, the barley is at the forefront with grist abounding and subtle spices pinging around the palate; **f23** oak-induced cocoa offers the perfect counter to the lively malt. A top quality cask ensures a layered sweet-dry finale; **b22.5** the gristy sugars are a pure joy! *48.4%. nc ncf sc. 681 bottles.*

Old Particular Highland Blair Athol 20 Year Old 1st fill sherry butt, cask no. DL9908, dist Apr 93, bott Aug 13 **(81) n20 t21 f20 b20.** Malty, clean and a little sharp. But among this flight of drams, this is the one which stubbornly refused to take off. *51.5%. nc ncf sc. 477 bottles.*

⬩ **That Boutique-y Whisky Company Blair Athol** batch 1 **(85.5) n22 t22 f20 b21.5.** The promising grassy start to this fades and finally bitters out. Very simple Speyside blending fodder with some pleasant moments. *48.9%. 35 bottles.*

Wemyss Malts 1991 Single Highland Blair Athol "Blackcurrant Coulis" barrel, dist 91, bott 14 **(86.5) n21.5 t22 f21.5 b21.5.** A very pleasant whisky intent to do simple, juicy things without really thinking much about complexity. A malty blending dram on the lightweight side for this distillery. *46%. sc. 338 bottles.*

The Whisky Agency Blair Athol 1989 dist 1989 **(88) n22** a fizzing mix of stout, bourbonesque tannin, all peppery and rich. A baser, thinner note on the malt gives shrill warning to original state of the spirit; **t22.5** an intriguing mix of dark sugars and resounding spice ensure a dapper delivery hardly short of character. But the body is woefully thin...; **f21.5** disappears quickly, leaving a few oaky, sugary tide marks; **b22** all the hallmarks of a whisky run fast through the stills, that near quarter of a century ago. But good oak has helped integrate it back into polite quaffing society. *50.8%.*

⬩ **Whisky Fair Blair Athol 26 Year Old** wine treated butt, cask no. 6794, dist 1988, bott 2015 **(66) n15 t22 f13 b16.** The scoring tells you all you need to know: the glory of the rich fruit is in stark contrast to the hefty sulphur present. *58.2%. 470 bottles. Signatory.*

BOWMORE
Islay, 1779. Morrison Bowmore. Working.

Bowmore Aged 12 Years db **(91) n22.5** light peats, the air of a room with a man sucking cough sweets; sweet pipe smoke; **t23.5** soft, beautiful delivery of multi-layered peats; lots of effervescent spices and molassed sugars; spices abound; **f22.5** much drier with sharper berries and barley; the peat still rumbles onwards, but has no problems with the light, sawdusty oaks; **b23.5** this new bottling still proudly carries the Fisherman's Friend cough sweet character, but the coastal, saline properties here are a notch or three up: far more representative of Islay and the old distillery style. Easily by far the truest Bowmore I have tasted in a long while with myriad complexity. Even going back more than a quarter of a century, the malt at this age rarely showed such relaxed elegance. Most enjoyable. *40%*

Bowmore Black Rock oak casks db **(87.5) n22.5 t22 f21 b22.** A friendly, full bodied dram whose bark is worse than its bite. Smoked toasted fudge is the main theme. But that would not work too well without the aid of a vague backdrop cinnamon and marmalade. If you are looking for a gentle giant, they don't come more wimpish than this. *40% WB15/336*

Bowmore "Enigma" Aged 12 Years db **(82) n19 t22 f20 b21.** Sweet, molassed and with that tell-tale Fisherman's Friend tang representing the light smoke. This Enigma hasn't quite cracked it, though. *40%. Duty Free.*

Bowmore "Darkest" Aged 15 Years db **(83) n20 t23 f19 b21.** In recent years a dram you tasted with glass in one hand and a revolver in the other. No more. But for the sulphur present, this would have been a much higher score. *43%*

Bowmore Gold Reef oak casks db **(79) n19.5 t21 f19 b19.5.** Simple, standard (and rather boring and safe) fare for the masses gagged by toffee. *43% WB15/280*

Bowmore "Mariner" Aged 15 Years db **(79) n19 t21 f19 b20.** There are two ways of looking at this. As a Bowmore. Which is how I have marked it. Or a something to throw down your neck for pure fun. Which is probably worth another seven or eight points. Either way, there is something not entirely right here. *43%. Duty Free.*

Bowmore Aged 17 Years db **(77) n18 t22 f18 b19.** For all the attractiveness of the sweet fruit on delivery, the combination of butt and cough sweet makes for pretty hard going. *43%*

Bowmore Aged 18 Years db **(79) n20 t21 f19 b19.** Pleasant, drinkable Fisherman's Friend style – like every Bowmore it appears around this age. But why so toffee-dull? *43%*

Bowmore Aged 23 Years Port Matured db **(86) n22 t22 f21 b21.** Have you ever sucked Fisherman's Friends and fruit pastels at the same time, and thrown in the odd Palma Violet for good measure...? *50.8%*

Bowmore Aged 25 Years db **(86) n21 t22 f21 b22.** Not the big, chunky guy of yore: the age would surprise you if tasted blind. *43%*

Bowmore Aged 30 Years db **(94) n23** intense burnt raisin amid the intense burnt peat; a deft rummy sweetness strikes an improbable chord with the sweetened lime; the oak is backward coming forward but binds beautifully with both peat and fruit; **t24** near flawless delivery showing a glimpse of Bowmore in a form similar to how I remember it some 25 years ago. The peat, though intense does have a hint of the Fisherman's Friend about it, but not so upfront as today. For all the peat, this is clean whisky, moulded by a craftsman into how a truly great Islay should be; **f23** dries sublimely as the oak contains the peat and adds a touch of coffee to it in unsugared form. Gentle oils cling tightly to the roof of the mouth; **b24** a Bowmore that no Islay scholar should be without. Shows the distillery at its most intense yet delicate; an essay in balance and how great oak, peat and fruit can combine for those special moments in life. Unquestionably one of the best Bowmores bottled this century. *43%*

Bowmore 1985 db (89) **n21.5 t24 f22 b21.5.** I may have tasted a sweeter Islay. Just not sure when. This whisky is so wrong..it's fantastically right...! *52.6%*

Bowmore 100 Degrees Proof db (90.5) **n22** low key smoke. Anyone who has been to Arbroath looking for where the Smokies are cured and homed in on the spot by nose alone will recognise this aroma...; **t23** delicate in all departments, including the peat. The barley is sweet but it is the tenderness of the oils which stars; **f22.5** long with a tapering muscovado finale; **b23** proof positive! A real charmer. *57.1%. ncf.*

Bowmore Devil's Cask db (87.5) **n22 t23 f21 b21.5.** Not really my style of whisky, for all its obvious fun...and this little devil doesn't really even to try and balance itself out. *56.9%*

⬦ **Bowmore Devil's Cask II** db (80.5) **n19.5 t22 f19 b20.** Another huge experience, like Devil's Cask I. And, also like that bottling, brimstone can be detected. Still not my cup of tea. *56.3%*

⬦ **Bowmore Laimrig Aged 15 Years** db (90.5) **n22.5** thumping oloroso smashed head first into Bowmore in its Fisherman's Friend mode. The result is unique...and not for the faint-hearted...; **t23.5** a genuinely attractive delivery which concentrates on the silky mouth-feel at first before getting on with the business of the molasses, dates and outrageous spice. And of course, the smoke...; **f22** some wonderful chocolate on show, comfortable with the now busy rather than raging spices and those dark, vaguely dirty, sugars; **b22.5** first things first: absolutely spot on sherry butts at work here with not a hint of an off note. But often it is hard to get smoke and sherry to gel. The exercise here is not without success, but you feel it is straining at every sinew to hit the high spots. *53.7%. 18,000 bottles.*

Bowmore Laimrig III db (92) **n23.5** so delicate is the ultra clean grape, I am guessing this is a sherry cask finish. Not usually a fan of smoke and grape, but when it is this delicate, what isn't there to like?; **t23.5** the softness found on the nose is continued on the palate. The sweetness is cleverly controlled and when the Fisherman's Friend personality arrives, it is quietly muffled, if not smothered to death, by a combination of silky grape, teasing spice and melting muscovado sugars; **f22.5** the oak now raises its profile, the deep vanillas and hint of honeycomb underlining a reasonable age; **b23** I must ask my research team: where the hell are Laimrigs I and II....? *53.7%*

Bowmore Legend db (88) **n22 t22.5 f22 b22.5.** Not sure what has happened here, but it has gone through the gears dramatically to offer a substantial dram with both big peat and excellent balancing molasses. Major stuff. *40%*

Bowmore Small Batch "Bourbon Cask Matured" db (86) **n22 t22 f21 b21.** A big improvement on the underwhelming previous Small Batch from this distillery, then called "Reserve", though there appears to be a naievity to the proceeding which both charm and frustrate. The smoke, hanging on the grist, is very low key. *40%*

Bowmore Small Batch Reserve db (80.5) **n20 t21 f19 b20.5.** With a name like "Small Batch Reserve" I was expecting a marriage between intense Kentucky and Islay. Alas, this falls well short of the mark. *40%*

Bowmore Tempest Aged 10 Years Small Batch Release V db (90.5) **n23** where Kildalton meets Kentucky...soft, some might say puny, smoke swept almost contemptuously aside as confident honey-bourbon notes claims lordship; **t23** at least the barley gets a brief look in as a wave of gristy sugars erupt for a salivating opening; the light smoke drifts aimlessly while red liquorice and thin ulmo honey coats the palate; **f21.5** vaguely smoked vanilla; bitters out; **b23** if you like your Islays on the subtle side but with a bold undercurrent, here you go..! *55.9%. ncf. WB15/279*

⬦ **Bowmore White Sands Aged 17 Years** db (88) **n20** not quite the most exciting Bowmore nose but a winner if you like hesitant peat and irrepressible caramel; **t22** chewy dates to start, then a slow working through the peat. Again, the caramel seems to have fingers everywhere, smothering the spices in particular; **f23** ridiculously soft mouth-feel. Now the spices have spread and try to nip but have no teeth. The sugars appear to be an amalgam of muscovado, molasses, maple syrup and caramel...but all watered down; **b23** a muzzled malt which shouldn't work – but somehow does. *43%*

Alexander Weine&distillate Bowmore 16 Year Old refill bourbon hogshead, cask no. 9646, dist 1996, bott 2013 (84.5) **n21.5 t22 f20 b21.** The intense sugars shape much of the mouth feel. But, ultimately, we are in pure Fisherman's Friend territory... *57.1%. sc. Cask strength.*

Blackadder Raw Cask 1997 16 Years Old Bowmore single oak hogshead, cask no. 1896, dist 13 Jun 97, bott Oct 13 **(85.5)** **n21** **t22.5** **f21** **b21.** Bitty and shapeless, there is a lot to commend the salivating delivery. But not much else stacks up. Busy and rather hot. 57.5%. nc ncf sc. 284 bottles, cask strength. WB15/058

Blackadder Raw Cask 2001 12 Years Old Bowmore single oak hogshead, cask no. 20063, dist 13 Mar 01, bott Oct 13 **(94)** **n23** punchy smoke: some mocha seasoned with ginger and allspice; **t24** stunning oils ensure the depth of the muscovado sugars reaches where they have best effect; the smoke appears to be part of the sugars and flying a little higher, too; **f23.5** smoked butterscotch; **b24** the old distillery back on top of its game. 58.5%. nc ncf sc. 312 bottles, cask strength. WB15/059

◈ **Cadenhead's Single Cask Bowmore 2001** bourbon cask **(95.5)** **n24** Bowmore...really...?? Someone has upped the peat content and smoke when producing the malt for this one. None of your Fisherman's Friends here: beautifully coastal and saline; **t24** silky textured: like a hammer thumping your taste buds through your very best shirt. Fabulous blizzard of varying phenolic tones, all intensified by a big liquorice kick; **f23.5** hickory and molasses...but still carrying a full phenolic theme; **b24** exceptionally heavy phenols for a Bowmore, But the balance is the stuff of legend.: one of the very best Bowmores I have had for many a year. 57.1%. sc.

◈ **Fadandel.dk Bowmore 16 Years Old** hogshead, cask no 800344, dist 25 Sep 98, bott 2 Oct 14 **(92.5)** **n23** so complex, you don't at first notice the enormity of the phenols; overly polished oak and liquorice grabs your attention before the peat does, which arrives in a plastic pouch...; **t23.5** crisp, intricate - and intimate – sugars straight off the blocks. The smoke is less direct, circling and occasionally touching base. Toasted fudge softens to the more buttery variety...and then, finally, the smoke, less like plastic now but still with an unusual refrain; **f23** buttery, with a soft peat tag; **b23** creamy, heavily peated for a Bowmore. And beautifully matured. 58.6%

◈ **Gleann Mór Bowmore 12 Year Old** dist May 03, bott Jun 15 **(93)** **n22.5** no Fisherman's Friend! No cough sweet! Just good old fashioned kippery peat at its freshest and most enticing; **t23.5** good heavens...!! A Bowmore...??? Wonderfully gristy and energetic with a salivating smokiness which certainly wakes you up; **f23.5** remains clean and sharp and lip-smackingly delicious; the late phenols now have a slight hickory feel to them; **b23.5** the most succulent and lively Bowmore I have encountered for a very long while! 53.3%. sc.

◈ **Gleann Mór Bowmore 30 Year Old** dist Mar 85, bott May 15 **(95.5)** **n23.5** a little thin and strained at first, as though the meagre smoke is trying to keep the oak at bay; when you pick up an orange blossom honey note, you know things are not what they first seem; **t24.5** an entirely different ball game now: this is when exotic fruit meets exotic smoke; the integration of orange blossom honey, manuka honey and smoked treacle is as mesmerising is it is beautiful; **f23.5** lightly peated ulmo honey; a vague oak tang; **b24** after what first appears as an underwhelming, if pleasant, nose, what happens next is spectacular...! 52.3%. sc.

◈ **Glen Fahrn Airline Nr 04 Bowmore 1997 Aged 14 Years** cask no. 800208 **(91)** **n22** **t23** **f23** **b23**. A neat and tidy Islay with a maltiness and oil profile more associated with Caol Ila. Little of the cough sweet characteristics of that era, so a welcome treat. Some typical molasses, though. 53.6%. sc. 101 bottles.

Montgomerie's Single Cask Collection Bowmore cask no. 085078, dist 24 Apr 90, bott Mar 13 **(92)** **n23** relaxed smoke but by no means horizontal. A lovely salty twang gives this a rock pool feel; a little marmalade, too; **t24** sublime texture has a near perfect meeting of smoke and sugar; most remarkably, the barley is still intact and readable; **f22** slow smoke fade; a tad bitter late on; **b23** resplendent in its deft smoke and refined sugars, an impressive Bowmore. 46%. nc ncf sc. WB15/125

◈ **Old Malt Cask Bowmore 12 Years Old** refill hogshead, cask no. 10919, dist Dec 01, bott Oct 14 **(88)** **n22** a drizzle of citrus on the blackjack candy and smoke; **t22.5** excellent marriage of smoke and sugar. The oak is more than ballast and weighs in with enriching waves; **f21.5** dries and thins; **b22** a satisfying Bowmore where the peat and sugar levels are a touch higher than normal. 50%. nc ncf sc. 204 bottles.

Old Malt Cask Bowmore Aged 14 Years refill hogshead, cask no. 10146, dist Sep 99, bott Oct 13 **(87.5)** **n21.5** **t22** **f22** **b22**. Pleasant enough. But never really has much to say or a point to make and gets lost in its own sugary, phenolic fug. 50%. nc ncf sc. 563 bottles.

◈ **Old Malt Cask Bowmore 16 Years Old** refill hogshead, cask no. 11211, dist Jun 98, bott Jan 15 **(95)** **n23.5** don't think I'll be the only one to spot a bit of exotic fruit on that undercooked phenol...; **t24.5** one of the most sumptuous deliveries from a Bowmore for a very long time. And, sure enough, arriving early are those exotic fruits, which work magnificently well with the muffled smoke notes; the gentle mix of ulmo honey and Demerara sugars don't hurt, either...;

f23 a vague spice, and a slight edge to the peat; **b24** hats off to a quietly classy little number. Bowmore looking a lot older than its 16 years... *50%. nc ncf sc. 234 bottles.*

Old Particular Islay Bowmore Aged 12 Years refill hogshead, cask no. 10284, dist Dec 01, bott Mar 14 **(86) n22 t21 f21.5 b21.5.** Curiously metallic, as if a new still or maybe condenser had been recently put in place. The gristy element and fudgy smoke remains untarnished, though. *48.4%. nc ncf sc. 421 bottles.*

◇ **Old Particular Islay Bowmore 15 Years Old** refill butt, cask no. 10583, dist Sept 99, bott Dec 14 **(94) n21.5** a bit of an arm wrestle between toffeed peat and a vague, unspecified fruitiness, during which the contents of the table are sent crashing to the floor; **t23.5** an outstanding landing of maple syrup and toasted, subtly-smoked fudge...; the spices arrive very early for a Bowmore and linger; **f25** a brilliant cocoa fruitcake which is intensely spiced and well smoked: just about the perfect finish...; **b24** while the nose represents an unsavoury battle between smoke and peculiar fruit notes, the remainder of this bottling is something to truly applaud and even includes a finish as good as any Bowmore you will find this and many other-a-year...A true classic. *48.4%. nc ncf sc. 655 bottles.*

◇ **Old Particular Islay Bowmore 16 Years Old** refill hogshead, cask no. 10448, dist Jun 98, bott Sept 14 **(92) n23.5** the oak ensure this is as minty as it is smoky: dry, powdery, quietly threatening, extra-strong Trebor mints in case you are wondering...; **t22.5** a dry delivery, too, with the sugars arriving in force only to counter the more excessive oak-n-smoke; **f23** lingers, with a little liquorice now adding to the depth; **b23** moderately peated and works comfortably with the good quality oak. *48.4%. nc ncf sc. 323 bottles.*

Old Particular Islay Bowmore 17 Years Old refill hogshead, dist Mar 96, bott Aug 13 **(88) n21 t23 f21.5 b22.5.** One of those quirks of whisky where someone appears to have tipped a bag of sugar into some peat...and ended up with a malt which works! *48.4%. nc ncf sc. 312 bottles. Douglas Laing & Co.*

Old Particular Islay Bowmore 25 Year Old refill hogshead, cask no 9906, dist Dec 87, bott Aug 13 **(80) n20 t21 f19 b20.** Indubitably from the unforgiving "Fisherman's Friend" period of Bowmore's production history. *50.2%. nc ncf sc. 234 bottles.*

Riverstown Bowmore Aged 16 Years oak hogshead, cask 2013-205, dist 13 Jun 97, bott Aug 13 **(94) n23.5** complex Bowmore making the most of its slightly above average peating level. A degree of Fisherman's Friend, but this has been checked, allowing the muscovado sugars a free hand; **t23.5** wow! And do those sugars let rip! A seriously full on degree of sugars, some in heather honey form, appears to somehow intensify the peat further; **f23.5** settles for a degree of complexity and sanity: a little mocha uses the muscovado well while strands of barley and Digestive biscuit can also be picked out; **b23.5** I think this is what is known by some as a honey cask...and for good reason. *56.1%. nc ncf sc. 251 bottles. WB15/123*

Scotch Malt Whisky Society Cask 3.216 Aged 18 Years refill hogshead, dist 06 Apr 95 **(90.5) n23** just down the lane from me is a pigstye. Some more agricultural aromas here are what may greet me on an evening stroll...; **t23** intense sugars on delivery: a kind of smoked Demerara; **f22** dry and spiced; **b22.5** a whisky which will you can stand your mucking out shovel up in... *56.1%. nc ncf sc. 266 bottles.*

Scotch Malt Whisky Society Cask 3.220 Aged 13 Years 1st fill barrel, dist 13 Oct 00 **(87.5) n21.5 t22.5 f21.5 b22.** Juicy, effervescent and lusty. *55.4%. nc ncf sc. 235 bottles.*

◇ **Scotch Malt Whisky Society Cask 3.228 Aged 26 Years** 2nd fill butt, dist 8 Dec 87 **(88) n21.5** Fisherman's Friend meets a strawberry chew; **t22.5** exceptionally sweet start for a Bowmore; a sultana layering seeing off the more excessive cough sweet effect; **f22** busy and a little furry around the gills; **b22.5** the relatively clean sherry butt has helped what was originally indifferent spirit. *46%. sc. 206 bottles.*

◇ **Scotch Malt Whisky Society Cask 3.230 Aged 26 Years** refill barrel, dist 11 Apr 88 **(83.5) n20 t22 f20.5 b21.** A curious marriage of Fisherman's friend and Palma Violets. Warming and sugary but works spasmodically. *50.5%. sc. 204 bottles.*

◇ **Scotch Malt Whisky Society Cask 3.236 Aged 16 Years** refill barrel, dist 25 Sept 98 **(87) n21.5 t22.5 f21 b22.** Lively and juicy yet with resounding oak. The modest smoke ramps up an attractive degree of spice while a secondary bourbon note adds further weight and complexity. *59.9%. sc. 141 bottles.*

◇ Scotch Malt Whisky Society Cask 3.238 Aged 17 Years refill butt, dist 25 Sept 97 **(93) n22** dull yet thick waves of half-hearted smoke and more confident fruit; **t24** delightful delivery: a huge wave of rich dark cherry and fruitcake is fringed by an ever-increasing degree of peat; **f23** late spices add extra verve to the already steady oscillations of the peat-fruit interplay; **b24** a patchwork of intense flavours which make for a pretty picture. A delicious dram by any standards. *56.5%. sc. 588 bottles.*

Signatory Vintage Cask Strength Collection Bowmore 1997 Aged 16 Years hogshead, cask no. 1911, dist 13 Jun 97, bott 07 Jul 13 (**93.5**) **n22.5** unassuming and polite to a fault, the smoke drifts in through the back door but has some presence once it has wiped its feet; **t24** astonishingly sweet, as though every atom of sugar from the grist has been stored up and allowed to tumble on to the taste buds; the smoke takes up a dual role of comforter and backbone; **f23** long, with the emphasis on crisp muscovado sugars sooted by peat smoke; the spices grow, glow, rumble and stay...; **b24** does the heart good to see a Bowmore offer this degree of top quality entertainment. Smoked a little over the norm, one suspects. 55.4%. nc sc. WB15/02

⟐ **Signatory Vintage Cask Strength Collection Bowmore 2000 Aged 14 Years** bourbon cask, cask no. 800093, bott Sept 14 (**91.5**) **n23** low level smoke –a mix of both peat and anthracite; delicate ulmo honey and butterscotch tart fill in the gaps; **t24** deft delivery despite the early spice; the softness is aided by a surprising gooseberry and melon fruitiness mingling with the barley and honey: some serious complexity at work; **f22** dries dramatically, but picks up the smoky trail again; **b22.5** one of the lighter and more delicate Bowmores you'll find this year. Don't expect a peaty giant. Really quite elegant. 54.4%. nc sc. 233 bottles. The Whisky Exchange Exclusive. WB16/002

Signatory Vintage Un-chillfiltered Collection Bowmore 2001 Aged 12 Years refill butt, cask no. 1365, dist 25 Sep 01, bott 06 Mar 14 (**77**) **n20 t22 f17 b18.** The usual gathering of suspects: Fisherman's Friends, molasses, Parma Violets. But despite the best attempts of decent spice and hickory, with its off-key fruit absolutely fails to make a coherent noise. 46%. nc ncf sc. 777 bottles. WB15/027

⟐ **Single Malts of Scotland Bowmore 15 Year Old** dist 1999 (**85.5**) **n20.5 t23 f20.5 b21.5.** An entirely enjoyable Bowmore which keeps things simple. A bit of the old Fisherman's Friend nose warns you this won't be a classic, but the light peat unites with the intense dark sugars and late butter very attractively. 55.2% WB16/012

Wemyss Malts 1982 Single Islay Bowmore "Loch Indaal Catch" hogshead, dist 82, bott 14 (**85.5**) **n21 t22 f21 b21.5.** Could have done with this liquid Fisherman's Friend when I had a cold a couple of months back.... 46%. sc. 165 bottles.

Wemyss Malts 1987 Single Islay Bowmore "Sweet Peat Posy" hogshead, dist 87, bott 14 (**89.5**) **n23** charmingly floral signature to the decent smoke; **t22** distinctive Fisherman's Friend tang; **f22.5** salty, spicy sharp finish. More FF and an extra shake of salt to wring out all the delicate fruit notes from the vanilla; **b22** Bowmore's old Fisherman's Friend style could be hit and miss. This one hits... 46%. sc. 231 bottles.

Wemyss Malts 1996 Single Islay Bowmore "Aniseed Pastille" hogshead, dist 96, bott 14 (**90**) **n21.5** lazy, remarkably peat-free. High vanilla dependency; **t23** unlike the nose, this takes off with a prodigious leap of juicy barley and grabs the attention. Mouth-watering and refreshing, the fudgy sugars and shy spice work well; **f22.5** still no smoke to mention. Dries as the vanilla grips; **b23** more or less an unpeated Bowmore which shows its malty teeth in a rare display. Always fascinating to see what lurks beneath the phenols. 46%. sc. 344 bottles.

⟐ **Wemyss Malts 1998 Single Islay Bowmore "Cacao Geyser"** butt, bott 2014 (**69**) **n16 t21 f15 b17** For all the liberal lashings of sugars and coastal saltiness, this is gruesomely off key. All accusing fingers point at the sherry butt. 46%. sc. 737 bottles.

Wemyss Malts 2001 Single Islay Bowmore "Peat Smoked Herring" hogshead, dist 01, bott 13 (**87**) **n21.5 t22 f21 b21.5.** Call me a stick-in-the-peat but I would have much rather seen this do its business in a blend than as a single malt. Know what I could have done with this to give some body. As a singleton, enjoyable for the smoke-encrusted grist but rathers lacks development other than some pleasing spice. Alays enjoyable, though, and worth the experience. But as for "Peat Smoked Herring" on the label. FFS, as they say... As a man who eats herring at least twice a week and tastes one helluva lot of peated whisky, possibly as much as anyone else on this planet, and grew up on kippers and Arbroath Smokies...I could honestly weep for the poor bemused punter...46%. sc. 405 bottles.

The Whisky Agency Bowmore 1998 dist 1998 (**87.5**) **n21.5 t22 f22 b22.** Harmony is something deeply hoped for but rarely attained thanks to both the egotistical grape and peat being at loggerheads; the anthracite side story is a pleasant one, though. Even so, a spotless sherry butt with not a hint of sulphur. But the entanglement between grape and smoke sometimes becomes a little too much of a test. 52.1%.

⟐ **Whisky-Fässle Bowmore 10 Year Old** hogshead, dist 2003, bott 2013 (**88.5**) **n22.5 t22 f22 b22.** Has something of the Fisherman's Friend cough sweet about it, though nothing like the 1993 vintage. But the bits which work beautifully are all done by smoke and sugars... 50.2%. nc ncf.

⟐ **Whisky-Fässle Bowmore 16 Year Old** hogshead, dist 1993, bott 2010 (**84**) **n21 t22 f20 b21.** A trawler full of Fisherman's Friend. 53.5%. nc ncf.

⟨⟩ **Whisky-Fässle Bowmore 18 Year Old** sherry cask, dist 1995, bott 2013 **(63) n16 t18.5 f14.5 b16**. Loads of smoke. Even more sugar. But totally sulphur wrecked. *54.9%. nc ncf.*

BRAEVAL
Speyside, 1974. Chivas Brothers. Working.

Càrn Mòr Strictly Limited Edition Braes of Glenlivet Aged 19 Years bourbon barrel, dist 1994, bott 2014 **(86.5) n21.5 t23 f20.5 b21.5**. When this distillery is good it is very good. The quality punctured only by residual oak bitterness. The delivery, though, offers a malty-citrus mix of the highest quality. *46%. nc ncf. 486 bottles. WB15/156*

⟨⟩ **Deerstalker Braeval Limited Release 1994 aged 19 years, 8 months (89) n23** subtle spices and even subtler fruit; a fat nose with a suety tang; **t23** outstanding delivery: typical Braeval intensity to the barley. Outstanding structure to sugars; **f21** a definite barrel-induced tang; **b22** almost a brilliant malt but a slight weakness to the cask takes the foot off the pedal. *48%. nc ncf.*

Directors' Cut Braes of Glenlivet Aged 25 Years refill hogshead, cask no. 10350, dist May 89, bott Jun 14 **(91.5) n22.5** complex and weighty: mainly toasty but some milky mocha softens; **t23** surprisingly salivating as an early malt blast catches the toasty tannins off guard; liberal burnt treacle tart and spices; **f23** fabulous chocolate mousse; **b23** a malt which knows how to go old with a spring in its step. *60.3%. nc ncf sc. 174 bottles.*

Gordon & MacPhail Connoisseurs Choice Braeval dist 1995, bott 2013 **(85) n21 t22 f21 b21** From the intensely grassy school of Speyside. Despite a short juicy phase, not quite as perky as you'd like from this distillery and fails to find a different groove. *46%. nc ncf. WB15/144*

Hepburn's Choice Braeval 2001 Aged 12 Years sherry, bott 2013 **(89) n22** barley, the whole barley and nothing but the barley...; **t23.5** clean, juicy malt intensifies into full Malteser mode; **f21.5** after an injection of tannin, a tired oak tang takes a little polish from the previous charming moments; **b22** the type of cask which allows the barley an unhindered life. *46%. WB15/062*

Hepburn's Choice 2001 Aged 12 Years sherry butt, dist 2001, bott 2014 **(84) n22 t21.5 f20 b20.5**. A bit like the coffee served to you in First Class on the 08:07am Wellingborough to London St Pancras. You thank them on being handed it, appreciate the first mouthful but on realising how insipid it is you decline their offer for a refill...*46%. nc ncf sc. 523 bottles.*

Old Particular Speyside Braeval 15 Year Old refill hogshead, cask no. 9989, dist Feb 98 bott Aug 13 **(85) n21 t22 f20.5 b21.5**. An interesting one: though the cask has a few wobbly moments, especially on the nose and finish, the malt compensates with some extra barley sugar intensity. *48.4%. nc ncf sc. 329 bottles. Douglas Laing & Co.*

The Pearls of Scotland Braeval 1991 22 Year Old cask no. 95119, dist Aug 91, bott Nov 13 **(92.5) n23.5** an irrepressible thread of ginger on no less confident field of tannin; superb malt which has blossomed in first fill ex-bourbon; **t22.5** some zinging spice as the oak holds all the aces; **f23.5** settles into intense cocoa backed handsomely by deft molasses; **b23** a high value oldie, no little thanks to a top quality cask. *52.9%.*

Signatory Vintage Single Malt Braeval 1998 Aged 14 Years bourbon barrels, cask no. 168894+168895, dist 12 Nov 98, bott 22 Mar 13 **(94.5) n23.5** gorgeous apples and pears beefs up the barley; **t24** a delivery from some kind of Speyside heaven: faultless barley which is at once firm yet yielding. The layering of the sugars, topped with soft ulmo honey is a joy; **f23** beautifully even oak input, allowing the barley and feint fruit safe passage; faultlessly clean to the very death; **b24** quintessential Speyside malt. Not overly complex. Just does what it does very beautifully helped by some exceptional oak. If you see it, grab it and be seduced... *43%. nc. 668 bottles. WB15/014*

⟨⟩ **Single Cask Collection Braeval 1997 17 Year Old** hogshead **(93) n23** clean, juicy barley with just the right degree of firmness. Subtle hazelnut oil thickens the expectation; **t24** intense, beautifully clean, barley concentrate. Molten muscovado sugars adds extra sparkle before a meringue light sweetness melts on the palate; **f22.5** dries gently while the barley somehow intensifies and pulses; **b23.5** when this distillery shines, it positively glistens... *54.7%*

The Whisky Agency Braeval 1994 dist 1994 **(86.5) n21.5 t22.5 f21 b21.5** Absolutely prime blending malt where the barley performs cartwheels, but little other excitement besides gentle spices. *52.9%.*

BRORA
Highlands (Northern), 1819–1983. Diageo. Closed.

Brora 25 Year Old 7th Release bott 2008 db **(96) n24 t24.5 f23.5 b24**. As the distillery closed in March 1983, if memory serves me correctly, this must be coming to the end of the road for the true 25-year-old. Those looking for the usual big peat show might be disappointed. Others, in search of majesty, sophistication and timeless grace, will be blown away. *56.3%*

Brora 30 Years Old db (**97**) n24 t25 f24 b24. Here we go again! Just like last year's bottling, we have something of near unbelievable beauty with the weight perfectly pitched and the barley-oak interaction the stuff of dreams. And as for the peat: an entirely unique species, a giant that is so gentle. Last year's bottling was one of the whiskies of the year. This even better version is the perfect follow-up. 56.4%

Brora 30 Years Old Special Release refill American and European oak db (**89**) n22 t23.5 f21.5 b22. Seeing as I was the guy who proudly discovered this whisky over 20 years ago, I take more than a keen interest. But like a loved and cherished old relative, you can still adore its personality and unique independence but be aware that it is slowly fading away... 54.3%. nc ncf. Diageo. 2958 bottles.

Brora 32 Years Old Special Release 2011 db (**89**) n22 t23 f22 b22. A strange bottling containing more natural caramels from a Brora than I have ever before seen. Obviously a dumbing down effect is inevitable but enough of the original beauty remains to enthral. 54.7%. nc ncf.

Brora 35 Years Old Special Release 2012 Refill American Oak, dist 1976 & 1977, bott 2012 db (**90.5**) n24.5 t22.5 f21 b22.5. Perhaps 90% of other Scottish malts would have failed under such an oaky onslaught. However, the pedigree of this distillery sees it through against the odd and the nose rewards a good hour's study. Not sure how much longer this guy can hold out for, though. 48.1%. nc ncf. Diageo.

◇ **Lombard Jewels of Scotland Single Malt Brora 1982** cask no. 876, dist 13 May 82, bott 2014 (**85**) n21 t22 f21 b21. Tangy oak and an odd, tingling weightiness which was once, I presume, the trademark smoke. Still retains some salivating qualities, though. 46.1%. sc.

BRUICHLADDICH
Islay, 1881. Rémy Cointreau. Working.

Bruichladdich 10 Years Old db (**90**) n22 beautifully clean and zesty, the malt is almost juvenile; t23 sweet, fruity then malty charge along the tastebuds that geets the mouth salivating; f23 the usual soft vanilla and custard but a bigger barley kick in the latter stages; b22 more oomph than previous bottlings, yet still retaining its fragile personality. Truly great stuff for a standard bottling. 46%

Bruichladdich 12 Years Old 2nd Edition db (**88**) n23 t22 f22 b21. A similar type of wine involvement to "Waves", but this is oilier in the old-fashioned 'Laddie style and lacks a little of the sparkle. The fruit on the finish is outstanding, though, and I don't think you or I would turn down a third glass... 46%

Bruichladdich 15 Years Old 2nd Edition db (**86**) n22 t23 f20 b21. Delicious, as usual, but something, possibly fruity, appears to be holding back the show. 46%

Bruichladdich 16 Years Old bourbon cask db (**89**) n22.5 t22.5 f22 b22. Plucked from the cask in the nick of time. In this state rather charming, but another Summer or two might have seen the oak take a more sinister turn. 46%

Bruichladdich 16 Years Old bourbon/Chateau d'Yquem cask db (**95**) n24 if you've got a good half an hour to spend, try using it intelligently by sticking your nose in this for a while: the grape is sweet and sultana juicy; the understated spices somehow hit just the right point to satisfy grape, oak and barley in one hit: some achievement... t23.5 sweet, as the nose suggests, but the arrival is not all about grape. That sweetness also contains pristine barley... f23.5 just so soft and subtle with the vanillas offering a discreet escort to the barley-grape marriage; b24 possibly the most delicate and understated of all the truly great whiskies of the year. Not one for the ice and water brigade. 46%

Bruichladdich 16 Years Old bourbon/Chateau Haut Brion cask db (**81.5**) n21 t21.5 f19 b20. fruity and busy for sure. But just not the kind of wine barrel effect that does much for me, I'm afraid, not least because of the background buzz on the palate. 46%

Bruichladdich 16 Years Old bourbon/Chateau Lafite cask db (**89**) n24 t22.5 f21.5 b21.5. Ridiculously soft. Could just do with an injection of something to propel it into greatness. 46%

Bruichladdich 16 Years Old bourbon/Chateau Lafleur cask db (**92.5**) n23 t23.5 f23 b23. So luminous on the palate, it's positively Lafleurescent... 46%

Bruichladdich 16 Years Old bourbon/Chateau Latour cask db (**84.5**) n21 t21.5 f21 b21. Enjoyable. But there is a strange aggression to the spice which doesn't altogether sit as comfortably as it might. The fruit heads off into not just grapey but citrus territory, but there is a always a but about the direction it takes... 46%

Bruichladdich 16 Years Old bourbon/Chateau Margaux cask db (**78.5**) n20.5 t20 f19 b19. Not 1st Cru Bruichladdich, I'm afraid. 46%

Bruichladdich XVII Aged 17 Years bourbon/renegade rum db (**92**) n23 t23.5 f22 b23.5. Always good to see the casks of drier, more complexly structured rums being put to such intelligent use. My sample doesn't tell me which rum casks were used, but I was getting vivid flashbacks here of Ruby-Topaz Hummingbirds flitting from flower to flower in the gardens of the now closed Eigflucht distillery in Guyana in the long gone days when I used to scramble around the warehouses there. That distinctive dryness though is pure Enmore, though some Barbadian rum can offer a similar effect. Something very different and a top quality experience. *46%. nc ncf.*

Bruichladdich 18 Years Old bourbon/cognac cask db (84.5) n23.5 t21 f20 b20. Big oak-spice buzz but thin. Sublime grapey nose, for sure, but pays a certain price, ultimately, for associating with such an inferior spirit... *46%*

Bruichladdich 18 Years Old bourbon/opitz cask db (80.5) n19 t22 f19.5 b20. Dry, complex; at times oak-stretched. *46%*

Bruichladdich 18 Years Old 2nd Edition bourbon/jurancon db (86) n22 t21.5 f21 b21.5. Plenty of fruit, including medium ripe greengages and slightly under-ripe grape. Juicy and sweet in the right places. *46%*

Bruichladdich Flirtation Aged 20 Years 2nd Edition db (86) n21 t22 f22 b21. Hi sugar! A Laddie for those with a sweet tooth. *46%*

Bruichladdich 21 Years Old oloroso cask db (76.5) n18.5 t21 f18 b19. Oops! *46%*

Bruichladdich Black Art 3rd Edition Aged 22 Years db (83) n22 t21.5 f20 b20.5. Where last year' Black Art II managed to get away with the odd slight off note due to its brain-exploding enormity, this year it just hasn't got what it takes to get over the hurdles. Some sumptuous fruit through the middle, but it just ain't enough... *48.7%. nc ncf.*

Bruichladdich 37 Years Old DNA 80% bourbon/20% sherry cask, aged in Le Pin wine casks db (87) n23.5 t22 f20.5 b21. Balance..? What balance...? Actually, somehow, this crazy thing does find some kind of equilibrium... *41%*

Bruichladdich 1984 Golder Still bourbon cask, db (88.5) n22 t23 f22 b21.5. A huge amount of natural caramels leached from the oak does the joint job of ensuring extraordinary softness and eroding the higher notes. Still, there is enough eye-rolling honey and spice to keep anyone happy and the rich bourbony character on delivery really is dreamy stuff. *51%*

Bruichladdich 1984 Redder Still db (95.5) n23.5 t24 f23.5 b24.5. Now it's finding whiskies like this that I became the world's first-full time whisky for. I dreamed of discovering drams which stretched my tastebuds & spoke to me with eloquence, charisma & unmistakable class. This is one such whisky: the style is highly unusual; the cleverness of the layering almost unique. This is the kind of near flawless whisky for which we were given tastebuds. Oh, & a nose... *50.4%*

Bruichladdich 1989 db (75.5) n20 t19 f17.5 b19. Ouch! *52.9%. Special bottling for Alberta.*

Bruichladdich Black Art 1990 Aged 23 Years 4th Edition cask no. 13/161 db (79) n20 t21 f18 b20. The same wobbly weaknesses found in the 3rd edition are back here in force once again. Big, juicy fruit notes will form a degree of compensation for some. *49.2%. nc ncf sc.*

Bruichladdich 1990 Aged 18 Years db (85.5) n22.5 t21 f21 b21. Enlivened by citrus and emboldened by soft salt. *46%*

Bruichladdich 1990 Aged 18 Years cognac cask db (81.5) n20.5 t21 f20 b20. Wouldn't be a far greater benefit to the spirit world if Cognac was matured in a Bruichladdich cask...? *46%*

Bruichladdich 1991 Aged 16 Years Chat Margaux finish db (94) n23 t25 f22.5 b23.5. A true Premier Cru malt...I have been almost certainly the most outspoken critic of whisky finishes: trust me, if they were all like this, you would never hear the merest clack of a dissenting typing key from me again... *46%*

Bruichladdich 1991 Valinch Anaerobic Digestion 19 Years Old bourbon & madeira casks db (96.5) n24.5 t24 f24 b24. About 20 minutes ago I could name you 250 excellent reasons to go and visit this distillery. I can now name you 251...A potential world whisky of the year that manages to do just about everything right...!!! *52.5% ncf sc. Only available at distillery.*

Bruichladdich 1992 Sherry Edition Pedro Ximénez Aged 17 Years bourbon/PX db (83) n22 t22 f18.5 b20.5. My word, that grape really does fly relentlessly at the taste buds. Probably the hardest sherry type to get right and here it works pretty well for the most part. *46%. nc ncf.*

Bruichladdich 1993 14 Years Old Bolgheri French oak db (85.5) n23 t21 f21.5 b20. The fabulous nose doesn't quite translate once on the palate. The natural caramels and barley combo never quite gets it together with the grape. Now the nose: that's a different matter! *46%*

Bruichladdich 1993 14 Years Old Sassicaia French oak db (83) n20 t21 f20.5 b21. From a too tight nose to a too limp body. Just not my sac... *46%*

Bruichladdich 1994 Valinch Blandola bourbon/Chateau d'Yquem casks, dist Sep 94 db (87) n21.5 t22.5 f21 b22. A bit muddled here and there but, like the distillery and staff, no shortage of personality. *55.3%. Available only from Bruichladdich's distillery shop.*

Bruichladdich 1994 "Kosher" Aged 12 Years db (85.5) n22 t21 f21 b21.5. Clean. What else, my dear? *46%*

Bruichladdich 1998 db (89) n22 t22.5 f22.5 b22. A truly unique signature to this but absolute class in a glass. *46%*

Bruichladdich 1998 bourbon/oloroso cask, dist 1998 db (87.5) n22.5 t22.5 f21 b21.5. Surprisingly conservative. But, joy of joys, not an atom of sulphur to be found...!! *46%*

Bruichladdich 1998 bourbon/Manzanilla cask, dist 1998 db **(82.5) n21 t21 f20 b20.5.** Fruity. But bitter where it should be sweet. 46%

Bruichladdich 1998 Ancient Regime db **(84.5) n22 t21.5 f20 b21** An easy, slightly plodding celebration of all things malty, caramelly, oily and vanillay... 46%

Bruichladdich 2001 Renaissance db **(91) n23** lively with the smoke and oak in particular going hammer and tongs; **t23** brilliant delivery! Varying fruit tones hit the palate running but there is a bit of barley reinforcement flexing some considerable muscle. But the star is the ubiquitous smoke which shows a gentle iron fist; **f22.5** a big surge of natural caramels but the spices make a scene; **b22.5** a Big Laddie. 46%

Bruichladdich 2001 The Resurrection Dram 23.10.01 bourbon cask, dist 2001, bott 2009 db **(90.5) n23 t23 f21.5 b23.** Now, be honest. How can you not have a first class Resurrection in the Bible...? 46%. 24,000 bottles.

Bruichladdich 2004 Islay Barley Valinch fresh sherry butt db **(89.5) n22.5 t24 f21 b22.** Yet another quite fabulous bottling form Bruichladdich, this one really cranking up the flavours to maximum effect. Having said all that, call me mad if you will...but seeing as this is Islay barley, would it not have been a good idea to shove it into a bourbon barrel, so we could see exactly what it tastes like? Hopefully that is on its way... 57.5%

Bruichladdich Infinity Second Edition bourbon/rioja db **(94) n24 t24 f23 b23.** Wasn't it Daffy Duck who used to put on his cape and shout: "Infinity and Beyond"? Oh, no... it was Buzz Lightyear. Anyways, he must have been thinking of this. And there's certainly nothing dethspicable about this one... 52.5%

Bruichladdich Infinity Third Edition refill sherry tempranillo db **(94.5) n24 t24 f23 b23.5.** I dare anybody who says they don't like smoky whisky not to be blown away by this. Go on...I dare you... 50%

Bruichladdich Islay Barley Aged 5 Years db **(86) n21 t22.5 f21.5 b21.** The nose suggests a trainee has been let loose at the stills. But it makes amends with an almost debauched degree of barley on delivery which lasts the entirety of the experience. Heavens! This is different. But I have to say: it's bloody fun, too! 50%. nc ncf.

Bruichladdich Islay Barley Rockside Farm 2007 bourbon, cask no. 13/159 db **(88) n22** so, so young! Maybe Islay barley, but it is still pretty green; very odd molecule of smoke here and there; **t22** juicy youthful barley; the final echoes of new make but otherwise absolutely pure, uncomplicated malt. Spices litter the palate, as do some hardening sugars and softer caramel; **f22** a few cocoa, mildly minty notes, though this seems more like the remnants of new make than cask; **b22** clean and chirpy. Great fun. 50%. nc ncf.

Bruichladdich Laddie Classic Edition 1 db **(89.5) n23 t23 f21 b22.5.** You probably have to be a certain vintage yourself to fully appreciate this one. Hard to believe, but I can remember the days when the most popular malt among those actually living on Islay was the Laddie 10. That was a staunchly unpeated dram offering a breezy complexity. Not sure of the age on this Retroladdich, but the similarities almost bring a lump to the throat... 46%

Bruichladdich Legacy Series 3 Aged 35 Years db **(91) n22 t22.5 f23.5 b23.** So they managed to find a whisky exactly the same age as Ladie distiller Jim. 40.7%

Bruichladdich Links "Carnoustie" 14 Years Old db **(78) n19 t20 f19 b20.** Hits some unexpected rough. 46%

Bruichladdich Links "Torrey Pines" 15 Years Old db **(89.5) n23 t22.5 f22 b22.** As clean as the perfect tee shot from the 15th... 46%

Bruichladdich Organic 2003 Anns An T-Seann Doigh Scottish barley db **(84.5) n22 t22 f20 b20.5.** Thick barley carrying soft smoke; slight bitterness threads in and out of the proceedings. 46%.

Bruichladdich Organic Multi Vintage bourbon db **(87.5) n22 t22 f20.5 b22.** Genteel. 46%

Bruichladdich Peat db **(89.5) n23** peat; **t22.5** peat; **f22** peat; **b22** peaty. 46%

Bruichladdich Rocks db **(82) n19 t22 f20 b21.** Perhaps softer than you'd imagine something called "rocks"! Beautiful little malty charge on entry. 46%

Bruichladdich Scottish Barley The Classic Laddie db **(78.5) n20 t21.5 f18 b19.** Not often a Laddie fluffs its lines. But despite some obviously complex and promising moves, the unusual infiltration of some sub-standard casks has undone the good of the local barley. If you manage to tune out of the off-notes, some sublime moments can still be had. 50%. nc ncf sc.

Bruichladdich Sherry Classic Fusion: Fernando de Castilla bourbon/Jerez de la Frontera db **(91) n23 t23 f22 b23.** What a fantastically stylish piece of work! I had an overwhelming urge to sing Noel Coward songs while tasting this: for the Dry Martini drinkers out there who have never thought of moving on to Scotch... 46%

Bruichladdich Waves db **(81.5) n20.5 t21.5 f19.5 b20.** Not sure if the tide is coming in or out on this one. Got various sugar and spice aspects which appeals, but there is something lurking in the depth that makes me a little uneasy... 46%

Bruichladdich WMD II - The Yellow Submarine 1991 db **(75) n20 t19 f18 b18.** This one just doesn't have the balance and sinks. 46%

Bruichladdich X4 db **(82) n18 t22 f21 b21.** Frankly, like no new make I have ever come across in Scotland before. Thankfully, the taste is sweet, malty and compact: far, far better than the grim, cabbage water nose. Doesn't really have the X-Factor yet, though. *50%*

Bruichladdich X4 +3 Quadruple Distilled 3 Aged Years bourbon db **(86) n21.5 t22 f21 b21.5.** It is as if the sugars in the barley have been reduced to their most intense form: this is all about huge barley of eye-watering intensity. A novel and not unattractive experience. *63.5%. nc ncf. 15,000 bottles.*

The Laddie Ten American oak db **(94.5) n24** a stunning balance between sea spray, the most delicate liquorice and hickory imaginable and blemish-free barley; **t23.5** no let down on delivery with the barley and delicate sugars hand in hand for the first three or four very big flavour waves; the middle has an oaky richness but not a single hint of weary dryness: gorgeously weighted and rich without over sweetening; **f23** at last the salts form, as do the vanillins and slightly coarser oaky notes. Retains that distinctly coastal feel; **b24** this, I assume, is the 2012 full strength version of an Islay classic which was the preferred choice of the people of Islay throughout the 70s, 80s and early 90s. And I have to say that this is already a classic in its own right.... *46%. nc ncf.*

Octomore 5 Years Old db **(96) n23.5 t24.5 f24 b24.** Forget about the age. Don't be frightened by the phenol levels. Great whisky is not about numbers. It is about excellent distillation and careful maturation. Here you have a memorable combination of both... *63.5%*

Octomore Edition 2.1 Aged 5 Years (140 ppm) bourbon cask, bott Jun 09 db **(94) n23 t24 f23 b23.** Talk about a gentle giant: as though your taste buds are being clubbed to death by a ton of smoky feathers. *62.5%. nc ncf. 15,000 bottles.*

Octomore Edition 2.2 "Orpheus" Aged 5 Years (140 ppm) bourbon/chateau Petrus, bott 2009 db **(96.5) n24 t24.5 f23.5 b24.5.** A standing ovation for this massive performance... the quite perfect way to bring up my 900th new whisky for the 2011 Bible. Everything works; the age and freshness of the barley, the controlled enormity of the smoke...even the entirely sulphur-free wine barrel. For those with a lot of hair on their chest...and want even more. *61%. 15,000 bottles.*

Octomore 3rd Edition Aged 5 Years db **(95) n24.5 t24 f23 b23.5.** I usually taste this late in the Bible writing cycle: it is so important to be rewarded at the end of a long journey. This hasn't let me down and here's the rub: how something which looms so large be made from so many traits so small...? *59%*

Octomore 4th Edition Aged 5 Years (167 ppm) db **(92) n21.5 t23.5 f23.5 b23.5** Choctomore, surely? *62.5%*

Octomore Edition 5.1 db **(91.5) n23 t22.5 f23 b23.** A slightly less complex version, probably because of the obvious lack of years. Great fun, though. *59.9%*

Octomore Edition 6.1 Aged 5 Years bourbon cask db **(91.5) n24** acrid smoke. Bonfires at my Dad's old allotment back in Surrey, it's leafy sweetness mixing with the chunkier peak reek; beyond that is a mix of Fisherman's Friend and cherry cough sweet. Also detectable, if you can spot it, is very young grist...the aroma of grist mashing...; **t23** a brief new make opening amid the big sugary delivery: concentrated Demerara concentrated again. The smoke is both chewy and also acts as a counter for the staggering grist sweetness; **f22** some late coconut cake carries the smoke and mocha; **b22.5** a slightly different Octomore, a little more tart than usual and wears its youth with pride. *57%*

Octomore Edition 6.1 Aged 5 Years Scottish Barley (167 ppm) db **(94) n23.5** peat so dense, at first appears as a wall of smoked hickory and burnt cocoa: it takes a while for a layer of smoke to drift off lightly enough for the peat to come across as...well, peat...! **t24** a one-off delivery which absolutely grips the palate: the peat is beyond concentrated. Some molasses filter through to reduce the singularity of the impact, but hardly diverts it from its course of feeling that you are engulfed in the dense smoke of a peaty bonfire...from which there is no escaping; **f24** now the peat reveals a lighter touch and a degree of layering. But it is all part of the same relentless story: balance here hardly comes into play....; **b22.5** talk about can't see the wood for the trees: here you can't see the peat for the moss. It appears that when you get to a certain degree of phenol saturation, the smokiness suggests less rather than more. On the nose that is. Then you taste it...and you are then in for the peatiest experience of your life... *57% WB15/314*

Octomore Edition 6.2 Aged 5 Years Cognac cask db **(90) n22.5** the peat is already crushed, the fruit strangles any possible movement; **t23.5** hard to imagine the smoke playing second fiddle, but it does: the sugars are so intense and the barley so salivating, for a few moments you even forget it is there; **f22** even tighter oak and crisp enough to break all your teeth; **b22** one of the sweetest bottlings from this distillery of all time. Some warming late spice, too; *58.2%.*

⟫ **Octomore Edition 7.1 Aged 5 years** (208 ppm) db **(96.5) n24** at first the wall of peat is so thick, it is opaque and barely noticeable. But as your nose acclimatises, it recognises the ever-gathering intensity of the phenols, its shape, its depth...its enormity! And then, finally, its scariness...!! **t24.5** certainly no doubts when it comes to delivery and immediate follow through. In some ways, the secondary fruit presence becomes the dominant theme. Hang on...it isn't fruit. No, it is concentrated sugars, as you might get from a mouthful of noble rot. This is pushed to the fore by the tidal wave of phenols. Then that peaty wave breaks and the "fruit" is lost under the crashing smoke; leaving splinters of mocha, fragments of liquorice, flotsam of citrus...; **f24** amid the swirl and haze of smoke, spices begin their serious work...; **b24** a gargantuan malt which will make short work of the feint hearted... This, also, was the whisky which Islay whisky maker par excellence Jim McEwen decided to bow out on. Farewell, Jim, my dear old friend of some 35 years. You have been to Scotch whisky what Jock Stein was to Scottish football; what Octomore is to Islay malt.... *59.5%*

Octomore 10 db **(95) n24** have I ever mentioned cowsheds? This is David and Ruth Archer's threatened milking parlour...but without the milk...awww nawooo..! **t24** as ever, smoke...like someone's set fire to the barn...awww nawooo!; **f23** the most intense of all finishes, as though the excess of the cowshed has been drained by marauding badgers... awww nawoooo! **b24** when I am tasting an Octomore, it means I am in the home straight inside the stadium after running (or should I say nosing and tasting) a marathon. After this, there is barely another 20 more Scotch malts to go and I am closing in on completing my 1,200 new whiskies for the year. So how does this fair? It is Octomore. It is what I expect and demand. It gives me the sustenance and willpower to get to that crossing line. For to tell you guys about a whisky like this is always worth it...whatever the pain and price. Because honesty and doing the right thing is beyond value. Just ask David Archer... *50%. nc ncf.*

Port Charlotte An Turas Mor Multi Vintage bourbon cask db **(85.5) n23 t22 f20 b20.5** Does much right, especially the intriguing bullying of the colossal peat over what probably passes for grape. But bitters out and struggles to find a balance or plot line to keep you wanting to discover more. *46%*

Port Charlotte Heavily Peated db **(94.5) n23** smoke comes scudding into the nose, vigorously, giving the joint effect of death by peat and acrid burnt toast; **t24** a youthful livewire delivery with a pretty surprising degree of maple syrup and treacle latching onto the phenols: the effect and balance is wonderful; pay attention and you'll spot some juicy fruit notes popping up here and there, too; **f23.5** the lack of major oak means the finish is fractionally lighter than it might be, but the smoke is now even and pretty soft despite the late spice; **b24** rearrange the following two words: "giant" and "gentle". *50%*

Port Charlotte PC6 db **(96.5) n24.5** ohhhhhh... arrrrrrrhh... mmmmmmmmmmm... oh, the peat, the peat... yessssss... oh my god... mmmmmmm... ohhhhhhh... **t24** first you get the smoky... oooohhhhhhh... arrrrrrrrr... then the sweeter... mmmmmmmm... arrrroooohhhh... **f24** it finishes with a more gentle arghoooo... mmmmmmm... oooophhhhhh... arrrrrrrrr... **24** not many whiskies have a truly unmistakable nose... and... but this is, this... is... this... mmmmmmm..., arrrrrhh. Ohhhhhhhh... *61.6%*

Port Charlotte PC7 dist 2001 db **(93.5) n24** dry. The most profound peat fire ashes: not for peaty amateurs... **t24** a few drops of sweetness added; a liquorice/molassed melt to the massive smoke: the phenols seems a lot higher than the 40ppm they talk about; **f22** drops down a gear or two as some bitterness creeps in, as does a secondary fizz to the spice; **b22.5** not quite as orgasmic as last year, sadly. But should still be pretty stimulating... *60.5%*

Port Charlotte PC8 bourbon, dist 2001, bott 2009 db **(88) n22 t23 f21 b22.** Enjoyable, but muted by PC standards... *60.5%. 30,000 bottles.*

Port Charlotte PC10 db **(96) n24** promises to be the best PC for a few years! There is a vague kumquat undercoat that does well having itself heard amid the formidable phenols. But the weight is just so enormous, yet somehow crushes nothing; **t24.5** stunning! You know the peat is omnipotent yet, miraculously, it is the sugar-honey mix which dictates play, especially the pace of flavour development. Some oils and caramels ensure excellent shape and body; **f23.5** the smoke works hard to re-establish itself but the oak still has much to say; **b24** just so right....!!! *59.8%*

Port Charlotte The Peat Project db **(95.5) n24.5** the smoke drifts through in varying degrees of intensity and types of mood. Whenever it darkens, a burst of citrus appears to brighten its countenance; **t24** soft sugars form a guard of honour as the smoke tip-toes into the arena. The peat does not seem so prominent here as it does on the nose, a light vanilla infusion also detracting from the smoke; **f23** dries slowly, allowing in a delicate cocoa oil intensity to the smoke; **b24** this is not peat for peat's sake. This appears to be crafted and layered, offering a pleasing timbre and unusual gracefulness. *46% WB15/339*

The Laddie Sixteen American oak db **(88) n22** huge natural caramels dipped in brine; **t22.5** very even and gentle with a degree of citrus perking it up; **f21.5** reverts to caramels before the tannins strike hard; **b22** oak 'n' salt all the way... *46%*

The Laddie Twenty Two db **(90.5)** n24 a breakfast plate of three pieces of toast: one with salted butter, another with ulmo honey and the last one with marmalade; light spices, too. Busy yet understated; t23 silky salted butters again on delivery immediately backed by intense barley sugar; f21.5 the oak cranks up significantly; b22 fabulous coastal malt, though the oak is a presence always felt. *46%*

Alexander Weine & Destillate Port Charlotte 10 Year Old fresh port wine cask, cask no. 646, dist 07 Jul 03 bott 06 Sep 13 **(95.5)** n24 one of those noses which stops you dead in your tracks. First you have to comprehend the enormity of the peat, then the intensity and clarity of the grape...and then the ease in which they combine. You know this s major piece of phenols when the peat comes across so dry and dusty; t24 the fabulous port is so juicy and fresh for a few moments the peat doesn't get a look in. When it goes it exacts revenge by sending in spices as intense as the dry smoke; the fruity sugars simply carry on regardless; f23.5 majors in spice. Very long with the dry, slight cocoa-shrouded peat always in play; b24 you know that I am no fan of big peat and big wine. But when something arrives in your glass this enormous, this magnificent...you will not hear a dissenting word from me. *60%. sc. cask strength.*

The Coopers Choice Bruichladdich 1992 Aged 20 Years hogshead, cask no. 3685, bott 2013 **(89.5)** n22 salted bananas; old garden sheds; t23.5 gorgeous juicy malt: salivation cannot be prevented; f22 several thick layers of caramel; b22 the early threat of over-aged oak is swept away by the juicy malt and toffee. Satisfying whisky. *46%. 365 bottles. WB15/303*

The Coopers Choice Port Charlotte 2004 Aged 9 Years hogshead, cask no. 1032, bott 2014 **(92)** n23.5 t23 f22.5 b23. Description is pointless: it's Port Charlotte.! That said, there is an extra injection of lime. And this cask appears to have brought the most out of the caramel because there are deadening toffee notes I have never seen in this make before. A dozing giant. *46%. 330 bottles. WB15/302*

The Maltman Port Charlotte Aged 12 Years bourbon cask **(94)** n23 the driest known peat soot known to mankind...; t23.5 yet sweetens dramatically on delivery as the big phenolic grist takes hold. From then on its melt in the mouth smoke, bolstered by an extra degree of golden syrup; f23.5 returns to a more even balance between sweet and dry. The smoke, though, is big and constant...; b24 with PC you know what you are going to get. Only the cask type impacts and here we have a lethargic bourbon cask happy for the peat to get on with it. *52.4%*

⟐ **Master of Malt Single Cask Bruichlddich 12 Year Old** first-fill bourbon cask, dist Jul 02, bott Nov 14 **(67)** n17 t18 f16 b16. A bourbon cask by name. A poor sherry butt by nature. *57.3%. sc. 114 bottles.*

⟐ **Master of Malt Single Cask Bruichlddich 12 Year Old** first-fill sherry hogshead, dist Jun 02, bott Nov 14 **(82)** n21.5 t21.5 f19 b20. Thumping fruitiness and a silk delivery. But a bitter furriness is not far below the tannin and sugar surface. *62.3%. sc. 86 bottles.*

⟐ **Old Particular Islay Bruichladdich 21 Years Old** refill hogshead, cask no. 10706, dist Nov 93, bott Feb 15 **(91.5)** n23 a busy, salty nose which – irrespective of where it has matured for the last two decades – shows an "ozone"-style freshness (what people regularly describe as ozone – as I have done here – does not smell like real ozone at all..!!) and a sharpish barley background; a little lemon zest also tags along, t23 no sign of wear and tear on delivery – the contrary in fact. The barley has located and magnified in full the lemon on the nose, so for a whisky of this age, the salivation levels are very high; f22.5 remains light and delicate but much more emphasis on barley and custard cream biscuit; b23 one of the old school 'Laddies, devoid of smoke but beautifully endowed with charm. *51.5%. nc ncf sc. 306 bottles.*

⟐ **Scotch Malt Whisky Society Cask 127.43 Aged 12 Years** refill barrel, dist 21 Jun 02 **(94)** n24.5 intriguing, enticing and delicious mix of peat reek and the type of coal smoke churned up by today's few remaining steam engines. All kinds of citrus notes bombard the phenols; t24 nowhere near as puckering as some Port Charlotte you might find: a roll call of delicate sugars and honey melt into the phenols and make for a thick yet gentle outpouring of controlled smoke. It is the buzz of the spices which reverberates most keenly, though; f22 surprisingly short or, rather, it falls off a cliff after being on such a high. The biscuit oakiness lasts longest; b23.5 anyone looking for a PC which blasts them onto another planet will be disappointed. Those looking for clever complexity will fall in love... *65%. sc. 228 bottles.*

That Boutique-y Whisky Bruichladdich batch 1 **(88.5)** n22 dried pickled cucumber, sun-dried tomato and must; t22.5 again a series of odd, slightly sharp notes to back up the intense juicy barley and salt; f22 malty and straightforward on one level, curiously dry on another; b22 it's Bruichladdich, Jim (McEwan). But not as we know it... *49.6%. 94 bottles. WB15/191*

⟐ **That Boutique-y Whisky Company Bruichladdich** batch 2 **(68)** n17 t18 f16 b17. Somehow the sulphur actually raises a bigger flag than the peat...that takes some doing! *52.7%. 226 bottles.*

BUNNAHABHAIN

Islay, 1881. Burn Stewart Distillers. Working.

Bunnahabhain 12 Years Old (Older Bottling) db **(80)** n19 t21 f20 b20. Pleasant in its own clumsily sweet, smoky way. But unrecognisable to the masterful, salty Bunna 12 of old. 43.3%. nc ncf.

Bunnahabhain Aged 12 Years db **(85.5)** n20 t23 f21 b21.5. Lovers of Cadbury's Fruit and Nut will adore this. There is, incongruously, a big bourbony kick alongside some smoke, too. A lusty fellow who is perhaps a bit too much of a bruiser for his own good. Some outstanding moments, though. But, as before, still a long way removed from the magnificent Bunna 12 of old... 46.3%. nc ncf.

Bunnahabhain Aged 16 Years Manzanilla Sherry Wood Finish db **(87)** n20.5 t23 f21.5 b22. The kind of undisciplined but fun malt which just makes it up as it goes along... 53.2%

Bunnahabhain Aged 18 Years (Older Bottling) db **(94)** n24.5 chestnut colour and, fittingly, roast chestnut on the fruitcake nose: the health-conscious might say there is too much salt in the mix, but it works perfectly here...; t24 outstanding oloroso with the clean, faultless grape dripping of the salty barley; the oak again offers a nutty background, while Demerara sugars form a crisp counter to the invading salt; burnt raisin underscores the fruitcake character; f22.5 light mocha, as a very slight bitterness steels its way in; b23 a triumph for the sherry cask and a reminder of just how good this distillery can be. It's been a long time since I've enjoyed a distillery bottling to this extent. 43%

Bunnahabhain Aged 18 Years db **(93.5)** n24 a sumptuous amalgam of lightly salted roasted hazelnut shimmering within its own oil. Oloroso bulging with toasted, slightly singed currants, a sliver of kumquat and topped by thick vanilla. Irresistible... t24.5 almost impossible to fault: the oloroso grandly, almost pompously, leads the way exuding thick, Christmas pudding depth; a light muscovado sugar top dressing counters the deeper, lightly salted vanillas which begin to emerge; f22 a very slight sulphury note sullies the tone somewhat, but there is still enough rich vanilla and spotted dick for some enjoyable afters; b23 only an odd cask has dropped this from being a potential award winner to something that is merely magnificent... 46.3%. nc ncf.

Bunnahabhain XXV Aged 25 Years (Older Bottling) db **(91.5)** n23 t23 f22.5 b23. An intense and fun-packed malt for those who like a fine sherry and a sea breeze. 43%

Bunnahabhain XXV Aged 25 Years db **(94)** n23 you almost need a blow torch to cut through the oloroso, so thick is it. A little tight thanks to a minor distortion to a butt, but I am being picky. Salty and seaweedy, the ocean hangs in the air...; t24 glorious weight and sheen to the delivery. The early balance is nearly perfect as the thick fruit is thinned by the proud barley. The early, contemplative sweetness, buttressed by a wonderful mixture of sultana and Demerara, gives way to the drier oaks and the tingly, chalky signs of a mildly treated butt; f23 despite the winding down of the sugars the residual fruit manages to overcome the small obstacles placed before it; b24 no major blemishes here at all. Carefully selected sherry butts of the highest quality (well, except maybe one) and a malt with enough personality to still gets its character across after 25 years. Who could ask for more...? 46.3%. nc ncf.

⬥ **Bunnahabhain Ceòbanach** db **(87.5)** n21.5 t22.5 f21.5 b22. An immensely chewable and sweet malt showing little in years but much in character. A charming liquorice and acacia honey lead then a developing, dry smokiness. Great fun. 46.3%

Bunnahabhain Cruach-Mhòna batch no.1 db **(83)** n17.5 t24.5 f21 b20. It appears that there is a new house style of being strangely off balance and less than brilliantly made, but making amends by offering a blistering maltiness which leaves one almost speechless. The delivery alone, with its light smokiness mixing in with the Demerara sugars and Grenadine spices, is the stuff of Islay legend. All else is skewed and out of sync. Unique, for sure. 50% nc ncf.

Bunnahabhain Darach Ùr Batch no. 1 db **(87)** n21.5 t22.5 f21 b22. Almost milkshake thick. Not exactly a technical triumph but high marks for entertainment value! 46.3%

Bunnahabhain Darach Ùr Batch no. 4 db **(95)** n24 good grief; as though matured in a barrel full of plump sultanas... but from the depth of sweetness, rather than the fruit...if you get my drift. Just a hint of spice as well as coconut and honey. Fabulous in a bourbon kind of salty, Hebridean way...; t24.5 as thick and richly-textured as any malt you'll find this year. Intense, lightly salted barley is a match for the brimming, fruit-like sweetness; with a salivation factor which disappears through the roof, wonderful bourbon over- and under-tones link wonderfully to the mega sugars attached to the vanilla; f23 much drier with a tangy, kumquat fade but plenty of vigorous spice; b23.5 because of my deep love for this distillery, with my association with it spanning some 30 years, I have been its harshest critic in recent times. This, though, is a stunner.. 46.3%. nc ncf.

Bunnahabhain Toiteach db **(78)** n19 t21 f19 b19. Cloying, sweet, oily, disjointedly smoky. Had you put me in a time capsule at the distillery 30 years ago, whizzed me forward to the present day and given me this, it would have needed some serious convincing for me to believe this to be a Bunna. 46%

Bunnahabhain Toiteach Un-Chillfiltered db **(75.5)** n18 t21 f17.5 b19. A big gristy, peaty confrontation on the palate doesn't hide the technical fault lines of the actual whisky. 46%. ncf.

❖ **Baffo Forever Bunnahabhain 2006 8 Years Old** dist 1 Dec 06 **(86)** n21 t22.5 f21 **b21.5**. Pretty full on, on the phenol front. Good early oils. The sweet-dry interplay should work better than it actually does. 46%. sc. 192 bottles. WhiskyAuction.com.

Berry's Own Selection Bunnahabhain 1987 Aged 26 Years cask no. 2451, bott 2014 **(96.5)** n23.5 not a distillery naturally suited to great age, this is very comfortable in its fruity clothes, loose fitting and, despite the odd patch here and there, mildly exotic; **t25** quite literally faultless: perhaps the softest delivery of the year with lush, understated exotic fruit and molasses and maple syrup. The oak is pretty ingrained but only the spices make a stand out contribution: you cannot find anything more completely balanced than this; **f23.5** naturally falls away a little but only as the oak takes the upper hand from the spent sugars; **b24.5** for my 900th new whisky for the 2015 Bible, a malt from a distillery I stayed at in the year this was distilled. It appears to have fared infinitely better over the years than me.... 49.8%. ncf ncf. WB15/242

Berry's Own Selection Bunnahabhain 2006 Aged 7 Years cask no. 800092, bott 2014 **(91.5)** n23.5 not for the ageists: luckily I am from a generation brought up on young smoky whisky rather than the geriatrics you see bottled today. So how can you not adore this lively, lemon-tinged smoky grist...? **t23.5** firm with more of that fabulous grist sensually caressing the palate; **f21.5** it is inevitable that a little imbalance should kick in, and it does towards the end, as a bitterness strikes; **b23** a handsome youth promising good things for the future. Oh, and on the subject of young 'uns, whilst writing these notes at 11.46pm on 28th July discovered fledgling willow warbler in my garden for the very first time, which for five minutes from my vantage point from under the apple tree where I am tasting today (shielded from the sun my trusty Panama and only my parrot Percy for company) I watched spellbound as it learned how to hunt solo. I shall raise a fitting toast with this fledgling Bunna...56.1%. ncf ncf. WB15/247

❖ **Chieftain's Bunnahabhain Aged 24 Years** hogshead, dist Oct 89, bott Jun 14 **(90.5)** n22 juicy apple leaks into the pear crumble. Much more youthful on the nose than the actual age; **t23** massive flooding of barley on delivery, then shockwaves of thickening oak; no shortage of barley sugar; **f22.5** a little spice begins to make a courteous mark adding extra life to the custardy oak; **b23** a rapier sharpness to the barley despite the great age. 43.6%. nc ncf.

The Coopers Choice Bunnahabhain 1990 Aged 23 Years hogshead, cask no. 8944, bott 2013 **(87)** n21 t22.5 f22 b21.5. A well mannered gentleman of a dram. But got to the stage in its life where the suits are frayed and ill-fitting and the comb-over detracts rather than adds. Some pretty tired oak intruding where not wanted. No denying the excellent toasted honeycomb, though. 46%. 345 bottles. WB15/304

Directors' Cut Bunnahabhain Aged 35 Years refill hogshead, cask no. 10348, dist Dec 78, bott Jun 14 **(89)** n23.5 exotic fruit of the most emboldened kind: kumquat and salty Tunnock's wafer give it some desirable depth; **t22.5** soft, melt-in-the-mouth milk chocolate then a steady increase of the oak; **f21.5** much drier, with remaining sugars holding the tannins at bay; **b21.5** never a relaxed dram, as the oak uses a tad too much force in making itself known. But the soft chocolate malt shake is a delight. 45.2%. nc ncf sc. 129 bottles.

Fine Malt Selection Bunnahabhain 33 Years Old cask no. 84, dist 1980, bott 2013 **(92)** n23.5 weighty oak. But a kind of salty chocolate raisin and fudge cake sees it beautifully through what might have been a crisis; **t22** much lighter delivery, first offering saline-soaked barley. Then a forest of splinters leaves you in no dout of its vintage. Minty chocolate revives the spirit(s); **f23.5** returns to a major fruit chocolate assault, aided by salty treacle; **b23** Bunna has rarely been a distillery given to old age: for me it reaches its peak in average casks in standard maturation conditions at 12 years. So I feared the worst. And although this has more than its fair share of splinters, it still retains enough class to warrant investigation. A genuine surprise package. 45%. James MacArthur & Co. Ltd.

❖ **Glen Fahrn Airline Nr 14 Bunnahabhain 1968 Aged 44 Years** refill oak **(91.5)** n23 t22.5 f23 b23. Rarely a distillery which ages well beyond 25 years, this one is a stand-out exception. Time has fashioned many intrinsic and delectable fruit notes. Certainly the oak refuses to take a backward step in its journey to Old Father Time. But there is enough solid vanilla and complex sugars –and darker honeys – to ensure the malt and salt make a difference. Ancient, but entirely charming. 41.2%. sc. 117 bottles.

❖ **Gordon & MacPhail The Macphails Collection Bunnahabhain 2006 (77)** n19 t20.5 f18.5 b19. Cloying sugars can't prevent the stranglehold of late bitterness. Technically, far more crosses than ticks. 43%

The Maltman Bunnahabhain Aged 10 Years sherry cask, cask no. 1003710, dist Dec 02, bott Apr 13 **(80)** n20 t21 f19 b20. Not sure this was a classic period for Bunna. An overly sweet soup of a dram which bitters out with a degree of meanness and aggression. *46%. sc ncf nc. 229 bottles. WB15/227*

⬧ **Malt Mountain Bunnahabhain 23 Year Old** hogshead, dist 1999, bott Feb 15 **(88.5) n22** a tiring, faltering nose were the oak is showing signs of stress. But, equally, there are lashings of sea spray and honey to keep it alive; **t22.5** dry, pounding tannin, then a charge of acacia honey and fudge; **f22** salt encrusted cocoa; **b22** the tide is just beginning to go out on this one. But deep deposits of honey steers it home. *44.1%*

Old Malt Cask Bunnahabhain Aged 16 Years refill hogshead, cask no. 10128, dist Aug 97, bott Oct 13 **(91) n22** sweet chestnuts and smoke; **t23** the sugars arrive as clearly and unhurried on the palate as the sweet waters tumbling down a highland stream; the smoke is demure and accentuates the muscovado; **f23** vanilla and gristy smoked barley play us out; **b23** how many of us are left, I wonder, who still do a bit of a mental double take every time we nose a smoked Bunna – so used were we for this distillery to be unsmoked. This chap is one of the better examples of recent years, showing an impressive clarity to the phenolic proceedings. *50%. nc ncf sc. 348 bottles.*

⬧ **Old Malt Cask Bunnahabhain 13 Years Old** sherry butt, cask no. 11240, dist Dec 01, bott Feb 15 **(84) n21.5 t22.5 f19 b21.** The welcoming sugars on delivery and all round bonhomie are all too short lived, especially when the finish starts cutting up rough. *50%. nc ncf sc. 308 bottles.*

Old Malt Cask Bunnahabhain Aged 25 Years refill hogshead, cask no. 9516, dist Nov 87, bott Feb 13 **(69) n18 t f19 f15 b17** Furry. Off key. Grim. *50%. nc ncf sc. 271 bottles. WB15/135*

⬧ **Old Masters Bunnahabhain 34 Year Old** cask no. 87, dist 1991, bott 2014 **(91) n23** sharp minty marmalade and myriad other signs of a great whisky having been left the odd summer too long, but plucked from the cask in the nick of time...; **t23.5** still soft and a slow deployment of random sugars which, crucially, see off the excesses of the oak; **f22** a little ulmo honey moves in to settle things. The tannin keeps on wailing their frustration and intent...; **b22.5** a Bunna hanging onto life like a hill walker might hang on to a cliff edge of the Paps opposite the distillery after having taken a tumble... *44.7%. sc. James MacArthur & Co Ltd.*

⬧ **Old Particular Islay Bunnahabhain 17 Years Old** refill hogshead, cask no. 10584, dist Aug 97, bott Dec 14 **(96.5) n24** majestic! Soft, layered, whispered peats amid brine, kumquat and ulmo honey: a **t24** ridiculously beautiful. The sugars, smoke and honey merge like a peaty orgasm without beginning or end... **f24** more of the same, except now a powdery, sooty spiciness. Still the kumquats sing and there is even some late barley on display with the mocha; **b24.5** any more coastal and this would come with its own lighthouse...A kind of Highland Park in disguise, one of the best peated versions from this distillery I have ever encountered in bottled form. *48.4%. nc ncf sc. 306 bottles.*

Provenance Bunahabhain Over 12 Years sherry butt, cask no. 10330, dist Winter 01, bott Spring 14 **(87.5) n21.5 t22.5 f22 b21.5.** Soft and easy going, this is a Bunna from the old non-peated school which leaks a fair bit of oak for its age but works charmingly especially when the salt and malt remain in tandem. *46%. nc ncf sc.*

Provenance Bunnahabain ' Young & Feisty' refill hogshead, cask no. 10175, bott Winter 2014 **(85) n21 t21.5 f21.5 b21.** Refreshing and almost puckeringly juicy. Well made and clean with some lovely oils helping the un-peated malt travel further. *Nc ncf sc. Douglas Laing & Co.*

⬧ **Romantic Rhine Collection Bunnahabhain 1987** sherry octave cask, cask no. 383560, dist 30 Jun 87, bott 18 Jul 12 **(96.5) n24 t24 f24 b24.5.** This is a wonderful whisky, reminding me of the old Bunnas I used to taste when I used to holiday each year at the distillery in the early 1980s. Except few could withstand the years as well as this has, though the saltiness reminds me of the rain being blown into my face during the frequent storms. Also, clean grape influence, as of old, yet with the malt always in pole position. Unusual, though, is the patience of the oak. Wonderful, truly wonderful... *55.2%. 72 bottles.*

Scotch Malt Whisky Society Cask 10.77 Aged 6 Years refill hogshead, dist 03 Oct 07 **(76.5) n19 t19.5 f19 b19.** Not that there is anything technically wrong with this dram: you are unlikely to find malts on such a stampede for the remainder of the year. It is just that young whiskies are like Bambi: they take a little time to find their feet. From one month to the next they could be looking OK one minute, then flat on their arse the next. This is a cask picked at entirely the wrong time either through ignorance or genius. Other than a learning curve for whisky students, there is not much point to it... *61.4%. ncf sc. 196 bottles.*

Signatory Vintage Cask Strength Collection Bunnahabhain 1997 Heavily Peated Aged 18 Years hogsheads, cask no. 5513+5514, dist 11 Dec 97, bott 08 Nov 13 **(94) n23** good saline edge to the powdery peat. A little chocolate Swiss roll alongside the smoky Blackjack; **t24** silky delivery. Fabulous sugars: seemingly a heather honey sweetness to the increasingly intense smoke, like a lightly oiled Highand Park on peaty overdrive; **f23** carries on without a hint of bitterness or tiredness. The vanillas do stack up, but so do the spices which buzz by the finale; **b24** curious how this was filled into cask on the same day as the Signatory UCF version. Yet this offers lustre and complexity. Because of the oils being broken up by reducing to 46? Or was the other one unlucky by simply having inferior wood? Probably a bit of both. *51.3%. nc. 527 bottles. WB15/001*

Signatory Vintage Un-chillfiltered Collection Bunnahabhain 1997 Heavily Peated Aged 15 Years hogsheads, cask no.5578+5579, dist 11 Dec 97, bott 05 Jul 13 **(87) n21 t22 f22 b22** Chocolate mint amid some smoky barley oil. The nose is problematic but saved by subtle citrus. *46%. nc ncf. 798 bottles. WB15/026*

◇ **The Single Malts of Scotland Bunnahabhain 25 Years Old** cask no. 4344, dist 1988, bott Mar 14 **(95.5) n24** the high quality of the original spirit glows from the nose: it takes a solid distillate to absorb these exotically fruity, salty notes with such ease; a ten minute nose for maximum effect as it grows and oxidises; **t24** a sharp delivery with the salt biting hard and the tannins digging as deep as the growing dark sugars will allow: a gorgeous mix of maple syrup and manuka honey forges a striking defence; **f23.5** long, now even slightly oily as the vanillas begin to make their mark. Unusually late on, the exotic fruit at last shows and to immediate outstanding effect; a few mocha nuggets – as well as a lump or two of molasses, make for a superb, lightly spiced finish; **b24** a Bunna from the time when I used to stay at the distillery on my annual vacation...and spend half of it working my way through samples direct from the casks in the warehouse. This is a wonderful example of a lost style of Bunna and from a Hoggy imparting a fruity panache you are unlikely to experience in a quarter of a century's time...Truly mind-bowing. *50.4%. 193 bottles. WB16/013*

That Boutique-y Whisky Bunnahabhain batch 2 **(78) n20 t21 f18 b19**. A bit of a train wreck: hard to see what this is trying to be or achieve. There appears to be smoke, some kind of fruit, all kinds of oils, treacle-type sugars and much else besides. Absolutely no structure or balance, other than the odd fleeting accidental moment. Tasted blind, would not have recognised this as my beloved Bunna in a million years. *45.3%. 156 bottles. WB15/198*

◇ **Wemyss Malts 1988 Single Islay Bunnahabhain "Kirsch Gateau"**, bott 2014 **(96.5) n24** rich oloroso well stocked in muscovado sugars and spice: something like a Christmas pudding but with more resonant liquorice-oaky moments; **t25** the kind of delivery you could stand a spoon in: thick, spices of varying intensity and warmth coming at you from all directions. The weight is just about perfect, as is the ratio of fruit to oak; a layer of manuka honey also helps keep the pounding, toasty oak under control; **f23.5** dries with a certain austerity and burnt raisin bitterness. But there is still enough sultana and mocha to make for a charming fade, with the spices now barely audible; **b24** I was actually at Bunna in 1988 when they took shipment of a consignment of oloroso butts. Some were not that great, I remember. This, though, is not only up to scratch but is a rare example of exactly how an unpeated high quality sherry Bunna should be...and for decades before had been. Such scarce magnificence. A malt to be revered, applauded and remembered. And taken around to the Scotch Whisky Association, the insufferably pompous ignorant press office in particular, and perhaps with a bottle of Yamazaki, to remind them – no, much more likely teach them - what a true unblemished sherry butt tastes like. *56%. sc. 442 bottles.*

Wemyss Malts 1991 Single Islay Bunnahabhain "A Thread of Smoke" butt, bott 14 **(88.5) n22** thumping oak washes over every aspect of the nose. Briny, sharp and fading, like an old wooden rowing boat, the remains of which are sinking after many years into the silt of an estuary; **t22** it needed some muscovado sugars on the delivery – at least – to make this work... and they arrive quite plentifully. The tannins work prodigiously hard to drag the experience off the edge, but fail; **f22.5** lovely butterscotch tart softens the edges of the worst of the oak, as does some chocolate fudge; salty to the very end; **b22** a distillery which struggles uncommonly with age and this cask comes from the Ancient Order of Bunnas. Just enough sweetness left in the tank to make this an elegant dram...but it is a close run thing. *46%. sc. 302 bottles.*

Wemyss Malts 1991 Single Islay Bunnahabhain "Oysters With Lemon Pearls" bott 14 **(87) n21 t23 f21 b22.** Bunna struggles with age like England batsman Robson struggles with the ball outside his off stump. This, had it been bottled just maybe three years back, would have been memorable. But the tannin on the nose is too assertive and the rich, briny malt and toffee has to work too hard to keep it under control on the palate. An enjoyable dram, not least because of the mocha...but all a bit too stretched and frantic. *46%. sc. 265 bottles.*

Wemyss Malts 1991 Single Islay Bunnahabhain "Seaweed On The Rocks" dist 1991 bott 2013 **(91.5) n23.5** sumptuous diced fruit with tinned pears to the fore. The vaguest (and surprising) smoke thickens out the sugary barley; **t23** lively from the off with enough salt to underline the coastal credentials. The smoke has vanished but plenty of spices amid the vivid sugars; **f22.5** medium length with a thinning crispness accentuating the oak; **b23** a fruity cove. Almost literally... *sc. 294 bottles.*

Wemyss Malts 1997 Single Islay Bunnahabhain "The Bosun's Dram" hogshead, dist 97, bott 13 **(88)** **n22** one of the peated crop showing some impressive salt and sea spray...; **t22.5** blisteringly sweet delivery but thin enough to avoid any cloying, though thickens with peat in a spicy fashion; **f22** salted spiced smoky vanilla; **b22** "Westering home with some Peat In the Air..." *46%. sc. 380 bottles.*

Wemyss Malts 1997 Single Islay Bunnahabhain "A Peaty Punch!" bott 2013 **(86.5)** **n21.5 t23 f21 b21.** Very pleasant if simple whisky. But there is a fascinating – and revealing – contrast between this and the Wemyss Bunna 1991 which starkly shows the strengths and weaknesses of the old and new style Bunnahabhain. Here we have just another peaty malt with an attractive gristy sweetness but not quite of the eminence or complexity of an Ardbeg or Lagavulin coasting in neutral. And a long way behind the classic un-peated style where the salt and delicate fruits can truly weave pictures of beauty. *46%. sc. 348 bottles.*

⬧ **Whisky-Fässle Bunnahabhain 22 Year Old** sherry cask, dist 1990, bott 2013 **(95.5)** **n24** salty, coastal...and old. No shortage of slightly overcooked, heavily raisined fruitcake...; **t24** surprisingly soft texture. But the great age is apparent, almost to the extent that you might expect to find the remains of odd dinosaur or two, as the layers are stripped away. However, this must have been one hell of a sherry butt all those years ago, because the fruit carries on giving, and kissing some of the bruised oak better. Excellent spices abound; **f23.5** amazingly, the worst of the tannins have now vanished and we are treated to a magnificently dexterous interplay between manuka honey and cherry jam tart...slightly overcooked, of course....; **b24** the sherry has done a first class preservation job on the wood. All the tannins are manageable, even if some are straining at the leash. Entirely sulphur-free. *52%. nc ncf.*

⬧ **Whisky-Fässle Bunnahabhain 23 Year Old** hogshead, dist 1991, bott 2015 **(96)** **n24** as salty as can be expected with the oak digging in with a series of comforting honey notes, heather-honey at the fore; **t24.5** that is absolutely brilliant: the salts have now infused with the tannins and balance magnificently with the chalky liquorice and hickory. The heather honey on the nose is reinforced; **f23.5** quietly magnificent: creamy butterscotch still carries that salty tang, originally light spices intensify; **b24** for a distillery which so often falls flat on its face when passing 18, this has carried its years with exceptional grace. A true Bunna classic for the serious Islayphile. *47.5%. nc ncf.*

CAOL ILA

Islay, 1846. Diageo. Working.

Caol Ila Aged 10 Years "Unpeated Style" bott Aug 09 db **(93.5)** **n24** a beautiful medley of pear and lime with a thin spread of peanut butter for good measure...not exactly what one might expect...!!! **t23.5** the barley is just so juicy from the kickoff: the citrus on the nose reappears, though any hopes of pear vanishes; the barley, so rarely heard in a Caol-Ila grows in confidence and intensity as the delivery develops; **f23** not as oily as you might expect, allowing extra oak to emerge; **b23** always fascinating to see a traditional peaty Islay stripped bare and in full naked form. Shapely and very high class indeed. *65.4%. Only available at the Distillery.*

Caol Ila Aged 12 Years db **(89)** **n23 t23 f21 b22.** A telling improvement on the old 12-y-o with much greater expression and width. *43%*

Caol Ila 12 Years Old Special Release 2011 db **(89)** **n21.5 t23.5 f22 b22.** A sideways look at a big distillery allowing the casks to have the loudest say over the malt: not at all common with this Islay. *64%. nc ncf.*

Caol Ila 14 Years Old Unpeated Style First fill ex-bodega European Oak Casks, dist 1997, bott 2012 db **(95.5)** **n22.5 t24 f23 b24.** What a night's entertainment to battle your way through this. In normal circumstances the astonishing machinations of this malt would be lost under a sea of peat. But the malt here – 14 going on 40 – never ceases to amaze. A whisky grey and hunched way beyond its years...but what a story it tells...! A malt that lives long on the palate...and in the memory... *59.3%. nc ncf.*

Caol Ila Aged 18 Years db **(80)** **n21 t20 f19 b20.** Another improvement on the last bottling, especially with the comfortable integration of citrus. But still too much oil spoils the dram, particularly at the death. *43%*

Caol Ila 1979 db **(74)** **n20 t19 f17 b18.** Disappointing. I could go on about tropical fruit yada, yada, yada. Truth is, it just conks out under the weight of the oak. Too old. Simple as that. *58.6%*

Caol Ila 1997 The Manager's Choice db **(93.5)** **n24 t23.5 f23 b23.** When this malt is not enveloped in taste bud-clogging oil, it really can be a little special. Here's further proof. *58%*

Caol Ila Moch db **(87) n22 t22 f21 b22.** Easy drinking, but I think they mean "Mocha"... 43%

Caol Ila Stitchell Reserve "Unpeated Style" bott 2013 db **(89) n23** breezy salt and spices lighten the fruity load; a rare pinch of allspice; **t24** so confident – possibly thanks to the backing of a near 60% abv leg up – the intense fruit enjoys a rare balance of silky sultana and drier grape skins; **f20** dries a little too vigorously; **b22** not really a patch on the 2012 bottling, mainly due to inferior sherry butts, any smoke which does appear is like a half-imagined movement in the shadows. The delivery, though, is superb! 59.6% WB15/344

◈ **Aflodal's Whisky Cool Islay 31 Year Old** cask no. 4682, refill bourbon barrel, dist 15 May 80, bott 1 Aug 11 **(90) n23 t22 f22.5 b22.5.** Your nose and palate has to adjust to this like your eyes do to the dark: first you can make out little, but, with time, shapes emerge. The nose seems far too salty, but after a while you realise that it is playing cat and mouse with the thick smoke. Likewise, the sugars on the palate seem a little too full of themselves, but eventually settle attractively in the soot. 46.6%. 100 bottles.

◈ **Alexander Murray & Co Caol Ila 2006 8 Years Old (84.5) n21.5 t22 f20 b21.** Very possibly the dullest, most one-dimensional Caol Ila of this age I have tasted for a decade or more. There is a big, though muted, peat explosion on delivery. But it is short and the smoke and any possible fires of passion are extinguished PDQ. I may be wrong, but this has all the hallmarks of a malt which has been caramelised. And if so, then heavily. 40%

◈ **Best Dram Caol Ila 9 Years Old** bourbon hogshead **(90.5) n23** the sooty smoke, unobstructed by much oak, goes a very long way...; **t23** sublime sugary oils coat the palate: the peat is obliged and sticks to it like a limpet; **f22** a youthful, green-ish tang is fully exposed. Lovely, though; **b22.5** a green, beautifully refreshing big smoked dram to start the day...and a reminder of how this malt displayed itself over three decades ago. 51.7%

Cooper's Choice for Limburg Fair Caol Ila 1982 dist 1982 (84.5) n21 t22.5 f20 b21. Tangy and tight, the smoke plays a supporting role to the slightly muddled oak and sugars. 52%.

◈ **Glen Fahrn Airline Nr 02 Caol Ila 1982 Aged 29 Years** cask no. 759 **(86.5) n21 t22 f21.5 b22.** Struggles to ultimately cope with the tannin. Some entertaining spice and smoke moments along the way; a good cocoa blast, too. 59.3%. sc. 232 bottles.

Gordon & MacPhail Cask Strength Caol Ila refill sherry butts, cask no. 308843 & 308845, dist 29 Aug 01, bott 07 Mar 14 **(90.5) n23** a dry, wonderfully powdery, peat sooty offering; **t23** the usual early gristy release of sugars then a return to charmingly smokier ways; **f22** just a little bitter oak bite. Much the smoked dried date sweetness is impressively underplayed; **b22.5** always fascinating to see this distillery immerge from its usual oily cloak. In part a much drier, grittier dram than normal, though more than enough balancing sweetness to please.. 59.2%.

◈ **Gordon & MacPhail Cask Strength Collection Caol Ila 2004 9 Years Old** refill sherry cask, cask no. 306655, bott Aug 14 **(77.5) n20 t22.5 f17 b18.** Even through the thick smoky fog of the intense peat, you can tell something is not quite right with the sherry butt. Just for maybe two or three seconds after the initial, off key, hit on the palate, you doubt yourself as the fruity sugars surge. But slowly, and very surely, the sulphur returns to do its worst... 58.5%. nc ncf sc. The Whisky Exchange exclusive. WB16/005

◈ **Gordon & MacPhail Cask Strength Caol Ila 2004 (82) n22.5 t21 f19 b19.5.** At first the sultanas and smoke on the nose work in acceptable synchronisation, especially due to some serious juiciness on offer. But there is a background weakness, and so it proves on the palate, the finish in particular showing a nagging degree of furriness. 60.1%

Gordon & MacPhail Connoisseurs Choice Caol Ila 2001 (91.5) n22 dry, slightly minty phenols; **t23.5** sharp grassy, salivating barley, as though a crisp Speysider has been blended into the peaty mix. The spices lead the counter attack while the smoke slowly envelopes, builds and intensifies...; **f23** lightly molassed peat, then vanilla; **b23** simple but very effective. 46%. WB15/112

◈ **Gordon & MacPhail Connoisseurs Choice Caol Ila 2003 (90) n23** something of the Bavarian lightly smoked sausage about this, except for the background gristy sugars; **t23** excellent mouth feel: nothing like as oily as it can be, but just enough body weight to handle the sugars with purpose. Chewy, although slightly less to get your teeth into than normal for a Caol Ila; **f21.5** bitters slightly, but now the smoke grows and oils develop...; **b22.5** paradoxically, understated...yet confident. 46%

Hepburn's Choice Caol Ila Aged 5 Years refill hogshead, dist 08, bott 14 **(92.5) n22.5** new make but with the new born nip strained out. The smoke is nothing more than pure grist. Rather lovely; **t24** oil like highly peated grist, the sugars have the big say on the juicy delivery, but the smoke forms the framework; **f23.5** more of the same, with a little spice arriving late; **b22.5** when little things like oak aren't about to interfere with new make Caol Ila for five years, what isn't there to like? 46%. nc ncf sc. 414 bottles.

⟡ **Hepburn's Choice Caol Ila Aged 5 Years** refill hogshead, dist 2008, bott 2014 **(94) n24** quite brilliant distillate already picking up a balancing act from the cask. Love the sooty, acidic, coal-smoky winter day wind, which enriches the calmer peaty phenols; **t23.5** ridiculously soft and silky for its age. The sugars positively bombard the taste buds while the phenols hang around menacingly; **f23** drier now with the fizz of dissolving candyfloss and vanilla treading on peaty toes; **b23.5** this is how the majority of blenders in Scotland see Caol Ila these days: a five-year-old of controlled feistiness radiating rich and elegant smoke in all directions with just enough oils to lengthen the finale. This really is an excellent version: just about faultless for its age. 46%. nc ncf sc. 381 bottles.

⟡ **Hunter Laing's Old & Rare Caol Ila Aged 30 Years** refill hogshead, dist Jan 84, bott Oct 14 **(96) n24** the smoke of a discharged rifle disappearing into a salty, coastal breeze...; **t24** beautiful two-toned attack with the almost aggressive peppery spice couched and soothed by the house oils; the sugars are just so subtle yet nimbly spruce up the thick vanillas...; **f24** every bit as long as you wish it to be: the smoke drifts aimlessly catching on the liquorice and molasses from time to time; **b24** puts Caol Ila onto a different plinth from the vast majority we have tasted before. Absolutely everything you could ask from this distillery at this age... and a whole lot more beside! 53.2%. nc ncf sc. 246 bottles.

Islay Single Malt Caol Ila 33 Years refill hogshead, cask no. 10159, dist Sept 1980, bott Dec 2013 **(95.5) n24** anthracite mixed in with peak reek. Almost a mix of a south Wales mining village from 30 years ago, or a winter (and summer!) cottage on Islay. Predominantly dry for all the ground muscovado sugars and hickory; **t24** a Catherine wheel of a delivery, with sparks and smoke flying in all directions. Helped by a bizarre lack of oils for this distillery, the shape and layering forms unhindered; chewey and no shortage of burnt fudge mixing with the weighty peat; **f23.5** long with a more toasty finale than normal. Again the sugars have much to say, but do so with quiet assertiveness though never speaking above the rumbling phenols; **b24** you will do well to find a Caol Ila in better nick than this over the next year or so. Absolutely tip top form and showing an unusual vibrancy thanks to some restraint with the oils and oak at its very best. Simply glorious. 58.8%. nc ncf sc. 136 bottles.

Montgomerie's Single Cask Collection Caol Ila cask no. 1477, dist 08 Feb 90, bott Mar 13 **(95) n23** minted chocolate...in smoke, of course...; **t24** mouth-watering and gorgeously refreshing; all kinds of spices fizz but softened by creamy butter milk plus a little liquorice, fudge and mocha; **f24** more of the same, with a slow fade; **b24** sharp, yet easy going, charming and fatally moreish. An understated gem. 46%. nc ncf sc. WB15/126

Old Malt Cask Caol Ila Aged 16 Years refill hogshead, cask no. 9512, dist Sep 96, bott Feb 13 **(95) n23.5** dry: the hearth being cleaned of the previous night's burnt peats; **t24** outstanding citrus attack on delivery – fresh and salivating. The peat arrives by the squadron load but the light oils carry some serious barley sugar; **f23.5** more like the drier nose now as diced coconut and fudge make for a chewy finish; the confident peat makes all the right noise; **b24** never one of Caol Ila's greatest fans (well, since it was rebuilt), I have to say this is a dram I could drink all day any day, simply because it is so subtle and understated....and without a single distilling or maturation blemish. Truly sublime. 50%. sc. 156 bottles.

Old Malt Cask Caol Ila Aged 17 Years refill hogshead, cask no. 10123, dist Sep 96, bott Oct 13 **(86.5) n21.5 t21.5 f22 b21.5** Pleasant, decently smoked, attractively spiced but the big natural caramels and vanillas blunt the experience. 50%. nc ncf sc. 324 bottles. WB15/132

Old Malt Cask Caol Ila Aged 17 Years refill hogshead, cask no. 10229, dist Sep 96, bott Jan 14 **(91) n23** anthracite and drying bombarding peat reek appear to take this above the normal 35ppm phenols. Dry and challenging; **t22** the sugars absent on the nose appear on the delivery, but soon spices enter the fray. The peat also appears to have a chocolate orange persona; **f23** long, drying, complex with the smoke appearing in all kinds of degrees of intensity; **b23** bare knuckle Caol Ila, with all the punches unencumbered by oil. 50%. nc ncf sc.

Old Malt Cask Caol Ila Aged 17 Years refill hogshead, cask no. 10446, dist Sep 96, bott Apr 14 **(95.5) n23.5** some sizzling spice is calmed by the soft smoke; **t23.5** textbook Islay: the peat waits a moment or two before revealing the full intensity of its hand, allowing a few vital seconds of sugared barley to sparkle. The oak offers an attractive mocha sub plot; **f23.5** a few saline notes hoist the coastal flag while the smoke drifts on in more layers than you'll ever be able to count; **b24** hats off to a bottling which shows the distillery in the most positive light possible. There is less oils than normal for here, allowing the peat to show a much more guile than is the norm. Not to be missed! And gentle and complex enough to convert the unbelievers... 50%.nc ncf sc. 354 bottles.

Old Malt Cask Caol Ila Aged 18 Years refill hogshead, cask no. 9913, dist Sep 94, bott Aug 13 **(88) n22.5** some decent citrus cuts through the smoke; **t21.5** only the midland spices pep up some standard malt; **f22** better finale with the smoke now layering, the spices persisting and the sugars softening; **b22** enjoyable. But could have been better...and a lot worse. *50%. nc ncf sc. 328 bottles.*

Old Malt Cask Caol Ila Aged 29 Years refill hogshead, cask no.10069, dist Jan 84, bott Oct 13 **(96.5) n24** dry smoke meets its light orange and minty match; **t24** the softest of oils hoist the phenols aloft, but it dries quickly to let in a wonderful minty mocha middle; **f24** dispenses with the coffee and concentrates fully on the chocolate; elegant, well balanced and allows that citrus to show through at the finish; **b24.5** one of the most chocolate-rich smokies you'll ever come across. Rare to find a whisky of this age so beautifully weighted and balanced: shows absolutely no signs of wear. Sublime. *50%. nc ncf sc. 131 bottles. WB15/136*

Provenance Caol Ila 'Young & Feisty' refill hogshead, cask no. 10178 **(77) n20 t19 f20 b18.** Young for sure. But not even remotely feisty. Fails to work on so many levels, though lack of body and balance are the main stumbling blocks. *46%. nc ncf sc.*

◇◇ **Provenance Caol Ila "Young & Feisty"** refill hogsheads, cask nos. 10423 & 10447, bott Summer 14 **(85.5) n21 t22 f21 b21.5.** A youthful, perhaps oversimplified, smoky gristfest. A squeeze of lemon makes it fresher still. *46%. nc ncf.*

◇◇ **Provenance Caol Ila Over 6 Years** refill hogshead, cask no. 10582, dist Autumn 08, bott Autumn 14 **(83.5) n20 t21.5 f21 b21.** Struggles to find its feet, but once it does, shows some degree of balance. Beyond the sweet smoke, don't expect too much else. *46%. nc ncf sc.*

◇◇ **Riegger's Selection Cask Strength Caol Ila 30 Year Old** rum cask finish, bott 23 Oct 14 **(88.5) n22** a tight nose with the profound smoke seemingly against some kind of glass ceiling...; **t23** a crisp, firm sugar is slowly overtaken by spice and oily smoke in equal measure; the oak tries to evolve but appears to be stopped in its tracks; **f21.5** bitters slightly despite the early sugar. The spices continue to throb; **b22** like most whiskies matured in rum, this feels as though it is in a straight jacket. Pleasant, but never quite opens up. *56.2%*

◇◇ **Old Malt Cask Caol Ila 18 Years Old** refill butt, cask no. 10874, dist Sept 96, bott Sept 14 **(88) n22.5** confident smoke, but lightened by citrus and vanilla: elegant despite its weight; half a mark lost due to a little tiredness showing through; **t23.5** brilliant spice buzz from the off. Countering sugars range from icing to dried maple syrup with the smoke harmonising according to plan; **f20.5** bounds along according to plan until the slight off-note on the nose is confirmed with a little milky buzz at the very death; **b22** an initially satisfying and beautifully weighted Islay malt undone late on by the discordant beginnings of an unhappy cask. *50%. nc ncf sc. 452 bottles.*

◇◇ **Old Malt Cask Caol Ila 18 Years Old** refill hogshead, cask no. 11407, dist Sept 96, bott Mar 15 **(95.5) n23.5** the usual distillery oils and quietly hefty phenols are delightfully interwoven; **t24** the delivery is as clean and precise as the nose; the smoke rams itself home with a thud, but little collateral damage. So the malt is still perceptible...and the oils find and cling to every nook and cranny on the palate; **f24** outrageously long, and now spicy yet with a late addition of citrus and icing sugars to help thin the malt enough to allow the developing vanillas to ensure a weighty finale; **b24** coming to the end of a long tasting day, I actually began marking this in my mind as a Caol Ila before actually seeing what the sample actually was....!!! So, a wonderful and unmistakable example of this distillery at its most relaxed and comfortable... *50%. nc ncf sc. 234 bottles.*

Scotch Malt Whisky Society Cask 53.197 Aged 18 Years refill hogshead, dist 24 Aug 95 **(91) n22** simplistic but very effective gristy peat reek; **t23** abounds with crisp sugars on delivery, then a beguiling degree of interwoven spice. The smoke is omnipresent; **f23** some tangy citrus among the embers; **b23** sweet and beautifully made. *574%. nc ncf sc. 253 bottles.*

Scotch Malt Whisky Society Cask 53.198 Aged 18 Years refill butt, dist 29 Aug 95 **(85) n21 t21.5 f21.5 b21** Less giving oak ensures the barley and peat show a degree of enforced astringency. *59%. nc ncf sc. 510 bottles.*

Scotch Malt Whisky Society Cask 53.201 Aged 18 Years refill butt, dist 29 Aug 95 **(86.5) n22 t22 f21 b21.5.** Some biting spices make this a Caol Ila to remember. The oils play a stranger role than usual, thickening things at the beginning but dying at the finale to allow the drier peat notes and some more bitter tanins to filter through. *60%. nc ncf sc. 575 bottles.*

Scotch Malt Whisky Society Cask 53.203 Aged 17 Years refill hogshead, dist 03 Sep 96 **(89) n22.5** quintessential Caol Ila: oily and pugnaciously smoky...; **t22** gristy and full of peaty resolve. Some mocha and hickory notes enrich; **f22.5** some searing spices at the death; **b22** some lovely complexity to this guy. *578%. nc ncf sc. 271 bottles.*

Scotch Malt Whisky Society Cask 53.205 Aged 22 Years refill hogshead, dist 17 Jan 92 **(95.5) n23.5** superb oak sets up the pea for a sweet, bluebell wood earthiness; a sublime drier sub-strata balances matters; **t23.5** for all the obvious oils, the oak, juicy barley and smoke puncture the sugary bubble easily...; **f24.5** a chewy, smoky finish with a slow development of dark sugars, fudge and cocoa; meanwhile the spices buzz laudibly; **b24** straight as a dye truly great whisky! *52.9%. nc ncf sc. 229 bottles.*

Scotch Malt Whisky Society Cask 53.206 Aged 18 Years refill hogshead, dist 24 Aug 95 **(85.5) n21.5 t21.5 f21 b21.5**. They've gone very easy on the smoke, rendering this lively but rather tart. *56.6%. nc ncf sc. 233 bottles.*

◇ **Scotch Malt Whisky Society Cask 53.216 Aged 21 Years** refill butt, dist 13 Jul 93 **(91) n24** understated magnificence: no doubt about the good age or the usual soft oils. Where it really comes into its own is in the rare balance involving the smoke, underlined by the gentle spice; **t22** the oak makes an early mark with no more than a hint of bitterness. But the smoke remains confident, helped by light oily cocoa sheen; **f22.5** the sugars disperse leaving a dry, smoky residue; **b22.5** a good quality malt which revels in its antiquity. *60.6%. sc. 597 bottles.*

◇ **Scotch Malt Whisky Society Cask 53.218 Aged 14 Years** refill hogshead, dist 16 Mar 00 **(83.5) n21 t21.5 f20 b21**. Average fare. Moderate smoke and a less than moderate cask. Youthful and juicy in part – but never takes off. *64.4%. sc. 242 bottles.*

◇ **Scotch Malt Whisky Society Cask 53.219 Aged 14 Years** refill hogshead, dist 16 Mar 00 **(81) n20.5 t22 f18.5 b20**. Very ordinary malt redeemed by a fresh juiciness on delivery. Not the greatest wood at work. *62.8%. sc. 254 bottles.*

Signatory Vintage Un-chillfiltered Collection Caol Ila 1996 Aged 17 Years hogsheads, cask no. 5572+5573, dist 04 Apr 96, bott 05 Jul 13 **(95) n23.5** dry, slightly sooty and toast slightly burned an hour ago. A little salt add piquancy so, naturally, matching pepper is around somewhere; **t24** very high quality delivery. The oak is already up and running and helps keep the early smoke in order. Spices pound from early on and even a dab of hickory offers a brief glimpse of something bourbony The high point, though, is the mid ground when the ulmo honey softens, caresses and ensures complexity and balance; **f23.5** lovely spice tingle and low level smoke on the butter shortcake; **b24** there is something irresistible – and sadly rare – about a Caol Ila that is sparing on the oil and big on complexity. Sublime spirit in a top hole cask. Superb. *46%. nc ncf. 729 bottles. WB15/024*

Wemyss Malts 1982 Single Islay Caol Ila "Smoke on the Water" hogshead, dist 82, bott 14 **(91) n22.5** minted weak peat reek; **t22.5** lively delivery, though some cracks show early from the big age. Enough oil around to gloss them over and allow the smoke and spice to build; **f23** hit genuine complexity: the smoke dissolves into a delicious mocha finale sweetened by surprising heather honey; **b23** a little touch of the Highland Parks on the finish helps this become a venerable and enjoyable dram. *46%. sc. 255 bottles.*

The Whisky Agency Perfect Dram Caol Ila 1995 (94.5) n23 sultry, gentle, delightfully sweet and above the norm degree of smoke for a Caol Ila; **t24** the usual C I oils have been limited here, allowing the smokiness full reign. Just so gentle and elegant, the vanillas and spices are in total harmony with the mouth-filling smoke; **f23.5** the spices intensify, as does the brittleness of the sugars; **b24** whoever was working out their 35ppm phenols must have been a little numerically dyslexic...some whopping peat here. *50.6%.*

◇ **Wilson & Morgan Barrel Selection Caol Ila 25 Year Old** oloroso sherry finish, cask no. 4707, 4708, dist 1990, bott 2015 **(78) n19 t21 f19 b19**. Too much tannin. Too much grape. And, in that context, too much smoke. And, of course, too much buzz from the sherry butt. *54.3%*

◇ **World of Orchids Caol Ila 1983 30 Year Old** bourbon cask, cask no. 4843 **(94.5) n24 t24 f23 b23.5**. Not just smoky...complex enough to be a three pipe malt should Sherlock Holmes try to unravel this one. The intertwangling of the citrus and borderline hefty oak really does keep you amused for tens of minutes on end. Not sure I have ever come across an oak infusion so borderline OTT, but never quite crosses the mark, either on nose or palate. A cask plucked in the final moments before it took on just a shade too much tannin. But for it to then run into citrus is almost unique. An amazing and joyous experience. *52.9%. sc. 204 bottles.*

CAPERDONICH
Speyside, 1898. Chivas Brothers. Closed.

Alexander Weine & Distillate Caperdonich 20 Year Old refill bourbon hogshead, cask no. 121120, dist 1992, bott 2013 **(86.5) n23 t22 f20 b21.5**. I remember back in 1992 wandering around this distillery and being told by its manager that, no matter how they tried, they had problems guaranteeing the quality of the distillate. The distillery has gone now, a victim of its own quirkiness and uneven temperament. This bottling gives some clues as to why, with a hotness which has nothing to do with spice. But there is a charismatic charm to the barley too. The oak, though, is all embracing. *54.7%. sc. Cask Strength.*

Berry's Own Selection Caperdonich 1995 Aged 18 Years cask no. 95076, bott 2014 **(86)** n22 t22 f20 b21. While tasting this, I have just been presented by my partner, Judy, a massive toad found in the garden minding its own business under a bush. This splendid fellow was a fat, rather ugly thing but brimming with personality. By contrast, this has its moments of beauty – with the barley sugar delivery for instance – but is rather devoid of character. I know which of the two kept my attention longer.... *46%. ncf ncf. WB15/241*

◇◇◇ **Single Cask Collection Caperdonich 1994 20 Year Old** sherry hogshead **(87.5)** n23 t22 f21 b21.5. The nose reminds me of a muesli I used to eat a decade ago built on apple, raisin and mixed nuts...but without the milk. The delivery is quite superb thanks to the controlled oiliness of the body and the charm of the intense grist. The finish, though, works hard to cut out a threatening bitterness. It succeeds, but could have done without the battle. *53.5%*

That Boutique-y Whisky Caperdonich batch 4 **(85)** n21.5 t22 f20 b21.5. Not a distillery to raise its head high above the parapet before it reaches at least 25, this shows good form – and no little banana - until the mean, limited finish. *48.1%. 79 bottles. WB15/197*

The Whisky Agency Caperdonich 1992 dist 1992 **(89.5)** n21.5 thin, rather strained, uninspiring oak; t24 one dimensional, ultra intense malt with a near faultless body you really want to explore: amazing and really quite beautiful...; f21.5 thins out once more, though a few warming spices filter through; b22.5 the whisky equivalent of getting a malty custard pie in the kisser.... *60.9%.*

The Whisky Cask Caperdonich Aged 20 Years bourbon hogshead, dist 1994, bott 2014 **(87)** n22 t22 f21 b22. Malty and salivating with plenty of barley sugar candy. A little bite but simplistic stuff. *54.7%. nc ncf.*

◇◇◇ **Whisky-Fässle Caperdonich 39 Year Old** sherry cask, dist 1972, bott 2011 **(86.5)** n21.5 t22.5 f21 b21.5. A typically placid Caper, showing a remarkable amount of fresh, almost grassy malt for a 20-year-old. Plenty of citrus, and spices, too. Delicious, though entirely unassuming. *45%. nc ncf.*

◇◇◇ **Whisky Tales Caperdonich Aged 20 Years** dist 1994, bott 2015 **(89.5)** n23 t23 f21.5 b22. From the famous Caperdonich school of exotic fruitiness. Except this one is a little oak-bloated and on its way down... *57%. nc ncf sc. 150 bottles.*

CARDHU
Speyside, 1824. Diageo. Working.
Cardhu 12 Years Old db **(83)** n22 t22 f18 b21. What appears to be a small change in the wood profile has resulted in a big shift in personality. What was once a guaranteed malt love-in is now a drier, oakier, fruitier affair. Sadly, though, with more than a touch of something furry. *40%*

◇◇◇ **Cardhu 18 Year Old** db **(88)** n22.5 soft, easy going – one might even say "safe". Attractive amalgam of clean fruit, citrus especially, and vanilla-drenched barley. But perhaps not enough subtle peaks and troughs to excite; t23 more of the same: soft, juicy malt but with a darker side as the fruit fills in the gaps; f20.5 way too bitter for its own good; b22 very attractive at first. But when you consider what a great distillery Cardhu is and how rare stocks of 18 year old must be, have to say that I am disappointed. The fruit masks the more intricate moments one usually experiences on a Cardhu to ensure an acceptable blandness and accounts for a poor finish. Why, though, it is bottled at a pathetic 40% abv instead of an unchillfiltered 46% – the least this magnificent distillery deserves – is a complete mystery to me. *40%*

Cardhu Amber Rock db **(87.5)** n22 t23 f21 b21.5. Amber is the right colour for this: it appears stuck between green and red, not sure whether to go or not. The delivery, in which the tangerine cream is in full flow reflects the better elements of the nose. But the finish is all about being stuck in neutral. Not helped by the useless 40% abv, you get the feeling that a great whisky is trying to get out. The odd tweak and we'll have a winner. That said, very enjoyable indeed. Just even more frustrating! *40%. Diageo.*

CLYNELISH
Highlands (Northern), 1968. Diageo. Working.
Clynelish Aged 15 Years "The Distillers Edition" double matured in oloroso-seco casks CI-Br: 169-1f, bott code L6264CM000 03847665, dist 1991, bott 2006 db **(79)** n20 t20 f19 b20. Big in places, distinctly oily in others but the overall feel is of a potentially brilliant whisky matured in unsympathetic barrels. *46%*

Adelphi Selection Clynelish Aged 17 Years dist 96, bott 14 **(92)** n22.5 oak through a loudhailer...good creamy Swiss roll filling keeps down the noise; t24 for the muscle on the tannin, the red liquorice and treacle mixing with the major spice makes this something to savour; f22.5 as the sugars wear thin, the slight over eagerness of the dry, toasty oak is again revealed...as is a big helping of powering cocoa; **b23** gargantuan, relatively brawny for a Clynelish but, as usual, just exploding with character. Slightly over aged but gets away with it with aplomb. *57.1%. ncf. 264 bottles. WB15/335*

Alexander Weine & Destillate Clynelish 24 Years Old refill bourbon hogshead, cask no. 4550, dist 1988, bott 2013 **(89) n23** remember when the icecream man used to pour some of that green sweet stuff on your vanilla cornet...? **t22** buzzing spices take no time to delve into the gathering, multi-layered sugars, most of a dark, smouldering variety; **f21.5** the tannins take few prisoners; the spices keep on buzzing...and a puff of smoke appears on the most distant horizon...; **b22.5** another malt caught in the tailwind of the oak. But the steering sugars see this oldie home. *48.8%. sc. Cask strength.*

Berry's Own Selection Clynelish 1997 Aged 16 Years cask no. 6871, bott 2014 **(94) n22.5** a salty, unsure nose. Directionless and half-hearted but enough lively malt and marmalade in there to offer hope...; **t24** which is soon rewarded: fabulous oils and spice combine for a seriously complex delivery, which only gets better as the ulmo honey and chocolate wafer gets to work; **f23.5** custard creams and raisin shortcake biscuits mix it with the ulmo honey; **b24** this poor thing had to follow the two Balvenie Single Barrels I reviewed...a very hard act to follow. The nose suggested it might bomb, but excellence will out in the end. *55.4%. ncf ncf. WB15/246*

⬦ **Cadenhead's Authentic Collection Clynelish Aged 24 Years** bourbon barrel, dist 1990, bott Oct 14 **(91.5) n23** a hint of smoke – just like Clynelish of yesteryear. But it is the earthy heath-honey which dominates; **t23** the honey (again of the heather and borage variety) needs no second invite: arrives early as if to keep the toastier tannins at bay; the sugar twinkles alongside the busy spices; **f22.5** as soon as the sugars fade, the deeper, drier oaks take up their positions; **b23** seems almost impossible to find a disappointing Clynelish these days... *40%. 156 bottles.*

Cadenhead's Clynelish 2014 Aged 24 Years dist 1990, bott Apr 14 **(92) n23.5** the volume is set on low: the ulmo honey, red liquorice, molasses just audible above the vanilla chatter; **t23** salivating barley – so fresh it mocks its 24 years in barrel; the sugars are constantly at arms against the encroaching oak, but attacks with a feather duster, merely tickling the intruder; excellent spices add some varoom; honey returns for the late mid-ground going into the finale; **f22.5** spiced Tunnock's wafers...; **b23** an exclusive to one shop. Lucky London: Millwall and this shy little charmer... *47.5%. 228 bottles. London exclusive. WB15/079*

Darkness! Clynelish Aged 16 Years Oloroso Cask Finish (90.5) n22.5 errr...oloroso...; **t22.5** errr....oloroso...with lots of spice. And I mean lots...; **f23** errr...oloroso. With a massive date and walnut swirl to the finish plus the inevitable spiced cocoa; **b22.5** no off notes from the sherry butt whatsoever. But a good example of more being less: far too much fruit completely overwhelms the usual Clynelish complexity. Still, brilliant chewiness to the fruit and the spice is uncompromising. Soothing, rich but overly simple – especially on the finish - so far as this distillery is concerned....yet still just so bloody delicious...! *54.9%. 94 bottles. WB15/200*

⬦ **Dun Bheagan Clynelish 16 Year Old** hogshead, dist Jul 97 **(95) n23.5** like sticking your nose into an ulmo honeycomb...except there is not a single sting; some distant sea-breeze salt...; **t23.5** the mouth-feel is sublime but soon your attention is taken by the spices. As well as the honey on toast and butterscotch tart; the mid-ground delights in a sublime Nice biscuit; **f24** appears at first to be fading. Then, somehow, the light honey notes return, accompanied now by gentle waves of oak-induced praline. The spices are no more than a distant tingle...all is understated. All is magnificent...; **b24** a mark of genius is when a whisky, already outstanding, improves on the finish. Here is one such whisky. *50.5%. nc ncf.*

Gordon & MacPhail Cask Strength Clynelish 1997 (89.5) n22 there is a rumble of sherry in this glass like there is a rumble of thunder outside my tasting room. Only there, there is far more water...this nose is also earthy as though mixing manuka honey with ginger, allspice and freshly trimmed beans: definitely unusual; **t23** massive delivery with several layers of jam amid the honey. Again the spices are at full throttle; thought I caught a furry off note...; **f21.5** and indeed I have, as confirmation is received that this has been matured in sherry butts, though the damage by the sulphur is pretty limited. **b23** almost a brilliant whisky. For Clynelish, certainly an oddball. *57.9%.*

The Maltman Clynelish Aged 15 Years bourbon cask **(96.5) n24.5** fabulous display of oak-based spice and dried orange peel: cedar and sandalwood sweetened by molassed liquorice: magnificent...and worth a good ten minutes' study before tasting...; **t24.5** the spices zing through from the first moment again with that sublime backdrop of distant, dark sugars: a malt which claims at first on the palate to be dry but then broadcasts the most astonishing degree of spice and subtle sugar complexity with deeper complexity offered by the high cocoa chocolate orange; **f23** long, long, long and enjoyed a slightly oily depth to that superb spiced chocolate orange; **b24.5** near perfect weight and layering, especially with the spices. An essay in poise and sophistication, the secret being the persistent, dry undertone: the fact so much has happened in just a single cask borders the incredible. *46%. WB15/215*

Old Malt Cask Clynelish Aged 15 Years refill hogshead, cask no. 9881, dist Jul 1997, bott Jun 2013 **(94) n23** the citrus prods the vanilla awake; **t24** now your taste buds get a wake up call as the muscovado and lemon sherbet dusted barley makes its stunning opening salvo; powdered custard cream biscuits fill the mid ground; **f23** a slow denouement of those astonishing barley and matching oak notes. Perhaps the most subtle spice attack of the year gets under way late on... **b24** just can't always trust a nose, can you? This one is dul by Clynelish's normally mesmeric standards. But the delivery....wow!!! *50%. nc ncf sc. 315 bottles.*

Old Malt Cask Clynelish Aged 16 Years refill hogshead, cask no. 10227, dist May 97, bott Dec 13 **(85) n20 t22 f20.5 b21**. Some usually limited oak for this distillery ensures a Clynelish a long way from its normal mark. Oddly enough, the smoke and spices are accentuated here, but the remainder is an off target mish-mash. *50%. nc ncf sc. 154 bottles.*

Old Malt Cask Clynelish Aged 16 Years refill hogshead, cask no. 10298, dist May 97, bott Feb 14 **(92) n22** beautiful suet pudding with salted acacia honey spread all over it; **t23.5** after a series of uninspiring malts, great to at last receive a delivery which makes the hairs stand on end: classic Clynelish, even if slightly understated. Elegant barley gets things off to a juicy start; the spices enter with aplomb and purpose; pear juice thins honey; **f23** more pear juice.. and even that crunchy texture to match. A lovely swirl of muscovado; **b23.5** the annual OMC Clynelish 16 has become a fixture of excellence in this Bible: if memory serves, this is bang on course with the others. *50%. nc ncf sc. 318 bottles.*

◈ **Old Malt Cask Clynelish 17 Years Old** refill hogshead, cask no. 11236, dist Apr 97, bott Feb 15 **(86.5) n23.5 t22 f20 b21**. Gets off to the usual Clynelish flying start of beauty, then an uncharacteristic cask bitterness creeps in. *50%. nc ncf sc. 280 bottles.*

◈ **Old Particular Highland Clynelish 18 Years Old** refill hogshead, cask no. 10580, dist Oct 96, bott Nov 14 **(94.5) n24** ridiculously subtle: everything works on the very edge of your radar. Light ulmo honey dovetails with butterscotch and slightly salty, very vaguely smoky tannin....less an aroma, more a teasing caress of the nose...; **t23.5** the softest delivery: butterfly-like take offs and landings of gentle muscovado sugars and vanilla; **f23** drier, a little spicier, occasionally maltier...that vaguest hint of smoke again...; **b24** even in a less than generous cask, there is still no diminishing the greatness of this malt. A beautiful dram: one of the most understated whiskies of the year. *48.4%. nc ncf sc. 390 bottles.*

◈ **Provenance Clynelish Over 7 Years** refill barrel, cask no. 10771, dist Summer 08, bott Summer 15 **(92.5) n23** this is seven...??? Though young, there is a precocious earthy weightiness to this which completely balances the light spice and gentle Zambian exotic honey; **t23.5** thick, absolutely creaking under the weight of intense gristy barley; vanilla already and even a hint of liquorice; **f23** a light spice buzzes, then oily, orange blossom honey-tinged barley; **b23.5** how can a malt this young have so many strings to its bow? It's like the junior school classroom beauty you know will grow up and one day break a thousand hearts... *46%. nc ncf sc.*

◈ **Romantic Rhine Collection Clynelish** oak hogshead & sherry octave, cask nos. 903, 666, dist 7 Jun 89, bott 26 Mar 12 **(93) n23.5 t24 f22 b23.5**. One of the fruitier Clynelishs you'll find at the minute: grape, pear juice and greengage also make delicate but complex entries, but that is nothing to the spices which, combining with the salt, makes for an orgy of salivation. A little bitter at the end, though. *52.9%. 70 bottles.*

Scotch Malt Whisky Society Cask 26.95 Aged 10 Years 1st fill barrel, dist 16 Jun 03 **(92.5) n23** unusually intense and busy for a Clynelish...even some hints of lobster and paprika here; **t24** wow...!!! Takes more time than there is in the day to understand the nature of this fruity-spicy beast. Mangoes and honeydew melon dominate early on. Really has absorbed some major tannin since the fruit is volumised by deft ulmo honey; **f22.5** could be a little too much oak, but soft smoke cushions the blows; the sugars are eaked out cleverly; **b23.5** has become a greybeard ahead of its time. But the fruity structure is compelling. *61.3%. nc ncf sc. 157 bottles.*

Scotch Malt Whisky Society Cask 26.101 Aged 9 Years 1st fill barrel, dist 03 Jun 04 **(94) n22** unusually mono syllabic with the tannins far too in control; **t24.5** ye gods!!! Nobody could expect that! The delivery rocks you off your chair and blows your socks off as the spices combust on impact. The depth charge stirs up some sedimentary sugars and the resulting soup is a spicy treat; **f23.5** the fade is a delicious run through of many of the tangier notes found in older bourbons; **b24** the dullness of the nose is a good decoy for the rampaging spice which follows....! *59.3%. nc ncf sc. 247 bottles.*

◈ **Scotch Malt Whisky Society Cask 26.102 Aged 29 Years** refill butt, dist 13 Dec 84 **(92.5) n22.5** a hint of lactose from the cask, revealing oak on its way out. Luckily, the house honey still manages to embrace it; **t24** not a single hint of a problem on the delivery: quite the opposite as the molassed sugars give an extra degree of weight while coconut jelly gives a slightly creamy feel; **f22** sugar-coated vanilla; just the faintest hint of oak degradation on the very finish; **b24** even though the oak is showing the first stages of tiring, this is still yet another astounding whisky from a truly world class distillery. *56%. sc. 416 bottles.*

Signatory Cask Strength Collection Clynelish 1995 Aged 17 Years refill sherry butt, cask no. 12794, dist 12 Dec 95, bott 23 Sep 13 **(91) n22.5** curious subtle smoke and gentle grape mix. Clean sherry butt at work...so even a bourbon-style edge from the oak is detected; **t23** two-toned spice – presumably two types, one from the oak, the other from the grape – dominate early on before a Cadbury's Fruit and Nut middle even apes its cotton wool texture; **f22.5** delicate fruit but mainly tannins which rather over dominate despite the Demerara; **b23** probably peaked two years earlier. Great to see a magnificent sherry butt offering zero negativity and allowing the character of the distillate to come through. *56.2%. sc nc. Cask hand picked by The Whisky Exchange. WB15/322*

Signatory Vintage Un-chillfiltered Collection Clynelish 1997 Aged 16 Years dist 29 Oct 97, bott 19 Feb 14, hogsheads, cask no. 12375+12376 **(85.5) n23 t21.5 f20 b21.** Even one of the world's great distilleries, such as Clynelish, struggles to hit the heights after spending 16 years in oak coming to the end of its useful life. But at least the nose is allowed to give a virtuoso display of sublimely subtle citrus and barley, enriched further by floral honey. *46%. nc ncf. 787 bottles. WB15/025*

The Single Malts of Scotland Clynelish Aged 18 Years hogshead, cask no. 10193, dist 31 Oct 95, bott 25 Mar 14 **(88.5) n22** a little light peat mingles with the silky vanillas; **t22.5** juicy with a few malty thrusts early on, then the expected spice which arrives in abundance; some boiled cooking apple tries to penetrate the tannins; **f22** dries, though retains that vaguely sweet oiliness. The tang of the tannins surrounds the malt and sugars like Indians around a waggon train of settlers; **b22** just a little too bold with the oak for true greatness. But plenty to see along the way. *57.5%. 265 bottles. WB15/294*

The First Editions Clynelish 1996 Aged 17 Years refill hogshead, dist 1996, bott 2014 **(96.5) n24.5** this is all about complexity and deftness. Just hints here, murmurs there...and the odd whisper, sometimes bolstered by a caress. Honey is at the vanguard, though in varying forms, most light and flickering, the odd shard of honeycomb momentarily adding a touch of weight before vanishing again...; citrus flickers, a sprinkling of salt amplifies; **t24.5** a delivery crafted by the gods: the spices arrive early and in force to show this is going to be no namby-pamby honeyfest. They buzz and spit, often truculently, yet do so without breaking the spell of the honey, in its myriad manifestations, being broken. Sublime oils help the honey-lemon sub strata flourish; salty with a butterscotch middle; **f23.5** only some late bitterness detracts vaguely from the elegance of the ever-drying finale, though the spices which started entirely unobtrusively now take on a more commanding roll; **b24** not sure if they should rename this distillery "Old Faithful". Just never, ever seems to let you down. Another beautifully, almost perfectly, crafted essay. *58.2%. nc ncf sc. 265 bottles.*

Wemyss Clynelish Malts 1997 Single Highland "Apple Basket" bott 2013. **(88) n22.5** under-ripe conference Pear and vanilla; **t23** charming and salivating in the first instant, thins rather too quickly though a dose of spices are welcome; **f20.5** dry, flaky oak; **b22** one of those casks which has been damaged by being reduced to 46%. The oils, so essential for the finish, have been split and the oak takes on too chalky a style as a result. *46%. Sc. 339 bottles.*

Wemyss Clynelish Malts 1997 Single Highland "Beach with a Sea View" hogshead, dist 97, bott 14 **(95) n23** coconut water and milky mocha; **t24** magnificent delivery – comes from nowhere as the nose doesn't hint at this. Outstanding weight, an early spice eruption then the ulmo honey coming thick and confidently. Malt is also intense, lightened by just a touch of citrus; **f24** a gentle saltiness gives a nod towards the oak but also helps highlight the long malt and bourbon biscuit dunked in coffee fade; **b24** probably the only distillery on this planet which can surprise like this does. Another gem of a malt from this distillery which, for my money, is now in the world's top three... *46%. sc. 371 bottles.*

Wemyss Clynelish Malts 1997 Single Highland "Cayenne Cocoa Bean" (91) n22 coconut water & pineapple; **t23** sweet citrusy kick off: Jaffa orange tamed by ulmo honey & butterscotch; **f23** a sugary fade and the coconut water returns as spices build; **b23** shows a bit more age than you might expect but still has that effortless Clynelish panache. *46%. sc.*

Wemyss Clynelish Malts 1997 Single Highland "Toffee Glaze" bott 13 **(95) n23.5** surging tannin. But is met with no shortage of red liquorice and, tellingly, light ulmo honey; **t24** a majestic delivery where the soft oils and molten golden sugars and spices counter the confident oak to a tee; the ulmo honey continues its impressive repair job; **f23.5** mocha towards the finish but the estery finale is almost more in keeping with a fine pot still rum; **b24** another gorgeous little essay from this most expressive of distilleries. *46%. sc. 258 bottles.*

⟐ **Whiskybroker Clynelish 17 Years** hogshead, cask no. 12380, dist 29 Oct 97 **(88.5) n22.5** a salty edge to the banana sandwich nose; young grassy malt, too...; **t22.5** salivating and unusually simple. The malt is intense and sharp; **f21.5** bitters slightly, but that salivation factor barely drops; **b22** not the usual honeyfest. But makes purposeful malt statements. *54.5%. sc.*

The Whisky Cask Clynelish bourbon cask, dist 1997, bott 2014 **(88.5) n23** earthy and oaky, the malt is working at full stretch to keep out the tannins. A soft honey undercurrent helps; **t22.5** for a few seconds on delivery we are treated to a malty brilliance: the unidentifiable honey, grist and oak are in perfect harmony; dries out rapidly; **f21.5** warming spices and hovering oak; **b21.5** creamy for a Clynelish with no shortage of oaky aggression. *52.5%.*

⟐ **Whisky-Fässle Clynelish 16 Year Old** sherry cask, dist 1996, bott 2013 **(95.5) n24** gooseberries, elderflower and toffee-apple vie with the orange blossom honey for top billing...and there is no clear victor...other than the lucky sod nosing this; **t24.5** typical Clynelish melt-in-the mouth texture. Also typically, the intense yet clean barley is soon visible. But it is soon adorned with myriad complex fruit and honey notes, each of them delicate and sensual; **f23** spices begin to make a mark, the honey gets into manuka weighty mode and the fruit a little towards burnt raisin. Sadly, just a little 'you know what' turns up very late in the day; **b24** an outstandingly beautiful butt, so to speak. And so close to being sulphur free. *53.3%. nc ncf.*

⟐ **Whisky-Fässle Clynelish 19 Year Old** hogshead, dist 1995, bott 2014 **(92.5) n23** orange blossom honey with a squeeze of lime; **t23.5** silky delivery with a sharp coppery edge. The honey takes a little longer to linger, though ulmo makes its way through eventually; **f23** the finale is surprisingly oily – with a curious mouth feel almost identical to its sister distillery Caol Ila...; **b23** a few extra oils to go with the honey. *52.7%. nc ncf.*

COLEBURN
Speyside, 1897–1985. Diageo. Closed.

⟐ **Glen Fahrn Airline Nr 01 Coleburn 1983 Aged 26 Years** cask no. 1465 **(88) n22 t22.5 f21.5 b22.** Always a bit of a shock when one of these comes along. Been about five years since I last tasted it in bottle form. This is very similar. Above average for the old house style, absolutely dripping with citrusy gristy sugars. *47.5%. sc. 179 bottles.*

The Whisky Agency Coleburn 26 Year Old dist 1983, bott 2009 **(88.5) n22 t23 f21.5 b22.** Coleburn is a rare whisky. A thoroughly enjoyable Coleburn is rarer still. So here's one you've just got to go and track down... *49.5%. The Whisky Agency, Germany.*

CONVALMORE
Speyside, 1894–1985. William Grant & Sons. Closed.

⟐ **Gordon & MacPhail Rare Old Convalmore 1975 (94) n23** first nose suggests OTT tannin. But a few sniffs and we begin to detect the outline of the barley. More oak, now via mild green mint tea. Graceful and confident; **t24** oh, how that took me back: a fabulous rush of barley (as in the old days) with a light honey sub-plot (also, as in the old days). The oak is attentive but not quite smothering, which allows the ulmo honey to slowly show its influence; chopped roast hazelnut adds a little further sweetness; that green tea still hops around; **f23** delightfully soft and beautifully poised: the light waves of mocha are a delicious inevitability...; **b24** the rarest of the rare. And in tasting, the flavour map took me back 30 years, to when I used to buy bottles of this from Gordon and MacPhail as a 10-year-old... probably distilled around 1975. The unique personality and DNA is identical on the palate as it was then; except now, of course, there is far more oak to contend with. Like finding an old lover 30 years further on: a little greyer, not quite in the same lithe shape as three decades earlier...but instantly recognisable and still very beautiful... *46%*

CRAGGANMORE
Speyside, 1870. Diageo. Working.

Cragganmore Aged 12 Years db **(81.5) n20 t21 f20 b20.5.** I have a dozen bottles of Cragganmore in my personal cellar dating from the early 90s when the distillery was first bottled as a Classic Malt. Their astonishing dexterity and charm, their naked celebration of all things Speyside, casts a sad shadow over this drinkable but drab and instantly forgettable expression. *40%*

Cragganmore Aged 14 Years The Distillers Edition finished in port casks, dist 1993, bott 2007 db **(85) n22 t21 f21 b21.** The tightly closed fruit on the palate doesn't quite match the more expansive and complex nose. *40%*

Cragganmore Distillers Edition double matured, dist 00, bott 13 db **(82.5) n21 t21.5 f20 b20.** Matured in toffee, one presumes. Hard to imagine a flatter, less inspiring malt from a great distillery if you tried. *40% WB15/313*

⬧ **Alexander Murray & Co Cragganmore 1994 19 Years Old (88.5) n22.5** attractive old fruitcake, perhaps with a little marmalade adding an understated sharpness; **t23** silky moist fruitcake with Demerara sugars; quite a creamy texture; **f21** dulls slightly and a slight degree of furry buzz; **b22** an unusual take on this great distillery. *40%*

Cadenhead's Authentic Collection Cragganmore-Glenlivet Cask Strength Aged 13 Years bourbon hogshead, dist 1999, bott Oct 13 **(85) n21 t23 f20 b21.** Tangy and intense, here's a fine example of excellent malt battling against sub-standard oak and almost winning the battle. Reveals a citrusy side. And the spices also helps paper over the cracks. Built for blending. *54.5%. 276 bottles. WB15/092*

Cadenhead's Wine Cask Cragganmore-Glenlivet Aged 21 Years Chateau Lafitte cask, dist 93, bott Jul 14 **(74) n17 t20 f18 b19.** I have had many bottles of Chateau Lafitte in my life of all kinds of vintages. In my cellar are many more. But I have never had one that shows the sulphur on this. Presumably a sulphur stick at work... *56.1%. 198 bottles. WB15/253*

Old Malt Cask Cragganmore Aged 16 Years refill hogshead, cask no. 9931, dist Mar 97, bott Aug 13 **(89) n23** lemon curd tart; **t22.5** another tyoe of tart: thi time eye-watering and salivatingly grassy; **f21.5** custard cram biscuits (as opposed to the lemon puffs on the nose); **b22** doesn't really try when it comes to complexity. Just does the simple things well. *50%.*

Old Malt Cask Cragganmore Aged 24 Years refill hogshead, cask no. 10375, dist Nov 89, bott Mar 14 **(87.5) n22.5 t23 f20.5 b21.5.** Those still around who remember the bracing sea-salty old Bunnas of three decades back will give this one a curious, sideway look. Inland Speysiders don't come more coastal and salty than this in style...so not sure where it has been matured. The oak has left little space for much else to breath. An early-morning malt to wake you up, much like a sea-front wave direct into the kisser. *50%. sc. 169 bottles.*

CRAIGELLACHIE
Speyside, 1891. John Dewar & Sons. Working.

⬧ **Craigellachie 13 Year Old** db **(88) n21.5** an old-fashioned nose, common among Speysiders 20 years back: a seasoned maltiness busied by a mixture of ex-bourbon casks of mixed age and fortune; **t23** astonishing volley of varied sugars. The gristy ones go first, settled by a layer of ulmo honey; **f21.5** the weaknesses of the barrels begin to show. But an impressive array of peppery spices offer a keen diversion; **b22** not technically the best. But those honey and spice tones are irresistible. *46% WB16/033*

⬧ **Craigellachie 17 Year Old** db **(84.5) n20 t23 f20 b21.5.** A slightly dirty, earthy nose is matched on the tangy finish. But there is no doubting the deliciousness of the silky delivery which is as chewy and fruity as a bar of toffee raisin fudge. *46% WB16/034*

⬧ **Craigellachie 23 Year Old** db **(91.5) n23.5** easy enough to say honey on toast: accurate, too. But it is the variation of honeys which impresses, along with the salt and pepper seasoning; **t23** ulmo honey, inevitably, leads the way. But it doesn't get far before a surge of ultra intense malt washes over it – remarkable considering its age. The oak, through vanilla, isn't far behind; **f22** a little bitter, perhaps from the worm tub sulphur trace. But still spicy and biscuity; **b23.5** expected a little house smoke on this (the malt made here in the early 1990s always had delicate phenol), but didn't show. The honey is nothing like so shy. *46% WB16/035*

⬧ **Hepburn's Choice Craigellachie Aged 9 Years** sherry butt, dist 2004, bott 2014 **(72.5) n17.5 t18 f19 b18.** Never finds balance nor synchronisation. Hefty, but at a point in its development where the distillate and oak are barely on the same page. The intriguing puff of smoke at the death is pure Craigellachie, though. *46%. nc ncf bottles. 786 bottles.*

Master of Malt Single Cask Craigellachie 8 Year Old refill sherry cask, dist Oct 06, bott Apr 15 **(84.5) n21 t21.5 f21 b21.** Thick and sticky malt. Like Batch 1, doesn't really possess the will to get beyond the big nut flavours. *64.1%. sc. 83 bottles.*

Old Malt Cask Craigellachie Aged 18 Years sherry butt, cask no. 10589, dist Nov 95, Jun 14 **(85) n21 t22.5 f20 b21.5.** A silky, rather quagmire-ish moist fruitcake number. After the dates and walnut on delivery, and the rather cloying treacle follow through, the finale shows a slight furry quality. *50%. nc ncf sc. 730 bottles.*

⬧ **Old Particular Speyside Craigellachie 22 Years Old** refill barrel, cask no. 10422, dist Feb 92, bott Aug 14 **(83) n22 t22 f19 b20.** Oak and age has filtered out the least appetising elements of what was obviously an originally aggressive, probably thuggish malt. Still ignites and fizzes on the plate, but masses of malt have combined with decent vanillas from an excellent cask such a spirit barely deserves. *51.5%. nc ncf sc. 181 bottles.*

◈ **Provenance Craigellachie Over 8 Years** sherry butt, cask no. 10552, dist Spring 06, bott Autumn 14 **(77) n19 t19 f20 b19**. Just doesn't get away with it at this age in a third fill cask. Thin and lacking in personality. 46%. nc ncf sc.

Signatory Vintage Single Malt Craigellachie 1999 Aged 14 Years, bourbon barrels, cask no. 148+149, dist 30 Aug 99, bott 26 Nov 13 **(88) n22.5** over-ripe, seasoned gooseberries; **t22.5** beautifully refreshing malt, though it is the mouth feel which steels the show; **f21** dries lopsidedly with some bitterness from the oak; **b22** a decent malt mostly in fine shape. 43%. nc. 614 bottles. WB15/018

Single Cask Collection 10 Year Old Craigellachie Rum Cask Finish bourbon barrel, finished in a rum cask, cask no. 162, dist 26 Jun 03, bott 08 Jul 13 **(87.5) n22 t22 f21 b21.5**. A pleasant, inoffensive whisky right enough. But a danger of finishing in rum is that a cask is left open to being sealed in a crisp sugary wrapping, which is what has happened here. Limited development results, especially on the finish. 54.4%. sc. 267 bottles.

The Single Malts of Scotland Craigellachie 16 Years Old hogshead, cask no. 7286, dist 14 Nov 96, bott 11 Nov 13 **(90.5) n22.5** a moment of smoke heralds a slightly salty maltiness; **t23.5** not sure if the light smoke on delivery is my imagination triggered by my nose. But excellent weight, not least from the treacle pudding; **f22** salty fudge; mint chocolate lolly; **b22.5** even before I looked to see what I was tasting next, that curious, quite unique puff of near invisible smoke told me this was a Craigellachie. A jolly, expansive dram from a usually neat and tidy distillery. 52.7%. 312 bottles. WB15/308

◈ **That Boutique-y Whisky Company Craigellachie** batch 1 **(85.5) n21 t22 f21 b21.5**. Pleasant enough. But on the nutty side and sharp. Good citrus side to the barley, though. 49.2%. 148 bottles.

◈ **That Boutique-y Whisky Company Craigellachie** batch 2 **(88) n22** clean, vanilla-bleached malt; **t22** salivating with an intense barley depth; **f22** again the vanilla tries to make a contribution but the malt ties them up; **b22** operates on cruise control. 50.1%. 75 bottles.

◈ **Wemyss Malts 2002 Single Speyside Craigellachie "Dark Treacle Fondant"** butt, bott 2014 **(68) n14 t21 f15.5 b17.5**. No idea how this made it past the sulphur police. Must have conned them with that delicious moment of fresh sweet grape on arrival. 46%. sc. 804 bottles.

DAILUAINE

Speyside, 1854. Diageo. Working.

Dailuaine 1997 The Manager's Choice db **(87.5) n21.5 t23 f21 b22**. One of the most enjoyable (unpeated!!) Dailuaines I've come across in an age. There is the usual distillery biff to this, but not without a honeyed safety net. Great fun. 58.6%

Dailuaine Aged 16 Years bott lot no. L4334 db **(79) n19 t21 f20 b19**. Syrupy, almost grotesquely heavy at times; the lighter notes of previous bottlings have been lost under an avalanche of sugary, over-ripe tomatoes. One for those who want a massive dram. 43%

◈ **Alexander Murray & Co Dailuaine 1997 16 Years Old (84.5) n20.5 t22 f21 b21**. A fudged issue. Literally. 40%

◈ **Cadenhead's Authentic Collection Dailuaine Aged 18 Years** dist 1997 **(73) n18 t19 f18 b18**. Dailuaine struggles in a half decent bourbon cask. In what appears to be a sulphur-treated wine cask, it has no chance at all... 54.4%

Càrn Mòr Strictly Limited Edition Dailuaine Aged 14 Years hogshead, dist 1999, bott 2013 **(90) n22.5** beautifully clean spirit with a real sparkle to the barley; the slightly tangy oak may prove problematic later; **t23.5** superb delivery: a gorgeous coconut in golden syrup thread breaking down into an umo honey and grist middle, helped along by clever, delicate spices; **f21.5** vanilla then bitters somewhat; **b22.5** this usually run of the still distillery offers little to get too excited about. But here is a rare exception. 46%. nc ncf. 653 bottles. WB15/158

Darkness! Dailuaine Aged 15 Years Pedro Ximenez Cask Finish **(73) n19 t19 f16 b18**. Dull-uaine more like. Not just flat and lifeless but even sports a suspect furriness on the finish. 53.9%. 96 bottles. WB15/220

◈ **Douglas Laing's Single Minded Dailuaine Aged 7 Years** sherry butt, dist Mar 07, bott Nov 14 **(78) n19 t20 f19.5 b19.5**. Malty, creamy, juicy and very young. Not exactly complex but would have made a good, unthreatening filler in the malt content of a light blend. 41.5%. sc.

◈ **Glen Fahrn Airline Nr 12 Dailuaine 1992 Aged 22 Years** bourbon barrel, cask no. 3126 **(88) n21.5 t23 f21.5 b22**. It's been some time since I last enjoyed a Dailuaine as much as I have this one. Though rough and ready on delivery, it explodes at every given opportunity with concentrated, gristy barley. Not technically brilliant, or the most complex, but offers enough richness to fully entertain. 53.1%. sc. 159 bottles.

Hepburn's Choice Dailuaine 2005 Aged 8 Years sherry butt **(83) n19 t22.5 f21.5 b20.** Designed to be shoved into a three year old blend, only the dazzling malt delivery, with its profound searchlit-starring barley, is up to true single malt billing. *46%. 393 bottles.*

Old Masters Dailuaine 13 Year Old dist 2001, bott 2014 **(88.5) n20** a touch of the sweaty armpits...; **t24** ...but makes up for it with a sensationally vibrant delivery of punchy barley. How explosively juicy was that!?! **f22.5** lovely chocolate mousse overcomes the more ambiguous oak notes; **b22** absolutely nothing simple or straightforward about this one. *61.3%.*

◈ **Old Particular Dailuaine 18 Years Old** refill hogshead, cask no. 10778, dist Apr 97, bott May 15 **(87) n21 t22.5 f21.5 b22.** A typically thin example of the distillery's output, with a very limited narrative. But the simple clarity of the juicy barley is something to be fully enjoyed. *48.4%. nc ncf sc. 240 bottles.*

Old Particular Speyside Dailuaine 16 Years Old bourbon barrel, cask no. 10207, dist Apr 1997, bott Jan 2014 **(88.5) n22 t23 f21 b22.** My glasses overfloweth with impressive Dailuaines. Not often that has happened over the last 25 years...*55.2%. nc ncf sc. 91 bottles.*

The Pearls of Scotland Dailuaine 1997 15 Year Old cask no. 15561, dist Dec 97, bott Nov 13 **(88) n21.5** rhubarb and custard with a major tannin injection; **t23.5** absolutely enormous and gob-smackingly beautiful delivery with just-so oils. The barley is on steroids and punches through the massive, well spiked and spicy oak; **f21** reverts to type with a thin, sugary underwhelming finale; **b22** a top dollar Dailuaine which sparkles quite dazzlingly early on. *55.9%. WB15/006*

◈ **Provenance Dailuaine Over 10 Years** sherry butt, cask no. 10551, dist Spring 04, bott Autumn 14 **(72) n18 t19 f17 b18.** Sweet and ungainly, there are good reasons why this has never been much marketed as a single malt. The odd fruit gum moment is not enough to redeem it. *46%. nc ncf sc.*

◈ **Provenance Dailuaine Over 12 Years** sherry casks, cask no. 10451, dist Autumn 01, bott Summer 14 **(86) n20.5 t21 f22.5 b22.** Attractively, clean, malty and rammed with Speyside juiciness. Silky and lightly spiced at the finish and abounding with youthfulness despite its age, this is almost the perfect late afternoon/early evening Friday dram to liven you up before the weekend begins. *46%. nc ncf sc.*

◈ **Romantic Rhine Collection Dailuaine Nieport** port cask finish, cask nos. 10167, 4236, dist 12 Aug 97 & 26 Mar 97, bott 20 Aug 12 **(89.5) n22.5 t23 f21 b23.** I thought this was Dailuaine as I'd never seen it before: then read the notes to see that this is Port finished. This is a distillery in need of a lift at the best of times, and here the Port casks have added not just an enriching sweet grape element, but spellbinding spices also. The finish gives the game away a bit, but excellent for the distillery. *55.4%*

Scotch Malt Whisky Society Cask 41.59 Aged 10 Years 1st fill barrel, dist 14 Jul 03 **(94.5) n23.5** gloriously uplifting barley with a major under-ripe Cox's apple freshness; **t24** stupendous delivery absolutely bursting with rich, salivating barley. There are some wonderful oak-induced spices (this has matured in an absolutely top-grade bourbon cask, by the way) with red liquorice delving into the rich esters; **f23** long with a wonderful "Nice" coconut biscuit signature...; **b24** always good to see a younger bottling from the SWMS. Especially when, as is the case here, it helps show a distillery in its very best light... A surprise dram which seems to be a liquid form of the sunny spring morning outside the sample room windows... *61.9%. 233 bottles.*

◈ **Scotch Malt Whisky Society Cask 41.61 Aged 33 Years** refill hogshead, dist 13 Dec 80 **(85.5) n21 t21 f22 b21.5.** Flinty and seemingly distilled from Speyside granite rather than malt. There is a degree of attractiveness to hard-faced barley which does eventually radiate a begrudging juiciness. *51.5%. sc. 130 bottles.*

DALLAS DHU
Speyside, 1899–1983. Closed. Now a museum.

Gordon & MacPhail Rare Vintage Dallas Dhu 1979 (94.5) n23 marginally earthy but probably only there for the fruit and nuts to grow in; green banana and toasted yam lead, pecan pie follows behind; **t23.5** how can barley melt in the mouth after 32 years? It defies logic and description. What makes it work so well, is that the base and baritone sugars from the oak never for a moment attempt to drown the tenor from the grist. Often that is the key to a whisky's success and here it is demonstrated perfectly: it means the complexity levels remain high at all times and the depth of oak controlled; **f23.5** long, with the vanilla enjoying a nutty depth, moving into a more deliciously praline oiliness. The tannins are firm enough to remind us that 1979 was a long time ago now but not a single hint of oaky degradation. Clear, confident, strident notes from first to last; **b24** I can hardly recall the last time a bottling from this distillery popped along – depressing to think I am old enough to remember when they were so relatively common when they were being sold on special offer! It was always a class act; it's closure an act of whisky vandalism, whether it be preserved as a museum or not. This, even after all these years, shows the extraordinary quality we are missing day in, day out. *43%*

DALMORE

Highands (Northern), 1839. Whyte and Mackay. Working.

The Dalmore 12 Years Old db **(90) n22** mixed dates: both dry and juicy; **t23** fat, rich delivery with a wonderful dovetailing of juicy barley and thick, rumbling fruit; **f22.5** lots of toffee on the finish, but gets away with it thanks to the sheer depth to the barley and the busy sherry sub-plot; **b22.5** has changed character of late yet remains underpowered and with a shade too much toffee. But such is the quality of the malt in its own right it can overcome any hurdles placed before it to ensure a real mouth-filling, rumbustious dram. *40%*

The Dalmore Dee Dram 12 Years Old db **(63.5) n15.5 t17 f14 b16.** Words fail me...*40%*

The Dalmore 15 Years Old db **(83.5) n21 t21 f20.5 b21.** Another pleasant Dalmore that coasts along the runway but simply fails to get off the ground. The odd off note here and there, but it's the blood orange which shines brightest. *40%*

The Dalmore 18 Years Old db **(76.5) n19 t21 f18 b18.5.** Heaps of caramel and the cask choice might have been better. *43%*

The Dalmore 21 Years Old db **(87) n22 t23 f20 b22.** Bottled elegance. *43%*

The Dalmore 25 db **(88) n23.5** hugely attractive with a sherry-trifle signature; **t22.5** a glossy delivery with the accent very much on fruit, plums in particular; an attractive degree of sharpness throughout; **f20** just a little dry with a tell-tale tang towards the end; **b22** the kind of neat and tidy, if imperfect, whisky which, were it in human form, would sport a carefully trimmed and possibly darkened little moustache, a pin-striped suit, matching tie and square and shiny black shoes. *42%. Whyte & Mackay Ltd.*

The Dalmore Forty Years Old db **(82) n23 t20 f19 b20.** Doubtless my dear friend Richard Paterson will question whether I have the ability to spot a good whisky if it ran me over in a ten ton truck. But I have to say here that we have a disappointing malt: I had left this too late on in writing this year's (2008) Bible as a treat. But it wasn't to be. A soft delivery: but of what? Hard to exactly pin down what's going on here as there is so much toffee and fruit that the oak and barley have been overwhelmed. Pleasant, perhaps, but it's all rather dull and passionless. Like going through the motions with an old lover. Adore the sherry-trifle/toffee mousse nose, though... *40%*

The Dalmore Astrum Aged 40 Years db **(89) n23.5 t21 f22 b22.5.** This guy is all about the nose. The oak is too big for the overall framework and the balance hangs by a thread. Yet somehow the overall effect is impressive. Another summer and you suspect the whole thing would have snapped... *42%*

The Dalmore Aurora Aged 45 Years db **(90.5) n25 t22 f21.5 b22.** Sophisticated for sure. But so huge is the oak on the palate, it cannot hope to match the freakish brilliance of the nose. *45%*

The Dalmore 50 Years Old db **(88) n21 t19 f25 b23.** Takes a while to warm up, but when it does becomes a genuinely classy and memorable dram befitting one of the world's great and undervalued distilleries. *52%*

The Dalmore Candela Aged 50 Years db **(96) n25 t24 f23.5 b23.5.** Just one of those whiskies which you come across only a handful of times in your life. All because a malt makes it to 50 does not mean it will automatically be great. This, however, is a masterpiece, the end of which seemingly has never been written. *50% (bottled at 45%).*

⬩ **The Dalmore Distillery Exclusive 2015** db **(85.5) n22.5 t22.5 f19.5 b21.** Dalmore, so often a thick and syrupy dram when house bottled, in thick and syrupy mode. The nose offers a sharp bite of greengage and fresh-out-of-the-oven fruitcake. But the lack of a malt perspective and, more fatally, the bitter finish, means excellence is a long way off. *48%. 450 bottles.*

The Dalmore Eos Aged 59 Years db **(95) n24.5** extraordinary pulsing of rich, dry sherry notes: nutty and polished oak in one of the finer Mayfair antique shops or clubs. The moistest, choicest Lubeck marzipan with a thread of Jaffa jam and, as the whisky settles into its stride, this moves to Jaffa cakes with heavy dark chocolate; very limited spice, but the salt levels grow..; **t24** ultra dry delivery despite the juices flowing from the very first moment: the grape is beautifully firm and holds together light oils and burgeoning oak which threaten to inject a weighty toastiness; the mid ground though is a triumph of glorious lightly molassed vanilla notes with strands of barley; spices buzz and fizz and add even further life; **f22.5** a light off-key bitterness knocks off a mark or two, but the cocoa and burnt raisin charge to the rescue; **b24** for those of you who thought this was a camera, let me put you in the picture. This is one well developed whisky, but by no means over exposed, as it would have every right to be after nearly 60 years. Indeed: it is one of those drams which utterly confounds and amazes. I specially chose this as the 1001st new whisky for the 2012 Bible, and those of us old enough to be young when most of its sister casks were hauled off for blending, there was an advert in the '60s which said: "1,001 cleans a big, big carpet...for less than half a crown." Well this 1001 cleans a big, big palate. But I can't see a bottle of this majestic malt going for as little as that... 44%

The Dalmore 62 Years Old db (95) n23 PM or REV marked demerara potstill rum, surely? Massive coffee presence, clean and enormous, stunning, topdrawer peat just to round things off; t25 this is brilliant: pure silk wrapping fabulous moist fruitcake soaked in finest oloroso sherry and then weighed with peat which somehow has defied nature and survived in cask all these years. I really cannot fault this: I sit here stunned and in awe; f24 perfect spices with flecks of ginger and lemon rind; b24 if I am just half as beautiful, elegant and fascinating as this by the time I reach 62, I'll be a happy man. Somehow I doubt it. A once-in-a-lifetime whisky – something that comes around every 62 years, in fact. Forget Dalmore Cigar Malt – even I might be tempted to start smoking just to get a full bottle of this. 40.5%

The Dalmore 1263 King Alexander III db (86) n22 t22.5 f20 b21.5. Starts brightly with all kinds of barley sugar, fruit and decent age and oak combinations, plus some excellent spice prickle. So far, so good...and obviously thoughtfully and complexly structured. But then vanishes without trace on finish. 40%

The Dalmore 1978 db (89.5) n23.5 t22 f21.5 b22.5. A seriously lovely old dram which is much weightier on the palate than nose. 47.1%. 477 bottles.

The Dalmore 1979 db (84) n21 t21.5 f20 b21.5. Hard to find a more rounded malt. Strangely earthy, though. 42%. 487 bottles.

The Dalmore 1980 db (81.5) n19 t21 f20.5 b21. Wonderful barley intensity on delivery does its best to overcome the so-so nose and finale. 40%

The Dalmore 1981 Amoroso Sherry Finesse amoroso sherry wood cask db (85.5) n21 t22 f21.5 b21. A very tight, fruity, dram which gives away its secrets with all the enthusiasm of an agent under torture. Enjoyable to a degree... but bloody hard work. 42%

The Dalmore Cabernet Sauvignon db (79) n22 t19 f19 b19. Too intense and soupy for its own good. 45%

The Dalmore Castle Leod db (77) n18.5 t21 f18.5 b19. Thumpingly big and soupy. More fruit than you can wave a wasp at. But, sadly, the sting comes with the slightly obvious off note. 46%

The Dalmore Ceti db (91.5) n24 a nose for fruitcake lovers everywhere: ripe cherries and blood orange abound and work most attractively with the slightly suety, muscovado enriched body...; t23.5 the nose demands a silky delivery and that's exactly what you get. Rich fruit notes form the principle flavour profile but the backing salivating barley and spice is spot on; the mid ground becomes a little saltier and more coastal...; f21.5 a vague bitterness to the rapidly thinning finale, almost a pithy element, which is slightly out of sync with the joys of before; b22.5 a Ceti which warbles rather well... 44.7%

The Dalmore Cigar Malt Reserve Limited Edition db (73.5) n19 t19.5 f17 b18. One assumes this off key sugarfest is for the cigar that explodes in your face... 44%

The Dalmore Cromartie dist 1996 db (78.5) n20 t22 f17.5 b19. Always hard to forecast what these type of bottlings may be like. Sadly there is a sulphur-induced bitterness and tightness to this guy which undermines the more attractive marmalade notes. 45%

The Dalmore Gran Reserva sherry wood and American white oak casks db (82.5) n22 t21.5 f19 b20. An improvement on the near nonentity this once was. But still the middle and finish are basic and lacking sophistication or substance outside a broad sweet of oaky chocolate toffee. Delightful mixture of blood orange and nuts on the approach, though. 40%

The Dalmore Valour db (85.5) n21 t22 f21 b21.5. Not often you get the words "Valour" and "fudge" in the same sentence. 40%. Whyte and Mackay. Travel Retail Exclusive.

The Dalmore Visitor Centre Exclusive db (95.5) n25 this isn't just about fruit: this is a lesson in a nosing glass in how the marriage and equilibrium between salt, sugars, barley and delicate fruit juices should be arranged. There is not an off note; no party dominates; the complexity is beguiling as the picture shifts and changes in the glass every few seconds. Also, how the weight of the whisky is essential to balance. It is, frankly, the perfect malt whisky nose... t24 so off we go on a journey around about fifteen fruit levels, half that number of sugar intensities and a fabulous salty counter. Close your eyes and be seduced...; f22.5 a minor blemish as a vaguely bitter note from the oak interjects. Luckily, the thick barley sugar is in there to repair the damage; remains salty to the very end; b24 not exactly the easiest distillery to find but a bottle of this is worth the journey alone. I have tasted some sumptuous Dalmores over the last 30-odd years. But this one stands among the very finest. 46%

Cadenhead's Single Cask Dalmore Aged 37 Years butt, dist 1976, bott 2014 (94) n24.5 nosed blind I would have sworn that was corn oil coming at me; certainly a bourbony stance in the way the oak has threaded tannin, kumquats, mocha and liquorice into the narrative; a little suet pudding and raisin, too, thinned slightly by a little fresh fruit salad: seriously wonderful; t24 busy with mocha and spice soon thrown into action, both genuinely getting a firm hold by the middle; still oily and the sugars help a little glazed ginger mix with the half-hearted fruit;

f22 huge degree of natural caramels make for a low key, slightly oily finish; b23.5 a heaven-sent nose sending you on all kinds of wild goose chases. And but for the mildly lazy finale, this might well have been a Bible a category ward winner. *46.2%. 150 bottles. WB15/106*

Cadenhead's Small Batch Dalmore Aged 24 Years bourbon barrels, dist 1989, bott 2013, (87.5) n23.5 t22 f21 b22. Starts beautifully both on nose and delivery but the bite and bitterness of the oak wins out towards the end. Some lovely sharp navel orange and custard delights. *46.6%. 312 bottles. WB15/068*

The Maltman Dalmore Aged 16 Years sherry finish, cask no. 3221, dist Oct 96, bott Apr 13 (87.5) n21.5 t23.5 f21.5 b21. The good news: despite a sherry finish, this is clean and 100% untroubled by sulphur. The bad news: from the slight sweaty armpit nose to the surprisingly fruit toffee finale, it is easy to see that, when bottled, the marrying process was in a state of slight imbalance. Even so, enjoy the spiced dates and the molasses – and all-round, unspoiled moist fruitcakiness: it does have some excellent moments. *46%. sc ncf nc. 298 bottles. WB15/218*

Montgomerie's Single Cask Collection Dalmore cask no. 3093, dist 19 Jun 1986, bott Sep 13 (87.5) n22 t23 f20.5 b22. A silky-soft offering, with superb citrus on the nose and a wonderfully salivating burst of juicy malt on delivery, backed by toasted fudge. Just a little too bitter at the death, though. *46%. nc ncf sc. WB15/129*

Old Particular Highland Dalmore 17 Years Old refill hogshead, cask no. 10206, dist Oct 1996, bott Jan 2014 (90) n22 lemon tart with a dash of custard; t23.5 kerpow...!!! Dalmore denuded at last. A spanking array of top drawer barley notes, all fresh and sparkling allowing full juiciness and depth to show. The barley steals the show, but the supporting cast of playful, custard cream vanilla are also worthy of a standing ovation; f22 gentle waves of light spices and citrus; b22.5 when one finally comes across a Dalmore matured in a decent cask and neither hindered, hidden nor bullied by the opaque fug of caramel, one could almost weep with joy...54.8%. nc ncf sc. 139 bottles. Douglas Laing & Co.

Single Cask Collection 1996 Dalmore 17 Year Old bourbon hogshead/sherry cask finish, dist 1996 (89.5) n22.5 from the suet pudding school of malt; t23 superb barley explosion on impact. Gentle gristy tones slowly bend into the vanilla; f22 much duller, but the oak has a gentle late message; b22 very little, if any, evidence of the sherry cask finish. And for that we can be truly thankful.... 53.5%. sc. *Single Cask Collection.*

Single Cask Collection 2000 Dalmore 13 Year Old Bourbon Hogshead/ HOMOK (Willi Opitz) finish, dist 2000 (90) n23 fizzes and zips with various, though mainly kumquat-style, citrus notes; some attractive salt-buttered toast, too; t23 deep and pungent delivery, again erring towards light citrus with maybe a touch of delicate, wild strawberry; f22 spices begin to mount as it dries; b22 never less than fresh and salivating. Almost like a chewy fruit pastel. *56.3%. sc.*

DALWHINNIE
Highlands (Central), 1898. Diageo. Working.

Dalwhinnie 15 Years Old db (95) n24 sublime stuff: a curious mixture of coke smoke and peat-reek wafts teasingly over the gently honied malt. A hint of melon offers some fruit but the caressing malt stars; t24 that rarest of combinations: at once silky and malt intense, yet at the same time peppery and tin-hat time for the tastebuds, but the silk wins out and a sheen of barley sugar coats everything, soft peat included; f23 some cocoa and coffee notes, yet the pervading slightly honied sweetness means that there is no bitterness that cannot be controlled; b24 a malt it is hard to decide whether to drink or bath in: I suggest you do both. One of the most complete mainland malts of them all. Know anyone who reckons they don't like whisky? Give them a glass of this – that's them cured. Oh, if only the average masterpiece could be this good. *43%*

Dalwhinnie 25 Years Old Special Release 2012 Rejuvenated American oak hogshead, dist 1987, bott 2012 db (92) n23.5 toasty with lashings of hickory and maple syrup. A little sappy but the busy saltiness lifts the barley; t23.5 a busy delivery of light sugars and spice; red liquorice and acacia honey combine beautifully. The spice rises as the oiliness increases; f22 thins as the impact of the oak lessens. Just the vaguest hint of smoke drifts in; b23 more from the mountains of Kentucky than central Scotland. Anyone with a bourbon bent and a sweet tooth will adore this. As will bee keepers. *52.1 %. nc ncf. Diageo.*

DEANSTON
Highlands (Perthshire), 1966. Burn Stewart Distillers. Working.

Deanston 6 Years Old db (83) n20 t21 f22 b20. Great news for those who remember how good Deanston was a decade or two ago: it's on its way back. A delightfully clean dram with its trademark honey character restored. A little beauty slightly undermined by caramel. *40%*

Deanston 12 Years Old db **(74)** n18 t19 f18.5 b18.5. It is quite bizarre how you can interchange this with Tobermory in style; or, rather, at least the faults are the same. *46%. ncf.*

Deanston Aged 12 Years db **(75)** n18 t21.5 f17.5 b18. The delivery is, for a brief moment, a malty/orangey delight. But the nose is painfully out of sync and finish is full of bitter, undesirable elements. A lot of work still required to get this up to a second grade malt, let alone a top flight one. *46.3%. ncf. Burn Stewart.*

Deanston Virgin Oak db **(90)** n22.5 does exactly what it says on the tin: absolutely brimming with virgin oak. To the cost of all other characteristics. And don't expect a bourbon style for a second: this is sharp-end tannins where the sugars have their own syrupy point of entry; t23 now those sugars dissolve with some major oak attached: many years back, I tasted a paste made from roasted acorns and brown sugar...not entirely dissimilar; f22.5 continues to rumble contentedly in the oakiest possible manner...but now with some fizzy spice; b22 quirky. Don't expect this to taste anything like Scotch... *46.3%*

Cadenhead's Small Batch Deanston Aged 19 Years butts, dist 1994, bott 2014 **(83)** n20.5 t21.5 f20 b21. A syrupy, unsubtle malt which paints on the sugar-coated barley with a spray gun. The odd fruit note, especially some diced, crunchy French apple. But counts for little when the jigsaw has been mis-printed. *56.4%. 846 bottles. WB15/067*

Marks & Spencer Deanston Aged 12 Years db **(84.5)** n20.5 t22 f21 b21. It's been a while since I found so much honeyed malt in a Deanston. Echoes of 20 years ago. *40%. UK.*

Old Malt Cask Deanston Aged 18 Years refill butt, cask no. 10428, dist Apr 96, bott Apr 14, **(73)** n19 t19 f17 b18. Tart and tangy, this was produced some of Deanston's grimmer production days. This, alas, seems to celebrate the fact. *50%. sc. 628 bottles.*

⟨⟩ **Old Particular Highland Deanston 20 Years Old** refill butt, cask no. 10426, dist Jun 94, bott Aug 14 **(78.5)** n20.5 t20 f19 b19. A good example of a malt distilled in haste. Hot, thin and, at times, has something of a grappa, pippy quality. *51.5%. nc ncf sc. 188 bottles.*

Robert Graham Deanstown 19 Year Old Highland Malt hogshead, cask no. 3139, dist 24 Jun 94, bott 13 Nov 13 **(92.5)** n23 vague strawberry thinly spread on toast while sugared shredded wheat buckles in the warm milk; t23.5 a touch of class to the delivery: just so oils really do crank up the massive malt; f22.5 residual muscovado sugars and maple syrup embattle the slight bitterness to the oak; b23.5 warms the heart to see a Deanston showing as well as this. It seems like a very long time ago... *46%. 201 bottles.*

Signatory Vintage Un-chillfiltered Collection Deanston 1997 Aged 16 Years refill sherry butt, cask no. 1347, dist 18 Jun 97, bott 05 Nov 13 **(89.5)** n21 a little weak on the oak front. But devoid of the dreaded S word and some half decent fruit gurgles contentedly; t24 now I didn't expect that! The fruit has combined rather beautifully with a light maple syrup muscovado mix and thrown in some Nice coconut biscuit for good measure. The spices rise with aplomb; f22 the spice carries on its good work as tasted mallows and fruit cake ends mingle with vanilla; b22.5 I'll be honest. I had marked this as an end-of-session potential dud, the last before a meal in order to restore my palate after twinning a less than auspicious distillery with a sherry butt: usually a sure-fire recipe for disaster. But it has twitted me. For both the butt and spirit are above average on both counts and make for enjoyable dramming. I do so love these little surprises! Breakfast is delayed... *46%. nc ncf sc. 786 bottles. WB15/022*

That Boutique-y Whisky Deanston batch 2 **(88)** n22 intense malt attractively balanced with chalky oak; t22.5 barley still dominates, even more so now, and bolstered by a surprising degree of oiliness; just after delivery, a brief burst of barley sugar offers the only sweetness on show; f22 oil-lengthened and keeps to the malty but oak-dusty path; b22 something of an oily soul, this. No faulting the crisp and sparkling barley which glistens most notable on delivery but could do with its old honey injection of three decades back – and now seemingly lost – which would have added so much more. *49.6%. 248 bottles. WB15/223*

⟨⟩ **Whiskyjace Deanston 15 Year Old** bourbon hogshead, dist 1997, bott 2013 **(83)** n21 t21.5 f20 b20.5. A hot, sugary dram. Malty, simple and thin but with a hint of citrus. *54.4%*

DUFFTOWN
Speyside, 1898. Diageo. Working.

Singleton of Dufftown 12 Years Old db **(71)** n18 t18 f17 b18. A roughhouse malt that's finesse-free. For those who like their tastebuds Dufft up a bit... *40%*

The Singleton of Dufftown "Sunray" db **(77)** n20 t20 f18 b19. One can assume only that the sun has gone in behind a big toffeed cloud. Apparently, according to the label, this is "intense". About as intense as a ham sandwich. Only not as enjoyable. *40%. WB15/121*

The Singleton of Dufftown "Tailfire" db **(79)** n20 t20 f19 b20. Tailspin, more like. *40%. WB15/122*

Cadenhead's Single Cask Dufftown-Glenlivet Aged 34 Years sherry butt, dist 1979, bott 2014 **(92.5)** n22.5 so, after three decades the weightiest spirit of Speyside emerges from a presumably still wet when filled sherry butt. It is a mess: a thick, undecipherable puddin' of a malt. Yet, you know what? With those juicy dates fighting against the grimy oils and the sugars being shovelled in to keep the bitterness out...I rather like it...; **t23** massive: filthy on the palate...but those sugars and plums...; **f24** and now a soup made mainly of molasses and spice....outrageous! **b23** since it arrived in my tasting lab yesterday, this bottle and I have been staring at each other like distrusting old foes wondering who was going to blink first. I remember being at the distillery about 30 years ago and tasting some three- and four- year old and saying "Christ!" to the warehouseman as I sampled the unbelievably oily, dirty whisky which had been placed into my nosing glass. It was then part of Bell's and it had been a long time since any money had been spent on the stills, which were being run into the ground... producing pretty poor distillate. The thing I have learned over the years, though, is that the worse the distillate when young, the better it can be after time has played all kinds of tricks on it. Just look at some of those ancient Fettercairns, for instance. So I give you at the end my preamble...and now I get to work... And, as I suspected, for its myriad faults, its coarseness and whisky depravity...I'd queue for a second glass. Must appeal to the whisky Neanderthal in me. Or maybe we all like a bit of rough now and then... *48%. 216 bottles. WB15/107*

Gordon & MacPhail Connoisseurs Choice Dufftown 2004 (82.5) n20 t21.5 f20 b21. Srypy thick sugars at first but a dullard by nature. *46%.*

Old Malt Cask Dufftown Aged 18 Years refill butt, cask no. 10378, dist Aug 95, bott Mar 14 **(83.5) n21 t21.5 f20 b21.** Bludgeons the taste buds into submission. Malty to the point of being almost opaque. *50%. sc. 589 bottles.*

⬧ **Scotch Malt Whisky Society Cask 91.20 Aged 37 Years** refill hogshead, dist 3 Jun 76 **(72.5) n19 t18 f18.5 b18.** A harsh malt which plays lip-service to the oak which is better than the all-round experience suggests. The initial spirit was so uncompromisingly tough and steely, though, there is little direction for this whisky to take – even at such great age. *46.9%. sc. 58 bottles.*

Signatory Cask Strength Collection Dufftown 1997 Aged 15 Years hogshead, cask no. 19488, dist 09 Dec 97, bott 30 Apr 13 **(83) n20.5 t21.5 f20 b21.** At times you actually feel you are spitting out splinters. Massive oak, but the usual sugary soup offers some kind of counter. *56.1%. nc sc. 309 bottles. WB15/142*

EDRADOUR
Highlands (Perthshire), 1837. Signatory Vintage. Working.

Edradour Aged 10 Years db **(79) n18 t20 f22 b19.** A dense, fat malt that tries offer something along the sherry front but succeeds mainly in producing a whisky cloyingly sweet and unfathomable. Some complexity to the finish compensates. *43%*

Edradour Ballechin The Discovery Series #3 Port Cask Matured Heavily Peated, First fill port casks db **(88) n21** a little bit of a smoky-fruit shambles; the peat, as phenolic as anything I've ever encountered, is actually aggressive; **t23** eye-watering delivery as the fruit appears to have a chiselled countenance. Mind you, it needs to: the smoke is borderline opaque; **f22** the taste buds are beaten into smoky submission...; **b22** for Peat Freaks and masochists only... *46%. nc ncf. 6,000 bottles. WB15/033*

Edradour Ballechin The Discovery Series #4 Oloroso Sherry Cask Matured Heavily Peated, First fill oloroso sherry butts db **(87) n22.5** simply huge smoke – a peat refinery on fire; **t23.5** you cannot but be taken aback by this entirely unique experience: the delivery begins smokily enough, then a wave of phenolic oils grab command; **f20** bitter and furry; **b21** one of the fattest malts of all time. Just trips with tarry oil... *46%. nc ncf. 6,000 bottles. WB15/034*

Edradour Ballechin The Discovery Series #5 Marsala Cask Matured Heavily Peated, First fill Marsala hogsheads db **(92) n23** usual big, soot-dry phenols – almost acidic. The fruit hardly gets a look in...; **t23.5** works superbly, with the sugars, phenols and grape sugars working in tandem; **f22.5** long with Demerara sugar working hard on the peat; moves into smoked Black Forest Gateaux mode – very Bavarian; **b23** challenging at first, not least because the oily spirit takes some navigating, but once you dip your shoulders under the peat, you are in...!!! Complex, well weighted and beautifully formulated. *46%. nc ncf. 6,000 bottles. WB15/035*

Edradour Ballechin The Discovery Series #6 Bourbon Cask Matured Heavily Peated, First fill bourbon barrels db **(90.5) n23** seriously dry: substantial peat presence given a pretty clear run other than a light floral sub note; **t23** big coppery charge to the smoke: the oils really carry weight and purpose – much more kippers than Arbroath Smokies; **f22** smoked cocoa butter; **b22.5** Edradour's tiny still give this ultra smoky malt a truly unique fingerprint. *46%. WB15/036*

Edradour Ballechin The Discovery Series #7 Bordeaux Cask Matured Heavily Peated First fill Bordeaux hogsheads db **(74) n20 t21 f16 b17.** A sweet, phenolic start...but goes horribly downhill from there... *46%. nc ncf. 6,000 bottles. WB15/037*

Edradour Ballechin The Discovery Series #8 Sauternes Cask Matured Heavily Peated, First fill sauternes hogsheads db **(82) n21 t22 f19 b20.** A bit like looking at the Mona Lisa through cracked glass. There is something so right with it, yet so very wrong. Massive peat enshrined in what might have been a truly stunning cask. But hardly for a moment do the two twains meet. *46%. nc ncf. 6,000 bottles. WB15/038*

Edradour Barolo Cask Matured Barolo hogsheads, dist March/April 06, bott Apr 14 db **(79.5) n19 t21.5 f19 b20.** Never entirely at ease with spirit or maturation level. The wide cut doesn't suit the indisciplined grape *46%. nc ncf. batch number: One, 2450 bottles. WB15/041*

Edradour Chardonnay Cask Matured chardonnay hogsheads, dist Dec 2003, bott Sep 2011 db db **(72) n18 t19 f17 b18.** Crushingly dry. Grim. *46%. nc ncf. batch number: One, 1600 bottles. WB15/043*

Edradour Dougie Maclean's Caledonia Selection Aged 12 Years db **(91) n23** about as thick as it gets: nose and fruit is soon dripping off your proboscis. A clean cask, but not sure the initial spirit was entirely spot on. Just can' get enough of those juicy, syrupy dates, though; **t23** genuine intensity now with the tannin matching the fruit blow for blow. Nothing sugars other than molasses could live with this company...and it doesn't; **f22** the lingering oils confirm a wide cut was made those dozen years back; **b23** gosh! Hold on to your hats. This is some ride.... *46%. nc ncf. WB15/044*

Edradour Port Cask Matured port hogsheads, dist June/July 2003, bott Mar 14 db **(91.5) n23** wonderful liveliness: the grape is fresh with trace sweetness embracing its more natural dry side; old sweet shops, of the jars of boiled candy variety; **t23.5** one of the lightest delivery I can remember in 30 years of tasting Edradour. Rarely have I seen the sugars so disentangled from the grain and grape; **f22** a little bitterness; slightly pithy as it dries; short; **b23** wonderful malt, make no mistake. Hardly any small still trace, allowing for a more expansive whisky. *46%. nc ncf. batch number: One, 2400 bottles. WB15/042*

Edradour Sauternes Cask Matured Sauternes hogsheads, dist Dec 03, bott Feb 13 db **(81) n19 t24 f18 b20.** For a few brief, glorious moments this malt soars to the heights obtained only by great Sauternes casks and looks imperiously down at everything else around. But to get there you have to go through a dodgy take off and an even bumpier landing... *46%. nc ncf. batch number: Three, 2150 bottles. WB15/039*

Edradour Straight From The Cask Aged 10 Years sherry butt, cask no. 530, dist 06 Dec 01, bott 21 Nov 12 db **(88.5) n22.5** nutty – a bit like a Harvey's Bristol Cream...only with the kick of a Scottish rather than Spanish mule. Intriguingly, the spice appears more oak – almost bourbon type – than fruit related; **t23** myriad sugars, and no shortage of intense grapey ones, hit early but it is the texture and overall mouth feel which wins the heart; vanillas creep in slowly; **f21** a little furry; **b22** some you know what. But otherwise sweet as a nut... *57.3%. sc. 984 bottles. WB15/051*

Edradour Straight From The Cask Barolo Cask Finish Aged 10 Years dist 28 May 02 in hogsheads, disgorged 28 Feb 11, finished in a Barolo hogshead, bott 15 Apr 13 db **(88) n22** between the grape and chunky original spirit, a nose dense enough to create its own gravitational pull... **t22.5** a series of thick, nondescript fruit notes clutter he taste buds; at last a juicy, spice-riddled, blast is detectable; **f22** some Columbian cocoa dulls any last chance of fruity sharpness; **b22** it packs a presence, that's for sure. *58.3%. 423 bottles. WB15/050*

Edradour Straight From The Cask Burgundy Cask Finish Aged 11 Years dist 08 May 02 in hogsheads, disgorged 24 Mar 11, finished in a Burgundy hogshead, bott 09 Dec 13 db **(89.5) n23.5** for those who like a little fruit in their spice...; **t22** hits you like a fruity custard tart in the face. The heftiness of the original spirit is never far from the surface...but those spices...! **f22.5** raisins dipped in cocoa; **b21.5** lurches around the palate like Ron Burgundy on a bender. Great fun, though. *58.6%. 429 bottles. WB15/048*

Edradour Straight From The Cask Chardonnay Cask Finish Aged 12 Years dist 30 Jun 00 in hogsheads, disgorged 22 Nov 08, finished in a Chardonnay hogshead, bott 11 Apr 13 db **(82.5) n20 t22 f20 b20.5.** Massive grape statement and no shortage of cocoa on the furry finish. But not my type of whisky, I'm afraid, and leaves me cold. *56.3%. 451 bottles. WB15/045*

Edradour Straight From The Cask Chateauneuf Du Pape Cask Finish Aged 11 Years dist 28 May 13 in hogsheads, disgorged 28 Feb 11, finished in a Chateauneuf Du Pape hogshead, bott 28 Nov 13 db **(94) n24** a dense nose, a bit like a bag of soft-centred fruit bon bons where one has broken allowing the sticky stuff inside to escape; some delicate salt and pepper raises the game further; **t24** hang on: these are fruit bon bons! A really jammy edge to this, some strawberry and greengage dives into the mix; **f22** forcefully dries as the spices rise and the vanilla gathers; a hint of cocoa and hickory challenges the dying fruit; **b24** had no idea Chateauneuf Du Papa 2002 was this good a vintage.... *57.6%. 440 bottles. WB15/049*

Edradour Straight From The Cask Marsala Cask Finish Aged 11 Years dist 28 May 02 in hogsheads, disgorged 28 Feb 11, finished in a Marsala hogshead, bott 04 Oct 13 db **(93.5) n23.5** deep, dry fruit. Seasoned grapes and crushed grape seeds; **t24** enormously salivating delivery, tinged with juicy malt as well as the more obvious grape; maple syrup brushes the edges before those more austere grape notes return; **f22.5** remains juicy but doesn't quite live up to the delivery thanks to a late uncompromising bitterness; **b23.5** good to see another sulphur-free wine cask. At its very height, quite stupendous. *58.6%. 603 bottles. WB15/047*

Edradour Straight From The Cask Port Wood Finish Aged 13 Years dist 23 Jan 2001 in hogsheads, disgorged 10 Dec 2010, finished in a port pipe, bott 20 Feb 2014 db **(95) n24** hard to imagine the grape being any more intense, yet opens out slowly. Like an unfurling petal, to reveal not just scalding peppers but soft ribbons of orange-caressed marzipan and Melton Hunt Cake at its most moist; **t24** a posse of sugars round up the heavier fruit notes and keep them quiet, allowing the spices and even barley to infiltrate the juicier elements. Slowly the oils and cocoa arrive...; **f23** undone slightly by the fatness of the spirit, the grape battles on manfully; **b24** one of the greatest Port Finishes for a very long time. *56.3%. 1010 bottles. WB15/046*

Edradour Super Tuscan Cask Matured Super Tuscan hogsheads, dist March/April 06, bott Apr 14 db **(81) n20.5 t23 f18 b19.5**. Not sure what a non-Super cask would have been like. Imbalanced from nose to finish, at least it boasts a rousing chocolate fruit and nut middle. *46%. nc ncf. Batch number: One, 2450 bottles. WB15/040*

Edradour Vintage 2006 oloroso sherry matured, cask no. 240, dist 1 Jun 06, bott 3 Sep 13 db **(91.5) n24** errrr...oloroso...and about as grapey and cherry fruitcakey as it gets...; no shortage of plum jam and spice, too; **t23** sharp, quivering effect on the palate as a mix of fruit and molasses get to work in earnest; **f21.5** just a little over bitter and toasty: things not quite tickety-boo; **b23** a big malt still dripping with the fresh contents of the handsome sherry butt. *59.2%. sc nc. Cask hand picked by The Whisky Exchange. WB15/282*

⬩ **Anam na h-Alba The Soul of Scotland Edradour 2000** bourbon & oloroso sherry casks, dist May 00, bott Aug 14 **(83.5) n21 t22 f20 b20.5**. Pretty clean sherry by today's standards and viscous in body. But lacking balancing sugars: something of a dullard. *46%. 310 bottles.*

Signatory Vintage Un-chillfiltered Collection Edradour 2002 Aged 10 Years cask no. 464, dist 13 Dec 02, bott 17 Jul 13 **(88.5) n22** moist fruitcake. No shortage of orange peel and dates have been pitched in; **t23** sensuous arrival with a big toasted fudge and raisin back up. Spices are bitty and warming; the dates hinted on the nose arrive in mid stream; **f21** thins quickly; late minor furriness; **b22.5** a much better than average butt for its day. A real small still intensity throughout. *46%. nc ncf sc. 774 bottles. WB15/021*

FETTERCAIRN

Highland (Eastern), 1824. Whyte and Mackay. Working.

Fettercairn 12 Year Old db **(66) n14 t19 f16 b17**. If the nose doesn't get you, what follows probably will...Grim doesn't quite cover it. 40%

Fettercairn 30 Years Old db **(73) n19 t18 f18 b18**. A bitter disappointment. Literally. 46.3%

Fettercairn 40 Years Old db **(92) n23** technically, not exactly how you want a 40-y-o to be: a bit like your old silver-haired granny knitting in her rocking chair...and sporting tattoos. But I also have to say there is no shortage of charm, too...and like some old tattooed granny, you know it is full of personality and has a tale to tell... **t24** I was expecting dates and walnuts... and I have not been let down. A veritable date and walnut pie you can chew on until your jaw is numb; the sharp raisiny notes, too, plus a metallic sheen which reminds you of its provenance...; **f22** those burned raisins get just a little more burned...; **b23** yes, everyone knows my views on this distillery. But I'll have to call this spade a wonderfully big, old shovel you can't help loving...just like the memory of me tattooed ol' granny... 40%. 463 bottles.

Fettercairn 1824 db **(69) n17 t19 f16 b17**. By Fettercairn standards, not a bad offering. Relatively free from its inherent sulphury and rubbery qualities, this displays a sweet nutty character not altogther unattractive – though caramel plays a calming role here. Need my arm twisting for a second glass, though. 40%

⬩ **Anam na h-Alba The Soul of Scotland Fettercairn 1995** bourbon cask, dist Jan 95, bott Feb 15 **(86.5) n21 t23 f21 b21.5**. Not normally a malt which impresses. But here you can only enjoy – and, to a degree, admire – the crisp juiciness of the barley sugar as well as the normal nuttiness. Have to say it: an enjoyable Fettercairn. *58.3%. 250 bottles.*

Gordon & MacPhail Connoisseurs Choice Fettercairn dist 1997, bott 2013 **(83) n21 t21.5 f19.5 b21**. Nutty, milky sweet (a little cloyingly at times, surprise, surprise...) and malty. A bit hot and a little oak bitterness at the death, as well as its usual house tang. That apart, perfectly drinkable. *46%. nc ncf. WB15/143*

Hepburn's Choice Fettercairn 2005 Aged 8 Years refill hogshead, bott 2014 **(79) n19 t21.5 f19 b19.5.** Goodness gracious... I have just been flung back nearly 30 years and I have returned to a Glasgow hotel room, my evening sanctuary while being seconded to Scotland for a national newspaper. I had invested in a bottle of Fettercairn of perhaps this very age in order to try and understand a cloying whisky argument I little agreed with...and here it seems to be again, like a ghost from the past, determined to haunt me and have the last, nagging word. I'll give it credit for its nutty, lopsided consistency over the passing three decades. Thing is: I was no fan of it then. I am still perhaps even less so today. 46%. nc ncf sc. 377 bottles.

Hepburn's Choice Fettercairn Aged 11 Years refill hogshead, dist 2002, bott 2014 **(79) n19 t20 f20 b20.** Nutty, malty and more rubber than a school pencil case. 46%. nc ncf sc. 384 bottles.

Master of Malt Single Cask Fettercairn 17 Years Old hogshead, dist 30 Oct 95, bott Jul 13 **(85) n22 t23 f19 b21.** By no means the Fettercairn horror show one always fears, despite the trademark rubbery qualities to the tail. The nose and delivery certainly come up trumps with an, at times, malty elegance which is able to make full use of the light molasses on offer. The oak also pitches in with a very acceptable, countering dryness. The finale, though, gives the game away... 579%. sc. 294 bottles. WB15/212

◇ **Master of Malt Single Cask Fettercairn 19 Year Old** sherry hogshead, dist 25 Oct 95, bott 25 Mar 15 **(86.5) n22 t22 f21 b21.5.** Plenty of nuttiness to the malt, but a thread of golden syrup on delivery to compensate. 60.1%. sc. 133 bottles.

Old Malt Cask Fettercairn Aged 18 Years refill hogshead, cask no. 10314, dist Nov 95, bott Feb 14 **(86) n21 t21.5 f22 b21.5.** Acceptably pleasant. The intense, cloying barley and sugar has been granted a spicy butterscotch and custard pardon by some very decent oak. 50%. sc. 268 bottles.

◇ **Provenance Fettercairn Over 8 Years** refill hogshead, cask no. 10571, dist Autumn 06, bott Autumn 14 **(66.5) n17 t18.5 f15 b16.** Weird. Just transported back 35 years or so when, in a hotel room, I tasted my first ever bottle of Fettercairn. It was an 8-y-o and offered the same gluey, nutty awfulness. At least it is consistent... 46%. nc ncf sc.

Provenance Fettercairn Over 10 Years one refill hogshead, cask no. 9653, dist Autumn 2000, bott Spring 2013 **(76) n20 t20 f17.5 b18.5.** Not unpleasant. But nutty, thin and varnish-like particularly towards the finish. For most distilleries, hardly one to write home about. For Fettercairn, a triumph. 46%. nc ncf sc. Douglas Laing & Co.

Provenance Fettercairn Over 10 Years refill hogshead, cask no. 10329, dist Winter 04, bott Spring 14 **(72) n17 t19 f18 b18.** As I feared: strip all the oak out of a Fettercairn and you can see it in all its naked, rubbery, cloying ugliness. 46%. nc ncf sc.

◇ **Provenance Fettercairn Over 11 Years** one refill barrel, cask no. 10416, dist Spring 03, bott Summer 14 **(67.5) n18 t18 f15 b16.5.** Thin, hot, nutty nonsense. Malty, too, but reminds me quite scarily of Littlemill in the final, grim days of its existence. 46%. nc ncf sc.

Signatory Cask Strength Collection Fettercairn 1995 Aged 18 Years bourbon barrel, cask no. 419, dist 22 Mar 95, bott 24 Oct 13 **(74.5) n21.5 t18.5 f17.5 b18.** The nose offers false hope (a false nose...?) as a genuinely attractive degree of relatively uncluttered barley comes across. But those hopes are dashed the moment the palate is struck and we are thrown back into familiar rubbery, over cloyingly sweet, sticky-bitter territory. Can't blame the bottlers: they tell it as it is. 58%. nc sc. 208 bottles. WB15/139

◇ **That Boutique-y Whisky Company Fettercairn** batch 1 **(79) n18 t22 f19 b20.** Nil points for quality and panache. But certainly something undeniably attractive about the malt-sugar mix on delivery with its usual nutty background. The finish is a bit fierce, but not too bad for this distillery. 50.5%. 170 bottles.

◇ **That Boutique-y Whisky Company Fettercairn** batch 2 **(85) n21 t22 f21 b21.** Malty, buttery and unusually coherent and attractive for a Fettercairn 52.4%. 58 bottles.

◇ **Whiskyjace Fettercairn 18 Year Old** bourbon hogshead, dist 1995, bott 2014 **(79.5) n21 t20 f19 b19.5.** Nowhere near as heavy and nutty as usual, and the malt swims along attractively until it hits some very bitter rocks towards the end. 56.9%

GLEN ALBYN
Highlands (Northern) 1846–1983. Diageo. Demolished.

Gordon & MacPhail Rare Vintage Glen Albyn 1976 (96) n22.5 salty and nippy. And the theme thunders into an early Kentuckian drawl, with red liquorice and hickory prominent; **t24.5** I am shaking my head in disbelief. Not through disappointment, but wonder! How can something of this antiquity still fill your mouth with so much juice? The barley still offers a degree of grassiness, though this is camouflaged by the softest bourbon characters I have seen in a long time. The honeycomb is in molten form, as is the vanilla which appears to carry with it a fabulous blend of avocado pear and ulmo honey; **f24.5** a pathetic degree of oaky bitterness tries to interrupt, but it is swept aside by the residual and very complex sugars. There remains some spicy activity and even some Kentuckian red liquorice and hickory, but that South American honey really does the business **b24.5** wow! My eyes nearly popped out of my head when I spotted this in my sample room. Glen Albyns come round as rarely as Scotsman winning Wimbledon. Well, almost. When I used to buy this (from Gordon and MacPhail in their early Connoisseur's Choice range, as it happens) when the distillery was still alive (just) I always found it an interesting if occasionally aggressive dram. This masterpiece, though, is something else entirely. And the delivery really does take us to places where only the truly great whiskies go... 43%

GLENALLACHIE
Speyside, 1968. Chivas Brothers. Working.

Glenallachie 15 Years Old Distillery Edition db **(81)** n20 t21 f19 b19. Real battle between nature and nurture: an exceptional sherry butt has silk gloves and honied marzipan, while a hot-tempered bruiser lurks beneath. 58%

Hepburn's Choice Glenallachie 2005 Aged 9 Years sherry butt **(71)** n17 t18 f18 b18. An ample, hideously off-key indicator as to why you'll find this distillery on no true blender's top dressing list. 46%. 299 bottles.

◈ **Hepburn's Choice Glenallachie Aged 9 Years** sherry butt, dist 2005, bott 2014 **(64)** n15 t17 f16 b16. Take one of the least impressive spirits distilled in Scotland and put it into a very poor cask....and the result is predictable. 46%. nc ncf sc. 431 bottles.

◈ **Master of Malt Single Cask Glenallachie 6 Year Old** refill sherry cask, dist Dec 08, bott Apr 15 **(77)** n19 t20 f19 b19. A hot, characterless malt that would be the cure for insomnia if it didn't burn your mouth out.. 64.3%. sc. 92 bottles.

◈ **Old Particular Speyside Glenallachie 15 Years Old** sherry butt, cask no. 10707, dist Mar 99, bott Mar 15 **(79)** n19 t20 f20 b20. Sweet, malty, clean, thin and one-dimensional. And very fresh and youthful for its age, too. 48.4%. nc ncf sc. 312 bottles.

◈ **Provenance Glenallachie Over 9 Years** sherry casks, cask no. 10404, dist Spring 05, bott Summer 14 **(73.5)** n18 t18 f19 b18.5. Malty, though astringent. Lacking any discernible charm or complexity. 46%. nc ncf sc.

◈ **Riegger's Selection Cask Strength Glenallachie 2004** cask no. 768, bott 28 May 15 **(80.5)** n21 t21 f19 b19.5. Never finds a happy place. Starts with a degree of malty control but slip-slides through its range as a fruity edge destabilises its fragile balance. 55.4%

◈ **That Boutique-y Whisky Company Glenallachie** batch 1 **(80.5)** n19 t21.5 f20 b20. Thin, austere and with a malt fixation. Yet there is enough clean malty charm to actually ensure a fleeting enjoyable moment or two. 51.7%. 219 bottles.

◈ **Villa Konthor Glenallachie 9 Years Old** refill sherry cask, dist 2005, bott 2015 **(73)** n18 t20 f17 b18. This is not a distillery which readily takes prisoners – even before it is filled into a sulphured butt. And when it is in this sugar-sharp, aggressive, slightly "dirty" state, I admit I am not sorry... 46%

◈ **World of Orchids Glenallachie 2004 9 Year Old** bourbon cask, cask no. 3004 **(89)** n22 t23 f22 b22. I really am bemused: the label says from bourbon barrel. But this is a malt swimming in lush fresh, spicy fruit – and entirely sulphur free, it should be added. And, furthermore, for a Glenallachie it is enjoyable. Not something that happens very often. If ever. Answers on a postcard, please... 59.3%. sc. 264 bottles.

GLENBURGIE
Speyside, 1810. Chivas Brothers. Working.

Glenburgie Aged 15 Years bott code L00/129 db **(84)** n22 t23 f19 b20. Doing so well until the spectacularly flat, bitter finish. Orangey citrus and liquorice had abounded. 46%

◈ **Master of Malt Single Cask Glenburgie 19 Year Old** refill sherry cask, dist 7 Jun 95, bott 7 Apr 15 **(93.5)** n23 good oils holding both the barley and red liquorice; a charming floral sub plot.; **t24** this distillery knows how to deliver, and it does here: an engulfing wave of thick, molasses and malt – heavier on the malt, though – ensures maximum salivation properties; a wonderful spice and citrus double bill really ups the intensity; **f23** several nods to the high quality oak which offers citrus-tinged vanilla and butterscotch; **b23.5** an irrepressible and irresistible high grade malt. 55.8%. sc. 151 bottles.

Old Malt Cask Glenburgie Aged 16 Years sherry butt, cask no. 10222, dist Jun 97, bott Dec 13 **(68)** n16 t18 f16 b18. You know that neighbour whose cat keeps crapping on your lawn? I think I've just found his Christmas present for you... Just awful oak. What more can you say? 50%. nc ncf sc. 449 Bottles.

❖ **Old Malt Cask Glenburgie 25 Years Old** refill hogshead, cask no. 11218, dist Jun 98, bott Feb 15 **(86.5) n21 t22.5 f21 b22**. A competent, malty spirit in a less competent cask. That said, some exotic fruit manages to do the rounds. *46.9%. nc ncf sc. 223 bottles.*

Old Particular Speyside Glenburgie Aged 18 Years refill hogshead, cask no. 10277, dist Jun 95, bott Mar 14 **(86.5) n21.5 t23 f21 b21.** An oily, intense beastie at its best shortly after delivery when the malt is piled on thick and with syrupy intent. Elsewhere, though, fails to develop as it might. *48.4%. nc ncf sc. 318 bottles.*

❖ **Old Particular Speyside Glenburgie 25 Years Old** refill hogshead, cask no. 10590, dist Jun 89, bott Dec 14 **(94) n24.5** one of the great noses from this distillery: a near perfect embrace of mint and tangerine coupling with a very comfortable malt-oak double bill. Genteel and elegant; **t23** much livelier on the palate and surprisingly oily, too. The spices take off like a domestic firework, not quite reaching the heights you hope, but the starburst is lovely nonetheless; **f22.5** back to mint, with some chocolate for company; **b23** high quality bottling of a high quality malt; you can see why it plays such a key role in complex and delicate whiskies like Ballantine's at this age... *49.3%. nc ncf sc. 242 bottles.*

The Pearls of Scotland Glenburgie 1995 17 Year Old cask no. 6281, dist Dec 95, bott Nov 13 **(92) n22** a few apples in the straw; **t23.5** how can a whisky show such intensity, yet hardly stretches itself? The delivery is a little juicy but the coconut-biscuit oakiness comes all the way from Nice; the sugars settle early, as do some pounding spices; **f23** really lovely oils stay on the biscuit theme, but now a style from Brazil...; **b23.5** nonchalantly superb. *54.1%*

❖ **Provenance Glenburgie Over 7 Years** refill hogshead, cask no. 10574, dist Autmun 07, bott Autumn 14 **(85.5) n21.5 t21.5 f21 b21.5.** Another couple of years and this would have been a memorable dram. The clarity of the barley is as seen through a prism, as it breaks up into its constituent parts, the sugars especially. Just a little too young in character for greatness, though. *46%. nc ncf sc.*

Signatory Cask Strength Collection Glenburgie 1983 Aged 29 Years hogshead, cask no. 9820, dist 23 Oct 83, bott 10 Jul 13 **(96.5) n24** gorgeously estery with all kinds of honeyed apple notes drifting about the glass with chunkier spiced muscovado, It is as if ulmo and manuka honey has been mixed and then set solid...; **t24.5** give yourself about twenty minutes for this one to pan out on the palate: the first half dozen notes almost defy description as nothing appears to want to take the lead; the mouth feel is luxurious to the point of eroticism, the weight of the sugars are just about perfect with a hypnotic alternation between toasty liquorice and lighter acacia honey; the mid ground is a see-sawing of sugars (and even a degree of grist!) and oak, with a slow introduction of spice; **f24** a little tangy at first, but this is checked as a spiced ulmo honey note hoves into view and the oiles congregate to block out anything negative; a little pineapple juice and few other semi wxotic fruit notes announce that great age is on display here...; **b24** seriously asks the question: why has Glenburgie, like Clynelish, never been made into a mainstream malt. Here is a classic example as to why as it is the first commercial bottling of its matured spirit I have seen in a while which properly reflects the quality of the blending samples I see in my lab. If you see one of these guys, don't leave the shop without it... *53.4%. nc sc. 197 bottles. WB15/141*

Signatory Vintage Single Malt Glenallachie 1996 Aged 16 Years hogsheads, cask no. 5235+5244, dist 17 Oct 96, bott 22 Feb 13 **(89) n22** polished barley; **t23** barley sugar with a real twinkle; **f22** gisty even towards the finish; good late butterscotch; **b22** Glenallachie this ship shape is a collectors' item. As clean as it gets. *43%. nc. 827 bottles. WB15/009*

Signatory Vintage Single Malt Glenburgie 1995 Aged 17 Years hogsheads, cask no. 6452+6453, dist 13 Jun 95, bott 05 Mar 13 **(87.5) n22 t22 f21 b21.5.** A little extra oil diminishes the more telling aspects of the barley. The nose may suggest some kind of peppery celery, but the delivery never moves far from simple malt. Good spices but needs to escape the vanilla skirt tails. *43%. nc. 882 bottles. WB15/008*

The Single Malts of Scotland Glenallachie 21 Years Old bourbon barrel, cask no. 588, dist 20 Feb 92, bott 13 Sep 13 **(91.5) n22.5** a touch of exotic fruit mixing with more prosaic diced pear; **t23.5** big kick to the delivery (as in the tradition of the distillery) but fascinating blend of heather and ulmo honey; red liquorice and a hint of hickory: well balanced and complex; **f22.5** an outstanding malt finale despite the oaky attention; **b23** good example of a malt that's a bit rubbish when young showing what's for in old age. *47.9%. 235 bottles. WB15/342*

That Boutique-y Whisky Glenburgie batch 1 **(90.5) n22** green barley; fresh with apple and barley water; **t24** fabulously salivating delivery where the malt is juicy and pitch-perfect. The sugars are refined – in both senses of the word –and play second fiddle to the ultra-intense malt; **f22** a slow movement towards oak-induced butterscotch tart – with the emphasis on the tart...; **b22.5** always a bit of a lucky dip with bottled versions of this distillery: very rarely match the consistency experienced in the blending lab. This one shows all its malty cards. 49%. 183 bottles. WB15/222

GLENCADAM
Highlands (Eastern), 1825. Angus Dundee. Working.

Glencadam Aged 10 Years db (95) n24 crystal clarity to the sharp, ultra fresh barley. Clean, uncluttered by excessive oak, the apparent lightness is deceptive; the intensity of the malt carries its own impressive weight and the citrus note compliments rather than thins. Enticing; t24 immediately zingy and eye-wateringly salivating with a fabulous layering of sweet barley. Equally delicate oak chimes in to ensure a lightly spiced balance and a degree of attitude; f23 longer than the early barley freshness would have you expecting, with soft oils ensuring an extended, tapering, malty edge to the gentle, clean oak; b24 sophisticated, sensual, salivating and seemingly serene, this malt is all about juicy barley and balance. Just bristles with character and about as puckeringly elegant as single malt gets...and even thirst-quenching. My God: the guy who put this one together must be a genius, or something... 46%

Glencadam Aged 12 Years Portwood Finish db (89.5) n22.5 t22.5 f22 b22.5. After coming across a few disappointing Port finishes in recent weeks, just wonderful to experience one as you would hope and expect it to be. 46%

Glencadam Aged 14 Years Oloroso Sherry Cask Finish bott May 10 db (95) n24 t23.5 f24 b23.5. What a total treat. Restores one's faith in Oloroso whilst offering more than a glimpse of the most charming infusion of fruit imaginable. 46%

Glencadam Aged 15 Years db (90.5) n22.5 soft kumquats mingle with the even softer barley. A trace of drier mint and chalk dust points towards the shy oak. Harmonious and dovetails beautifully; t23 sharp, juicy barley - almost fruity - fuses with sharper oak. The mouth-watering house style appears to fatten out as gentle oils emerge and then give way for a spicy middle; f22 long, with those teasing, playful spices pepping up the continued barley theme. Dries as a 15 year old ought to but the usual bitterness is kept in check by the prevailing malt; b23 the spices keep the taste buds on full alert but the richness and depth of the barley defies the years. Another exhibition of Glencadam's understated elegance. Some more genius malt creation... 46%

◈ **Glencadam Aged 17 Years Triple Cask Portwood Finish** db (93.5) n23 that is one beguiling and sexy nose: so many layers of fruit and of varying intensity; the background is choc-a-bloc (almost literally) with vanilla and natural caramels in the shape of chocolate fudge; t24.5 is it the mouth feel which blows you away most? Or the way the lush, fruitcake notes take on an extra dimension – especially when the intense dark chocolate begins to form? One of the flavour profiles of the year...; f22 some dry, bitter powdery notes emphasise the wine casks, but the fruit-chocolate-alcohol mix really does underline the innate greatness and profound beauty of this whisky; b24 a 17-year-old whisky truffle. A superb late night or after dinner dram, where even the shadowy sulphur cannot spoil its genius. 46%. nc ncf. 1128 bottles.

Glencadam Aged 21 Years "The Exceptional" bott 2011 db (94) n23.5 t24 f23 b23.5. This distillery is emerging out of the shadows from its bad old Allied days as one of the great Scottish single malt distilleries. So good is some of their whisky, this "exceptional" bottling is almost becoming the norm. 46%. nc ncf.

Glencadam 30 Years Old Single Cask 1982 Limited Edition cask no. 730, dist 10 Jun 82, bott Oct 12 db (96) n25 t24 f23 b24. A rare bottling from a country at war. This was distilled in the very final days of the Falklands War when the conflict was at its most ferocious. Anyone finding a bottle of this can raise a glass to honour the memory to the gallant who are no longer with us. On both sides. 46%. nc ncf sc.

Abbey Whisky Glencadam Aged 22 Years Limited Edition Release dist 1991, bott 2014 (92) n22.5 a pretty old but unspoiled cask at work allows the barley maximum freedom at least cost to its freshness. A little toasted yam is on offer to represent age, but the grassy gristiness remains intact; t24 absolutely sublime delivery with the barley offering a sharpness which is as eye-watering as it is vivid; the spices which follow are the perfect counter point; the maple syrup appears to crystallise; f22 a little glassy with a big sheen to the mouth feel; a little bitterness creeps in, but there is enough barley sugar about to do the job; b23.5 in the right conditions this is one of the most salivating malts in the world. This sparkling little gem is a wonderful exponent. Fresh-faced and adorable. 55.3%.

Berry's Own Selection Glencadam 1991 Aged 22 Years cask no. 4765, bott 2014 (95) n23 delicate barley with a hint of gooseberry; a distant hint of Trebor mints; t24 gorgeously refreshing, outrageously sharp yet still a gooseberry theme, though the barley and, later, chocolate limes offer complexity; f23.5 the oak has spoken and speaks as dry as dust; b24.5 oh, if only Brechin City could play football as well as its next door neighbour, Glencadam, makes whisky....Champions League: bring it on...! 53.3%. ncf ncf. WB15/249

Gordon & MacPhail Connoisseurs Choice Glencadam dist 1991, bott 2013 **(88) n21.5** just a little over reliant on vanilla and natural caramel; **t23** much more life on delivery: a mix of citrus and crisp sugars sets the tone; soft but with excellent spice; **f21.5** the spices overcome the Allied bitterness; **b22** the limitations of the oak prevent you from see Glencadam at full throttle. Some lovely moments, though. *46%. nc ncf. WB15/150*

⬦ **Gordon & MacPhail Connoisseurs Choice Glencadam 1993 (96) n24** the nose with nearly everything – except spice: stewed gooseberries, freshly cut rhubarb, malt grist, vanilla and custard, molten sugar on porridge...and, if you look carefully, even topped off with anthracite dust for a bit of weight...; **t24.5** one of the best malt deliveries of the year: both weight and texture are borderline perfect and the fresh salivating properties of the cleanest possible barley defies belief. The ulmo honey is there, but acacia honey is in pole position; just love the way some phenols drift but never settle; **f23.5** medium length. No bitterness, no surge of over oakiness; a late delivery of distant phenol - that anthracite again – and with it comes some ultra belated and very delicate spice; **b24** one of the most dependable malts on the circuit: rare to come across a dud these days. This one is fabulous even by Glencadam's exceptionally high standards. World class whisky. *46%*

Hepburn's Choice Glencadam 2004 Aged 10 Years refill hogshead, dist 2004, bott 2014 **(87.5) n21.5 t22 f22 b22.** As one dimensional whiskies go, this is up there with the best of them: in being both delicious...and one dimensional. Actually, I suppose the big spice kick late on is a second dimension. Otherwise, it's the house style juicy barley at its new-make juiciest as the oak from this third fill cask barely registers at all. *46%. nc ncf sc. 177 bottles.*

Old Malt Cask Aged 18 Years refill hogshead, cask no. 4581, dist Nov 95, bott Feb 14 **(90) n22.5** apples and pears....with the accent on the pears; **t23** gets the sugars in early and, better still, makes them of a gristy type. Which means that the ever-growing oak is comfortably contained and the complexity increases...; the barley is juicy despite the years and the spices busiest early on; **f22** some very clever oils ensure a dessert feel to the finale, which includes some sugary diced coconut; **b22.5** creamy, complex and luxurious. Both well made and matured. *50%. sc. 162 bottles.*

⬦ **Provenance Glencadam Over 10 Years** refill hogshead, cask no. 10596, dist spring 04, bott autumn 14 **(92) n23** a lovely interplay between pears and papaya. The malt is dabbed with acacia honey; **t23** worth getting for the first ten seconds on the palate alone: crystalline, juicy barley still touched with honey and now honeydew melon, too; **f22.5** a little spicy moment or two before the oaky fade; **b23.5** Glencadam is one of the little-known Highland gems and there is enough elegant nuances in the script for this to cordially entertain and quietly charm you before your evening meal. *46%. nc ncf sc.*

GLENCRAIG
Speyside, 1958. Chivas Brothers. Silent.

⬦ **Cadenhead's Single Malt Glencraig 31 Years Old (92) n22.5** light – hints of green apple and even a few feints getting into the act, which is odd, as you'd expect the whole to be a lot weightier. A unique nose from a one-off distillery...; **t23.5** much heavier now, confirming the minor flaws detected on the nose. But still a beautifully delicate fruitiness working beautifully with the intense, biscuity malt; the sugars and light honeys bide their time before arriving – and make themselves count when they do; **f23** still a few feints to be had. But so delightful are the sugary, gristy tones – and the developing lemon and butterscotch – you really don't mind. Indeed, you welcome them, as they provide the oils which ensure a finish much longer than you might ever have believed; **b23** well done Cadenhead in coming up with one of the last surviving Glencraig casks on the planet. The feintiness shows why it was eventually done away with. But this is a malt with great distinction, too. *50.8%*

GLENDRONACH
Highlands, 1826. The BenRiach Distillery Co. Working.

⬦ **GlenDronach 8 Year Old The Hielan** db **(82) n20 t22 f20 b20.** Intense malt. But doesn't quite feel as happy with the oil on show as it might. *46%*

The GlenDronach Aged 8 Years "Octarine" db **(86.5) n23.5 t23 f19 b21.** Juicy yet bitter: a bipolar malt offering two contrasting characters in one glass. *46%. nc ncf.*

⬦ **The Glendronach 2003 11 Year Old** pedro ximinez sherry puncheon, cask no. 3568, dist Jan 03, bott Nov 14 db **(94.5) n23** no notes to guide me, alas... looks like a PX butt at work here: the sugars, like the grape are crisp and tight, locking in both the vanilla and barley; **t24** yep, def PX!! Those sugars...only a vivid spice can punch its way though. The midground offers up chocolate and toffee...for about five minutes...then raisin fudge; **f24** total confirmation of PX...only now do we get the real picture, as the tightness loosens and the fruit begins to have some kind of a say. A little maple syrup and butterscotch tries to equal the spices; **b23.5** helped by a superb, entirely sulphur free butt, this malt is as clean as it rich as it is memorable as it is excellent. *53.3%. 625 bottles. The Whisky Shop exclusive.*

The GlenDronach 12 Years Old db **(92) n22** some pretty juicy grape in there; **t24** silky delivery with the grape teaming with the barley to produce the sharpest delivery and follow through you can imagine: exceptionally good weight with just enough oils to make full use of the delicate sweetness and the build towards spices and cocoa in the middle ground is a wonderful tease; **f22.5** dries and heads into bitter marmalade country; **b23.5** an astonishingly beautiful malt despite the fact that a rogue sherry butt has come in under the radar. But for that, this would have been a mega scorer: potentially an award-winner. Fault or no fault, seriously worth discovering this bottling of this too long undiscovered great distillery *43%*

The GlenDronach Aged 12 Years "Original" db **(86.5) n21 t22 f22 b21.5**. One of the more bizarre moments of the year: thought I'd got this one mixed up with a German malt whisky I had tasted earlier in the day. There is a light drying tobacco feel to this and the exact same corresponding delivery on the palate. That German version is distilled in a different type of still; this is made in probably the most classic stillhouse on mainland Scotland. Good, enjoyable whisky. But I see a long debate with distillery owner Billy Walker on the near horizon, though it was in Allied's hands when this was produced. *43%*

The GlenDronach Aged 12 Years db **(83) n20 t22.5 f20.5 b20**. Glendronach at 12 is a whisky which has long intrigued me...for the last three decades, in fact. Always felt Allied had problems dealing with it, though when it was right it was sumptuous. Here it is a distance from being right: odd tobacco notes creeping into the fray, though that rings a bell with this distillery as I'm sure the old "Original" showed a similar trait. A very decent malty middle but elsewhere it flounders somewhat. *43%. nc ncf.*

The GlenDronach Original Aged 12 Years Double Matured db **(88) n23 t21 f22 b22**. Vastly improved from the sulphur-tainted bottling of last year. In fact, their most enjoyable standard distillery bottling I've had for many years. But forget about the whisky: the blurb on the back is among the most interesting you are likely to find anywhere. And I quote: "Founder James Allardice called the original Glendronach, 'The Guid Glendronach'. But there's no need to imitate his marketing methods. The first converts to his malt were the 'ladies of the night' in Edinburgh's Canongate!" Fascinating. And as a professional whisky taster I am left wondering: did they swallow or spit... *40%*

◇ **GlenDronach 12 Year Old Sauternes** db **(93.5) n23** the fruit, with an edgy, rounded sharpness – if that makes sense – is in tip-top condition. The malty background remains profound; **t24** the delivery of your dreams: a near perfect marriage between light grape and chunkier barley...with a wonderful vanilla-oak border to both: the result is salivating...; **f23** long, still deep with the fruit – marmalade – taking a bigger part in the play, despite the malty curtain coming down; **b23.5** despite the magnificently delicate fruit, it is the malt which wins on points. Superb! *46%*

The GlenDronach 14 Years Old Sauternes Finish db **(78.5) n18 t22 f19 b19.5**. That unique Sauternes three dimensional spiced fruit is there sure enough...and some awesome oils. But, with so much out of key bitterness around, not quite I had hoped for. *46%. nc ncf.*

The GlenDronach 14 Years Old Virgin Oak db **(87) n22.5 t22 f21 b21.5**. Charming, pretty, but perhaps lacking in passion... *46%. nc ncf.*

The GlenDronach 15 Years Old db **(77.5) n19 t18.5 f20 b20**. The really frustrating thing is, you can hear those amazingly brilliant sherry butts screaming to be heard in their purest voice. Those alone, and you could, like the 12-y-o, have a score cruising over the 95 mark. I can't wait for the next bottling. *46%*

The GlenDronach 15 Years Old db **(83) n20 t22 f20 b21**. Chocolate fudge and grape juice to start then tails off towards a slightly bitter, dry finish. *40%*

The GlenDronach 15 Years Old Moscatel Finish db **(84) n19 t22.5 f21.5 b21**. Such is the intensity of the grape, its force of life, it makes a truly remarkable recovery from such a limited start. But it is hard to be yourself when shackled... *46%. nc ncf.*

The GlenDronach 15 Years Old Tawny Port Finish db **(84.5) n21 t22 f20.5 b21.5**. Quite a tight fit for the most part. But when it does relax, especially a few beats after delivery, the clean fruit fairly drips onto the palate. *46%. nc ncf.*

The GlenDronach Aged 15 Years "Revival" db **(88.5) n22 t23 f21.5 b22**. Unambiguously Scottish... A fantastically malty dram. *46%*

The GlenDronach 18 Years Old db **(96.5) n24** groaning under the weight of sublime, faultless sherry and peppers; **t24** puckering enormity as the saltiness thumps home. Black forest Gateaux complete with cherries and blended with sherry trifle. The spices have to be tasted to be believed. The sugars range from Demerara to light molasses; **f24** again the sugars are in perfect position to ramp up the sweetness, but the grape, vanilla and spices are the perfect foil; **b24.5** the ultimate sherry cask whisky. Faultless and truly astounding! *46%. nc ncf.*

The GlenDronach Aged 18 Years "Allardice" db **(83.5) n19 t22 f21 b21.5.** Huge fruit. But a long-running bitter edge to the toffee and raisin sits awkwardly on the palate. *46%*

The GlenDronach Batch 10 1995 18 Years Old Pedro Ximenez sherry puncheon, cask no. 3025, dist 25 Oct 95 db **(88.5) n22.5 t22 f22 b22.** Yippee for the sulphur-free sherry butt. But PX whisky can labour a point somewhat... *51.1%. sc.*

The GlenDronach Batch 10 1996 18 Years Old Pedro Ximenez sherry puncheon, cask no. 1487, dist 16 Feb 96 db **(94) n23** oddly enough, this displays both youth and unusual old age in equal measures: definitely a strand of eucalyptus amid the vibrant, juicy grape; **t23.5** having been worn down by the deathly plod of dryness marching from one end of a PX whisky to the other, rather taken aback by the vitality of the grape, the confidence of the sugars – some surprisingly gristy – and the complexity of the layering of the fruit...; **f23.5** dries, but well within its own structure and with oak-induced spice and mocha really taking up important position; **b24** I hold my hand up and admit I am surprised by the excellence of this whisky. An exercise in layering and elegance. For once the sugars are soft enough to allow the whisky to breathe. *54.1%. sc.*

The GlenDronach Batch 10 1994 19 Years Old Pedro Ximenez sherry puncheon, cask no. 326, dist 16 Dec 94 db **(92.5) n21** typically tight and non-expansive...the PX calling card on the nose. As you have guessed, I am not a fan, though it is the nature of the beast...; **t23.5** among the most sharp, salivating deliveries you'll find this year; for once there appears to a be malty element to this and maybe it is this which really makes the complexity levels almost jump off the scale. The mid ground is a touch nutty with good vanilla and clean, even interplay between malt and fruit; spices buzz contentedly; **f24** a light spiced throbbing does no harm. Genuine sophistication here with a dry peachy tone slightly lightening the hefty grape mood while the sugars dovetail between light grist and thinned muscovado; **b24** if only the nose could be a little less unforgiving and expansive we'd have a stunning all rounder of a sherry butt. Again, absolutely sulphur-free. *53.5%. sc.*

The GlenDronach Batch 10 1994 19 Years Old Pedro Ximenez sherry puncheon, cask no. 3397 dist 23 Sep 1994 db **(89.5) n21** astonishingly estery and a bit of the dunder pit about this...; **t23** a kind of thicker version of cask 326, but with a less relaxed attitude towards the sugars; **f23** dry: almost hickory infused grape; **b22.5** more than a single element of this had me whizzing back to Jamaica. A degree of high ester rum here and there. But one wnders: how can such a sweet wine create such a dry whisky? *53.8%. sc.*

The GlenDronach 21 Years Old db **(91.5) n23.5** thumping sherry of the old fruitcake school; a serious number of toasty notes including hickory of a bourbon style; **t23.5** no less lush delivery than the nose portends; the follow up layerings of burnt raisin and cremated fudge are pretty entertaining; **f22** like burnt toast, a touch of bitterness at the death; **b22.5** a quite unique slant on a 21-year-old malt: some aspects appear very much older, but some elements of the grape occasionally reveal a welcome youth. Memorable stuff. *48%. nc ncf.*

The GlenDronach Batch 10 1993 21 Years Old Oloroso sherry butt, cask no. 494, dist 19 Feb 93 db **(96.5) n23.5** a nose I used to enjoy in the warehouses of Macallan back in the early '90s. The grape is intense and clear, soft and pulling its finger towards itself, indicating that you must follow...how can you not....? **t24.5** this is where you come close to swooning: the butt is, indeed, faultless. No sulphur ambush here: instead just a complex and, frankly, mind-blowing procession of fruit notes of varying intensity and sweetness, seekigly topped with spiced butterscotch; **f24** the chewiness continues...the spice continues...the grape still offers both depth and juice...and a little vanilla remds you of its age...; **b24.5** yet another faultless sherry butt from Glendronach with not an atom of sulphur. I must be dreaming, or, miraculously, I have found myself back amongst the great sherried whiskies of 25 years ago... Now, compare this to the 1992 cask 199 Glendronach and you will see how far Scotch whisky has descended in a single generation. And why I am at war with the SWA and the apologist self-styled "whisky writers" and publishers and know-nothing, worthless, egocentric bloggers who cover up this shocking decline. *55.8%. sc.*

The GlenDronach Batch 10 1992 22 Years Old Oloroso sherry butt, cask no. 199, dist 29 May 92 db **(68.5) n17.5 t19 f15 b17.** A sherry butt of its time, alas... *59.4%. sc.*

The GlenDronach Batch 10 1991 22 Years Old PedroXimenez sherry puncheon, cask no. 1346, dist 02/11/1991 db **(91.5) n22** held in a molassed sugar and dry, pip-infested grape concentrate embrace, the malt is nowhere to be seen...; **t23** much softer delivery with an intense under-ripe greengage tartness blending in well with the more expansive molasses; grape juice begins to spill freely while the sugars lighten in tone; **f23.5** as the grape wears off a Danish marzipan in dark chocolate mask is worn; **b23** a delicious clean sherry butt with no sulphury hanky-panky whatsoever. *52.1%. sc.*

The GlenDronach Batch 10 1990 24 Years Old PX sherry puncheon, cask no. 2970, dist 13/06/90 db **(94) n23** low key. A kind of toffee and raisin thing going on; also, a bag of those liquorice allsorts with the coffee-coloured sugar bits; the vaguest hint of something smoky, too; **t23.5** the oak strikes first and pretty hard. Enough grape and spice is around to cushion the blow. There is also a controlled explosion of sugars, plus – surprisingly - a little ulmo and heather honey. Vanilla dominates the middle; even a tad earthy; **f23.5** slightly angled and skew, not least because of the unexpected earthiness. The usual tight sugars are refusing to straighten the picture but the praline-lined caramel wafer works wonders; **b24** faultless sherry butt and a whisky which never quite works out the direction it is headed. Which kind of equals complexity. And makes for a very enjoyable experience....and a top rate malt. *51.3%. sc.*

◈ **GlenDronach Cask Strength** Batch 4 db **(92.5) n23** the odd liquorice note; sweet chestnut and spice; **t24** a fizzer! The malt comes at you on delivery in its thickest, most intense form; huge but controlled oak, too...more bourbon notes of liquorice and hickory. The molasses are inevitable as is the spice; the natural toffee-fudge softness is a surprise; **f22** vanilla – and more toffee; **b23** After the absorbing delivery, the complexity levels go down a bit. But still a belter! *54.7%*

The GlenDronach Grandeur Aged 31 Years db **(94.5) n23.5** dry, mildly peppery vanilla; crushed golden raisin counter-plot; **t24** spice-dusted grapes explode on the palate on entry; the mouth-feel plays a key role as the early lushness carries the fruit only so far before it begins to break up, allowing a fabulous spicy complexity to develop; **f23.5** beautiful intertwangling between those golden raisins and coffee. The spices are never far away...; **b23.5** just one hell of an alpha sherry butt. *45.8%*

The GlenDronach Aged 33 Years oloroso db **(95) n24 t24 f23 b24.** Want to know what sherry should really nose like: invest in a bottle of this. This is a vivid malt boasting spellbinding clarity and charm. A golden nugget of a dram, which would have been better still at 46%. *40%*

The GlenDronach Batch 10 2002 12 Years Old Pedro Ximenez sherry puncheon, cask no. 1500, dist 11 Jun 02 db **(94.5) n23.5** another clean butt and a less than dogmatic insistence on tight, humourless sugar-crushed lines. Instead there is enticing plum jam, the vaguest hint of malt and a spreading of molten muscovado sugar; the roast horse (not sweet) chestnut is an interesting complexity; **t24** yea gods! A sweat PX Glendronach!!! And beautifully so: with fingers of lightly molassed muscovado caressing in all directions, the spices massaging teasingly and the oak proferring red liquorice; the fruit takes a back seat, but you are aware in the rear view mirror; **f23** dries but now towards dark liquorice and Black Jacks; **b24** confirmation, were it required that PX usually feels far more at home alongside younger malt that the old stuff. Quite brilliant. *56.7%. sc.*

The GlenDronach Cask Strength batch 2 Oloroso & Pedro Ximenez sherry casks db **(94) n23 t24.5 f23 b23.5.** For those who like their sherried malts to take not a single prisoner. Immense, magnificent and quite unique in flavour profile. *55.2%. nc ncf.*

GlenDronach Cask Strength Batch 3 db **(90) n21.5** very tight and not exactly finding the balance it sought. Dry for all the obvious fruitiness, with a distinctly crushed pip edge...in some ways closer to a Cognac style than whisky; improves and opens a little after about 20 minutes airing; **t23** again, tight on delivery. When it does relax, it does so slowly allowing only a gradual release of juice and welcome sugars. The spices do pulse attractively throughout and man mark the sugars; **f22.5** so dry. Again back to a pithy countenance with the brief flirtation with Nicaraguan coffee. The sugars have been soundly defeated; **b23** after last year's Batch 2, I had laid a knife and fork out in my lab for this and tucked a napkin into my shirt. However, this proved just a little more aloof, austere and sophisticated. *54.9%.*

GlenDronach Grandeur 24 Year Old Batch 5 db **(93.5) n23** a busybody nose: fussing around the oak one moment, some traces of toasted malt the next....; **t24** a lush delivery, as soft as you like. Thick, almost syrupy malt and then a constant pulse of spice which warms by the moment; **f23** spiced butterscotch tart; and rather tart towards the finale, too...; **b23.5** one to stand your spoon up in. Enormous whisky. *48.9%.*

The GlenDronach Single Cask 1971 Aged 42 Years batch 8, Pedro Ximenez sherry puncheon, cask no. 1246, dist 15 Feb 71, bott May 13 db **(92.5) n22** spiced toffee apple; creosote drying next door; **t23.5** the oak doesn't wipe its feet before entering. But the wall of robust fudgy sugar and treacle is up to absorbing any excess. Busy and chewy; **f23.5** much more settled and last some distance. A light build up of spice turns this even more into a fruity boiled cough sweet; **b23.5** the PX cask leaves so little room for the malt to get a word in. The spices, though, make this when it could so easily have just tipped over the oaky edge. Curiously delicious and different. *44.6%. nc ncf sc.*

The GlenDronach Single Cask 1990 Aged 22 Years batch 8, Pedro Ximenez sherry puncheon, cask no. 2971, dist 13 Jun 90, bott May 13 db **(86) n21 t22.5 f21 b21.5**. Although a relatively healthy puncheon, there is tightness here where the sugars, for all their intense fruit and fudginess, strangle other development. Enjoyable. But... 50.8%. nc ncf sc.

The GlenDronach Single Cask 1991 Aged 21 Years batch 8, Pedro Ximenez sherry puncheon, cask no. 5409, dist 22 Nov 91, bott May 13 db **(81) n20 t21 f20 b20**. A steady stream of treacle. 49.8%. nc ncf sc.

The GlenDronach Single Cask 1992 Aged 21 Years batch 8, oloroso sherry butt, cask no. 145, dist 22 May 92, bott May 13 db **(96) n23.5** excellent balance between the lightweight spice and the grape; citrus darts in and out to ensure subtlety while the heavier oak offer ballast; **t24.5** the delivery of dreams: as near as damn it perfect weight with the grape as juicy as you like and the balancing oils full of malty intent. The sugars are molassed but thin enough for the buttery vanillas to make it to the middle; **f24** much lighter, with a sultana-laced butterscotch sign off; **b24** call me old fashioned, but I really do think there is a vast difference in the quality between whisky matured in good oloroso and PX. The trouble with PX is that it is so intense it often snuffs out the complexity which can make a good whisky great. Here, you can see so many aspects of the malt which has been lost in previous vintages: this is sherried Highland malt of the very highest calibre. 58.1%. nc ncf sc.

The GlenDronach Single Cask 1993 Aged 20 Years batch 8, oloroso sherry butt, cask no. 3, dist 15 Jan 93, bott May 13 db **(90.5) n22** pretty heavy and tight. But at its best, a fruitcake on steroids; **t24** melt in the mouth – while your mouth melts into the malt thanks to the spices; sublime range of sugars, topped with manuka honey and dates; **f21.5** a little furry and dull towards the end; **b23** a very slight blemish on the butt, but there are enough stunning moments to make this one to savour. 52.9%. nc ncf sc.

The GlenDronach Single Cask 1994 Aged 19 Years batch 8, oloroso sherry butt, cask no. 101, bott May 13 db **(96) n24** a half hour nosing job, this. Apart from the crisp toffee apple and pepper and steamed ginger spice, just look out for the interaction of the bourbon-style liquorice and carrot juice; ulmo honey is on the prowl, also; **t24.5** that is perfect weight and an equally perfect match between the silky fruit and the spice and vanilla led oak; heather honey and molasses thicken the fruitcake; **f23.5** back to ulmo honey and butterscotch, with a confident sultana thread and continuing spice; **b24** proof that great, unspoiled sherry butts were getting into Scotland during this period. And what proof! Magnificent. 58.4%. nc ncf sc.

The GlenDronach Single Cask 1996 Aged 17 Years batch 8, Pedro Ximenez sherry puncheon, cask no. 1490, dist 16 feb 96, bott May 13 db **(76) n19 t20 f18 b19**. Syrupy and too many spent matches. 53.1%. nc ncf sc.

The GlenDronach Single Cask 2002 Aged 10 Years batch 8, Pedro Ximenez sherry puncheon, cask no. 1988, dist 3 Jul 02, bott May 13 db **(94.5) n23.5** probably the cleanest PX puncheon I have yet nosed that's available commercially. Dense, of course. But sufficiently light enough to allow a little coffee and spice to wander in and out; **t23** quite feminine? Sugars and spice and all things nice...; **f24** where the delivery jars sensationally for a moment, this is probably the highlight: the toasted sugars come through in varying degrees of intensity, as does the pulsing spice. Is there even a hint of malt in there...? My imagination, surely...; **b24** a superior PX cask in that it is not so heavy as to blot out some of the more quixotic elements of the whisky and is as clean as a whistle and as spicy as a poppadom. The best PX puncheon I have found on the market in my lifetime. 55.6%. nc ncf sc.

Abbey Whisky GlenDronach Aged 20 Years cask no. 33, dist 1993, bott 2013 **(96.5) n24** not a single atom of sulphur means a treat in store: spiced, vaguely erfumed with lavender and clove and intense oloroso of your dreams proffering a near Guyana pot still rum heaviness and intensity; **t24.5** one of the few whiskies this year I really struggled to spit. That sticky molasses Demerara rum style hits hard and early: something akin to concentrated Melton Hunt Cake but with twice the number of toasted raisin; a wonderful nip and bite ensures this is no sherried softy; **f24** toasty...a mix of high percentage cocoa chocolate liberally dotted with burnt raisins; a last minute sign of some S-word treatment...but little or no damage done; **b24** faultless sherry butt. Glendronach at full throttle....and very few whiskies can come close to that! Those into heavy Demerara pot still rum will make be drawn like a moth to a flame to this gorgeous beast! 59.1%. sc.

❖ **Abbey Whisky GlenDronach Aged 20 Years** Pedro Ximenez sherry puncheon, cask no. 3400, dist 1994, bott 2014 db **(94) n24** pretty old fruit cake alert: lashings of molasses and a few dried dates working alongside beautifully weighted spices to make for a classic aroma; **t24** the estery kick off guides you along pot still rum lines at first. But it gets off that track as the burnt raisin begins to kick in, as do the very warming spices. Just classic oloroso mingling with top quality barley; **f22.5** dries with vigour as well as a hint of mocha. But the spices take some quelling; **b23.5** a dusky and beautiful sherry butt at work. 54.8%. sc. 672 bottles.

Cadenhead's Small Batch Glendronach Aged 23 Years bourbon hogsheads, dist 90, bott 13 (86) n21.5 t22.5 f20 b22. Nothing wrong with the heather-honey, viscous distillate. The oak has a few niggles, though, and detracts rather than spoils. Nothing wrong with the intensity of the malt content though. 49.5%. 534 bottles. WB15/260

GLENDULLAN (see also below)
Speyside, 1972. Diageo. Working.
Glendullan Aged 8 Years db (89) n20 t22 f24 b23. This is just how I like my Speysiders: young fresh and uplifting. A truly charming malt. 40%

Singleton of Glendullan 12 Years Old db (87) n22 t22 f21 b22. Much more age than is comfortable for a 12-y-o. 40%

◈ Singleton of Glendullan Liberty db (73) n17 t19 f18 b19. For showing such a really unforgiving off key bitter furriness, it should be clamped in irons... 40% WB16/036

◈ Singleton of Gendullan Trinity db (92.5) n24 truly exceptional nose: Turkish Delight means things are looking rosy here while the weight is provided by a distant, indistinct smokiness which may be down to the molasses at play; t23 not such a complex or cleverly weighted delivery, and even a little bitter oak gets in on the act. But there is no denying the intensity of those sugars again, nor their crispness. The way they melt into the barley is exceptional; f22.5 the bitterness retains, but some fluttering spices help compensate; b23 designed for airports, this complex little beauty deserves to fly off the shelves... 40% WB16/037

Old Malt Cask Glendullan Aged 14 Years refill hogshead, cask no.10124, dist Oct 99, bott Oct 13 (93) n23.5 what a beautiful mix between clean, alluring barley and citrus, mainly clementines; a little lavender freshens it up even further; t24 just about a perfect impact on delivery: the malts are salivating, the sugars are crisp and clean, the vanilla unembittered... wow!!! f22 here's the dull bit in Glendullan...the oak injects a little natural caramel but a few spices compensate; b23.5 at last! A Glendullan how I normally see it in the blending lab, rather than when tasting bottlings for the Bible. Of late they have been pretty ordinary and hardly representative. This one is much truer to its known quality among the pros, mainly due to this crisp malt being presented in decent oak for a change. 50%. nc ncf sc.336 bottles.

GLENDULLAN (see also above)
Speyside, 1898–1985. Closed.
Glendullan 1978 Rare Malt db (88) n23 t22 f21 b22. Sherlock Holmes would have loved this one: he would have found it lemon-entry. 56.8%

GLEN ELGIN
Speyside, 1900. Diageo. Working.
Glen Elgin Aged 12 Years db (89) n23 t24 f20 b22. Absolutely murders Cragganmore as Diageo's top dog bottled Speysider. The marks would be several points further north if one didn't get the feeling that some caramel was weaving a derogatory spell. Brilliant stuff nonetheless. States Pot Still on label – not to be confused with Irish Pot Still. This is 100% malt... and it shows! 43%

Cadenhead's Glen Elgin-Glenlivet Aged 22 Years dist 1991, bott Oct 13 (94) n23.5 does whisky come any more molassed than this...? Under-ripe greengages and over-ripe should add weight, but here they lighten..; t24 every bit as massive as on the nose: the sugars, a mix of molasses and treacle, arrive as a thick wall, guarded along the top by spikey spices. When you do surmount it a thick field of ulmo honey mingles with the typical Glen Elgin high intensity barley comes into view; f22.5 big, if relatively quiet. But an excellent cask means the tannins offer a degree of butterscotch...with glazed sugar and spices, of course...! b24 a bit more than a must for those with a sweet tooth: I thinking we are entering new territory so far continuous intensity goes. There is a vague hint of fruit but it is blasted from insignificance into irrelevance... 56.8%. 498 bottles. WB15/078

The Coopers Choice Glen Elgin 1995 Aged 17 Years sherry finish, cask no. 9043, bott 2013 (93.5) n22 a black cherry pie straight in the kisser..; t24 fabulously silky but unravels into something a lot more interesting as honeydew melon and heather honey gets involved in the Dundee cake and toasted honeycomb: big....! f23.5 the spices and honeycomb work well; b24 a blemish-free sherry butt, thankfully. And the malt has enough character to see off its slightly smothering presence. A dram to end an exhausting day with...as I am doing now, having just tasted the 950th new whisky of the 2015 Bible... 46%. 360 bottles. WB15/299

Old Particular Speyside Glen Elgin 21 Year Old 2nd fill sherry butt, cask no. 10185, dist Jun 92, bott Dec 13 (94) n23.5 mmmm!! Glazed ginger and fudgy tannin. Beautifully weighted and then brought to life with a sprinkling of pepper; t23 both voluptuous and eruptious... the ginger and spice combine to make a massive statement, all the more remarkable when the juicy barley is taken into account; **f24** lingers and fizzes. One of the great controlled spice explosions of the year is a class act to the end; **b23.5** what a way to start the day...!! *51.5%. nc ncf sc. 219 bottles. Douglas Laing & Co.*

⟫ **Scotch Malt Whisky Society Cask 85.30 Aged 15 Years** refill hogshead, dist 6 Oct 99 **(89.5) n23** a little essay in understated complexity: busy, slightly nutty oak offers the nippy, spicy counter to the lemon-drizzled barley; **t22.5** more austere than the nose, but the sugars offer a little twinkle here and there; **f22** dries, almost to an eye-watering degree. But this is good oak and the finale fits impressively; **b22.5** a pretty standard, unremarkable cask as far as a Glen Elgin is concerned: which means it's bloody good stuff... *56.6%. sc. 321 bottles.*

Wemyss Malts 1995 Single Speyside Glen Elgin "Eastern Promise" bott 2013 **(84) n21.5 t21.5 f20 b21.** After a Douglas Laing Glen Elgin which is perfect as morning's first dram, this oaky incarnation is one to take to bed.... for it is all rather over-tired. *46%. sc. 363 bottles.*

GLENESK
Highlands (Eastern), 1897–1985. Diageo. Demolished.
Duncan Taylor Collection Glenesk 1983 cask no. 4930 **(89.5) n22 t23 f22 b22.5.** By far the best Glen Esk I've tasted in years. Perhaps not the most complex, but the liveliness and clarity are a treat. *52.1%*

GLENFARCLAS
Speyside, 1836. J&G Grant. Working.
Glenfarclas 8 Years Old db **(86) n21 t22 f22 b21.** Less intense sherry allows the youth of this malt to stand out. Mildly quirky as a Glenfarclas and enormous entertainment. *40%*

Glenfarclas 10 Years Old db **(80) n19 t20 f22 b19.** Always an enjoyable malt, but for some reason this version never seems to fire on all cylinders. There is a vague honey sheen which works well with the barley, but struggles for balance and the nose is a bit sweaty. Still has distinctly impressive elements but an odd fish. *40%*

Glenfarclas 12 Years Old db **(94) n23.5** a wonderfully fresh mix of grape and mint; **t24** light, youthful, playful, mouthwatering. Less plodding honey, more vibrant Demerara and juiced-up butterscotch; **f23** long, with soft almost ice-cream style vanillas with a grapey topping; **b23.5** a superb re-working of an always trustworthy malt. This dramatic change in shape works a treat and suits the malt perfectly. What a sensational success!! *43%*

Glenfarclas 15 Years Old db **(85.5) n21.5 t23 f20 b21.** One thing is for certain: working with sherry butts these days is a bit like working with ACME dynamite...you are never sure when it is about to blow up in your face. There is only minimal sulphur here, but enough to take the edge off a normally magnificent whisky, at the death. Instead it is now merely, in part, quite lovely. The talent at Glenfarclas is unquestionably among the highest in the industry: I'll be surprised to see the same weaknesses with the next bottling. *46%*

Glenfarclas 17 Years Old db **(93) n23** just so light and playful: custard powder lightens and sweetens, sultana softens, barley moistens, spice threatens...; **t23** the relaxed sherry influence really lets the honey deliver; delightfully roasty and well spiced towards the middle; **f23** when I was a kid there was a candy – pretend tobacco, no less! – made from strands of coconut and sweetened with a Demerara syrup. My, this takes me back...; **b24** an excellent age for this distillery, allowing just enough oak in to stir up the complexity. A stupendous addition to the range. *40%*

Glenfarclas 18 Years Old db **(84) n21 t22 f20 b21.** Tight, nutty and full of crisp muscovado sugar. *43%. Travel Retail Exclusive.*

Glenfarclas 21 Years Old db **(83) n20 t23 f19 b21.** A chorus of sweet, honied malt and mildly spiced, teasing fruit on the fabulous mouth arrival and middle compensates for the few blips. *43%*

Glenfarclas 25 Years Old db **(84) n20 t22 f20 b22.** A curious old bat: by no means free from imperfect sherry but compensating with some staggering age – seemingly way beyond the 25-year statement. Enjoys the deportment of a doddering old classics master from a family of good means and breeding. *43%*

Glenfarclas 30 Years Old db **(85) n20 t22 f21 b22.** Flawed yet juicy. *43%*

Glenfarclas 40 Years Old db **(94) n23** old Demerara rum laced with well aged oloroso. Spicy, deep though checked by vanilla; **t23** toasty fruitcake with just the right degree of burnt raisin; again the spices are central to the plot though now a Jamaican Blue Mountain/Mysore medium roast mix makes an impressive entrance; **f24** long, with the oak not just ticking every box, but doing so with a flourish. The Melton Hunt cake finale is divine... **b24** couldn't help but laugh: this sample was sent by the guys at Glenfarclas after they spotted that I had last year called their disappointing 40-year-old a "freak." I think we have both proved a point... *46%*

Glenfarclas 50 Years Old db **(92) n24** Unique. Almost a marriage between 20-y-o bourbon and intense, old-fashioned sherry. Earthy, weighty stuff that repays time in the glass and oxidization because only then does the subtlety become apparent and a soft peat-reek reveal itself; **t23** an unexpected sweet – even mouthwatering - arrival, again with a touch of peat to add counter ballast to the intense richness of the sherry. The oak is intense from the middle onwards, but of such high quality that it merely accompanies rather then dominates; **f22** warming black peppers ping around the palate; some lovely cocoa oils coat the mouth for a bitter-sweet, warming and very long finish; **b23** Most whiskies cannot survive such great age. This one really does bloom in the glass and the earthy, peaty aspect makes it all the more memorable. It has taken 50 years to reach this state. Give a glass of this at least an hour's inquisition, as I have. Your patience will be rewarded many times over. 44.4%

Glenfarclas 105 db **(95.5) n23.5** the youthful grape comes in clean, juicy bunches; the herbs and spices on a rack on the kitchen wall; **t24** any lovers of the old Jennings books will here do a Mr Wilkins explosive snort as the magnificent barley-grape mix is propelled with the force of dynamite into the taste buds; survivors of this experience still able to speak may mention something about cocoa notes forming; **f24** long, luxurious, with a pulsing vanilla-grape mix and a build up of spices; light oils intensify and elongate; **b24** I doubt if any restorative on the planet works quite as well as this one does. Or if any sherry cask whisky is so clean and full of the joys of Jerez. A classic malt which has upped a gear or two and has become exactly what it is: a whisky of pure brilliance... 60%

Glenfarclas 2000 Vintage bott 2014 db **(76) n18.5 t22.5 f17 b18.** Surprisingly youthful in part. Wonderful early coffee and spice before the dull, bitter furriness kicks in... 43%.

◈ **Glenfarclas The Family Casks 1955** sherry butt, cask 2216 db **(95.5) n23.5** after nearly half an hour we at last get some kind of true but indelible picture as the fog clears and we can see the red liquorice and hickory tumbling in quiet battle with the barley...; **t24** astonishing. The tannins are way out of control, yet the sugars and spices gang together to bring them back into line. One of the most memorable counterpoints in this and many preceding years' whisky lexicon; **f23** more tired now as the tannins pile in for the finale; that said, the cocoa and Demerara fight back against the tannins is something to behold; **b24** a malt in its 60th year really has no right to survive. Remember, when the cask was filled, it wasn't designed to reach this kind of antiquity. T'was expected that this fellow would end up in a blend or possibly – though much more unlikely – as a single malt more than 50 years earlier...! So I will forgive the tiredness as the oak gains hold. It is natural and to be expected. Instead, I will savour those fruity depths on both nose and delivery and the beguiling development of the faint honey notes which guarantee and maintain the complexity to be found. This, after all these ridiculous years, is imperfect perfection... 45.4%. sc.

◈ **Glenfarclas The Family Casks 1956** sherry hogshead, cask 1767 db **(95.5) n24** a ridiculous nose for a malt this age. There is a tannin, fact. But it pales into insignificance compared to the mesmerising complexity of the butterscotch, ulmo honey and Black Jack candy which form the most beautifully constructed sweetness to counter the drier aspects of the oak; **t24** those sugars can't help themselves! They are there at the delivery and as if on the lookout for damaging oak, flood the palate by latching onto the improbable gristiness which still lingers after nearly 60 years! **f23** a slow dissolving of the barley while the tannin resides in butterscotch and vanilla. Where the late ulmo honey and spices come from is anyone's guess... **b24** age and logic defying Speyside whisky. Proves that great distillate in outstanding wood can comfortably withstand the test of time... 43.8%. sc.

◈ **Glenfarclas The Family Casks 1957** sherry hogshead, cask 2110 db **(96.5) n24** blueberries, blackberries, toasted raisins and semi-dried dates ...; **t24** sumptuous, borderline aggressive, delivery of fruit and spice. The age is non-negotiable...it is old....and some! For the tannins appear to have given up any notion of taking over the cask and add their considerable, spicy weight behind the almost impenetrable fruit...; concentrated mocha (decidedly coffee rich) makes an elegant contribution to the mid ground, though it is the intensity of the molasses which secures the overall balance; **f24** the earlier coffee has now progressed to high class latte; the big fruitcake theme continues and, somehow, the molasses use their intense weight to keep those marauding tannins at bay: indeed, if you imagined a great old whisky, this is more or less exactly how it would be in your mind's eye...astonishing! **b24.5** I chose this as my 1,000th new dram for the Jim Murray's Whisky Bible 2016 as I was born in 1957 and there are very few casks of my vintage still untapped worldwide....and because Glenfarclas have some astonishingly super-quality malts in their warehouse. Well I struck lucky with this, as it ticks every single box that a great malt might, and there is not a single cross to be found. And to a very special person who should have enjoyed this celebration of a malt with me tonight, all I can say is: Mazel Tov .... 50.3%. sc.

◈ **Glenfarclas The Family Casks 1958** sherry hogshead, cask 2061 db **(88) n22.5** a nose with cobwebs...creaking oak and ancient Melton Hunt Cake reinforced with extra burnt raisins...; **t21.5** borderline OTT burnt Christmas pudding, but the heavy molasses, squeezed dry of all their lingering sweetness, give just enough life to see it through; **f22** settles into a slightly more comfortable position as the more bitter notes are cancelled by the more confident late sugars; **b22** a substantially old whisky; in its really aged and imperfect way, it's all rather beautiful... *41.7%. sc.*

⬙ **Glenfarclas The Family Casks 1959** sherry hogshead, cask 3226 db **(80) n22 t21.5 f17 b19.5**. Quite possibly the darkest uncoloured whisky I have ever encountered...and if I didn't know any better, from the evidence of the mammoth bitterness of the finish and the deep black colour, I'd say some iron had got into this somewhere along the line (a nail dropping into the cask, for instance, sometime in the last 56 years, that kind of thing) ...Maybe the best mixer for a Rusty Nail, ever! Despite this, the early fruit is monumental. *55.2%. sc.*

⬙ **Glenfarclas The Family Casks 1961** sherry hogshead, cask 3056 db **(93) n23.5** the tannin levels are in the red zone and threatening to blow the gauge. Fortunately, just enough mind-blowingly intense fruit fill in the cracks. Not a nose for the squeamish and a must for heavy duty pot still rum lovers...; **t24** the sugars have the foresight to arrive early to cushion the oaky impact. Vaguely burnt...but the molasses combined with tasted raisins. Despite this, the body is one of silk, helped by a surprising ulmo honey sub plot; **f22.5** as the sugars tire, the more bitter notes begin to gather...; **b23** like all whiskies of this age, needs about 15 minutes to breathe and reveal its true self: drink direct after pouring and you will be missing the fun. Who buys this kind of malt? Well, I know some very rich Spurs supporters who would pour themselves a double of this any day... *46.7%. sc.*

⬙ **Glenfarclas The Family Casks 1962** sherry hogshead, cask 3246 db **(94) n23.5** rock hard molasses and a minty depth absolutely creaks of high quality old age; **t24** the last remnants of intense, concentrated grape disappear under the ever-emerging mix of barley and oak-soaked ulmo honey. The spices are neat and respectful; **f22.5** toasty and creaking like the timbers of an old ship; **b24** the resin cuts into the whisky like a diamond drill. Remember always to give these whiskies a good ten minutes to breathe in the glass before tasting, otherwise the results can be a little tight and you get only a quarter of the picture. Most remarkable here is the closer aspect to an old bourbon whisky than an ancient sherry butt. *43.4%. sc.*

⬙ **Glenfarclas The Family Casks 1963** sherry hogshead, cask 3541 db **(95.5) n24** just love that salty nip to the nose. Something of the dank old warehouse to this one in the long lost days when all sherry butts were clean and sulphur was something you got rid of at all costs; fabulous mocha sub thread; **t24** splendidly soft and alluring. The grape is of the burnt raisin variety, found in an old fruitcake, for there is a wonderful date, nut and molasses depth to this also; **f23.5** still salty, while chunky sugars and the dates just keep on giving; **b24** a malt which defies the years. This must have been matured in oak which today is almost impossible to find. Ensure when you've finished your glass you leave it beside your bed overnight. Should you wake in the early hours, remember to give it a sniff... *47.4%. sc.*

⬙ **Glenfarclas The Family Casks 1964** sherry butt, cask 4725 db **(84) n22 t22 f19 b21**. Grape and date abounds. But much too tight for its own good. Especially late on. *46.4%. sc.*

⬙ **Glenfarclas The Family Casks 1965** sherry butt, cask 4512 db **(91) n23.5** lashings of ulmo honey and there needs to be, as there is a feeling of fatigue....; **t23.5** the ulmo stays true and does all it can to blunt the oaky attack; **f22** thin now with waxy vanilla; **b22** three years ago or so, this might have been a whisky to die for. But for the ulmo honey it would be a spent force: there is no doubting it is a malt in descent. That said, some magnificent moments to fully savour... *51.8%. sc.*

⬙ **Glenfarclas The Family Casks 1966** sherry butt, cask 4198 db **(96.5) n23.5** as fresh, rich, generous and precise as the commentary of my late, lamented old friend Ken Wolstenholme; **t25** so much honeyed grape still; the oak never quite crosses the line, but this still goes into extra time; **f24** there's some sugary vanilla running on to the pitch: they think it's all over. It is now... **b24** when England beat West Germany 4-2 in 1966 to win the World Cup, the Scots were so delighted that they put much of their finest whisky in to their very best casks so, nearly 50 years on, we can still celebrate that special day. It was a very fine gesture. Thank you. *50.6%. sc.*

⬙ **Glenfarclas The Family Casks 1967** sherry butt, cask 6359 db **(96.5) n23.5** thumping, uncompromising grape; big age statement from the butt, also, by throwing in some unusually Kentucky type moves... **t24.5** powering, towering oak early on. The tannins positively whip the taste buds into submission before settling back and allowing the Melton Hunt Cake to take up the reins...; **f24** dusky sherry and dark cherry helped along with molasses and liquorice; **b24.5** heavy duty on both fruit and oak front. And neither compromising balance or quality. Quite magnificent: almost the ultimate aged heavy sherry dram. *52%. sc.*

◇ **Glenfarclas The Family Casks 1969** refill sherry butt, cask 2458 db **(87.5) n20.5 t21 f24 b22**. Ultimately, a beautiful whisky which appears to have fallen between two stalls. Has hit that point where the oaks are having to be slightly over aggressive to see off the quiet dominance of the high class grape. The result is a rough passage as the palate is assaulted by marauding, OTT oak. And then a sublime follow through as harmony is achieved with the aid of subtler spice and mocha, which seems to be in complete accord with the molasses and dates. A challenging but rewarding experience. *56.2%. sc.*

◇ **Glenfarclas The Family Casks 1970** sherry hogshead, cask 2026 db **(78) n19 t22 f18 b19**. By no means the first thing I've encountered with a 1970 vintage that promised so much but, after flattering to deceive, was ultimately a heart-breaking let down. Looks great from a distance and is wonderful when first encountered on the palate. But on close inspection proves old, haggard and bitter with not a single trace of lingering sweetness. No amount of patience sees any improvement as time progresses, alas. *53%. sc.*

◇ **Glenfarclas The Family Casks 1974** refill sherry hogshead, cask 4077 db **(87) n22.5 t21 f22 b21.5**. When it comes to oaky brinkmanship, this can show others how it should be done. The odd moment of chewing pencils, but just enough sugar lasts the course for sufficient balance. Watch out at the death for some late chocolate cupcake. *43.9%. sc.*

◇ **Glenfarclas The Family Casks 1978** 4th fill sherry hogshead, cask 746 db **(89.5) n22** the tannins leave a few battle scars...; **t22.5** cocoa and hickory vie with the spices. But it's all about age; **f22.5** a Zambia honey saltiness, depth and subtle sweetness emerges; **b22.5** so oaky and old, the whisky has growth rings... *46.2%. sc.*

◇ **Glenfarclas The Family Casks 1980** refill sherry hogshead, cask 1411 db **(94.5) n23.5** from the exotic fruit school of Speyside malts. Shows serious age...and quality...; **t24** at first you can't divert your attention away from the silky depth of the exotic fruit, the most intense of Seville marmalade and lightest of smoke notes. When you do, you realise that perhaps the oak is offering just a little too much tannin. Then, finally, you work out that it's the trade off... and a fabulous one at that; **f23.5** plenty of weighty tannins. A few more puffs of smoke...and a long malty/salty/fruity fade; **b23.5** some whiskies can show their age, yet be more sexy than ever before. You get the feeling this cask has peaked. *48%. sc.*

◇ **Glenfarclas The Family Casks 1983** refill sherry hogshead, cask 49 db **(73) n18 t20 f17 b18**. One assumes this was "refreshed" in a newer cask somewhere along the line. Anyway, sulphur has slipped in from somewhere. *53%. sc.*

◇ **Glenfarclas The Family Casks 1985** refill sherry hogshead, cask 2593 db **(96.5) n24** deft, now-you-see-it, now-you-don't smoke unites with rare harmony with the cleanest, most fabulously weighted grape. Seemingly neither sweet nor dry, yet both...; **t24** oh...heavens! That is ridiculously beautiful. Again, smoke dances playfully behind the sultana while vanilla, butterscotch and ulmo honey all play handsome parts; **f24** ridiculously complex and long. Enters into the Maryland biscuit territory: chocolate, dark sugars, nuts...but light fruit added also. Oh, and some spiced smoke...; **b24.5** one of the most supremely balanced Glenfarclases of all time. As beautifully mesmerising as it is memorable. If only all whisky was like this.... *49%. sc.*

◇ **Glenfarclas The Family Casks 1987** refill sherry butt, cask 1477 db **(69) n17 t19 f15 b18**. Big juicy grape. Bigger sulphur. *51.1%. sc.*

◇ **Glenfarclas The Family Casks 1988** refill sherry hogshead, cask 1993 db **(93.5) n24** curiously coastal – akin to the old Hoggies I used to sample at Bunna in the early '80s. Fabulous saltiness to the old Dundee cake...; a slight dollop of heather honey for good measure; **t24** that honey shows early, as does the salt. But still more than enough salivating sultanas in its train...; **f22** a little drier, especially with the oak making a vanilla-rich stand. And furrier. Late malt offers a grassy alternative to the grape; **b23.5** G is for juicy... F is for fruity... *56.4%. sc.*

◇ **Glenfarclas The Family Casks 1992** 4th fill sherry butt, cask 5850 db **(93) n23** busy and beautiful: the oak has dug its toasted heals in to ensure the grape doesn't get all its own way...; **t24** mmmm! Just...yes!!! Something of the boiled fruit candy about this, except there is some cough sweets in there also to arrest the sweetness and up the spices; **f22.5** busy and buzzy; **b23.5** a dry giant of a dram. *50.9%. sc.*

◇ **Glenfarclas 1994** db **(95.5) n23.5** an intense layering of rich sultanas and dessert-type wine; **t24.5** a delivery to die for (or kill, if you can't buy a bottle!): the cleanest, juiciest grape on the vine, at times eye-wateringly juicy and proud enough to absorb the continuing waves of toasty oak; a few sharper sauternes and marmalade notes mingle before the oils begin to form; **f23.5** dries and bitters with a degree of enthusiasm, but the spices move in to compensate while the cocoa and vanilla mops up the rest; **b24** very close in character and quality with to distillery's latest official 1994 release. Which means it's not far off God's gift to present day sherried malt whisky... *43%. 1200 bottles. The Whisky Shop exclusive.*

◇ **Glenfarclas The Family Casks 1994** 4th fill sherry butt, cask 4319 db (**95**) **n24** I could nose that near dessert-sweet yet lightly salted grape forever: sherry trifle, but with some absolutely top ranking wine...; **t24** the nose suggests delicate. The delivery, a series of fruit and biscuit whispers, confirms it. Then crisp grape in a slightly oily field; **f23.5** a vague tightening but the oak offers a light chocolate almond fade; **b24** such understated elegance! *56%. sc.*

◇ **Glenfarclas The Family Casks 1995** sherry hogshead, cask 2283 db (**82.5**) **n21 t22 f19 b20.5**. The fruit appears to be thrown like paints on a canvas by a troubled artist. Not so troubled, though, as the tight, furry finish. *47.8%. sc.*

◇ **Glenfarclas The Family Casks 1996** sherry butt, cask 1493 db (**94**) **n23.5** fascinating: a gorgeous mix of old and new. Some slightly crusty grape notes merging with fresher marmalade and thin vanilla; **t24** wow! Just so salivating. The fruit is dusted in cocoa and spice but always juicy and even leading into some major malt moments; **f23** drier, a little tighter fruit-wise while the vanilla has formed a glossy sheen. The spices work to the finish; **b23.5** almost exemplary sherry butt whiskying. *55.6%. sc.*

◇ **Villa Konthor Glenfarclas Vintage 2000** sherry butt no. 3639 filled 8 Jun 00, refill sherry hogshead no. 6394 filled 18 Dec 00, bott 2015 db (**90.5**) **n23** lots of grapes and gooseberries. A real dessert wine sweetness at times here; **t24** one of the best deliveries of a "modern" sherry butt I have encountered this year. The fruit is bulging from every nook and cranny, ranging from bubblegum chewy to a far more stylised and juicy green grapeyness; **f21** a little bitter furriness slowly filters through; **b22.5** always a reason to celebrate when you encounter an almost (but not quite) clean sherry butt. *46%. 1050 bottles. The Whisky Fair, Limburg.*

Cadenhead's Authentic Collection Glenfarclas Aged 25 Years bourbon hogshead, dist 1988, bott Oct 2013 (**95**) **n24** so complex – love it. A mild mocha element adds weight: gooseberries, glazed cherries and lemon cream Swiss roll ensures the fun; the barley is concentrated barley concentrate...; **t24** buttery malt is swathed in lightly fizzing, gorgeously spiced barley sugar; the intensity is almost beyond description; **f23** here comes the cream to the Swiss roll, very sticky and jammy; **b24** just adore the way Cadenhead gets out to the world a wonderful side of the incomparable Glenfarclas distillery we would not otherwise often see. Probably the liveliest 25-year-old I will taste this year! *53.7%. 222 bottles. WB15/275*

◇ **Cadenhead's Authentic Collection Glenfarclas Aged 25 Years** bourbon cask, dist 1990 (**92**) **n21.5** such busy bourbon noises: the oak pulls all the strings and like a marionette tends to dance around a little ungainly; **t23** much better now: the oak-bestowed spices strike early to form a superb counter point to the mocha and Demerara sugars; **f24** long and mega complex: more mocha, a little Lubeck marzipan and a few late strands of hickory...almost showing as many bourbon traits as Scotch; **b23.5** just as how this light spirit allows sherry to have its merry way with it, so great American oak can shape this into something special, too... *52.6%*

Cadenhead's Authentic Collection Glenfarclas Aged 41 Years bourbon hogshead, dist 73, bott July 14 (**94.5**) **n22.5** the tannins have taken over the asylum: oak, intense to the point of paranoia, dictate shape and form. Even the marmalade is tannin-based and slowly sweetens to soften all the edges; **t24.5** the sugary marmalade arrives immediately but it is the malt which opens up. Coconut cake mix has Demerara mixed into it, then a butter cream which also offers soft oils; a little bourbon biscuit chocolate cream is added to the mix; **f23.5** dries as the tannin returns. But enough cake mix survives to ensure a comfortable finale; lovely late spices tingle; **b24** thankfully, the dreamy palate makes a lie of the nose which suggests we have one overly tired dram. However, it appears it was the strength of the whisky which suggested it was time to bottle, not the zealous oak. One important suggestion: leave it in the glass for 25-30 mins before tasting to allow it to open to its fullest potential. *40.7%. 186 bottles. WB15/270*

Riegger's Selection Eagle of Spey Glenfarclas 1993 (**96.5**) **n24.5 t24.5 f23 b24.5**. You will have to pass a few bottlings to find one from this distillery so fruity yet not from a sherry butt. An absolute masterpiece from this outstanding distillery. *53.6%.*

◇ **Romantic Rhine Collection Green Meadows 1993** bourbon hogshead, cask no. 605, dist 4 Mar 93, bott 20 Oct 12 (**92**) **n23 t23.5 f22 b23.5**. Until the cask begins to fragment slightly at the very death, we have a malt which is entirely content in its own skin: its light body allowing the flavours to possess an ethereal quality, especially in the barley and honey tones. Beautifully delicate and fragile, even the lightest saline moment has an important impact. Charming. *52.2%. 605 bottles.*

Scotch Malt Whisky Society Cask 1.178 Aged 11 Years 1st fill barrel, dist 07 Jun 02 (**92.5**) **n23** hefty malt revels in the barley fest; **t23** salivates like a bottled Glenfarclas has rarely salivated before. Fresh grist which refuses to let up; just adore the developing spices; **f23** impressive spiced cocoa; **b23.5** this is the flip side of Glenfarclas: relatively young and showing its malty rather than fruity plumage. A bit of a treat. *56.8%. nc ncf sc. 232 bottles.*

Scotch Malt Whisky Society Cask 1.179 Aged 27 Years refill hogshead, dist 03 Dec 86 **(89.5)** n23 a thin layering of ulmo honey on toast; t23 the delivery pings with voluptuous barley at times tantalising, others tangy; f21 dries as oak gains hold; b22.5 another superb blending malt slightly highjacked by oak. *472%. nc ncf sc. 201 bottles.*

◇ **Scotch Malt Whisky Society Cask 1.184 Aged 24 Years** refill hogshead, dist 8 Nov 89 **(91)** n24 there is no escaping the lightness of the big stills. But here it has created room for a mix of barley, fruit meringue (with a dusting of icing sugar), apple pie and vaguely spiced butterscotch. The kind of aroma where you'd like to have the glass attached to your head all day...; t23 much sharper on delivery than Ed Miliband...and more interesting too. The barley is in molten form; f21.5 little body to see off a slight oaky bitterness; b22.5 for a malt with little body, the curves are very juicy indeed. *52.9%. sc. 49 bottles.*

◇ **Scotch Malt Whisky Society Cask 1.185 Aged 30 Years** refill hogshead, dist 16 May 84 **(86.5)** n22 t22 f21 b21.5. A pleasant, if thin chap full of mouth-watering barley and sugars but, curiously, has something of slivovitz about it. Agreeable oak at work. *54.4%. sc. 190 bottles.*

◇ **Scotch Malt Whisky Society Cask 1.188 Aged 28 Years** refill hogshead, dist 3 Dec 86 **(86)** n22 t22 f20.5 b21.5. For a malt pushing 30 years, enjoys a remarkable freshness about it. An agreeable mix of salivating barley and pear. But the oak could be a little more interested. *47%. sc. 208 bottles.*

◇ **Whisky Fair Glenfarclas 14 Year Old** sherry butt, cask no. 3639, dist 2000, bott 2015 **(92.5)** n23.5 hefty fruit and militant spice. The more you nose, the more intense and unfathomable it becomes; t23.5 a gorgeous volley of spicy, treacled grape kicks the delivery off to a fine and juicy start...and allows the nose to the letter. Toffee apple begins to lighten the effect; f22.5 lazier spice, a few waves of malt, more toffee apple...and then the spices arrive in Mark II form, much busier and more aggressive; b23 not exactly technically spic-and-span. But what wonderfully chewy fun... *52.1%. Distillery bottled for The Whisky Fair.*

GLENFIDDICH
Speyside, 1887. William Grant & Sons. Working.

Glenfiddich 12 Years Old db **(85.5)** n21 t22 f21 b21.5. A malt now showing a bit of zap and spark. Even displays a flicker of attractive muscovado sugars. Simple, untaxing and safe. *40%*

Glenfiddich 12 Years Old Toasted Oak Reserve db **(92.5)** n22.5 t23.5 f22.5 b24. Another bottling to confound the critics of Glenfiddich. This is as fine an essay in balance, charm and sophistication as you are likely to find in the whole of Speyside this year. Crack open a bottle... but only when you have a good hour to spend. *40%*

Glenfiddich Caoran Reserve Aged 12 Years db **(89)** n22.5 t22 f21.5 b23. Has fizzed up a little in the last year or so with some salivating charm from the barley and a touch of cocoa from the oak. A complex little number. *40%*

◇ **Glenfiddich Cask Collection Select Cask** db **(78.5)** n19 t22.5 f18 b19. Bourbon and wine casks may be married together...but they are on course for a messy divorce. The honeymoon on delivery is pretty rich and exotic. But it is all too short-lived as things soon turn pretty bitter. *40% WB16/041*

◇ **Glenfiddich Cask Collection Reserve Cask** db **(83)** n20 t22 f20 b21. Soft, chewy, occasionally sparkling but the overdose of toffee and a disappointing degree of late furriness means its speech is distinctly limited in its topic. *40% WB16/040*

Glenfiddich Rich Oak Over 14 Years Old new American & new Spanish oak finish db **(90.5)** n23 t22 f23.5 b22. From the moment you nose this, there is absolutely no doubting its virgin oak background. It pulls towards bourbon, but never gets there. Apparently European oak is used, too. The result is something curiously hinting at Japanese, but without the crushing intensity. Delicious, thoughtful whisky and one to tick off on your journey of malt whisky discovery. Though a pity we don't see it at 46% and in full voluptuous nudity: you get the feeling that this would have been something really exceptional to conjure with. *40%*.

Glenfiddich 15 Years Old db **(94.5)** n23 such a deft intermingling of the softer fruits and bourbon notes...with barley in there to remind you of the distillery; t23 intense and big yet all the time appearing delicate and light; the most apologetic of spices help spotlight the barley sweetness and delicate fruits; f24.5 just so long and complex; something of the old fashioned fruit salad candy about this but with a small degree of toffee just rounding off the edges; b24 if an award were to be given for the most consistently beautiful dram in Scotland, this would win more often than not. This under-rated distillery has won more friends with this masterpiece than probably any other brand. *40%*

Glenfiddich Aged 15 Years Cask Strength db **(85.5)** n20 t23 f21 b21.5. Improved upon the surprisingly bland bottlings of old, especially on the fabulously juicy delivery. Still off the pace due to an annoying toffee-ness towards the middle and at the death. *51%*

Glenfiddich Distillery Edition 15 Years Old db (93.5) n24.5 t24 f22 b23. Had this exceptional whisky been able to maintain the pace through to the finish, this would have been a single malt of the year contender - at least. 51%. ncf.

Glenfiddich Aged 15 Years Solera Reserve (see Glenfiddich 15 Years Old)

Glenfiddich 18 Years Old db (95) n23.5 the smoke, which for long marked this aroma, appears to have vanished. But the usual suspects of blood orange and various other fruit appear to thrive in the lightly salted complexity; t24.5 how long are you allowed to actually keep the whisky held on the palate before you damage your teeth? One to really close your eyes and study because here we have one of the most complex deliveries Speyside can conjour: the peat may have gone, but there is coal smoke around as the juicy barley embeds with big fat sultanas, plums, dates and grapes. Despite the distinct lack of oil, the mouthfeel is entirely yielding to present one of the softest and most complete essays on the palate you can imagine, especially when you take the bitter-sweet ratio and spice into balance; f23 long, despite the miserly 40% offered, with plenty of banana-custard and a touch of pear; b24 at the moment, the ace in the Glenfiddich pack. If this was bottled at 46%, unchilfiltered etc, I dread to think what the score might be... 40%

Glenfiddich Age Of Discovery Aged 19 Years Bourbon Cask Reserve db (92) n23.5 t24 f22 b22.5. For my money Glenfiddich turns from something quite workaday to a malt extraordinaire between the ages of 15 and 18. So, depending on the casks chosen, a year the other side of that golden age shouldn't make too much difference. The jury is still out on whether it was helped by being at 40%, which means the natural oils have been broken down somewhat, allowing the intensity and richness only an outside chance of fully forming. 40%

Glenfiddich Age Of Discovery Aged 19 Years Madeira Cask Finish db (88.5) n22.5 t22.5 f21 b22.5. Oddly enough, almost a breakfast malt: it is uncommonly soft and light yet carries a real jam and marmalade character. 40%

Glenfiddich 21 Years Old db (86) n21 t23 f21 b21. A much more uninhibited bottling with loads of fun as the mouth-watering barley comes rolling in. But still falls short on taking the hair-raisingly rich delivery forward and simply peters out. 40%

Glenfiddich 30 Years Old db (93.5) n23 always expect sherry trifle with this: here is some sherry not to be trifled with... salty, too; t23.5 the juiciest 30-y-o I can remember from this distillery for a while: both the grape and barley are contributing to the salivation factor...; the mid ground if filled with light cocoa, soft oils and a delicate hickory-demerara bourbon-style sweetness; f23.5 here usually the malt ends all too briefly. Not this time: chunky grape carries on its chattering with the ever-increasing bourbon-honeycomb notes; a vague furry finale...; b23.5 a 'Fiddich which has changed its spots. Much more voluptuous than of old and happy to mine a grapey seam while digging at the sweeter bourbon elements for all it is worth. Just one less than magnificent butt away from near perfection and a certain Bible Award... 40%

Glenfiddich Rare Collection 40 Years Old db (86.5) n22.5 t23 f20 b21. A quite different version to the last with the smoke having all but vanished, allowing the finish to show the full weight of its considerable age. The nose and delivery are superb, though. The barley sheen on arrival really deserves better support. 43.5%

Glenfiddich 50 Years Old db (97) n25 we are talking 50 years, and yet we are still talking fresh barley, freshly peeled grape and honey. Not ordinary honey. Not the stuff you find in jars. But the pollen that attracts the bees to the petunia; and not any old petunia: not the white or the red or pink or yellow. But the two-toned purple ones. For on the nose at least this is perfection; this is nectar... t24 a silky delivery: silky barley with silky, watered down maple syrup. The middle ground, in some previous Glenfiddich 50-year-olds a forest of pine and oak, is this time filled with soft, grassy barley and the vaguest hint of a distant smoke spice; f24 long, long, long, with the very faintest snatch of something most delicately smoked: a distant puff of peat reek carried off on the persistent Speyside winds, then a winding-down of vanillas, dropping through the gears of sweetness until the very last traces are chalky dry; b24 for the record, my actual words, after tasting my first significant mouthful, were: "fuck! This is brilliant." It was an ejaculation of genuine surprise, as any fly on the wall of my Tasting Room at 1:17am on Tuesday 4th August would testify. Because I have tasted many 50-year-old whiskies over the years, quite possibly as many as anyone currently drawing breath. For not only have I tasted those which have made it onto the whisky shelves, but, privately, or as a consultant, an untold number which didn't: the heroic but doomed oak-laden failures. This, however, is a quite different animal. We were on the cusp of going to press when this was released, so we hung back. William Grant blender David Stewart, whom I rank above all other blenders on this planet, has known me long and well enough to realise that the surrounding hype, with this being the most expensive whisky ever bottled at £10,000 a go or a sobering £360 a pour, would bounce off me like a pebble from a boulder. "Honestly, David," he told my chief researcher with a timorous insistence, "please tell Jim I really think this isn't too oaky." He offered almost an apology for bringing into the world this 50-year-old babe. Well, as usual David Stewart, doyen of the blending lab and Ayr United season ticket holders, was absolutely spot on. And, as is his want, he was rather understating his case. For the record, David, next time someone asks you how good this whisky is, just for once do away with the Ayeshire niceness installed by generations of very nice members of the Stewart family and tell them: "Actually, it's bloody brilliant if I say so myself! And I don't give a rat's bollocks what Murray thinks." *46.1%*

Glenfiddich Malt Master's Edition double matured in oak and sherry butts db (84) n21 t22 f20 b21. I would have preferred to have seen this double matured in bourbon barrels and bourbon barrels... The sherry has done this no great favours. *43%*

Glenfiddich Millennium Vintage dist 2000, bott 2012 db (83.5) n21.5 t22 f20 b20. Short and not very sweet. Good juicy delivery though, reminiscent of the much missed original old bottling. *40%*

GLEN GARIOCH
Highlands (Eastern), 1798. Morrison Bowmore. Working.

Glen Garioch 8 Years Old db (85.5) n21 t22 f21 b21.5. A soft, gummy, malt – not something one would often write about a dram of this or any age from Geary! However, this may have something to do with the copious toffee which swamps the light fruits which try to emerge. *40%*

Glen Garioch 10 Years Old db (80) n19 t22 f19 b20. Chunky and charming, this is a malt that once would have ripped your tonsils out. Much more sedate and even a touch of honey to the rich body. Toffeed at the finish. *40%*

Glen Garioch 12 Years Old db (88.5) n22 t23 f21.5 b22. A significant improvement on the complexity front. The return of the smoke after a while away was a surprise and treat. *43%*

Glen Garioch 12 Years Old db (88) n22.5 t22.5 f21.5 b22. Sticks, broadly, to the winning course of the original 43% version, though here there is a fraction more toffee at the expense of the smoke. *48%. ncf.*

Glen Garioch 15 Years Old db (86.5) n20.5 t22 f22 b22. In the bottling I sampled last year the peat definitely vanished. Now it's back again, though in tiny, if entertaining, amounts. *43%*

Glen Garioch 21 Years Old db (91) n21 a few wood shavings interrupt the toasty barley; t23 really good bitter-sweet balance with honeycomb and butterscotch leading the line; pretty juicy, busy stuff; f24 dries as it should with some vague spices adding to the vanilla and hickory; b23 an entirely re-worked, now smokeless, malt that has little in common with its predecessors. Quite lovely, though. *43%*

Glen Garioch 1797 Founders Reserve db (87.5) n21 t22 f22.5 b22. Impressively fruity and chewy: some serious flavour profiles in there. *48%*

Glen Garioch 1958 db (90) n24 t21 f23 b22. The distillery in its old smoky clothes: and quite splendid it looks! *43%. 328 bottles.*

Glen Garioch 1995 db (86) n21 t22 f21.5 b21.5. Typically noisy on the palate, even though the malty core is quite thin. Some big natural caramels, though. *55.3%. ncf.*

Glen Garioch 1997 db (89) n22 unusually salty, dry and subtle; t22.5 just a few semi-gristy sugars make a minor noise while the barley appears in intense bursts but happy to duck behind the oak; some early barley wine oils early on; f22 a charming fade of caramelised barley; b22.5 had you tasted this malt as a 15-year-old back in 1997, you would have tasted something far removed from this, with a peaty bite ripping into the palate. To say this malt has evolved is an understatement. *56.5%. Whisky Shop Exclusive. 204 bottles.*

Glen Garioch 1997 db (89.5) n22 t23 f22 b22.5. I have to say: I have long been a bit of a voice in the wilderness among whisky professionals as to regards this distillery. This not so subtly muscled malt does my case no harm whatsoever. *56.7%. ncf.*

⋙ **Glen Garioch 1998** db (89.5) n21 ok, not exactly the perfect nose but, the slight taint apart, the depth of the dates is pretty startling; t23.5 a thick, three-course malt which needs a knife and fork to get through. An astonishing mix of date and grape yet still with a malty background to ensure a honeyed sweetness keeps out any unwelcome guests; f22.5 yes, some spoiling sulphur, certainly. But, again, we have the date-malt combo sticking to the ulmo-manuka honey blend and lasting a ridiculous amount of time...; b23 with dates this good, a chocolate-loving, non-Islamic Tuareg will adore this one...one of the best flawed whiskies I have tasted in a while... *48% WB16/039*

⋙ **Glen Garioch The Renaissance Aged 15 Years** db (79) n19 t23 f18 b19. Oh...so close to absolute brilliance, this one. Certainly one of the top ten most complex whiskies this year and you need your taste buds turned up to maximum alertness to be able to tackle the depth and myriad intricacies of this malt. However, I suspect the casks plucked from the warehouse for bottling didn't match those in the blending lab: the nose and finish reveal a furry, bitter off note which does the damage. *51.9% WB16/038*

Glen Garioch 1999 db (64) n16 t17 f15 b16. Massively sulphured. *56.3%. ncf.*

Glen Garioch Sherry Cask Matured Oloroso sherry casks, batch no. 30, dist 1999, bott 2013 db **(79) n19 t23 f18 b19**. The usual sherry problems arise. Which is enough to make you weep, because for a few glorious seconds on delivery (about the third to the fifth taste beats in) the impact and beauty of the oloroso matches anything experienced in Scotland this year. But the s-word wins, as it so often does, in the end. *56.3%. ncf. WB15/157*

Glen Garioch Virgin Oak db **(93) n22** a salty, unsmoked bacon feel to this with quietly controlled tannins and hickory; **t23.5** a series of complex sugar notes are first to arrive. Then come in second, third and fourth, the complexity levels rising by the second; grated coconut and Brazilian biscuit works well with the maple syrup; **f24** now the complexity peaks with modest spices cranking up the vanilla and countering the light layer of ulmo and manuka honey blend; **b23.5** Glen Garioch as probably never seen before and at its most beautifully complex. *48%*

◈ **Alexander Murray & Co Glen Garioch 1991 22 Years Old** **(84) n21.5 t22 f20.5 b20**. The nose and delivery show great promise, what with a salty edge and a toffee-apple moment. But impossible to recognise the regional style, let alone distillery or age, as the unrelenting semi-fruity fudge gums up everything. *40%*

Berry's Own Selection Glen Garioch 1989 Aged 24 Years cask no. 7854, bott 2014 **(89.5) n22.5** understated smoke and passion fruit; **t23** fabulous delivery: muscovado sugar and deft smoke make a malty soup interesting; salivating sweet juicy barley; **f21.5** thins and warms but the sugars continue; **b22.5** fascinating bottling which captures the spirit of that period, with the smoke apparent but reduced from what it once was. And a little bite from the lively spirit. *53.8%. ncf ncf. WB15/250*

Directors' Cut Glen Garioch Aged 21 Years refill hogshead, cask no. 10353, dist Apr 93, bott Jun 14 **(84.5) n21.5 t21 f21 b21**. Expected some smoke on this. Instead, got the malty, fireball version of that era...and some pretty full on oak, too. *57.4%. nc ncf sc. 213 bottles.*

The First Editions Glen Garioch 1993 Aged 20 Years **(95.5) n23.5** a Fisherman's Friend-Worther's Original cross...; **t24.5** that is how I like to see a Geery on to the palate: like a fast bowler's ball on to my bat...true, fast, clean and with no little zip. Absolutely creams the taste buds with a gorgeous barley-sugar-butterscotch mix while other sugars, mainly maple syrup, giving a delicate, cleansing effect despite the bite and spice....just so fantastically malty and juicy...to the nth degree; **f23.5** still some fizz, but settles into a more medium-paced vanilla-textured finale; **b24** could drink this all day and every day. If you know what I mean. A stunner. *58.2%. nc ncf sc.*

◈ **Kingsbury Gold Glen Garioch 23 Year Old 1990** hogshead, cask no. 10398 **(92) n23** oddly fruity for both the distillery at that date, and the cask type. But there is a distant smokiness which ensures not just intensity, but balance; **t23.5** none of the old Garioch fire water on delivery: the opposite in fact, as the taste buds are kissed and bathed in silky malt concentrate. Again, a few phenols hang around, converting slowly into sensational spice notes; **f22.5** soft muscovado sugars infiltrate the spices and vanillas. The malt continues to massage the palate while some very late redcurrants infuse the finish; **b23** this was the first of the new style Garioch. And probably the last which ensured smoke was, as it had always previously been, part of its makeup. *55.9%. 213 bottles.*

Kingsbury Silver Glen Garioch 19 Year Old cask no. 345, dist 1993 **(84) n20 t22 f21 b21**. A good example of decent though not entirely convincing malt being filled into a decent though not entirely convincing cask. The mottled effect on the taste buds results, though when the barley sparkles it makes the duller moments bearable. *46%. nc ncf sc. 284 bottles.*

The Last Drop Glen Garioch 47 Year Old hogshead, cask no. 662 dist 23 Mar 67 **(96) n24** you will do well to find a another nose like this over the next year or five: profound, chunky oak thinned and tamed by sharp kumquat notes and finally defused by the friendliest – slightly cocoa-softened – peat reek. For it to be this confident now, it must have been a peaty monster some half a century ago...; in its lighter, relaxed mode the oak pulses out soft liquorice and hickory; **t23.5** a slight eye-watering moment as the tannins bite with intent on delivery. But again the smoke and citrus come rushing to the rescue and now we go from salvation into salivation mode as even remnants of barley make an impact; now creamy, fudgy and liquorice bourbony and helped further by the thinnest layer of smoked molasses; **f24** so long...and a delightful tangle of oaky roots and peaty off-shoots make way first for the citrus then a fabulous pounding spiciness; **b24.5** when this distillery produced the whisky in the bottle before me it was making probably the smokiest malt on mainland Scotland. Which is just as well for this grizzled old greybeard. Because things preserve rather well in peat – and this Glen Garioch is no exception. Just a standard low- or non-peated malt would have vanished behind the layers of tannins which have formed a crust around some of the lighter components of the dram. But here the smoke softens the oaky blows until they become only caresses. It is a quite extraordinary - and in many ways lucky – experience. *45.4%.*

⟡ **Liquid Treasures Glen Garioch 24 Year Old** dist 1991, bott 2015 **(88) n22.5** toffee orange; **t22.5** sharp delivery where both oak and barley bite deep with spices joining in; the oak holds the mid-ground as the tannins ensure dryness rules; **f21** dull toasted fudge; **b22** the natural caramels appear a little too active. 51.9%. 229 bottles.

Master of Malt Single Cask Glen Garioch 20 Year Old (87.5) n21 t23 f21.5 b22. Magnificent delivery of concentrated barley. A minor oak niggle prevents development. But for those into intense malt...you'll be pouring a second glass! 58.8%. sc.

Montgomerie's Single Cask Collection Glen Garioch cask no. 8555, dist 12 Nov 90, bott Mar 13 **(87) n21 t22 f22 b22.** Made at an interesting period in the distillery's period when they were just trying to work out who they were. Once, it had been a peaty malt which added not just smoke to a blend but a degree of ruggedness. Here it is undergoing a makeover. The smoke has vanished. And rather rip at the throat as of yore, is rather too tame and vanishes, albeit pleasantly, behind the skirts of fudgy toffee. 46%. nc ncf sc. WB15/128

⟡ **Old Malt Cask Glen Garioch 20 Years Old** refill hogshead, cask no. 10899, dist Oct 94, bott Oct 14 **(85.5) n22.5 t21 f21 b21.** Enjoy the Spotted Dick pudding nose. The delivery and follow through is a paper-thin malty mess by comparison, though the icing sugars do pretty well. 50%. nc ncf sc. 322 bottles.

Old Particular Highland Glen Garioch 21 Years Old refill hogshead, cask no. 9901, dist May 92, bott Aug 13 **(88) n21.5** a little gingerbread amid the toasty barley; **t23** quietly aggressive delivery with a beautiful and salivating build up of oily barley; **f21.5** returns to the toasty nose with a lovely pulse of spice lingering; **b22** at times quite irresistible for all its rough edges. 51.5%. nc ncf sc. 122 bottles. Douglas Laing & Co.

The Pearls of Scotland Glen Garioch 1989 cask no. 7855, bott Jun 14 **(83.5) n20 t21.5 f21 b21.** From that razor-blade-hot-as-Hades-slap-on-the-wallpaper-paste school of Geery. Still, plenty to enjoy with its intense maltiness and Demerara input. 56%. sc.

Single Cask Collection 1993 Glen Garioch 20 Year Old bourbon hogshead, dist 1993 **(87) n21 t23 f21 b22.** An infuriating "Geery". Flips with alarming and confusing regularity between a juicy, malty big boy and a thin, austere wimp of a dram. It is a bit of a distillery character trait. Finally settles on wimpy alternative. 55.1%. sc. Single Cask Collection.

⟡ **Spirit & Cask Glen Garioch 1993** hogshead, bott 2014 **(92) n22** some of the malt notes are vigorous and youthful, even today...; **t23.5** gorgeous bite to the delivery, with a high quality malt follow through. Decidedly barley sugarish at times...; **f23** excellent oak arrival with a gorgeous Milky Way style milk chocolate/nougat edge; **b23.5** having just been tasting a bunch of single malts in a caramel straightjacket, so wonderful to taste one unfettered and free. Wonderfully malty and salivating. 52.5%. 260 bottles.

That Boutique-y Whisky Glen Garioch batch 1 **(85) n21 t22 f21 b21.** Very straight up and down blending malt. Pleasant barley which shows brief vitality before the natural caramels take hold. 50.6%. 284 bottles. WB15/225

Wemyss Glen Garioch Malts 1989 Single Highland "Brandy Casket" bott 13 **(86) n22 t22 f20.5 b21.5.** A curious remnant from a lost Geery style. The smoke hammers its phenolic point home hard and the spices nip and nibble delightfully. But there is also an underlying austerity to this, too, which prevents it from entering the next level. 46%. Sc.

Wemyss Glen Garioch 1989 Single Highland "Fruit Bonbons" hogshead **(91.5) n22 t23.5 f23 b23.** The spirit from the stills at this time had a "fire water" reputation which now, as is so often the case, means we have a malt which is wilful and complex and able to take the two decades of maturation comfortably in its stride. 46%. sc. 325 bottles.

Wemyss Glen Garioch Malts 1989 Single Highland "Peaches and Cream" hogshead, dist 89, bott 14 **(92) n22** pretty tired but just enough smoke and vanilla to paper over the cracks; **t23.5** mouth-filling, oily and attractively sharp. Deft peat ensures both substance and gristy sweetness to make for a chewy experience; **f23** smoked mocha with a lovely piece of Battenberg cake; **b23.5** improves as it goes along, helped by the peaty remnants. Ends up as a delicious whole. 46%. sc. 357 bottles.

GLENGLASSAUGH
Speyside, 1875. The BenRiach Distillery Co. Working.
Glenglassaugh 21 Year Old db **(94) n23.5** elegant and adroit, the lightness of touch between the citrus and barley is nigh on mesmeric: conflicting messages of age in that it appears younger and yet you feel something has to be this kind of vintage to hit this degree of aloofness. Delicate and charming...; **t24.5** again we have all kinds of messages on delivery: the spices fizz around announcing oaky intentions and then the barley sooths and sweetens even with a degree of youthful juiciness. The tastebuds are never more than caressed, the sugar-sweetened citrus ensuring neither the barley or oak form any kind of advantage; impeccably

weighted, a near perfect treat for the palate; **f22.5** white chocolate and vanilla lead the way as the oak begins to offer a degree of comparative austerity; **b23.5** a malt which simply sings on the palate and a fabulous benchmark for the new owners to try to achieve in 2030...!! *46%*

Glenglassaugh 26 Years Old db **(78.5) n19 t21.5 f18.5 b19.5.** Industrial amounts of cream toffee here. Also some odd and off key fruit notes winging in from somewhere. Not quite the gem I had hoped for. *46%*

Glenglassaugh 1986 28 Years Old Batch 1 hogshead, cask no. 2101, dist 19 Feb 86, db **(93) n23.5** sublime fruit intervention on the rampant honey. Moist cherry fruit cake and vanilla also show well; **t24** and off goes those honey tones again. A fabulous marriage between soothing ulmo and grittier manuka. A little maple syrup says hello; **f22.5** bitter marmalade as the tannins begin to show form; **b23** a spotless cask which has more grey hairs than you might expect for its age. Superb, though. *43.7%. sc.*

Glenglassaugh Master Distillers' Selection Aged 28 Years dist 1983 db **(93) n23** seville orange and vanilla. But not quite that simple...don't get me started on the antique leather...; **t24** the body is of the type you might see on a Scandinavian beach in high summer: beautiful tone and delicate curves in all the right places. The barley myriad juices; the oak conjures several layers of vanillas, including a light covering of ulmo honey; **f22.5** just bitters out slightly, though remains busy; **b23.5** knowing Norway as I do, glad to see these lovely people are getting their money's worth! *49.8%. nc ncf sc. Norway exclusive. 400 bottles.*

Glenglassaugh 30 Year Old db **(89) n23 t23 f21 b22.** Sheer poetry. Or not... *43.1%*

Glenglassaugh 30 Year Old db **(87) n22.5 t23 f20 b21.5.** A gentle perambulation around soft fruitcake. Moist and nutty it still has a major job on its hands overcoming the enormity of the oak. The buzzing spices underline the oak involvement. Meek, charming though a touch furry on the finish. *44.8%.*

Glenglassaugh Rare Casks Aged Over 30 Years db **(86) n22 t21 f21.5 b21.5.** Nearly four decades in an oak cask has resulted in a huge eruption of caramels. Soft oils and citrus abounds but it is the oak which dominates. *43%. nc ncf sc. Actual age 36 years. 280 bottles.*

Glenglassaugh 1963 51 Years Old cask no. 3301 db **(88) n23.5** cherry cough sweets: a dram that should help you breathe more easily...; **t22.5** oddly enough it remains medicinal as the intensity of the tannins almost carve out a creosote-ish bite; some sugars – again something akin to black cherry juice – does all it can to stem the oaky tide; steady weight and pace to development; **f20** burnt toast meets burnt coffee: slowly, all meaningful sweetness is consumed by the rampant oak; **b22** a shame this wasn't bottled a few years back: there are some magnificent phases here. The nose and delivery possess their own morbid beauty and the battle of the fruity sugars against the passage of time is of heroic status. The final moments, though, are a little painful. *41.7%*

Glenglassaugh 1978 35 Years Old Batch 1 sherry hogshead, cask no. 1803, dist 06 Oct 78 db **(95.5) n23.5** a light brushing of kumquat but vanilla dominates. Slightly milky nougat. Elegant, clean and some delightful hints of moist fruitcake; **t24** its age beats it chest on entry with a distinctive oaky yodel. But the marzipan and ulmo honey mix really does make you purr...; **f22** so, so gentle. A vague hint of something fruity. A gentle statement of spice, more deft vanilla and again a fruitiness which slips through your grasp...; **b24** truly exceptional. *41.6%. sc.*

Glenglassaugh 1978 35 Years Old Batch 1 port hogshead, cask no. 1810, dist 06 Oct 78 db **(93) n23** a slightly feminine perfume, decidedly tangerine and celery-based; **t23.5** so soft on delivery. The oak is old enough to possess a sheen; the barley confident enough to still generate a degree of salivation; **f23** long with the complexity levels rising. The main theme now, though, revolves around cocoa..with a little coconut grated into the mix. The vanilla is strictly Walnut Whip fondant...complete with walnut; **b23.5** one of those quiet, unassuming chaps who takes about half an hour to fully fathom. Worth the effort, though. *42.9%. sc.*

Glenglassaugh 1975 38 Years Old Batch 1 Oloroso sherry hogshead, cask no. 7301, dist 03 Sep 75 db **(94.5) n23.5** entirely intact: the dry, sophisticated grape remains firm and allows only limited passages of oak to intervene. Very gentle; **t23.5** good sugar presence to cap that inherent dryness. The fruits are simple, clean, occasionally salivating and rarely make any effort to steer away from a grape effect; **f23.5** remains dry but spices now buzz in to elongate the finale; **b24** a classy, understated little malt, one that does all it can to pass under the radar,. Sorry – but you've been outed! Also, at its best after being allowed to breathe in glass for a good half hour. *40.7%. sc.*

Glenglassaugh 1975 38 Years Old Batch 1 Moscatel hogshead, cask no. 7801, dist 18 Jun 75, db **(89) n21.5** the grape works hard to polish up some uncomfortable old oak; **t21.5** still lacks shape on delivery and we are several layers in before a milky chocolate embrace comes to its rescue; **f22.5** now comfortable with soft tannins meeting the fruit in the eye; **b22.5** a more voluptuous, expansive version of cask 7301. But in being so, has somewhere lost its finesse and complexity down the line. Oh, not the similarity of the cask numbers: probably from being tucked away in an inaccessible part of an old warehouse... 42.4%. sc.

Glenglassaugh 40 Year Old db (**87.5**) n21.5 t23.5 f21 b21.5. Not entirely sure what it is with this one. I wasn't too happy about my 40th birthday, I remember, and this appears to have had the same mind-set. Hasn't quite extracted some of the better qualities of the oak, so never entirely gets its game together. A few flashy clothes (mainly in the form of a brief outbreak of stunning exotic fruit) and bling. But, underneath, for all its occasionally exotic patter a bit of a dullard, really. And then, maybe late of an evening, when less analytical, I see this in a slightly different light and home in on its good points, jettisoning the bad – then it is worth half a dozen points more. Entirely a mood and/or moment thing. 42.5%.

Glenglassaugh 1973 40 Years Old Batch 1 Manzanilla sherry puncheon, cask no. 6801, dist 05 Dec 73 db (**74**) n22 t20 f15 b17. A particularly lingering and unwanted drying note has gone traipsing over what looks like fabulous sherry. Some lovely fleeting moments, but will be tarnished for some. I was caught off guard on this one due to the overt richness of the nose. 52.1%. sc.

Glenglassaugh 1972 41 Years Old Batch 1 refill sherry butt, cask no. 2114, dist 25 Oct 72 db (**87.5**) n23 t23 f20 b21.5. The nose has the malt's age tattooed in oak across it. But there is big grape with no intention of yielding on delivery and for a while is an essay on style. Sad, then, that it should bitter out on the finish with no less single mindedness. 50.6%. sc.

Glenglassaugh Aged 43 Years db (**91**) n23.5 a nose of rare clarity for its age. Or it is once it has been in the glass for a good 15 minutes. Then the wrinkles vanish and we are left with a vibrant, juicy nose offering a sweetness that runs the full gamut from fruit to biscuit... Not surprisingly there is a death by chocolate feel to this one, too. And even a little smoke; not entire free of the odd gremlin, but not too much damage done; t24 you really don't spit this kind of whisky, however professional you are. Not sure if the silkworm has been bred yet that can produce something as silky as this guy. A few random spices here, a splash of walnut oil there; f21 a slight Achilles heel: some weaknesses show as a mild bitterness leaks in. But I am not quibbling; b22.5 another ridiculously magnificent malt from a distillery which should never have been closed in the first place... 48.7%. nc ncf.

Glenglassaugh 45 Years Old 1968 Batch 1 sherry hogshead, cask no. 1601, dist 07 May 68 db (**96**) n23.5 intense orange peel, almost like that you might find in a gin. Slight spotted dog puddin', though the full blown fruitcake effect slowly grows...with a bit of extra tannin where you hope the Demerara might be...; t23.5...and, likewise, the oak rams a few splinters home early on. But as the oils settle and some sugar does slowly start to sooth, the true story and elegance of this malt can at last be recognised and told... f24.5 what a finish! This is nigh on perfection. Not an off note; barely an atom of detectable sulphur (if it has been touched up in a new cask it, miraculously, got away with it): just outstanding, as it how seems, very lightly smoked, spirit maturing for 45 years in a sherry butt the way they once were and we can only hope against hope will be again one day. Look, and it is there somewhere: a little liquorice and marzipan; black cherries, a squirt of sweetening ulmo honey, Melton Hunt Cake kept in the larder for a good four or five years; vanilla snd butterscotch in small spoon fulls...on and on and on it goes....all the way back to 1968! b24.5 it may be hanging on for grim death at times against the oak, but what emerges is something you'll remember forever. 44.3%. sc.

Glenglassaugh 1973 Family Silver db (**95**) n23 t24 f24 b24. From first to last this whisky caresses and teases. It is old but shows no over-ageing. It offers what appears a malt veneer but is complexity itself. Brilliant. And now, sadly, almost impossible to find. Except, possibly, at the Mansefield Hotel, Elgin. 40%

Glenglassaugh The Chosen Few 1978 db (**94**) n24 the nose of a malt which has seen probably more summers than it should have done. But it has picked up a creamy, orange blossom honey tan along the way; the multiple vanilla tones are seasoned beautifully with a soft saltiness. Enough to make one swoon...; t23 despite the early sugars, the delivery is dominated with over-aged oak: punchy tannins which creak around the palate. Thankfully there is enough spotted dog pudding encased in sugar – and coconut cream – to see off the aged excess; f23.5 settles now with a few spices adding to the sweetened Carnation evaporated milk; b23.5 hate to say it, and almost impossible to believe: but Mhairi McDonald has not seen off the years quite as well as Ronnie Routledge. Even so, still some looker! 46.5%.

Glenglassaugh Evolution Ex-Tennessee Cask db (**87**) n22 crème brule; t22.5 an ever increasing melting degree of muscovado sugars stirred into the vanilla; f21 the fondant of a Walnut Whip battling with some random barley and oak notes; b21.5 a Bambi of a dram, youthfully stumbling around seeking balance with limited success. Interesting: the 10cl sample bottle here tells me only it is ex-Tennessee cask. I'd be willing to bet a wad of this is Dickel over Daniel any day. The giveaway is the fact that the punchier tannins are not in evidence – suggesting older maturation in the US. Nor is the residual oiliness which usually makes its mark. Having said all that, I'm sure someone will now tell me this is a JD cask! 57.2%.

Glenglassaugh Evolution db (85) n21 t22 f21 b21. Cumbersome, oily and sweet, this youngster is still evolving. 50%.

Glenglassaugh Madeira db (93) n23.5 spices rarely come sexier: busy, pulsing and of varying tone and heat; mainly appear to be oak led, though the sultana concentrate makes its mark, also; t23.5 thick grape dulls the expected grape kick; the sugars, at first beaming, are also quickly subdued, though of a lightly molassed style; supremely chewy, though, with just so sugar impact; f22.5 a gorgeous creamy mocha with a tea spoon of molasses; a slightly muffled, furry finale; b23.5 a deliciously rich but surprising malt in that the spices fanfared on the nose never quite arrive. Love it, warts and all. 44.8% nc ncf sc. 437 bottles.

Glenglassaugh The Manager's Legacy No.1 Jim Cryle 1974 db (90.5) n21.5 citrus and various salty, herbal notes try to prop up a crumbling castle as an incoming tide of oak begins to wash it away...; t23.5 where did that come from? Early oak, but then a magnificent recovery in the form of sharp old orange peel and a salty, mega malty thrust. Some dried fruit, mainly old dates and plums, build further bridges and as the saline quality intensifies, the juicier it all becomes; f22.5 long with spices and plenty of cream toffee; b23 talk about blowing away the cobwebs! The nose trumpets all the hallmarks of a tired old malt in decline. What follows on the palate could not be more opposite. Don't you just love a surprise! 52.9%. nc ncf sc.

Glenglassaugh The Manager's Legacy No.2 Dod Cameron 1986 refill sherry butt, dist Dec 86 db (92) n23.5 the sherry residue must have been as thick as tar when they billed this butt: an enormous welter of pithy and juicy grape married with the aroma one might expect at a Fruitcake Fest. The odd roasty bitter note counters the sweeter Demerara tones. Wow! t24 a near perfect delivery with that thick grape arriving hand-in-hand with sublime spices; again a burnt toast bitterness battles it out with some macho sugars; f22 back to a more Dundee cake style, with a few natural caramels thrown in; b23.5 did anyone mention this was from a sherry butt...? A vague, mildly out of kilter, bitterness knocks the odd mark off here and there, but a dram to kick the shoes off to and savour. 45.3%. nc ncf sc. 500 bottles.

Glenglassaugh The Manager's Legacy No.3 Bert Forsyth 1968 db (89) n22 t23 f22 b22. A kind of upside down whisky: usually the big oaks arrive at the death. Here they are all upfront... An excellent whisky that, by rights, should never be... 44.9%. nc ncf sc. 300 bottles.

Glenglassaugh The Manager's Legacy No.4 Walter Grant 1967 refill sherry hogshead, dist May 67 db (86.5) n19.5 t22 f23 b22. Despite the oaky wounds to the nose, the palate is far more open and somehow reaches a degree of depth and complexity which makes for an excellent and unexpected experience. 40.4%. nc ncf sc. 200 bottles.

Glenglassaugh Massandra Connection 1978 35 Years Old Madeira Finish db (94.5) n24.5 the softest and most silky aroma it is possible to imagine. A whisper of buzzing spice reminds you this is a living thing, otherwise you are likely to drift off with the sultry, juicy spices into a happy oblivion; t24 and a delivery to match. The rarest of styles: both velvety on delivery yet broadcasting enough fresh juiciness to leave you in no doubt it means business as far as complexity is concerned. The spices rattle apologetically, the sugars drift towards molasses. Then...a little bitterness...; f22.5 ah, an unwelcome tang on the long, soft finish...; b23.5 last year's Massandra created a rod for its own back, so beguilingly beautiful was it. This one has done all it can, very quietly, though somewhat suavely to live up to the expectation. A marginally less clean-cut cask this time, though. 41.7%.

Glenglassaugh Massandra Connection 1973 41 Years Old Sherry Finish db (86.5) n20.5 t22 f22 b22. Plenty of nibble on this for such a relatively weak cask strength malt. The grape appears to have such a hard time overcoming the obvious tiredness of the cask, it has little scope to draw pretty pictures. Pleasant but borderline austere. 44.5%.

Glenglassaugh Muscat Finish db (94) n23 the nose appears to be hit continuously with an oak stave. The blows are softened only by a thick layer of boiled plums and under-ripe dates; t23.5 salivating to the point of near incontrollable dribbling...as juicy as any malt you'll taste this year. But, unusually, oak-weighted, too, with that sucked back of pencil unmistakable in its sheer woodiness. Even so, it works..beautifully! And not least because of a fabulous mocha, rum and raisin middle; f24 at last softens, though the fruits, aided by lemon-topped marzipan, rumble on; the butterscotch fade is truly classic; b23.5 you'd expect any Muscat finish to be over the top...and it is. Great to see a whisky named after a former Millwall hardman...wasn't it...? 44.1% nc ncf sc. 308 bottles.

Glenglassaugh Red Port db (85) n22 t22 f20 b21. Loads of homemade redcurrant jam on toast here. Excellent texture, good age but an off key finish. 50.2%. nc ncf sc.

Glenglassaugh Revival new, refill and Oloroso sherry casks db (75) n19 t20 f17 b19. Rule number one: if you are going to spend a lot of money to rebuild a distillery and make great whisky, then ensure you put the spirit into excellent oak. Which is why it is best avoiding present day sherry butts at all costs as the chances of running into sulphur is high. There is some stonkingly good malt included in this bottling, and the fabulous chocolate raisin is there to see. But I look forward to seeing a bottling from 100% ex-bourbon. *46%. nc ncf.*

Glenglassaugh Sherry db **(87) n21.5** pure sherry trifle...with an extra dollop of custard; **t22.5** rampant tannins are impressively quelled by a viscous layer of clean, unambiguous sherry which, after untangling, offers greengage and spice; **f21** long, with those oak notes calming down into gentler cocoa tones; no shortage of raisin, too...; **b22** at first the sherry is over dominant, but once it relaxes the complexity and enjoyment levels rise. Technically, a bit of a nightmare. But the impact of the sherry is compelling. *53.3% nc ncf sc. 328 bottles.*

Glenglassaugh The Spirit Drink db **(85) n20 t22 f21.5 b21.5**. A pretty wide margin taken on the cut here, it seems, so there is plenty to chew over. Richly flavoured and a tad oily, as is to be expected, which helps the barley to assert itself in midstream. The usual new make chocolaty element at work here, too, late on. Just great to see this distillery back in harness after all these years. And a great idea to get the new spirit out to the public, something I have been encouraging distilleries to do since my beard was still blue. Look forward to seeing another version where a narrower cut has been made. *50%. 8,160 bottles.*

Glenglassaugh The Spirit Drink Fledgling XB db **(91) n22 t23.5 f22.5 b23**. The barley arrives unblemished and makes a proud, juicy stand. A surprising degree of early natural caramel. Prefer this over the peat, to be honest, and augers well for the distillery's future. *50%*

Glenglassaugh The Spirit Drink Peated db **(89.5) n22 t23 f22 b22.5**. Enjoyable and doesn't appear close to its 50%abv. But it's not about the bite, for there is a welcome citrus freshness to this, helped along the way by a peatiness which is big but by no means out to be the only important voice. *50%*

Glenglassaugh The Spirit Drink That Blushes to Speak Its Name db **(85) n22 t21.5 f21 b21**. Not whisky, of course. New make matured for a few months in wine barrels. The result is a Rose-looking spirit. Actually takes me back to my early childhood – no, not the tasting of new make spirit. But the redcurrant aroma which does its best to calm the new make ruggedness. Tasty and fascinating, though the wine tries to minimalise the usual sweetness you find in malt spirit. *50%*

Glenglassaugh Torfa db **(90) n23.5** not stinting on the phenols: the peat appears to have been shovelled into the furnace like a fireman feeding coals to the Flying Scotsman; **t22.5** crisp, sugary delivery with some meaningful smoke layering. Some Parma Violet candy nuzzles alongside the treacle-cocnut; **f22** good phenolic grist fade; **b22** appears happy and well suited in its new smoky incarnation. *50%.*

◈ **Anam na h-Alba The Soul of Scotland Glenglassaugh 1978** port hogshead, dist 06 Oct 78, bott 28 Jan 15 **(90.5) n23.5** complex. The oak is a tad tired, but the light ulmo honey-marzipan-coconut-Jameson Raspberry Ruffles Chocolate bar (nothing to do with the whiskey!) more than makes amends; **t21.5** sharp delivery, a little wobbly until the grape takes a more even road; **f23** that's more like it: the fruit is now soft and graceful, allowing the barley and butterscotch plenty of legroom; **b22.5** age is creeping in. But retains a touch of class. And not a sulphur atom in sight... *41.9%. 310 bottles.*

GLENGOYNE
Highlands (Southwest), 1833. Ian Macleod Distillers. Working.

Glengoyne 10 Years Old db **(90) n22** beautifully clean despite coal-gas bite. The barley is almost in concentrate form with a marmalade sweetness adding richness; **t23** crisp, firm arrival with massive barley surge, seriously chewy and textbook bitter-sweet balance; but now some oils have tucked in to intensify and lengthen; **f22** incredibly long and refined for such a light malt. The oak, which made soft noises in the middle now intensifies, but harmonises with the intense barley; an added touch of coffee signals some extra oak in recent bottlings; **b23** proof that to create balance you do not have to have peat at work. The secret is the intensity of barley intertwangling with oak. Not a single negative note from first to last and now a touch of oil and coffee has upped the intensity further. *40%*

Glengoyne 12 Years Old db **(91.5) n22.5** salty, sweet, lightly fruity; **t23** one of the softest deliveries on the market: the fruit, gristy sugars and malt combine to melt in the mouth: there is not a single hint of firmness; **f23** a graduation of spices and vanilla. Delicate and delightful...; **b23** the nose has a curiously intimate feel but the tasting experience is a wonderful surprise. *43%*

Glengoyne 12 Years Old Cask Strength db **(79) n18 t22 f19 b20**. Not quite the happiest Glengoyne I've ever come across with the better notes compromised. *57.2%. nc ncf.*

Glengoyne Aged 14 Years Limited Edition oloroso cask db **(77) n19 t20 f19 b19**. A vague sulphur taint. But rather underpowered anyway. *40%. nc. Marks & Spencer UK.*

Glengoyne 15 Years Old db **(73.5)** n18 t19 f18 b18.5. Some sub-standard, left-out-in-the-rain oak crept in from somewhere. Ouch. 40%. *Travel Retail exclusive.*

Glengoyne 15 Years sherry casks db **(81)** n19 t20 f21 b21. Brain-numbingly dull and heavily toffeed in style. Just don't get what is trying to be created here. Some late spices remind me I'm awake, but still the perfect dram to have before bed – simply to send you to sleep. Or maybe I just need to see a Doctor... *43%. nc. Ian Macleod Distillers.*

Glengoyne 17 Years Old db **(86)** n21 t23 f21 b21. Some of the guys at Glengoyne think I'm nuts. They couldn't get their head around the 79 I gave it last time. And they will be shaking my neck not my hand when they see the score here...Vastly improved but there is an off sherry tang which points to a naughty butt or two somewhere. Elsewhere mouth-watering and at times fabulously intense. *43%*

Glengoyne 18 Years first-fill sherry casks db **(82)** n22 t22 f18 b20. Bunches of lush grape on nose and delivery, where there is no shortage of caramel. But things go downhill once the dreaded "s" word kicks in. *43%. nc. Ian Macleod Distillers.*

Glengoyne 21 Years Old db **(90)** n21 closed and tight for the most part as Glengoyne sometimes has a tendency to be nose-wise, with the emphasis very much on coal gas; t22 slow to start with a few barley heads popping up to be seen; then spices arrive with the oak for a slightly bourbony feel. Gentle butterscotch and honey add a mouth-watering edge to the drier oaks; f24 a stupendous honey thread is cross-stitched through the developing oak to deliver near perfect poise and balance at finish; b23 a vastly improved dram where the caramel has vanished and the tastebuds are constantly assailed and questioned. A malt which builds in pace and passion to delivery a final, wonderful coup-de-grace. Moments of being quite cerebral stuff. *43%*

Glengoyne 21 Years Old Sherry Edition db **(93)** n22 t24 f23 b24. The nose at first is not overly promising, but it settles at it warms and what follows on the palate is at times glorious. Few whiskies will match this for its bitter-sweet depth which is pure textbook. Glengoyne as few will have seen it before. *43%*

⬦ **Glengoyne 25 Year Old** db **(95.5)** n24 an old-fashioned, sopping-with-oloroso nose, resplendent in orange peel and molasses; t24.5 voluptuous and curvy in all the right places, hard not to be turned on by a delivery like this. Being pedantic, the sherry is slightly OTT and two decades ago I would have marked this down as being a little too gushing in grape. But such is the rarity of finding un-ruined sherry butts at work, one is easily tempted to turn a blind eye and just enjoy this soaking-moist fruitcake moment; f22.5 slightly bitter as the ancient tannins begin to dig in; b23.5 a beautiful sherry-matured malt from the pre-cock up sulphur days. Not a single off note of note and a reminder of what a sherry cask malt meant to those of us who were involved in whisky a quarter of a century ago... *48% WB16/042*

Glengoyne 40 Years Old db **(83)** n23 t21 f19 b20. Thick fruit intermittently pads around the nose and palate but the oak is pretty colossal. Apparent attempts to reinvigorate it appear to have backfired. *45.9%*

Glengoyne Cask Strength batch no. 002 db **(85.5)** n20 t23.5 f20.5 b21.5. Perhaps only the single slightly off-key cask has found its way into this. But it plays out far better on the palate than it does the nose, though you get the feeling that there is a grinding in the gears as it tries to run through its set-pieces. Love the lilting richness of the delivery, though, with its honey concentrate and bubbling, jammy fruit. A spicy chap, too. So close to a classic. *58.9%. nc. WB15/119*

⬦ **Glengoyne Cask Strength** batch 003 db **(81)** n19 t20 f20 b20. Dull, disjointed, a tad furry and bitter. Though at cask strength, refuses to fire on all cylinders. *58.2%*

Glengoyne Port Cask Finish 1996 db **(74)** n17 t20 f18.5 b18.5. Decent fruit on delivery, but elsewhere proof that in whisky there is no such thing as any port cask in a storm... *46%*

Glengoyne Teapot Dram db **(86.5)** n23 t22 f20.5 b21. The nose, for its obvious fault, still has a truly classic oloroso-style depth. However, the light sulphur stain is not so easily covered up once tasted. A slightly cracked teapot, I'm afraid. *58.8%. nc ncf. Distillery exclusive.*

Glengoyne Vintage 1996 db **(70)** n16 t18 f18 b18. Creamy, but off key. *43%. nc ncf. USA.*

Glengoyne Vintage 1997 db **(68)** n16 t18 f17 b17. The "S" word strikes. And with a vengeance. *43%. nc ncf. German release.*

Glengoyne 'Glen Guin' 16 Year Old Shiraz Finish db **(79)** n18.5 t20 f19.5 b20. Some oily depth here. *48%*

Glengoyne Burnfoot db **(84)** n21 t21 f21.5 b21. A clodhopping bruiser of a malt. Good honey, though. *40%. Duty Free Market.*

Hepburn's Choice Glengoyne Aged 7 Years sherry butt, dist 07, bott 14 **(84.5)** n21 t22.5 f21 b20. Less new make and more embryo malt. This must have been not only filled into a third fill cask but kept for seven years at the bottom of the warehouse. But apart from the wobbly nose, this youngest-ever seven-year-old ever bottled still charms with its Nesquik banana milkshake sweetness and the vivid beauty of its all-round maltiness. *46%. nc ncf sc. 774 bottles.*

Ian Macleod Glengoyne 25 Years Old db **(94.5)** n23 the grape may be a little tight but the marmalade really comes into its own: bursting with hints of spice and no more, as well as ground toasted hazelnuts; **t24** sumptuous delivery which gets increasingly more salivating as the grape plot thickens; some toasty depth, but only for a little more marmalade to be spread over it...just so beautifully weighted...; **f23.5** now really upping the spiciness, but also a late butterscotch and crème brule signature...showing the oaks have more to say than just something spicy; light oils keep the elegance levels on a high; **b24** by far and away the best Glengoyne sherry butts I have come across for a very long time. One worth tracking down. *48%.*

Old Malt Cask Glengoyne Aged 16 Years refill hogshead, cask no. 10302, dist Sep 97, bott Feb 14 **(86)** n21 t22 f21 b22. Doesn't even try to tax you with matters regarding complexity and shape. Simply dolls out gristy, sugar-coated malt by the cask-load with rich intensity, but in a cask which offers scant support. *50%. sc. 285 bottles.*

◈ **Old Particular Highland Glengoyne 17 Years Old** refill hogshead, cask no. 10697, dist Sept 97, bott Feb 15 **(86.5)** n21 t22 f21.5 b22. An unusual firmness to the barley for this distillery with a degree of hickory as the only clue to its age. *48.4%. nc ncf sc. 348 bottles.*

◈ **Premier Barrel Selection Glengoyne Aged 7 Years (85)** n20 t22 f21.5 b21.5. An exceptionally well made malt with a starburst of salivating young, gristy barley. The cask has hardly moved the maturation on at all but a real sugar-laden, chewy mouthful for all that. Some seriously sticky oils late on the finish. *46%. nc ncf sc. 863 bottles.*

◈ **Provenance Glengoyne Over 7 Years** refill hogshead, cask no. 10566, dist Spring 07, bott Autumn 14 **(82)** n21 t21 f20 b20. Here's a malt to make your eyes water! So young, it's voice is yet to break, and although there is distinct new spirit feel to this, just enough natural caramel to give it a presence. *46%. nc ncf sc.*

◈ **Scotch Malt Whisky Society Cask 123.9 Aged 16 Years** 1st fill butt, dist 9 Jul 98 **(93)** n23 has someone poured me a Harvey's Bristol Cream...? **t24** No, because, unlike the nose, a distinctive malty note mixes with the thick oloroso; **f23** a little bitterness kicks in, but no discernible taint. Spices abound and we are now firmly in mocha territory now, as well as Cadbury's Fruit and Nut...; **b23** one that slipped through the net at Jerez: no sulphur spoil whatsoever. Unusual for this distillery. *56.6%. sc. 608 bottles.*

◈ **Scotch Malt Whisky Society Cask 123.10 Aged 9 Years** 1st fill barrel, dist 5 May 05 **(86.5)** n22 t22 f21 b21.5. The outline of this malt will take those of us long enough in the tooth back about quarter of century when Glengoyne made a fuss about being an unpeated malt – and that all their oak was ex-bourbon. An annoying bitterness creeps in though just to stifle the barley as it was getting into full flow. *57.6%. sc. 238 bottles.*

◈ **Scotch Malt Whisky Society Cask 123.11 Aged 9 Years** 1st fill barrel, dist 5 May 05 **(95.5)** n23.5 subtle and understated: the barley thinks it has the upper hand, but the gentle sawdusty tones of oak fade in to diminish the sharpness: sublime in its simplicity; **t24** again, it is the barley which gets off to a flyer: both juicy yet with a much thicker undertone it only slowly allows in citrus and a spicy buzz which morphs into a drier, biscuity oakiness; **f23.5** ridiculously long for a malt which pretends to be so slight. The barley just keeps on going, eventually becoming buttery, though with added sugar rather than salt. The last piping spicy notes are truly classic; **b24.5** a malt which grows into its task, its complexity....and greatness. A minor gem. *57%. sc. 231 bottles.*

◈ **Whisky Tales Glengoyne Aged 15 Years** sherry cask, dist 1998, bott 2014 **(83)** n22.5 t23 f18.5 b19. What a quite extraordinary malt. For a start, any semblance to this being whisky has been almost 100% obliterated by the overwhelming indulgency of the sherry itself, presumably oloroso, of which I suspect some was still in the cask when this was bottled. Yes, the finish is bitter and unkempt and there is hardly any balance to speak of. But it is hard not to enjoy the outrageous richness of the cold coffee nose and the fruit infested delivery. *51%. nc ncf sc. 289 bottles.*

GLEN GRANT
Speyside, 1840. Campari. Working.

Glen Grant db **(87)** n21.5 t23 f21 b21.5. This is a collector's malt for the back label alone: truly one of the most bizarre I have ever seen. "James Grant, 'The Major'" it cheerfully chirrups, "was only 25 when he set about achieving his vision of a single malt with a clear colour. The unique flavour and appearance was due to the purifiers and the tall slender stills he designed and the decision to retain its natural colour…" Then underneath is written: "Farven Justeter Med Karamel/Mit Farbstoff"" Doh! Or, as they say in German: "Doh!" Need any more be said about the nonsense, the pure insanity, of adding colouring to whisky. 40%

Glen Grant 5 Years Old db **(89) n22.5 t22 f21.5 b23.** Elegant malt which has noticeably grown in stature and complexity of late. 40%

Glen Grant Aged 10 Years db **(96) n23.5** OK: let's take turns in counting the rungs on the barley ladder here….the usual crisp aroma, but softened by deft, if unspecific fruitiness (maybe the distant aroma of a very old orange and by no means unpleasant!), myriad vanilla and butterscotch notes can do without the toffee one; **t24** magnificent! A malty delivery which simultaneously melts in the mouth, yet offers granite-like barley that crashes into your teeth; the star, perhaps are the sugars which vary from caster, through golden syrup and pans out somewhere in the muscovado range – curiously honey-free, though; **f23.5** a tad tangy, though the caramel returns to turn out the lights after the butterscotch and marzipan say goodnight..; **b24** unquestionably the best official 10-y-o distillery bottling I have tasted from this distillery. Absolutely nails it! Oh, and had they bottled this at 46% abv and without the trimmings…my word! Might well have been a contender for Scotch of the Year. It won't be long before word finally gets around about just how bloody good this distillery is. 40% ⊙ ⊙

Glen Grant Aged 16 Years bott Mar 10 db **(91.5) n23** a lovely under-ripe banana sharpness to this while the malt snuggles up to the crunchy green apple; a playful molecule of smoke wafts around; t23.5 salivating, fresh, slightly green …and that's just the first few nano-seconds of the delivery! Next comes a lengthy, relaxed wave of oilier barley, with a coppery, honeyed depth; tangy vanilla fills the middle ground; **f21.5** medium length, more oils and barley but with a degree of bitterness; **b22** again the finish doesn't do justice to the earlier jousting on the nose and palate. The label talks about orchard fruits, and they are absolutely spot on. Apples are order of the day, but not sure about the ripe bit: they appear slightly green to me… and that suits the nature of the crisp malt. A gorgeous whisky I fully expect to see improve over coming batches: it's one that has potential to hit superstar status. 43%

Glen Grant Distillery Edition Cask Strength Aged 20 Years cask no. 17165, dist 12 Feb 92, bott 14 Aug 12 db **(95.5) n23.5** oranges and roasted hazelnuts…and distant peat…?; **t24** busy delivery but the improbable smoke on the nose is confirmed on the palate, the peats clinging to the oils on which barley, as usual, abounds. More marmalade which works well with the buttery element. Amazing shape and complexity, all helped by the usual, unique clarity of this glorious distillery; **f23.5** so, so long, with the spices picking up where the smoke leaves off; cream jam doughnuts come to mind late on; **b24.5** I can only assume that this was matured in a cask which once held a high phenol Islay. The underlying peat is as intriguing as it is delicious! Glen Grant as you may never have seen it before…and will definitely want to see again. 55.7%.

Glen Grant 40 Year Old db **(83.5) n22.5 t21 f20 b20.** Probably about ten summers too may. The nose threatens an oakfest, though there are enough peripheral sugars for balance and hope. Sadly, on the palate the cavalry never quite gets there. 40%.

Glen Grant Cellar Reserve 1992 bottled 2008 db **(94.5) n23 t24 f24 b23.5.** One of the great world distilleries being revealed to the us in its very finest colours. They tend to be natural, with no colourings added, therefore allowing the extraordinary kaleidoscope of subtle sweetnesses to be deployed and enjoyed to their fullest. I defy you not to be blown away by this one, especially when you realise there is not a single big base note to be heard… 46%. nc ncf.

Glen Grant 50 Year Old db **(96.5) n24** heavyweight malt: toasted hazelnut and fruit combine with ridiculous ease; the spryness of the spice is amazing; a few old black cherries bob around on the breeze; **t24** silky delivery with early oak signs, but these are little more than polite enquiries. Delicate molasses and black cherry combine to match the drier elements of the oak; half way through, a surprising blast of juicy malt pierces the darkness; **f24** like on delivery, the weight of the piece is extraordinary: near perfect, in fact. Just a slight hint of smoke for the first time and this sits well with the chocolate and cherry pie served up with cream on the finish. Naturally, a little treacle is mixed in for effect; **b24.5** I really don't know how G&M keep coming up with these golden oldies. The quality of the oak must have been pretty exceptional. Sexier than any 50-year-old has the right to be. For those celebrating their 50th birthday or wedding…well you'd only regret it if you missed out. 40%

Glen Grant 170th Anniversary db **(89) n23.5 t23.5 f20 b22.** The odd mildly sulphured cask has slipped through the net here to reduce what was shaping to be something magnificent. Still enjoyable, though. 46%

Glen Grant Five Decades bott 2013 db **(92) n24** the kind of aroma which leaves you transfixed: the trademark crisp, juicy barley is there in force, but the darker, deeper tones rumble with a spiced orange lead: sublimely complex; **t23.5** the delivery is full of the usual malty zest for life. There is a unique clarity to the barley of Glen Grant and here, on delivery and for a few a few moments after, this goes into overdrive. The mid ground is more muddled with tannin and burnt raisin making their presence felt; **f21.5** tangy marmalade; **b23** a nose and delivery of astonishing complexity. Hardly surprising the fade cannot keep up the pace. 46%

Glen Grant The Major's Reserve bott Mar 10 db **(85.5) n21.5 t23 f20 b21.** Forget about the so-so nose and finish. This is one of those drams that demands you melt into your chair on delivery, such is the fresh beauty of the malt and stunning honeycomb threads which tie themselves around every taste bud. Pity about the ultra dry, caramel-rich finish, but apparently nearly all the sherry butts have now been used up at the distillery. Thank gawd for that. 40%

Cadenhead's Small Batch Glen Grant-Glenlivet Aged 15 Years bourbon hogsheads, dist 97, bott 13 **(88) n23** unusually oily. Fresh malt, still with a hint of green grassiness; **t22.5** oils apparent early on delivery; malt and icing sugar evolve at equal rate; Madeira cake oakiness hits mid-ground; **f21** bitters and dries slightly; **b21.5** usually a crisp, brittle malt, this is the oiliest from this distillery I've seen for at least a decade. 46%. 924 bottles. WB15/265

◈ **Cadenhead's Small Batch Glen Grant Aged 24 Years** sherry butt **(94.5) n23** not a single off note from the fruit, thus revealing a rare unsullied sherry butt. The spices are polite and try not to raise themselves above the malt- toasted sultana mix; **t24** a delivery to die for: not sure if the weight of a whisky can be any more sexy or alluring than this. Silky malt enjoys an outstanding balance between gristy remnants and lightly toasted oak; Lubeck marzipan waits in the nutty wings and a little ulmo honey attaches itself to the light sultana; **f23.5** a pathetic attempt to dry and die is thwarted by the beautiful seams of sugar and busy spice; **b24** great malt in an outstanding sherry butt. So clean, you won't even need to wash your glass afterwards... 55.5%

Cadenhead's Authentic Collection Glen Grant Cask Strength Aged 24 Years bourbon barrel, dist 1989, bott Oct 13 **(83.5) n21.5 t21.5 f20.5 b20.** Glen Grant, as Gordon & MacPhail have shown continuously for the last three decades, can be bottled at very great age with very great success. Sometimes, though, a mixing of casks is required to keep the bolder oak influences at bay. Here we have a cask that was probably too good for long termism. The degree of tannin has thrown out of kilter all else and balance has vanished from the map. There are some major marmalade moments as well as some sugar-spice interplay. But this is a tweezers whisky... 58%. 156 bottles. WB15/084

The First Editions Glen Grant 1994 Aged 19 Years refill hogshead, dist 1994, bott 2014 **(93.5) n23** oak plays a deft hand here, merely offering a drying chain to shackle the lively barley; **t24** hard to imagine a Speysider being more Speyside-like at this age. So clean you can almost polish your teeth with it. How the sugars and barley appear to be in such perfect harmony is a wonder to behold; **f23.5** much more inclined to vanilla; **b23.5** a malty study in crunchy sugars. Adorable. 55.5%. nc ncf sc. 256 bottles.

Gordon & MacPhail Distillery Label Glen Grant 40 Year Old (83.5) n22.5 t21 f20 b20. Probably about ten summers too many. The nose threatens an oakfest, though there are enough peripheral sugars for balance and hope. Sadly, on the palate the cavalry never quite gets there. 40%

Gordon & MacPhail Distillery Label Glen Grant 50 Year Old (96.5) n24 heavyweight malt: toasted hazelnut and fruit combine with ridiculous ease; the spryness of the spice is amazing; a few old black cherries bob around on the breeze; **t24** silky delivery with early oak signs, but these are little more than polite enquiries. Delicate molasses and black cherry combine to match the drier elements of the oak; half way through, a surprising blast of juicy malt pierces the darkness; **f24** like on delivery, the weight of the piece is extraordinary: near perfect, in fact. Just a slight hint of smoke for the first time and this sits well with the chocolate and cherry pie served up with cream on the finish. Naturally, a little treacle is mixed in for effect; **b24.5** I really don't know how G&M keep coming up with these golden oldies. The quality of the oak must have been pretty exceptional. Sexier than any 50-year-old has the right to be. For those celebrating their 50th birthday or wedding...well you'd only regret it if you missed out. 40%

Gordon & MacPhail Glen Grant 1948 66 Year Old cask no. 1369 **(96) n24** improbably charming and delicate after all this time: a light caress of smoke helps you to forgive any over eagerness by the oak – the tannin is confident but softened not just by the smoke but a gentle marmalade sharpness; **t24** an immediate puff of smoke on delivery is a fabulous time machine to take you back to a day when Speyside malts were smokier and more fuller bodied than they are today. Aping the nose, the tannins are next through, and for a few moments are sharp, aggressive almost, and threaten to spoil the party. But, like on the nose, they are reigned back, this time by a delicious milk chocolate, though only after there has been a telling burst of molasses to ensure there will be enough sweetness for the duration; **f23.5** long, with the oak threat now falling silent thanks to a spent, rounded feel one often finds in very old rum casks in South America. The compensation is a delicate, gently sweetened mocha which leaves a gorgeous, tang-less and clean last impression; **b24.5** when this was being made, my parents were getting married (they had me late!), Millwall were in the process of being relegated from the second tier under the auspices of manager Jack Cock and the Ealing classic, Whisky Galore, was being filmed on Barra. So what better whisky to choose as my 1,111 new dram for the 2015 Bible? Hearty congratulations to Gordon and MacPhail – and the extraordinary Glen Grant distillery, and those hardy, war-bitten souls who made this malt two generations ago – on somehow defying the odds and logic and, 66 years on, giving us a whisky experience which leaves you cooing with delight. My last little taste shall be to those lost men of Glen Grant distillery, 1948. I salute your memories, sirs, fittingly with your very own magnificent craftwork. *46.6%. sc.*

Hepburn's Choice Glen Grant 2004 Aged 10 Years refill hogshead, dist 2004, bott 2014 **(88) n22.5** sound barley enlivened by citrus; **t22.5** young and youthful – a few years below its actual age. But the barley is crisp, profound, clean and just so enjoyable... **f21** just a little tangy from the half-hearted oak; **b22** a distillery which rarely disappoints....even in probably a third-fill cask. *46%. nc ncf sc. 390 bottles.*

The Maltman Glen Grant Aged 17 Years bourbon cask **(95) n23** fabulous: crisp and flinty as type, yet somehow radiates the malt beautifully, allowing the fresh greenness to intermingle with both the drier, chalkier oak and a more cereal-rich maltiness: just so understated! **t24.5** salivating barley appears rampant on three or four different levels of intensity and sweetness. Seemingly simple, yet for a Speysider just about all you can ask of it...; **f23.5** the malt pulses with a little salt taking the sharpness of the grains higher than the delicate oak; **b24** can't help wondering if this distillery provides the perfect Speyside malt... *46% WB15/219*

Old Malt Cask Glen Grant Aged 18 Years refill hogshead, cask no.9920, dist Apr 95, bott Aug 13 **(94.5) n24.5** wow...so subtle and sexy. This could charm its way into the stoniest heart. Perhas by being both more flinty with the barley and more delicate with the citrus than nearly any other malt you might find this year. One to dab behind the ears, if not drink...; **t23.5** simplistically sexy and salivating. The barley really has much to say; **f23** a slow realisation of spices; **b23.5** now, find any whisky refusenik who condemns whisky out of hand and if, after a mouthful or three of this, they cannot be shewn the error of their misguided ways then they deserve a life of Cognac and vodka... *50%. nc ncf sc. 178 bottles.*

Old Particular Speyside Glen Grant Aged 18 Years refill hogshead, cask no. 10283, dist Apr 95, bott Mar 14 **(94) n23.5** deft smoke, rather unlike a Glen Grant, may be the ghostly echoes from an old Islay cask. But the firmness of the grain and crispness of sugars confirms, indubitably, which distillery this hails from; **t24.5** a truly textbook delivery. The clarity of the malt, oak and orbiting sugars cannot be truer, reflected in the extraordinary salivating qualities it displays. The barley appears to be polished and cleaned to a startling degree; meanwhile the crunchiness of the sugars presents the oaks in their most dignified light; **f22.5** medium length but always precise and crisp, with a late vaguely smoky fade; **b23.5** a scary malt: quite beautiful – yet without ever seeming to try. *48.4%. nc ncf sc. 282 bottles.*

◈ **Old Particular Speyside Glen Grant 20 Years Old** refill hogshead, cask no. 10703, dist Oct 94, bott Feb 15 **(94) n23.5** even after all these years, a charming youthfulness persists; **t24** beautiful enough to make you groan aloud! Such subtlety to the barley, offering a juicy introduction but with layers of firmer barley below. The oak enters by a back door which, despite the age, doesn't creak; **f23** stunning Brazilian biscuit and just enough oil to broadcast the last gristy sweetness as far as possible. A slow build of sizzling spice reminds you the oak still has much to say; **b23.5** so right for so many reasons... *51.5%. nc ncf sc. 270 bottles.*

◈ **Scotch Malt Whisky Society Cask 9.100 Aged 12 Years** 1st fill barrel, dist 21 Aug 02 **(89) n23.5** a curious mix of sandalwood and Victorian polished oak floors leaves no doubt which path this malt has followed; **t23.5** an early blast of salivating barley and massively spiced oak make for a monumental entry. The oak carries on piling on the weight...; **f20.5** very dry with a failed attempt of muscovado and cocoa to make an impression; the spice continues; **b21.5** doubtlessly excellent malt. But, for me, second fill bourbon tends to show this distillery in its most dazzling light. The dryness to the finale underlines how easily it is to overcook genius: was probably at its prime aged about seven or eight. *59.9%. sc. 215 bottles.*

Scotch Malt Whisky Society Cask 9.77 Aged 25 Years refill butt, dist 25 May 88 **(79) n19 t20 f20 b20.** Off key, tangy and a little hot. *56.9%. nc ncf sc.*

Scotch Malt Whisky Society Cask 9.85 Aged 16 Years dist 03 May 97 **(94.5) n23.5** defies the years with oak-repellent barley. Fresh, clean and crisp; **t24** the delivering sugars boast an almost bourbon quality, though the barley which engulfs slams home the pedigree; spices fill the mid-ground; **f23.5** one of the better finishes of any Speyside of this age. There are enough sugars in the bank to let in the oak, sluice-like, for a tapering, high quality finale; **b23.5** a deceptively complex malt very at home at this good age. *55.3%. nc ncf sc. 290 bottles.*

The Single Malts of Scotland Glen Grant Aged 22 Years bourbon barrel, cask no. 35936, dist 13 Mar 92, bott 25 Mar 14 **(94) n22** bit of a slovenly nose: lazy malt with a half-hearted attempt to generate spice and complexity; **t24.5** yes...!!! That's more like it: pure Glen Grant! The mixed sugars explode simultaneously with the barley on impact. The usual firmness is rammed home, making the sensation almost unique to this delivery. As the spices settle a vague hint of smoke forms, then a succession of treacle and spiced liquorice; **f23.5** long with a fabulous singed feel: treacle on overdone toast. Some oils surface from somewhere and spread an ulmo and manuka honey mix to the finish; **b24** talk about mixed messages! The nose gives no hint of the magic to be unleashed on the palate. A true stunner. *578%. WB15/295*

That Boutique-y Whisky Glen Grant batch 1 (91) n21.5 rather un Glen Grant-y kind of nose: uncharacteristically yielding in part, though the mix of green malt and butterscotch is familiar to the blending lab; **t24** delivery of the day so far: a starburst of ultra clean salivating malt, seemingly intensified by the unusual oils and icing sugar; **f22.5** slightly tangy as the oak make inroads but the barley pulses; **b23** has loosened its belt and nowhere near as starched as normal. But that delivery...wow!! *50.1%. 138 bottles. WB15/210*

Wemyss Malts 1995 Single Speyside Glen Grant "In a Bluebell Wood" bott 14 **(88.5) n22** surprisingly hefty oak. A few toasted almond, marmalade on toast and fudge notes offer balance; **t23** eye-watering impact. The oak really does come at you. But a concentrated gristy sweetness counters, getting the ol' saliva glands going; **f21.5** dries a tad too austerely; decent late spice; **b22** such a good distillery that, even when a cask struggles to live up to its normal standards, still has enough quality and surprises in the locker to make for a lovely dram. *46%. sc.*

GLENGYLE
Campbeltown, 2004. J&A Mitchell & Co. Working.

Kilkerran Single Malt db **(80) n19 t20 f21 b20.** Glyngyle's first offering doesn't rip up any trees. And maybe the odd flaw to its character that you won't see when the distillery is fine-tuned. But this is the first-ever bottling from this brand new Campbeltown distillery and therefore its chances of being a worldbeater as an untried and untested 3-y-o were pretty slim. I will be watching its development with relish. And with heart pounding... *46%.*

Kilkerran Single Malt bott 22 May 07 db **(84) n20 t21 f22 b21.** Sadly, I was out of the country and couldn't attend the Coming of Age of Kilkerran, when its first casks turned three and became whisky. Very kindly, they sent me a bottle as if I was there and, therefore, these are the notes of the very first bottling handed out to visitors. Interestingly, there is a marked similarity in distillery style to the 46% bottling in that the malt offers a crescendo of quality. This is only three year old whisky, of course, and its fingerprints will alter as it spends longer in the cask. *62%. nc ncf.*

Kilkerran 'Work in Progress' db **(88) n22.5 t22 f21.5 b22.** Doing very well. *46%*

Kilkerran Work In Progress 5 Bourbon Wood db **(90.5) n22.5** dry, toasty phenols sweetened by a smattering of smoky grist; **t23.5** takes a few waves, but finally the sugars are unleashed and rain down as crisp Demarara; the smoke swirls around placidly, though there is a slightly acidic bite to the peat; **f22** medium length, delicately smoked with a milky mocha fade; **b22.5** that ever-decreasing number of us who were around when Port Ellen could be tasted as a bit of a youngster will immediately spot more than the odd passing similarity. *46%. WB15/098*

Kilkerran Work In Progress 5 Sherry Wood db **(86) n21 t22.5 f21 b21.5.** Sometimes you can have too much of a good thing. Almost a form of smoke and grape cancelling the other up, leaving the path for some powerful sugars to look pretty but do little for the balance. *46%. WB15/097*

Kilkerran Work In Progress 6 Bourbon Wood db **(92.5) n23.5** the peat is more astringent and demanding: tighter with less will to share the limelight with the sweeter elements, though it does allow a firm and clean fruit note entry; **t23** mouth filling with both soft oils and then puffs of peat reek; sharp and angular on the palate despite the oil, it is obvious the peat is both of a high phenol content but of a singular bent; the muscovado sugars slowly leek into the plot, but they seem controlled; **f22.5** pulsing spices as the smoke keeps its foot on the throat of the sugars; **b23.5** an intriguing dram offering a style of peated malt like nowhere else in Scotland. Where WIP 5 had something of the Port Ellen about it, this has no such pretentions. Austere and disciplined, the precision of the sugar and fruit is a thing at which to marvel. *46%. WB15/100*

Kilkerran Work In Progress 6 Sherry Wood db **(88.5) n21.5** whoosh!!! The peat is slapped on over the undercoat of grape; **t23** the phenols must be nearing record level for Campbeltown because the poor old sherry is a-hollorin'-an'-a-shoutin'...and you can barely hear a thing; **f22** busy spice amid the smoke; **b22** less lugubrious than WIP5, and though things here are painted with a wallpaper brush, there is some fun to be had for sure. 46%. WB15/099

GLEN KEITH
Speyside, 1957. Chivas Brothers. Working (re-opened 14th June 2013).

Glen Keith 10 Years Old db (80) n22 t21 f18 b19. A malty if thin dram that finishes with a whimper after an impressively refreshing, grassy start. 43%

Cadenhead's Single Cask Glen Keith-Glenlivet Aged 29 Years bourbon hogshead, dist 85, bott 14 (93.5) n24 lightly salted ginger beer and sandalwood; even a light hint of smoke; a stratum of peach, lychee and over-ripe papaya underscores the big age; t24 a yummy delivery full of oaky vim of a mainly herbal kind. The tannins bite hard but cannot get further than the treacle and maple syrup which accompanies the barley sugar; a soft, vaguely smoky buzz of spice; f22 long, a little bitter but the toffee plays out attractively; b23.5 offers great age for a GK but without too many recriminations. So complex... 47.5%. 108 bottles. WB15/257

Gordon & MacPhail Connoisseurs Choice Glen Keith dist 1996, bott 2013 (86) n21 t21.5 f22 b21.5. Puckering, juicy malt and lemon zest. A well used cask means Keith just never grew up... 46%. nc ncf. WB15/148

◇ **Gordon & MacPhail Connoisseurs Choice Glen Keith 1997** (92) n22 profound oak kept honest by fudgy maple syrup; t23.5 huge delivery: the sugars – mainly manuka honey – politely go first to cushion the oaky impact. But some sublime mocha notes filter through, with praline for good measure; a little dry molasses; excellent bite; f23 though you are picking splinters from between your teeth, those rich molasses notes do their job brilliantly; b23.5 for those who like some whisky in the oak. That said, those oaky sugars make for one massive and delicious dram. 46%

◇ **Master of Malt Single Cask Glen Keith 19 Year Old** dist 8 Nov 95, bott 30 Mar 15 (82) n21 t21 f20 b20. More tangy second hand and second class cask spoiling the show. The barley tries to sparkle, but the battle is unequal. 56.6%. sc. 192 bottles.

◇ **Old Malt Cask Glen Keith 18 Year Old** refill hogshead, cask no. 11405, dist May 97, bott May 15 (84.5) n21 t23 f19.5 b21. Recovers well from the oak-tangy nose. The delivery almost redefines salivating and there is certainly nothing wrong with the juiciest conceivable barley. The tired wood returns late on, though. 50%. nc ncf sc. 329 bottles.

Old Malt Cask Glen Keith Aged 20 Years refill hogshead, cask no. 10147, diss Sept 93, bott Oct 13 (89) n21.5 grassy and about as lightweight as any 20-y-o you'll nose this year. Clean and malty, though...; t23 and that clarity on the nose transfers perfectly on the palate with a stunning injection of grassy, zesty, salivating malt...; f22 thin, vanilla clad but lightly spiced, too; b22.5 good to see this unfashionable distillery show itself in such a good light. 50%. nc ncf sc. 318 bottles.

◇ **Old Particular Glen Keith 21 Years Old** refill hogshead, cask no. 10793, dist Sept 93, bott May 15 (84) n22 t21 f20 b21. Distinctly on the sharp side. Which is good for the salivation levels. But doesn't really develop as one might hope, remaining on the thin side throughout. 51.5%. nc ncf sc. 270 bottles.

Old Particlur Speyside Glen Keith 20 Year Old refill hogshead, cask no. 9953, dist Jul 93, bott 2013 (87) n21 t23 f21 b22. One of those classic drams which should, with half a dozen similar casks, be used in a 21-y-o blend to add the zip and malty sparkle to the weightier complexity. On its own a tasty, juicy, highly intense and well-made malt but lacking depth and desired acidity. 51.5%. nc ncf sc. 274 bottles. Douglas Laing & Co.

The Pearls of Scotland Glen Keith 1995 18 Year Old cask no. 171224, dist Nov 95, bott Nov 13 (88) n22 adroitly complex with vague puff of smoke add some bllast to the citrusy lead; t22.5 promises citrus on the nose and juicy lemon obliges early on; a surprising degree of oil; f21.5 oak casks a heavy shadow over the more delicate elements; b22 a satisfying dram for a malt of such age from this distillery. 56%

That Boutique-y Whisky Glen Keith batch 1 (90) n22 freshly-made paper with a gristy overtone; t23.5 superb delivery with rare clarity to the malt delivery. Light sugars and a little ulmo honey spreads the sweetness and ups the complexity; f22 a simple but beautifully clean oak-barley fade; b22.5 concentrates on doing the little it does exceptionally well. 51.2%. 176 bottles. WB15/234

◇ **That Boutique-y Whisky Company Glen Keith batch 2** (95) n24 delicate cut-glass grassy malt. Clean and shimmering with malty clarity: both entices you to taste...but wants to keep you nosing, too...; **t24** every bit as salivating and sweet as the nose promises. The oak offers just enough to ensure the malt doesn't have it all its own way...but the sugars attached to the barley...oh...my....word...!!! **f23** a little bitterness tries to creep in, but the malt works like a swan – serene above yet working like blazes below – to keep everything as it should be...; **b24** just like that girl at the dinner party who wears just the right quietly classy and elegant clothes, has her hair cut in perfect sympathy with the contours of her face and, when speaking, comes across quietly yet clearly and wittily...absolutely irresistible... *44%. 85 bottles.*

◇ **That Boutique-y Whisky Company Glen Keith batch 3** (87) **n20 t24 f21 b22.** The nose tells, mainly, of poor old casks which had hung around the distillery for a while before being used. But the delivery and follow on sing with a heavy-beating heart of sublime malt. Amazing contradictions. *47.8%. 61 bottles.*

The Whisky Agency Perfect Dram Glen Keith 1992 (90) **n22.5** attractively malty and delicate; some tangy citrus and promise of complex bourbon notes to come further down the line; **t24** the highlight by some way: a superb lift off of intense malt followed by a plethora of a gorgeously well- defined sugars and ever-intensifying vanilla-led bourbon-oak notes. A little citrus leaks into the ongoing malt; biscuit, chewy middle. The weight and pace is truly wonderful; **f21** typically thin, pasty finale; **b22.5** hmmm! Dangerous to flaunt yourself as "perfect" anything. But as far as a Glen Keith goes from this particular era, this ain't half bad. *46.6%.*

◇ **Whisky-Fässle Glen Keith 20 Year Old** barrel, dist 1992, bott 2013 (87.5) **n22 t22.5 f21 b22.** For a light spirit not naturally given to old age, this has withstood the ravages of time a bit like a Hollywood star, but without the makeovers. The fruit is still in the citrus rather than exotic stage – not sure Glen Keith is capable of exotic – and manages to sharply see off the oak which you know wants to give it a final knock out clout. A surprise, death-defying package which is seriously enjoyable. *51.8%. nc ncf.*

GLENKINCHIE
Lowlands, 1837. Diageo. Working.
Glenkinchie 12 Years Old db (85) **n19 t22.5 f21.5 b22.** The last 'Kinchie 12 I encountered was beyond woeful. This is anything but. Still not firing on all cylinders and can definitely do better. But there is a fabulous vibrancy to this which nearly all the bottlings I have tasted in the last few years have sadly lacked. Impressive. *43%*

Glenkinchie Aged 15 Years The Distillers Edition Amontillado finished, dist 1992, bott 2007 db (94) **n23.5 t24 f23 b23.5.** Now this is absolutely top class wine cask finishing. One of my last whiskies of the night, and one to take home with me. Sophisticated, intelligent and classy. *46%*

Glenkinchie 20 Years Old db (85.5) **n21 t22 f21.5 b21.** When I sampled this, I thought: "hang on, haven't I tasted this one before?" When I checked with my tasting notes for one or two independents who bottled around this age a year or two ago, I found they were nigh identical to what I was going to say here. Well, you can't say its not a consistent dram. The battle of the citrus-barley against the welling oak is a rich and entertaining one. *58.4%*

Glenkinchie 1992 The Manager's Choice db (78) **n19 t22 f18 b19.** Has a lot going for it on delivery with a barley explosion which rocks you back in your chair and has you salivating like a rabies victim. But the rest of it is just too off key. *58.1%. Diageo.*

THE GLENLIVET
Speyside, 1824. Chivas Brothers. Working.
The Glenlivet Aged 12 Years db (79.5) **n22 t21 f18 b18.5.** Wonderful nose and very early development but then flattens out towards the kind of caramel finish you just wouldn't traditionally associate with this malt, and further weakened by a bitter, furry finale. *40%*

The Glenlivet Aged 12 Years Old First Fill Matured db (91) **n22.5 t22.5 f23 b23.** A quite wonderful whisky, far truer to The Glenlivet than the standard 12 and one which every malt whisky lover should try once in their journey through the amber stuff. Forget the tasting notes on the bottle, which bear little relation to what is inside. A gem of a dram. *40%*

The Glenlivet Excellence 12 Year Old db (87) **n22 t21.5 f22 b21.5.** Low key but very clean. The emphasis is on delicate. *40%. Visitor Centre and Asian exclusive.*

The Glenlivet The Gaurdians' Chapter db (81.5) **n20 t21 f20 b20.5.** Read the chapter – but can make neither head nor tail of it. A brief moment of honeyed enjoyment. But nothing else really adds up. Just doesn't gel. *48.7%. WB15/120*

The Glenlivet 15 Years of Age db (80) **n19 t21 f20 b20.** Undeniable charm to the countless waves of malt and oak. But don't expect much in the way of complexity or charisma. *40%*

The Glenlivet Alpha db (92) **n23.5 t24 f21.5 b23.** You get the feeling some people have worked very hard at creating a multi-toned, complex creature celebrating the distillery's position at the centre of Speyside. They have succeeded. Just a cask selection or two away from a potential major Bible award. Maybe for the next bottling.... *50%*

The Glenlivet French Oak Reserve 15 Years of Age Limousin oak casks db **(91) n**22.5 **t**23 **f**22.5 **b**23. I have to say that after tasting nearly 800 cask strength whiskies, to come across something at the ancient 40% is a shock to the system. My taste buds say merci... And, what is more, a bottle of this shall remain in my dining room for guests. Having, a lifetime ago, lived with a wonderful French girl for three years I suspect I know how her country folk will regard that... Oh, and forgive a personal message to a literary friend: Bobby-Ann...keep a bottle of this beside the Ancient Age... 40%

The Glenlivet Nadurra Aged 16 Years batch no. 0712U, bott 07/12 db **(95.5) n**24 **t**24 **f**23.5 **b**24. So rare to find a big corporate dram like this showing every sign of grey-bearded cherry picking. A wise whisky, where care has been taken to wring every last drop of complexity from this great malt. 55.5%.

The Glenlivet Nadurra Aged 16 Years batch no. 0313W, bott 03/13 db **(88.5) n**21.5 a simple mix of vanilla and barley; **t**23 oily (maybe too oily) delivery of tart barley and spice; the malt expands out in ever-increasing circles until a familiar mocha character is found; **f**22 spiced butterscotch; **b**22 an enjoyable enough whisky which would be more than acceptable to most distilleries. But palls by comparison with other Nadurras. 54.8%.

The Glenlivet Nadurra Aged 16 Years batch no. 0114A, bott 01/14 db **(94.5) n**23 huge barley sugar statement; **t**24.5 wow! Some delivery as the intense ulmo honey and most concentrated form of grassy barley combine to make the eyes water: glorious in its enormity; **f**23 coconut biscuit speckled with salt; **b**24 confident, rich, full-bodied and clean: exactly how a Nadurra should be. And as though this is a distilled, concentrated definition of Speyside whisky. Fabulous. 55.3% WB15/312

⬦ **The Glenlivet Nàdurra First Fill Selection** batch no. FF0714, first fill American white oak casks, bott 07/14 db **(95.5) n**23.5 mmmm! A naughtily spicy cove: a real nose tingle. No question the oak leads the way with a dry flourish; the sweeter barley is left in its wake...; **t**24.5 a sumptuously rich delivery. And though the oils are healthy, never is there a threat to the complexity. The spices on the nose arrive just after the malt has made a sweet opening. But then we hit a massive crescendo as the dry tannins thud home almost with a degree of aggression: all this in the first half dozen beats. Red liquorice and treacle pudding fills the mid ground; walnut oil subtly adds a further oaky presence; **f**23.5 a long interweaving between the oak and barley, although it is the malt which fades faster...; **b**24 now that is what I call a whisky... 63.1%. ncf.

The Glenlivet Nàdurra Oloroso Matured batch no. OL0314, bott 03/14 db **(73) n**19 **t**21 **f**16 **b**17. Present generation first fill sherry butts at work here...so I'll let you guess. Meanwhile, those immune to sulphur will find this rich and many a fruity dream come true. 48%.

⬦ **The Glenlivet Nàdurra Oloroso Matured** batch no. OL0614, first fill oloroso sherry casks, bott 06/14 db **(71) n**17 **t**20 **f**17 **b**17. Easy to see how good this might have been. But in the end, sulphur wins – or, rather, loses – the day. 60.7%. ncf.

The Glenlivet Aged 18 Years bott Feb 10 db **(91) n**22 attractive mixture of honeycombed bourbon and fruitcake; **t**23.5 oh...just didn't expect that...!! Fabulous, honey-sweet and slightly sharp edge to the barley: excellent weight and mouthfeel with the honeycomb on the nose making slow but decisive incursions; **f**23 a very slight technical flaw drops it half a point, but there is no taking away from the improbable length of the dissolving honey and barley...some gentle chewing is required, especially with the late juices and vanilla arriving; **b**23 a hugely improved bottling seriously worth discovering in this form. Appears to have thrown off its old shackles and offers up an intensity that leaves you giving a little groan of pleasure. 43%

The Glenlivet Archive 21 Years of Age batch 1012L db **(95.5) n**24 so soft, so teasing, you might have to go to a local university and pick up some kind of aroma detector to aid your nose: Turkish delight and distant banana lead the sweeter elements while lime chews and lemon-drizzled lychee leads the fruit; even the drier vanilla tones are only half-hearted, as this entire scene is played out in whispers and innuendo; **t**24 the delivery is so soft, you can hardly detect its landing: I could give a plethora of varying tones, some being barely audible to the taste buds. But, really, it is the understated effect which counts so importantly; **f**23 it took me three hours to confirm a slight degree of sulphur. That is because I nosed and tasted alongside the XXV for comparison, and that, too, had creeping sulphur: it is not immediately detectable, as it is in relatively low amounts. A shame – this might have been one of the top three whiskies of the year...; **b**24.5 possibly the most delicate whisky of this and many years: a kind o' Ballantine's 17, but in single malt form... 43%.

⬦ **The Glenlivet Conglass 14** db **(92.5) n**22 a curious fresh paper/vanilla nose and, while you try to work out if the sweetness or dryness is dominant, the spices enter from a side entrance; **t**23 no doubt about who dominates now: the sugars take off vividly in a maple syrup/ulmo honey direction while the gristy barley also has a major presence; **f**23.5 ahhh...

now it settles for the complexity to totally enchant: the vanillas have stood firm while the sugars have slowly weakened...now a lovely mocha thread weaves in, with just a sprinkle of vanilla; **b24** a joyous barley and high quality oak interplay: probably what this distillery does best of all. *59.8% WB16/043*

❧ **The Glenlivet Founder's Reserve** db **(78.5) n20 t21.5 f18 b19**. Really can't believe what a shy and passionless whisky this is (not to mention flawed). The strength gives the game away slightly as to where the malt is positioned. But I had hoped for a little more than malty tokenism. *40%*

The Glenlivet XXV Twenty Five Years of Age Batch No. 0913A, finished in first fill OLOROSO sherry casks db **(93.5) n24** nutty, sassy, elegant but showing just a little smirk and attitude. Dried dates and cock-a-snook spice. Yet all set within walls of quiet reflection; **t24** mouth-filling, soft with fruit and malt in equal measures; the oils and spices border perfection; **f22** some cocoa and butter cream. But, alas, late on a little sulphur niggle, too; **b23.5** probably one dodgy sherry butt away from immortality: some of the passages here are lifetime memorable. *43%.*

The Glenlivet Master Distiller's Reserve db **(86.5) n22.5 t22 f20.5 b21.5**. I chose this as my 800th whisky to taste for the 2012 Bible against the Founder's Reserve on the strength of the nose over the first 30 seconds. Oh, well. Shows you the pricelessness of time when evaluating a whisky... *40%*

The Glenlivet Single Cask Inveravon Aged 21 Years cask no. 10667, bott 25 Oct 11 db **(96.5) n24** sophisticated: obviously bourbon cask, but the malt still somehow conjures up a number of fruit notes, including salted cucumber and lime. Delicate, hushed liquorice and hazelnut tones and polite spice. Everything is so understated; **t24** no disappointment on delivery. The weight is sublime: just enough oil to carry the more powerful fruit notes towards the growing cocoa without there being a gap; the spices are equal and busy; **f24** happy to sign off with a simple Neapolitan ice cream vanilla and chocolate finish; **b24.5** this was a single cask for the Taiwanese market I think. Time to get a flight to Taipei...this is Glenlivet at its absolute best. *54.6%*

Cadenhead's Glenlivet (Minmore) Wine Cask Aged 24 Years Claret cask, dist 1988, bott Feb 2013 **(93) n22.5** attractive balance between spice and firm, almost non-porous oak; **t23.5** juicy barley lead; spiced fruit follows not too far behind. The middle is softly toffee; **f23.5** the spices now really hammer the point home; a light Venezuelan cocoa assists the fade; **b23.5** how good is that? A cask from France without a trace of sulphur! A genuine – and rather delicious – collectors' item. *53.9%. 258 bottles. WB15/075*

Cadenhead's Single Cask Glenlivet (Minmore) Aged 25 Years bourbon hogshead, dist 88, bott 14 **(89) n22.5** toffee apple, which was bitten into half an hour ago...; **t22** succulent fudge and treacle tart; and tart barley, too; **f22** all about the molasses and warming, busy spice. Oh...and the toffee...; **b22.5** every last atom of natural caramel appears to have been extracted from the cask. *54.5%. 252 bottles. WB15/258*

Montgomerie's Single Cask Collection Glenlivet cask no. 13643, dist 12/06/89, bott Sep 13 **(91.5) n23.5** a beauty! Myriad deft sweet notes, some borderline Muscat grape mixes with a marzipan; a rising degree of eucalyptus highlights the age; **t23** sugars up and running fast, solidly ensuring against the lurking oak; attractive bite despite the natural caramels; **f22.5** plenty of vanilla, but those deft sugars keep on working; **b22.5** a complex malt which embraces it age lines comfortably. *46%. nc ncf sc. WB15/127*

❧ **Scotch Malt Whisky Society Cask 2.87 Aged 21 Years** refill hogshead, dist 14 Apr 92 **(88) n23** a series of citrus notes – ranging from lime to grapefruit – balance the tannins beautifully; **t22** intense barley to start, with all the accompanying sugars, but this soon vanishes to be replaced by some major oaky waves, underlined by the growing spice; **f21** disappointingly bitter as the oak yields just a little too much; **b22** this bottling has captured that crucial few months when the oak has just taken over from the barley for control and the last say... *51.7%. sc. 194 bottles.*

GLENLOCHY
Highlands (Western), 1898–1983. Diageo. Closed.

Gordon & MacPhail Rare Old Glenlochy 1979 (95) n23.5 proudly displays its age with major, but entirely acceptable, oak involvement. A pretty salty affair, lifted by delicate kumquat & wild strawberry (two fruits usually associated with oak) though the natural caramel & nibbling spice also balance beautifully; **t24** ridiculously soft delivery, even though the oak insists on at least a dual starring role. The deft & fleeting malt moments are really quite monumental & with the milky chocolate gathering in intensity, the entire piece seems to become like a Malteser liqueur; **f23.5** the spices which had a little attitude early on now drift serenely about the melted Malteser. A hint of late butterscotch, but the malt holds firm. Or should that be soft? **b24** it has been many years since a bottle from this long lost distillery turned up and that was such a classic, I can remember every nuance of it even now. This shows far greater age, but the way with which the malt takes it in its stride will become the stuff of legend. I held back on tasting this until today, August 2nd 2013, because my lad David this afternoon moved into the first home he has bought, with new wife Rachael and little Abi. It is near Fort William, the remote west coast Highland town in which this whisky was made, and where David will be teaching next year. His first job after moving in, though, will be to continue editing this book, for he worked on the Whisky Bible for a number of editions as researcher and editor over the years. So I can think of no better way of wishing David a happy life in his new home than by toasting him with what turned out to be a stunningly beautiful malt from one of the rarest of all the lost distilleries which, by strange coincidence, was first put up for sale exactly 100 years ago. So, to David, Rachael & little Abigail... your new home! And this time I swallowed.. *46%. ncf.*

GLENLOSSIE
Speyside, 1876. Diageo. Working.

Cadenhead's Authentic Collection Glenlossie-Glenlivet Cask Strength Aged 20 Years bourbon hogsheads, dist 1993, bott Feb 14 **(94.5) n23** an astonishing lucidity to the barley even after all these years; fruit salad with a stick of celery; **t24.5** three dimensional malt: any cleaner and your teeth would sparkle. Incredibly sharp, crisp and salivating, the sugars are crunchy and of a crystalline quality. The spices positively hiss and singe the palate; **f23** returns to a softer barley sugar countenance, but a little pear juice helps...; **b24** fruitier than a barrow boy down East Lane.... Magnificent! *53.3%. 252 bottles. WB15/083*

Cadenhead's Single Cask Glenlossie-Glenlivet Aged 48 Years bourbon hogsheads, dist 66, bott 14 **(91) n22.5** a little oxidisation and warming takes the edge off the sharper end of the tannin attack: even a little ulmo honey comes out to play; **t23.5** again, the tannins are crawling over every inch of this. But the light liquorice and treacle teams with the creamy fudge to repair the time damage; **f22** salty, spicy...and just generally bloody old! But the sugars keep it breathing...; **b23** When you consider this was distilled in the year Harold Wilson was prime minister of Great Britain, England won the World Cup (no, we did.... honestly....I remember it!), when virtually all of Scotland's dual carriageways of today were simple, ambling roads offering a bottleneck from town to town, I saw Millwall play for the very first time...and I was still two years short of tasting my first whisky, and you realise we are approaching something close to pre-history. So the fact a malt like Glenlossie, not renowned for its propensity to last overly long in the cask, can still come up with the goods, even if a little tarnished and dented, really does make this worth a good 45 minutes in the glass before drinking. A dram that deserves as much time as you've got...and a little more besides. *43.5%. 168 bottles. WB15/254*

Gordon & MacPhail Connoisseurs Choice Glenlossie dist 1995, bott 2013 **(96) n24** cucumbers and celery get this off to an unusual but complex start with spice, naturally, in the mix; as the nose opens the complexity of the varied honeys becomes apparent, as does the delicate smoke; **t24** mouth-watering delivery, but quickly thickens as the honey takes hold. A mix of heather and acacia grip and then mingles with the growing maple syrup; a soft earthiness begins to add weight; **f24** a deft touch of smoke appears to be the crowning glory to the delicate vanillas and walnut cake; **b24** getting harder and harder to find a dud Lossie these days: glad people are getting a chance to be in on one of the best kept secrets in Scotland... This one is truly glorious: absolutely exceptional even by the distillery' very high standards. *46%. nc ncf. WB15/149*

Gordon & MacPhail Connoisseurs Choice Glenlossie 1997 (74) n17 t21 f18 b18. I had put this to one side, earmarked as a special treat. But what a disappointment. The nose and finish are off key in such a way, one has no difficulty recognising the culprit. *46%.*

◈ **Romantic Rhine Collection Glenlossie 1992** hogshead & sherry octave, cask no. 892622, dist 16 Sept 92, bott 16 Jan 12 **(96) n24.5 t24 f23.5 b24**. The kind of Speysider you wait to come along like a single man waits for that perfect woman. Sensual and sophisticated, the aroma bounds with honeycomb and pollen, ensuring a balancing dryness all encrusted in beeswax. The weight on delivery is something of wonder, the gentleness of the barley-rich sweeter tones something of splendour. Understated honey rules, but with a yielding hand, allowing the light liquorice and hickory to form subtle depth. As on the finish, the oak is sprinkled lightly, as are the spices, while the age is underlined with a light desiccated, dry coconut edge to the vanilla. A must get bottling of a ridiculously hard-to-find distillery. *51%. 69 bottles.*

Scotch Malt Whisky Society Cask 46.24 aged 20 Years refill hogshead, dist 30 Sep 93 **(92.5) n23** interesting and unusual mix of green barley, green tea and minted liquorice; **t23.5** lively, salivating delivery at first hints at youth. But a few waves of controlled tannin refocuses the mind...: just love the layered structure...; **f23** the semi-lush body carries the darker sugars onward to meet the developing natural caramels and drier toast; **b23** Lossies from the SMWS are a bit thin on the ground...but this is worth waiting for! Has no problems taking off... *53.8%. nc ncf sc. 260 bottles.*

Signatory Vintage Un-chillfiltered Collection Glenlossie 1992 Aged 16 Years hogshead, cask no. 3439, dist 18 Nov 92, bott 17 Jan 13 **(94.5) n24** despite the school room plasticine, it is the massive and magnificent Lubek marzipan which dominates, creaking under the weight of diced almond. Spices are required for balance and oblige; honey is represented by a blend of ulmo and heather; sweetened lime completes the treat; **t23.5** you'd expect one of the above to come out top on delivery. Instead, it is the barley. Carries a degree of oak bitterness (less when you taste at body temp) but any excesses there are dealt with by the rampant sugars; **f23** reverts to a more conservative creamy fudge finale; **b24** puts the Glossie in Genlossie. Masterful stuff. *46%. nc ncf sc. 378 bottles. WB15/023*

Signatory Cask Strength Collection Glenlossie 1992 Aged 20 Years hogshead, cask no. 3443, dist 18 Nov 92, bott 03 Apr 13 **(94) n23.5** busy, waxy, weighty: a malt making a big statement. The oak has an old, been round the block feel, even to the point you are sure you can pick up dank, lichen-crusted walls. There is evidence of apple and barley, but this is so enormously muddled and complex; **t24** the honey, notable by its absence on the nose, arrives by the jar full here. But it does not have a clear run in goal and even some gristy sugars and rich vanilla manage to make their mark. Chewey...; **f23** quite a salty finale. Remains heavy, oily and dense to the far from bitter end; **b23.5** a marathon of a malt. Enormous and seemingly goes on forever. *57.1%. nc sc. 274 bottles. WB15/140*

GLEN MHOR
Highlands (Northern), 1892–1983. Diageo. Demolished.

Glen Mhor 1976 Rare Malt db **(92.5) n23 t24 f22 b23.5.** You just dream of truly great whisky sitting in your glass from time to time. But you don't expect it, especially from such an old cask. This was the best example from this distillery I've tasted in 30 years...until the Glenkeir version was unleashed! If you ever want to see a scotch that has stretched the use of oak as far it will go without detriment, here it is. What a pity the distillery has gone because the Mhor the merrier... *52.2%*

Cadenhead's Single Malt Glen Mhor Aged 31 Years hogshead, dist 82, bott Jul 14 **(94.5) n24** an exotic blast of pineapple cube candy, grapefruit and dried lychee topped, surprisingly, with a delicate puff of smoke; tannins issue a constant hum; **t23** a thick stick of oak beats the taste buds on delivery, but that calms sufficiently to allow amazing spices to launch beautifully; indeed, there is even a mouth-watering maltiness still to be found – astonishing! Early on, a degree of cocoa takes hold and, thanks to some treacle and oil, sits comfortably on the palate; **f24** more well balanced milky, lightly sweetened cocoa with that hint of smoke returning to accompany the spice; **b23.5** a malt which pushes itself about in an oak constructed Zimmer frame, reaching its destination in ungainly fashion but always well groomed and dressed elegantly. This charming ghost of this long lost distillery is about as good as you could hope for. *52.9%. 186 bottles. WB15/267*

GLENMORANGIE
Highlands (Northern), 1843. Glenmorangie Plc. Working.

Glenmorangie 10 Years Old db **(94) n24** perhaps the most enigmatic aroma of them all: delicate yet assertive, sweet yet dry, young yet oaky: a malty tone poem; **t22** flaky oakiness throughout but there is an impossibly complex toastiness to the barley which seems to suggest the lightest hint of smoke; **f24** amazingly long for such a light dram, drying from the initial sweetness but with flaked almonds amid the oakier, rich cocoa notes; **b24** you might find the occasional "orange variant", where the extra degree of oak, usually from a few too many first-fill casks, has flattened out the more extreme peaks and toughs of complexity (scores about 89). But these are pretty rare – almost a collector's item – and overall this remains one of the great single malts: a whisky of uncompromising aesthetic beauty from the first enigmatic whiff to the last teasing and tantalising gulp. Complexity at its most complex. *40%*

Glenmorangie 15 Years Old db **(90.5) n23** chunky and fruity: something distinctly sugar candy about this one; the barley's no slouch, either; and, just to raise the eyebrows, just the faintest waft of something smoky...; **t23** silky, a tad sultry, and serious interplay between oak and barley; a real, satisfying juiciness to this one; **f22** dries towards the oaky side of things, but just a faint squeeze of liquorice adds extra weight; **b22.5** exudes quality. *43%*

Glenmorangie 15 Years Old Sauternes Wood Finish db **(68) n16 t18 f17 b17**. I had hoped – and expected – an improvement on the sulphured version I came across last time. Oh, whisky! Why are you such a cruel mistress...? *46%*

Glenmorangie 18 Years Old db **(91) n22** pleasant if unconvincing spotted dick; **t23** sharp, eye-watering mix of fruit and mainly honeyed barley; nutty and, with the confident vanillas, forming a breakfast cereal completeness; **f23** Cocoa Krispies; **b23** having thrown off some previous gremlins, now a perfect start to the day whisky... *43%*

Glenmorangie 25 Years Old db **(95.5) n24** it's strap yourself in time: this is a massive nose with more layers, twists and turns than you can shake a thief at. Soft, mildly lush Lubec marzipan is sandwiched between fruit bonbons and myriad barley tones. Worth taking half an hour over this one, and no kidding... **t24** the clarity on the nose is matched here. Every single wave of flavour is there in crystal form, starting, naturally, with the barley but this is soon paired with various unidentified fruits. The result is salivation. Towards the middle the oak shows form and does so in various cocoa-tinged ways; every nuance is delicately carved, almost fragile, but the overall picture is one of strength; **f23.5** medium length with the cocoa heading towards medium roast Java **b24** every bit as statesmanlike and elegant as a whisky of this age from such a blinding distillery should be. Ticks every single box for a 25-year-old and is Morangie's most improved malt by the distance of Tain to Wellingborough. There is a hint of genius with each unfolding wave of flavours with this one: a whisky that will go in 99/100 whisky lover's top 50 malts of all time. And that includes the Peatheads. *43%*

Glenmorangie 30 Years Old db **(72) n17 t18 f19 b18**. From the evidence in the glass the jury is out on whether it has been spruced up a little in a poor sherry cask – and spruce is the operative word: lots of pine on this wrinkly. *44.1%*

Glenmorangie Vintage 1975 db **(89) n23 t23 f21 b22**. A charming, fruity and beautifully spiced oldie. *43%*

Glenmorangie Artein Private Edition db **(94) n24 t23.5 f23 b23.5**. If someone has gone out of their way to create probably the softest Scotch single malt of the year, then they have succeeded. *46%. ncf.*

Glenmorangie Artein Private Edition 15 Years Old db **(91) n23 t23.5 f21.5 b23**. A truly sensual and complex dram, gorgeously weighted underplaying the fruit and wine aspect to a disarming degree. *46%. ncf.*

Glenmorangie Artisan Casks db **(93) n23 t23.5 f23 b23.5**. If whisky could be sexed, this would be a woman. Every time I encounter Morangie Artisan, it pops up with a new look, a different perfume. And mood. It appears not to be able to make up its mind. But does it know how to pout, seduce and win your heart...? Oh yes. *46%*

Glenmorangie Astar db **(88) n21 t23 f22.5 b22**. Decidedly strange malt: for quite a while it is as if someone has extracted the barley and left everything else behind. A star is born? Not yet, perhaps. But perhaps a new breed of single malt. *57.1%*

Glenmorangie Burgundy Wood Finish db **(72) n17.5 t19.5 f18 b18**. Sulphured whisky de table. *43%*

Glenmorangie Burr Oak Reserve db **(92) n24 t24 f22 b22**. Fades on the finish as a slightly spent force, but nose and arrival are simply breathtaking. Wouldn't be out of place in Kentucky. *56.3%*

Glenmorangie Cellar 13 Ten Years Old db **(88.5) n22 t22.5 f22 b22** oh, if only I could lose weight as efficiently as this appears to have done... oh, I have! My love and thanks to Nancy, Nigel and Ann Marie. *43%*

Glenmorangie Companta Clos de Tart & Rasteau casks, dist 27 Jan 99, bott 14 Nov 13 db **(74) n17 t20 f18 b19**. "I don't think you'll be a fan of this one, Jim" said the Glenmorangie blender to me, letting me know the sample was on its way. How right he was. Have to say there is some breath-taking fruit to be had before the sulphur does its worst. *46%. ncf.*

Glenmorangie Dornoch db **(94) n23.5** light and sea breezy: grist on a coastal wing. The gristiness extends to the sugars which stick to a simple but effective path. The secret to its charm, though, is the clarity and layering... **t23** even on delivery the malt arrives on all levels and in different hues, ranging from sweet and fresh to a duller, oak-dried digestive biscuit – but quite tightly bound; **f23.5** a beautiful unravelling: those tighter notes relax offering a procession of further biscuity, malty themes – not without a light sprinkling of salt – and then a denser malt extract feel; **b24** a rare Glenmorangie which this time does not put the emphasis on fruit or oak influence. But this appears to concentrate on the malt itself, taking it through a routine which reveals as many angles and facets as it can possibly conjure. Even if the casks are from a central warehouse, at times a seascape has been created by a light salty influence – so befitting the whisky's name. A real treat. 43%

Glenmorangie Ealanta 1993 Vintage db (97.5) n24 a near faultless nose, as one might expect from ultra high quality oak and supremely well-made distillate. A kind of elite Stranahan's nose, all black tie and wing collars and without the oils. Here, a mesmerising mix of dried orange peel and lychee flips for the leading role with gristy barley sugar and butterscotch seasoned with drying allspice and a few shavings of hickory: monumental...! t24 the delivery, tasted blind, is bourbon! The nose whispers it, the palate sings it proudly! A gorgeous intertwining of black and red liquorice leaves no doubt. Most amazing is the weight: just an astonishing degree of oils and sugars with the grist seemingly mixed with an 80% Venezuelan cocoa and molassed and muscovado sugar mix (actually, leaning more towards the muscovado); f24.5 one of the longest finishes to any Scotch this year and borderline perfection. The sugars are supremely weighted, their trick being not to interfere with the complex permutation of vanilla and barley. I cannot remember a fade so wonderfully orchestrated – like the final dying notes of a Vaughan Williams masterpiece – and so entirely free of distracting side issues of weakness and interference. Assisted perfectly by the lightest but most welcome degree of oil; b25 when is a bourbon not a bourbon? When it is a Scotch single malt...And here we have potentially the World Whisky of the Year. Free from the embarrassing nonsense which passes for today's sherry butt, and undamaged by less than careful after use care of second-hand bourbon casks, we see what happens when the more telling aspects of oak, the business end which gives bourbon that extra edge, blends with the some of the very finest malt made in Scotland. Something approaching one of the best whiskies of my lifetime is the result... 46%

Glenmorangie Elegance db (92) n22 quite herbal and soothing; t24 the thinnest layer of icing sugar coats the silk-soft malt; every bit as gentle as the nose suggests; f22 medium to short with some attractive rolling vanilla; b24 a surprise package that is not entirely dissimilar to the Golden Rum, only a tad sweeter. 43%

Glemorangie Finealta db (84.5) n21 t22 f20.5 b21. Plump and thick, one of the creamiest malts around. For what it lacks in fine detail it makes up for in effect, especially the perky oaky spices. 46%

Glenmorangie Lasanta sherry casks db (68.5) n16 t19 f16 b17.5. The sherry problem has increased dramatically rather than being solved. 46%

Glenmorangie Lasanta Aged 12 Years sherry cask finish db (93) n23.5 a dry exhibition of fruit – or perhaps an exhibition of dry fruit. Either way, quietly rich and showing the range of old fruit cake depths I had hoped to find on the original Lasanta; really love the stewed plums and spotted dick; t24 wonderfully soft delivery, backed handsomely by a two-toned sherry fruitiness, with dry and cream being just about on equal terms. The sugars appear both fruit and cask borne, though it is the deeper Eccles cake and treacle notes which carry furthest; f22 a fluffy dryness and numbing to the tip of the tongue reveals that not every sherry butt used here was faultless, but there is enough of a chocolate and walnut butter cream sideshow to distract; b23.5 a delightful surprise: every bottling of Lasanta I'd ever tasted had been sulphur ruined. But this new 12-y-o incarnation has got off to a flying start. Although a little bit of a niggle on the finish, I can live with that in the present climate. Here's to a faultless second bottling... 43%

⬦ **Glenmorangie Legends The Duthac** db (91.5) n23.5 a big yet tight nose: the sugars are rigid, the tannins unusually confident; t23.5 a nutty delivery, confirming wine casks. But again, those nuts are encased in crisp sugars, then a softer cocoa follow through and gorgeous light nutty liquorice; f21.5 a slight 's-word' furriness takes some of the gloss off the excellence, b23 not spoken to their blender, Bill Lumsden, about this one. But he's been busy on this, though not so busy as to get rid of the unwelcome you-know-what from the wine casks. Educated guess: some kind of finish involving virgin oak, or at least first fill bourbon, and sherry, probably PX on account of the intensity of the crisp sugar. 43%. ncf.

Glenmorangie Madeira Wood Finish db (78) n19.5 t20.5 f19 b19. One of the real problems with wine finishes is getting the point of balance right when the fruit, barley and oak are in harmony. Here it is on a par with me singing in the shower, though frankly my aroma would be a notch or two out. 43%

Glenmorangie Margaux Cask Finish db (88) n22 t22 f22 b22. Even taking every whisky with an open mind, I admit this was better than my subconscious might have considered. Certainly better than the near undrinkable Ch. Margaux '57 I used to bring out for my birthday each year some 20-odd years ago... 46%

⬦ **Glenmorangie Milsean** db (94) n23 the odd kumquat does battle with a big vanilla oak kick...; t23.5 opens up far more on delivery than it does on the nose: juicy barley goes on full salivating duty. Light spices pulse while a tangy marmalade (thick cut) ramps up the sharpness;

f23.5 the marmalade bitterness continues, but slowly morphs into a cocoa theme. Superb weight and pace to the development, helped by the malt being on standby at all times...; **b24** a quite beautiful malt which goes out of its way to put the orangey in 'Morangie... 46%

Glenmorangie Nectar D'or Sauternes Finish db **(94) n23** delicate cinnamon on toast and a drizzle of greengage and sultana; **t24** refreshing and dense on the palate as the bitter-sweet battle goes into overdrive; excellent weight and body; **f23** remains clean and precise, allowing some custard onto the apple strudel finale; **b24** great to see French casks that actually complement a whisky – so rare! This has replaced the Madeira finish. But there are some similar sweet-fruit characteristics. An exercise in outrageously good sweet-dry balancing. 46%

Glenmorangie Quinta Ruban Port Finish db **(92) n24** typical Morangie complexity, but the grape notes added act almost like a prism to show their varied hues; **t23** fruit and spice about as the oak goes in search of glory: barley stands in its way; **f22** light, deftly sweetened and juicy to the end; **b23** this replacement of the original Port finish shows a genuine understanding of the importance of grape-oak balance. Both are portrayed with clarity and confidence. This is a form of cask finishing that has progressed from experimentation to certainty. 46%

Glenmorangie Sherry Wood Finish db **(84) n23 t21 f20 b20.** Stupendous clean sherry nose, then disappoints with a somewhat bland display on the palate. 43%

Glenmorangie Signet db **(80.5) n20 t21.5 f19 b20.** A great whisky holed below the waterline by oak of unsatisfactory quality. Tragic. 46%

Glenmorangie Sonnalta PX db **(96.5) n24** now this works: has that heavy-handed feel of a sweet sherry butt (or five) at work here, usually the kiss of death for so many whiskies. But an adroit praline sub-plot really does the trick. So with the malt evident, too, we have a three-pronged attack which somehow meshes in to one. And not even the merest hint of an off-note...goodness gracious: a new experience...!!! **t24** Neanderthal grape drags its knuckles along the big vanilla floor before a really subtle light Columbian coffee kick puts us back on course; sharper vanillas from some awkward oak threatens to send us off course again but somehow it finds a settled, common ground; **f24.5** now goes into orgasmic overdrive as Demerara sugar is tipped into some gorgeous, cream-lightened mocha. This is obviously to wash down the Melton Hunt cake which is resplendent in its grape and roast nut finery. It is the perfect whisky finish... **b24** remains a giant among the tall stills. A mesmeric whisky... 46%

Glenmorangie Taghta db **(92) n23** a soft infusion of dates and chocolate; **t23** fresh and salivating: a barley juiciness gives way to a slow amplification of oak; the sugars are of a lightly molassed bent, helping to inject life into a pithy sub-current; **f23** there have been hints of chocolate throughout and here it offers a more precise outline of a fruit and chocolate theme. Remains soft and deft to the last...; **b23** a curious Glenmorangie which, unusually, appears not to be trying to make a statement or force a point. This is an old Sunday afternoon film of a dram: an old-fashioned black and whitie, (home grown and not an Ealing, or Bogie or Edward G Robinson) where, whether we have seen it before or not, we know pretty much what is going to happen, in a reassuring kind of a way... 46%

Glenmorangie Traditional db **(90.5) n22** orange blossom, barley sugar and chalk dust; **t23** delicate delivery revelling in gentle complexity: really playful young-ish malt makes for a clean start and middle; **f22.5** soft mocha notes play out a quiet finish; **b23** an improved dram with much more to say, but does so quietly. 57.1%

◈ **Glenmorangie Tayne** db **(87.5) n21 t22.5 f22 b22.** Tangy back story. But also a curious early combination between butterscotch and Werther's Original candy. The malt – topped with a splash of double cream – in the centre ground, though, is the star showing. 43%

◈ **Glenmorangie Tùsail Private Edition** db **(92) n24.5** if you sniff this too hard, you might break the whisky into a thousand pieces... just so gentle, wafer-thin shards of barley, butterscotch, boiled pear, vanilla, marzipan...and all watched over by brittle spices; **t23** the delivery mirrors the nose: the first six or seven waves are simply sketches of most of the things you find in the aroma, yet with no weight or substance at all...the mid-ground becomes little more simple and vanilla-driven, though with a delicate ulmo honey thread; **f21.5** lightweight vanilla and barley; only the spices make a noise; bitters very slightly at death; **b23** doesn't quite live up to the nose. But that would have been a big ask! From the Understated School of Glenmorangie. 46%. ncf.

GLEN MORAY
Speyside, 1897. La Martiniquaise. Working.

Glen Moray Classic 8 Years Old db **(86) n20 t22 f21 b23.** A vast improvement on previous bottlings with the sluggish fatness replaced by a thinner, barley-rich, slightly sweeter and more precise mouthfeel. 40%

Glen Moray 10 Years Old Chardonnay Matured db **(73.5) n18.5 t19 f18 b18.** Tighter than a wine cork. 40%

Glen Moray 12 Years Old db **(90)** n22.5 gentle malt of varying pitch and intensity; t22 a duller start than it should be with the vanilla diving in almost before the barley but the juicy, grassy notes arrive in good time; f23 long, back on track with intense malt and the custardy oak is almost apologetic but enlivened with a dash of lime: mmmmm... pure Glen Moray! b22.5 I have always regarded this as the measuring stick by which all other malty and clean Speysiders should be tried and tested. It is still a fabulous whisky, full of malty intricacies. Something has fallen off the edge, perhaps, but minutely so. Still think a trick or two is being missed by bottling this at 40%: the natural timbre of this malt demands 46% and no less.... 40%

Glen Moray 16 Years Old db **(74)** n19 t19 f18 b19. A serious dip in form. Drab. 40%

Glen Moray 16 Years Old Chenin Blanc Mellowed in Wine Barrels db **(85)** n20 t22 f22 b21. A fruity, oak-shaded dram just brimming with complexity. 40%

Glen Moray 20 Years Old db **(80)** n22 t22 f18 b18. With so much natural cream toffee, it is hard to believe that this has so many years on it. After a quick, refreshing start it pans out, if anything, a little dull. 40%

◈ **Glen Moray 25 Year Old Port Cask Finish** batch 2 db **(95)** n23.5 for all the fruit flying about, there is a massive bourbon-style oak richness to this. Very unusual light/heavy duel personality which really takes your breath away...; t23.5 ...and no less complex on delivery, again with the fruit trying to run away with it, but the spices having none of it. The malt part seems lightweight, the oak and fruit offers greater intensity; f24 unusual, as the length of the finish – which is impressive – does not overly depend on oils. Instead, the oak now moves into a spicier phase, which lengthens the enjoyment considerably – and unexpectedly. And the biggest surprise of all...? The very late juiciness which belies the quarter of a century in wood; b24 some quite first rate port pipes are involved here. Absolutely clean as a whistle and without any form of off-note. A distillery I have a very soft spot for showing very unusual depth – and age. Brilliant. 43%. 3295 bottles.

Glen Moray Aged 25 Years Portwood Finish Rare Vintage Limited Edition bott code. 3153, dist 1986 db **(87.5)** n22.5 t22 f21 b22. Just get the feeling that the Port pipe has not quite added what was desired. 43%

Glen Moray 30 Years Old db **(92.5)** n23.5 it's probably the deftness of the old-fashioned Speyside smoke in tandem with the structured fruits that makes this so special; t23.5 for a light Speysider, the degree of barley to oak is remarkable: soft, oil-gilde d barley is met by a wonderful, if brief, spice prickle; f22.5 deft layering of vanilla and cocoa; a sprinkle of muscovado sugar repels any darker oak notes; b23 for all its years, this is comfortable malt, untroubled by time. There is no mistaking quality. 43%

Glen Moray 1959 Rare Vintage db **(91)** n25 t23 f21 b22. They must have been keeping their eyes on this one for a long time: a stunning malt that just about defies nature. The nose reaches absolute perfection. 50.9%

Glen Moray 1962 Very Rare Vintage Aged 42 Years db **(94)** n23 t24 f23 b24. The first temptation is to think that this has succumbed to age, but a second and a third tasting reveal that there is much more complexity, integrity and balance to this than first meets the tastebuds. The last cask chosen by the legendary Ed Dodson before his retirement from the distillery: a pretty perceptive choice. A corker! 50.9%. sc.

Glen Moray 1984 db **(83)** n20 t22 f20 b21. Mouthwatering and incredibly refreshing malt for its age. 40%

Glen Moray 1989 db **(86)** n23 t22 f20 b21. Doesn't quite live up to the fruit smoothie nose but I'm being a little picky here. 40%

Glen Moray 1992 Single Cask No 1441 sherry butt db **(74)** n17 t21 f18 b18. Oops! Didn't anyone spot the sulphur...? 596%

Glen Moray 1995 Port Wood Finish bott Dec 2009 db **(95.5)** n23 a surprising liquorice base to the healthy spiced fruit; t24 vivid grape: clean, intense and, for a while, dominant. The oak surges back with a few tricks of its own, the most impressive being a liquorice-hickory thrust and a soothing custardy topping. Meanwhile, the grape offers spice and a sheen; f24.5 a wonderful array of spicy chocolate and raisin notes that appear to continue indefinitely. Needs to be tasted to be believed. b24 possibly the most satisfying wine finish of the year. 56.7%

Glen Moray 1995 Single Sherry Cask sherry butt db **(56)** n15 t14 f13 b14. So stunned was I about the abject quality of this bottling, I even looked on the Glen Moray website to see if they had said anything about it. Apparently, if you add water you find on the nose "the lingering soft sulphury smoke of a struck match." Well, here's the news: you don't need water. Just open the bottle and there's Rotorua in all it's stink bomb finery. And errr...hullo, guys... some further news: that means it's a bloody faulty, useless cask. And has no right to be put anywhere near a bottling hall let alone set loose in a single bottling. This, quite frankly, is absolutely rank whisky, the type of which makes my blood boil. I mean, is this really the best cask that could be found in the entire and considerable estate of Glen Moray..???? Am I, or is it the whisky world going mad...? *59.6%*

Glen Moray Classic db **(86.5)** n22 t21.5 f21.5 b21.5. The nose is the star with a wonderful, clean barley-fruit tandem, but what follows cannot quite match its sure-footed wit. *40%*

◈◈ **Glen Moray Peated** db **(87.5)** n21.5 t22.5 f21.5 b22. Really never thought I'd see this distillery, once the quintessential Speyside unpeated dram, gone all smoky... A little bit of a work in progress. And a minor word to the wise to their blenders: by reducing to 40% you've broken up the oils a shade – but tellingly - too much, which can be crucial in peaty whiskies. Up to 46% next bottling and I think you'll find things fall into place – and not apart... Some minor erotic moments, though, especially on the fourth or fifth beats, when the sugars and smoked vanilla do work well together. Too fleeting, though. *40%*

◈◈ **Glen Moray Port Cask Finish** db **(89.5)** n21 a bit of a mess: the lack of integration between the harsh fruit, confused thin vanillas and seemingly young barley has been exposed through the weak structure of the spirit. Untidy and sharp...; t21.5 not a great delivery, either. Still no telling narrative...then, suddenly, it clicks! Maybe an injection of sugars has made the difference because the fruit is now identifiable as fruit while the spice offer extra dimensions; f23.5 my word: that chocolate fruit and nut....ridiculously yummy. The late Demerara sugars do no harm, either; b23.5 a malt which has to somehow work its way to the exit...and finally does so with supreme confidence and a touch of class along the way... *40%*

Glen Moray Wine Cask Edition bott Sep 09 db **(83.5)** n20 t23 f20 b20.5. When in full flow this is just bursting with some of the juiciest fruit you are likely to encounter. But a familiar bitter buzz brings down the value. How sad. *59.7%*

◈◈ **Adelphi Glen Moray 22 Year Old** **(86.5)** n21.5 t23 f20.5 b21.5. A thick, glutinous malt bounding with fruity, nutty tones. But there is an annoying, nagging bitterness, too. The highlight is the delivery, a thing of viscous, fruit-sugary intensity. What follows, though, is just a little too bitty for its own good. Other than the late cocoa, that is... *56.6% WB16/010*

Adelphi Selection Glen Moray 27 Years Old cask no. 1931, dist 86, bott 13 **(87)** n21.5 t21 f22.5 b21.5. A brave and, at times, nuclear battle against old age, mainly using molasses in the front line. But when you are fighting time there can be only one winner. Some of the early spice and later cocoa notes are an absolute treat, though. *56.8%. ncf sc. WB15/413*

Blackadder Raw Cask Glen Moray 1995 18 Years Old single oak hogshead, cask no. 2510, dist 21 Mar 95, bott Apr 13 **(92)** n22 a real oaky buzz , but enough sugars for balance; t24 oily from the off, allowing some pretty major citrus and banana notes to develop. A little golden syrup helps master the intense tannin; f23 long, oil-deendent with the oak straining at the least but just about muzzled; b23 not a distillery naturally given to passing this many summers. But this is rather lovely, at times wonderful, despite the obvious oak encroachment. *54.9%. nc ncf sc. 211 bottles. WB15/162*

Cadenhead's Small Batch Glen Moray-Glenlivet Aged 15 Years bourbon hogsheads, dist 1998, bott 2013 **(84)** n20 t21.5 f21 b21.5. Both citrus and barley is working flat out to get results. Certainly manages to get the juices flowing, but a less than magnificent cask means an underlying bitterness knocks things a little off key. *46%. 684 bottles. WB15/087*

Cadenhead's Glen Moray Wine Cask Aged 21 Years Claret cask, dist 1992, bott Feb 14 **(95)** n23.5 elegant mix between lightly spiced greengage and more basic boiled fruit sweets, with a lemon drop thrown in for extra bite; t24 one of the cleanest deliveries of the year: the oak may be present, but the fruit and sugar is crisp and linear, the spices confident and clear; the mid ground at last reveals a little vanilla and tannin to the growing oil; f23.5 really good age showing now, but the quality of the oak is faultless. This means the fruits can still trill their top notes, while the spices rumble and the cocoa builds; b24 highly unusual example of Glen Moray, the least oak-damaged I have ever encountered at this age. Brilliant. Literally. *55.4%. 216 bottles. WB15/077*

Darkness! Glen Moray Aged 22 Years Oloroso Cask Finish **(85.5)** n22 t22.5 f21 b20. One can only presume that there is some malt in there somewhere...The nose takes me right back to my Fleet Street days when a famous old wine bar there served up the most outrageously OTT oloroso sherry matured whisky I had ever come across. Until now... *578%. 88 bottles. WB15/201*

◈◈ **Hepburn's Choice Glen Moray Aged 8 Years** refill hogshead, dist 2007, bott 2015 **(77)** n19 t20 f19 b19. Fat, oily, sweet with the malt finally coming through as a thick syrup, though one with a tangy finish. Hardly Glen Moray in its finest voice. *46%. nc ncf sc. 182 bottles.*

Hepburn's Choice Glen Moray 2001 Aged 12 Years refill hogshead, dist 01, bott 14 **(91)** n22.5 fresh, lively maltiness boasting a citrus-vanilla backdrop; t23 massive malt: clean, salivating, gristy. The sugars are understated and light; f22 heavier finale as the vanilla returns; **b23** absolutely classic for the distillery at this age: a case where simplicity can be quietly beautiful. 46%. nc ncf sc. 193 bottles.

Old Malt Cask Glen Moray Aged 21 Years refill hogshead, cask no. 9935, dist Oct 91, bott Aug 13 (85) **n21 t22 f21 b21.** I can see why it's the Glen Moray 21....! Pleasant enough, but the oak has injected some major natural caramels which have rubbed out the usual juicy aspects of this malt. 50%. nc ncf sc. 165 bottles.

⟡ **Old Particular Glen Moray 15 Years Old** refill hogshead, cask no. 10420, dist Jun 99, bott Aug 14 (93) **n23.5** clean barley intertwangled with orange blossom honey and bourbon-style spices; **t23** the oak leads still, but it's a speech of understatements and innuendo as it heads in a bourbony direction but never arrives: the delicate malt is always blocking the path; **f23** much maltier now – but the spices do warm up to a late toasty bourbon style; **b23.5** the subtlest of malts which is absolutely true to the distillery. Excellent. 48.4%. nc ncf sc. 332 bottles.

⟡ **Provenance Glen Moray Over 12 Years** refill hogshead, cask no. 10578, dist summer 02, bott autumn 14 (77) **n19 t20 f19 b19.** A tired bourbon cask ensures too much new make character for a malt this age. Grassy malt, though. 46%. nc ncf sc.

Scotch Malt Whisky Society Cask 35.102 Aged 39 Years refill hogshead, dist 19 Feb 74 (85.5) **n22 t22 f20 b21.5.** Never a distillery designed for such great age, the oak ultimately proves all-conquering. But there are some pretty skirmishes along the way and I admit to being somewhat enthralled between the battle between the golden syrup and highly toasted tannin, with some pungent marmalade (and, later, chocolate-orange) notes, like me, looking on from a distance. Another cask which could have served so much better in a blend but at least a couple of hundred whisky lovers will get the chance see what happens when a lightweight malt pulls out all the stops to survive 30 years against the odds. 52.1% 180 bottles.

Scotch Malt Whisky Society Cask 35.107 Aged 19 Years 1st fill toasted oak hogshead, dist 11 Nov 94 (87.5) **n22 t22.5 f21 b22.** Probably from a first fill cask, the tannins have taken just too big grip. Compelling, but ultimately limited as a single cask. 58.7%. nc ncf sc. 204 bottles.

Scotch Malt Whisky Society Cask 35.108 Aged 12 Years 1st fill butt, dist 17 May 01 (85.5) **n22.5 t22 f20 b21.** A surprising bottling, this, with the oak really cutting up rough against the trademark charming, gentle and elegant barley and grapey fruit. A shame after such a pleasing deft nose. 60.5%. nc ncf sc. 230 bottles.

Scotch Malt Whisky Society Cask 35.109 Aged 28 Years refill hogshead, dist 19 Mar 85 (88.5) **n23** bananas and custard, suet pudding base; **t22.5** a bit like dipping your shoulders under the tepid water, the oak doesn't appear half as bad as it seems on initial impact; the barley holds its position impressively against the oaky advance and even manages to fight back and regain ground; a vague gristiness appears to be even throughout; **f21** some deft spice enriches the sugar-tannin fade; **b22** complex whisky, though more by luck than judgement. 46.8%.

Scotch Malt Whisky Society Cask 35.110 Aged 17 Years 1st fill designer barrel, dist 17 Dec 96 (95) **n24** very high class: all is softness and whispers with a crème brule and butterscotch tart mix topped with a squeeze of tangerine; a serious nod towards top grade bourbon here; **t23** gorgeously salivating with the barley gliding around on the lush, spiced acacia honey; **f24** the spices pulse while the citrus-honey sweetness embraces the coconut milk and other sign of high quality oak; **b24** a demure and spellbinding essay in balance. A truly must bottling for this distillery. 496%. nc ncf sc. 97 bottles.

Scotch Malt Whisky Society Cask 35.111 Aged 12 Years refill chardonnay hogshead, dist 27 Nov 01 (83) **n20 t22 f20 b21.** A dumpy, off-key fruitiness has the odd bright moment but it's just all too discordant. 59.4%. nc ncf sc. 256 bottles.

⟡ **Scotch Malt Whisky Society Cask 35.131 Aged 19 Years** 1st fill toasted oak hogshead, dist 11 Nov 94 (94) **n23.5** lively, fully spiced and reeking of bourbon...; **t24** wonderful delivery: at once full on tannin, so weighty and toasty, yet so much malty citrus spilling into every crevice of the palate; **f22.5** dries quickly as the big oak takes hold; **b23** I'm pretty sure I saw these casks when they were just a few weeks old at the Glen Moray distillery, freshly filled and bursting with mystery and promise. Some may think there is far too much bourbon character for its own good. But for me...absolutely delicious!! 55.1%. sc. 271 bottles.

⟡ **Scotch Malt Whisky Society Cask 35.132 Aged 19 Years** 1st fill toasted oak hogshead, dist 17 Nov 94 (91) **n23** adopts a comfortable bourbon-style liquorice and manuka honey theme; **t23** the sugars have been teased and collected from the oak, with butterscotch-hickory the earthier flavour profile on show; **f22.5** long, and toasty to the very end. Some decent mocha notes; **b22.5** massively tasty. But just a little too much oak indulgence possibly. 56.1%. sc. 248 bottles.

⟡ **Scotch Malt Whisky Society Cask 35.134 Aged 20 Years** 1st fill toasted oak hogshead, dist 11 Nov 94 (89) **n23** brittle Demerara sugar, manuka honey and a mix of back and red liquorice...this is Speyside malt...? **t22** the bourbon theme continues as the tannins take grip and even nip a little too harshly; **f22** long, dry but punctuated by the odd moment of molasses; **b22** one of Kentucky's finest malts...oh, hang on a minute.... *56.5%. sc. 270 bottles.*

That Boutique-y Whisky Glen Moray batch 1 **(84.5) n21 t22 f21 b21.5.** Kind of a near 50%abv chocolate toffee bar. *49.1%. 176 bottles. WB15/208*

GLEN ORD
Highlands (Northern), 1838. Diageo. Working.

Glen Ord Aged 12 Years db **(81) n20 t23 f18 b20.** Just when you thought it safe to go back...for a while Diageo ditched the sherry-style Ord. It has returned. Better than some years ago, when it was an unhappy shadow of its once-great self, but without the sparkle of the vaguely-smoked bottling of a year or two back. Nothing wrong with the rich arrival, but the finish is a mess. I'll open the next bottling with trepidation... *43%*

Glen Ord 25 Years Old dist 1978 db **(95) n24 t24 f23 b24.** Some stupendous vatting here: cask selection at its very highest to display Ord in all its far too rarely seen magnificence. *58.3%*

Glen Ord 28 Years Old db **(90) n22 t23 f22 b23.** This is mega whisky showing slight traces of sap, especially on the nose, but otherwise a concentrate of many of the qualities I remember from this distillery before it was bottled in a much ruined form. Blisteringly beautiful. *58.3%*

Glen Ord 30 Years Old db **(87) n22 t21 f23 b21.** Creaking with oak, but such is the polish to the barley some serious class is on show. *58.8%*

Singleton of Glen Ord 12 Years Old db **(89) n22.5 t22.5 f22 b22** a fabulous improvement on the last bottling I encountered. Still possesses blood oranges to die for, but greatly enhanced by some sublime spices and a magnificent juiciness. *40%*

Singleton of Glen Ord 32 Year Old db **(91) n23.5 t23 f22 b22.5.** Delicious. But if ever a malt has screamed out to be at 46%, this is it. *40%*

 Fadandel.dk Glen Ord 15 Years Old dist 1997, bott 2012 **(93.5) n22.5** a well used second- or even third-fill cask has left the sharp citrus and malt unmolested; **t24** ...and the most Salivating Whisky of the Year goes to....; **f23.5** that astonishing juicy malt-citrus combination continues until, at last, a little chalky oak catches up. Thinned ulmo honey merges with a touch of late maple syrup: just so fresh and clean...; **b23.5** with Glen Ord being a key malt for so many top blends, hard to imagine there'll ever be scope for this to become a big player on the single malt stage. A great pity, as this gorgeous bottling testifies... *50.7%*

Liquid Library Glen Ord 1997 ex-bourbon hogshead, dist 97, bott 11 **(84) n22 t21 f20 b21.** A pretty tired cask even before it was filled back in 1997, the oak involvement here is virtually trace. *50.4%. The Whisky Agency.*

Old Particular Highland Glen Ord 16 Years Old refill hogshead, cask no. 9954, dist Apr 1997, bott Aug 2013 **(94) n23.5** one of those teasing noses which keeps you spellbound and in its thrall for seemingly hours A near perfect marriage of ridiculously light peat and green and over-ripe banana. At once chunky...yet light. How does it do that....? **t24** juicy delivery with the malt entering on many levels of intensity and complexity. A string of oak offers both backbone and further density; the mid-ground retains its pulsing, fresh malt and the lightest layer of smoke; **f22.5** some light esters hang on creating almost a Jamaican rum style; **b24** staggeringly beautiful, effortlessly complex whisky. *48.4%. nc ncf sc. 396 bottles.*

GLENROTHES
Speyside, 1878. Edrington. Working.

Glenrothes 2001 dist 25 May 01, bott 13 db **(72) n16 t21 f17 b18.** The sulphur in Spain makes this whisky very plain. *43% WB15/297*

The Glenrothes Alba Reserve db **(87.5) n22 t22 f21.5 b22.** You know that smartly groomed, polite but rather dull chap you invariable get at dinner parties? *40%*

 The Glenrothes Elders' Reserve db **(75.5) n19 t20.5 f17.5 b18.5.** Now when I was a young man, young man, Scotch single malt whisky tasted a lot better than this, you know. Well, could hardly have tasted worse, could it?! That nice young Mr Lloyd George wouldn't have put up with this rubbish, oh no. He would have sent in the troops and nationalised the industry, that's what he would have done. Hung anyone guilty of using sherry butts stinking of sulphur. Or shot 'em. Only fair. These young blenders... Blenders?!? Don't know they are born... In my day.... *43% WB16/046*

 The Glenrothes Manse Reserve db **(74) n18.5 t20 f17 b18.5.** More like Mansfield Reserves... *43% WB16/045*

 The Glenrothes Minister's Reserve db **(91) n22.5** trace sulphur, but by Genrothes standards this is pretty amazing: the grape really does come through with a spring in its juicy step; **t23.5** absolutely top dollar sherry at work: a gorgeous sultana-laden sweetness but backed by the most luscious mouth feel, aided by a little liquorice from the oak; **f22** a little manuka honey fights off successfully the late bitterness from the obligatory dodgy butt; **b23** I think the Minister had a little word with someone upstairs... 43% WB16/047

⬦ **The Glenrothes Sherry Cask Reserve** db **(68) n16 t19 f16 b17**. Inevitable, I suppose... The tragedy is that before some bloke stuffed lighted sulphur candles into these sherry butts, thereby ruining them and the whisky which would later mature in them, they were obviously the dog's...; and had they been left unmolested we would have been nosing and tasting something of intense brilliance. Exasperating doesn't even begin to cover it. 40% WB16/044

⬦ **Anam na h-Alba The Soul of Scotland Glenrothes 1988** bourbon cask, dist Mar 88, bott Jun 14 **(94) n23.5** barley with a squeeze of blood orange; salty; not just spices, but the odd herb, too...; **t24** fabulous delivery: the oak really is up for it, but doesn't possess a single degree of bitterness or tautness. The tannins still retain their sugars, which merge merrily with the malt: spot on balance between light ulmo honey and salt; **f23** a beautiful caramelised biscuit fade, complete with spice and even distant, molasses-sweetened cinnamon **b23.5** very high class Speyside. 53.4%. 92 bottles.

Cadenhead's Small Batch Glenrothes-Glenlivet Aged 24 Years bourbon barrels, dist 1989, bott 2013 **(96.5) n23.5** toasted hazelnuts, natural caramels...a kind of Topic candy but with spice taking the place of milk chocolate; a little kumquat...not unlike what might be found at Four Roses; **t23.5** superb delivery: a wide range of sugars, from juicy icing sugar to muscovado adding real depth to the intense grist and breath-taking spice; ridiculously and quite staggering fresh; the ulmo honey builds early on, revealing itself into a more earthy, heather-honey style later; **f25** long, with evidence of a high copper content (maybe a new part of a still or condenser at work) which gives a certain polish to the cocoa. But it doesn't end there: we are seemingly whisked away to Kentucky, for the late honey, liquorice and hickory gives a distinctly top-notch bourbon feel: no bad thing; **b24.5** always thought Glenrothes to be a little over-rated (though obviously not helped by its sherry butt regime of the last two decades), but this is unreconstituted quality. The tasting notes attached to the bottle bangs on about fruit, I have just noticed (I never read anything like that until mine are done and dusted). I haven't a clue as to what they are going on about...if this hasn't all the hallmarks of a ultra-high quality bourbon cask or probably two, taking into account the degree of complexity, I really don't know what does. 56.9%. 360 bottles. WB15/071

⬦ **Chapter 7 Glenrothes 1997 17 Year Old** bourbon hogshead, cask no. 15721 **(91) n22.5** a big spice nip hovers over the fruit-like juices. Something of the cake shop about this one; **t23** fresh for its years, with that non-specific fruit note really making the most of the sugars and growing butterscotch; **f22** a quieter fade, drying as the oak gently outmuscles the malt; **b23.5** richer and more heavily bodied than many Glenrothes. 54.5%. sc. 219 bottles.

Cheiftan's Glenrothes Aged 13 Years sherry butt, cask no. 3400/3401, dist Mar 99, bott Feb 13 **(68) n17 t19 f16 b17**. Absolutely standard of its cask type from this period from this distillery. Alas. 46%. 1896 bottles. WB15/163

The Coopers Choice Glenrothes 1997 Aged 16 Years hogshead, cask no. 15715, bott 2014 **(85.5) n22.5 t22 f20 b21**. Par for the course Glenrothes: starts well with a big malty proclamation...and fades almost without trace. Still, if you like a bit of blood orange and boot polish to your nose. Go for it. 46%. 300 bottles. WB15/300

⬦ **Glen Fahrn Airline Nr 09 Glenrothes 1992 Aged 19 Years** bourbon hogshead, cask no. 108 **(92) n22.5 t23 f23.5 b23**. A delicate, elegantly structured and rhythmically balanced malt, showing an unusual light phenol sub-plot for a Glenrothes, amid fresher apples and intense barley. 52.1%. sc. 124 bottles.

⬦ **Gordon & MacPhail The Macphails Collection Glenrothes 1971 (94) n22** a tiring malt, as the tannins have a firm grip. But the toasted raisins are of the best fruit cake tradition; **t23.5** not often you get eucalyptus on the delivery. But the grape is so rich, it is handled with tact and respect. The tannins continue to drive forward, but now muffled by the delicious grape; **f24.5** hits the high spots, as salt and spice combine to big up the high quality fruitcake style moistened with the very best molasses; **b24** threatens to run to old age fast. But instead we get a master class in age management by the fruit. Sublime. 43%

Master of Malt Single Cask Glenrothes 25 Years Old refill, dist 20 Jun 88, bott 18 Feb 14 **(87) n23 t22.5 f20 b21.5**. An old chap with no major faults to speak of and, in many ways, a remarkably unscathed dram for its age. However, while the Digestive biscuit note adds a morish roughage, it is a little too toffee dependent. 54.2%. sc. 50 bottles. WB15/213

⬦ **Master of Malt Single Cask Glenrothes 26 Year Old** refill bourbon hogshead, dist Jun 88, bott Sep 14 **(92.5) n23** huge salty barley surge, the complexity supplied by lemon and liquorice; **t24** probably the most concentrated form of barley I have encountered this year! Almost like an oak-stained barley wine; **f22.5** much drier: the liquorice has the last word; **b23** had to look twice to ensure I had the correct sample: unusually confident and intense for this distillery. *53.4%. sc. 40 bottles.*

Old Malt Cask Glenrothes Aged 16 Years refill hogshead, cask no. 10435, dist Dec 97, bott Apr 14 **(92.5) n23** clean with a proud butterscotch tart theme. The barley is still fresh and at times concentrated; **t23.5** I defy you to count how many different style of natural toffee you can find on this...; in thin layering of ulmo honey sits well with the maple syrup and persistent malt; **f23** a little spiced cocoa on the fading barley sugar; **b23** given the right cask, shows what a lovely malt this distillery is capable of producing. Engaging and irresistible. *50%. sc. 361 bottles.*

◈ **Old Particular Speyside Glenrothes 17 Years Old** refill hogshead, cask no. 10564, dist Sept 97, bott Dec 14 **(84.5) n22.5 t22.5 f19 b20.5**. Sets off with an impressive kaleidoscope of malt and honey on nose and delivery. But the finish is as bitter as it is disappointing. *48.4%. nc ncf sc. 266 bottles.*

◈ **Old Particular Speyside Glenrothes 11 Years Old** sherry hogshead, cask no. 10792, dist May 04, bott May 15 **(72) n18 t20 f16 b18**. Has a couple of strengths: the muscle on the grape and the depth of the sugars. It has a major weakness, also. No prizes for guessing what.... *48.4%. nc ncf sc. 250 bottles.*

◈ **The Pearls of Scotland Golden Pearl Collection Glenrothes 1988** cask no. 7856, dist Jun 88, bott Sept 15 **(95.5) n24** exotic fruit territory has been entered into here, so old age is confirmed. Just a little smoke drifting about, too; **t24** that is, quite simply, brilliant! Kumquats and red liquorice confront the big spice and ulmo and Zambian honey mix...and decides to blend rather than fight...; **f23.5** some trace phenols add even more weight to the honey-tipped vanilla; late on, the malt intensifies by delicious degrees; **b24** not just competent. But effortlessly beautiful, too. *50.6%. sc.*

Provenance Glenrothes 'Over 9 Years sherry butt, cask no. 10191, dist Spring 2004, bott Winter 2014 **(76) n19 t22 f16.5 b18.5**. Mildly sulphured, and for a Glenrothes very mildly early on. Good to see a youngster at play here and the unmistakable oloroso has some blisteringly good moments early on. But the lack of sophistication to be offered by slow maturation added to the eventual uncomfortable powderiness of the treated butt leads to a disappointing, though inevitable, decline. *61.2%. nc ncf sc. Douglas Laing & Co.*

◈ **Provenance Glenrothes Over 10 Years** sherry butt, cask no. 10542, dist Spring 04, bott Autumn 14 **(62) n12 t18 f16 b16**. A trademark Glenrothes heavily sulphured sherry butt. *46%. nc ncf sc.*

◈ **Scotch Malt Whisky Society Cask 30.81 Aged 23 Years** refill hogshead, dist 24 Sept 90 **(91.5) n23** well mannered oak softens the crunchy barley; sexy non-specific fruit; **t22.5** firm from the first moment with a mix of white and Demerara sugars; **f23** spices up beautifully... almost bread pudding dipped in chocolate; **b23** fantastically crisp and juicy. *56%. sc. 206 bottles.*

◈ **Scotch Malt Whisky Society Cask 30.83 Aged 34 Years** refill hogshead, dist 03 Jul 80 **(82.5) n22 t21.5 f19 b20**. Just enough sugars and juiciness to take the edge off the over enthusiastic oak. *45.8%. sc. 178 bottles.*

◈ **Scotch Malt Whisky Society Cask 30.84 Aged 34 Years** refill hogshead, dist 24 Apr 80 **(88) n23.5** massive oak. Yet the exotic fruit hits just the right chords...; **t22.5** early muscovado sugar and under-ripe greengage compliments the hairy-chested oak; **f20.5** dries a tad too aggressively as the sweetness tails off; **b21.5** an uneven and often unequal performer. But the array of fruit and sugar does entertain when needed. *44.5%. sc. 213 bottles.*

◈ **Scotch Malt Whisky Society Cask 30.86 Aged 21 Years** refill barrel, dist 9 Sept 93 **(90) n23** a beautifully subtle lemon and tangerine mix with the butterscotch; **t22.5** impressive balance between unlikely depth of barley juice and the more crusty dryness; **f22** the spices really kick in hard as the oak bites; **b22.5** fresh and pulsing with vitality despite the lengthening, confident oak. *50.3%. sc. 186 bottles.*

◈ **Signatory Glenrothes 1989 (89) n22** moist fruitcake, though still a little doughy and undercooked; **t23.5** soft delivery with major fruit and molasses. But then hits a wonderful crescendo as the cocoa is driven home; **f21.5** becomes remarkably soporific with fruit fudge... and a little furriness at the finish; **b22** one of the better refill sherry butts to come this distillery's way for a while. Maybe a one-paced, slightly dreary dram after the gorgeous delivery, but always great – and highly unusual - to see a fruity version of this distillery relatively untainted. *54.1% Wb16/18*

◈ **Single Cask Collection Glenrothes 2002 12 Year Old** bourbon hogshead **(85.5) n21.5 t22.5 f20 b21.5**. Juicy and malty with stellar barley sugar quality. Refuses to expand out, though. *54.8%. sc.*

The Single Malts of Scotland Glenrothes Aged 23 Years bourbon barrels, cask no. 35484, dist 12 Nov 90, bott 25 Mar 14 **(80.5) n21.5 t21.5 f18.5 b18**. While the barley is thick enough to chisel through, the slight milkiness and bitterness present suggests the cask failed to make it through the 23 years... 49.4%. 210 bottles. WB15/291

Speyside Single Malt Glenrothes 26 Years 2nd fill sherry butt, dist Jun 1987, bott Dec 2013 **(89) n22** massive barley sugar signature; some sherbet lemons rather undermine the age but the overall experience is invigorating; **t23** barley at its most pumped up, fresh and salivating – hard to believe it has spent over quarter of a century in the barrel; **f22** slightly tart and tired oak but again the freshness of the barley, coupled with some fizzy candy-like properties, make this something to behold! **b22** by no means a run of the distillery Glenrothes. Not sure if this has been distilled or made in a sweet shop... 53.3%. nc ncf sc. 288 bottles.

That Boutique-y Whisky Glenrothes batch 1 **(89) n22.5** charming lemon curd tart and custard; clean malt; **t22.5** viscous, lightly sweetened malt on delivery, a vanilla and barley mix follows; **f22** diced Nice coconut biscuit; **b22** well mannered, non-taxing...and very attractive. 47.9%. 235 bottles. WB15/189

⚜ **Whiskybroker Glenrothes 17 Years** hogshead, cask no. 15721, dist 15 Oct 97 **(93) n22.5** a graceful intertwangling of punchy, spicy tannins, molasses and bold barley; **t24** excellent delivery: a gorgeous mixture of oaky weight which ensure stature and a more nimble maltiness revealing surprising life; all backed up by serious spices, matching the Demerara sugars and red liquorice blow for blow; **f23** a very elegant array of vanillas and spice; **b23.5** another example of why putting Glenrothes into fresh sherry should be counted as a national crime... 54.5%. sc.

The Whisky Cask Glenrothes Aged 22 Years sherry butt, dist 1990, bott 2012 **(91.5) n22 t23 f22.5 b23**. Just so great to enjoy the unusual experience of savouring an unspoiled sherried Glenrothes. 53.8%. nc ncf.

⚜ **Whiskyjace Glenrothes 26 Year Old** bourbon cask, dist 1988, bott 2014 **(92.5) n23.5** a yummy nose which pushes all the right malty buttons; irresistible citrus, too; **t23** high flying juiciness shows spiced barley at its busiest; **f22.5** pays its respects to the gathering oak, but with a refreshing drizzle of citrus on the vanilla; **b23.5** this distillery really can impress when matured in good oak, as is the case here. 53.4%

⚜ **Wilson & Morgan Barrel Selection Glenrothes 25 Year Old** oloroso sherry finish, cask no. 1609, 1610, dist 1990, bott 2015 **(73) n18 t20 f17 b18**. There are good reasons why the words "Glenrothes" and "oloroso" in the same sentence make me twitch. Taste this and discover why... 53.3%. 396 bottles.

GLEN SCOTIA
Campbeltown, 1832. Loch Lomond Distillers. Working

Glen Scotia 2005 9 Year Old Heavily Peated cask no. 136, bourbon cask db **(92.5) n23 t23.5 f23 b23**. Peaty malts which nose like a farmyard can go either way...and usually to extremes. This settles into a beautifully compact, fabulously distilled dram where the barley gets an equal airing to the massive smoke. The sugars are on song from first to last and help bring out the best of the late cocoa. Brilliant stuff helped by the lack of aggressive oak. 57.7%. nc ncf. Taiwan exclusive.

Glen Scotia Aged 10 Years bourbon cask, bott Dec 12 db **(90.5) n22.5 t23.5 f22 b22.5**. Fabulous to see Scotia back in this excellent nick again. 46%. nc ncf.

Glen Scotia 12 Years Old db **(73.5) n18 t19 f18 b18.5**. Ooops! I once said you could write a book about this called "Murder by Caramel." Now it would be a short story called "Murder by Flavours Unknown." What is happening here? Well, a dozen years ago Glen Scotia was not quite the place to be for consistent whisky, unlike now. Here, the caramel is the only constant as the constituent parts disintegrate. 40%

Glen Scotia Aged 12 Years bourbon cask, bott Dec 12 db **(89) n22 t22 f23 b22**. Simplistic but delicious. 46%. nc ncf.

Glen Scotia 1999 14 Year Old Heavily Peated cask 528, bourbon cask db **(89) n22.5 t22 f22.5 b22**. Elegant peat and showing excellent sugars a third of the way in. At times a little thin and on the fierce side with fast still spirit burn rather than spice. But genuinely pleasing overall. 55.9% nc ncf. Taiwan exclusive.

Glen Scotia 14 Year Old Peated bourbon cask db **(87) n21.5 t22 f21.5 b22**. A very straight bat played by this one: a malty up and downer with few frills others than a slow though ineffective build up of smoke. 50%. nc ncf.

Glen Scotia Aged 16 Years bourbon cask, bott Dec 12 db **(87) n22 t22 f21 b22**. Signs of a less than brilliant distillate which has been ironed out to some good effect in the cask. 46%. nc ncf.

Glen Scotia Aged 18 Years bourbon cask, bott Dec 12 db (77) n20 t21 f17 b19. Malty but hot as Hades: a reminder of a less than glorious period in the distillery's history. 46%. nc ncf.

Glen Scotia Aged 21 Years bourbon cask, bott Dec 12 db (86.5) n21.5 t22.5 f21 b21.5. Appears nothing like its age: the very vaguely smoked malt is entirely on top and offers little deviation. A playful spice reminds you oak is involved somewhere. 46%. nc ncf.

Glen Scotia 1989 23 Years Old cask 310, bourbon cask db (96) n24 t24 f24 b24. Obviously a cherry-picked cask, as this is stunning. A riot of delicate honey notes trying to outdo each other. Majestic ulmo honey leads the way with heather honey not far behind. Light spice flickers like a butterfly on a lavender bush. Off note free and about as good a Glen Scotia I have ever seen. Like the other new Glen Scotias, arrived too late for full tasting notes. 55.6% nc ncf.

Glen Scotia Legends of Scotia 1st Release "Picture House" 10 Year Old Heavily Peated bourbon cask db (85.5) n21 t21 f22 b21.5. Not exactly a B Movie. But doesn't have you on the edge of your seat, either. Some smoke meanders along the thin plot line with little to say while weight takes on only a walk on part. Occasionally complex, but you'll be asleep before the lights come on... 50%. nc ncf. 6,000 bottles.

Glen Scotia Legends of Scotia 2nd Release "Murfield" Heavily Peated bourbon cask db (94.5) n23 t24 f23.5 b24. The nose has about as much smoky power as me teeing off from the 5th: virtually none. But it apologetically creaks into action on the palate and actually plays a delicate and sophisticated game with the peat no more than shadowing the muscovado and liquorice. Again, a little ulmo honey shows to add understated sweetness and body. With such genius at play less Muirfeld, more Tynecastle, I'd say... 50%. nc ncf. 6,000 bottles.

◇ **Glen Scotia Single Cask Distillery Edition 001** cask no. 196, dist Dec 02, bott May 15 db (94) n23 the oak kicks up some busy spice. The malt swirls around a bit, but is upstaged by the oak in every quarter, to the extent that a few bourbon notes are detectable; the vaguest degree of smoke can be detected, also...; t24 a much more co-operative delivery, with the barley pretty apparent. But, again, those superb liquorice-manuka honey bourbon notes are soon apparent; f23.5 relaxes now and stretches. So even a slight sawdusty note creeps into the sugars which have no problem lasting the pace; meanwhile, those spices just keep on gently stinging; b23.5 a delicious malt which makes the most of what is available. Love it! 56.1%. sc.

◇ **Glen Scotia Victoriana** db (89.5) n23 adore the malt and oak stripes with vague citrus weaving in and out at random. Very soft...; t23 initially, thick manuka honey at play, then a spice wave. Malty and keeps the oak at arm's length. That's until the toffee invades the midground; f21.5 now the toffee dominates as the sugars from the heavy char take on a chewy, slightly one-dimensional theme; b22 an unusual malt for a cask strength. Beyond the nose there is limited layering, instead concentrating on the malt-toffee intertwangling. 51.5%

The Pearls of Scotland Glen Scotia 1992 22 Year Old cask no. 35, dist Jan 92, bott Feb 14, (91) n22.5 the malt is still evident, if a little surly; the oak is layered and sweetened with yam; t23.5 an indulgent but enjoyable lift off with the sugars showing early, like molten sugar on porridge. But the chewy, creamier fudge is sublime; the barey is unmolested and intense; f22.5 the oaks reappear on a custardy ticket, though doing nothing to reduce the barley effect; b23 a few clues here that that spirit may have been a bit of a tough guy when first distilled. But over 20 years in a top quality cask has set it on a blameless path...48.7%.

Scotch Malt Whisky Society Cask 93.59 Aged 14 Years refill barrel, dist 31 Jul 99 (94.5) n24 uncommonly delicate and dry, and charms its way around the nose with its well-mannered, lightly salted smokiness; t23.5 probably more heavily smoked than you might first think. First on the scene are gorgeous gristy sugars while the smoke builds quietly and unobtrusively. Some cocoa residue arrives with the pinging spices; f23 delicate vanilla and smoke entwines; b24 an understatedly attractive smoky Scotia which disarms more than overpowers with peat. A semi-silent classic... 60.8%. nc ncf sc. 193 bottles.

GLEN SPEY
Speyside, 1885. Diageo. Working.

Glen Spey Aged 12 Years db (90) n23 the kind of firm, busy malt you expect from this distillery plus some lovely spice; t22 mouthwatering and fresh, a layer of honey makes for an easy three or four minutes; f22 drier vanilla, but the pulsing oak is controlled and stylish; b23 very similar to the first Glen Spey I can remember in this range, the one before the over-toffeed effort of two years ago. Great to see it back to its more natural, stunningly beautiful self. 43%

Glen Spey Special Release 2010 21 Years Old sherry American oak cask, dist 1988 db (94.5) n23 t24 f23.5 b24. Glen Speys of this age tended to find their way into blends where they would beef up the sweeter malt content. Sometimes they were used to impart clean sherry or at least fruit, but otherwise give nothing of themselves. This bottling tends to take both strands and then ties them up in a complex and compelling fashion. Wonderful. 50.4%. nc ncf. Diageo.

◈ **Anam na h-Alba The Soul of Scotland Glen Spey 1988** bourbon cask, dist Jun 88, bott Mar 14 **(89) n22** very simple nose: clean, with some well-shuffled vanilla and barley; **t23.5** begins a deliciously salivating course as the malt hits full throttle. Development pegged back by marauding toffee notes; **f21.5** vanilla and fudge; **b22** the natural toffees extracted from the oak make for a quiet bottling. 47.3%. 180 bottles.

Cadenhead's Small Batch Glen Spey-Glenlivet Aged 17 Years bourbon hogsheads, dist 1995, bott 2013 **(90) n23** the lightest trace of smoke – probably due to the history of a pre-used hogshead – adds surprising extra weight to the perky tannin and usual floral earthiness. The gooseberries show the barley in good form, though; **t22.5** salivating as the sharp, tangy barley cuts through the soft oils; both gristy and pithy in equal measures, it doesn't take long for the spices to say "hi"; **f22** tangy oak but the firm barley retains control; **b22.5** a few decades back this was not a difficult malt to locate, either as a proprietor-bottled youngster or among the independents. By no means the case today, which is a shame: few do light but fruity and juicy Speysider quite like this distillery. 46%. 948 bottles. WB15/088

Hepburn's Choice Glen Spey Aged 11 Years sherry butt, dist 02, bott 14 **(85.5) n21 t22 f21 b21.5.** Another of those juicy, somewhat oak-free malts Hunter Laing specialise in, where you see the whisky naked, warts and all. Just a light citric tang to this, but there is no tannin to disguise the minor butyric, either. Still, salivating and lively with a curious grappa finale. 46%. nc ncf sc. 816 bottles.

◈ **Old Malt Cask Glen Spey 18 Years Old** refill hogshead, cask no. 11192, dist Jan 97, bott Jan 15 **(95) n23.5** outstanding oak and citrus mix, indicating genuine happiness between the oak and malt sections. A little banana and mango smoothie in there, too...; **t23.5** mmmm.... those fabulous malt notes: salivating, intense, seemingly clean barley. But there is not much else happening besides: the oak starts nonchalantly, but begins to warm to the task....perhaps helped by the subtle spices; **f24** a top-drawer finish: the quality of the oak is remarkable, and the delicate latte coffee infusion invites the malt to carry on with its sumptuous unravelling; **b24** one of those rare malts which just gets better as it goes along. Hard to imagine such a light and sometimes transparent malt having so many tricks up its sleeve...and not even the hint of a suggestion of a flaw or off note. My kind of Speysider. 50%. nc ncf sc. 297 bottles.

Old Particular Speyside Glen Spey Aged 15 Years refill hogshead, cask no. 10286, dist Apr 99, bott Apr 14 **(85.5) n21 t23 f20.5 b21.** Pleasantly clean, though strictly limited malt thanks to the old cask employed. But the after-delivery, a combination gristy malt and concentrated, unhindered sugars, is sheer joy. 48.4%. nc ncf sc. 324 bottles.

GLENTAUCHERS

Speyside, 1898. Chivas Brothers. Working.

◈ **Alexander Murray & Co Glentauchers 1996 17 Years Old (84) n21 t22 f20.5 b20.5.** Not unpleasant. Perfectly drinkable, in fact. But 'Tauchers is one of my favourite of all Speyside distilleries, producing a dancing malt as it waltzes and jives around your taste buds. Here, though, we have a malt which, after the first few lively seconds, is stripped of its personality and zest, vanishing into a toffee-chocolate depression. 40%

◈ **Cadenhead's Authentic Collection Glentauchers Aged 38 Years** bourbon barrel, dist 1976 **(95.5) n23.5** you expect to get a disarming mix of gentle exotic fruit and pure untainted barley sugar...and that's exactly what arrives at your nostril's door; **t24** and that pristine clarity translates onto the palate as the barley forms a crystalline mass. The sugars are sublime in their non-egocentric role, offering molassed support to paper over any cracks; **f23.5** some understandable fatigue from the barrel, but nothing which detracts or harms. Dries and ramps up the spices before the vanilla takes grip; **b24.5** a quite brilliant bottling which helps further the name of this understated and truly great distillery. You can see why this malt is so greatly prised by blenders, especially those creating ultra high class aged blends. 50.8%

Càrn Mòr Strictly Limited Edition Glentauchers Aged 18 Years bourbon barrels, dist 1996, bott 2014 **(91) n23** soft William pear serenaded by vanilla; **t23.5** a juicy quasi-fruity sprint off the gun before settling into an intensely malty theme; **f22** slight oak bitterness, but good spice, too; **b22.5** the type which makes you sigh thanks to its delicious simplicity. 46%. nc ncf. 443 bottles from 2 casks. WB15/052

◈ **Chapter 7 Glentauchers 1996 18 Year Old** bourbon barrel, cask no. 3809 **(89.5) n22** malt, yeast and vanilla in equal measures; **t23** fizzing delivery: ultra-salivating and malty; **f22.5** the oak makes a dry re-entry for a quite suave finale; **b22** curiously yeasty and bubbly. 48.3%. sc. 173 bottles.

◈ **Endangered Drams Glentauchers 16 Year Old** dist 1996, bott 2013 (94) n23.5 t23.5 f23 b24. Unusually sharp and fruity for a 'Tauchers, but that doesn't detract from its usual supremely-weighted complexity. About as busy as a Speysider ever gets, and that fruit offers extra weight here, too. Excellent, chocolate-bitter orange late middle. 55.2%

Gordon & MacPhail Cask Strength Glentauchers 1995 (76) n17 t20 f19 b20. I have been banging the gong longest of all for Gentauchers being one of the greatest yet-to-be-discovered distilleries of the world. But not even this distillery's brilliance can fully overcome the curse of lightly sulphured sherry butts... 58.3%.

◈ **Gordon & MacPhail Distillery Label Glentauchers 1996** (81) n21 t21.5 f19 b19.5. After the unalloyed magnificence of their 1994 bottling, I was drooling into this glass in anticipation. But talk about after the Lord Mayor's show... This is a disappointingly dull creature with absolutely none of the spark not only of the 1994 edition, but from what you'd expect from this distillery in general. Offers a few honey notes on delivery by way of compensation. But that's your lot. The furriness from the midpoint onwards dominates, alas. 43%

Hepburn's Choice Glentauchers Aged 8 Years sherry butt, bott 2014 (74.5) n20 t19 f17.5 b18. Usually hard to go wrong with a Glentauchers, one of the world's most consistent spirits. Unless the oak has a personality disorder, of course... 46%. nc ncf sc. 310 bottles.

The Maltman Glentauchers Aged 15 Years bourbon cask, cask no. 3854, dist Jul 97, bott Apr 13 (90.5) n22.5 sliced green banana and gooseberry; t23 fresh barley, of the barley sugar variety; f22.5 vanilla and crisp, gristy barley: simple but effective...; b22.5 after a day of tasting finishes of every shape and hue, oh! the sheer unalloyed joy of finding excellent distillate having grown up in a respectable bourbon cask... 46%. sc ncf nc. 298 bottles. WB15/214

Master of Malt Single Cask Glentauchers 15 Year Old (96) n23 egg custard tart...with a gristy layering; t25 one of the deliveries of the year: mouth-watering explosion of barley at its gristiest – and fortified with a citrus-muscovado sugar mix; f24 elegant oak in slight sherbet-fizzing form. Of course, the barley has the final word; b24 a great distillery, magnificently and truly faultlessly portrayed. Not a weakness nor off note: hard to see this distillery in a better light. 55.1%. sc.

◈ **Old Malt Cask Glentauchers Aged 18 Years** refill barrel, cask no. 11149, dist Feb 96, bott Dec 14 (91.5) n22.5 the oak character dominates, but nowhere near over aged and with the malt sturdy, a shade musty perhaps, but proud; t23 a few tramlines of sugar on the malty-oaky road; f23 some late fizz shows the barley still has some teeth. The malt retains its integrity despite the oaky spine; b23 I remember when I was learning about Speyside whisky in the late '70s. And a few malts came across as confident and vibrant without frills and absolutely vital for older blends to show malty steel. This takes me right back to the kind of whiskies I was introduced to then. Timeless. 50%. nc ncf sc. 169 bottles.

The Pearls of Scotland Glentauchers 1996 17 Year Old cask no. 3616, dist Jun 96, bott Nov 13 (94) n23.5 such a relaxed Speyside-style nose: the balance between the oak and crisp barley is nigh spot on, with neither determined to overpower the other. Simple, but effective...; t23.5 just the right kind of bite – the kind of bite which every bender worth his salt is looking for in a blended scotch. So it is no coincidence that this is a malt truly prized by the grey beards of the lab. This manifests itself in a rushing wave of sprightly barley, at once jagged and soft with salivates, and continues to do so as a light mocha on the oak begins to shape; f23 like the nose, but in pulses and now with soft oils rather than celery...; b24 even when as a relaxed as this, a 'Tauchers is just such balm for the soul. A true little gem. 47.7%.

◈ **Spirit of Caledonia Glentauchers 18 Years Old** (88) n22 salty, malty and a little cask tang; t23 eye-wateringly sharp delivery with salivating malt and crisp sugars; f21 a little tangy, as the nose warns; b22 deliciously lively and survives a mediocre cask. Just. 50.2%.

That Boutique-y Whisky Glentauchers batch 1 (91.5) n22 apple tart...with custard... and maybe a little hay thrown in on top; t23.5 intense malt from the off with crystallised muscovado sugars adding extra crunch; f23 firm and flinty; the light malty oil gather a little spice; b23 shouts "top grade Speyside blending fodder" at every opportunity. 50.7%. WB15/224

Wemyss Malts 1992 Single Speyside Glentauchers "Liquorice Spiral" bott 13 (92) n24 sensual and soft, this just has to be just about the epitome of high grade blending Speyside, so far as a nose is concerned. The barley is ripe and sugar coated and anyone old enough to remember Black Jack and Fruit Salad candy in its pomp will be cheerfully transported back to their childhood; t23 the nose suggests "salivating". And salivating it is...to a dribblesome degree. The citrus notes are also evident as well as the tangy barley. Vanilla begins to fill the middle ground; f22 biscuity and dries as the oak shows some puny muscle; b23 another minor gem from one of the most trustworthy malts in the business. 46%. sc. 339 bottles.

⬦ **Whisky-Fässle Glentauchers 18 Year Old** barrel, dist 1996, bott 2014 **(84.5)** n21 t22.5 f20 b21. Would never have recognised this as a 'Tauchers had I tasted it blind. All kinds of toffee at work and though there is a brief glimpse of the usual malty landscape on delivery, what follows is pretty dull and disappointing. *51.9%. nc ncf.*

GLENTURRET
Highlands (Perthshire), 1775. Edrington. Working.

Glenturret Aged 8 Years db **(88)** n21 t22 f23 b22. Technically no prizewinner. But the dexterity of the honey is charming, as this distillery has a tendency sometimes to be. *40%*

The Glenturret Aged 10 Years db **(76)** n19 t18 f20 b19. Lots of trademark honey but some less than impressive contributions from both cask and the stillman. *40%*

The Glenturret Aged 15 Years db **(87)** n21 t22 f22 b22. A beautifully clean, small-still style dram that would have benefitted from being bottled at a fuller strength. A discontinued bottling now: if you see it, it is worth the small investment. *40%*

The Famous Grouse 1986 Glenturret Glasgow 2014 Limited Edition dist 86, bott 14 db **(95)** n24 about as chunky a Glenturret as I can remember: chocolate fudge in tandem with apricot and kumquat. The sugars are no less heavy with treacle and pears in close proximity; t24 every bit as rounded and chewy as the nose suggests. This distillery always has honey somewhere and it arrives as a blend of manuka and – ensuring the depth and mouth feel – ulmo honeys make a huge impact and add even thicker layers of complexity; f23 maybe a slight tang to the finish from some kind of wine cask. It was expected but nowhere near as damaging as I had feared. Again, the chocolate fudge is back on the menu doing all it can to see off the late but prevailing furry bitterness; b24 I honestly can't remember the last time I experienced a Glenturret this good – even taking into account its blemish. A PB and Gold medal performance... *46.4%. 1,800 bottles. WB15/409*

⬦ **Gordon & MacPhail The Macphails Collection Glenturret 2001** **(82.5)** n22 t22.5 f19 b19. You'll love the rich honey nose and dates and walnuts on delivery. Some substantial whisky at play here. But one or two rogue casks inject a furry bitterness which, not unlike a single wind turbine in an area of glorious British countryside, pointlessly spoils the beauty. *43%*

⬦ **The Pearls of Scotland Glenturret 1994** cask no. 213, dist May 94, bott May 15 **(83)** n21 t22.5 f19 b20.5. Serious honey abounds. But can't entirely overcome the milkiness of the over-tired cask. *55%. sc.*

Signatory Vintage Single Malt Glenturret 1993 Aged 20 Years hogsheads, cask no. 173, dist 19 Apr 93, 07 Feb 14 **(81)** n20.5 t21 f19 b20.5. Borderline feinty with the cut adding a few extra oils offering kumquats in nougat. Big whisky from a tiny distillery, but struggles beyond the early barley-honey mix. *43%. nc sc. 376 bottles. WB15/019*

GLENUGIE
Highlands (Eastern). 1834–1983. Whitbread. Closed.

Deoch an Doras Glenugie 30 Years Old dist 1980, bott 2011 db **(87)** n22 t23.5 f19.5 b22. Now there's something I didn't expect to see again: a distillery bottling of Glenugie. Well, technically, anyway, as Glenugie was part of the Chivas group when it died in the 1980s. As far as I can remember they only brought it out once, either as a seven- or five-year-old. I think that went to Italy, so when I walked around the old site just after it closed, it was a Gordon and MacPhail bottling I drank from and it tasted nothing like this! Just a shame there is a very slight flaw in the sherry butt, but just great to see it in bottle again. *52.13%. nc ncf.*

GLENURY ROYAL
Highlands (Eastern), 1868–1985. Diageo. Demolished.

Glenury Royal 36 Years Old db **(89)** n21 t23 f22 b23. An undulating dram, hitting highs and lows. The finish, in particular, is impressive: just when it looks on its last legs, it revives delightfully. The whole package, though far from perfect, is pretty astounding. *50.2%*

Glenury Royal 40 Year Old Limited Edition dist 1970, bott 2011 db **(84)** n20.5 t20 f22 b21.5. Glenury is these days so rare I kept this back as a treat to savour as I neared the end of the book. The finale throws up a number of interesting citrus equations. But the oak, for the most part, is too rampant here and makes for a puckering experience. *59.4%. 1,500 bottles.*

⬦ **Lombard Jewels of Scotland Single Malt Glenury Royal 1973** cask no. 6867, dist 21 Jun 1973, bott 2014 **(86.5)** n22 t22.5 f22 b20. Always great to happen across old timers like this and delve into the last of their finite stocks. The romantic in me wants to big up the shards of honey embedded in the oak. But the professional must report that, for its charm and gritty determination to stay lively and fresh, the oak has imparted a dry sawdusty trait which plays a major part in the whisky's character, with the exception of a moment or two just after the initial delivery. Even the milky cocoa finale is dictated by the tannin. Charming, though. *40%. sc.*

HAZELBURN *(see Springbank)*

HIGHLAND PARK
Highlands (Island–Orkney), 1795. Edrington. Working.

Highland Park Dark Origins db **(80)** n19 t23 f18 b20. Part of that Dark Origin must be cocoa, as there is an abundance of delicious high grade chocolate here. But the other part is not so much dark as yellow, as sulphur is around on the nose and finish in particular - and does plenty of damage. Genuinely disappointing to see one of the world's greatest distilleries refusing to play to its strengths and putting so much of its weight on its Achilles heel. *46.8%. ncf.*

Highland Park Einar db **(90.5)** n23 soft, warmingly smoky, toffee apple; t23 fresh, salivating delivery but bordered by tannin and imbued with spice; vague heather honey; f22 dry with the tannins and spices buzzing to the end; b22.5 a curious style of HP which shows most of its usual traits but possesses an extra sharpness. *40% WB15/328*

Highland Park Freya 1st fill ex-bourbon casks db **(88.5)** n22 t23 f21.5 b22. The majestic honey on delivery makes up for some of the untidier moments. *52.10%.*

Highland Park Harald db **(74.5)** n19 t20 f17 b18.5. Warrior Harald has been wounded by sulphur. Fatally. *40% WB15/337*

Highland Park Sigurd db **(96)** n23.5 clever, delicate layering of exotic fruit lurking behind gentle smoke, all heightened by a shake of salt; t24.5 truly beautiful delivery which nutshells HP at its most intense: the smoke is rounded and only marginally intense, the heather-honey forms the centre point and is equally as circular in its shape and motion around the palate. Yet all along, there is that exotic fruit, omnipresent, but so easy to miss. And, if that is not enough, the mouth feel is simply perfection...; f23.5 just when you need spice, you really get it...; b24.5 breath-taking, star-studded and ridiculously complex reminder that this distillery is capable of serving up some of the best whisky the world can enjoy. *43%*

Highland Park Svein db **(87)** n22 t22 f21.5 b21.5. A soft, friendly dram with good spice pick up. But rather too dependent on a tannin-toffee theme. *40% WB15/318*

Highland Park 8 Years Old db **(87)** n22 t22 f22 b21. A journey back in time for some of us: this is the orginal distillery bottling of the 70s and 80s, bottles of which are still doing the rounds in obscure Japanese bars and specialist outlets such as the Whisky Exchange. *40%*

⬥ **Highland Park 10 Year Old Ambassador's Choice** db **(74)** n17.5 t20 f17.5 b19. Some of the casks are so badly sulphured, I'm surprised there hasn't been a diplomatic incident... *46%*

Highland Park Aged 12 Years db **(78)** n19 t21 f19 b19. Let's just hope that the choice of casks for this bottling was a freak. To be honest, this was one of my favourite whiskies of all time, one of my desert island drams, and I could weep. *40% WB16/048*

Highland Park Saint Magnus Aged 12 Years 2nd edition db **(76.5)** n18.5 t21 f19 b19. Tight and bitter 2nd edition. *55%*

Highland Park Aged 15 Years db **(85)** n21 t22 f21 b21. Had to re-taste this several times, surprised as I was by just how relatively flat this was. A hill of honey forms the early delivery, but then... *40%*

Highland Park Earl Magnus Aged 15 Years 1st edition db **(76.5)** n20 t21 f17.5 b18. Tight and bitter. *52.6%. 5976 bottles.*

Highland Park Loki Aged 15 Years db **(96)** n24 heather honey milling around in a confident, but soft, plume of smoke – but a curious different type of lighter heather! Usual stewed apples at play, but sweetened by the honey rather than sugar; a little stem ginger amid the hickory and vanilla, too; t24 wonderful HP silkiness, a rasping snort of barley is captured and enwrapped by the heather-ish-honey while those ginger-led spices are pitched at the smouldering smoke; f23.5 tangy marmalade changes the fruity dimension, but the comforting oils continue to ensure a gentle mouth feel, despite the best efforts of some late herbal interaction. The smoke continues on its cheery but quietly deep way...; b24.5 the weirdness of the heather apart, a bit of a trip back in time. A higher smoke ratio than the bottlings of more recent years which now converts to the distillery will be unfamiliar with, but reverting to the levels regularly found in the 1970s and 80s, probably right through to about 1993/94. Which is a very good thing because the secret of the peat at HP was that, as puffed out as it could be in the old days, it never interfered with the overall complexity, other than adding to it. Which is exactly the case here. Beyond excellent! *48.7%. Edrington.*

Highland Park 16 Years Old db **(88)** n23 t23 f20 b22. I tasted this the day it first came out at one of the Heathrow whisky shops. I thought it a bit flat and uninspiring. This sample, maybe from another bottling, is more impressive and showing true Highland Park colours, the finish apart. *40%. Exclusively available in Duty Free/Travel Retail.*

Highland Park Thor Aged 16 Years db **(87.5)** n22.5 t23.5 f19 b22.5. Now, from what I remember of my Norse gods, Thor was the God of Thunder. Which is a bit spooky seeing as hailstones are crashing down outside as I write this and lightning is striking overhead. Certainly a whisky built on power. Even taking into account the glitch in one or two of the casks, a dram to be savoured on delivery. *52.1%. 23,000 bottles.*

Highland Park Aged 18 Years db **(95.5) n23.5** a thick dollop of honey spread across a layer of salted butter; in the background the ashes of a peat fire are emptied; **t24** eye closing beauty: immediate glossy impact of rich, vaguely metallic honey but upped in the complexity stakes by the subtle intense marbling of peat; the muscular richness, aided by the softness of the oil ensures that maximum intensity is not only reached but maintained; **f24** long continuation of those elements found in the delivery but now radiating soft spices and hints of marzipan; **b24** if familiarity breeds contempt, then it has yet to happen between myself and HP 18. This is a must-have dram. I show it to ladies the world over to win their hearts, minds and tastebuds when it comes to whisky. And the more time I spend with it, the more I become aware and appreciative of its extraordinary consistency. The very latest bottlings have been astonishing, possibly because colouring has now been dropped, and wisely so. Why in any way reduce what is one of the world's great whisky experiences? Such has been the staggering consistency of this dram I have thought of late of promoting the distillery into the world's top three: only Ardbeg and Buffalo Trace have been bottling whisk(e)y of such quality over a wide range of ages in such metronomic fashion. Anyway, enough: a glass of something honeyed and dazzling calls... *43%*

Highland Park Aged 21 Years db **(82.5) n20.5 t22 f19 b21.** Good news and bad news. The good news is that they appear to have done away with the insane notion of reducing this to 40% abv. The bad news: a sulphured sherry butt has found its way into this bottling. *47.5%*

Highland Park Aged 25 Years db **(96) n24** big aged oak amid the smoke and honey: it appears something a lot older has got in here...; uniquely complex and back to its very best; **t24** silky and confident, every usual box is ticked – or even double ticked. Much more honey and smoke than I have seen here for a while and it's not all about quantity. What quality! **f24** long with amazing degrees of oil, almost of the bourbony-corn variety! Helps keep those mind-bending honeys coming! **b24** I am a relieved man: the finest HP 25 for a number of years which displays the distillery's unmistakable fingerprints with a pride bordering on arrogance. One of the most improved bottlings of the year: an emperor of a dram. *48.1%*

Highland Park Aged 30 Years db **(90) n22** a fascinating balancing act between juicy fruit and very tired, splintered oak; **t22.5** the age waters the eye, so powerful is the oak. But it settles into an oily sweetness displaying both a lazy smokiness and burnt raisin; **f23** some real complexity here with oils filling in the drier vanilla moments; **b22.5** a very dramatic shift from the last bottling I tasted; this has taken a fruitier route. Sheer quality, though. *48.1%*

Highland Park 40 Years Old db **(90.5) n20.5** tired and over-oaked but the usual HP traits are there in just enough force to save it from failing with an extra puff of something smoky diving in to be on the safe side; **t22.5** even after 40 years, pure silk. Like a 40-year-old woman who has kept her figure and looks, and now only satin stands in the way between you and so much beauty and experience...and believe me: she's spicy...; **f24** amazing layering of peat caresses you at every level; the oak has receded and now barley and traces of golden syrup balance things; **b23.5** I have to admit to picking splinters from my nose with this one. Some of the casks used here have obviously choked on oak, and I feared the worst. But such is the brilliance of the resilience by being on the money with the honey, you can say only that it has pulled off an amazing feat with the peat. Sheer poetry... *48.3%*

Highland Park 50 Years Old dist Jan 60 db **(96.5) n24.5** mint, cloves and a thin coat of creosote usurp the usual deft heather and smoke to loudly announce this whisky's enormous age. Don't bother looking for honey, either. Well, not at first... However, there is a growling sweetness from the start: deep and giving up its part molten Demerara-part treacle character with miserly contempt, as though outraged by being awoken from a 50-year slumber. Of course, as the whisky oxidises there is a shift in pattern. And after about ten minutes a wine effect – and we are talking something much more akin to a First Growth Bordeaux than sherry - begins to make a statement. Then the sugars transmogrify from treacle to molasses to manuka honey; **t24** certain sugars present on the delivery, though at first hard to quite make out which. Some surprising oil ensures suppleness to the oak; there is also a wonderful marriage, or perhaps it is a threesome, between old nutty fruitcake, tangy orange-enriched high quality north European marzipan, and ancient bourbon...; **f24** silky with some wonderful caramels and toasted fudge forming a really chewy finale. As well as ensuring any possible old-age holes are plugged; **b24** old whiskies tend to react to unchartered territory as far as time in the oak is concerned in quite different ways. This grey beard has certainly given us a new slant. Nothing unique about the nose. But when one is usually confronted with those characteristics on the nose, what follows on the palate moves towards a reasonably predictable path. Not here. Truly unique – as it should be after all this time. *44.8%. sc. 275 bottles.*

Highland Park 1973 bott 2010 db **(96) n24** what could be better than a standard HP nose, complete with all that delicate smoke and honey? An HP nose with a decent smidgeon of high quality bourbon! Well that's what those extra years in the cask has gone and given you; **t25** mouth-watering barley enters the arena hand-in-hand with pristine acacia honey. Directly behind is two-tone smoke: one firm, lightly peated and spiced, the other a softer, billowing safety net; the middle ground concerns molten manuka honey and muscovado sugar thickened with vanilla and then the lightest hint of mocha. Frankly, perfect...; **t23** lighter, lengthy with toffee and liquorice; **b24** now that, folks, is Highland Park and make no mistake! 50.6%

Highland Park Vintage 1978 db **(95.5) n24** some thumping oak is of such high quality it only adds to the mix, rather than detracts. The smoke level is pretty high considering it's had so long in the cask and this helps fend off any oaky excess. Elsewhere tangy kumquats mix with physalis and greengages. The usual honey has given way to soft molasses; **t24** I hope the flight is a long one if you have bought this Duty Free: you really need a good hour alone with this guy to begin to understand his foibles and complexities. The delivery offers a surprising degree of sharpness and life, in which those citrus notes formulate. Then a gentle mixing of delicate, vaguely weary smoke and an almost bourbony red liquorice and light honeycomb mix...; **f23.5** a very light oiliness has formed and provides all that is required to give an extra polish to those soft oaky tones. An equally understated mocha and molasses creamy sweetness ties up the loose ends; **b24** if you are buying this in Duty Free, a tip: get it for yourself...it's too good for a gift!! This purrs quality from first to last. And is quite unmistakably Highland Park. A noble malt. 47.8%. Available in Global Travel Retail.

Highland Park 1997 "The Sword" db **(79.5) n19 t23 f18 b19.5.** Shows its cutting edge for only a brief while on delivery – when it is quite spectacular. Otherwise, painfully blunted. 43%. Available in Taiwan.

Highland Park Earl Haakon db **(92) n22.5 t24 f22.5 b23.** A fabulous malt offering some of the best individual moments of the year. But appears to run out of steam about two thirds in. 54.9%. 3,300 bottles.

Highland Park Hjärta db **(79.5) n18.5 t22 f19 b20.** In part, really does celebrate the honeycomb character of Highland Park to the full. But obviously a major blemish or two in there as well. 58.1%. 3924 bottles.

Highland Park Leif Eriksson bourbon and American oak db **(86) n22 t22 f21 b21.** The usual distillery traits have gone AWOL while all kinds of caramel notes have usurped them. That said, this has to be one of the softest drams you'll find. 40%. Edrington.

Highland Park New Make Spirit Drink dist Feb 10, bott Mar 10 db **(85.5) n21 t22 f21 b21.5.** Doesn't boast the usual degree of ultra rich texture of new make HP – even when reduced – and though sweet, malty and enjoyable, with its few extra metallic molecules not exactly how I recently tasted new make HP in a blending lab. A curious choice. 50%. Venture Whisky Ltd.

Adelphi Selection Highland Park 26 Years Old cask no. 10112, dist 86, bott 13 **(95.5) n23.5** HP in that delightful form when you can actually pick up pollen...; **t24** some people say they can't find heather honey on HP. No? Give this a go...; **f23.5** just so long...and it's a fair way in before the very first puff of smoke is detected. By then your taste buds have already weaved their way through myriad minor flavour hints and statements, the delicate spices having the greatest amount to say and gaining confidence from the late smoke; a full mark docked for a slightly tangy but persistent, tongue-tingling finale; **b24.5** one of the most complex bottlings of the year showing HP's ability to mesmerise the taste buds and blow the mind. 44%. ncf & sc. 240 bottles. WB15/414

❖ **Aflodal's Whisky Highland Park Mansie 1998** cask no. 5793, refill bourbon barrel, dist 3 Jun 98, bott 20 Dec 10 **(84.5) n21 t23 f20 b20.5.** A salty chap with a big malt lift on delivery. Honey in short supply: a tightness on the finish as the oak takes a stranglehold. 49.7%. 188 bottles.

❖ **Alexander Murray & Co Highland Park 2000 13 Years Old Cask Strength (92) n22 t23.5 f23 b23.5.** A light smoke and a blast of tannin is detectable on the nose, but not the usual heather-honey. However, the delivery excels with the smoke encircling the intense malt like Apaches around a wagon train. Gorgeous layers of marzipan and vanilla, both with a smoky hook, carry on forward, with a light ulmo honey sweetness as back up. An attractive, increasingly spiced chocolate fudge sees the malt to its ever-warming conclusion. Very impressive and absolutely delicious. 56.1%

Gordon & MacPhail Cask Strength Highland Park first fill Bourbon barrels, cask no. 2809, 2810, 2811 & 2812, dist 18 Apr 05, bott 07 Mar 14 **(95.5) n23.5** the presence of the heather honey makes you smile: it is a cliché come true. But there it is, though without its usual lightly smoked accompaniment. Thought eh delicate spice might well be peat induced; **t25** OK. That's it...I might as well pack it in for the week. I am not likely to find a better delivery and follow through between now and the ending of writing this Bible...and seeing as this is the

624th new whisky of the 2015 edition (and so far the best), I am unofficially one short of being halfway through. This is the sweetest a whisky can get without being cloying, the smokiest without being heavy, the spiciest without being aggressive: it is, truly...perfection; **f23.5** long, with toasted honeycomb; the spices massage and warm and even so far in the malt filters through, a little smoked, still with those traces of heather honey....it is like all your dreams and fantasies in a 70cl bottle...; **b23.5** I think the first HP I ever tasted was an 8-y-o from Gordon and MacPhail. That was something in the region of 40 years ago. It wasn't even half way to being this good, though. As it was at 40% and the added caramel filled in and homogenised all the interesting features. This 8-year-old, seemingly distilled by bees and matured in a hive might be the perfect whisky for Brentford supporters to celebrate their return to the second tier of English football after a very long time. And one for the blending lab at HP, as here is proof that sherry butts are not remotely required to impart greatness in their core brands. Just care. This is a whisky of a lifetime. *59.1%. WB15/111*

The MacPhail's Collection from Highland Park 1988 (88) n23 ginger and Turkish delight make a change from the usual honeyed offering, but emphasises the age. Spices, naturally; **t22.5** after a bright display of barley pretty rabid caramels soften the texture by overshadowing the usual complexity; again honey absent, but some toasty fudge instead; **f21** soft, dry and toasty but essentially flat-lining; **b21.5** pleasant, but drab. Very flat for a HP with the usual signature smoke and heather honey conspicuous by their absence...and an absence which doesn't make the hard grow fonder. *43%.*

Old Malt Cask Highland Park Aged 17 Years cask no. 9903, dist Sep 96, bott Sept 13 **(94) n23.5** Ok, so it doesn't have the usual heather-honey. But that lurking hint of smoke? Those deftly layered barley tones? The neat and tidy, liquorice-leaning tannins? Don't tell me what Highland Park has done for us...; **t24** well, no doubting the honey now. The ulmo variety is up there loud and clear with the peat offering a low rumble in the background; the barley also has a delicious input; **f23** citrus drizzled, delicately smoked vanilla, enlivened with peek-a-boo, spice; **b23.5** simple genius cannot be denied. *50%. nc ncf sc. 206 bottles.*

⬧ **Old Malt Cask Highland Park 18 Years Old** refill hogshead, cask no. 10897, dist Sept 96, bott Sept 14 **(96) n24** one of the most gentle and polite noses of the year: heather, vague smoke and not so vague honey are all present and correct. But none are falling over themselves to dominate: as it should be; **t24** such joy. Near perfect mouth feel, with the oils putting a silky edge to the more thrusting oak. But it is that puff of smoke which leaves you in no doubt where you are...and the heather honey confirms as if making fun of itself. But...oh, that texture....!!! **f23.5** the oak shows a few signs of wear as a little tang bites into the comfort zone. But it is minor, and some late salty notes helps focus the mind on other things...like the late-arriving, bitty and busy spices for instance; **b24.5** probably the best age for this distillery. And when matured in this type of high quality cask, the purring of satisfaction can be heard afar. Sensational: a true representation and celebration of one of the world's great distilleries. *48.8%. nc ncf sc. 132 bottles.*

Old Malt Cask Highland Park Aged 17 Years refill hogshead, cask no. 10313, dist Sep 96, bott Feb 14 **(90) n23** the feeble but compelling smoke locked into the heather honey can mean only one distillery....; **t23.5** gorgeous medium weight honeyed barley given a little extra depth by the spiced smoke and minty cocoa; **f21** spicy; just a little lingering bitterness; **b22.5** the distillery more or less nut-shelled... *50%. sc. 296 bottles.*

Old Particular Highland Park Aged 17 Years refill hogshead, cask no. 10230, dist Sep 96, bott Apr 14 **(92.5) n22** here we go: heather honey spread on light, golden toast; **t24** more emphasis on the barley on delivery, then a light honeyed footfall. The smoke drifts in as an afterthought; **f23** roasty, almost like a Guinness but without the hops; the smoke lingers awhile; **b23.5** that heather honey really isn't a cliché. But it is the deftness of the smoke which steals the show. *48.4%. nc ncf sc. 324 bottles.*

Old Particular Highland Park 18 Years Old refill hogshead, cask no. 10161, dist Nov 95, bott Dec 13 **(92) n22** the sugars are suppressed by tight smoky citrus; **t22.5** opens up to better effect on delivery as the barley offers both juiciness and depth; a light smokiness flickers around; **f24** its finest hour for the malt Churchill loved. At last all the boxes are ticked, especially the peaty one, with aplomb and even the lengthening oak is weighted perfectly with the juicier elements; **b23.5** HP lovers will not be disappointed. *48.4%. nc ncf sc. 332 bottles. Douglas Laing & Co.*

⬧ **Old Particular Highland Park 18 Years Old** refill hogshead, cask no. 10589, dist Sept 96, bott Nov 14 **(95.5) n23.5** the distillery nutshelled...!!!! **t24** you'll have no problem finding smoke and heather-honey on the nose. And none here either. Extra spices are injected early probably to prevent you from floating off on a pink cloud somewhere; **f23.5** the salty finale underscores the extra dryness infused by the tannins as well as the coastal location; **b24.5** truly magnificent. A real must have for Highland Park lovers out there. 48.4%. nc ncf sc. 450 bottles.

Scotch Malt Whisky Society Cask 4.186 Aged 22 Years dist 31 May 91 **(96.5) n24** ever nosed heather honey? Here's your chance. But please take the smouldering toast from the cask into account, please; oh, and the peat is found in degrees not often seen in latter day casks; **t24** one distillery and one distillery only offers this citric tartness to the honey and soft smoke which embrace so charmingly; **f24** the smoke drifts, the oak thickens and engrosses, spices assemble, the honey flirts...all is well in this sublime bottling; **b24.5** absolutely had to laugh when nosing this. Among of group of whiskies waiting inspection, I nosed without studying the source of the sample: "Bloody hell," I thought. "This is a old Highland Park impersonating an old Highland Park at a old Highland Park gathering" You will be hard pressed to find a bottling so true to the distillery's nature as this... 52.2%. nc ncf sc. 250 bottles.

Scotch Malt Whisky Society Cask 4.189 Aged 13 Years 1st fill barrel, dist 24 Aug 00 **(88.5) n22** a quiet HP skimping on the smoke and focussing on the vanilla; **t23** tangy and boisterous, a wave of citrus breaks over the saltier malt; **f21.5** a spicy oak reprise; **b22** coastal but short of the required smoke. 59.5%. nc ncf sc. 278 bottles.

⬦ **Scotch Malt Whisky Society Cask 4.197 Aged 14 Years** 1st fill barrel, dist 15 Oct 99 **(93) n23** a little salty and shy; light smoke drifts through; **t23** you don't get more heather honey-ish than this delivery; the smoke ambles into position; **f23.5** now some massive complexity as the honey, smoke and spices all fall into place; **b23.5** quietly agreeable and seems to up the volume without you even noticing... 56.4%. sc. 201 bottles.

⬦ **Scotch Malt Whisky Society Cask 4.199 Aged 14 Years** 1st fill barrel, dist 15 Oct 99 **(95.5) n24.5** beautiful balance between the light peat and gentle tannin on one hand and the heather honey on the other – perhaps with a saline, coastal thread binding them together; **t24** a delivery of your dreams: salivating, yet thick with honeyed barley; the smoke evolves into mocha, but all in slow moton...; **f23** long, graceful, with the sugars melting on the palate; **b24** quintessential HP... 56.2%. sc. 148 bottles.

That Boutique-y Whisky Highland Park batch 2 **(90.5) n22.5** some serious oak at work muffles the smoke; almost an estery, pot still rum-like sweetness; **t23** again the oak really does come charging at you. And, again, an estery mouth feel saves the day, helped along by some building spice; **f22.5** a lovely spice glow works well with the late arriving malt... but the oak never goes away; **b22.5** top heavy with oak and missing its trademark honey accompaniment. Lovely, though! 46%. 386 bottles. WB15/207

IMPERIAL

Speyside, 1897. Chivas Brothers. Silent.

Imperial Aged 15 Years "Special Distillery Bottling" db **(69) n17 t18 f17 b17.** At least one very poor cask, hot spirit and overly sweet. Apart from that it's wonderful. 46%

Gordon & MacPhail Imperial 1995 (87.5) n21.5 t23 f21 b22. Impressively sweet, with more grist than you might believe possible for a malt this old. Good spice involvement, too. Light, limited but delicious. 43%

Signatory Vintage Cask Strength Collection Imperial 1995 Aged 18 Years hogsheads, cask no. 50143+50144, dist 21 Aug 95, bott 07 Jan 14 **(84.5) n21 t21.5 f21 b21.** Not sure Imperial was being filled into the world's greatest oak by this stage of its declining life when its spirit was already not what it once was. The result is an ultra malty dram trying to say much but being gagged at every turn. 51.9%. nc. 573 bottles. WB15/003

Signatory Vintage Un-chillfiltered Collection Imperial 1995 Aged 18 Years hogsheads, cask no. 50280+50281, dist, 18 Sep 95, bott 27 Nov 13 **(86) n21 t22 f21.5 b21.5.** A lively, tangy Imperial, though by no means at its most imperious. Only sweet-toothed grist lovers need apply... 46%. nc ncf. 692 bottles. WB15/020

⬦ **Whisky Fair Imperial 19 Year Old** hogshead, cask no. 50174, dist 1995, bott 2015 **(90) n22** rich cream toffee and even some surprising raisin; **t23** ooo-wow! Didn't expect that! A major juicy barley nip to the delivery before the oak rolls in with wave upon wave of toffee; **f22** the vaguest hint of smoke adds depth to the caramel-rich finale; **b23** good to see what is usually an unremarkable distillery in relatively sparkling form. 46%. 323 bottles.

INCHGOWER

Speyside, 1872. Diageo. Working.

Inchgower 1993 The Manager's Choice db **(84.5) n21 t21.5 f21 b21.** Like your malts subtle, delicate, clean and sophisticated? Don't bother with this one if you do. This has all the feel of a malt that's been spray painted onto the taste buds: thick, chewy and resilient. Can't help but like that mix of hazelnut and Demerara, though. You can stand a spoon in it. *61.9%*

›› **Cadenhead's Authentic Collection Inchgower Aged 25 Years** bourbon hogshead, dist 1989, bott Jan 15 (**87.5**) **n21 t23 f21.5 b22**. As a blender, you'd love this bare-chested warrior of a malt to stir things up a little. As a single malt, it is something of a white-knuckle ride. Nutty on the nose, it is profound and rough hewn on delivery with intense, dark-sugared grist. The finish, though, is pure sandpaper! Fun stuff. *52.6%. 210 bottles.*

›› **Gleann Mór Inchgower 35 Year Old** dist Feb 80, bott Jun 15 (**88**) **n22.5** a sexy bit of rough: a little dirty but liquorice and molasses mean there's a sweet edge to the experience; **t22.5** and it becomes a free-for-all romp on the palate, those unrefined sugars now leading the way and getting thicker by the moment as a little rubber is donned; **f21** a dirty, sticky ending...; **b22** the distinctive, trademark earthiness of this malt is there to see even after 35 years in the barrel. I actually visited this distillery in the year this was made, 1980, and remember discovering for the first time the almost rubber-chewy properties of its malt. So powerful was that character, it has hardly changed in the many passing years. *54.1%. sc.*

Gordon & MacPhail Connoisseurs Choice Inchgower 1998 (**85.5**) **n21 t22.5 f21 b21.** Flavoursome if one dimensional. Soupy and syrupy with a big juicy barley kick at first. Tangy finish. *46%.*

›› **Gordon & MacPhail Connoisseurs Choice Inchgower 2000** (**86.5**) **n21 t22.5 f21 b21.** In so many ways, this is classic Inchgower, virtually unchanged to how it was when bottled at this age 35 years ago. Still one of the chewiest malts around and enough delicious rough edges for this to taste more like an old-fashioned blend than a single malt. And that's a good thing, by the way. *46%*

›› **Hepburn's Choice Inchgower 14 Years Old** sherry butt, dist 2000, bott 2014 (**75**) **n18 t19 f19 b19.** For all – no, probably because – of its obvious faults, this makes for an interesting malt. Not often Jack Daniel's is compared to a scotch single malt, but it would be fair to do so here. JD possesses a slightly dirty character due to its inefficient second distillation. There is a recognisably similar dirtiness to this, also: big oils and clammy on the palate, the impurities from the distillate spread abundantly about. Some JD lovers might well enjoy this. *46%. nc ncf sc. 377 bottles.*

Montgomerie's Single Cask Collection Inchgower cask no. 31032, dist 11 Oct 90, bott Mar 13 (**94**) **n23.5** someone has spilled a tin of molasses in a liquorice factory...; elsewhere a lovely pollen attack; **t24** massive delivery: pounding spice cuts through the usual distillery oils. A fabulous mix of treacle and maple syrup is toned down by dry coconut shavings and vanilla; **f23.5** a long line of ulmo honey, liquorice and those outstanding spices; **b24** impressively above the norm for an Inchgower. Inching towards excellence all the way through - pretty damn delicious. *46%. nc ncf sc. WB15/131*

Old Malt Cask Inchgower Aged 18 Years refill hogshead, cask no. 9983, dist Jan 95, bott Aug 13 (**85.5**) **n21.5 t21.5 f21.5 b21.** Typically soupy and dense. But the Demerara sugars come out loud and clear. *50%. nc ncf sc. 242 bottles.*

›› **Old Malt Cask Inchgower 18 Years Old** sherry butt, cask no. 10920, dist Nov 95, bott Oct 14 (**85.5**) **n21 t21 f22 b21.5**. A real Inchgower of the old school: a touch dirty but the malt is pretty fired up and form a decent partnership with the stinging spices. *50%. nc ncf sc. 347 bottles.*

›› **Old Malt Cask Inchgower 18 Years Old** sherry butt, cask no. 11402, dist Nov 95, bott Mar 15 (**83**) **n21.5 t22 f19 b20.5**. Solid, punchy and no shortage of the house style dirty molassed sugar. A bit oily on the finish. *50%. nc ncf sc. 370 bottles.*

›› **Old Particular Inchgower 16 Years Old** refill hogshead, cask no. 10414, dist Aug 00, bott Oct 14 (**85**) **n21 t21 f22 b21**. Biting, sharp and one of the few single malts which can probably cut its way through diamonds. Yet the crunchy barley juice and molassed sugar combo overcomes the obvious weaknesses in the clarity of the narrative. A bit messy – but strangely delicious. *48.4%. nc ncf sc. 774 bottles.*

The Whisky Agency Inchgower 1985 dist 1985 (**81**) **n21 t21 f19 b20**. Typical Inchgower in sludgy, shapeless form showing big malt intent but a slovenly attitude. *50.8%.*

›› **The Whisky Cask Inchgower Aged 14 Years** bourbon cask, dist 1999, bott 2013 (**90**) **n22** a slight creosote bite amid the molasses; **t23** no prisoners taken here: the spices and spirit nip in equal measure but those intense sugars, helped by manuka honey, bathe the wounds deliciously; **f22.5** stays rough and basic all the way...with warming liquorice for a final, growling flourish; **b22.5** full on fighting whisky: not even the vaguest attempt at subtlety...but it works fabulously well in its own way. *56.1%. nc ncf.*

INVERLEVEN

Lowland, 1938–1991. Demolished.

Deoch an Doras Inverleven 36 Years Old dist 1973 **(94.5) n24** just one of those noses where you think twice about tasting: not because it is bad, but quite the opposite...you really don't want the experience to end. Exotic fruit sitting comfortably with bigger oak notes and the juiciest of grassy malt; **t23.5** a slightly ungainly delivery but after the first three or four flavour waves settles into a more rhythmic pulsing of light golden syrup, fresh barley, cocoa and spices; a bourbon sub text is deliciously fascinating; **f23** exemplary dovetailing of the finer details of the malt, with the spices now showing a little more keenly; **b24** as light on the palate as a morning mist. This distillery just wasn't designed to make a malt of this antiquity, yet this is to the manor born. 48.85%. nc ncf. Chivas Brothers. 500 bottles.

ISLE OF ARRAN

Highlands (Island–Arran), 1995. Isle of Arran Distillers. Working.

⟡ **Isle of Arran Machrie Moor 5th Edition** bott 2014 db **(91.5) n22.5** I think last year they displayed a unique sage seed honey sweetness: well, they've gone and done it again! This time, though, the smoke makes just a slightly deeper imprint; **t24** if lightly peated grist is your thing, knock yourself out on this! Helped handsomely by the clever citrus intervention and even the odd sprig of mint and mocha; **f22** an annoying degree of bitterness is contributed by the oak, but a slightly creamy hazelnut and milk chocolate finale is assisted by the last, lingering dregs of smoke; **b23** a few tired old bourbon barrels have taken the score down slightly on last year. But the spirit itself is nothing short of brilliant. 46% WB16/049

The Arran Malt 10 Year Old db **(87) n22.5 t22.5 f20 b22.** It has been a while since I last officially tasted this. If they are willing to accept some friendly advice, I think the blenders should tone down on raising any fruit profile and concentrate on the malt, which is amongst the best in the business. 46%. nc ncf.

The Arran Malt 12 Years Old db **(85) n21.5 t22 f20.5 b21** Hmmmm. Surprise one, this. There must be more than one bottling already of this. The first I tasted was perhaps slightly on the oaky side but otherwise intact and salt-honeyed where need be. This one has a bit of a tang: very drinkable, but definitely a less than brilliant cask around. 46%

The Arran Malt 12 Years Old Cask Strength Batch 1 bott Sep 11 db **(78) n21 t22 f17 b18.** There is no questioning that Arran is now one of Scotland's Premier League quality malts. But the strength of their whisky is in their bourbon casks, not so much their sherry. And to create a batch like this was tempting fate. The sulphur present is by no means huge, but it takes only a single off butt to spoil the party. 54.1%. nc ncf. 12,000 bottles.

The Arran Malt Aged 12 Years Cask Strength batch no. 2, bott 09/12 db **(80) n21 t22 f18 b19.** A better dram than their 2011 bottling with a little extra depth, nuttiness and sweetness and small degree less sulphur. But there is still enough on the finish in particular to make the difference between the great whisky it should be, and this essay in off-key ordinariness it actually is. 53.6%. nc ncf. 13,200 bottles. WB15/114

The Arran Malt Aged 14 Years db **(89.5) n22 t23.5 f21.5 b22.5.** A superb whisky, but the evidence that there has been a subtle shift in emphasis, with the oak now taking too keen an interest, is easily attained. 46%. ncf.

The Arran Malt 15 Years Old sherry hogshead, dist 21 Jul 97, bott 30 Apr 13 db **(90) n22** banana and custard; oak marauds everywhere...quietly; **t23** gorgeous, silky delivery with a major oaky statement but glazed with barley sugar; **f22** chocolate mint; **b23** a truly lovely whisky which, as is often the case from this distillery, has somewhat become prematurely grey as the oak has made its mark. But enough light fruit and sugar abound to make for a treat. 50.7%. 230 bottles. Whisky Shop Exclusive.

The Arran Malt Aged 17 Years db **(91.5) n23.5** the grape assumes a non-aggressive stance, allowing the sweeter elements to flourish. Freshly bitten toffee apple and vaguely salty barley dust make for a delightful and understated signature; **t23.5** the sharpness on delivery is helped by the crisp sugars which crunch about a bit before melting into the grist. The fruit, mainly dates and dry, over-ripened plums, is subdued and makes way for the more intense pollen-honey middle; **f21.5** only a very minor furry notes reminds you sherry is at work here but a late salty vanilla helps; **b23** "matured in the finest ex-Sherry casks" trills the back label. And, by and large, they are right. Maybe a single less than finest imparts the light furriness to the finish. But by present day sherry butt standards, a pretty outstanding effort. 46%. nc ncf. 9000 bottles. WB15/152

The Arran Malt 1996 Single Cask ex-sherry puncheon, cask no. 96/1327, dist 1996, **(89) n21 t23.5 f22 b22.** Arran showing a very different face here. The early copper of the young stills is still apparently evident as there is a metallic kick to this. Slightly knocks the decent sherry influence off kilter. 55.8%. sc.

The Arran Malt Ambassador's Choice db (87.5) n22 t22 f21.5 b22. So heavy with oak I was amazed I could pick the nosing glass up... 46%

The Arran Malt Amarone Cask Finish db (94.5) n23 t24 f23 b23.5. As cask finishes go, this one is just about perfect. 50%. nc ncf.

The Arran Malt Bourgogne Finish db (74) n18 t19 f18 b19. Arran Malt Vinegar more like... 56.4%

The Arran Malt Chianti Classico Riserva Cask Finish db (85) n19 t23 f21 b22. Mamma mia: there eeza poco zolfo ina mia malto!! Butta chicco d'uva, ee eez eccellente! 55%

The Arran Malt Devil's Punch Bowl Chapter No. 2 Angels & Devils db (87.5) n22 t24 f20 b21.5. When Chapter I was launched, the whisky was what it said on the tin...for it offered little more than brimstone. I gave the devil a poke in the eye for going to the trouble of undermining one of the world's greatest distilleries with contemptuous sulphur. And it appears someone has taken heed. For this is an almost unimaginable improvement over the previous bottling. Is this entirely without blemish? The finish suggests not. But, clearly, much greater diligence has been taken in cask selection. To the extent that those lucky ones who do not possess the genetic make up to detect sulphur will have a hell of a time. Even those of us who cannot be but astonished by the beauty of the intense, mollassed fruit. With even more judicious care in the cherry picking of casks next time round, this could be a monster whisky that will give any devil a run for his money. 52.3%. 6,660 bottles. WB15/153

The Arran Malt Fino Sherry Cask Finish db (82.5) n21 t20 f21 b20.5. Pretty tight with the bitterness not being properly compensated for. 50%

The Arran Malt Fontalloro Wine Cask Finish db (84.5) n20 t22 f21.5 b21. For a wine cask, the malt really does sing. 50%

The Arran Malt Lepanto PX Brandy Finish db (85) n22 t22 f20 b21. Tight, unusually thin for an Arran, but some lovely sweet fruit amid the confusion. Pretty oaky, too. 59%

The Arran Malt Madeira Wine Cask Finish db (77.5) n19 t21 f18.5 b19. The odd exultant moment but generally flat, flaky and bitter. 50%

The Arran Malt Millenium Casks db (94) n23.5 the nutty, honeyed overture has as much in common with bourbon as it does a single malt scotch; there is a soft Turkish Delight fruitiness, too as well as fruit pastel candy. As I nose this a female great spotted woodpecker is tucking into the feeder outside my tasting room window: had I the window open she might have come in attracted by the sweet oak wafting from the glass... t24 absolutely beautiful delivery with the malt leading healthily and though all is seemingly soft and controlled, has a bite like Lois Suarez. A mix of heather honey and thin manuka works a treat; f23 more nuttiness, now of a marzipan type, a pinch of salt plus a little unwelcome furriness from a renegade sherry cask; b23.5 at times hits some dizzying heights. Superbly complex the late fault line. 53.5%. nc ncf. 7,800 bottles. WB15/154

The Arran Malt "The Sleeping Warrior" bott 2011 db (84.5) n19 t22.5 f21.5 b21.5. Zzzzzzzz. 54.9%. nc ncf. 6000 bottles.

The Peated Arran "Machrie Moor" 1st release db (86.5) n22 t22 f21 b21.5. A bit of a surprise package: I have tasted many peated Arrans over recent years, the majority voluptuous and generous in their giving. Yet this one is strangely aloof. The flavours and nuances have to be sought rather than presented for inspection and there is a hardness throughout which makes for a very solid dram. That said, it has many fine qualities, too. And the mouth-watering unravelling of its slightly cough-sweetish intensity is great entertainment. A fascinating, mixed bag. 46%. nc ncf. 9000 bottles.

The Peated Arran "Machrie Moor" Fourth Edition 14 ppm, bott 2013 db (95.5) n23 delicate rape seed honey and powder-puff peat; t23.5 playful oil, nor polite smoke cannot curtail the sharpness of the mouth-watering malt; f24.5 slow spice buzz moves towards a wonderful light molasses and chocolate finale. Ridiculously long...and so much happening... so many whispering layers even so late on; b24.5 a masterful, gentle but wonderfully complex whisky. A complete gem. 46%. nc ncf. 12,000 bottles. WB15/343

⬧ **Anam na h-Alba The Soul of Scotland Arran 1996** 1st fill sherry cask, dist Aug 96, bott Mar 15 (84.5) n22 t22 f19.5 b21. For those who love their grapes by the bunch. The first few moments on delivery are sublime, but the sugars can never quite overcome the nagging bitterness which follows. 55%. 280 bottles.

Berry's Own Selection Arran 1997 Aged 16 Years cask no. 5, bott 2014 (75) n19.5 t22 f16 b17.5. Dry, nutty with an exceptionally rich delivery. But sulphur tainted. 56.9%. ncf ncf. WB15/237

⬧ **Cadenhead's Authentic Collection Isle of Arran Aged 16 Years** bourbon cask, dist 1998 (95) n23.5 has this cask been stored in a shoreline cave for the last 16 years...? t24 eye-watering delivery: the salt and barley are both in concentrate form and combine for a delivery you're not likely to forget...; the midground has space to allow a little manuka honey and marzipan to perform a little duet; **f23.5** salted chocolate hazelnut closes the show; **b24** a salty dog which howls most beautifully.... 54.8%

Cadenhead's Small Batch Arran Aged 16 Years 1 Hogshead and 1 butt, dist 1997, bott 2013 **(92) n23** sharp lemon softened by orange blossom honey; complex earthy, salted celery and vanilla; **t23.5** big, full-bodied delivery. Oil and what seems (however unlikely) as a brief flicker of smoke adds further weight; spices and mocha on one level, more orange blossom honey on another; **f22.5** the cocoa is now very intense as it dries; just a slight furriness; **b23** a busy tapestry of salt and honey. 46%. 792 bottles. WB15/089

Càrn Mòr Strictly Limited Edition Arran Aged 16 Years hogsheads, dist 1997, bott 2014 **(92.5) n23** probably what you get when you stir marmalade into honey...and then add a pinch of salt; **t24** succulent, soothing and quietly rich delivery. Citrus early on. Peaks, though, on about the fourth to seventh waves when the sugars hot perfect pitch and in total harmony with the tannin; a short blast of Worther's Originals; **f22.5** long, soft with a slow build up of salt 'n' spice; **b23** a very simple joy... 46%. nc ncf. 568 bottles from 2 casks. WB15/053

✧ **Glen Fahrn Airline Nr 06 Arran 1996 Aged 15 Years** cask no. 776 **(95.5) n24 t24 f23.5 b24.** A bottle of this should be sent to every blending lab in Scotland with a neck tag reading: "how a malt whisky should taste." Exemplary in every detail, and probably benefitting from the extra copper backbone offered by the then new stills. Even after the 15 years the barley is beautifully unblemished, but it is the interplay between the perfectly aligned sugars and uplifting salt which makes you drop your jaw. A little ulmo honey is the counterpoint to the spices. Only a vague cask degradation towards the end prevents this from scooping prizes. 56.2%. sc. 236 bottles.

Gordon & MacPhail Connoisseurs Choice Arran dist 2000, bott 2013 **(89) n22** malty; light layer of honey; **t23** identical to nose, except more juicy than might be expected and an excellent burst of barley sugar; **f22** hangs on to the vanilla; **b22** simplistic by Arran standards but attractive. 46%. nc ncf. WB15/146

Master of Malt Single Cask Arran 17 Years Old refill, dist 5 Aug 1995, bott 4 Feb 2014 **(94) n23.5** a delicate citrus sheen to the slightly salt-breezed barley; the spiced oak nips attractively; **t23.5** intense, salivating and sound. Excellent muscovado sugar development; the saltiness is now rather Digestive biscuit in style; **f23** dries quickly as a little spice moves in; a light coating of oil patches up the cracks; **b24** lovely, composed malt and, though the passing years are beginning to stretch its finer points, this is still a work of whisky art. 53.6%. 100 bottles. WB15/231

Old Malt Cask Arran Aged 16 Years port finished puncheon, cask no. 9901, dist Sep 98, bott Jul 13 **(82) n19 t22 f20 b21.** The tangy nose points accusingly to an off-key cask. Which is a shame: there is enough salty acacia and ulmo honey to have made for a dram of purely memorable proportions. Does have some symphonic early moments all the same. 50%. sc. 330 bottles.

Old Particular Highland Arran 17 Years Old refill hogshead, cask no. 9983, dist Feb 96, Aug 13 **(89) n22** moody in its old age (old for Arran, that is). Only at body temperature does its nature sweeten; **t22** trimmed and clipped delivery by Arran standards with only some of the usual small still body which normally serves it so well. Still, the malts are neat, crisp and almost crunchy; **f22.5** expands in complexity as the vanillas gather momentum; **b22.5** a malt which begrudgingly fills the bottle – and palate - at this age. Enjoyable and high quality, but not quite the complex charmer it would have been half a dozen years before. 48.4%. nc ncf sc. 318 bottles.

✧ **Old Malt Cask Arran 18 Years Old** refill hogshead, cask no. 10852, dist Dec 95, bott Aug 14 **(89) n22** complex and elegantly honeyed. Even so, the oak is, at times, a little too stark and dry; **t23** beautiful delivery with the extra weight and sheen of a young still ensuring a slight metallic edge; **f22** good late spice; a little cocoa but the oak is tiring; **b22** the unmistakable tang of a malt slightly beyond its best as the oak has a louder say than it once did. Charming, nonetheless. And always interesting to see my little baby now sporting a few grey hairs... 50%. nc ncf sc. 299 bottles.

✧ **Old Particular Highland Arran 18 Years Old** refill hogshead, cask no. 10470, dist Aug 96, bott Sept 14 **(91.5) n22** no shortage of copper, apples, coconut and molten icing sugar; **t23** succulent, desirably oiled delivery on the palate. A curious mix between grist and esters: very chewy, though the oak starts rattling the cage; **f23.5** massive copper surge is met by intriguing spice; **b23** probably filled into an older cask as the oak is slightly jaded, which is not uncommon of this new distillery as it reaches relatively old age. Enjoys some outstanding moments on the voyage, though. 48.4%. nc ncf sc. 117 bottles.

Scotch Malt Whisky Society Cask 121.66 Aged 15 Years refill barrel, dist 07 Sep 98 **(93) n23.5** maple syrup and a slice of lime brushed with salt; **t23.5** spectacular mouth feel: the softest of oils allows the salivating butterscotch and barley to do its thing; **f23** the oak cranks up a little; **b23** the way in which it keeps its sweetness in such delicate voice is a thing of wonder. 55.5%. nc ncf sc. 273 bottles.

Scotch Malt Whisky Society Cask 121.68 Aged 14 Years refill hogshead, dist 02 Dec 99 **(89) n23 t22 f22 b22.** Great whisky on its way down as the tannins don the captain's armband. *55.1%. nc ncf sc. 273 bottles.*

Scotch Malt Whisky Society Cask 121.70 Aged 13 Years refill hogshead, dist 01 Jan 2000 **(94.5) n23.5** controlled oak; a hint of Kellogg's Cornflakes in heavily sugared gold top milk; **t24** crisp Demerara sugars encrust toasted barley; the salivation factor rises sharply; **f23.5** despite the close attention of the oak, the spices and toasted almond flakes leave you purring; **b23.5** such a delicate, complex malt: someone will one day wake up to the fact that it peaks at around twelve. This is still pulsing with brilliance though I suspect had it been bottled two or three years ago it would have enjoyed legendary status. *54.7%. nc ncf sc. 307 bottles.*

Scotch Malt Whisky Society Cask 121.71 Aged 14 Years refill hogshead, dist 02 Dec 99 **(92.5) n23** suet and blood orange; **t23** a spectacular delivery which hits you like some kind of full-frontal celebration of bourbon but soon calms to offer a more malty, saline crusted coastal picture; **f23** a light, vaguely zesty citrus fleeting moment which you must look out for is probably the highlight; late on the oak gathers; **b23.5** a busy number which just never stops working the palate. *54.9%. nc ncf sc. 224 bottles.*

That Boutique-y Whisky Arran batch 3 **(74.5) n18.5 t19 f18.5 b18.5.** Unusually cumbersome for an Arran with a little too much oil and feint. Malty, a touch salty but a distinct lack of sweetness and charisma. Now just checking back, I see Batch 1 was of the same ilk... *51.5%. 728 bottles. WB15/221*

⬖ **That Boutique-y Whisky Company Arran** batch 4 **(91.5) n22.5** big malty kick...pretty sharp and incisive, too; **t23** good grief...!! You are sent into full puckering mode as the most biting barley pounds on your taste buds and needles them relentlessly. The malt intensity would go off most known charts...; **f23** excellent oak at work as a degree of tannin and coconut biscuit comes into play...; **b23** bring a handkerchief for this one: so sharp it'll make your eyes water...deliciously compelling stuff, though. *52%. 1270 bottles.*

ISLE OF JURA

Highlands (Island–Jura), 1810. Whyte and Mackay. Working.

Isle Of Jura Aged 10 Years db **(79.5) n19 t22 f19 b19.5.** Perhaps a little livelier than before, but still miles short of where you might hope it to be. *40%*

Jura Elixir Aged 12 Years Fruity & Spicy db **(77) n18 t21 f18 b20.** Fruity, spicy and a little sulphury, I'm afraid. Those who can't spot sulphur will love the caramel-fruitcake enormity. *40%*

Isle of Jura Mountain of Gold 15 Years Old Pinot Noir cask finish db **(67.5) n15 t18 f17 b17.5.** Not for the first time a Jura seriously hamstrung by sulphur - for all its honeyed sweetness and promise: there are some amazingly brilliant casks in there tragically wasted. And my tastebuds partially crocked because of it. Depressing. *46%. 1366 bottles.*

Isle of Jura Mountain of Sound 15 Years Old Cabernet Sauvignon finish db **(81) n20 t21.5 f19.5 b20.** Pretty quiet. *43%*

Isle of Jura The Sacred Mountain 15 Years Old Barolo finish db **(89.5) n21.5 t24 f21.5 b22.5** Hoo-bloody-rah! One of the three from this series has actually managed to raise my pulse. Not, it must be said, without the odd fault here and there. But there really is a stunning interaction between grape and barley that sets the nerves twitching: at its height this is about as entertaining a malt as I've come across for some time and should be on everyone's list for a jolly jaunt for the taste buds. Just when I was beginning to lose faith in this distillery... *43%*

Isle Of Jura Aged 16 Years db **(90.5) n21.5** salty, coastal, seaweedy, but with an injection of honey; **t23.5** carries on from the nose perfectly and then ups the stakes. The delivery is malt dependent and rich, the salty tang a true delight; **f23** all kinds of vanillas and honeys carried on a salty wind; **b23** a massive improvement, this time celebrating its salty, earthy heritage to good effect. The odd strange, less than harmonious note. But by far and away the most improved Jura for a long, long while. *40%*

Isle of Jura Aged 21 Years 200th Anniversary db **(74) n19 t19 f18 b18.** Don't know what to say. Actually, I do. But what's the point...? *44%*

Isle of Jura 21 Years Old Cask Strength db **(92) n22 t24 f23 b23.** Every mouthful exudes class and quality. A must-have for Scottish Island collector... or those who know how to appreciate a damn fine malt *58.1%*

Isle of Jura 30 Years Old db **(89) n22.5 t22.5 f22 b22.** A relaxed dram with the caramel dousing the higher notes just as they started to get very interesting. If there is a way of bringing down these presumably natural caramels - it is a 30 years old, so who in their right mind would add colouring? - this would score very highly, indeed. *40%*

Isle of Jura 40 Years Old finished in oloroso wood db **(90) n23** a different species of Jura from anything you are likely to have seen before: swamped in sherry, there is a vague, rather odd smokiness to this. Not to mention salty, sea-side rockpools. As a pairing (sherry and smoke), the odd couple... which works and doesn't work at the same time. Strange... **t22** syrupy sweet delivery with thick waves of fruit and then an apologetic 'ahem' from the smoke, which drifts in nervously. Again, everything is awkward... **f22** remains soft and velvety, though now strands of bitter, salty oak and molasses drift in and out; **b23** throw the Jura textbooks away. This is something very different. Completely out of sync in so many ways, but... 40%

Jura Elements "Air" db (76) n19.5 t19 f18.5 b19. Initially, I thought this was earth: there is something strangely dirty and flat about both nose and delivery. Plenty of fruits here and there but just doesn't get the pulse racing at all. 45%

Jura Elements "Earth" db (89) n23.5 t22 f21.5 b22. I haven't spoken to blender Richard Paterson about these whiskies yet. No doubt I'll be greeted with a knee on the nuts for declaring two as duds. My guess is that this is the youngest of the quartet by a distance and that is probably why it is the best. The peat profile is very different and challenging. I'd still love to see this in its natural plumage as the caramel really does put the brakes on the complexity and development. Otherwise we could have had an elementary classic. 45%

Jura Elements "Fire" db (86.5) n22.5 t21.5 f21 b21.5. Pleasant fare, the highlight coming with the vaguely Canadian-style nose thanks to a classic toffee-oak mix well known east of the Rockies. Some botanicals also there to be sniffed at while a few busy oaky notes pep up the barley-juiced delivery, too. Sadly, just a shade too toffee dependent. 45%

Jura Elements "Water" db (73.5) n18.5 t19 f18 b18. Oranges by the box-full trying to get out but the mouth is sent into puckering spasm by the same sulphur which spoils the nose. 50%

Jura Prophecy profoundly peated db (90.5) n23.5 something almost akin to birchwood in there with the peat and salt; there is a wonderful natural floral note as well as coastal elements to this one; **t23** impressively two-toned: on one side is the sharper, active barley and peat offering an almost puckering youthfulness and zest; on the other, a sweeter, lightly oiled buzz...a treat; **f22** thins as the vanillas enter; **b22** youthful, well made and I prophesize this will be one of Jura's top scorers of 2011... 46%

Jura Superstition db (73.5) n17 t19 f18 b18.5. I thought this could only improve. I was wrong. One to superstitiously avoid. 43%

Jura Tastival db (79) n20 t22 f18 b19. Light, complex, multi-layered, varying strata of subtle....oh...oh! Sorry, dozed off and had a dream about being let loose in a Jura warehouse and lab. Sorry where was I? Oh yes; Jura Tastival. Thick, black, impenetrably sweet raisin fudge and dates. Otherwise furry and characterless...indeed, a clone of so many other previous Juras, alas. Zzzzzz. 44%. 3000 bottles. Whisky Festival Exclusive 2014. WB15/285

Jura Turas-Mara db (82.5) n20.5 t22 f19 b21. Some irresistible Jaffa Cake moments. But the oils are rather too severe and tangy. 42%. Travel Retail Exclusive.

⁂ **Douglas Laing's Single Minded Jura Aged 8 Years** sherry butt, dist Apr 06, bott Sept 14 (80) n18.5 t21.5 f20 b20. Young malt, clean and juicy, despite the indifferent nose, but with very limited development. A pleasant wafer biscuit sweetness, though. 41.5%

Hepburn's Choice Jura 2006 Aged 8 Years refill butt (80) n19 t21.5 f19.5 b20. Fat, malty but lacking couth. 46%. sc. 598 bottles.

⁂ **Old Malt Cask Jura Aged 21 Years** refill hogshead, cask no. 10817, dist Oct 92, bott Aug 14 (88.5) n20.5 a slight (smoked!) apple brandy buzz to this; **t22.5** excellent body. The barley is dense, the oils well marshalled. Again, a slight pithy quality before the oak begins to play its hand; **f22.5** dry with the vaguest hint of smoke; **b23** a malt where the sum is better than its parts. Lots of pleasing maltiness to tuck into. 50%. nc ncf sc. 249 bottles.

⁂ **Old Malt Cask Jura 24 Years** Old refill hogshead, cask no. 11383, dist Feb 91, bott Mar 15 (92.5) n23.5 wonderfully delicious marriage between a bourbon-like honeysuckle and liquorice mix and a saltier, vaguely zesty tang; **t23.5** beautiful weight thanks to a mix of oils and coppery sheen...and that's before we get to the excellent manuka honey – salty maltiness. And then the spices turn up...; **f22.5** long, spiced and impressive honey fade; **b23** big, complex Jura showing almost at its best... 46.8%. nc ncf sc. 259 bottles.

⁂ **Romantic Rhine Collection Jura 1992** sherry octave, cask no. 780841, dist 14 Nov 92, bott 21 Jun 11 (74) n18 t19 f18 b19. The good whisky days on Jura are thin on the ground. This isn't one of them. Decidedly furry. 50.9%. 68 bottles.

⁂ **Signatory Cask Strength Collection Jura 1989 Heavily Peated Aged 23 Years** bourbon barrel, cask no. 30708, dist 17 Dec 89, bott 10 May 13 (87.5) n22 t21.5 f22 b22. Pleasant enough, and at times thoroughly enjoyable, but this must go down as one of the least heavily peated "heavily peated" whiskies in history. The fact that the tannin has just as much to say as the smoke speaks volumes. Perhaps a bit too heavy on the oak, in fact, but the soft oil does stir the sugars in attractively. 57.6%. nc sc. 196 bottles. WB15/137

KILCHOMAN
Islay, 2005. Kilchoman Distillery Co. Working.

Kilchoman 2007 Vintage dist 2007, bott 2013 db **(95.5) n24.5** surely one of the great peat noses of the world now. This is like grist in the palm of your hand: sweet, dripping with coastal air, salty and dank....yet at the same time tuning into another band width astringent, dry and sooty. The balance is truly exceptional...; **t24** stunning hazelnut crème wafer ensures the sugars are out in force early, the majority of them muscovado based. The drier, sooty peat can add so much acidity and dust, but no more; **f23** citrus joins the fun as the peats now fizz with light spice and the vanilla appears from under a smoky hood; **b24** credit where credit is due. This malt has moved on in quality expedientially from one vintage to the next since its first unsteady, Bambiesque, feinty bottlings. Not hint of feints now. But excellence is writ large... 46%. WB15/116

⋙ **Kilchoman 100% Islay The 5th Edition** db **(95.5) n23.5** young phenols let the gristy barley fall all over the nose without much ballast keeping them in line. Despite the obvious wet-behind-the-ears character, some vanilla still gets through and allows the Zambian forest honey to share the stage; **t24** big peat, yet this is the softest of softies on delivery, ulmo honey now taking control. The smoke offers a dual role of integrating with the sugars and offering an embracing, friendly, oily backdrop; **f24** the character style of central American coffee makes a later entry than normal, but intertwines with the smoke to magnificent effect...; **b24** 100% stunning. 50%. nc ncf.

Kilchoman Loch Gorm sherry cask, dist 07, bott 13 db **(92.5) n23.5** anyone who has squelched through the blackest peat bog on a stormy Islay day will recognise parts of this earthy aroma; fruit has tightened the smoky, slightly coal tar creosote aspect; **t23.5** ridiculously soft landing on the palate with those now familiar oils soon aboard and to all parts of the palate; one of the oiliest middles I have tasted in a Scotch; **f22.5** big smoked raisin fudge; **b23** it is never a good idea to be Gorm-less...especially when a whisky is quite this scarily enormous. On this and other evidence, it could be that Kilchomen is not just challenging Caol Ila as the oiliest malt on Islay, but may well have surpassed it. 46%. nc ncf.

Kilchoman Machir Bay bott 2012 db **(93) n23** fireside peat ash wrapped in sherry; **t23.5** beautifully distilled barley and grist – both youthful and soon weighed down with a little vanilla – tapping out some major peaty notes; just a little bitter as it appears the oak has been forced slightly. The sultana fruit maximises the juiciness; **f23** long with a wonderful ulmo honey depth and the now restrained peat taking a support role rather than the lead; **b23.5** it is over 30 years since I first tried to play football on the sands of Machir Bay. I did it because with the winds never ceasing, it was, like a latter day Canute, an attempt at the impossible. A bit like trying to get to the bottom of this malt, in fact. In some respects it works, in others I feel a degree of sherry may just have knocked out some of the more complex characters in an attempt to soften. It is, however, much more successful than my failed attempts at playing "Keepie Uppie" against the perennial winds of Machir Bay... 46%. nc ncf.

Kilchoman Machir Bay oloroso sherry butt finish, bott 13 db **(90.5) n23** as fat as an Islay goose with the wine helping to turn this chunky; **t22.5** how sweet it is: to be loved by those who want their palate caked Caol Ila style in thick oil with the phenols subdued and trying to get out from under the weight of the juicy sultanas; **f22** the oiliest coffee ever; **b23** I think this was more honeyed last time, but the sultanas ring a bell. Another very different but high quality offering from Kilchomen. 46%. nc ncf.

Kilchoman Machir Bay bott 2014 db **(92) n23** soft, teasing, engulfing smoke lightened further by grapefruit; **t24** pleasing grist offers bold sugars which melt in the mouth and an intensifying peat which gathers like storm clouds on the horizon; **f22** the storm wanders in another direction leaving a slightly bitter oakiness washed up on the beach alongside some sugar and spice; **b23** some 25 years ago, Machir Bay would be where my children and I tried to play blow football: it was us against the impossible, relentless winds which howled off the sea with a will and singularity of mind that could not be tamed. There was only ever one winner. So, interesting to see that they have created a malt to reflect those very rare days when you can explore the length of it untroubled by nature. As lovely as this whisky is, I think I would have enjoyed it more had it reflected the Bay in all its fury... 46%. ncf nc. WB15/27

⋙ **Kilchoman Machir Bay** bott 2015 db **(94.5) n23** acidic, dry, peat and anthracite bite...; **t24** fat, oily, mouth-filling then a slow disambiguation between the initially wrapped up smoke and the ever intensifying sugars. And as the sugars expand, so the countering big spices begin to take control; **t23.5** that warming spice lingers, but so do those phenols. The oak provides late, controlled bitterness; **b24** a thudding, thumping dram hitting you like a Dave Mackay tackle. Big peat, perfectly representing a big malt. 50%. nc ncf.

⋙ **Kilchoman Port Cask Matured** dist 2010, bott 2014 db **(96) n23.5** the phenol levels may be through the roof and the smoke may be dry enough to make your contact lenses fall out, yet.... The fruit finds the perfect perch to sing a beautiful song, its feathers unruffled; **t24** gosh! One of the smoke-fruit mixes of the year: ashy – a kind of blend of peat and anthracite dust. These are at such high levels, it should obliterate most cask influences. But, again, the grape shows such beautiful purpose and clarity that it offers all the required sugars without coming into conflict; **f24** despite the intensity of the peat, the grape ensures a beautifully soft landing and allows the spices room to manoeuvre; **b24.5** a rare occasion when smoke and fruit find outstanding harmony. And for its age...just ridiculously good. *55%. ncf nc.*

❖ **Kilchoman Port Cask Matured Aged 5 Years** cask 285, dist 2009, bott 2014 db **(92.5)** **n23** spiced fruit cake; a dry peat reek plays second fiddle; **t24** juicy landing and then a massive explosion of spices and sugar – mainly dark and brooding; the pet begins to get louder as a little tannin arrives, too; **f22.5** the fruit loses its sugars just a little too quickly; **b23** delicious but a rare Kilchoman where the fruit rules the roost.. *58.3%. Abbey Whisky exclusive.*

Kilchoman Sherry Cask Release bott 2011 db **(83)** **n21.5 t21.5 f19 b21.** The thumping peat and at times almost syrupy sherry is just too much of a good thing. *46%. nc ncf.*

Kilchoman Single Cask Release bourbon, cask no.473/2008, dist 25 Sep 08, bott 16 Sep 13 db **(95.5)** **n23.5** a hint of Fisherman's Friend adds a menacing sharpness to the otherwise serenely sweet peat; **t24** quite outstanding mouth feel on delivery: the palate is a blur of smoke and dark sugars, though midway in, ash and coal dust bites; **f24** as long as demanded for a malt this big; the peat now layering in both intensity and sweetness. The spices buzz cleverly and almost below the taste buds' radar; **b24** most of the whiskies I have tasted from this distillery this year have been truly exceptional. Here is another one. 61%. ncf nc. Bottled in celebration of the 5th year of The Whisky Show. The Whisky Exchange. WB15/278

Kilchoman Vintage 2006 bott 2012 db **(93.5)** **n24 t23.5 f22.5 b23.** A sweetly peated triumph. *46%. nc ncf.*

Master of Malt Single Cask Kilchoman 5 Years Old (96) **n24** delicate smoke and marmalade: that's basic. Where this works in is the complexity lurking behind the phenols: minor dabs of ginger and allspice keeping things warm and dry; **t24.5** the smoke is up there but again happy to play second fiddle to the much more integrated grain and oak notes which dovetail sugar and spice and all things nice...a feminine whisky one might say..; **f23.5** light oils towards the end...; **b24** the smoke keeps a lower than usual profile. No bad thing: the intricacy of the oak in particular takes some believing. A wonder malt. *596%. sc.*

That Boutique-y Whisky Kilchoman batch 1 **(95)** **n24** if you want to know what just about faultless heavily peat grist is like, try this: a wonderful mix of salty sea spray and peat reek on the wind; **t24** the sweetness promised on the nose arrives immediately; the sugars play out from gristy melt-in-the-mouth icing sugar through to muscovado. Always, though, it is handcuffed to smoke; **f23.5** much drier with the sugars seemingly spent and a little nudge towards light vanilla; **b24** sublimely made and maturing comfortably. When whisky is this good, age matters not a jot. *55.5%. 272 bottles.*

KINCLAITH
Lowlands, 1957–1975. Closed / Dismantled.
Mo Ór Collection Kinclaith 1969 41 Years Old first fill bourbon hogshead, cask no. 301453A, dist 28 May 69, bott 29 Oct 10 **(85.5)** **n22 t22 f20.5 b21.** Hangs on gamely to the last vestiges of life, though the oak, without being overtly aggressive, is squeezing all the breath out of out of it. *46%. nc ncf sc. Release No. 2. The Whisky Talker. 164 bottles.*

KNOCKANDO
Speyside, 1898. Diageo. Working.
Knockando Aged 12 Years dist 94 db **(86)** **n22 t22 f21 b21.** An unusually light bottling. Here you get full exploration of the attractive, malty skeleton. But Knockando has a tendency towards dryness and the casks here oblige rather too well. A delicate dram all the same. *43%*

Knockando Aged 12 Years dist 1995 db **(71.5)** **n16 t19 f18 b18.5.** If there was an award for Worst Nose of the Year, this must be somewhere in the running. *43%*

Knockando Aged 12 Years dist 1996 db **(76)** **n18 t20.5 f18.5 b19.** Disappointing. As someone who knows this distillery perhaps as well as anyone working for its current owners, I had hoped for a dry, sophisticated dram to send me into various degrees of ecstasy. Instead, I am left lamenting a few poor casks which have distorted what this distillery stands for. *43%*

Knockando Aged 18 Years sherry casks, dist 1987 db **(77)** **n19 t21 f18 b19.** Bland and docile. Someone wake me up. *43%*

Knockando 25 Years Old Special Release 2011 db **(77)** **n20 t22 f16 b19.** One or two renegade sherry butts away from what would have been a memorable whisky. *43%. nc ncf.*

Knockando 1990 db **(83)** n21 t22 f20 b20. The most fruity Knockando I've come across with some attractive salty notes. Dry, but a little extra malty sweetness these days. *40%*

KNOCKDHU

Speyside, 1894. Inver House Distillers. Working.

AnCnoc 12 Year Old db **(94.5)** n24 so complex it is frightening: delicate barley; delicate spices; delicate butterscotch-vanilla, delicate citrus... and all the while the lightest discernible sugars melt into the malt; **t23** it had to be salivating... and is! Yet there is enough oaky-vanilla roughage to ensure the citrus and barley don't get their own way; **f23.5** a slow but telling arrival of spices fit hand in glove with the complex cocoa-barley tones; **b24.5** a more complete or confident Speyside-style malt you are unlikely to find. Shimmers with everything that is great about Scotch whisky... always a reliable dram, but this is stupendous. *40%*

AnCnoc 13 Year Old Highland Selection db **(85)** n21 t23 f20 b21. A big Knockdhu, but something is dulling the complexity. *46%*

AnCnoc 16 Years Old db **(91.5)** n22 sharp, pithy, salty, busy...; **t23.5** those salts crash headlong into the taste buds and then give way to massive spice and barley; soft sugars and vanilla follow at a distance; **f23** salted mocha and spice; **b23** unquestionably the spiciest AnCnoc of all time. Has this distillery been moved to the coast..? *46%*

◈ **AnCnoc 18 Years Old** db **(88.5)** n22.5 a curious mix of prickly spice and buttered raisin shortcake; **t23** the palate is swamped by malt and vanilla; malt sharp and two-toned, as though the third fill bourbon casks more than equal first. But the middle is a little dull, with fruit fudge the order of the day; **f21** disappointingly short of charisma: monotone fruit, perhaps, but badly lacking in lengthening sugars; **b22** cleaner sherry at work here. But again, the contours of the malt have been flattened out badly. *46%. nc ncf.*

AnCnoc 22 Year Old db **(87)** n22 t21.5 f22 b21.5. Often a malt which blossoms before being a teenager, as does the fruits of Knockdhu; struggles to cope comfortably with the inevitable oakiness of old age. Here is such a case. *46%. Inverhouse Distillers.*

◈ **AnCnoc 24 Years Old** db **(94)** n23 deep...and gets deeper. Dates and spiced toasted raisin dominate, leading to a heavy, dense fruitcake feel...; **t24.5** so no surprises: thick Melton Hunt cake, with extra lashing of molasses are quickly to the fore...and linger. The spices begin early but multiply even when the manuka honey begins to kick in; ulmo honey, then Lubeck marzipan and sultana enrich the middle ground; **f22.5** dulls slightly as the sugars wear thin, but now some dough with the plums, dates and spices aplenty; there is, if you are wondering, a slight furry tang – but pretty low key; **b24** big, broad-shouldered malt which carries a lot of weight but hardly veers away from the massively fruity path. For sherry loving whisky drinkers everywhere... *46%. nc ncf.*

AnCnoc 26 Years Old Highland Selection db **(89)** n23 t22 f23 b21. There is a little flat moment between the middle and finish for which I have chipped off a point or two. That apart, superb. *48.2%*

AnCnoc 30 Years Old db **(85)** n21 t23 f19 b22. Seat-of-the-pants whisky that is just on the turn. Still has a twinkle in the eye, though. *49%*

AnCnoc 35 Years Old db **(86)** n21 t21 f22.5 b21.5. Tries to take the exotic fruit route to antiquity but headed off at the pass by a massive dollop of natural caramels. The slow burn on the spice is an unexpected extra treat, though. *43%*

AnCnoc 35 Years Old bourbon and sherry casks db **(88)** n22.5 t22 f21.5 b22. The usual big barley sheen has dulled with time here. Some attractive cocoa notes do compensate. *44.3%. nc ncf.*

◈ **AnCnoc 1975** bott 2014 db **(90)** n23.5 creaking, crumbling oak at every turn. Fortunately there's enough sugar at play – a blend of maple syrup and molasses – to see off any negative points. When some form of equality is established, the rich fruitcake comes out to play...; **t23** all kinds of timber notes up front but the fruit gushes in quickly to form a lush cushion. Two year old Melton Hunt Cake with fully burned raisin; **f21.5** just a little bit of awkward bitterness – and an odd furriness – joins the fruit; **b22.5** if it showed any more signs of age, it'd need its own Zimmer frame. But the deep, fruity sugars are a superb restorative. *44.2%. nc ncf.*

An Cnoc 1993 db **(89)** n22 t21 f24 b22. Quite an odd one this. I have tasted it a couple of times with different samples and there is a variance. This one takes an oakier path and then invites the barley to do its stuff. Delicious, but underscores the deft touch of the standard 12-year-old. *46%*

AnCnoc 1994 db **(88.5)** n22.5 t22.5 f21.5 b22. Coasts through effortlessly, showing the odd flash of brilliance here and there. Just get the feeling that it never quite gets out of third gear... *46%. ncf.*

AnCnoc 1995 db **(84.5) n21 t22 f20.5 b21.** Very plump for a Knockdhu with caramel notes on a par with the citrus and burgeoning bourbon. Some barley juice escapes on delivery but the finish is peculiarly dry for the distillery. *46%*

AnCnoc 1999 db **(95.5) n24** ridiculously delicate with a heather honey backbone from which certain light liquorice and citrus notes hang. Rarely is good age so cleverly revealed, or disguised, or spices so polite; even a hint of light smoke for goodness sake; **t24** both firm yet silky delivery, the two contrasting tones continuing throughout. The spices buzz while a little maple syrup thins that prominent heather honey; a decent puff of vanilla; **f23.5** pretty lengthy, helped by the spice and the muscovado-topped butterscotch; a late milky chocolate flourish does no harm; **b24** I noticed as I was putting the bottle away that on their back label their description includes "Colour: soft, very aromatic with a hint of honey and lemon in the foreground" and "Nose: amber with a slight yellow hue." Which would make this malt pretty unique. But this is worth getting for far more than just the collectors' item typo: this is brilliant whisky – one of their best vintage malts for a very long time. In fact, one of their best ever bottlings...period. *46%. nc ncf. WB15/160*

⬙ **AnCnoc 2000** bott Sept 14 db **(87) n21.5 t23 f21.5 b21.5.** Knockdhu whisky is at its best in a judicious mix of ex-bourbon barrels, as it is they which can fully exploit – and allow unrestricted access to show - the abnormal complexity of the malt. It appears sherry butts have been introduced here. And though there is no OTT sulphur, a flattening process – similar to that experienced when caramel is inserted – has occurred. Some lovely chocolate fruit and nut notes, and all round enjoyable stuff. But the higher complexity has been trimmed. *46%. nc ncf.*

⬙ **AnCnoc Barrow** 13.5 ppm phenols db **(88) n22** a light, almost skinny nose: the phenols are profound, but mainly because they appear to be hanging off very little; **t21** still positively anorexic, even on delivery. The peats again appear to have a disproportionate say in matters as there is so little body; **f23** only now do we move into the realms of seriously good whisky. Whatever oils there are have finally found each other to form some kind of depth, and with it comes the balancing malt and light tannins (in the form of liquorice); **b22** a quite peculiar Knockdhu. The usual subtle richness of texture is curiously absent. As are friendly sugars. The strange angles of the phenols fascinate, however. *46%. nc ncf. Exclusive to travel retail.*

⬙ **AnCnoc Black Hill Reserve** db **(81) n20 t22 f19 b20.** The furriness threatened on the nose and realised at the finish does this great distillery no favours at all. *46%. nc ncf. Exclusive to travel retail.*

⬙ **AnCnoc Cutter** 20.5 ppm phenols db **(96.5) n24** sexily lush ground, full of molten brown sugars, on which the peat can build its foundations; the salt gives a unambiguous coastal feel...though the casks may have been matured inland; **t24** distinctly Islay style - Ardbeg to be precise – as the phenols have now picked up a charmingly citrus edge, while the smoke varies in pace, weight and sweetness to constantly change theme as the complexity rises; some wonderful oils surge early on ensuring good weight throughout; **f24** the oils are now spent, though light sugars – some gristy - linger. The smoke still circles, now accompanied by spice. Vanilla arrives, replacing the citrus. Long and satisfying...; **b24.5** brilliant! An adjective I am far more used to associating with anCnoc than some of the others I have had to use this year. The most Ardbeg-esque mainland malt I have ever encountered. *46%. nc ncf.*

AnCnoc Flaughter 14.8 ppm phenols db **(88.5) n23** dense malt with something of distant kippers; **t22** soft oils, several layers of malt of varying intensity. But a quite piquant smokiness; **f21.5** surprisingly hard smoke and even harder sugars. Something to break your teeth on; **b22** interesting to compare the relative heavy handedness of this against the Rutter. A lovely whisky this may be, but has nothing like the poise or balance. *46%. ncf nc. WB15/345*

AnCnoc Peter Arkle Limited Edition db **(87.5) n22.5 t22.5 f20.5 b22.** A floral nose, with lavender and honeysuckle in abundance. Also offers dried orange peel. But the malt doesn't move on from there as one might hope, becoming just a little too sugary and caramel stodgy for the malt to do itself justice. All that said, a great dram to chew on for a few minutes! *46%. ncf nc. WB15/321*

AnCnoc Rutter 11 ppm phenols db **(96.5) n24.5** citrus with a twist of peat...; the most delicately yet meaningfully smoked nose on the market today **t24.5** a delivery from heaven: melt-in-the mouth sugary grist continues with its lemony dress. While all around smoke plays, at times hardly audibly, in the background; **f23.5** fabulous finale: no bitterness, no angst or mess. Just the most elegant and charming fade of grist and smoke, perhaps with a dusting of honeyed cocoa on the way down; **b24** I remember vividly, at this great distillery's

Centenary party exactly 20 years ago this summer, mentioning to the then distillery manager that I thought that the style of the malt produced at Knockdhu was perfectly geared to make a lightly malted peat along the lines of its neighbour, Ardmore. Only for a few weeks of the year I ventured. I'm pretty certain this malt was not a result of that observation, but it is heartening to see that my instincts were right: it's a sensation! *46%. ncf nc. WB15/320*

LADYBURN
Lowlands, 1966–2000. William Grant & Sons. Closed.

Mo Ór Collection Rare Ayrshire 1974 36 Years Old first fill bourbon barrel, cask no. 2608, dist 10 May 74, bott 1 Nov 11 **(89.5) n22 t23.5 f22 b22.5**. I had a feeling it'd be this distillery when I saw the title on the label... it couldn't be much else! Fascinating to think that I was in final countdown for my 'O' levels when this was made. It appears to have dealt with the passing years better than I have. Even so, I had not been prepared for this. For years during the very early 1990s Grant's blender David Stewart sent me samples of this stuff and it was, to put it mildly, not great. Some were the oakiest malt I ever tasted in my life. And, to compound matters further, the distillery's own bottling was truly awful. But this cask has re-written history. *46%. nc ncf sc. Release No. 4. The Whisky Talker. 261 bottles.*

LAGAVULIN
Islay, 1816. Diageo. Working.

Lagavulin 12 Years Old 8th release, bott 2008 db **(94.5) n24 t24.5 f22.5 b23.5**. Sensational malt: simply by doing all the simple things rather brilliantly. *56.4%*

Lagavulin 12 Years Old 10th release, bott 2010 db **(94.5) n23.5 t24 f23.5 b23.5**. Keeps on track with previous Releases. Though this is the first where the lowering of the ppms from 50 to 35 really do seem noticeable. Quite beautiful, nonetheless. *56.5%*

Lagavulin 12 Years Old Special Release 2011 db **(96.5) n24.5 t24 f23.5 b24.5**. So the peat may not pound as it did when the Whisky Bible began life in 2003: the phenols are noticeably lighter here. But it is not all about size: balance and complexity still reign supreme. *57.5%. nc ncf.*

Lagavulin 12 Years Old Special Release 2012 Refill American oak casks, bott 2012 db **(95) n23 t24 f24 b24**. Truly wonderful. A very clever, sympathetic and professional choice of casks from this superstar distillery. *56.1%. nc ncf. Diageo.*

Lagavulin 16 Years Old db **(95) n24** morning cinders of peat from the fire of the night before: dry, ashy, improbably delicate. Just a hint of Demerara sweetness caught on the edge; **t24** that dryness is perfectly encapsulated on the delivery with the light sugars eclipsed by those countless waves of ash. A tame spiciness generates a degree of hostility on the palate, but the mid-ground sticks to a smoky, coffee-vanilla theme; **f23** light spicy waves in a gentle sea of smoke; **b24** although i have enjoyed this whisky countless times socially, it is the first time for a while I have dragged it into the Tasting Room for professional analysis for the Bible. If anyone has noticed a slight change in Lagavulin, they would be right. The peat remains profound but much more delicate than before, while the oils appear to have receded. A different shape and weight dispersal for sure. But the sky-high quality remains just the same. *43%*

Lagavulin The Distillers Edition batch lgv.4/502, dist 97, bott 13 db **(94.5) n25** two toned peat with Arbroath Smokies battling buttery kippers for supremacy; salty, soft and seemingly with some kind of indecipherable fruit number lurking in the near opaque background; **t23.5** probably the silkiest delivery you'll come across this year. Voluptuous, moist date drowned in smoke descends into a molassed mass; **f22** fades a little too fast as the vanilla bring matters to a surprisingly tangy conclusion; **b24** hugely enjoyable. In some ways simply too dense to maximise the distillery's enormous complexity. The nose, however, deserves legendary status and its presence on the palate offers something exceptional, even if the flavours have been daubed on, rather than finely painted. *43% WB15/309*

Lagavulin Aged 16 Years The Distillers Edition PX cask, dist 1991, bott 2007 db **(83) n22 t21 f20 b20**. I have oft stated that peat and sherry are uncomfortable bed-fellows. Here, the two, both obviously from fine stock and not without some individual attraction, manage to successfully cancel each other out. One is hard pressed to imagine any Lagavulin this dull. *43%*

Lagavulin 21 Years Old Special Release 2012 dist 1991, bott 2012 db **(92.5) n23.5 t23.5 f23 b22.5**. The impact of the fruit is truly delicious in its sweet juiciness, but the smoke means complexity is slightly subdued. Fantastic whisky, though...and rather sweet. *52%. nc ncf. Diageo.*

Lagavulin Special Release 2010 12 Years Old db **(94) n24.5 t24 f22 b23.5**. Bloody hell! This is some whisky...! *56.5%. nc ncf.*

◈ **Gleann Mór Lagavulin 10 Year Old** dist Mar 05, bott Apr 15 **(94) n24** who needs to actually drink a whisky when you can nose something like this? Absorbing because the nose appears less peat encumbered than it actually is. Then you realise it is the subtlety of the balance and weight and the clever positioning of the marshmallow and citric sweetness which play olfactory tricks: this is big...; **t23.5** big indeed! The delivery is all about comforting sugars, lightly oiled and gristy, then the smoke sweeps home abreast of biting spices. The mellow sweetness of the grist is a constant cushion; **f23** at last a little tannin arrives, but its presence is fleeting and barely registers. A light citrus-smoke plays us out; **b23.5** even without being troubled by pesky things such as...oooh, oak, for instance, this bottling shows just how profoundly good the basic Lagavulin spirit is. *53.2%. sc.*

LAPHROAIG
Islay, 1815. Beam Inc. Working.

Laphroaig 10 Years Old db (**90**) **n24** impossible not to nose this and think of Islay: no other aroma so perfectly encapsulates the island – clean despite the rampaging peat-reek and soft oak, raggy coast-scapes and screeching gulls – all in a glass; **t23** one of the crispiest peaty malts of them all, the barley standing out alone, brittle and unbowed, before the peat comes rushing in like the tide: iodine and soft salty tones; **f20.5** the nagging bitterness of many ex-Allied bourbon casks filled during this period is annoyingly apparent here... **b22.5** has reverted back slightly towards a heavier style in more recent bottling, though I would like to see that old oomph at the very death. Even so, this is, indisputably, a classic whisky. The favourite of Prince Charles apparently: he will make a wise king... *40%*

Laphroaig 10 Years Old Original Cask Strength db (**92**) **n22** a duller nose than usual: caramel reducing the normal iodine kick; **t24** recovers supremely for the early delivery with some stunning black peppers exploding all over the palate leaving behind a trail of peat smoke; the controlled sweetness to the barley is sublime; **f23** again there is a caramel edge to the finish, but this does not entirely prevent a fizzing finale; **b23** caramel apart, this is much truer to form than one or two or more recent bottlings, aided by the fresh, gristy sweetness and explosive spices. Wonderful! *55.7%*

Laphroaig Aged 15 Years db (**79**) **n20 t20 f19 b20.** A hugely disappointing, lacklustre dram that is oily and woefully short on complexity. Not what one comes to expect either from this distillery or age. *43%*

Laphroaig 18 Years Old db (**94**) **n24** multi-layered smokiness: there are soft, flightier, sweeter notes and a duller, earthier peat ingrained with salt and leather; **t23.5** perhaps it's the big leg-up from the rampant hickory, but the peat here offers a vague Fisherman's Friend cough sweet quality more usually associated with Bowmore, except here it comes in a milder, Demerara-sweetened form with a few strands of liquorice helping that hickory to a gentler level; **f23** soft oils help keep some late, slightly juicy barley notes on track while the peat dances off with some spices to niggle the roof of the mouth and a few odd areas of the tongue; **b23.5** this is Laphroaig's replacement to the woefully inadequate and gutless 15-year-old. And talk about taking a giant step in the right direction. Absolutely brimming with character and panache, from the first molecules escaping the bottle as you pour to the very final ember dying on the middle of your tongue. *48%*

Laphroaig Aged 25 Years db (**94**) **n23** the clean - almost prim and proper - fruit appears to have somehow given a lift to the iodine character and accentuated it to maximum effect. The result is something much younger than the label demands and not immediately recognisable as Islay, either. But no less dangerously enticing... **t24** the grapes ensure the peat is met by a salivating palate; particularly impressive is the way the sweet peat slowly finds its footing and spreads beautifully; **f23.5** no shortage of cocoa: a kind of peaty fruit and nut chocolate bar... **b23.5** like the 27-y-o, an Islay which doesn't suffer for sherry involvement. Very different from a standard, bourbon barrel-aged Laphroaig with much of the usually complexity reined in, though its development is first class. This one's all about effect - and it works a treat! *40%*

Laphroaig Aged 25 Years Cask Strength 2011 Edition oloroso and American oak casks db (**96.5**) **n24 t24.5 f24 b24.** Quite possibly the finest bottling of Laphroaig I have ever encountered. And over the last 35 years there have been a great many bottles... *48.6%*

Laphroaig Aged 30 Years db (**94**) **n24 t23 f23 b24.** The best Laphroaig of all time? Nope, because the 40-y-o is perhaps better still... just. However, Laphroaig of this subtlety and charm gives even the very finest Ardbeg a run for its money. A sheer treat that should be bottled at greater strength. *43%*

Laphroaig Aged 40 Years db (**94**) **n23 t24 f23 b24.** Mind-blowing. A malt that defies all logic and theory to be in this kind of shape at such age. The Jane Fonda of Islay whisky. *43%*

◈ **Laphroaig Au Cuan Mòr** db (**95**) **n24** the even peat appears to have a rich, fruity tint to it. But it is the influence of the bourbon barrel which stars, seemingly forging a seamless alliance with the more provocative notes to harmonise them and bring them into a charmingly

Kentuckian fold; **t24** it will be hard to locate a more serene delivery on the palate for any peated malt this year. The fruit is entirely sulphur-free and polite enough to, rather than row with the smoke, combine with it to give a featherbed mouth-feel. The oak is profound and should clatter into the taste buds. But the smoke and fruit provide the buffers; **f23** drier, with a gentle smoked fruit-chocolate finale; **b24** you don't need to squint at the back label to be told that first fill bourbon barrels are at work here: this is where Kentucky, Jerez and Islay merges with breath-taking ease and harmony. 48%. *Travel retail exclusive.*

Laphroaig Cairdeas bourbon barrels and Amontillado seasoned traditional hogsheads, bott 2014 db **(92.5) n22.5** ashy...with a few dabs of TCP; **t23** something seemingly youthful bites and bites hard: the light muscovado sugars melt; a little lavender creeps up from nowhere; **f23.5** now pretty dry with the lavender and peat on equal terms; **b23.5** as dry as Laphroaig gets. Rather beautifully made and so delicate you feel it might simply crumble in your mouth. 51.4%.

Laphroaig Càirdeas Origin quarter casks, bott 2012 db **(89) n24 t22.5 f20.5 b22.** Started like a train and hit the buffers for the finish. Still, early on it is quite superb. 51.2%. *ncf.*

Laphroaig PX Cask bourbon, quarter and Pedro Ximenez casks db **(96) n23.5 t24.5 f24 b24.** I get the feeling that this is a breathtaking success despite the inclusion of Pedro Ximenez casks. This ultra sweet wine is often paired with smoky malt, often with disastrous consequences. Here it has worked, but only because the PX has been controlled itself by absolutely outstanding oak. And the ability of the smoke to take on several roles and personas simultaneously. A quite beautiful whisky and unquestionably one of the great malts of the year...in spite of itself. 48%. *Travel Retail exclusive.*

Laphroaig Quarter Cask db **(96) n23** burning embers of peat in a crofter's fireplace; sweet intense malt and lovely, refreshing citrus as well; **t24** mouthwatering, mouth-filling and mouth-astounding: the perfect weight of the smoke has no problems filling every crevice of the palate; builds towards a sensationally sweet maltiness at the middle; **f24** really long, and dries appropriately with smoke and spice. Classic Laphroaig; **b25** a great distillery back to its awesome, if a little sweet, self. Layer upon layer of sexed-up peatiness. The previous bottling just needed a little extra complexity on the nose for this to hit mega malt status. Now it has been achieved... 48%

Laphroaig Select db **(89) n22** not just full of smoke, but vitality, too. Certain aspects of the sweetness are slightly more aligned to bourbon with a red liquorice flourish to the gristy smoke; **t22** soft – almost too soft – as the smoked toffee becomes decidedly fudgy; **f23** more of the same, only a hint of cocoa and Demerara plus some late oil and spice; **b22** missed a trick by not being unchillfiltered at 46%. An apre-taste squint at the back label revealed some virgin oak casks had been used here, which explains much! 40%. WB15/117

Laphroaig Triple Wood ex-bourbon, quarter and European oak casks db **(86) n21 t21.5 f21.5 b21.** A pleasing and formidable dram. But one where the peat takes perhaps just too much of a back seat. Or, rather, is somewhat neutralised to the point of directional loss. The sugars, driven home by the heavy weight of oak, help give the whisky a gloss almost unrecognisable for this distillery. Even so, an attractive whisky in many ways. 48%. *ncf.*

◇ **Aflodal's Whisky The Famous Leapfrog** cask no. 70260, refill hogshead, dist 17 Jun 99, bott 22 Dec 10 **(96.5) n24** if you heard a bump, that was me falling off my seat after swooning: ticks every box with its majestic, nimble yet uncompromisingly gruff and growling peat. At once minty and sweet yet also salty and hickory-laden, dry and deep; **t25** every last hint of sugar, each and every ppm of phenols, every single oak facet, both dry and vanilla-rich, gather for the opening ceremony on the palate, then marching off in varying degrees of intensity for the lightly oiled, mega-satisfying mid-ground; **f23.5** the perfection of the arrival is a hard act to follow. Still beautiful – and none of the usual bitterness from old Laphroaig bourbon casks – the light spices and deft vanilla make for a much more demure, almost shy, finale. Yet still quite salty, seaweedy and lovely...; **b24** any more coastal and this dram will have a tide while in the glass. Laphroaig at its most true and epic. 51.5%. 323 bottles.

◇ **Cadenhead's Authentic Collection Laphroaig Aged 16 Years** bourbon cask, dist 1998 **(96.5) n24** Laphroaig in a nutshell; or, rather, in a tasting glass: evaporating rock pools with briny kelp nearby. Nearby, a cottage keeps a peat fire on the go, the reek drifting on the wind. Yes, it's summer on Islay...; **t24.5** much sweeter delivery than the nose ever suggests: a mix of Demerara sugar and heavily smoked grist. All helped along by a subtle oiliness and balanced by a drier, ashy note; **f23.5** the dryness grows, though slowly and without drama and with the sugars keeping track throughout; **b24.5** if anyone wants to know what a quintessential Laphroaig looks like, let them have a gargle with this...it's near perfection, I tells you.. 57.5%

◇ **Chieftain's Laphroaig Aged 12 Years** refill sherry hogshead, dist Feb 03, bott Feb 15 **(93) n22.5** almost opaque as a nose: the thick peat and thicker sherry lets little else pass;

t23 usually, the delivery on such chunky whiskies are disappointing. This, however, bucks the trend with the sugars lifting the hefty gloom and lightening the chewability; **f23** the oak forces a way through and ensures some superb spices; **b23.5** a real heavyweight of a malt, thankfully basting untainted sherry. 48%. nc ncf. The Village (Germany) limited edition.

Cheiftain's Laphroaig Aged 14 Years hogshead, cask no. 8601/8604, dist Sep 98, bott Feb 13 **(90) n23** dry, powdery...like sticking your head up a peat sooted chimney (and believe me, I've done it often enough...); **t22.5** an early burst of typical gristy sugars, then a move towards mocha; **f22** quiet: returns to a smoky powdery dryness; **b22.5** curious, as there is hardly a bite of spice to be had. Intriguing, as you feel the malt is operating very much within its capabilities. 44.3%. 1518 bottles. WB15/164

 Douglas of Drumlanrig Laphroaig 13 Year Old refill sherry butt, dist Mar 02, bott Apr 15 **(94.5) n24.5** the glass brimmeth over with dry, nose-twitching, gristy peat reek like Dr Jekyl's test tubes brimmeth over with foreboding vapour...; **t24** cripes and yikes! That is some delivery. The sugars are regimental and at you from the first moment. But the phenols, first sparsely populated amongst them, begin to gather in force and take control. But is not a gentle skirmish: this is a full-on battle...; **f23** borderline bitter towards the end, as this distillery sometimes has a tendency towards. But the peat still marches on, ignoring the half-hearted vanillas along the way; **b23.5** yep! That's Laphroaig, indubitably. 56.8%. Loch Fyne Whiskies exclusive.

 Dun Bheagan Laphroaig 20 Year Old hogshead, dist May 94 **(89) n22** a trademark and unmistakable Laphroaig nose: dry, salty and seaweedy, with a genuine buzz to the iodine. Also a coded message that the oak will bitter out later...; **t23** spot on for the distillery, age and cask type. A loose lushness helps bind the peat; as salty as a seadog; **f21.5** bitters out...; **b22.5** should satiate most peat whisky lovers. 49%. nc ncf.

 Glen Fahrn Airline Nr 10 Laphroaig 1998 Aged 14 Years cask no. RF7981 **(96) n23.5 t24 f23.5 b25**. Always wonderful to find a malt rich in Laphroaig DNA not undone by the bitterness of a poor cask. Here oak and smoke are in harmony and ensure a complex intricacy to the liquorice and phenols. A rare case of the magic of the distillery captured showing every element of its greatness. One of the finest – and, but for the oil, most true – commercially bottled casks from the distillery I have ever tasted. 54.1%. sc. 236 bottles.

Hepburn's Choice Laphroaig Aged 11 Years refill hogshead, dist 02, bott 2014 **(90) n22.5** soot dry, with matching attractively acrid phenols; **t22** every atom of the 35ppm phenols arrives on delivery or very soon after. Light oil blends well with the light ulmo honey; **f23** gorgeous build up of smoked chocolate; **b23** does the simple things exceedingly well. Clean and helped by an impeccably behaved cask. 46%. nc ncf sc. 151 bottles.

 Hunter Laing's Old & Rare Laphroaig Aged 24 Years refill hogshead, dist Mar 90, bott Jul 14 **(84) n21 t22 f20 b21**. The nose clambers through the smoke, warning of a less than perfect bourbon barrel. And this is confirmed on delivery and, especially, the finish. The burn and prickle is not spice. 51.9%. ncf sc. 285 bottles.

 Old Malt Cask Laphroaig 12 Years Old refill butt, cask no. 11511, dist Jun 92, bott Apr 15 **(89) n23** a coastal cowshed overlooking rock pools with the tide out; **t22.5** sharp delivery rattling with salty smoke and cocoa; **f21.5** a little thin and bitter perhaps; **b22** a particularly salty version. 50%. nc ncf sc. 332 bottles.

Old Malt Cask Aged 14 Years refill butt, cask no. 10432, dis Apr 00, bott Apr 14 **(81.5) n20.5 t21 f20 b20**. A trademark old Allied bitter barrel des for this, its signature legible on the nose. Never happy, there are still plenty of sugars among the smoke. 50%. sc. 731 bottles.

 Old Malt Cask Laphroaig Aged 14 Years refill hogshead, cask no. 10809, dist Jun 00, bott Aug 14 **(90) n23** someone threw lavender into the smouldering peat; pretty gristy; **t23.5** polite peat. The sugars are big and brassy; **f21** dries as the oaky vanilla grips. Slight milkiness; **b22.5** a typical Allied cask does this no favours, or flavours. But the overall experience is delightful. 50%. nc ncf sc. 351 bottles.

 Old Malt Cask Laphroaig 14 Years Old refill hogshead, cask no. 10984, dist Sept 00, bott Oct 14 **(90) n22** there is a little sharpness and attitude but the depth of the farm-yardy phenols is so deep and true, this can be forgiven; **t23** promiscuous sugars wrap themselves teasingly around any peat-shrouded taste bud; **f22.5** much drier now, with the oak having its moment or three; **b22.5** absolutely yummy! 50%. nc ncf sc. 284 bottles.

 Old Malt Cask Laphroaig Aged 14 Years refill barrel, cask no. 11151, dist Jun 00, bott Dec 14 **(94.5) n23** classical Laphroaig: no more, no less... **t24** outstandingly noisy on the palate: not content with having massive peat to deal with, the taste buds have to deal with a fanfare of sugar and then a blast of warming, prickly spice – which is not very Laphroaigish at all...; **f23.5** gallops off into a very even and smoky sunset...; **b24** the kind of Islay you can drink all day, any day. And though par for the course in many ways, offers the odd welcome surprise which sets it apart. *50%. nc ncf sc. 295 bottles.*

◈ **Old Malt Cask Laphroaig 14 Years Old** refill hogshead, cask no. 11209, dist Jun 00, bott Jan 15 **(88) n23** dry, sooty, nippy peat-reek; **t22.5** sweet delivery even with a touch of liquorice amid the chewy phenols; **f20.5** bitters out comprehensively; **b22** for age and cask type, it pans out exactly as can be expected. *50%. nc ncf sc. 305 bottles.*

Old Malt Cask Laphroaig Aged 15 Years refill hogshead, cask no. 9932, dist Apr 98, bott Aug 13 **(95) n24** classically coastal with all kinds of saline rock pools mixing with the peat reek; a bit of a stunner... **t23.5** melt-in-the-mouth Demerara sugars gells sublimely with the slightly lighter than expected smoke; **f23.5** now the spices begins to orbit the late hickory, all played out on a smoky bed; **b24** intense and comfortably lives up to the distillery's reputation, throwing in the odd surprise for good measure. *50%. nc ncf sc. 212 bottles.*

Old Malt Cask Laphroaig Aged 15 Years refill butt, cask no. 10167, dist Mar 99, bott Jun 14 **(80.5) n21 t21.5 f19 b19**. An untidy mish-mash of a malt which boasts smoke aplenty. But another agent causes annoying disharmony. *50%. nc ncf sc. 292 bottles.*

Old Malt Cask Laphroaig Aged 16 Years refill hogshead, cask no. 10260, dist Oct 97, bott Dec 13 **(77) n19 t21 f18 b19**. Welcome to an old-fashioned Allied Domecq dud bourbon cask. Perhaps the slightly Fisherman's Friend-style distillate is not helping, but this is a pretty rough ride. *50%. nc ncf sc. 322 bottles.*

Old Malt Cask Laphroaig Aged 17 Years refill hogshead, cask no. 10125, dist Oct 96, bott Oct 13 **(86.5) n22 t21.5 f21.5 b21.5**. The smoke is a little dull and though plenty to chew at, liquorice in particular, this is rather hotter whisky than it should be. *50%. nc ncf sc.*

◈ **Old Particular Islay Laphroaig 14 Years Old** refill butt, cask no. 10694, dist Feb 01, bott Feb 15 **(92.5) n24.5** a sensually smoky nose with "Laphroaig" written through it like a stick of rock might have "Brighton". So coastal you can hear the gulls mewing, so salty you wonder if it needs some vinegar to even it up; **t23** a sweet, sugary arrival which still cannot lessen the impact of the peat; chewy yet seemingly devoid of oils; **f22** the lingering smoke almost conceals the cask's latent bitterness; **b23** impossible not to enjoy and savour... *51.5%. nc ncf sc. 636 bottles. Feis Ile 2015 bottling.*

Old Particular Islay Laphroaig Aged 15 Years refill hogshead, cask no. 10273, dist Mar 99, bott Mar 14 **(95) n23.5** firm in both its gristiness and oak involvement. Clean and almost chiselled in its smoky profile; **t24** spot on delivery with a fabulous interplay between the liquorice and Demerara bourbon notes and the forthright, unerring smoke; **f23.5** long, with a biscuit edge to the tapering smoke and moist ginger cake finale; **b24** beautifully disciplined and attractively sweet. *48.4%. nc ncf sc. 288 bottles.*

◈ **Provenance Laphroaig Over 8 Years** one refill hogshead, cask no. 10407, dist autumn 05, bott summer 14 **(94.5) n23.5** sharp, acerbic phenols of top farmyard quality; **t24** brilliant delivery: young, feisty but already wonderfully even in its sugar-smoke ratio; **f23** fabulous mint chocolate finale as the smoke and spice circle; **b24** I'd love a few casks of this in a blend I design: it'd make such an impact! But pretty much on the money as a singleton, too. Superb. *46%. nc ncf sc.*

Scotch Malt Whisky Society Cask 29.148 Aged 18 Years refill barrel, dist 04 Apr 95 **(90.5) n22** smoke-charged with the peat having that morning after in the Highland hearth feel; **t22.5** harp delivery with the sugars almost combustable; tangy melon fills the mid-ground; **f23** long, lightly oiled and surprisingly delicate; **b23** quietly goes about its subtly citrusy business. *60.6%. nc ncf sc. 206 Bottles.*

Scotch Malt Whisky Society Cask 29.151 Aged 24 Years refill butt, dist 09 Nov 89 **(85.5) n21.5 t22 f21 b21**. Top heavy with oak, giving the smoke a restricted space to work its magic. *50.7%. nc ncf sc. 311 bottles.*

Scotch Malt Whisky Society Cask 29.154 Aged 23 Years refill hogshead, dist 12 Oct 90 **(89) n23** a sprig of mint amid the smoke underlines the age; **t22** a short burst of younf gristiness holding on for grim death, then an avalanche of smoky oak; **f22** soft oils preserve the sugars...thankfully; **b22** a big, proud malt trying not to vanish under the oak. *49.9%.*

◈ **Scotch Malt Whisky Society Cask 29.158 Aged 14 Years** refill butt, dist 14 Apr 00 **(69) n17 t19 f16 b17**. Sweet, smoky, but fatally sulphur riddled. *61.7%. sc. 584 bottles.*

Signatory Cask Strength Collection Laphroaig Aged 15 Years refill sherry butt, cask no. 700393, dist 22 Sep 98, bott 23 Sep 13 **(96.5) n24** so farmyardy...with allotment bonfires thrown in for stunning effect; **t24.5** a truly exceptional clean sherry butt offers a fruity gloss to the smoky gristy sugars and spices. With a light oil to hand, the mouth feel and weight are spot on, as ulmo honey and treacle combine; **f23.5** minty chocolate as well as chocolate raisin. But all this couched in wonderfully dry peat ash...; **b24.5** if I have ever tasted a better sherry-peat combination, it escapes my mind. Look what happens when you have a sulphur free case: magic and malty miracles... *60.8%. sc nc. 551 bottles. WB15/298*

Signatory Cask Strength Collection Laphroaig Aged 17 Years hogshead, cask no. 8519, dist 26 Nov 96, bott 07 Jan 14 **(88) n22.5** light clan peat; citrus fresh; **t22** sweet, thin acacia honey, a little marzipan...and the remainder is peaty grist; **f21.5** drier, smokey; **b22** a cask which has done the rounds makes only a marginal contribution. So this is fresh stuff, but not quite so complex or heavy as it might be. *50.7%. nc sc. 271 bottles. WB15/138*

⬦ **Whisky Fair Laphroaig 16 Year Old** sherry hogshead, dist 1998, bott 2015 **(87) n24 t22 f19 b22.** A rare case of fruit and phenols working merrily in tandem, with the smoke in particular having a certain swagger. But it appears that it is the oak, rather than treated sherry, which makes the finish bitter and hard going. Some beautiful moments to treasure early on, though. *46%. 246 bottles.*

LINKWOOD
Speyside, 1820. Diageo. Working.

Linkwood 12 Years Old db **(94.5) n23.5** gorgeous malt absolutely bursting at the seems with barley-rich vitality; citrus and anthracite abound; **t24** a quite stunning delivery with some of the clearest, cleanest, most crystalline malt on the market. The sugars are angular and decidedly Demerara; **f23** a long play out of sharp barley which refuses to be embattled by the oaky vanillas; light spices compliment the persistent sugars; **b24** possibly the most improved distillery bottling in recent times. Having gone through a period of dreadful casks, it appears to have come through to the other side very much on top and close to how some of us remember it a quarter of a century ago. Sublime malt: one of the most glittering gems in the Diageo crown. *43%*

Linkwood 26 Year Old port finish dist 1981, bott 2008 db **(85) n20 t24 f20.5 b20.5.** Can't say that either nose or finish do it for me. But the delivery is brilliant: the enormity and luxurious sweetness of the grape leaves you simply purring and rolling your eyes in delight. *56.9%*

Linkwood 26 Year Old rum finish, dist 1981, bott 2008 db **(89.5) n23.5 t23.5 f21 b21.5.** A real touch of the rum toffee raisin candy to this one. *56.5%*

Linkwood 26 Year Old sweet red wine, dist 1981, bott 2008 db **(89) n22.5 t23 f21 b22.** Juicy, spicy: doesn't stint on complexity. *56.5%*

Linkwood 1974 Rare Malt db **(79) n20 t21 f19 b19.** Wobbles about the palate in search of a story and balance. Finds neither but some of the early moments, though warming, offer very decent malt. The best bit follows a couple of seconds after – and lasts as long. *55%*

⬦ **Adelphi Selection Linkwood 24 Years Old** cask no. 3535 **(86) n21 t23.5 f20 b21.5.** A malt with plenty of bounce and charisma, especially on delivery, when the fruit-tinged sugars go into overdrive and spices make the most of the palate-hugging depth. But the overall feeling is of a self-concious malt, never quite happy in the direction it is going, especially when the more bitter, off-key notes arrive towards the end. *57.5% WB16/007*

Berry's Own Selection Linkwood 1999 Aged 14 Years cask no. 11971, bott 2014 **(93) n23** wickedly sharp! **t23.5** oh my word...! The barley is so lively and puckering: enough oil and lemon-soaked sugar to deeply satisfy; **f23** a little bitterness to the tang, but that barley just keeps on coming, now with zesty flourish; **b23.5** a wonderful malt brimming with character. Speyside nutshelled. *46%. ncf ncf. WB15/244*

Berry's Own Selection Linkwood 1987 Aged 26 Years cask no. 1043, bott 2013 **(96.5) n24.5** a nose I could nose all day, had I the time: fabulous blood orange meeting moist Lubec marzipan head on; a fiendishly clever layering of delicate herbs; the fruitiness reforms into a wonderful exotic mush, caressing, cajoling, teasing, reminding you of its past, whispering about the delights yet to come...; **t24** the weight, the pace of flavour development, the degree of malt, its juiciness, of residual sugar of vanilla and natural caramel from the oak, the spices...all just about perfect for its age; **f23.5** concentrates on the vanillas, allowing any tanginess from the cask to filter through; **b24** there is not a competent professional blender in the world who might not resort to murder to get a parcel of malt like this in his 25-year-old blend. This would be the apex of the top dressing, the cherry on the cake, the box of subtle delights that could tip a creation from excellence to magnificence. *46%. ncf ncf. WB15/239*

Cadenhead's Authentic Collection Linkwood-Glenlivet Cask Strength Aged 12 Years bourbon hogsheads, dist 2001, bott Oct 13 **(89.5) n22** fresh, clean and faultless. The barley sparkles while the vanilla and spice does its thing quietly; **t23** salivating delivery with beautiful oscillation between the sharp barley, lingering sugars and spice; **f22** yet more barley, with a little late fudge and marzipan; some late bitterness; **b22.5** exemplary Linkwood at it most −Glenlivetish...! *57%. 246 bottles. WB15/082*

Cadenhead's Authentic Collection Linkwood-Glenlivet Cask Strength Aged 12 Years bourbon hogsheads, dist 2001, bott Feb 14 **(90) n22.5** a few apples amid the tannins; **t23**

light oils close ranks to keep in and magnify the enormity of the barley and spice; the mid ground is surrpsiignly juicy and offering over-ripe pear; **f22** late muscovado shadows the tannins; **b22.5** leave in glass a good half hour to unfold. Complex and surprisingly big. *57.8%. 294 bottles. WB15/085*

Cadenhead's Small Batch Linkwood-Glenlivet Aged 26 Years dist 1987, bott 2014 **(95.5) n24** one of the cleanest amalgamations of delicate fruit and barley you'll encounter for a while; **t25** one of the best deliveries this year: the barley is three dimensional and lit by a laser-sharp spotlight. For about ten seconds, oak, sugar, fruit and malt, all brought to the height of their flavour profiles by a liberal dose of salt, come together for an orgasmic blast which leaves the head spinning in delight...; **f22.5** the afterglow seems a little tame by comparison; the vanillas bob and weave but a slight tang shows the oaks are beginning to wither; **b24** when Linkwood is on top form, few Speysiders comes close. *56.8%. 972 bottles. WB15/259*

Duncan Taylor Dimensions Linkwood Aged 22 Years oak casks, cask no. 8326, dist 10/90, bott 04/13 **(94) n24** an astonishing nose in which my daily uncooked vegetable salad has been chopped up and mixed with Melton Hunt fruit cake at its most ridiculously moist and rich. With a little pepper added, of course...hang on, this kind of reminds me....(see summary)...; **t23.5** a plethora of dark sugars mingle with thick fruit and juicy barley. Still the spices buzz...; **f23** more spiced moist fruitcake; **b23.5** had to say, this got me scrambling to my 2014 Bible checking up Linkwood. And there was a DT bottling from a sister cask showing a very similar nonconventionalist style. Only this goes off on a different, fruitier tangent altogether. Staggeringly lovely. *48.7%. nc ncf sc. 237 bottles. WB15/115*

⋄ **Endangered Drams Linkwood 21 Year Old** dist 1991, bott 2013 **(91) n22 t23 f23 b23.** Really lovely Linkwood which chugs along, carrying a bit of weight and never really changing its sluggish pace. Thick, chewy, as fruity as it is malty and enriched by a little molasses which goes a long way. *50.8%*

Gordon & MacPhail Exclusive Single Malt Linkwood refill sherry hogshead, cask no. 5018, dist 08 Dec 88 **(97.5) n25** dry lead thanks to some well-muscled tannins. Lovely spices inject extra life into the sharp pineapple candy; some moist parkin cake underlines the age; even deeper notes babble underneath...; **t24** good weight of early, surprising, barley alongside a sturdier volley of spices. A procession of exotic fruits is topped off by custard and a few volts of tannin; the odd atom of smoke drifts around deliciously; **f24** the smoke persists and give extra life and depth, as well as captures the darker sugars to ensure the oak remains contented and positive; the late mocha tops it off magnificently; **b24.5** just like the proprietor of SWC, has aged with sophistication, elegance...and a touch of spice. Also, surrounded by smoke... A tip or two. Allow to sit in the glass for at least ten minutes to breathe. Nose and taste only at body temperature. Not a degree below. And do not add water. That way you will experience one of the most complete single casks ever bottled. *55.3%. nc ncf sc. 229 Bottles. Exclusive to the Soho Whisky Club. WB15/066*

Kingsbury Silver Linkwood 24 Year Old cask no. 568, dist 1989 **(85) n20.5 t23.5 f20.5 b21.** What seems like a thumping heavyweight oloroso butt has its weaknesses on both nose and finish. But there is no denying the delivery which is of the Harvey's Bristol Cream variety and is stashed with some serious grapey treasures. A flawed diamond, indeed... *46%*

Montgomerie's Single Cask Collection Linkwood cask no. 6713, dist 05 Dec 89, bott Mar 13 **(89.5) n22.5** just dig the diced apple and over-ripe pear; **t23** beautifully clean and busy delivery with the sugar and spice at the vanguard. Most of the sugars are gristy but the pear returns...even with that curious grittiness you get from the fruit...; **f22** tangy and heading towards a vanilla and Walnut Whip fondant finale; **b22** in many ways a modest whisky. But what it does right can be breath-taking. *46%. nc ncf sc. WB15/130*

⋄ **Old Malt Cask Linkwood Aged 15 Years** refill hogshead, cask no. 10828, dist Oct 98, bott Aug 14 **(87.5) n20 t23 f22 b22.5**. The higgledy-piggledy nose is more than compensated by a thoroughly entertaining malty richness on delivery, fully backed by complex spices and light molasses. Good oils, too. Hugely satisfying on the palate. *50%. nc ncf sc. 351 bottles.*

Old Malt Cask Linkwood Aged 16 Years sherry butt, cask no. 10068, dist Nov 96, bott Oct 13 **(91.5) n22.5** fresh, almost gristy but weighted by excellent vanilla and the lightest (and most surprising) smoke; **t23** mouth-watering with an alloy of fresh barley and crisp sugars; **f23** long, heading down the vanilla route but some late Manuka honey and liquorice intervene; **b23** an understated little gem. *50%. nc ncf sc.407 bottles.*

Old Masters Linkwood 14 Years Old cask no. 11980, dist 2001, bott 2014 **(77) n20 t20 f18 b19**. Never gets into step, let alone stride. Tart and as hot as Hades as the stills were obviously full steam ahead when this cut was taken. Then, to add insult to injury, it was then filled into a poor cask which bitters out unpleasantly at the end. Not even remotely up to usual Old Masters high standard. 58.1%. *James MacArthur & Co. Ltd.*

‹›» **Old Particular Speyside Linkwood 17 Years Old** refill hogshead, cask no. 10413, dist Jun 97, bott Aug 14 **(78) n19 t22 f18 b19.** Juicy, charming and effervescent on delivery but the nose and slightly milky finish tells tales against the quality of the oak. 48.4%. *nc ncf sc. 401 bottles.*

Scotch Malt Whisky Society Cask 39.91 Aged 22 Years refill hogshead, dist 29 Oct 90 **(88.5) n21.5 t22 f22.5 b22.** A little fruit here goes a long, long way... 48.5%. *nc ncf sc. 226 bottles.*

Scotch Malt Whisky Society Cask 39.92 Aged 23 Years refill hogshead, dist 29 Oct 90 **(82) n20 t22 f19.5 b20.5.** Tasting this absent-mindedly (a nuthatch had just descended on to a tree in my garden), the first words to form in my mind was: "United Distillers." Absolutely typical of their cask policy at the time. Showing some oaky strain but a vague fruitiness somehow proffers an alarmingly discordant note. 49.4%. *nc ncf sc. 226 bottles.*

Scotch Malt Whisky Society Cask 39.93 Aged 29 Years refill hogshead, dist 04 Sep 84 **(83) n21.5 t21 f20 b20.5.** There are times when oak can be a little too sturdy...and here is one. The odd bitterness, too, where you hope the sugars would play. 57.9%. *nc ncf sc.*

Scotch Malt Whisky Society Cask 39.94 Aged 23 Years refill hogshead, dist 29 Oct 90 **(88.5) n22 t23 f21.5 b22.** Shows the odd scar of passing time but not half bad. 44.7%. *nc ncf sc. 196 bottles.*

Scotch Malt Whisky Society Cask 39.96 Aged 29 Years refill hogshead, dist 04 Sep 84 **(87.5) n22 t22.5 f21 b22.** Outwardly, a close relation to 39.93. Except this one works on many more levels. Including a more luxuriant, estery mouth feel countering the purposeful oak plus some charming spices which punctuate at every opportunity. 55%. *nc ncf sc. 131 bottles.*

Scotch Malt Whisky Society Cask 39.97 Aged 23 Years refill hogshead, dist 29 Oct 90 **(87.5) n21.5 t23 f21.5 b22.** Though clearly designed as a blending malt this cask has its moments in the sun. Especially on delivery when, for about fifteen mercurial seconds, all the elements - including the slight but welcome ulmo honey - combine beautifully. Spice on the finish, but a little tangy too. 45.9%. *nc ncf sc. 228 bottles.*

Scotch Malt Whisky Society Cask 39.99 Aged 23 Years refill hogshead, dist 30 Apr 90 **(94) n23** here you get a compelling sense of the passing years with the oak, though wilting slightly, being supported by an attractive boiled sweet fruitiness and playful spice. A really good balance...; **t24** a sublime mouth feel is matched by the most charming combination of intense, salivating barley, light muscovado sugars, liquorice and fresh black peppers; good esters and fabulous weight; **f23.5** there was something inevitable that butterscotch tart develops, but this is heftily spiced, with the odd sultana dropped in for good measure! **b23.5** this one operates on an entirely different level to the other SWMS Linkwoods I have tasted this year. This, uniquely, is very high class. 58.9%. *nc ncf sc. 222 bottles.*

Signatory Vintage Single Malt Linkwood 1995 Aged 18 Years cask no. 652+653, bott 13 **(95.5) n24.5** all bells and whistles at full blast as we enter a delicately fruity world. Cox's apples and Williams pears make for a great combination, especially alongside gooseberries fit to burst. But there is also a succession of cake and pudding notes...walnut plus spotted dog and sticky toffee. Glorious. **t24** silky delivery, with the suet from the spotted dog pudding prevalent. The barley is grassy, juicy and fresh; the spices nibble rather than bite; natural caramels thicken and sweeten; **f23** long, with the buttery barley spreading further. The sugars are molten and a little nutty; the tannins offer up further spices; **b24** great whisky. Simple as. 43%. *nc. WB15/013*

‹›» **Signatory Vintage Cask Strength Collection Linkwood 1985 Aged 28 Years** American oak hogshead, cask no. 4538, dist 1985, bott Sept 14 **(85.5) n22 t22 f20 b21.5.** Not every cask achieves greatness at this ripe old age. It has a good stab at it – especially with the earthy bluebells and spices on the nose and the elegant muscovado sugars on delivery. But the massively dry oak is uncompromising and relentless ....as might be expected. 53.4%. *nc sc. 161 bottles. The Whisky Exchange Exclusive. WB16/003*

Speyside Single Malt Linkwood Aged 30 Years hogshead, cask no. 8250, dist Jan 84, bott Mar 14 **(92) n23.5** even after such a long time the oak ad barley appear to be holding hands in unison. All is understated yet quietly confident, with soft ground cashews mixing beautifully with the deft bluebell and primrose floral tones; **t23.5** the underlying sweetness of the nose is quickly apparent: gentle sugars with a gristy hue make way for sparkier, spicier, oak-stained depth; **f22** tires a little and dries, but the big tannins stay alive thanks to a sprinkling of Demerara; **b23** just so attractive in so many way. 52.7%. *sc. 69 bottles.*

‹›» **Wemyss Malts 1995 Single Speyside Linkwood "Honeysuckle Bower"** hogshead, bott 2014 **(84) n22.5 t21.5 f20 b20.** The promise from the dusted marshmallow nose is not realised as an unsympathetic cask takes its toll. Some good early, uncomplicated, barley to be had on the palate, though. 46%. *sc. 332 bottles.*

Wemyss Malts 1997 Single Speyside Linkwood "Citrus Burst" bott 13 **(88)** n22.5 an old oak chair sandpapered down; a squeeze of lime from somewhere; **t22.5** almost a lemon sherbet explosion on delivery....; **f21** ....and here's the liquorice. Plus mega dry oak for good measure; **b22** those looking for a fizzy Speysider will be in their element. *46%. sc. 363 bottles.*

◇ **The Whisky Barrel Linkwood 1990 Burns Malt 24 Years Old** cask no. 3540 **(84.5)** n22 t21.5 f20 b21. Despite the attractive green apple and pear on the nose and delivery, the thin finish doesn't quite step up to the pulpy plate. Sharp, fresh, almost eye-watering delivery. Can't help but love the marzipan though. But very young for its age. *51.7%*

◇ **Whiskybroker Linkwood 26 Years** hogshead, cask no. 1828, dist 4 Apr 89 **(83)** n22 t21.5 f19 b20.5. Malty, sharp and, at times, searingly hot. Sparse and off key on the finish, also. *53.1%. sc.*

◇ **Whiskyjace Linkwood 12 Year Old** bourbon hogshead, dist 1999, bott 2012 **(87.5)** n22.5 t22 f21.5 b21.5. Get beyond the aggression and late nagging bitterness and this has a few charming tricks up its sleeve, not least the light smoke apparent on the nose and delivery. Good minty cocoa, too. *61.7%*

LITTLEMILL
Lowland, 1772. Loch Lomond Distillers. Demolished.

Littlemill 21 Year Old 2nd Release bourbon cask db **(87)** n22 t21.5 f21.5 b22. So thin you expect it to fragment into a zillion pieces on the palate. But the improvement on this as a new make almost defies belief. The sugars are crisp enough to shatter on your teeth, the malt is stone hard and fractured and, on the finish, does show some definite charm before showing its less attractive teeth....and its roots... Overall, though, more than enjoyable. *47%. nc ncf.*

◇ **Littlemill 25 Year Old** db **(92.5)** n22 perhaps a little reminder of the once flame-thrower nose, but this is more like a popgun amid the slightly (and characteristically) glue-like maltiness; **t24** the malt excels here in a way those of us intimately familiar with this distillery 25 years ago could scarcely imagine. Even moves into mocha and then praline mode as the intensity of the barley flies off the scale; **f23** long, with a pleasing spice pulsing alongside the flatter vanillas; **b23.5** another example of a malt which was practically undrinkable in its fiery, punkish youth but that is now a reformed, gentle character in older age. *52%*

Littlemill 1964 db **(82)** n21 t20 f21 b20. A soft-natured, bourbony chap that shows little of the manic tendencies that made this one of Scotland's most-feared malts. Talk about mellowing with age... *40%*

Littlemill 1990 Vintage Aged 22 Years bott 2013 db **(91)** n23 despite a light flame licking at the nose there is enough honey and sugar on the barley to persuade you to dive in head first; **t23** peppered barley attacks the taste buds with gusto, leaving behind a trail of tannins and honey; **f22.5** butterscotch and watered-down napalm in equal measures; **b22.5** a very tasty bit of rough. *50.6%. nc ncf. Glen Contrine Bonded Warehouse Ltd.*

◇ **Chieftain's Littlemill Aged 22 Years** hogshead, dist Feb 92, bott Jun 14 **(82)** n19.5 t21.5 f20 b21. Some attractive sugar-barley moments. But never manages to quite grow out of its aggressive youth. *50.7%. nc ncf.*

◇ **Glen Fahrn Airline Nr 03 Littlemill 1989 Aged 22 Years** cask no. 007 **(84)** n20 t22.5 f20.5 b21.5. Well, you can't say it is lacking in character. Almost like a distilled breakfast cereal: nutty, milky, intense grain and with a light cover of sugar. The lactose note is the old cask just beginning to break up. *55.1%. sc. 310 bottles.*

Gordon & MacPhail Rare Old Littlemill 1985 (89) n22 slightly gluey in the grand tradition of Littlemill but some exotic fruit sticks, too; **t23.5** so ridiculously soft on delivery with sme kind of non-specific fruit curling up cosily with the barley. Juicy and surprisingly fresh; **f21.5** diminishes as it thins out like Dr Jekyll returning to be Mr Hyde....; **b23** this is so soft in part, you cannot help but laugh when you know exactly what brand of firewater this would have been in the cask 25 years ago. A lovely treat. *46%.*

Lowland Single Malt Littlemill Aged 25 Years refill hogshead,cask no. 10349, dist Nov 88, bott Jun 14 **(87.5)** n21.5 t23 f21 b22. Good to see a Littlemill celebrate its quarter century in style. The obvious limitations are more than made up for by the odd elaborate and/or elegant flourish. But it is the texture plus the biting intensity of the barley, coupled with the happy link between the brown sugars and vanilla-rich oak which makes this a winner. *56.2%. sc. 225 bottles.*

The Pearls of Scotland Littlemill 1991 bott Jun 14, cask no. 112 **(83.5)** n20 t22 f20.5 b21. More than most, alas, this has retained many of the aspects which made this distillery an impossible one to continue as a commercial concern. However, among the obvious chinks and cracks there can be found a few attractive pieces of mosaic, especially when the crisp muscovado sugars enter into play. *52.9%. sc.*

The Pearls of Scotland 1988 25 Year Old cask no. 132, dist Oct 88, bott Feb 14 **(87) n22 t23 f20.5 b21.5.** This is like a shuffling old man walking with a stoop and telling the guys in the pub of his former hell-fire days. For when he was young he would have thought nothing of grasping your throat and ripping out your tonsils and setting a flame-thrower to the remainder of your mouth. Now, just a quiet, malt-and-gooseberry sort of guy who will do nothing to offend. *43.5%.*

The Pearls of Scotland 1988 25 Year Old cask no. 134, dist Oct 88, bott Feb 14 **(85) n21.5 t22 f20.5 b21.** Some gentle oils bathe where the last remnants of the scalding spirit bites. Some attractive barley, but all a little too brusque. *476%.*

◈ **Romantic Rhine Collection Littlemill** bourbon hogshead, cask no. 6, dist 22 Oct 89, bott Aug 11 **(82) n19 t21 f21 b21.** The house weird glue style is in force. As is the tangy nuttiness. Good sugars, though. *55.1%. 153 bottles.*

The Whisky Agency Littlemill 1990 (90) n22 soft cardboard containing a pithy fruitiness and malty, nutty mix; **t24** gorgeously salivating opening movement followed by a procession of malty notes, all of varying intensity but always superb; **f22** much thinner with its signature pastiness; **b22** you have to doff your cap to this old fellow: undrinkable when in its youth and prime; unmissable in its dotage. *52.4%.*

The Whisky Cask Littlemill 1st fill sherry butt, cask no. 601 **(90.5) n23.5** ultra-attractive fruitiness appears to mingle the apple and pear house style with the juicy grape from the sherry butt. Beautiful, yet unassuming; **t23** crisp and salivating. Again the fruits enjoy star status, but there is room enough for the malt to shine; **f21.5** just a little grunting from the more negative aspects of the initial spirit. But can be forgiven; **b22.5** amazing; you get probably the worst-made spirit of 1992, put it into a first fill sherry butt at a time they were arriving from Spain in hideously sub-standard condition and what so you get? A quietly delicious whisky. *53%.*

The Whisky Cask Littlemill Aged 21 Years bourbon hogshead, dist 1992, bott 2013 **(88.5) n22** fruity, apples especially and topped with over-ripe pear; **t22** juicy chewing gum, Some of the wallpaper paste of old can just about be detected but icing sugars compensate attractively; **f22.5** some genuine complexity here with a malty blast catching the light oak-led vanilla full on; **b22** odd how a malt once undrinkable in its youth can offer such charm as a greybeard... *49.9%. nc ncf.*

◈ **Whisky-Fässle Littlemill 22 Year Old** hogshead, dist 1992, bott 2014 **(86) n21.5 t22 f21 b21.5.** The limitations of this whisky may be there for all to see and the gluey properties on display. But there remains an attractive malty crunchiness to the protective crisp sugars. *50.3%. nc ncf.*

◈ **Whisky-Fässle Littlemill 23 Year Old** sherry cask, dist 1988, bott 2012 **(89.5) n23 t23.5 f21 b22.** Filled into sherry in the last days before they became tainted with dire and disastrous sulphur. The weird notes on the finish show the spirit was, as to be expected, of poor quality. But this faultless old school cask proves that if you pour rubbish into an excellent cask it stands a chance of becoming a half decent whisky. Yet you can pour the greatest spirit distilled in the word into a sulphured sherry butt...and you get rubbish. *52.4%. nc ncf.*

◈ **Whisky-Fässle Littlemill 23 Year Old** hogshead, dist 1990, bott 2014 **(84) n21 t22 f20 b21.** For those who like their whisky stark, uncomplicated and with very little development. *57.2%. nc ncf.*

◈ **Whisky-Fässle Littlemill 24 Year Old** hogshead, dist 1989, bott 2014 **(72.5) n18.5 t20 f16 b18.** Ablaze with flavours and aromas not normally associated with good Scotch single malt. It's as though the distiller ran a course showing students not what to do with a pot still... *476%. nc ncf.*

LOCH LOMOND

Highlands (Southwestern), 1966. Loch Lomond Distillers. Working.

◈ **Glengarry 12 Year Old** db **(92.5) n22.5** the citrus edge cannot hide the big barley presence. Weighty, without being oily and cumbersome; **t23.5** good grief: it is like sucking on a tablet of concentrated malt! The oak also makes its mark, but acts no more than a prop and inserter of warming, though controlled, spice. And faint molasses; **f23** more of the same with those spices peddling to the end; **b23.5** probably the most intense malt on the market today. Astonishing. And stunning. *46%. ncf.*

Inchmurrin 12 Years Old db **(86.5) n21.5 t22 f21.5 b21.5.** A significantly improved dram which is a bit of a malt soup. Love the Demerara injection. *40%*

Inchmurrin Aged 15 Years bourbon cask, bott Dec 12 db **(86) n22 t21.5 f21 b21.5.** Slightly tangy with an edge to the cask which interferes with the usual malty procession. *46%. nc ncf.*

Inchmurrin Aged 18 Years bourbon cask, bott Dec 12 db **(92.5) n22.5 t23.5 f23.5 b23.** Loch Lomond distillery in its brightest colours. 46%. nc ncf. Glen Catrine Bonded Warehouse Ltd.

Inchmurrin Aged 21 Years bourbon cask, bott Dec 12 db **(90) n22 t23 f22.5 b22.5.** This has spent 21 years in a very exceptional cask. Not exactly breathtaking complexity, but what it does is completed with aplomb. 46%. nc ncf. Glen Catrine Bonded Warehouse Ltd.

◈ **Inchmurrin Loch Lomond Island Collection 12 Year Old** db **(87) n21.5 t22 f21.5 b22.** A thick malty offering with a weighty grist and maple syrup infusion. Big and clumsy. 46%. ncf.

Loch Lomond Organic 12 Year Old bourbon cask db **(83.5) n19 t20 f23 b21.5.** A malty beast. But in some respects has more in common with a German still than a traditional pot. Definite loss of feint. 48%. nc ncf.

◈ **Loch Lomond Original** bourbon casks db **(81.5) n20 t21 f20 b20.5.** Hmmm. Surprisingly feinty, though the really wide cut does ensure a huge number of flavours. A distinctly German style to this. 40%

Loch Lomond 14 Year Old Peated bourbon cask db **(83) n21 t21.5 f20.5 b20.** Lomond can do a lot, lot better than this. Huge malts but entirely out of sync and never comfortable with the oils present. This isn't the Loch Lomond I know and love. 46% nc ncf.

Loch Lomond 18 Years Old db **(78.5) n19 t21 f19 b19.5.** A demanding, oily malt which is a long way from technical excellence but is no slouch on the chocolate nougat front. 43%

Loch Lomond 21 Years Old db **(89.5) n22.5 t23 f22 b22.** A little while since I last tasted this, and pretty close to exactly how I remember it. Seems to revel in its own enormity! 43%

◈ **Scotch Malt Whisky Society Cask 112.8 Aged 14 Years** refill barrel, dist 27 Sept 00 **(92) n22.5** a few drips of lemon ensures a sharpness to the buttery barley; **t23** eye-watering clarity to the malt makes for a juicy delivery and midterm; **f23** thickens, as a very high quality bourbon cask dissolves a biscuity richness into the heart of the shimmering barley. Very satisfying and long finale...; **b23.5** the distillery resplendent in all its maltiest finery. 57.8%. sc. 182 bottles.

That Boutique-y Whisky Inchmurrin batch 1 **(83) n21 t21 f20 b21.** The label calls it about right: for despite the trace manuka honey and blood orange, this is a bit of a soup. 54.7%. 543 bottles. WB15/195

LOCHSIDE
Highlands (Eastern), 1957–1992. Chivas Brothers. Demolished.
The Cooper's Choice Lochside 1967 Aged 44 Years cask no. 807 **(96.5) n24.5** yep. Pretty close to perfection. At first it is the softest of smoke which gets you primed. Then the pastel-shaded fruit begins to take shape, perhaps drawing from the honey blossom honey which is weighted by the butterscotch oak and Nice biscuits; **t24.5** again the smoke makes a very early foray, but it is a ghostly one and does a masterful job of keeping anchored the lighter fruit tones. Astonishingly after all these years the barley is still capable of a big juicy volley. While the oak, though arriving early, is of the most benign type offering a seemingly impossible layering of delicate tannins which emboldens and enriches; **f23.5** just a little thinner here with the oat now showing a slightly more austere trait. However, that priceless and ultra-complex smoke ensures the finale is one of quiet dignity; **b24** it is amazing that I had to travel 6,000 miles to find this in British Columbia. But, this is the kind of whisky you would travel four times that kind of distance to experience. Easily one of the top ten single casks I have tasted in the last five years. 41.5%. 354 bottles.

LONGMORN
Speyside, 1895. Chivas Brothers. Working.
Longmorn 15 Years Old db **(93) n23** curiously salty and coastal for a Speysider, really beautifully structured oak but the malt offers both African violets and barley sugar; **t24** your mouth aches from the enormity of the complexity, while your tongue wipes grooves into the roof of your mouth. Just about flawless bitter-sweet balance, the intensity of the malt is enormous, yet – even after 15 years – it maintains a cut-grass Speyside character; **f22** long, acceptably sappy and salty with chewy malt and oak. Just refuses to end; **b24** these latest bottlings are the best yet: previous ones had shown just a little too much oak but this has hit a perfect compromise. An all-time Speyside great. 45%

Longmorn 16 Years Old db **(84.5) n20.5 t22 f21 b21.** This was one of the disappointments of the 2008 edition, thanks to the lacklustre nose and finish. This time we see a cautious nudge in the right direction: the colour has been dropped fractionally and the nose celebrates with a sharper barley kick with a peppery accompaniment. The non-existent (caramel apart) finale of yore now offers a distinct wave of butterscotch and thinned honey...and still some spice. Only the delivery has dropped a tad...but a price worth paying for the overall improvement. Still a way to go before the real Longmorn 16 shines in our glasses for all to see and fall deeply in love with. Come on lads in the Chivas lab: we know you can do it... 48%

◇ **Adelphi Selection Longmorn 22 Years Old** cask no. 48510 **(93.5) n22.5** the odd sign of a tiring cask. But those rich semi-bourbon notes so far extracted do a good job of maximising honeyed depth; **t23.5** an opulent, busy delivery: the sugars are absolutely firing, somehow showing signs of rich malt, too. The vanillas arrive pretty early...and stay; **f23.5** carries on the toasted sugar theme for an age; **b24** this cask has not been sitting idle in the warehouse: one suspects some deep charring at play to extract this kind of toasty depth. Stunningly delicious. *53.6% WB16/008*

Adelphi Selection Longmorn 28 Years Old cask no. 9907, dist 85, bott 14 **(94.5) n23.5** ridiculously elegant for its age: the tannins have made no meaningful incursions other than a citrus butterscotch note and half-hearted spice. Elsewhere the barley enjoys sharing the spotlight with angel cake; **t24** a Longmorn...at nearly 30...? Wow! One of the first never to grind my taste buds down with over excited oak. It's the barley which still sings clearly and trills sweetly and without falter; **f23** after the cake and tart notes earlier, I had anticipated chocolate sponge on the very finish...... and what do you know...! **b24** not normally a distillery that raises my pulse once the years pile on. This, though, is exceptional for its age. A must get Longmorn. *50.6%. ncf sc. 247 bottles. WB15/415*

Alexander Weine & Destillate Longmorn 22 Years Old refill bourbon hogshead, cask no. 8646, dist 90, bott 13 **(93) n23.5** very high quality mix diced glazed fruit and Bakewell pudding; **t24** best Longmorn delivery for some time! Textbook mouth feel carrying confident barley sugar, some rampant oak but controlled by maple syrup and liquorice; **f22.5** elegant with a fine spice fade and toasty, creamy fudge; **b23** nectar... *55.1%. sc. cask strength.*

Berry's Own Selection Longmorn 1988 Aged 24 Years cask no. 14385, bott 2013 **(94) n24** a wonderful array of ultra-delicate mixed fruit notes, all so well married that you can barely pick one from another. But some old conference pear mixes seamlessly with Sharon fruit skin, backed by a banana paste and manuka honey; **t24** hardly seems possible, but more silky on delivery than nose. Less fruit apparent now, but a wide selection of medium to dark sugars; **f22.5** bitters slightly as the oak tires; **b23.5** a malt which evolved on to regal status. And the kind of malt which is the mainstay for the more imperious Ballantine's and Royal Salute brands. *46%. ncf ncf. WB15/245*

Berry's Own Selection Longmorn 1992 Aged 20 Years cask no. 149091, bott 2013 **(86) n22 t22.5 f20 b21.5.** Something of a curate's egg, this. Starts its journey on the palate as an essay of sweet, friendly, gently oiled benignity and ends its trek as a rock hard, slightly bitter figure of malevolence. But the good moments are very good... *50.9%. ncf ncf. WB15/248*

Best Dram Longmorn 21 Years Old refill sherry, dist 92, bott 13 **(87.5) n21 t23.5 f22.5 b23.** Tries to fight off its age like a nudist flings off its clothes. But in the end, an arthritic joint means the oaky coat is a little too heavy. Bottled two years earlier this would have been an astonishing malt... *48.8%. ncf. 121 bottles.*

Chivas Brothers Cask Strength Edition Longmorn Aged 18 Years batch no. LM 18 009, dist 95, bott 13 **(85.5) n20 t22.5 f21 b21.5.** Disappointing when you think about what they must have available. The dull nose is not much more exciting on the toffee-thick finale. Lacks complexity but at least the delivery affords a jazzed up spicy maltiness. *53.1%. sc ncf. WB15/319*

◇ **Distiller's Art Longmorn Aged 21 Years** refill butt, dist 1999, bott 2015 **(89.5) n21.5** shows a degree of unsympathetic oak; **t23.5** salty and content with the intense, gristy malt smashing enthusiastically against the taste buds on delivery; the mid ground offers some spectacular citrus on the barley – so refreshing yet rich! **f22** like the nose, a little off key but that can be forgiven thanks to the lovely chocolate which wanders into the frame; **b22.5** tangy on both the nose and finish, this is Longmorn not quite at maximum tide. Even so, some of the quality and complexity is so outstanding, it is impossible not to be swept away by it... *48%. ncf sc. 271 bottles.*

Hepburn's Choice Longmorn Aged 11 Years bourbon barrel, dist 03, bott 14 **(87) n22 t22.5 f20.5 b22.** Malty, zesty and vibrant, the barley gives an impressive one-man show in this production until the tanginess of a weary cask intervenes. *46%. nc ncf sc. 351 bottles.*

Old Malt Cask Longmorn Aged 18 Years refill hogshead, cask no. 9885, dist Dec 94, bott Jun 13 **(95) n23.5** hard to know which is the firmer: the barley or the vanilla. The subtle tannin-led spices are a dream; **t24** magnificent! The delivery ticks every box you can think of, and a few more besides. Gorgeous weight, yet never too lofty or threatening. Very much in the hands of the oak – the spices ensure that – but complexity is the key word here. Just above dexterity...; **f23.5** a wonderful spectrum of dark sugars...and teasing spice; **b24** the kind of bottle which will keep you good company on the coldest of winter nights... 50%. nc ncf sc. 321 bottles.

◇ **Old Malt Cask Longmorn Aged 19 Years** refill hogshead, cask no. 10818, dist Dec 94, bott Aug 14 **(94) n22.5** buttery – only lightly salted – with the odd primrose amid the Werther's Originals. All rather malty and pleasant; **t23.5** much more spice and fizz than apparent on the nose: a lively chap, to put it mildly; **f24** settles quite beautifully into a much more docile, sugar-laden malt fest. The oaks arrive late and further the elegance; **b24** an adorable cask which gets the recipe almost bang on. 50%. nc ncf sc. 297 bottles.

Old Masters Longmorn 16 Years Old cask no. 156778, dist 96, bott 13 **(91) n22 t23.5 f22.5 b23.** Anyone with a love for malt shakes or Malteser candy will probably take no prisoners to get their hands on this one. Truly idiosyncratic. 56.3%. sc.

Old Masters Longmorn 17 Years Old dist 96, bott 14, cask no. 156779 **(94.5) n23** the vaguest of smoke mingles with the oak but thinned slightly by the more conventional citrus and honey; **t24** excellent delivery: spot-on weight and the timing for the oak to intervene in the sugar and malt fest; the mid ground is a "Milky Way" candy mix of milk chocolate and delicate malty nougat; light ulmo honey arrives at the midpoint; **f23.5** gentle oak returns to lead the way back home, but the malt and honey still have delicate, understated parts to play; **b24** Longmorn in its most classic pose. 57.1%. James MacArthur & Co. Ltd.

Old Particular Speyside Longmorn 21 Years Old refill hogshead, cask no. 10264, dist May 93, bott May 14 **(91.5) n22.5** light, vaguely floral with a busy barley-vanilla interplay; **t23** amazingly clean for its age, a little young, too; the barley is juicy and bristling with life: the sugars are of a gristy nature; **f23** oil develops and allows the malt full weight; **b23** the type of malt a blender rubs his hands about: here is a perfect insight into how a whisky like Ballantine's can feel so demure at such a great age. 51.5%. nc ncf sc. 246 bottles.

◇ **Old Particular Speyside Longmorn 22 Years Old** refill hogshead, cask no. 10461, dist May 92, bott Aug 14 **(90) n22** has no trouble showing its age with some weighty oak at work. Spicy and peppery – almost sneezably so...; **t23.5** punchy, spicy and salivating. The mid-ground is deliciously clean barley concentrate; **f22** the oak hangs around and becomes a little tangy; **b22.5** for those who enjoy a little sawdust sprinkled on their excellent, intensely malty whisky. 60.1%. nc ncf sc. 254 bottles.

◇ **Old Particular Longmorn 20 Years Old** refill hogshead, cask no. 10772, dist Dec 94, bott May 15 **(93) n23** delicate spices ensure a twist to the ultra clean and intense barley; **t23.5** stunning barley sugar on delivery. Ulmo honey adds the sweet cream, then a blossoming of busy spice; **f23** by magic, oils appear which makes the lengthy malt and digestive biscuit finish even longer; **b23.5** a friendly old cask has added nothing but complex spice. The result is a whisky of rare maltiness to be savoured all day every day...!! 48.4%. nc ncf sc. 252 bottles.

◇ **Provenance Longmorn Over 11 Years** refill barrel, cask no. 10544, dist Spring 06, bott Autumn 14 **(92) n23** a little heather-honey ensures depth to the butterscotch and clean malt; **t23** intricate sugars – mainly fudge and muscovado – interplay with the semi-gristy, semi-tasty malt. A light liquorice and coconut note does the midground no harm at all; **f22.5** dries as the oaks guarantee length and weight; **b23.5** anyone into Maltesers should buy a case...! I really do wish the owners would bottle at around 12 years (similar to this), rather than the over-aged, over-coloured stuff we normally get. This is high quality malt. 46%. nc ncf sc.

◇ **The Queen of the Moorlands Rare Cask Ipstones Edition Longmorn 1992 Aged 21 Years (93) n22.5** just a slight hint of tiredness from this one, with the odd lactic note coming through. But completely compensated for by a thin but compelling chocolate honeycomb theme enriched further by a semi-bourbon liquorice signature; **t23.5** a quite gorgeous delivery as the honey is again ensuring depth and a counterpoint to the toasty spices; again, that little tiredness leaks through, but is almost contemptuously dismissed by the charismatic honey; **f23** long, a vague milkiness...but that lingering spice and honey teases and seduces, even at the end; **b24** rarely has a malt with, strictly speaking, a slight technical flaw, been quite so entertaining. But, there again, you rarely find honey quite this switched on. Some serious Highland Park tendencies at play here. 56.2%. sc.

◇ **Romantic Rhine Collection Longmorn 1996** refill hogshead & sherry octave, cask no. 422964, dist 25 Jun 96, bott 20 Jan 12 **(87.5) n22 t22.5 f21 b22.** A creamy, butter-kissed but, ultimately, dry version of Longmorn, where the malt flourishes despite the oak keeping the sugars to a minimum. 53.8%. 706 bottles.

◇ **Scotch Malt Whisky Society Cask 7.104 Aged 24 Years** 2nd fill barrel, dist 11 Dec 89 **(92) n22.5** a thick, fruity nose: something of the Melton Hunt cake about this one. Slightly frothy, too, with a light creaminess enriching the experience; **t23.5** the spices show first, then a succession of dark sugars; **f22.5** bitters slightly and a touch pithy, too. Very late on, a lemon-malt softness emerges; **b23** apparently from a bourbon cask. You could have fooled me. 52.6%. sc. 200 bottles.

⟨⟩ **Scotch Malt Whisky Society Cask 7.111 Aged 11 Years** 1st fill barrel, dist 22 Sept 03 **(94.5) n24.5** a friendly buzz suggests we are in for a lively experience further down the line. A gorgeous mix of fruit salad candy and butterscotch; **t24.5** try to keep the groans of joy down so you don't upset the neighbours. The sugars could not be any better balanced alongside the rich barley. Perfection; **f22** bitters out disappointingly: the oak's fault, not the spirit; **b23.5** if this isn't evidence that this malt is usually bottled past its sell by date, I don't know what is. Spectacular! 60.1%. sc. 183 bottles.

⟨⟩ **Scotch Malt Whisky Society Cask 7.113 Aged 24 Years** 2nd fill port barrique, dist 11 Dec 89 **(92.5) n23** lemon sherbet and spiced butterscotch; **t23.5** ridiculously juicy for its age with that sherbet-like fizz gathering tantalisingly; **f23** a light bitterness is coped with by the continuous fresh barley; **b23** a well used cask has allowed the malt to relax and fully stretch out. 51.7%. sc. 147 bottles.

⟨⟩ **Signatory Vintage Cask Strength Collection Longmorn Aged 22 Years** hogshead, cask no. 48488, dist 1992, bott Sept 14 **(89) n22** a little salt is mixed in with the sweet vanilla; **t23** massive barley sugar concentrate, maybe with a nod to Werther's Originals; **f22** does little to veer off its earlier course, other than become just a shade toastier; **b22** highly revved up on the sugar front. Perhaps short on development and complexity. But a joy, all the same. 51.4%. nc sc. 224 bottles. The Whisky Exchange Exclusive. WB16/004

Signatory Vintage Single Malt Longmorn 1996 Aged 17 Years 1st fill sherry butts, cask no. 72325, dist 01 May 96, bott 06 Aug 13 **(77) n19 t21 f18 b19.** Fails to find any form of meaningful harmony, though there are a brief few intriguing moments post-delivery when the background salivatory sharpness cannot be attributed to either grape or grain. Furry. But above all, dull. 43%. nc sc. 869 bottles. WB15/010

The Single Malts of Scotland Longmorn Aged 21 Years hogshead, cask no. 110979, dist 11 Sep 92, bott 25 Mar 14 **(95) n23.5** dusty sweet shops of the early '60s! Boiled candy in jars; oak floor polish; Demerara-sweetened high value cocoa; **t24** silky delivery of malt. Below stairs, the mocha-enriched dark sugars play while the spices strike up; **f23.5** spiced creamy fudge and toasted honeycomb; **b24** absolutely beautiful, evocative malt. A rare treat of a dram. 49.7%. 293 bottles. WB15/293

The Single Malts of Scotland Longmorn 22 Years Old cask no. 12289, dist 90, bott 14 Sep 13 **(89.5) n22.5** a puff of smoke heralds an otherwise malty nose; **t23** good fresh, mouth-watering properties: the barley takes up all the leading positions. Slowly drier vanillas begin to emerge; **f22** just a hint of coconut biscuit and marzipan bolsters the finale; **b22** a very decent Longmorn which does the simple things attractively. 48.1%. 199 bottles. WB15/305

Speyside Single Malt Longmorn Aged 25 Years refill hogshead, cask no. 10368, dist Apr 89, bott Jun 14 **(94) n23** diced hazelnut, polished oak floors, Shredded Wheat (though shouldn't it be barley...?); **t24** a two-tiered experience: first, young malt gushes into view, complete with gristy sugars and full salivating impact...then the oak arrives...; **f23.5**...and it's the oak all the way on the finish, though the Digestive Biscuit and retained sugars ensures balance is preserved; **b23.5** the degree of control throughout is breath-taking. It is like the marathon runner who has times his use of energy to the second to maximise everything available. Simple. But superb. 54.2%. sc. 183 bottles.

Wemyss Malts 1992 Single Speyside Longmorn "Coconut and Sandalwood" dist 1992 bott 2013 **(74) n19 t23 f15 b17.** "Coconut and Sandalwood" says the label, presumably listing about the only two things you can't find in what would minor classic had it not been for a flaw in the cask. When at its best, in some ways more like a busy small-grain bourbon than a scotch with the oak playing all kinds of delicious tricks. What a shame, though. 46%. sc. 330 bottles.

⟨⟩ **Whisky-Fässle Longmorn 21 Year Old** hogshead, dist 1992, bott 2013 **(95) n24 t24.5 f23 b23.5.** For students of whisky, there is a good case for buying this with their bottle of Glen Keith from the same vintage if you can afford it. You can then see why one is regarded by blenders as top dressing for their high quality older blends, and the other simply as fodder to make up the numbers. No prizes for working out which is which. The depth and interaction between the ulmo honey and the still beautifully intact barley is something at which to marvel... 51.1%. nc ncf.

THE MACALLAN
Speyside, 1824. Edrington. Working.

The Macallan 7 Years Old db **(89) n23 t23 f21 b22.** An outstanding dram that underlines just how good young malts can be. Fun, fabulous and in recent bottlings has upped the clarity of the sherry intensity to profound new heights. 40%

The Macallan Fine Oak 8 Years Old db (82.5) n20.5 t22 f20 b20. A slight flaw has entered the mix here. Even so, the barley fights to create a distinctive sharpness. However, a rogue sherry butt has put paid to any hopes the honey and spice normally found in this brand. 40%

The Macallan 10 Years Old db (91) n23 oloroso appears to be the big noise here, but clever, almost meaty, incursions of spice offer an extra dimension; fruity, yet bitter-sweet: dense yet teasingly light in places; t23 chewy fruit and the old Macallan silk is back: creamy cherries and mildly under-ripe plum ensures a sweet-sour style; f21.5 traces of vanilla and barley remind us of the oak and barley, but the fruit reverberates for some while, as does some annoying caramel; b23.5 for a great many of us, it is with the Mac 10 our great Speyside odyssey began. It has to be said that in recent years it has been something of a shadow of its former great self. However, this is the best version I have come across for a while. Not perhaps in the same league as those bottlings in the 1970s which made us re-evaluate the possibilities of single malt. But fine enough to show just how great this whisky can be when the butts have not been tainted and, towards the end, the balance between barley and grape is a relatively equal one. 40%

The Macallan 10 Years Old Cask Strength db (85) n20 t22 f22 b21. Enjoyable and a would give chewing gum a run for its money. But over-egged the sherry here and not a patch on the previous bottling. 58.8%. Duty Free.

The Macallan Fine Oak 10 Years Old db (90) n23 finely tuned and balanced: everything on a nudge-nudge basis with neither fruit nor barley willing to come out and lead: really take your time over this to maximise the entertainment; t22.5 brimming with tiny, delicate oak notes which just brush gently, almost erotically, against the clean barley; f21.5 drier, chewier and no less laid-back; b22 much more on the ball than the last bottling of this I came across. Malts really come as understated or clever than this. 40%

The Macallan Sherry Oak 12 Years Old db (93) n24 thick, almost concentrated grape with a stunning degree of light spices. Topped with boiled greengage; t23.5 clean sherry is heralded not just by vanilla-thickened grape but a deft muscovado sweetening and a light seasoning of spice; f22.5 cocoa, vanilla and fudge. Remains clean and beautifully layered; b23 I have to say that some Macallan 12 I have tasted on the road has let me down in the last year or so. This is virtually faultless. Virtually a time machine back to another era... 40%

The Macallan 12 Years Old Sherry Oak Elegancia db (86) n23 t22 f20 b21. Promises, but delivers only to an extent. 40%

The Macallan Fine Oak 12 Years Old db (95.5) n24 faultless, intense sherry light enough to allow the fabulous apple and cinnamon to blend in with the greengage and grape; t24 a near perfect entry: firm, rummy sugars are thinned by a barley-grape double act; juicy just enough vanilla to ensure structure and layering; f23.5 delicate spice keeps the finish going and refuses to let the muscovado-grape take control; b24 a whisky whose quality has hit the stratosphere since I last tasted it. I encountered a disappointing one early in the year. This has restored my faith to the point of being a disciple... 40%

Macallan Gran Reserva Aged 12 Years db (92) n23 massive cream sherry background with well matured fruit cake to the fore: big, clean, luxurious in a wonderfully old-fashioned way. Oh, and a sprinkling of crushed sultana just in case the grapey message didn't get across... t24 a startlingly unusual combination on delivery: dry yet juicy! The ultra fruity lushness is dappled with soft spices; oak arriving early-ish does little to alter the path of the sweetening fruit; just a hint of hickory reveals the oak's handiwork towards the middle; f22 dry, as oloroso does, with a vaguely sweeter edge sparked by notes of dried date; the delicate but busy spices battle through to the toffeed end; b23 well, you don't get many of these to the pound. A real throwback. The oloroso threatens to overwhelm but there is enough intrigue to make for a quite lovely dram which, as all good whiskies should, never quite tells the story the same way twice. Not entirely without blemish, but I'm being picky. A Macallan soaked in oloroso which traditionalists will swoon over. 45.6%

The Macallan Fine Oak 15 Years Old db (79.5) n19 t21.5 f19 b20. As the stock of the Fine oak 12 rises, so its 15-y-o brother, once one of my Favourite drams, falls. Plenty to enjoy, but a few sulphur stains remove the gloss. 43%

The Macallan Fine Oak 17 Years Old db (82) n19.5 t22 f19.5 b21. Where once it couldn't quite make up its mind on just where to sit, it has now gone across to the sherry benches. Sadly, there are a few dissenters. 43%

The Macallan Sherry Oak 18 Years Old db (87) n24 t22 f20 b21. Underpowered. The body doesn't even come close to matching the nose which builds up the expectancy to enormous levels and, by comparison to the Independents, this at 43% appears weak and unrepresentative. Why this isn't at 46% at the very least and unambiguously uncoloured, I have no idea. 43%

The Macallan 18 Years Old dist 1991 db (87) n22 t22.5 f21 b21.5 Honestly: I could weep. Some of the sherry notes aren't just textbook...they go back to the Macallan manuals of the early 1970s. But the achievable greatness is thwarted by the odd butt of you know what... 43%

The Macallan Fine Oak 18 Years Old db **(94.5) n23.5** classic cream sherry aroma: thick, sweet but enlivened by a distinct barley sharpness; **t24** juicy, chewy, clean and intense delivery. Strands of honey and syrup help pave the way for vanillas and spices to get a grip; the complexity levels are startling and the weight just about spot on; **f23** a degree of blood orange bitterness amid the cocoa and raisin; the spices remain lazy, the texture creamy; **b24** is this the new Fine Oak 15 in terms of complexity? That original bottling thrived on the balance between casks types. This is much more accentuated on a cream sherry persona. But this sample is sulphur-free and quite fabulous. 43%

The Macallan Fine Oak 21 Years Old db **(84) n21 t22 f20 b21.** An improvement on the characterless dullard I last encountered. But the peaks aren't quite high enough to counter the sulphur notes and make this a great malt. 43%

The Macallan 25 Years Old db **(84.5) n22 t21 f20.5 b21.** Dry with an even drier oloroso residue; blood orange adds to the fruity mix. Something, though, is not entirely right about this and one fears from the bitter tang at the death that a rogue butt has gained entry to what should be the most hallowed of dumping troughs. 43%

The Macallan Fine Oak 25 Years Old db **(90) n22** coal dusty: the plate of old steam engines; a speckle of raisin and fruitcake; **t23.5** despite the early signs of juicy grape, it takes only a nanosecond or two for a much drier oak-spiced spine to take shape; the weight is never less than ounce perfect, however; **f22** puckering, aged oak leaves little doubt that this is a malt of advanced years, but a few liquorice notes ensure a degree of balance; **b22.5** the first time I tasted this brand a few years back I was knocked off my perch by the peat reek which wafted about with cheerful abandon. Here the smoke is tighter, more shy and of a distinctly more anthracitic quality. Even so, the sweet juiciness of the grape juxtaposes gamely with the obvious age to create a malt of obvious class. 43%

The Macallan Fine Oak 25 Years Old db **(89) n23 t23 f21 b22.** Very similar to the Fine Oak 18. However, the signature smoke has vanished, as I suppose over time it must. Not entirely clean sherry, but much remains to enjoy. 43%

The Macallan Fine Oak 30 Years Old db **(81.5) n22 t22 f18 b19.5.** For all its many riches on delivery, especially those moments of great bourbon-honey glory, it has been comprehensively bowled middle stump by the sherry. Gutted. 43%

The Macallan 40 Years Old dist 10 May 61, bott 09 Sep 05 db **(90) n23 t23 f22 b22.** Very well-rounded dram that sees off advancing years with a touch of grace and humour. So often you think the oak will take control, but each time an element intervenes to win back the balance. It is as if the dram is teasing you. Wonderful entertainment. 43%

The Macallan 50 Years Old dist 29 Mar 52, bott 21 Sep 05 db **(90) n25 t23 f19 b23.** Loses it at the end, which is entirely excusable. But until then, a fabulous experience full of passion and complexity. I nosed and tasted this for over an hour. It was one very rewarding, almost touching, experience. 46%

The Macallan Millennium 50 Years Old (1949) db **(90) n23 t22 f22 b23.** Magnificent finesse and charm despite some big oak makes this another Macallan to die for. 40%

The Macallan Lalique III 57 Years Old db **(95) n24.5 t23 f23.5 b24.** I chose this as my 1,000th new whisky tasted for the 2012 Bible not just because of my long-standing deep love affair with this distillery, but also because I honestly felt it had perhaps the best chance to offer not just a glimpse at the past but also the possibility of a whisky experience that sets the hairs on the back of my neck on end. I really wasn't disappointed. It is almost scary to think that this was from a vintage that would have supplied the whiskies I tasted when getting to first discover their 21-year-old. Then, I remember, I thought the malt almost too comfortable for its age. I expected a bit more of a struggle in the glass. No less than 36 years on, the same thing crosses the mind: how does this whisky find it so easy to fit into such enormous shoes? No experience with this whisky under an hour pays sufficient tribute to what it is all about. Checking my watch, I am writing this just two minutes under two hours after first nosing this malt. The score started on 88.5. With time, warmth, oxidation and understanding that score has risen to 95. It has spent 57 years in the cask; it deserves two hours to be heard. It takes that time, at least, to not just hear what it has to say to interpret it, but to put it into context. And for certain notes, once locked away and forgotten, to be slowly released. The last Lalique was good. But simply not this good. 48.5%

The Macallan 1824 db **(88) n24 t23.5 f19 b21.5.** Absolutely magnificent whisky, in part. But there are times my job is depressing...and this is one of them.. 48%

The Macallan 1824 Estate Reserve db **(90.5) n22** excellent clean grape with an intriguing dusting of mint; **t23** almost a Jamaican pot still rum sheen and sweetness; beautiful weight and even some barley present; **f22.5** satisfying, gorgeously clean with very good vanilla-grape balance; **b23** don't know about Reserve: definitely good enough for the First Team. 45.7%

The Macallan 1824 Select Oak db **(82) n19 t22 f20 b21.** Soft, silky, sometimes sugary... and tangy. Not convinced every oak selected was quite the right one. 40%

The Macallan 1851 Inspiration db **(77)** n19.5 t19.5 f19 b19. Flat and uninspirational in 2008. 41%

The Macallan 1937 bott 1969 db **(92)** n23 an outline of barley can eventually be made in the oaky mist; more defined as a honeyed sweetness cuts in. Fingers of smoke tease. When nosing in the glass hours later the fresh, smoky gristiness is to die for ... and takes you back to the mill room 67 years ago; t22 pleasantly sweet start as the barley piles in – even a touch of melon in there; this time the oak takes second place and acts as a perfect counter; f24 excellent weight with soft peat softening the oak; b23 subtle if not overly complex whisky where there are few characters but each play its part exceptionally well. One to get out with a DVD of Will Hay's sublime Oh Mr Porter which was being made in Britain at the same time as this whisky and as Laurel and Hardy were singing about a Lonesome Pine on the other side of the pond; or any Pathe film of Millwall's FA Cup semi-final with Sunderland. 43%

The Macallan Gran Reserva 1981 db **(90)** n23 t22 f22 b23. Macallan in a nutshell. Brilliant. But could do with being at 46% for full effect. 40%

The Macallan Gran Reserva 1982 db **(82)** n21 t22 f20 b19. Big, clean, sweet sherry influence from first to last but doesn't open up and sing like the '81 vintage. 40%

Macallan Cask Strength db **(94)** n22 t24 f24 b24. One of those big sherry babies; it's like surfacing a massive wave of barley-sweetened sherry. Go for the ride. 58.6%. USA.

The Macallan Estate Reserve db **(84)** n22 t22 f20 b20. Doh! So much juice lurking about, but so much bitterness, too. ...grrrrr!!!! 45.7%

The Macallan Fine Oak Master's Edition db **(91)** n23 one of the most delicate of all Macallan's house noses, depending on a floral scented theme with a sweetish malty tinge to the dank bracken and bluebells; t23 so salivating and sensual! The tastebuds are caressed with sugar-coated oaky notes that have a devilish buzz about them; f22 more malt and now vanilla with a bitter cocoa death... b23 adorable. 42.8%

The Macallan Fine Oak Whisky Maker's Selection db **(92)** n22 t23 f23 b24. This is a dram of exquisite sophistication. Coy, mildly cocoaed dryness, set against just enough barley and fruit sweetness here and there to see off any hints of austerity. Some great work has gone on in the lab to make this happen: fabulous stuff! 42.8%. Duty Free.

The Macallan Gold sherry oak cask db **(89.5)** n22 t23.5 f21.5 b22.5. No Macallan I have tasted since my first in 1975 has been sculpted to show the distillery in such delicate form. 40%

The Macallan Oscuro db **(95.5)** n24.5 t24 f23 b24. Oh, if all sherried whiskies could be that kind - and taste bud-blowingly fabulous! 46.5%

The Macallan Ruby sherry oak cask db **(92.5)** n23 t24 f22 b23.5. Those longer in the tooth who remember the Macallan 10 of 30 years ago will nod approvingly at this chap. Perhaps one butt away from a gong! 43%

The Macallan Sienna sherry cask db **(94.5)** n23 t24 f23.5 b24. The pre-bottling sample presented to me was much more vibrant than this early on, but lacked the overall easy charm and readily flowing general complexity of the finished article. A huge and pleasing improvement. 43%

The Macallan The Queen's Diamond Jubilee db sherry cask matured **(94)** n23.5 t23 f24.5 b23. A wonderful, high quality sulphur-free zone where Macallan unashamedly nails its sherried credentials to the union flag. 52%. 2012 bottles. UK exclusive.

The Macallan Royal Marriage db **(89)** n23.5 t22.5 f21 b22. Some amazing moments to remember. 46.8%

The Macallan Select Oak db **(83)** n23 t21 f19 b20. Exceptionally dry and tight; and a little furry despite the early fruitiness. 40%

The Macallan Whisky Makers Edition db **(76)** n19 t20 f18 b19. Distorted and embittered by the horrific "S" element... 42.8%

The Macallan Woodlands Limited Edition Estate Bottling db **(86)** n21 t23 f21 b21. Toffee towards the finish brings a premature halt to a wonderfully mollased early delivery. 40%

Darkness! Macallan Aged 15 Years Pedro Ximenez Cask Finish (85.5) n21.5 t22 f21.5 b20.5. Mixed feelings here. A clean sherry influence, which is great. But the PX is so tightly bound with thick sugar that expression, complexity and balance all take a right pounding. Good spices, though. And I'm sure some will regard this as some kind of Macallan orgasm. Whatever turns you on... 52.3%

⬧ **The First Editions Author's Series No. 1 Macallan Aged 21 Years** refill barrel, cask no. 11213, dist Jun 93, bott Mar 15 (95.5) n24 t24 f23.5 b24. This is weird! I have just tasted this whisky, surely. As near as damn it identical to the Old and Rare Macallan 21-year-old. Except there appears to be a little extra alcohol intensity and bite. Oh...even though they are the same strength, apparently... 54.8%. sc. 99 bottles.

Gordon & MacPhail Speymalt Macallan 1972 (93) n23 heady, heavy-duty stuff with the oak furthest up the flagpole. The tannins may be hefty but there is enough Spotted Dog pudding and molten sugar on porridge to form a salute; **t23.5** a fabulous example of the small still syndrome enjoyed by Macallan, as this is tight and intense, sharp and punchy despite the gentle rounding polishing of the last 40-odd years. A lovely mix of intense malt and juicy non-specific fruitiness; a layer of muscovado sugar stands guard and charges in when required; **f23** a little oak buzz but the late mocha charms; **b23.5** the astonishing sugar reserves bring this old timer back from the dead on more than one occasion. *43%*.

Gordon & MacPhail Speymalt Macallan 1994 (91.5) n23 banana cake is crumbled into concentrated, lightly oiled barley; **t24** you expect intense...and you get intense. The malt, as the nose suggests, is in concentrated form but he sugars and spice fix around to give a colourful third dimension; there are layers of citrus, too, each of varying depth and sweetness; **f22** tangy; **b22.5** a busy malt which never quite decides the path it wishes to take, but lets you in for an enjoyable journey nonetheless. *43%*.

Gordon & MacPhail Speymalt Macallan 2005 (84.5) n20.5 t22 f21 b21.5. Sweet, malty, sharp in places; the nose and finish reveals a distinct tang. OK, but I expect a lot better. *43%*.

◇ **Gordon & MacPhail Speymalt Macallan 2006 (74.5) n19 t20.5 f16 b18.** Bitter, dull. Usual suspect – poor oak - guilty. *43%*.

Heiko Thieme's 1974 Macallan 65th Birthday Bottling cask no. 16807 dist 25 Nov 74 bott Jul 08 **(94) n23** the clarity of the sherry takes some believing: this malt has obviously been in a good clean home for the last 34 years: not a single off note and the balance between grape, oak, spice and sweetened tomato puree is exceptional...; **t23** the arrival is sharp, both in terms of barley and grape. At first it looks shocked to have escaped the cask, or is hunting around for the alcohol to tie it together. But soon it finds harmony, helped along the way by a stunning chocolate and raisin middle which leads to some sweetening molasses; **f24** now enters into a class of its own. We all know about the fruitcake cliché: well here it is in glorious roasted raisin brilliance. Melton Hunt cake and trifle combined; the length makes a mockery of the strength. And it looks as though someone forgot to go easy on the burnt cherry. The vanillas are deft, the coffees are medium roast; **b24** this is not whisky because it is 38%abv. It is Scottish spirit. However, this is more of a whisky than a great many samples I have tasted this year. Ageism is outlawed. So is sexism. But alcoholism isn't....!! Try and become a friend of Herr Thieme and grab hold of something a little special. *38% 238 bottles.*

◇ **Hunter Laing's Old & Rare Macallan Aged 21 Years** refill barrel, dist Jun 93, bott Mar 15 **(95.5) n24** wow! Speyside at its most concentrated: the barley is both thick yet, on another level, bordering on juicy and light. Almond oil appears to cling to the nose, as does kumquats and freshly picked peas; **t24** almost a mirror image of the nose. That barley...there is simply no getting to the bottom of it; **f23.5** long, with those oils clinging fast. The oak is spice free but projects mocha afar...; **b24** one of the best Macallans I have encountered for a very long while. The weight of the malt emphasis beautifully the small size of the stills. Intense yet so complex and beautifully balanced. *54.8%. ncf sc. 100 bottles.*

◇ **Hunter Laing's Old & Rare Macallan Aged 30 Years** cask no. 14651, dist Apr 85, bott May 15 **(93.5) n23.5** a little lavender and the first sign of eucalyptus date stamps this malt. Dry date sweetness does likewise; **t24** a mix of exotic fruit and more prosaic dates and molasses makes for a chewy sweetie; **f22.5** duller as the vanillas begin to take hold, though a squadron of spices have now been scrambled; **b23.5** a clean cask making for a simple but deliciously effective malt. *48.3%. nc ncf sc. 212 bottles.*

Old Malt Cask Macallan Aged 15 Years refill hogshead, cask no. 9458, dist Oct 97, bott Feb 13 **(92) n23** thick barley seems as though it is stuck fast to the red liquorice. High quality oak at play...and the pedigree of the initial spirit is pretty impressive, too; **t23.5** classic small still intensity here with the oils tight and copper giving both a lustre and sharpness to the barley. As intense as Speyside malt gets; **f22.5** thins out as the vanilla arrives, though the copper lingers; **b23** Macallan at its most malty and muscular. Really beautiful, if simplistic. *50%. sc. Douglas Laing & Co. 329 bottles.*

Old Malt Cask Macallan Aged 15 Years refill hogshead, cask no. 991, dist Oct 97, bott Sep 13 **(90) n21.5** pretty one dimensional, with the barley at full throttle; **t23** strap yourself in for this one: the malt starts of gently enough, but then bursts through the gears until you have barley concentrate impacting on every taste bud! Wowww....!!! **f22.5** settles down somewhat to allow the tad salty vanillas back into the match; **b23** this mac shows its small still muscle to full effect. Impressive. *50%. nc ncf sc. 210 bottles.*

◇ **Old Malt Cask Macallan Aged 16 Years** refill hogshead, cask no. 10819, dist Oct 97, bott Aug 14 **(83.5) n21 t21.5 f20 b21.** Pretty dry throughout, with plenty of chalky vanilla to tuck into. When at its most rampant, custard tart abounds. *50%. nc ncf sc. 302 bottles.*

Old Malt Cask Macallan Aged 20 Years bourbon barrel, cask no. 10290, dist Jun 93, bott Feb 14 **(93) n23** apples and pears freshly diced, topped with a squeeze of lemon. The tannins look on seemingly bemused and powerless...; **t23.5**....though they don't hang around on delivery. Red liquorice to the fore, though soon swamped by salivating barley and muscovado sugar. A little orange hangs about; **f23** long, softy oiled and not a degree of light molasses and toffee as the tannins begin to make their mark; **b23.5** ironically, a Macallan not from a wine cask, yet turns out to be as fruity as you'll find! A real treat. *50%. nc ncf sc. WB15/134*

⬦ **Old Particular Speyside Macallan 21 Years Old** refill hogshead, cask no. 10586, dist Jun 93, bott Dec 14 **(88.5) n22.5** tries to take an exclusively fruity path, but a puff of smoke dashes that plan; pithy and lots of crushed pips; **t23** excellent, warming delivery. Surprising early volley of spice; a major must influence; **f21** a little on the tight side; **b22** not quite where it should be in terms of cask quality, but escapes major damage and has enough fruit in reserve for a busy and busty experience. *51.5%. nc ncf sc. 290 bottles.*

⬦ **The Pearls of Scotland Golden Pearl Collection Macallan 1989** cask no. 17894, dist Sept 89, bott Sept 15 **(85.5) n21 t22.5 f21 b21**. The small still intensity is here in abundance. But a bitter cask weaves a course through the malt. Never finds its rhythm despite the brief golden syrup delivery. An untidy malt. *46%. sc.*

The Pearls of Scotland Macallan 1989 24 Year Old cask no. 17895, dist Sep 89, bott Feb 14 **(94.5) n23** a little bit of a fruit salad thing going on here...and they haven't spared the pears; **t24** just massive intensity to the malt. There are some coppery sub-plots here, but it is hard to get away from the salivating qualities of the barley; **f23.5** long, with those barley tones stretching and stretching until they are sure to break. The spice is remarkably calm, the texture remains a little like the pear juice apparent: bitty refreshing and sweet; **b24** a fine example of small style syndrome... dense, vaguely metallic and delightful! *46.5%.*

MACDUFF
Speyside, 1963. John Dewar & Sons. Working.

Glen Deveron Aged 10 Years dist 1995 db **(86) n19 t23 f23 b21**. The enormity of the third and fourth waves on delivery give some idea of the greatness this distillery could achieve perhaps with a little more care with cask selection, upping the strength to 46% and banning caramel. We'd have a malt scoring in the low to mid 90s every time. At the moment we must remain frustrated. *40%*

Gordon & MacPhail Connoisseurs Choice Macduff 2000 (95.5) n23.5 a blend of praline and Jaffa Cake....almost impossible to extract your nose from; **t24** oooh....!!! That is one erotic delivery: near perfect texture which glides around the palate. Where it touches a fabulous hazelnut cream cake (yes, they do exist...though, sadly not common enough!) mingles with lustrous barley. Heather honey and muscovado sugar do the rest...; **f24** now drifts into ulmo honey topped with praline. Then more chopped hazelnuts. Simply sublime...; **b24** you'll go nuts for this. But, then, it is the nuttiest dram you'll encounter this year. Stunningly made and matured. *46%.*

⬦ **Hepburn's Choice Macduff Aged 6 Years** refill hogshead, dist 2008, bott 2015 **(71) n18 t19 f17 b18**. Neither cask nor spirit work particularly well on their own and here two negatives certainly don't make a positive. *46%. nc ncf sc. 454 bottles.*

Master of Malt Single Cask Macduff 15 Year Old (90.5) n23 surprisingly salty malt; **t23** the saline feel kicks in immediately: very sharp, slightly tangy barley. A little banana and citrus adds depth; **f22** stays on the malty theme, but that tang goes up an extra notch; **b22.5** not remotely complex. And the oak might be better. But the malty acrobatics are something else. *56.9%. sc.*

Old Malt Cask Macduff Aged 21 Years refill hogshead, cask no. 9909, dist Dec 91, bott Aug 13 **(87) n22 t21.5 f22 b21.5**. As a blending malt, invaluable. The tartness of the barley would add some malty punch; the finish would be enriched by a light, glossy honey. *50%. nc ncf sc. 262 bottles.*

Old Particular Speyside Macduff 14 Years Old refill butt, cask no. 10358, dist Dec 99, bott May 14 **(81.5) n20 t22 f19.5 b20**. MacRough. *48.4%. nc ncf sc. 587 bottles.*

The Pearls of Scotland Macduff 1997 24 Year Old cask no. 5232, dist Sep 97, bott Nov 13 **(89) n22** the accent firmly on the barley, but a little peach, too; **t22** early acacia honey is dwarfed by the spice attack; the barley displays some youthful traits; **f22.5** reverts to a softer honeyed, juicy barley style before drying with a vanilla flourish; **b22.5** a bit of a honeyed carry on... *54.4%. WB15/007*

⬦ **Provenance Macduff Over 8 Years** refill hogshead, cask no. 10773, dist Autumn 06, bott Summer 15 **(87) n21.5 t22.5 f21.5 b21.5**. Positively pre-pubescent. The near complete absence of colour confirms what your nose and taste buds have already told you: oak from a presumably very old cask has barely troubled this malt. Nearer new make than the finished article, but so rich and juicy is the barley and so delicate is the honey, this can still be fully enjoyed. *46%. nc ncf sc.*

Signatory Vintage Un-chillfiltered Collection Macduff 1997 Aged 16 Years hogsheads, cask no. 4077+4078, dist 12 Jun 97, bott 13 Nov 13 (88.5) n22 some nagging tired oak tries to disrupt the honey ceremony; t23 superb delivery of wonderful weight and thinned acacia honey. A little spice advances and retreats...; f21.5 standard, and annoying, oak-induced bitterness; b22 possibly distilled by bees...with the odd wasp. *46%. nc ncf. 692 bottles. WB15/030*

That Boutique-y Whisky Macduff batch 1 (93) n23.5 the clarity of the vanilla and butterscotch suggests the oak is top notch. The squeeze of lime amid the barley water suggests unsullied youth; t23.5 mouth-watering barley – literally of the thirst quenching variety. Thinned maple syrup has a little ulmo stirred in for extra depth; f22.5 perfect oaky footprints offer extra weight and depth but with no bitter recrimination. At last the spices begin to throb; b23.5 youthful, fresh and brimming with all kinds of citrus and sugars. Delightful. *52%. 340 bottles. WB15/190*

Wemyss Malts 2002 Single Speyside Macduff "Lead On Macduff!" dist 2002 bott 2013 (61) n15 t16 f15 b16. Thanks to the hideously rank sulphur, a duff Macduff, Macduff... *46%. sc. 46%. 854 bottles.*

MANNOCHMORE
Speyside, 1971. Diageo. Working.
Mannochmore Aged 12 Years db (84) n22 t21 f20 b21. As usual the mouth arrival fails to live up to the great nose. Quite a greasy dram with sweet malt and bitter oak. *43%.*

Mannochmore 1998 The Manager's Choice db (71.5) n18 t18 f17.5 b18. A very bad cask day... *59.1%*

Cadenhead's Authentic Collection Mannochmore Aged 17 Years bourbon hogshead, dist 96, bott Jul 14 (91) n23 lemon and lime in equal measure; the barley positively sparkles; t23.5 the nose points to clean, intense, salivating barley and that's what you get: in droves; f22 a little allspice cuts down the gristy sugars; a little tang from the wearying oak; b22.5 yet another lovely, high quality cask from Cadenhead. *52.5%. 174 bottles. WB15/255*

◇ **Cadenhead's Mannochmore Port Cask Aged 32 Years** dist 1982, bott Jan 15 (89) n22.5 clean and fruity: over-ripe greengage and spice; t22.5 those spices arrive early and usher in wave upon wave of yet more fruit; f22 drier, but neither the malt or oak make much of a mark, other than a late hint of cocoa. The pithy fruit continues charmingly; b22 hardly gets out of second gear for a malt of such age. But a deliciously comfortable, if predictable, ride nonetheless. *54.7%. 186 bottles.*

Gordon & MacPhail Connoisseurs Choice Mannochmore 1994 (95.5) n24 quietly enormous. The oak puffs out its chest to offer marzipan lined with a little orange filling – most cake like! But the barley counters with a juicy grassiness which makes you purr, as this is both clean yet complex; t24 if you locate a more spotless exhibition of intense yet clean and sugary barley this year, give me a call...; the lilting poise of the oils beggars belief; f23.5 the oaks return to add spice and coconut macaroon. Naturally, golden syrup accompanies it; b24 full of vitality, charm and class. Quite irresistible. *46%.*

MILLBURN
Highlands (Northern), 1807–1985. Diageo. Demolished.
Millburn 1969 Rare Malt db (77) n19 t21 f18 b19. Some lovely bourbon-honey touches but sadly over the hill and declining fast. Nothing like as interesting or entertaining as the massage parlour that was firebombed a few yards from my office twenty minutes ago. Or as smoky... *51.3%*

MILTONDUFF
Speyside, 1824. Chivas Brothers. Working.
Miltonduff Aged 15 Years bott code L00/123 db (86) n23 t22 f20 b21. Some casks beyond their years have crept in and unsettled this one. But some real big salty moments to savour, too. *46%*

Cadenhead's Single Malt Miltonduff-Glenlivet Aged 20 Years dist 1994, bott Jun 2014 (82) n21 t22 f19 b20. An "Allied Distillers" trait cask with more residual bitterness than is good for it. An untidy dram that hits the ground limping... *50.4%. 246 bottles. London exclusive. WB15/272*

Cadenhead's Small Batch Miltonduff-Glenlivet Aged 24 Years bourbon hogheads, dist 90, bott 14 (95) n23.5 Ok, this must be Miltonduff in Franklin County, Kentucky. Every part of this nose screams bourbon from the honeycomb to the liquorice. Wonderful...; **t24** maybe a fleeting trace of malt just after the big sugar delivery. But blink and you'll miss it because the spices are there in number, gentle yet determined and accentuating those muscovado honey and treacle notes; **f23.5** well, ya'll all be enjoying this elegant sweetened tannin finish. The malt has thrown in the white flag and scarpered leaving all those toasty sugar notes to be on their lonesome; **b24** probably a first fill bourbon at play as there is more 'ye-harr' to this than 'och-eye'. Bit of a Kentucky belle. *55.3%. 474 bottles. WB15/256*

Gordon & MacPhail Rare Vintage Miltonduff 1984 (85) **n21.5 t21.5 f21 b21.** Overcooked on the oak, alas. Even the spikey nose is a bourbon, sniffed blind. Has a few moments of brilliance when the barley shines and the spices bite. But would have done a way better job in a blend than as a singleton. *43%.*

Hepburn's Choice Miltonduff Aged 7 Years sherry butt, dist 07, bott 14 (75) **n18 t20 f18 b19.** More duff than Milton for the nose, finish and balance. Paradise has certainly been lost. *46%. nc ncf sc. 805 bottles.*

Kingsbury Silver Miltonduff 18 Year Old cask no. 2796, dist 1995 (89.5) **n22** some overcooked oak but the lemon-drizzled barley is divine; **t23** impeccably salivating and clean; **f22** toasty with a butterscotch topping; **b22.5** a distillery in its usual effortless sumptuous mood. *46%. nc ncf sc. 166 bottles.*

Old Malt Cask Miltonduff Aged 18 Years refill barrel, cask no. 10120, dist Feb 95, bott Oct 13 (91) **n22** peat! What on earth, literally, is that doing there...? **t23** clean, gristy, citrus enhanced barley which fair pings about the palate and enjoys full salivations levels; **f23** smoked mocha; a bit of a Cornish cream tea finish....but with a dollop of smoke, too; the residual spices tingle; **b23** a fully fledged peated Miltonduff. With the parent distillery owning nothing on Islay, they did get their Speyside distilleries to produce a peaty whisky for bending purposes. Can't remember finding a Miltonduff of this type, however. As intriguing as it is delicious! *50%. nc ncf sc.228 bottles.*

Old Particular Speyside Miltonduff 17 Years Old 2013 refill hogshead, cask no. 9904 dist Mar 1996 bott Aug (81.5) **n20 t21 f20.5 b20.** A staple of the all-conquering Ballantine's 17 has been housed in some under-performing oak thus allowing almost unfettered access to a youthfulness rarely seen in usually thicker, more cerebral malt than this. Lightweight and juicy, save some very late cocoa. *48.4%. nc ncf sc. 319 bottles. Douglas Laing & Co.*

⟡ **Old Particular Speyside Miltonduff 22 Years Old** refill butt, cask no. 10592, dist Jul 92, bott Dec 14 (70) **n16 t21 f16 b17.** I could weep. Because while this is the sulphured butt which puts the "duff" in to Miltonduff, there is a four or five second explosion on the palate which reveals that, before it was treated, this, untainted, was once an emperor among oloroso casks... *51.5%. nc ncf sc. 440 bottles.*

⟡ **Provenance Miltonduff Over 8 Years** refill puncheon, cask no. 10405, dist Autumn 05, bott Summer 14 (92.5) **n22.5** all the hallmarks of a young bourbon: the oak dominates with layers of gutsy tannins; **t23.5** a soft body but a bold personality. Doesn't take long for the oak-structured spices to really fizz. But the wonderful muscovado sugars and light liquorice forms the perfect backdrop; **f23** a long parade of spices and oak-stained malt: gorgeous; **b23.5** you can ask little more from an 8-y-o Speysider. Bubbles in the glass with class and character. *46%. nc ncf sc.*

⟡ **Old Malt Cask Miltonduff Aged 20 Years** refill hogshead, cask no. 11205, dist Feb 95, bott Feb 15 (91.5) **n20.5** disappointing: indifferent and a little too much wallpaper paste for its own good...; **t23.5** wow...!! I was expecting a thin dram devoid of character. Instead, this rumbles onto the palate with an oily depth and the barley positively bursting with muscle. The saltiness of a Digestive biscuit dunked into concentrated malt; **f24** long, with an almost late night malt drink intensity to this, balanced and lengthened further by a delicate Demerara sugar and ulmo honey mix: sensational...; **b23.5** you know those whiskies which absolutely knock you off your feet with the beauty of its nose and then lets you down on the palate? Well, this is the exact opposite... Considering the aroma, really a thing of rare wonder. *50%. nc ncf sc. 259 bottles.*

Scotch Malt Whisky Society Cask 72.38 Aged 28 Years refill hogshead, dist 27 Nov 84 (94) **n23.5** a little bit of glue has got into the attractive vanilla and barley scene; elsewhere some bourbon notes play around with the lavender honey; **t23** sumptuous delivery with the accent always in the salivating barley...even after all these years...!! **f24** elegant, complex finale with the barley preferring a clean crispness, rounded by delicate maple syrup and a vanilla/butterscotch finale; **b23.5** the kind of bottling which leaves you in no doubt why this malt is sought after for being at the heart of the very finest bended scotch. *50.1%. nc ncf sc.*

Scotch Malt Whisky Society Cask 72.39 refill hogshead, dist 03 Nov 81 **(95)** n23.5 myriad barley notes range from pristine and untouched to those engulfed in rich oaky depth; **t24** lush yet lively the barley doesn't just explode on the palate but brings with it a host of vanilla tones which reverberate around the palate with delightful abandon; **f23.5** tangy, but only from the barley pulsing in a big tannin afterglow **b24** like Noel Cowerd in The Italian Job a whisky which positively glows in its age and veneration. *51.1%. nc ncf sc. 185 bottles.*

Scotch Malt Whisky Society Cask 72.40 Aged 31 Years refill hogshead, dist 03 Nov 81 **(90)** n21.5 massive oak but a Horlicks maltiness attracts; **t23.5** enormous delivery with thick oils combining with extraordinary barley and beefsteak tannin; some kumquats not just fill the middle ground but positively give it the kiss of life; **f22** a memorable and enthralling essay in spiced tannin and vanilla; **b23** delightful whisky but one slightly in danger of being over engrossed in its own oaky dominance. The saving grace is a sublime citrus tones which steers an orangey path to greatness. *50.7%. nc ncf sc. 239 bottles.*

Scotch Malt Whisky Society Cask 72.41 Aged 9 Years 1st fill white wine hogshead, dist 23 Sep 04 **(85)** n21.5 t22 f21 b21.5. Now this is the thing about single cask youngish malts: to get the best job out of a whisky of this age you need a squadron of casks, not just the lone flyer. In itself a competent, attractively spiced and lively cove. But perhaps lacking in depth, weight and overall complexity. *59.8%. nc ncf sc. 199 bottles.*

Signatory Vintage Un-chillfiltered Collection Miltonduff 1995 Aged 18 Years bourbon barrels, cask no. 4112+4113+4114, dist 23 Feb 95, bott 18 Mar 13 **(89)** n22 those who have travelled out to enjoy the World Cup in Brazil, though presumably very few will be Scots, might happen across a local coconut-based biscuit with an almost identical aroma; **t23** magnificent early barley, helped along by butterscotch and ulmo honey; red liquorice - then warms...; **f22** a light spice perks up the finish by numbers; **b22** very good blending fodder unleashed upon a lucky public. *46%. nc ncf. 870 bottles. WB15/031*

That Boutique-y Whisky Miltonduff batch 1 **(86)** n21 t22 f21.5 b21.5. Funny how, as generously malty as this dram is, if I get a speck of botanical where it shouldn't, my nose and taste buds focus on that to the cost of all else. A bit like the tongue on a chipped tooth. *51.4%. 122 bottles. WB15/226*

The Whisky Cask Miltonduff Aged 21 Years first fill sherry butt, dist 1992, bott 2013 **(76.5)** n19 t22.5 f17 b18. A shame: no shortage of honey and fruit from this great distillery. But the S word rears its ugly head just enough to spoil the party. Those immune will find this an outstanding dram. *56.7%. nc ncf.*

◈ **Villa Konthor Miltonduff 19 Years Old** ex bourbon cask, dist 1995, bott 2015 **(92.5)** n24.5 a mini lesson in brilliance: the oak influence is apparent in the most busy of understated spices; so subtle, they could easily slip below the radar. No less shy is the mysterious array of fruits not normally associated with bourbon casks, especially the gooseberry. And if the oak has any thoughts of injecting a restrictive dryness, the heather and mild orange blossom honey soon puts paid to that. A nose which could be easily overlooked...and at your loss...; **t23** the demure delivery of ultra rich malt is soon engulfed in a series of light fruit tones and then liquorice – there is something of the old British fruit salad and Blackjack farthing candy about this; **f21.5** a regrettable degree of old Allied cask bitterness just slightly stains the finish; **b22.5** the greatness of this distillery is best witnessed on the superb nose. Worth 15 minutes of anyone's time... *46%*

◈ **Whisky-Fässle Miltonduff 18 Year Old** barrel, dist 1995, bott 2014 **(85)** n21.5 t22 f20.5 b21. Unusually aggressive for a Miltonduff – the distiller must have had a date with the local golf course. Not all bad, as honey is there in abundance. But the Allied-style bitter cask finish doesn't help much. *51.2%. nc ncf.*

◈ **Whiskyjace Miltonduff 21 Year Old** refill sherry hogshead, dist 1989, bott 2011 **(94.5)** n23 beautiful coastal saline feel, complete with light ozone kick; even, yet complex tannins; **t24.5** superb delivery: fabulous layering of honey, with both ulmo honey and acacia to the fore. Red liquorice and golden syrup, with only the vaguest hint of pear; **f23** long vanilla and butterscotch fade, a little dryness to match the honey; massive spice presence on the fade; **b24** so hard to find a refill sherry hoggy which offers this degree of honey. No off notes and so much to love. Sublime. *50.1%*

MORTLACH
Speyside, 1824. Diageo. Working.
Mortlach Aged 16 Years db **(87)** n20 t23 f22 b22. Once it gets past the bold if very mildly sulphured nose, the rest of the journey is superb. Earlier Mortlachs in this range had a slightly unclean feel to them and the nose here doesn't inspire confidence. But from arrival on the palate onwards, it's sure-footed, fruity and even refreshing... and always delicious. *43%*

Mortlach 18 Year Old db **(75) n19 t19 f18 b19.** When I first tasted Mortlach, probably over 30 years ago now, it really wasn't even close to this. Something went very wrong in the late '80s, I can tell you...*43.4%. Diageo.*

Mortlach 25 Year Old db **(91.5) n23** just love the lemon grass alongside the liquorice and hickory; **t23.5** thick and palate-encompassing. The sugars are pretty toasty with a light mocha element in play; **f22.5** crisp finale with a return of the citrus, sitting confidently with the late spice; **b22.5** much more like it. The sugars may be pretty full on, but there is enough depth and complexity for a narrative to be told. Very much a better Mortlach on so many levels. *43.4%. Diageo.*

Mortlach 32 Years Old dist 1971 db **(88) n22 t22 f22 b22.** Big and with attitude... *50.1%*

Mortlach Rare Old db **(79) n20 t21 f19 b19.** Not rare enough... *43.4%. Diageo.*

Mortlach Special Strength db **(79.5) n20 t21.5 f19 b19.** Does whisky come any more cloyingly sweet than Mortlach...? Not in my experience.... *49%. Diageo.*

Cadenhead's Sherry Cask Mortlach Aged 25 Years sherrywood, dist 88, bott July 14 **(68) n16 t19 f16 b17.** Huge grape and the 'S' word in equal measure battle it out. But there is only one loser. *56.8%. 576 bottles. WB15/269*

⬥ **Crom Mortlach 16 Years Old Warlords & Warriors Edition Thorgrim's Shield** hogshead, dist Oct 97, bott Apr 14 **(85.5) n22.5 t21.5 f20.5 b21.** Typically sweet and macho and comes complete with you usual tangy weaknesses. *52.3%. sc.*

Gordon & MacPhail Rare Vintage Mortlach 1981 (90) n23.5 various exotic fruit with Chinese gooseberry at the vanguard; **t23** slightly papery start with the broken down oak getting in first. But then we return to fruity normal service and the barley juices up to a serious degree as the sugars begin to dissolve; diluted honeycomb moves into the mid-ground; **f21.5** slightly bitty, with the oak becoming papery and a little too dry; **b22** really don't even begin to understand why this is at 43%abv rather than at least 46 and preferably at cask strength. Reducing to this strength after so many years has broken down the vital oils holding the aged elements together and subtracted from what might have been a great experience. *43%.*

Gordon & MacPhail Rare Vintage Mortlach 1984 (89) n23 slightly dirty, almost coal dust-like, as the aromas from a burning anthracite fire. But it is sweetened by a syrup including outrageously over-ripe figs and plums; **t22** silky delivery and then an avalanche of some the most eye-watering sugars and fruits you can imagine. Curiously, never hits liqueur mode and the malt positively sparkles; **f22** long, back to those over-ripe fruit and now some serious spice; **b22** ridiculously sweet and soupy in typical Mortlach fashion. But, against the odd, this one works rather well! *43%.*

⬥ **Hepburn's Choice Mortlach Aged 7 Years** refill hogshead, dist 2007, bott 2014 **(85.5) n21 t22 f21 b21.5.** For a malt that has been matured in older-than-normal second fill cask or, more likely, a standard third fill, enjoys some surprising buttery nuances to bring entertainment to the semi-new make. Every bit as salivating as you'd expect it to be and so light even a discreet puff of peatiness can be located. A typical Mortlach of mixed messages. *46%. nc ncf sc. 384 bottles.*

Hepburn's Choice Mortlach Aged 9 Years refill hogshead, dist 04, bott 14 **(88) n22** young, expansive malt; slight bubble gum; lemon zest; **t23** fresh-faced but builds into barley sugar intensity; juicy juicy throughout; **f21** citrus and flaky vanilla; **b22** a fascinating and juicy insight into a malt which has changed style in the last decade. *46%. nc ncf sc. 380 bottles.*

⬥ **Hepburn's Choice Mortlach Aged 10 Years** refill hogshead, dist 2004, bott 2015 **(83.5) n21 t21 f21 b20.5.** Settles for a display of thick, creamy sugars. Cloying, but with the good grace to offer up late spice and barley, though the old unkempt house style is evident throughout. *46%. nc ncf sc. 153 bottles.*

The Maltman Mortlach Aged 14 Years bourbon cask, cask no. 10998, dist Oct 98, bott Apr 13 **(84.5) n22 t23 f19.5 b20.** Ticks all the boxes for those looking for a big malty Speysider. But suffers from a lack of complexity and guile, unspiced heat and a thin finale. *46%. sc ncf nc. 376 bottles. WB15/228*

Old Malt Cask Mortlach Aged 13 Years refill hogshead, cask no. 10200, bott Dec 13 **(94) n23.5** delicate peat reek on the breeze; **t23** juicy, lively barley dashes haphazardly around the palate; **f23.5** more vanilla and citrus now...and a return to a lightly spiced smoke; some late praline adds to the puzzlement; **b24** effervescent, fresh and works the palate continually. A surprise treat with massive entertainment value.. *50%. nc ncf sc. 319 bottles.*

Old Malt Cask Mortlach Aged 18 Years refill hogshead, cask no. 9882, dist Jun 95, bott Jun 13 **(86) n22 t22.5 f20.5 b21.** Juicy, honest, majorly malty and very simple Speysider. *50%. nc ncf sc. 279 bottles.*

⟐ **Provenance Mortlach Over 8 Years** refill hogshead, cask no. 10560, dist Spring 06, bott Autumn 14 **(87) n21.5 t22 f22 b21.5**. A massively enjoyable, honest whisky. Simple, well constructed, pleasantly weighted blending fodder which cleans the palate beautifully. *46%. nc ncf sc.*

⟐ **Riegger's Selection Cask Strength Mortlach 20 Year Old** 2nd fill cask, bott 19 Mar 15 **(85.5) n21 t22 f21 b21.5**. Typical of the distillery from this era. Dense, like a bowl of porridge with molten sugar on top. *55%*

⟐ **Romantic Rhine Collection Mortlach** sherry octave, cask no. 796872, dist 30 Sept 93, bott 7 Feb 11 **(85) n20.5 t22.5 f21 b21**. Laid on with a trowel, the sugars almost make your jaw ache, so dense and chewy are they. But the spices work beautifully on this and make amends for the obvious fault lines elsewhere. *56.6%. 71 bottles.*

Scotch Malt Whisky Society Cask 76.112 Aged 27 Years refill hogshead, dist 24 Apr 86 **(85) n21.5 t22 f20.5 b21**. Astonishingly dense and sweet....almost sickly so: similar to an over the top Bakewell tart. Without the late spices it would flounder. Almost like walking through a sugar plantation without a map...*58.2%. nc ncf sc. 284 bottles.*

Scotch Malt Whisky Society Cask 76.115 Aged 18 Years refill butt, dist 19 Jul 95 **(85.5) n21 t22 f21 b21.5**. Massively sweet and about as subtle as being biffed over the head with a stick of sugar cane. *56.7%. nc ncf sc. 535 bottles.*

Scotch Malt Whisky Society Cask 76.116 Aged 26 Years refill hogshead, dist 07 Apr 87 **(84.5) n20.5 t22 f21 b21**. A slightly sub-standard cask ensures a tartness to the experience As is the wont with Mortlach the sugars are way out of control, though the intensity if the malt and some late spices tries to save the day... *48.4%. nc ncf sc. 239 bottles.*

Signatory Vintage Single Malt Mortlach Aged 13 Years hogsheads, cask no. 7900+7901, dist 28 May 99, bott 05 Mar 13 **(90) n22.5** gentle, gristy malt; a little maple syrup adds weight; **t23** the juiciest barley delivery imaginable. Limited complexity back up so the squeeze of citrus is welcome; **f22.5** keeps right on that juicy malt road; **b22.5** absolutely middle of the road Speyside. But it does it all rather well. One of the most lightweight Mortlachs I have encountered for a very long while. *43%. nc. 851 bottles. WB15/011*

Signatory Vintage Un-chillfiltered Collection Mortlach Aged 17 Years cask no. 4092+4093, bott Apr 13 **(86) n21.5 t22 f21.5 b22**. Mortlach in its usual syrupy mode. Just a little too cloying for its own good, though it does have a few juicy moments. *46%. nc ncf. WB15/032*

Wemyss Malts 1998 Mortlach Single Speyside "Pastille Bouquet" dist 1998 bott 2013 **(88.5) n22** light sawdust sprinkled on vanilla; **t22.5** massive barley thrust with a slow unravelling of sugars; **f22** thickens as the grist intensifies; **b22.5** well constructed, unmistakable Speyside. Some serious weight towards the finish, too. *46%. sc. 325 bottles.*

⟐ **Wilson & Morgan Barrel Selection Mortlach 15 Year Old** sherry butt, cask no. 2, dist 1999, bott 2014 **(87) n21.5 t22.5 f21 b22**. Not distilled during Mortlach's greatest era and the stodginess of the spirit is apparent throughout. But this isn't too bad a sherry butt and although the finish is tight and toffeed, there is plenty of good grape to go round. *56.6%. sc. 622 bottles.*

⟐ **World of Orchids Mortlach 2006 7 Year Old** cask no. 18 **(85.5) n21.5 t22.5 f20 b21.5**. A ponderous, plodding Mortlach totally devoid of subtlety and dexterity: every facet of its personality is splashed on with a large brush. But personality it certainly possesses; and sugars, which vary in style from heavy to mammoth, though the juicy dates do offer a comparatively subtle variation. *53.9%. sc. 330 bottles.*

⟐ **Xtra Old Particular Mortlach 22 Years Old** sherry butt, cask no. 10578, dist Sept 92, bott Dec 14 **(88) n23** OK...been doing this a few years, as you know. Not quite nosed anything like this. Almost a thick paste of greengage jam mixed in with a bourbon-doused fruitcake which may have been in a cupboard with a few boxes of matches for a while. Big. Challenging. And odd...; **t23** one of the thickest, least compromising deliveries you'll find this year. Not exactly subtle, the grape appears to be in concentrate, crushed into maximum intensity by blocks of solid molasses; massively spiced, somewhat flawed...but unquestionably delicious; **f19.5** some late sulphur; **b22.5** OK, technically all over the shop. But...well, whatever that was...it was different! *571%. nc ncf sc. 225 bottles.*

MOSSTOWIE
Speyside, 1964–1981. Chivas Brothers. Closed.

Rare Old Mosstowie 1979 (84.5) n21.5 t21 f21 b21. Edging inextricably well beyond its sell by date. But there is a lovely walnut cream cake (topped off with brown sugar and spices) to this which warms the cockles. Bless... *43%. Gordon & MacPhail.*

NORTH PORT
Highlands (Eastern), 1820–1983. Diageo. Demolished.

Brechin 1977 db **(78)** n19 t21 f18 b20. Fire and brimstone was never an unknown quantity with the whisky from this doomed distillery. Some soothing oils are poured on this troubled – and sometimes attractively honeyed – water of life. *54.2%*

OBAN
Highlands (Western), 1794. Diageo. Working.

Oban 14 Years Old db **(79)** n19 t22 f18 b20. Absolutely all over the place. The cask selection sits very uncomfortably with the malt. I look forward to the resumption of normality to this great but ill-served distillery. *43%*

Oban Aged 15 Years The Distiller's Edition db finished in Montilla Fino casks, dist 1992, bott 2007 **(90)** n22.5 t23 f22.5 b22. This isn't all about complexity and layering. It's about style and effect. And it pulls it off brilliantly. *43%*

Oban Aged 15 Years The Distiller's Edition db finished in Montilla Fino casks, dist 1993, bott 2008 **(91.5)** n22 nutty, tight, a little musty; **t24** much more assured: the dryness of the grape sports beautifully against the obviously more outgoing and sweeter barley: excellent balance between the two; **f22.5** perhaps the Fino wins, as it dries and embraces the oak quite happily; **b23** delicate and sophisticated whisky. *43%*

⬩⬩⬩ **Oban Little Bay** db **(87.5)** n21 t23 f21.5 b22. A pleasant, refreshing simple dram. Clean and juicy in part and some wonderful oak-laden spice to stir things up a little. Just a little too much chewy toffee near the end, though. *43%*

PITTYVAICH
Speyside, 1975–1993. Diageo. Demolished.

Pittyvaich Aged 12 Years db **(64)** n16 t18 f15 b15. It was hard to imagine this whisky getting worse. But somehow it has achieved it. From fire-water to cloying undrinkability. What amazes me is not that this is such bad whisky: we have long known that Pittyvaich can be as grim as it gets. It's the fact they bother bottling it and inflicting it on the public. Vat this with malt from Fettercairn and neighbouring Dufftown and you'll have the perfect dram for masochists. Or those who have entirely lost the will to live. Jesus... *43%. Flora and Fauna.*

PORT ELLEN
Islay, 1825–1983. Diageo. Closed.

Port Ellen 1979 db **(93)** n22 mousy and retiring; a degree of oak fade and fruit on the delicate smoke **t23** non-committal delivery but bursts into stride with a series of sublime, peat-liquorice waves and a few rounds of spices; **f24** a surprising gathering of oils rounds up the last traces of sweet barley and ensures an improbably long – and refined – finish; **b24** takes so long to get out of the traps, you wonder if anything is going to happen. But when it does, my word...it's glorious! *57.5%*

Port Ellen 31 Years Old Special Release refill American & European oak, dist 1978, bott 2010 db **(88.5)** n22 t23 f22 b21.5 shows some serious cracks now, though that can't be helped; this whisky was never made for this type of age. Still some moments to close the eyes and simply cherish, however; *54.6%. nc ncf. Diageo. Fewer than 3000 bottles.*

Port Ellen 32 Years Old Special Release 2011 db **(88.5)** n22.5 t22.5 f22 b22. Really feeling its age, though there are many superb passages of play. *53.9%. nc ncf.*

Port Ellen 32 Years Old Special Release 2012 Refill American and European oak casks, dist 1979, bott 2012 db **(88.5)** n23 t23.5 f20 b22. Some mesmerising moments. Not sure what the finish is all about, though. *52.5 %. nc ncf. Diageo.*

Directors' Cut Port Ellen Aged 35 Years refill hogshead, cask no. 10355, dist May 79, bott Jun 14 **(94)** n22.5 the trademark gristy nose has given way over the decades to a minty one, though here infused with lemon tea and hickory where once the smoke might have been; **t23** sharp delivery full of fired-up, juicy malt. The oak really does hound and pound but the teamwork between first, the apologetic muscovado then the more confident smoke ensures there's plenty of life and complexity in the slightly salty old dog; **f24** only on about the third tasting does the minty mocha begin to make enough noise to drown out the tannin. Ends up as a genuinely classy fade where balance, somehow, has been clawed back; **b24.5** a great distillery whose few remaining casks are now, sadly, coming to the end of their life. But this one just hangs in their enough to show that greatness and genius is still to be found in abundance. You'll find it only on about the third or fourth taste, as this is a dram the palate must acclimatise to. Ensure your tastebuds are in top notch nick before you take this one on... and no smoking, water or strong food. It is a dram which deserves and demands you to be at the top of your game. *51.1%. nc ncf sc. 162 bottles.*

❧ **That Boutique-y Whisky Company Port Ellen batch 5** (95.5) n24 a time-defying beauty to this aroma: the smoke is both intense, yet relaxed and elegant. The sugars come from both the grist and the oak. The pace of the changing notes is slow, the citrus breathing defiant youth into the equation; t24 try not to groan in pleasure: I challenge you! The sugars are, in that unique Port Ellen way, simply melting on the tongue. The spices rattle and roll around the palate; and at last some clove notes give the game away regarding this whisky's age; f23.5 long, the spices keep rocking...; b24 rolls back the years, like rolling back the sheets to find a naked beauty slumbering, never to wake... *471%. 89 bottles.*

PULTENEY
Highlands (Northern), 1826. Inver House Distillers. Working.

Old Pulteney Aged 12 Years db (90.5) n22 pungent, busy and full of zesty zap. Enough salt to get your blood pressure up; t23 beautifully clean barley, again showing little shortage of saltiness, but thriving in its zesty environment; f22.5 the vanillas and cocoa carry out an excellent drying operation. The sea-breeze saltiness continues to hang on the taste buds...; b23 a cleaner, zestier more joyous composition than on the old 43%, though that has less to do with strength than overall construction. A dramatic whisky which, with further care, could get even closer to the truth of this distillery. *40%*

Old Pulteney Aged 12 Years db (85) n22 t23 f19 b21. There are few malts whose finish dies as spectacularly as this. The nose and delivery are spot on with a real buzz and panache. The delivery in particular just bowls you over with its sharp barley integrity: real pulse-racing stuff! Then... toffee...!!! Grrrr!!! If it is caramel causing this, then it can be easily remedied. And in the process we'd have a malt absolutely basking in the low 90s...! *43%*

Old Pulteney Aged 15 Years db (91) n21 pretty harsh and thin at first but some defter barley notes can be detected; t24 an attention-grabbing, eye-wateringly sharp delivery with the barley in roasty mood and biting immediately with a salty incision; the barley-sugar effect is mesmerising and the clarity astonishing for its age; f23 long, with those barley sugars working overtime; a slight salty edge there but the oak behaves impeccably; b23 only on about the fourth or fifth mouthful do you start getting the picture here: enormously complex with a genuine coastal edge to this. The complexity is awesome. *54.9%*

Old Pulteney Aged 17 Years db (95) n22 tight but does all that is possible to reveal its salty, fruity complexity with pears and lemons to the fore; t25 one of the softest, most beautifully crafted deliveries in the whisky world. Absolutely faultless as it picks the most fabulous course among the honeyed vanilla and barley which is so delicate words simply cannot do justice; f24 near perfect balance between the vanillas and delicate honeys; b24 the nose confirms that some of the casks at work here are not A1. Even so, the whisky performs to the kind of levels some distillers could only dream of. *46%*

Old Pulteney Aged 21 Years db (97.5) n25 if you had the formula to perfectly transform salt, citrus, the most delicate smoke imaginable, sharp barley, more gristy barley, light vanilla, toasty vanilla, roasted hazelnut, thinned manuka honey, lavender honey, arbutus blossom and cherry blossom, light hickory, liquorice, and the softest demerara sugar into the aroma of a whisky, you still wouldn't quite be able to recreate this perfection...; t24 the sugars arrive: first gristy and malt-laden, then Demerara. This is followed by a salty, nerve-tingling journey of barley at varying intensity and then a slow but magnificently complete delivery of spice...; f24 those spices continue to buzz, the vanillas dovetail with the malt and the fruit displaying a puckering, lively intensity. Ridiculously long fade for a malt so seemingly light, the salts and spices kiss the taste buds goodnight...; b24.5 by far and away one of the great whiskies of 2012, absolutely exploding from the glass with vitality, charisma and class. One of Scotland's great undiscovered distilleries about to become discovered, I think... and rightly so! *46%*

Old Pulteney 30 Years Old db (92) n23.5 fabulous mix of Jaffa cake and bourbon, seasoned by a pinch of salt; t23.5 an early, unexpected, wave of light smoke and silkier oak gives immediate depth. But stunning, ultra-juicy citrus and barley ensures this doesn't get all big and brooding; f22 thinner and oakier with a playful oak-spice tingle; plenty of vanilla controls the drier aspects; b23 I had to laugh when I tasted this: indeed, it had me scrambling for a copy of the 2009 Bible to check for sure what I had written. And there it was: after bemoaning the over oaking I conjectured, "As Pulteney has the fascinating tendency to radically shift style over not too long a period, I can't wait for the next instalment." And barely a year on, here it is. Pretty far removed from last year's offering and an absolute peach of a dram that laughs in the face of its 30 years... *45%*

Old Pulteney 35 Year Old db (89) n23 the dry ginger doesn't do anything to make this feel younger than its 35 years; a meeting place of various forms of tannin, some sweeter than others. But it is those delicate muscovado sugars alongside the manuka honey, alongside the ginger, which are key; t21.5 much harder to keep it together on the palate:th attractive mouth feel is undermined by the drier oa elements, some of which are very dry; **f22.5** some lovely mint chocolate does offer great charm; **b22** a malt on the perimeter of its comfort zone. But there are enough gold nuggets included to make this work. Just. *46%. Inverhouse Distilleries.*

Old Pulteney Aged 40 Years db (95) **n23.5** gosh! That's pretty aged stuff with the exotic fruit hanging on by a fingernail. Some major bourbon notes now evident – and lip-smacking; **t23.5** massive delivery, again with tannins coming from every angle. But a mix of liquorice, dates, burnt raisin and honey cope well while spices tingle; **f24** settles for a long essay of happy old bourbon-style led whisky; **b24** this malt still flies as close to the sun as possible. But some extra fruit, honey and spice now grasps the tannins by the throat to ensure a whisky of enormous magnitude and complexity *51.3%*

Old Pulteney 1990 Vintage American oak ex bourbon & Spanish oak ex sherry butts. db (85) **n21 t23 f21 b20.** As you know, anything which mentions sherry butts gets me nervous – and for good reason. Even with a World Great distillery like Pulteney. Oddly enough, this bottling is, as near a dammit, free of sulphur. Yee-hah! The bad news, though, is that it is also untroubled by complexity as well. It reminded me of some heavily sherried peaty jobs...and then I learned that that ex Islay casks were involved. That may or may not be it. But have to say, beyond that first big, salivating, lightly spiced moments on delivery you wait for the story to unfurl...and it all turns out to be dull rumours. *46%. Inverhouse Distilleries.*

Old Pulteney Clipper American ex bourbon and ex sherry casks db (93) **n23** slightly less salty than you might expect, but enough to tease the more complex tones from the delicate oak and raise the spice profile; citrus-soaked grist give the malt a big platform; **t24** fabulous delivery: so light yet salivating and packed with many layers of sugar, including acacia and ulmo honey; **f22.5** extra weight as the oak kicks in, mainly of a toffee-fudge style; and as the salt returns, a little manuka honey now, of course...; **b23.5** looks like honey, tastes like honey. Most un-Pulteney like. The most delicate and disarming bottling from this distillery I can remember. *46%. ncf nc. 2013-14 commemorative bottle. WB15/276*

Old Pulteney Duncansby Head Lighthouse bourbon and sherry casks db (90.5) **n23** Manor House cake; blood oranges; **t23** stunning weight: the malt is weighed down by a toffee sponge pudding with the odd toasted raisin thrown in here and there; **f22** toasted fudge and raisin; **b22.5** beginning to wonder if Pulteney is into making whisky or cakes. And malt straight from the oven. *46% WB15/329*

⬦ **Old Pulteney Dunnet Head Lighthouse** bourbon & sherry casks db (90.5) **n22** moody and broody, this is heavy going with only a hint of dusty heather honey lighting the way; **t23.5** much more expansive on delivery, showing true Pulteney depth and layering, especially when those light honey notes transfer from the nose; the sugar-spice interplay is excellent; **f22** salted caramel-vanilla and slightly tangy; dulls quickly despite the spice's best efforts; **b23** loads to chew over with this heavyweight. *46%. nc ncf. Exclusive to travel retail.*

Old Pulteney Isabella Fourtuna WK499 2nd Release db (89) **n23** coconut cake, anyone? Or moist Battenburg? **t23** a brilliant bit-blow of Madeira cake with an extra dollop of malty icing sugar; **f21.5** bread pudding – but someone forgot to add the sugar; **b22** this sailing lark...a piece of cake! *46%. Travel retail exclusive. WB15/324*

Old Pulteney Noss Head Lighthouse bourbon casks db (84) **n22.5 t22 f19 b20.5.** If Noss Head was as light as this dram, it'd be gone half way through its first half decent storm. An apparent slight overuse of third and less sturdy second fill casks means the finale bitters out considerably. A shame, as the nose and delivery is about as fine a display of citrus maltiness as you'll find. *46%. Travel retail exclusive. WB15/327*

Old Pulteney Pentland Skerries Lighthouse db (85) **n21 t22 f20.5 b21.5.** A chewy dram with an emphasis on the fruit. Sound, evens enjoys the odd chocolate-toffee moment. But a little sulphur, apparent on the nose, creeps in to take the gloss off. *46%. WB15/323*

Old Pulteney WK209 db (71) **n68.5 t18 f16.5 b17.** Could well be liked by the Germans. *46%*

Old Pulteney WK217 db (88.5) **n21 t22 f23 b22.5.** The WK series is named after the old fishing vessels which used to be based in the town's harbour. I suspect old WK217 rarely had a day at sea in waters as calm as this softy of a malt. *46%*

Gordon & MacPhail Rare Vintage Old Pulteney 1982 (87.5) **n21 t22.5 f22 b22.** So oak-soaked there even a degree of creosote on the nose. The oak involvement makes for a tart experience to the very death, but I adore the battle put up by the barley and banana to keep this alive and kicking. *43%.*

ROSEBANK

Lowlands, 1840–1993. Diageo. Closed. (But if there is a God will surely one day re-open)

Rosebank Aged 12 Years db (95) **n24 t24 f23 b24.** Infinately better than the last bottling, this is quite legendary stuff, even better than the old 8-y-o version, though probably a point or two down regarding complexity. The kind of whisky that brings a tear to the eye... for many a reason... *43%. Flora and Fauna.*

Rosebank 21 Years Old Special Release db **(94) n24** fabulous interplay between apple and berry fruits, though it's the pear juice which acts as the sweetening agent; a nose to spend a good 20 minutes over; **t23.5** at once fizzing and busy while soft and caressing; natural caramels combine with coconut oil to offer the weightier sheen; **f23** dries but never bitters; healthy vanilla all the way **b23.5** can any Lowland be compared to a fully blossomed Rosebank? This is whisky to both savour and worship for this is nectar in a Rose... *53.8%. nc ncf.*

Rosebank 22 Years Old Rare Malts 2004 db **(85) n22 t23 f19 b21.** One or two Rosebank moments of joyous complexity but, hand on heart, this is simply too old. *61.1%*

Rosebank 25 Years Old db **(96) n24.5 t23.5 f24 b24.** I had to sit back, take a deep breath and get my head around this. It was like Highland Park but with a huge injection of sweetened chocolate on the finale and weight – and even smoke – from a Rosebank I had never quite seen before. And believe me, as this distillery's greatest champion, I've tasted a few hundred, possibly thousands, of casks of this stuff over the last 25 years. Is this the greatest of all time? I am beginning to wonder. Is it the most extraordinary since the single malt revolution took off? Certainly. Do I endorse it? My god, yes! *61.4%*

Gordon & MacPhail Rare Old Rosebank 1989 **(85.5) n21 t22 f21 b21.5.** The once dazzling greatness of this malt has been sacrificed on the alter of time. Enjoyable whisky, but significantly limited by the degree of involvement from the vanilla and natural caramels which dominate completely. Eye-watering at times, but the juicy moments are a plus. *46%.*

◇ **Romantic Rhine Collection Rosebank** refill barrel, cask no. 6492, dist Feb 90, bott Feb 11 **(90.5) n22 t23 f22.5 b23**. An unusual, busy saltiness for a Rosebank. But the weight and pace of the slow infusion of acacia honey makes for a beautiful malt, treading carefully through the oaky ruins. *50%. 120 bottles.*

Scotch Malt Whisky Society Cask 25.65 Aged 22 Years refill barrel, dist 01 Jul 91 **(89.5) n23.5** some sharp rhubarb crumble with exotic fruit on a side plate.. The custard is extra thick...; **t23** the oak lets rip from the first moment, like a cry of despair and lament for a lost soul.... The layerings of muscovado sugars sooth and comfort, though; **f21** bitters out; **b22** the odd spell of magic, but a malt now on the way down. *50%. nc ncf sc. 220 bottles.*

Scotch Malt Whisky Society Cask 25.66 Aged 23 Years refill hogshead, dist 14 Nov 90 **(96) n23.5** red liquorice abounds - perhaps a little nearer bourbon these days... **t24** a stunner: literally! You are stopped in your tracks as the beaty of this malt first grips you, then seduces. The early spices help. Ripping into the tastebuds but immediately undoing any damage with intimate caresses of muscovado and Demerara sugars **f24** now enters in mocha territory, with a toasty sugar fade which last seemingly forever...; **b24.5** you'll be hard-pressed to find a spicier, sweeter single malt than this all year. Wat a way for this distillery to bid its farewells. A world classic. *57.9%. nc ncf sc. 206 bottles.*

◇ **Scotch Malt Whisky Society Cask 25.66 Aged 23 Years** refill hogshead, dist 14 Nov 90 **(94) n23** beautifully weighted. Old school butterscotch tart; the barley bounds along playfully with a jaunty sharpness; **t24** explosive barley again, this time backed by a crisper sugar tone than that found on the nose; **f23** thinks about bittering out but decides against it as the oak offers a more fudge-laden alternative; remains lively salivating almost to the very end – when the last minute spices take over; **b24** a truly great whisky when young, it is holding out impressively. There is life in this dead distillery still. *57.8%. sc. 157 bottles.*

◇ **Scotch Malt Whisky Society Cask 25.69 Aged 23 Years** refill barrel, dist 1 Jul 91 **(90) n22** pretty dull and conservative, though the delicate bourbon note is attractive; **t23** a busy delivery reminding me of the malt whisky made at Midleton in Ireland some decades ago. Juicy only for the first few waves, it settles into a much more even maltiness after; **f22.5** a good quality oak cask has added just the right degree of tannin to strengthen rather than rule the barley note; **b22.5** much less inclined to go the sugar or honey route you might expect but sets a course flatly amid the barley. *52.5%. sc. 35 bottles.*

ROYAL BRACKLA
Speyside, 1812. John Dewar & Sons. Working.

Royal Brackla Aged 10 Years db **(73) n18 t20 f17 b18.** A distinct lowering of the colours since I last tasted this. What on earth is going on? *40%*

Adelphi Selection Royal Brackla 16 Years Old dist 97, bott 14 **(94) n24** you feel like applauding at the near perfect marriage between grassy-fresh barley, freshly squeezed lime and the slice of kumquat which tops it off. A delicate spice prickle underlines just how fragile this fabulous nose is; **t23** as mouth-watering as the nose announces. Barley holds court and a succession of light sugars see off the rising oak; **f23.5** a little ulmo honey seeps into the proceedings, ensuring a controlled gentle sweetness to match the vanilla; **b23.5** uncommonly superb! *56.8%. ncf. 268 bottles. WB15/315*

Gordon & MacPhail Connoisseurs Choice Royal Brackla 1998 (87) n22 t22 f21.5 b21.5. A slightly more adventurous bottling than their '97 version thanks to the three-way dogfight between abrasive oak, the attractively honeyed barley and the coppery sheen at the death. *46%*.

⬦⬦ **Romantic Rhine Collection Royal Brackla** hogshead & sherry octave, cask no. 933512, dist 26 Sept 97, bott 13 Feb 12 **(92.5)** n22 t23.5 f23 b23.5. Any malt which bases its flavour profile on a mix of barley sugar, acacia honey and ulmo honey is probably going to be a winner. A slight vegetable aroma is evident, but the light sprinkling of salt and late citrus ensure there is a pulse to the very end. *55.6%. 73 bottles.*

⬦⬦ **Scotch Malt Whisky Society Cask 55.24 Aged 20 Years** 2nd fill hogshead, dist 21 Feb 94 **(94)** n24 all the notes are confident, clear and clean. It is an honourable tie between the higher hints of ulmo honey and more moody mocha; t24 a wonderful pulsing honey note maximises the clean barley; f22.5 dries, as it should after two decades, with a visit to deposits of oak which ensure a just-so degree of gravitas; intense spice lingers; **b23.5** not a single off-note: an essay in elegance. *52.7%. sc. 189 bottles.*

ROYAL LOCHNAGAR
Highlands (Eastern), 1826. Diageo. Working.

Royal Lochnagar Aged 12 Years db **(84)** n21 t22 f20 b21. More care has been taken with this than some other bottlings from this wonderful distillery. But I still can't understand why it never quite manages to get out of third gear...or is the caramel on the finish the giveaway...? *40%*

Cadenhead's Royal Lochnagar Rum Cask Aged 17 Years dist 1996, bott 13 **(89.5)** n23 ethereal and translucent, you know what you are nosing is good but it is hard to pin the tail on the donkey: crisp muscovado sugars, for certain, spices pinging around like a bat after moths – for sure. But it is earthy, too, with a slight vegetable note, like the smell of the stem of a freshly cut tulip. It is all these things...and sometimes none...; t23.5 no doubts about the delivery: a cascade of molten sugary grist with even bigger spices, at tis with the nip of a midge, directly behind; acacia honey and maple syrup sooths the pain; f21 tails off through a little cask bitterness; **b22**. little Royal Lochnager like you have never quite seen her before... *57.4%. 606 bottles. WB15/076*

Old Malt Cask Royal Lochnagar Aged 16 Years cask no. 10588, dist Aug 97, bott Jun 14 **(94)** n24 now there's a nose...! Wonderful shifting pattern of interwoven marzipan, ulmo honey, barley sugar, lemon zest, Blackjack candy and diced macadamia nuts; t23.5 the delivery is superbly executed and evolves with the same complexity as the nose, though here the oak add a controlling dryness and spice; the weight, oils and slight copper tang is sublime; f23 some barley, zesty citrus and milky mocha; **b23.5** it is some 30 years since I spotted a ring ouzel half way up a hill very near the Lochnagar distillery, the only time I have ever seen one. Unlike that elusive bird, there is nothing black and white about this. Absolutely champions its small stills by offering here a malt of regal depth and virtuosity. *50%. nc ncf sc.*

ST. MAGDALENE
Lowlands, 1798–1983. Diageo. Demolished.

Linlithgow 30 Years Old dist 1973 db **(70)** n18 t18 f16 b18. A brave but ultimately futile effort from a malt that is way past its sell-by date. *59.6%*

SCAPA
Highlands (Island–Orkney), 1885. Chivas Brothers. Working.

Scapa 12 Years Old db **(88)** n23 t22 f21 b22. Always a joy. *40%*

Scapa 14 Years Old db **(88)** n22 t22.5 f21.5 b22. Enormous variation from bottling to bottling. In Canada I have tasted one that I gave 94 to: but don't have notes or sample here. This one is a bit of dis-service due to the over-the-top caramel added which appears to douse the usual honeyed balance. Usually, this is one of the truly great malts of the Chivas empire and a classic islander. *40%*

Scapa 16 Years Old db **(81)** n21 t20.5 f19.5 b20. For it to be so tamed and toothless is a crime against a truly great whisky which, handled correctly, would be easily among the finest the world has to offer. *40%*

Scapa 'the' Orcadian 16 Years Old db **(87.5)** n22 t22 f21.5 b22. A thin wisp of honey is key to the weight and balance of this malt. *40%. For the Swiss market.*

Gordon and MacPhail Distillery Label Scapa 2001 (94.5) n23 the fresh, slightly fruity aromas of a high class bakery on first opening its doors; the barley is so, so young...but equally unblemished; **t24** the delivery is near perfect: a light oil helps spread the juiciest of salty barley notes, young and chock-a-bloc with gristy sugars; a very light, cooling mintiness to the vanilla; **f23.5** more of the same, the oils ensuring a long fade and high quality oak offering weight and keeping things on track; **b24** showing Scapa exactly as it should be. One of the easiest drinking malts currently in the market place, and quite probably the most moreish. Genius. And dangerous... *43%*

SPEYBURN
Speyside, 1897. Inver House Distillers. Working.
Speyburn 10 Year Old db (82) n20 t21 f20.5 b20.5. A tight, sharp dram with slightly more emphasis on the citric. A bit of toffee on the finale. *40%*

Speyside 12 Years Old db (85) n22 t22 f20.5 b21.5 Copious honey and malt on delivery. Simplistic, effective but a tad bitter on finish. *40%*

Speyburn Aged 25 Years db (92) n22 t24 f23 b23. Either they have re-bottled very quickly or I got the diagnosis dreadfully wrong first time round. Previously I wasn't overly impressed; now I'm taken aback by its beauty. Some change. *46%*

Speyburn Bradan Orach db (76.5) n19 t20 f19.5 b18. Fresh, young, but struggles to find a balance. *40%*

Gordon and MacPhail Connoisseurs Choice Speyburn 1989 (82.5) n21 t21.5 f20 b20. A kind of Speyside version of malt gruel. *46%. ncf.*

◇ **Gordon & MacPhail Connoisseurs Choice Speyburn 1991** (94) n23.5 unusually dense for Speyburn: excellent oak has rubbed off just enough to give some depth to the barley while crisp barley sugar adds lustre; **t23.5** gorgeously clean and salivating. The barley is beautifully defined and untainted by the years. The oak is gentle and slightly powdery. But it's the gracefulness of the light sugars – pepped by outline spice – which sets this whisky off; **f23** just a little (acceptably) tired oak buzz towards the end, but clean barley sugar persists; the slow intensifying of the spice is masterful; **b24** not a distillery you'd expect to negotiate two decades with such panache. About as enjoyable as anything I've seen from this distillery for a very long while. *46%*

◇ **Provenance Speyburn Over 8 Years** sherry butt, cask no. 10437, dist Autumn 05, bott Summer 14 (86) n20.5 t22 f21.5 b22. A little while since I've seen a Speyburn with this degree of oomph and body at any age. A much broader church for denser malt notes than it once was, while still light enough to easily take onboard the oak to ensure some genuine layering and depth to the finish, and even some intermittent honey. Impressed! *46%. nc ncf sc.*

THE SPEYSIDE DISTILLERY
Speyside, 1990. Speyside Distillers. Working.
The Speyside 10 Years Old db (81) n19 t21 f20 b21. Plenty of sharp oranges around; the malt is towering and the bite is deep. A weighty Speysider with no shortage of mouth prickle. *40%*

The Speyside Aged 12 Years db (81) n19 t22 f19.5 b20.5. Unusual to find feints to this degree after twelve years. Some short-lived honey...but it's hard work! *40%*

Spey 12 Years Old limited edition, finished in new oak casks db (85.5) n21.5 t23 f19.5 b21.5. One of the hardest whiskies I have had to define this year: it is a curious mixture of niggling faults and charming positives which come together to create a truly unique scotch. The crescendo is reached early after the delivery with an amalgamation of acacia honey, barley sugar and butter notes interlocking with something bordering classicism. However, the nose and finish, despite the chalky oak, reveals that something was lacking in the original distillate or, to be more precise, was rather more than it should have been. Still, some hard work has obviously gone into maximising the strengths of a distillery that had hitherto failed to raise the pulse and impresses for that alone. *40%. nc. 8,000 bottles.*

The Speyside Aged 15 Years db (75) n19 t20 f18 b18. A case of quantity of flavours over quality. *40%*

Spey 18 Years Old ltd edition, fresh sherry casks db (82.5) n19 t23.5 f19 b21. What a shame this malt has been brushed with sulphur. Apparent on nose and finish, it still can't diminish from the joy of the juicy grape on delivery and the excellent weight as the liquorice and treacle add their gentle treasures and pleasures. So close to a true classic. *46%. nc.*

Spey Chairman's Choice db (77) n19 t21 f18 b19. Their Chairman's Choice, maybe. But not mine... *40%*

Spey Royal Choice db (87) n21 t23 f21 b22. "I'll have the slightly feinty one, Fortescue." "Of course, Your Highness. Would that be the slightly feinty one which has a surprising softness on the palate, a bit like a moist date and walnut cake? But with a touch too much oil on the finish?" "That's the blighter! No ice, Fortescue!" "Perish the thought, Sir." Or water, Forters. One must drink according to the Murray Method, don't you know!" "Very wise, Sir." 46%

Spey Tenné finished in Tawny Port casks db **(90) n22.5** the usual Spey character, but made short work of by a crisp, boiled sweet fruitiness; **t23** softer than marshmallow, which is odd as it has a kind of mallow quality about it: creamy, sugary and melt-in-the-mouth; the cherry-grape fruits are omnipresent; **f22** long, rings out every last drop of sweetness before entering a lightly oiled, bitter phase; **b22.5** upon pouring, the handsome pink blush tells you one of three things: i) someone has swiped the whisky and filled the bottle with Matheus Rose instead; ii) I have just located where I put the pink paraffin or iii) this whisky has been matured in brand spanking new port casks. Far from a technical paragon of virtue so far as distilling is concerned. But those Tawny Port casks have brought something rather magical to the table. And glass. 46%. nc. 18,000 bottles.

Cadenhead's Small Batch Speyside-Glenlivet Aged 18 Years 1 sherry butt & 1 hogshead, dist 95, bott 14 **(95.5) n23.5** I am as bowled over as I am nonplussed: thick, juicy dates, a pinch on the nose of anthracite gas, succulent grape and Turkish delight in a high cocoa chocolate casing: this is Speyside distillery...???? **t24.5** the workings of a faultless sherry butt, entirely untroubled by brainless ruination by sulphur, allows the distillery's usual generous width of cut a free hand to add a light nougat and toasted honeycomb; **f23.5** back to the kind of dates plus Cadbury fruit and nut chocolate which makes you check your waistline after each mouthful; **b24** unquestionably the best bottle of Speyside distillery whisky I have ever encountered. Having a sublime sherry butt at work has done it no harm at all. Whatever you do, find this whisky and add to your collection. Gawd knows when you might find another like it! 62.8%. 738 bottles. WB15/262

⬦ **Distiller's Art Speyside Aged 21 Years** sherry butt, dist Oct 93, bott 2015 **(76) n21 t21 f16 b18**. Lots of sugary flavours, of course, but the oily, undesirables flood through, too, ensuring a rough finish. 48%. nc ncf sc. 150 bottles.

⬦ **Old Malt Cask Speyside 21 Years Old** sherry butt, cask no. 11404, dist Oct 93, bott Mar 15 **(88) n22.5** a thick nose, mixing intense barley and a vague fruit-sweetness; **t22.5** attractively silky with soft, safe layers of sugary vanilla before a few spices pep up the proceedings; **f21** the spices fade as a more bourbony theme is pursued; just becomes a little more chewy and "dirty" towards the finish; **b22** a pretty big whisky which, though a long way from faultless, has plenty of entertainment value. 50%. nc ncf sc. 164 bottles.

Old Particular Highland The Speyside Distillery 17 Years Old sherry butt, cask no. 10097, dist Nov 96, bott Jan 14 **(91.5) n22** an apple surprise; **t23** massively rich with the pomanian theme being stepped up and even chivvied along as the spices arrive with apple pie panache; **f23** superb oils help meld the fruits with the Demerara sugars. The spices hold firm...; **b23** so rare to find Speyside in this kind of nick. It fair warms the cockles... 48.4%.

⬦ **Old Particular Highland Speyside 18 Years Old** refill bourbon, cask no. 10441, dist Apr 96, bott Sept 14 **(94) n23.5** fruity and pithy. A lovely sheen to the barley which can still be found, but the freshness and dexterity of the fruit and gentle spice impresses above all; **t24** oh.... now that's quite wonderful...!! So juicy with spiced barley exploding all over the palate, then a wonderful display of ginger, burnt raisins, toasted fudge and Dundee cake. Magnificent...; **f23** an excellent equilibrium between the dry oak and lemon drizzled granular honey; **b23.5** one of the best samples I have tasted from Speyside distillery inside either my tasting room or blending lab. Had to look twice to ensure I had picked up the right glass: some people, including myself, will have to look at this distillery in a slightly different light if there are other casks like this through the years. 48.4%. nc ncf sc. 829 bottles.

⬦ **Villa Konthor Speyside Distillery 21 Years Old** refill cask, dist 1993, bott 2014 **(86) n23 t22.5 f19 b21.5**. Usually, I feel a little sorry for any independent bottler who lands up with a cask of this, as, for a while, Speyside's output was not always the best. Here, though, there are reasons to celebrate. At times the malty intensity hits something which borders beauty. Okay, the finish is predictably limited. But, until then, there is much to commend this bottling for. 43%

The Single Malts of Scotland Speyside 18 Years Old sherry butt, cask no. 0018, dist 02 May 95, bott 29 Oct 13 **(94) n24** sweet, intense sultana; a little ginger and pepper, too. Fabulous; **t23** thick, glutinous malt enriched by that outrageously fresh and bright sherry; **f23.5** long: sherry trifle and chocolate cup cake happily united. Oh, with an extra dollop of treacle; **b23.5** a sherry butt that hasn't been within ten miles of a sulphur candle...and just look at the spectacular results! Beautiful... 52.3%. 600 bottles. WB15/316

⬦ **Svenska Eldvatten Speyside 1994** ex bourbon hogshead, dist Nov 94, bott Sept 14 **(95) n23.5** not sure you can find oak playing a fuller yet entirely non-intrusive role: the toasty tannins outweigh barley, while there is some nip and bite to the French toast sugars; **t24** a real buzz on the initially soft delivery. Molten icing sugars meet spicy tannins head on, while the malt is in pure and concentrated form. What's more, it has taken on the first signs of exotic fruit...just delicious...; **f23.5** long with the vanilla and butterscotch in control but the barley still has much to say. The spice pulse is almost mesmerising...; **b24** what a pleasant surprise: a genuinely high quality malt from a distillery which doesn't always deliver. The exceptional oak has a lot to do with it. *55.6%. sc.*

SPRINGBANK
Campbeltown, 1828. J&A Mitchell & Co. Working.

Hazelburn Aged 8 Years bourbon cask, bott 2011 db **(94.5) n23** green apple represents the more dashing aspect of the very young barley; **t24** fabulously solid barley; intense and complete. The youth shimmers on the palate, the malt mixing contentedly with pleasing early butterscotch; elsewhere there is a real richness seemingly imparted from the stills themselves; **f23.5** confirmation of an excellent cask in use here as the lightly spiced vanilla enjoys the odd strand of honey; more light metals breaking into the lengthy barley; **b24** a very curious coppery sheen adds extra lustre and does no harm to a very well made spirit filled into top grade oak. For an eight year old malt, something extra special. *46%*

Hazelburn Aged 12 Years fresh sherrywood, bott 2012 db **(85.5) n22 t21 f21.5 b21.** At times nutty. At others, oily. And is that the vaguest hint of phenol I spot bouncing around at one stage...? But overall a malt which does not, at this juncture in its life, seem entirely at ease with either itself or the cask. Some lovely moments of lucidity but for the most part it's an interrupted work in progress. Still, this is the 666th new whisky I have tasted for the 2013 Bible, so it was likely to have a little bit of devil in it... *46%*

Hazelburn Rundlets & Kilderkins Aged 10 Years dist Nov 03, bott Jan 14 db **(95.5) n24** firm and oak-enriched there is a fascinating halfway house between light coconut cake, moistened in syrup, and walnut bread. Further sweetness is provided by a gentle orange blossom honey; **t24** the delivery is just as intense as the nose gives hope for. Except the honey is more up front than expected and arrives abreast of the spiced tannin; wonderfully dry in part, with a soft cocoa powder edge, but golden syrup returns delicately and deliciously; **f23.5** the tannins try to get a charge going but those fabulous sugars stand fast; **b24** Rundlets. Kilderkins. There's a blast from the past: a name I had seen now and then from my vast library of 19th and early 20th century literature on whisky and distilling, and only a handful of times in warehouses in nearly 40 years of distillery hopping. But here we have a malt matured in these tiny casks. And though the barrels may be small, the whisky they are responsible for really is quite huge. The kind of multi-faceted whisky I could so easily drink all day every day, if you know what I mean... *50.1%. 12,000 bottles. WB15/101*

Hazelburn Rundlets & Kilderkins Aged 11 Years dist Nov 01, bott Jan 13 db **(95.5) n23.5** dry and farm-yardy there is a lovely interplay between peat fire and byre; the sub plot is salty and citrusy but the whole ensemble is quite harsh and austere; **t24.5** hells bells! Where did that come from? Much juicier and sweeter on delivery with early spice and then more extended oak and smoke: at times borderline perfection; oils out simplifies towards the middle; **f23.5** dries again and moves towards a slightly citrusy edge; cocoa, and spicy peat account for the fade; **b24** a fascinating comparison with the Hazelburn sister bottling. Doubtless the Peat Freaks will have this down as a clear winner. But, to me, the smoke in giving so much also subtracts some of the more intricate moments found on the non-peated version, even allowing for a ten second purple patch which is as good as whisky can get. A battle which goes the full 15 rounds, but the Hazelburn, just a little lighter on its feet and with a devastating jab, wins narrowly on points. But, if you have the opportunity, grab both bottlings and compare. It will be one of the best whisky moments you'll have this year. *51.7%. nc ncf. 9,000 bottles. WB15/118*

Longrow Aged 10 Years db **(78) n19 t20 f19 b20.** This has completely bemused me: bereft not only of the usual to-die-for smoke, its warts are exposed badly, as this is way too young. Sweet and malty, perhaps, and technically better than the marks I'm giving it – but this is Longrow, dammit! I am astonished. *46%*

Longrow Aged 10 Years 100 Proof db **(86) n20 t23 f22 b21.** Still bizarrely smokeless – well, maybe a flicker of smoke as you may find the involuntary twitching of a leg of a dying fly – but the mouthfeel is much better here and although a bit too oily and dense for complexity to get going, a genuinely decent ride heading towards Hazelburn-esque barley intensity. Love it, because this oozes class. But where's the ruddy peat...?! *57%*

Longrow Red 11 Year Old Port cask db **(85.5) n21.5 t21 f22 b21.** I know some people will take a bottle of this to bed with them...to cuddle rather than drink. But, for me, this is just too astringent with a coal gas fierceness to both nose and delivery which doesn't quite sit with the fruit. Passages to enjoy, especially at the end when some kind of compromise is reached. But otherwise just too in your face. *51.8%. 9,000 bottles.*

Longrow Red Aged 11 Years Australian Shiraz Cask Peated six years in refill bourbon hogsheads & five years in fresh Shiraz casks db **(91)** **n23** an airless blockbuster: all done by smoke and shiraz; **t23** thick, almost impenetrable delivery: blackcurrant jam in a smoke chamber; **f22.5** tangy, still dense though fair dinkum honey seeps out at the end; **b22.5** strewth! No surprise that a combination of peat and shiraz has biffed out the complexity. But enough goodies to go round. Just. *53.7%. ncf. 9000 bottles. WB15/252*

Longrow 14 Years Old refill bourbon and sherry casks db **(89)** **n24 t23.5 f19 b22.5**. Again, a sherry butt proves the Achilles heel. But until then, a charmer. *46%*

Longrow Aged 18 Years (94.5) n25 my work for the day has stopped: I will not nose a better whisky today, this week, this month, this year... The playfulness, the disarmingly relaxed state of the smoke, even in the face of some pretty major tannins, is something you might regret never experiencing. The heather honey offers a slight Highland Park outlook to this, except no HP has ever been so deep, so meaningful, so absolutely perfect to nose...; **t23** the sugars dissolve on impact, some seemingly extracted from manuka honey, others from molasses. The smoke swirls around the palate, and tunnels down into the taste buds now and again, creating a light but busy spice drop; **f23** now ulmo honey stretches the sweetness as the drier elements of the oak begin to bite a tad, mixing with the peat to u the spices further...; **b23.5** if you gently peat a blend of ulmo, manuka and heather honey you might end up with something as breathtakingly stunning as this. But you probably won't... *46%. WB15/103* ⊙ ⊙

Longrow CV bott 2012 db **(91)** **n24 t24.5 f19.5 b23**. For a few moments this is heading onto the shortlist of potential Whisky Bible award winners, but a familiar furry rumble – a bit like the distant thunder currently heard from my tasting room – means vital points are lost. Even so, the nose and delivery are something very special, indeed. *46%*

Longrow Limited Edition 18 Years Old db **(82)** **n21 t22 f19 b20**. Spicy. Smoky. But a long way from its usual brilliant self. A cask, presumably a sherry one, has done it no favours at all. *46%. WB15/104*

Springbank Aged 9 Years dist Feb 04, bott Oct 13 db **(94)** **n24** a smoky Springbank? Looks like it, though the message is confused by the spiced fruit. Somewhere in the tumult Cape Gooseberry puree calls. But still surprisingly sooty; **t24.5** good grief...!!! The taste buds are impaled by the enormity of the delivery. Again we have a sooty start, but while your head is getting around that you are overwhelmed by dynamite-laced spice and a kind of concentrated apple and pear juice-barley sugar thingy. Pretty much unique and by the fifth mouthful, delicious...; **f22** bitters slightly but the rumble of spice is very noisy; **b23.5** can you have too much of a good thing? When you combine an undercooked malt like Springbank at half the age it is usually comfortable at being with the intense impact of these very fresh Barolo casks, then the onrush of flavours is almost too much. Certainly harmony takes a bit of a ding. Still, if you are looking for something different and quite memorable... and after a while confusion makes way for awe...! *54.7%. 11,000 bottles. WB15/074*

Springbank Aged 10 Years db **(89.5)** **n22 t23 f22 b22.5**. Although the inherent youthfulness of the 10-y-o has not changed, the depth of body around it has. Keeps the taste buds on full alert. *46%*

Springbank Aged 10 Years (100 Proof) db **(86)** **n21.5 t22 f21 b21.5**. Trying to map a Springbank demands all the skills required of a young 18th century British naval officer attempting to record the exact form and shape of a newly discovered land just after his sextant had fallen into the sea. There is no exact point on which you can fix...and so it is here. A shifting dram that never quite tastes the same twice, but one constant, sadly, is the bitterness towards the finale. Elsewhere, it's one hell of a journey...! *57%*

Springbank Aged 12 Years Cask Strength db **(89)** **n21.5** tangy fruit; **t24** superb delivery: rather thick; almost overwhelming, but enough mocha escapes to lighten the load; the sugar and treacle mix takes some believing; **f22** Cadbury's dairy fruit...with an injection of spice and tannin; just a little too bitter for greatness; **b22** does well to untangle itself at critical times to make for an OTT but wonderfully intense superheavyweight whisky. *50.3%. WB15/073*

Springbank Aged 12 Years Cask Strength db **(87)** **n21.5 t23.5 f21 b21**. Springbank is such an enormous whisky that for decades the 12 has usually struggled to cope with successfully making sense of all it has to offer. This is borderline going under its own weight, with so much fruit, oil and toffee-tannin to disperse on the palate. Best just to sit back and role with the delivery which offers more different types of sugar than you probably knew existed. Have a white flag at the ready, though.... *52.3%. WB15/072*

Springbank Aged 15 Years db **(88.5)** n22.5 t22 f22 b22. Last time I had one of these, sulphur spoiled the party. Not this time. But the combination of oil and caramel does detract from the complexity a little. *46%*

Springbank Aged 16 Years 10 years in refill bourbon, 6 years in fresh Madeira, cask no. 07/178-3, dist Jun 97, bott Oct 13 db **(93)** n23 liquorice laced with honeycomb; t23 an eye-watering spice attack is a dramatic contra to the gushing barley sugar; f23.5 settles into a more sober and satisfying treacle tart finish; b23.5 a superb malt which, early on, does little quietly, but is at its best when in sedate contemplation. *56%. sc ncf nc. WB15/266*

Springbank Aged 18 Years db **(90.5)** n23 busy in the wonderful Springbank way; delicate greengage and date; nippy; t23 yummy, mouthwatering barley and green banana. Fresh with excellent light acacia honey; f21.5 fabulous oak layering, including chocolate. A little off-key furriness from a sherry butt late on; b23 just one so-so butt away from bliss... *46%*

Springbank Aged 21 Years db **(90)** n22 vague, un-Springbank-like smoke adds more weight than the oak; a few berries doing the rounds; t23 silky delivery where the barley momentarily dominates then gristy malt and accompanying maple syrup goes into overdrive; the spices are compact and confident; f22.5 long, a surprising trace of tapering and very distant smoke, all enlivened by ripe gooseberries; the spice carries on growling; b22.5 a few years ago I was at Springbank when they were bottling a very dark, old-fashioned style 21-year-old. I asked if I could take a 10cl sample with me for inclusion in the Bible; they said they would send it on, though I tasted a glass there and then just for enjoyment's sake. They never did send it, which was a shame. For had they, they most probably would have carried off World Whisky of the Year. This, though very good, is not quite in the same class. But just to mark how special this brand has always been to me, I have made this the 500th new single malt scotch and 700th new whisky in all of the 2015 Whisky Bible. *46%. WB15/096*

Cadenhead's Authentic Collection Hazelburn Aged 12 Years bourbon hogshead, dist 02, bott July 14 **(89)** n23 a poke in the eye and up the nose with a tannin stick: toasted mallows and, though from a bourbon cask, a hefty degree of fruitcake, too; t22 tigerish oak claws at you while piranha-esque spice nips and nibbles; only juicy malt concentrate bathes the wounds; f22 in some ways, too oaky. But allow the butterscotch and molasses to drift across you and the minty mocha finale makes sense; b22 chunky, dense whisky with a dazzling number of oaky layers for a mere 12-year-old... *54.1%. 294 bottles. WB15/271*

◇ **Cadenhead's Authentic Collection Longrow 12 Years Old** sherry cask, dist 2002 **(65.5)** n16 t18 f15.5 b16. Just no on so many levels. The sherry butt provides a clue as to why... *53.1%*

◇ **Dà Mhìle Organic Springbank Director's Cut 23 Years Old** cask no. 233 **(91)** n22.5 salty and typically deep. The interwoven acacia honey and oil, nutty fudge forms a weighty tapestry alongside the waxed oak floors; a few citrus notes try to offer a lighter side; t23 a huge delivery: there appears to be no gaps in flavour or mouth feel, with those big oils from the wide cut thickening a chewy malt further; the oak plays it quietly at first, but soon gets into a weighty stride; the malty nuttiness is topped with molasses; f22.5 those unmistakable feints tingle. But the malt is now in its element and jousting contentedly with the vanilla-rich oak; b23 the first Da Mhile where the oak is in the driving seat. The complexity levels remain magnificently high and the road it takes is a panoramic one. *50%*

Kingsbury Gold Springbank 20 Year Old cask no. 381, dist 93 **(92)** n22.5 the oak creaks like the door to a mansion but some red liquorice and redcurrants join the vaguest hint of smoke to ensure balance; t23.5 a stunning delivery with a slow dissolving of heather honey alongside the spice: quite outstanding body; f22.5 a slow, gently spiced, butterscotch and (natural!) caramel fade; b23.5 tip your cap to understated, gentle genius. *53.6%. nc ncf sc.*

◇ **Lombard Jewels of Scotland Single Malt Springbank 1969** cask no. 15, dist 1969, bott 2014 **(90.5)** n22.5 massive oak – enough to kill most other malts from 100 paces. But lurking is an intense salty barley concentrate: not a nose for the lily-livered; t22.5 again, the oak is first to show and in force. But that barley remains firm, even inveigling some softer sugars into the fray, some of them vaguely honeyed; f23 a little mocha and malt shake; the oak has retreated, defeated, allowing the softer tones to stretch; b22.5 Springbank is one of the few distilleries on this planet to absorb this degree of tannin and still present something that delights. *40.6%. sc.*

The Maltman Springbank Aged 16 Years first fill port, cask no. 212 **(88)** n23.5 t23.5 f19.5 b21.5. A very curious malt: it's as if some iron has got into the system somehow, though the whisky is not black enough. A faulty whisky which is rather delicious. *51.2%*

The Maltman Springbank Aged 17 Years sherry cask **(88.5)** n23 t23.5 f20 b22.5. A profound malt to get sherry lovers smacking their lips. *50.1%*

Scotch Malt Whisky Society Cask 27.105 Aged 13 Years refill sherry hogshead, dist 31/03/2000 **(73.5)** n19 t20.5 f16 b18. Too young and cramped. And a butt which offers no help at all. *53.9%. Nc ncf sc. 288 bottles.*

◇◇ **Scotch Malt Whisky Society Cask 27.106 Aged 13 Years** refill hogshead, dist 30 Apr 00 **(93)** n23 a huge nose groaning under the weight of the crystalline molasses and thicker liquorice. Some kind of dull, nonspecific phenol note also contributes; sweet despite the constant rumble of the oak; t24 the sugars are confirmed on delivery: this is thick almost semi-tarry in its mouth feel, confirming the phenols evident on the nose. Chewy, with the feeling the malt has a long way to go age-wise before its begins to thin out for full complexity, though some blood orange does lighten the load slightly; f23 a light saltiness mixes well with the late buzz of spice; b23 as refill hogsheads go, this behaves like a first fill bourbon. For its age, ridiculously rich in flavour and texture and dark in colour. *50%. sc. 294 bottles.*

◇◇ **The Whisky Barrel Springbank 1996 Burns Malt 18 Years Old** cask no. 491 **(87.5)** n23.5 t22 f20.5 b21.5 Finest fruitcake on the nose and plenty of promising salt. But the palate dries a little too vigorously and almost to furriness. *56.3%.*

◇◇ **Whiskybroker Springbank 18 Years** sherry hogshead, cask no. 491, dist 18 Oct 96 **(86)** n21 t23.5 f20 b21.5. Springbank at 18 and 21 can, in the right conditions, be the best whisky in the world at any particular moment. The light sulphur buzz here means these aren't the right conditions... That said, for about seven or eight glorious seconds, the delivery gives you some idea of what is possible: the concentrated manuka honey with mocha background is quite magnificent. *56.3%. sc.*

STRATHISLA
Speyside, 1786. Chivas Brothers. Working.

Strathisla 12 Years Old db **(85.5)** n21.5 t22 f21 b21. A slight reduction in strength from the old bottling and a significant ramping up of toffee notes means this is a malt which will do little to exert your taste buds. Only a profusion of spice is able to cut through the monotonous style. Always sad to see such a lovely distillery so comprehensively gagged. *40%.*

Strathisla Distillery Edition 15 Years Old db **(94)** n23 flawlessly clean and enriched by that silky intensity of fruity malt unique to this distillery; t23 the malt is lush, sweet and every bit as intense as the nose; a touch of toffeespice does it no harm; f24 just so long and lingering, again with the malt being of extraordinary enormity: these is simply wave upon wave of pure delight; b24 what a belter! The distillery is beautiful enough to visit: to take away a bottle of this as well would just be too good to be true! *53.7%.*

◇◇ **Gordon & MacPhail Rare Vintage Strathisla 1967 (92)** n22.5 no shortage of age jabbing at you. But grape first soothes and then guides you to a softer date-like fruitiness; t23 a svelte fruitiness is momentarily bludgeoned by determined oak, including hickory, giving a double-layered attack. Finally a compromise merges the two styles, with an oily mocha as peacemaker. As those fruitcake notes gather, so do spices and even bigger cocoa; f23.5 true harmony at last: the spices are now in full flow while late manuka honey sees off any last oaky uprising; b23 holds up beautifully for its antiquity. Perhaps more equally confrontational than truly balanced, but class tells in the end for the experience is charming. *43%*

Gordon & MacPhail Strathisla 1999 bott 2013 **(83.5)** n22 t21 f20 b20.5. Odd that a bottling which for many years you could showcase as a "that's the way to do it" malt has been off the boil for a while now. There is a charming honey-pollen element to the nose, but beyond that balance is at a premium as the cask types clash. *43%. WB15/109*

STRATHMILL
Speyside, 1891. Diageo. Working.

Cadenhead's Authentic Collection Cask Strength Strathmill Aged 18 Years bourbon hogshead, dist 1995, bott Feb 14 **(87.5)** n22 t23 f21 b21.5. Crusty barley offers good gristiness and ultra juiciness. Lovely malt, as you'd expect from Strathmill, with excellent spice kick, too. But the oak tires slightly injects a late bitterness. Just revere the delivery, though! *54.4%. WB15/080*

◇◇ **Crom Strathmill 26 Years Old The Angry Moon** refill bourbon barrels, refill sherry butt finish, dist Mar 88, bott Mar 14 **(92)** n23.5 it's all there: salty butter on toast, Zambian honey, raisin-infested fudge, marzipan...and so much more. Not entirely flawless...but wow! t24 the beauty and completeness of the weight could bring a tear to the eye: the malty fudge melts on the palate, though not before forming an enormously rich bank of flavours and textures; f21 Okay, not entirely free from sulphur...but it is pretty low key and takes a while to rumble through. By then you will have become acquainted with the light heather honey and sherry trifle; b23.5 when you read refill sherry finish, you cannot help but fear the worst. But make no mistake: this is a belter from this massively underrated distillery. *50.4%. sc.*

Gordon & MacPhail Connoisseurs Choice Strathmill 1999 bott 2013 **(94.5) n23.5** slowly roasting yams, a splodge of custard and a quite a few half-hearted bourbon notes, especially the diluted molasses; **t24** soft delivery, with the light, malty oils rolling over the palate on a cushion of light maple syrup; delicate shades of mandarin and Jammy Dodger biscuits; **f23** superb oak means there is no bitterness, allowing the vanillas and sugars to continue the friendly glide towards the fade; **b24** there is no substitute for good old-fashioned simple complexity...if you know what I mean...! 46%. nc ncf. WB15/147

Gordon & MacPhail Connoisseurs Choice Strathmill 2000 (89) n22 grassy barley; **t22.5** fresh, concentrated barley juice; gristy with a twist of citrus; **f22** a simple play out of sugar barley and butterscotch; **b22.5** un-taxing but the kind of clean, intense barley-rich malt any blender worth his salt would be licking his lips at...46%.

◈ **Gordon & MacPhail Connoisseurs Choice Strathmill 2002 (95) n23.5** playful and fleeting malt spars with the green toffee apple and delicate spice; **t24.5** a fabulously intricate delivery: as though all the atoms have not quite made molecules and tiny, buzzing flavour capsules dust the palate... the barley causes maximum salivation while the sugars grow in to delicate acacia honey modules; soft vanillas and more sawdusty oak tones ensure balance; **f23** a little taste oil helps further the spice and eek out the sugars; **b24** this is just how Speyside should do complexity. Simply and irresistibly brilliant! 46%

Old Malt Cask Strathmill Aged 21 Years refill hogshead, cask no. 10122, dist Dec 91, bott Oct 13 **(91) n22** plenty of Kentucky at work here with the liquorice and hickory giving depth to the vanilla. The barley is not outdone, though...; **t23** the oak yoke is discarded on delivery and the barley is at full blast; **f23** just adore those gristy sugars which have somehow survived all these years; some lemon to the late vanilla; **b23** simple, but so elegant with it! 50%.

◈ **Old Malt Cask Strathmill 25 Years Old** refill butt, cask no. 10978, dist Oct 89, bott Oct 14 **(95) n24.5** a 15 minute nose: take as much time as you can with this. This is Speyside elegance at its most deft and adroit. Many of the nose elements can be found in a high class chocolate box, especially one that has cherries, nougat, caramel and Danish marzipan. The only thing missing is cocoa, but the ulmo honey compensates...; **t23.5** melt-in-the-mouth malt. Though from a single cask, there is a fascinating structure tied to this, as some of the barley elements seem pretty young, while others, especially those tied up with the oak, are much nearer their age; the spice buzz is at almost perfect pitch; **f23** gentle oak forages around the palate, seemingly finding a fair bit of salt. The sugars remain shy but on hand when needed; **b24** such a classy act! 50%. nc ncf sc. 468 bottles.

◈ **Old Particular Speyside Strathmill 21 Years Old** refill hogshead, cask no. 10585, dist Jan 93, bott Dec 14 **(91) 22.5** fascinating mix between seasoned, mildly bourbon-style sweetness and new make barley; **t22.5** an explosive launch: a real bit of nibble and bite to the barley, followed by spiced lime and pineapple; **f23** the oak begins to make sense of the darker, muscovado sugars while the barley reasserts itself late on; **b23** a distillery which does excellence and balance effortlessly. As it shows. 51.5%. nc ncf sc. 320 bottles.

Robert Graham Strathmill 22 Year Old Speyside Malt hogshead, cask no. 3795, dist 09 Sep 91 bott Oct 2013 **(82.5) n20 t22 f20 b20.5.** Strathmill is a wilting flower of a malt which bruises easily. When kept for this number of years, the cask has to be spot on. The oak here makes too many of its flaws apparent to be a force for good. 46%. 232 bottles.

Single Cask Collection 23 Year Old Strathmill Sherry Butt sherry butt, cask no. 2258, dist 07 May 90, bott 04 Jul 13 **(96) n24.5** elegant dry sherry, entirely free from both sulphur or oloroso weightiness; beautiful nuttiness, the only sweetness maybe from some top notch Lubek marzipan; a real gem of a nose which takes me back to a previous distilling era in Scotland; **t23.5** the delivery is both firm yet somehow rounded with the grape again nothing other than sophistication. The weight is in keeping with the dexterity of the malt, which somehow allows the juicier elements of the barley through while keeping them under control with a crisp fruitiness; spice begins to pulse, though in a typically understated style; **f23.5** rounding off one of the casks of the year is a dull, throbbing spice meeting perfectly the covert sweetness and drying vanillas; **b24.5** in the Spring of 1990, J&B blender Jim Milne and I nosed some sherry butts just prior to them being filled at Strathmill. They were clean and fresh, like this one. I wonder... 51.3%. sc. 470 bottles.

That Boutique-y Whisky Strathmill batch 1 **(86.5) n21.5 t22.5 f21 b21.5.** Not a Strathmill style I am particularly familiar with (and I'd thought I'd seen the lot!): beyond the intense barley, there is, on the nose especially, a drier, vegetable note. It's not unpleasant. But just seems out of place. Still, deliciously juicy and malty in part. 48.2%. 167 bottles. WB15/206

The Whisky Agency Strathmill 1976 dist 1976 **(95) n23.5** the oak throbs gently, offering a nutty – and sometimes coconutty – depth, lightened by seemingly being dipped into maple syrup. Elsewhere a little malt and vaguest of smoky notes stirs...; **t24.5** a ridiculously sweet and caressing delivery with no effort to make any kind of oaky statement or claim. Again the coconut has a big say, still serenaded by delicate sugars; the spices are at the vanguard of the symphony and remain, though in lesser intensity, throughout; **f23** the dryness which slowly assembles is in perfect keeping with the delicate sugars. But the ace is the light puff of smoke which offers just the right amount of lingering ballast; **b24** this was the year my beloved Millwall, helped in no small part by my dear old friends Barry Kitchener and John Seasman, completed a run of 15 unbeaten games – and conceding only four goals in the process - to somehow claw promotion back to the second tier from the mid-table invisibility. Later that year we walloped Chelsea 3-0, with my dad standing proudly beside me as another great mate, Terry Brisley, sent the most lethal of all bullet headers past Peter Bonetti to complete the route. It was also the year when I played a game of cricket in which I could hardly see the ball bowled at me through a blizzard of ladybirds during a blistering heat wave that rendered England's green and pleasant land brown. And it was, above all, the year an unassuming Speyside distillery filled into cask a malt destined for a blend at four years old, most probably J&B, yet somehow – against every odd possible - lived on into antiquity with charming good grace. 47%.

TALISKER

Highlands (Island–Skye), 1832. Diageo. Working.

Talisker Aged 10 Years db (93) **n23** Cumberland sausage and kipper side by side; **t23** early wisps of smoke that develop into something a little spicier; lively barley that feels a little oak-dried but sweetens out wonderfully; **f24** still not at full throttle with the signature ka-boom spice, but never less than enlivening. Some wonderful chocolate adds to the smoke; **b23** the deadening caramel that had crept into recent bottlings of the 10-y-o has retreated, and although that extraordinary, that wholly unique finale has still to be re-found in its unblemished, explosive entirety, this is much, much closer to the mark and a quite stupendous malt to be enjoyed at any time. But at night especially. 45.8%

Talisker 12 Years Old Friends of the Classic Malts db (86) **n22 t21.5 f21 b21.5**. Decent, sweet, lightly smoked...but the explosion which made this distillery unique - the old kerpow! - appears kaput. 45.8%

Talisker Aged 14 Years The Distillers Edition Jerez Amoroso cask, dist 1993, bott 2007 db (90.5) **n23 t23 f22 b22.5**. Certainly on the nose, one of the more old-fashioned peppery Taliskers I've come across for a while. Still I mourn the loss of the nuclear effect it once had, but the sheer quality of this compensates. 45.8%

Talisker Aged 20 Years db (95) **n24 t24 f23 b24.** I have been tasting Talisker for 28 years. This is the best bottling ever. Miss this and your life will be incomplete. 62%

Talisker 25 Years Old db (88) **n22.5 t22 f21.5 b22.** Pretty taken aback by this one: it has taken a fancy to being a bit of a Bowmore, complete with a bountiful supply of Fisherman's Friends. 45.8%

Talisker 25 Years Old db (88.5) **n23 t22 f21.5 b22.** Another Talisker almost choked with natural caramels. Chewy and undoubtedly charming. 54.8%

Talisker 25 Years Old db (92) **n23.5 t24 f22.5 b22.5**. Fabulous stuff, even though the finish in particular is strangely well behaved. 58.1%

Talisker 30 Years Old db (93.5) **n23** complex and slightly bitty, lemon-lightened phenols, sitting comfortably atop a pile of buttery egg custard tart. A lot sexier than it sounds...! **t24** the citrus leads the way here, too. It helps intensify the juiciness of the barley, though a countering liquorice and crunchy Demerara sugar sweetness amplifies the age. The smoke is restrained though not beyond offering a spice throb; **f23** just a few shuddering oaky passes, but the smoke, sugar, spice and even a little salted butter ensure the fade is long and satisfying; **b23.5** much fresher and more infinitely entertaining than the 25 year old...!!! 45.8%

Talisker 30 Years Old db (84.5) **n21 t21.5 f21 b21.** Toffee-rich and pretty one dimensional. Did I ever expect to say that about a Talisker at 30...? 53.1%

Talisker 1977 Special Release 2012 American and European oak refill casks, bott 2012 db (86.5) **n22 t21 f22.5 b21** Distilled just two years after I first visited the distillery, I remember being told that they bottled their whisky at 8-years-old as they felt it was the optimum age of the maturing malt. The manager pointed to some very old casks in a warehouse there but said they were for blending, as it tastes better that way rather than as a singleton. Interesting to hear those works echo around my head now. Certainly this is a malt of character, but over the time the majority of the peat has vanished and huge oak has taken its place. The highlight is somewhere near the end, when the sugars have at last come to terms with the tannins and a gorgeous, vaguely smoky mocha theme strikes up. 54.6%. nc ncf.

Talisker 57 Degrees North db (95) **n24** salty, smoky, coastal, breezy. The distillery's location in a nose... **t24.5** peat encased in a muscovado sugar, in the same way as a fly might be enveloped in amber, melts to allow the slow blossoming of a quite beautiful and peaty thing...; **f23** some welcome whip and bite; the smoke and vanillas hang in there and even the odd hint of mocha puffs around a bit; **b23.5** a glowing tribute, I hope, for a glowing whisky... 57%

Talisker Dark Storm charred oak db **(92) n22** some pretty chunky peat and spice is blown around the glass, certainly big enough to take the muscovado sugars and red liquorice head on...; **t23.5** the sugars on the nose appear to multiply on delivery, as does the bourbon-style tannin-led liquorice and hickory. The smoke takes a bit of time to get back into the game, as if hiding behind the sofa until safe to come out again but mildly reasserts itself; **f23** even the sugars buckle under the oaky strain. But all is fresh and balanced enough to come good, even with some very late spices; **b23.5** much more like it! Unlike the Storm, which appeared to labour under some indifferent American oak, this is just brimming with vitality and purpose. 45.8%.

Talisker Port Ruighe db **(88) n22 t22 f22 b22.** Sails into port without changing course 45.8%.

⬧ **Talisker Skye (85) n21 t22 f21 b21.** The sweetest, most docile Talisker I can ever remember with the spices working hard in the background but weirdly shackled. More Toffee Sky than Vanilla... 45.8% WB16/051

Talisker Storm db **(85.5) n20 t23 f21 b21.5** The nose didn't exactly go down a storm in my tasting room. There are some deft seashore touches, but the odd poor cask –evident on the finish, also - has undone the good. But it does recover on the palate early on with an even, undemanding and attractively sweet display showing malt to a higher degree than I have seen any Talksker before. 45.8%.

Hepburn's Choice Talisker Aged 6 Years refill hogshead, dist 08, bott 14 **(92.5) n22.5** a little tame compared to days of yore with the smoke noticeable by its half-heartedness with the emphasis now on vanilla and butterscotch; **t23.5** certainly a bite on delivery. But where a decade or two ago those spices would have roared into your throat, rendering you speechless for a minute or two, now they buzz with intent. Malty, juicily so, with a lovely muscovado sugar backdrop; **f23** at last the smoke builds enough to register but, ironically softens as it does so; cocoa and smoke fill the last moments; **b23.5** sadly, I am one of those long enough in the tooth to remember the only Talisker you could find was an 8-year-old distillery bottling (unless you were lucky enough to happen upon a Gordon and MacPhail 1950s vintage). So seeing this at such a seemingly young age in bottled form is nothing new. But it also confirms that the peat from this distillery is nowhere near as telling as it once was. All that said, still a very classy act. 46%. nc ncf sc. 410 bottles.

⬧ **Hepburn's Choice Talisker Aged 6 Years** refill hogshead, dist 2008, bott 2014 **(88.5) n23** quite fabulous: youthful with a dusting of cocoa on the amplified smoke; **t21.5** thin beginnings and sugar dependent; fattens up towards the middle ground but cannot shake off its youth; the smoke is pretty much unobstructed; **f22** smoky and a tad oily. But little sign of any oak; a lighter than normal spice rumble; **b22** the minimal oak determines the intensity of the peat. 46%. nc ncf sc. 362 bottles.

⬧ **Hepburn's Choice Talisker Aged 6 Years** refill hogshead, dist 2008, bott 2015 **(91) n22.5** very lightly grilled kippers; **t23** chunkier and more honey-compacted than other Taliskers I have tasted of late: gently smoked ulmo honey is something to celebrate; **f22.5** lightens further as the vanilla and spices arrive; **b23** young, gently done and all delightfully charming. 46%. nc ncf sc. 483 bottles.

⬧ **Kingsbury Gold Talisker 5 Year Old 2008** bourbon cask, cask no. 10264 **(80.5) n20 t21.5 f19 b20.** Malty, salivating, sparsely peated and thin. And at a point in its development where balance has been lost. 594%. 287 bottles.

⬧ **Premier Barrel Selection Talisker Aged 5 Years (87) n23 t22 f22 b22.** Attractive light citrus dovetails amiably with the smoke. That's the nose. The palate is not quite so well charmed by the youthful, lightweight, gristy-sweet but undercooked palate. 46%. nc ncf sc. 463 bottles.

⬧ **Provenance Talisker Over 6 Years** refill hogshead, cask no. 10699, dist winter 08, bott spring 15 **(94.5) n24** surprisingly high phenols on the gorgeously gristy malt; **t23.5** lightly oiled and heavily sugared, there is even an irresistible spoonful of ulmo honey to counter the surprisingly thick smoke; **f23.5** the spices arrive later on the spirit than it once did, and with slightly less intensity. But they are here to impress and lengthen the already long finish. The sugars, however, just keep on striding...; **b23.5** Talisker was traditionally a malt bottled young – usually at 8-years-old - and it stands its ground here with so little effort it borders arrogance. Even taking into account its youth, the phenol levels appear higher than normal. Unquestionably a gem of a bottling. 46%. nc ncf sc.

Provenance Talisker Young & Feisty refill hogshead, cask no. 10227 & 10229, bott Spring 14 **(87) n22 t22.5 f21 b21.5.** Should actually be called Young, Sweet, Smoky and slightly Fiesty... 46%.

TAMDHU
Speyside, 1897. Ian Macleod Distillers. Working (re-opened 3rd March 2013).

Tamdhu db **(84.5)** n20 t22.5 f21 b21. So-so nose, but there is no disputing the fabulous, stylistic honey on delivery. The silkiest Speyside delivery of them all. *40%*

Tamdhu Aged 10 Years oak sherry cask db **(69.5)** n17 t18.5 f17 b17. A much better malt when they stick exclusively to ex-bourbon casks, as used to be the case. *40%*

Tamdhu Aged 18 Years bott code L0602G L12 20/08 db **(74.5)** n19 t19 f18 b18.5. Bitterly disappointing. Literally. *43%*

Tamdhu 25 Years Old db **(88)** n22 t22 f21 b23. Radiates quality. *43%*

◇ **Tamdhu Batch Strength** db **(80)** n19.5 t21.5 f19 b20. A chunky bruiser of a dram. What it misses in sophistication, it makes up for with a brooding sugary, spicy oomph... *58.8%*

Cadenhead's Tamdhu-Glenlivet Port Cask Aged 22 Years dist 1991, bott Feb 2014 **(95.5)** n24 lively, gripping, fruity, perky, fresh, clean and about as clear in its Port signals as any whisky you'll find; t24.5 a fabulous delivery, ripping into your taste buds with determination and clarity of purpose which fair – and literally – takes the breath away. The spices are extraordinary, as they are profound, bite in throat like a great whisky of yesteryear, but never uncouth or over dominating. However, it is the early sugar-grape mix on delivery which, for a few moments, offers one of the great whisky experiences of the year; f23 much more oak oriented, so a big chunk of cocoa compliments rather well; b24 can't remember the last time I tasted a Tamdhu this stunningly dressed up and with so many places to go. A belter! *57%. 258 bottles. WB15/081*

Cadenhead's Small Batch Tamdhu-Glenlivet Aged 22 Years bourbon hogsheads, dist 91, bott 14 **(87.5)** n21.5 t22.5 f22 b21.5. Hangs its very large hat on punchy sugars, but complexity is lost to the big toffee-coffee element. Pleasant, chewy and one for those who have a sweet tooth while liking a bit of bite to their dram. *56%. 522 bottles. WB15/264*

◇ **Glen Fahrn Airline Nr 08 Tamdhu 1984 Aged 28 Years** cask no. 2832 **(89)** n22 t23 f22 b22. Charming and fruit-edged from age as the oak offers its most exotic notes. Silky and sensuous, the obvious limitations of the distillate is overcome by the magnificence of the cask. *56.2%. sc. 132 bottles.*

Hepburn's Choice Tamdhu 2005 Aged 8 Years refill hogshead, dist 05, bott 14 **(80)** n20 t21 f19 b20. As young whiskies mature, they tend to peak and trough. This is not peaking. The sweaty armpit nose is interesting... *46%. nc ncf sc. 381 bottles.*

The Macphail's Collection from Tamdhu 1971 (91.5) n22 Nice coconut biscuits dunked in weakish milky tea, but gripping on for dear life against the oaky scars; some citrus does offer some alleviation; t23 now that is classy! Somehow the oils have survived the last 40-odd years to smear citrus-tinged maple syrup all over the palate. Astonishing...; f23 not a single hint of bitterness or over indulgent oak. Just more vanilla and citrus...and ths delicate sugars, of course; b23.5 must admit: been a little let down by some of the older whiskies this year. But this unassuming guy has stepped u to the plate and done Speyside proud. *43%.*

◇ **Old Malt Cask Tamdhu 16 Years Old** refill hogshead, cask no. 10923, dist Mar 98, bott Oct 14 **(77)** n19 t20 f19 b19 . Just the thing for those who like a bit of malty rough... *50%. nc ncf sc. 279 bottles.*

Old Malt Cask Tamdhu Aged 23 Years refill hogshead, cask no. 10585, dist May 91, bott Jun 14 **(90)** n22.5 apples. With a hint of apples, with a heavy apple undercurrent, lightened slightly with...apples...; t23 ....juicy....ummmm...apples? f22.5 the oak arrives to offer some lovely crusty late notes...apple pie...? b22 cor(e)! Not dissimilar to some whiskies I have seen matured in cider brandy warehouses. Must leave some of this out for the great spotted woodpecker in my garden. *50%. nc ncf sc. 215 bottles.*

◇ **Old Particular Speyside Tamdhu 16 Years Old** refill hogshead, cask no. 10360, dist Jun 98, bott Jun 14 **(87.5)** n21.5 t22 f22 b22. Set up as a blending malt, there is no second guessing the game plan to make this a big malt player. Well made, decently matured, if a little young for its years. No shortage of vanilla, though. *48.4%. nc ncf sc. 324 bottles.*

◇ **Old Particular Speyside Tamdhu 16 Years Old** refill hogshead, cask no. 10452, dist Jun 98, bott Aug 14 **(88.5)** n22 clean barley with a teasing honey edge; t23 about as lively a malt you'll find from this distillery: the grassy malt has real grit and bite; attractively salivating; f21.5 the delicate oak quietens the barley; b22 what a playful, elegant little dram. *48.4%. nc ncf sc. 291 bottles.*

Provenance Tamdhu Over 8 Years refill hogshead, cask no. 10293, dist Summer 05, bott Spring 2013 **(87.5)** n22 t22.5 f21 b22. Spiffing stuff, chaps. A deliciously juicy, malty ball bowled directly on the middle stump but with too little deviation to cause the taste buds any trouble. *46%. nc ncf sc.*

◇◇◇ **Provenance Tamdhu Over 8 Years** refill hogshead, cask no. 10570, dist autumn 06, bott autumn 14 **(87) n22 t22 f21.5 b21.5**. A slight whisky it may be, but the maltiness is attractive and pretty well held together by the uncluttered oak. Lovely lemon-honey backdrop. *46%. nc ncf sc.*

Speyside Single Malt Tamdhu Aged 25 Years sherry butt, cask no. 10297, dist Sep 88, bott Mar 14 **(68.5) n18 t19 f15 b16.5**. A sherry butt from a distillery once owned by Highland Distillers. You don't have to be Sherlock Holmes to work out what has gone wrong here... *50.1%. sc. 288 bottles.*

◇◇◇ **Whisky-Fässle Tamdhu 25 Year Old** hogshead, dist 1988, bott 2013 **(92.5) n22.5 t24 f22 b22**. This distillery often made ordinary whisky. But when it got it right, as here, few malts can be so spectacularly barley rich. It is as if the stills are paying homage to the distillery's maltings.... *50.7%. nc ncf.*

◇◇◇ **Whiskyjace Tamdhu 20 Year Old** bourbon hogshead, dist 1991, bott 2011 **(94.5) n24** I could nose that all day: the malt – produced on site – really does have massive dignity and presence. The complexity is enormous, with various boiled candy aromas on show, rhubarb, cinnamon and cough sweets. Light ulmo honey thickens it up; **t23.5** all kinds of spices on delivery. But entirely in harmony with the intense, juicy and brittle barley; **f23** long, still peppery and juicy to the very end; **b24** for a distillery which doesn't enjoy the best of reputations, this sticks two fingers up to its detractors...myself included. Superb! *50.5%*

TAMNAVULIN
Speyside. 1966. Whyte and Mackay. Working.
Tamnavulin 1966 Aged 35 Years cream sherry butt db **(91) n24 t22 f23 b22**. For those who love great old sherry, this is an absolute. Perhaps too much sherry to ever make it a true great, but there is no denying such quality. *52.6%*

Cadenhead's Small Batch Tamnavulin-Glenlivet Aged 22 Years bourbon hogsheads, dist 1992, bott 2014 **(85) n21.5 t22 f20.5 b21**. Very good malt in part but a distinct feel of sugared porridge, too. The oak has obvious limitations, though the metallic feel to the Crunchie bar candy is rather attractive. *52.9%. 432 bottles. WB15/263*

Directors' Cut Tamnavulin Aged 25 Years refill hogshead, cask no. 10352, dist May 89, bott Jun 14 **(90.5) n22** a puff of smoke sweetens the minty tannin; **t22.5** silky again, with a light smokiness softening the oak; **f23** Love Heart candy adds a slightly sweet fizz to the coffee-hued vanilla. Still that vague smokiness persists, aided now by a late but busy spice; **b23** a delightful dram where lots of little things make a much bigger whole. Satisfying. *48.8%. nc ncf sc. 78 bottles.*

◇◇◇ **Old Malt Cask Tamnavulin Aged 21 Years** refill butt, cask no. 11150, dist Dec 93, bott Dec 14 **(86.5) n21 t21.5 f22 b22**. Exceptionally malty, with an excellent spice build, though the oak is shy for the age. *50%. nc ncf sc. 318 bottles.*

The Single Malts of Scotland Tamnavulin 21 Years Old hogshead, cask no. 5849, dist 06 Dec 91, bott 14 Sep 13 **(85) n22.5 t21.5 f20 b21**. Promises much on the nose with its surprisingly fresh maltiness. But after rubbing your hands for what is to come next, the palate is met by a juicy delivery, then an uncompromising cask tang. *48.2%. 328 bottles. WB15/340*

TEANINICH
Highlands (Northern), 1817. Diageo. Working.
Gordon & MacPhail Connoisseurs Choice Teaninich 2006 (86.5) n22 t22 f21 b21.5. Sugary and unsophisticated, has all the bells and whistles required for a very decent blending malt, though one from a decent cask. Lots of spice and busyness, though thins out a little too quickly. *46%.*

Highland Single Malt Teaninich Aged 40 Years refill hogshead, cask no. 10234, dist Dec 73, bott Mar 14 **(91) n23** has the brooding, quasi creosote quality of a whisky which has seen a dozen summers too many. But a dense, liquorice-crusted Demerara tarriness appears to offer balance...and hope...; **t21** sugary, but yep...too oaky...; **f24** the most extraordinary thing: after a bout of semi-excrutiating tannin, it suddenly relaxes and bursts out into a series of chocolate fruit creams in the style of Quality Street or Roses, the orange centres in particular; **b22** the whisky which came back from the dead. *48.9%. sc. 156 bottles.*

Old Particular Highland Teaninich 30 Years Old refill hogshead, cask no. 9900, dist Dec 82, Bott Aug 13 **(95.5) n24** gosh! A malt which stops you in your tracks: three styles of whisk(e)y are all in evidence here – single malt, Irish pot still and bourbon. Just love the glorious cumquat and peat topping; **t24** spectacular weight to this. Light oils fill the mouth and allow a spiced maltyness to infiltrate the layered, intense yet charming oak, all the while a playful smokiness cranking up the weight; some sublime hickory and maple syrup champions the late middle ground; **f23** dries as rich chocolate builds; **b24.5** some people in the industry give this distillery a bit of a hard time. A couple of mouthfuls of this will makes them understand why, 30 years ago, I rated this distillery so highly. Magnificent! *49.3%. nc ncf sc. 198 bottles. Douglas Laing & Co.*

Scotch Malt Whisky Society Cask 59.48 Aged 30 Years refill hogshead, dist 08 Nov 83 **(90) n23** the exotic fruit draws attention to the 30-plus years in the cask; **t22.5** impressive fruit – including pears and rhubarb – compliments the buttery vanilla; **f22** thinks about over-drying but enough sugars hang on; **b22.5** a malt at the end of its age range but enjoys this last hurrah of excellence. *51.3%. nc ncf sc. 158 bottles.*

◈ **Scotch Malt Whisky Society Cask 59.49 Aged 30 Years** refill hogshead, dist 08 Nov 83 **(87) n22 t22 f21.5 b21.5.** A very similar animal to 59.48, except here the oak has gained just too austere a control of matters with a resulting decrease in complexity and balance, despite the best efforts of the esters. Enjoyable as a pre-prandial moment, though. *49.3%. nc ncf sc.*

◈ **Scotch Malt Whisky Society Cask 59.51 Aged 30 Years** refill hogshead, dist 8 Nov 83 **(84.5) n21.5 t22 f20 b21.** No shortage of character. And one with some witty lines written for it. But this is about as outrageously salivating and eye-watering as you can find without really offering any depth or complexity. A tart blending malt essentially. But one which has its moments in the spotlight. *51.5%. sc. 140 bottles.*

◈ **World of Orchids Teaninich 2007 7 Year Old** bourbon cask, cask no. 456 **(96) n23.5** there are so many deep tannin notes dancing around that you feel almost hypnotised. Presumably a little-used first fill or even virgin cask at work here: the bourbon tones outnumber the malt ones....; **t24.5** inevitably a string of tannin-thickened sugars arrives first, soon joined by oilier, concentrated malts. Begins with muscovado before moving on to maple syrup then a touch of spiced treacle; **f24** long, meandering spices, toasty butterscotch, then, to top it all, moves into a coffee cake mode...; **b24** the kind of beauty which leaves you almost speechless. This youngster was matured in one of the best casks in Scotland... *59.7%. sc. 300 bottles.*

TOBERMORY

Highlands (Island–Mull), 1795. Burn Stewart Distillers. Working.

Ledaig Aged 10 Years db **(85.5) n20 t22.5 f21.5 b21.5.** Almost a Bowmore in disguise, such are its distinctive cough sweet qualities. Massive peat: easily one of the highest phenol Ledaigs of all time. But, as usual, a slight hiccup on the technical front. Hard work not to enjoy it, though. *46.3%. nc ncf.*

Ledaig Aged 10 Years db **(63) n14 t17 f15 b17.** What the hell is going on? Butyric and peat in a ghoulish harmony on nose and palate that is not for the squeamish. *43%*

Ledaig Aged 12 Years db **(90) n23** serious farmyard aromas – and as someone who spent three years living on one, believe me...borderline butyric, but somehow gets away with it, or at least turns it to an advantage; **t23.5** the staggering peat on the nose is no less remarkable here: chunky, clunking, entirely lacking poise and posture. And it obviously doesn't give a damn...; **f21.5** strange gin-type juniper amid the smoke; **b22** it has ever been known that there is the finest of lines between genius and madness. A side-by-side comparison of the Ledaig 10 and 12 will probably be one of whisky's best examples of this of all time... *43%*

◈ **Ledaig Dùsgadh 42 Aged 42 Years** db **(96) n25** perfection: the peat – once fierce and unfettered – is now restrained and purring in aged contentment. The moist fruitcake must have a Dundee connection as nuts abound. Spices are muted, the molassed sugars thick and inert. We have found an idyllic whisky spot...; **t24.5** you expect the gentlest of deliveries – and you are not disappointed. The oak has stirred like a deaf old uncle shouting above the rest, unaware of the disruption caused, but is mollified and shushed by a thin comforting blanket of peat, supported by some juicy sugars; **f22.5** bitters slightly towards the finish, but compensated by busy spices which rise as all else fades; **b24** it has to be about 30 years ago I tasted my first-ever Ledaig – as a 12 year old peated malt. This must be from the same stocks, only this has been housed in exceptional casks. Who would have thought, three decades on, that it would turn into some of the best malt bottled in a very long time. A smoky experience unlikely to be forgotten. *46.3%*

Tobermory Aged 10 Years db **(67.5) n16 t17 f17.5 b17.** A less than brilliantly made malt totally bereft of character or charm. I have no idea what has happened here. I must investigate. Frankly, I'm gutted. *40%*

Tobermory 10 Years Old db **(73.5) n17.5 t19 f18 b19.** The last time I tasted an official Tobermory 10 for the Bible, I was aghast with what I found. So I prodded this sample I had before me of the new 46.3% version with all the confidence Wile E Coyote might have with a failed stick of Acme dynamite. No explosions in the glass or on my palate to report. And

201

though this is still a long way short, and I'm talking light years here, of the technical excellence of the old days, the uncomplicated sweet maltiness has a very basic charm. The nose and finish, though, are still very hard going. 46.3%

Tobermory Aged 10 Years db (85) n20 t22.5 f21 b21.5 Bracing, nutty and malty the oils perhaps overdo it a little but there are enough sugars on hand to steer this one home for an enjoyable experience overall. 46.3%. nc ncf.

Tobermory Aged 15 Years db (93) n23.5 dripping with fresh, clean, ultra high quality oloroso there remains enough tangy malt to underscore the island location; t23.5 a fabulous marriage of juicy grape and thick, uncompromising malt. It is an arm wrestle for supremacy between the two...but it is the delicate spices which win; f23 salty chocolate raisin; b23 a tang to the oils on both nose and finish suggests an over widened middle. But such is the quality of the sherry butts and the intensity of the salt-stained malt, all is forgiven. 46.3%. nc ncf.

Tobermory Aged 15 Years Limited Edition db (72.5) n17 t18 f19 b18.5. Another poorly made whisky: the nose and delivery tells you all you need to know. 46.3%

⬥ **Alexander Murray & Co Tobermory 1994 19 Years Old** (78) n19 t19 f20 b20. Poorly made malt. Not even a few slabs of fudge can save it. 40%

Best Dram Ledaig 9 Years Old bourbon barrel, dist 05, bott 14 (89) n22.5 unsophisticated, pile-it-high peat; youthful gristiness lurks at every corner; t22 yet even bigger peat than the nose, though that seems hardly possible; the sugars take a while to register; f22.5 dry, ultimately spicy; b22 one of the most heavily peated Ledaigs I've found in a while, though younger than its years. 52.2%. ncf. 182 bottles.

Cadenhead's Sherry Cask Tobermory Aged 19 Years sherrywood, dist 95, bott July 14 (67) n15 t20 f16 b16. Riddled with sulphur. 54.2%. 498 bottles. WB15/268

⬥ **Cadenhead's Small Batch Ledaig Aged 21 Years** bourbon cask, dist 1992 (78.5) n19 t21 f19 b19.5. Intensely malty, threateningly sugary, barely smoky and, alas, distilled to a pretty mediocre standard. 53.6%

Càrn Mòr Strictly Limited Edition Ledaig Aged 7 Years hogshead, dist 2005, bott 2013 (89) n22.5 a citrusy smokiness which never shakes off its youth but the peat intensifies; t22.5 lightly oiled, rather beautifully made ad still offering major citrus notes on the juicy malt; f22 thins slightly, but the smoke remains intact and quietly delicious, having sweetened slightly; b22 oh, for the promise of youth... So lovely to for once see this malt uncluttered by oak. 46%. nc ncf. 785 bottles. WB15/155

The Coopers Choice Ledaig 2005 Aged 8 Years hogshead, cask no. 0062, bott 2014 (91.5) n23 sharp, pungest, acidic, rather acrid peak reek....love it! t23 softer on delivery than nose thanks to a big oil surge. The gristy sugars have a field day as the smoke envelops; f22.5 more accent on vanilla and a little citrus; b23 I really do adore young Ledaigs which allow the grist to do its thing. Oily enough to woo Caol Ila fans. 46%. 400 bottles. WB15/301

Dramboree 2014 Ledaig 8 Years Old sherry butt, cask no. 900173 (87) n22 t21 f22 b22 Says this is from the Ledaig distillery. I think they mean Tobermory. Don't mind the strength, but there is some heat coming from elsewhere other than the alcohol. No sulphur on the sherry – hurrah! But the big peat and grape are in a bit of a grapple which blasts balance and complexity out of the window. Still, great fun and the perfect dram to sort out any plaque. 58.8%. WB15/410

⬥ **First Edition The Freedom of 811 Ledaig 2004 10 Years Old** bott 2014 (94.5) n23.5 the dry, ashy phenols suck you into the glass; t24 magnificent delivery: the smoke is full on but there is more than enough sugar to cope. What's more, the sweetness ranges from grist to ulmo honey, with the vanillas also being gorgeously spruce and confident; f23.5 the major sugars now spent, the ashy finish is beautifully structured and paced; b23.5 one of the best younger Ledaigs I have had for many a year. A dram from the old Ledaig school... 46%. 192 bottles. WhiskyAuction.com

⬥ **Glen Fahrn Airline Nr 07 Tobermory 1995 Aged 17 Years** cask no. 446 (85.5) n21 t22 f21 b21.5. A typically indifferent Tobermory of so-so distillation quality. But a decent cask has helped highlight the richness of the malt itself, while helping to paper over some cracks. 56.8%. sc. 236 bottles.

Gordon and MacPhail Connoisseurs Choice Ledaig 1994 (90) n21.5 t23.5 f22 b23. Probably the most miserly peated Ledaig of all time. But don't let that worry you: the chocolate chip mint is a stunner...! 46%. ncf.

Gordon & MacPhail Connoisseurs Choice Ledaig 1996 (82) n20 t21 f20.5 b20.5. Occasionally the Ledaig from Tobermory became a smoky renegade. Here is such an example: thin and seemingly missing some copper from the system. Even the peat fails to make any kind of a positive impact save, perhaps, for its contribution towards a degree of soft mocha. Astringent and underwhelming. 46%.

⊰⊱ **Gordon & MacPhail Connoisseurs Choice Ledaig 1999 (69) n15 t19 f17 b18**. Though well peated, the phenols aren't enough to disguise the rough, occasionally syrupy distillate at the core. Rare to find this degree of feints in Scotch whisky. *46%*

Gordon & MacPhail Exclusive Single Malt Ledaig sherry hogshead, cask no. 469, dist 23 Oct 97, bott Oct 13 **(86.5) n21 t23.5 f21 b21**. Has you gripping your seat...not in excitement but trying to hold on tight. Hardly brilliant distillate here and the peat is thrust at you like clods of turf and anthracite eggs hitting you slap on the nose: it is all rather austere, brutal and distinctly farmyardy. Peaks on delivery when a bevvy of sugars, mainly molasses and maple syrup combined, overcome the covert bitterness and soften the peaty blows. The finish is mildly less brutal, and even offers black cherries to counter the bittering oak. For peat freaks, you'll find this a hard-faced, icy-hearted lover. But you'll probably return to her for more...*58.6%. nc ncf sc. 263 bottles, bottled exclusively for The Vintage House. WB15/065*

The Maltman Tobermory Aged 16 Years sherry cask, cask no. 5010, dist Jun 96, bott Apr 13 **(71.5) n16.5 t19 f18 b18**. More distilling faults in this than you can wave a whisky thief at. Feinty though sweet. *43%. sc ncf nc. 233 bottles. WB15/217*

Master of Malt Single Cask Ledaig 7 Year Old (94) n23.5 fresh, citrusy, medium-peated grist. And...that's all folks...! **t24** wonderful buttery quality to the intense gristy sweetness. A little lemon lightens and sharpens; **f23** the oak cannot resist adding a touch of bitterness, but is kind about it. A spice buzz is kept to a barely audible hum by the low blanket of smoke; **b23.5** a distillery style beautifully captured. *61.9%. sc.*

Master of Malt Single Cask Tobermory 18 Years Old refill, dist 22 Nov 95, bott 4 Feb 14 **(88.5) n21** intense malt compensates for the odd blemish on the distillate; **t22.5** unusually flinty for a Tobermory, but the degree of muscovado-sugared malt rises to impressive proportions; **f22** a little salt raises the sharpness of the grain while the oak offers a buttery touch; **b22** a better than expected malt given the nose. For its obvious technical faults it is impossible not to enjoy the overall richness of the picture. *53.9%. 100 bottles. WB15/230*

Old Malt Cask Tobermory Aged 19 Years refill hogshead, cask no. 9910, dist Apr 94, bott Aug 13 **(81.5) n20 t21.5 f20 b20**. Smoky, but stringent and eye-watering, too. Those stills were running at a lick when this was made... *50%. nc ncf sc. 170 bottles.*

⊰⊱ **Old Malt Cask Tobermory 18 Years Old** cask no. 11235, dist Oct 96, bott Feb 15 **(87.5) n21.5 t22.5 f21.5 b22**. A wizard malty jape. Forget any pretentions to whisky greatness: this is just a dram which has hardly grown up for its age but instead is set upon all kinds of barley-rich fun and spicy adventures. If you can't enjoy this, then you need to chill out a bit. *50%. nc ncf sc. 314 bottles.*

Old Malt Cask Ledaig Aged 20 Years refill hogshead, cask no. 9858, dist Mar 93, bott Jun 13 **(89) n22** an usually sweet nose for a Ledaig, the delicate honey tones holding sway over the crushed Digestive biscuits and earthier floral notes; **t22** mild hint of glazed ginger amid the tannin; **f22.5** a lovely ginger buzz, crystalline sugars and the vaguest of phenolic fades; **b22.5** a juicy little trip with an almost apologetic degree of smoke. *50%. nc ncf sc.*

⊰⊱ **Old Malt Cask Tobermory Aged 20 Years** refill hogshead, cask no. 10827, dist Apr 94, bott Aug 14 **(90) n22** a hefty cut once, the excesses have died over two decades in the barrel. Remains malty; **t22.5** chewy, with the remnants of the light feints to the fore. But the intensity of the barley, seasoned with salt makes for a salivating joy, too; **f23** fabulous layering, not least due to a metallic seam. Serious butterscotch and pastry at the death; **b22.5** work had recently been carried out on one of the stills or condenser: there is a lot of copper floating around the palate. Suitably sharp and rich. *50%. nc ncf sc. 309 bottles.*

Old Particular Highland Tobermory 18 Years Old refill butt, cask no. 10361, dist Feb 96, bott May 14 **(84.5) n21 t22 f21.5 b21**. Salted celery nose and profound malt throughout on the palate. But never quite raises its game high enough. *48.4%. nc ncf sc. 314 bottles.*

Old Particular Highland Leidaig Aged 21 Years refill hogshead, cask no. 10263, dist Mar 1993, bott Mar 2014 **(95.5) n24** the astonishing complexity signals a whisky of importance and no little greatness: perfect fruit and spices commensurate with age, mainly of a kumquat theme but heightened in effect by the gorgeous coastal saltiness; **t24** wonderful...truly wonderful. That coastal effect is not lost on delivery, though plays its hand quietly, content in allowing the delicate fruit to intermingle with the rich barley and multi-layered oakiness; the sugars purr gentle...; **f23.5** gentle vanillas and ever-intensifying cocoa tones, some distinctly Cuban; **b24** one of the best fruit plucked from Tobermory for many a year. Sublime. *50.9%.*

⊰⊱ **Old Particular Ledaig 14 Years Old** refill hogshead, cask no. 10789, dist May 01, bott Jun 15 **(83.5) n21.5 t22 f19 b21**. Shame. Trace elements of milky oakiness reveal on the nose a weakness in the cask despite the very high – and slightly Fisherman's Friend style – phenols. The growing tang on the finish confirms it. *48.4%. nc ncf sc. 330 bottles.*

⟨⟩ **Romantic Rhine Collection Ledaig 7 Years Old** Heavily Peated bourbon hogshead, dist 29 Sept 97 (**91**) n24 t23.5 f21 b22.5. Unlikely you will find a better non-Islay peated nose this year: a mesmerising balance between coal and peat reek, the sweet-dry ration constantly making micro-adjustments to keep in unison, like a bird's head staying perfectly still on a swaying branch. The delivery, with its complex citrus sweetness, is almost as good, but the finish bitters out. 48%. 72 bottles.

The Single Malts of Scotland Tobermory Aged 19 Years hogshead, cask no. 5174, dist 14 Dec 1994, bott 25 Mar 2014 (**74**) n18 t19 f18 b19. Furry, sweet but off key. 55.8%. WB15/311

⟨⟩ **Spirit of Caledonia Ledaig 8 Years Old** (**88.5**) n22.5 busy nose bursting with big phenols: the oak seems a little dodgy; t23 sweet and oily but a real bite and juiciness to the grist; f21 oily still, but an annoying tang; b22 a generally sound Ledaig: this one has many components – especially the oiliness - similar to Caol Ila. 58.8%. Mr Whisky.

⟨⟩ **Spirit & Cask Ledaig** hogshead, dist 2005, bott 2015 (**91**) n23 thumping, unrefined peat still to be taken down a peg or two by the oak; t23.5 oils and sugars ganging together from the off. They need to, as the peat tries to own it all it can see...; f22 a light, buttery vanilla and deft spices emerge as the smoke runs out of steam; b22.5 raw and young, but enough sugars to ensure a gentle landing. 48%. 324 bottles.

⟨⟩ **Svenska Eldvatten Tobermory 1994** ex px sherry butt, dist Mar 94, bott Sept 14 (**85.5**) n21 t22 f21 b21.5. Sadly, not quite the highest ranking distillate you'll find, so the intense malt theme doesn't get the all round backing it deserves. Certainly mouthwatering and bursting with barley. 54.8%. sc.

⟨⟩ **Svenska Eldvatten Ledaig 1997** ex bourbon hogshead, dist Oct 97, bott Sept 14 (**87**) n22 t22 f21.5 b21.5. Love the mildly minty nose to this one, which impressively uplifts the smoke. But there is no getting away from the rough edge and overall coarseness to the malt itself, becoming rather thin towards the end. 50.3%. sc.

That Boutique-y Whisky Ledaig batch 1 (**91.5**) n24 pure smoked grist: astonishing. Ignore the soft feint niggle and breathe in something remarkable...; t23.5 decently peated grist with the sugars dissolving on the tongue. A little golden syrup adds lustre to the sweetness; f21.5 bitters slightly and the oils mount; b22.5 technically, not the most gifted malt. But blunders along beautifully, helped by its disarming peat profile. 571%. 217 bottles. WB15/209

⟨⟩ **That Boutique-y Whisky Company Ledaig** batch 2 (**84**) n19 t22.5 f21 b21.5. Pretty major peat at work. But this is rough stuff: not so much spicy as not particularly well made. The stills have been run fast on this one, hence the lack of rounded edges. The sugars ensure there is plenty to enjoy, as does the smoke and oils. The kind of malt to have after coming home on a freezing cold day when the barbed rain has been battering your face without mercy. This will be either kill or cure. 50.2%. 99 bottles.

That Boutique-y Whisky Tobermory batch 2 (**76**) n18 t19 f20 b19. Follows pretty much in the same footsteps as Batch 1, except the finish enjoys an extra smudge of decent barley. 53.9%. 73 bottles. WB15/196

That Boutique-y Whisky Tobermory batch 3 (**76.5**) n18.5 t20 f19 b19. Malty, hot but another one that sinks without trace like the wrecks off Tobermory... 48.1%. WB15/233

⟨⟩ **Trader Joe's Isle of Mull Single Malt 1996 17 Years Old** (**83.5**) n21.5 t21 f20.5 b20.5. Possibly not the greatest distillate to start off with. But does island whisky come any duller than this? 40%. Alexander Murray & Co.

⟨⟩ **Villa Konthor Ledaig 9 Years Old** ex bourbon cask, dist 2005, bott 2015 (**91.5**) n23 firm phenols offer little in the way of flare or fancy footwork. Peat at its most acidic and effective; t23.5 the sugars missing on the nose are found here in abundance. As is the lush malty softness. The smoke works on an alternative level and in a different key; f22 lingering sugars met by growing vanilla; b23 a very competent Ledaig, especially for the period. 46%

⟨⟩ **The Whisky Barrel Tobermory 1994 Burns Malt 20 Years Old** cask no. 188063 (**89.5**) n21 technically a bit off, partially through the oak plus a wider cut than is usually wise. Very suety; t23 that generous cut ramps up the malt intensity to delightful levels. The oil cling limpet-like to the palate, ensuring the spices have a slight searing quality; f22.5 the hefty oils turn a little bitter, but a coppery sheen compensates; b23 achieves fleeting moments of brilliance. Coppery in places but the oily spice positively sings. 51.1%

⟨⟩ **Whisky-Fässle Ledaig 7 Year Old** hogshead, dist 2005, bott 2013 (**93**) n23.5 t24 f22 b23.5. Someone went nuts on the peating level with this one: phenols are practically crawling out of the glass! For all its youthful, smoky muscle, this is a thing of beauty and wonder. Superb! 55.2%. nc ncf.

⟨⟩ **Whisky-Fässle Ledaig 8 Year Old** hogshead, dist 2005, bott 2014 (**88**) n22 a little bit of oak tang is brushed aside by the chunky phenols; t23 sharp, young, lively barley - but oily peat remains the master; **f21** that tang is confirmed; **b22** decent. A better cask and this would have been a cracker. *53.3%. nc ncf.*

⟐ **Wilson & Morgan Barrel Selection Ledaig 2005** oloroso sherry finish, cask no. 800069/70/71/72/75/76, dist 2005, bott 2015 **(77.5) n19 t21.5 f18 b19**. The irony that so much excellent grape is visible is not lost on us. Sadly, the whisky is as the sulphur takes hold. *48.5%*

⟐ **Wilson & Morgan Barrel Selection Tobermory 18 Year Old** sherry finish, dist 1997, bott 2015 **(84.5) n23 t21.5 f19 b21**. Most entertainment is provided on the nose, where the peat enjoys a piercing acidic quality. Beyond that, the smoke and fruit never quite hit it off as they might, while a tang on the finish does few favours either. *54.3%*

⟐ **Whiskyjace Tobermory 18 Year Old** bourbon hogshead, dist 1994, bott 2012 **(80) n18 t22 f19 b21**. The nose tells you exactly what you are in for and it doesn't let you down. Or, rather, it does... Poor oak makes for a sharp aroma; the delivery is more intense still. There are some magic moments to the mountainous malt, but it is the problem with both spirit and barrel which grabs most. *60.6%*

TOMATIN
Speyside, 1897. Takara, Shuzo and Okura & Co. Working.

⟐ **Cù Bòcan The Bourbon Edition** fully matured in bourbon casks db **(84) n21.5 t22 f20 b20.5**. The malt battles hard to overcome the poor cask bitterness. But fails. *46%*

⟐ **Cù Bòcan The Sherry Edition** fully matured in sherry casks db **(83) n20 t22 f20 b21**. For several magic seconds, the delivery and first four or five flavour waves after offer delicious malt polished by high grade grape. But it is all far too short-lived as off-key notes abound on the nose and finish. *46%*

⟐ **Cù Bòcan The Virgin Oak Edition** fully matured in virgin oak casks db **(94.5) n23.5** subtly rich and strangely coastal: varying levels of honey intensity intertwangled with a light and uplifting saltiness. Darker sugars point the honey towards manuka, though the ulmo undercurrent ensures a beguiling softness; **t23.5** no surprises with the honey coming first: its sweetness is kept in check by equal amounts of vanilla and oaky chalkiness. A little red liquorice takes the side road towards hickory; ulmo and butterscotch counter the gnawing spices; **f23.5** dries, becomes a tad oilier as the malt makes its mark. But it is those buzzing spices amid the dying rays of honey which push the correct buttons; **b24** don't expect a quiet little whisky to nuzzle into. This chap has attitude, and no little complexity. Magnificent use of differing honey styles: overall a delightful box of tricks. *46%*

Cù Bòcan Highland Single Malt virgin oak, bourbon & sherry casks db **(85.5) n21 t21 f22 b21.5**. An old fashioned dram: the type Pitt the Younger, or Pitt the Embryo might remember... and appreciate. Appears to be nearer new make than fully matured Scotch: the big player is the oak which, almost, bourbon-like, shovels cart loads of caramel and muscovado into the mix. Green...and engrossing. *46%*

Cù Bòcan Highland Single Malt 1989 Vintage db **(95.5) n23** what the....??? A peaty Tomatin! And classy, too...; **t24** sure, the peat is first to show...and glistens as it does so. But where the hell has all that juicy fruit come from. Fruit and peat...not usually happy marriage. But here it is bliss...; **f24.5** now dries slightly to allow the smoke to have a slightly sharp tang,as though the phenls have risen to surprisingly high levels. Still the fruit is on song, like the citrus jelly which accompanies some of the better marzipans...; **b24** the last Cu Bocan I got my nose around, I likened to Pitt the Younger. Well, the only pit here would be a peat one... This is not only absolutely superb whisky, but a bit of a shock, too...Indeed, I am stunned! *53.2%. ncf.*

Tomatin 12 Years Old db **(85.5) n21 t21.5 f22 b21**. Reverted back to a delicately sherried style, or at least shows signs of a touch of fruit, as opposed to the single-minded maltfest it had recently been. So, nudge or two closer to the 18-y-o as a style and shows nothing other than good grace and no shortage of barley, either. *40%*

⟐ **Tomatin 12 Year Old** finished in Spanish sherry casks db **(91.5) n23** an uplifting clean grape note adds lustre to the more prosaic butterscotch and vanilla; **t23.5** beautiful delivery where both malt and fruit lift off hand-in-hand; **f21.5** the malt shines longer, while a buttery note develops. The late bitterness is a shame; **b23.5** for a great many years, Tomatin operated under severe financial restrictions. This meant that some of the wood brought to the distillery during this period was hardly of top-notch quality. This has made life difficult for those charged with moulding the stocks into workable expressions. I take my hat off to the creator of this: some great work is evident, despite the finish. *43%*

Tomatin 14 Year Old Port Finish db **(92.5) n23** under-ripe greengage shows some nip and spice; **t24** salivating, as a Tomatin delivery so ften is. But here we get all juiced up by succulent fruit, helped along by glazed muscvado; f22.5 the fruit tails off allowing the vanilla and spice an easy ride; b23 allows the top notch port a clear road. 46%. ncf.

Tomatin Aged 15 Years ex bourbon cask, bott 2010 db (86) n21 t22 f21.5 b21.5. One of the most malty drams on the market today. Perhaps suffers a little from the 43% strength as some of the lesser oak notes get a slightly disruptive foothold. But the intense, juicy barley trademark remains clear and delicious. 43% Tomatin Distillery

Tomatin 15 Years Old bourbon barrels and Spanish Tempranillo wine casks db (88.5) n22 t23 f21 b22.5. Not free from the odd problem with the Spanish wine casks but gets away with it as the overall complexity and enjoyment levels are high. 52%

Tomatin Aged 18 Years db (85) n22 t21 f21 b21. I have always held a torch for this distillery and it is good to see some of the official older stuff being released. This one has some serious zing to it, leaving your tastebuds to pucker up - especially as the oak hits. 40%

Tomatin 18 Years Old db (88) n22.5 t22 f21.5 b22. What a well-mannered malt. As though it grew up in a loving, caring family and behaves itself impeccably from first nose to last whimpering finale; 43%

Tomatin Aged 18 Years sherry finish, bott 2010 db (92.5) n22.5 busy, thick milkshake maltiness with a touch of fruitcake; t23.5 cream sherry: creamy + sweet barley + fruity = cream sherry...; f23 very long with a touch of controlled spicy fizz to the proceedings. But that indomitable barley signature sings to the end; b23.5 finished in quite superior sherry butts. A malt brimming with character and quality. What a treat! 46%. ncf. Tomatin Distillery

Tomatin 25 Years Old db (89) n22 t23 f21.5 b22.5. Not a nasty bone in its body: understated but significant. 43%

Tomatin 30 Years Old db (91) n22 if there was a hint of the exotics in the 25-y-o, it's here, five years on, by the barrel load. Evidence of grape, but the malt won't be outdone, either; t23 silky and sultry, there is every suggestion that the oak is thinking of going too far. Yet such is the purity and intensity of the malt, damage has been repaired and/or prevented and even at this age one can only salivate as the soft oils kick in; f23.5 probably my favourite part of the experience because the sheer deliciousness of the chocolaty finale is awesome; b22.5 malts of this age rarely maintain such a level of viscosity. Soft oils can often be damaging to a whisky, because they often refuse to allow character to flourish. Yet here we have a whisky that has come to terms with its age with great grace. And no little class. 49.3%

Tomatin 30 Year Old European & American oak casks db (85.5) n21 t21 f22.5 b21. Unusually for an ancient malt, the whisky becomes more comfortable as it wears its aged shoes. The delivery is just a bit too enthusiastic on the oaky front, but the natural caramels soften the journey rather delightfully. 46%. ncf.

⬧ **Tomatin 36 Year Old American & European oak** db (96.5) n24 the elegant, slightly erotic and truly exotic fruit means one thing only...; t24.5 which happens to be confirmed by the even more exotic fruit delivery: great age! The mid ground is both firm with the oak also evident with the butterscotch theme, and soft - the malt still extant having laid down a yielding carpet. A little mocha and praline seep into the mix; but the fruits just keep on giving; f23.5 not a hint of bitterness, no stewed pencils of exhausted oak. Just a slow re-run of all that has gone before, though now only in shadowy form...except for the busy but behaved spices...; b24.5 the difference between old oak and the newer stuff is brilliantly displayed here. Make no mistake: this is a masterpiece of a malt. 46%

Tomatin 40 Years Old db (89.5) n21.5 t22 f23 b23. Not quite sure how it's done it, but somehow has made it through all those oaky scares to make for one very impressive 40-y-o!! Often it shows the character of a bourbon on a Zimmer. 42.9%

Tomatin 1981 Single Cask db (93.5) n24 classic nutty old sherry; dried dates and burnt raisin...the label really doesn't need to mention the type of cask...; t23.5 further indelible hallmarks of an eye-watering dry oloroso, the oak offering a degree of bitter orange but only after the clipped, spiced delivery; f22.5 brooding molasses offering stingy amounts of sweetness to counter that late bitterness; b23.5 a hand-picked beautifully rip cherry from Tomatin, one that essentially has to be tasted at body temperature for very best results. Even then, still one of the driest sherry butts you'll find this year. 43.2%.

Tomatin Highland 1988 Vintage db (86.5) n22 t22 f21 b21.5. Few whiskies in the world shows off its malty muscle like Tomatin and here, briefly, it goes into overdrive. For the most part, a happy meeting of slightly salty malt and oak. 46%. ncf.

⬧ **Tomatin 1988** Batch 2, bourbon & port casks db (95.5) n23.5 a firmness to the grape plus a degree of ye olde fruitcake; t24.5 lush, with seemingly malt at first but soon overtaken by a huge swirl of clean fruit – mainly grape, ripe greengage and fat, sweet gooseberries burst at the skin; the undercurrent is thin acacia honey; f23.5 drier cocoa but with molasses and fudge; b24 another stunner from Tomatin. Complex, beautifully clean and delicious! 46%

≪ **Tomatin Cask Strength** Batch 1, bourbon & sherry casks db **(77) n19 t20 f19 b19.** I could weep: these sherry butts are dripping with juice. But then, sulphur-tainted, lead to the whisky's downfall... *57.5%*

≪ **Tomatin Contrast Bourbon Casks** from 1973, 1977, 1988, 2002, 2006 db **(94.5) n24** sublime layering: the oak is captured in many phases and poses, so the characteristics stretch from the more youthful citrus notes, through dank, sea-salt caves right along to the first hints of exotic fruit. Spices nip and kiss playfully, butterscotch and heather honey vie to fill in any gaps...; **t24** my word! That is just such a satisfying delivery: a little oil, but not enough to disguise the busy honey, manuka and heather at the fore. Instead, it cushions the arrival of those inevitable spices and surprisingly solid malt notes; **f22.5** a slight bittering towards the end; the sugars are so nimble and beautifully poised, they compensate almost immediately wherever needed; **b24** this is exceptionally fine malt whisky boasting an advanced degree of structure and complexity. If you don't have half an hour to spare to do it justice, don't even open the bottle... *46%. Packaged with sherry edition.*

≪ **Tomatin Contrast Sherry Casks** from 1973, 1977, 1988, 2002, 2006 db **(87) n21 t22 f22 b22.** Certainly a contrast with the bourbon, not least on the complexity front. No damaging off notes, even if the nose is a little tight. But though the grape makes itself heard, it never spreads its wings and flies in this curiously muted offering.. *46%. Packaged with bourbon edition.*

≪ **Tomatin Whisky Meets Sherry Oloroso** finished in oloroso sherry casks db **(78) n22 t20 f17 b19.** So powerful is the grape that the nose promises all you desire. Sadly, the bitterness on delivery and beyond makes for a punishing experience. *57.9%. Packaged with PX edition.*

≪ **Tomatin Whisky Meets Sherry Pedro Ximenez** finished in PX sherry casks db **(84) n20.5 t22.5 f20 b21.** No shortage of spice. And enough sugar to cause any number of cavities. But the casks, alas, have been very mildly tainted with you-know-what. That said, those (lucky ones?) who cannot detect sulphur will probably have their minds blown by this one, especially once the grape goes into overdrive.. *53.4%. Packaged with oloroso edition.*

≪ **Anam na h-Alba The Soul of Scotland Tomatin 2006** 1st fill sherry cask, dist Jan 06, bott Feb 14 **(73.5) n18 t20 f17 b18.5.** A dram which crashes around the taste buds like a blind F1 driver at Monaco. Unappealingly sweet, weird phenol-type never finds harmony with the fruit and inevitable sulphur. Just weird. *54.2%. 96 bottles.*

≪ **Cadenhead's Authentic Collection Tomatin Aged 25 Years** bourbon cask, dist 1989 **(84.5) n21.5 t22 f20 b21.** When you need a dose of malt concentrate in your life, you don't have to look any further than a Tomatin. In this instance, a slightly off key cask has just undermined the star quality with a tangy input. *51.9%*

Cadenhead's Small Batch Tomatin Aged 19 Years bourbon hogshead, dist 1994, bott 2014 **(89) n22** dry, borderline austere with a grainy barley and spice outer shell: a bender's delight; **t22.5** honeycombed, juicy barley **f22.5** impressively clean oak but still that simple gristiness presses home; **b22** malt at the max. The complexity is down to the kind oak rather than any magic within the spirit. A simple, very decent quality Tomatin nutshelled, really. *46%. WB15/090*

≪ **Gordon & MacPhail Connoisseurs Choice Tomatin 1996 (82) n19 t22 f20 b21.** Undone somewhat by a hint of butyric and an oak-bitter finish. But you might love the gooseberry and lychee combination. *46%.*

≪ **Gordon & MacPhail Connoisseurs Choice Tomatin 1997 (89.5) n22.5** unmistakable signs of elegant aging as the exotic fruits take control; **t22.5** soft and luscious at first, then grips you and warms beautifully. A superb mix of drier oak notes and those joyous fruity tones; good background barley still; **f22** drier and spicier as the oak grips tighter; **b22.5** slips onto your palate and cuddles up to your taste buds like a lover slips into bed and cuddles up with you on a cold night... *46%*

≪ **Old Malt Cask Tomatin Aged 20 Years** refill hogshead, cask no. 11143, dist Oct 94, bott Dec 14 **(92) n21.5** perhaps heavy on the dry tannin; **t23** early Demerara sugars give way to the inevitable; delightfully oily, though, and very weighty; **f23** spiced mint-chocolate ice cream. In an oaky wafer... **b23.5** Heavy on the oak. But surprisingly refreshing – as well as complex – at times. A lot of whisky... *50%. nc ncf sc. 233 bottles.*

Old Masters Tomatin 16 Years Old cask no. 5969, dist 1997, bott 2014 **(92.5) n24** a zesty fruit salad, including raw rhubarb. Estery and sharpened with fresh spring grass: one of the brightest noses you'll fine! **t23.5** from the nose you expect max salivation...and you get it. Fabulously grassy, sugar-coated malt; **f22** quietens as vanilla and butterscotch find a home; very late cocoa; **b23** a cut glass malt. *56.4%. James MacArthur & Co. Ltd.*

Old Particular Speyside Tomatin 20 Years Old refill hogshead cask no. 9984, dist Jan 93, bott Aug 13 **(84.5) n21 t22 f20.5 b21.** Concentrates on the house big malt theme. But a few spices tag along to enliven procedings. *51.5%. nc ncf sc. 211 Bottles. OLP0037.*

The Pearls of Scotland Tomatin 1998 cask no. 3667, bott Jun 14 **(88)** n22.5 refreshing, despite a stodgy spotted dog pudding touch. The sugars are like molten Demerera on lightly salted porridge; **t23** wonderfully clean and intense barley which becomes more concentrated as it continues; the salt begins to open up the tannins as the spices arrive; **f20.5** more excellent malt which takes an age to wither away; beware the mild "milky" fault at the end which suggests the cask had reached the end of its useful life in the final year or two of maturation; **b22** a dram which splashes malt about it like an artist may throw paint at his canvas. *52.4%. sc.*

⟨⟩ **Single Cask Collection Tomatin 2006 9 Year Old** bourbon barrel **(91)** n22 the vague strains of peanut butter on toast drifting in from a distant kitchen. Green, drying grass but not the usual malty intensity...; **t23.5**...until the delivery! Ye gods!! Malt rarely comes maltier than this, while butterscotch rumbles around contentedly...; so salivating...and shows little sign of letting up; **f22.5** duller, but the malt still eclipses the growing oak; **b23.5** for me, this is a much underrated distillery, not least because it can produce, as it has done here, the almost definitive malty whisky... The kind of malt a blender might kill for. *55.7%*

The Whisky Cask Tomatin Aged 8 Years sherry cask, dist 2004, bott 2013 **(77)** n19 t23 f17 b18. Extra marks for the incredible intensity of the malt and sweet grape on delivery. Stunning. But this is from a contemporary sherry butt. So I'll let you guess what happens next... *58.6%. nc ncf.*

⟨⟩ **World of Orchids Tomatin 2004 8 Year Old** bourbon cask, cask no. 456 **(73)** n18 t20 f17 b18. Though this is from a bourbon cask, the result is of the profoundly negative sherry variety. Presumably, at some time in the cask's history it was treated with an ersatz sherry mix to turn it into a sherry-type cask, a practise used in the industry but not widely mentioned. Sadly, most of these had a sulphur tinge. *58.6%. sc. 119 bottles.*

TOMINTOUL

Speyside, 1965. Angus Dundee. Working.

Tomintoul Aged 10 Years db **(83.5)** n21 t20 f21.5 b21. Has bucked up recently to offer a juicy, salivating barley thrust. Yet still a little on the thin side, despite some late oak. *40%*

Tomintoul Aged 12 Years Oloroso Sherry Cask Finish db **(73.5)** n18.5 t19 f18 b18. Tomintoul, with good reason, styles itself as "The Gentle Dram" and you'll hear no argument from me about that one. However, the sherry influence here offers a rough ride. *40%*

Tomintoul Aged 12 Years Portwood Finish db **(87.5)** n22 t22 f21.5 b22. As Portwood finishes go, a real lightweight allowing the barley plenty of room to flex its juicier muscles. *46%. nc ncf.*

Tomintoul Aged 14 Years db **(91)** n23.5 t23 f21.5. This guy has shortened its breath somewhat: with the distinct thinness to the barley and oak arriving a little flustered and half-hearted rather than with a confident stride; b23 remains a beautiful whisky full of vitality and displaying the malt in its most naked and vulnerable state. But I get the feeling that perhaps a few too many third fills, or under-performing seconds, has resulted in the intensity and hair-raising harmony of the truly great previous bottlings just being slightly undercooked. That said, still a worthy and delicious dram! *46%. nc ncf.*

Tomintoul Aged 16 Years db **(94.5)** n24.5 a fruity concoction of apples and pears topped with vanilla ice cream; even the vaguest hint of something smoky...one of the noses of the year; **t23.5** every bit as gentle as the label promises, as the light oils coat the palate with a fabulously intense and delicately sweetened barley skin. The skeleton is playful oak; **f23** a wonderful, multi-layered interplay between malt and oak-vanillas. Long, curiously spice-free, increasingly dry but hugely sophisticated; **b23.5** confirms Tomintoul's ability to dice with greatness. *40%*

Tomintoul Aged 21 Years db **(94)** n24 has all the hallmarks of a malt which contains casks a lot older than the stated age: the fruit is of the exotic variety and the manner in which those fruit and defter floral notes effortlessly intertwine confirms not just the magnificence of quality but also familiarity between oak and malt **t24** silky and soft with the balance of the light sugars to barley almost perfect; the vanillas grow, as they should, but the freshness to the barley never diminishes **f22.5** a beautiful butterscotch and custard confection **b23.5** just how good this whisky would have been at cask strength or even at 46 absolutely terrifies me. *40%.*

⟨⟩ **Tomintoul Aged 25 Years** db **(95)** n25 the day has just begun and the sun is barely up. But I will be hard pushed to find a more quaint and gorgeously balanced nose between now and sunset. The aroma would not be out of place in the garden outside my window, a sensual breeze of orange blossom and floral scents. Ulmo honey thinly spread on toast is about as heavy as it gets; **t24** no less subtle is the array of sweet notes on delivery, melting, meringue-like, into every crevice; the malt at times stacks up to make a short Speyside-themed speech; **f23** bitters slightly, though to no great detriment, as the oak quietly takes command. The malt and vague fruitiness drifts inexorably to the finale; **b23.5** a quiet masterpiece from one of Scotland's criminally underappreciated great distilleries. 43%

Tomintoul Aged 27 Years db **(87) n22 t22.5 21.5 b21.** The last time I saw a colour like this was on antique expert David Dickinson's face. Still, lots of charm and character to go round... and on the whisky, too. 40%

Tomintoul Aged 33 Years db **(95.5) n24.5 t24.5 f23 b24.** The point about whiskies of this age is that sometimes you have to deal with what you are given. Some 33 years ago a blender didn't decide to put these to one side for a single malt; this was made to be blended away and have arrived at this point with a pleasing randomness: the casks used here escaped the call of the warehouse foreman. Which means this breathtakingly beautiful 33 Year Old Tomintoul bares virtually no resemblance to the last one I tasted. Which is what makes this job of mine, at times, so bloody fascinating. 43%.

Tomintoul With A Peaty Tang db **(94) n23 t24 f23 b24.** A bit more than a tang, believe me! Faultlessly clean distillate that revels in its unaccustomed peaty role. The age is confusing and appears mixed, with both young and older traits being evident. 40%

⫸ **Tomintoul 1976 Vintage** bott 2013 db **(94.5) n25** stupendously classic Speyside style old timer's exotic fruit: you have to have reached a massive age to find something as juicily soft and alluring as this! **t22** all's well with the sweet, fruity-malty delivery...before the oak hits you so hard, your eyes water. But the malts fight back – aided by their fruitiest notes to soften the impact; **f23.5** to complete the recovery, we are thrown back into fruity mode – this time jelly babies without the dusting of sugar plus more exotic papaya, even with that attractive bitterness it possesses...; **b24** when you get that amount of exotic fruit on the nose, you know there is going to be a massive oaky kickback somewhere. However, this copes brilliantly and even has something fruitier up its sleeve further down the line. This can be taken as one of your five fruits a day... 40%

Darkness! Tomintoul Aged 18 Years Oloroso Cask Finish (91.5) n23 huge fruitcake: Melton Hunt Cake at its moistest, though with separate layers of Sumatra coffee and Venezuelan cocoa...intriguing; **t23** a mixed, noisy bag on delivery but settles towards a spiced, high cocoa chocolate raisin treat...; **f22.5** more of the same, but with extra oils and vanilla; **b23** luscious sherry with not a sulphur of atom in sight...! 52.7%. 95 bottles. WB15/204

⫸ **Glen Fahrn Airline Nr 05 Tomintoul 1968 Aged 43 Years** cask no. 4227 **(95.5) n24 t24.5 f23 b24.** Exotic fruit par excellence! Everything one might hope from such an aged Speysider. The tannins are a shade over eager at the death. But until then, the movement through the phases of vanilla, blood orange and kumquats, oily barley and cocoa tick every box of expectation. Sublime. 48.1%. sc. 180 bottles.

⫸ **Master of Malt Single Cask Tomintoul 19 Year Old** dist 1 May 95, bott 1 Apr 15 **(87) n21.5 t22.5 f21.5 b21.5.** Boasts a similar type of fruitiness to their Batch 2. Quite a short, thin finish follows a refreshing, though European-style body and spirit. Youthful for its near two decades. 54.6%. sc. 186 bottles.

⫸ **Old Ballantruan** db **(89.5) n23.5** ye gods!! This is packing some peat!! Young it may be...but...well...ye gods!! **t23** sugars are falling over themselves to engage before the tidal wave of peat arrives. They just about manage it...; **f21** becomes fractionally too bitter as the vanilla and lime retreats, despite the phenols; **b22** profound young malt which could easily be taken for an Islay. 50%. ncf.

⫸ **That Boutique-y Whisky Company Tomintoul** batch 2 **(88) n22** gorgeous (and curious) mix of grape must and grist; **t23** fresh, salivating and something of the east European slivovitz; **f21.5** continues on the sugary-fruity theme; **b21.5** malts rarely come much cleaner. An odd distinctive fruitiness more akin to brandy. 54.1%. 71 bottles.

TORMORE
Speyside, 1960. Chivas Brothers. Working.

Tormore 12 Years Old db **(75) n19 t19 f19 b18.** For those who like whisky in their caramel. 40%

Tormore Aged 14 Years batch no. A1308, bott 2013 db **(83.5) n21 t21.5 f20.5 b20.5.** Toffeed, flat and inoffensive. Good dram to have last thing at night: chances are you'll be asleep before you finish the glass... 43% WB15/326

⫸ **Tormore Aged 16 Years** batch no. B1309, bott 09 2013 db **(95) n23.5** a husky nose: deep with an oaky roughage, underlined by spice. But on another plane there is a softer, oilier, dark-sugared, vaguely kumquat-ish hue, too...; **t24** this is Tormore....? Wow! Succulent maws are topped with complex but effective spices. But as the ulmo honey moves in the complexity levels rise accordingly. Stunning butterscotch tart and red liquorice towards the still lightly oiled middle and cocoa can soon be expected...; **f23.5**...which arrives bang on cue and on time like a Japanese bullet train! Not so much predictable, but following the path of great whisky. The cocoa shimmers on different levels of intensity, with an occasional citrus moment. The spices grumble gorgeously; **b24** Tormore as I have never seen it before. The label talks about the "long and dry" finish. It does the bottling such a disservice: this is magnificently complex with cocoa notes a thing of sheer beauty. A landmark bottling for Tormore. *48%*

Tormore Aged 15 Years "Special Distillery Bottling" db **(71)** n17 t18 f19 b17. Even a supposed pick of choice casks can't save this from its fiery fate. *46%*

⟳ **Best Dram Tormore 19 Years Old** hogshead **(91)** **n23** nuts and dates...what the... thought this was from a hoggie...?? **t23.5** an implausible delivery – really not out of the usual Tormore canon. Those dates and nuts on the nose are now joined by juicy figs and greengages. Some mocha drifts through, and a little dollop of ulmo honey arrives and vanishes; **f21.5** not entirely flawless with its nagging, buzzing off note. But still a lot of liquorice and raisin going on besides...; **b23** a genuinely pleasant surprise. This is just bursting out of the glass with class and character... *499%*

⟳ **Chapter 7 Tormore 1995 19 Year Old** bourbon hogshead, cask no. 20159 **(94.5)** **n23.5** a real attitude between the oak and malt: fascinating and intriguing..; the oak (a little nimbler thanks to some kumquat and pear juiciness) appears to be landing some knock out blows...; **t24** Tormore...? Really...? I mean...really...??? A massive delivery where the obvious fault line between the barley and tannin turns into a magnitude 8 quake, spices ripping into the taste buds without mercy. Huge...but the barley and oak are in two different camps. Meanwhile dark, satanic sugars run amok, even the odd hint of manuka honey in there....before the barley battles back; **f23** you can't really follow that. And the finish doesn't even try: it just lets nature take its course. A light descending of vanilla and butterscotch from the mountainous heights of the massive sugars. Then, at last, the barley again makes its mark...before, finally, spiced cocoa: just so mmmmmm!!! **b24** for a Tormore, this is right up there. No: despite its usual rough and ready antics, this is beyond all possible expectation. But just dig that delivery! Groovy, baby! *55.7%. sc. 209 bottles.*

Gordon & MacPhail Connoisseurs Choice Tormore 1996, bott 2011 **(86)** n22 t21 f22 b21. Can't say this is an example of how scotch should be distilled, but pans out well thanks to decent oak. *46%. nc ncf. WB15/151*

Gordon & MacPhail Cask Strength Tormore 1999 (90.5) **n22** custard cream tart meets lemon merengue pie; **t23.5** hugely intense eye-watering barley, crunchy sugar with a lovely gooseberry edge; **f22** bitters out a tad, but the barley sugar remains on top; **b23** lays it on thick with the barley. Attractive. *58%.*

⟳ **Cadenhead's Small Batch Tormore Aged 30 Years** dist 1984 **(82)** n20 t21.5 f20 **b20.5**. The Speyside style chiselled in stone; the aggressively smouldering delivery on the palate...the total refusal to harmonise beyond the gripping spices...Yes, no mistaking this as a Tormore,,! *53.8%*

⟳ **Old Malt Cask Tormore 26 Years Old** sherry butt, cask no. 10665, dist Nov 88, bott Apr 15 **(95.5)** **n23** oddly thin for a sherry butt, but no off notes. Nutty and enticing; **t24** superb delivery: probably not oloroso as that nuttiness continues (impressively, mind), though now accompanied by gentle greengage and grape. Oils build and we slowly move into moist fruitcake territory; light on the sugars, though the odd toasted cherry turns up; **f24** long, with an impressive continuation but now backed confidently by spice; **b24.5** beautifully elegant and sophisticated: an absolute class act. And it is not often in 30 years I have said that about Tormore... *50%. nc ncf sc. 183 bottles.*

The Pearls of Scotland Tormore 1995 17 Years Old cask no. 20097, dist Dec 95, bott Nov 13 **(86.5)** n21.5 t22 f20.5 b22. Quite well made, malty, sweet, fruity, spicy, technically OK. Wholly likeable. Yet, for some reason (maybe because there appears to be no spine), somehow fails to get the adrenalin going... *476%.*

Signatory Vintage Single Malt Tormore 1995 Aged 18 Years hogsheads, cask no. 3885+3886, dist 27 Apr 95, bott 07 Feb 14 **(85.5)** n21.5 t22 f21 b21. Clean, sweet, unchallenging malt. Perfectly acceptable. Easily drinkable. Safe. Just give me a nudge if it starts to do something. *43%. nc. 779 bottles. WB15/012*

The Single Malts of Scotland Tormore 25 Years Old bourbon barrel, cask no. 603, dist 03 Feb 8, bott 14 Feb 13 **(94.5)** **n23** freshly toasted hazelnut embedded in chocolate mousse; someone is burning the toast in the kitchen next door; **t23.5** yep; burnt toast. On delivery. Or, rather burnt French toast as there is plenty of sugar to compensate. Under all this noise, malt throbs away contentedly; **f24** long with the most profound toasted fudge you'll ever find; the spices carry on merrily, the oils thicken and the general feel of excellent bourbon accentuates; **b24** from the colour and strength, you'd be thinking this had been matured in

Kentucky. And as for the flavour profile...OK, what have you done with the real Tormore...that guys nothing like as handsome as you! Never seen anything like it from this distillery in 30 years! A fabulous freak of a dram. *64.2%. 194 bottles. WB15/306*

◇ **That Boutique-y Whisky Company Tormore** batch 2 (83.5) **n**20.5 **t**22 **f**20 **b**21. After it makes its malty statement, it has little else to say. Steely hard but the spices help. *51.4%. 103 bottles.*

Wemyss Malts 1988 Single Speyside Tormore "Floral Trellis" barrel, dist 1988, bott 2014 (85) **n**21 **t**22 **f**21 **b**21. Pleasant though thin, malty, and too simplistically toffee dependent for greatness. *46%. sc. 286 bottles.*

TULLIBARDINE
Highlands (Perthshire), 1949. Tullibardine Ltd. Working.

Tullibardine 1992 Rum Finish bott 2009 db (89.5) **n**22 **t**23 **f**22.5 **b**22. Cracking stuff! *46%*

Tullibardine 1993 bott 2009 db (91.5) **n**22 **t**23.5 **f**23 **b**23. Intrinsically sweet barley. But spellbindingly charming all the way. *40%*

Tullibardine 1993 Moscatel Finish bott 2007 db (92.5) **n**23.5 **t**23.5 **f**23 **b**22.5. This really is how wine casks should integrate. A minor stunner. *46%*

Tullibardine 1993 Oloroso Sherry Finish bott 2008 db (89) **n**23 **t**23 **f**21 **b**22. Almost a trip down Memory Lane: once a pretty standard sherry butt, but now a treat. *46%*

Tullibardine 1993 Pedro Ximénez Sherry Finish bott 2009 db (87) **n**21 **t**23 **f**20.5 **b**22.5. Sticky and enjoyable. *46%*

Tullibardine 1993 Port Finish bott 2008 db (83.5) **n**21.5 **t**21 **f**20 **b**21. A bumbling, weighty kind of dram with indistinct shape and purpose, even to the extent of displaying a more bourbony gait than a fruity one. Enjoyable, decently spiced but limited in scope. *46%*

Tullibardine 1993 Sauternes Finish bott 2008 db (84.5) **n**22 **t**22 **f**20 **b**20.5. Sleepy and soft with the expected major grape input. Yet rather flattens out too early and to too great a degree. Pleasant, but a little disappointing, too. *46%*

Tullibardine Aged 20 Years db (92.5) **n**22.5 busy and can't decide which weight to adopt; ethereal hazelnut and citrus rise above the languid tannins; **t**24 no doubting the richness of body and the exceptional weight: first it is scorched yet juicy barley by the cartload, then thudding oak with just enough ulmo honey to oil the wheels. And then rampaging spice; **f**22.5 settles for more prosaic butterscotch but the spices continue to bristle; **b**23.5 while there are whiskies like this in the world, there is a point to this book... *43%*

Tullibardine Aged 25 Years db (86.5) **n**22 **t**22 **f**21 **b**21.5. There can be too much of a good thing. And although the intricacies of the honey makes you sigh inwardly with pleasure, the overall rigidity and fundamentalism of the oak goes a little too far. *43%*

Tullibardine 225 sauternes cask finish db (85) **n**20 **t**22.5 **f**21 **b**21.5. Hits the heights early on in the delivery when the honey and Lubeck marzipan are at full throttle. *43%*

Tullibardine 228 Burgundy cask finish db (82) **n**21 **t**22 **f**18 **b**21. No shortage of bitter chocolate. Flawed but a wow for those looking for mega dry malt. *43%*

Tullibardine 500 sherry cask finish db (79.5) **n**19 **t**21 **f**19 **b**20.5. The usual problems from Jerez, but the grape ensures maximum chewability. *43%*

Tullibardine Aged Oak bott 2009 db (86) **n**21.5 **t**21 **f**22 **b**21.5. Aged oak maybe. But early on this is all about the malt which is faultless. Major oaky buzz later. *40%*

Tullibardine Aged Oak Edition bott 2010 db (88) **n**21 **t**22 **f**22.5 **b**22.5. Beautifully made malt which is full of life. *40%. nc.*

Tullibardine Banyuls Finish bott 2011 db (68) **n**16 **t**18 **f**17 **b**17. I saw the sulphur coming on this. A steaming mug of intense black coffee and a cool glass of taste bud restorative coconut water wait in the wings. *46%. nc ncf.*

Tullibardine Banyuls Finish bott 2012 db (71) **n**17 **t**19 **f**17 **b**18. A minor tragedy: take away the sulphur and you have what would have been a serious juicefest. Not for the first time with a banyuls cask, I could cry! *46%. nc ncf.*

Tullibardine John Black db (84.5) **n**20 **t**21.5 **f**22 **b**21. Young, clean and bursting with all kinds of delicious maltiness. An almost perfect first dram of the day. *40%. nc.*

Tullibardine Pure Pot new make db (90.5) **n**24 **t**23 **f**21.5 **b**22. Pure delight! Not whisky, of course, but a great example of how new make malt should be. *69%*

Tullibardine Sauternes Finish bott 2012 db (90.5) **n**22 **t**23 **f**22.5 **b**23. The spices attached to the richness of the body makes for a very satisfying and quite intriguing malt. *46%. nc ncf.*

Tullibardine Sovereign bourbon barrel db (89.5) **n**22.5 a kind of 'what's what' of bourbon aromas: an entire regiment of delicate oaky tones from the standard butterscotch through to polished oak floors. But all tinged with a green-ish barley note. Always light and a little chalky; **t**23 the nose is transferred almost in identical form to the delivery: more light sugars at play here and a little nutty, too; **f**21.5 a slight tang to the fading milky Sugar Puffs; **b**22.5 beautifully salivating despite the intricate oak notes. *43%*

Tullibardine Vintage Edition Aged 20 Years dist 1988, bott 2008 db **(86) n22 t22 f21 b21.** The malt sparkles on the nose and delivery. Fades as caramels kick in. 46%

⟨⟩ **Anam na h-Alba The Soul of Scotland Tullibardine 1989** bourbon cask, dist Apr 89, bott May 15 **(84) n21 t22.5 f19 b20.5**. The earthy, dank moss nose suggests not all is right with the barrel, as the sharp, tangy, ill-at-ease finale certifies. The massively intense barley on delivery is exceptional, though. 53.3%. 36 bottles.

Old Malt Cask Tullibardine Aged 23 Years cask no. 10453, bott 14 **(95) n23.5** beautiful structure and weight: a little toasty, but welcomes the nutty spread. Excellent salt to sugar ratio; **t24** sublime delivery with near perfect weight and poise and some ramped up barley. The oils are delicate, the sugars playful and the quasi-bourbon style liquorice adding just the right degree of tostesterone; **f23.5** a late settling of some sugary scores as the light muscovado overpowers the fudgy oak; **b24** an early morning reminder why I can really love this job. 50%. sc.

The Pearls of Scotland Tullibardine 1990 cask no. 6115, bott Jun 14 **(94) n23.5** borderline bourbon in style with nut and toasted honeycomb amid the red liquorice; **t24** superb delivery: the mouth feel, approach and realisation of the soft molassed sugars. Their intermingling with the liquorice and light hickory; the weight...and pace of change....the stamp of rich malt to remind you this is Scotch...classy! **f23** more bourbon-style notes hang in there, especially the sugar-oak and red liquorice; **b23.5** top drawer whisky which embraces the oak like a Kentuckian. 51.7%. sc.

⟨⟩ **Provenance Tullibardine Over 7 Years** refill barrel, cask no. 10767, dist Summer 08, bott Summer 15 **(84) n21 t21.5 f20.5 b21**. Decidedly green, sugary and youthful. Struggles to find body beyond the malt and would have benefited from being at cask strength. 46%. nc ncf sc.

⟨⟩ **Spirit & Cask Tullibardine** barrel, dist 2007, bott 2015 **(85) n21 t22 f21.5 b21.5**. Young, malty and refreshing. 46%. 294 bottles.

UNSPECIFIED SINGLE MALTS (CAMPBELTOWN)

Cadenhead's Campbeltown Malt (92) n22 t24 f23 b23. On their home turf you'd expect them to get it right... and, my word, so they do!! 59.5%

Cadenhead's Classic Campbeltown (92) n23 t24 f22 b23. What a dram! Must be what they gave Lazarus... 50%

UNSPECIFIED SINGLE MALTS (HIGHLAND)

⟨⟩ **Alexander Murray & Co Bon Accord Highland Single Malt (82.5) n21 t21.5 f20 b20.** Fudge whisky. Pleasant, but way too simple. 40%

⟨⟩ **Alexander Murray & Co Highland Single Malt 1964 49 Years Old (88) n22 t23 f21.5 b21.5**. For a malt bottled on the cusp of its 50th anniversary of being distilled, beyond the delivery it is hard to find a narrative here. Often malts of this age are simply too oaky and lopsided to be of any significance on the greatness front. This certainly has its fair share of tannin, and even a hint of bourbon on the nose. But it is the reticence of the malt to give much of a clue to what's been happening all these years which is perplexing: I cannot remember a bottled whisky of this age which is so comprehensively gagged on the mid-ground and finish. The delivery has a bit more going for it, and at times you can almost chew the golden syrup-dripping sawdust. And the spices at the death are superb. No doubting it has some genuinely lovely moments, and if you are looking for a very old malt which simply exudes soft, aged, occasionally charming benevolence, then this could be for you. But, overall, it is all so frustratingly fuddled and fudged. 40%

⟨⟩ **Alexander Murray & Co Highland Single Malt 1995 19 Years Old (85) n21 t22 f21 b21.** Agreeably spiced toffee. 40%

⟨⟩ **Trader Joe's Highland Single Malt 1996 17 Years Old (86.5) n21.5 t22 f21.5 b21.5**. Some serious juiciness and spice on the delivery. The spices last the course. 40%.

UNSPECIFIED SINGLE MALTS (ISLAND)

Master Of Malt Island Single Malt (91.5) n22.5 t23 f22.5 b23.5. Don't know about Lord of the Isles. More like Lord of the Flies...Fruit flies, that is...! They would be hard pressed to find even an over-ripe mango any juicier than this gorgeous malt... 40%

UNSPECIFIED SINGLE MALTS (ISLAY)

Blackadder Peat Reek Raw Cask Islay single oak hogshead, bott Jul 13 **(88.5) n23** rich in phenols and sugar cane juice. Oily, too; **t23** big and chewy arrival, but still allows the sugars a pretty full hand. The oak is bit niggardly but banana and vanilla still hold out; **f21** finally bitters out on the oak; **b21.5** a more sympathetic hoggy and this would have scored very highly. 60.6%. nc ncf sc. 216 bottles. WB15/060

Blackadder Smoking Islay cask. BA2013/450, bott Jun 13 **(88) n22** on the nose, more like Fighting Islay: the peat is pretty spiced up and gives the old schnoz a sharp biff; **t23** the palate becomes a playground for energetic young sugars; **f21** slightly overly aggressive on the bitterness front; spice tries to compensate; **b22** attractive, but not quite up to the usual very high standards for this bottling. *55%. nc ncf sc. 386 bottles. WB15/161*

Blackadder Smoking Islay Raw Cask cask no. BA2013/449 **(92.5) n24** brilliant nose. Very high phenols offering Parma violets (flowers, not candy), celery and accompanying pepper, salted liquorice, hickory and, cleverly hidden, smoked treacle; **t23.5** the more sugary elements have enough power to hold off the creeping, drying smoke for a while. It is the massive spice which really focusses the attention; **f22** dries and bitters. But the dark, buttery, cake-mix, sugars combine with the smoke to see off the worst; **b23** almost a curious re-run of Blackadder's Peat Reek, with the fun threatening to end as the bitterness of the cask bites, adder-like. But just many good points compensate. Really lovely. *59.9%. nc ncf sc. 318 bottles. WB15/061*

⬧ **Cask Islay (91.5) n22.5** ashy and dry. Oh, and smoky; **t23** soft oils dissolve to be replaced by lively spice, citrus and polite Demerara sugar. Oh, and some smoke...; **f22.5** good length thanks to the remaining oil with a light smattering of vanilla. The sugars also linger...as does the smoke; **b23** does what it says on the tin. *46%. A.D. Rattray*

Celtique Connexion Origine Islay Affiné Sauternes cask dist 1999, bott 2013 **(95.5) n23** huge smoke is somehow contained in a creamy, sultana studded crust; **t24** soft and voluptuous, the peat arrives confidently, spices in hand; silky fruit soon takes command displaying a fine array of varied sugars; **f24** a finish marginally longer than the Channel Tunnel...an offering an even more comfortable ride; dries into a sooty peat finale; **b24.5** that rarest of beasts: a heavily peated malt happy to mature in a wine cask. Not surprised it required a spotless Sauternes cask to do the job. Mind-blowingly glorious. *46%*

⬧ **Douglas Laing's Single Minded Islay Aged 6 Years (84.5) n21 t22.5 f20 b21.** Oily, sweet and moderately smoky. Don't look for complexity. Or a particularly great finish, either. *48.4%. nc ncf.*

Elements of Islay AR4 (93.5) n23.5 t23.5 f23 b23.5. Massive oak infusion: the slow burn of smoke leaves no doubt to distillery. Clever oily-dry interplay plus hickory and cocoa-orange. *58.1% WB15/341*

⬧ **Elements of Islay Ar5 (76) n19 t20 f18 b19.** One element too many in this fruity and off-key version. *57.8% WB16/017*

⬧ **Elements of Islay Bn5 (82.5) n19.5 t22 f20 b21.** Peat a'plenty, but perhaps a few too many tangy moments than is desirable. *54.9% WB16/014*

Elements of Islay BN6 (80) n20 t22 f19 b19. Simply too sweet and cloying for its own good. Zero complexity as the molasses, golden syrup and manuka honey go ballistic. Off key finale. *56.9% WB15/346*

Elements of Islay BR5 (96) n24 t24.5 f23.5 b24. An unpeated masterpiece of the Laddie old school. Possibly the most complete and harmonious alloy of honeys bottled this year. Genius. *53.8% WB15/296*

Elements of Islay BW3 (90.5) n22.5 t23.5 f22 b22.5. A playful Bowmore showing a copper sharpness amid the more languid smoke. Fabulous delivery: acacia and ulmo honey starring. *51.6% WB15/289*

⬧ **Elements of Islay Bw4 (87) n22 t22.5 f20.5 b22.** Low peated and highly sugared; the spices are more than welcome. *51.6% WB16/016*

⬧ **Elements of Islay CI7 (91) n22 t23.5 f22.5 b23.** At times thick enough to be like dementedly peated clotted cream...with vanilla and Demerara sugar stirred in. *58.5% WB16/015*

Elements of Islay CL6 (94) n23 t24 f23 b24. Less oil means more balance for this stunning Caol Ila. The major citrus element cuts through the peat; light sugar and malt salivates. *61.2% WB15/290*

Elements of Islay LG4 (87.5) n22 t23 f21 b21.5. Typical huge Lagavulin but untypical sharpness on delivery & sweet finish. The phenols are of a smoked mackerel variety. *55.7% WB15/287*

Elements of Islay LP4 (89) n22.5 t22.5 f22 b22. Profound peat at its earthiest. A tangy delivery but then soothing, as muscovado sugars & vanillas arrive. A gentle giant. *54.8% WB15/286*

Elements of Islay LP5 (92) n23.5 t22.5 f22 b22. Elements is right for this Laphroaig: what we are getting here is the malt at its gristiest with the sugars releasing the smoke beautifully. *52.4% WB15/288*

Finlaggan Old Reserve Cask Strength (94) n23 t23.5 f23.5 b24. I can imagine even people who proclaim to not like peaty whisky slowly falling in love with this...it is so enormous, that it would be a case of kill or cure. *58%. The Vintage Malt Whisky Co Ltd.*

Mystery Lochside (95) n24.5 t24 f22.5 b24. The kind of malt that deserves all the time you can afford it. It will repay you handsomely, especially on the nose and delivery and will never come at you at the same speed or angle. Subtle and sublime.

Port Askaig Harbour Aged 19 Years (94) n23.5 t23.5 f23 b24. One of those gorgeous offerings which basks in its simplicity, but takes what it does to the max. 50.4%.

⟷ **Smokey Joe Islay Malt** (94.5) n23 high level phenols are broadcast on an oily, salty, coastal wind...; t24 the delivery, snug in its peaty overcoat, is good...the following waves of smoke are truly exceptional. A just-so degree of dark sugar and liquorice embrace the phenols...; f23.5 a vague bitterness, but caught in its tracks by the gradual ascent of delicious cocoa notes; b24 a high quality Islay ticking all the required boxes. 46%

Wemyss Aged 30 Years Islay "Heathery Smoke" hogshead, bott Aug 11 (95.5) n24 t24 f23.5 b24. One of those magical malts which never noses or tastes the same twice and always offers a different perspective and new facets each time it is sampled. A true gem. 46%. sc. 272 bottles. USA exclusive.

⟷ **Whisky Fair Islay Malt 8 Year Old** bourbon hogshead, dist 2007, bott 2015 (88.5) n22.5 simple, straightforward, clean, powdery, spicy phenols; t22 very youthful, juicy delivery. Simple and straightforward with attractive butterscotch in the midground; f22....errr... straightforward...? b22 clean, gristy and irresistibly charming. 54.4%. 144 bottles.

⟷ **Wilson & Morgan House Malt Single Islay Malt** cask no. 6158, 6266, dist May 06, bott Jan 15 (86.5) n23 t22.5 20 b21. The nose is a success with its Arbroath Smokies on newly-baked bread. Oily and pugnacious. But the strangely metallic and off-key finish leaves you scratching your head... 43%

UNSPECIFIED SINGLE MALTS (LOWLAND)

Tweeddale Single Lowland Malt Scotch Whisky 14 Years db (89) n21.5 sharp citrus and basic vanilla; t23.5 lively, clean and salivating, the grist positively pulses; f22 back to simple vanilla basics...but attractively done; b22 busy, bustling, elegant and old-fashioned...like a small borders town. 62%. nc ncf sc. Stonedean Ltd.

UNSPECIFIED SINGLE MALTS (SPEYSIDE)

⟷ **Alexander Murray & Co Speyside Single Malt 1972 41 Years Old** (90) n22.5 t23 f22 b22.5. The fascinating nose is worth a good ten minutes of anyone's time: earthy, pungent, with some fruit and nut amid the oak. But you can't escape the tannin on the palate, as this reached its prime maybe a decade earlier. Even so, as oaky mountains go, this is scalable and there are some half decent views when you get to the top. 40%

⟷ **Glen Fahrn Airline Nr 13 Red Baron of Speyside 1971 Aged 40 Years** bourbon cask (87.5) n22 t21 f22.5 b22. I'd say this is the product of big stills. Because a lightweight body to the malt has allowed the oak to run riot. Thankfully, enough muscovado and maple syrup has been extracted for tannins to be controlled. More Kentucky than Speyside, but with none of the depth, richness and complexity of a good bourbon. 51.7%. sc. 139 bottles.

⟷ **Kirkland Speyside 20 Year Old** (88) n22 an enticing, marginally complex nose: tannins and creamy chocolate mix comfortably while gentle spices massage; t23 attractive delivery with a supine mouth feel. The spice is gentle but upfront while a soft toffee and raisin theme develops; f21 a little tangy and fades a shade too fast; b22 pleasant and workmanlike. 40%. Bottled for Costco. Alexander Murray & Co.

⟷ **Malt Mountain Speyside Region 20 Year Old** dist 1994, bott 2015 (89) n22 fat, sugar-laden gooseberries being gently boiled; t24 sumptuous mouth feel; divine arrival of over-ripe greengage, gooseberry, vanilla and spices almost at the very same moment; f20 back to a drier, lightly salted gooseberry tart...but some cask taint, as well; b23 not flawless, but the depth and freshness of the fruit is astonishing...and stunning! 52.4%

Master of Malt Speyside 30 Years Old 6th edition (95) n24.5 textbook balance and dexterity to the oak. Like opening up an old herb and spice cupboard and the last reverberations of a hundred cakes and stews made many years ago come quietly drifting back...; t24 no less delicate on delivery. Probably made in a big still as there is little oil or metallic residue, leaving the oak to, again, lead the way, both in weight and depth of layering; the sweetness is confined to a light mintiness and a vague grist presence, but after the brief initial barley juice outpouring, it is the drying oak which dominates; f22.5 so light, the fade is over quickly but not without delicate spice and overall elegance; b24 Hmmmm. My 13th whisky of the day...and this comes from bottle number 13 of 238. The omens may be bad but in fact it has proved to be the best of the session so far. From the understated school of Speysiders where subtlety is key. 43.7%. 238 bottles. WB15/229

Master Of Malt Speyside 40 Years Old 2nd Edition (95) n23.5 t24 f23.5 b24. Magnificent. has no problem mastering the years. *43%.*

Master Of Malt Speyside 50 Years Old 3rd Edition (96.5) n24 t23.5 f24.5 b24.5. Like many an old 'un, it seems to forget where it's going for a while. But when it reaches its destination, it just charms you to death. *43%.*

⬦ **Old Malt Cask Probably Speyside's Finest 28 Years Old** sherry butt, cask no. 11272, dist Nov 86, bott Feb 15 (96) n24 a seemingly quiet nose, but on concentrated listening, far more is going on than first meets the nostril: the fruit is little more than a whisper, but the honey notes star, with a blend of manuka and rape constantly fidgeting about; t24.5 so subtle: a charming re-run of the nose with almost the same points arriving with similar timing. Only the spice is more outgoing, while the mouth feel is gently oiled and exceptionally soft; f23.5 drier, of course, as 28 years worth of oak is intent on making some impression. But still we are in the land of caresses and hints...; b24 a clean bill of health for this quietly intriguing and drop-dead gorgeous sherry bottling. *48%. nc ncf sc. 285 bottles.*

Old Malt Cask Probably Speyside's Finest Distillery wine finished refill hogshead, cask no. 10376, dist Nov 92, bott Mar 14 (74) n18 t20 f17 b19. Tart, furry, woefully off key: I think Speyside can do a little better than this. *50%. sc. 152 bottles.*

Old Masters Queen of Spey 12 Year Old dist 2001, bott 2013 (89.5) n22 an attractive thread of anthracite smoke weaves in and out of the fresh ear and gristy malt; t23 much, much younger on delivery than its 14 years, with a hint of new make. But the mix of intense juicy barley and spice is gorgeous; f22 a little oak bite and nibble but vanilla dominates; b22.5 an unspecified single malt of very specified freshness and beauty. *56.8%.*

⬦ **Riegger's Selection Cask Strength Eagle of Spey 1993** sherry cask finish, bott 24 Dec 13 (87.5) n22.5 t23 f20 b22. A joyful, fruity –and beautifully juicy – ride until we get to the very bitter finish. *52.9%*

⬦ **Spirit & Cask El Máximo No. 7 sherry butt,** dist 2008, bott 2015 (86.5) n21.5 t22 f21.5 b21.5. A clean sherry butt. No sulphur, so bravo! But because of the age, the fruit, malt and oak haven't yet found a happy medium. Not unpleasant - indeed, at times very pleasant - just plucked from the cask at the wrong time. *65%. 675 bottles.*

⬦ **Trader Joe's Speyside Single Malt 2001 12 Years Old** (85) n21.5 t22.5 f20 b21. For a moment on both nose and delivery it appears this little bird can sing, especially when the muscovado sugars kick off early and appear to ignite the grist. But the caramel middle and fade are a disappointment. *40%. Alexander Murray & Co.*

⬦ **Whisky-Fässle Speyside Malt 6 Year Old** sherry butt, dist 2008, bott 2014 (85) n21 t22 f21 b21. A sweet and syrupy cove. The spices appear to be the harbinger of something a little less desired. Superficially enjoyable but never finds a rhythm or happy medium. *46.9%. nc ncf.*

⬦ **Whisky-Fässle Speyside Malt 20 Year Old** sherry butt, dist 1994, bott 2015 (96) n23 doughy. Jam doughnut...? t24 oh, oh, oh....!!! That's how a sherry cask should be: a few tantalising glimpses of malt, but the rest is clean, beautifully spiced and rounded fruit...; f24.5 the freshness of the juicy dessert wine continues, until finally met by weightier, liquorice-edged oak. Such full on complexity...; b24.5 old school sherry cask – as clean as a whistle. And one which not only hits all the high notes but possesses the ability to stay on the mark. Just fantastic stuff! *53.2%. nc ncf.*

UNSPECIFIED SINGLE MALTS (GENERAL)

Blackadder Black Smoke Vat No. 2 First Venom bott Sep 13 (95) n23.5 fudge with juicy raisin; slight hint of greengage; t23.5 superb delivery: the barley is in full concentrated mode and after a toffee-laden interlude returns, alongside a wave of grape to make for a delightful, mouth-watering juiciness; f24 spiced grape...which can't entirely escape the toffee encasement; some attractive praline and mocha mix to finish; b24 great to find a malt finished in sherry and has not paid the price...pure entertainment. *56.9%. nc ncf. 474 bottles.*

Blackadder The Legendary Cask Strength (93) n23 delicate, (non-salted) buttery tones link with boiled pear and creamy custard....yummy! t24 if there are awards for the softest cask strength deliveries, this would be up there. A playfully light oil adds lustre to the intense barley and toffee tones which dominate; a gorgeous layer or two of ulmo honey absorbs and punches the spices try to give; f23 very light tannin adds depth, but it is a slow fade of all that has gone before...; b23 if the legendary Blackadder, complete with trusted sword, reappeared through the "swirling mists of time" and came back as a whisky, I think he'd prefer to be something a little more butch than this essay of gentility bordering on femininity. *58.1%. WB15/055*

Blackadder The Legendary 20 Years Old cask no. LT132013-02 (87.5) n22 t22 f21.5 b22. Appears to have spent a significant part of the passing 20 years trapping all the soft caramel notes it can find. This overcomes the more stark oakiness, but at the cost of complexity. Hardly challenging but very pleasant, though. *46%. nc ncf sc. WB15/057*

Chieftain's The Cigar Malt Aged 20 Years sherry butt, dist May 93, bott Sept 13 (86.5) **n21 t23 f21 b21.5** From a 90% clean sherry butt (the finish gives the game away a bit), a whisky you can puff on, apparently. Not being a smoker – and never having ever been one – I have no idea what this is about. But as a single malt, a pleasant enough experience, though strictly limited in its scope and desires and the real fun bit revolves around the impressively rich delivery. *51.8%. ncf nc. Ian Macleod Distillers Ltd.*

◇ **Saar Whisky Bliesgau 2007** bott 2015 (83.5) **n22 t22.5 f19 b20.** A beautiful start with sugars abounding. But the finish is a little too tangy. *53.2%. ncf sc.*

◇ **Saar Whisky Gruwehewwel 2007** bott 2015 (96.5) **n24.5** textbook phenolic nose: dry and ashy yet clever muscovado sugars ensuring softness and balance; **t24** again the sugars get up close and personal early on. And they need to for the peat is as outlandishly big as it is majestic **f23.5** long, elegant, the sugars and oils lasting long enough to ensure a peaty complexity carries on for a very good while; **b24.5** just outstandingly good, fault-free peaty whisky. One of the great independent bottlings of the year. *51.9%. ncf sc.*

◇ **Saar Whisky Mandelbachtal 2007** bott 2015 (93.5) **n23.5** just so honeyed: heather honey, ulmo honey, rape honey all there in varying amounts and to differing depths. But excellent slightly salted butterscotch tart to keep the sugars in check; **t23.5** and there they are again: a surge of lightly oiled honeys – mainly heather honey, as on the nose – beautifully shaped by the Brazilian biscuit-style flour of the oak; **f23** drier, saltier, lingering beeswax; **b23.5** distilled by bees. *52.7%. ncf sc.*

◇ **Saar Whisky Schwenker 2005** bott 2015 (89) **n22.5** beautiful dry, salty peat. A charmer; **t23** early gristy peat, then a slow blossoming of ever intensifying phenols; sugars are sprinkled liberally; **f21.5** just a little biter at death; **b22** a competent, easy going malt for peat lovers. *53.7%. ncf sc*

◇ **Spirit & Cask Maximum Peat 2008 No. 14 butt**, bott 2015 (95) **n23.5** dry, acidic peat...errr, to the max...!! **t24** huge marriage of phenols, muscovado sugar and ulmo honey.... sublime! **f23.5** dry, tingling smoke with a light vanilla coating; that said, enough lingering sugars to ensure balance throughout; **b24** this may be from a butt, but let me reassure you: this kicks ass...!! No sulphur nonsense present here. *61.6%. 624 bottles..*

Scottish Vatted Malts
(also Pure Malts/Blended Malt Scotch)

◇ **Angels' Nectar** (81) **n21 t21 f19 b20.** This angel has a bitter tooth... *40%*

100 Pipers Aged 8 Years Blended Malt (74) **n19 t20 f17 b18.** A better nose, perhaps, and some spice on arrival. But when you consider the Speysiders at their disposal, all those mouth-wateringly grassy possibilities, it is such a shame to find something as bland as this. *40%*

Ballantine's Pure Malt Aged 12 Years bott code. LKAC1538 (88.5) **n22.5 t23 f21 b22.** No sign of the peat being reintroduced to major effect, although the orange is a welcome addition. Remains a charmer. *40%. Chivas.*

Bell's Signature Blend Limited Edition (83.5) **n19 t22 f21 b21.5.** The front label makes large that this vatted malt has Blair Athol and Inchgower at the heart of it as they are "two fine malts selected for their exceptionally rich character". Kind of like saying you have invited the Kray twins to your knees up as they might liven it up a bit. Well those two distilleries were both part of the original Bell's empire, so fair dos. But to call them both fine malts is perhaps stretching the imagination somewhat. A robust vatting to say the least. And, to be honest, once you get past the nose, good back-slapping fun. *40%. 90,000 bottles.*

Berrys' Best Islay Vatted Malt Aged 8 Years (82) **n20 t21 f20 b21.** Smoky, raw, sweet, clean and massive fun! *43%. Berry Bros & Rudd.*

Berry's Own Selection Blue Hanger 5th Release bott 2010 (81) **n20 t21 f20 b20.** Not a lot – but enough – sulphur has crept in to take the edge of this one. *45.6%. ncf.*

Berry's Own Selection Islay Reserve 2nd Edition (86.5) **n22 t22 f21 b21.5.** Maybe an Islay reserve but has enough smoky weight and hickory/chocolate charisma to be pushing for the first team squad. *46%. nc ncf. Berry Bros & Rudd.*

Berry's Own Selection Speyside Reserve 2nd Edition (79.5) **n21 t21.5 f18 b19.** Some excellent early sharpness and honey depth but falters. *46%. nc ncf. Berry Bros & Rudd.*

Big Peat Batch 30 (92) **n23 t22 f23.5 b23.5.** That's much more like it! This is far more how I expect this dram to be. *46%. nc ncf. Douglas Laing & Co.*

Big Peat Batch 31 (90.5) **n23** love it: superb mix of allotment bonfire and peat reek. Some young spirit offering great energy; **t22** gristy sweet delivery pounded by spicy attitude; a blast of hickory and cocoa; **f22.5** the smoke rumbles along, but there is no letting up in intensity of peat or spice; **b23** good to see it has maintained its cheery high standard. Youthful, boisterous and challenging throughout. *46%. nc ncf. Douglas Laing & Co.*

The Big Smoke 40 (83) **n22 t21 f20 b20.** Pure grist. *40%*

The Big Smoke 60 (92) **n23 t23.5 f22.5 b23.** Much more delicate and in touch with its more feminine self than was once the case. A real beauty. *60%. Duncan Taylor & Co.*

Black Face 8 Years Old (78.5) **n18.5 t22 f19 b19.** A huge malt explosion in the kisser on delivery, but otherwise not that pretty to behold. *46%. The Vintage Malt Whisky Co Ltd.*

Burns Nectar (89.5) **n22 t22 f23 b22.5.** A delight of a dram and with all that honey around, "Nectar" is about right. *40%*

Carme 10 Years Old (79) **n21.5 t20 f18.5 b19.** On paper Ardmore and Clynelish should work well together. But vatting is not done on paper and here you have two malts cancelling each other out and some less than great wood sticking its oar in. *43%*

Cask Islay Vatting No. 1 (89) **n23 t22 f22 b22.** Those looking for a soft, smoky, inoffensive little Islay to keep them company had better look elsewhere... *46%. ncf. A.D. Rattray Ltd.*

Castle Rock Aged 12 Years Blended Malt (87) **n22.5 t23 f19.5 b22.** Stupendously refreshing: the finish apart, I just love this style of malt. *40%*

Cearban (79.5) **n18 t21.5 f20 b19.** The label shows a shark. It should be a whale: this is massive. Sweet with the malts not quite on the same wavelength. *40%. Robert Graham Ltd.*

Celtique Connexion Sauternes 16 Years Old dist 1995, bott 2012 (95) **n24 t24 f23 b24.** Not many whiskies make me cough, and hardly any at all at just 46%abv. But this, though only because the intensity caught me by surprise. And what a pleasant one! This horse chestnut-coloured malt is one you are unlikely to forget in a hurry. As sweetly balanced and beautiful to enjoy as Josh Wright's stunning volley for Millwall at Burnley in February 2012.... *46%. nc ncf.*

Clan Campbell 8 Years Old Pure Malt (82) **n20 t22 f20 b20.** Enjoyable, extremely safe whisky that tries to offend nobody. The star quality is all on the complex delivery, then it's toffee. *40%. Chivas Brothers.*

Clan Denny (Bowmore, Bunnahabhain, Caol Ila and Laphroaig) (94) **n24 t23 f23 b24.** A very different take on Islay with heavy peats somehow having a floating quality. Unique. *40%*

Clan Denny Islay (86.5) **n21.5 t23 f21 b21.** A curiously bipolar malt with the sweetness and bitterness at times going to extremes. Some niggardly oak has taken the edge of what might have been a sublime malt as the peat and spices at times positively glistens with honey. *46.5%. nc ncf sc. Douglas Laing & Co.*

Clan Denny Speyside (87) **n22 t22 f21 b22.** A Tamdhu-esque oiliness pervades here and slightly detracts from the complexity. That said, the early freshness is rather lovely. *46%*

Compass Box Canto Cask 10 bott Jul 07 (86.5) **n20.5 t21 f23.5 b21.5.** One the Canto collection which slipped through my net a few years back, but is still around, I understand. Typical of the race, this one has perhaps an extra dollop of honey which helps keep the over vigorous oaks under some degree of control. Sublime finish. *54.2%. nc ncf. 200-250 bottles.*

Compass Box Eleuthera Marriage married for nine months in an American oak Hogshead (86) **n22 t22 f20 b22.** I'm not sure if it's the name that gets me on edge here, but as big and robust as it is I still can't help feeling that the oak has bitten too deep. Any chance of a Compass Box Divorce...? *49.2%. Compass Box for La Maison du Whisky.*

Compass Box Flaming Heart second batch, bottling no. FH16MMVII (95.5) **n23.5 t24.5 f23 b24.5.** The Canto range was, I admit, a huge over-oaked disappointment. This, though, fully underlines Compass Box's ability to come up with something approaching genius. This is a whisky that will be remembered by anyone who drinks it for the rest of their lives as just about the perfect study of full-bodied balance and sophistication. And that is not cheap hyperbole. *48.9%. nc ncf. 4,302 bottles.*

Compass Box Flaming Heart 4th Edition bott Aug 12 (95) **n23.5 t24.5 f23 b24.** Vatted malt at its very best. A genuine celebration of great Scotch malt whisky. *48.9%. 9,147 bottles.*

Compass Box Flaming Heart 10th Anniversary bott Sep 10 (92) **n24 t23 f22 b23.** This one, as Flaming Heart so often is, is about counterweight and mouth feel. Everything appears just where it should be... *48.9%. nc ncf. 4186 bottles.*

⟨◇⟩ **Compass Box The Lost Blend** (95.5) **n23** there are gristy, vanila notes....but these cower as the peat begins to grasp hold of the situation and ushers in the spice; **t23.5** sensuously soft, sweet and oily: a little gristiness returns but the spices are proinent; a thin layer of ulmo honey breaks free of the smoke; **f24.5** an elegant finish allowing all parties an even say. Vanilla and caramel naturally complete the tale, though not before high class marzipan makes its welcome mark. The smoke lingers contentedly and without threat; **b24.5** I may be wrong, but I have a feeling that when the nose and flavour profile was being constructed, a little extra smoke than first planned was added. Seems that way by the manner in which the phenols just pipe up a little louder than it first seems... *46%*

Compass Box Lady Luck bott Sep 09 (91) **n22 t24 f23 b22.** Just a shade too sweet for mega greatness like The Spice Tree, but quite an endearing box of tricks. *46%.*

Compass Box Oak Cross bott May 10 **(92.5) n23 t24 f22.5 b23**. The oak often threatens to be just too big a cross to bear. But such is the degree of complexity, and cleverness of weight, the overall brilliance is never dimmed. Overall, a bit of a tart of a whisky... 43%. nc ncf.

Compass Box The Peat Monster bott May 10 **(82) n21.5 t21.5 f19 b20**. It is as though Victor Frankenstein's creation has met Bambi. Monsters don't come much stranger or more sanitised than this... 46%. nc ncf.

Compass Box The Peat Monster first fill and refill American Oak Casks, bott 18 Aug 12 **(94) n23.5 t23.5 f23 b24**. Wonderful to see peat working on so many levels. The sugars are perhaps more judicially used this time around. 46%. nc ncf.

◇ **Compass Box The Peat Monster Cask Strength (89) n23.5** fascinating arm wrestle between the drier, ashy notes and a more expansive peatiness, rich in dark sugars; some delicate citrus furthers the complexity; **t23** superb weight: just the right amount of oils help maximise the heather honey; the smoke is happy to hint rather than holler; **f20.5** just a little bit of oak bitterness but countered by the persistent sweetness; the smoke now blends with the spices; **b22** plenty of peat between your teeth but deserving of some better oak. 57.3%.

Compass Box The Peat Monster Reserve (92) n23 t23.5 f22.5 b23. At times a bit of a Sweet Monster...beautiful stuff! 48.9%

Compass Box The Peat Monster Tenth Anniversary Release bott Sept 13 **(95) n24** it has retained its sooty style from last year, though has bent at the knee to allow a little extra light brown sugar to soften the more eye-watering, sharper elements of the peat; **t24** a very clever delivery: both muscovado sugar and thick smoke are battling for early supremacy with neither having the heart for the kill. The oils enter and side with the muscovado, spreading around the palate, aided with a cocoa-bitter edge, while the smoke patrols and watches; **f23** a little bitter now, with a slight return to an acrid bite; slight sootiness foils attempts by the vanilla to gain a foothold; **b24** here we appear to see a mix, or compromise, between the sweeter bottling of two years ago and last year's searing dryness. And, unlike most compromises, this one works... 48.9%. 5,700 bottles.

Compass Box The Spice Tree first-fill and refill American oak. Secondary maturation: heavily toasted new French oak **(95.5) n24.5 t24.5 f23 b23.5**. Having initially been chopped down by the SWA, who were indignant that extra staves had been inserted into the casks, The Spice Tree is not only back but in full bloom. Indeed, the blossom on this, created by the use of fresh oak barrel heads, is more intoxicating than its predecessor – mainly because there is a more even and less dramatic personality to this. Not just a great malt, but a serious contender for Jim Murray Whisky Bible 2011 World Whisky of the Year. 46%

Compass Box The Spice Tree Inaugural Batch (93) n23 t23 f23 b24. The map for flavour distribution may be drawn for the first time here: an entirely different whisky in shape and flavour emphasis. And it is a map that takes a long time to draw... 46%. 4150 bottles.

Co-operative Group (CWS) Blended Malt Aged 8 Years (86.5) n22 t22 f21 b21.5. Much, much better! Still a little on the sticky and sweet side, but there is some real body and pace to the changes on the palate. Quite rich, complex and charming. 40%

◇ **Crom Westport 16 Years Old Warlords & Warriors Edition Thulsa's Choice** bourbon hogshead, dist Oct 97, bott Feb 14 **(92) n23** bananas in custard – a kind of trifle but without the sherry...; **t24** wow! Ulmo and acacia honeys blended with a smidge of spice. A few vanilla notes reprise the custard effect; **f22.5** a little drier and tighter as the oak gets a little more agressive; **b23.5** a genuine treat! Someone has done a great job finding complimentary casks... 53.7%. sc.

Cutty Sark Blended Malt (92.5) n22 t24 f23 b23.5. Sheer quality: as if two styles have been placed in the bottle and told to fight it out between them. What a treat! 40%.

◇ **Deerstalker Blended Malt Highland Edition (94) n23.5** top quality nose: the malt shows no great age but there is fresh, grassy barley by the bushel and a vague suggestion of some phenols to ensure weight; **t23.5** cut-glass clarity to the barley on delivery and as squeaky clean as the nose states. And just like the nose, some phenols come lurking up from the depths to guarantee length...; **f23** ...which is accomplished; **b24** a quite beautiful whisky by any standards. 43%

Douglas Laing's Double Barrel Ardbeg & Aultmore (85) n21.5 t22.5 f20 b21. Fruity, juicy and fulsome, the smoke has an adroit presence. But, ultimately, a little too tangy for its own good. 46%.

◇ **Douglas Laing's Double Barrel Ardbeg & Craigellachie (95) n24** moody and brooding, the smoke, despite the gentle veins of molasses, positively scowls from the glass; **t24** my word! What a delivery! Intense and massive, it somehow lands on the palate with all the force of a feather. Soon, though, the peat input gathers momentum, deepened in its intensity by a chocolate-liquorice injection; **f23** delicate spice buzz on the smoke; bitters out a little; **b24** I doubt if any whisky I taste today will display the same simmering beauty as this. *46%. ncf.*

Douglas Laing's Double Barrel Ardbeg & Glenrothes 8th Release (85.5) **n22.5 t22 f20 b21.** Nothing like as perky as the bottling I tasted last year: the Glenrothes appears to blunt the more intricate machinations of the Ardbeg after a beautifully choreographed nose and very early delivery. *46%*

Douglas Laing's Double Barrel Ben Nevis & Caol Ila (87.5) **n22.5 t22 f21 b22.** One of the lightest coloured malt whiskies I have ever seen bottled so, unsurprisingly, oak appears to play no part in either nose or flavour profile other than a very late tang at the finish. The Ben Nevis has thinned both the oils and smoky intensity if the Islay, which shows a delicate charm on both nose and delivery in particular. *46%.*

⬦ **Douglas Laing's Double Barrel Bowmore & Inchgower** (69) **n16.5 t18 f17 b17.5.** Too dry and austere with very little smoke to bind the two styles. Not happy bedfellows at all. *46%. ncf.*

Douglas Laing's Double Barrel Braeval & Caol Ila Aged 10 Years (78) **n18 t21 f20 b19.** The Mike and Bernie Winters of double barrelled whisky. *46%. Douglas Laing & Co Ltd.*

Douglas Laing's Double Barrel Caol Ila & Braeval 4th Release (92.5) **n23 t23.5 f22.5 b23.5.** After a few failures with this combination, a hit. A real egg and bacon of a vatted malt with the two personalities this time complimenting each other beautifully. *46%*

Douglas Laing's Double Barrel Caol Ila & Tamdhu (86.5) **n22 t22.5 f21 b21.** Positively shimmers on the palate while the smoke blasts its way through any encumberences. But there is something a little too youthful about the malt and too inhibited about the oak to make the most of the occasion. *46%.*

Douglas Laing's Double Barrel Glenallachie & Bowmore 1st Release (89) **n22 t22.5 f22 b22.5.** The delicate smoke of the Bowmore has tamed the wilder elements of the Glenallachie. A good mix. *46%*

Douglas Laing's Double Barrel Highland Park & Bowmore (95) **n23 t24.5 f24 b23.5.** The vital spark of fury to this one keeps the palate ignited. A standing ovation for such a magnificent performance on the palate. *46%. Douglas Laing & Co Ltd.*

⬦ **Douglas Laing's Double Barrel Islay & Highland** (91.5) **n23** delicate smoke hangs above the weightier malt; **t23** a volley of gristy sugars is sprinkled with a dusting of peat; **f22.5** dries and spices up slightly; **b23** a charmingly understated and mellifluous dram. *46%. ncf.*

Douglas Laing's Double Barrel Ledaig & Bowmore (87) **n22.5 t22 f21.5 b21.** About as sweet a marriage as you are likely to find. For some, it may be too sweet! *46%*

Douglas Laing's Double Barrel Macallan & Laphroiag 5th Release (93) **n23.5 t24 f22.5 b23.** As if born to be together. *46%*

Douglas Laing's Double Barrel Macallan & Laphroaig Aged 9 Years (83.5) **n21 t22 f20 b20.5.** Curiously muted. Sweet with the natural caramels outweighing the smoke. *46%*

Douglas Laing's Double Barrel Mortlach & Laphroaig 2nd Release (83.5) **n20 t22 f20.5 b21.** Compared to the Ardbeg/Glenrothes match, about as subtle and delicate as a smoky custard pie in the face. Hot and snarling fare. *46%*

Douglas Laing's Double Barrel Mortlach & Laphroaig 3rd Release (82.5) **n22.5 t21 f19 b20.** Its sweet nose and soft touch in the opening seconds promises so much, but fails to deliver – especially on the finish. *46%*

Douglas Laing's Double Barrel Mortlach & Laphroaig 4th Release (85.5) **n21.5 t21.5 f21 b21.5.** All kinds of sugars heading off every which way. Juicy and punchy, interests and entertains without harmonising. *46%*

⬦ **Douglas Laing's Double Barrel Speyside & Lowland** (84) **n21 t21.5 f20.5 b21.** Pleasant, sweet, exceptionally new makey throughout but, while simple and unchallenging, always refreshing. *46%. ncf.*

Douglas Laing's Double Barrel Talisker & Craigellachie 2nd Release (94.5) **n23 t24 f23.5 b24.** These two malts go together like bacon & eggs. And very smoky bacon at that... *46%*

⬦ **Douglas Laing's Rock Oyster** (84.5) **n21 t21.5 f21 b21.** So hugely salty – and weirdly phenolic into the bargain – not quite sure what it's done for my blood pressure... *46.8%*

Duncan Taylor Regional Malt Collection Islay 10 Years Old (81) **n21 t22 f19 b19.** Soft citrus cleanses the palate, while gentle peats muddies it up again. *40%*

Duthies Campbletown Region Blended Malt Scotch Whisky (76) **n18 t21 f18 b19.** Off key and furry: one suspects the hand of a naughty sherry butt...Those not troubled by such things will lap up the rich delivery in particular. *46%. WB15/360*

Duthies Highland Region Blended Malt Scotch Whisky (85) **n22.5 t22 f20 b21.** Nose stars with its sweet; untoasted marshmallow. Delivery has attractive nip to the barley; accent on the malt; exceptionally creamy but then bitters out. Competent and pleasant other than an unforgiving bourbon cask. *46% WB15/361*

219

Duthies Islay Region Blended Malt Scotch Whisky (94) n23.5 mid-range peat....top range oil; a few gorgeous dry sooty moments; t23.5 sweet delivery with the sugars, Demerara topping the bill, arriving before the smoke. Though only just, for that makes quite a noise, like thunder after a flash of sugary lightning; f23 the oils unravel and coat the palate with a smoky top dressing...which lasts a fair while; b24 has no great pretentions to enormity of complexity. But just displays a decent degree of peat in a thoroughly enjoyable and classical Islay manner. 46% WB15/359

Duthies Lowland Region Blended Malt Scotch Whisky (89.5) n22 lovely citrus freshens up the barley; t22 the barley jags into the palate from various, unsatisfied angles until settling on a light massaging style full of lightly sugared, soothing oils; f23 happier now, reverts to citrus and simple, caressing vanilla; b22.5 a classic gentle pre-prandial top up. 46% WB15/356

The Famous Grouse 10 Years Old Malt (77) n19 t20 f19 b19. The nose and finish headed south in the last Winter and landed in the sulphur marshes of Jerez. 40%. Edrington Group.

The Famous Grouse 15 Years Old Malt (86) n21 t22 f21.5 b21.5. Salty and smoky with a real sharp twang. 43%. Edrington Group.

The Famous Grouse 15 Years Old Malt (86) n19 t24 f22 b21. There had been a hint of the "s" word on the nose, but it got away with it. Now it has crossed that fine – and fatal – line where the petulance of the sulphur has thrown all else slightly out of kilter. All, that is, apart from the delivery which is a pure symphony of fruit and spice deserving a far better introduction and final movement. Some moving, beautiful moments. Flawed genius or what...? 40%

The Famous Grouse 18 Years Old Malt (82) n19 t21.5 f21 b20.5. Some highly attractive honey outweighs the odd uncomfortable moment. 43%. Edrington Group.

The Famous Grouse Malt 21 Years Old (91) n22 t24 f22 b23. A very dangerous dram: the sort where the third or fourth would slip down without noticing. Wonderful scotch! 43%.

The Famous Grouse 30 Years Old Malt (94) n23.5 t24 f23 b23.5. Whisky of this sky-high quality is exactly what vatted malt should be all about. Outrageously good. 43%

⬦ **Glenn** (89.5) n22 no shortage of nip and nibble on the grassy nose: t23 clean, salivating and fresh. Gets even more malty as it progresses on the palate, the oak making a low-key, vaguely honeyed entrance about half way in; f22 the oak takes a tangy twist; b22.5 a forceful malt. Seems as though at least two strands of the thread are trying to outdo each other. Enjoyable, but erratic towards the end. 50%. Svenska Eldvatten.

Glenalmond 2001 Vintage (82.5) n22 t21.5 f19 b20. Glenkumquat, more like: the most citrusy malt I have tasted in a very long time. 40%. The Vintage Malt Whisky Co Ltd.

Glenalmond "Everyday" (89.5) n21.5 t23.5 f22 b22.5. They are not joking; this really is an everyday whisky. Glorious malt which is so dangerously easy to drink. 40%

Glen Brynth Aged 12 Years Blended Malt (87) n22.5 t23 f19.5 b22. Deja vu...! Thought I was going mad: identical to the Castle Rock I tasted this morning, right down to the (very) bitter end ..!!! 40%. Quality Spirits International.

Glenbrynth Blended Malt 12 Years (87.5) n22.5 t22.5 f21 b21.5. Heavyweight malt which gets off to a rip-roaring start on the delivery but falls away somewhat from the mid ground onwards. 43%. OTI Africa.

Glenbrynth Ruby 40 Year Old Limited Edition (94) n23.5 t24 f23 b23.5. Has all the hallmarks of a completely OTT, far too old sherry butt being brought back to life with the aid of a livelier barrel. A magnificent experience, full of fun and evidence of some top quality vatting at work, too. 43%. OTI Africa.

Glendower 8 Years Old (84) n21.5 t21 f20.5 b21 Nutty and spicy. 43%

The Glenfohry Aged 8 Years Special Reserve (73) n19 t19 f17 b18. Some of the malt used here appears to have come from a still where the safe has not so much been broken into, but just broken! Oily and feinty, to say the least. Normally I would glower at anyone who even thought of putting a coke into their malt. Here, I think it might be for the best.. 40%

⬦ **Glen Talloch Blended Malt Aged 8 Years** (85.5) n21 t23 f20.5 b21. An invigorating and engulfing vatting, full of intrinsic barley tones on delivery. But the caramel is too strident for further complexity. 40%

Glen Turner Heritage Double Wood Bourbon & Madeira casks, bott code. L311657A (85.5) n21.5 t22 f21 b21. A very curious amalgamation of flavours. The oak appears to be in shock with the way the fruit is coming on to it and offers a bitter backlash. No faulting the crisp delivery with busy sugar and spice for a few moments brightening the palate. 40%.

Glen Turner Pure Malt Aged 8 Years L525956A (84) n20 t22 f22 b20. A lush and lively vatting annoyingly over-dependent on thick toffee but simply brimming with fabulously mouth-watering barley and over-ripe blood oranges. To those who bottle this, I say: let me into your lab. I can help you bring out something sublime!! 40%

Glen Orchy (80.5) n19.5 t21.5 f19.5 b20. Not exactly the most subtle of vatted malts though when the juicy barley briefly pours through on delivery, enjoyable. 40%. Lidl.

Glen Orchy 5 Year Old Blended Malt Scotch Whisky (88.5) n22 t22.5 f22 b22. Excellent malt plus very decent casks equals light-bodied fun. 40%. Lidl.

Glen Orrin (68) n16.5 t17.5 f17 b17. In its favour, it doesn't appear to be troubled by caramel. Which means the nose and palate are exposed to the full force of this quite dreadful whisky. 40%.

Glen Orrin Six Year Old (88) n22 t23 f21 b22. A vatting that has improved in the short time it has been around, now displaying some lovely orangey notes on the nose and a genuinely lushness to the body and spice on the finish. You can almost forgive the caramel, this being such a well balanced, full-bodied ride. A quality show for the price. 40%

Hedges and Butler Special Pure Malt (83) n20 t21 f22 b21. Just so laid back: nosed and tasted blind I'd swear this was a blend (you know, a real blend with grains and stuff) because of the biting lightness and youth. Just love the citrus theme and, err...graininess...!! 40%

Highland Harvest Organic Blended Malt 7 Casks batch 002 **(86.5)** n21.5 grassy, single-minded maltiness; t22.5 juicy, clean barley; muscovado sugar; f21 some late citrus; b21.5 not even remotely complex. But pleaant enough. 40% WB15/371

◈ **Highland Journey Blended Malt (94.5)** n23.5 a lovely mix of very lightly minted butterscotch with small dabs of acacia and ulmo honey. Delightfully indolent; t23.5 when I taste this much honey I am always reminded of Perthshire. That mix of acacia and ulmo on the nose was not a ruse; some curious young notes appear to lighten the intensity a little; f23.5 the journey ends, as it began and continued, without a single jolt. Very late, understated spices offer an unexpected viewpoint at the end of the line; b24 I have been on some memorable Highland journeys in my life, but few have been quite as comfortable as this one. 46.2%. Hunter Laing & Co.

Imperial Tribute (83) n19.5 t21.5 f21 b21. I am sure – and sincerely hope – the next bottling will be cleaned up and the true Imperial Tribute can be nosed and tasted. Because this is what should be a very fine malt... but just isn't. 46%. Spencer Collings.

Islay Trilogy 1969 (Bruichladdich 1966, Bunnahabhain 1968, Bowmore 1969) Bourbon/Sherry **(91)** n23 t23 f22 b23. Decided to mark the 700th tasting for the 2007 edition with this highly unusual vatting. And no bad choice. The smoke is as elusive as the Paps of Jura on a dark November morning, but the silky fruits and salty tang tells a story as good as anything you'll hear by a peat fire. Take your time...the whiskies have. 40.3%. Murray McDavid.

J & B Exception Aged 12 Years (80) n20 t23 f18 b19. Very pleasant in so many ways. A charming sweetness develops quickly, with excellent soft honeycomb. But the nose and finish are just so...so...dull...!! For the last 30 years J&B has meant, to me, (and probably within that old company) exceptionally clean, fresh Speysiders offering a crisp, mouth-watering treat. I feel this is off target. 40%. Diageo/Justerini & Brooks.

J & B Nox (89) n23 t23 f21 b22. A teasing, pleasing little number that is unmistakably from the J&B stable. 40%. Diageo.

John Black 8 Years Old Honey (88) n21 t22.5 f22.5 b22. A charming vatting. 40%

John Black 10 Years Old Peaty (91) n23 salty and peaty; t23 soft and peaty; f22 delicate and peaty; b23 classy and er...peaty. 40%. Tullibardine Distillery.

John McDougall's Selection Islay Malt 1993 (94.5) n23.5 t24.5 f22.5 b24. Complex, superbly weighted and balanced malt which just keeps you wondering what will happen next. 54.7%.

Johnnie Walker Green Label 15 Years Old (95) n24 t23.5 f23.5 b24. God, I love this stuff...this is exactly how a vatted malt should be and one of the best samples I've come across since its launch. 43%. Diageo.

Jon, Mark and Robbo's The Rich Spicy One (89) n22 t23 f22 b22. So much better without the dodgy casks: a real late night dram of distinction though the spices perhaps a little on the subtle side... 40%. Edrington.

Jon, Mark and Robbo's The Smoky Peaty One (92) n23 t22 f23 b24. Genuinely high-class whisky where the peat is full-on yet allows impressive complexity and malt development. A malt for those who appreciate the better, more elegant things in life. 40%. Edrington.

The Last Vatted Malt bott Nov 11 **(96.5)** n24 t25 f23.5 b24. Being an American, Compass Box founder and blender, John Glaser, knows a thing or two about pouring two fingers of whisky. So I join John in raising two fingers to the SWA and toast them in the spirit they deserve to thank them for their single-minded and successful quest to outlaw this ancient whisky term. 53.7%. nc ncf. 1,323 bottles.

◈ **The Loch Fyne The Living Cask 1745 (94.5)** n23.5 an intriguing two-toned nose which, if you concentrate on one side, offers firm smokiness giving further edge to the unyielding malts; and from the other angle is a complete softie...! t23.5 the delivery takes the path of the second option with an immediate eiderdown softness on delivery but doesn't duck out of juicy and, at times, forceful barleysugar then Fisherman Friend notes...all very sweet shop; f23.5 remains silky; now with a few spices joining the rolling smoke; b24 one of the best whiskies ever created at quarter to six in the evening....and one quite impossibe not to love. 46.3%

⟐ **The Loch Fyne The Living Cask** Batch One **(92) n22** the harsh smoke generates little more than a wispy buzz; the banana, ulmo honey, gristy malt and growing spice is the perfect foil; **t23.5** a volley of intense sugars, further enlivened by prickly spice makes for a memorable kick off. The smoke continues to drift and offer anchor; unusually, the texture actually becomes silkier as the flavours develop; **f23** a series of liquorice, fudge and crisp sugar notes, all on top of a blend of genteel and tangy phenols, makes for an easy exit; **b23.5** absolutely charming. 46.3%

Mackinlay's Rare Old Highland Malt (89) n22 t22 f22 b23. Possibly the most delicate malt whisky I can remember coming from the labs of Whyte and Mackay. Thought it still, on the palate, must rank as heavy medium. This is designed as an approximation of the whisky found at Shackleton's camp in the Antarctic. And as a life-long Mackinlay drinker myself, it is great to find a whisky baring its name that, on the nose only, briefly reminds me of the defter touches which won my heart over 30 years ago. That was with a blend: this is a vatted malt. And a delicious one. In case you wondered: I did resist the temptation to use ice. 47.3%

Master of Malt Reference Series I (82) n19.5 t23 f19 b20.5. Not quite the happiest of bunnies at times, as it occasionally struggles to find a balance in the face of big, not entirely desired, oils. That said, nothing to stop you embracing the enormity of the date & sugar-drizzled barley soon after delivery & during the period it has escaped a certain feintiness. 47.5% WB15/349

⟐ **Master of Malt Reference Series I.1 (87.5) n21 t23 f21.5 b22**. No enormous age – or at least oak involvement - as confirmed by the nose. But some wonderful moments as the juicy, clean barley hits the palate running. 47.5%

⟐ **Master of Malt Reference Series I.2 (93) n23** the delicate smokiness is accentuated by the crispness of the barley sub strata; **t23** the barley is first to hit, juicy and clean; delicate sugars dissolve merrily; **f23.5** the phenols slowly reassert themselves, but never at the cost of the delicate barley tones; **b23.5** a charming marriage between Fisherman's Friend phenols and balletic barley. 47.4%

⟐ **Master of Malt Reference Series I.3 (91) n22** dry, oak-steered with a nod towards mocha; **t22.5** a deft, peaceful delivery with no drama but loads of development; **f23.5** lightly sweetened cocoa powder makes for a fabulous ending: reminiscent of Merlin lollies of yesteryear ; **b23** it's all about the chocolate... 47.1%

Master of Malt Reference Series II (84.5) n20 t22 f21.5 b21. The oils have been toned down for this one, though the sugars have reached shrieking point. Malty, but perhaps a tad too cloying for its own good. 47.5% WB15/350

⟐ **Master of Malt Reference Series II.1 (88) n21** nothing wrong with it: just dull and uninspiring; **t23** a rich seam of malt appears to be of an oily disposition; **f22** again, technically sound. Plenty of rich malt and all that plus a hint of spice; **b22** an oily cove... 47.5%

⟐ **Master of Malt Reference Series II.2 (87) n22 t22.5 f21 b21.5**. Soft lemon drizzle on chunky malt plus an enjoyable volley of sugary grist early on. 47.4%

⟐ **Master of Malt Reference Series II.3 (89) n21.5** floral – a dank bluebell wood; **t22.5** mouth-filling malt. Playful oils and a steady ramping up of the malt intensity; **f22.5** something of a malt cereal about the finale; a little butterscotch tart thickens the effect; **b22.5** reminiscent of a Kentucky maltshake. 47.2%

Master of Malt Reference Series III (88) n22 fruit and nut...in abundance; **t23** salty beginnings on delivery then sugary shockwaves with the malt riding the surf; **f21** calms at last for the spices to form and the fruit/oak/malt elements to gel quite impressively before the warming fade; a slight fuzziness on the finale; **b22** still one for the sweet toothed, but you don't need a diagram at the back to tell you some decent age has been added to this vatting. The odd blemish, but great fun. 47.5% WB15/351

⟐ **Master of Malt Reference Series III.1 (89.5) n22.5** a squeeze of blood orange and grapefruit set the malt off beautifully; **t23** thrusts malt at the taste buds like a politician rams his party line down your earholes; **f21.5** a little vanilla and spice, though the malt lingers; a tad bitter late on; **b22.5** if you like your malt malty, vote for this. 47.7%

⟐ **Master of Malt Reference Series III.2 (92.5) n22.5** earthy, yet enticingly malty. And thick...; **t23** superb Malteser style delivery: massive malt with an attractive milk chocolate element; **f24** good grief!! That malt just doesn't know when to call it a day. A little ulmo honey has joined in to intensify the sweetness slightly; even some late spice adds to the ultra late complexity; **b23** similar to III.1, except without the bitter bits. 47.5%

⟐ **Master of Malt Reference Series III.3 (78) n19.5 t21.5 f18 b19**. Fruity, fat, sweet. A tad furry. And somewhat one-dimensional. 47.5%

Matisse 12 Year Old Blended Malt (93) n23.5 t23 f22.5 b23. Succulent, clean-as-a-whistle mixture of malts with zero bitterness and not even a whisper of an off note: easily the best form I have ever seen this brand in. Superb. 40%. Matisse Spirits Co Ltd.

Matisse Aged 12 Years (79) n17 t21 f20 b21. Not sure if some finishing or re-casking has been going on here to liven it up. Has some genuine buzz on the palate, but intriguing weirdness, too. Don't bother nosing this one. 40%. The Matisse Spirits Co Ltd.

Milroy's of Soho Finest Blended Malt (76) n18 t19 f20 b19. Full flavoured, nutty, malty but hardly textbook. 40%. Milroy's of Soho.

Moidart Aged 10 Years (89.5) n23 wonderfully clean and blends malty promise with youth; t23 superb! The delivery is rich in oils which makes the light, gristy-citrus notes just a little heavier; salivating and satisfying; f21.5 some of the more well-used casks radiating a degree of tiredness which slightly detracts from the delicate malts; b22 just love the fresh, crystal clarity of this whisky. 46% WB15/358

Mo'land (82) n21 t22 f19 b20. Extra malty but lumbering and on the bitter side. 40%.

Monkey Shoulder batch 27(79.5) n21 t21.5 f18 b19. Been a while since I lasted tasted this one. Though its claims to be Batch 27, I assume all bottlings are Batch 27 seeing as they are from 27 casks. This one, whichever it is, has a distinctive fault found especially at the finale, which is disappointing. Even before hitting that point a big toffeed personality makes for a pleasant if limited experience. 40%. William Grant & Sons.

"No Age Declared" The Unique Pure Malt Very Limited Edition 16-49 Years (85) n22.5 t19.5 f22 b21. Very drinkable. But this is odd stuff: as the ages are as they are, and as it tastes as it does, I can surmise only that the casks were added together as a matter of necessity rather than any great blending thought or planning. Certainly the malt never finds a rhythm but maybe it's the eclectic style on the finish that finally wins through. 45%. Samaroli.

Norse Cask Selection Vatted Islay 1992 Aged 16 Years hogshead cask no. QWVIM3, dist 92, bott 09 (95) n24 t24 f23 b24. The recipe of 60/35/5 Ardbeg/Laphroaig/Bowmore new make matured in one cask is a surprise: the oiliness here suggests a squirt of Caol Ila somewhere. This hybrid is certainly different, showing that the DNA of Ardbeg is unrecognisable when mixed, like The Fly, with others. Drinkable...? Oh, yes...!! Because this, without a single negative note to its name, is easily one of the whiskies of the year and a collector's and/or Islayphile's absolute must have. 56.7%

Norse Cask Selection Vatted Islay 1991 Aged 12 Years (89) n24 t23 f21 b21. Fabulous, but not much going in the way of complexity. But if you're a peat freak, I don't think you either notice...or much care...!! 59.5%. Quality World, Denmark.

Old St Andrews Fireside (88.5) n22 t22.5 f21.5 b22.5. Beautifully driven... 40%.

Old St Andrews Nightcap (89) n21.5 t24 f21 b22.5. Some delightful weight and mass but perhaps a bit too much toffee takes its toll. 40%. Old St Andrews Ltd.

Old St Andrews Twilight (94.5) n24 t23.5 f23 b24. Less Twilight as Sunrise as this is full of invigorating freshness which fills the heart with hope and joy: Lip-smacking Scotch malt whisky as it should be. Anyone who thinks the vatted malt served up for golf lovers in these novelty bottles are a load of old balls are a fair way off target... 40%. Old St Andrews Ltd.

The Pearls of Scotland Burnside 1992 20 Year Old cask no. 7350, dist Dec 92, bott Nov 13 (85) n22 t22 f20 b21. You can tell this is 99% Balvenie: it just has real problems handling the oak at this age. Nothing too much wrong with the nose for those into over-ripe banana. And the delivery boasts excellent mouth feel and early sugars until the merciless tannin bites deep. 55.8%.

Poit Dhubh 8 Bliadhna (90) n22.5 t23.5 f21.5 b22.5. Though the smoke which marked this vatting has vanished, it has more than compensated with a complex beefing up of the core barley tones. Cracking whisky. 43%. ncf. Pràban na Linne.

Poit Dhubh 12 Bliadhna (77) n20 t20 f18 b19. Toffee-apples. Without the apples. 43%. ncf. Pràban na Linne.

Poit Dhubh 21 Bliadhna (86) n22 t22.5 f21 b20.5. Over generous toffee has robbed us of what would have been a very classy malt. 43%. ncf. Pràban na Linne.

The Pot Still Scotch Vatted Malt Over 8 Years Old (90) n22 t24 f22 b22. Such sophistication: the Charlotte Rampling of Scotch. 43.5%. ncf. Celtic Whisky Compagnie, France.

Prime Blue Pure Malt (83) n21 t21 f21 b20. Steady, with a real chewy toffee middle. Friendly stuff. 40%

Prime Blue 12 Years Old Pure Malt (78) n20 t20 f19 b19. A touch of fruit but tart. 40%

Prime Blue 17 Years Old Pure Malt (88) n23 t21 f22 b22. Lovely, lively vatting: something to get your teeth into! 40%

Prime Blue 21 Years Old Pure Malt (77) n21 t20 f18 b18. After the teasing, bourbony nose the remainder disappoints with a caramel-rich flatness. The reprise of a style of whisky I thought had vanished about four of five years ago 40%

Queens & Kings Robert The Bruce (88) n21 the light smoke seems to be neutered by toffee; **t23.5** the brilliant delivery lifts the malt out of the doldrums. Smoked manuka honey to the fore; much, much better! **f21.5** some dull cocoa and spice, but oak bitterness, too; **b22** a bit of a wobbly vatting, where the part of the peat and its effects have not been thoroughly thought through. *54%. Mr Whisky.*

Rattray's Selection Blended Malt 19 Years Old Batch 1 Benrinnes sherry hogsheads **(89.5) n22 t23.5 f21.5 b22.5.** Absolutely love it! Offers just the right degree of mouth-watering complexity. not a malt for those looking for the sit-on-the-fence wishy-washy type. *55.8%. Auchentoshan, Bowmore, Balblair & BenRiach. A.D. Rattray Ltd.*

Sainsbury's Malt Whisky Finished in Sherry Casks (70) n18 t19 f16 b17. Never the greatest of the Sainsbury range, it's somehow managed to get worse. Actually, not too difficult when it comes to finishing in sherry, and the odd sulphur butt or three has done its worst here. *40%. UK.*

Scottish Collie (86.5) n22 t23 f20.5 b21. A really young pup of a vatting. Full of life and fun but muzzled by toffee at the death. *40%. Quality Spirits International.*

Scottish Collie 5 Years Old (90.5) n22.5 t23 f22 b23. Fabulous mixing here showing just what malt whisky can do at this brilliant and under-rated age. Lively and complex with the malts wonderfully herded and penned. Without colouring and at 50% abv I bet this would have been given a right wolf-whistle. Perfect for one man and his grog. *40%.*

Scottish Collie 8 Years Old (85.5) n22 t21.5 f21 b21. A good boy. But just wants to sleep rather than play. *40%. Quality Spirits International.*

Scottish Collie 12 Years Old (82) n20 t22 f20 b20. For a malt that's aged 84 in Collie years, it understandably smells a bit funny and refuses to do many tricks. If you want some fun you'll need a younger version. *40%. Quality Spirits International.*

Scottish Leader Imperial Blended Malt (77) n20 t20 f18 b19. Now don't be confused here: this isn't Imperial malt from Speyside. And although it says Blended, it is 100% malt. What is clear, though, is that this is pretty average stuff. *40%. Burn Stewart.*

Scottish Leader Aged 14 Years (80) n21 t21 f19 b19. A cleaner, less peaty version than the no-age statement vatting, but still fails to entirely ignite the tastebuds *40%. Burn Stewart.*

Scott's Selection Burnside 1994 (93) n23.5 t24 f22.5 b23.5. I may well be wrong. But I think this is the first time I have seen a Burnside, which is a cask of Balvenie spoiled as a single malt by having a spoonful of same age Glenfiddich added to it, in a commercial bottling rather than as a sample in my blending lab! Believe me: it was well worth waiting for...! *56.7%.*

Sheep Dip (84) n19 t22 f22 b21. Young and sprightly like a new-born lamb, this enjoys a fresh, mouthwatering grassy style wth a touch of spice. Maligned by some, but to me a clever, accomplished vatting of alluring complexity. *40%*

Sheep Dip 'Old Hebridean' 1990 dist in or before 1990 **(94) n23 t24 f23.5 b23.5.** You honey!! Now, that's what I call a whisky...!! *40%. The Spencerfield Spirit Co.*

The Six Isles Pomerol Finish Limited Edition French oak Pomerol wine cask no. 90631-90638, dist 03, bott 10 **(85.5) n19 t23 f21.5 b22.** What makes the standard Six Isles work as a vatted malt is its freshness and complexity. With these attributes, plus the distinctive distilleries used, we consistently have one the world's great and truly entertaining whiskies. With this version we have just a decent malt. The wine finish has levelled the mountains and valleys and restricted the finish dramatically, while the nose doesn't work at all. Perfectly drinkable and the delivery is extremely enjoyable. But as a Six Isles, delighted it's a Limited Edition. *46%.*

S'Mokey (88) n22.5 t22 f21.5 b22. Delicate, sweet and more lightly smoked than the nose advertises. *40%.*

Smokey Joe Islay Malt (87) n21.5 t22 f21.5 b22. A soft, soporific version of a smoky Islay. No thumping of waves here: the tide is out. *46%. ncf. Angus Dundee Distillers.*

Speyside Mysteria 24 Years Old Blended Malt bourbon cask, dist 90, bott 14 **(90) n22.5** hangs on against the advancing years with gritty determination...and a dollop of gooseberry jam; **t23.5** fruity delivery: black cherry preserve and strawberry jam and cream Swiss roll, aided by delicate ulmo honey; **f21.5** just a little too much oak, perhaps; **b22.5** a malt which has lived a long and rich life...and has plenty of wrinkles to show for it. *54.2%. ncf.*

Spirit of Caledonia Flaitheanas 18 Years Old (94) n23.5 oak shavings and tannin-based spices quietly and attractively dominate: so elegant..; **t24** superb arrival of both spice and ulmo honey, then a slow malty infusion; **f23** long, with butterscotch in the driving seat; **b23.5** now that is a proper vatted malt...!!! *578%. Mr Whisky.*

Sweet Wee Scallywag Sherry butts & bourbon hogsheads **(72) n23.5** oak shavings and tannin and a sulphured Scallywag at that...! *46%. ncf. Douglas Laing & co.*

Tambowie (84.5) n21.5 t21.5 f20.5 b21. A decent improvement on the nondescript bottling of yore. I have re-included this to both celebrate its newly acquired lightly fruited attractiveness...and to celebrate the 125th anniversary of the long departed Tambowie Distillery whose whisky, I am sure, tasted nothing like this. *40%. The Vintage Malt Whisky Co Ltd.*

⟨⟩ **That Boutique-y Whisky Company Blended Malt #2** batch 1 (72) n17.5 t19 f17.5 b18. Unmolested , the grape would have been spectacular, especially with the big cocoa finish. But the cask has done its damage. 48.3%. 370 bottles.

Treasurer 1874 Reserve Cask (90.5) n23 t23 f22.5 b22. Some judicious adding has been carried out here in the Robert Graham shop. Amazing for a living cask that I detect no major sulphur faultlines. Excellent! 51%. Live casks available in all Robert Graham shops.

Triple Wood Blended Malt Scotch Whisky (77) n17.5 t22 f18.5 b19. At least one wood too many. Tangy...for all the wrong reasons. 42%. Lidl.

Vintner's Choice Speyside 10 Years Old (84) n21.5 t22 f20 b20.5. Pleasant. But with the quality of the Speysiders Grants have to play with, the dullness is a bit hard to fathom. 40%.

Waitrose Pure Highland Malt (86.5) n22 t22 f20.5 b22. Blood orange by the cartload: amazingly tangy and fresh; bitters out at the finish. This is one highly improved malt and great to see a supermarket bottling showing some serious attitude...as well as taste!! Fun, refreshing and enjoyable. 40%

Wemyss Velvet Fig (64) n15 t19 f15 b15. Either vatted by someone who smokes 20 a day minimum or on purpose for the German and Chinese market which appears to enjoy this sort of thing. I eat a lot of figs which, on song, are sweet and spicy. This isn't. Although another "S" word plays a very big, debilitating, part... 46%. ncf.

Wemyss Vintage Malt The Peat Chimney Hand Crafted Blended Malt Whisky (80) n19 t22 f20 b19. The balance is askew here, especially on the bone-dry wallpapery finish. Does have some excellent spicy/coffee moments, though. 43%. Wemyss Vintage Malts Ltd.

Wemyss Vintage Malt The Smooth Gentleman Hand Crafted Blended Malt Whisky (83) n19 t22 f21 b21. Not sure about the nose: curiously fishy (very gently smoked). But the malts tuck into the tastebuds with aplomb showing some sticky barley sugar along the way. 43%

Wemyss Vintage Malt The Spice King Hand Crafted Blended Malt Whisky (84) n22 t22 f20 b20. Funnily enough, I've not a great fan of the word "smooth" when it comes to whisky. But the introduction of oily Caol Ila-style peat here makes it a more of a smooth gentleman than the "Smooth Gentleman." Excellent spices very late on. 43%. Wemyss Vintage Malts.

⟨⟩ **Whisky-Fässle Burnside 24 Year Old** barrel, dist 1989, bott 2014 (71) n18 t21 f15 b17. Exceptionally sweet, but this is a cask on the turn: the good tannins have been extracted and we are now entering into less than briliant lactose-type notes. You will find it takes quite a while to clean your palate after this. 51.1%

Whyte & Mackay Blended Malt Scotch Whisky (78) n19 t22 f18 b19. You know when the engine to your car is sort of misfiring and feels a bit sluggish and rough...? 40%. Waitrose.

Wild Scotsman Scotch Malt Whisky (Black Label) batch no. CBV001 (91) n23.5 t23.5 f21 b23. The type of dram you drink from a dirty glass. Formidable and entertaining. 47%

Wild Scotsman Aged 15 Years Vatted Malt (95) n23 t24 f24 b24. If anyone wants an object lesson as to why you don't screw your whisky with caramel, here it is. Jeff Topping can feel a justifiable sense of pride in his new whisky: for its age, it is an unreconstituted masterpiece... 46% (92 proof). nc ncf. USA.

William Grant & Sons Rare Cask Reserves 25 Years Old Blended Malt Scotch Whisky (82) n21 t22 f19 b20. Mouth-filling, chewy and mildly fruity, doesn't quite grow on the decent start offered and finishes untidily. 47%. Exclusive to The Whisky Shop.

⟨⟩ **Wilson & Morgan Barrel Selection Speybridge** sherry wood, dist 2001, bott 2015 (94) n23.5 the malt has a distinctly vanilla-rich slant, but it is the gentle, clean grape which dominates; t24 the golden syrup and spices need no invitation to head the cast and ensure a sweet and caressing delivery. The fruit tones turn up only when the sugars have receeded; f23 a slow spice burn plus a gentle tang. Butterscotch tart represents the oak; b23.5 almost spot on sherry butts at work here. No sulphur involvement to speak of, so you can simply concentrate on the embracing beauty of the sugars. And so rare to encounter a sherried malt with no bitterness on the finish whatsoever. 45.9%

⟨⟩ **Wilson & Morgan Barrel Selection Westport** sherry wood, dist 1997, bott 2014 (93.5) n23.5 dripping with sweet grape and green toffee-apple; t24 close on perfection for a present day sherry butt delivery. The taste buds are caressed by grape of initially rare clarity, clean enough to allow the molten Demerara sugars full range to mingle with the grist; f22.5 tightens up ever so slightly, but the spices buzz away beautifully; b23.5 oh...!!! The charm of virtually clean sherry butts!! Almost no sulphur here....just magnificent whisky! 48%

Mystery Malts

Chieftain's Limited Edition Aged 40 Years hogshead (78) n22 t22 f16 b18. Oak-ravaged and predictably bitter on the death (those of you who enjoy Continental bitters might go for this..!). But the lead up does offer a short, though sublime and intense honey kick. The finish, though... 48.5%. Ian Macleod.

Scottish Grain

It's a bit weird, really. Many whisky lovers stay clear of blended Scotch, preferring instead single malts. The reason, I am often told, is that the grain included in a blend makes it rough and ready. Yet I wish I had a twenty pound note for each time I have been told in recent years how much someone enjoys a single grain. The ones that the connoisseurs die for are the older versions, usually special independent bottlings displaying great age and more often than not brandishing a lavish Canadian or bourbon style.

Like single malts, grain distilleries produce whisky bearing their own style and signature. And, also, some display characteristics and a richness that can surprise and delight. Most of the grains available in (usually specialist) whisky outlets are pretty elderly. Being made from maize and wheat helps give them either that Canadian or, depending on the freshness of the cask, an unmistakable bourbony style. So older grains display far greater body than is commonly anticipated.

Light whiskies, including some Speysiders, tend to adopt this North American stance when the spirit has absorbed so much oak that the balance has been tipped. So overtly Kentuckian can they be, I once playfully introduced an old single grain Scotch whisky into a bourbon tasting I was conducting and nobody spotted that it was the cuckoo in the nest ... until I revealed all at the end of the evening. And even had to display the bottle to satisfy the disbelievers. Younger grains may give a hint of oncoming bourbon-ness. But, rather, they tend to celebrate either a softness in taste or, in the case of North British, a certain rigidity. Where many malts have a tendency to pulverise the taste-buds and announce their intent and character at the top of their voice, younger grains are content to stroke and whisper.

Scotch whisky companies had a relaxed attitude to marketing their grains. William Grant had made some inroads with Black Barrel, though with nothing like the enthusiasm they unleash upon us with their blends and malts. But Diageo have raised the bar and the grain whisky tempertature by spending probably more than my beloved Millwall have in their history forked out for players by signing up David Beckham to be the face of their new Haig Club grain brand. If his fee did not trump Millwall's historical spend, then the massive budget they appear to have set aside for a glamorous advertising campaign probably will have. Hopefully younger grains, rather than the massive-impact pensioner ones that can normally be found kicking about, will be accepted for being the quality product they unquestionably are. Even if other companies follow suit, I cannot see them trying to make quite the same impact as Diageo are trying with Beckham. For many distillers, trying to find enough grain whisky for their existing blend portfolio is proving challenging enough.

In Ireland, Cooley have in the past forged a healthy following with their introduction of grain whiskies at various ages. They have shown that the interest is there and some fresh thinking and boldness in a marketing department can create niche and often profitable markets. Edrington entered the market with a vatted grain called Snow Grouse, designed to be consumed chilled and obviously a tilt at the vodka market. The first bottling I received, though, was disappointingly poor and I hope future vattings will be more carefully attended to. All round, then, the news for Scottish grain lovers has not been good of late with the demolition of mighty Dumbarton and, controversially, closure of Port Dundas itself. With the expansion of Cameronbridge and a 50% stake in North British, Diageo obviously believe they have all the grain capacity they require.

The tastings notes here for grains cover only a few pages, disappointingly, due to their scarcity. However, it is a whisky style growing in stature, helped along the way not just by Cooley but also by more Independent bottlers bringing out a succession of high quality ancient casks. There has even been an organic grain on the market, distilled at the unfashionable Loch Lomond Distillery. Why though, it has to be asked, does it take the relatively little guys to lead the way? Perhaps the answer is in the growing markets in the east: the big distillers are very likely holding on to their stocks to facilitate their expansion there.

At last the message is getting through that the reaction to oak of this relatively lightweight spirit - and please don't for one moment regard it as neutral, for it is most certainly anything but - can throw up some fascinating and sometimes delicious possibilities. Blenders have known that for a long time. Now public interest is growing. And people are willing to admit that they can enjoy an ancient Cambus, Caledonian or Dumbarton in very much the way they might celebrate a single malt. Even if it does go against the grain...

Single Grain Scotch
CALEDONIAN

Clan Denny Caledonian 45 Years Old bourbon barrel, cask no. HH6294, dist 1965 **(89) n22** t23.5 f21.5 b22. For all its obvious tiredness, there is plenty of rich character. *46.1%. nc ncf sc.*

Clan Denny Caledonian 45 Years Old refill hogshead, cask no. HH6228, dist 1965 **(96) n23.5 t25 f23.5 b24.** Super Caley...my prayers have been answered... *476%. nc ncf sc.*

Clan Denny Caledonian Aged 45 Years bourbon barrel, cask no. HH7501, dist 1965 **(94) n23.5 t24 f23 b23.5.** Anyone who managed to get their hands on the very oldest maturing stocks of Barton bourbon from twenty years ago (and there were very few of us who managed it) would recognise it immediately. The similarities are uncanny. *473%. nc ncf sc.*

Scotch Malt Whisky Society Cask G3.3 Aged 26 Years refill barrel, dist 29 Apr 86 **(87) n21.5 t22 f21.5 b22.** A straight up and downer other than the unusual coastal twang. *56%.*

CAMBUS

Clan Denny Cambus Vintage Aged 25 Years refill hogshead, cask no. HH9320 **(96.5) n24 t24.5 f23.5 b24.5.** Nosed blind, this would be mistaken for absolutely top notch Canadian, and in particular the finer output from the now entirely lost LaSalle Distillery. But that rarely engaged its sugars in such a breathtakingly, almost outrageously, attractive way. One of the grain bottlings that will be remember among those in the know until the last one amongst us follow the Path of LaSalle...and, no less tragically, Cambus. *53.1%. ncf sc.*

◈ **The Clan Denny Cambus Aged 25 Years** refill hogshead, cask no 10595, dist 1988 **(96) n24** the tapestry of delicate sugars are woven faultlessly into the corn-rich buttery neo bourbon silk. A kind of mix between high class Canadian and mid-aged top-drawer bourbon; **t24** one can only purr as the sugars and honeys flit around the palate. A welcome tautness to the proceedings, ensuring a crispness to the ulmo honey-butterscotch blend; **f24** long, unusual depth to the oils of the grain, confirming corn domination. The liquorice-cocoa fade presses all the right buttons; **b24** just about the perfect grain from the perfect distillery. *58.1% sc.*

Clan Denny Cambus Aged 36 Years bourbon barrel, cask no. HH7252, dist 1975 **(89.5) n22 t23.5 f22 b22.** Flawless grain limited only by its simplicity. *52.1%. nc ncf sc.*

Clan Denny Cambus 45 Years Old refill bourbon barrel, cask no. HH5638, dist 1965 **(88.5) n22 t23 f21.5 b22.** A grain which has learned to deal with the impact of age in its very own, sweet way... *45.9%. nc ncf sc. Douglas Laing & Co.*

Clan Denny Cambus 47 Years Old bourbon barrel, cask no. HH7029, dist 1963 **(97) n24.5 t25 f23 b24.5.** If this wasn't a Scotch single grain, it might just qualify as Bourbon of the Year. Proof that where a whisky is made, matured, or from makes absolutely no difference: it is the quality which counts. And there will be very few whiskies I taste this year that will outgun this one in the quality stakes... *49.7%. nc ncf sc. Douglas Laing & Co.*

Clan Denny Cambus Aged 48 Years bourbon barrel, cask no. HH 7863, dist 1963 **(93) n24 t23 f22.5 b23.5.** No wonder they closed down the Cambus distillery; they must've plain gone and shipped it to Kentucky... *49.5%. nc ncf sc. Douglas Laing & Co.*

◈ **The Pearls of Scotland Cambus 1988** cask no. 59232, dist Sept 88, bott May 15 **(89) n22.5 t23.5 f21 b22.** A déjà vu moment here: "I've tasted this one before." Looked through my notes for the Sov Cambus 26-y-o...and found they were distilled in the same month. Peas in a pod. The notes for that are spot on for here, except this has a bit of extra oily toffee... *478%. sc.*

◈ **Scotch Malt Whisky Society Cask G8.5 Aged 25 Years** refill hogshead, dist 12 Jun 89 **(93.5) n22** exceptionally quiet by Cambus standards: clean, vaguely peppery and an even vaguer celery note; **t24** erupts into life to cofound the nose: spices starburst about the palate to offer the perfect counter to the ulmo honey and Lubeck marzipan theme; a touch of rummy esters at work in the midground; **f23.5** the near perfect cask influence allows for the sweetness to lessen in a beautifully timed fade. The last notes of Brazilian coconut and German caramelised biscuit could not be better; **b24** the politeness of the nose gives little indication of the outstanding experience on the palate which awaits. *59.6%. sc. 240 bottles.*

◈ **The Sovereign Cambus Aged 50 Years** refill bourbon barrel, cask no 11031, dist Aug 64, bott Nov 14 **(89.5) n22.5** no shortage of oak, or polished oak floors. Someone in the last 50 years has trod some dried dates into them...; **t23.5** a surprising degree of oil holds out against the tannin, capturing the sugars and refusing to let them go; **f21.5** a few bitter notes, as might be expected, but the buttery ones carry the dark sugars furthest; some last minute spices and a furry buzz...; **b22** not quite a picture of whisky wisdom and at times fails to find the adequate balance. But, the very last moments apart, and for a whisky which was hardly expected to reach more than three years, a remarkable old survivor. *49.2% nc ncf sc.*

◈ **The Sovereign Cambus Aged 26 Years** refill hogshead, cask no 11116, dist Sept 88, bott Nov 14 **(89.5) n23** pretty floral for a Cambus; corn thick but a bit of bite, too; **t23.5** usual silky start, plus the standard opening of delicate sugars to be associated with Cambus; **f21** dries and bitters out just a little too quickly; **b22** a fabulous spirit looked for better support from the cask than it received. Some pretty mercurial and magical moments, though. *46.9% nc ncf sc.*

◇ **The Sovereign Cambus Aged 40 Years** refill hogshead, cask no. 11266, dist Feb 75, bott Feb 15 (95) **n23** a wonderful and possibly unique mix of corn whisky and Shredded Wheat cereal; the sugars are of the dark variety, the tannin more Canadian than Kentucky in style; **t24** corn oil coats the palate with a friendly, ulmo-honeyed swoosh; then the sugars and spices come out to play. Elements of fruit pastilles juice things up further while the oak is content in a buttery role; **f23.5** not a trace of bitterness or tiredness of any sort. Just a gentle wind down of the more intense flavours of before, with maybe only a further nod to the oak in its buttered toast finale; **b24.5** just about defies belief that a whisky can reach this number of years and still retain sugar-honey at its core. Remarkable and majestic whisky from a once remarkable and majestic distillery. *57.7%. nc ncf sc. 114 bottles.*

◇ **The Sovereign Cambus Aged 30 Years** refill hogshead, cask no. 11591, dist Feb 85, bott May 15 (93) **n23** remember that coconut "tobacco" candy moistened with treacle when we were very, very young...?; **t23.5** taste buds are met with a wall of lightly oiled, but beautifully seasoned tannin, but covered in golden syrup; the oaky spices punch through beautifully; **f23** a slow dissolving of the sugars and tannins; **b23.5** satisfying whisky on just about every level bar the certain knowledge there is little more of this nectar still to come. *53.4%. nc ncf sc.*

CAMERONBRIDGE

Cadenhead's Small Batch Cameronbridge Aged 24 Years bourbon hogsheads, dist 1989, bott 2013 (92) **n21.5** slightly aggressive oak becalmed by vanilla; **t23.5** weighty delivery for a grain: indeed, more malt-like with decent oils and a delicious dollop of ulmo honey and butterscotch; **f23** a little busier as the tannins rev up the spices; **b23.5** a pleasing grain with idea above its supposedly lowly station. Kicks the crap out ofa great many single malts it is supposed to kow-tow to. *46%. 618 bottles. WB15/167*

Clan Denny Cameronbridge Aged 21 Years refill butt, cask no. HH7541, dist 1990 (85.5) **n21.5 t22 f20.5 b21.5.** Creamy textured and sweet. Possibly filled into an old – and tired - Islay cask as there is the odd strand of smoke. *58.2%. nc ncf sc. Douglas Laing & Co.*

Clan Denny Cameronbridge Aged 38 Years refill barrel, cask no. HH9488 (94) **n23.5 t24 f22.5 b24.** A Canadian and corn whiskey orgy. And a bit of a turn on it is, too...*52.4%. sc.*

Clan Denny Cameronbridge 45 Years Old bourbon, cask no. HH6805, dist 1965 (78) **n21 t20 f18 b19.** Even grains can feel the cold hand of Father Time on their shoulder... *40.5%. nc ncf sc.*

Rare Auld Grain Cameronbridge 32 Years Old cask no. 3597, dist 1979 (92) **n23 t23.5 f22.5 b23.** Anything but the norm. *48.8%. sc. Duncan Taylor & Co.*

Signatory Single Grain Collection Cameronbridge 1995 dist 31 Jan 95, bott 18 Mar 14 (87) **n22 t22 f21.5 b21.5.** Although with nearly 20 years on the clock, living nearly two decades in presumably a third fill cask has done little for colour or complexity: it has the demeanour of a grain very much younger. The good news is that this is still high quality oak, so although a simple dram the mix of sugars and light vanilla is a pleasing one. *43%. WB15/170*

The Sovereign Single Cask Cameronbridge 1990 cask no. 9860, dist 1990, bott Jun 13, (88) **n22 t22 f22 b22.** Monosyllabic but a joyous ride for all that. *59.2%. sc.*

CARSEBRIDGE

Clan Denny Carsebridge 29 Years Old 1st fill hogshead, cask no. HH6609, dist 1981 (82) **n22 t22 f18 b20.** The intensity of the corn is profound. So too, alas, is the bitter retribution of the tired cask. *53.1%. nc ncf sc. Douglas Laing & Co.*

Clan Denny Carsebridge Aged 30 Years refill hogshead, cask no. HH7780, dist 1981 (91.5) **n21.5 t23.5 f22 b23.5.** Is there such a thing as a juicy 30-year-old grain? On this evidence, indubitably. *59.1%. nc ncf sc. Douglas Laing & Co.*

Clan Denny Carsebridge Aged 45 Years bourbon barrel, cask no. HH7500, dist 1965 (95) **n24 t24 f23 b24.** As we so often see in Kentucky and Canada, old grains maturing in high quality casks rank among the world's best whiskies: here's a stunning example. *44.7%. nc ncf sc.*

Clan Denny Carsebridge Aged 47 Years refill barrel, cask no. HH9489 (91) **n23.5 t23.5 f22 b22.** A simple grain, despite the antiquity, doing the easy things attractively. *45.3%. sc.*

DUMBARTON

Clan Denny Dumbarton Aged 48 Years refill hogshead, cask no. HH9345 (96.5) **n25 t24 f23.5 b24.** Truly great. Forget this being a grain: excellence is excellence. Full stop. *50.1%. sc.*

◇ **The Last Drop Dumbarton 54 Year Old** 2nd fill bourbon barrel, dist 19 Jan 61 (96) **n24.5** no splinters apparent on this golden oldie. Instead, we see a little coconut water adding lustre to the corn bread. Reminds me of Waterloo, one of the lost original distilleries of Canada, as there is a subtle layering which ensures the weight is neither too hefty nor restrictive. A once common nose world-wide, now just about unique...; **t24.5** an unmistakable Canadian-style corn and oak marriage in which the ulmo honey melts with the golden syrup but still can't outperform the clean corn oils. The spices are at exactly the right volume; **f23** a little bitterness from the old cask creeps in. But the spices counter immediately, and even up their game as we near the end; **b24** Dumbarton here displays, with an ease almost bordering arrogance, why it is the doyen of grain whiskies. It is no coincidence that the greatest ancient blended whiskies I have tasted include liberal amounts of Dumbarton. As you can see here, it has the ability to be firm enough for backbone to form, yet soft enough to ensure a yielding countenance, too. A grain, glorying in its 55th year. *43.5%. sc. 34 bottles.*

❖ **The Sovereign Dumbarton Aged 50 Years** refill hogshead, cask no 11227, dist Dec 64, bott Feb 15 **(91) n22.5** a light interplay between corn and polite oak. Clean, quiet and undemonstrative; **t23** soft, silky corn is massaged by ulmo honey...; **f22.5** the sugars meander through some bittering oak; **b23** despite the late tanginess, the overall elegance of this grain after half a century takes some believing. *43.8% nc ncf sc. 93 bottles.*

❖ **The Sovereign Dumbarton Aged 50 Years** refill hogshead, cask no 11592, dist Dec 64, bott May 15 **(96.5) n24** a comfortable marriage of fruit and oak, neither dominating the other. Dates, prunes and nose-tickling spices. The dark sugars are lurking in the recesses; **t24.5** now that is staggering: the weight of the mouth feel could hardly be better – after 50 years it is astonishing. No aggression, and though the tannins are apparent early, there is not a single splinter. Just silk made from corn and fruit tones woven throughout...; **f24** mocha – a bit heavier on the coffee – sweetened with a dollop of manuka honey. The spices pick up the pace during the very long fade; **b24** an astonishing bottling. No wonder why Ballantine's ancient blends are that little bit special. For this a fabulous example as to why this was the king of all Scotland's grain distilleries until its brainless dismantling, one of the most grievous injuries inflicted on blended Scotch in living memory. *49.1% nc ncf sc. 162 bottles.*

GARNHEATH

Clan Denny Garnheath 43 Years Old refill hogshead, cask no. HH6642, dist 1967 **(94) n24.5 t23.5 f22.5 b23.5.** What a treat: not just a whisky as rare as budgie teeth, but one in tip-top nick for its age. A rare delight. *44.4%. nc ncf sc. Douglas Laing & Co.*

The Coopers Choice Golden Grains Garnheath 1967 45 Years Old (94.5) n23.5 t24 f23.5 b24. I remember the last time I tasted Garneath it was Atlanta corn whiskey coming back at me from the glass. Now we have top grade bourbon... *42%. nc ncf sc.*

GIRVAN

The Girvan Patent Still No. 4 Apps db **(87) n21.5 t22 f21.5 b22.** A first look at probably the lightest of all Scotland grain whiskies. A little cream soda sweetens a soft, rather sweet, but spineless affair. The vanillas get a good, unmolested outing too. *42% WB15/369*

Cadenhead's Small Batch Girvan Aged 33 Years bourbon barrels, dist 1979 bott 2013 **(85) n22 t23 f19 b21.** Some parts of this are light and citrusy enough to be a gin or flavoured rum. The fact this is 33 years old at times defies belief. But where it does work is on delivery when the citrus notes are under control thanks to the butterscotch tart. Then the sugars go on a rampage. *46% 222 bottles. WB15/165*

Clan Denny Girvan Aged 21 Years refill barrel, cask no. HH9451 **(92) n23 t23.5 f22.5 b23.** Complex, busy and compelling. *59.6%. sc.*

Clan Denny Girvan 45 Years Old refill hogshead, cask no. HH6276, dist 1965 **(90) n23 t23.5 f21.5 b22.5.** Laid on with a golden trowel. *47.3%. nc ncf sc.*

Clan Denny Girvan 45 Years Old refill hogshead, cask no. HH6923, dist 1965 **(88.5) n23 t23 f20.5 b22.** Simplistic, certainly. But as you get older, you learn to appreciate the more simple things in life... *45.3%. nc ncf sc. Douglas Laing & Co.*

Clan Denny Girvan Aged 46 Years refill hogshead, cask no. HH7669, dist 1965 **(94.5) n23 t24 f23.5 b24.** Sublime. *49.7%. nc ncf sc. Douglas Laing & Co.*

❖ **Old Masters Girvan 26 Year Old** cask no. 57869, dist 1988, bott 2015 **(88.5) n22** oily, spicy and busy; **t23** beautifully rich delivery where the honey is given full scope to dominate; sweetened vanilla abounds, too; the silky texture impresses no less; **f21.5** a little sharp, as though copper deprived; **b22** a curious Girvan, showing a distinctive Strathclyde style tartness at times at the end, but excellent compensating honey for the remainder. *59.8%. sc.*

❖ **A.D. Rattray Girvan** cask no. 2 dist 1964 **(95.5) n23.5** toasty with natural fudge notes now gathered from the cask. Non specific fruit give a cake-like quality. But there is no sign of degeneration...; **t24** sumptuous and luxurious, the spices and vanillas dominate hand-in-hand. A light brushing of ulmo honey guarantees the complex sweetness, though again there is a light jammy fruitiness leaking in from somewhere; **f23.5** dries into toasted fudge. The corn oils offer the most ridiculously gentle fade after half a century you could imagine; **b24.5** even after half a century, not a hint of an off note. *47.1%*

Riegger's Selection Girvan 1964 bourbon cask, cask no. 86, dist 64, bott Feb 11 **(87) n22.5 t22.5 f20 b22.** Lovers of corn whisky will enjoy many aspects of this oldie. *48.7%. nc ncf sc.*

Scotch Malt Whisky Society Cask G7.5 Aged 28 Years hogshead, dist 84 **(91) n23.5 t23.5 f22 b22.** Keep bottling gems like this and they'll have to form the Grain Whisky Society. *58.9%.*

⬧ **The Sovereign Girvan Aged 26 Years** refill hogshead, cask no 11119, dist Oct 88, bott Nov 14 **(90.5) n22** touch of the rum about this...with a vague hint of smoke on the horizon; **t23** delivery is sublime, showing magnificent texture and unexpected weight. The sugars are of the acacia honey variety. Serious depth; **f22.5** takes an attractively spicy turn and with the light praline development sees off the slight oak bitterness; **b23** a spicy cove which may well have matured for the last quarter of a century in a former Islay cask as there are some feeble smoke notes attached. *56.3% nc ncf sc. 283 bottles.*

INVERGORDON

⬧ **Best Dram Invergordon 23 Years Old** hogshead **(87) n22 t23 f20.5 b21.5.** Not quite the best hoggie to have carried grain, as the finish clearly testifies. But there's no faulting the silky delivery, or the myriad sugar notes – the golden syrup in particular. *50.7%*

The Clan Denny Invergordon Aged 26 Years North American Oak, cask no. 10250, dist 1998 **(92) n22 24 f22.5 b23.5.** Perhaps should be exported to Canada. True Canadian lovers will swoon at this: so similar to the now lost La Salles distillery in its final days. *50.6%.*

Clan Denny Invergordon Vintage Aged 46 Years barrel, cask no. HH9077 **(91.5) n24 t23 f22 b22.5.** About a quiet a dram you could wish to bring into your house. Open late at night... it will disturb nobody. *44.2%. sc. Douglas Laing & Co.*

Duncan Taylor Octave Invergordon 38 Years Old cask 520883, dist 1972 **(86.5) n24 t21 f20 b21.5.** Serious Demerara sugars knit tightly into the intense vanilla. A few bitter notes amid the booming spice. The nose excels and conjures myriad bourbon images. *47.8%. sc.*

⬧ **Master of Malt Single Cask Invergordon 23 Year Old** refill sherry hogshead, dist Apr 91, bott Jul 14 **(77.5) n22 t21.5 f16 b18.** Very similar to their Invergordon Batch 3, perhaps with a kinder nose – which makes the bitter finish even more disappointing. Not sure of the point of sherry and grain: the Invergordon doesn't have enough about it to make a mark on the grape while the bitterness carries on unchecked... *52.8%. sc. 82 bottles.*

⬧ **Old Masters Invergordon 23 Year Old** cask no. 77733, dist 1991, bott 2014 **(89) n22.5** intense vanilla-corn mix – expect to see the Rockies when I look out of my tasting room window...; **t23** gorgeous texture: spices arrive early to ensure immediate complexity with the honeyed corn oils; **f21** a little on the oak-bitter side; **b22.5** presumably distilled from maize, as this has "Canadian" stamped all over it... *59.1%. sc. James MacArthur & Co Ltd*

The Pearls of Scotland Invergordan 1972 bott May 14 **(96) n23.5 t24 f24.5 b24.** Really don't quite understand why the distillery is not bringing out its own bottlings when it has gems of drams like this to choose from. This, for its age, is astonishing. *43.4%.*

⬧ **The Pearls of Scotland Invergordon 1972** dist Dec 72, bott Apr 15 **(90.5) n23.5** a big Canadian signature here, with light liquorice and muscovado sugars lining with the big corn; **t22.5** pure silk: a featherbed delivery full of corn and acacia honey; **f22** a complete take over by the corn; **b22.5** amazing that something so old can be so simple and untaxing! *46.6%*

⬧ **The Pearls of Scotland Invergordon 1997** cask no. 105, dist Apr 97, bott May 15 **(95) n24** much firmer nose than usual Invergordon. And spicier. The sugars are crisp and clean, of a Demerara style; **t24** wow!! A stunning delivery – an ulmo honey and maple syrup mix, bought down to earth by highly spiced vanilla. The silky texture is textbook...; **f23.5** long, with those sugars and spices never knowing when to stop...; **b24** yet another true pearl of a grain unleashed by Pearls of Scotland. Congrats – you guys have absolutely excelled! *59.1%. sc.*

Rare Auld Grain Invergordon 38 Years Old cask no. 96251, dist 1972 **(88.5) n22.5 t22.5 f21.5 b22.** Ramrod straight and beyond the nose eschews any grand design of complexity. *44%. sc. Duncan Taylor & Co.*

Scotch Malt Whisky Society Cask G5.7 Aged 19 Years refill hogshead, dist 20 May 93 **(92) n24 t23 f22 b23.** For those who like a little whisky in their oak....Outrageous. But somehow works! *64.6%. sc. 234 bottles.*

Single Cask Collection Ivergordon Aged 24 Years bourbon barrel, cask no. 18589, dist 22 Feb 1988, bott 22 Aug 2012 **(89.5) n21.5 t23.5 f22 b22.5.** Softly, softly all the way. *55.5%. nc*

The Sovereign Single Cask Invergordon 1964 cask no. 9861, dist 1964, bott Jun 13 **(92.5) n23.5 t23 f22.5 b23.5.** High voltage Canadian style whisky of yesteryear... *43.7%. sc.*

The Sovereign Single Cask Invergordon 1992 cask no. 10155, dist 1992, bott Nov 13 **(87)** n22 t22 f21.5 b22. Very quiet: as though trained for a silent part in a blend. Some spice does make a noise, though. 60.4%. sc.

The Sovereign Single Cask Invergordon Aged 25 Years cask no. 10699 dist 1988, bott Jul 14 **(94.5)** n23 t24 f23.5 b24. Ignore the fact this is grain and not malt. Just grab yourself a bottle of something rather beautiful... 58.1%. sc.

◈ **The Sovereign Invergordon Aged 50 Years** refill bourbon barrel, cask no 11047, dist Nov 64, bott Nov 14 **(90.5)** n23.5 gentle corn oil, entirely at peace with its age in life: no bitterness or spice...just a simple triangulation between the corn, the vanilla oak and the laziest of balancing sugars; t22 laid back to the point of not giving a damn about its age. The corn dominates, but can barely be bothered....; f22.5 long, soft, languid...still after all these years just bursting out with Indian corn intensity...; b23 hangs on in there...and finally reaches its biblical time in the cask gracefully... 42.5% nc ncf sc. 252 bottles.

◈ **The Sovereign Invergordon Aged 30 Years** refill butt, cask no. 11237, dist Oct 84, bott Feb 15 **(93.5)** n24.5 the clarity of the fruit is matched only by the ease of its balance with the deeper, spiced cocoa notes of the oak. Simultaneously light yet deep, I'm not sure spices come any more subtle and desirable than this; t24 enjoys the usual distillery mellowness and yield, allowing the heftier fruit notes to be cushioned in their fall by the silkier grain; f22 a little tiredness of the cask allows in the odd burnt toast bitter note; b23 refilled into a sherry butt which dates before the days of the big sulphur cock-up...and it shows in the beauty of its soul... 59.6%. nc ncf sc. 687 bottles.

That Boutique-y Whisky Invergordan batch 2 **(88.5)** n22 lightly spiced toffee; t23 a Demerara-treacle mix melts as the spices evolve; f21.5 vanilla and toffee; b22 unassuming, easy going and just-so spiced. 58.3%. 160 bottles. WB15/347

◈ **That Boutique-y Whisky Company Invergordon** batch 3 **(79)** n21.5 t22 f17 b18.5. On the nose, blind, one would take this for a rum whisky made on a continuous still with insufficient sulphur-killing copper in the system – and the poor, bitter finish would bear this out. Absolutely nothing wrong with the big fruity delivery, though. 49.8%. 60 bottles.

Wemyss Malts 1988 Single Grain Invergordon "Caribbean Crème" barrel, bott 2014 **(88)** n22 the distillery's trademark softness wafts from the glass like feathers caught in the breeze. Delicately sweet, a little oily...not unlike the fondant in a chocolate Swiss Roll....; t23.5 remarkably tart launch, almost a citrus kick before the oak and corn begin to lay claim to the taste buds; f20.5 bitterish and a little dull; b22 somewhat moody. But when in good form, chewy and balanced. 46%. sc. 171 bottles.

Wemyss Malts 1988 Single Grain Invergordon "Lemon Cheesecake" barrel, dist 88, bott 14 **(90)** n22.5 t23 f22 b22.5. Classic Invergordon pudding-type grain. 46%. sc. 220 bottles.

Wemyss Malts 1988 Single Grain "Vintage Strawberry Punnet" barrel, dist 88, bott 14 **(92.5)** n22 t24 f23 b23.5. From a non-committal nose to a delivery which speaks volumes. Fabulous! 46%. sc. 242 bottles.

◈ **The Whisky Barrel Invergordon 2006 Burns Malt 7 Years Old** oloroso cask, cask no. 901446 **(91)** n23 fresh and fruity, but tight and even vaguely smoked; t23 that weird smoke turns up early, only to give way to burnt raisin and Melton Hunt cake; f23 some cocoa and diced hazelnut; at times quite sharp; b23 Cadbury's Fruit and Nut, the beauty of which will be lost on American candy executives. Admittedly, Invergordon as I have never seen it before in some 40 years tasting...though at times feeling as though it is operating in a strait jacket..!! Off the wall, but a joy! 61.5%

◈ **The Whisky Barrel Invergordon 2006 Burns Malt 7 Years Old** px cask, cask no. 901446 **(84)** n21 t22 f20 b21. Crisp, uniform and with a rumbling dark sugar singularity. A little tainted on the finish, though. 60.2%

◈ **Wilson & Morgan Barrel Selection Invergordon 30 Year Old** sherry wood, dist 1984, bott 2015 **(68)** n17 t21 f14 b16. I'd be amazed if this spent its life in only the one sherry butt since 1984 – a dreadful flavour profile such as this didn't exist in those halcyon days. Sulphur apart, the delivery has an unusual gin quality to it, though for a brief moment on arrival it sparkles quite wonderfully. 57%

LOCH LOMOND

◈ **Loch Lomond Single Grain** db **(93)** n23 crisp sugars are willing to absorb the vanilla; t23.5 indeed, the sugars on the nose are indicative of a sweet grain, for the delivery centres around the maple syrup lead. The oak is something like most anchors at work: barely visible to invisible; f23 the oaks do have a say, though you have to wait a while on the long finale. A little spice arrives, too; b23.5 elegant grain; keeps the sweetness controlled. 46%

Master of Malt Single Cask Loch Lomond 16 Year Old (89) n22 t23 f21.5 b22.5. On this evidence, Loch Lomond is filled with malt and malt alone.... *62.7%. sc.*

⟐ **Master of Malt Single Cask Loch Lomond 18 Year Old** sherry hogshead, dist Dec 94, bott Apr 15 (92.5) n23 big, chunky: the impressive oak may spread its trunk but there are sugars and spices to meet its demands; t24 easily the most dense grain of the year. There appear to be malt notes abounding, the sugars shine and sparkle with even a layer of ulmo honey for good measure; f22 thinner and much more vanilla dependent; b23.5 a five course meal with all the trimmings and silver service. For a grain, malty and massive. *60.5%. sc. 96 botts.*

That Boutique-y Whisky Loch Lomond batch 1 (89.5) n22 glorious but delicate citrus; soft toffee; t23.5 the salivation index goes flying off the page as the citrus and malt combine beautifully before a heavier treacle toffee trait moves in; f22 tangy toffee; b22 a sometimes unloved and often misunderstood distillery, shown here to excellent fruity effect with the yeast ensuring the citrus is working at full blast. *52.4%. 191 bottles. WB15/348*

Rhosdhu 2008 Cask No. 2483 re-char bourbon, dist 17/03/08, bott 27/07/11 (86.5) n22 t22 f21 b21.5. Delicately clean barley with a touch of lemon and, though engagingly soft, is not beyond showing some sugary teeth. *45%. nc ncf sc.*

Rhosdhu 2008 Cask No. 2484 bourbon barrel, dist 17/03/08, bott 27/07/11 (84) n21.5 t21.5 f20.5 b21. The barley battles with some aggressive oak, even at this tender age. The spice count is pretty high. *45%. nc ncf sc.*

LOCHSIDE

The Coopers Choice Lochside 1964 47 Years Old sherry, bott 12 (95.5) n24.5 t24 f23.5 b23.5. There are still some around who remember 1964 as a very special year in Montrose. First, their distillery, Lochside, was working. Secondly, they were receiving top quality sherry butts, long before the days they were ruined by reckless, unforgivable – and unforgiving - sulphur treatment. And, thirdly, for a while their football team enjoyed rare success on the park. In fact, in 1964 the guys at the distillery would have seen their blue-hooped heroes thrash neighbours Forfar 5-0 (having already murdered them 8-2 earlier in the season) would have made the short journey to next door Brechin for victory there as well as seen their lads annihilate Raith 8-3 and Stenhousemuir 7-1 back on home soil. The only thing they were denied was victory over the upstarts down the coast at Arbroath. But you can't have everything. Obviously happy workers make happy whisky. Amazing how those goals – and sound sherry butts - of 1964 can come back and heighten our enjoyment now. *41.5%. ncf sc.*

NORTH BRITISH

Berry's Own Selection North British 2000 cask no. 4312, bott 2011 (87.7) n22 t22.5 f21. Bitters thanks to some indifferent oak; b22 neutral whisky....? I don't think so. *46%. nc ncf sc.*

Cadenhead's Small Batch North British Aged 24 Years bourbon barrel, dist 1989, bott 2014 (94) n23.5 molten honeycomb, coconut and golden syrup...wow!! All on top of usual spices and butterscotch. Kind of Canadian on stilts; t24 the nose...in pure fluidity; f23 more of the same...with extra spice, including Canadian Ginger Ale; b23.5 made on another continent, and we might have had Canadian Whisky of the Year.. *46%. 240 bottles. WB15/168*

Darkness! North British Aged 18 Years Oloroso Cask Finish (89.5) n22 clean, uninterrupted olosoro waves a thick, fruity flag; t22.5 sweet, thick on the fruit and pith; a slow arrival of spice; developing juiciness; f23.5 at last some complexity as the spices layer superbly with the sherry trifle; b21.5 a rule of thumb is that putting grain into fresh sherry tells you far more about the cask than the distillate. And it hangs true here. Very good cask, by the way... *50.4%. 94 bottles. WB15/352*

⟐ **Deerstalker Limited Release North British 1994 aged 20 years 3 months** (91) n22.5 beautiful rhubarb and custard...while going easy on the sugars; t23 must be rhubarb tart – as few grains arrive on the palate quite as tart as this. Eye-wateringly lively with what appears to be a corn oil sheen offering the softer tones; f22.5 at last the sugars arrive, with a reintroduction of the custard. So soft, with the taste buds being massaged in oils to the very end; b23 a grain which has more life and complexity than a great many malts. Superb! *48%.*

Director's Cut North British Aged 52 Years first fill hogshead, cask no. 10356, dist 1962 (85) n23 t22.5 f19.5 b20. As you can see from the strength, this oldie was bottled just in the nick of time. Hard to imagine that when this was made, just the other side of the distillery walls, Hearts were sitting top of the Scottish League, their Tynecastle ground packed every other week, and that year won the League Cup. Now as I taste this, they are acclimatising to life in a lower league being watched by only a fraction of that once solid support. Curiously, in 1962 they got off to a bright start and then faded badly at the end. Odd that 52 years on a cask of whisky filled just a few yards away did exactly the same thing... *41.1%. sc. 195 bottles.*

Master of Malt North British 18 Years Old bourbon, cask no. 309896, dist 23 Dec 94, bott 1 Apr 13 **(77) n17.5 t22 f18 b19.5.** From around this time some blenders were bemoaning the sulphurous qualities of N B. Even taking into account the oily, sugary charge on the palate, you can see why. This, I have just discovered, is the 777th new whisky for the 2014 Bible. And it scores 77...how weird is that! But this 777, a very lopsided grain, never takes off. *52.3%.*

◇ **Master of Malt Single Cask North British 20 Year Old** refill bourbon barrel, dist Dec 94, bott Apr 15 **(84.5) n21.5 t22 f20 b21.** Quirky stuff, with a degree of gin-like botanicals floating around. Pleasant, but never quite reaches satisfying... *51.7%. sc. 115 bottles.*

The Pearls of Scotland North British 1994 18 Year Old cask no. 309880, dist Dec 94, bott Nov 13 **(89) n22 t22.5 f22 b22.5.** Simple fayre, but enough honey to make a single malt, let alone grain, proud. *52.6%.*

Signatory Single Grain Collection North British 1997 dist 14 May 97, bott 28 Nov 13 **(92.5) n22.5** surprisingly hefty: looks like an ex Islay cask has been involved somewhere: the mocha has a puff of smoke in there; **t23** beautiful delivery aided by the softest of oils coating the palate with a thin layer of ulmo honey and vanilla; **f23** yet more ulmo honey (could have been distilled in Chile!) weighted by the hint of smoke and spreading of molasses; **b24** the vague, distant smokiness adds further intrigue to a fine grain whisky. *43%. WB15/169*

◇ **The Sovereign North British Aged 52 Years** refill hogshead, cask no 10883, dist May 62, bott Sept 14 **(92) n23.5** the corn almost bulges on the nose as it gathers full intensity to overcome the French toast oakiness; **t23** mouth-watering and fresh, totally making a lie of its age. The corn oils drip with toasty sugars, the sweetness forever gathering in intensity; **f22.5** long, the spices upping the ante; **b23** yet another grain whisky at 50 which not only defies the years, but asks searching questions of the wood deployed today in which whisky is matured. For an oldie, in many ways still a relative youngster... *40.8% nc ncf sc. 155 bottles.*

◇ **The Sovereign North British Aged 25 Years** refill bourbon barrel, cask no. 11226, dist Sept 89, bott Feb 15 **(86.5) n22 t22.5 f20.5 b21.5.** A steady-as-she-goes, moderate grain with all the emphasis on the natural caramels and deeper molassed sugars. *59.7% nc ncf sc.*

The Sovereign Single Cask North British 1962 cask no. 9930, dist 1962, bott Aug 13 **(94.5) n24 t23 f24 b23.5.** Bottlings such as these really do re-draw the map of truly great whisky... And as for this: one of the most gentle rides you will ever enjoy around a whisky bottle, entirely sans bumps; indeed, a 50-year-old without a single wrinkle...*57.2%. sc.*

That Boutique-y Whisky Company North British batch 1 **(73.5) n18 t19 f18 b18.5.** Didn't know they were making gin at North British. What the bloody hell is this...? *51.1%.*

◇ **That Boutique-y Whisky Company North British** batch 2 **(87) n22 t22.5 f21 b21.5.** Hard to imagine a grain being more sweet and lush than this one on delivery, helped on the complexity front by a squeeze of citrus. As is so often the case with sweet whiskies, severe bitterness follows later. An enormous degree of Canadian character to this, especially on the nose, *49.3%.*

NORTH OF SCOTLAND

Clan Denny North Of Scotland Vintage Aged 38 Years barrel, cask no. HH9078 **(94.5) n23 t24 f23.5 b24.** Fascinating how some grains, like the Cambus, head in a Canadian style of direction, while this is pure Kentucky. And superb Kentucky at that... *52%. sc.*

◇ **The Pearls of Scotland North of Scotland 1971** dist Dec 71, bott Apr 15 **(95.5) n25** oh, that nose...sublime! About as soft as it gets and if you find a kinder infusion of tannins amid light sugars this year, then please let me know. A fruitiness has developed, but we are talking pastel tones of genteel understatement. Lime, greengage, pink grapefruit, peach...all are there. And so too are the spices which quietly announce the great age of this grain. As polite and enticing as a whisky nose ever gets...and shows virtually every malt of this age a thing or two. Perfection; **t23.5** the grapefruit arrives upfront and offers more bite and aggression in the first three seconds than you get in 20 minutes of nosing. Still no sign of the oak wanting to spoil the party. The vanillas merge with butterscotch; **f23** again, a grapefruit tartness begins to descend, the spicy buzz is distant; **b24** what a beautifully elegant old lady...and one with virtually no wrinkles... *43.6%*

PORT DUNDAS

Port Dundas 20 Years Old Special Release 2011 db **(90) n21.5 t22 f23.5 b23.** Can a whisky be a little too silky. This one tries, especially on the non-committal nose and over friendly delivery. But once the spices rise, things get very interesting... *57.4%. nc ncf sc.*

Cadenhead's Small Batch Port Dundas Aged 25 Years bourbon hogshead, dist 88, bott 14 **(96) n24.5** presumably distilled from corn as this is like an ultra high quality Canadian: red liquorice, sweetened tannin, a mix of over-ripe greengage and kiwifruit, but, above all, lightly peppered corn oil; **t24** the oils sit and balance on the palate like a tightrope walker above the

Grand Canyon; the sugars are barely believable varying from ulmo honey to muscovado; just so refined...; **f23.5** the oak performs somersaults, balancing a little bitterness with a further array of sugars which now head towards lighter manuka honey and maple syrup; the corn oil never relents for a moment; **b24** as grain whisky goes, and Port Dundas in particular, just about perfect. Certainly represents one of the best three nose and delivery combinations of the year. *46%. 246 bottles. WB15/363*

◈ **The Sovereign Port Dundas Aged 25 Years** refill hogshead, cask no 10876, dist Oct 88, bott Sept 14 **(93) n23.5** anyone over a certain age will remember the smell of the dedicated pipe tobacco/sweetshop...this takes me right back...; **t24** massive delivery: spices explode on impact while maple syrup dribbles over the taste buds; **f22** tires and bitters out quite rapidly; **b23.5** what a treat! *58.5% nc ncf sc. 246 bottles.*

◈ **The Sovereign Port Dundas Aged 25 Years** refill hogshead, cask no 11593, dist Feb 90, bott May 15 **(84) n22 t21.5 f20 b20.5**. A promising outburst of attractive early sugars is done in by the encroaching bitterness. *51.9% nc ncf sc. 236 bottles.*

◈ **The Sovereign Port Dundas Aged 36 Years** refill hogshead, cask no 11052, dist Jan 78, bott Nov 14 **(95.5) n24** a magnificent soup-like amalgamation of Bakewell pudding, buttered muffins and corn oil; **t24** thick corn oil has plenty of molten muscovado sugar and ulmo honey stirred in; **f23.5** long sizzling spice embraces the vanilla; **b24** a classy, though intense, act which makes the perfect late night dram. *59.7% nc ncf sc. 177 bottles.*

The Sovereign Single Cask Port Dundas 1978 cask no. 9864, dist 1978, bott Jun 13 **(96.5) n24 t24 f24 b24.5**. One can assume only that this matured in an old Islay cask. For phenolic fingerprints are all over this, but so subtly and fleeting that this is one hell of a turn on. Intriguing, entertaining, beautifully made and matured. A grainy dream... *58.1%. sc.*

The Sovereign Single Cask Port Dundas 1978 cask no. 10431, dist 1978, bott Apr 14 **(94.5) n23.5 t24 f23 b24**. The Mounted Police are probably tracking this down: it appears to have escaped from Canada...And he's big enough to spot from miles away. A grain which puts so many malts to shame. *58.7%. sc.*

STRATHCLYDE

Cadenhead's Small Batch Strathclyde Aged 24 Years bourbon barrels, dist 1989, bott 2013 **(79.5) n20.5 t22 f18 b19**. Quaffable enough – providing you don't concentrate too hard on what's going on on your palate. Two dozen years ago there wasn't enough copper in the distilling system by half. And even all these years on, it shows! A bit of an Allied bitter cask doesn't help, either. *46%. 504 bottles. WB15/166*

Chivas Brothers Cask Strength Edition Strathclyde Aged 12 Years batch no. ST 12 001, dist 01, bott 13 **(88.5) n22 t23 f21.5 b22**. The back label informs us: "You may notice a slight natural haze for when you add water or ice. This is perfectly natural." I am sorry but there is nothing natural about adding ice... *62.1%. ncf nc. WB15/370*

◈ **The Clan Denny Strathclyde Aged 9 Years** sherry butt, cask no. 10710, dist 2005 **(86) n21 t21 f22 b21.5**. Relax. No nasty notes despite the cask: all is good. But the grain itself doesn't make quite enough impact against the sherry influence for the balance to be quite right. Loads of sugar and spice at work - all rather like a fruit pastille with attitude. *55.7%. sc.*

Clan Denny Strathclyde Aged 38 Years refill barrel, cask no. HH9486 **(88) n23.5 t22 f20.5 b22**. Appears to be wheated grain as opposed to corn. Very early if so. *55.5%. sc.*

◈ **The Pearls of Scotland Strathclyde 1988** cask no. 62111, dist Jun 88, bott May 15 **(95.5) n23.5** hugely impressive –and confusing: think it is corn, but there are enough belligerent spices to suggest this could be from early wheat mash. Not often I get confused on this, but an infusion of particularly dark weighty sugars has muddied the waters; **t24** and there's those big spices attacking at full pelt while the profound sugars try to soften the blows. Light oil... but is it corn? Probably not...; **f23.5** medium length as the oak now gathers traction. No off notes, no tiredness: very pleasant and impressive...; **b24.5** the full on nature of this little beast means it has coped with the encroaching years without breaking sweat... *55.5%. sc.*

Scotch Malt Whisky Society Cask G10.1 Aged 23 Years refill hogshead, dist 31 Aug 89 **(94) n24 t23 f23.5 b23.5**. If only the majority of malts could offer such clarity from the cask! *59.6%. sc.*

The Sovereign Single Cask Strathclyde 1977 cask 9912, dist 1977, bott Aug 13 **(95) n23 t24 f24 b24**. Those who fell in love with Macallan all those years back because of its faultlessly silky sherry influence are about to have their hearts won again. It'll be love at first flight... *58.1%. sc.*

◈ **The Sovereign Strathclyde Aged 25 Years** refill hogshead, cask no 10875, dist Feb 89, bott Sept 14 **(83) n21 t22.5 f19 b20.5**. A roaring blast of sugars early on does its best to compensate for the clear deficiencies in the body and balance. A combo of lack of copper and a typical Allied cask means the finish is lacking somewhat. *59.7% nc ncf sc. 186 bottles.*

⬦ **Xtra Old Particular Strathclyde 40 Years Old** refill hogshead, cask no. 10598, dist Oct 74, bott Dec 14 **(87) n22.5 t23 f20 b21.** In many ways more rum in character than whisky! The Strathclyde is lost under a syrupy, sticky mass which makes the bitter finish all the more accentuated. *55.4%. nc ncf sc. 150 bottles.*

UNSPECIFIED SINGLE GRAIN

Haig Club toasted oak casks **(89) n21.5** soft, non-commital, medium aged, medium oaked...safe...; **t23** attractive degree of sharpness early on but soon reverts to full supine mode once the oils begin to gather. The vanilla on the oak infuses enough to ensure the levels of sweetness are contained; **f22.5** gentle cream fudge and vanilla with a pleasant spice fade; **b22** when I first saw this, I wasn't quite sure whether to laugh or cry. Because 25 years ago bottles of single grain whisky were the unique domain of the flat cap brigade, the miners and other working class in the Kirkcaldy area of Scotland. Their grain, Cameron Brig, would be drunk with a splash, mixed with Coke or ginger, or even occasionally with Irn Bru, or straight and unmolested as a chaser to the ubiquitous kegged heavy, McEwan's lager or a bottle of Sweetheart stout. When I suggested to the hierarchy at United Distillers, the forerunners of Diageo, that in their finer grains they had a product which could conquer the world, the looks I got ranged from sympathy for my lack of understanding in matters whisky to downright concern about my mental wellbeing. I had suggested the exquisite Cambus, now lost to us like so many other grain distilleries in those passing years, should be brought out as a high class singleton. It was pointed out to me that single grain was, always had been and always will be, the preferred choice of the less sophisticated; those not wishing to pay too much for their dram. Fast forward a quarter of a century and here sits a gorgeously expensive bottle in a deep cobalt blue normally associated with Ballantine's and a very classy, heavyweight stopper. In it is a grain which, if the advertising is to be believed, is the preferred choice not of the back street bar room idlers carefully counting their pennies but of its major ambassador David Beckham: it is the drop to be savoured by the moneyed, jet-set sophisticates. My, oh my. Let's not call this hype. Let's just say it has taken some genius exec in a suit half a lifetime – and probably most of his or hers - to come around to my way of thinking and convince those in the offices on the floor above to go for it. Wonder if I qualify for 10 percent of profit for suggesting it all those years back...or, preferably, five percent of their advertising budget. Meanwhile, I look forward to watching David pouring this into some of his Clynelish and Talisker. After all, no-one can Blend it like Beckham... 40%. WB15/408

Lady of the Glen Twenty Four Year Old (89.5) n21.5 t23 f22.5 b22.5. Squelchy-sift Invergordon at its sugary best. *56%. Hannah Whisky Merchants.*

Scottish Spirits Single Grain 3 Years Old (Canned) **(82.5) n21 t21.5 f20 b20.** An absolutely standard, decent quality grain whisky with an attractive sweetness and latent youthful zesty fizz. Ill-served, however, by what I presume is caramel to give it a clichéd scotch look which dulls the finish in particular. In its natural form, this would have scored a lot higher. *40% (80 Proof).*

Tweeddale Single Lowland Grain Scotch Whisky Aged 16 Years (88) n23 t22 f21 b22. A quiet speech of understatement. *46%. nc ncf sc. Stonedean.*

Vatted Grain

Compass Box Hedonism first fill American oak cask, bott 20 Feb 13 **(84) n22 t22 f19 b20.** Just too fat, too sweet and too bitter at the finale to work to great effect. Some decent oak on both nose and delivery, though. *43%. nc ncf. Compass Box Whisky Company.*

Compass Box Hedonism Maximus (93.5) n25 t22.5 f23 b23. Bourbon Maximus... *46%*

⬦ **Compass Box Hedonism Quindecimus (88.5) n22.5** a drizzle of lemon on custard; **t22** simple sugars and a little oil; **f22** even late on, a hint of juiciness; **b22** sweet and refreshingly ordinary grain. Well made and unspectacularly delicious. *46%*

The Last Vatted Grain bott Nov 11 **(88.5) n23 t22 f21.5 b22.** Not just sad that the term "vatted" is now pointlessly outlawed on the bottle. But also that half of the four grain distilleries used in this vatting are equally consigned to history. *46%. nc ncf. Compass Box.*

William Grant & Sons Rare Cask Reserves 25 Years Old Blended Grain Scotch Whisky (92.5) n23 t23.5 f23 b23. A really interesting one, this. In the old days, blenders always spent as much time vatting the grains together as they did the malts, for if they did not work well as a unit it was unlikely harmony would be found in their blend. A long time ago I was taught to, whenever possible, use a soft grain to counter a firmer one, and vica versa. Today, there are far fewer blends to choose from, though 25 years ago the choice was wider. So interesting to see that this grain is soft-dominated with very little backbone at all. Delicious. But screams for some backbone. *47%. Exclusive to The Whisky Shop.*

Scottish Blends

For the first time in my career, I got a bit of an ear-bashing from a dissatisfied customer at one of my blind whisky tastings. And, of all things, it was because I had not included a blended Scotch in the line-up. My-oh-my! How times change.

Actually the guy was good natured about it, especially when I told him it was because the samples had been lost in transit, but his sense of loss was real. Apparently, he had attended one of my tastings a few years before, arriving as a self-confessed malt snob. He left converted to the blended whisky cause... to the extent it was now his favourite whisky style. As much as it is annoying when things go slightly wrong at an event, I still felt a thrill that more hardcore whisky lovers find experimenting in blends every bit as enjoyable as finding new malts. This implies blended scotch is as good as single malt. And, for my money, that is entirely the case; and if the blender is really doing his or her job, it should often be better. However, that job is getting a little harder each year. Once it was the standard joke that a sulphured sherry butt that had once been marked for a single malt brand would be dumped into a large blend where it would work on BP Chief executive Tony Hayward's "drop in the ocean" principle. However, there is now a lot more than just the odd off sherry butt finding their way in and blenders have to take guard that their blends are not being negatively affected. Certainly, during the course of writing the Whisky Bible I discovered this was becoming a much more common occurrence from the 2010 edition onwards. Indeed, one or two brands which a few years back I would have expected to pick up awards on a regular basis have been hit badly: disappointing and a great loss to whisky lovers.

As if to drive home this point, this year's Blend of the Year, from the irrepressable Last Drop Company, consisted of malt and grain from the year 1965. It had not, thankfully, been rounded off in new sherry to "freshen it up". Had they done, it probably wouldn't have been top Scotch.

Over 90 out of every 100 bottles of Scotch consumed is a blend, and therefore rather common. That has brought about some cold-shouldering from certain elitist whisky lovers who convince themselves a blend must be inferior. Well, not in my books. In fact, perhaps the opposite is true. Until you get to grips with blends you may well be entitled to regard yourself knowledgeable in single malts, but not in Scotch as a whole. Blends should be the best that Scotland can offer, because with a blend you have the ability to create any degree of complexity. And surely balance and complexity are the cornerstones of any great whisky, irrespective of type.

Of course there are some pretty awful blends created simply as a commodity with little thought going into their structure – just young whiskies, sometimes consisting of stock that is of dubious quality and then coloured up to give some impression of age. Yes, you are more likely to find that among blends than malts and for this reason the poorest blends can be pretty nasty. And, yes, they contain grain. Too often, though, grain is regarded as a kind of whisky leper – not to be touched under any circumstances. Some writers dismiss grain as "neutral" and "cheap", thus putting into the minds of the uninitiated the perception of inferiority.

But there really is nothing inferior about blends. In fact, whilst researching The Bible, I have to say that my heart misses more than one beat usually when I received a sample of a blend I have never found before. Why? Well, with single malts each distillery produces a style that can be found within known parameters. With a blend, anything is possible. There are myriad styles of malts to choose from and they will react slightly differently with certain grains.

For that reason, perhaps, I have marked blends a little more strictly and tighter than I have single malts. Because blends, by definition, should offer more.

The most exciting blends, like White Horse 12 (why is that, like Old Parr 18, restricted mainly to Japan?) Grant's and the perennially glorious Ballantine's show bite, character and attitude. Silk and charm are to be appreciated. But after a long, hard day is anything better than a blend that is young and confident enough to nip and nibble at your throat on its way down and then throw up an array of flavours and shapes to get your taste-buds round? Certainly, I have always found blends ultimately more satisfying than malts. Especially when the balance, like this year's Scotch Blend of the Year, The Last Drop 50-year-old, simply caresses your soul. They do more: they paint pictures on the palate, flavour-scapes of extraordinary subtlety and texture. No two bottles are ever exactly the same, but they are usually close enough and further illustrate the fascination of a beautifully orchestrated variation on a theme.

With Blended Scotch the range and possibilities are limitless. All it takes is for the drinker not just to use his or her nose and taste-buds. But also an open mind.

Scottish Blends

100 Pipers (74) n18.5 t18 f19 b18.5. An improved blend, even with a touch of spice to the finish. I get the feeling the grains are a bit less aggressive than they for so long were. I'd let you know for sure, if only I could get through the caramel. 40%. Chivas.

Aberdour Piper (88.5) n22 t23 f21.5 b22. Always great to find a blend that appears to have upped the stakes in the quality department. Clean, refreshing with juicy young Speysiders at times simply showing off. 40%. Hayman Distillers.

⬦ **Alexander Murray & Co Monumental Blend 30 Years Old** (89.5) n23.5 Now there's a nose! The oak is quietly prominent with gorgeous layering of kiwifruit jam and moist Lubeck marzipan...wow!! Lurking somewhere appears to be a hint a four-fifths-hidden smoke...; **t23** the softest delivery imaginable: a combination of soft oils and molten sugars. Again, the tannins are pretty upfront, but the clever semi fruitiness – something akin to glace cherries on a sponge; **f21** a little messy by comparison: tangy and toffeed; **b22** forget the average finish, the nose and delivery are a treat. 40%

Antiquary 12 Years Old (92) n23.5 t23.5 f22 b23 A staggering about turn for a blend which, for a very long time, has flown the Speyside flag. 40%. Tomatin Distillery.

Antiquary 21 Years Old (93) n23.5 t23.5 f23 b23 A huge blend, scoring a magnificent 93 points. But I have tasted better, and another sample, direct from the blending lab, came with even greater complexity and less apparent caramel. A top-notch blend of rare distinction. 43%

Antiquary 30 Years Old (86) n22 t23 f20 b21. Decidedly odd fare but the eccentric nose and early delivery are sublime, with silky complexity tumbling over the palate. 46%

⬦ **The Antiquary Blended Scotch Whisky** (81) n20 t21 f20 b20. A slightly richer version than its predecessor, Antiquary Finest, this still could do with some extra complexity from the malts to help distract from the monotony of the firm grain. Clean and enjoyable, though. 40%

Antiquary Finest (79.5) n20 t21 f19 b19.5. Pleasantly sweet and plump with the accent on the quick early malt delivery. 40%. Tomatin Distillery.

Arden House Scotch Whisky (86) n19.5 t22 f22.5 b22. Another great bit of fun from the Co-op. Very closely related to their Finest Blend, though this has, for some reason or other, a trace of a slightly fatter, mildly more earthy style. If only they would ditch the caramel and let those sweet malts and grains breathe! 40%. Co-Operative Group.

Asda Blended Scotch Whisky (76.5) n19 t21 f17.5 b19. A scattergun approach with sweet, syrupy notes hitting the palate early. Beware the rather bitter finish, though. 40%

Asda Extra Special 12 Years Old (78) n19 t21 f19 b19. Pleasantish but dragged down by the dreaded S word. 40%. Glenmorangie for Asda.

The Bailie Nicol Jarvie (B.N.J) (95) n24 t24 f23 b24. I know my criticism of BNJ, historically one of my favourite blends, over the last year or two has been taken to heart by Glenmorangie. Delighted to report that they have responded: the blend has been fixed and is back to its blisteringly brilliant, ultra-mouth-watering self. Someone's sharpened their ideas up. 40%

⬦ **Ballaglass Blended Scotch Whisky** (85) n21 t22 f21 b21. Perfectly enjoyable, chewy – but clean – blend full of toffee and fudge. Very good weight and impressive, oily body. 40%.

Ballantine's Aged 12 Years (84.5) n22.5 t22 f19 b21. Attractive but odd fellow, this, with a touch of juniper to the nose and furry bitter marmalade on the finish. But some excellent barley-cocoa moments, too. 43%. Chivas.

Ballantine's 12 Years Old (87) n21 t22 f21 b23. The kind of old-fashioned, mildly moody blend Colonel Farquharson-Smythe (retired) might have recognised when relaxing at the 19th hole back in the early '50s. Too good for a squirt of soda, mind. 40%. Chivas Bros.

Ballantine's 17 Years Old (97.5) n24.5 deft grain and honey plus teasing salty peat; ultra high quality with bourbon and pear drops offering the thrust; a near unbelievable integration with gooseberry juice offering a touch of sharpness muted by watered golden syrup; **t24** immediately mouthwatering with maltier tones clambering over the graceful cocoa-enriched grain; the degrees of sweetness are varied but near perfection; just hints of smoke here and there; **f24** lashings of vanilla and cocoa on the fade; drier with a faint spicey, vaguely smoky buzz; has become longer with more recent bottlings with the most subtle oiliness imaginable; **b25** now only slightly less weighty than of old. After a change of style it has comfortably reverted back to its sophisticated, mildly erotic old self. One of the most beautiful, complex and stunningly structured whiskies ever created. Truly the epitome of great Scotch. 43%. ⊙

Ballantine's Aged 17 Years Limited Edition Miltonduff Signature Distillery (91.5) n22.5 t24 f21.5 b23.5. The usual alto libretto of the Ballantine's 17 has been replaced here by a much weightier composition, even though the usual subtle smoke is missing. Using sherry butts is to enter a minefield in this day and age, one I'm afraid, there is no clear path through. The ones here are of mixed quality, but the overall effect is pleasing. 43%

Ballantine's Aged 21 Years (93) n24 t24 f22 b23 One of the reasons I think I have loved the Ballantine's range over the years is because it is a blenders' blend. In other words, you get the feeling that they have made as much, and probably more, as possible from the stocks available and made complexity and balance the keystones to the whisky. That is still the case, except you find now that somehow, although part of a larger concern, it appears that the spectrum of flavours is less wide, though what has been achieved with those available remains absolutely top drawer. This is truly great whisky, but it has changed in style as blends, especially of this age, cannot help but doing. *43%*

Ballantine's Aged 30 Years (94) n23.5 t24 f23.5 b23.5. Quite a different animal to that which I tasted last year...and the year before. Having come across it in three different markets, I each time noted a richer, more balanced product: less a bunch of old casks being brought together but more a sculpted piece from preferred materials. That said, I still get the feeling that this is a work in progress: a Kenny Jackett-style building of a team bit by bit, so that each compartment is improved when it is possible, but not to the detriment of another and, vitally, balance is maintained. *43%*

Ballantine's Finest (96) n24 a playful balance and counter-balance between grains, lighter malts and a gentle smokiness. The upped peat of recent years has given an extra weight and charm that had been missing; t24 sublime delivery: the mouthfeel couldn't be better had your prayers been answered; velvety and brittle grains combine to get the most out of the juicy malts: a lot of chewing to get through here; f23.5 soft, gentle, yet retains its weight and shape with a re-emergence of smoke and a gristy sweetness to counter the gentle vanillas and cocoa from the oak b24.5 as a standard blend this is coming through as a major work of art. Each time I taste this the weight has gone up a notch or two more and the sweetness has increased to balance out with the drier grain elements. Take a mouthful of this and experience the work of a blender very much at the top of his game. *40%. Chivas Bros.* ⊙

Ballantine's Limited brown bottle, bott code D03518 (94.5) n23.5 t24 f23 b24. When it comes to Ballantine's I am beginning to run out of superlatives. The last time I tasted Limited, I remember being disappointed by the un-Ballantine's-like bitter finish. Well, from nose to finale, there is a barely perceptible trace of a rogue cask costing half a point from each stage: indeed, it may have cost it World Whisky of the Year. But so magnificent are all those keeping it company there has been no such falling at the last hurdle here. This bottle, rather than finding its way back into my warehouse library, will be living at my home for offering an ethereal quality unmatched by any other whisky in the world. *43%. Chivas.*

Ballantine's Limited 75cl royal blue bottle (89) n22 t24 f21 b22. Hadn't tasted this for a little while but maintains its early style and quite glorious delivery. *43%*

Ballantine's Limited Release no. J13295 (95.5) n24.5 just so soft...ridiculously so. You have to listen hard to what is happening here...only perfect silence will do. Then you will pick up fluting fruit calls which are absorbed by the delicate smoke. The sugars and honey mix shyly but effectively, all this seemingly glazed. A hint of spice wakes you if you are being caressed to sleep; t25 there is no point in trying to describe the indescribable. Just about the best delivery I have experienced from a blended whisky with the fruit and grains seemingly having a telepathic understanding of each other's movements; f22 annoying bitters out and a slight furriness attaches to the late smoke; b24 I absolutely take my hat off to the blender. When it comes to the weight, complexity, subtlety, suaveness, balance, pace of flavour development, charm and just all-round yessss!!!!ness, I am not sure how the delivery can be bettered. A slight mix of exhausted bourbon cask (allowing some bitterness) and a degree of perhaps sherry-induced furriness means the finish can't quite reach those heights of seemingly effortless perfection and rob this of the World Whisky of the Year for this Bible it most likely would have picked up. But for the combination of nose and delivery I will take those losses. Yet again a Ballantine's which just makes me purr and celebrate the greatness some whiskies can reach. *43%.*

◆ **Ballantine's Limited Release no. L40055** (96.5) n24 sherry can be as dry as it might be sweet, and here the grape is in its most austere form of dryness. Excellent use of Speyside malts in particular generates both the sugars and the fuller structure and oils; the vaguest degree of phenol also makes for a both ethereal yet weighty experience; t25 a silky landing, though hard to tell if that is through the malt or delicate, yielding fruit: that really is a sign of exceptional blending! Astonishingly, one starts salivating on very first contact with the palate and the spices, never more than a buzzing murmur, begin their important work nanoseconds later. The mid-ground is a busy mesh of malt, vanilla and delicate fruit notes before the cocoa begins to make an impact; you try to count the flavour waves, but on the third or fourth time of trying, give up: there are simply too many; f23 there is a vague furriness which shows that not every cask was perhaps reaching perfection, though it must have been only the odd one or two. Despite this the peek-a-boo played between the still slightly juicy malt and the aloof grape keeps the senses entertained and the mind enthralled; b24.5 a vaguely weightier incarnation than the last bottling I came across, and here the oils have a much more emboldening role. Indeed, this is a more embracing and confiding version, increasing even more the slightly austere part of its character, and, in doing so, just slightly upping the degree of sophistication. Even though this is only by fractions, it is enough to make it not only a world class whisky, but one of the great whiskies of 2015. And without that late, lightly furry finish, that audible whisper of a taint, almost certainly World Whisky of the Year. *40%*

Ballantine's Master's (82) n21 t22 f19 b20. Excellent lively grain and chewy malt, but the always suspect, grain-drizzled finish has become even more nondescript in recent bottlings. *40%*

Ballantine's Rare Limited (89.5) n23.5 t22.5 f21.5 b22 A heavier, more mouth watering blend than the "Bluebottle" version. *43%. ncf. Chivas.*

Barley Barony (83) n21.5 t21 f20 b20.5. Faintly furry finish follows from firm, fruity front. *40%.*

Bell's Original (91) n23 t22.5 f22.5 b23 Your whisky sleuth came across the new version for the first time in the bar of a London theatre back in December 2009 during the interval of "The 39 Steps". To say I was impressed and pleasantly surprised is putting it mildly. And with the whisky, too, which is a massive improvement on the relatively stagnant 8-year-old especially with the subtle extra smoky weight. If the blender asks me: "Did I get it right, Sir?" then the answer has to be a resounding "yes". *40%*

Bells 8 Years Old (85) n21.5 t22.5 f20 b21. Some mixed messages here: on one hand it is telling me that it has been faithful to some of the old Bells distilleries – hence a slight dirty note, especially on the finish. On the other, there are some sublime specks of complexity and weight. Quite literally the rough and the smooth. *40%. Diageo.*

Benmore (74) n19 t19 f18 b18. Underwhelming to the point of being nondescript. *40%*

Berrys' Blue Hanger 30 Years Old 3rd Release bott 2007 (90.5) n23 t22.5 f22.5 b22.5 Much improved version on the last, closer to the original in every respect. Excellent. *45.6%.*

Big "T" 5 Years Old (75) n19 t20 f18 b18. Still doesn't have the finesse of old and clatters about the tastebuds charmlessly. *40%. Tomatin Distillery.*

Black & White (91) n22 t23 f22.5 b23.5 This one hasn't gone to the dogs: quite the opposite. I always go a bit misty-eyed when I taste something this traditional: the crisp grains work to maximum effect in reflecting the malts. A classic of its type. *40%. Diageo.*

Black Bottle (74.5) n18 t20.5 f17 b18. Barely a shadow of its once masterful, great self. *40%*

Black Bottle 10 Years Old (89) n22 t23 f22 b23 A stupendous blend of weight and poise, but possessing little of the all-round steaming, rampaging sexuality of the younger version... but like the younger version showing a degree less peat: here perhaps even two. Not, I hope, the start of a new trend under the new owners. *40%*

Black Dog 12 Years Old (92) n21 t23 f24 b24. Offering genuine sophistication and élan. This minor classic will probably require two or three glass-fulls before you take the bait... *42.8%*

Black Dog Century (89) n21 t23 f23 b22. I adore this style of no-nonsense, full bodied bruising blend which amid the muscle offers exemplary dexterity and finesse. What entertainment in every glass!! *42.8%. McDowell & Co Ltd. Blended in Scotland/Bottled in India.*

Black Grouse (94) n23 t24 f23 b24. A superb return to a peaty blend for Edrington for the first time since they sold Black Bottle. Not entirely different from that brand, either, from the Highland Distillers days with the smokiness being superbly couched by sweet malts. *40%*

The Black Grouse Alpha Edition (72.5) n17 t19.5 f17 b18. Dreadfully sulphured. *40%*

Black Knight (85.5) n21 t22 f21 b21.5. More of a White Knight as it peacefully goes about its business. Not many taste buds slain, but just love the juicy charge. *43%. Quality Spirits Int.*

Black Ram Aged 12 Years (85) n21 t23 f21 b20. An upfront blend that gives its all in the chewy delivery. Some major oak in there but it's all ultra soft toffee and molasses towards the finish. *40%. Vinprom Peshtera, Bulgaria.*

Blend No. 888 (86.5) n20 t21.5 f23 b22. A good old-fashioned, rip-roaring, nippy blend with a fudge-honey style many of a certain age will fondly remember from the 60s and 70s. Love it! *40%. The House of MacDuff.*

Boxes Blend (90) n22.5 t23.5 f21 b23. A box which gets plenty of ticks. *40.9%. ncf.*

Broadford (78.5) n19 t19.5 f20 b20. Boringly inoffensive. Toffee anyone? *40%. Burn Stewart.*

Buchanan's De Luxe 12 Years Old (82) n18 t21 f22 b21. The nose shows more than just a single fault and the character simply refuses to get out of second gear. Certainly pleasant, and some of the chocolate notes towards the end are gorgeous. But just not the normal brilliant show-stopper! *40%. Diageo.*

Buchanan's Red Seal (90) n22 t23 f22 b23 Exceptional, no-frills blend whose apparent simplicity paradoxically celebrates its complexity. *40%. Diageo.*

Budgen's Scotch Whisky Finely Blended (85) n21 t22 f21 b21. A sweet, chunky blend offering no shortage of dates, walnuts, spice and toffee. A decent one to mull over. *40%*

Cadenhead's Putachieside Aged 12 Years (91) n23 no shortage of citrus and vanilla: fresh, and the flaky, puff-pastry topping is fitting; t23 the sugars and oils make an early assault. A little bitterness from the oak creeps in; f22 malty-lemon sawdust; b23 not tasted

239

for a while and delighted to re-discover this understated little gem. Also, has to be one of the best labels of any scotch going... 40% WB15/357

Cadenhead's Creations Light Creamy Vanilla Aged 17 Years batch no. 1, bott 2014 **(91)** n22 mainly oranges and lemons, the only weight coming from the faintest echo of smoke; **t23** a miniature painting of subtlety and, though a blend, a powerful juicy barley theme, with digestive biscuit and Tunnock's teacake filling also playing a major role; **f23** the grain gets to work, though the backdrop is caramelised biscuit and sugar cubes; the fade brings together all the natural caramels on show...and late spice; **b23** just adore clean, refreshing blends like this: says so much while appearing to do so little. For the record: Ardmore, Auchroisk, Caperdonich, and Clynelish are the malts involved, while Invergordon represents the grain. 46%. ncf nc. WB15/362

Callander 12 Years Old (86) n21 t22 f21.5 b21.5. No shortage of malt sparkle and even a touch of tangy salt. Very attractive and enjoyable without ripping up trees. 46.3%. Burn Stewart.

Campbeltown Loch (94) n23 soft, creamy vanilla: Jammy Dodger biscuit; **t24** rousingly salivating with some extraordinary young malt allowing the grain in only by degree. The grain is no less lush and the creaminess apparent on the nose shows here, too; **f23.5** wonderful sugars enjoy a light vanilla and lemon glow; **b23.5** over 30 years ago, this blend was one of my preferred drams at home. Not seen it for a while, so disappeared from The Bible. Found again and though it has changed a little in structure, its overall excellence takes me back to when I was a young man. 40% WB15/355

Campbeltown Loch Aged 15 Years (88) n22.5 t22.5 f21 b22 Well weighted with the age in no hurry to arrive. 40%. Springbank Distillers.

Cambletown Loch 21 Years Old db **(83)** n21 t23 f19 b20 Neither the nose or finish are much to write home about, the latter being a little tangy and bitter. But the delivery is rich and comforting: like a Digestive biscuit dunked in coffee. A seemingly decent malt content and a bit of toffee before the furry finale. 46%. WB15/102

Castle Rock (81) n20 t20.5 f20 b20.5. Clean and juicy entertainment. 40%

Catto's Aged 25 Years (85.5) n22 t22.5 f19.5 b21.5. A hugely enjoyable yet immensely frustrating dram. The higher fruit and spice notes are a delight, but it all appears to be played out in a padded cell of cream caramel. One assumes the natural oak caramels have gone into overdrive. Had they not, we would have had a supreme blend scoring well into the 90s. Elsewhere the increased furriness on the finale has not improved matters.40% ⊙

Catto's Deluxe 12 Years Old (79.5) n20 t21.5 f18 b20. Refreshing and spicy in part, but still a note in there which doesn't quite work. 40%. Inverhouse Distillers.

Catto's Rare Old Scottish (92) n23.5 t23.5 f22 b23 Currently one of my regular blends to drink at home. Astonishingly old-fashioned with a perfect accent on clean Speyside and crisp grain. In the last year or so it has taken on a sublime sparkle on the nose and palate. An absolutely masterful whisky which both refreshes and relaxes. 40%. James Catto & Co.

Chequers Deluxe (78.5) n19.5 t20 f19 b20. Charm, elegance, sophistication...not a single sign of any of them. Still if you want a bit of rough and tumble, just the job. 40%. Diageo.

Chivas Regal Aged 12 Years (83.5) n20.5 t22.5 f20 b20.5. Chewy fruit toffee. Silky grain mouth-feel with a toasty, oaky presence. 40%. Chivas.

Chivas Regal Aged 18 Years (73.5) n17.5 t20 f17.5 b18.5. The nose is dulled by a whiff of sulphur and confirmation that all is not well comes with the disagreeably dry, bitter finish. Early on in the delivery some apples and spices show promise but it is an unequal battle against the caramel and off notes. 40%

Chivas Regal 25 Years Old (95) n23 t23.5 f24 b24.5. Unadulterated class where the grain-malt balance is exemplary and the deft intertwangling of well-mannered oak and elegant barley leaves you demanding another glass. Brilliant! 40%

⋙ **Chivas Regal Extra (86)** n20 t24 f20.5 b21.5. Chivas, but seemingly from the Whyte and MacKay school of thick, impenetrable blends. The nose may have the odd undesirable element and the finish reflects those same trace failings. But if chewy date and walnuts in a sea of creamy toffee is your thing, then this malt is for you. This, though, does show genuine complexity, so I have to admit to adoring the lush delivery and early middle section: the mouth-feel is truly magnificent. Good spice, too. Flawed genius comes to mind. 40%

Clan Campbell (86.5) n21.5 t22.5 f21 b21.5. I'll wager that if I could taste this whisky before the colouring is added it would be scoring into the 90s. Not a single off note; a sublime early array of Speysidey freshness but dulls at the end. 40%. Chivas.

Clan Gold 3 Year Old (95) n23.5 t24 f23.5 b24. A blend-drinkers blend which will also slay the hearts of Speyside single malt lovers. For me, this is love at first sip... 40%

Clan Gold Blended 15 Years Old (91) n21.5 t23 f23.5 b23 An unusual blend for the 21st century, which steadfastly refuses to blast you away with over the top flavour and/or aroma profiles and instead depends on subtlety and poise despite the obvious richness of flavour. The grains make an impact but only by creating the frame in which the more complex notes can be admired. 40%

Clan Gold Blended 18 Years Old (94.5) n23 t24 f23.5 b24. Almost the ultimate preprandial whisky with its at once robust yet delicate working over of the taste buds by the carefully muzzled juiciness of the malt. This is the real deal: a truly classy act which at first appears to wallow in a sea of simplicity but then bursts out into something very much more complex and alluring. About as clean and charming an 18-year-old blend as you are likely to find. 40%

Clan MacGregor (92) n22 t24 f23 b23 Just gets better and better. Now a true classic and getting up there with Grant's. 43%

Clan Murray Rare Old (84) n18 t23 f21 b22. The wonderful malt delivery on the palate is totally incongruous with the weak, nondescript nose. Glorious, mouth-watering complexity on the arrival, though. Maybe it needs a Murray to bring to perfection... 40%. Benriach Distillery.

Clansman (80.5) n20.5 t21 f19 b20. Sweet, grainy and soft. 40%. Loch Lomond.

Clansman (78.5) n20 t21.5 f18 b19. Plenty of weight, oil and honey-ginger. Some bitterness, too. 43%. Loch Lomond Distillers.

The Claymore (85) n19 t22 f22 b22. These days you are run through by spices. The blend is pure Paterson in style with guts etc, which is not something you always like to associate with a Claymore; some delightful muscovado sugar at the death. Get the nose sorted and a very decent and complex whisky is there to be had. 40%. Whyte & Mackay Distillers Ltd.

Compass Box Asyla 1st fill American oak ex-bourbon, bott May 10 (93) n24 t24 f22.5 b23.5 If you can hear a purring noise, it is me tasting this... 40%. nc ncf.

Compass Box Asyla Marriage nine months in an American oak barrel (88) n22 t23 f21 b22 A lovely blend, but can't help feeling that this was one marriage that lasted too long. 43.6%. Compass Box Whisky for La Maison du Whisky in commemoration of their 50th Anniversary.

Compass Box Delilah's Limited Release American oak, bott Jul 13 (89.5) n23 t22 f22 b22.5. A clean and satisfying blend which ramps up the sugars when need be. I'll be surprised if you get to the point where you couldn't take any more... 40%. 6400 bottles.

Compass Box Delilah's Limited Release Small Batch American oak (92.5) n23 the tannins arrive early, offering a delicate spice, but it is the weak acacia honey whisky dominates; but all hush-hush and understated; t23.5 this time the hney shoulders the tannins to one side. The grain is of the soft, yielding variety offering succour and comfort...like a soft pillow or gentle breast at the end of a hard day's tasting...; f23 tangy as the tannins begin to bite...and much warmer now thanks to busier spice. The bourbn effect I had been waiting for fails to materialise...though the is the odd Canadian strain here and there...; b23 blends rarely come more honeyed, or even sweeter, than this with every last sugary element seemingly extracted from the oak. My only sorrow for this whisky, given its American theme, was that it wasn't bottled as a 101 (ie 50.5% abv) instead of the rather underpowered 80 proof – because you have the feeling this would have become pretty three dimensional and leapt from the glass. And then down your throat with serious effect. 40%. nc ncf. WB15/171

Compass Box The Entertainer Limited Edition bott Aug 12 (88.5) n21.5 t22.5 f22 b22. A pleasant blend, though the tanginess is perhaps a little too sharp. 46%. Compass Box Whisky Company. 1000 bottles. Commissioned by Selfridges.

Compass Box The General bott Nov 13 (95) n24 t24 f23 b24. I have never encountered a bend quite like this one. The grain's part in the act appears only to give breathing space to the more delicate notes: a pretty worthy cause. Commanding and unambiguously brilliant. 53.4%. ncf nc. 1,698 bottles.

Compass Box Great King St. Artist's Blend (93) n24 t23 f22.5 b23.5. The nose of this uncoloured and non-chill filtered whisky is not dissimilar to some better known blends before they have colouring added to do its worst. A beautiful young thing this blend: nubile, naked and dangerously come hither. Compass Box's founder John Glaser has done some memorable work in recent years, though one has always had the feeling that he has still been learning his trade, sometimes forcing the issue a little too enthusiastically. Here, there is absolutely no doubting that he has come of age as a blender. 43%. nc ncf.

Compass Box Great King Street Experimental Batch #00-V4 bott Sep 13 (93) n22.5 t24 f23 b23.5. A blend combining astonishing vibrancy with oaky Russian roulette. Not a dram to do things by halves... 43%. 3,439 bottles.

Compass Box Great King Street Experimental Batch #TR-06 bott Sep 13 (92) n22 the most dense of all the GKS I have yet tasted. All, including batch 00-V4 have shewn signs of younger malts offering a bright outlet. This, though, is a distant rumble, like highway traffic a mile off, of tannin, toast and smoke; t23.5 unlike on the nose, the first to display is a sweet, buttery maltiness, mixed with the gentle elements of the grain. And there is sweet smoke, too which holds the middle until the tannins return; f23 long, oily, with a smoked Demerara theme. The oak, though, rumbles and grumbles on; b23.5 I think this one's been rumbled... 43%.

⟡ **Compass Box Great King Street Glasgow Blend** (88.5) n22 playful phenols delight, but a strange wrong un of a note detracts and distracts; t23.5 some clever interplay on delivery: the smoke appears to have its own way early on, but the grain clears a path of clarity, along which brighter, more honeyed notes occasionally travel; f21 soft oils ensure a gentle landing, but those odd discordant notes detected on the nose bob up again, especially at the death; b22 just the odd note seems out of place here and there: delicious but not the usual Compass Box precision. *43%*

Consulate (89) n22 t22 f22.5 b22.5. One assumes this beautifully balanced dram was designed to accompany Passport in the drinks cabinet. I suggest if buying them, use Visa. *40%*

Co-operative Finest Blend (92.5) n23.5 t23 f22.5 b23.5 A fabulous and fascinating blend which has divested itself of its peaty backbone and instead packed the core with honey. Not the same heavyweight blend of old, but still one which is to be taken seriously – and straight – by those looking for a classic whisky of the old school. *40%*

Co-operative Premium Scotch 5 Years Old (91.5) n22 t24 f22.5 b23 From the nose I thought this blend had nosedived emphatically from when I last tasted it. However the delivery remains the stuff of legend. And though it has shifted emphasis and style to marked degree, there is no disputing its overall clout and entertainment value remains very high. *40%*

Craigellachie Hotel Quaich Bar Range (81) n20 t21 f20 b20. A delightful malt delivery early on, but doesn't push on with complexity as perhaps it might. *40%*

Crawford's (83.5) n19 t21 f22 b21.5. A lovely spice display helps overcome the caramel. *40%.*

Cutty Black (83) n20 t23 f19 b21. Both nose and finish are dwarfed and flung into the realms of ordinariness by the magnificently substantial delivery. Whilst there is a taint to the nose, its richness augers well for what is to follow; and you won't be disappointed. At times it behaves like a Highland Park with a toffeed spine, such is the richness and depth of the honey and dates and complexity of the grain-vanilla background. But those warning notes on the nose are there for good reason and the finish tells you why. Would not be surprised to see this score into the 90s on a different bottling day. *40%. Edrington.*

Cutty Sark (78) n19 t21 f19 b19. Crisp and juicy. But a nipping furriness, too. *40%*

Cutty Sark Aged 12 Years (92) n22 t24 f23 b23 At last! Cutty 12 at full sail...and blended whisky rarely looks any more beautiful! *40%. Edrington.*

Cutty Sark Aged 15 Years (82) n19 t22 f20 b21. Attempts to take the honey route. But seriously dulled by toffee and the odd sulphured cask. *40%. Edrington.*

Cutty Sark Aged 18 Years (88) n22 t22 f22 b22 Lost the subtle fruitiness which worked so well. Easy-going and attractive. *43%*

Cutty Sark Aged 25 Years (91) n21 t23.5 f22.5 b23 Magnificent, though not quite flawless, this whisky is as elegant and effortlessly powerful as the ship after which the brand was named... *45.7%. Berry Bros & Rudd.*

Cutty Sark Storm (81.5) n18 t23.5 f19.5 b20.5. When the wind is set fair, which is mainly on delivery and for the first six or seven flavour waves which follow, we really do have an astonishingly beautiful blend, seemingly high in malt content and really putting the accent on ulmo honey and marzipan: a breath-taking combination. This is assisted by a gorgeous weight to the silky body and a light raspberry jam moment to the late arriving Ecuadorian cocoa. All magnificent. However, the blend, as Cutty sadly tends to, sails into sulphurous seas. *40%. Edrington.*

Demijohn's Finest Blended Scotch Whisky (88) n21 t22 f23 b22 A fun, characterful blend that appears to have above the norm malt. Enjoy. *40%. Adelphi.*

Dew of Ben Nevis Blue Label (82) n19 t22 f20 b21. The odd off-key note is handsomely outnumbered by deliciously complex mocha and demerara tones. Ditch the caramel and you'd have a sizzler! *40%. Ben Nevis Distillery. Replacement for Dew of Ben Nevis Millennium Blend.*

Dew of Ben Nevis Special Reserve (85) n19 t21 f23 b22. A much juicier blend than of old, still sporting some bruising and rough patches. But that kind of makes this all the more attractive, with the caramel mixing with some fuller malts to provide a date and nuts effect which makes for a grand finale. *40%. Ben Nevis Distillery.*

Dew of Ben Nevis Supreme Selection (77) n18 t20 f20 b19. Some lovely raspberry jam swiss roll moments here. But the grain could be friendlier, especially on the nose. *40%*

Dewar's Special Reserve 12 Years Old (84) n20 t23 f19 b22. Some s... you know what... has crept onboard here and duffed up the nose and finish. A shame because elements of the delivery and background balance shows some serious blending went on here. *40%*

Dewar's 18 Years Old (93) n23 t24 f22.5 b23.5 Here is a classic case of where great blends are not all about the malt. The grain plays in many ways the most significant role here, as it is the perfect backdrop to see the complexity of the malt at its clearest. Simply magnificent blending with the use of flawless whisky. *43%. John Dewar & Sons.*

Dewar's 18 Year Old Founders Reserve (86.5) n22.5 t22 f20.5 b21.5. A big, blustering dram which doesn't stint on the fruit. A lovely, thin seam of golden syrup runs through the piece, but the dull, aching finale is somewhat out of character. *40%. John Dewar & Sons.*

Dewar's Signature (93) n24 t23.5 f22 b23.5. A slight departure in style, with the fruit becoming just a little sharper and juicier. Top range blending and if the odd butt could be weeded out, this'd be an award winner for sure. 43%

Dewar's White Label (78.5) n19 t21.5 f19 b19. When on song, one of my preferred daily blends. But not when like this, with its accentuated bitter-sweet polarisation. 40%

Dhoon Glen (85.5) n21 t22 f21 b21.5 Full of big flavours, broad grainy strokes and copious amounts of dark sugar including toffee. 40%. Lombard Brands Ltd.

Dimple 12 Years Old (86.5) n22 t22 f21.5 b21. Lots of sultana; the spice adds aggression. 40%.

Dimple 15 Years Old (87.5) n20 t21 f24 b22.5. Only on the late middle and finish does this particular flower unfurl and to magnificently complex effect. The texture of the grains in particular delight while the strands of barley entwine. A type of treat for the more technically minded of the serious blend drinkers among you. 40%. Diageo.

Drummer (81) n20 t21 f20 b20. Big toffee. Rolos...? 40%. Inver House Distillers.

Drummer Aged 5 Years (83) n19 t22.5 f20.5 b21. The nose may beat a retreat but it certainly gets on a roll when those fabulous sharp notes hit the palate. However, it deserves some stick as the boring fudge finishes in a cymbal of too much toffee. 40%. Inver House.

Duncan Taylor Auld Blended Aged 35 Years dist pre 70 (93) n23 t24 f22 b24 An infinitely better dram than previous bottlings, due mainly to the fact that the dangers of old oak appear to have been compensated for. 46%. 131 bottles.

Duncan Taylor Collection Black Bull 12 Year Old (88.5) n22.5 t22.5 f21.5 b22 Black Bulls enjoy a reputation for being dangerous. So does this: once you pour yourself a glass, it is difficult not to have another...and another... 50%. Duncan Taylor & Co Ltd.

Duncan Taylor Collection Black Bull Deluxe Blend Aged 30 Years (93) n24 t24 f22 b23. This pedigree Black Bull doesn't pull its horns in... 50%. Duncan Taylor.

Duncan Taylor Collection Rarest of the Rare Deluxe Blend 33 Years Old (94) n24 t24 f22 b23. Outstanding and astounding blended whisky. An absolute must for blend lovers... especially those with a bourbony bent. 43.4%

Duncan Taylor Collection Black Bull 40 Year Old batch 1 (86.5) n23 t21 f21.5 b21. Almost certainly whisky which had dipped below 40%abv in the cask has been included in this blend. That would account for the occasional spasm of ultra intense natural caramels, a kind of tell-tale fingerprint indicating this is likely to have been done. The nose is exotic fruit; the delivery is a battle to keep the oak at bay. One which is happily won. 40.2%

Duncan Taylor Collection Black Bull 40 Years Old batch 2 (94) n23 t24 f23 b24. Just sit back and marvel at something so old...yet so young at heart. 41.9%. Duncan Taylor & Co.

Duncan Taylor Collection Black Bull Special Reserve batch 1 (86) n21 t22.5 f21 b21.5. Juicy in just the right areas. Some charming spice and vanilla, too. 46.6%

Duncan Taylor Black Bull Special Reserve batch 2 (87.5) n23 t23.5 f19 b22. Has seriously upped the fruit and spice from the original version to make for a compelling blend. 50%

Duncan Taylor Smokin' (85) n21 t22 f21 b21. On one hand phenolic, on the other surprisingly lightweight. Attractively sweet and friendly, though. 40%. Duncan Taylor.

The Famous Grouse (89) n22 t23 f21.5 b22.5 It almost seems that Grouse is, by degrees, moving from its traditional position of a light blend to something much closer to Grant's as a middle-weighted dram. Again the colouring has been raised a fraction and now the body and depth have been adjusted to follow suit. Have to say that this is one very complex whisky these days: I had spotted slight changes when drinking it socially, but this was the first time I had a chance to sit down and professionally analyse what was happening in the glass. A fascinating and tasty bird, indeed. 40%. Edrington Group.

The Famous Grouse Aged 16 Years Special 2013 Edition (84) n22 t22 f19 b21. A completely different type of Grouse which on one hand offers a pretty comprehensive guide of the sugar shelves, yet somehow manages, for all its apparent esters, to bitter out violently at the finish. Intriguing, to put it mildly. 40%. Edrington Group.

The Famous Grouse Gold Reserve (90) n23.5 t23 f21.5 b22 Great to know the value of the Gold Reserve is going up...as should the strength of this blend. The old-fashioned 40% just ain't enough carats. 40%. Edrington Group.

⬦ **The Famous Grouse Married Strength** (82.5) n19 t22 f20 b21.5. The nose is nutty and toffeed. But despite the delightful, silky sweetness and gentle Speyside-style maltiness which forms the main markers for this soft blend, the nose, like the finish, also shows a little bitter furriness has, sadly, entered into the mix. Not a patch on the standard Grouse of a decade ago. 45.9% WB16/019

⬦ **The Famous Grouse Mellow Gold** sherry & bourbon casks (85) n20 t23.5 f20 b21.5. While the nose and finish tell us a little too much about the state of the sherry butts used, there is no harm tuning into the delivery and follow though which are, unquestionably, beautiful. The texture is silk normally found on the most expensive lingerie, and as sexy as who you might find inside it; while the honey is a fabulous mix of ulmo and orange blossom. 40%

The Famous Jubilee (83.5) n21.5 t22.5 f18.5 b21. A heavyweight, stodgy, toffee-laden kind of blend a long way from the Grouse tradition. With its ham-fisted date and walnut middle I would have sworn this was the work of another blender entirely. There are redeeming rich honey tones that are a joy. But the dull, pulsing sulphur on the finish has almost an air of inevitability. I promise you this: go back 60 years, and there would have been no blend created with this signature...not only did the style not exist, but it would have been impossible to accomplish. 40%. Edrington.

The Formidable Jock of Bennachie (82) n19 t22 f21 b20. "Scotland's best kept secret" claims the label. Hardly. But the silky delivery on the palate is worth investigating. Impressive roastiness to the malt and oak, but the caramel needs thinning. 40%. Bennachie Scotch Whisky.

Fort Glen The Blender's Reserve Aged 12 Years (88.5) n21.5 t23 f21.5 b22.5 An entirely enjoyable blend which is clean and boasting decent complexity and weight. 40%

Fort Glen The Distiller's Reserve (78) n18 t22 f19 b19. Juicy, salivating delivery as it storms the ramparts. Draws down the portcullis elsewhere. 40%. The Fort Glen Whisky Company.

Fraser MacDonald (85) n21 t21.5 f21 b21.5. Some fudge towards the middle and end but the journey there is an enjoyable one. 40%. Loch Lomond Distillers.

Gairloch (79) n19 t20 f20 b20. For those who like their butterscotch at 40% abv. 40%

Glen Brynth (70.5) n18 t19 f16 b17.5. Bitter and awkward. 43%

Glenbrynth 8 Year Old (88) n21.5 t22 f22.5 b22. An impressive blend which improves second by second on the palate. 40%. OTI Africa.

Glenbrynth Pearl 30 Year Old Limited Edition (90.5) n22.5 t23.5 f21.5 b23 Attractive, beautifully weighted, no off notes...though perhaps quietened by toffee. Still a treat of a blend. 43%. OTI Africa.

Glen Gray (84.5) n20 t22.5 f21 b21. A knife and fork blend you can stand your spoon in. Plain going for most of the way, but the area between delivery and middle enjoys several waves of rich chocolate honeycomb...and some of the cocoa resurfaces at the finale. 43%

Glen Lyon (85) n19 t22.5 f22 b21.5. Works a lot better than the nose suggests: seriously chewy with a rabid spice attack and lots of juices. For those who have just retired as dynamite testers. Unpretentious fun. 43%. Diageo.

Glen Orrin Aged 5 Years (77) n19 t21 f18 b19. Glen Orrible more like. A step up from the no age statement version, thanks mainly to a very delicate underlying smokiness. But the core malt is still of that ilk that will drive people to bourbon. 40%. Aldi.

Glen Orin 30 Years old Blend (95) n24 the grains have made a first-class job of drawing out the most lively vanillas and when fully warmed in the hand the delightfully sharp marmalade is at its zenith. The malt is no less graceful and dovetails majestically and at times almost covertly, injecting a delicate maple syrup sweetness to soften the richer elements of the grassy barley; **t24** crisp, firm grain ensures a cracking delivery and a very old-fashioned style. Despite its early ramrod rigidity, it softens slowly – almost tantalizingly - with first mouth-watering barley then a volley of the vanillas promised on the nose. The sugars are delicate, still offering a degree of maple but more inclined now towards a thin layer of acacia honey; **f23** the same grainy crispness which makes the delivery so strident ensures a less dramatic, more peaceful finale. Here, the influence of the oak is underlined with a drier, chalkier feel to the persistent vanillas. A light barley frame ensures that drier oak, patiently sculpted over three decades, is seen to its fullest advantage; **b24** a clean, charming blend from the old school and of a style too rarely seen today, alas. The accent, as it should be, is on the grain, and its very brittleness accentuates just how delicate this whisky is. A perfect pre-prandial dram to be taken straight and at body temperature, without water or ice, so its astonishing complexity can be fully explored. Or very late at night when you might find time for all its mysteries to unravel. Top notch Scotch where subtlety is the watchword. Delicacy and understatement is the key; yet with enough life and juiciness to entertain even the most fatigued taste buds. Truly outstanding. 40%. Aldi

◈ **Glen Talloch Choice Rare & Old (85.5) n20.5 t22.5 f21 b21.5.** A very pleasing sharpness to the delivery reveals the barley in all its Speyside-style finery. The grain itself is soothing, especially when the caramel notes kick in. 40%. ncf.

◈ **Glen Talloch Gold Aged 12 Years (85) n21 t22 f21 b21.** Impressive grain at work insuring a deft, velvety caress to the palate. Mainly caramel speaking, despite the age, though there is an attractive spice buzz towards the thin-ish finish. 40%

Glory Leading Blended Scotch Whisky 30 Years Old American oak casks **(93) n22.5** apple; some grain bite shows that all is not fully aligned; **t23** more relaxed on delivery, though concentrates on treacle tart (with custard) and spice; **f23.5** now makes much more sense as a little smoke and spice adds to the mix yet allows the malt a good platform and the grains a much clearer voice; **b24** a big, clever, satisfying blend which just gets better and better... though not too sure about the Crystal Palace style eagle on the label. Even so, love it! 43%

Golden Piper (86.5) n22 t21 f22 b21.5. A firm, clean blend with a steady flush through of diverse sugars. The grain does all the steering and therefore complexity is limited. But the overall freshness is a delight. *43%. Whisky Shack.*

Grand Sail (87) n21 t22 f22 b22. Sweet, attractive with enough bite to really matter. *40%*

Grand Sail Aged 10 Years (79) n20 t22 f18 b19. Pleasant and at times fascinating but with a tang that perhaps the next vatting will benefit from losing. *40%. China market.*

Grand Sail Rare Reserve Aged 18 Years (94) n23 t24 f23 b24. A truly beautiful whisky which cuts effortlessly and elegantly through the taste buds. *40% Angus Dundee. China market.*

Glenross Blended (83) n20 t22 f20 b21. Decent, easy-drinking whisky with a much sharper delivery than the nose suggests. *40%. Speyside Distillers.*

Glen Simon (77) n20 t19 f19 b19. Simple. Lots of caramel. *40%. Quality Spirits International.*

The Gordon Highlanders (86) n21 t22 f21 b22. Lush and juicy, there is a distinctive Speysidey feel to this one with the grains doing their best to accentuate the developing spice. Plenty of feel good factor here. *40%. William Grant & Sons.*

Grand Macnish (79) n19 t21 f19 b20. Welcome back to an old friend...but the years have caught up with it. Still on the feral side, but has exchanged its robust good looks for an unwashed and unkempt appearance on the palate. Will do a great job to bring some life back to you, though. *43%. MacDuff International Ltd.*

Grand Macnish 12 Years Old (86) n21 t22 f21.5 b21.5. A grander Grand Macnich than of old with the wonderful feather pillow delivery maintained and a greater harmonisation of the malt, especially those which contain a honey-copper sheen. *40%. MacDuff.*

Grant's Aged 12 Years bott 30/09/10 (89.5) n23 t23 f21.5 b22 Can't argue too much with the tasting notes on the label (although I contend that "full, rich and rounded" has more to do with its body than taste, but that is by the by). Beautiful whisky, as can be reasonably expected from a Grant's blend. If only the sharpness could last the distance. *40%.*

Grant's Cask Edition No.1 Ale Cask Finish Edinburgh ale casks (88.5) n22 t23 f21.5 b22. always loved this concept: a whisky and chaser in one bottle. This was has plenty of cheer in the complex opening, but gets maudlin towards the end. *40%. William Grant & Sons.*

Great McCauley (81) n20 t20.5 f20 b20.5. Reminds me of another whisky I tasted earlier: Castle Rock, I think. Identical profile with toffee & spice adding to the juicy & youthful fun. *40%.*

Green Plaid 12 Years Old (89) n22 t23 f22 b22 Beautifully constructed; juicy. *40%.*

Guneagal Aged 12 Years (85.5) n21 t22.5 f20.5 b21.5. The salty, sweaty armpit nose gives way to an even saltier delivery, helped along by sweet glycerine and a boiled candy fruity sweetness. The finish is a little roughhouse by comparison. *40%. William Grant & Sons.*

Haddington House (85.5) n21 t21.5 f22 b21. Mouth-watering and delicate. *40%*

Haig Gold Label (88) n21 t23 f22 b22 What had before been pretty standard stuff has upped the complexity by an impressive distance. *40%. Diageo.*

Hankey Bannister (84.5) n20.5 t22 f21 b21. Lots of early life and even a malt kick early on. Toffee later. *40%. Inverhouse Distillers.*

Hankey Bannister 12 Years Old (86.5) n22 t21.5 f21 b22. A much improved blend with a nose and early delivery which makes full play of the blending company's Speyside malts. Plenty of toffee on the finish. *40%. Inverhouse Distillers.*

Hankey Bannister Regency 12 Year Old (84.5) n22.5 t22 f19 b21 Plenty of honey and some fine, silky structuring. Just a tad too bitter and furry on the finish, though. *40%.*

Hankey Bannister 21 Years Old (95) n23.5 a fruity ensemble, clean, vibrant and loath to show its age t24 as juicy as the nose suggests, except for the odd rumble of distant smoke; a firm, barley-sugar hardness as the grains keep control; f23.5 the arrival of the oak adds further weight and for the first time begins to behave like a 21-y-o; long, now with decent spice and with some crusty dryness at the very death; b24 with top dressing like this and some obviously complex secondary malts, too, how can it fail? *43%.*

Hankey Bannister 25 Years Old (91) n22.5 t24 f21.5 b23 Follows on in style and quality to 21-year-old. Gorgeous. *40%*

Hankey Bannister 40 Years Old (89) n22 t23 f22 b22. This blend has been put together to mark the 250th anniversary of the forging of the business relations between Messrs. Hankey and Bannister. And although the oak creaks like a ship of its day, there is enough verve and viscosity to ensure a rather delicious toast to the gentlemen. Love it! *44%. Inverhouse.*

Hankey Bannister 40 Year Old (94) n23.5 t23.5 f23 b24. Pure quality. The attention to detail is sublime. *44.3%. Inverhouse Distillers.*

Hankey Bannister Heritage (84.5) n21 t22 f20.5 b21. So softly spoken sometimes you struggle to hear it. Makes a juicy, malty chuntering mid-way through, though. *46%.*

Hankey Bannister Heritage Blend (92) n23 despite the evidence of sherry the spiced chocolate fudge keeps you spellbound; t24 at moments like this, one's taste buds are purely in love. They are being caressed, serenaded and kisses by the most glorious of old grains, encrusted with a Speyside-syle maltiness which makes you purr with pleasure; f22 the weakness on the nose returns, though sparingly. Outstanding late Malteser candy style confirms a very decent malt depth; **b23** just so soft and sensual... *46%. Inverhouse Distillers.*

Harveys Lewes Blend Eight Year Old (89.5) n23 a tightness to the grape cannot entirely outdo the beauty of the soft fruit and delicate smoke combining; **t23.5** excellent grain choice ensures a velvety delivery on the palate, helped along by dates and nuts and a marvellous succession of dark sugar notes, Demerara leading the way. The malt content is evident beyond the fruit and delivers a Brazilian-style biscuit sweetness; sublimely chewy; **f20.5** only a single dodgy (sulphured) sherry butt, most probably – but that's all it takes! - within the malt content of the blend plus some enthusiastic caramelisation detracts from a superb experience...; **b22.5** when a blend is this good you can forgive them the missing apostrophe... A superb whisky, despite its unfortunate hiccup, from a gem of a British brewery. *40%.*

Hedges & Butler Royal (92) n22.5 t23.5 f23 b23 Massively improved to become a juicy and charming blend of the very highest order. *40%*

High Commissioner (88.5) n22.5 t22.5 f20.5 b22.5 Now I admit I had a hand in cleaning this brand up a couple of years back, giving it a good polish and much needed balance complexity. But I don't remember leaving it in quite this good a shape. Just a bitter semi-off note on the finish, otherwise this guy would have been in the 90s. What a great fun, three-course dram this is... *40%. Loch Lomond Distillers.*

Highland Baron (85.5) n21 t22 f21 b21.5. A very clean, sweet and competent young blend showing admirable weight and depth. *40%. Loch Lomond Distillers.*

Highland Bird (77) n19 t19 f19 b20. I've has a few of these over the years, I admit. But I can't remember one quite as rough and ready as this... *40%. Quality Spirits International.*

Highland Black 8 Years Old Special Reserve (85.5) n22 t22.5 f20 b21. A lovely blend which has significantly improved since my last encounter with it. A touch too much grain on the finish for greatness, perhaps. But the nose and delivery both prosper from a honey-roast almond sweetness. *40%. Aldi.*

Highland Dream 12 Years Old bott Jan 05 **(94.5) n23.5 t24 f23 b24.** Now that is what I call a blend! How comes it has taken me two years to find it? A wet dream, if ever there was one... *43%. J & G Grant. 9000 bottles.*

Highland Dream 18 Years Old bott May 07 **(88.5) n22.5 t22.5 f21.5 b22.** Perhaps doesn't get the marks on balance that a whisky of this quality might expect. This is due to the slight over egging of the sherry which, while offering a beautiful delivery, masks the complexities one might expect. Lovely whisky, and make no mistake. But, technically, doesn't match the 12-year-old for balance and brilliance. *43%. J & G Grant. 3000 bottles.*

Highland Earl (77) n19 t20 f19 b19. Might have marked it higher had it called itself a grain: the malt is silent. *40%. Aldi.*

Highland Gathering Blended Scotch Whisky (78) n19 t20 f19 b20. Attractive, juicy stuff, though caramel wins in the end. *40%. Lombards Brands.*

Highland Glendon (87.5) n21.5 t22.5 f21.5 b22 An honest, simple but effectively attractive blend. *43%. Quality Spirits International.*

Highland Harvest Organic Scotch Whisky (76) n18 t21 f19 b18. A very interesting blend. Great try, but a little bit of a lost opportunity here as I don't think the balance is quite right. But at least I now know what organic caramel tastes like... *40%*

Highland Mist (88.5) n20.5 t23 f22.5 b22.5 Fabulously fun whisky bursting from the bottle with character and mischief. Had to admit, broke all my own rules and just had to have a glass of this after doing the notes... *40%. Loch Lomond Distillers.*

Highland Piper (79) n20 t20 f19 b20. Good quaffing blend – if sweet - of sticky toffee and dates. Some gin on the nose – and finish. *40%*

Highland Pride (86) n21 t22 f21.5 b21.5. A beefy, weighty thick dram with plenty to chew on. The developing sweetness is a joy. *40%. Whyte & Mackay Distillers Ltd.*

Highland Queen db **(88.5) n22** classic grain, clean, soft and a little toffeed; **t22.5** no less classically silky and soft: again a bit toffee heavy, but not so much that you can't revel in this brief burst of Speyside-style malt bursting through for a quick, juicy blast; **f22** long and remains silky soft; b22 this is a young blend, so maybe the controlled toffee inclusion can be forgiven as the whole works beautifully well. An improved whisky to be sure. **40%** ⊙ ⊙

Highland Queen Blended Scotch Whisky (86.5) n22 t21 f21.5 b22. Lots of grains at play here. But what grains?! Clean and crisp with a superb bite which balances the softening mouth feel attractively. Old fashioned and delicious. *40%*

Highland Queen Aged 8 Years Blended Scotch Whisky (90) n22.5 t23.5 f21.5 b22.5. Lots of entertainment value from a high quality whisky. The blender has done a great job in the lab. *43%*

Highland Queen Aged 12 Years Blended Scotch Whisky (87) n22 t22 f21 b22. A polite, slightly more sophisticated version of the 8-year-old...but without the passion and drama! *40%*

Highland Reserve (82) n20 t21 f20 b21. You'll probably find this just off the Highland Way and incorporating Highland Bird and Monarch of the Glen. Floral and muddy. 40%

Highland Reserve Aged 12 Years (87) n21 t22 f22 b22 Anyone who has tasted Monarch of the Glen 12 will appreciate this. Maybe a bit more fizz here, though, despite the big caramel. 43%. Quality Spirits International.

Highland Warrior (77.8) n19 t19 f19.5 b20. Just like his Scottish Chief, he's on the attack armed with some Dufftown, methinks... 40%. Quality Spirits International.

Highland Way (84) n19 t20.5 f22.5 b22. This lovely little number takes the High Road with some beautiful light scenery along the way. The finish takes a charming Speyside path. 40%

Inverarity Limited Edition cask no. 698, dist 1997, bott 2009 **(84.5)** n20.5 t22 f21 b21. A heady, heavy-duty blend where honeycomb rules on the palate and thick dates offer a more intense sweetness. But don't go looking for subtlety or guile: those whose palates have been educated at the Whyte and Mackay school of delicate sophistication will have a ball. 40%

Islay Mist 8 Years Old (84) n20 t22 f21 b21. Turned into one heavy duty dram since last tasting a couple of years back. This appears to absorb everything it touches leaving one chewy, smoky hombre. Just a little tangy at the end. 40%. MacDuff International Ltd.

Islay Mist 12 Years Old (90) n22 t23 f22 b23 Adore it: classic bad cop - good cop stuff with an apparent high malt content. 40%

Islay Mist 17 Years Old (92.5) n22.5 t23.5 f23 b23.5 Always a cracking blend, this has improved of late into a genuine must have. 40%. MacDuff International Ltd.

Islay Mist Delux (85) n21.5 t22 f21.5 b20. Remains a highly unusual blend with the youthful peat now more brilliant than before, though the sugar levels appear to have risen markedly. 40%

Isle of Skye 8 Years Old (94) n23 t24 f23.5 b23.5. Where once peat ruled and with its grain ally formed a smoky iron fist, now honey and subtlety reigns. A change of character and pace which may disappoint gung-ho peat freaks but will intrigue and delight those looking for a more sophisticated dram. 40%. Ian Macleod.

Isle of Skye 21 years Old (91) n21 t23.5 f23 b23.5 What an absolute charmer! The malt content appears pretty high, but the overall balance is wonderful. 40%. Ian Macleod.

Isle of Skye 50 Years Old (82.5) n21.5 t21 f20 b20. Drier incarnation than the 50% version. But still the age has yet to be balanced out, towards the end in particular. Early on some distinguished moments involving something vaguely smoked and a sweetened spice. 41.6%

The Jacobite (78.5) n18 t18.5 f22 b20. Neither the nose or delivery are of the cleanest style. But comes into its own towards the finish when the thick soup of a whisky thins to allow an attractive degree of complexity. Not for those with catholic tastes. 40%. Booker.

Jackson McCloud Premium Blended Scotch Whisky (81) n20 t21 f20 b20. Absolutely standard fare, full of grainy bite and caramel. 40%. Galleon Liqueurs.

Jackson McCloud Rare Batch Blended Scotch Whisky (85.5) n20 t22.5 f22 b21. Pleasant, but with little or no effort to overcome the dominating grain. As it happens, it turns out to be pretty decent silky grain with some attractive fruit notes. 40%. Galleon Liqueurs.

James Alexander (85.5) n21 t21.5 f21.5 b21.5. Some lovely spices link the grassier Speysiders to the earthier elements. 40%. Quality Spirits International.

James King (76.5) n20 t18 f20 b18.5. Young whiskies of a certain rank take their time to find their feet. The finish, though, does generate some pleasant complexity. 43%

James King Aged 5 Years (85) n21 t21.5 f21 b21.5. Very attractive, old fashioned and well weighted with a pleasing degree of fat and chewy sweetness and chocolate fudge. Refreshingly good quality distillate and oak have been used in this: I'd drink it any day. 40%

James King 8 Years Old (78.5) n18.5 t21.5 f19 b19.5. Charming spices grip at the delivery and fine malt-grain interplay through the middle, even showing a touch of vanilla. But such a delicate blend can't fully survive the caramel. 43%. Quality Spirits International.

James King 12 Years Old (81) n19 t23 f19 b20. Caramel dulls the nose and finish. But for some time a quite beautiful blend soars about the taste buds offering exemplary complexity and weight. 40%. Quality Spirits International.

James King 15 Years Old (89) n22 t23 f21.5 b22.5. Now offers extra spice and zip. 43%

James King 21 Years Old (87.5) n20.5 t23.5 f22 b22. Attractive blend, but one that could do with the strength upped to 46% and the caramel reduced if not entirely got rid of. One of those potentially excellent yet underperforming guys I'd love to be let loose on! 43%

James Martin 20 Years Old (93) n21 t23.5 f24.5 b24. I had always regarded this as something of an untamed beast. No longer: still something of a beast, but a beautiful one that is among the most complex found on today's market. 43%. Glenmorangie.

James Martin 30 Years Old (86) n21.5 t22 f21 b21.5. Enjoyable for all its exotic fruitiness. But with just too many creaking joints to take it to the same level as the sublime 20-y-o. Even so, a blend worth treating with a touch of respect and allowing time for it to tell some pretty ancient tales... 43%. Glenmorangie.

J&B Jet (79.5) n19 t20 f20.5 b20. Never quite gets off the ground due to carrying too heavy a load. Unrecognisable to its pomp in the old J&B days: this one is far too weighty and never properly finds either balance or thrust. 40%. Diageo.

J&B Reserve Aged 15 Years (78) n23 t19 f18 b18. What a crying shame. The sophisticated and demure nose is just so wonderfully seductive but what follows is an open-eyed, passionless embrace. Coarsely grain-dominant and unbalanced, this is frustrating beyond words and not worthy to be mentioned in the same breath as the old, original J&B 15 which, by vivid contrast, was a malty, salivating fruit-fest and minor classic. 40%. Diageo.

J&B Rare (88.5) n21.5 t22.5 f22 b22.5 I have been drinking a lot of J&B from a previous time of late, due to the death of their former blender Jim Milne. I think he would have been pretty taken aback by the youthful zip offered here: whether it is down to a decrease in age or the use of slightly more tired casks − or both − is hard to say. 40%. Diageo.

Jim McEwan's Blended Whisky (86.5) n20 t22 f22.5 b22. Juicy and eye-watering with clever late spices. 46%. Bruichladdich.

John Barr (85.5) n20 t22 f21.5 b22. I assume from the big juicy dates to be found that Fettercairn is at work. Outwardly a big bruiser; given time to state its case and it's a bit of a gentle giant. 40%. Whyte & Mackay Distillers Ltd.

Johnnie Walker Black Label 12 Years Old (95.5) n23.5 pretty sharp grain: hard and buffeting the nose; a buffer of yielding smoke, apple pie and delicate spice cushions the encounter; **t24.5** if there is a silkier delivery on the market today, I have not seen it: this is sublime stuff with the grains singing the sweetest hymns as they go down, taking with them a near perfection of weighty smoke lightened by brilliantly balanced barley which leans towards both soft apple and crème broulee; **f23.5** those reassuringly rigid grains re-emerge and with them the most juicy Speysidey malts imaginable; the lovely sheen to the finish underlines the good age of the whiskies used; **b24** here it is: one of the world's most masterful whiskies back in all its complex glory. A bottle like this is like being visited by an old lover. It just warms the heart and excites. 40%. Diageo.

Johnnie Walker Blue Label (88) n21 t24 f21 b22 What a frustrating blend! Just so close to brilliance but the nose and finish are slightly out of kilter. Worth the experience of the mouth arrival alone. 43%. Diageo.

Johnnie Walker Blue Label The Casks Edition (97) n24.5 t24.5 f23.5 b24.5. This is a triumph of scotch whisky blending. With not as much as a hint of a single off note to be traced from the tip of the nose to tail, this shameless exhibition of complexity and brilliance is the star turn in the Diageo portfolio right now. Indeed, it is the type of blend that every person who genuinely adores whisky must experience for the good of their soul....if only once in their life. 55.8%.

Johnnie Walker Double Black (94.5) n23 t23.5 f24 b24. Double tops! Rolling along the taste buds like distant thunder, this is a welcome and impressive addition to the Johnnie Walker stable. Perhaps not as complete and rounded as the original Johnnie Walker Black... but, then, what is it? 40%.

Johnnie Walker Explorers' Club Collection The Gold Route (89) n23.5 t24 f19.5 b22. Much of this blend is truly the stuff of golden dreams. Like its Explorer's Club stable mate, some attention has to be paid to the disappointing finish. Worth sending out an expedition, though, just for the beautiful nose and delivery... 40%. Diageo.

Johnnie Walker Explorer's Club Collection 'The Royal Route' (93) n24.5 that's just how a blended whisky's nose should be: understated, clever, complex without being showy, multi-faceted and ambiguous enough to have to constantly changing your mind as to whether it is the lightly smoked mocha or the more ethereal citrus and jasmine which is leading the way. I'll let you decide...; **t24** soft to the point of surrender, the grains allow the malts to melt into them in the sexiest way imaginable; the accomodating smoke drifts and swirls, light Demerara sharpens, a thin layer of ulmo honey fattens and enriches; **f21.5** just the odd injudicious use of cask results in an unwelcome late bitterness which has robbed this of a gong: otherwise this would have been challenging for a spot in the world's top three. So, eye-wateringly bitter marmalade and furry...such a shame....; **b23** a fabulous journey, travelling first Class most of the way. But to have discovered more, could have been bottled at 46% for a much more panoramic view of the great whiskies on show. 40%. Diageo

Johnnie Walker Explorers' Club Collection The Spice Road (84.5) n22 t23.5 f18 b21. Sublime delivery of exceptionally intense juiciness: in fact, probably the juiciest blend released this year. But the bitter, fuzzy finish reveals certain casks haven't helped. 40%.

Johnnie Walker Gold Label Reserve (91.5) n23 t24 f22 b23. Moments of true star quality here, but the finish could do with a polish. 40%. Diageo.

Johnnie Walker King George V db **(88)** n23 t22 f21 b22 One assumes that King George V is no relation to George IV. This has genuine style and breeding, if a tad too much caramel. 43%

Johnnie Walker Platinum Label Aged 18 Years (88) n22 t23 f21 b22. This blend might sound like some kind of Airmiles card. Which wouldn't be too inappropriate, though this is more Business than First... 40%. Diageo.

Johnnie Walker Red Label (87.5) n22 t22 f21.5 b22. The ongoing move through the scales quality-wise appears to suggest we have a work still in progress here. This sample has skimped on the smoke, though not quality. Yet a few months back when I was in the BA Business Lounge at Heathrow's new Terminal Five, I nearly keeled from almost being overcome by peat in the earliest JW Red I had tasted in decades. I found another bottle and I'm still not sure which represents the real Striding Man. 40%. Diageo.

⟫ **Johnnie Walker Select Casks Aged 10 Years Rye Cask Finish** (90) n22.5 curiously, more Canadian than ol' Kentucky! The rye definitely nibbles deepest and earliest. But there is a distinctive corny feel I didn't expect which begins to dominate. Also, look out for a sharp tangerine and ground pistachio note. Very different; t23 a curious delivery: both hard and soft tones try to baffle the taste buds. The predominant note is one of crisp sugars, not surprisingly tinged with a deep tannin note; citrus still to be had; f21.5 a little bitter and sketchy once the sugars wear thin; the spices, though, are sincere and busy; b23 with the use of first fill bourbon casks and ex-rye barrels for finishing, hardly surprising this is the Johnnie Walker with the most Kentuckian feel of them all. Yet it's even more Canadian, still. 46% (92 Proof)

Johnnie Walker X.R Aged 21 Years (94) n23.5 t24 f23 b23.5. How weird: I nosed this blind before seeing what the brand was. My first thought was: "mmm, same structure of Crown Royal XR. Canadian??? No, there's smoke!" Then looked at what was before me and spotted it was its sister whisky from the Johnnie Walker stable. A coincidence? I don't think so... 40%.

Kenmore Special Reserve Aged 5 Years bott code L07285 (75) n18 t20 f19 b18. Recovers to a degree from the poor nose. A must-have for those who prefer their Scotch big-flavoured and gawky. 40%

Kingsbury Gold Mhain Baraille 1980 32 Year Old diss 1980 (92) n23 t23.5 f22.5 b23. A distinguished blend with just a little grey around the temples... A rather brilliant first bending attempt by Kingsbury after all these years. 47.3%. nc ncf. Cask Strength. 424 bottles.

⟫ **King Glenorsen** (81) n20 t21 f20 b20. Pleasant and easy drinking enough. But the young grains dominate completely. Designed, I think, to be neutralised by ice. 40%

King Robert II (77) n19 t19 f20 b19. A bustier, more bruising batch than the last 40 per cent version. Handles the OTT caramel much better. Agreeably weighty slugging whisky. 43%.

Kings Blended 3 Years Old (83) n21 t21.5 f20 b20.5. A young, chunky blend that you can chew forever. 40%. Speyside Distilleries.

· **King's Crest Blended Whisky 25 Years Old** (83) n22 t22 f19 b20. A silky middle weight. The toffee-flat finish needs some attention because the softly estered nose and delivery is a honey-rich treat and deserves better. 40%. Speyside Distilleries.

⟫ **Kirkland Blended Whisky 21 Year Old** (84.5) n21 t22 f20.5 b21. Frustrating stuff: hard to see what's going on through all the caramel. 40%. Bottled for Costco.

⟫ **Kirkland Blended Whisky 24 Year Old** (87) n22 t22 f21.5 b21.5. A weighty blend with some attractive oaky moments on the nose to underscore the age and chewy fudge after the hefty, though controlled, tannin arrival. Mild mocha on the fade. 40%.

Label 5 Aged 18 Years (84.5) n20.5 t22 f21 b21. A big mouthful and mouth-feel. Has changed course since I last had this one. Almost a feel of rum to this with its estery sheen. Sweet, simple, easy dramming. 40%. La Martiniquaise, France.

Label 5 Classic Black (75) n18 t20 f18 b19. The off-key nose needs some serious re-working. Drop the caramel, though, and you would have a lot more character. Needs some buffing. 40%. The First Blending for La Martiniquaise, France.

Label 5 Classic Black bott code L3060 (84.5) n20.5 t22 f21 b21. A better whisky than when last tasted with more even use of the date and walnut theme. Caramel still substantial, but complexity levels are higher. 40%. La Martiniquaise, France.

Label 5 Classic Black bott code L3084 (83.5) n20 t21.5 f21 b21. Like L3060. Except the nose is even harsher and here the grain have a much more jarring effect. 40%.

Label 5 Classic Black bott code L3144 (85) n20.5 t22 f21 b21.5. Stays in the same areas as two previous bottlings, but slightly better use of spices. Still needs a nose job, though... 40%.

⟫ **Label 5 Gold Heritage** (92) n22.5 a tad milky, but compensated by delicate honey and date sugar notes, without being particularly fruity... well, except for the crushed physalis, maybe...; t23.5 the grain is as soft as it can possibly come, dissolving on the palate, but not before harmonising sublimely with coconut and some meandering smoke atoms seemingly attached to a maple syrup/molasses blend. The malts also have a melt-in-the mouth quality, leaving behind a gorgeously weighted degree of fine cocoa; f22 a few struggling barrels leave a lactic imprint. But the spices gang together to form a delightful diversion while the Walnut

Whip vanilla and walnut oil combo takes you to the exit; **b24** a very classy blend very skilfully constructed. A stunningly lovely texture, one of the very best I have encountered for a while, and no shortage of complexity ensures this is a rather special blend. I'll even forgive the dulling by caramel and light milkiness from the tired bourbon barrel. The overall excellence outweighs the odd blemish. *40%*

Label 5 Reserve No. 55 sherry cask finish, bott code B-3695 **(89) n22 t23 f21.5 b22.5.** The last one of these I have a couple of years back was a sulphur-damaged disaster. This is anything but. A real bold treat. *43%. La Martiniquaise, France.*

Label 5 Reserve No. 55 sherry cask finish, bott code F-4482 **(87) n20.5 t22.5 f22 b22.** Lacking the suave sweetness of the B-3695 bottling, but excellent spice. *43%.*

Label 5 Reserve No. 55 Single Cask sherry cask finish, bott code no. E-1067 **(75) n19 t20 f18 b18.** The cordite on the nose suggests fireworks. But somehow we end up with a damp squib. *43%. La Martiniquaise, France.*

Label 5 Aged 12 Years bott code L307157A **(82) n21 t20 f21 b20.** Heavy duty date and walnut. Loads of caramel, too. For those looking for a weighty and chewy, rather complex dram. *40%. Glen Turner.*

Lang's Supreme Aged 5 Years (93.5) n23.5 t23.5 f23 b23.5. Every time I taste this the shape and structure has altered slightly. Here there is a fraction more smoke, installing a deeper confidence all round. This is blended whisky as it should be: Supreme in its ability to create shape and harmony. *40%. Ian Macleod Distillers Ltd.*

The Last Drop 1965 American Standard Barrel **(96.5) n24** ridiculously pliable nose: the grain used is clearly made from corn which, with the great age, means a distinct Canadian/bourbon trait impresses; the spices are playful and occasionally an apologetic puff of smoke reminds you this is a blend, not a grain...; **t24.5** the corn oils pave the way for a fabulous delivery – not entirely unlike a breakfast cereal with a dollop of honey to sweeten things up. The oak offers a precision to the weight and spice; **f23.5** again, a hint of smoke takes you away from the North American feel to this. The honey remains perfectly measures to ensure the encroaching oaky vanilla never dominates; **b24.5** almost impossible to imagine a blended whisky to be better balanced than this. If there is a cleverer use of honey or less intrusive oak in any blended whisky bottled in the last year, I have yet to taste it. An award winner if ever I tasted one. Magnificent doesn't quite cover it... *48.6%. Morrison Bowmore. The Last Drop Distillers Ltd.*

◇ **The Last Drop 50 Year Old** Sherry Wood **(97) n24** a curious mix of cherry drop candy and shoe polish: pungent, fruity and lively. None of the tired oak you might expect to turn up arrives, though the vanillas do have the odd few grey hairs; **t24.5** those cherry drops are there on impact, intensely so, with a further oily spiciness making for a busy, warming and juicy experience; the midground is still controlled by the fruit – a little more burnt raisin in style now – but those spices are the forerunner of a much toastier effort from the oak; **f24** here's the thing: you expect those gathering oak tones to turn a tad tired and worn. But they never do. Instead, the spices buzz and a little manuka and heather honey face the oak to inject just that small degree of sweetness required for a happy ending; **b24.5** you'd expect, after half a century in the cask, that this would be a quiet dram, just enjoying its final years with its feet up and arms behind its head. Instead we have a fairly aggressive blend determined to drive the abundant fruitiness it still possesses to the very hilt. It is backed up all the way by a surprising degree of warming, busy spice. There is a hell of a lot of life in this beautiful ol' dog... *51.2%*

Lauder's (74) n18 t21 f17 b18. Well, it's consistent: you can say that for it! As usual, fabulous delivery, but as for the rest...oh dear. *40%. MacDuff International Ltd.*

Lauder's Aged 12 Years (93.5) n23 t24 f23 b23.5 This is every bit as magnificent as the standard Lauder's isn't. *43%*

The Loch Fyne (89.5) n22 t23 f21.5 b23. This is an adorable old-style blend....a bit of a throwback. But no ruinous sherry notes...just clean and delicious. Well, mainly... *40%*

Loch Lomond Blended Scotch (89) n22 t22.5 f22 b22.5 A fabulously improved blend: clean and precise and though malt is seemingly at a premium, a fine interplay. *40%*

◇ **Loch Lomond Reserve** db **(86.5) n21.5 t22 f21.5 b21.5.** A spongy, sweet, chewy, pleasant blend which is more of a take as you find statement than a layering of flavours. *40%*

Lochranza (83.5) n21 t21.5 f21 b20. Pleasant, clean, but, thanks to the caramel, goes easy on the complexity. *40%. Isle of Arran.*

Lochside 1964 Rare Old Single Blend (94.5) n24 t23.5 f23 b24. A unique and entirely fitting tribute to a distillery which should never have been lost. *42.1%. nc ncf.*

Logan (78.5) n19 t19 f20 b19.5. Entirely drinkable but a bit heavy-handed with the grains and caramel. *40%. Diageo.*

Lombard's Gold Label (85) n21 t22 f21 b21. Big and chewy, not as complex as of old but those who like chunky toffee will be in for a treat. *40%. Lombard Brands Ltd.*

Lord Elcho (76) n19 t20 f18 b19. Oh, Lord...! *40%. Wemyss Malts.*

Lord Elcho Aged 15 Years (84) n21 t21 f21 b21. A straight wicket with no turn at all. A degree of coppery sharpness and caramel, but low key. *40%. Wemyss Malts.*

Lord Hynett (88.5) n21.5 t23 f22 b22 Just perfect after a shitty day. *40%.*

Lord Hynett (87) n22 t22 f21.5 b21.5. An honest, beautifully made blend with a welcome degree of attitude. *43%. Loch Lomond Distillers.*

Lord Scot (77.5) n18.5 t20 f19.5 b19.5. A touch cloying but the mocha fudge ensures a friendly enough ride. *40%. Loch Lomond Distillers.*

Lord Scot (86.5) n20 t22 f22.5 b22. A gorgeously lush honey and liquorice middle. *43%*

The Lost Distilleries batch 2 **(94) n22.5 t24 f23.5 b24.** Whoever lost it better find it again: this is how you dream every whisky should be. *53.2%.*

⬦ **The Lost Distilleries Blend** Batch 6 **(91) n23.5** huge grain presence....some old grain, too, with corn oils abounding. The vague fruity sweetness, not unlike stewed and lightly sweetened rhubarb, has much more to do with the grain than the oak: no, the oak is responsible for the custard...; **t23** soft, silky, lithe...the corn oils are working at full speed, the light sugars working flat out to keep pace; **f22** spices arrive for a late wake up call. A little tiredness from the oak, but dealt with quickly; **b22.5** the Lost Malt as well: completely grain dominant – but wonderfully lush and tasty. *49.3%*

Mackessack Premium Aged 8 Years (87.5) n21.5 t23 f21.5 b21.5. Claims a high Speyside content and the early character confirms it. Shoots itself in the foot, rather, by overdoing the caramel and flattening the finish. *40%. Mackessack Giovenetti. Italian Market.*

Mac Na Mara (83) n20 t22.5 f20 b20.5. Absolutely brimming with salty, fruity character. But just a little more toffee and furriness than it needs. Enjoyable, though. *40%*

Mac Na Mara Rum Finish (93) n22 t24 f23 b24 High quality blending, and the usage of the rum appears to have retained the old Mac Na Mara style. *40%. Praban na Linne.*

MacQueens (89) n21.5 t22.5 f22.5 b22.5. I am long enough in the tooth now to remember blends like this found in quiet country hotels in the furthest-flung reaches of the Highlands beyond a generation ago. A wonderfully old-fashioned, traditional one might say, blend of a type that is getting harder and harder to find. *40%. Quality Spirits International.*

Master of Malt 8 Years Old (88) n22.5 t22.5 f21 b22. Understated and refined. *40%*

Master Of Malt 8 Year Old Blended Whisky (83.5) n21 t22 f20.5 b20. Never quite makes up its mind what it wants to do, or where it wants to go. A few intriguing vaguely Irish Pot Still-style moments on delivery, though. *40%*

Master of Malt Blended 10 Years Old 1st Edition (84.5) n21.5 t22.5 f20 b20.5. A pleasant enough, though hardly complex, blend benefitting from the lovely malty, then silky pick-up from delivery and a brief juicy barley sharpness. But unsettled elsewhere due, mainly, to using the wrong fit of grain: too firm when a little give was needed. *47.5%. ncf. WB15/353*

Master Of Malt St Isidore (84) n21 t22 f20 b21. Sweet, lightly smoked but really struggles to put together a coherent story. Something, somewhere, is not quite right. *41.4%*

Master Of Malt World Whisky Day Blend (86) n21.5 t22 f21 b21.5. Limited complexity and depth but it gets the Orange Aero bit right.... *40.18%. Master Of Malt.*

Matisse 12 Years Old (90.5) n23 t23 f22 b22.5 Moved up yet another notch as this brand continues its development. Much more clean-malt oriented with a Speyside-style to the fore. Majestic and charming. *40%. Matisse Spirits Co Ltd.*

Matisse 21 Years Old (86) n23 t22 f20 b21. Begins breathtakingly on the nose, with a full array of exotic fruit showing the older bourbon casks up to max effect. Nothing wrong with the early delivery, which offers a touch of honeycomb on the grain. But the caramel effect on the finish stops everything in its tracks. Soft and alluring, all the same. *40%*

Matisse Old (85.5) n20 t23 f21 b21.5. Appears to improve each time I come across it. The nose is a bit on the grimy side and the finish disappears under a sea of caramel. But the delivery works deliciously, with a chewy weight which highlights the sweeter malts. *40%*

Matisse Royal (81) n19 t22 f20 b20. Pleasant, if a little clumsy. Extra caramel appears to have scuppered the spice. *40%. Matisse Spirits Co Ltd.*

McArthurs (89.5) n22 t22.5 f22 b23 One of the most improved blends on the market. The clever use of the peat is exceptional. *40%. Inverhouse Distillers.*

Michael Jackson Special Memorial Blend bott 2009 **(89) n24 t22.5 f20.5 b22.** Whenever Michael and I had a dram together, his would either be massively sherried or equally well endowed with smoke. This is neither, so an odd tribute. Even so, there is more than enough here for him to savour. *43%. Berry Bros & Rudd. 1000 bottles.*

Mitchell's Glengyle Blend (86.5) n21.5 t22 f21.5 b21.5. A taste of history here, as this is the first blend ever to contain malt from the new Campbeltown distillery, Glengyle. Something of a departure in style from the usual Mitchell blends, which tended to put the accent on a crisper grain. Interestingly, here they have chosen one at least that is soft and voluptuous enough to absorb the sharper malt notes. *40%. Springbank Distillers.*

Monarch Of The Glen Connoisseurs Choice (80) n20 t21 f19 b20. Has changed shape a little. Positively wallows in its fat and sweet personality. *40%. Quality Spirits International.*

Monarch Of The Glen Connoisseurs Choice Aged 8 Years (76.5) n19 t20.5 f18 b19. Leaves no doubt that there are some malts in there... *40%. Quality Spirits International.*

Monarch Of The Glen Connoisseurs Choice Aged 12 Years (88) n21.5 t22.5 f22 b22. Charming, fruity and a blend to put your feet up with. *40%. Quality Spirits International.*

Monarch Of The Glen Connoisseurs Choice Aged 15 Years (83) n21 t22 f19 b21. Starts off on the very same footing as the 12-y-o, especially with the sumptuous delivery. But fails to build on that due to toffee and bitters at the death. *40%. Quality Spirits International.*

Montrose (74.5) n18 t20 f18 b18.5. A battling performance but bitter defeat in the end. *40%.*

Morrisons The Best 8 Years Old (87) n21 t23 f22 b21. Some of the traces of its excellence are still there, it remains highly drinkable, but that greatness has been lost in a tide of caramel. When, oh when, are people going to understand that you can't just tip this stuff into whisky to up the colour without causing a detrimental effect on the product? Is anybody listening? Does anyone care??? Someone has gone to great lengths to create a sublime blend – to see it wasted. Natural colour and this'd be an experience to die for. *40%*

Morrisons Fine Blended Whisky (77) n18.5 t21 f18.5 b19. Sweet, chewy; rough edges. *40%.*

Muirhead's (83) n19 t22 f23 b21. A beautifully compartmentalised dram that integrates superbly, if that makes sense. *40%. MacDonald & Muir.*

Muirhead's Blue Seal (83) n21 t21 f20.5 b20.5. Goes to town quite heavily on the grain. If this is the new version of the old McDonald and Muir brand, then this is a lot oilier, with a silkier mouthfeel. *40%. Highland Queen Scotch Whisky Company.*

The Naked Grouse (76.5) n19 t21 f17.5 b19. Sweet. But reveals too many sulphur tattoos. *40%.*

Northern Scot (68) n16 t18 f17 b17. Heading South bigtime. *40%. Bruce and Co. for Tesco.*

Old Crofter Special Old Scotch Whisky (83) n18 t22 f21 b22. A very decent blend, much better than the nose suggests thanks to some outstanding, velvety grain and wonderfully controlled sweetness. *40%. Smith & Henderson for London & Scottish International.*

Old Masters "Freemason Whisky" (92) n24 t23 f22 b23. A high quality blend that doesn't stint on the malt. The nose, in particular, is sublime. *40%. Supplied online. Lombard Brands*

Old McDonald (83.5) n20 t22 f20.5 b21. Attractively tart and bracing where it needs to be with lovely grain bite. Lots of toffee, though. *43.%. The Last Drop Distillers. For India.*

Old Mull (84.5) n22 t21 f20.5 b21. With dates and walnuts clambering all over the nose, very much in the house style. But this one is a shade oilier than most – and certainly on how it used to be – and has dropped a degree or two of complexity. That said, enjoyable stuff with the spices performing well, as does the lingering sweetness. *40%*

Old Parr 12 Years Old (91.5) n21.5 t23.5 f23 b23.5 Perhaps on about the fourth of fifth mouthful, the penny drops that this is not just exceptionally good whisky: it is blending Parr excellence... *40%. Diageo.*

Old Parr Aged 15 Years (84) n19 t22 f21 b22. Absolutely massive sherry input here. Some of it is of the highest order. The nose, reveals, however, that some isn't... *43%*

Old Parr Classic 18 Years Old (84.5) n21 t21.5 f21 b21. A real jumbled, mixed bag with fruit and barley falling over each other and the grains offering little sympathy. Enough to enjoy, but with Old Parr, one expects a little more... *46%. Diageo.*

Old Parr Superior 18 Years Old batch no. L5171 **(97)** n25 t25 f23 b24. Year in, year out, this blend just gets better and better. This bottling struck me as a possible Whisky of the Year, but perhaps only an outsider. Familiarity, though, bred anything but contempt and over the passing months I have tried to get to the bottom of this truly great whisky. Blended whisky has long needed a champion. This grand old man looks just the chap. This is a worthy, if unexpected (even to me), Jim Murray' Whisky Bible 2007 World Whisky of the Year. *43%.*

Old Smuggler (85.5) n21 t22 f21 b21.5. A much sharper act than its Allied days with a new honeyed-maple syrup thread which is rather delightful. Could still do with toning down the caramel, though, to brighten the picture further. *40%. Campari, France.*

Old St Andrews Clubhouse (82) n18 t22 f21 b21. Not quite the clean, bright young thing it was many years back. But great to see back in my nosing glass after such a long while and though the nose hits the rough, the delivery is as sweetly struck as you might hope for. *40%*

Old Stag (75.5) n18.5 t20 f18.5 b18.5. Wants shooting. *40%. Loch Lomond Distillers.*

The Original Lochian Aged 8 Years (80.5) n19 t21 f20 b20.5. Doused in caramel. So much so it's like a toffee and nut bar. One to chew until your fillings fall out, though the spices compensate on the finish to a degree. Pleasant and sweet, but don't expect great refinement. *40%. Tesco.*

The Original Mackinlay (83) n19 t21 f22 b21. A hard nose to overcome and the toffee remains in force for those addicted to fudge. But now a degree of bite and ballast appears to have been added, giving more of a story to the experience. 40%. *Whyte & Mackay Distillers Ltd.*

Passport (83) n22 t19 f21 b21. It looks as though Chivas have decided to take the blend away from its original sophisticated, Business Class J&B/Cutty Sark, style for good now, as they have continued this decently quaffable but steerage quality blend with its big caramel kick and chewy, rather than lithe, body. 40%. *Chivas.*

Passport v (91) n23 23.5 f22 b22.5. Easily one of the better versions I have come across for a long time and impressively true to its original style. 40%. *Bottled in Brazil.*

Passport v (91) n22.5 t22 f23.5 b23.5. A version closer to original style with markedly less caramel impact and grittier grain. An old-fashioned treat. 40%. *Ecuador.*

Parkers (78) n17 t22 f20 b19. The nose has regressed, disappearing into ever more caramel, yet the mouth-watering lushness on the palate remains and the finish now holds greater complexity and interest. 40%. *Angus Dundee.*

Prince Charlie Special Reserve (73) n17 t20 f18 b18. Thankfully not as cloyingly sweet as of old, but remains pretty basic. 40%. *Somerfield, UK.*

Prince Charlie Special Reserve 8 Years Old (81) n18 t20 f22 b21. A lumbering bruiser of a dram; keeps its trademark shapelessness but the spices and lush malt ensure an enjoyable experience. 40%. *Somerfield, UK.*

Queen Margot (86) n21 t22 f21.5 b21.5. A lovely blend which makes no effort to skimp on a spicy depth. Plenty of cocoa from the grain late on but no shortage of good whiskies put to work. 40%. *Wallace and Young for Lidl.*

Queen Margot v (83.5) n20.5 t22 f20 b21. Same brand, but a different name on the back label. And certainly a different feel to the whisky with the grains having harsher words than before. 40%. *Clydesdale Scotch Whisky Co for Lidl.*

Queen Margot Aged 8 Years (89) n22 t22.5 f22 b22.5. A satisfying blend with a delicious clarity to the light malts and high class grains. Just the right touch of sweetness, too. 40%.

Queen Margot Aged 8 Years (84) n20.5 t21 f21.5 b21. Here's the variant. Darker in colour I notice and a bit of a dullard and simpleton by comparison, though not without an acceptable degree of charm. Much weightier. 40%. *Clydesdale Scotch Whisky Co for Lidl.*

Real Mackenzie (80) n17 t21 f21 b21. As ever, try and ignore the dreadful nose and get cracking with the unsubtle, big bruising delivery. A thug in a glass. 40%. *Diageo.*

Real Mackenzie Extra Smooth (81) n18 t22 f20 b21. Once, the only time the terms "Real Mackenzie" and "Extra Smooth" were ever uttered in the same sentence was if someone was talking about the barman. Now it is a genuine descriptor. Which is odd, because when Diageo sent me a sample of their blend last year it was a snarling beast ripping at the leash. This, by contrast, is a whimpering sop. "Killer? Where are you...???" 40%. *Diageo.*

Red Seal 12 Years Old (82) n19 t22 f20 b21. Charming, mouthwatering. But toffee numbs it down towards the finish. 40%. *Charles Wells UK.*

Reliance PL (76) n18 t20 f19 b19. Some of the old spiciness evident. But has flattened out noticeably. 43%. *Diageo.*

Robert Burns (85) n20 t22.5 f21 b21.5. Skeletal and juicy: very little fat and gets to the mouthwatering point pretty quickly. Genuine fun. 40%. *Isle of Arran.*

Robertson's of Pitlochry Rare Old Blended (83) n21 t20 f21 b21. Handsome grain bite with a late malty flourish. Classic light blend from Pitlochry's landmark whisky shop. 40%

The Royal & Ancient (80.5) n20 t21.5 f19 b20. Has thinned out dramatically in the last year or so. Now clean, untaxing, briefly mouth-watering and radiating young grain throughout. 40%

Royal Castle (84.5) n20 t22 f21 b21.5. From Quality Street, or Quality Spirits? Sweet and very well toffeed! 43%. *Quality Spirits International.*

Royal Castle 12 Years Old (84.5) n21 t22 f20 b20.5. Busy nose and delivery with much to chew over. Entirely enjoyable, and seems better each time you taste it. Even so, the finish crumbles a bit. 40%. *Quality Spirits International.*

Royal Clan Aged 18 Years (85) n21.5 t21 f21.5 b21. For those giving up gum, here's something to really chew on. Huge degree of cream toffee and toasted fudge which makes for a satin-soft blend, but also one which ensures any big moves towards complexity are nipped in the bud. Very enjoyable, all the same. 40%. *Quality Spirits International.*

Royal Household (90.5) n21.5 t23 f23 b23 We are amused. 43%. *Diageo.*

Royal Park (85) n21.5 t22.5 f20 b21. Pretty generic with an attractive silky sheen, Demerara sugars and decent late spice swim around in an ocean of caramel. 40%

Royal Salute 21 Years Old (92.5) n23 t23.5 f23 b23.5 If you are looking for the velvety character of yore, forget it. This one comes with some real character and is much the better for it. The grain, in particular, excels. 40%. *Chivas.*

Royal Salute 62 Gun Salute (95.5) n24.5 prunes and apples plus a little cinnamon. And grapes, of course. All this in a bed of seemingly natural caramels. It is a smoke-free environment where every oak note is rounded and friendly, where you fancy you can still find the odd mark of barley and yet although being a blend, the grain is refusing to take it down a bourbon path, despite the peek-a-boo honeycomb; **t24** the oak is relatively full on, but early on adds a toasty quality to the marmalade and plum jam. The mid ground casts off any sherry-like clothes and heads for a more honey-rich, vaguely bourbon style without ever reaching Kentucky; **f23** the fade is on the gentle side with sugars dissolving against a slightly bittering background as some of the oak rebels, as you might expect at least one or two of these old timers to do. At the very death comes the one and only sign of smoke...that is some parting shot; **b24** how do you get a bunch of varying whiskies in style, but each obviously growing a grey beard and probably cantankerous to boot, to settle in and harmonise with the others? A kind of Old People's Home for whisky, if you like. Well, here's how...*43%. Chivas.*

Royal Salute The Diamond Tribute (91) n23.5 t23 f21.5 b23. Ironic that a diamond is probably the hardest natural creation, yet this whisky is one of man's softest... *40%. Chivas.*

Royal Salute The Hundred Cask Selection Limited Release No. 7 (92) n22 t23.5 f23 b23.5 As blends go, its entire countenance talks about great age and elegance. And does so with a clipped accent. *40%. Chivas.*

Royal Silk Reserve (93) n22 t24 f24 b23 I named this the best newcomer of 2001 and it hasn't let me down. A session blend for any time of the day, this just proves that you don't need piles of peat to create a blend of genuine stature. A must have. *40%*

Sainsbury's Basics Blended Scotch Whisky (78.5) n19 t20.5 f19.5 b19.5. "A little less refined, great for mixing," says the label. Frankly, there are a lot of malts out there far less enjoyable than this. Don't be scared to have straight: it's more than decent enough. *40%*

Sainsbury's Scotch Whisky (84.5) n20 t22 f21 b21.5. A surprisingly full bodied, chewy blend allowing a pleasing degree of sweetness to develop. No shortage of toffee at the finish – a marked improvement on recent years. *40%. UK.*

Sainsbury's Finest Old Matured Aged 8 Years (86) n21.5 t21 f22 b21.5. A sweet blend enjoying a melt-in-the-mouth delivery, a silky body and toffee-vanilla character. The spices arriving towards the end are exceptionally pleasing and welcome. *40%. UK.*

Sandy Mac (76) n18 t20 f19 b19. Basic, decent blend that's chunky and raw. *40%. Diageo.*

Scots Earl (76.5) n18 t20 f19 b19.5. It's name is Earl. And it must have upset someone in a previous life. Always thrived on its engaging disharmony. But just a tad too syrupy now. *40%.*

Scottish Chief (77) n19 t19 f19 b20. This is one big-bodied chief, and not given to taking prisoners. *40%. Quality Spirits International.*

Scottish Collie (77) n19 t19 f19 b20. Caramel still, but a Collie with a bit more bite. *40%*

Scottish Collie 12 Years Old (85) n22 t22 f20 b21. On the cusp of a really classy blend here but the bitterness on the finish loses serious Brownie points. *40%. Quality Spirits Int, UK.*

Scottish Collie 18 Years Old (92) n24 t23 f22 b23. This, honey-led beaut would be a winner even at Crufts: an absolute master class of how an old, yet light and unpeated blend should be. No discord whatsoever between the major elements and not a single hint of over-aging. Superb. *40%. Quality Spirits International, UK.*

Scottish Glory dist 2002, bott 2005 **(85) n21 t21 f22 b21.** An improved blend now bursting with vitality. The ability of the grain to lift the barley is very pleasing. *40%. Duncan Taylor.*

Scottish Leader Original (83.5) n17.5 t22.5 f21 b22.5. About as subtle as a poke in the eye with a spirit thief. The nose, it must be said, is not great. But I have to admit I thoroughly enjoy the almost indulgent coarseness from the moment it invades the palate. A real chewathon of a spicy blend with a wicked, in-yer-face attitude. Among all the rough-'n-tumble and slap-'n-tickle, the overall depth, weight, balance and molassed charm ain't half bad. *40%. Burn Stewart.*

Scottish Leader Aged 12 Years (91) n22.5 t23 f22 b22.5 Absolutely unrecognisable from the Leader 12 I last tasted. This has taken a plumy, fruity route with the weight of a cannonball but the texture of mallow. Big and quite beautiful. *40%. Burn Stewart.*

Scottish Leader 30 Years Old (87) n23.5 t21.5 f20.5 b21.5 A little too docile ever to be a great whisky, but the nose is something rather special. A bit of attention on the finish and this could be a real corker. *40%. Burn Stewart.*

Scottish Leader Select (91.5) n23 t23.5 f22.5 b22.5 Don't make the mistake of thinking this is just the 40% with three extra percentage points of alcohol. This appears to be an entirely different bottling with an entirely different personality. A delight. *43%. South African Market.*

Scottish Leader Select (74) n18.5 t19 f18 b18.5. I assume the leader is Major Disharmony. *40%.*

Scottish Leader Supreme (72.5) n17 t19 f18 b18.5. Jings! It's like an old-fashioned Gorbals punch-up in the glass – and palate. *40%. Burn Stewart.*

Scottish Piper (80) n20 t20 f20 b20. A light, mildly- raw, sweet blend with lovely late vanilla intonation. *40%*

Scottish Prince (83.5) n21 t22 f20 b20.5. Muscular, but agreeably juicy. *40%*

Scottish Reel (78.5) n19 t19 f20 b19.5. Non fussy with an attractive bite, as all such blends should boast. *40%. London & Scottish International.*

Scottish Rill (85) n20 t20.5 f22.5 b22. Refreshing yet earthy. *40%. Quality Spirits Int.*

Sheep Dip Amoroso Oloroso 1999 Oloroso sherry casks, bott Mar 12 **(92)** n23.5 t24 f21 b23.5. More like Sherry Dip than Sheep Dip. Actually, chocolate dip wouldn't be too far off the mark, either. To create this, malt which had spent three years maturing in bourbon cask was then shipped to Jerez where it spent a further nine years in presumably fresh sherry. It was worth the trouble... *41.8%. Spencerfield Spirits.*

Something Special (85) n21.5 t22 f20.5 b21. Mollycoddled by toffee, any murderous tendencies seem to have been fudged away, leaving just the odd moment of attractive complexity. You suspect there is a hit man in there somewhere trying to get out. *40%. Chivas.*

Something Special Premium Aged 15 Years (89) n22 t23 f21 b23 Fabulous malt thread and some curious raisiny/sultana fruitiness, too. A blend-lover's blend. *40%.*

Spar Finest Reserve (90.5) n21.5 t22.5 f23.5 b23 One of Britain's best value for money blends with an honest charm which revels in the clean high quality grain and earthier malts which work so well together. *40%*

Spirit of Freedom Aged 30 Years (91) n23.5 though the age says 30, you get the feeling something a hell of a lot older is in there! A ripe aroma on every front from ancient oak to passion fruit just about on the turn; t22.5 yet: it's old!! Silky, vaguely coppery and crisp, crystalline Demerara sugar; f22 dry, flaky almost sawdusty oak; b23 a blend created to mark the 700th anniversary of Bannockburn has a battle of its own against so many aging casks. Somehow, it just about wins. *46%. 2014 bottles. WB15/364*

Stewart's Old Blended (93) n22.5 t24 f23 b23.5 Really lovely whisky for those who like to close their eyes, contemplate and have a damned good chew. *40%*

Storm (94) n23 t23.5 f24 b23.5. A little gem of a blend that will take you by storm. *43%.*

Swords (78) n20 t21 f18 b19. Beefed up somewhat with some early smoke thrusting through and rapier grains to follow. *40%. Morrison Bowmore.*

Talisman 5 Years Old (85.5) n22 t22 f20.5 b21. Unquestionably an earthier, weightier version of what was once a Speyside romp. Soft peats also add extra sweetness. *40%*

Teacher's 50 - 12 Years Old batch 2-16, bott Sep 11 **(85.5)** n20.5 t22.5 f21.5 b21. Once, before entering the Indian bottling hall, this must have been a strutting peacock of a Scotch blend. But after being doused in a far too liberal amount of caramels it has been reduced to a house sparrow: outwardly common and dull but at least with an engaging personality. The usual Teacher's smoke shows itself only at the death, alas. And all else is a silky honeyed sweetness pleading for an extra degree of complexity. The very complexity, indeed, which was almost certainly there before being coloured to death. If they could sort out the caramel levels in the bottling hall, this would be a blend that would put on a spectacular display... *42.8%*

Teacher's Aged 25 Years batch 1 **(96.5)** n24 at first this Teacher's lectures malt to you; not any old malt, but delicately smoked and as light with citrus as it is heavy with phenol. Then slowly the grains emerge, offering weighted consistency to the sweeter, maple syrup elements, until there is a satisfying fusion between the two....; t24.5 not sure one can quite nose silk, though that's what it appeared to be. But you can certainly spot it on the palate, and that's exactly what we have on delivery: every atom, be it smoky or marmalade orangey, simply melts in the mouth though unusually for a 25-y-o, it does not leave an oaky residue; f23.5 long, spicy, a little tangy; b24.5 only 1300 bottles means they will be hard pushed to create this exact style again. Worth a go, chaps: considering this is India bound, it is the karma sutra of blended scotch. *46%. Beam Inc. 1300 bottles. India & Far East Travel Retail exclusive.*

Teacher's Highland Cream (90) n23 t23 f22 b22 Not yet back to its best but a massive improvement on the 2005 bottlings. Harder grains to accentuate the malt will bring it closer to the classic of old. *40%*

Teacher's Highland Cream v **(90)** n23 t22.5 f22 b22.5 A very curious, seriously high grade, variant. Although the Ardmore distillery is on the label, it is the only place it can really be seen. Certainly - the least smoky Teacher's I've come across in 35 years of drinking the stuff: the smoke is there, but adds only ballast rather than taking any form of lead. But the grain is soft and knits with the malts with ease to make for a sweeter, much more lush version than the rest of the world may recognize. *40%*

Teacher's Origin (88.5) n22 t23.5 f21 b22 A fascinating blend among the softest on the market today. That is aided and abetted by the exceptionally high malt content, 65%, which makes this something of an inverted blend, as that, for most established brands, is the average grain content. What appears to be a high level of caramel also makes for a rounding of the edges, as well as evidence of sherry butts. The bad news is that that has resulted in a duller finish than perhaps might have been intended, which is even more pronounced given the impressive speech made on delivery. Lovely whisky, yes. But something, I feel, of a work in progress. Bringing the caramel down by the percentage points of the malt would be a very positive start... *42.8%. ncf.*

Té Bheag (86) n22 t21 f21.5 b21.5. Classic style of rich caramels and bite. *40%. ncf.*

Tesco Finest Reserve Aged 12 Years (74) n18.5 t19 f18 b18.5. The most astonishing thing about this, apart from the fact it is a 12 year-old, is that it won a Gold "Best in Class" in a 2010 international whisky competition: it surely could not have been from the same batch as the one before me. Frankly, you have to go a long way to find a whisky as bland as this and for a 12-y-o it is monumentally disappointing. 40%.

Tesco Special Reserve Minimum 3 Years Old (78) n18.5 t21.5 f19 b19. Decent early spice on delivery but otherwise anonymous. 40%. Tesco.

Tesco Value Scotch Whisky (83) n19 t21 f22 b21. Young and genuinely refreshing whisky. Without the caramel this really would be a little darling. 40%

Traquair (78) n19 t21 f19 b19. Young, but offering a substantial mouthful including attractive smoke. 46%. Burn Stewart.

That Boutique-y Whisky Blended Whisky #1 batch 1 **(72) n18 t19 f17 b18.** Fuzzy, furry and generally out of sorts. 50.3%. 148 bottles. WB15/354

The Tweeddale Blend Aged 10 Years (89.5) n22 t23.5 f21.5 b22.5 The first bottling of this blend since World War 2, it has been well worth waiting for. 46%. ncf. 50% malt. Stonedean.

The Tweeddale Blend Aged 12 Years bott code 28, Feb 13 **(95) n23.5 t24 f23 b24.5** For the tasting notes see the 2011 bottling above. Very, very similar, except more crisp grain on the nose and a slightly more clever use of citrus throughout. How heart-warming to see a blend not just keep faithfully to its style, but appears to somehow up the quality a fraction. A treat of a whisky experience. 46%. nc ncf. Stonedean. 3rd release.

◈ **The Tweeddale Blended Scotch Whisky Aged 14 Years** batch 5 **(92) n22.5** zesty and grassy, this really does give your nose a tweak; **t23.5** the massive degree of salivation is no surprise after that nose: the barley goes into Speyside-style overdrive, revealing all its malty charms simply and cleanly. The citrus notes have a say throughout; **f23** here it changes from the last bottling, the complexity and spices at a premium with the yielding grains having the major say and ensuring the softest landing imaginable; **b23** I was salivating just at the prospect of this one, as I remember what a fresh article Batch 4 was. Well, this is even sharper in some places...yet curiously far more laid back and docile in others. 46%. nc ncf.

Ushers Green Stripe (85) n19 t22.5 f21.5 b22. Upped a notch or two in all-round quality. The juicy theme and clever weight is highly impressive and enjoyable. 43%. Diageo.

VAT 69 (84.5) n20 t22 f21 b21.5. Has thickened up in style: weightier, more macho, much more to say and a long way off that old lightweight. A little cleaning up wouldn't go amiss. 40%

◈ **Walton Royal Blend Deluxe Reserve (91.5) n22.5** the unusual experience of encountering a blend which hoists and then flies the peaty flag with gay abandon: smoky and exceptionally soft; **t23** and yes....there it is again: the smoke building slowly into something substantial, but only after the spongy grains have made a sugary entrance; **f23** remains soft, not very complex but friendly and adds some late cocoa and spice to the lingering smoke; **b23** it's amazing what a dose of good quality peaty whisky can do to a blend. Certainly ensures it stands out as a deliciously chewy – and smoky – experience. 43%

White Horse (90.5) n22 t23 f22.5 b23 A malt which has subtlety changed shape. Not just the smoke which gives it weight, but you get the feeling that some of Diageo's less delicate malts have been sent in to pack a punch. As long as they are kept in line, as is the case here – just – we can all enjoy a very big blend. 40%. Diageo.

White Horse Aged 12 Years (86) n21 t23 f21 b21. enjoyable, complex if not always entirely harmonious. For instance, the apples and grapes on the nose appear on a limb from the grain and caramel and nothing like the thoroughbred of old. Lighter, more flaccid and caramel dominated. 40%. Diageo.

Whyte & Mackay 'The Thirteen' 13 Year Old (92) n22.5 t23.5 f23 b23. Try this and your luck'll be in...easily the pick of the W&M blended range. 40%. Whyte & Mackay Distillers Ltd.

Whyte & Mackay Luxury 19 Year Old (84.5) n21 t22 f20 b21.5. A pleasant house style chewathon. Nutty, biting but with a tang. 40%. Whyte & Mackay Distillers Ltd.

Whyte & Mackay Supreme 22 Year Old (87) n21 t23 f20.5 b22.5. Ignore the nose and finish and just enjoy the early ride. 43%

Whyte & Mackay Oldest 30 Year Old (87.5) n23 t23 f20 b21.5. What exasperating whisky this is. So many good things about it, but... 45%

Whyte & Mackay Original Aged Blended 40 Years Old (93) n23 t24 f22 b24. I admit, when I nosed and tasted this at room temp, not a lot happened. Pretty, but closed. But once warmed in the hand up to full body temperature, it was obvious that Richard Paterson had created a quite wonderful monster of a blend offering so many avenues to explore that the mind almost explodes. Well done RP for creating something that further proves, and in such magnitude, just how warmth can make an apparently ordinary whisky something bordering genius. 45%

Whyte & Mackay Special (84.5) n20 t23 f20 b21.5. If you are looking for a big-flavoured dram and with something approaching a vicious left uppercut, this might be a useful bottle to have on hand. The nose, I'm afraid, has not improved over the years but there appears to be compensation with the enormity and complexity of the delivery, a veritable orgy of big, oily, juicy, murky flavours and tones if ever there was one. You cannot but like it, in the same way as you may occasionally like rough sex. But if you are looking for a delicate dram to gently kiss you and caress your fevered brow, then leave well alone. 40%

William Grant's 12 Years Old Bourbon Cask (90.5) n23 t22.5 f22 b23. Very clever blending where balance is the key. 40%

William Grant's 15 Years Old (85) n21 t23 f20 b21. Grain and, later, caramel dominates but the initial delivery reveals the odd moment of sheer genius and complexity on max revs. 43%

William Grant's 25 Years Old (95.5) n23.5 some serious oak, but chaperoned by top quality oloroso, itself thinned by firm and graceful grain; t24 sheer quality: complexity by the shovel-load as juicy fruits interact with darting, crisp barley; again the grain shows elegance both sharpening increasingly mouth-watering malt and softening the oak; f24 medium length, but not a single sign of fatigue: the sweet barley runs and runs and some jammy fruits charm. Just to cap it all, some wonderful spices dazzle and a touch of low roast Java enriches; b24 absolutely top-rank blending that appears to maximize every last degree of complexity. Most astonishing, though, is its sprightly countenance: even Scottish footballing genius Ally MacLeod struggled to send out Ayr Utd. sides with this kind of brio. And that's saying something! A gem. 40%

William Grant's 100 US Proof Superior Strength (92) n23 t24 f22 b23. A fruitier drop now than it was in previous years but no less supremely constructed. 50% (100 US proof)

William Grant's Ale Cask Reserve (89) n21 t23 f22 b23. A real fun blend that is just jam-packed with jagged malty notes. The hops were around more on earlier bottlings, but watch out for them. Nothing pint-sized about this: this is a big blend and very true in flavour/shape to the original with just a delicious shading of grain to really up the complexity. 40%

William Grant's Family Reserve (94) n25 t23 f22 b24. There are those puzzled by my obvious love affair with blended whisky - both Scotch and Japanese - at a time when malts are all the rage. But take a glass of this and carefully nurture and savour it for the best part of half an hour and you may begin to see why I believe this to be the finest art form of whisky. For my money, this brand - brilliantly kept in tip-top shape by probably the world's most naturally gifted blender - is the closest thing to the blends of old and, considering it is pretty ubiquitous, it defies the odds for quality. It is a dram with which you can start the day and end it: one to keep you going at low points in between, or to celebrate the victories. It is the daily dram that has everything. 40%

William Grant's Rare Cask Reserves 25 Years Old Blended Scotch Whisky (88) n22.5 busy without offering a narrative. Punchy, salty notes, dried dates and a vague fruitiness; t23 confident delivery: silky textured and mouth-filling; a little ulmo honey mingles with dull fruit and butterscotch; f20.5 fudgy and furry; b22 an appealing blend that appears to be designed to come at you as a concept rather than allowing the different instrumentalists to have the odd solo. Not helped by what appear to be some less than perfect casks. 47%.

William Grant's Sherry Cask Reserve (82) n20 t22 f20 b20. Raspberry jam and cream from time to time. Attractive, but somewhat plodding dram that's content in second gear. 40%

William Lawson's Finest (85) n18.5 t22.5 f22 b22. Not only has the label become more colourful, but so, too, has the whisky. However that has not interfered with the joyous old-fashioned grainy bite. A complex and busy blend from the old charm school. 40%

William Lawson's Scottish Gold Aged 12 Years (89) n22 t23 f22 b22. For years Lawson's 12 was the best example of the combined wizardry of clean grain, unpeated barley and good bourbon cask that you could find anywhere in the world: a last-request dram before the firing squad. Today it is still excellent, but just another sherried blend. What's that saying about it it's not being broke...? 40%

Windsor 12 Years Old (81) n20 t21 f20 b20. Thick, walloped-on blend that you can stand a spoon in. Hard at times to get past the caramel. 40%. Diageo.

Windsor Aged 17 Years Super Premium (89) n23 t22 f22 b22. Still on the safe side for all its charm and quality. An extra dose of complexity would lift this onto another level. 40%

Windsor 21 Years Old (90) n20 t23 f24 b23. Recovers fabulously from the broken nose and envelopes the palate with a silky-sweet style unique to the Windsor scotch brand. Excellent. 40%. Diageo.

Ye Monks (86) n20 t23 f21.5 b21.5. Just hope they are praying for less caramel to maximize the complexity. Still, a decent spicy chew and outstanding bite which is great fun and worth finding when in South America. 40%. Diageo.

Yokozuna Blended 3 Years Old (79.5) n18.5 t20.5 f20 b20.5. It appears the Mongols are gaining a passion for thick, sweet, toffeed, oily, slightly feinty whisky. For a nation breastfed on airag, this'll be a doddle... 40%. Speyside Distillers. Mongolian market.

Irish Whiskey

Of all the whiskies in the world, it is Irish which probably causes most confusion amongst both established whisk(e)y lovers and the novices.

Ask anyone to define what is unique to Irish Whiskey – apart from it being made in Ireland – and the answers, if my audiences around the world at my tastings are anything to go by, are in this order: i) It is triple distilled; ii) It is never, ever made from peat; iii) They exclusively use sherry casks; iv) It comes from the oldest distillery in the world; v) It is made from a mixture of malted and unmalted barley.

Only one of those answers is true: the fifth. And it is usually the final answer extracted from the audience when the last hand raised sticks to his guns after the previous four responses have been shot down.

There was no shortage of Blarney when the Irish were trying to market their whiskey back in the 1950s and early 60s. Hence the triple distilled/non-peated myth was born. The Irish had had a thin time of it since the 1920s and seen their industry decimated. So the marketing guys got to work.

As much of Ireland is covered in peat, it is hardly surprising that in the 19th century smoky whiskey from inland distilleries was not uncommon. Like Scotland. Some distilleries used two stills, others three. Like Scotland. Sherry butts were ubiquitous in Ireland before World War 2. Just as they were in Scotland. And there are distilleries in Scotland older than Bushmills, which dates from 1784 (and certainly not 1608 as some still rabidly believe). However, the practice of using malted and unmalted barley, begun so less tax had to be paid on malted grain, had died out in the Lowlands of Scotland, leaving it for Ireland to carry on alone.

It is hard to believe, then, that when I was researching my Irish Whiskey Almanac way back in 1993, Redbreast had just been discontinued as a brand leaving Green Spot, an ancient gem of a bottling from Mitchell and Son, Dublin's legendary fine class wine and spirit merchants, as the sole surviving Pure Irish Pot Still Whiskey. At first Redbreast's owners refused to send me a bottle as they regarded it as a pointless exercise, seeing as the brand had gone. After I wrote about it, first in my Almanac and then in newspapers and magazines elsewhere, they had no option other than to reverse their decision: interest had been whetted and people were asking for it once more.

When it was relaunched, the Pot Still came from Midleton. The Redbreast they were discontinuing was Pure Pot Still from the long defunct original Jameson Distillery in Dublin. Jameson may once have been locked in commercial battle with their neighbouring Power's distillery, but they united in the late 19th century when they brought out a book called: "The Truth About Irish Whiskey" in which they together, along with other Dublin distillers, fought against blended and other types of what they considered adulterated whiskey to tell the world that the only true Irish whiskey was Pure Pot Still. The last direct descendent of the true Irish distilling DNA from that era is Barry Crockett. We first met nearly a quarter of a century ago when he took me around the very Midleton Distillery in whose grounds he had been born long before the present plant of 1975 had been as much as a glint in an accountant's eye. Barry, myself, Irish Distillers blender Barry Walsh and Green Spot owners Mitchell and Son were then the only people in the entire industry who knew just how great true Irish pot still whiskey was and the deadly threat it was under with Redbreast having been discontinued.

In recent years the production capacity at Midleton has been increased significantly. Enough for pure Pot Still brands to be marketed in a way perhaps that have not been seen since the 1920s. The only thing to have prevented a World Whiskey of the Year Award in the Bible is some unfortunate echoes of less than perfect sherry butts used in maturation. The spirit itself ranks among the finest made anywhere on this planet.

So no surprise that the only thing which could overtake the Redbreast 21-year-old for Irish excellence this year was another pure Pot Still, Midleton Dair Ghaelach, which out-rares the long-established Midleton Rare as well as out performs that Premium Blend by a considerable margin. Recent whiskeys from Midleton have been at the vanguard of using virgin oak outside of Kentucky and Tennessee. Here you even have the added bonus of Irish oak at work, too, ensuring perhaps one of the most truly Irish whiskeys of all time; certainly this century. For not since the earliest days of distilling on the Green Isle when barrels would have been made from scratch by local coopers, or later perhaps bought from a local brewery, has there been a demand for Irish oak. These are deliciously fascinating days in Ireland...

Pure Pot Still
MIDLETON (old distillery)

Midleton 25 Years Old Pot Still db **(92) n24 t24 f21 b23**. A really enormous whiskey that is in the truest classic Irish style. The un-malted barley really does make the tastebuds hum and the oak has added fabulous depth. Interesting when tasted against an American rye – the closeness of the character is there to be experienced, but also the differences. A subtle mature whiskey of unquestionable quality. Superb. *43%*

Midleton 30 Years Old Pot Still db **(85) n19 t22 f22 b22**. A typically brittle, crunchy Irish pot still where the un-malted grains have a telling say. The oak has travelled as far as it can without having an adverse effect. A chewy whiskey which revels in its bitter-sweet balance. An impressively tasty and fascinating insight into yesteryear. *45%*

Midleton 1973 Pure Pot Still db **(95) n24 t24 f23 b24**. The enormous character of true Irish pot still whiskey (a mixture of malted and unmalted barley) appears to absorb age better than most other grain spirits. This one is in its element. But drink at full strength and at body temp (it is pretty closed when cool) for the most startling – and memorable effects. I have no idea how much this costs. But if you can find one and afford it... then buy it!! *56%*

MIDLETON (new distillery)

Green Spot db **(94.5) n23.5 t24 f23.5 b23.5**. This honeyed state has remained a few years, and its sharpness has now been regained. Complex throughout. Unquestionably one of the world's greatest branded whiskies. *40%. Irish Distillers for Mitchell & Son, Dublin.*

⬦ **Green Spot Château Léoville Barton** finished in Bordeaux Wine Casks db **(83.5) n21.5 t22.5 f19 b20.5**. Have a kind of proprietarily, fatherly feel about Green Spot, as it was an unknown whiskey outside Ireland until revealed to the world 21 years ago in my Irish Whiskey Almanac. And fitting this is finished in Ch. Leoville Barton as I have a fair bit of that from the 70s and 80s in my cellar – and the creators of Green Spot was Dublin's oldest wine shop. However, after all that, have to say that this is a disappointment. There are warning signs on the nose and confirmation on the finish that the wine barrel did not escape the dastardly sulphur treatment. Which means it is dull where it should be bright, though the delivery does reach out for complexity and there are some excellent light cocoa moments. But the sulphur wins. *46%*

Master Distiller's Selection Single Pot db (94) n23.5 something about the cake shop about this: sweet with random honey, apples, citrus and flour notes mixing together eloquently and enticingly; t23.5 the first two waves are soft and welcoming. What follows is a ram-rod firm thwack of barley, which is as crunchy as it is chewy. Slowly, some fruit notes unravel, mainly of the plummy type, though the odd pear shows its hand. The spices are beginning to warm; f23 maybe some sherry at work as there is a vague furriness now. But the spices and the crisp barley remain on course to the end; b24 at the sweeter end of the Pot Still spectrum. The use of fruit as a background noise, rather than a lead, is a masterstroke. 46%. 500 bottles. ncf.

Midleton Barry Crockett Legacy db (94) n23.5 t24.5 f22.5 b23.5. Another fabulous Pot Still, very unusual for its clever use of the varied ages of the oak to form strata of intensity. One very sophisticated whiskey. 46%. ncf.

◈ **Midleton Dair Ghaelach** db (97) n23.5 a plethora of bourbon-style liquorice and honey – though, here, closer to heather honey. Polished oak floors, melt-on-the-nose grain... and so it goes on...and on...and on... An odd hybrid of Kentucky and Irish...but a thoroughbred, of course...; t25 that is probably one of the great deliveries of the year. Absolutely abounds in pot still character, both being hard as nails and soft as a virgin's kiss. But the way it interacts with the ulmo honey/red liquorice/heather-honey-vanilla/embracing grain is something of a once in a lifetime experience. And, what's more, barely a hint of spice throughout...; f24 just long, gorgeously silky and soft and a delicious furtherance of the spellbinding flavour compounds of before...; b24.5 for heaven's sake. This is just too ridiculously beautiful...and so unmistakably Irish for all the virgin oak. Truly world class. 58.1%

Midleton Single Pot Still Single Cask 1991 cask no. 48750, dist Nov 91, bott Oct 12 db (96.5) n23.5 usual mix of beech honey, manuka honey and an indistinguishable fruit-like sweetness, somewhere between pear and strawberry; a fascinating blend of bourbon and rye styles; t24 just one of those deliveries you pray for: magnificent mouth feel and weight, just about perfect in fact. Then that unique iron rod of sweet barley couched in velvet. The salivation levels are off the scale, while the hard-nosed unmalted barley offers up their standard crisp honey tones. The enormous age is supported by a crypto-bourbon attack of liquorice and hickory; f23.5 softens, elongates and really kicks in with more bourbon/rye-style molasses, though this only adds weight to the strawberry and chocolate mousse towards the very death; b24.5 like the majority of Pot Still whiskeys, takes a little time to settle in the glass: always give it time to breath and come alive. When it finally does...just....wow!! 54.1%. ncf. Irish Distillers. Warehouse No. M09, exclusive to The Whisky Exchange.

Midleton Single Pot Still Single Cask 1994 cask no. 74060, dist 15 Nov 94 db (93) n23 t23 f23.5 b23.5. Probably a mod pot as opposed to a heavy one. A charming bottling, though if only they had been braver and gone for full cask strength... 46%. ncf Irish Distillers. Exclusive to the Celtic Whiskey Shop.

Paddy Centenary Edition db (93) n22 t23.5 f24 b23.5. This 7-year-old Pure Pot Still whiskey really is a throwback. All Paddy's original whiskey from this era would have been from the old Midleton distillery which sits, in aspic, beside the one opened in 1975. Even with the likelihood of oats being in the mash in those days, still can't believe the original would have been quite as sweet on the palate – and soul – as this. 43%

Powers John's Lane Release Aged 12 Years db (96.5) n24 unmistakable. Unique. Utopian. Irish pure pot still at its most embracing and magnificent. That bizarre bipolar character of rock hard grain so at home in the company of silky, molten honey. Some light, non-specific fruit – a bit like boiled sweets in a candy shop. But a vague menthol note, too...; t25 as Irish whiskey goes: perfection! The delivery can come only from Irish Pot Still – I have encountered it nowhere else. And it is a replay of the nose: soft, dissolve-on-the-palate honey and elsewhere strands of something much firmer – hardening more and more as it moves to the middle ground; f23.5 wonderful fade: a distant medium roast Java, the Lubec marzipan which you just knew would be coming; a little caramel; some orangey notes... b24 this is a style of Irish Pot Still I have rarely seen outside the blending lab. I had many times thought of trying to find some of this and bottling it myself. No need now. I think I have just tasted Irish Whiskey of the Year, and certainly one of the top five world whiskies of the year. 46%

Powers John's Lane Release Aged 12 Years bott 13 Nov 12 db (91) n24 t23.5 f21 b22.5. Researchers some time ago discovered the American accent is derived from an Irish one (and the Canadian from Scots). As pure Irish pot still is the foundation stone of all Irish whiskey, there is no little irony that so many aspects of this bottling is more recognisable as Kentuckian than it is from Cork. Only a slightly off beam cask undermines the finish a tad. Otherwise, superb. 46%. Irish Distillers.

Powers Signature Release bott code. L3065 db (91) n23.5 t22.5 f22 b23. When I first tasted pure pot still over three decades ago, virtually all that I came across was maturing in oloroso butts. Often, the quality of the casks was better than the spirit from the dilapidated distilleries which produced it. Here again the sherry butts are of the highest quality. Maybe one is below par and this is evidenced, very vaguely, on the finish. But, overall, superb! 46%

⟡ **Powers Signature Release** db **(92.5) n23** complex: a great deal of bourbon-style tannin digs deep, assisted by the rigidity of the grain. Something sherry-related lurks in the shadows; **t24** a truly beautiful delivery: marmalade on toast and a quick burst of spices. A little ulmo honey has been stirred into the pot (still!) but it is the combination of tannin and barley which sparks off a fabulously juicy phase; **f22** the ulmo honey moves closer towards vanilla, but then a rapid drying process occurs as a dulling, tingling furriness from the sherry takes effect – a shame...; **b23** I have lately become a little nervous of Irish matured in sherry. At the turn of this century there was plenty in the warehouse and sulphur was not a problem. Something has changed, for now it is. Here, there is not much, but just enough to it take the edge off what had been, until then, a wonderful experience. Hopefully in future bottlings this can be more carefully monitored and the oak profile adjusted. If so, greatness awaits... *46%. ncf.*

Redbreast Aged 12 Years bott 7 Jan 13, bott code: L3007 db **(89) n22 t23.5 f21.5 b22.** This one took me aback. One of the softest Irish pot stills I have encountered, in or outside a lab. Delicious, but displaying very little of the trademark steel which sets this whiskey apart. *40%. Irish Distillers.*

Redbreast Aged 12 Years Cask Strength batch B1/11 db **(96) n24.5** just about the ultimate in Irish whiskey noses. Absolutely rock hard: you feel you could cut diamonds with an aroma like this. It is curiously fruity in that unique Irish Pot Still way, and not just from the obvious sherry involvement, yet shows clearly it's a relation to another whiskey style: American rye. A little hint of mint and lavender goes a long way and offers the only softness in this glorious bitter-sweet aroma; **t24.5** my, oh my, oh my, oh my...one of those deliveries which takes your breath away and it is a few moments before you can compose yourself to think. Or, in my case, to compose myself to compose. The first thing is the sweetness which is never apparent on the nose: here we have the crunchiest Demerara sugar meeting even crunchier muscovado; then a litany of varied fruit and quasi-rye juicy bits...mmmmmm; **f23** majestically long and moves in fabulously mysterious chocolatey ways - chocolate and raisin to be more precise - generating even more salivating moments right until the big chocolate sponge/sherry trifle finale. Late spices, even the faintest possible bitterness of a rogue treated sherry butt, though for once it does no serious damage, other than costing it a possible place in the world's top three. The vanillas come into action for the first time here, too...; **b24** this is Irish pot still on steroids. And sporting an Irish brogue as thick as my great great grandfather John Murray's. To think, had I not included Redbreast in Jim Murray's Irish Whiskey Almanac back in 1994, after it had already been unceremoniously scrapped and discontinued, while championing the then entirely unknown Irish Pot Still cause this brand would no longer have been with us. If I get run over by a bus tomorrow, at least I have that as a tick when St Peter is totting up the plusses and minuses... And with the cask strength, he might even give me two... *577%. ncf. Irish Distillers.*

Redbreast Aged 12 Years Cask Strength Edition batch B1/12 bott 4 Apr 12, bott code: L2095 db **(97) n23 t24 f24 b24.5.** For the sake of space, it is best I refer you to the tasting notes for Batch B1/11. Except here there is less fruit and absolutely no off notes. It is, as Irish whiskey is concerned, nigh-on perfection. *58.6%. ncf. Irish Distillers.*

⟡ **Redbreast Aged 12 Years Cask Strength** batch no. B1/13 db **(95.5) n24** quintessential pot still: a double bill of soft and rock hard notes, one vanishing behind the other and, occasionally, co-starring. There is a blood orange and marmalade fruitiness, plus a liquorice and molasses weightiness; **t24** salivating delivery, to the point where I am nearly drooling all over the computer. A slight note from the odd cask dulls matters, but the sparkle is so profound elsewhere it doesn't matter for now. Crystalline Demerara sugars conjure up a bit of sweet smokiness, as does the rumbling liquorice and vanilla...and even Fisherman's Friend cough sweet; **f23.5** the cough sweet continues while the odd degree of bitterness creeps in. But that is more than offset by the magnificently long cocoa and praline tail... **b24** oh, for that bitterness. A potential World Whisky of the Year otherwise? Perhaps... *59.9%. ncf.*

Redbreast 15 Years Old db **(94) n23 t24 f23 b24.** For years I have been pleading for Irish Distillers to launch a pot still at 46%, natural colour and unchillfiltered. Well, I've got two out of three wishes. And what we have here is a truly great Irish whiskey and my pulse races in the certain knowledge it can get better still... *46%. ncf. France.*

Redbreast Aged 21 Years db **(96) n24** so rare to find age so obvious on a nose, yet so positive in all it does. The pot still is easily recognised with its unique firmness and playful bite, surrounded by a vague fruitiness and encrusted muscovado. But the honey astonishes: so deft and calming, offering acacia in sweetness and heather in floral weight; a half mark is lost though for a light dustiness revealing, surely, added caramel; **t25** perfection: at once the palate is met by a two-toned delivery - a voluptuous silkiness enwrapping steel-hard spine which a great pot still whiskey demands. The sugars melt first, then the malt and this opens the way for a delicate spice to throw a deft contrast against the cough-sweet style mentholated citrus and honey; f23 concentrates now on the more simple aspects; the vanilla-honey balance, the fading malt, the chalkiness of the cask against the buzzing spice....though, sadly that buzzing goes on to reveal the weakest of sulphur inputs, and all the standard off-key bitterness which follows; b24 I have tasted no shortage of 21-year-old pot still before in my career, but that was some time back when the whiskey in question was usually from the original Jameson distillery in Dublin, or Power's. I also managed to get my hands on some old stuff from the original Midleton as well as Tullamore Dew and few others. That old spirit had been made at a time when those distilleries were in the process of being closed down and the quality was nothing like it once was. This, I admit, is the first I can remember from Midleton's rebuilt distillery and it knocks the spots of the Jameson and Power's. Those did not have the balance or the insouciance so far as the honey involvement was concerned or the all-round world-class star quality which positively radiates from the glass. Hopefully this gentle giant amongst the world's truly great whiskies and near blue print for the perfect pot still Irish is here to stay. Only for the next bottling absolutely no need for the pointless caramel and the damaging sherry, both which contribute in tarnishing the dazzling sheen. There are times when less is so significantly more. 46%. ncf. WB15/417

⟐ **Redbreast Mano a Lámh** db **(85) n22.5 t22.5 f19 b21**. Curious that on an all sherry butt bottling, the most enjoyable flavour profile is a spiced chocolate one which begins about four or five beats after the original big, soppy, lush delivery. No prizes for guessing why the score goes down towards the finish. By the way: love the robin on the label – a kind of weird cross between an immature and adult robin with the face of a white wagtail thrown in. Like the whiskey type: unique! 46%. ncf.

Yellow Spot Aged 12 Years bourbon, sherry and Malaga casks db **(88.5) n23.5 t22.5 f20 b22.5**. If anything, just a shade too many wine casks used which somewhat drowns out the unique IP character. Reminds me of when Barry Walsh was working on the triple maturation theme of the Bushmills 16, probably about 15 years ago. Not until the very last days did all the components click. Just before then, it went through a phase like this (though obviously with malt, not IPS). Knowing current blender Billy Leighton as I do, I can see this whiskey improving in future batches as lessons are learned. not that there isn't already much to enjoy... 46%.

OLD COMBER

Old Comber 30 Years Old Pure Pot Still (88) n23 t24 f20 b21. A classic example of a whiskey spending a few Summers too many in wood: increasing age doesn't equal excellence. That said, always very drinkable and early on positively sparkles with a stunning mouthfeel. Out of respect for the old I have made the markings for taste cover the first seven or eight seconds... 40%

Single Malt
COOLEY

Connemara bott code L9042 db **(88) n23 t22.5 f20.5 b22**. One of the softest smoked whiskies in the world which though quite lovely gives the impression it can't make its mind up about what it wants to be. 40%

Connemara Aged 8 Years db **(85) n22.5 t21.5 f20 b21**. Another Connemara lacking teeth. The peat charms, especially on the nose, but the complexity needs working on. 46%

Connemara Aged 12 Years bott code L9024 db **(85.5) n23 t21.5 f20 b21**. The nose, with its beautiful orange, fruity lilt, puts the shy smoke in the shade. 40%

Connemara Cask Strength bott code L9041 db **(90) n21.5 t23 f22 b22.5**. A juicy negative of the standard bottling: does its talking on the palate rather than nose. Maybe an absence of caramel notes might have something to do with that. 57.9%

Connemara Distillers Edition db **(86) n22 t22.5 f20 b21.5**. When I give whisk(e)y tastings around the world, I love to include Connemara. Firstly, people don't expect peated Irish. Secondly, their smoked whisky stock is eclectic and you never quite know what is going to come out of the bottle. This is a particularly tight, sharp style. No prisoners survived... 43%

Connemara Turf Mór Limited Edition Small Batch Collection bott code L10215 db **(94) n23.5 t23.5 f23.5 b23.5**. At Burnley FC, the wine served in their boardroom is The Claret's Claret, naturally. I will not be surprised to find this the whiskey on offer... The tasting notes to this just about perfectly match the ones above. 58.2%

Cooley Poitín Origin Edition dist 26 July 2011, rotation 232/11 db **(92.5) n23.5 t23 f23 b23**. Full bloodied and rumbustious, this is high quality new make Irish that absolutely thumps the salivation button on palate. And, apparently, a mix of malted and unmalted barley in the traditional Irish Pot Still style....though this neither noses nor tastes anything like the new spirit from Midleton. The label waffles on about 1,000 years of Irish tradition. But the use of unmalted barley came into use only when distillers found a way of avoiding tax on the malted stuff. Were there taxes on alcohol in Ireland 1,000 years ago...? 65%

Inish Turk Beg Maiden Voyage db **(91.5) n22 t23.5 f22.5 b22.5** Brooding and quite delicious. 44%

Locke's Aged 8 Years bott code L9005 db **(88) n22.5 t22 f22 b21.5.** A beautiful malt at probably this distillery's optimum age. 40%

Locke's Aged 8 Years Crock (92) n23 t24 f22 b23. Much, much better cask selection than of old: some real honey casks here. A crock of gold...! 40%

Locke's Aged 10 Years Premier Crew cask no. 713, dist Feb 00, bott Jul 10 db **(88) n22 t23 f21 b22.** The cask does its best to try and spoil the barley fun. Here's a tip: stick to younger malts. Cooley is brilliant and relatively undiscovered at between seven and nine years. And there is less time for cask to bite back... 46%. Cooley for The Irish Whisky Society. 292 bottles.

◈ **Scotch Malt Whisky Society Cask 117.4 Aged 22 Years** refill sherry hogshead, dist 16 Sept 91 **(94.5) n24** huge clean fruit just bursting with juice; the background noise suggests very old oak - old enough to offer a second fruity string to the bow....this time of the exotic variety; **t23.5** perhaps the most silky texture of any Cooley I have ever encountered – and I have sampled quite literally thousands of their casks. Despite the age, the salivation factor rockets through the roof, the spice cow-towed by the juiciness of it all; **f23** some real complexity here as the fruit settles down and the malt actually comes out to play with its buttery, biscuit friends; **b24** the oldest unpeated Cooley I have ever encountered. And fully upholds my belief that this was a malt built for age, unlike its triple-distilled counterpart north of the border. 50.3%. sc. 266 bottles.

◈ **Scotch Malt Whisky Society Cask 117.5 Aged 22 Years** refill sherry hogshead, dist 16 Sept 91 **(94) n23.5** a pithy, fruity number, clean and clever despite its antiquity. The fruit element is clear, but takes a humbled stance, allowing the oak to show its equally understated depth; **t23** much more lively and assertive on delivery – indeed, the magnitude of the flavour profile arrives as a shock. The spices are seismic, the grape – compared to the nose – tight and borderline aggressive; **f24** cools and calms down into something far more genteel as the oak begins to show a certain bourbon degree of honeycomb and liquorice. But the fruit is never far away...; **b23.5** good grief. A tempestuous ride – a genuine rollercoaster which somehow offers subtlety amid the fireworks. Well done SMWS for landing three of the best Irish whiskeys you'll taste for many a year. 55.5%. sc. 236 bottles.

◈ **Scotch Malt Whisky Society Cask 118.3 Aged 22 Years** 2nd fill barrel, dist 14 Oct 91 **(96) n24** fading beauty: early peated malt designed for their Connemara brand could sometimes be of low phenolic value. This appears to be of that style, but what remains is bolstered by the first movements of an exotic fruit concerto.; **t23.5** ...and it is that very same exotic fruit which shows first, though hand-in-hand with delightfully explosive spice: a little pineapple and mango marry together despite those peppery spices, though now it is the peat's turn to slowly creep into the picture; **f24.5** one of the great finishes of the year: the smoke has transformed into a mint-chocolate fade with the spices gaining a second, busier wind; a little desiccated coconut and caramelised biscuit fits delightfully with those lingering fruit tones; **b24** presumably a different number (118) has been given to Cooley's peated malt, though made in the same stills. Odd. Anyway, whatever it is...it's bloody magnificent. 579%. sc. 206 bottles.

Tullamore Dew Single Malt 10 Years Old db **(91.5) n23 t23 f22.5 b23.** The best whiskey I have ever encountered with a Tullamore label. Furtively complex and daringly delicate. If only they could find a way to minimise the toffee... 40%. William Grant & Sons.

The Tyrconnell Aged 10 Years Madeira Finish bott code L8136 db **(91) n23 t23 f22 b23.** Not quite the award-winning effort of a few years back, as those lilting high notes which so complimented the baser fruit tones haven't turned up here. But remains in the top echelon and still much here to delight the palate. 46%

The Tyrconnell Single Cask 11 Year Old db **(95.5) n23.5 t25 f23 b24.** Well, if there weren't enough reasons to go to Dublin, you now have this... 46%. sc. Exclusive to the Celtic Whiskey Shop.

Clonmel Peated Aged 8 Years (86) n22 t23 f20 b21. Take the toffee away and you would have one hell of an Irish. Claims to be "Pure Pot Still". It isn't (in Irish terms): it's malt. 40%

Craoi na Mona Irish Malt Whiskey (68) n16 t18 f17 b17. I'm afraid my Gaelic is slipping these days: I assume Craoi na Mona means "Feinty, badly made smoky malt"... (that's the end of my tasting for the day...) 40%

◈ **Glendalough Single Malt Irish Whiskey Aged 7 Years** bourbon casks **(79) n18 t22 f20 b19.** Disappointing on so many levels. Malt at Cooley at 7-year-old, should, if the casks are picked assiduously, be vibrant and brimming with barley and vitality. That only happens for the odd moment or two on delivery. The nose reveals some pretty poor barrels at work while two much toffee flattens the experience. Love the spice, though. 46%. ncf.

⬦⬦⬦ **Glendalough Single Malt Irish Whiskey Aged 13 Years** bourbon casks **(90)** n22.5 fresh dates sprinkled, like a Shrove Tuesday pancake, with sugar and lemon...and a touch of lime, too; **t23** superb texture: the barley bristles with oaky spice while the light oils help get the spices established; **f21.5** dies slightly as the oak dries vividly and toffee kicks in; a touch milky, too; **b23** a rather beautiful whiskey, spilling over with spices. A few tired casks evident, though. *46%. ncf.*

Glen Dimplex (88) n23 t22 f21 b22. Overall, clean and classically Cooley. *40%*

Liquid Sun Cooley 1999 bott 2012 **(87) n22 t22 f21.5 b21.5** awash with natural caramels and enjoyable in a horrible way...without the horrible. *53.2%. nc ncf sc. The Whisky Agency.*

Magilligan Cooley Pure Pot Still Single Malt (91) n22 t22 f24 b23. A touch of honey for good measure ...or maybe not..!! *43%. Ian MacLeod Distillers.*

Magilligan Irish Whiskey Peated Malt 8 Years Old (89) n21 t23 f22 b23. Such a different animal from the docile creature that formally passed as Magilligan peated. Quite lovely...and very classy. *43%. Ian Macleod Distillers.*

Merry's Single Malt (83) n20 t22 f20 b21. Ultra-clean barley rich nose is found on the early palate. The finish is flat, though. *40%*

Michael Collins Irish Whiskey Single Malt db **(68) n17 t18 f17 b16.** Bloody hell, I thought. Didn't anyone get my message from last year? Apparently not – and it's our fault as the tasting notes above were accidentally edited out before they went in. Sorry. But the caramel in the latest bottling has been upped to take the whisky from deep gold to bronze. Making this among the most over-coloured single malt I have tasted in years. Please guys. For the love of whiskey. Please let us taste exactly what a great malt this could be. *40% (80 proof)*

Milroy's of Soho Single Malt Cooley Aged 11 Years first fill bourbon, cask no. 3442, dist 22 Oct 01, bott 5 Nov 12 **(91) n23.5 t23 f22.5 b23.** Seriously enjoyable. Just what the doctor ordered...! *46%*

Sainsbury's Single Malt Irish Whiskey bott code L10083/16 **(87.5) n22 t22 f21.5 b22.** Classic Cooley showing its big, malty depth. *40%*

Shannahan's (92) n23 t22 f24 b23. Cooley natural and unplugged: quite adorable. *40%*

Slieve Foy Single Malt Aged 8 Years bott code L9108 **(88) n23 t22.5 f21 b21.5.** Never deviates from its delicate touch. *40%. Cooley for Marks & Spencer.*

Vom Fass Cooley Irish Single Malt 8 Years Old (88) n22 t22.5 f21.5 b22. A very decent, if undemonstrative, example of the distillery at an age which well suits. *40%*

The Wild Geese Single Malt (85.5) n21.5 t21 f22 b21. "A Rare Blend of Pure Aged Irish Malt Whiskies" says the front label. Yet it is a single malt. Confusing. And very unhelpful to a whisky public already being totally bamboozled by the bizarre and misguided antics of the Scotch Whisky Association. It is not a blend. It is a mixing of Cooley malt whiskey, as I understand it. The back label's "Smoother Because We Distil it Longer" is also a bit of a blarney. It's made in a pot still and whilst it is true that if you distil faster (by higher temperatures) you could well end up with "hot" whiskey, I am not aware of this being distilled at a significantly slower rate than at either Bushmills or Midleton. Or do they mean the cut of the run from the spirit still is longer, which would impart more oils – not all of them great? Just ignore the Wild Goose chase the labels send you on and enjoy the malt, with all its failings, for what it is (and this is pretty enjoyable in an agreeably rough and ready manner, though not exactly the sniff of Irish whiskey purists): which in this case for all its malt, toffee and delicate smoke, also appears to have more than a slight touch of feints - so maybe they were right all along...!!! *43%. Cooley for Avalon.*

OLD KILBEGGAN

Kilbeggan Distillery Reserve Malt matured in quarter casks, batch no. 1, bott Jun 10 db **(89) n22.5 t22.5 b22.** An endearingly soft malt to see Kilbeggan distillery back into the whiskey world. Shame it has been reduced to 40%, as this one demanded to be at least 46% - indeed, preferably naked - and allowing those delicate, elegant but marginalised characters a chance to bloom. But welcome back...and I look forward to many an evening with me tasting you as you blossom, as I am sure you will. It has been nearly 20 years since I first discovered the beauty of Kilbeggan Distillery and I have countless times since dreamed of that moment. *40%. 1500 bottles. Available only in the distillery gift shop.*

The Spirit of Kilbeggan 1 Month (90.5) n22 t23 f23 b22.5. Wow!! They are really getting to grips with the apparatus. Full bodied and lush small still feel to this but radiating complexity, depth, barley and cocoa in equal measures. The development of the oils really does give this excellent length. Impressed!! *65.5%*

The Spirit of Kilbeggan 1 Year (85) n20.5 t21 f22 b21.5. A veritable Bambi of a spirit: a typical one year old malt which, as hard as it tries, just can't locate its centre of gravity. Even so, the richness is impressive and some highly sugared chocolate mousse near the end is a treat. *62.7%*

The Spirit of Kilbeggan 2 Years (84) n20 t21 f22 b21. A tad raw and a little thin. There is some decent balance between oak and malt, but the overall feeling is that the still has not yet been quite mastered. *60.3%*

OLD BUSHMILLS

Bushmills Aged 10 Years matured in two woods db (**92.5**) **n23 t23 f23 b23.5.** Absolutely superb whiskey showing great balance and the usual Antrim 19th century pace with its favour development. The odd bottle of this I have come across over the last couple of years has been spoiled by the sherry involvement. But, this, as is usually the case, is absolutely spot on. 40%

Bushmills Select Casks Aged 12 Years married with Caribbean rum cask db (**95**) **n23** unusual moist rum and raisin cake effect: effective and just enough spice to deliver extra complexity. Just the very slightest hint of bourbon, too; **t24** adorable malt richness; biscuity and stupendously seasoned yet always remains fresh and mouthwatering. The sweetness is very cleverly controlled; **f24** there are just so many layers to this: the oak is a growing force, but restricts itself to a vanilla topping; **b24** one of the most complex Bushmills in living memory, and probably since it was established in 1784. 40%

Bushmills Aged 16 Years db (**71**) **n18 t21 f15 b17.** In my days as a consultant Irish whiskey blender, going through the Bushmills warehouses I found only one or two sulphur-treated butts. Alas, there are many more than that at play here. 40%

Bushmills Aged 21 Years db (**95.5**) **n24.5** this remains something of a Chinese puzzle on the nose: just how do all those different notes , sometimes soft and rounded, sometimes hard and angular, many of them fruity, manage to intertwine...yet never clash? And why can you never detach one without another clinging on to it. If Sherlock Holmes tried to solve it, this would be a three pipe conundrum...except the use of tobacco would ruin the experience. Just marvel at the greengage and physalis, the flaked vanilla and liquorice, the ulmo honey and hickory... so much else besides; **t24** as melt-in-the-mouth as a whiskey can be: amazingly juicy barley offers the cutting edge and lead while a plethora of delicate sugars dissolve on impact; the fruit is served as a perpetual mixed salad; **f23.5** this is where I am really impressed. Despite all the complexity of the nose and delivery, at the finish the Bushmills trademark flaky vanilla and delicate barley comes through...a signature unique to one distillery in the world; **b24** an Irish journey as beautiful as the dramatic landscape which borders the distillery. Magnificent. 40%

Clontarf Single Malt (**90.5**) **n23 t23 f22 b22.5.** Beautiful in its simplicity, this has eschewed complexity for delicious minimalism; 40%. Clontarf Irish Whiskey Co.

Connemara Original Peated Single Malt db (**81.5**) **n21 t21.5 f19 b20.** It's been about a week since I last tasted a whisk(e)y at 40% abv...a shock to the system! Also a bit of a while since the first thing I got off the nose and last thing on the finish was caramel. Not the Connemara I witnessed being launched in a blaze of defiant glory those decades back. This rather meek, pleasant, safe, lightly smoked version appears to have been sanitised. Today's Connemara it may sadly be. Original Connemara it is most certainly NOT...! 40%

The Irishman Single Malt bottle no. E2496 (**83**) **n20 t21 f21 b21.** Highly pleasant malt but the coffee and toffee on the finish underline a caramel-style whiskey which may, potentially, offer so much more. 40%. Hot Irishman Ltd.

The Irishman Single Malt 12 Years Old 1st fill bourbon barrels, casks no. 70691 & 70692, bott Nov 2012 (**88**) **n22 t22.5 f21.5 b22.** Very pleasant but, ultimately, docile thanks to the caramels at work. Putting my Irish blender's hat on for a moment, I think the whiskey would had offered a lot more had it been carefully selected first and second fill bourbon casks at play, rather than two very similar B1s. 43%. ncf. Hot Irishman Ltd.

The Irishman Small Batch Single Malt batch no. 1703/2013, sherry and bourbon casks (**86.5**) **n22 t22 f21 b21.5.** A pleasant, sticky malt with early fudge and raisin sweetness and then an over dependence on a single caramel note. 40% WB15/403

Knappogue Castle Aged 12 Years bourbon cask matured (**90**) **n23.5 t23 f21 b22.5.** The massive toffee influence deflects from the huge character elsewhere which springs a few surprises. 40%. Castle Brands Group.

Single Grain
COOLEY

Greenore 6 Year Old bott code L9015 db (**89**) **n23.5 t22.5 f21 b22.** Very enjoyable whiskey. But two points: cut the caramel and really see the baby sing. And secondly, as a "Small Batch" bottling, how about putting a batch number on the label...? 40%. Cooley.

Greenore 8 Year Old bott code L8190 db (**86.5**) **n20 t22 f23 b21.5.** The vague hint of butyric on the nose is more than amply compensated by the gradual build up to something rather larger on the palate than you might have expected (and don't be surprised if the two events are linked). The corn oil is almost a meal in itself and the degree of accompanying sugar and corn flour is a treat. 40%. Cooley.

Greenore 15 Years Old bott code L8044 db (**90**) **n23 t22.5 f22 b22.5.** The advent of the Kilbeggan 15 reminded us that there must be some grain of that age around, and here to prove it is a superb bottling of the stuff which, weirdly, is a lot better than the blend. Beautiful. 43%

Greenore 18 Years Old db (**91**) n22.5 t22.5 f23 b23. This continuous still at Cooley should be marked by the State as an Irish national treasure. One of the most complex grains you'll ever find, even when heading into uncharted territory like this one. 46%. ncf. 4000 bottles.

GLENDALOUGH

◇◇ **Glendalough Double Barrel Irish Whiskey** first aged in American bourbon casks, then Spanish oloroso casks (**88.5**) n22.5 vague fruit, mainly of pears; t23 succulent mouth feel with a juicy surge of barley and spice; f21 dulls out but remains silky, though dry; b22 a very pleasant malt but rather vague and at time a little dull. 42%

TEELING

◇◇ **Teeling Single Grain Irish Whiskey** (**94**) n23.5 how can something be this clean yet so complex? A beautiful marriage of custard and kumquats with a touch of astringent rhubarb tart for good measure; t23.5 much sweeter as ulmo honey shows first before slowly giving way to a jam Swiss roll sweetness and oiliness; f23 more of the same, but more quietly...; b24 presumably Cooley grain – as good as anything of its ilk on this planet. And showing it has enough about it to combine to stunning effect with some high quality wine casks. I've just had that Teeling feeling....wonderful! 46%. ncf.

◇◇ **Teeling Single Malt Irish Whiskey** (**80.5**) n20 t22 f19 b19.5. Sometimes in a whiskey, complexity can be overdone – especially if different wine casks are in use. Then finding the balance, the very essence, can be a nightmare. I have but a small sample before me here and know nothing of the make-up of this malt....other than what my taste buds are telling me. It appears like a multi-cask style, but one – probably the sherry - has not been of the highest standard. A dangerous game...and always worth remembering in whiskey that less can so often be more... 46%

UNSPECIFIED SINGLE MALT S

◇◇ **Black Corbie Boyne Single Malt 2001** refill sherry cask, cask no. 15283, dist 18 Sept 01, bott 09 Feb 15 (**93**) n23 full blown fruitcake at its most lush; t24 the palate is awash with an all consuming tidal wave of thick grape and greengage, maple syrup and treacle mix, a bit more molasses for good measure...and about as many spices as you can possibly fit in; f23 once the sugars begin to fade, a bitterness emerges – rather like the severely burnt raisins on a fruitcake; b23 balance doesn't really come into it: there is hardly any. Like Gyles Brandreth warming to a tale, this is all about effect! Just such great fun! 57.1%. sc. 221 bottles.

◇◇ **Dublin in the Rare Ould Times Single Malt Irish Whiskey Aged 10 Years** bourbon barrel (**81.5**) n21 t21 f19 b20.5. It was a rare old time when they made single malt whiskey like this in Dublin, for they hardly ever did. The city was the centre of Pot Still Irish and though single malt was not unknown there, it was a scarce order at the bar. When it did come along, it is hard to believe it would have been this kind of age. And, indeed, this malt would have been happier had it been a couple of years younger: the bourbon barrel at work here has allowed little malty punch to get through, while the toffee middle and finish is disappointingly dull. 40%. Bottled by Glendalough Distillery for Pete St John.

◇◇ **Hotel Essener Hof Single Malt Irish Whisky Aged 16 Years** ex rum cask (**85.5**) n21.5 t22.5 f20.5 b21. The trouble with some ex-rum casks is that they don't allow the malt to breathe or develop its own personality: whisky in a sugar-toffee straight jacket, if you like. That has happened here, though the spices are a treat. 55.7%. 211 bottles.

◇◇ **Jack Ryan Single Malt Irish Whisky Aged 12 Years** bourbon cask (**92.5**) n23.5 mainly oak on the rise: playful diced toasted hazelnut intermingles with lemongrass and orange blossom honey; t23 early barley offers a fresh, semi-juicy delivery; the malt is confident, elegant and clean and handles the spice with tact; f22.5 the inevitable cocoa notes arrive in force. But the malt lingers; b23.5 deft, very clean malt whisky where decent bourbon wood adds all kinds of beautifully paced complexity. Not even a hint of an off note. Impressive. 46%

◇◇ **Limburg Dramclub Irish Malt 6 Year Old** dist 2009, bott 2015 (**89**) n22 lightly smoked: exceptionally clean, with little more than hints of smoke or oak; t23 delightful delivery: probably the most salivating smoked malt you'll come across this year as the gristy sugars are left to their own devices; f22 a tad thin, thanks to the lack of oaky input; b22 a young, shy malt and as clean as it comes. 51.4%. 141 bottles.

◇◇ **Whisky-Fässle Irish Single Malt 10 Year Old** hogshead, dist 2003, bott 2014 (**71**) n18 t21.5 f15 b16.5. A strangely soapy dram. The finish really is in distress. Malty on delivery. But as for the rest....bejabers! 49.5%. nc ncf.

Blends

Bushmills 12 Years Old Distillery Reserve db **(86) n22.5 t22.5 f20 b21.** This version has gone straight for the ultra lush feel. For those who want to take home some 40% abv fruit fudge from the distillery. *40%*

Bushmills 1608 anniversary edition **(94) n23.5 t23.5 f23 b24.** This whiskey is talking an entirely different language to any Irish blend I have come across before, or any blend come to that. Indeed, nosed blind you'd not even regard it a blend: the malt calls to you like a Siren. But perhaps it is the crystal malt they have used here which is sending out such unique signals, helping the whiskey to form a thick cloak of roasty, toasty, burnt toffeed, bitter-sweetness which takes your breath away. What a fabulous whiskey! And whether it be a malt or blend, who cares? Genius whiskey is genius whiskey. *40%*

Bushmills 1608 400th Anniversary (83) n21 t21.5 f20 b20.5. Thin-bodied, hard as nails and sports a peculiarly Canadian feel. *46%. Diageo.*

Bushmills 1608 db **(87) n22 t23 f20 b22.** A blend which, through accident, evolution or design, has moved a long way in style from when first launched. More accent on fruit though, predictably, the casks aren't quite what they once were. Ignoring the furriness on the finish, there is much to enjoy on the grape-must nose and how the fruit bounces off the rigid grain on delivery. *46%*

Bushmills Black Bush (91) n23 t23 f21.5 b23.5. This famous old blend may be under new management and even blender. But still the high quality, top-notch complexity rolls around the glass and your palate. As beautiful as ever. *40%*

Bushmills Original (80) n19 t21 f20 b20. Remains one of the hardest whiskeys on the circuit with the Midleton grain at its most unflinching. There is a sweeter, faintly maltier edge to this now while the toffee and biscuits qualities remain. *40%*

Cassidy's Distiller's Reserve bott code L8067 **(84.5) n21.5 t22 f20 b21.** Some salivating malt on flavour-exploding delivery, but all else tame and gentle. *40%. Cooley.*

Clancey's bott code L8025 **(87) n22 t21 f22 b22.** Remains an excellent blend for all the toffee. The spice balance excels. *40%. Cooley for Wm Morrison.*

Clontarf Classic Blend (81) n20 t22 f19.5 b19.5. A hard as nails blend softened only by the heavy use of caramel which, though chewy, tends to obliterate any complexity from elsewhere. Ouch! 40%. Castle Brands Group.

Delaney's (85.5) n20 t21.5 f22 b22. Young, clean, citrusy, refreshing and proud. Thoroughly enjoyable and dangerously moreish. *40%. Cooley for Co-operative UK.*

Delaney's Special Reserve (84) n21.5 t20.5 f22 b21. An attractive blend with a big late spicy blast. The toffee dominates for long periods. *40%. Cooley for Co-operative Group.*

Feckin Irish Whiskey (81) n20 t21 f20 b20. Tastes just about exactly the feckin same as the Feckin Strangford Gold... *40%. The Feckin Drinks Co.*

Golden Irish bott code L7064 **(93) n23 t23 f23.5 b23.5.** By far one of the most enjoyable Irish blends around. Simple, but what it does, it does deliciously well. *40%. Cooley.*

The Irishman Superior Irish Whiskey bott code L6299L059 **(93) n23 t23 f23 b24.** What a quite wonderful blend: not of the norm for those that have recently come onto the market and there is much more of the Irish Distillers about this than most. Forget about the smoke promised in the tasting notes on the label...it gives you everything else but. And that is one hell of a lot!! *40%. Hot Irishman Ltd.*

Jameson (95) n24.5 Swoon...bizarrely shows even more Pot Still character than the Redbreast I tasted yesterday. Flinty to the point of cracking. The sherry is there but on reduced terms, allowing the firm grain to amplify the unmalted barley: truly brilliant; **t24** mouthwatering delivery and then wave upon wave of diamond-hard barley and grain; the odd eclectic layer of something sweetish and honeyed, but this is eye-watering stuff; **f22.5** an annoying touch of caramel creeps in, costing points, but even beyond that you still cannot other than be charmed by the layering of cocoa, barley and light grape; **b24** I thought I had detected in bottlings I had found around the world a very slight reduction in the Pot Still character that defines this truly classic whiskey. So I sat down with a fresh bottle in more controlled conditions...and was blown away as usual. The sharpness of the PS is vivid and unique; the supporting grain of the required crispness. Fear not: this very special whiskey remains in stunning, truly wondrous form. *40%*

Jameson 18 Years Old Limited Release bott 08/10/14 **(93.4) n24** one of the first high quality Irish whiskeys I've encountered where you are drawn in by bourbon-style tannins – virgin oak, perhaps? - rather than by the unique pot still experience. There are pot still echoes, reverberating the ulmo honey and thin lime marmalade; mega complex, fascinating and beautiful; **t23.5** so no let down on delivery. Indeed, it is even better for the first 12 to 15 seconds as the clear and thin honey melts into the hickory and liquorice; **f22.5** just bitters slightly at the end with a furry flourish; **b23.5** I've always found an Irish beauty irresistible... *40%*

Jameson 12 Years Old Special Reserve (88) n22 t23 f21 b22. Much more sherry than of late and the pot still makes inroads, too. Just needs to lose some of the caramel effect; *40%*

Jameson 18 Years Old Limited Release bott 08/10/14 (93.4) n24 one of the first high quality Irish whiskeys I've encountered where you are drawn in by bourbon-style tannins – virgin oak, perhaps? - rather than by the unique pot still experience. There are pot still echoes, reverberating the ulmo honey and thin lime marmalade; mega complex, fascinating and beautiful; t23.5 so no let down on delivery. Indeed, it is even better for the first 12 to 15 seconds as the clear and thin honey melts into the hickory and liquorice; f22.5 just bitters slightly at the end with a furry flourish; b23.5 I've always found an Irish beauty irresistible... *40%*

Jameson Black Barrel (91.5) n23 t23 f22.5 b23. Here's the problem faced by any Jameson blender: the column still grain from Midleton is the hardest on the palate made anywhere in the world. So how do you get it to mould into what you want? Usually you can't, so you have to make the whiskeys around it reflect and deflect for maximum effect. And that's what's going on here: a brittle whisky where the pot still element is magnified very cleverly indeed. Lovely stuff: New Yorkers are a lucky bunch! *40%. NY exclusive.*

Jameson Gold Reserve (88) n22 t23 f20 b22. Enjoyable, but so very different: an absolute re-working with all the lighter, more definitively sweeter elements shaved mercilessly while the thicker oak is on a roll. Some distance from the masterpiece it once was. *40%*

Jameson Signature Reserve (93) n23.5 t23.5 f22.5 b23.5. Be assured that Signature, with its clever structuring of delicate and inter-weaving flavours, says far more about the blender, Billy Leighton, than it does John Jameson. *40%. Irish Distillers.*

Kellan American oak cask (84) n21 t22 f20 b20. Safe whisky which is clean, sweet and showing many toffeed attributes. Decent spices, too. *40% (80 Proof). Cooley.*

Kilbeggan bott code L7091 db (86) n21 t22 f21.5 b21.5. A much more confident blend by comparison with that faltering one of the last few years. Here, the malts make a significant drive towards increasing the overall complexity and gentle citrus style. *40%. Cooley.*

Kilbeggan 15 Years Old bott code L7048 db (85.5) n21.5 t22 f21 b21. My word! 15 years, eh? How time flies! And on the subject of flying, surely I have winged my way back to Canada and am tasting a native blend. No, this is Irish albeit in sweet, deliciously rounded form. However, one cannot help feeling that the dark arts have been performed, as in an injection of caramel, which, as well as giving that Canadian feel has also probably shaved off some of the more complex notes to middle and finish. Even so, a sweet, silky experience. *40%. Cooley.*

Kilbeggan 18 Year Old db (89) n23 t21.5 f22.5 b22. Although the impressive bottle lavishly claims "From the World's Oldest Distillery" I think one can take this as so much Blarney. It certainly had my researcher going, who lined this up for me under the Old Kilbeggan distillery, a forgivable mistake and one I think he will not be alone in making. This, so it appears on the palate, is a blend. From the quite excellent Cooley distillery, and it could be that whiskey used in this matured at Kilbeggan... which is another thing entirely. As for the whiskey: apart from some heavy handedness on the toffee, it really is quite a beautiful and delicate thing. *40%*

Kilgeary bott code L8063 (79) n20 t20 f19 b20. There has always, and still proudly is, something strange about this blend. Cold tea on the nose and a bitter bite to the finish, sandwiches a brief flirtation with something sweet. *40%. Cooley.*

Locke's bott code L8056 (85.5) n21 t22 f21.5 b21. Now, there you go!! Since I last really got round to analysing this one it has grown from a half-hearted kind of a waif to something altogether more gutsy and muscular. Sweeter, too, as the malts and grains combine harmoniously. A clean and pleasant experience with some decent malt fingerprints. *40%*

Michael Collins A Blend (77) n19 t20 f19 b19. Michael Collins was known as the "big fellow". This pleasant, impressively spiced dram, might have enjoyed the same epithet had it not surrendered to and then been strangled by caramel on the finish. *40% (80 proof). Cooley.*

◇ **Midleton Very Rare 30th Anniversary Pearl Edition** db (91) n23.5 one of the best Midleton noses over the last decade: toffee at a minimum with the emphasis on a sexy, soft and come-hither alluring bourbon notes, especially of the red liquorice variety; one presumes the harder middle note is the pot still; t24 brilliant delivery and follow-through: the pot still is first to crash land into the taste buds, followed by a gorgeous passion fruit sharpness. The Pot Still forms its usual backbone, but then a bitterness creeps in; the passion fruit continues, joined now by soft pear and vanilla; f21 bitter and slightly out of sync; b22.5 the nose and delivery will go down in Irish whiskey folklore... *53.1%*

Midleton Distillery Reserve (85) n22 t22 f20 b21. A whiskey which, for all its muscovado sweetness offers some memorable barley moments. *40%. Irish Distillers Midleton Distillery only. Changes character slightly with each new vatting. This one is some departure.*

Midleton Very Rare 1984 (70) n19 t18 f17 b16. Disappointing with little backbone or balance. *40%. Irish Distillers.*

Midleton Very Rare 1985 (77) n20 t20 f18 b19. Medium-bodied and oily, this is a big improvement on the initial vintage. *40%. Irish Distillers.*

Midleton Very Rare 1986 (79) n21 t20 f18 b20. A very malty Midleton richer in character than previous vintages. 40%. Irish Distillers.

Midleton Very Rare 1987 (77) n20 t19 f19 b19. Quite oaky at first until a late surge of excellent pot still. 40%. Irish Distillers.

Midleton Very Rare 1988 (86) n23 t21 f21 b21. A landmark MVR as it is the first vintage to celebrate the Irish pot-still style. 40%. Irish Distillers.

Midleton Very Rare 1989 (87) n22 t22 f22 b21. A real mouthful but has lost balance to achieve the effect. 40%. Irish Distillers.

Midleton Very Rare 1990 (93) n23 t23 f24 b23. Astounding whiskey: one of the vintages every true Irish whiskey lover should hunt for. 40%. Irish Distillers.

Midleton Very Rare 1991 (76) n19 t20 f19 b18. After the Lord Mayor's Show, relatively dull and uninspiring. 40%. Irish Distillers.

Midleton Very Rare 1992 (84) n20 t20 f23 b21. Superb finish with outstanding use of feisty grain. 40%. Irish Distillers.

Midleton Very Rare 1993 (88) n21 t22 f23 b22. big, brash and beautiful – the perfect way to celebrate the 10th-ever bottling of MVR. 40%. Irish Distillers.

Midleton Very Rare 1994 (87) n22 t22 f21 b22. Another different style of MVR, one of amazing lushness. 40%. Irish Distillers.

Midleton Very Rare 1995 (90) n23 t24 b21 b22. They don't come much bigger than this. Prepare a knife and fork to battle through this one. Fabulous. 40%. Irish Distillers.

Midleton Very Rare 1996 (82) n21 t22 f19 b20. The grains lead a soft course, hardened by subtle pot still. Just missing a beat on the finish, though. 40%. Irish Distillers.

Midleton Very Rare 1997 (83) n22 t21 f19 b21. The piercing pot still fruitiness of the nose is met by a countering grain of rare softness on the palate. Just dies on the finish when you want it to make a little speech. Very drinkable. 40%. Irish Distillers.

Midleton Very Rare 1999 (89) n21 t23 f22 b23. One of the maltiest Midletons of all time: a superb blend. 40%. Irish Distillers.

Midleton Very Rare 2000 (85) n22 t21 f21 b21. An extraordinary departure even by Midleton's eclectic standards. The pot still is like a distant church spire in an hypnotic Fen landscape. 40%. Irish Distillers.

Midleton Very Rare 2001 (79) n21 t20 f18 b20. Extremely light but the finish is slightly on the bitter side. 40%. Irish Distillers.

Midleton Very Rare 2002 (79) n20 t22 f18 b19. The nose is rather subdued and the finish is likewise toffee-quiet and shy. There are some fabulous middle moments, some of flashing genius, when the pot still and grain combine for a spicy kick, but the finish really is lacklustre and disappointing. 40%. Irish Distillers.

Midleton Very Rare 2003 (84) n22 t22 f19 b21. Beautifully fruity on both nose and palate (even some orange blossom on aroma). But the delicious spicy richness that is in mid launch on the tastebuds is cut short by caramel on the middle and finish. A crying shame, but the best Midleton for a year or two. 40%. Irish Distillers.

Midleton Very Rare 2004 (82) n21 t21 f19 b21. Yet again caramel is the dominant feature, though some quite wonderful citrus and spice escape the toffeed blitz. 40%.

Midleton Very Rare 2005 (92) n23 t24 f22 b23. OK, you can take this one only as a rough translation. The sample I have worked from here is from the Irish Distillers blending lab, reduced to 40% in mine but without caramel added. And, as Midleton Very Rares always are at this stage, it's an absolute treat. Never has such a great blend suffered so in the hands of colouring and here the chirpiness of the pot still and élan of the honey (very Jameson Gold Label in part) show just what could be on offer given half the chance. Has wonderful natural colour and surely it is a matter of time before we see this great whiskey in its natural state. 40%

Midleton Very Rare 2006 (92) n22 t24 f23 b23. As raw as a Dublin rough-house and for once not overly swamped with caramel. An uncut diamond. 40%

Midleton Very Rare 2007 (83) n20 t22 f20 b21. Annoyingly buffeted from nose to finish by powering caramel. Some sweeter wisps do escape but the aroma suggests Canadian and insufficient Pot Still gets through to make this a Midleton of distinction. 40%. Irish Distillers

Midleton Very Rare 2008 (88.5) n22 t23 f21.5 b22. A dense bottling which offers considerably more than the 2007 Vintage. Attractive, very drinkable and without the caramel it might really have hit the heights. 40%. Irish Distillers.

Midleton Very Rare 2009 (95) n24 t24 f23 b24. I've been waiting a few years for one like this to come along. One of the most complex, cleanest and least caramel-spoiled bottlings for a good few years and one which makes the pot still character its centre piece. A genuine celebration of all things Midleton and Barry Crockett's excellence as a distiller in particular. 40%. Irish Distillers.

Midleton Very Rare 2010 (84) n21 t22 f20 b21. A case of after the Lord Mayor's Show. Chewy and some decent sugars. But hard to make out detail through the fog of caramel. 40%

Midleton Very Rare 2011 (81.5) n22.5 t20 f19 b20 Another disappointing version where the colour of its personality has been compromised for the sake of the colour in the bottle. A dullard of a whiskey, especially after the promising nose. 40%. Irish Distillers.

Midleton Very Rare Irish Whisky 2012 db (89.5) n22 t23 f22 b22.5. Much more like it! After a couple of dud vintages, here we have a bottling worthy of its great name & heritage. 40%.

Midleton Very Rare Irish Whisky 2014 db (78.5) n20.5 t22 f17 b19. Hmmm. Somehow we have missed the 2013 Midleton Very Rare...only the second of all the Midleton Rares to get away - ever. We shall try to remedy that for Jim Murray's Whisky Bible 2016. Must say how odd it looks to see Brian Nation's signature scrawled across the label and not Barry Crockett's. Also, I was a bit worried by this one when I saw the depth of orange hue to this whiskey. Sadly, my fears were pretty well founded. Toffee creaks from every corner making for a mainly flat encounter with what should be an uplifting Irish. Some lift at about the midway point when something, probably pot still, throws off the shackles of its jailer and emerges briefly with spice. But all rather too little, especially in the face of a dull, disappointingly flawed, fuzzy finale. Midleton Very Rare should be, as the name implies, a lot, lot better than this safe but flabby, personality bypassed offering. The most frutrating aspect of this is that twice I have tasted MVR in lab form just prior to bottling. And both were quite stunning whiskeys. That was until the colouring was added in the bottling hall. 40% WB15/416

Millars Special Reserve bott code L8069 (86) n21 t22 f21.5 b21.5. Now that's some improvement on the last bottling of this I found, with spices back with abandon and grains ensuring a fine mouthfeel. Even the chocolate fudge at the death is a treat. 40%. Cooley.

Morrisons Irish Whiskey bott code L10028 (78) n19 t20 f19 b20. Sweet, pleasant and inoffensive. 40%. Wm Morrison Supermarket.

Paddy (74) n18.5 t20 f17.5 b18. Cleaned its act up a little. Even a touch of attractive citrus on the nose and delivery. But where does that cloying sweetness come from? As bland as an Irish peat bog but, sadly, nothing like so potentially tasty. 40%. Irish Distillers.

Powers (91) n23 t24 f22 b22. Is it any coincidence that in this bottling the influence of the caramel has been significantly reduced and the whiskey is getting back to its old, brilliant self? I think not. Classic stuff. 40%. Irish Distillers.

Powers Gold Label (87) n22 t22 f21 b22. The solid pot still, the very DNA of what made Powers, well, Powers is vanishing in front of our very noses. Yes, still some pot still around, but nothing like so pronounced in the way that made this, for decades, a truly one-off Irish and one of the world greats. Still delightful and with many charms but the rock hard pot still effect is sadly missed. What is going on here? 40%. Irish Distillers.

Power's Gold Label (96) n23 a bold mixing between caramel and Powers' famous high potstill content. Here the potstill even appears to have an edge which cuts effortlessly through the grains and toffee...; t24.5 oh gosh! That is just such a fabulous delivery: a biting, jolting Irishness that is entirely unique to the genre. The sugars and honeys arrive easily and are profound – maple syrup linking arm in arm with the crisp post still to ensure some serious thrust and counter-thrust moment...; f24 there appears to be plenty of caramel on this fella, yet somehow it is discarded and counts for virtually nought as the pot still runs rings around anything trying to prevent it making a ful impact. How do those sugars keep so lively and going for so long...? b24.5 a slightly dfferent breed. This is not all about minute difference in strength...this is also about weight distribution and flavour pace. It is a subtly different blend... and all the better for it...Make no mistake: this is a truly classic Irish. 43.2% ⊙ ⊙

Redbreast Blend (88) n23 t23 f20 b22. Really impressed with this one-off bottling for Dillons the Irish wine merchants. Must try and get another bottle before they all vanish. 40%.

Sainsbury's Blended Irish Whiskey (86.5) n22 t22 f21 b21.5. A beautifully relaxed blend showing pretty clearly – literally, thanks to an admirable lack of colouring - just how good the Cooley grain whiskey is even at no great age. Clean with a deceptively busy and intense flavour profile. Far too good for the cola the back label says this should go with... 40%. UK.

St Patrick bott code L030907 (77) n19 t20 f19 b19. Good grief! No prisoners here as we have either a bitter oakiness or mildly cloying sweetness, rarely working in tandem. A few gremlins for the Kremlin. 40%. Cooley for Russia.

Strangford Gold (81) n20 t21 f20 b20. A simplistic, exceptionally easy drinking blend with high quality grain offering silk to the countering spice but caramel flattens any malt involvement. 40%. The Feckin Drinks Co.

◈ **Teeling Small Batch Irish Whiskey** (87.5) n21 t23 f21.5 b22. Pleasant enough, and again showing high class grain. But a sharper liquorice/phenol note is out of kilter here and disrupts the natural flow of things, especially on the finish. 46%. ncf

The Teeling Whiskey Company Poitin (85) n21 t22 f21 b21. Intense and makes the eyes water to the required levels. Much cleaner, if not as sweet, though a lot safer than the illegal stuff I've tasted over there for the last 20-odd years! 61.5%

Tesco Special Reserve Irish Whiskey bott code L8061 (89.5) n21.5 t23.5 f22 b22.5. A cracker of a blend which allows the malts full scope to do their juicy bit. Possibly more malt than usual for a Cooley blend, but as they say: every little bit helps. 40%. Cooley.

Tullamore Dew (85) n22 t21.5 f20.5 b21. The days of the throat being savaged by this one appear to be over. Much more pot still character from nose to finish and the rough edges remain, attractively, just that. 40%. Campbell & Cochrane Group.

Tullamore Dew 10 Years Old (81.5) n21 t21.5 f19 b20. A bright start from this new kid on the Tullamore block. Soft fruit and harder pot still make some kind of complexity, but peters out at the death. 40%. Campbell & Cochrane Group.

Tullamore Dew 12 Years Old (84.5) n21.5 t21.5 f20 b21.5. Silky thanks to some excellent Midleton grain: there are mouthwatering qualities here that make the most of the soft spices and gentle fruit. An improved whiskey, if still somewhat meek and shy. 40%. Campbell & Cochrane Group.

Tullamore Dew Black 43 (85) n19 t22 f22.5 b21.5. "Black". Now there's an original name for a new whisky. Don't think it'll catch on, personally: after all, who has ever heard of a whisky being called "This or That" Black...?? But the whiskey might. Once you get past the usual Tullamore granite-like nose, here even more unyielding than usual, some rather engaging and complex (and especially spicy) things happen, though the caramel does its best to neuter them. 43%. William Grant & Sons.

Tullamore Dew Heritage (78) n20 t21 f18 b19. Tedious going with the caramel finish a real turn off. 40.0%. Campbell & Cochrane Group.

⟳ **Uisce Beatha Real Irish Whiskey** ex-Bourbon cask (81) n21 t20.5 f19.5 b20. The label blurb claims this is soft and subtle. That is, about as soft and subtle as if distilled from granite. Hard as nails with dominant grains; takes no prisoners at the death. 40%

Waitrose Irish Whiskey (86.5) n21.5 t22 f21.5 b21.5. Cooley's grain whiskey, about as good a grain made anywhere in the world, is in fine voice here. Pity some toffee stifles it slightly. 40%

Walker & Scott Irish Whiskey "Copper Pot Distilled" (83) n20 t22 f20 b21. A collectors' item. This charming, if slightly fudgy-finished blend was made by Cooley as the house Irish for one of Britain's finest breweries. Sadly, someone put "Copper Pot Distilled" on the label, which, as it's a blend, can hardly be the case. And even if it wasn't a blend, would still be confusing in terms of Irish whiskey, there not being any traditional Irish Pot Still, that mixture of malted and unmalted barley. So Sam's, being one of the most traditional brewers in Britain, with the next bottling changed the label by dropping all mention of pot still. Top marks, chaps! The next bottling can be seen below. 40%. Sam Smith's.

Walker & Scott Irish Whiskey (85) n21 t22 f21 b21. Oddly, sharper grain has helped give his some extra edge through the toffee. A very decent blend. 40%

The Wild Geese Classic Blend (80.5) n20 t21 f19.5 b19. Easy going, pretty neutral and conservative. If you are looking for zip, zest and charisma you've picked the wrong goose (see below). 40%. Cooley for Avalon.

The Wild Geese Limited Edition Fourth Centennial (93) n23 t23.5 f23 b23.5. A limited edition of unlimited beauty. One of the lightest, subtle, intriguing and quite simply disarming Irish whiskeys on the market. As a bird and whiskey lover, this is one goose that I shall be looking out for. 43%. Cooley for Avalon.

The Wild Geese Rare Irish (89.5) n22 t23 f22 b22.5. Just love this. The Cooley grain is working sublimely and dovetails with the malt in the same effortless way wild geese fly in perfect formation. A treat. 43%. Cooley for Avalon.

Writers Tears (93) n23.5 t24 f22 b23.5. Now that really was different. The first mix of pure Pot Still and single malt I have knowingly come across in a commercial bottling, but only because I wasn't aware of the make up of last year's Irishman Blend. The malt, like the Pot Still, is, I understand from proprietor Bernard Walsh, from Midleton, but the two styles mixed shows a remarkably similar character to when I carried out an identical experiment with pure pot still and Bushmills the best part of a decade ago. A success and hopefully not a one off. Which is more than I can say for the label, a whiskey collectors – sorry, collector's – item in its own right. There is a wonderfully Irish irony that a whiskey dedicated to Ireland's extraordinary literary heritage should be represented by a label, even a brand name, so punctually inept; it's almost brilliant. The reason for the Writers (sic) Tears, if from the spirits of James Joyce, Samuel Beckett, George Bernard Shaw, Oscar Wilde and perhaps even Maurice Walsh, author of The Quiet Man whose even quieter grandson, Barry, became a legendary blender at Irish Distillers, will be open to debate: we will never know whether they laughed or cried. As far as the actual whiskey is concerned, though, I am sure they, to a man, would have no hesitation but to pen the most luminous and positive critiques possible. 40%. Writers Tears Whiskey Co.

American Whiskey

It is now exactly ten years since a bourbon won the coveted title of Jim Murray's Whisky Bible World Whisky of the Year. And you might think that with Kentucky going a record-equalling three years without the top award the greatest days may be in the past. Wrong.

For the consistency of the great bourbon and ryes means that year on year it is found in the top three world whisky spots - sometimes occupying all positions. And it's probably for that reason on my tours around the globe I am asked by whisky shop owners and distributors if I know any good Kentucky and Tennessee brands, or contacts in their marketing departments, so they might bring a great bourbon onboard. Because at last, after years of being in the shadow of Scotch whisky, bourbon and rye are being rightly recognised for their greatness, diversity and sometimes enormity. Certainly, their consistency is the very thing which is winning over so many friends.

In some ways, though, it is this very consistency of quality which is holding back some distillers from loosening the stranglehold Buffalo Trace holds when it comes to top-ranking bourbon and rye. How apt is their brand name George T Stagg. For of the 26 Awards given by the Whisky Bible for either top bourbon or number one rye, Buffalo Trace has snaffled up a staggering 23 of them...! Indeed, it had been seven years since they last reliquinshed one of the top titles, when Heaven Hill in 2006 unleashed a 23-year-old rye from seemingly beyond the grave. I can still remember and describe its nose and taste to this day, so extraordinary was it! Well, Heaven Hill have done it again. They have ended the Sazerac dominance with their Pikesville rye which not only landed them the best rye prize, but also American Whisky of the Year. And came within touching distance of being crowned World Whisky of the Year, having to settle for runner-up instead. And all this with a rye made at an entirely different distillery to the one where they made their legendary Rittenhouse 21- and 23-year-olds.

However, if we look at the Whisky Bible's main American award winners by listing below the Bourbon of the Year, the Rye and micro-distillery (when awarded), you can see just how ruthlessly dominant and breathtakingly consistant Buffalo Trace has been.

2004: George T Stagg - Sazerac 18 - McCarthy's Oregon Single Malt
2005: George T Stagg - Sazerac 18 - McCarthy's Oregon Single Malt
2006: George T Stagg - Sazerac 18 - McCarthy's Oregon Single Malt
2007: Buffalo Trace Experimental - Rittenhouse 21 - McCarthy's OSM
2008: George T Stagg - Old Potrero Hotaling's - Old Potrero Hotaling's
2009: George T Stagg - Rittenhouse 23 - Stranahan's Colorodo Single Malt
2010: George T Stagg - Sazerac 18 - N/A
2011: William Larue Weller - Thomas Handy Sazerac - N/A
2012: George T Stagg - Thomas Handy Sazerac - N/A
2013: William Larue Weller - Thomas Handy Sazerac - Balcones Brimstone
2014: William Larue Weller - Thomas Handy Sazerac -Cowboy Texas Bourbon
2015: William Larue Weller - Sazerac 18 - Arkansas Single Barrel Bourbon
2016: William Larue Weller - Pikesville - Triple Eight Notch

Yet for someone who has been deeply involved in Kentucky whiskey for the best part of 25 years, and during that time probably its loudest international advocate, it is hard to see how two other truly World Class distilleries, Jim Beam and Four Roses, have failed somehow to burst the Buffalo Trace bubble. I have watched as the quality of the whiskey from these distilleries has improved year on year, especially Four Roses who, for two decades, blossomed under the wise council, insight, energy, sure touch and integrety of Jim Rutledge. Both distilleries have battered at BT's unyielding walls and it is hard to imagine that a hairline crack isn't forming somewhere: but I haven't seen it yet. That said, Buffalo Trace have a little trick up their sleeve with their sister Tom Moore distillery in Bardstown showing just what truly complex whiskeys can be produced there, given time to develop in the barrel, something the previous owners refused point blank to do.

On the subject of Jim Rutledge, on 1st September 2015, just as we were editing this latest edition of the Whisky Bible, Jim finally called it a day at Four Roses. It so happened that I was at the distillery on the very day he sat in the manager's chair for the first time, the seat still warm from Ova Haney's dozen or so years of tenure. And from day one Jim set about ending an era where the Lawrenceburg plant was content in producing a light, delicately structured and quite safe bourbon that was increasingly finding its way into foreign rather than home markets. Slowly, but surely, the new manager changed that. To the extent that by the end of his two-decade tenure Four Roses had risen from being a pretty, but rather insignificant distillery into a pretty significant distillery even among the world's most elite. He did this by sticking abidingly to the century-old rules which governed exactly what bourbon whiskey was. He was not interested in frills or marketing gimmicks: the only thing he believed that counted was the excellence of the bourbon he bottled. He and I share an identical and unyielding belief that bourbon is defined by quality and tradition which takes a lot more skill to perfect than playing around with different cask finishes. Bourbon is unique and great for a time-honoured reason. Jim Rutledge, to whom this edition of the Whisky Bible is dedicated, invested a life and career proving that to be manifestly true.

Bardstown
   Heaven Hill
   Tom Moore
Frankfort
   Buffalo Trace

Woodford Reserve
Louisville
   Early Times
   Bernheim
   Stitzel Weller

Bourbon Distilleries

Bourbon confuses people. Often they don't even realise it is a whiskey, a situation not helped by leading British pub chains, such as Wetherspoon, whose bar menus list "whiskey" and "bourbon" in separate sections. And if I see the liqueur Southern Comfort listed as a bourbon one more time I may not be responsible for my actions.

Bourbon is a whiskey. It is made from grain and matured in oak, so really it can't be much else. To be legally called bourbon it must have been made with a minimum of 51% corn and matured in virgin oak casks for at least two years. Oh, and no colouring can be added other than that which comes naturally from the barrel.

Where it does differ, from, say Scotch, is that the straight whiskey from the distillery may be called by something other than that distillery name. Indeed, the distillery may change its name which has happened to two this year already and two others in the last three or four. So, to make things easy and reference as quick as possible, I shall list the Kentucky-based distilleries first and then their products in alphabetical order along with their owners and operational status.

BUFFALO TRACE Leestown, Frankfort. Sazerac. Operating.

BROWN-FORMAN Shively, Louisville. Brown-Forman. Operating.

FOUR ROSES Lawrenceburg. Kirin. Operating

HEAVEN HILL BERNHEIM DISTILLERY Louisville. Heaven Hill. Operating.

JIM BEAM Boston and Clermont. Fortune Brands. Operating.

MAKER'S MARK Loretto. Fortune Brands. Operating.

TOM MOORE Bardstown. Sazerac. Operating.

WILD TURKEY Lawrenceburg. Campari Group. Operating.

WOODFORD RESERVE Near Millville. Brown-Forman. Operating.

Bourbon

◈ **1792 Sweet Wheat Kentucky Straight Bourbon** db (94.5) n23.5 rich honeycomb threatened by spice: a brilliant, almost dizzying interweaving of grain and oak; t24 mmmm!!! That delivery! Just too good! The corn oils are present enough to ensure a soft landing, but sufficiently light to allow the small grains full scope (something peculiar to these stills, whoever operates them); the spices ramp up slowly but not insignificantly; f23 in fifth gear here, cruising from honeyville to downtown cocoa; excellent slow dry build, arrested by the lingering manuka; b24 Barton had long been one of the wasted distilleries of the world, its product once bottled and sold way before its intricate, busy bourbon was able to sing to its fullest potential. Under the new management of Sazerac, we are now consistently seeing the greatness from this distillery that for decades was found only in its 6-year-old. This is a wheated, honeyed stunner. 45.6% (91.2 proof)

Ancient Ancient Age 10 Star (94.5) n23 t24 f23.5 b24. A bourbon which has slipped effortlessly through the gears over the last decade. It is now cruising and offers so many nuggets of pure joy this is now a must have for the serious bourbon devotee. Now a truly great bourbon which positively revels in its newfound complexity: a new 10 Star is born... 45%

Ancient Age Bonded (92) n23 t24 f23 b23. Unmistakably Buffalo Trace... with balls. 50%

Ancient Ancient Age 10 Years Old (96) n23.5 t24 f24 b24.5. This whiskey is like shifting sands: same score as last time out, but the shape is quite different again. Somehow underlines the genius of the distillery that a world class whiskey can reach the same point of greatness, but by taking two different routes...However, in this case the bourbon actually finds something a little extra to move it on to a point very few whiskeys very rarely reach... 43%

Big Bottom Straight Bourbon 91 (95) n23 tight, in that small grain dominates over the corn, while making the most of its oils, and the oak is chunky, salty and chocolaty; t24 again, a big salty tang to this, but this then serves to bring out the enormity of the grains, in which the corn has fought back pole position; the middle is full of honey, liquorice and burgeoning spices; f24 and now the small grains are back behind the wheel for a tantalisingly complex finale; b24 stupendous bourbon. 45.5% (91 proof) ncf.

Big Bottom Straight Bourbon 111 (85.5) n21.5 t21.5 t20.5 f22.5 b21. An aggressive bourbon and that has nothing to do with the strength. The delivery is tart and lopsided. The sharpness recedes towards the middle and, finally, the lights shine as the praline and mocha enter the fray on the spicy finish. 55.5% (111 proof) ncf.

◈ **Blade & Bow** batch SW-B1 (84) n21.5 t21.5 f20 b21. A simple, if at times massively sweet, offering which minimises on complexity. 45.5%

◈ **Blade & Bow DeLuxe** batch WLCFSS-2 (88.5) n22.5 major liquorice contribution; t22.5 manuka honey and molasses counter the big toasty notes; f21 as the sugars fade, the toast burns...; b22.5 a steady ship which, initially, is heavy on the honey. 46%

Blanton's (92) n21.5 t24 f23 b23.5. If it were not for the sluggish nose this would be a Whisky Bible Liquid Gold award winner for sure. On the palate it shows just why little can touch Buffalo Trace for quality at the moment... 40%

Blanton's Gold Original Single Barrel (96.5) n24 t24.5 f24 b24. It is improbable that a whiskey this enormous and with so many star turns can glide so effortlessly over the palate. One of the best Blanton's in years, this is true Gold standard... 46.5% (93 Proof)

Blanton's Takara (91.5) n24.5 t23 f22 b22. Not quite how many people might envisage a bourbon: certainly not butch enough to keep the wild west gunslingers happy. No this is a bourbon which searches for your feminine side. And being so light, leaves itself open for any off-key bitter notes which might just happen along the way. 49% (98 proof)

Blanton's Uncut/Unfiltered (96.5) n25 t24 f23.5 b24. Uncut. Unfiltered. Unbelievable. 65.9%

◈ **Booker's 7 Years 2 Months 28 Days** batch no. 2015-03 db (92.5) n23 big in intensity by normal standards: modest by Booker's. Less rigid tannin than normal – more emphasis on softer liquorice and friendly rye; t23.5 makes amends on delivery where normal service is resumed. All kinds of manuka honey and maple syrup is at play. The rye range is a little muted as fudge and hickory storm the mid-ground; f22.5 distinctly light with toffee notes intertwangled with deft liquorice; b23.5 one very gentle giant. 63.6% (1272 Proof)

◈ **Booker's 7 Years 5 Months** batch no. C2014-05 db (95) n24 the essence of Jim Beam: almost clotted rye as sweet custard powder radiates. Strangely gentle outwardly, but is wilfully withholding a massive punch; t24 ker-powww!! And there it is! Right on delivery, the rye notes thud relentlessly against the taste buds as corn oil clings to the palate, allowing spices to sizzle contentedly. Intense molasses and hickory deal firmly with the deep oak which has just made its play while all the time there is a honeyed beat; f23 oaky splinters and mocha fatten out the thinning, corn-rich, finale; b24 not for the simpering or squeamish. There's an oaky ambush to deal with. And if you ain't man (or woman) enough, then best to mosey on over to the sarsaparilla counter... 63.95%

✧ **Booker's Big Man, Small Batch 7 Years 2 Months 16 Days** batch no. 2015-01 db **(89.5)** n22 presumably from the buzzard's roost: the amount of tannin floating around the nose is almost scary for its age...; **t23** sugars appear early. But they are pretty burnt and the toasty notes continue to arrive in droves. Liquorice concentrate and hickory reminds you this has been distilled in Kentucky, not cooked by King Alfred; **f22** the cindered sugars and intense cocoa powder are enough to make your eyes water...; **b22.5** the driest Booker's I've happened across for a good while: probably ever. Matured for seven years in a warehouse located somewhere near the centre of the sun, one assumes... 64.35% (128.7 Proof)

Bowman Brother's Virginia Straight Bourbon (90) n21 t23 f23 b23. Quietly confident and complex: a bit of a gem waiting to be discovered. 45% (90 proof)

Buffalo Trace (92.5) n23 t23 f23.5 b23. Easily one of the lightest BTs I have tasted in a very long while. The rye has not just taken a back seat, but has fallen off the bus. 45%

Buffalo Trace Single Oak Project Barrel #132 (r1yKA1 see key below) db **(95)** n24 t23.5 f23.5 b24. This sample struck me for possessing, among the first batch of bottlings, the classic Buffalo Trace personality. Afterwards they revealed that it was of a profile which perhaps most closely matches their standard 8-year-old BT. Therefore it is this one I shall use as the tasting template. 45% (90 Proof)

Key to Buffalo Trace Single Oak Project Codes

Mash bill type: r = rye; w = wheat
Tree grain: 1 = course; 2 = average; 3 = tight
Tree cut: x = top half; y = bottom half
Warehouse type: K = rick; L = concrete

Entry strength: A = 125; B = 105
Seasoning: 1 = 6 Months; 2 = 12 Months
Char: All #4 except * = #3

Buffalo Trace Single Oak Project Barrel #1 (r3xKA1*) db **(90.5)** n22 t23 f23 b22.5. Soft corn aroma, buttery, big sugars building, silky texture, long. 45% (90 Proof)

Buffalo Trace Single Oak Project Barrel #2 (r3yKA1*) db **(91.5)** n23 t23 f22.5 b23. Bright rye on nose and delivery. Juicy red liquorice and soft corn oil to chew on... 45%

Buffalo Trace Single Oak Project Barrel #3 (r2xKA1) db **(90.5)** n22.5 t23 f22.5 b22.5. Nutty, dry aroma; apple fruitiness and brown sugars. 45% (90 Proof)

Buffalo Trace Single Oak Project Barrel #4 (r2yKA1) db **(92)** n23 t23 f23 b23. Exceptionally crisp; sharp rye, honeycomb, big liquorice. 45% (90 Proof)

Buffalo Trace Single Oak Project Barrel #5 (r2xLA1*) db **(89)** n23 t22.5 f21.5 b22. Dullish after a rye-intense and busy nose. Early muscovado followed by vanilla and spice. 45%

Buffalo Trace Single Oak Project Barrel #6 (r3yLA1*) db **(90)** n22.5 t22 f23 b22.5. Toast with salted butter and maple syrup. Prickly, mildly aggressive spice throughout. 45%

✧ **Buffalo Trace Single Oak Project Barrel #7** (r3xLA1) db **(90.5)** n23 t22.5 f22.5 b22.5. Prominent rye on nose and delivery; tannin rich, toasty with big liquorice fade. 45%

Buffalo Trace Single Oak Project Barrel #8 (r3yLA1) db **(92.5)** n23 t23 f23.5 b23. Crisp rye aroma. Fruity, firm, salivating. Spiced toffee and muscovado; toasty. 45% (90 Proof)

Buffalo Trace Single Oak Project Barrel #9 (r3xKA2*) db **(90)** n22 t22.5 f23 b22.5. Marmalade on singed toast. Soft oils: slow release of natural caramels and mocha. 45%

Buffalo Trace Single Oak Project Barrel #10 (r3yKA2*) db **(93)** n23.5 t23.5 f22.5 b23.5. Rich, delicate rye. Complex, busy body; rye oils; tannins; slow sugar build. Bitters. 45%

Buffalo Trace Single Oak Project Barrel #11 (r3xKA2) db **(94.5)** n23 t24 f23.5 b24. Pronounced accent on rye, especially on delivery. Oak nose upfront; good muscovado fade. 45%.

Buffalo Trace Single Oak Project Barrel #12 (r3yKA2) db **(92)** n24 t23 f22.5 b22.5. The floral, supremely balanced nose isn't matched on the palate in weight or complexity. 45%

Buffalo Trace Single Oak Project Barrel #13 (r3xLA2*) db **(89.5)** n22 t23 f22 b22.5. Soft, yielding tactile. Early juicy, rye stance, slow build of duller light vanilla. Late spice. 45%

Buffalo Trace Single Oak Project Barrel #14 (r3yLA2*) db **(95)** n24 t24 f23 b24. Chocolate rye nose and body; silky texture; brown sugar and vanilla; rye-rich sweet finish. 45%

Buffalo Trace Single Oak Project Barrel #15 (r3xLA2) db **(90.5)** n22.5 t23 f22 b23. Mouth feel concentrates on sugars and spices, which grow well. Fruity on nose and finish. 45%.

Buffalo Trace Single Oak Project Barrel #16 (r3yLA2) db **(91.5)** n22.5 t23.5 f22.5 b23. Explosive delivery: big spices, juicy, firm rye. Silky middle butterscotch & ulmo honey finish. 45%.

Buffalo Trace Single Oak Project Barrel #17 (r3xKB1*) db **(88.5)** n21.5 t22.5 f22.5 b22. Liquorice nose; oily body sweetens; big vanilla, caramel; dull spice. 45% (90 Proof)

Buffalo Trace Single Oak Project Barrel #18 (r3yKB1*) db **(92.5)** n23 t23 f23.5 b23. Full bodied from nose to finish. Cocoa mingles with rye and rich corn oil. Deep, intense, even. 45%

Buffalo Trace Single Oak Project Barrel #19 (r3xKB1) db **(93)** n23 t23.5 f23 b23.5. Solid, crisp rye hallmark on nose, delivery. Sugars firm and fractured. Precise whiskey. Salivating. 45%.

✧ **Buffalo Trace Single Oak Project Barrel #20** (r3yKB1) db **(95)** n23.5 t24 t23 b23.5. Buttery nose; profound rye kick on delivery, ulmo honey body; complex toasty fade. 45%

◈ **Buffalo Trace Single Oak Project Barrel #21** (r3xLB1*) db **(92)** n23 t23 f23 b23. Estery, clipped rye nose; salivating delivery, dark sugars, moderate spice. *45%*

◈ **Buffalo Trace Single Oak Project Barrel #22** (r3yLB1*) db **(91)** n22 t23.5 f22.5 b23. Corn/rye mix nose with manuka honey; silky corn oil throughout. Sweet, soft. *45%*.

Buffalo Trace Single Oak Project Barrel #23 (r3xLB1) db **(89)** n21 t22.5 f22.5 b23. Massive spices throughout; juicy, rye-dominated middle. Soft corn oil and rounded. *45%*.

Buffalo Trace Single Oak Project Barrel #24 (r3xLB1) db **(90)** n22 t23 f22.5 b22.5. Big liquorice nose and delivery; toffee raisin; big corn oil; medium spice; even ulmo honey. *45%*

Buffalo Trace Single Oak Project Barrel #25 (r3xKB2*) db **(90.5)** n22.5 t23 f22.5 b22.5. Much more accent on the rye and a slow revealing of rich caramels and Demerara. *45%*

Buffalo Trace Single Oak Project Barrel #26 (r3yKB2*) db **(89.5)** n22 t23.5 f22 b22. A sugary volley follows a shy nose. Quietens quickly; small grains add complexity. *45%*

Buffalo Trace Single Oak Project Barrel #27 (r3xKB2) db **(95.5)** n23 t24 f24.5 b24. Bold timber on nose and delivery; hickory and liquorice evident; a big spiced honey finale. *45%*

Buffalo Trace Single Oak Project Barrel #28 (r3yKB2) db **(94.5)** n23 t24 f23.5 b24. Sublime balance between sugars and grains on body. Controlled spice; layered cocoa. *45%*

Buffalo Trace Single Oak Project Barrel #29 (r3xLB2*) db **(91)** n23 t22.5 f23 b22.5. Crisp rye nose; more precise grain. Excellent spices. *45% (90 Proof)*

Buffalo Trace Single Oak Project Barrel #30 (r3yLB2*) db **(95.5)** n23.5 t24 f24 b24. One of the most delicate yet: crisp rye and sugars, minty forthright oak. Clean yet deep. *45%*

Buffalo Trace Single Oak Project Barrel #31 (r3xLB2) db **(87.5)** n22 t22 f21.5 b22. Dull, rumbling and herbal; oily caramel and sugars. Soft. *45% (90 Proof)*

Buffalo Trace Single Oak Project Barrel #32 (r3yLB2) db **(90.5)** n23.5 t23 f21.5 b22.5. Soft corn oils dominate. Buttery, molten muscovado. Late hickory. Bitterish finish. *45%*

Buffalo Trace Single Oak Project Barrel #33 (w3xKA1*) db **(94.5)** n24 t23.5 f23 b24. Huge, busy baking spiced cake; muscovado sugar delivery; remains sweet, silky and spicy; *45%*

Buffalo Trace Single Oak Project Barrel #34 (w3yKA1*) db **(90)** n21.5 t23.5 f22.5 b22.5. Lazy nose but big succulent spiced molasses on delivery, with a mint cocoa finale. *45%*

Buffalo Trace Single Oak Project Barrel #35 (w3xKA1) db **(89.5)** n22 t22 f23 b22.5. Soft mint, yeasty; soft toffee delivery, builds in spice. *45% (90 Proof)*

Buffalo Trace Single Oak Project Barrel #36 (w3yKA1) db **(91.5)** n23 t23 f22.5 b23. Vague rum and toffee; bold, salivating, slow spice. *45% (90 Proof)*

Buffalo Trace Single Oak Project Barrel #37 (w3xLA1*) db **(90)** n21 t23 f22 b22. Typical big spice beast. Complex, doughy middle with accent on butterscotch and citrus. *45% (90 Proof)*

Buffalo Trace Single Oak Project Barrel #38 (w3yLA1*) db **(87.5)** n22 t23.5 f20.5 b21.5. Fizzy, busy nose matched by massive spice attack on delivery. Bitter, thin finish. *45% (90 Proof)*

◈ **Buffalo Trace Single Oak Project Barrel #39** (w3xLA1) db **(87)** n21.5 t22 f21.5 b22. Oak dominated: a degree of bitterness runs from nose to finish. Spices build slowly. *45%*

Buffalo Trace Single Oak Project Barrel #40 (w3xLA1) db **(93)** n23 t23 f23.5 b23.5. Soft, spiced cake, big citrus; silky, oily, bananas and golden syrup; late spice, balancing bitters. *45%*

Buffalo Trace Single Oak Project Barrel #41 (w3xKA2*) db **(92.5)** n22 t23 f23.5 b24. Less spice than expected. Docile start, builds in intensity. Buttery, big sugars. Balanced. *45%*

Buffalo Trace Single Oak Project Barrel #42 (w3yKA2*) db **(85.5)** n22 t21.5 f21 b21. Tight nose opens slowly; sultana pudding with maple syrup. Sweet, late bitterness. *45%*

Buffalo Trace Single Oak Project Barrel #43 (w3xKA2) db **(89)** n22 t23 f22 b22. Dates & plum nose; succulent fruit with broad maple syrup & molasses flourish. Big late spice. *45%*.

Buffalo Trace Single Oak Project Barrel #44 (w3yKA2) db **(89)** n23 t23 f21 b22. Spice rack nose; superb warm liquorice eruption on palate but dull finale. *45%*

Buffalo Trace Single Oak Project Barrel #45 (w3xLA2*) db **(87)** n23 t22 f21 b21. Ginger and allspice nose; body thick corn oil and toffee. Short finish. *45%*.

Buffalo Trace Single Oak Project Barrel #46 (w3yLA2*) db **(88)** n21.5 t22 f22.5 b22 Doughy aroma. Big corn oils and sugars. Late spice growth. Big vanilla. Quietly complex. *45%*

Buffalo Trace Single Oak Project Barrel #47 (w3xLA2) db **(88.5)** n22.5 t22 f22 b22. Floral, waxy aroma; sugars dominate on palate with vanilla-butterscotch-ulmo theme. *45%*.

Buffalo Trace Single Oak Project Barrel #48 (w3yLA2) db **(90.5)** n22 t23 f22.5 b23. Sound, rounded from first to last. Greater accent on sugar intensity and vanilla inclusion. *45%*.

Buffalo Trace Single Oak Project Barrel #49 (w3xKB1*) db **(93)** n24 t23 f23 b23. Chocolate spice, apples, oaky aroma; treacle pudding, soft oils; banana and custard; bitters. *45%*

Buffalo Trace Single Oak Project Barrel #50 (w3yKB1*) db **(88)** n21.5 t23 f21.5 b22. Flat nose. Muscovado delivery. Slow spices. Late liquorice. Even. Limited depth. *45% (90 Proof)*

Buffalo Trace Single Oak Project Barrel #51 (w3xKB1) db **(89.5)** n23 t23 f21.5 b22. Firm and well spiced from start. Oils play bigger role as sugar develops. *45%*.

◈ **Buffalo Trace Single Oak Project Barrel #52** (w3yKB1) db **(87.5)** n21.5 t22 f22 b22. Yeasty nose; blend of molasses and toffee on delivery then slow spice increase. *45%*

⟡ **Buffalo Trace Single Oak Project Barrel #53** (w3xLB1*) db **(91)** n22 t23 f23 b23. Full bodied on nose and palate. Toasty, big liquorice and molasses. Even and elegant. 45%

⟡ **Buffalo Trace Single Oak Project Barrel #54** (w3yLB1*) db **(89)** n22 t23 f22.5 b22.5. Crisp sugars and coconut nose; big molassed delivery, nutty and gentle oil. Late vanilla. 45%

Buffalo Trace Single Oak Project Barrel #55 (w3xLB1) db **(89)** n22 t22 f23 b22. Mocha nose with sturdy tannin and vanilla early on delivery. Red liquorice and vanilla late on. 45%.

Buffalo Trace Single Oak Project Barrel #56 (w3yLB1) db **(91)** n24 t22.5 f22 b22.5. Chocolate vanilla and tannins; soft, slow build up of spice, oily; bitters. 45% (90 Proof)

Buffalo Trace Single Oak Project Barrel #57 (w3xKB2*) db **(94)** n23 t23.5 f23.5 b24. Immediate spice kick on nose and delivery. Caramels and marmalade. Busy, balanced. 45%

Buffalo Trace Single Oak Project Barrel #58 (w3yKB2*) db **(90.5)** n22.5 t23 f22.5 b22.5. Liquorice and Fisherman's Friend nose; molassed middle and big spice finish. 45%

Buffalo Trace Single Oak Project Barrel #59 (w3xKB2) db **(92)** n22 t23.5 f23 b23.5. Lighter Fisherman's Friend; roasted fudge; busy small grains attack. Mega complex. 45%

Buffalo Trace Single Oak Project Barrel #60 (w3yKB2) db **(87.5)** n22.5 t22.5 f21 b21.5. Aggression to spice nose; tame delivery and body. Soft corn oil and muscovado. 46%

Buffalo Trace Single Oak Project Barrel #61 (w3xLB2*) db **(94.5)** n24 t23 f23.5 b24. Classic spiced wheat; Demerara sugars and spices abound. Big. 45% (90 Proof)

Buffalo Trace Single Oak Project Barrel #62 (w3yLB2*) db **(88)** n22 t22.5 f21.5 b22. Caramel is leading theme; soft, big wheated spice. Oily. 45% (90 Proof)

Buffalo Trace Single Oak Project Barrel #63 (w3xLB2) db **(95.5)** n24 t22.5 f24 b24.5. Subtle dates, spice, cocoa; gentle, oily, perfect spice build. Ultra complex. 45% (90 Proof)

Buffalo Trace Single Oak Project Barrel #64 (w3yLB2) db **(91)** n22.5 t23.5 f22.5 b23. Citrus nose. Big oak and spice delivery; treacle tart and liquorice. Softens into caramel. 45%

Buffalo Trace Single Oak Project Barrel #65 (r2xKA1) db **(91)** n23.5 t22 f23 b22.5. Small grain nose; crunchy muscovado, corn oil; liquorice, vanilla; late spice. Complex. 45%

Buffalo Trace Single Oak Project Barrel #66 (r2yKA1*) db **(88.5)** n22.5 t22.5 f21.5 b22. Dry tannin dominates on nose and palate; good spice kick and treacle. Short finish. 45%

Buffalo Trace Single Oak Project Barrel #67 (r2xKA1) db **(89.5)** n22 t23 f22 b22.5. Blandish nose; tart, tight, sharp, some toffee raisin. 45% (90 Proof)

Buffalo Trace Single Oak Project Barrel #68 (r2yKA1) db **(92)** n22.5 t23 f23.5 b23. Rye depth; deeper, warmer spices, liquorice and light molasses. 45% (90 Proof)

Buffalo Trace Single Oak Project Barrel #69 (r2xLA1*) db **(94.5)** n23 t24 f23.5 b24. Crisp, sharp rye on nose and delivery. Jagged muscovado and spice. Goes down a treat... 45%

Buffalo Trace Single Oak Project Barrel #70 (r2yLA1*) db **(91.5)** n22.5 t23 f23 b23. Yielding caramel and vanilla. Rye and hot spice breaks up the sleepy theme. 45% (90 Proof)

⟡ **Buffalo Trace Single Oak Project Barrel #71** (r2xLA1) db **(92)** n22.5 t23 f23.5 b23. Busy, small grain and citrus nose; rye backbone then darker sugars and tannin. 45%

Buffalo Trace Single Oak Project Barrel #72 (r2yLA1) db **(89)** n22.5 t23 f21.5 b22. Floral nose; juicy, tangy, citrus. Liquorice, sugary vanilla. Bitter marmalade finish. 45%

Buffalo Trace Single Oak Project Barrel #73 (r2xKA2*) db **(87.5)** n21.5 t22 f22 b22. Tight, unyielding nose. Initially crisp rye then thick vanilla and baked apple blanket. 45%

Buffalo Trace Single Oak Project Barrel #74 (r2yKA2*) db **(88)** n22 t22 f22 b22. Corny nose; more corn oil early on; syrup, huge rye sure on finish; bitters slightly. 45% (90 Proof)

Buffalo Trace Single Oak Project Barrel #75 (r2xKA2) db **(91.5)** n23 t22.5 f23 b23. Clean with accent firmly on grain throughout. Spiced minty mocha middle and fade. 45%

Buffalo Trace Single Oak Project Barrel #76 (r2yKA2) db **(89)** n22.5 t22.5 f22 b22. Bristling rye on nose and delivery; fruity edge then dullish spiced fudge and mocha. 45%

Buffalo Trace Single Oak Project Barrel #77 (r2xLA2*) db **(88)** n22 t23 f21 b22. Busy, bitty nose; sugary blast on delivery; spice follow through then vanilla overload. 45%.

Buffalo Trace Single Oak Project Barrel #78 (r2yLA2*) db **(89)** n22.5 t22 f22.5 b22.5. Small grain busy nose; light spice to oils; light rye, late sugars; chewy caramels. 45% (90 Proof)

Buffalo Trace Single Oak Project Barrel #79 (r2xLA2) db **(93)** n23 t23.5 f23 b23.5. Juicy crisp sugars. Toasty with slow liquorice burn. Creamed spiced hickory fade. Complex. 45%.

Buffalo Trace Single Oak Project Barrel #80 (r2yLA2) db **(91.5)** n23 t22.5 f23 b23. Broad oily strokes on nose, delivery. Simple vanilla tannins and ulmo honey. 45%.

Buffalo Trace Single Oak Project Barrel #81 (r2yKB1*) db **(94)** n23 t23 f24 b24. Candy shop fruitiness; delicate oils and flavour development; big yet subdued brown sugars. 45%

Buffalo Trace Single Oak Project Barrel #82 (r2yKB1*) db **(91.5)** n22.5 t23.5 f22.5 b23. Liquoice, manuka honey; lurid rye bite and lychee fruitiness; mocha and Demerara. 45%

Buffalo Trace Single Oak Project Barrel #83 (r2xKB1) db **(92)** n22.5 t23 f23.5 b23. Sharp, angular grain, rye dominant. Softer salty praline fade. 45%.

⟡ **Buffalo Trace Single Oak Project Barrel #84** (r2yKB1) db **(94)** n23.5 t24 f23 b23.5. Hefty nose mixing tannin, rye and hickory. Huge sugar and corn oil theme. 45%.

◇◇◇ **Buffalo Trace Single Oak Project Barrel #85** (r2xLB1*) db **(88.5)** n21.5 t22.5 f22 b22.5. Shy nose of soft vanilla; firm body with more vanilla and butterscotch; low level sugar. *45%*

◇◇◇ **Buffalo Trace Single Oak Project Barrel #86** (r2yLB1*) db **(90)** n22.5 t22 f23 b22.5. Salty, sweaty nose; sharp delivery with rye, red liquorice dominant; spiced mocha finish. *45%*

Buffalo Trace Single Oak Project Barrel #87 (r2xLB1) db **(93.5)** n22.5 t23.5 f23.5 b24. Citrus-led nose; slow, corn oil start then explosive grain; rye, liquorice & honey to the fore. *45%*

Buffalo Trace Single Oak Project Barrel #88 (r2yLB1) db **(89)** n23.5 t22 f21.5 b22. Hickory, rye nose; liquorice delivery big caramel surge; bitters on finish. *45% (90 Proof)*

Buffalo Trace Single Oak Project Barrel #89 (r2xKB2*) db **(89.5)** n22 t22.5 f22 b22.5. Rye radiates on nose and delivery. Big spice surge to the middle. Late mocha, liquorice. *45%*

Buffalo Trace Single Oak Project Barrel #90 (r2yKB2*) db **(94)** n23.5 t24 f23 b23.5. Big tannin, cocoa and caramel throughout. Major peppery spice. Complex. *45% (90 Proof)*

Buffalo Trace Single Oak Project Barrel #91 (r2xKB2) db **(86.5)** n21.5 t22 f21.5 b21.5. Half-cooked: dull caramel throughout. Short spice peak. Sweet, oily, lacking complexity. *45%*

Buffalo Trace Single Oak Project Barrel #92 (r2yKB2) db **(91)** n22 t23 f23 b23. Silky texture. Big corn oil but intense tannin thinned by beech honey. Hickory and maple syrup. *45%*

Buffalo Trace Single Oak Project Barrel #93 (r2xLB2*) db **(89)** n22.5 t22 f22 b22.5. Soft rye and sugars; juicy grain, tangy citrus, muscovado. *45% (90 Proof)*

Buffalo Trace Single Oak Project Barrel #94 (r2yLB2*) db **(92.5)** n22.5 t24 f23 b23. Rich, hefty. Slightly salty, crisp rye. Light caramel, hint of Guyanese rum. Delicate spice. *45%*

Buffalo Trace Single Oak Project Barrel #95 (r2xLB2) db **(94)** n23 t23.5 f23.5 b24. Citrus, banana; soft vanilla, profound rye sharpness, spices. Big. *45% (90 Proof)*

Buffalo Trace Single Oak Project Barrel #96 (r2yLB2) db **(89)** n22 t23.5 f21.5 b22. Bright, grainy delivery in contrast to oily nose and finish. Heavy, dry molasses at the death. *45%*

Buffalo Trace Single Oak Project Barrel #97 (w2xKA1*) db **(87)** n22.5 t22 f21.5 b21.5. Toffee apple nose; heavy corn oil, light muscovado sugar, bitters out; *45% (90 Proof)*

Buffalo Trace Single Oak Project Barrel #98 (w2yKA1*) db **(93)** n23 t23.5 f23 b23.5. Peppers on at full blast on nose and delivery; big oily liquorice and treacle counter. *45%*

◇◇◇ **Buffalo Trace Single Oak Project Barrel #99** (w2xKA1) db **(86.5)** n22 t22 f21 b21.5. Malty, vanilla; thin maple syrup, caramel. Dull. *45% (90 Proof)*

Buffalo Trace Single Oak Project Barrel #100 (w2yKA1) db **(94)** n23 t23.5 f23.5 b24. Busy, green, fresh; big juicy, vanilla, muscovado, spices. *45% (90 Proof)*

Buffalo Trace Single Oak Project Barrel #101 (w2xLA1) db **(96)** n23.5 t24 f23.5 b25. Unerring chocolate and mint aided by even muscovado, vanilla and spice. Hugely complex. *45%*

Buffalo Trace Single Oak Project Barrel #102 (w2yLA1*) db **(88.5)** n22 t22 f22.5 b22. Insane tannin on nose; overcooked caramel. Massive sugar-spice mix. *45% (90 Proof)*

◇◇◇ **Buffalo Trace Single Oak Project Barrel #103** (w2xLA1) db **(89)** n22.5 t22 f22 b22.5. Early spice on nose; prominent brown sugars on deliver; corn oil follow through. *45%*

Buffalo Trace Single Oak Project Barrel #104 (w2xLA1) db **(91)** n23 t23 f22.5 b22.5. Apple, cinnamon; light spice; corn oil; vanilla and ulmo honey; spices, bitters out. *45%*

Buffalo Trace Single Oak Project Barrel #105 (w2xKA2*) db **(89)** n22.5 t22 f22.5 b22. Spiced, lively nose; hot cross buns; oils and sugars build slowly; spices intensify at end. *45%*

Buffalo Trace Single Oak Project Barrel #106 (w2yKA2*) db **(92.5)** n24 t23 f23 b23.5. Mega complex nose: busy sugars and spices; silky texture; nougat, caramel. *45%*

Buffalo Trace Single Oak Project Barrel #107 (w2xKA2) db **(93.5)** n23.5 t23 f23 b24. Bold, rich nose; pepper bite; thick body: maple syrup, molasses, cocoa. Classic wheat recipe. *45%*

Buffalo Trace Single Oak Project Barrel #108 (w2yKA2) db **(94)** n22.5 t24 f23.5 b24. Soft, delicate. Ulmo honey leads the sugars; corn oil but complex liquorice and lavender. *45%*

Buffalo Trace Single Oak Project Barrel #109 (w2xLA2*) db **(87.5)** n21.5 t23.5 f21 b21.5. Dull nose and finish. Delivery lush, souped-up spiced caramel-toffee fudge. *45%*

Buffalo Trace Single Oak Project Barrel #110 (w2yLA2*) db **(90)** n22 t22.5 f22.5 b23. Intense caramel; liquorice and toffee middle, citrus and salt; caramel finish. *45% (90 Proof)*

Buffalo Trace Single Oak Project Barrel #111 (w2xLA2) db **(89)** n22.5 t22.5 f22 b22. Intriguing sugar operatic. Vary from castor to muscovado. Countering spices make it work. *45%*

Buffalo Trace Single Oak Project Barrel #112 (w2yLA2) db **(90)** n21.5 t23 f22.5 b23. Caramel fudge lead. Usual whited spice before heavier, liquorice development. *45%.*

Buffalo Trace Single Oak Project Barrel #113 (w2xKB1*) db **(88)** n22.5 t22 f22 b21.5. Big vanilla nose; minor spice, oily, buttery vanilla. Simple. *45% (90 Proof)*

Buffalo Trace Single Oak Project Barrel #114 (w2yKB1*) db **(90)** n22 t23 f22 b23. Elements of citrus. Oily corn. Controlled spice. Earthy and sweet. *45% (90 Proof)*

Buffalo Trace Single Oak Project Barrel #115 (w2xKB1) db **(88.5)** n22 t22.5 f22 b22. An even mix of corn oil and persistant light sugars. Low level spice until finish. A tad dull. *45%.*

◇◇◇ **Buffalo Trace Single Oak Project Barrel #116** (w2yKB1) db **(90.5)** n22 t22 f23.5 b23. Caramelised biscuit nose; polite, corny start; finish rich with hickory, manuka honey. *45%*

◈ **Buffalo Trace Single Oak Project Barrel #117** (w2xLB1*) db **(82.5)** n20 t20.5 f22 b20. Weird pineapple nose; fruity delivery with spices trying to escape. Entirely different. *45%*

◈ **Buffalo Trace Single Oak Project Barrel #118** (w2yLB1*) db **(86)** n20.5 t21.5 f22 b22. Fruity (less than 117); big toffee body, busy spice, developing ulmo honey. Soft. *45%*

Buffalo Trace Single Oak Project Barrel #119 (w2xLB1) db **(93.5)** n22.5 t24 f23.5 b23.5. Spices from nose to fade, accompanied by chewy burnt fudge. French toast finale. Big. *45%*

Buffalo Trace Single Oak Project Barrel #120 (w2xLB1) db **(89.5)** n23 t22 f22.5 b22. Controlled oak throughout. Intermittent dry vanilla. Delicate sugars. *45% (90 Proof)*

Buffalo Trace Single Oak Project Barrel #121 (w2xKB2*) db **(89)** n22.5 t23 f21.5 b22. Citrusy corn oil apparent and dominates. Sugars rampant, spices shy. Rather flat finale. *45%*

Buffalo Trace Single Oak Project Barrel #122 (w2yKB2*) db **(93)** n22 t23.5 f23.5 b24. Serious wheat-spice with cocoa back up. Demerara sugars evenly spread. Complex. *45%*

Buffalo Trace Single Oak Project Barrel #123 (w2xKB2) db **(85.5)** n21 t22 f21 b21.5. One of the dullest yet: limited sparkle despite light spice. Big caramel. *45% (90 Proof)*

Buffalo Trace Single Oak Project Barrel #124 (w2yKB2) db **(90.5)** n22.5 t23 f22.5 b22.5. The startling, extra sugars over #123 impact hugely. Juicy; oak (liquorice) support. *45%*

Buffalo Trace Single Oak Project Barrel #125 (w2xLB2*) db **(93)** n24 t22 f22.5 b22.5. Heavy oak, spices; firm, juicy. Softer caramel fade. *45% (90 Proof)*

Buffalo Trace Single Oak Project Barrel #126 (w2yLB2*) db **(90)** n22 t23 f22.5 b22.5. Floral nose (primroses); elaborate delivery of spice and creamed mocha plus molasses. *45%*

Buffalo Trace Single Oak Project Barrel #127 (w2xLB2) db **(85.5)** n21.5 t22 f21 b21. Off balance, citrus; juicy at first, bitters later. *45% (90 Proof)*

Buffalo Trace Single Oak Project Barrel #128 (w2yLB2) db **(89)** n21.5 t22 f22.5 b22.5. Conservative nose, OTT spice on delivery. Molassed dates and walnut. *45% (90 Proof)*

Buffalo Trace Single Oak Project Barrel #129 (r1xKA1*) db **(88)** n22.5 t22 f22 b22. Firm grainy, tannin nose; nougat, nutty, corn oil; clean but dim vanilla fade. *45% (90 Proof)*

Buffalo Trace Single Oak Project Barrel #130 (r1yKA1*) db **(92.5)** n22 t23.5 f23 b24. Macho: cloaked in oak. Kumquats on nose, oily, punchy tannins on sharp, silky delivery. *45%*

Buffalo Trace Single Oak Project Barrel #131 (r1xKA1) db **(92.5)** n23 t23 f23.5 b23. Relaxed vanilla, light tannin; corn oily, icing sugars, marzipan. *45% (90 Proof)*

Buffalo Trace Single Oak Project Barrel #132
See above.

Buffalo Trace Single Oak Project Barrel #133 (r1xLA1*) db **(89)** n22.5 t23 f21 b22.5. Small grain busyness does the business: rye leads the dark sugar procession. Bitters out. *45%*

Buffalo Trace Single Oak Project Barrel #134 (r1yLA1*) db **(91.5)** n22 t23.5 f23 b23. Velvet delivery: big spice cushioned by muscovado and butterscotch. Mixed honey finale. *45%*

◈ **Buffalo Trace Single Oak Project Barrel #135** (r1xLA1) db **(92.5)** n23 t23 f23.5 b23. Chocolatey theme, except on firm, grainy nose. Silky oils, intense flavours, rye rigidity. *45%*

Buffalo Trace Single Oak Project Barrel #136 (r1yLA1) db **(92)** n23.5 t22.5 f23 b23. Liquorice on nose and delivery. Spicy. Richer oils. Demerara. Spice. *45% (90 Proof)*

Buffalo Trace Single Oak Project Barrel #137 (r1xKA2*) db **(90.5)** n22 t23.5 f22 b23. Fruity opening with a hardening rye presence and emphasis on muscovado. Late cocoa. *45%*

Buffalo Trace Single Oak Project Barrel #138 (r1yKA2*) db **(87)** n22.5 t21.5 f21.5 b21.5. Marzipan, citrus nose; dull delivery, slow build of muscovado and vanilla. Soft. *45%*

Buffalo Trace Single Oak Project Barrel #139 (r1xKA2) db **(88)** n22.5 t22 f21.5 b22. More or less flatlines throughout. Big corn oil with limited spice and cocoa. *45%*

Buffalo Trace Single Oak Project Barrel #140 (r1yKA2) db **(93)** n23 t24 f23 b23. Classic bourbon: citrus-rich nose, thumping spicy molassed liquorice-hickory delivery. *45%*

Buffalo Trace Single Oak Project Barrel #141 (r1xLA2*) db **(90)** n23.5 t22 f22.5 b22. Busy nose & finish. Corn dominates the mid ground. Sugar, spice growth. Complex finale. *45%*

Buffalo Trace Single Oak Project Barrel #142 (r1yLA2*) db **(89.5)** n22.5 t22.5 f22 b22.5. Light tannin nose; oils, liquorice, spice bite. More corn oil. Sugars, spicy vanilla. *45%*

Buffalo Trace Single Oak Project Barrel #143 (r1xLA2) db **(88.5)** n22.5 t22.5 f21.5 b22. Hickory drifts in and out of narrative. Light rye & vanilla. Very soft – overly gentle. *45%*

Buffalo Trace Single Oak Project Barrel #144 (r1yLA2) db **(91)** n23 t23 f22.5 b22.5. Tannin led. Bristling dark sugars. Oily with comforting vanilla. *45%*.

Buffalo Trace Single Oak Project Barrel #145 (r1xKB1*) db **(91)** n22.5 t22 f23.5 b23. Nougat, cocoa; busy small grains; oily corn; spiced chocolate. *45% (90 Proof)*

Buffalo Trace Single Oak Project Barrel #146 (r1yKB1*) db **(93)** n23 t24 f22 b24. Rye dominates with clarity and aplomb. Crystal clean nose and delivery: Dundee cake. *45%*

Buffalo Trace Single Oak Project Barrel #147 (r1xKB1) db **(93)** n23.5 t23 f23.5 b23. Macho rye & tannins. Toasty & dry delivery; liquorice, sugars, soft spice gain ascendency. *45%*.

◈ **Buffalo Trace Single Oak Project Barrel #148** (r1yKB1) db **(94)** n22.5 t24 f23.5 b24. Quiet aroma but intense delivery. Big sugar up front, liquorice and manuka honey fade. *45%*

⬩ **Buffalo Trace Single Oak Project Barrel #149** (r1xLB1*) db **(92)** n22.5 t23.5 f23 b23. Massive tannin influence. Heavy nose; heavier body with toasty liquorice and cocoa. 45%

⬩ **Buffalo Trace Single Oak Project Barrel #150** (r1yLB1*) db **(93)** n23 t23.5 f23 b23.5. Huge tannin softened by big dark sugars, hickory, sharp rye notes. Long, chewy finish. 45%

Buffalo Trace Single Oak Project Barrel #151 (r1xLB1) db **(91.5)** n22 t23 f23.5 b23. Diced citrus; light body with busy grains. Powerful dark sugars gain upper hand. 45%

Buffalo Trace Single Oak Project Barrel #152 (r1yLB1) db **(81.5)** n21 t20.5 f20 b20.5. Vaguely butyric; harsh, hot fat corn, light rye; bitters out. 45% (90 Proof)

Buffalo Trace Single Oak Project Barrel #153 (r1xKB2*) db **(94)** n23.5 t23.5 f23 b24. Complex nose, delivery. Big spice with crisp, juicy rye. Praline, delicate oils. Big but elegant. 45%

Buffalo Trace Single Oak Project Barrel #154 (r1yKB2*) db **(92)** n22.5 t23 f23 b23.5. Rye dominates. Hard on palate; yet burnt raisin, lychee and muscovado soften. 45% (90 Proof)

Buffalo Trace Single Oak Project Barrel #155 (r1xKB2) db **(93)** n23 t24 f22.5 b23.5. Fierce spice. Dynamic rye shapes all directions. Hickory and manuka honey combine. 45%

Buffalo Trace Single Oak Project Barrel #156 (r1yKB2) db **(85.5)** n22 t21 f21.5 b21. Doesn't work. Spices too hot. Caramels and oils negate development. 45% (90 Proof)

Buffalo Trace Single Oak Project Barrel #157 (r1xLB2*) db **(84.5)** n21 t21.5 f20.5 b21. Vague butyric; sharp, juicy corn with slow rye build. Bitter. 45% (90 Proof)

Buffalo Trace Single Oak Project Barrel #158 (r1yLB2*) db **(88)** n22 t22 f22 b22. Another brawny, corn-oily, oaky effort. Excellent cocoa, citrus and spice development. 45%

Buffalo Trace Single Oak Project Barrel #159 (r1xLB2) db **(88)** n20.5 t22.5 f22 b22.5. Vague butyric; firm sugars then watery, confident spices, soft honey. Complex. 45% (90 Proof)

Buffalo Trace Single Oak Project Barrel #160 (r1yLB2) db **(92.5)** n23.5 t23 f22 b23. A salty style with fruity, crisp rye right behind. Steady and firm. 45% (90 Proof)

Buffalo Trace Single Oak Project Barrel #161 (w1xKA1*) db **(87)** n21 t22 f22 b22. Cream caramel candy; juicy corn, oily; more caramel, Light spice. 45% (90 Proof)

Buffalo Trace Single Oak Project Barrel #162 (w1yKA1*) db **(88.5)** n22 t22 f22.5 b22. Cream soda and minty fudge. Early treacle kick then settles for simple life. 45%

Buffalo Trace Single Oak Project Barrel #163 (w1xKA1) db **(90)** n23 t22.5 f22 b22.5. Citrus, bubble gum; spiced muscovado sugars at first, bitters. 45% (90 Proof)

Buffalo Trace Single Oak Project Barrel #164 (w1yKA1) db **(94.5)** n23.5 t23 f24 b24. Citrus and vanilla; massive spice, building. Demerara. Warm and complex. 45% (90 Proof)

Buffalo Trace Single oak Project Barrel #165 (w1xLA1*) db **(91.5)** n22.5 t23 f23 b23. Lively, spice dominated. Ulmo honey offers superb back up. 45% (90 Proof)

Buffalo Trace Single Oak Project Barrel #166 (w1yLA1*) db **(91)** n22 t23 f23 b23. Heady, leathery. Sublime spice middle; molasses and liquorice enrich the tail. 45% (90 Proof)

Buffalo Trace Single Oak Project Barrel #167 (w1yLB1) db **(94)** n23.5 t23.5 f23 b24. Demerara, rummy; intense liquorice, hickory; dark sugars and big spice. 45% (90 Proof)

⬩ **Buffalo Trace Single Oak Project Barrel #168** (w1xLA1) db **(89.5)** n22 t23 f22 b22.5. Clean, spiced nose; juicy grains with toffee and raisin. Mocha and liquorice on finish. 45%

Buffalo Trace Single Oak Project Barrel #169 (w1xKA2*) db **(94)** n23.5 t23.5 f23 b24. Spice, lavender & leather on delivery; spicy nose. Honey & corn oil follow through. 45% (90 proof)

Buffalo Trace Single Oak Project Barrel #170 (w1yKA2*) db **(92.5)** n22.5 t23 f23.5 b23.5. Sweet, spiced nose; firm, spicy delivery; Demerara and ulmo honey. 45% (90 Proof)

Buffalo Trace Single Oak Project Barrel #171 (w1xKA2) db **(88.5)** n22 t23 f21.5 b22. Friendly corn oils dominate. Estery. Dry finish after sugar and spice crescendo. 45%

Buffalo Trace Single Oak Project Barrel #172 (w1yKA2) db **(90.5)** n22.5 t23 f22.5 b22.5. Tannins prevalent on nose and spiced delivery. Good bite, esters and oils. Late mocha. 45%

Buffalo Trace Single Oak Project Barrel #173 (w1xLA2*) db **(91)** n23.5 t23 f22 b22.5. Bold nose & delivery: honeycomb, tannins. Liquorice & vanilla middle; good spice balance. 45%

Buffalo Trace Single Oak Project Barrel #174 (w1yLA2*) db **(89)** n22 t22.5 f22.5 b22. Delicate oak; juicy corn, liquorice, light spices, buttery corn. Bitter marmalade. 45% (90 Proof)

Buffalo Trace Single Oak Project Barrel #175 (w1xLA2) db **(91.5)** n21.5 t23 f24 b23. Lazy nose, juicy delivery. Big vanilla profile. Buttery caramel; light honey & spice. Long. 45%

Buffalo Trace Single Oak Project Barrel #176 (w1yLA2) db **(89)** n21.5 t22.5 f22.5 b22.5. Light caramel aroma; sharp, juicy (rye-esque) delivery with mocha & butter toffee finale. 45%

Buffalo Trace Single Oak Project Barrel #177 (w1xKB1*) db **(87)** n21.5 t22 f22 b21.5. Vaguely spiced corn oil; soft, nutty, marzipan sweetness, citrus. Late mocha. 45% (90 Proof)

Buffalo Trace Single Oak Project Barrel #178 (w1yKB1*) db **(88.5)** n22.5 t23 f21.5 b21.5. Complex marzipan and Demerara nose and delivery; runs out of things to say. 45%

Buffalo Trace Single Oak Project Barrel #179 (w1xKB1) db **(88)** n21 t22 f22.5 b22.5 Dull caramel nose. Toffee caramel continues on palate. Late fudge sweetness. Growing spice. 45%

⬩ **Buffalo Trace Single Oak Project Barrel #180** (w1yKB1) db **(92)** n22 t23.5 f23 b23.5. Molasses/cough sweet nose; scrambled grains and citrus; thickens with corn at end. 45%

◈ **Buffalo Trace Single Oak Project Barrel #181** (w1xLB1*) db **(94.5) n22.5 t24.5 f23 b23.5**. Silky chocolate fudge delivery with perfect spice. Nose more austere, finish intense. 45%

◈ **Buffalo Trace Single Oak Project Barrel #182** (w1yLB1*) db **(86) n21.5 t21.5 f22 b21**. Nose over fruity; profound sugars but tart, thin body. Vanilla and mocha on finish. 45%

Buffalo Trace Single Oak Project Barrel #183 (w1xLB1) db **(95.5) n24 t24 f23.5 b24**. Intense. Brilliant fudge/honey/molasses delivery; cocoa finish; perfect spices: mini Weller! 45%.

Buffalo Trace Single Oak Project Barrel #184 (w1yLA1) db **(93) n23.5 t23 f23 b23.5**. Tannins, walnut oil; nutty, corn oils. Light spice, firm Demerara. Late fruity spice. Complex. 45%

Buffalo Trace Single Oak Project Barrel #185 (w1xKB2*) db **(92.5) n23 t23.5 f23 b23**. Dry, riveting nose; liquorice dominates the palate. Cocoa, hickory enlivened by sugars. 45%

Buffalo Trace Single Oak Project Barrel #186 (w1yKB2*) db **(90) n23 t22.5 f22 b22.5**. Rampant spice from delivery onwards. Burnt fudge and toasted raisin. 45% (90 Proof)

Buffalo Trace Single Oak Project Barrel #187 (w1xKB2) db **(88) n22 t22 f22 b22**. Exceptionally even and caramel rich. Unbalanced tannin and lack of spice. 45% (90 Proof)

Buffalo Trace Single Oak Project Barrel #188 (w1yKB2) db **(90) n21.5 t23.5 f22.5 b22.5**. Lazy nose. Bright delivery; citrusy corn oil and muscovado. Late mocha and liquorice. 45%

Buffalo Trace Single Oak Project Barrel #189 (w1xLB2*) db **(88.5) n24 t22 f21 b21.5**. Complex citrus, delicate yet big; tart, sweet, fresh, strangely off balance. 45% (90 Proof)

Buffalo Trace Single Oak Project Barrel #190 (w1yLB2*) db **(94) n23.5 t24 f23 b23.5**. Ulmo/manuka honey mix on nose and delivery; silky corn oil; spiced mocha. Complex. 45%

Buffalo Trace Single Oak Project Barrel #191 (w1xLB2) db **(94.5) n23 t23.5 f24 b24**. Big, spicy, classic; firm wheaty spiciness, juicy, thick caramels. Complex. 45% (90 Proof)

Buffalo Trace Single Oak Project Barrel #192 (w1yLB2) db **(94.5) n23 t24 f23.5 b24**. Demerara rum nose; heavy, dry liquorice body; late spice; molassed butterscotch finish. 45%

Buffalo Trace Experiment #7 Heavy Char charred white oak, dist 21 Jan 97, bott Oct 12 db **(77) n20 t21.5 f17 b18.5**. The very nature of experiments means that, sometimes, they go wrong. Perhaps a bit harsh for this one which, to be more precise, has not gone right. The nose has an almost bizarre sherry feel to it, the fruitiness really striking home on the attractive delivery. From then on, it's downhill, leaving an unattractive tang at the death. 45%

Buffalo Trace Experimental Collection 12 Year Old Bourbon From Floor #1 dist 11/29/01, barreled 11/30/01, bott 3/12/14, still proof: 140, entry proof: 125, warehouse/ floor: K/1, rick/ row/slot:1/1/1-4, charred white oak, age at bottling, 12 years, 3 months, evaporation: 27% db **(91.5) n23.5** alive with small grain bittiness; manuka honey; a tad salty; **t23** sweet delivery: soft corn oils and polite spice; German coffee biscuit; **f22.5** a slight bitterness as the sugars can't stretch that far; **b22.5** delicate bourbon with limited fight. 45%.

◈ **Buffalo Trace Experimental Collection 12 Year Old Wheated Bourbon From Floor #1** dist 04/24/02, barrelled 04/26/02, bott 11/03/14, still proof: 130, entry proof: 125, warehouse/ floor: K/1, rick/row/slot: 1/3/1-5, age at bottling: 12 Years, 6 Months, evaporation: **(88.5) n22** relatively inert: muscovado sugar and vanilla dominates; a hint of cough sweet; **t22** sharp tannins; the vanillas are missing their normal sugars; **f22.5** dry, liquorice enriched and, at last, some late muscovado sugars and melt-in-the-mouth caramelised biscuit **b21.5** pleasant, but feels as though it is lurching around; not entirely convincing. 42% db 45%

◈ **Buffalo Trace Experimental Collection 12 Year Old Wheated Bourbon From Floor #5** dist 04/24/02, barrelled 04/26/02, bott 11/03/14, still proof: 130, entry proof: 125, warehouse/ floor: K/5, rick/row/slot: 51/1/1-5, age at bottling: 12 Years, 6 Months, evaporation: **(91) n22** Fisherman's Friend cough sweet; light molasses; **t23** salivating as the small grains are unleashed. Again, a hickory-liquorice cough sweet sharpness throbs through; **f22.5** late spice helps keep the salivation going to the very end; **b23.5** a gorgeously weighted whiskey and the pace of development on the palate is sublime. 47% db 45%

◈ **Buffalo Trace Experimental Collection 12 Year Old Wheated Bourbon From Floor #9** dist 04/24/02, barrelled 04/26/02, bott 11/04/14, still proof: 130, entry proof: 125, warehouse/ floor: K/9, rick/row/slot: 44/1/1-5, age at bottling: 12 Years, 6 Months, evaporation: **(89) n23** white chocolate, liquorice cough sweet, molasses, light spices. Big, but everything in perspective; **t21.5** duller than the nose hints at: massive degree of natural caramel; **f22.5** yet more caramel, with soft vanilla; good spice fade; **b22** technically very good, but a little overly simple and single paced. 51% db 45%

Buffalo Trace Experimental Collection 12 Year Old Bourbon From Floor #5 dist 11/29/01, barreled 11/30/01, bott 3/12/14, still proof: 140, entry proof: 125, warehouse/ floor: K/5, rick/row/slot:51/1/21-24, charred white oak, age at bottling, 12 years, 3 months, evaporation: 25% db **(91) n22** corn oil and citrus; a touch minty with a hint of eucalyptus;

t23 quite a heavy delivery: much more rich, molassed tannin than Floor #1, and a greater depth to the natural caramels, too; **f23** pulsing spices; **b23** though heavier, lacks some of the grace and complexity of its lower-matured stablemate. *45%.*

Buffalo Trace Experimental Collection 12 Year Old Bourbon From Floor #9 dist 11/29/01, barreled 11/30/01, bott 3/12/14, still proof: 140, entry proof: 125, warehouse/floor: K/9, rick/row/slot:44/1/13-16, charred white oak, age at bottling, 12 years, 3 months, evaporation: 49% db **(95.5) n24** big profound bourbon with liquorice softened by molasses; **t24** from the very first moment of delivery, this sings "massive, absolutely top quality bourbon" to you from every one of its countless layers; we are talking various types of liquorice, Fisherman's Friend cough sweets, treacle, dried molasses, dried dates and biting spice...and so much more, including a layering of ulmo honey in tanden with manuka; **f23.5** though quieter, the sugars not only stretch further but remain in harmony with the heavier tannins: the rumble goes on seemingly forever....thankfully! **b24** floorless...and confirms about bourbon maturation what we already know. And this distillery in particular... *45%.*

Cadenhead's World Whiskies Heaven Hill Aged 17 Years bott 14, **(93.5) n24.5** hard to imagine a more complete or classic bourbon aroma at this age: massive tannin toned down and beatified by a dollop of manuka honey, marzipan and toasted fudge....no shortage of corn apparent, too; **t23** rich, dripping with corn oil and molasses with a slow burnt toast, thick liquorice growth; **f23** a light ulmo honey layering sticks to the corn oil; **b23** although it says "distilled at Heaven Hill Bardstown," the distillery was by then a burnt out husk and production had shifted to various other distilleries around Kentucky who were happy to distil to contract, or sell spare parcels of maturing distillate to help plug the huge stock gap. Not sure exactly where this single cask was from but has a certain touch of the Old Forester from Louisville, which often displayed the heavy liquorice and honey character apparent here. *58%. WB15/378*

Calhoun Bros Straight Bourbon (84.5) n20.5 t22 f21 b21. Very different! A much wider cut than the norm on straight bourbon whisky results in an oily fellow which you can chew until your jaws ache. Massively toasty, vanilla gorged and intense. *43% (86 proof)*

Charter 101 (95.5) n23.5 t24.5 f23.5 b24. Now here is a whiskey which has changed tack dramatically. In many ways it's like the Charter 101 of a year back. But this bottling suggests they have turned a warehouse into a giant beehive. Because few whiskeys offer this degree of honey. You can imagine that after all these years, rarely does a whiskey genuinely surprise me: this one has. No wonder there is such a buzz in the bourbon industry right now... *50.5%*

Clarke's Old Kentucky Straight Sour Mash Whisky Bourbon (88.5) n22.5 t22 f22 b22. Honest and hugely impressive bourbon. The rich colour – and remember straight bourbon cannot be falsely coloured – tells its own tale. *40%. Aldi.*

Colonel E H Taylor Barrel Proof (91) n23.5 t23 f22 b22.5. A big boy which turns out to be a bit of a softy in the end... *67.25% (134.5 Proof). nc ncf.*

⬥ **Colonel E H Taylor Cured Oak (93.5) n23** one assumes the cured oak has resulted in a maximising of early sugars being released in maturation. Because this nose has more in common with a Caribbean pot still rum than it does whiskey. Or whisky...; **t24** and, as predicted, sugars of all forms and denominations gather on delivery: one of the sweetest starts to a bourbon for this and many a year. But there is much more besides, especially a veritable creaminess to the vanilla which is bursting out in all directions; **f23** a dissenting vague bitterness lasts for a second or two before it is shackled and led away by the remaining sugars; **b23.5** not sure about the oak being cured: coming from Buffalo Trace, I doubt if there was anything wrong with it in the first place...In many ways a much quieter than normal and delicate bourbon with the tannins harnessed and led to a path quite different from the normal toasty/liquorice style. *50%. (100 Proof)*

Colonel E. H. Taylor Old Fashioned Sour Mash (94) n24 t23.5 f23 b23.5. When they say "old fashioned" they really aren't joking. This is a style which takes me back to my first bourbon tasting days of the mid 1970s. And, at the moment, it is hard to name another bourbon offering this unique, technically brilliant style. Outstanding! *50% (100 Proof)*

Colonel E H Taylor Single Barrel (93) n23.5 t23 f23 b23.5. An exceptionally bright barrel that's a bit of a tease. *50% (100 Proof)*

Colonel E.H. Taylor Small Batch (94.5) n23 pretty effortlessly classic: a friendly layering of crisp sugars and teasing spice as well as a thin hint of mint and eucalyptus; the natural vanillas are out in force, too; **t24** pretty perfect weight: the oils have just enough clout to ensure the sugars remain in check and on the Demerara side of things; the small grains do stir, also, and herald the arrival of the toastier elements; **f23.5** long, again with the sweetness in harmony with the butterscotch tart and late peppery bite; **b24** from first nose, to last, the exemplary high quality of this bourbon is not for a second in dispute. *50% (100 Proof)*

Cougar Bourbon Aged 5 Years (95) n25 t24 f23 b23. If Karl Kennedy of Neighbours really is the whisky buff he reckons he is, I want to see a bottle of this in his home next to Dahl. By the way: where is Dahl these days...? (And by the way, Karl, the guy who married you and Susan in London is a fan of mine. So you had better listen up...!) *37% (74 proof). Foster's Group, Australia.*

Daniel Stewart 8 Years Old (92.5) n22 t23 f23.5 b24. Stellar sophistication. Real complexity here, and, as 8-year-olds go, probably among the most complex of them all. A deep notch up on the previous bottling I encountered. *45%*

Eagle Rare Aged 10 Years Single Barrel (89) n21.5 t23 f22 b22.5. A surprising trip, this, with some dramatic changes en route. *45%*

Eagle Rare 17 Years Old bott Spring 2013 db (94) n23 wonderful chocolate fudge; thick and toasty; t24 ker-pow! By far and away the biggest landing by this rare Eagle for quite some time. Almost aggressive in its bite, which entirely suits the intensity of the spice which sits prettily with the manuka honey and treacle; f23 tones down quite quickly and we are back to the lovely chocolate fudge found on the nose; b24 a much more profound bottling than the 2012 edition with the accent firmly on the heavy, chocolatey sugars. Shows BT to enormous advantage and is, above all, great fun. *45%. Buffalo Trace Antique Collection.*

◈ **Eagle Rare 17 Year Old** bott Spring 2014 db (95) n23 has someone thrown a sprig of mint into that famous chocolate fudge...? t24 sensual delivery with the corn oils licking around the taste buds in a rather sexy manner. The sugars keep apace with a mollassed depth; f23.5 late spice harmonise with that lovely sweetened corn oil. As the oak rumbles back into play the chocolate fudge returns...; b23.5 one of the most relaxed and confident Eagle Rares I've encountered for a while. More telling sugar around than usual and a little less weighty. *45%.*

Elijah Craig Barrel Proof Bourbon 12 Years of Aging db (95.5) n23.5 heavy duty and fudgy, the fruits are all about plums fit to burst and the sweetness from molasses and reduced manuka honey; t24 Batman would love the ker-pow factor to this. Everything so intense and the balancing sugars and the enormity of the liquorice make this one to remember. Spices punctuate at every point...just astonishing...; f24 slightly overcooked toast with treacle spread and washed down with a sublime Javan coffee; b24 not sure when I saw a darker bourbon at 12 years commercially available. Remember that in straight bourbon colour represents interaction between spirit and barrel. So expect big oak presence and you will not be disappointed! A bourbon for bourbon lovers with very hairy chests – male or female. *67.1% (134.2 proof) ncf.*

Elijah Craig 18 Years Old Single Barrel barrel no. 3328, dist 8/9/91 (94.5) n25 t23.5 f22.5 b23.5. Masterful. Don't even bother opening the bottle unless you have an hour to spend. *45%*

Elijah Craig 21 Year Old Single Barrel barrelled 26/11/90, barrel no. 41 db (95.5) n23.5 the busy nose shows no discomfort despite the major age: a real jumble of seasonings ranging from the nonchalantly sweet toasted honeycomb through to the much more abrupt ginger and coriander mix and diced, dried orange peel. A light sprinkling of salt brings everything out to the full; t24 and, of course, it is that oak-weighted seasoning which shows first, semi explosively and almost like botanicals of a dry gin. The sugars, flanked by minute amounts of ulmo honey, take their time to evolve and thread their way into the complex tapestry; f23.5 still mainly dry with the vanillas building alongside the increasingly peppery spices; light corn oil helps spread the limited sugar and honey; b24.5 even by bourbon's high standards, this is a thing of rare beauty and of a type. One of the most subtle and sophisticated bottlings you'll ever find at this age and one for those who prefer their Martinis and gins dry. And I mean very dry.... *45%.*

◈ **Elijah Craig Aged 23 Years Single Barrel** barrel no. 26, barrelled 2.26.90 db (87) n21 t23 f21 b22. The citrus on this old boy is working overtime to ensure a degree of freshness combats the encroaching years. But it is a somewhat unequal battle and, finally, as was inevitable, slips under the tide of ancient oak like a man pushing a boulder up an interminable hill finally falls, spent, to the ground for the great rock to run over him on its way back downhill. That said, plenty of magic moments to be getting on with here, especially on delivery when there's a greater evenness between the light muscovado sugars and the more dogged tannins. Of course, the tannins win out in the end as the nose accurately forecast, with a bitter –ish fade. But there is no shortage of understated elegance and charm along the way. *45%*

Elmer T Lee Single Barrel (91) n22 t23.5 f(22.5) b23. A sturdy, dense bourbon with above average sweetness. So effortless, it is hard to immediately realise that greatness has entered your glass. *45%*

Elmer T. Lee Single Barrel Bourbon 1919 - 2013 db (96.5) n24.5 BT at its most genteel and delicate: an evening breeze of honeysuckle, rain-washed roses and orange blossom. Below that, a darker, earthier depth – a rich aroma from which much might grow; t24 quite brilliant. A disguised delivery moving your senses in one direction thanks to a rumbling, growling, tannin-rich preamble, then suddenly switches tack and offers a flutier, juicier, more highly charged, spice-ridden essay of small grains and a few kumquats; f24 perhaps the most chocolate-rich finish of any whisky this year. And we are not talking Hershey but high quality oily cocoa bean of a distinctly South American hue: wow! b24 I left this as the 1,145th and final new whisk(e)y to be tasted for the 2015 Jim Murray's Whisky Bible. Elmer, once a neighbour of mine, loved his garden and more than once I helped him safely remove squirrels without them being hurt in any way. Which makes this whiskey, seemingly gentle but with a backbone of American steel - yet on the nose flowing with floral notes, a touching and entirely apposite marker to his memory. And it delights me to say that I know, with absolute certainty, he would have been blown away by this barrel of glorious complexity. Elmer: with a glass of this rare genius I salute your memory, my friend. *46.5%*

Evan Williams 23 Years Old (94) n22 t23.5 f24.5 b24. Struts his stuff, refusing to allow age to slow him or dim the shine from his glowing grains. Now oak has taken its toll. This seems older than its 23 years... Or so I first thought. Then a light shone in my soul and it occurred to me: hang on...I have wines going back to the last century. For the older ones, do I not allow them to breathe? So I let the whiskey breathe. And, behold, it rose from the dead. This Methuselah of a whiskey had come alive once more...and how!! *53.5%*

Evan Williams Single Barrel 2004 Edition barrel no. 1, dist 19/03/2004, bott 16/11/2013 db (89.5) n22 relatively simplistic: ulmo honey and vanilla enlivened by a faint dash of tangerine peel; t24 profound early sugars, mainly of an icing and syrupy variety. The spices are dull, though weighty and plod and prod rather than stimulate; f21.5 thins and vanillas out with surprising abruptness; b22 demure: wouldn't say boo to a goose. *43.3%. 19th in the series.*

Four Roses 125th Anniversary Small Batch Bourbon OBSV - 18 years, OBSK - 13years, OESK- 13 years db (96.5) n24 how can something so big and rich be equally as delicate and complex? Quintessential bourbon aroma with manuka honey, liquorice, treacle, black cherry, coffee and toasted honeycomb all dipping in and out, or forming a whole....; t24.5 the rye I couldn't find on the nose has saved itself for the crisp, juicy, controlled, sweetened delivery. Corn oils have formed now and hold the dark sugars and magnificent spices beautifully; f24 toasty, medium roast Java coffee, then a slow fade in which the sugars counter the gathering tannin-led bitterness; b24 nosing and tasting a whiskey like this and, after a morning of sulphur-ruined horrors, I am reminded why I still do this job. A celebration of bourbon; a triumph of blending. *51.6%. ncf. 12468 bottles. WB15/385*

Four Roses 2013 Limited Edition Single Barrel #3-4P Aged 13 Years db (97) n24.5 anyone who knows Fox's Party Rings biscuits from the UK will get this nose immediately. It involves vanilla and rich muscovado sugar and a little molasses for good measure. But then there is the light liquorice, too, and the ulmo honey spread on a thin slice of moist gingerbread. Magnificent. And truly classic...; t24.5 a Four Roses feminine touch for it is sugar and spice and all things nice on delivery. The molasses ensure a crispness t the manuka honey and liquorice follow through, but then softens as the lightly oiled vanillas ad caramels arrive; the biting spice ensures that the classical aspect of this bourbon is sustained; f24 long, oily molasses and treacle complicated by a seemingly rye-like crisp fruitiness; b24 in that great horse racing state of Kentucky, the home of the Derby, only one distillery is seriously threatening Buffalo Trace's position of supreme bourbon maker. Coming fast up on the rails is Four Roses. Here is another truly sensational bottling. In many ways this is the quintessential bourbon displaying just about every character you can as for. The fact that so much has come from just a single barrel is truly astonishing, as usually you require several mixed together to offer such a rich and classic diversity on nose and palate. Indeed, this is probably the best single barrel bourbon I have ever encountered...from anywhere. *63.4%. WB15/173*

⬧ **Four Roses Limited Edition 2014 Small Batch** (94) n23.5 a fascinating marriage of younger and older liquorice tones....and I mean red, not black...; t24 such a soft embodiment of sponge-like corn absorbes the bolder tannins, leaving the coconut-tinged, buttercream and maple syrup an uncomplicated and unchallenged path through the midground; f23 surprsing low key, again with the younger tones being given a surprising degree of latitude; b23.5 a little youthful undercurrent means, as beautiful as this whiskey is, it doesn't quite hit the heights of the 2013 verion. Still a beauty, though...; *60% approx 11,200*

Four Roses 2014 Limited Edition Single Barrel Aged 11 Years Recipe OESF db (88.5) n22 busy small grain plus a touch nougat and eucalyptus to accompany the honeycomb; t23.5 light delivery though the intensity builds as the manuka honey and liquorice build up a head of steam; developing spice; f21 unusaly thin finale, with a little lime to accompany the vanilla; b22 a pretty quiet cask refusing to scale the highest peaks. *60%.*

George T. Stagg (97.5) n24 t25 f24 b24.5. Astonishing how so much oak can form and yet have such limited negative impact and so few unpleasant side notes. These tasting notes took nearly four hours to compile. Yet they are still in a simplified form to fit into this book... George T Stagg is once again... staggering. *71.5% (143 Proof). ncf.*

George T. Stagg (Barrel Proof) db (95) n24 a big parade of rye and creamy toffee make a curious juxtaposition; toffee apple against the ever-intensifying spice also make for another big match; t24 just like on the nose, the delivery is a battle between rye grain and caramel supremacy, only now with no quarter given: salivating, mainly crisp and, again, echoing the nose, spices gather and intensify to startling effect; **f23** an outbreak of vanilla and butterscotch, topped by liquorice and molasses, makes for a relatively supine finish; **b24** quite beautiful bourbon of the top order. But not quite so breathtakingly complex and brain-shatteringly vivid as Staggs of past times. *64.1%. Buffalo Trace Antique Collection.*

George T. Stagg Limited Edition (96.5) n24 it is as if someone has come up with the quintessential bourbon aroma...and then multiplied it by itself. This is huge, yet the small grains are busy enough to ensure the complexity levels go spinning off the chart. Even a few apples at play. Interestingly low in oils for a Stagg; **t24.5** if you want to know what a big game bourbon should taste like, just take a small mouthful of this. The rye ensures a degree of sharpness present; there are eye-wateringly bright sugars and some serious toasted honeycomb; the tannins nibble; at last the oils form though the spices allow them only so far; **f24** beautifully toasty, all kinds of mocha and hickory and even the outlines of a rather overcooked blackberry tart; **b24** as spectacular as a sunset from the hilltop village of Coldharbour in my beloved Surrey *71.4% (142.8 proof). ncf.*

⬙ **George T. Stagg (96.5) n24.5** when I die it is unlikely I'll go to heaven. But if wherever I go smells like this, then I'll be happy enough. The rye in the mash pulls the strings here, ensuring a clipped sweetness and vague fruitiness to proceedings. Concentrated dates and crispy Demerara sugars combine with a mocha middle for something rather special...; oh, and the spices...mmmm....those spices....; **t24** salivating...which you would hardly expect from something of 138 proof...then opens out into a more complex, truly labyrinthine. Coffee fudge dominates alongside the rye...and for a very long time; **f24** the usual liquorice and hickory fade; **b24** the alcohol by volume of one of the sexiest whiskeys on the planet is 69...and it goes down a treat. Much harder to spit than swallow...*69.05% Buffalo Trace Antique Collection.*

Hancock's Reserve Single Barrel (92) n25 t23 f21.5 b22.5. A slightly quieter example of this consistently fine brand. The nose, though, is the stuff of wet whiskey dreams... *44.45%*

⬙ **I.W. Harper Kentucky Straight Bourbon (87.5) n22 t22 f21.5 b22.** The puckeringly dry delivery and finish forms the toast for the well spiced light sugar sandwich. *41% (82 Proof)*

⬙ **I.W. Harper Kentucky Straight Bourbon 15 Year Old (94.5) n23.5** a well-balanced nose: the small grains are all but dancing a jig while light ulmo honey and butterscotch put a friendly face on the oak; **t23.5** the first note or two threatens an explosion – and then there are second thoughts. Instead, we have an almost genteel procession of half-hearted but brilliantly weighted sugars bathed in soft corn oil. The spice rises quickly and falls even faster...; **f24** those oils ensures a ridiculously long finish. Which means the praline is given all the time it needs to strut its stuff, as does the curiously salty oak notes...; the spices hum gently, but just loud enough to be heard; **b23.5** class in a glass. *43% (86 Proof)*

Jefferson's Reserve batch no. 84 **(91) n23 t23.5 f22 b23.** Once a 15-year-old, no age statement here. But this has seen off a few Summers, sweetening with each passing one. *45.1%.*

Jim Beam Black Double Age Aged 8 Years (93) n23 t24 f22.5 b23.5. Rather than the big, noisy, thrill-seeking JB Black, here it is in quiet, reflective, sophisticated mode. Quite a shift. But no less enjoyable. *43% (86 proof)*

⬙ **Jim Beam Bonded 100 Proof** db **(92.5) n22.5** a little lazy at first, but by degree begins to reveal light layers of small grain and slightly larger oak...; **t23.5** soft, vaguely sugared start... then the small grains go berserk. The mouth is peppered with shotgun blasts of rye-infused small grain and then complex sugars, wide-ranging in style; so beautifully busy; **f23** now a sublime toastiness kicks in, making the most now of the molasses and chicory; **b23.5** takes its time to get going. But when it does, it just won't shut up.... Complex and compelling, the toastiness takes time to make itself felt but does so with panache. *50%*

⬙ **Jim Beam Signature Craft Brown Rice 11 Year Old** db 45% **(78) n20.5 t21 f18 b18.5.** A whiskey I nosed and tasted before looking to see what it was. And immediately alarm bells rang and I was reaching to inspect the bottle in a state of panic and shock. RICE!!! Well that explains the unsatisfying simplicity to the finish where, really, only oak can be heard....apart from the wallpaper paste, that is. And the fact the whiskey never quite gets off the ground despite an attractive cocoa thread. Or was that actually real cocoa...? Sorry, but in the great name of Jim Beam, this is one that should have just stayed in the lab. *(90 Proof)*

⬙ **Jim Beam Signature Craft Soft Red Wheat 11 Year Old** db **(92) n22** buttery with touches of seasoned oak and lightly spiced liquorice; **t23.5** mouth-filling delivery yet with a sugary crispness. The spices go to town almost immediately, offering an almost spiced fruit loaf feel; **f23** happy to take its time to disappear and rolls out the sugars for a last, gently spiced hurrah...; **b23.5** a beautifully weighted bourbon making a big deal of the sugar-spice interplay. Hugely enjoyable and at times fascinating. *45% (90 Proof)*

⬙ **Jim Beam Signature Craft Small Batch Quarter Cask Finished 3rd Release** db **(92) n23.5** delicate for any type of quarter cask: emphasis on citrus and subtlety rather than thumping oak; **t23.5** soft delivery with beautifully weighted molten sugar and oils forming a match for the early spicy attack; light hickory forms the backbone; **f22** a touch grainy with a little rye bite on the semi-thin finale; **b23** quarter casks are not normally associated with deftness and poise. This one certainly is. Elegant, if a little lightweight at the end. *43% (86 Proof)*

Jim Beam Signature Craft Aged 12 Years db **(92.5) n23** gorgeous roasted coffee and liquorice. The rye pokes through gamely; **t23.5** soft delivery with a wonderful toasted fudge quality. Takes time for the rye to arrive but it does as the spices mount; **f23** softly spiced with plenty of creamy mocha; **b23** classic Beam: big rye and massive fruit. Quite lovely. *43% WB15/386*

John B. Stetson Straight Bourbon Whiskey (92) n23.5 t23.5 f22 b23. Absolutely love it! Quality: I take my hat off to you...*42%*

John E. Fitzgerald Larceny (94) n23 t23.5 f23.5 b24. If this doesn't win a few converts to wheated bourbon, nothing will. A high quality, stunningly adorable whiskey, pulsing with elegance and personality. Every drinks cabinet should have this wonderful new addition to the bourbon lexicon. *46%*

John J Bowman Virginia Straight Bourbon Single Barrel (94) n23 t24 f23 b24. One of the biggest yet most easily relaxed and beautifully balanced bourbons on the market. *50%*

Johnny Drum (Black Label) (89.5) n22 t23 f21.5 b23. How often does that happen? The same whiskey, different strength, virtually same quality (though this has a little more depth) but gets there by a slightly different route. *43%*

Johnny Drum (Green Label) (89) n22.5 t23 f21 b22.5. Much more honey these days. Worth making a bee-line for. *40%*

Johnny Drum Private Stock (90.5) n22.5 t23 t22.5 f23 b22.5. One of those bourbons where a single glass is never quite enough. Great stuff! *50.5% (101 proof)*

Kentucky Vintage batch 08-72 **(94.5) n23.5** delicate to the point of brittle. Playful spice prickles as the small grains dance and tease; beautiful citrus notes are just showing off; **t24.5** the whole thing just melts in the mouth. No grating oak nor rabid spices. No bitter char. Just an intricate and delicate mix of grain and vanilla interweaving...and then melting along with some accompanying butterscotch and muscovado sugar. Quite stunning; **f23** both the bitterness and spices grow. But all is balanced and genteel; **b23.5** staggered! I really didn't quite expect that. Previous bottlings I have enjoyed of this have had hair attached to the muscle. This is a very different Vintage, one that reaches for the feminine side of a macho whiskey. If you want to spend an hour just getting to know how sensitive your taste buds can be, hunt down this batch... *45%*

Knob Creek Aged 9 Years (94.5) n23.5 almost arrogantly consistent: you know pretty well what you are going to get...and there it is. In this classic whiskey's case a whole bunch of honeycomb and vanilla, always more delicate than it first appears...; **t24** salivating delivery with rye and barley absolutely hammering on the palate. The corn oil is there not for flavour but effect – it is a fabulous mixture of dates and Demerara rum having the biggest say; **f23.5** wonderfully long with the oak toastiness now really beginning to bite...; **b23.5** no whiskey in the world has a more macho name, and this is not for the faint-hearted. Big, hard in character and expansive, it drives home its point with gusto, celebrating its explosive finish. *50%*

Maker's Mark (Red Seal) (91) n22.5 t23.5 f22 b23. The big honey injection has done no harm whatsoever. This sample came from a litre bottle and the whiskey was darker than normal. What you seem to have is the usual steady Maker's with a helping hand of extra weight. In fact this reminds me of the old Maker's Gold wax. *45%*

Maker's 46 (95) n23.5 crushed toasted hazelnuts dappled with honeycomb and delicate hickory; beautifully even and well mannered; **t24.5** quite superb: an initially thick, intense delivery which fans out in directions; excellent weight as those honeycomb notes go into overdrive; a dotting of wheaty and oaky spices but it's the way the softest of silky and highly complex flavours crash feather-like into the taste buds which cranks up the points; **f23** surprisingly light and simplistic with the accent firmly on vanilla; **b24** some people have a problem with oak staves. I don't: whisky, after all, is about the interaction of a grain spirit and oak. This guy is all about the nose and, especially, the delivery. With so much controlled honey on show, it cannot be anything other than a show-stopper. Frankly, magnificent. I think I've met my Maker's... *47% (94 proof)*

⟐ **Michter's No. 1 Bourbon (87) n23 t22.5 f20 b21.5.** This one is mainly a nose job: all kinds of heavy liquorice and diced kumquat. But there is also a brooding tannin menace lurking in the shadows, which revel themselves more fully – and with a tad of bitterness - on delivery and finish. *45.7%*

Noah's Mill batch 10-170 **(93) n23.5 t23.5 f23 b23.** This monster of a bourbon just rumbles along on the palate like one of the four thunderstorms I have encountered in Kentucky today... *57.15%*

Noah's Mill batch 13-81 **(93.5) n23** gorgeous glazed almonds; a little citrus & cold coffee; **t23.5** oddly enough, doesn't taste like the nose: much more macho, with the full blooded hickory & Demerara; enormous weight & depth; assorted honey notes begin to form; **f22.5** gentle finale, reverting back to the style of the aroma. Excellent vanilla on sugars & weightier liquorice; **b23.5** a full bodied classic bourbon which undulates over the palate. 57.15% (114.3 proof)

Old Fitzgerald Very Special 12 Years Old (93) n24 t23.5 f22.5 b23. There is always something that makes the heart sing when you come across a whiskey which appears so relaxed in its excellence. At the moment my heart is in the shower merrily lathering itself... 45%

Old Grand-Dad (90.5) n22 t23 f23 b23.5. This one's all about the small grains. A busy, lively bourbon, this offers little to remind me of the original Old Grand-Dad whiskey made out at Frankfort. That said, this is a whisk(e)y-lover's whiskey: in other words the excellence of the structure and complexity outweighs any historical misgivings. Enormously improved and now very much at home with its own busy style. 43%

Old Grand-Dad Bonded 100 Proof (94.5) n22.5 light rye spices and citrus fruit pop around the glass. One of those weighty yet delicate bourbons, but here the small grain appear at full throttle; **t24** impossible not to be blown away. Exactly like the nose, you are expecting from first impact thundering, almost bullying oak. Instead your taste buds are mesmerised by a fabulous infusion of busy rye: a thousand tiny, crisp explosions in every quarter of the mouth followed by a layering of coconut strands dipped in lightly charred, molten sugars...; **f23.5** very toasty with the oak now unflinchingly taking the rye on; **b24.5** obviously Old Grand-dad knows a thing or two about classy whiskey: this is a magnificent version, even by its own high standards. It was always a winner and one you could bet your shirt on for showing how the small grains can impact upon complexity. But this appears to go a stage further. The base line is a touch deeper, so there is more ground to cover on the palate. It has been a whiskey-lover's whiskey for a little while and after a few barren years, has been inching itself back to its great Frankfort days. The fact that Beam's quality has risen over the last decade has played no insignificant part in that. 50% (100 proof)

Old Rip Van Winkle 10 Years Old (93) n24 t23 f23 b23. A much sharper cookie than it once was. And possibly a Maryland Cookie, too, what with the nuts and chocolate evident. As graceful as it is entertaining. 45% (90 Proof). Buffalo Trace.

Old Weller Antique 107 (96) n24.5 only pour this one if you have a good half hour to spare: the nose absolutely mesmerises as it changes shape and depth continuously. The honeys are soft and graceful, never dominating but rounding edges. The spices are well mannered yet condiment. The fruit takes the direction of apple and mango. Together they create a near faultless harmony; **t24** the wheat is vibrant, pressing bold spices into a honeyed core. The layering accentuated by the liquorice and hickory which balance the sweeter elements with rare panache; **f23.5** long with varying textures of oak. Never dries too much while refusing to allow the bountiful sugars the upper hand. All the time the spices throb... **b24** this almost blew me off my chair. Always thought this was pleasant, if a little underwhelming, in the past. However, this bottling has had a few thousands volts past through it as it now comes alive on the palate with a glorious blending of freshness and debonair aging. One of the surprise packages of 2012. 53.5% (107 proof)

Orphan Barrel 'Barterhouse' 20 Years Old (91) n22.5 elegant, almost playful, lavender and mint notes combine to give the softest outline to the big tannins; **t22.5** mouth-watering delivery despite age with only a gentle degree of spice. The oak bites but ample molasses absorb the shockwaves; **f23** the over-eagerness of the oak is stifled only by that impressive, dry molasses. The spice doesn't lose confidence...; **b23** to think: this was still white dog when I first visited Old Stitz! 45.1%.

◈ **Orphan Barrel Forged Oak (87)** n22 t22 f21 b22. Decent bourbon, but a little stiff and mechanical in its development. The finish has a tad too much toast for its own good. Still, a good chewing bourbon. 45.25%

◈ **Orphan Barrel Lost Prophet** batch tul-tr-1 **(92)** n22.5 hickory and butterscotch pair off beautifully; **t23.5** and in steams the liquorice, the old fashioned way, with molasses as its sidekick; **f23** comfortable as the spices rise; **b23** markedly more relaxed than Forged Oak and understands the value of good sugar-spice interplay. 45.05%

Orphan Barrel 'Old Blowhard' 26 Years Old (95) n23.5 fabulous, classic old bourbon: like the stuff I used to get from the inside of ancient barrels many years ago, seemingly still having something of the char on the nose as well as the profound burnt honeycomb and liquorice; **t24** brilliant delivery: thick almost rummy Demerara, liberally laced with spice, vanilla and toasted coconut; **f23.5** a sharp, almost acrid intensity to the toastiness now. But near sludgy molasses and manuka honey finds just enough sweetness to guarantee balance; **b24** I do get my hands on a few samples of very old bourbon, but this seems to have a style more recognisable in the 1980s and early to mid '90s than now. Time warp whisky in every sense. Wonderful! 45.35%. Bottled in Tullahoma, aged 26 years, "found in Stitzel Weller".

◈ **Orphan Barrel Rhetoric 21 Year Old** batch 0109-67 **(94.5)** n23.5 fabulous intensity from the get go: toasty and honeyed in the classic way with the small grains taking over the show to fizz and simper; **t24** gosh....this really is something a little special: the sugars stand tall and proud, despite being swamped by lush corns oils bathed in liquorice-coated tannins: the sweetness, as with all great bourbons, appears to be in league with the spices; **f23** dries but without bitterness and in perfect pace with the growing vanilla; **b24** a bourbon drinker's bourbon. How's that for rhetoric...? *45%*

Pappy Van Winkle's Family Reserve 15 Years Old (96) n24.5 the usual blood oranges by the cartload...the lilting mix of plum juice and white bread kneaded until it has become a sweet, sugary ball. All that plus a shy spiciness and some broad oak. But what makes it all work is the lightness of the mix...so big..yet so delicate...; **t23.5** lush but with those threatening oaks on the nose exploding on impact. For a moment just a little OTT, but then several huge waves of cocoa-lined vanilla and marmalade puts the world to rights again...; **f24** long and back to unbridled elegance. Cocoas flit around, as do those wheated softly, softly spices and layers of thinned manuka honey... stunning...; **b24** at a book signing in Canada earlier this year a Bible enthusiast asked me which well-aged, wheated bourbon he should look for. I told him Pappy 15. He looked at me quizzically and said: "Well, that's what I thought, but in the Bible you have it down as rye-recipe." I told him he was wrong... until I checked there and then. And discovered he was right. Of course, Pappy has always been wheated and the lushness on the palate and spices radiating from it has always confirmed this. I'll put it down to not spitting enough. Or perhaps the speed at which I type whilst tasting. Sometimes you mean one thing – then another word comes out. Like when a member of my staff asks for a pay rise. I mean no. But somehow say yes. So apologies to any other I fooled out there. For not only is this a wheated bourbon. With its improbable degree of deftness for something so big, it has edged up a notch or two into a truly world great whiskey...whatever the recipe. *53.5% (107 proof)*

Parker's Heritage Collection "Promise of Hope" Single Barrel 10 Years db **(95) n24** hard to imagine how so much complexity can evolve from a single barrel...a deep aroma lightened by sublime layering of sugars, mainly muscovado, aided and abetted by watered maple syrup. Gentle hints of orange and marzipan add depth and direction **t24** this has "Parker Beam" stamped all over the taste buds: a man who prefers his whisky lush, sweet and profound; a whiskey which the average north American bear would make a lethal swipe for, so full it is of yummy honey. But it needs the injection of almost perfectly infused spices to launch this to the next level and act as the perfect counter to the blend of ulmo and manuka honeys which, combining with the liquorice, make for a sublime experience of riches engulfing the palate; **f23** thins as the corn oils accelerate, but the spices persist; **b24** in an age when masters Distillers assume that noble title after about ten minutes in the job and for marketing reasons alone, it is touching to find a whiskey bottled in honour of a genuine Master Distiller, a man who has probably forgotten more about whiskey than the majority of the recent intake have so far learned. It is no less touching that part of the money raised from the sale of this whiskey will go to ALS charities, a condition under which Parker Beam now labours. *48%.*

Parker's Heritage Collection Sixth Edition Master Distillery's Blend Of Mashbills Aged Since 2001 db **(94.5) n24** my word! The small grains have a field day: the rye really ups the crisp fruit levels while the wheat shovels on the spice; elsewhere its big, sweetened liquorice to confirm the dozen years in barrel; **t23.5** the sugars arrive as though blasted from a cannon: hard as rock and crystalline they positively burrow into the taste buds and if explosives are required the wheat provides it with some wicked spices; that all said, the mid-ground is a depositary for the more elegant, teasing by-products; **f23** settles contentedly along a vanilla route. Some burnt toasty notes, as expected; the sugars more even now, almost quiet with a lovely fried yam fade...and spice, of course! **b24** shows plenty of muscle, but subtlety and sophistication in equal measures, too. *63.5% (127 proof). ncf.*

Parker's Heritage Collection Wheated Mash Bill Bourbon Aged 10 Years (97) n24 t24 f24.5 b24.5. Hard to find the words that can do justice. I know Parker will be immensely proud of this. And with every good reason: I am working exceptionally hard to find a fault with this either from a technical distillation viewpoint or a maturation one. Or just for its sheer whiskeyness...A potential World Whisky of the Year. *62.1% (124.2 Proof). ncf.*

⬦ **Redemption High Rye Bourbon (74.5) n19 t20 f17.5 b18.** Hugely disappointing bottling. Vaguely butyric, and its failure to reach any high point of quality is really driven home by the car-crash finish, complete with less than pleasant tang. Seriously needs to redeem itself next time round. *46%*

Ridgemont Reserve 1792 Aged 8 Years (94.5) n23.5 throbbing, pulsing oak is kept comfortably in check with a soft honey and mint restraint. Fabulous depth and even a hint of salt to season the effect; **t24** Barton's unique rye and Demerara combo is in full swing here and contrasts fascinatingly with the deeper, vaguely bitterish oak notes; **f23.5** back to a vanilla and rye thread here, oscillating with the house brown sugars; the pulsing of the spice is sublime; **b23.5** now here is a whiskey which appears to have come to terms with its own strengths and, as with all bourbons and malts, limitations. Rarely did whiskey from Barton reach this level of maturity, so harnessing its charms always involves a bit of a learning curve. Each time I taste this it appears a little better than the last...and this sample is no exception to the rule. Excellent. *46.85% (93.7 Proof)*

Rowan's Creek Batch 13-88 **(82)** n20 t21.5 f20.5 b20. A modest bourbon short on complexity and weight but big on spice and delicate sugars. *50.05% (100.1 proof)*

Russell's Reserve Single Barrel (94) n23.5 t24 f23 b23.5. Old-fashioned, thick as treacle bourbon. Delicious. *55%. ncf. Wild Turkey.*

Russell's Reserve Small Batch 10 Year Old (92.5) n24.5 t23 f22 b23. Had the quality and complexity on the palate followed on from the nose I may well have had the world's No 1 whisky for 2012 in my glass. Just slum it with something quite wonderful, instead. Still waiting for an official explanation as to why this is a miserly 90 proof, when Jimmy Russell's preferred strength is 101, by the way... *45%. Wild Turkey.*

Smooth Ambler Old Scout Straight Bourbon Aged 7 Years bott 13 **(94.5)** n23.5 brilliant nose: the rye compartment is next door to the clean, crisp Demerara. Fruity, sharp and pulsing; t23.5 fresh, again showing its rye recipe credentials to the full. Fabulous clarity with a Jim Beam style intensity to the sugared liquorice; f23.5 long, with a beautifully controlled sweetness and late, elegant hickory flourish; b24 there is an argument that if you wanted to present someone with a bottle of bourbon to show them all its main and unique characteristics, this should be the one: very useful, indeed. 'Andy Ambler – a lion among the scouts. *49.5% WB15/372*

Smooth Ambler Old Scout Straight Bourbon 10 Years Old batch 2, bott 4 May 13 **(95.5)** n24 fruity: citrus and pear juice-calmed; light vanilla and even lighter spice; t24 one of the softest bourbon deliveries at this strength I have encountered for a good while: the sugars are of the melt-on-impact variety, thickened only by the lightest touch of ulmo honey and broadened by a slow evolving of cream fudge and molasses. The liquorice is playful and the oak is from the butterscotch school; f23.5 quietens further. A spicy buzz rumbles and forms the backdrop to the slowest possible fade of the delivery; b24 one of the most delicate and sophisticated bourbons of the year. Absolutely every aspect of this glorious whisky is disarmingly understated...how un-American! *50% WB15/374*

Spring 44 Straight Bourbon batch 2 **(84.5)** n21 t22.5 f20.5 b20.5. A straight Kentucky bourbon blended from two distinctly different rye recipe styles. The result is something very different, indeed – and sadly doesn't always work. In short, chocolate orange meets Yorkshire Tea. Odd. *45% (90 proof)*

Spring 44 Single Barrel Bourbon batch 2, barrel no 8 **(93)** n22 t23.5 f23.5 b24. Pure entertainment. Ticks many of the boxes the Spring 44 bourbon misses. And, to be brutally honest, barrels properly blended should always outperform a single one. *50% (100 proof)*

Stagg Jn (91.5) n22.5 t24 f22.5 b22.5. A whiskey of staggering brinkmanship. Who will blink first? The massive oak or the taste buds. To be honest, this is the kind of bourbon that sorts out the men from the boys, the women from the girls. Doesn't have quite enough covering sweetness of varying type and intensity to match the complexity found in the original Stagg. One that needs a very long time to get to the bottom of. *67.2% (134.4 proof)*

⁘ **Trails End Bourbon 8 Year Old (87)** n21.5 t22.5 f21.5 b21.5. A light bourbon, where the end of the trail begins early. The citrus outpoints the tannins all too easily. *45% (90 Proof). Hood River Distillers, Inc.*

Very Old Barton 90 Proof (94) n23 t24 f23.5 b23.5. One of the most dangerously drinkable whiskeys in the world... *45% (90 proof)*

Very Old Barton 6 Years Old (92) n23 t23 f23 b23. One of those seemingly gifted bourbons that, swan-like, appears to glide at the surface but on closer inspection has loads going on underneath. *43%*

Virgin Bourbon 7 Years Old (96.5) n24 so Wild Turkey-esque in style it is almost untrue: just loads of honey spilling out of the glass, backed up by big rye and leathery oak; t24.5 hold on to the arm of your seats...the mouth feel is massive with chocolate honeycomb surrounded by juicy dates and figs; liquorice has been piled high with really thick molasses...quite incredible; f24 the corn oils carry the sugars to the very end. But like distant thunder beyond the limestone hills, comes the spices and that liquorice, now with a touch of hickory, rumbling to the last...; b24 this takes me back nearly 40 years to when I first began my love affair with bourbon and was still a bit of a whisky virgin. This was the very style that blew me away: big, uncompromising, rugged...yet with a heart of honeyed gold. It is the type of huge, box-ticking, honest bourbon that makes you get on your hands and knees and kiss Kentucky soil. *50.5% (101 proof)*

Virgin Bourbon 15 Years Old (92.5) n23.5 t23 f23.5 b23. The kind of bourbon you want to be left in a room with. *50.5% (101 proof)*

Virginia Gentleman (90.5) n22 t23 f23 b23.5. A Gentleman in every sense: and a pretty sophisticated one at that. *40% (80 Proof)*

Weller 12 Years Old (93) n24 t23.5 f22.5 b23. Sheer quality. And an enormous leap in complexity and grace from the 7-y-o. *45%*

Western Gold 6 Year Old Bourbon Whiskey (91.5) n22 heavy liquorice and faintly burnt toast; dry and debonair; **t23** early spice pricks through the light layering of manuka honey and hickory. Overall, deep, though with the Demerera acting as peacekeeper as the spices continue to thrust; **f22.5** soft oils and light buzzing spice; **b23** taken from barrels sitting high in the warehouse, that's for sure. You get a lot for your six years... *40%*.

Wild Turkey 101 (91) n22 t23.5 f22.5 b23. By far the best 101 I have tasted in a decade: you simply can't do anything but go weak at the knees with that spice attack. *55.5% (101 proof)*

Wild Turkey American Spirit Aged 15 Years (92) n24 t22.5 f22.5 b23. A delightful Wild Turkey that appears under par for a 100 proofer but offers much when you search those nooks and crannies of your palate. *50.0% (100 proof)*

Wild Turkey Rare Breed bott code L0049FH **(94) n22.5 t24.5 f23 b24.** It is hard to credit that this is the same brand I have been tasting at regular intervals for quite a long while. Certainly nothing like this style has been around for a decade and it is massively far removed from two years ago. The nose threatens a whiskey limited in direction. But the delivery is as profound as it is entertaining. Even on this bottling's singular though fabulous style, not perhaps quite overall the gargantuan whiskey of recent years. But, seeing as it's only the nose which pegs it back a point or two, still one that would leave a big hole in your whiskey experience if you don't get around to trying. *54.1%*

Willett Pot Still Reserve barrel no. 2421 **(95.5) n24.5 t23 f24 b24.** Another fabulous whiskey from Willett. You can so often trust them to deliver and here they have given us a bourbon showing serious oak injection, yet a sweetness which counters perfectly. *47%*.

William Larue Weller (97) n24 t24 f25 b24. Among the best wheated mash bill bourbon I have ever encountered. Why some whiskeys work better than others is the stuff of long debate. The reason for this particular bottling is relatively simple: you have an almost breathless intensity, yet somehow the constituent parts of the complexity can be individually identified and savoured. That is quite rare in any whiskey with this degree of weight. *67.4% ncf.*

William Larue Weller (97.5) n24 weightier than last time out, though only fractionally, and here much more dependent on a coffee framework backed by wonderfully crystallised dark sugars. Plenty of hickory and little cough sweet thicken the soup; **t24.5** it is probably impossible to get more types of dark sugars into the delivery of whiskey. This is so mesmerizing, you find yourself chuckling as the taste buds are asked to identify the myriad sugar and honey styles which pass through. I have counted eight with some form of certainty...though I'm sure I've missed a few, too; **f24** to make this whiskey work, you now need the finale to be moderately dry...to the point of sophistication. And that is exactly what you get. You can almost taste the char, though it is, like on the nose, the hickory which shapes the finish, comfortably cradling the spices which are dying to burst out; **b25** for any whiskey with a proof of 123.4, the only way is up...! Last year's Whisky Bible World Whisky of the Year Runner-up is going for the full title big time, no holds barred. Again, this is absolutely supreme class. *61.7% (123.4 proof). ncf. Buffalo Trace Antique Collection.*

William Larue Weller dist Spring 2001 db **(97.5) n24.5** almost too profound for words: you nose this as you might peel an onion, simply by stripping away layer upon layer. The sugars are of the heaviest duty imaginable: a mix of treacle and molasses. But this is met by a toasty almost meaty thrust of oak and spice. So dense, outwardly, but give it time and you will be royally entertained; **t24.5** no less massive on delivery. As ever, the sugars are in mesmerising form; thick, dark, brooding, restrained and holding onto the chunky oak to somehow up the intensity. Like on the nose, it is the dark sugars which perform, now with some manuka honey entering the fray; the spices, now buzzing and nipping, are truly glorious, **f24** just a fraction more restrained and simplistic than before. The oak has made more of a fist of this and is determined to end the complexity of the sugars; **b24.5** I always save this as one of the last whiskeys I taste for each Bible. In life you always need something to look forward to... *68.1%*.

⬦ **William Larue Weller (97) n24** which dominates? The wheat-induced spices? The burnt golden syrup? The liquorice-molasses mix? None? All...? **t24.5** just a slow drip-dripping of spices and acacia honey, then manuka. Probably the silkiest mouth feel to any wheated whiskey on the planet and unquestionably the most glorious intertwangling of honey-dripping dark sugars and even thicker but non-threatening tannins you'll encounter in this and many other years. For all this, salivating and just dripping with fresh juices; **f24** the spices continue surprisingly tamely but all those notes found earlier continue but in a lower key...; **b24.5** just one of those whiskeys which makes sense of life, of whiskey. A collection and collaboration of flavours and shapes on the palate which simply beguile... *70.1% (140.2 proof).*

Woodford Reserve Batch 98 (85.5) n23 t21.5 f20 b21. The promise of the nose, full of the kind of liquorice and molassey lovers of Old Forester rightly drool over will be as disappointed as I at the bitterness which digs in hard from the mid-point onwards. *43.2%*.

Woodford Reserve Batch 115 (90) n22 soft, delicate. Perhaps missing some complexity; mainly lemon-soaked vanilla; **t22** soft delivery; some citrus and coconut water amid the deeper tannin; **f23** late praline with no shortage of oily depth and demerera; really lovely spices come into their own as the story unfolds; **b23** for those who prefer their bourbons a little nutty and creamy. And spicy... *43.2%*

Woodford Reserve Batch 124 (87) **n22.5 t22 f21 b21.5.** Pleasant enough bourbon. Perhaps the tannins could do with a little muzzling, as they have too much to say when there are so few counter notes. The thickness of the oils hardly helps, either. Enjoyable squeezes of citrus and do enjoy the cocoa and lime theme. *43.2%*

Woodford Reserve Batch 126 (87.5) **n21.5 t23 f21.5 b22.** A very tame bourbon poodling along the Bourbon Highway at a steady 40mph. A slight over dependence on sugars make for a limitation in complexity, badly requiring some of the oak prevalent in batch 124 to make things happen. This lack of body allows a degree of over bitterness at the end. But plenty of citrus and at the late middle a welcome, if short-lived, burst of mocha. With plenty of Demerera, of course... *43.2% . WB15/172*

Woodford Reserve Distiller's Select batch 95 (91) **n23 t23 f22 b23.** Few bourbons so beautifully pits sweet against dry to such excellent effect. *43.2%*

⬦ **Woodford Reserve Double Oaked** (95) **n24.5** oh-my-word...!!! The best nose from Woodford Reserve yet: it appears enormous, yet has been muffled so the intensity is controlled and spreads gorgeously. Dried dates mix with fig rolls, red liquorice and hickory. Not a single note, though, tries to upstage another...; **t23.5** soft delivery, as it just had to be, though the spices arrive earlier than might be expected. Even so, those lush fruit notes soften the more intense liquorice and molasses; **f23** thins, leaving the lighter sugars and spices to play out the end game; a little bitterness creeps in at the death; **b24** the old Labrot and Graham Distillery has just entered a new phase of excellence since its reopening. Well done blender on creating a bourbon not just of beauty but of great significance. *43.2% WB16/052*

Woodford Reserve Master's Collection Four Grain (95) **n24 t24 f23 b24.** Sod's law would have it that the moment we removed this from the 2006 Bible, having appeared in the previous two editions without it ever making the shelves, it should at last be belatedly released. But a whiskey worth waiting for, or what? The tasting notes are not a million miles from the original. But this is better bourbon, one that appears to have received a significant polish in the intervening years. Nothing short of magnificent. *46.2%*

Tennessee Whiskey
BENJAMIN PRICHARD
Benjamin Prichard's Tennessee Whiskey (83) **n21.5 t21 f20 b20.5.** Majestic fruity rye notes trill from the glass. Curiously yeasty as well; bounding with all kinds of freshly crushed brown sugar crystals. Pleasant enough, but doesn't gel like Prichard's bourbon. *40%*

GEORGE DICKEL
George Dickel Superior No 12 Brand Whisky (90.5) **n22.5 t23 f22.5 b22.5.** A different story told by George from the last one I heard. But certainly no less fascinating. *45%*

JACK DANIEL
Jack Daniel's 120th Anniversary of the White Rabbit Saloon (91) **n22.5** lighter ulmo honey to this, which just lowers the temperature and intensity of the liquorice. Complex stuff...; **t23.5** magnificent delivery: early corn oil carries the deft molasses; both black and red liquorice slowly builds but the middle is pure vanilla; **f22** a mix of dry molassed notes and a little muscovado. Excellent late balance; **b23** on its best-behaved form. After the delivery, the oils are down a little, so not the usual bombastic offering from JD. Nonetheless, this is pure class and the clever use of sugars simply make you drool... *43%. Brown-Forman.*

Jack Daniel's Holiday Select 2013 Limited Edition db (91.5) **n23** probably the most well-seasoned nose I have ever experienced from JD. Less oil apparent allowing the herbs, spices and black cherry free rein. Almost as though perfumed...surely not...! **t23** remarkably dry delivery with the tannins biting deep and with very little sugar for support. Those which do come through are of the molassed variety; **f22.5** back to the spicy, seasoned style apparent on the nose; **b23** just never seen a JD like this...some pretty well cooked barrels in play here. Doubtless all this is by judicious barrel choice. Now the Americans are tampering with their casks, for the first time ever I began to wonder if the flavouring wasn't all natural. I am sure it is, but see what happens once you begin trying to change the rules...? *49% WB15/381*

Jack Daniel's Old No.7 Brand (Black Label) (92) **n23 t23 f22.5 b23.5.** Actually taken aback by this guy. The heavier oils have been muzzled and the points here are for complexity...that should shock a few old Hell's Angels I know. *40%*

Jack Daniel's Master Distiller Series No 1 db (90.5) **n24** wonderful dose of extra tangy kumquat over the normal JD signature; something of the fruity cough sweet about this one;

t22 a massive, pleasantly oiled mix of molassed fudge and liquorice; **f22** drier, toastier hickory; **b22.5** no mistaking the JD pedigree. Just a few telling extra degrees of fruit. *43% WB15/387*

⬦ **Jack Daniel's Rested Tennessee Rye** batch 2 **(88.5) n22** oily and lightly honeyed. Beyond the house style liquorice, surprisingly docile...; **t23** and there is no explosion on the palate, either. Just a dull thud as the fruity rye notes collide with the taste buds. There are some gentle spices sprinkled here and there, plus a little ulmo honey to accompany the liquorice; **f21** and now all is quiet, except for that light spice buzz and muscovado sugar. The bitterness of the oils strike late on; **b22.5** possibly the most intriguing whiskey of the year: America's most flavour-enhancing stills take on the world's most flavoursome grain. The result is surprisingly well mannered, though the oils from both the stills and grain do help obliterate any meaningful complexity. Probably the only world whiskey type I have never tasted in a warehouse at full strength (though I now intend to correct that). Instinct tells me a trick has been missed by not making this a 101...Oh, and one important thing. Normally I suggest you take your whiskey at body temperature. This is one whiskey which needs to be tasted at normal room temperature to keep the oils to a minimum and allow the rye maximum airtime. *40% WB16/022*

Jack Daniel's Single Barrel 12-5660 bott 15 Oct 12 db **(92.5) n23.5** such clarity to the crystallised Demerara sugar, even though some molasses seems to have got into the act; slight cloves and hickory fumble the mocha's blouse buttons; **t23.5** silk delivery, very much putting the onus on the crisp sugars to forge a bright palm, along which the very light oils (certainly lighter than of old) travel, as well as a gentle fruit rye kick which acts as the rudder; **f22.5** much gentler than of yore with some spices amid the vanillas; **b23** I'll tell you something about JD. A number of "whisky specialist" I know rubbish this whiskey. With a passion. In fact, they can barely bring themselves to call it whiskey at all. But their single barrel range really does show what magnificent stock they have maturing in their warehouses. As this random bottling testifies... Magnificent stuff. And sod the so-called experts, I say...just enjoy it! *45%*

⬦ **Jack Daniel's Single Barrel Holiday Select 2014 (93) n23.5** only one distillery on this planet produces a nose this oily and heavy, so full of the joys of liquorice, hickory and molasses; **t23** if you ever want to know what a nose tastes like, try this...; **f23** long, supremely chewy and thick enough to stand Syke's Hydrometer in; the manuka honey on the finish is rather wonderful...; **b23.5** if anybody puts a Coke in this, they want shooting. JD, warts 'n' all... Magnificent! One gripe: a single barrel, but no way of knowing which barrel...grrrrr!!! *48% WB16/020*

Corn Whiskey

Dixie Dew (95) n22.5 corn whiskey...???? Really...??? The corn oils form a bit of a sweet blob, but elsewhere it is all about graduated degrees of cocoa and hickory...and all rather lovely. **t24** good grief!! Have not tasted a profile such as this: healthy corn oils but then a welter of Columbian Santander Cacao and rye-rich spices interject. Absolutely unique and astonishing...; **f24** the corn plays out its long farewell but the spices don't listen and take up the main ground; a few juicy sultanas fly in...from goodness knows where; **b24.5** I have kept in my previous tasting notes for this whiskey as they serve a valuable purpose. The three matured corn whiskeys I have before me are made by the same distillers. But, this time round, they could not be more different. From Mellow Corn to Dixie we have three whiskeys with very differing hues. This, quite frankly, is the darkest corn whiskey I have ever seen and one of world class stature with characteristics I have never found before in any whiskey. Any true connoisseur of whisk(e)y will make deals with Lucifer to experience this freak whiskey. There is no age statement...but this one has gray hairs attached to the cob... *50%*

Georgia Moon Corn Whiskey "Less Than 30 Days Old" (83.5) n21.5 t22 f20 b20. If anyone has seen corn whiskey made – either in Georgia or Kentucky – then the unique aroma will be instantly recognisable from the fermenters and still house. Enjoyable stuff which does exactly what it says on the jar. *50%*

J. W. Corn (92.5) n23 t23.5 f23 b23. In another life this could be bourbon. The corn holds the power, for sure. But the complexity and levels are so far advanced that this – again! – qualifies as very high grade whiskey. Wonderful that the normal high standard is being maintained for what is considered by many, quite wrongly, as an inferior spirit. *50%*

Mellow Corn (83) n19 t21 f22 b21. Dull and oily on the nose, though the palate compensates with a scintillating array of sweet and spicy notes. *50%*

Single Malt Rye
ANCHOR DISTILLERY

Old Potrero Single Malt Straight Rye Whiskey Essay 10-SRW-ARM-E (94) n24 t23 f24 b23 The whiskey from this distillery never fails to amaze. With the distillery now under new management it will be fascinating to see what lands in my tasting lab. Even at 75% quality we will still be blessed with astonishing whiskeys. *45% (90 proof)*

Straight Rye

Benjamin Prichard's Tennessee Rye Whiskey (86) n20 t21.5 f23 b21.5. Bit of a scruffy nose, but polishes up pleasantly. The rye itself is not of the sharp variety and at times is hard to identify. But the ulmo honey and lush butterscotch offer the gloss at the finish. 43%

Bulleit 95 Rye (96) n25 only the rye from the Lawrenceburg Indiana distillery can conjure a perfect rye aroma such as this...and that is exactly where it is from. Cinnamon and crunchy muscovado sugar crystal on green apple...so soft...so rigid...so unique...; t24.5 exactly as the nose is fashioned, so is the delivery. At once liltingly soft yet absolutely granite hard...the rye offers both fruity and spicy branches...both lead to a salivating trunk; f22.5 echoes of firm grain and fruit but pretty quick by comparison to what has gone on before...23.5 this is a style of rye, indeed whiskey, which is unique. Buffalo Trace makes an ultra high-quality rye which lasts the course longer. But nothing compares in nose and delivery to this...in fact few whiskies in the world get even close... 45%. Straight *95% rye mash whiskey.*

Colonel E.H. Taylor Straight Rye (97) n24 how can a breezy whiskey, seemingly so light and full of sparkle, also have such an intensely dark side? The rye grains appear to have a spotlight on them following their every elegant movement; the spices, at first docile, build and build. Yet all the time, the grain appears to revel in its cut-glass sugary clarity. A little mystifying, too, as the vague clove and eucalyptus lurking in the background reveals an oak presence found nowhere else in the tasting experience; t24.5 almost all you want from a rye: so clean, so intent in purpose, that the grain seems to transform into Demerara granules with the most polite oils and (for the oak) ulmo honey notes spreading all far and wide and with sensational eight; f24 all is left to the muscovado sugar and quietly persistent ulmo honey to ensure no bitterness or any other wayward notes can infringe upon the charmingly sweet and still lively finish; b24.5 reminds me of the younger ryes when Sazerac Handy first hit the shelves, with the emphasis on the clarity of the grain and the fallout of oak and spice. Really, a bottle which should never be left on a liquor store shelf. 50%

Cougar Rye (95) n25 t24 f23 b23. The Lawrenceburg, Indiana Distillery makes the finest rye I have ever tasted - and that is saying something. Here is a magnificent example of their astonishing capabilities. Good luck hunting the Cougar. 37%. *Foster's Group, Australia.*

Crater Lake Rye Whiskey Batch no. JA 08 db (83.5) n20 t22 f20.5 b21. A distinctly warming, peppery whiskey with an obvious high rye content. Would do itself better justice as a 100 proof whiskey as here the oils are broken down a little too enthusiastically, allowing unhelpful freedom to a tobacco note. Good early use of dark sugars, though. One to keep an eye on. 40%.

Devil's Bit Seven-Year-Old Single Barrel (93.5) n22.5 t24 f23 b24. A must-find rye from one of the most impressive small distilleries in the world. 47.7%. *Edgefield Distillery.*

High West 12 Years Old Rye (92.5) n22 t24 f23 b23.5. A very clever rye which will hit a chord of appreciation for those who savour this whiskey style. 46%

High West Whiskey Rendezvous Rye Batch 12431 db (94.5) n23.5 sharp, classic rye. Hard as nails and brittle on the nose, the fresh fruity rye leaps from the glass; t24 and that sharpness translates perfectly on the palate. A younger style than before, with far more salivating grain. The molasses is something else; f23 still profound and sharop b24 after a few disappointing batches, this one appears to have found that vital spark. It could be a whole new set of whiskeys, a change of one barrel, or even the same whiskey re-stirred before bottling. It doesn't matter: something has clicked. 46%. ncf. WB15/176

⟐ **Jim Beam Pre-Prohibition Style Rye** db (95) n23 crisp muscovado and rye: clean, precise and slightly dazzling; t24.5 brilliant delivery: the old-fashioned juicy crispness on the palate of a Jim Beam rye has been restored, despite a background fudgy smokiness which dovetails with amazing finesse; a little manuka honey goes a long, long way; f23.5 long, with the spices now grabbing hold. Fabulous mocha makes the most of the lingering sugar and fading rye; b24 very similar to how Jim Bean Yellow Label was over 20 years ago. In other words: simply superb! 45% (90 Proof)

⟐ **Knob Creek Straight Rye Whiskey (92.5)** n23.5 classic rye firmness: a light dose of citrus and mango tries to gently thin the intensity; t23.5 salivating small grain action with the rye making its biggest mark at the base of the tongue. For all the light oils and juiciness, there is no escaping the crispness at the centre, or the surrounding spices; f22.5 an attractive rye-vanilla mix, with just a late frisson on liquorice; b23 a slightly more genteel rye than I expected, if you compare standard Knob Creek to their usual bourbon. 50%

⟐ **Michter's No. 1 Straight Rye (95.5)** n23.5 fabulous cut glass clarity to the rye, sparkling with almost crystalline sugars; t24 crunchy, rock hard and palate teaming with rye particles of the most clean and uncompromising style; the oils are clever and couched amid the juicier, fruity notes; f24 drier now, though the spices pick up as the tannins begin to get a grip; but the grain absolutely refuses to take a back seat; b24 truly classic rye whiskey. The stuff which makes one write swoonerisms... 42.4%

Pappy Van Winkle's Family Reserve Rye 13 Years Old (94) n24 outwardly, the aroma basks in a crisp rye flourish: scratch below the surface and there are darker, more sinister oaky forces at work; t23.5 crisp, almost crackling rye offers both the fruity-clean and burned fruitcake options; f23 dulls out a bit as the liquorice/toffee oak takes hold but remains alluringly spicy and sensual; b23.5 uncompromising rye that successfully tells two stories simultaneously. A great improvement on the Winkle rye of old. 478%

◈ **Pikesville Straight Rye Whiskey Aged at Least 6 Years** (97.5) n24.5 textbook: the fruitiness of the rye shimmers on the nose; a light spice tingles in Demerara rum fashion. Carry on nosing and you will, if patient and able enough, find unusual depths to which few whiskies reach. The tantalising chocolate-liquorice at about three quarters depth is one of the aromas of the year; t24.5 after that nose, the delivery just had to be majestic. And it is. The rye grain fair rattles against the teeth, the sugars – crystalline, dark and tinged with both molasses and muscovado – help bring its salivating qualities to maximum. Then those spices...those wonderful, bustling, fizzing spices...; f24 a lovely mix between ulmo and Zambian forest honey keeps the sweetness lingering to the end. The rye, of course, continues to sparkle and spice its way to the last embers of the fade...which is a long way away...; b24.5 the most stunning of ryes and the best from Heaven Hill for some time. 55% (110 Proof)

◈ **Redemption Riverboat Rye** (78) n19 t21 f19 b19. Dry, weirdly off key and oily – and holed below the water line. 40%

◈ **Redemption Rye** (85.5) n22 t22.5 f20 b21. The tobacco nose is a bit of a poser: how did that get there? Or the spearmint, which helps as you try to chew things over in your mind. The big rye wave on delivery is supported by mixed dark sugars. But there is something ashy about the finish. 46%

Rittenhouse Very Rare Single Barrel 21 Years Old (91) n25 t23 f21 b22. I may be wrong, but I would wager quite a large amount that no-one living has tasted more rye from around the world than I. So trust me when I tell you this is different, a genuine one-off in style. By rights such telling oak involvement should have killed the whisky stone dead: this is like someone being struck by lightning and then walking off slightly singed and with a limp, but otherwise OK. The closest style of whisky to rye is Irish pot still, a unique type where unmalted barley is used. And the closest whiskey I have tasted to this has been 35 to 50-year-old pot still Irish. What they have in common is a massive fruit base, so big that it can absorb and adapt to the oak input over many years. This has not escaped unscathed. But it has to be said that the nose alone makes this worthy of discovery, as does the glory of the rye as it first melts into the tastebuds. The term flawed genius could have been coined for this whisky alone. Yet, for all its excellence, I can so easily imagine someone, somewhere, claiming to be an expert on whiskey, bleating about the price tag of $150 a bottle. If they do, ignore them. Because, frankly, rye has been sold far too cheaply for far too long and that very cheapness has sculpted a false perception in people's minds about the quality and standing of the spirit. Well, 21 years in Kentucky equates to about 40 years in Scotland. And you try and find a 40-year-old Scotch for £75. If anything, they are giving this stuff away. The quality of the whiskey does vary from barrel to barrel and therefore bottle to bottle. So below I have given a summary of each individual bottling (averaging (91.1). The two with the highest scores show the least oak interference...yet are quite different in style. That's great whiskey for you. 50% (100 proof). ncf

Barrel no. 1 (91) n25 t23 f21 b22. As above. 50%
Barrel no. 2 (89) n24 t23 f20 b22. Dryer, oakier. 50%
Barrel no. 3 (91) n24 t23 f22 b22. Fruity, soft. 50%
Barrel no. 4 (90) n25 t22 f21 b22. Enormous. 50%
Barrel no. 5 (93) n25 t23 f22 b23. Early rye surge. 50%
Barrel no. 6 (87) n23 t22 f20 b22. Juicy, vanilla. 50%
Barrel no. 7 (90) n23 t23 f22 b22. Even, soft, honeyed. 50%
Barrel no. 8 (95) n25 t24 f23 b23. The works: massive rye. 50%
Barrel no. 9 (91) n24 t23 f22 b22. Sharp rye, salivating. 50%
Barrel no. 10 (93) n25 t24 f22 b22. Complex, sweet. 50%
Barrel no. 11 (93) n24 t24 f22 b23. Rich, juicy, spicy. 50%
Barrel no. 12 (91) n25 t23 f21 b22. Near identical to no.1. 50%
Barrel no. 13 (91) n24 t24 f21 b22. Citrus and toasty. 50%
Barrel no. 14 (94) n25 t24 f22 b23. Big rye and marzipan. 50%
Barrel no. 15 (88) n23 t22 f21 b22. Major oak influence. 50%
Barrel no. 16 (90) n24 t23 f21 b22. Spicy and toffeed. 50%
Barrel no. 17 (90) n23 t23 f22 b22. Flinty, firm, late rye kick. 50%
Barrel no. 18 (91) n24 t24 f21 b22. Big rye delivery. 50%
Barrel no. 19 (87) n23 t22 f21 b21. Major coffee input. 50%
Barrel no. 20 (91) n23 t24 f22 b22. Spicy sugar candy. 50%

Barrel no. 21 (94) n24 t23 f24 b23. Subtle, fruity. 50%
Barrel no. 22 (89) n23 t22 f22 b22. Mollased rye. 50%
Barrel no. 23 (94) n24 t23 f24 b23. Soft fruit, massive rye. 50%
Barrel no. 24 (88) n23 t22 f21 b22. Intense oak and caramel. 50%
Barrel no. 25 (93) n25 t22 f23 b23. Heavy rye and spice. 50%
Barrel no. 26 (92) n23 t23 f23 b23. Subtle, delicate rye. 50%
Barrel no. 27 (94) n25 t23 f23 b23. Delicate rye throughout. 50%
Barrel no. 28 (96) n25 t24 f23 b24. Salivating, roasty, major. 50%
Barrel no. 29 (88) n23 t22 f21 b22. Hot, fruity. 50%
Barrel no. 30 (91) n24 t23 f22 b22. Warming cough sweets. 50%
Barrel no. 31 (90) n25 t22 f21 b22. Aggressive rye. 50%

Rittenhouse Rye Single Barrel Aged 25 Years (93.5) n24.5 t24 f22 b23. This is principally about the nose: a thing of rare beauty even in the highest peaks of the whiskey world. The story on the palate is much more about damage limitation with the oak going at bit nuts. But remember this: in Scottish years due to the heat in Kentucky, this would be a malt well in excess of 50 years. But even with the signs of fatigue, so crisp is that rye, so beautifully defined are its intrinsic qualities that the quality is still there to be clearly seen. Just don't judge on the first, second or even third mouthful. Your taste buds need time to relax & adjust. Only then will they accommodate and allow you to fully appreciate and enjoy the creaky old ride. At this age, though, always worth remembering that the best nose doesn't always equal the best tasting experience... 50% (100proof).

Barrel no. 1 (93.5) n24.5 t24 f22 b23. As above. 50%
Barrel no. 2 (88) n22 t24 f20 b22. Intense. Crisp, juicy; a tad soapy, bitter. 50%
Barrel no. 3 (89.5) n23 t23.5 f21.5 b21.5. Fabulously crisp. Fruity. Mollassed. 50%
Barrel no. 4 (85) n21.5 t21.5 f21 b21. Subdued fruit. Massive oak. 50%
Barrel no. 5 (90.5) n25 t22.5 f21.5 b21.5. Complex. Mega oaked but spiced, fruity. 50%
Barrel no. 6 (91.5) n24.5 t22 f23 b22. Tangy. Honeyed and hot. Spiced marmalade. 50%
Barrel no. 7 (83.5) n20 t22 f20.5 b21. Treacle toffee amid the burnt apple. 50%
Barrel no. 8 (90) n23.5 t23.5 f21 b22. Flinty, teeth-cracking rye. Crème brulee. 50%
Barrel no. 9 (91) n23.5 t23.5 f22 b22. Massive ryefest. Mocha coated. 50%
Barrel no. 10 (86.5) n22 t23 f20 b21.5. Early zip and juice. Tires towards caramel. 50%
Barrel no. 11 (89) n24 t22 f21 b22. Honeycomb. Hickory. Caramel. Oil. 50%
Barrel no. 12 (84.5) n22.5 t21 f20 b21. Delicate. Vanilla and caramel. Light. 50%
Barrel no. 13 (89.5) n22.5 t23 f22 b22. Succulent. Yet rye remains firm. 50%
Barrel no. 14 (88) n22 t23 f21 b22. Very similar to 13 but with extra caramel. 50%
Barrel no. 15 (86) n21 t23 f20.5 b21.5. Lazy grain. Warming but flat. Caramel. 50%
Barrel no. 16 (92) n23 t23 f23 b23. Sculpted rye: sugared fruit; a twist of juniper. 50%
Barrel no. 17 (86.5) n22.5 t21.5 f21 b21.5. Fizzy, fruity spice calmed by caramel. 50%
Barrel no. 18 (91) n23.5 t23.5 f21.5 b22.5. Pristine rye. Spice. Juicy molasses. Crisp. 50%
Barrel no. 19 (96) n24 t23.5 f24.5 b23.5. Concentrated honeycomb and chocolate. 50%
Barrel no. 20 (89.5) n23 t22 f22.5 b22. Cream toffee. Fruit and spice. 50%
Barrel no. 21 (85) n21 t20 f23 b21. Severe oak delivery. Recovers with mocha toffee. 50%
Barrel no. 22 (81) n20 t20 f21 b20. Mild sap. Fruity. Oily. 50%
Barrel no. 23 (94) n23.5 t24 f23.5 b23. Rich. Fruity. Juicy. Clean. Corn oil. Cocoa. 50%
Barrel no. 24 (88.5) n22.5 t22 f21 b22. Huge vanilla. Slow spice. 50%
Barrel no. 25 (88) n22.5 t21.5 f22 b22. Custard and sugared fruit. Sharpens. 50%
Barrel no. 26 (90.5) n22 t23 f23 b22.5. Classic crisp rye. Big, manageable oak. 50%
Barrel no. 27 (88) n23 t22 f21.5 b21.5. Huge, honeyed oak. Oily. Dries at end. 50%
Barrel no. 28 (91) n22.5 t23.5 f22.5 b22.5. Exemplary honeycomb-rye delivery. Spices. 50%
Barrel no. 29 (94) n23.5 t24 f23 b23.5. Juicy rye; crisp sugar-vanilla-hickory fade. 50%
Barrel no. 30 (94.5) n23 t24 f24 b23.5. Thick rye. Cocoa. Spices. 50%
Barrel no. 31 (79) n21 t20 f19 b19. Lethargic. Bitter. 50%
Barrel no. 32 (88) n21.5 t22.5 f22 b22. Relaxed honeycomb. Hint of mint. 50%
Barrel no. 33 (88.5) n22.5 t22 f22 b22. Powering oak-rye battle. 50%
Barrel no. 34 (84) n23 t21 f20 b20. Thick oak throughout. Corn oil. 50%
Barrel no. 35 (93.5) n22.5 t23.5 f24 b23.5. Big rye. Demerara-hickory. Complex. 50%
Barrel no. 36 (77) n21 t19 f18 b19. Bitter oak. 50%

Russell's Reserve Rye 6 Year Old Small Batch bott. code L0194FH) (93.5) n24 t23.5 f22.5 b23.5. Lost none of its wit and sharpness: in fact has improved a notch or two in recent times. 45%

Sazerac Kentucky Straight Rye Whiskey 18 Years Old bott 2012 (95.5) n24 t23 f24 b24.5. Unquestionably showing a different side to its personality this time out, allowing the rye to show its fruity personality to the full. 45%

Sazerac Rye 18 Year Old bott Fall 2013 db (97) n24.5 if you are studying whiskey and need to know exactly how a straight rye should nose, stick your beak above a glass of this: sparkling grain, crisp, refined, unsullied by caramel and crystalline; t24.5 heavier now than the nose: the oak has made inroads and forges a delightful partnership with the light oils. Again, the sweetness is spot on, just enough muscovado to make the rye almost three dimensional in its sharpness; **f24** settles for a softer touch now, though the spices compensate. Hard to imagine a better rye-oak balance, though; **b24** another stir of the pot and up comes Sazerac 18 polished and wallowing in its own enormity. Rye whiskey exactly how it should be. *45%.*

⬧ **Sazerac Rye 18 Year Old** bott Spring 2014 db **(96.5) n24.5** a little less oil than normal means getting a particularly vivid sight of the rye in all its crisp, subtly fruity pomp; a bit like how the stars are brighter when you view them away from the lights. Last year was a little less sharp, if memory serves, but again the weight of the spice and the tannin simply cannot be bettered; also with this little less oil we can now recognose something of the herb garden...; **t24.5** dark and deep on the palate, there is a mischievous chocolate character abroad and this chimes in stunningly with the crunchy grain and promiscuous pices; **f23.5** the oak lays down the law slightly, with the spices its gun-happy deputy. The rye is now hiding a little; **b24** always one of the great and most fascinating whiskeys on the planet - essentially the same stuff year after year - plays out with each roll of the bottling dice. Here someone has cut off much of the oil...with stunning results. Way better than last year's offering and much closer to its old self. *45%. Buffalo Trace Antique Collection*

Smooth Ambler Old Scout Straight Rye Aged 7 Years batch 17, bott 9 Nov 13 **(82) n21 t22 f19 b20.** Now this is odd. What do you get when you combine the characteristics of rye and gin? Something, probably, like this. Never been to these guys in West Virginia, though I'll try and make a point of paying a visit when next in that stunning state. No idea if they are involved with gin. But something about the botanical feel to the nose and finish in particular suggests they might. Perhaps a bottling problem for this single batch? Intrigued. *49.5% WB15/373*

Sonoma County Rye pot distilled from grain db **(83.5) n21 t21.5 f20 b21.** Sweet nougat, heavy duty, wide-cut oily. Quite German in style. *48%. 1512 Spirits. WB15/384*

Thomas H. Handy Sazerac Straight Rye Whiskey (97.5) n24 heavy on the spice and honey and quite light on the flinty rye which can often be found here. Entangled, enticing, beguiling....; **t24.5** hold on to your hats, the chair...nail yourself to the ground...this is going to be some ride. The rye appears to have been to the gym and grown a few extra muscles: this is big and the spice will demolish the lily-livered beyond comprehension. The rye grains are always at the centre, even when a little liquorice forms towards the midpoint; **f24.5** long and now back to the grain once more with the varying sugar strains head in all directions; a slightly dry finish as, at last, the oak gets a word in but the countering sweetness is ulmo honey at its deftest; **b24.5** this was World Whisky of the Year last year and anyone buying this on the strength of that will not be disappointed. Huge whiskey with not even the glimmer of a hint of an off note. Magnificent: an honour to taste and rye smiles all round... *66.2%. ncf.*

⬧ **Thomas H. Handy Sazerac Straight Rye (95.5) n24** about as herbal as I've ever known this brand: crushed green leaves, including eucalyptus, make for a sharpness which isn't the usual crisp rye character you might expect; **t24** not so much enters the mouth as kisses it: for something around 130% proof you expect a thudding entry - instead, you get a controlled explosion with no casualties. All relatively free of angst or burn and concentrates on the delightful marriage between the intense grain and the calmer, sweeter ulmo honey. The oak pulses in the background, but without recourse to a full spice attack; **f23.5** curious how these big oils seem to carry with it so much natural caramel...makes for the softest finish you imagine for a whiskey so gargantuan...; **b24** perhaps because this has become something of a softie, without all those usual jagged and crisp rye notes, it doesn't quite hit the spot with quite the same delicious drama. Still a beauty, though. *64.6%*

Thomas H. Handy dist Spring 2007 db **(93) n22.5** a charming nose, but dull by Thomas Handy standards with the usual bright rye being outmuscled by some intimidating caramel; **t24.5** much more like it on delivery with the rye, gleaming but still not quite at its brightest, now thudding heavily on the palate; less juicy than normal: mocha sweetened by fudge and treacle; **f23** a quiet, restrained finale with toffee again to the fore; **b23** can't remember the last time I found so much natural caramel at every turn of a Thomas Handy. *64.2%.*

Whistlepig Aged 10 Years db **(88) n21 t22 f23 b22.** Having tasted this after the Sazerac beasts, this could have disappeared without trace. But had enough sharpness and rye freshness to make for a very pleasant and worthwhile experience. *50% (100 proof)*

⬧ **WhistlePig Old World 12 Year Old** European casks **(87) n23 t23.5 f20 b20.5.** What a tragedy! The spirit itself is magnificent. The grain positively glistens on both nose and delivery and is on a par with Kentucky's finest. Sadly, a pretty rough finish thanks to the cask...which is always the danger when dealing with European wine barrels. *45% (90 Proof)*

Willett Family Estate Bottled Single Barrel Rye 4 Years Old Barrel no 45 (94) n23.5 t24 f23 b23.5. Truly satisfying rye which has in style more than a passing resemblance to the old Jim Beam yellow label rye of about 15 years ago. *55%*

Straight Wheat Whiskey

Bernheim Original (91.5) n22 t23 f23 b23.5. By far the driest of the Bernheims I have encountered showing greater age and perhaps substance. Unique and spellbinding. *45%*

◆ **Parker's Heritage Collection Original Batch Kentucky Straight Wheat Whiskey Aged 13 Years** db **(95.5)** n23.5 quite a firm, feisty nose threatening spice on all fronts. A little starchy as well as toasty. The sugars seem surrounded and unable to offer more than a softening to the citrus; **t24** a mesmeric delivery, full of soft, bready oils and liquorice....for about a second and a half. Then the spices are in like Flint; or maybe the flint is in like spices... because this has suddenly become a rock hard, brittle bourbon softened only by background oil and a manuka honey-cocoa mix; **f23.5** more manuka and mocha, though the spices have left leaving a much more serene fade, while the liquorice and hickory underline the age to the relaxed finale; **b24.5** not sure if they get Bassett's Liquorice Allsorts in the US. But, if they did, they would immediately recognise the brown ones in this...though in an insanely beautiful mutated form. So, so delicious....! *63.7%. ncf.*

American Microdistilleries

ALASKA DISTILLERY Wasilla, Alaska

Alaska Outlaw Whiskey (78.5) n20 t20 f19 b19.5. A surprisingly clean whiskey with a thin body and even thinner finale. So clean, in fact, that if you put it in a dirty glass, it'll probably end up sparkling. *40%*

ALLTECH Lexington, Kentucky.

Pearse Lyons Reserve (85) n22 t21 f21 b21. A fruity, grainy, pleasant whisky with the higher notes citrus dominant. Never quite finds a place to land or quite tells its story. Attractive but incomplete. *40% (80 proof)*

Town Branch Kentucky Straight Bourbon (88.5) n22.5 red liquorice, under-ripe greengages, nutmeg and polished oak floors...mmmm! **t21.5** a soft landing with lashing of vanilla and muscovado; **f23** thickens out as the treacle and liquorice re-emerge; some kumquats, too; **b22** a delicious Kentucky bourbon of considerable depth and charm. I think they have found their niche: bourbon. In Kentucky. Go for it, guys! *40% (80 proof)*

AMERICAN CRAFT WHISKEY DISTILLERY Redwood Valley, California.

Low Gap Bavarian Hard Wheat Aged 2 Years dist 31 Dec 10, bott 23 Jan 13 **(76.5)** n18 t21 f18.5 b19. There appears to be butyric on the nose and the finish bitters uncompromisingly. Despite the odd juicy, spicy high spot, not this distillery's finest moment. *43.1%*

ARIZONA DISTILLING Tempe, Arizona

Desert Derum Wheat Whiskey 10 gallon cask barrelled 2013 **(89)** n22 toasted...toast! A few old barrels comes to mind, too; **t22.5** the delivery lulls you somewhat , as the sugars and oils are playful. Then....whuuumph!!! Along comes the spice, rammed home with the full weight of the oak; **f22** still a little oaky bitter, the spices sizzle, the sugars sooth...; **b22.5** a desert storm of a whiskey. The small barrel punches some pretty towering tannins into the mix, but credit to the distiller for producing a spirit with enough balls to take it. *46%. ncf.*

Desert Durum Wheat Whiskey Batch no. 2 db **(87.5)** n21.5 t23 f21.5 b21.5. Another hairy-chested gung-ho whiskey which pins you back in your chair. And my notes for the first edition fits this one equally as well. Except here it loses out slightly by having a slightly too wide cut, meaning the feints bite on the nose and finish. But still about as macho as a whiskey gets. And as chocolatey, too. *46%.*

BAINBRIDGE ORGANIC DISTILLERS Bainbridge Island, Washington

Battle Point Organic Washington Wheat Whiskey (88.5) n21 surprisingly placid with a light spice nibble; **t23** brilliant delivery, full of quick-tempered spicy attitude. The oils are sublime and the sugars mostly of a muscovado bent; **f22** some vanilla and butterscotch show light oaky intent while the sugars remove the spices completely; **b23** soft and satisfying. The spices demanded from wheat whiskey, though short-lived, hit all the right spots. Very well made and impressive. *43%*

BALCONES DISTILLERY Waco, Texas.

Balcones Crooked Texas Bourbon Barrel American Oak, cask no. 3017, bott 21/01/14 db **(96)** n24 black cherry and toasted honeycomb; **t24.5** more black cherry – entire tree-fulls of it. That toasted honeycomb is also evident but is dwarfed by the impact of the liquorice and molasses combination; **f23.5** much drier with spiced mocha on slightly burnt toast... with a glazed cherry on top... rare to find so many sugars completing the journey; **b24** like a concentrated form of bourbon, though with far more sugars evident than is normal. Profound. And ridiculously yummy. *62.8%. ncf. no age statement.*

Balcones Fifth Anniversary Single Barrel Texas Straight Malt American oak, Brimstone Resurrection finish, cask no. 2696, bott 20/12/13 db **(93) n23.5** the lively and forthright barley must manfully step up to the plate to make any impact on the dizzying depth of the oak: it does; **t24** near perfect weight on delivery: rarely do the sugars of the oak and concentrated, juicy riches of barley gather together so gorgeously; **f22.5** spiced, molassed and feeling the effects of the usual wide cut; **b23** you could stand a knife and fork as well as a spoon up in this. The depth of sugar is startling. *58.3%. ncf. no age statement. 204 bottles.*

Balcones Fifth Anniversary Single Barrel Texas Straight Bourbon American oak cask no. 1613, bott 05/07/13 db **(91.5) n23.5** fascinating nose: it is as if someone and blended together all the heavier, impenetrable sugars and honey, those deep brown chappies, and tied it together with a spicy, molassed bow...; **t23.5** the delivery needs a cutlass to hack your way through: massive oils from a dangerously generous cut ensure there is a persistent fizz to the toasty fudge; **f21.5** and it fizzes feintily onwards... **b23** just so profound. Had the cut been just a little more niggardly, might well have had an award-winner here. But early days for this great but young distillery: they will learn. *64.2%. ncf. no age statement. 176 bottles.*

Balcones Fifth Anniversary Single Barrel Texas Straight Bourbon v.ii American oak, cask no. 1142, bott 11/18/13 db **(93.5) n23.5** red liquorice enjoys top billing as the sugars veritably crunch across the nose; you can count the layers of oak as you might tree rings...; **t24.5** ye gods...!!! All my Christmasses and birthdays have come at once. The kind of delivery which sends you back in your chair through shock, then into a slump as you melt into its profound beauty. It is the harmony between the depth and softness of touch which ethralls. The usual generous cut ensure the oils are there to support the weight of the fudgy, molassed sugars; maple syrup tries to thin out the hickory; **f22** vague feints cling to the throat as the drier vanilla-oak elements mop up the remaining sugars; **b23.5** a bourbon version of a Texas steak: pleasing fat, full of succulent red juice and absolutely bloody enormous... *65.7%. ncf. 167 bottles.*

Balcones Fifth Anniversary Single Barrel Brimstone Resurrection Straight Corn Whisky American oak, cask no. 1200, bott 2013 db **(94) n23** huge, strangely uncluttered, big char effect held together superbly with elegant honeyed layerings amid the corn oil; **t24** immense delivery as thick as a sea fog with the sugars showing enormous strength despite their polite interplay with the manuka-ulmo honey blend; the liquorice begins to form just as quietly; **f23.5** a bourbon-style spice kick begins to build, though the corn oil refuses to recede; **b23.5** when you start your tasting day 5.30am, as I do, there are fewer whiskies more capable of waking you up - or sending you straight back to bed – than this. Absolutely shakes the body and mind into submission... Beautiful. *60.5%. ncf. no age statement. 167 bottles.*

BALLAST POINT San Diego, California
Devil's Share Single Malt Aged Four Years (batch 001) **(84) n20 t22.5 f20.5 b21.** Enough feints on the nose and finish to take the gloss off an attractive first bottling from Ballast Point. Beyond the nougat, plenty of honey around to enjoy. But every distiller should remember that to move from a decent to a very good whiskey, the devil is in the detail... *46%*

BENJAMIN PRICHARD'S DISTILLERY Kelso, Tennessee.
Benjamin Prichard's Lincoln County Lightning Tennessee Corn Whiskey (89) n24 t22.5 f21 b22. Another white whiskey. This one is very well made and though surprisingly lacking oils and weight has more than enough charm and riches. *45%*

BERKSHIRE MOUNTAIN DISTILLERS Great Barrington, Massachusetts.
Berkshire Bourbon Whiskey (91.5) n23 t23.5 f23 b23. A bourbon bursting with character: I am hooked! Another micro-gem. *43%*

BRECKENRIDGE DISTILLERY Breckenridge, Colorado.
Breckenridge Colorado Bourbon Whiskey Aged 2 Years (86) n22.5 t22 f20.5 b21. Full of character, big-hearted, chewy, slightly rugged bourbon where honey and cocoa thrives; spices make a distinct impact. How apposite that probably the one and only town in Colorado named after a Kentuckian should end up making bourbon. Being close on 10,000 feet above sea level you'd think ice would come naturally with this. But it does pretty well without it, believe me... *43%*

CATOCTIN CREEK DISTILLERY Loudoun County, Virginia.
Catoctin Creek Cask Proof Roundstone Rye Organic Single Barrel Whisky batch B12E1 **(88.5) n21 t23 f22 b22.5.** A truly huge rye that, from a technical standpoint, fails its exams. But through a combination sheer delicious belligerence and chutzpah has your taste buds swooning. Great fun! *58%. Distilled from 100% rye. 134 bottles.*

CEDAR RIDGE DISTILLERY Swisher, Iowa.

◈ **Twelve Five Rye** recipe: rye, corn & malted barley, batch no. 131304-A db **(87.5) n23** **t22.5 f20.5 b21.5.** Some seriously big rye at work here and the nose is something to enjoy if not marvel at. Once the distillers can just narrow the middle cut, this will be a rye of serious magnitude. As it is, the feints just take the edge off an otherwise impressive rye. *47.5%*

CHARBAY DISTILLERY Napa Valley, California.

Charbay Hop Flavoured Whiskey release II, barrels 3-7 **(91) n22 t22 f23 b24.** Being distilled from beer which includes hops, it can – and will - be argued that this is not beer at all. However, what cannot be disputed is that this is a rich, full-on spirit that has set out to make a statement and has delivered it. Loudspeaker and all. *55%*

CLEAR CREEK DISTILLERY Portland, Oregon.

McCarthy's Oregon Single Malt Aged 3 Years batch W12-01, bott 7 May 2012 **(95) n24 t23 f24 b24.** I doubt if you could find, outside of the tropics, such a relatively young whisky with so vibrant and complex a personality. *42.5%*

McCarthy's Oregon Single Malt Aged 3 Years batch W13-01 bott Feb 13 **(93.5) n23.5** no one does smoky bacon quite like Clear Creek...; **t23** smoke arrives upfront, vanishes for a second then regroups. The intervening moments are filled with thick fudge and vanilla; **f23.5** the spice and sugars which had been around since the first moments now get a chance to shine in the smoke...if you see what I mean...; **b23.5** McCarthy's in its usual irresistible form. *42.5%*

McCarthy's Oregon Single Malt Aged 3 Years batch W13-02 **(90.5) n22** a very modest degree of smoke this time round, with the sugars also curiously absent; **t22.5** silky delivery with the accent firmly on the fudge; toasty dry middle; **f23** the smoke and spice take time to gather, but when they arrive, they do so with some zip and intent; **b23** one of the lighter bottlings I have come across over the years. The spices, though, don't take a day off. Failed to grab hold of any 2014 bottlings. But will chase them down for the 2016 edition. *42.5%*

◈ **McCarthy's Oregon Single Malt Aged 3 Years** batch W14-01 Bott Sept 8 2014 **(96) n24** the house style smoky bacon sizzles with perhaps a little extra degree of phenol this time. There is almost an Islay – now lost young Port Ellen aspect to this...though the sea-breeze salt is replaced by a drier tannin; **t24** if you find a softer, cleaner, malt-true delivery in the US this year, lease let me know. The sugars from the grist spill over every aspect of the delivery and follow through. The smoke treads softly, but covers al the ground to be discovered. The overall texture borders perfection as it is both soft and firm, yet neither...; **f23.5** a beautifully adroit interplay between vanilla and a slightly tingly smoke; the oaks buzz at the death; **b24.5** Steve McCarthy's hands may not still be on the tiller. But they might well as be: this plots the same course he charted a great many years back in American micro distilling's very earliest days. Still the guiding star by which all other micro distilleries must follow: a kind of World Whiskey mile and sign post.... *42.5%*

COLORADO GOLD DISTILLERY Cedaredge, Colorado.

Colorado Gold Straight Bourbon Over Two Years Old Single Barrel bott 8 Oct 11 **(86.5) n21 t23 f21 b21.5.** A bit of a whippersnapper of a bourbon. The nose and finish may lack depth. But it is a whiskey bursting with personality and the delivery is an understated treat. A light mocha thread weaves in and out of the muscovado. Fun. *40%*

COPPER FOX DISTILLERY Sperryville, Virginia.

Copper Fox "Rye Whisky" Aged 14 Months bott 11 Jul 13 **(91) n22.5** crisp, meaningful rye with bells on. Minty spice and earthy, too; **t23** those rye notes really do gang together. Sublime firmness; all you could wish for. The mint is back for the middle, pleasantly cradled in chocolate; **f22.5** soft oils, and a few muscovado notes trill with the rye; **b23** when is rye whisky not a rye whisky? When it is matured in ex-bourbon barrels, rather than virgin oak for a start. Like this whisky. So the quote marks are mine, not the label's. That said, purely from a tasting perspective: beautiful! Probably as good a rye type yet to come out of Sperryville. Just need to work on the label... *45%*

Wasmund's Single Malt Whisky 13 Months Old batch 94 **(94.5) n23** the cherry wood both offers tannin and sweetness in equal measure, while the apple grapples with the spice; **t23.5** sublime oils and sugars on delivery making the weight spot on and enough sweetness around to absorb the big tannin session which crashes like a tree in a forest; the middle now really concentrates on the ulmo honey, complete with light waxy train; **f24** almost perfect. The smoke has gathered softly, the honey glows, the wood elements join the heavier phenols to create the base...gorgeous! **b24** distiller Rick Wasmund gets flavours into and out of his whisky like a magician conjures a dove from a hat. Here he has exceeded himself by removing the taughtness which comes with over aging or overdoing the apple and cherry wood smoke. Here he has called it right. Superb. *48% (96 Proof) ncf*

Wasmund's Single Malt Whisky 14 Months Old Batch No. 52 (91.5) n22 t23 f23 b23. Makes a huge lightly honeyed statement: superb! *48%. ncf.*

CORNELIUS PASS ROADHOUSE DISTILLERY Hillsboro, Oregon.

McMenamins C.P.R. White Owl Distillery (93) n23.5 t23 f23 b23.5. Top dollar White Dog. Huge amount of copper helps expose all the honey available, especially on the nose. Superbly distilled and surging with barley and spice. *49.3%*

CORSAIR ARTISAN DISTILLERY Nashville, Tennessee.

Corsair Rye Moon (85) n20 t22.5 f21 b21.5. A sweet, well-weighted white dog with surprisingly little bite. The odd intense, crystalline rye moment is a joy. *46% (92 proof)*

Corsair Aged Rye (73.5) n18 t18 f19 b18.5. Hot and anarchic, not as well made as the Rye Moon. But has enough playful character to keep you guessing what's coming next. *46%*

Corsair Triple Smoke (92.5) n24 t23 f22 b23.5. The odd technical flaw, to pick nits. But, overall, a lovely whiskey with a curiously polite smoke style which refuses to dominate. Teasingly delicate and subtle...and different. *40%*

DAD'S HAT RYE DISTILLERY Bristol, Pennsylvania

◇ **Dad's Hat Pennsylvania Rye** db **(89.5) n22** a heavyweight hat with a wide brim, for the middle cut has been generous, allowing every dimension of the rye essence to have its say; **t23.5** all the usual suspects tumble about the palate: ripe rye, rich molasses and crisp Demerara sugar. I get the feeling that the early rye made in those lost distilling towns of the state I used to frequent and research would once have made whiskey which would have tasted something very similar to this; **f21.5** oily and tangy thanks to that overgenerous middle...but still a massive rye residue; **b22.5** being a hat-wearing man all my adult life, the world's first international champion for rye whiskey and a parent, this whiskey should fit me to a T. *45% WB16/023*

◇ **Dad's Hat Pennsylvania Rye** Finished in Vermouth Barrels db **(86.5) n22 t22 f21 b21.5.** A strange hybrid between powerful rye whiskey and Swedish aquavit. *47% WB16/024*

DARK CORNER DISTILLERY Greenville, South Carolina

Dark Corner Moonshine Corn Whiskey (77.5) n18.5 t22 f18 b19. Full blooded sweet corn on delivery. But could do with some extra copper elsewhere. *50%*

DARK HORSE DISTILLERY Lenexa, Kansas

Dark Horse Reserve Bourbon Less Than Four Years Old Batch 2 **(93) n23** huge vanilla and toffee apple; ticks every bourbony box with a lovely toasted honey buzz; **t23.5** exceptional. The tannins arrive in tandem with the molasses. The liquorice is clean and deep, the manuka honey keeps a watchful eye. A slow spice arrival; **f23** back to colossal vanilla with a spiced cream toffee finale; **b23.5** Even though they appear to have used oak chips to bolster the overall richness of this bourbon, there is no taking away that this is the closest any whiskey produced by a microdistiller comes to the true Kentucky style. But even there, there are few which display so much vanilla. *44.5% (89 proof)*

Dark Horse Reunion Rye Less Than Four Years Old Batch 2 **(89) n22** rye on heat and a hint of clove; **t23** the rye grain is so sharp you can cut your tongue on it: it is first to hit the taste buds and the last to leave. There is a little more extra oil than desired, bringing toasted honeycomb; **f22** big oils again, though remains juicy and spicy; **b22** another enormous, and truly memorable, offering from Dark Horse which is unambiguous in its style. Here, though, the cut was perhaps a little over generous (costing a point or two) with the very sharpest notes sacrificed. That said: just so big and delicious! *44.5% (89 proof)*

Long Shot White Whiskey bourbon mash **(88.5) n22 t22.5 f22 b22.** Seriously good, honest white dog: well made and gives the corn a free hand to shine. Love it. *40% (80 Proof)*

DISTILLERY 291 Colorado Springs, Colorado.

291 Colorado Bourbon Whiskey Aspen Stave Finished distilled from a bourbon mash, aged less than 2 years, barrel no. 1 db **(91) n23** decent rye kick to the recipe; confident, thick and complex; a vague hoppy note; **t23.5** thicker and meatier than your average bourbon due to the fat oils. But the honeycomb and molasses play their part, as does the rye amid the soft grains which at times pulses on the palate and is occasionally pleasingly crisp; **f22** lots of spice buzz from the softening oil; **b22** the usual house style of taking the cut as far as it can go and maybe a fraction more: serious brinkmanship but, again, some very serious whiskey, too. Excellent! *50%*

291 Colorado Whiskey Aspen Stave Finished rye malt mash, barrel no. 21 db **(86) n23.5 t21.5 f20 b21.** A pretty wide cut on the still means every element from the rye has been magnified. But so has much else. Which means a dry whiskey at its happiest when nosing. A huge rye curiously still dry despite the massive honeycomb. Astonishingly herbal, too. *50%*

291 Colorado Whiskey Aspen Stave Finished distilled from a rye malt mash, aged less than 2 years, barrel no. 22 db **(92) n24** dazzling, crisp rye: far cleaner than barrel 21. Classically sharp and strengthened by sublime muscavado notes; **t23** full bodied delivery, this time revealing a little extra from the cut. The rye screams from every direction, bolstered by the extra oils, though the sharpness has now been blunted; **f22** dries a little as the spices and cocoa take position; **b23** wow! A rye whiskey for those who prefer theirs warts and all. 50.5% and 50.8% (two bottlings). *50.8%*

291 Colorado Whiskey Aspen Stave Finished distilled from a rye malt mash, aged less than 2 years, barrel no. 23 db **(91.5) n22** a big whoosh of tannin actually outguns the rye – which take some doing; **t23** the cut is generous, but not wide enough to do damage. Instead the rye, alternately hard as diamond or soft as silk, swoops around the palate with rare abandon. Heavy, pleasantly oiled and spiced enough to show the oak back at work again; **f23** enters into wonderful chocolate mousse territory; **b23.5** a rye of broad sweeps rather than the usual pinpoint, rapier thrusts. Technically not as good as barrel 22, but.... *50.8%*

291 Colorado Rye Whiskey White Dog Aged Less than a week, batch 10 **(86.5) n21 t21 f23 b21.5.** A much tamer version of the last one I got my hands on. The rye gets bullied by other factors more easily, too. The finish, though, is superb. 50.8% *(101.7 proof)*

291 Colorado Whiskey Aspen Stave Finished rye malt mash, barrel no. 2 **(94) n23 t24 f23.5 b23.5.** A superb, enigmatic rye which ticks every box: they are obviously fast learners! *50.8%*

American Whiskey Aged 3 months **(73) n18 t19 f18 b18.** Busy. Spices aplenty. But nothing sits right. 43% *(86 proof)*

Bad Guy Bourbon aged 379 days barrel # 1 **(95.5) n23.5 t24.5 f24 b24.** Arguably the most astonishing whisky of its age worldwide of the year. That a whiskey just a year old can be this good is obscene. But just proves: the bad guys always win... *56.1%*

Black Mountain Colorado Bourbon aged 9 months barrel #1 **(87) n22 t21.5 f22 b21.5.** Oily and in your face, despite the big colour, it has been unable to entirely shrug of the white dog bark. That said, the sheer abandon of the cough sweet sugars combined with surging spice – with cinnamon and cloves prevalent - makes for gripping sipping. 46% *(92 proof)*

DELAWARE PHOENIX DISTILLERY Walton, New York.

Rye Dog Batch 11-1 (78.5) n19 t21.5 f18 b19. Sweet, distinctive rye tang but a little short on copper sheen. 50% *(100 proof)*

DOWNSLOPE DISTILLING Centennial, Colorado.

Double Diamond aged 3 Years American/French oak batch RV-003 dist 1 June 2010 **(91.5) n22.5** all kinds of fruit and fruitcake covers the nose, but burnt raisin mostly; the oak is profound...; **t22** and on the delivery, also, though it settles quickly into a more creamy mocha-style; the fruit forms a healthy sub stratum; **f23** the spices grab hold and give the fudge and raisin attitude; finishes with chocolate milkshake; **b24** the degree of oak is a challenge. But in the end you finish shaking your head in wonderment as to how so many vastly different and unlikely aspects of a whiskey somehow fit together. Good going, guys! 50.5% (101 proof)

DRY FLY DISTILLING Spokane, Washington

Dry Fly Bourbon 101 (88) n21.5 t23 f21.5 b22. A well made bourbon which, with a bit of extra complexity, would stand above some of its Kentucky colleagues. *50.5%*

Dry Fly Cask Strength Straight Wheat Whiskey (94.5) n23 busy aroma, similar to the Washington wheat bottling with toasted Hovis, except here a couple of slices have been forgotten for a minute or so in the toaster; **t24** beautifully intense sugar and spice on delivery. The same rich sugar cane, except with a little molten muscovado in the mix as well; a cake mix with gentle oils and a squeeze of citrus forms the middle; **f23.5** back to lightly salted butter on brown toast...with a drizzle of sugars; **b24** quite beautiful whiskey. One every whisky lover should experience to further their understanding of this multi-faceted spirit. 60%

Dry Fly Port Finish Wheat Whiskey (89) n22 t23 f22 b22. If you mixed whiskey and jam you might end up with this little charmer. 50% *(100 proof)*

Dry Fly Straight Triticale Rye Wheat Hybrid (86) n22 t22 f21 b21. Pleasant and easy going. But very surprising degree of natural caramels fill in the gaps and shaves off the higher notes expected from the rye. 44% *(88 proof)*

Dry Fly Washington Wheat Whiskey (89) n22 t22 f22.5 b22.5. Hugely impressive, well weighted and balanced and a much better use of wheat than bread, for instance... *40%*

EASTSIDE DISTILLING Portland, Oregon
Burnside Bourbon 4 Year Barrel-Aged bott 2012 **(92) n24 t23.5 f22 b22.5.** "Put some sideburns on your face!" screams the back label. Well, a whiskey far too gracious to put hairs on your chest though it would be a close shave to choose this or a Kentucky 4-y-o as one of the best young bourbon noses of the year...Just bristles with charm. *48%*

EDGEFIELD DISTILLERY Troutdale, Oregon.
Edgefield Hogshead Whisky 100% malted barley, batch 12-B **(94) n23.5** chocolate and Lubec marzipan; honeycomb nougat; a little kumquat accumulates with air; **t24** superb texture with an almost perfect degree of oil. The barley has as much scope as it needs to shine; there is a juicy element as well as a weightier oakiness, inevitably heading towards a heather-honey sweetness; **f23** an elegant fade with more nougat honey and mocha; still heavy on the oils; **b23.5** been a little while since I lasted tasted Edgefield. At that time they were seriously getting their act together. Now they deserve star billing in any bar. This is sheer quality and even though the cut is very fractionally wide, the two years in new oak has ensured something bordering magnificence. *46%*

FEW SPIRITS DISTILLERY Evanston, Illinois.
FEW Bourbon Whiskey batch 13-808, aged in charred new oak barrels for less than four years db **(86) 13-808 n21 t22 f21.5 b21.5.** A thick, chewy bourbon with a vague hint of botanicals on the nose and a delivery leaving little to the imagination. The small grains are busy while little has been spared on the liquorice and molasses content. Reduce the oils a little and this would be a belter. *46.5% WB15/377*

◈ **FEW Bourbon Whiskey Cask Strength** batch 14-62 db **(84.5) n20 t22 f21 b21.5.** A wider cut than usual has ramped up the sugars for maximum effect. Decidedly oily and no little butterscotch on the fade. *58.7% WB16/021*

FEW Rye Whiskey batch 13-910, aged in charred new oak barrels for less than four years db **(87) n22 t22 f21.5 b21.5.** Few! What a scorcher! Big fresh rye fills every crevice of the palate, the house style oils ensuring it hangs around, too. The buzzing spice at the finale is indicative of the wide-ish cut which ensures a busy tang to the salivating, ultra juicy rye. Still not quite one for the purist, but the entertainment level is high. *46.5% WB15/375*

FEW Single Malt Whisky batch 10-13, aged in reused cooperage for one year db **(84.5) n21.5 t20 f22 b21.** This writing year, 2014, marks the 40th anniversary of when I first tasted an American single malt: it was in Maryland and I have made locally by a rye distillery. That was, I remember, a very simple, malty affair. This, by stark contrast, isn't. First you have to get through a nutty phase before the barley makes itself heard, but when it does, it is eloquent in its sheer maltiness. As usual, the oils have a big say. *46.5% WB15/376*

FINGER LAKES DISTILLING Burdett, New York.
Glen Thunder Corn Whiskey (92.5) n23.5 t23 f23 b23. Beautifully distilled, copper rich, Formula 1 quality, absolutely classic corn white dog. *45% (90 proof)*

White Pike Whiskey Aged 18 Minutes (91) n22.5 t23.5 f22 b23. Top notch white dog more full of flavour than any pike you are ever likely to catch. Maybe 19 minutes in cask might have just taken the edge of the complexity. So well done, boys. Beautifully made distillate, even if slightly copper challenged, where the grains really do stand and be counted and the sugars are slick and sing to you. Created from organic spelt, corn and malted wheat ostensibly as a mixing spirit: that would be a waste. *40%*

FLORIDA FARM DISTILLERS Umatilla, Florida
Palm Ridge Reserve Handmade Micro Batch Florida Whiskey orange and oak wood Less the 1 Year Old batch 29 **(94.5) n23** big rye signature to the nose: fruity, light and easy on the corn oils. Some hints of marzipan, trimmed apple and very old marmalade; aggressive tannin; **t24** I doubt if I will experience a more gentle landing on the palate for any US whiskey this year. Just enough oil to absorb the impact of the small grains and, again, the ryes run riot ensuring a juicy, spicy theme throughout. A little Parma Violet candy represents an earthiness which balances the complex, non-specific fruit doing the rounds; **f23.5** no great age to this guy (and I wrote that before I spotted the admitted maturation!), but the way the ulmo, manuka and orange-blossom honeys combine, depth is maintained; **b24** I can see why everyone heads to Florida in the winter: obviously to try and grab one of the meager 6,000 bottles of this on offer each year. This is beautifully crafted, truly adorable whiskey where fruit appears to constantly have its hand on the tiller. And rather than blast in like a Hurricane from the sea, it breezes gently around the glass and palate with an easy elegance. I have relatives in Florida: about time I gave them another visit... *45% (90 proof)*

GARRISON BROTHERS Hye, Texas.

Garrison Brothers Texas Straight Bourbon 2010 Aged Two Years Spring 2013 **(91)** n23 t23 f22 b23. A fascinating bourbon, made from local organic corn, which for a two-year-old is simply brimming with personality. The intensity and balance of the sugars and more bitter toastiness is a constant delight. Still room for improvement, but just love this magnificent stuff. Mind you, still waiting for the Hye Rye... 47%

Garrison Brothers Texas Straight Bourbon 2010 Aged Two Years dist 2010, bott Spring 2014 db **(91.5)** n22.5 a staggering degree of maple syrup sweetens the trademark high end bourbon development; waxy and nutty; t23.5 hard to imagine a bourbon packing so many intense flavour traits hitting the palate so softly. The silky delivery seems to underscore the rich mocha and honeycomb; f22.5 a tad bitter from light feints which reveal themselves late on. Some accompanying spices, too; b23 has not come close to outgunning their Cowboy bourbon which re-wrote the manual as far as micro distilleries are concerned. But there is still so much to savour here. Delicious. 47%.

Cowboy Bourbon Texas Straight Bourbon Whiskey Aged Three Years (96) n23.5 could be a blueprint for a solid bourbon aroma: beautifully waxy and nutty with a gathering of ever more intensifying tannins, the spice always well proportioned; t24 massive. Not exactly Stagg like, as this has some very helpful sweetness to lessen the impact. And there is obviously less age involved. But, again, the weight and pace of the heavier notes, the citrus-studded hickory, even hints of burnt fruit cake (presumably from the rye) are all set to ensure maximum flavour fulfillment; treacle tinged with ulmo honey; f24 now lightens to allow the liquorice and Sumatra coffee to mix and relax; the treacle lessens to Demerara and manuka honey; the waves just keep on lapping for a ridiculously long finish; b24.5 I always know when I have a truly great whiskey on my hands: it takes every ounce of my professionalism to spit it out! This has, and make no mistake, raised the bar for bourbon made by the micro distillers: it is truly world class, three year old or not. In fact the name is a misnomer: there are no cowboys at work here. This is darned tootin' fine whiskey. Yesiree! 68%. 600 bottles.

GOLDEN NORTHWEST DISTILLERY Bow, Washington.

Golden Artisan Spirits Single Barrel Cask Strength (88) n20.5 a little gruff, but redeemed by some coconut and maple syrup; t22.5 and it's the maple syrup which is first out of the trenches backed by decimated coconut drenched in manuka honey; f23 the highpoint by a distance as the honey is joined by deep liquorice...and welcome spice; b22 much more like it! Not exactly textbook but excellent body and some lovely honey touches. 62.3%

Golden Reserve Samish Bay Single Malt (85.5) n20 t23 f21 b21.5. From the nougat, molasses and chocolate school of distilling. Some honeycomb around, too. Actually, quite like its roughhouse antics on the palate. 40% (80 proof)

Samish Bay Peated Single Malt (79) n19 t20 f20 b20. The lightest smoke imaginable is somewhat overshadowed by the nougat and honey feints. Pleasant if a bit rough and unready. 43% (86 proof)

GRAND TRAVERSE DISTILLERY Traverse City, Michigan

Bourbon Whiskey (88.5) n21 a bit of youth makes for a slightly green, peppery aroma with limited harmony....; t22 which cannot be said of the delivery. Young, for sure, but small-grain punchy and with chocolate honeycomb. The spices sprint off from the start while muscovado sugars form; f23 we are now in deepest bourbon territory; thick liquorice, huge surges of vanilla, hints of molasses; b22.5 an absolute charmer which just gets better as it goes along. 46% (92 proof)

Ole George Straight Rye Whiskey (80) n19 t21 f20 b20. Hard to mark this one. As a rye, it marks relatively low. As a gin, it would be higher. Not sure why, but there seems to be all kinds of botanical aromas and flavours involved here. Pleasant as a spirit – and I love the mouth feel. But the flavour make up is skewed. 46.5% (93 proof)

GREAT LAKES DISTILLERY Milwaukee, Wisconsin.

KinnicKinnic A Blend of American Whiskies (87) n21.5 t22.5 f21 b22. The bitterness is replaced by an extra dollop of nougat and honey. 43% (86 proof)

HIGH WEST DISTILLERY Park City, Utah.

High West Silver Oat (86) n20 t22 f22 b22. A white whiskey which at times struggles to find all the copper it needs. But so delicious is that sweet oat – a style that has enjoyed similar success in Austria – that some of the technical aberrations are forgiven. Soft and friendly. 40%

HOUSE SPIRITS DISTILLERY Portland, Oregon

Westward Oregon Straight Malt Whiskey 2 Years Old batch 1 **(92.5) n23** a coating of vanilla to the intense barley and maple syrup; **t23.5** superb degree of oils ensure the barley clings thickly to the plate. Ulmo honey and light hickory intermingle as the spices begin a gentle journey; **f23** the spices now fizz a little and a delicate, non-specific fruit tang attaches to the big barley; the vanillas are confident and creamy; just a tad too much lasting bitterness; **b23.5** two years old, perhaps. But absolute star quality with the barley pulsing at every turn: just so satisfyingly mouth-filling and palate teasing. Another great whiskey from Portland. 45%

KINGS COUNTY DISTILLERY Brooklyn, New York.

Kings County Moonshine Corn Whisky (92) n23 t23 f23 b23. Absolutely spot on corn whiskey: sweet, clean, berry-fruity, very well made; does exactly what it says on the tin. 40%

KOVAL DISTILLERY Chicago, Illinois.

⬦ **Koval Single Barrel Four Grain Whiskey** barrel no. 412. Mashbill: Oat, Malted Barley, Rye, Wheat db **(83) n20.5 t23 f19.5 b20**. The nougat and chocolate on the nose suggests we have a feinty beast at work here. And that sometimes spells good news on the palate – especially the delivery. And so it proves here, as the taste buds positively shrink under a barrage of intense flavour blows, softened only by basic sugars. Equally, the nose points to a finish that is likely to be rough hewn. And it doesn't disappoint. Or, rather, it does. But cherish that amazing delivery where the oats shine particularly brightly. And best take a seat while you encounter this briefly delicious grainy onslaught. 47%. sc.

Koval Single Barrel Four Grain Whiskey cask no. 613, organic. Mashbill: Oat, Malted Barley, Rye, Wheat db **(88.5) n21.5 t23 f21.5 b22.5**. At times a seriously complex whiskey: a delightful experience. 47%. sc.

⬦ **Koval Single Barrel Millet Whiskey** db **(88) n22** the honeycomb and chocolate perhaps have more to do with the distillation technique and oak than the grain. For that, there appears to be a quite different sweet toastiness altogether; **t23** a beautiful and charming lift off: maple syrup sugars cascade into the much darker mooded oak-grain mix. These offer a flavour depth quite different to any other whisky type. The actual flavour itself cannot be compared exactly with another tasting experience: the grain has perhaps a vague oat porridge quality as its nearest marker. But this is deeper, with some of the smallest and most busy mini spices you'll ever encounter; **f21** a little bitter and oily as the sugars wear thin; **b22** I always wondered what my Myer's Parrot, Percy, sees in this stuff. If you want half an hour's peace and quiet, just hand him a small sprig of millet and he will munch contentedly on it, carefully inspecting, protecting and feasting on every single grain, not a single one seemingly wasted. Now I know. A gorgeously intense grain balances its unique flavour profile with delicate honey. Result: one happy palate. And one miserable parrot...for all his pleading he ain't getting his beak around this truly unique dram. 40%

⬦ **Koval Single Barrel Bourbon Whiskey** cask no. 378 db **(89.5) n22.5** full on with the oils but also massive manuka honey, liquorice and rye influence, too; **t23** usual Koval whiskey pie in the face delivery: enormous toasty depth on delivery before a gentle spreading of the honey. Then it flares into an bourbon of huge intensity, with varying Demerara sugar notes heading in all directions; **f21** busily spiced but overly oily; **b22** as usual, the wide-ish cut has ensured maximum intensity. Some of the bourbon tones are about as classic Kentucky as they have so far achieved. 47%. sc.

Koval Single Barrel Organic Bourbon Whiskey cask no. 506, db **(86.5) n21.5 t22 f21.5 b21.5**. Koval's whiskeys are nothing if not idiosyncratic. Hard to pick out a traditional, recognised bourbon character here. The nose abounds with citrus, the delivery eye-watering sugars until some drying feints appear at the death. Attractive but don't expect something Kentuckian in style. 47%. sc.

Koval Single Barrel Organic Rye Whiskey cask no. 531, db **(77) n19 t20 f19 b19**. Organic maybe. But, sadly, not orgasmic. Unbelievably sweet and flat with little or no rye sharpness whatsoever. 40%. sc.

LOST SPIRITS DISTILLERY Monterey County, California.

Leviathan III Under 4 Years db **(86) n21 t22 f22 b21**. Not sure I am a great fan of three things wishing to dominate at once: peat, fruit and oak. In the end there is too much cancelling of each other out. Pleasant enough, though, and very sweet. 53%. sc.

Umami Under 4 Years Peat smoked barley fermented in salt water. db **(94) n23** that sharp smoky bacon type smoke those who drink McCarthy's from Oregon will immediately recognise: something of a west coast thing...; **t24** some peat whiskies sooth and caress the palate: this arrives like an exocet blasting any phenols any taste buds which dare show its head above he parapet; quite possibly the spiciest arrival of any malt whisky made in the

USA to date; **f23** calms as the fruits begin to find room to show; a tad off key towards the finish, though rights itself as the molasses arrives. But then mixing sherry and peat is a very brave thing to do...; **b24** a chair with arms rests essential: you will be gripping them for dear life! If you are seeking a gentle, delicate little flower of a malt you have found the wrong bottle. This is a heat exuding missile...and your palate will be well and truly a-salted... *59%*.

MISSISSIPPI RIVER DISTILLERY Le Claire, Indiana
Cody Road Bourbon 2013 Batch 1 **(91.5) n23.5** toasted brown wheat bread with a perfectly understated sublime manuka- and ulmo honey sweetness. Wow! **t23** the delivery offers both spice and molten muscovado sugars in equal measure; the midground thickens and becomes almost doughy; **f22** a little bitterness counters the continuing sugars; **b23** you really don't need to be told this is a wheat recipe bourbon! A fabulously made whiskey of rare character. *45% (90 proof)*
Cody Road Rye 2013 Batch 4 **(86.5) n23 t22.5 f20 b21.** The clean, fruity unambiguous rye on the nose is stunning. There is nothing too shoddy about the crisp, juicy grain on delivery, either. Just bitters out a little too enthusiastically from the midpoint onwards. *40%*

MOYLAN'S DISTILLING COMPANY Petaluma, California.
Moylan's 2004 Cherry Wood Smoked Single Malt Cask Strength (94) n24 easily one of the most subtle of all America's micro distillery whiskeys and is unusual in not trying to make an early statements of intent. The smoke does no more than furnish a thin, earthy gloss to the delicate array of lightly fruited vanillas: absolutely beguiling; **t23.5** more of the same: a distinctive sharp kumquat note injects life into the vanilla; **f23** long yet without a hint of oil with light spices and cocoa playing happily together; again there is a faint, fruity glass to the finale; **b23.5** a top drawer, quite beautifully distilled and matured, malt which goes much easier on the smoke than you'd expect but is bubbling with personality...and quality. Bravo! *49.5%*

NEW HOLLAND BREWING COMPANY Holland, Michigan.
Beer Barrel Bourbon (86.5) n21.5 t22 f21.5 b21.5. A distinctly different bourbon, not least because it has been finished for three months in beer barrels. This really only becomes evident on the latest moments of the finish, when a slightly hoppy roast barley character emerges. The base Indiana-originating bourbon is decent enough, though you get the feeling the higher notes and rough edges have been blunted by the beer. *40% (80 proof)*
Bill's Michigan Wheat (85.5) n22 t21 f21.5 b21. A wheat whisky named in honour of an old friend of mine, Bill Owens, a shining beacon in the world of micro distilling. Kind of a fitting tribute, too, as the somewhat oily and bitter marmalade characteristics are always more likely to be found on a small still than from the big Kentucky boys. *45% (90 proof)*
Brewer's Whiskey Malt Whiskey Aged Six Months batch 3 **(87) n21.5 t22.5 f21 b22.** In the previous Bible, we had batch 1 of their Double Down Barley: this is, effectively batch 3. A better working this time, though the late finish is still challenging. *45% (90 proof)*

PEACH STREET DISTILLERS Pallisade, Colorado.
Colorado Straight Bourbon Aged More Than Two Years batch 40 **(92.5) n22.5** sharp hickory and caramel, flinty fruit and almost Indian-style spiced nuts; **t23.5** has that soothing mouth-feel on delivery of the oozy inside of a throat lozenge, except the flavours differ dramatically. For the odd moment you feel that malt is present, but soon we go into familiar manuka honey territory, as well as liquorice; the spices pick up pace with aplomb; **f23** a quality finale, with the spices gently raging, the rye notes riling and other familiar bourbon tones tantalising...; **b23.5** the last bottle I tasted was around the batch 20 mark and was an impressive intro to this distillery. Remarkably, this batch enjoys an almost identical thumb print. But now there is much more sharpness and definition. Superb! *46% (92 proof)*

RANGER CREEK DISTILLING, San Antonio, Texas
Ranger Creek .36 Texas Bourbon (93) n23 mega honey & liquorice: superbly weighted; **t23.5** again huge liquorice, perhaps pepped by the odd aniseed ball, before manuka honey and treacle weigh in; there are chewy vanillas to break up the intensity as well as chocolate toffee; **f23** scorched honeycomb & marzipan with just the right amount of sugars to make for a comfortable finale; **b23.5** I would so love to get back to Texas and have this wash down a plate-filling, half cooked ribeye. It's pretty obvious they have used small barrels to create a gentle giant like this – even before you find confirmation on the bottle. This comes under their Small Caliber series of whiskeys. Don't you believe it: this is a howitzer of a bourbon. *48% (96 proof)*
Ranger Creek Rimfire Mesquite Smoked Texas Single Malt batch 1 **(85) n21.5 t22 f20.5 b21.** As I have never tasted anything smoked with mesquite before – especially whiskey – I will have to guess that it is the tree of the semi-desert which is imparting a strange, mildly

bitter tang on the finish. Whether it is also responsible for the enormous degree of creamed toffee, I am also not sure. Enjoyable, fascinating even...but something the ol' taste buds need a bit of acclimatising to. *43% (86 proof)*

RANSON SPIRITS Sheridan, Oregon.

◈ **Ranson The Emerald 1865 Straight American Whiskey** Batch 002 malted barley, unmalted barley, malted rye, malted oats. **(87.5) n22 t22.5 f21 b22.** The mash bill screams: "Irish whiskey". The oils found everyone screams: "Oi! Let those foreshots run another five minutes...!!!" If this was cleaned up a little we would have a whiskey everyone would be talking about. Because, taking the feints out of the equation, the interplay and weight of those complex grains really make for the most delicious experiences. Indeed, even with its faults, this provides one fabulous ride on the palate. On the cusp of being an American great. *43.8%*

Whipper Snapper Oregon Spirit Whisky (86.5) n21.5 t22 f21.5 b21.5. A curiously thin offering for all the obvious corn apparent. Some walnut oil and light Demerara do offer some meat on the vanilla. *42%*

ROCK TOWN DISTILLERY Little Rock, Arkansas.

Arkansas Young Bourbon Whiskey batch 12 **(89) n22.5 t22 f22 b22.5.** gentle, sweet and all-round adorable. *46% (92 proof)*

Arkansas Bourbon Whiskey Batch 23 db **(89) n22 t22 f22.5 b22.5.** These guys have a tendency to do bourbon rather well. Again, a generous cut slightly oils up proceedings. But the magnitude of the liquorice/hickory/molasses combination is real stand-your-spoon-up-in fun. No insipid half-hearted stuff here. *46%.*

Arkansas Rye Whiskey Batch 5 db **(80) n21.5 t21 f19 b19.5.** A powerful whiskey with a determined rye bent. But like so many microdistiller's ryes, falls into the trap of over-widening the cut. This can be either from the fact they don't have much to distill from, so try maximise their resources. Or so powerful is flavour of the spirit, they have not yet worked out exactly where the middle is. Sometimes it is a bit of both. *46%.*

Arkansas Single Barrel Reserve Bourbon Whiskey cask #163 db **(90) n22.5** the tannins queue up, but happy to let the dark sugars ahead first...; **t22** liquorice concentrate, lightened by hickory; the molasses rolls in like sea mist; **f23** bitters sufficiently for major complexity, especially when the spiced vanilla enters the fray; **b22.5** major bourbon with the passive aggressive oak pulling the strings. *57.81%.*

Arkansas Single Barrel Reserve Bourbon Whiskey cask #167 db **(89.5) n22 t23 f22 b22.5.** As 163. Except here the sugars take far more of the load, resulting in a lighter and slower finish, but only after a bigger tannin crescendo. *57.14%.*

Arkansas Single Barrel Reserve Bourbon Whiskey cask #173 db **(87.5) n22 t22 f21.1 b22.** This guy has hairs on it. The tannins are a little too up front for the overall good of the bourbon, meaning some displaced sugars. The black cherry is irresistible, however. If you like a whiskey with its own built in tooth picks, this is for you. *56.93%.*

Arkansas Single Barrel Reserve Bourbon Whiskey barrel #181, cask strength db **(92.5) n22 t23 f23.5 b24.** Odd isn't it: I castigate cask 173 for over exuberant use of oak...and here is a bourbon in which you can count the tree rings...and I am praising it to the hilt. The secret is the balance: for every log of tannin to chew on there is magnificent blend of sugars, vanillas and fruits to counter it. The liquorice and molasses have to be experienced to be believed. And though this is OTT on the tannin, somehow it works rather beautifully. *56.2%.*

Arkansas Single Barrel Reserve Bourbon Whiskey barrel #190, cask strength db **(96.5) n23.5 t24 f24.5 b24.5.** The only bourbon I have ever tasted which comes close to this in profile is 23 years of age and from Heaven Hill distillery. This breaks every rule in the book... or, rather, appears content to have re-written the rules. This is absolutely enormous whiskey. It is beautifully made with not a hint of an off note, so the cut must be nigh on perfection. The oak it has matured in is top dollar, and they have extracted every cent's worth of its favourable aspects: the liquorice is borderline creosote yet so thick are the molasses, so clever is the use of manuka honey, so compelling the toasted honeycomb and so busy the spices, the balance and bitter-sweet interplay could hardly be bettered if created on computer rather than in cask. Unquestionably one of the great microdistillery bourbons of all time: a bottling which will put Arkansas and Rock Town in particular on the world whisky map. *56.08%.*

Hickory Smoked Whiskey db **(82.5) n21 t20 f21 b20.5.** Nowhere near as good as the last smoked offering I had from them. A tobacco note has replaced the bacon. Some pleasant Ovaltine and muscovado notes towards the finale. *45%.*

◈ **Rock Town 5th Anniversary Arkansas Straight Bourbon Whiskey #4** char white oak casks, bott Apr 15 db **(92) n22.5** busy spice, presumably wheat, and a mix of muscovado sugar and maple syrup. Heavy oils: signs of a generous cut; **t24** good grief! Probably the biggest whiskey I'll taste today. All kind of corn oils run rampant, though some enticing barley notes offer an unexpected salivating quality. The oak pounds hard, with some major liquorice notes; **f21** yes, a little too well oiled but the sugars fade gracefully; **b22.5** thought my taste buds were deceiving me on delivery with an unexpected barley kick. On inspection, it does boast 20% malted barley: intriguing as well as delicious. *50% (100 proof). ncf. 971 bottles.*

◇◇◇ **Rock Town Arkansas Single Barrel Reserve Hickory Smoked Whiskey** new charred oak barrels, barrel no. 165 db **(89.5) n21.5** uncertain and nervous: the tobacco note doesn't know whether to advance or retreat; **t22.5** light molasses turn into sharper Demerara notes as the half-hearted tobacco note is finally crushed; **f23.5** sublime finish, wallowing in milk chocolate mousse; **b22** that's a lot better. Overcomes the tobacco moment with far more sugars than I have seen in the past. *56.2%. ncf.*

◇◇◇ **Rock Town Arkansas Single Barrel Reserve Hickory Smoked Whiskey** new charred oak barrels, barrel no. 169 db **(90.5) n22.5** though thinner, the clarity of the sugar-smoke mix attracts; **t23** soft, melting sugars – then a wave of pugnacious oak. The smoke drifts in via the back door while the sugars make themselves at home; the bite suggests stills running a little warmly; **f22.5** buttery, lightly smoked pancake; **b22.5** a concept finally at ease with itself, though this is slightly more aggressive distillate. *55.9%. ncf.*

◇◇◇ **Rock Town Arkansas Rye Single Barrel Reserve Bourbon Whiskey** new charred oak barrels, barrel no. 22 db **(88.5) n21.5** feinty, as is the house style for their rye. But this one does appear to be distilled from rye concentrate...; **t23.5** good grief! I have picked myself off the floor after coming under attack from the most intense rye I have seen in years: I was wrong about their 4-year-old! And if the rye doesn't get you, the thick, tannin-rich oak certainly will; **f21.5** the tannins linger, clinging to the oils from the wide cut; **b22** ye gods! A veritable thug of a whiskey, which merrily beats your taste buds up without breaking sweat. Yet, so many intense rye moments to savour! *56.6%. ncf.*

◇◇◇ **Rock Town Four Grain Sour Mash Bourbon Whiskey** new charred oak barrels db **(81) n20 t21 f20 b20.** Perhaps a tad too much sour in the sour mash... *46%*

◇◇◇ **Scotch Malt Whisky Society Cask B3.1 Aged 3 Years** new charred oak, dist 15 Jul 11 **(93.5) n22.5** toasty, but never aggressively so as the house-style tannins queue quietly to have their say; **t23.5** chewy oils ensure maximum bang for your buck from the liquorice and molasses. The spices are far more up front than normal; **f23.5** ridiculously good age on this for such a youngster, as those toasty notes singing on the nose return for an encore; the lingering manuka honey-molasses and spice mix is mesmeric; **b24** as ever, Rock Town single barrel bourbon rocks... *53.9%. sc. 238 bottles.*

ROGUE SPIRITS Newport, Oregon
Dead Guy Whiskey Aged One Month (73) n21 t22 f14 b16. Salt and honey, especially on delivery, make for a lovely opening gambit. The finish, alas, takes you via the graveyard. *50%*

Shatoe Rogue Oregon Single Malt Aged 3 Months (76.5) n18.5 t19 f20 b19. Needs a bit more copper to brighten the experience. The growing sugars help. *40% (80 proof)*

ROUGHSTOCK DISTILLERY Bozeman, Montana.
◇◇◇ **Montana Pure Malt** db **(88.5) n21** no doubting the barley, but the sweetness of fried yam is a little unusual; **t22** oily, then a rich, vaguely spiced barley sugar coating; **f22** custard powder, then gristy barley of growing intensity; **b23** a rich offering where the barley is in deep, concentrated form. A better made spirit than their wheat whiskey, there appears to be tighter control of the stills. The result is a distinctive, confident and well-made malt which harmonises rather beautifully. *45% WB16/026*

◇◇◇ **Montana Spring Wheat Whiskey** db **(85.5) n21 t22 f21 b21.5.** Goes for the flavours in no half-hearted manner: the tobacco on the nose suggests the grains will be carried on big oils. And they really are, though the spices are subdued for a wheat whiskey while the sugars are broadcast widely. A genuine chewing whiskey! *45% WB16/025*

Roughstock Black Label (92.5) n22.5 t23.5 f23 b23.5. A very beautiful malt whiskey very well made which underlines the happy marriage between barley and virgin oak. A stunner! *64%*

ST GEORGE SPIRITS Alameda, California.
Breaking & Entering Bourbon New American charred oak, bott 08/08/2013 db **(82) n21.5 t21.5 f19 b20.** An arresting first attempt by St George. Vaguely butyric , but through the oils can be located some very decent bourbon strains. Needs a bit of tinkering, though. *43%. Batch no.130824/ 19,900 bottles.*

St Georges Single Malt Lot 12 bott 20/04/2012. db **(88.5) n22 t22.5 f22 b22.** Unquestionably their maltiest every offering, having now for the most part eschewed their traditional fruit style. Maybe the odd crack on the distillate is apparent, but the intensity of the barley more than compensates. *43%. Approximately 3,500 bottles.*

St Georges Single Malt Lot 13 bott 14/08/2013. db **(91)** n22.5 slightly overcooked butterscotch tart; light acacia honey and caramel; **t23.5** huge delivery: a thick cascade of toffeed malt thumps against the taste buds and takes time to unravel. As it does, the barley in is full salivating mode while toasted fudge adds weight; **f22** long with a late spice buzz and vanilla finale; **b23** technically by far and away their best bottling for a very long time – both in production and maturation, even though not quite perfect. Genuinely high quality single malt. And delicious with it, too... *43%. Approximately 3,000 bottles.*

❖ **St George's Single Malt Lot 14** db **(89)** n22.5 an absent-minded sniff of this soon sent me to California: the apple-fruitiness really is unique among American whiskeys; **t22.5** dazzlingly fresh and eye-watering: the barley is delicate and easily absorbs the slightly overcooked gooseberry tart on offer; **f22** a whole plethora of vanillas; **b22** not quite so complex as some of their bottlings, but there is no getting away from their engaging and delicious house style. *43%*

SAINT JAMES SPIRITS Irwindale, California.
Peregrine Rock (83.5) n21 t20.5 f21.5 b20.5. Fruity and friendly, the wine and smoke combo work well-ish enough but the thumping oak injection highlights that maybe there isn't quite enough body to take in the aging. Perhaps less time in the barrel will reduce the bitter orange finale. *40%*

SANTA FE SPIRITS Santa Fe, New Mexico.
Colkegan Single Malt Whisky once used American white oak batch no.2. db **(73)** n18 t20 f17 b18. I have been looking forward to seeing the latest from Santa Fe after encountering their strange Coyote whisky. This is another encounter which has me scratching my head wondering how some of the flavours were achieved – I really must get down to New Mexico to check this out: they are achieving results using just malt and oak I have never before seen. Can't say I go a bundle on the nose, or the finish come to that, with so much caramel and unidentified spice. Reminds me of some local whiskies I run across in India. *46%.*

STEIN DISTILLERY Joseph, Oregon.
Straight Rye Whiskey Aged 2 Years cask no. 7 **(88)** n23 t22 f21 b22. A whiskey which offers up the grains to the full spotlight. A little more care with the cut and we have something special on our hands. *40%*

STONE BARN BRANDYWORKS DISTILLERY Portland, Oregon.
Hard Eight Unoaked Rye Whiskey (86.5) n22.5 t21.5 f21 b21.5. The excellent fruity-rye nose does not quite show the width of the cut which creates a buzzing oiliness. Good brown sugar balance. *40%*

STRANAHAN DISTILLERY Denver, Colorado.
Stranahan's Colorado Whiskey Small Batch dist Dec 05, cask no. 225 **(94.5)** n24 t23.5 f23 b24. Absolutely magnificent; a malt which never stays still in the glass. By the way, boys: the message on the label to me brought a lump to my throat. Thank you. *47% (94 Proof). sc.*

Stranahan's Colorado Whiskey Batch #100 (93) n23.5 nutty: walnut oil and top quality north European marzipan; **t23** textbook oils show both malt and vanilla in a rich light. Biscuity...; **f23** the finish takes a surprise turn towards tangy marmalade **b23.5** a three course meal of a malt. And leaves you wanting seconds... *47% (94 Proof)*

Stranahan's Colorado Whiskey Batch #101 (87.5) n22 t22 f21.5 b22 More playing dare with the cut. Here it pays off as the oils go into molasses overdrive. A dessert whiskey. *47%*

Stranahan's Colorado Whiskey Batch #102 (92) n22.5 t23 f23 b23.5. Superb whisky of almost perfect weight and pace. *47% (94 Proof)*

Stranahan's Colorado Whiskey Batch #103 (88) n21 t22.5 f22 b22.5 Another vanilla, butterscotch and honey-ladened gem once the light feints are overcome. *47% (94 Proof)*

Stranahan's Colorado Whiskey Batch #104 (84.5) n21 t21.5 f21 b21 Just a little tight with the crisp sugars outflanked by the slightly bitter, blood-orange feints. *47% (94 Proof)*

Stranahan's Colorado Whiskey Batch #105 (90) n22 t22 f23 b23 Interesting to see them continue along this orangey-citrus route. Malts show integrity. Spiced. Complex. *47%*

Stranahan's Colorado Whiskey Batch #106 (86) n21.5 t22 f21 b21.5 Back to the big oils and cumbersome sugars and nougat. Marmalade on the finale, though. *47% (94 Proof)*

Stranahan's Colorado Whiskey Batch #109 (92) n22 t23.5 f23 b23.5 Beautifully flighted malt with a rich seam of molassed sugars and raisins. Vanilla topping and spice. *47%*

Stranahan's Colorado Whiskey Batch #110 (91.5) n22 t23 f23 b21.5 Lovely interplay between crispy grain and even crispier sugars. Two-toned . Juicy and gorgeously spiced. *47%*

Stranahan's Snowflake Cab Franc (95.5) n24 t24.5 f23 b24. A celebration of great whiskey, and a profound statement of what the small distilleries of the USA are capable of. *47%. sc.*

Stranahan's Snowflake Desire dist 3 Jan 07 **(94.5) n24 t24 f23 b23.5.** These guys do know how to pick a good barrel... And, frankly, make an exceptional whiskey... 47%. sc.

Stranahan's Snowflake Mount Shavano **(85.5) n22 t21 f21.5 b21** The malt vanishes under a cartload of plums. Flat. 47% (94 Proof)

Stranahan's Snowflake Mount Silverheels **(89) n22.5 t22 f22.5 b22** Another fruity job showing a pithy dryness in tandem with liquorice and treacle. A real mouthful of a malt. 47%

Stranahan's Snowflake Paladise/Grand Mesa dist Apr 05 **(94) n23 t24 f23 b24.** Seriously impressive. I know this distillery makes something a little special, but this is such a sure footed move away from the norm I am stunned. This is my first-ever Stranahan Snowflake... so named because it simply dissolves on touch...? 47%. (94 Proof). sc.

Stranahan's Snowflake Solitude dist Mar 08 **(93) n23 t23 f23.5 b23.5** I chose this as my 1,111th new whisky of the 2012 Bible, because there is a lot of ones in that. And when you spend three months on your own, virtually cut off from all others, one is number you get used to. So sampling a whisky called "Solitude" strikes home...whatever it tastes like. 47%. sc.

Stranahan's Snowflake Tempranillo **(91) n21.5 t22 f24 b23.5** A bold malt with a liquorice and greengage delivery backed by a big treacle middle. Molasses wherever you look! 47%. (94 Proof)

SQUARE ONE BREWERY & DISTILLERY St. Louis, Missouri

J J Neukomm Missouri Malt Whisky Single Barrel **(88.5) n21** sharp, smoky, intriguing – but a bit of a mess; **t23** juicy sugars with seemingly cherry at the heart make for soft footfall on delivery, but the intensity of the malt really surprises; **f22** rabidly spicy and threatens to bitter out. But cherry drops to the rescue; **b22.5** it was like being transferred back to Sperryville, Virginia, where Copper Fox whiskey is made. The cherry wood smoked malt has a highly distinctive voice, and here it is again. Except this really does appear to have dark cherry notes at work on the palate. Annoyingly, although single barrel, there is no distinguishing reference number. 45% (90 proof)

TUTHILLTOWN SPIRITS Gardiner, New York.

Hudson Baby Bourbon Year 13 Batch E1 **(86) n21 t21.5 f22 b21.5.** A big, heavy duty bourbon. Feinty, though nothing like as oily as some previous bottlings I've encountered from these guys over the years. Enough toasted honeycomb and liquorice for this to make a few lovely noises. 46%. WB15/174

Hudson Four Grain Bourbon Year 13 Batch E1 **(90.5) n22.5** busy with a small grain attack but the weightier cocoa and manuka honey hits the spot; **t22** a tad oily from the generous cut but this is overcome by a series of outlandish waves of muscovado sugar, maple syrup and treacle combining with the classic bourbon liquorice and hickory notes **f23** settles into a more delicate phase where complexity returns and the small grains are back on track; **b23** a really excellent whiskey, despite the odd technical weakness, which concentrates on complexity... and succeeds. An accomplished, big-hearted bourbon. 46%. WB15/175 **Hudson Manhattan Rye** pot-distilled from rye grain, year 13, batch E2 **(89) n23** the rye flies at you: does what it says on the tin. A little feinty, but the firmness of the rye outmuscles it; **t22.5** a macho arm wrestle between thick rye and treacle; **f21.5** bitters as the feints show their hand slightly; **b22** rich, dense and pretty impressive. 46% WB15/383

TRIPLE EIGHT DISTILLERY Nantucket, Massachusetts.

The Notch Aged 8 Years dist 2000, bott Aug 08 db **(93) n24 t23.5 f22.5 b23.** Very few distilleries make their international bow with a single malt this sublime and superbly constructed. $888 dollars a bottle it may be, but for a taste of America's very first island malt... well, is there really a price? A head turner of a whisky, and every time it's towards the glass. Do we have a world classic distillery in the making...? 44.4% (88.8 proof)

The Notch Aged 8 Years db **(95.5) n24.5 t24.5 f23 b23.5.** Only six bottles of this were produced for a special dinner at the distillery. It is possible one escaped. I admit I had a hand in putting this one together, selecting samples from about half a dozen casks on the warehouse and blending them to certain percentages. Perhaps the closest it might be compared to is a Cardhu, though with a touch extra fruit. For the doubters, proof that this distillery is quite capable of whisky of the very highest calibre. 40% (80 proof)

◇ **The Notch Aged 10 Years** cask no. 009-025 dist 2001, bott 2011 db **(95.5) n23.5** I almost had to pinch myself here: there is an exotic fruit kick to this that one normally associates with ancient Speyside malt whiskies. Yet here it is, indubitably, after ten years on Nantucket... Just so obscenely elegant...; **t24.5** the clarity of the barley, the interplay between the top quality malt and the creamy, caressing layer of ulmo honey...good, grief...you could almost weep with joy; **f23.5** and now, a little predictably (though in a good way) the oak has just enough influence to take us into milky mocha territory. A light sprinkling of muscovado sugars adds some weight; and there is – and there had to be – the complex spice, too...; **b24** this is the 19th malt whisky I have tasted today. The previous 18 have been from Scotland. Yet this, unquestionably, is head and shoulders above them all. In fact, it is a good foot above most whiskies you will ever taste in your lifetime... *46%*

⬩⬩⬩ **The Notch Aged 12 Years** cask no. 026-055 dist 2002, bott 2014 db **(96.5)** n24 the extra two years in the cask has meant that where before we were in the land of the exotic fruit, now we are entering bourbon country...; t24.5 spices arrive early, apparently loaded with liquorice and hickory. There is a small grain buzz to this while the sugars are deeper, darker and a little more subdued; f23.5 toasty, outwardly dry, still spicy and still those dark, aged bourbon notes pick around; then the ulmo honey reveals it is still around after all these years; b24.5 interesting to see this great whisky cope, as we all must do, with the passing of time. The quiet understatement and elegance of the 10-y-o has given way to a more brash and assertive, oak-stained version. Not that that is a criticism, as it does it with the usual Triple Eight panache. On the 8th of August 2008 (just two days after I had completed the 2009 Whisky Bible) I gave a speech at the distillery predicting that, from the samples I had tasted in their warehouses, this new venture was on course to be one of the great malt whisky distilleries of the world. I am heartened that, for once in my life, I got something right... *48%*

WESTLAND DISTILLERY Seattle, Washington.

⬩⬩⬩ **Westland American Single Malt Whiskey Peated** bott Sept 15 db **(91.5)** n23 a dry, powdery peatiness is enlivened by a sprig of mint; t23 muscovado sugar melts on delivery, followed by lightly peated barley grist. After the dry nose, now attractively juicy; f22.5 gently smoked vanilla; b23 lightly peated, polite and safe.. The gristy sugars refuse to be thwarted. *46% (92 Proof). nc ncf.*

⬩⬩⬩ **Westland American Single Malt Whiskey Sherry Wood** bott Dec 14 db **(81)** n20 t21 f20 b20. Pleasant and fruity, but a certain bitter tang pervades on both nose and finish which do no favours. *46% (92 proof). nc ncf.*

Westland American Single Malt Whiskey dist Jun 11, bott Sept 14 db **(95)** n23.5 even with the complex, buzzing oaky notes the marriage between profound citrus-tinted vanilla and intense barley is a happy one; the overt bourbon tones does give the malt an extra flourish; t24.5 you rather lovely little smoothie, you....! Hard to imagine I'll find many deliveries as silky soft as this, especially taking into account the overall weight. Just so salivating, you don't know whether to swallow or kiss it...; the sugars offer prefect weight to the malt, mainly of a maple syrup theme, but something more heavy and toasty besides; f23 back to vanilla – custard cream biscuits, to be precise; b24 the label makes the dangerously bold claim that this is a whisky which "can stand with the best whiskies in the world". As it happens, their pride may not be entirely misplaced... *46%. nc ncf.*

⬩⬩⬩ **Westland American Single Malt Whiskey Single Cask 115** Oregon oak cask, bott 2/10/15 db **(95.5)** n24.5 give it a good 20 minutes in the glass and ensure it is at body temperature. What you will then find will be an aroma like no other whisky in this, and probably any other world. And for those of you who have been to Guyana and crawled around the warehouses there to sample the very finest aged Demerara rum, you will suddenly be transported back to South America...astonishing! t24 again the sugars dominate. Not just any old sugars. But viscous Demerara and molasses; f23.5 more big rummy tones... and warming, honeyed spice; b23.5 the malt gets lost under the pungency of the massive oak influence. Oregon oak must contain more sugar compounds than any other tree on this planet. Not that I'm complaining... This is the perfect whisky for rum lovers. *55% (110 proof). sc.*

⬩⬩⬩ **Westland American Single Malt Whiskey Single Cask 118** Oregon oak cask, bott 2/10/15 db **(87.5)** n23.5 t23 f20 b21. Has just crossed that invisible line taking it from greatness – like cask 115 – to just very good. Too much tannin makes for a more sinewy and bitter experience, though the manuka honey delights. *55% (110 proof). sc.*

⬩⬩⬩ **Westland American Single Malt Whiskey Single Cask 177** ex-bourbon cask, bott 2/9/15 db **(94.5)** n24 needs time to oxidise and warm in the glass to maximise the manuka honey at play; a little red liquorice and hickory hints at a light bourbon character, too; t24.5 thick, powerful delivery with molasses and spices at the fore. A beautiful praline depth topped by an almost cake-like marzipan and honey frame. Calms slightly into a more Highland Park style heather honey-earthy character while the spices bubble along delightfully; f22.5 bitters slightly at the death; b23.5 bold, assertive single malt trying to stick to a honeyed theme. Fabulous quality! *62.5% (125 Proof). sc.*

⬩⬩⬩ **Westland American Single Malt Whiskey Single Cask 187** ex-bourbon cask, bott 2/9/15 db **(92.5)** n22.5 clean and gentle nose: old polished oak floors, with playful spice and a lick of acacia honey; t23.5 and it is the honey which comes out quickest, never heavy or challenging: just adds a sweet sheen to the grassy, highly salivating barley; f23 more heather honey now as a few spices buzz in. Very elegant oaky fade; b23.5 hugely impressive single malt whisky where the emphasis is on clear honey... *62.5% (125 proof). sc.*

⟐ **Westland American Single Malt Whiskey Single Cask 274** new oak cask, bott 2/10/15 db **(75.5)** n18 t20.5 f18 b19. A strange animal, this. Never sits right either on nose or finish, apart from an impressive malt hurrah soon after delivery (which itself is far from harmonious). And none of the new oak fingerprints I'd expect to find. By comparison with the usually high standards of this distillery, a real disappointment. *55% (110 Proof). sc.*

⟐ **Westland American Single Malt Whiskey Single Cask 350** ex-bourbon cask, bott 2/10/15 db **(91)** n22.5 malty, but also tangy. Not quite so honeyed as the norm...; t23.5 until it hits the palate, where acacia honey is spread over digestive biscuit; soft oils, malt and spice flit around delightfully; f22 some late cocoa on the dry-ish finish; b23 a more sombre offering but excellent complexity. *62.5% (125 Proof). sc.*

Westland Deacon Seat American Single Malt Whiskey dist Jun 11, bott Aug 13 db **(82)** n21 t22.5 f18.5 b20. Sweet – perhaps a little overly so early on. Soft in the house style. But way too flat and furry especially at the death. Sorry. No great fan of the effect the fruitiness has on this guy. *46%. 5000 bottles.*

Westland First Peated American Single Malt Whiskey dist Dec 11, bott Jan 14 db **(89)** n22.5 a wonderfully different style of peated malt: the phenols positively ping off the thrusting tannin. The smoke does envelope gently, but there is a rigidity to the main theme, and a little kumquat, too; t23.5 charming delivery which, like the nose, makes a point of entering new whiskey territory. The sugars are crisp and of a molassed disposition; the oak is forthright, firm and hickory fuddled. Before and after the briefest burst of spice the smoke doesn't appear sure whether to thrust or sit back and massage: in the end it does both...deliciously...; f21 some cocoa-dusted liquorice rounds off a quite idiosyncratic malt; b22 a very acceptable first forage into the smokier depths of the world's whiskies. If, in future bottlings, they can do something about the rock hard, unyielding finale they really will have something special here. *46%. nc ncf.*

WILLIE HOWELL SPIRITS

WH32137 (73.5) n15 t21 f18.5 b19. As big and intense as you'd expect from any spirit with a cut as wide as this. Very sweet corn oil ensures an uplifting body. *42.5%*

WOODINVILLE WHISKEY CO. Woodinville, Washington

Mash Bill No 9 Bourbon Batch 2 **(90)** n22 no shrinking violet here. And on the subject of violets: pretty floral, though the spice rack has much to say too. Genuinely oak-laden and busy; t23.5 if the nose has a lot to say, this positively grinds out the speeches and proclamations. Massive whiskey choc-a-bloc with varied citrus notes of different weights and density. The spices are outwardly delicate but cluster into something serious and meaningful, though the corn has a slightly miserly quality; f22 thins a shade too fast, though the natural caramels and residual sugars do their best to keep the party going; b22.5 a bourbon quite impossible not to love. Excellent fare from a new distillery to watch! *46%*

WOODSTONE CREEK DISTILLERY Cincinnati, Ohio.

Woodstone Creek 10 Year Old Peated Malt (92) 24 23 22 23. Just read the previous tasting notes. There is nothing I can either add nor subtract. Quite, quite wonderful... *46.25%*

YAHARA BAY DISTILLERY Madison, Wisconsin.

Sample No 1 (87) n22.5 t22 f20.5 b22. A disarmingly elegant whiskey. *40%*

American/Kentucky Whiskey Blends

Ancient Age Preferred (73) n16.5 t19 f19.5 b18. A marginal improvement thanks mainly to a re-worked ripe corn-sweet delivery and the cocoa-rich finish. But still preferred, one assumes, by those who probably don't care how good this distillery's whisky can be... *40%*

Beam's Eight Star (69.5) n17 t18 f17 b17.5. If you don't expect too much it won't let you down. *40%*

Bellows (67) n17 t17.5 f16 b16.5 Just too thin. *40%*

Calvert's Extra (79) n19 t20 f20 b20. Sweet and mega-toffeed. Just creaking with caramel but extra marks for the late spice. *40%*

Carstair's White Seal (72) n16.5 t18.5 f19.5 b17.5 Possibly the cleanest blend about even offering a cocoa tang on the finale. Pleasant. *40%*

Kentucky Dale (64) n16 t17 f15 b16. Thin and spineless, though soft and decently sweet on delivery. The grain spirit completely dominates. *40%*

Kessler (84.5) n20 t21 f22 b21.5. "Smooth As Silk" claims the label. And the boast is supported by what is in the bottle: a real toffee-mocha charmer with a chewy, spicy depth. *40%*

PM Deluxe (75) n18 t18 f19 b18. Pleasant moments as the toffee melts in the mouth. *40%*

Sunny Brook (79.5) n20 t21 f19 b19.5. An entirely agreeable blend with toffee and lightly oiled nuts. Plus a sunny disposition... *40%*

Whiskey Distilled From Bourbon Mash

Angels Envy Bourbon Finished in Port Barrels (84) n20 t22 f21 b21. Almost like a chocolate raisin candy and fruitcake. Silky textured and juicy. *43.3% (86.6 proof)*

Angels Envy Cask Strength Bourbon Finished in Port Barrels Cask Strength (86.5) n21.5 t24 f20 b21. The problem with cask finishing most things, and bourbon in particular it seems, is that something is lost in the complexity - especially the small grain interaction, as well as balance between the spirit and oak - which is not quite compensated for with the lushness of extra fruit. Much better than the standard bottling, though, and the juiciness and cushioned enormity on delivery and spice at the midpoint is certainly worth discovering. *60.5%*

Big Bottom Straight Bourbon Finished in Port Casks 91 (86.5) n21.5 t24 f20 b21. Subtract over enthusiastic toastiness and withering dryness and for a while we have a genuinely stunning mouth feel backed by spectacular spiced apricot and ulmo honey. The odd few moments of genius there. *45.5% (91 proof) ncf*

Big Bottom Straight bourbon Finished in Zinfandel Casks 91 (85) n21 t22 f21 b21. A flat nose and delivery comes alive about eight or nine flavour waves in when the fruit comes to a compromise with the grains. The burnt raisin finish is just a little too bitter. *45.5% ncf.*

Woodford Reserve Master's Collection Four Wood db (78.5) n20 t22.5 f18 b18. As much as they seem to want to kid us that this is bourbon – and let us be in no doubt: it isn't – it would help their misguided cause if whatever this was being offered proved an attractive experience. Apart from the immediate honey-rich delivery which is very pleasant indeed, the nose and finish have all the charisma of a 59-year-old train spotter going home to his empty house to make his sandwiches for the next day. Flat, characterless and spectacularly devoid of complexity. Basically, all the things bourbon cannot normally be accused of... *47.2% WB15/379*

Whiskey Distilled From Malt Mash

Woodford Reserve Master's Collection Classic Malt distilled from a malt mash db **(79.5) n20 t21 f19 b19.5.** Ok. So let me get my head around this. If their label and neck blurb is to believed, a spirit distilled from malt in the US and placed into used casks is a "whiskey distilled from a bourbon mash" while, as written on another product, a bourbon transferred into used casks is a bourbon. That appears to be Woodford's stance. Sorry, guys. Don't buy that argument for a second. If anyone argued that there appears to be more politicising, tactical manoeuvring and precedential games being played here as there is careful fermentation, distilling and blending, it would be hard to disagree. Says it is malt. But doesn't help by saying malt what. Presumably barley, as the nose offers nothing other than freshly cut hay. Which in a Scotch or Irish might be regarded as a problem, often pointing an accusing finger at fermentation. Sadly, the drinking experience, as sweet as it is, doesn't get much better. *45.2% WB15/382*

Whiskey Distilled From Rye Mash

Angels Envy Rye Finished in Caribbean Rum Casks (78) n18.5 truly a unique nose in my 24 years of professional tasting and 38 years of sampling the world's whisk(e)ys. Kind of perfumed burnt orange and toasted vanilla mallow filling in the rye peaks...; **t20.5** what the hell...?? Yes, the rye bites through the clutter, and does it well. But there is still a bizarre background noise that just about defies description. Oily, sugary...odd; **f20** a soft, lightly pulsing oil; **b19** frankly, I was hardly expecting to have any teeth left after this sample. The hardest, most crisp of all whiskeys is rye. And if you want to give any whisk(e)y an extra degree of exoskeleton, then just finish it in a rum cask. And here we have the two together : yikes! Some twenty years ago I gave then Jack Daniel's blender Lincoln Henderson his first-ever taste of peated whisky: a Laphroaig. He hated it! I think he's waited a long time to return the compliment by showing me a style I did not know could exist. Beyond fascinating. Weird, even - hence the full tasting notes. One for the ladies with this liqueur-style smoothie. *50%*.

Other American Whiskey

Abraham Bowman Double Barrel Bourbon dist 12/06 bott 03/14. db **(85) n23 t23 f19 b20.** What does double barrel mean here? Well, in this instance thankfully it does not involve sherry or other wine casks. This is bourbon x2: the spirit is matured in virgin oak for a few years before being dumped into a fresh one. So this really is bourbon. If the great Truman Cox, the former distiller at Bowman, was still with us I'd have fun telling him why I think this is not something that has been done too often in the past. Not least because of the double dose of oak-induced sugars which means, sadly, a cloying, over-the-top sweetness and overall lack of charm and complexity. The saving grace on the palate is the delivery which packs enough spicily explosive punch to cut through the concentrated sugar candy to create something meaningful, if only temporarily so. The uncompromisingly dry finish is way off beam, so to speak, and even off-handedly bitter. One hundred proof, I'm afraid, that you can have too much of a good thing. If you do end up with a bottle, do make the most of the nose and test it only after it has aired and oxidised for about 20 minutes: it is like dipping your head into the spice cupboard in which the ginger has been knocked over and spilled. Ginger beer barrel...who needs it? *50%.*

◇ **Abraham Bowman Pioneer Spirit Coffee Finished Bourbon** Release No. 11 dist 03/10/06, bott 4/10/15 db **(71) n19 t18 f17 b17**. Dry, aggressive, unbalanced...I think I'd rather just wake up and smell the whiskey... *673% (134.6 Proof)*

Abraham Bowman Pioneer Spirit 'Gingerbread Beer Finished Bourbon' charred white oak, dist 21/04/2006 bott 14/08/2013 db **(89) n22** most ginger cake lurks at ever corner of this dry, gently spiced nose...; **t22** again, a dry delivery with a build up of yapping if dull spice; big tannin signature though the hickory finds it hard to make its mark **f23** even drier – almost like toasted brown bread. The ginger, now more pronounced, shimmers...; **b22** as gingerbread beer finished whiskey goes, rates highly... *45%.*

◇ **Abraham Bowman Pioneer Spirit Vanilla Bean Flavored Whiskey** dist 04/16/07, bott 11/03/14 db **(79) n21 t20 f19 b19**. Sharp, tangy and.... weird. Think I prefer my whiskey vanilla notes to come from the oak. *45% (90 Proof)*

Abraham Bowman Virginia Limited Edition Whiskey "Port Finished Borboun" dist 30/03/01 bott 17/08/13. db **(84.5) n20 t23 f20.5 b21**. I imagine this at one time was an entertaining bourbon. However, it reaches us as something of a dullard. The nose is instantly forgettable with the fruit and grains cancelling the other out; likewise the finish does little to stretch the imagination or taste buds other than some persistent spices. Only on delivery does this work as we are treated to a virtuoso display of dark sugars and jam vying for top spot. But the question needing answering for me is simple: why are the Americans trying to ape the Scots at a time when, quality-wise, Kentucky boots are firmly trod on kilted windpipes? *50%.*

Buffalo Trace White Dog Mash #1 (93) n23 t23 f24 b23. Exceptionally high quality spirit, fabulously weighted, neither too sweet nor dry and with the distinctive cocoa character of the very best grain distillate. Beats the crap out of vodka. "White Dog" is the name for spirit which has run off the still but not yet been bottled: "New Make" in Scotland. It is not, therefore, whiskey as it has not been in any form of contact with oak. But what the hell... It must be at least 15 years ago that I told the old plant manager, Joe Darmond, that he should bottle this stuff as it would sell fast. BT brought it out initially for their distillery shop...and now it is in demand worldwide?! If you are reading this, what did I tell you? and about rye come to that! *62.5%*

High West Son of Bourye blend of bourbon & rye **(95) n23** the rye notes are as crunchy as a muscovado sugar driveway; **t24.5** the kind of salivation factor that brings you to your knees in a state of grainy euphoria. The radiating brown sugars are as clean as they are exemplary; **f23.5** only now does the bourbon get a word in edgeways, though can offer only a half-hearted honey, caramel and liquorice mix; the spices are sublime; **b24** this son, presumably called Ryebon, is a stunningly stylish chap which comprehensively eclipses its lackluster parent... *46%*

High West Campfire rye, bourbon & Scotch malt, batch no. 3 **(93) n23.5 t22.5 f23.5 b23.5**. An enchanting, hugely complex dram...the sort of thing I conjure up in my tasting room every day, in fact, by mixing differing whisky styles from around the world. Here the rye dominates by some margin, creating the backbone on which the sweeter bourbon tones hang. The peated malt ensures a wonderful background rumble. Well blended...and great fun! *46%*

High West Whiskey American Prairie Reserve Blend of Straight Bourbon batch 13DQ3 db **(91) n22.5** warm and rich, there is an unusually heavy copper content; red currents sits well with the spiced honeycomb; the hefty tannins in a brand called Prairie Reserve add a degree of irony; **t23** exceptionally dry, tingling delivery with the sugars apparent but usually keeping their distance; **f23** cream fudge and a return to a heftier type of tannin; **b23** not often you find a predominantly dry bourbon...must have something to do with the Prairie...which ten percent of post tax profit will help to preserve. *46%. ncf. WB15/177*

◇ **Michter's No. 1 American Whiskey (84.5) n21 t21.5 f21 b21**. Sugar-coated, oily and easy going. About as friendly as any whiskey you'll find this year *41.7%*

◇ **Michter's No. 1 Sour Mash (86) n22 t22 f21 b21**. A pleasant, clean, light whiskey: perhaps too clean at times. Good mocha throughout, with the accent on the coffee. *43%*

◇ **WhistlePig Old World 12 Year Madeira Finish** European casks **(88) n21.5** hard, unyielding but attractive rye; **t23.5** explosive delivery with spices going off like gelignite. But the sugars from the grain and yielding fruit form an unexpectedly attractive chocolatey mix; **f21** on the short and thin side; bitters out; **b22** not sure how this can be called a straight rye. But as a whiskey experience, certainly has its merits. *45%. (90 Proof)*

◇ **WhistlePig Old World 12 Year Port Finish** European casks **(74) n18 t20 f18 b18**. Oily, dense and bitter *45%. (90 Proof)*

◇ **WhistlePig Old World 12 Year Sauternes Finish** European casks **(79.5) n21 t22.5 f18 b18**. Has its brief moments of fun, mainly on delivery, when the rock-hard rye tries to keep out the surrounding, swamping fruit. But a very poor finish and very little balance throughout. *45%. (90 Proof)*

Canadian Whisky

The vastness of Canada is legendary. As is the remoteness of much of its land. Anyone who has not yet visited Gimli, which sits serenely on the shores of Lake Manitoba more or less bang in the middle of the country and in early Spring, venture a few miles out into the wilderness has missed a trick.

Because there, just a dozen miles from the remotest distillery of them all, Gimli, you can stand and listen to the ice crack with a clean, primeval crispness unlike any other thing you will have experienced; a sound once heard by the very first hunters who ventured into these uncharted wastes. And hear a distant loon call its lonely, undulating, haunting, song, its notes skudding for miles along the ice and vanishing into the snow which surrounds you. Of all the places on the planet, it is the one where you will feel a sensation as close to nature - and insignificance - as you are likely to find.

It was also a place where I felt that, surely, great whisky should be made. But in the early days of the Gimli distillery there was a feeling of frustration by the blenders who used it. Because they were simply unable to recreate the depth and complexity of the legendary Crown Royal brand it had been built to produce in place of the old, now closed, distilleries to the east. When, in their lab, they tasted the new Crown Royal against the old there were furrowed brows, a slight shaking of heads and an unspoken but unmistakable feeling of hopeless resignation.

To understand why, we have to dispense with the nonsense which appears to have been trotted out by some supposed expert in Canadian whisky or other

BRITISH COLUMBIA

ALBERTA

MANITOBA

Vancouver

Calgary

Alberta

Okanagan

Palliser

Gimli

Key
- ● Major Town or City
- ▲ Distillery
- † Dead Distillery

who has, I have been advised by quite a few people I meet at my tastings, been writing somewhere that Canada has no history of blending from different distilleries. Certainly that is now the perceived view of many in the country. And it is just plain wrong: only a maniac would write such garbage as fact and completely undersell the provenance of Canadian whisky. Crown Royal, when in its pomp, was a meticulous blending of a number of different whiskies from the Seagram empire and by far the most complex whisky Canada had to offer.

The creases in the furrowed brows deepened as the end of the last century aproached. Because the key distilleries of LaSalle, Beuþre and Waterloo were yielding the very last of their stocks, especially top quality pure rye, and although the much lighter make of Gimli was of a high standard, they had not yet been able to recreate the all round complexity as when adding the fruits of so many great distilleries together. The amount of experimentation with yeasts and distilling speeds and cutting times was a wonder to behold. But the race was on: could they produce the diversity of flavours to match the old, classic distilleries which were now not just closed but in some cases demolished before the final stocks ran dry?

When I had sat in the LaSalle blending lab for several days in the 1990s and worked my way through the near extinct whiskies in stock I recognised in Beupre a distillery which, had it survived, probably might have been capable of producing something as good, if not better, than anything else on this planet. And it was clear just what a vital contribution it made to Crown Royal's all round magnificence.

So I have monitored the Crown Royal brand with interest, especially since Gimli and the brand was acquired by Diageo 15 years ago. And anyone doubting that this really was a truly great whisky should have accompanied me when I visited the home of my dear and now sadly lost friend Mike Smith and worked our way through his astonishing Crown Royal collection which showed how the brand's taste profile had evolved through the ages.

And, at last, it appears all that hard work, all those early days of experimentation and fine tuning at Gimli have paid off. For while the standard Crown Royal brand doesn't yet quite live up to its starry past, they have unleashed upon us a whisky which dazzles, startles and engulfs you in its natural beauty like an early spring morning on Lake Manitoba. The whisky is called Crown Royal Northern Harvest Rye. It is not only the best Canadian to be found in the market today, it is this year's Jim Murray's World Whisky of the Year: in my view currently the best whisky on the planet. The fact it should have achieved this at a time when Canadian whisky is at a nadir, with far too many brands dependent on adding too many unacceptble things as accepted flavouring agents, is providential. It shows that keeping the grains at a maximum and allowing them to be the flavouring agents - like Alberta Premium - is not just keeping true to the old Canadian traditions, but the way to go to drag it back onto the world's stage and give it a leading role. Walter Jonke and the other old Canadian blenders I knew understood this. Let this be a lesson to the present generation.

QUEBEC

Glenora

ONTARIO

NOVA SCOTIA

Valleyfield

●Quebec
●Montreal

Canada Mist   ●Toronto
            Kittling Ridge
      Walkerville

Canadian Single Malts
GLENORA

Glen Breton db (81) n19 t21 f20 b21. Ultra sweet malt, in almost concentrated form with a tantalising whiff of smoke hanging around; mildly spiced and slightly oily, soapy finish. 43%

Glen Breton Ice Aged 10 Years db (85.5) n21.5 t21 f22 b21. Tasting both a full strength bottled Canadian, and one that had been matured in Icewine barrels, I was nearly blown through the back of my seat and into the wall. One of the biggest shocks to hit you on the Canadian whisky scene today, there is no denying that this whisky offers sufficient panache and lucidity to genuinely impress. Hardly an exercise in perfect balance, it certainly celebrates the art of surprise and, late on, charm. The cocoa-dusted butterscotch really is a rare treat and, thanks to the fruity world it finds itself in, a truly unique and enjoyable experience. 57.2%

Glen Breton Rare db (80) n18 t21 f20 b21. Caramel nose a bit soapy but the buttery, sweet malt, with its vanilla fizz, makes for a pleasant experience. 43%

Glen Breton Rare Aged 10 Years bott 10 db (89.5) n22 t23 f22 b22.5. An impressive whisky: one of the best bottlings of this age for some while and showing the malt at full throttle. 43%

Glen Breton Rare Aged 14 Years db (92) n23.5 t22.5 f23 b23. What is there not to enjoy? Some exceptionally good casks involved here. 43%

Glen Breton Battle Of The Glen Aged 15 Years Special Edition db (94) n23.5 t23.5 f23 b24. I really did know they were capable of bottling something this good: there isn't a single barrel of this vintage I have not tasted in their warehouse at one time or another during its maturation cycle. This watermark bottling from then is an essentially sweet whisky, tasting all the sweeter as it marks the little distillery's victory over the Goliath that is the Scotch Whisky Association in their rightful battle to retain the right to use the name of their brand. Just sometimes there is evidence there just may be a god... 43% 4200 bottles.

Glen Breton Rare Cabot Links Reserve Aged 19 Years db (86.5) n21 t22.5 f21 b22. You know when astronomers build a super-powerful new telescope that gives them a clearer view of when the universe began. This bottling is a bit like that... taking us back to the days of the Glen Breton Big Bang. Lots of dramatic barley to view. But, naturally, all the more basic and primitive elements are there on show, also... 46%

OKANAGAN SPIRITS CRAFT DISTILLERY

Laird of Fintry Single Malt Whisky French & American oak. db (84) n21 t22 f20 b21. A tangy, aromatic whisky where the oak appears to have a disproportionate say. Interesting marmalade depth. 40%. First Batch. 264 bottles.

POTTER DISTILLING CO.

Cadenhead's World Whiskies Canada Potter Distilling Co. Aged 24 Years Bourbon barrel, bott Feb 14 (94.5) n23 though from a bourbon cask and distilled from corn, you cannot escape a delicate fruit note, as though from boiled candy. This suggests the cask might have spent some time in the distant past maturing in a warehouse in Canada with fruit distillate alongside; t24 gorgeous delivery with the corn ramping up both the flavour profile and the oils; the sugars are a mix of maple syrup and ulmo honey. Again, that vague unspecified fruitiness catches the palate offering a silky hue; f23.5 now the spices are in play yet the salivation levels do not drop despite the polite oak intervention via the drying vanilla; b24 a true classic of the Canadian rye style...though of course without any rye at all. As a whisky, a little bit of a mystery. When at Potter distillers in British Columbia about 17 years ago, I remember then they had no maturing stock of their own as they did not distil large enough quantities. But they did have casks of maturing Canadian whisky they had bought in from the nearby Okanagan Distillery which, for a while, had made Canadian Club for the west coast and Far East market. No guarantees, but chances are it could be that – and they did make very good whisky there, evidenced by the outstanding old Bush Pilot single cask brand. 56.5%. 126 bottles. WB15/178

STILLWATERS DISTILLERY

Stalk & Barrel Single Malt Whisky cask 11 db (87.5) n21.5 t22 f22 b22. Attractively intense barley has all the space it requires to flourish thanks to a well distilled spirit impressively cut. Only a lack of complexity fails to crank the score a little higher. But if it's a malt whisky you want, with the accent on the malt, here's your man. 62.3%. sc.

Stalk & Barrel Single Malt Whisky cask 13 db (77) n20 t21 f17 b19. Not quite the delight that is cask 11. Not sure if that is because the weaker strength means the water has broken up the oils a little bit too much for their own good, exposing a few feints. Or if the cut wasn't quite as carefully made this time round. Still plenty of malt to get on with, though. 46%. sc.

Canadian Blended Whisky

Alberta Premium (95.5) n24 throbbing, pulsing rye on a variety of levels: full and juicy, dull and dusty, firm and flinty. Unique and unmistakable; **t25** my first whisky of the day – and it needs to be. The tastebuds are given such a working over that they need to be fully tuned and fit to take this on. Again it is all about the rye: the first three flavours to pound the mouth are all rye-related. The very first are juicy with a minute sweetness. The second, hanging onto the coattails of the first are Rockies hard and brittle, clattering into the tastebuds with zero yield. Next comes a quick follow through of explosive peppers, but again leaving in their wake a semi-sweet juicy, fruitiness, almost certainly from the malted rye. No other whisky unleashes this combination of grainy punches around the palate. The words beautiful and complex don't even begin to do this whisky justice; **f22.5** dulls even more, probably because of the needless caramel added, but there is slightly more depth than before thanks most probably to the malted rye. The spices continue to fizz as the Demerara-tipped vanillas make their mark; **b24** it has just gone 8am and the Vancouver Island sky is one of clear blue. My windows are open to allow in some chilly, early Spring air and, though only the first week of March, an American robin sits in the arbutus tree, resplendent in its now two-toned leaves, calling for a mate, as it has done since 5.15 this morning, his song blending with the lively trill of the house finches and the doleful, maritime anthem of the gull. It seems the natural environment of Alberta Premium, back here to its rye-studded best after a couple I tasted socially in Canada last year appeared comparatively dull and restrained. I am tasting this from Bottle Lott No L93300197 and it is classic, generating all I expect and now demand. A national treasure. *40%*

Alberta Premium 25 Years Old (95) n24 t23 f23 b25. Faultless. Absolutely nothing dominates. Yet every aspect has its moment of conquest and glory. It is neither bitter nor sweet, yet both. It is neither soft nor hard on the palate yet both elements are there. Because of the 100% rye used, this is an entirely new style of whisky to hit the market. No Canadian I know has ever had this uncompromising brilliance, this trueness to style and form. And, frightening to think, it could be improved further by bottling at least 46% and un-chillfiltered. For any whisky lover who ever thought Canadian was incapable of hitting the heights among the world's greats. *40%. Alberta Distillers.*

Alberta Premium 30 Years (88.5) n23 t23.5 f20 b22. It doesn't take much to tip the balance of a whisky this delicate on the nose and delivery. Five extra years in the cask has nudged the oak just a little too far. However, savour the nose and delivery which are to die for. *40%*

Alberta Premium Dark Horse (84) n18 t22 f22 b22. The blurb on the back says it is crafted for the "next generation of whisky connoisseur". Fine. But personally, I'd always shape a whisky for the true connoisseurs of today... I have not spoken to the blending team at Alberta to discuss this and, as the book has to be finished within a week or two, I won't get a chance. But this is the most extraordinary development in Canadian I have seen for a while. The nose is not great: it really does seem as though fruit cordial has been given the lead role. But the taste really does challenge, and I have to say there are many aspects I enjoy. It is as though some peated malt has been added to the mix as the finish does have distinctive smokiness. And the balance has been expertly worked to ensure the sugars don't dominate while the spices are persistent. But if it falls down anywhere, the over reliance on the fruit apart, it is the fact that Alberta makes the best spirit in Canada by a very great distance....yet someone has forgotten to ensure that fact is made clear in the taste and the nose especially. *45%*

⬦ **Alberta Rye Whisky Dark Batch Blended Rye (86) n19 t23 f22 b22.** A veritable fruitcake of a whisky – and about as moist and sultana-laden as you'll ever find. Not sure about that bitter-tobacco most un-Canadian nose, though. *45% (90 Proof)*

Alberta Springs Aged 10 Years (83) n21 t21 f20 b20. Really appears to have had a bit of a flavourectomy. Sweet but all traces of complexity have vanished. *40%.*

Barton's Canadian 36 Months Old (78) n19 t20 f19 b20. Sweet, toffeed, easy-going. *40%*

Bowman's Canadian Whisky (90.5) n22 t22 f23.5 b23. A delicious blend for chocoholics. *40%*

Black Velvet (78) n18 t20 f20 b20. A distinctly off-key nose is compensated for by a rich corn and vanilla kick on the palate. But that famous spice flourish is a distant memory. Another big caramel number. *40%*

Campbell & Cooper Aged a Minimum of 36 Months (84.5) n21.5 t22 f20 b21. Huge flavour profile. An orchard of oranges on the nose and profound vanilla on delivery. *40%*

Canadian Club 100 Proof (89) n21 t23 f22 b23. If you are expecting this to be a high-octane version of the standard CC Premium, you'll be in for a shock. This is a much fruitier dram with an oilier body to absorb the extra strength. An entertaining blend. *50%.*

⬦ **Canadian Club Chairman's Select 100% Rye (81.5) n21 t21.5 f20 b19.** A bemusing whisky. The label proudly announces that here we have a whisky made from 100% rye. Great news: a Canadian eagerly anticipated. But the colour – a deep orange – looks a bit suspicious. And those fears prove well founded when the taste buds, as well as the nose, go looking for the rye influence in vain. Instead we have a massive toffee effect, offset by some busy spice. Colouring has ruined many a great whisky...and here we have a painful example. What a waste of good rye... *40%*

Canadian Club Premium (92) n23 t22.5 f23 b23.5. A greatly improved whisky which now finds the fruit fitting into the mix with far more panache than of old. Once a niggardly whisky, often seemingly hell-bent on refusing to enter into any form of complexity: but not now! Great spices in particular. I'm impressed. *40%*

Canadian Club Aged 6 Years (88.5) n21.5 t22 f22.5 b22.5. Not at all bad for a Canadian some purists turn their nose up at as it's designed for the American market. Just brimming with mouth-watering enormity and style. Dangerously moreish. *40%*

Canadian Club Reserve Aged 10 Years (86) n20 t22 f21.5 b22. Odd cove, this. The nose is less than welcoming and offers a hotchpotch of somewhat discordant notes giving a jumbled message and less than well defined statement of intent. Decent delivery, though, shifting through the gears with some impressive and sultry fruit tying in well with a rare grain onslaught found in Canadian these days. The finish, though, just can't steer away from the rocks of bitterness, alas. Again, as so often appears to be the case with CC, the spices star. *40%*

Canadian Club Classic Aged 12 Years (91.5) n22 t24 f21.5 b23.5. A confident whisky which makes the most of a honeycomb theme. *40%*

Canadian Club Small Batch Classic 12 Aged 12 Years batch C12-020 (75.5) n21 t22.5 f15 b17. A syrupy whisky which talks a great game on the back label, but fails to deliver in reality. Big fruit, perhaps a little too heavily accented as other avenues of complexity are limited. The bitter, tangy finish is not great at all. *40%*

Canadian Club Aged 20 Years (92.5) n24 t21 f23.5 b23. In previous years, CC20 has ranked among the worst whiskies I have tasted, not just in Canada, but the world. Their current bottling, though, is not even a distant relation. Sure, it has a big sherry investment. But the sheer elan and clever use of spice make this truly magnificent. Possibly the most pleasant surprise in my latest trawl through all Canada's whiskies. *40%*

Canadian Club Sherry Cask batch no. SC-018 (76) n18 t20 f20 b18. Twice as strong as you can normally buy Sherry yet somehow has only half the body. As I say, I really don't know what to make of this. Nor do I get the point. *41.3%*

Canadian Five Star Rye Whisky (83) n21 t22 f20 b20. An entirely tame, well behaved Canadian which celebrates the inherent sweetness of the species. That said, the immediate impact on the palate is pretty delicious with a quick, flash explosion of something spicy. But it is the deft, satin-soft mouthfeel which may impress most. *40%*

Canadian Hunter (85.5) n20.5 t21 f22 b22. Remains truly Canadian in style. The toffee has diminished, allowing far more coffee and cocoa to ensure a delightful middle and finish. *40%*

Canadian Mist (78) n19 t20.5 f18.5 b20. Much livelier than previous incarnations despite the inherent, lightly fruited softness. *40%*

Canadian Pure Gold (82) n21.5 t20.5 f20 b20. Full-bodied and still a notably lush whisky. The pure gold may have more to do with the caramel than the years in cask but the meat of this whisky still gives you plenty to chew over. I especially enjoy the gradual building of spices. *40%*

Canadian Spirit (78) n20 t20 f19 b19. A real toffee-fest with a touch of hard grain around the edges. *40%. Carrington Distillers (Alberta Distillers).*

Caribou Crossing Single Barrel (84) n20 t22.5 f20 b21.5. While the nose offers an unholy battle between some apple-fruity rye notes and dry, dusty caramel, there is a real pulsating delivery with the sharper spices helped along the way by the silkiness of the body. Though the caramel offers a toffee-fudge backdrop, a countering dry date sweetness does more than enough to keep it at bay. However, the finish dulls out as the caramel gains the upper hand, though the twitching spices do ensure a light, throbbing beat. An enjoyable Canadian, undoubtedly, I am somewhat perplexed by it. There is no reference to the barrel number so you won't know if you are buying from different casks. Also, if it is single barrel what is the point of the caramel? If it is to make all the casks taste the same, or similar, then why not just blend them together. A badly missed opportunity. *40%. Sazerac.*

Centennial 10 Year Limited Edition (88.5) n21.5 t23 f22 b22. Retains its usual honey-flavoured breakfast cereal style, but the complexity has increased. Busy and charming. *40%*

Century Reserve 8 Years Old Premium (82) n20 t21 f20 b21. Clean vanilla caramel. *40%*

Century Reserve Custom Blend 15 Years Plus (88.5) n21.5 t22 f23 b22. After two days of being ambushed in every direction, or completely steamrollered by Canadian caramel, my tastebuds are in total shock. Caramel kept to an absolute minimum so that it hardly registers at all. Charming and refined drinking. *40%*

Century Reserve 21 Years Old (91.5) n23.5 t23 f23 b22. Quite beautiful, but a spirit that is as likely to appeal to rum lovers as whisky ones. *40%*

Century Reserve Custom Blend lot no. 1525 (87) n21.5 t22 f21.5 b22. An enjoyable whisky which doesn't quite reach its full potential. *40%*

Corby's Canadian 36 Months Old (85) n20 t21 f22 b22. Attractive with fine bitter-sweet balance and I love the late spice kick-back. 40%. Barton. Interesting label: as a keen ornithologist, I had no idea there were parrots in Canada. Must be related to the Norwegian Blue.

Crown Royal (86) n22 t23.5 f19.5 b21. The Crown has spoken and it has been decreed that this once ultra grainy old whisky is taking its massive move to a silky fruitiness as far as it can go. It was certainly looking that way last time out; on this re-taste (and a few I have unofficially tasted) there is now no room for doubt. If you like grape, especially the sweeter variety, you'll love this. The highpoint is the sublime delivery and starburst of spice. The low point? The buzzy, unhappy finale. The Grain Is Dead. Long Live The Grape! 40%

Crown Royal Black (85) n22 t23 f18.5 b21.5. Not for the squeamish: a Canadian which goes for it with bold strokes from the off which makes it a whisky worth discovering. The finish needs a rethink, though. 45%

Crown Royal Cask No 16 Finished in Cognac Casks (85.5) n21.5 t21 f22 b21. Clean cut and very grapey. The nose is unique in the whisky world: it is one of Cognac. Otherwise struggles to really find its shape and rhythm. A perfect Canadian for those who prefer theirs with an air of grace and refinement but very limited depth. In fact, those who prefer a Cognac. 40%

⬦ **Crown Royal Hand Selected Barrel** (90) n22 quintessential Canadian: corn oil and vanilla; t23 concentrated corn oil relieved by ulmo honey, spice and the inevitable toffee; f22.5 corn oil...and toffee. Thankfully the spice carries on buzzing; b22.5 more Canadian than a punch in the kisser from an ice hockey player. 51.5%

Crown Royal Limited Edition (87) n22 t22.5 f20.5 b22. A much happier and productive blend than before with an attractive degree of complexity but the more bitter elements of the finish have been accentuated. 40%

⬦ **Crown Royal Northern Harvest Rye** (97.5) n25 the rye is not just profound and three dimensional, but has that extraordinary trick of allowing new elements to take their place: rarely does ulmo honey and manuka honey link arms when rye is around, but they do here, yet never for a second diminish the sharpness and presence of the grain; t24.5 salivating and sensual on delivery, hardly for a second are we not reminded that rye is at work here. And it makes itself heard loudly through the stiff backbone from which all the softer, sugary notes emanate. Crunchy and at times bitter, though in a pleasant controlled way from the grain, rather than a questionable cask; f23.5 quietens rapidly, though only for a moment or two before the spices begin to pulse again and vanillas take up their comfortable positions; b24.5 this is the kind of whisky you dream of dropping into your tasting room. Rye, that most eloquent of grains, not just turning up to charm and enthral but to also take us through a routine which reaches new heights of beauty and complexity. To say this is a masterpiece is barely doing it justice. 45%

Crown Royal Special Reserve (96) n24 a clean and attractively spiced affair with cinnamon and the faintest pinch of allspice leading the way: rye at work, one presumes; the fruit is clean and precise with weightier grape overshadowing a green apple freshness; t24 a spicier element to the usual rye and fruit delivery, much more in keeping with the nose, but that fabulous, contrary mouth-feel of harder grain and softer fruit continues to do the business. The spices build slowly but with an impressive evenness and determination: one of the most outstanding Canadians on the palate of them all; f24 the finish has been tidied up and with stunning effect: no more sawdust and eye-watering dryness. Both grain and soft fruit ensure a magnificently mouth-watering end to an amazing journey; b24 complex, well weighted and simply radiant: it is like looking at a perfectly shaped, gossamer clad Deb at a ball. The ryes work astonishingly well here (they appear to be of the malted, ultra-fruity variety) and perhaps to best effect after Alberta Premium, though now it is a hard call between the two. 40%

Crown Royal XR Extra Rare lot no. L7064 N4 (93.5) n24 t23 f23 b23.5. Just about identical to the previous bottle above. The only difference is on the finish where the rye, fortified with spice, decides to hang back and battle it out to the death; the toffee and vanilla make a controlled retreat. Either the same bottling with a slightly different stance after a few years in the bottle, or a different one of extraordinary high consistency. 40%

Crown Royal XO (87.5) n22 t21 t22.5 b22. With an XO, one might have hoped for something eXtraOrdinary or at least eXOtic. Instead, we have a Canadian which carried on a little further where their Cask No 16 left off. Always a polite, if rather sweet whisky, it falls into the trap of allowing the Cognac casks a little too much say. Only on the finish, as the spices begin to find channels to flow into, does the character which, for generations, set Crown Royal apart from all other Canadians begin to make itself heard: complexity. 40% WB15/398

Danfield's Limited Edition Aged 21 Years (95) n24 t24 f23.5 b23.5. A quite brilliant first-time whisky. The back label claims this to be small batch, but there is no batch number on the bottle, alas. Or even a visible bottling code. But this is a five star performer and one of this year's whiskies of the world. 40%

Danfield's Private Reserve (84.5) n20 t21.5 f22 b21. A curious, non-committal whisky which improves on the palate as it goes along. An overdose of caramel (yawn!!) has done it no favours, but there is character enough for it to pulse out some pretty tasty spice. Seamless and silky, for all the toffee there underlying corn-rich clarity is a bit of a turn on. 40%

8 Seconds Small Batch (86) n20 t22 f22.5 b21.5. Fruity, juicy, luxurious. And perhaps one of the few whiskies on the market anywhere in the world today which could slake a thirst. 40%

Forty Creek Barrel Select (86.5) n21.5 t22 f21 b21.5. Thank goodness that the sulphur taint I had found on this in recent years has now vanished. A lush, enjoyable easy-goer, this juices up attractively at the start and ends with an almost sophisticated dry pithiness. 40%

Forty Creek Confederation Oak Reserve lot 1867-B **(94.5) n23.5 t24 f23.5 b23.5.** Those who tasted the first batch of this will be intrigued by this follow up. The shape and intensity profile has been re-carved and all now fits together like a jigsaw. 40%

Forty Creek Copper Pot Reserve (91.5) n23 t23.5 f22 b23. One of the beauties of John hall's whiskies at Forty Creek is that they follow no set pattern in the whisky would: they offer flavour profiles really quite different from anything else. That is why they are worth that bit of extra time for your palate to acclimatise. Here you are exceptionally well rewarded... 43%

Forty Creek Double Barrel Reserve lot 247 **(86) n21.5 t22.5 f20.5 b21.5.** Juicy ride with plenty to savour early on. But something is slightly off balance about the finish. 40%

Forty Creek Port Wood Reserve lot 61 **(95.5) n24.5** oh my word! Very highest quality Turkish Delight with some pretty top score chocolate; the fruit hangs off the frame full of juice and muscovado sugars. It demands spices...and gets them – with the right pizzazz! **t24** the delivery is pure silk in texture and the most stunning fruit and spice on delivery. Hard to know whether to suck as it melts in the mouth, or chew as the background depth is outrageously nutty, with more cocoa to thicken. It is the astonishing spice that really mesmerises, as it is of almost perfect intensity; **f23** dries into an attractive crushed grape pip dryness, again with the spices lingering; **b24** John P Hall has got his ducks in a row. Magnificent! 45%

Forty Creek Three Grain (76) n19 t20 f18 b19. Not quite as well assembled as some Three grains I have come across over the last few years. There is a lopsidedness to this one: we know the fruit dominates (and I still haven't a clue why, when surely this of all whiskies, just has to be about the grains!) but the bitterness interferes throughout. If there have been sherry casks used here, I would really have a close look at them. 40%

Fremont Mischief Whiskey batch MPJ-0803, bott 11 **(77) n19 t20 f19 b19.** Though this was from the Mischief distillery in Seattle, USA, the whiskey was produced in Canada. Overly sweet, overly toffeed and bereft of complexity. Like Alberta Springs on a very bad day. 40%

Gibson's Finest Aged 12 Years (77) n18 t20 f19 b20. Unlike the Sterling, going backwards rather than forwards. This is way too syrupy, fruity and toffee impacted. Despite the very good spice, almost closer to a liqueur than a true whisky style. 40%

Gibson's Finest Rare Aged 18 Years (95.5) n24 close your eyes and sniff and you would swear you have a bourbon-rye mix: simultaneously crisp and soft, the sharpness of the rye and apple-style fruitiness is sublime and as enticing as it gets; **t24.5** and a perfect transfer onto the palate: spectacularly juicy with all kinds of clean rye and corn notes bobbling around in a gorgeous gentle Demerara sugar backdrop; **f23.5** impressive vanilla and long strands of grain and bitter liquorice; **b23.5** so far ahead of both Sterling and the 12, it is hard to believe they are from the same stable. But make no mistake; this is pure thoroughbred: truly world class. 40%

Gibson's Finest 100th Grey Cup Special Edition (87) n21 t23 f21 b22. When the label tells you there is a hint of maple, they aren't joking... 40%

Gibson's Finest Canadian Whisky Bourbon Cask Rare Reserve (89) n23 t21 f23 b22. A much better version than the first bottling, the depth this time being massively greater. 40%

Gibson's Finest Sterling (86.5) n22 t22.5 f20.5 b21.5. A massively improved Canadian that had me doing the equivalent of a tasting double take: had to look twice at this to check I had the right stuff! Much firmer now in all the right places with the corn making sweeping statements, the golden syrup melting into all the required crevices and spices exploding at the appropriate moments. Just need to sort the heavy toffee and bitter finish out and this would be up in the Canadian Premier League. 40%

Gibson's New Oak (88) n22 t21 f23 b22. Distinctly different from any other Canadian doing the rounds: the oak influence makes a wonderful and clever impact. 40%

Highwood Pure Canadian (84) n20 t21 f22 b21. A decent, ultra-clean Canadian with markedly more character than before. Certainly the caramel has been seriously reduced in effect and the wheat ensures a rather attractive spice buzz while the cane juice sweetness harmonises well. Perhaps most delightful is the wonderful and distinct lack of fruit. 40%

Hiram Walker Special Old (93) n22.5 t24 f23 b23.5. Even with the extra degree of all-round harmony, this remains the most solid, uncompromising Canadian of them all. And I love it! Not least because this is the way Special old has been for a very long time with obviously no intentions of joining the fruity bandwagon. Honest, first class Canadian. 40%

James Foxe (77.5) n20 t19.5 f19 b19. James could do with putting some weight on... *40%*

Lord Calvert (72.5) n21 n19 t18.5 f17 b18. Truly eccentric aristocracy, this. Comes from the most noble of homes, Alberta Distillery, and the pedigree of the rye is evident in patches on both nose and delivery. Then marries something very fruity well beneath its class. *40%*

Lot No 40 Malted Rye Whisky (93) n24 the intensity of the malted rye element powers through, offering several variations of sharp honey concentrate, from manuka down to acacia. The tannins are pretty staggering for a Canadian and much more of the Kentucky/Indiana style. Simplistic yet so devastatingly beautiful... **t23.5** there we go....like a rocket of rye, firing off in three stages with the softer intensity of the oilier malted rye being propelled by the far more rigid unmalted into orbit; about half way through they meld and then the cocoa-vanilla oak stage bursts through, as well as a playful spiciness which dries towards a serious dark chocolate middle; **f22.5** being a miserable git, I'd say the oak tries too hard for world dominance here, allowing the bitterness to slightly overpower and over dry the crisper, toastier brown sugars. But on the other hand, those cocoa notes are pretty gorgeous and just enough oil allows it to level out across the palate; **b23** an old friend – almost a long lost son – has returned and has brightened up my glass with colossal Canadianness. This is of a style unique to this country, though here the high levels of oak have perhaps dimmed the flame of the rye slightly. Welcome home, my son...!!! *40%*

Masterson's 10 Year Old Straight Rye batch 003 **(96.5)** n24 fizzing with fruity finesse, there is little doubting the grain involved here; almost a bubble gum sweetness to the fruit and through the melting softness lurks a note as firm and sharp as a sabre; **t24** just about as mouth-watering as it is spellbinding, the taste buds are immediately immersed in a stellar degree of crisp, sparkling rye notes; vanilla pods pop as it soaks in the juicy, clean rye; **f24** if you want to see an almost perfect degree of spice at work in a whisky, you really can't do better than savour the finish of this gorgeous bottling. Helped along by deft oil, the crystalline sugars and light vanillas just carry on their hypnotic dance; **b24.5** a magnificent whisky without any shadow of doubt. Rye is my favourite whisky type and this displays the style to a degree of excellence which is truly memorable in terms of a commercial bottling. Someone has done an outstanding job in selecting these casks. Interesting, however, that they don't actually state on the bottle that this is Canadian and confuse things a little further by spelling it "whiskey". My understanding is that this is unmalted rye from the outstanding Alberta Distillery in Calgary. What is certain is that this is a true classic of its style. And not so much Masterson's but Masterful. *45%*

McGuinness Silk Tassel (79.5) n20 t21 f19.5 b19. Silk or satin? The corn oils offer a delightful sheen but still the caramel is over enthusiastic. *40%*

McLoughlin and Steele Blended in the Okanagan Valley (87.5) n22 t22 f21.5 b22. As straight as a die: a Canadian Rye... without any discernible rye. *40%. McLoughlin and Steele.*

Mountain Rock (87) n22 t20.5 f22.5 b22. Still a soft Canadian cocking a melt-in-the-mouth snook at its name. But this time the fruit is just over anxious to be heard and a degree of its old stability has been eroded. *40%. Kittling Ridge.*

Okanagan Spirits Rye (88.5) n23 t22.5 f21 b22. A crisp, quite beautiful whisky with a youthful strain. Sort the thin finish out and we'd have something to really remember! Not, by the way, a whisky distilled at their new distillery. *40%*

◈ **Pendleton 1910 Aged 12 Years Rye (83)** n21 t22 f20 b20. Pleasant enough. But if it wasn't for the small degree of spice pepping up this fruitfest, it would be all rather too predictable. *40%*

Pendleton Let'er Buck (91.5) n22.5 t23 f22.5 b23.5. A significantly improved whisky from the ultra-sweet, nigh on syrupy concoction of before. Here the surprisingly complex and sensual grains take star billing, despite the caramel: it almost makes a parody of being Canadian, so unmistakable is the style. For those who affectionately remember Canadian Club from 20-30 years ago, this might bring a moistening of the eye. *40% (80 proof). Hood River Distillers.*

◈ **Pendleton Midnight (78)** n20 t21 f18 b19. Soft and soothing. But far more rampant fruit than grain. In fact, hard to detect the grain at all... *45% (90 Proof).*

◈ **Pike Creek (92)** n22 an 'appeeling' nose: orange peel, mostly; **t23.5** so soft on delivery, you are not sure it has even arrived on your palate. The fruit flavours display first before moving into the realms of delicious chocolate mousse; **f23** more mousse, but now without the fruit; **b23.5** a whisky that is more effect over substance, for this really has to be the softest, silkiest world whisky of 2015. And if you happen to like your taste buds being pampered and chocolate is your thing, this Canadian has your name written all over it. *40%*

Pike Creek 10 Years Old finished in port barrels **(80)** n21.5 t22.5 f17 b19. The delivery is the highlight of the show by far as the fruit takes off backed by delicate spices and spongy softness. The nose needs some persuading to get going but when fully warmed, gives a preview of the delivery. The furry finish is a big disappointment, though. *40%*

Potter's Crown (83) n19 t21.5 f21.5 b21. Silky and about the friendliest and most inoffensive whisky on this planet. The dusty aroma and thick, chewy toffee backbone says it all but still impossible not to enjoy! *40%*

Potter's Special Old a blend of 5 to 11 year old rye whisky **(91) n23.5 t23 f22 b22.5**. More Canadian than a hockey punch-up – and, for all the spice, somewhat more gentle, too. *40%*

Rich and Rare (79) n20 t20 f20 b19. Simplistic and soft. One for toffee lovers. *40%*

Rich and Rare Reserve (86.5) n19.5 t21 f23.5 b22.5. Actually does what it says on the tin, certainly as to regard the "Rich" bit. But takes off when the finish spices up and even offers some ginger cake on the finale. Lovely stuff. *40%*

Royal Canadian (87.5) n22 t22.5 f21 b22. Now there's a whisky which is on the up. *40%*

Royal Canadian Small Batch (88) n22 t22.5 f21.5 b22. A big Canadian with a pleasing silk and steel pulse. *40%. Sazerac.*

Royal Reserve (84.5) n19 t22.5 f21.5 b21.5. No question that the delivery is much richer, fresher and entertaining than before with the spices, dovetailing with subtle fruit, ensuring a complexity previously lacking - especially at the death. Frustratingly, the caramel seems to be biting deeper on the nose, which has taken a backward step. A much more enjoyable and satisfying experience, though. *40%*

Royal Reserve Gold (94.5) n24 t23.5 f23 b24. Retains its position as a classy, classy Canadian that is an essay on balance. Don't confuse this with the much duller standard bottling: this has been moulded in recent years into one of the finest – and among its country's consumers - generally most underrated Canadians on the market. *40%*

Sam Barton Aged 5 Years (83.5) n19 t21.5 f22 b21. Sweet session whisky with a lovely maple syrup glow; some complexity on the finish. Friendly, hospitable: impossible not to like. *40%.*

Schenley Golden Wedding (92) n22 t24 f22 b23. Like a rare, solid marriage, this has improved over time. Always consistent and pleasant, there now appears to be a touch of extra age and maturity which has sent the complexity levels up dramatically. Quite sublime. *40%*

Schenley OFC (90) n22 t22.5 f23 b22.5. Notice anything missing from this whisky? Well the 8-year-old age statement has fallen off the label. But this is still a truly superb whisky which would benefit perhaps from toning down the degree of sweetness, but gets away with it in spectacular fashion thanks to those seductive oils. Not as complex as the magnificent old days, but a whisky that would have you demanding a refill nine time out of ten. *40%*

Seagram's Canadian 83 (86.5) n21 t22 f21.5 b22. A vastly improved blend which has drastically cut the caramel to reveal a melt-in-the-mouth, slightly crisp grain. There are some citrusy edges but the buttery vanilla and pleasing bite all go to make for a chic little number. *40%*

Seagram's VO (91) n22 t23.5 f22.5 b23. With a heavy heart I have to announce the king of rye-enriched Canadian, VO, is dead. Long live the corn-dominant VO. Over the years I have seen the old traditional character ebb away: now I have let go and have no option other than to embrace this whisky for what it has become: infinitely better than a couple of years back; not in the same league as a decade ago. But just taking it on face value, credit where credit is due. This is an enjoyably playful affair, full of vanilla-led good intention, corn and complexity. There is even assertive spice when needed and the most delicately fruity edge...though not rye-style. Thoughtfully blended and with no little skill, I am impressed. And look forward to seeing how this develops in future years. A treat which needs time to discover. *40%*

Still Waters Special 1•11 Blend batch 1204, bott 2012 **(92) n23.5 t22 f22.5 b23**. If the boys at Still Waters distillery end up with a whisky as enjoyable as this when theirs has matured, Canadian whisky will have flourished. *40%. 1200 bottles.*

Tangle Ridge Aged 10 Years (69) n18.5 t19.5 f15 b16. Decidedly less in your face than of old, unless you are thinking custard pies. For all the cleaned up aroma and early injection of spiced sultana, the uncompromisingly grim finish remains its usual messy self. An unpleasant reminder as to why I only taste this when it's Bible time... *40%*

Tesco Canadian Whisky (75) n18 t18 f20 b19. Sweet, clean, uninspiring. *40%*

Western Gold Canadian Whisky (91) n23 t23 f22.5 b22.5. Clean and absolutely classic Canadian: you can't ask for much more, really. *40%*

White Owl (77.5) n19 t19.5 f20 b19. White whisky: in others words, a whisky the same colour as water. To both nose and taste somewhat reminds me of the long gone Manx whisky which was casks of fully matured scotch re-distilled and bottled. Sweet and pleasant. But I doubt if connoisseurs will give two hoots... *40%*

Windsor (85.5) n21 t22 f21 b21.5. A whisky you could usually bet your week's wages on for consistency and depth. Here, though, the usual rye fruity, crispness has been dumbed down and though there are enough spices to make this a pleasant affair, the impact of the caramel is a tad too significant. The usual custard sweetness has also changed shape and dry vanilla at the death is the compromise. *40%*

Windsor (86) n20 t21 f23 b22. Pleasant but the majority of edges found on the Canadian edition blunted. Some outstanding, almost attritional, spice towards the middle and finale, though. Soft and desirable throughout: a kind of feminine version of the native bottling. *40%*.

J.P. Wiser's 18 Year Old db **(94) n22.5** dusty, fruity, busy. Soft, fruity sawdust to the sugars; **t24** excellent early bite, though the oils make their mark early. Salivating and silky despite the spice build and a little cocoa to accompany the fruit; f23.5 comfortable, with a pleasing acceleration of spice; b24 exceptionally creamy but maintains the required sharpness. 40%.

J.P. Wiser's De Luxe (86) n20 t22.5 f21.5 b22. Still nothing like the classic, ultra-charming and almost fragile-delicate Wiser's of old. But this present bottling has got its head partly out of the sand by injecting a decently oaked spiciness to the proceedings and one might even fancy detecting shards of fruity- rye brightness beaming through the toffeed clutter. Definitely an impressive turn for the better and the kind of Canadian with a dangerous propensity to grow on you. If they had the nerve to cut the caramel, this could be a cracker... 40%

J.P. Wiser's Legacy (95) n24 t24.5 f22.5 b22.5. When my researcher got this bottle for me to taste, she was told by the Wiser's guy that I would love it, as it had been specially designed along the lines of what I considered essential attributes to Canadian whisky. Whether Mr Wiser was serious or not, such a statement both honoured and rankled slightly and made me entirely determined to find every fault with it I could and knock such impertinence down a peg or two. Instead, I was seduced like a 16-year-old virgin schoolboy in the hands of a 30-year-old vixen. An entirely disarming Canadian which is almost a whisky equivalent to the finest of the great French wines in its rich, unfolding style. Complex beyond belief, spiced almost to supernatural perfection, this is one of the great newcomers to world whisky in the last year. It will take a glass of true magnificence to outdo this for Canadian Whisky of the Year. 45%

J.P. Wiser's Red Letter 2013 Release Virgin oak finish, cask 6075 db **(90.5)** n22 t24 f22 b22.5. The axis of this blend has moved away from a classical style recognisable three decades ago to a more contemporary fruity number. Alas. Superb delivery, though. 45%. ncf.

⬥ **J.P. Wiser's Red Letter 2014 Release** Virgin Oak Finish **(91)** n22.5 soft fruit and toffee mix with a major vanilla sub plot; t23.5 a more complex, slightly busier delivery than the nose suggests. Again, a silky entry, though this time harbouring a deceptively busy and spicy second wave. The toffee returns a little too quickly, but the manuka honey is welcome; f22 mildly toasty with vanilla and more toffee; b23 top end Canadian still eschewing the busy grain route of when the brand was reintroduced in favour of a silkier profile. Less well defined but perhaps now easy-drinking for the masses. A letter always worth opening, though. 45%. ncf.

J.P. Wiser's Reserve (75) n19 t20 f18 b18. The nose offers curious tobacco while the palate is uneven, with the bitterness out of tandem with the runaway early sweetness. In the confusion the fruit never quite knows which way to turn. A once mighty whisky has fallen. And I now understand it might be the end of the line with the excellent Wiser's Small Batch coming in to replace it. So if you are a reserve fan, buy them up now. 43%

⬥ **J.P. Wiser's Rye (84.5)** n21 t22 f20.5 b21 Sweet, soft and easy going. The delivery is classic Canadian, with an enjoyable corn oil-vanilla oak mix which initially doesn't go easy on the sugars. The finish, though, is more brittle toffee. 40%

J.P. Wiser's Small Batch (90.5) n21.5 t24 f22 b23. A real oddity with the nose & taste on different planets. The fruity onslaught promised by the drab nose never materialises and instead we are treated to a rich, grainy explosion. It's the spices, though, that take the plaudits. 43.4%

J.P. Wiser's Special Blend (78) n19 t20 f19 b19. A plodding, pleasant whisky with no great desire to offer much beyond caramel. 40%

⬥ **J.P. Wiser's Spiced Torched Toffee (35)** n9 t9 f8 b9 Whisky by name and law. But an absurdly sweet liqueur indeed. As an adorer of true whisky all I can say is this is to Canadian what the Coen brothers' remake of The Ladykillers was to the 1955 Ealing original... 43%

J.P. Wiser's Spiced Whisky Vanilla db **(51)** n16 t12 f11 b12. The policy of the Whisky Bible is to not accept any spiced distillate as, by definition, being whisky. Only Canadian can escape that ban, as they are allowed to put up to 9.09% of whatever into their spirit and still call it whisky. That does not mean to say I am going to like it, though. And, believe me when I tell you I really can't stand this cloyingly sweet liqueur-like offering. Indeed, it may have "whisky" on the label, but this is about as much that great spirit as I am the next Hollywood pin up. 43%

Canadian Wheat Whisky

Masterson's 12 Year Old Straight Wheat Whiskey batch 001 **(92)** n23 some spices, but not what I was expecting. Much lighter and more vanilla based. Gentle, but with a bit of attitude...; t23 soft and silky, the maple syrup makes the running while the spices lag behind. A little heather honey springs from nowhere as the oaky vanillas begin to gather momentum; f22.5 drier, yet remains delicate and quietly complex; b23.5 chose this as my 1,000th new whisk(e) y for Jim Murray WB 2015 because a couple of years back I uncorked their Rye...and tasted everything a great Canadian should be: indeed, it was a contender for my World Whisky of that year. Here I have their new wheat bottling. Not the blockbuster the rye bottling was: rye when distilled and matured to its fullest possibilities probably cannot be touched by any other grain. But this is a soft, melodious whisky, perfect for ending any day on a quiet high... 50% WB15/380

Japanese Whisky

How fitting that in the age when the sun never sets on where whisky is produced it is from the land of the Rising Sun that the finest can now be found.

Japan last year, for the first time ever, won Jim Murray's World Whisky of the Year with its insanely deep and satisfying Yamazaki Sherry Cask(s) 2013, a result which caused predicted consternation among more than a few. And a degree of surprise in Japan itself. The industry has followed that up this year by commanding 5th spot with a very different but truly majestic specimen of a malt showing a style unique to Japan. How impressive.

It reminded me of when, about 15 years ago, I took my old mate Michael Jackson and a smattering of non-friends on a tour of the Yoichi distillery on Hokkaido, pointing out to them that here was a place where a malt could be made to mount a serious challenge to the best being made anywhere in the world. While there, a local journalist asked me what Japanese distillers could learn from Scotland. I caused a bit of a sharp intake of breath – and a pathetically gutless but entirely characteristic denial of association by some whisky periodical executive or other who had a clear idea which side his bread was buttered – when I said it was the other way round: it was more what the Scots could learn from the Japanese.

The reason for that comment was simple: the extraordinary attention to detail and tradition that was paid by Japanese distillers, those at Yoichi in particular, and the touching refusal to cut costs and corners. It meant that it was the most expensive whisky in the world per unit of alcohol to produce. But the quality was astonishingly high – and that would, surely, eventually reap its rewards as the world learned to embrace malt whisky made away from the Highlands and islands of Scotland which, then, was still to happen. Ironically, it was the Japanese distillers' habit to ape most things Scottish – the reason why there is a near century-old whisky distilling heritage there in the first place - that has meant that Yoichi, or the magnificent Hakushu, has yet to pick up the Bible's World Whisky of the Year award I expected for them. Because, sadly, there have been too many bottlings over the last decade tainted by sherry butts brought from Spain after having been sulphur treated. So I was also pleasantly surprised when I first nosed – then nosed again in near disbelief – then tasted the Yamazaki 2013 sherry offering. There was not even the vaguest hint that a single one of the casks used in the bottling had been anywhere near a sulphur candle. The result: something as close to single malt perfection as you will have found in a good many years. A single malt which no Scotch can at the moment get anywhere near and, oddly, takes me back to the Macallans of 30 years ago.

A Japanese custom of refusing to trade with their rivals has not helped expand their export market. Therefore a Japanese whisky, if not made completely from home-distilled spirit, will instead contain a percentage of Scotch rather than whisky from fellow Japanese distilleries. This, ultimately, is doing the industry no favours at all. The practice is partly down to the traditional work ethics of company loyalty and an inherent, and these days false, belief that Scotch whisky is automatically better than Japanese. Back in the late 1990s I planted the first seeds in trying to get rival distillers to discuss with each other the possibility of exchanging whiskies to ensure that their distilleries worked more economically. So it can only be hoped that

Yamazaki

●Osaka

●Fukuoka

the deserved lifting of last year's Jim Murray's Whisky Bible World Whisky of the Year crown, and the hitherto unprecedented international press it received has helped put the spotlight back on the great whiskies coming from the east. Because unless you live in Japan, you are likely to see only a fraction of the fabulous whisky produced there. The Scotch Malt Whisky Society should have a special medal struck as they have helped in recent years with some memorable bottlings from Japan, single cask snapshots of the greatness that is still to be be fully explored and mapped. A two-pronged attack would be useful: one by whisky outlets to actively track down and stock the widest Japanese stock they can afford, though because of the clamour for all things Yamazaki this now at last appears to be hapening. And the distillers themselves, always on the conservative side of marketing, probably through a misplaced lack of belief, show us what they have.

And I don't mean just with malts. Because, even better still would be if the outside world could have at last access to the higher class blends produced there. But the Japanese whisky industry have themselves been slow coming forward. Just perhaps, with Yamazaki atop the world's whisky very own Mount Fuji, there are the first signs that they are at last ready to unleash upon us those hidden, majestic whiskies of Japan.

Single Malts
CHICHIBU

Chichibu 'The Peated' 2013 dist 2010 bott 2013 db **(96.5) n24.5** a dry intensity to this, perhaps suggesting a high phenol content. Earthy and a little floral – not unlike bluebell woods – or freshly watered African violets. Deep, intense and very intact; **t24.5** anyone old enough to remember the original, now demolished, Caol Ila will recognise a returning ghost: the similarity is startling. Sublimely weighted, gently spices and the peat offering both the background and the lead, though operating on different levels; the sugars levels, and their ability to dissolve then reappear is a thing of beauty; **f23** long thanks to the most subtle of oils with smoke drifting off the cocoa; some late oaky bitter tang; **b24.5** clean, elegant, does exactly what it says on the tin...and a lot, lot more besides... 53.5%.

Chichibu 'On The Way' dist 2010 bott 2013 db **(93) n23.5 t24 f22.5 b23**. A malt which has already travelled far... 58.50%.

Chichibu Port Pipe dist 2009 bott 2013 db **(66) n17 t18 f15 b16**. A port pipe in an awful, off-key storm. 54.5%. Number One Drinks Company.

Golden Horse Chichibu Aged 12 Years bott 08 db **(95.5) n24 t24.5 f23 b24**. Immaculate, faultless (OK, nearly faultless), whisky. And, rarely for Japanese, bottled at exactly the right age. Had this not been bottled in 2008, a contender for World Whisky of the Year. Guys! You have to get this to me sooner!!! For the record, it kind of took me back to the mid 1970s when I was first studying whisky, for here I felt I was learning about this distillery for the very first time... Oh, and for the best effects: don't bother warming in the glass – just pour...and score... 56%

Ichiro's Malt Chichibu Floor Malted 2009 **(85.5) n22 t22.5 f20 b21**. Big, pre-pubescent malt and barley statement, but barely in unison. Bitterness on the finish is unchecked. 50.5%.

Ichiro's Chichibu Peated 2009 **(91.5) n23 t23.5 f22 b23**. You can stand your chopsticks up in this one...works so beautifully in so many department. 50.5%

Number One Asama 1999/2000 **(71) n17 t19 f16 b19**. Sulphured. 46%

Scotch Malt Whisky Society Cask 130.1 Aged 4 Years 1st fill barrel. dist 16 Jun 09. **(94.5) n23 t24 f23.5 b24**. Not sure anyone on this planet does milky malt like Chichibu. Another remarkable whisky from them. 62%. nc ncf sc. 227 Bottles.

FUJI GOTEMBA 1973. Kirin Distillers.

The Fuji Gotemba 15 Years Old db **(92) n21 t23 f24 b24**. Quality malt of great poise. 43%. Kirin.

HAKUSHU 1973. Suntory.

Hakushu Single Malt Whisky Aged 12 Years db **(91.5) n22.5 t23.5 f22.5 b23**. About identical to the 43.3% bottling. Please see those tasting notes for this little beauty. 43.5%

Hakushu Single Malt Aged 12 Years db **(91) n22 t23 f23 b23**. An even more lightly-peated version of the 40%, with the distillery's fabulous depth on full show. 43.3%

The Hakushu Single Malt Whisky Aged 15 Years Cask Strength db **(95) n24 t23 f24 b24**. Last time round I lamented the disappointing nose. This time perhaps only a degree of over eagerness from the oak has robbed this as a serious Whisky of the Year contender. No matter how you look at it, though, brilliant!! 56%

The Hakushu Single Malt Whisky Aged 25 Years db **(93) n23 t24 f23 b23**. A malt which is impossible not to be blown away by. 43%

Hakushu Single Malt Whisky Aged 25 Years bott 2011 db **(91) n23.5 t23.5 f21 b23**. Just one slightly off butt away from total magnificence. 43%

⬥ **The Hakushu Single Malt Whisky Sherry Cask** bott 2014 db **(96.5) n24.5** there we have it: a masterclass in what clean, untainted sherry butts are all about. A thousand levels of fruit intensity without a single off note – or even peculiar but unmistakable background hint of an off note which points to a sulphur problem at the very end of a whisky - when nearly all the other flavours have vanished. It is not there. The only problem, being over picky, is that the character of the distillery itself is hard to locate: the concentrated dates, plums and raisins, topped, naturally, with warming spice, means the malt itself has vanished somewhat...; **t24** there we go. Find a comfortable chair for this one...it is going to take a very long time. Wave upon wave of fruitiness, of varying degrees of intensity, roll and then crash over the palate. In its quiet moments, that's the odd toasted honeycomb mingling with butterscotch and vanilla bits – something other than fruit are apparent...; **f24** long, elegant, gorgeously clean...but even more late toasted raisin...; **b24** theoretically, this should have been World Whisky of the Year. After all, Yamazaki – a distillery I regard as very slightly eclipsed in quality by Hakushu – won it last year using, like this, strictly unsulphured sherry butts. This is magnificent. One of the great whiskies of the year, for sure. However, the intensity of the grape has just strayed over that invisible line by a few molecules between being a vital cog and a shade too dominant. It is the finest of lines between genius and exceptional brilliance. *48%. ncf.*

Scotch Malt Whisky Society Cask 120.05 Aged 17 Years 1st fill barrel, dist Dec 91 **(94)** n23 t24 f23.5 b23.5. Amazingly, this is a less than perfect cask deployed. But so absurdly good was the spirit filled into it, you barely notice...or care. *59%. 104 bottles.*

◈ **Scotch Malt Whisky Society Cask 120.7 Aged 14 Years** 1st fill Bota Corta, dist 30 Sept 99 **(95.5)** n24 a scary mix of not so much staves of oak as bloody great planks of them, but their deleterious effects appear nullified by enough grape to keep my parrot quiet for a year...; t25 after a mouthful of this, not sure if I have the mental wherewithal to find the right words to describe this. Let's just say, that if you tell me you have found a more imposing mix of clear sweet, yet spiced grape along with liquorice-studded old oak this year...then I won't believe you....; f22.5 as the sugars wear thin, the bitterness of the oak increases. The spices find a compromise; b24 if I ever developed a twitch, it will be from being told I am about to taste a whisky matured in some wine cask or other: over the years it has about the same effect as when Herbert Lom was told he would have to spend time with Inspector Clouseau. Here, though, my fears were unfounded. Over-aged for sure, but otherwise sweet as a nut. So good and so big, it is almost terrifying... *55.5%. sc. 517 bottles.*

◈ **Scotch Malt Whisky Society Cask 120.8 Aged 13 Years** 2nd fill hogshead, dist 31 Dec 00 **(85.5)** n21 t23 f20 b21.5. Some typical Hakushu flourishes but done down by a disappointing cask which added too much tired tang than is appreciated. Unusually salty and sharp, this should have been destined for a blend. *63.1%. sc. 250 bottles.*

Suntory Pure Malt Hakushu Aged 20 Years db **(94)** n23 t24 f23 b24. A hard-to-find malt, but find it you must. Yet another huge nail in the coffin of those who purport Japanese whisky to be automatically inferior to Scotch. *56%*

HANYU

Ichiro's Malt Aged 20 Years (95.5) n24 t24 f23.5 b24. No this finish; no that finish. Just the distillery allowed to speak in its very own voice. And nothing more eloquent has been heard from it this year. Please, all those owning casks of Hanyu: for heaven's sake take note... *57.5%.*

Ichiro's Malt Aged 23 Years (92.5) n23 t23.5 f23 b23. A fabulous malt you take your time over. *58%*

Scotch Malt Whisky Society Cask 131.2 Aged 13 Years 1st fill barrel. dist 30 Jun 00. **(87)** n22 sweeping ultra rich fruitcake statements, heavy on the toasted raisin. The odd flicker of a sulphur fault; t22.5 swashbuckling grape, with a spices rampaging all over the deck. Loses points in the mid-ground as the fault on the nose begins to appear; f20.5 a faulty sulphur gene; b22. A malt which almost gets away with it. Despite the obvious and regrettable flaw, this really does have some outstanding attributes. *55%. nc ncf sc. 646 bottles.*

KARUIZAWA 1955. Mercian.

Karuizawa Pure Malt Aged 17 Years db **(90)** n20 t24 f23 b23. Brilliant whisky beautifully made and majestically matured. Neither sweetness nor dryness dominates, always the mark of a quality dram. *40%*

The Spirit Of Asama sherry cask **(71.5)** n17 t19 f17 b18.5. Sulphur hit. *48%.*

The Spirit Of Asama sherry cask **(75)** n18 t20 f18 b19. Lots of sultanas. Sweet. Pleasant in part. But it isn't just Scotland suffering from poor sherry butts. *55%.*

Scoth Malt Whisky Society Cask 132.1 Aged 28 Years refill butt. dist 30 Aug 84 **(96.5)** n23.5 t24.5 f24 b24.5. Long overdue on the SMWS portfolio, this is another Japanese malt which, with the care and attention of its make and maturation, put many of its Scottish counterparts to shame. What a way to make your SMWS debut!! *59.8% nc ncf sc. 229 bottles.*

Scotch Malt Whisky Society Cask 132.2 Aged 22 Years refill butt. diss 04 Sep 91. **(92.5)** n23.5 gristy peat spread over lime marmalade on toast; t24 the delivery, with its near perfect layering of smoke and its intense ulmo honey and concentrated grist is the stuff of Japanese fable; f22 bitters slowly at the death; b23 a rare case of peat and light fruit working for the benefit of the other. Superb. *62.4% nc ncf sc. 335 Bottles.*

Scotch Malt Whisky Society Cask 132.3 Aged 20 Years refill butt. diss 21 Jul 93 **(94.5)** n23.5 t24 f23 b24. Pure fun as a malt, no little complexity and keeps the taste buds on their toes from beginning to end. *61.1% nc ncf sc. 344 Bottles.*

Scotch Malt Whisky Society Cask 132.4 Aged 17 Years refill butt. diss 08 Jul 96 **(92)** n23 t24 f22 b22.5. Not just a sherry influence, but something of a big Demerara rum about this one. If you like your whisky naturally spiced, then you'll forever regret missing out on this. *61.7% nc ncf sc. 346 Bottles.*

Scotch Malt Whisky Society Cask 132.5 Aged 14 Years refill butt. diss 25 Jun 1999 **(69)** n17 t19 f16 b16. Not just sulphured, but cloying, too. *58.6% nc ncf sc. 495 Bottles.*

Scotch Malt Whisky Society Cask 132.6 Aged 12 Years refill butt. diss 32 Dec 2000. **(84.5)** n21 t23 f19 b21.5. Fabulous delivery. Surprisingly youthful in some ways, with echoes of a new make maltiness, but there is a vividity to the barley which really deserves better than the nose appears a little perfunctory and dull and a finish which is disappointingly tangy. *63% nc ncf sc.*

KIRIN

Kirin 18 Years Old db **(86.5)** n22 t22 f21.5 b21. Unquestionably over-aged. Even so, still puts up a decent show with juicy citrus trying to add a lighter touch to the uncompromising, ultra dense oak. As entertaining as it is challenging. *43%. Suntory.*

KOMAGATAKE

Komagatake 1992 Single Cask American white oak cask, cask no. 1144, dist 1992, bott 2009 db **(93.5)** n24.5 t23 f22.5 b23.5. You know when you've had a glass of this: beautiful and no shrinking violet. *46%. Mars.*

MIYAGIKYO (see Sendai)

NIKKA (Coffey Still)

Nikka Whisky Single Coffey Malt 12 Years db **(97)** n23.5 t25 f24 b24.5. The Scotch Whisky Association would say that this is not single malt whisky because it is made in a Coffey still. When they can get their members to make whisky this stunning on a regular basis via their own pots and casks, then perhaps they should pipe up as their argument might then have a single atom of weight. *55%*

◈ **Scotch Malt Whisky Society Cask G12.1 Aged 11 Years** re-charred hogshead, dist 6 Mar 03 **(89.5)** n22.5 whisky? Or toffee candy...? t23 silky-soft with only a nod towards the barley. Instead we are treated to the cream toffee and fudge; a short burst of spice offers some welcome pep; f22 more lightweight cream toffee; b22 coming via a Coffey still, the malt has been distilled to a high strength leaving more room to emphasis the barrel influence. The high degree of toffee shows it is mission accomplished. *58.9%. sc. 246 bottles.*

SENDAI 1969. Nikka.

Scotch Malt Whisky Society Cask 124.03 Aged 13 Years refill butt, dist 20 Jul 99 **(88)** n22.5 t22 f21 b21.5. Seriously feisty. I'm off to chew a jalapeno to cool down... *61.9%. nc*

◈ **Scotch Malt Whisky Society Cask 124.4 Aged 17 Years** 1st fill butt, dist 22 Aug 96 **(94)** n24 where do you start with the fruit, apart from prize Melton Hunt Cake? Certainly the dates are juicy and the sultanas a little burnt. I think there is some oak in there somewhere...; t24 brilliant delivery with sublime bitter-sweet toasty-roasty delivery. Yes, there is oak there, and it comes up as hickory straight after the burnt raisin on delivery; f23 still toasted – burnt toast, in fact. But with a plum jam (that's gone easy on the sugar) covering it thickly; b23 if there is a complaint to be made, it is that, at times, one might forget that this is a whisky at all, resembling instead a glass of highest quality oloroso. *60%. sc. 479 bottles.*

◈ **Scotch Malt Whisky Society Cask 124.5 Aged 23 Years** 1st fill hogshead, dist 12 Dec 90 **(96)** n23.5 countless layers: the majority oak-based, but so many hues and tones, ranging from chalky to sub-bourbon; big dry dates to spicy fruitcake – without the fruit but with plenty of molasses; t24.5 hold on tight: molasses concentrate has been dipped in tannin juice. Somehow, while the spices pepper you and the oak makes you draw breath, barley pops up out of nowhere for a juicy interlude...; f24 time and time again you think it is going OTT with the oak, then those molasses notes, as well as dark chocolate, intervene... brinkmanship of the sexiest kind...; b24 this isn't just how to grow old gracefully, but with style while making one hell of a statement! *66.7%. sc. 142 bottles.*

SHIRAKAWA

Shirakawa 32 Years Old Single Malt (94) n23 t24 f23 b24. Just how big can an unpeated malt whisky get? The kind of malt that leaves you in awe, even when you thought you had seen and tasted them all. *55%. Takara.*

WHITE OAK DISTILLERY

White Oak Akashi Single Malt Whisky Aged 8 Years bott 2007 db **(74.5)** n18.5 t19.5 f17.5 b19. Always fascinating to find a malt from one of the smaller distilleries in a country. And I look forward to tracking this one down and visiting, something I have yet to do. There is certainly something distinctly small still about his one, with butyric and feintiness causing damage to nose and finish. For all the early malty presence on delivery, some of the off notes are a little on the uncomfortable side. *40%*

YAMAZAKI 1923. Suntory.

The Yamazaki Single Malt Whisky Aged 12 Years bott 2011 db **(90) n23 t22 f22.5 b22.5.**
A complex and satisfying malt. 43%

◈ **The Yamazaki Single Malt Aged 18 Years** db **(96) n23** a sublime blend of Java and Sumatra coffees, enriched by vanilla and even toastier tannins. The sugars, a mix of treacle and maple syrup try not to steal the show, but nearly do...; **t24.5** oh, oh, oh...!!!! Possibly the softest yet most compelling delivery this year: the grape is doused in busy, ever intensifying spice, the toasty vanillas in those subtle sugars spotted on the nose. Overripe plums, juicy dates, stewed prunes...and all the time the spice buzzes, the sugars salivate; **f24** long, with just a slow wind down of the previously intense fruit notes. The juices just keep on gushing, but met almost perfectly with toasty, slightly milky mocha notes; the final strands are praline wafer...with chocolate fruit and nut, too; **b24.5** for its strength, probably one of the best whiskies in the world. And one of the most brilliantly and sexily balanced, too... All told, one glass is equal to about 45 minutes of sulphur-free satisfaction... 43%

Suntory Pure Malt Yamazaki 25 Years Old db **(91) n23 t23 f22 b23.** Being matured in Japan, the 25 years doesn't have quite the same value as Scotland. So perhaps in some ways this can lay claim to be one of the most enormously aged, oak-laden whiskies that has somehow kept its grace and star quality. 43%

◈ **The Yamazaki Single Malt Whisky Mizunara** Japanese oak cask, bott 2014 db **(97) n25** the unmistakable and one off aroma of Japanese oak: a form of slightly aggressive bourbon where the spices are as busy as the light liquorice and hickory. But the malt has a massive presence, though you have to look for it first. The sugars are typically crisp for this style of oak and there is something of the Malteser chocolate candy about this, too: absolutely unique; **t24** the sugars ram home first – a peculiar mix of crystallised heather and ulmo honey with molasses – but the sweetness immediately limited by the more toffeed and tannic qualities of the intense oak. Polite spices are not too far behind and they, too, have a vaguely American quality, only a little more prickly. A delicate oil ensures the sugars cover as much distance as possible; **f23.5** late on, the spices pulse a backdrop to the vaguely bittering oak; **b24.5** no other malt offers this flavour profile. And as there are now very few Japanese oak casks still in the industry it is a malt worthy of as long a time as you can afford it. A very special whisky of very high quality. 48%

The Yamazaki Single Malt Whisky Puncheon bott 2013 db **(87) n22 t22 f21 b22.** Not to be confused with former Millwall footballer Jason Puncheon who scored a hat-trick against Crystal Palace a couple of years back. Does not possess his guile, balance or explosive finish. Even so, a pleasant dram even if you'd like to see it do more than just offer a sugary glow offset by some half decent spices. 48%. ncf. WB15/179

The Yamazaki Single Malt Whisky Sherry Cask bott 2013 db **(97.5) n24.5** when they say sherry, they are not joking: huge oloroso signature, nutty, thick, dry as rounded as a snooker ball. A nose that was not uncommon in the warehouses of Scotland three decades ago, but now as rare as...well, an unsulphured sherry butt...; **t24.5** every bit as silky as the nose promises. The sugars, spices, plum walnut cake and moist Melton Hunt Cake combine for something rather special; **f24** long, juicy dates, more walnuts, sultanas as big as a small planet...a light, teasing spice; **b24.5** one of the first sherry casks I have seen from Japan not in any way, shape or form touched by sulphur for a very long time. It is as if the oloroso cask was still half filled with the stuff when they filled with Yamakazi spirit. If anyone wants to find out roughly what the first Macallan 10-year-old I had in 1975 tasted like, then grab a bottle of this... 48%. ncf. WB15/180

◈ **The Yamazaki Single Malt Whisky** db **(86) n22 t22 f21 b21.** A tame, malty affair which, after the initial barley burst on delivery, plays safety first. 43%

◈ **Scotch Malt Whisky Society Cask 119.13 Aged 10 Years** 1st fill barrel, dist 31 May 03 **(94) n23** Brazil nut oil and toasted hazelnuts...getting the picture? **t23.5** crisp muscovado sugar met head on by intense, peppery spice and caramelised biscuit; **f24** at last the malt filters through...but still with a spicy guard. The tannins begin to get a bit toasty; **b23.5** excellent distillate in a quality cask: can't go wrong! 60.2%. sc. 149 bottles.

◈ **Scotch Malt Whisky Society Cask 119.14 Aged 11 Years** 1st fill Bota Corta, dist 30 Apr 03 **(96.5) n24** big coffee overture...hang on, am I in Japan or Guyana here? This is virtually rum in style...! **t24.5** more of the same: big fruit beginnings, juicy with a mix of dates and prunes. But in comes that Demerara spicy coffee kick...with toasty tannins drying out the middle ground; **f24** ridiculously long. And with the fruit and coffee interweaving. Each time it looks like getting too bitter, somehow those sugars intervene...amazing! **b24** tasted blind, I probably would have mistaken this for a the very highest quality – and very old - pot still Demerara rum. 53.9%. sc. 538 bottles.

YOICHI 1934. Nikka.

Yoichi Key Malt Aged 12 Years "Peaty & Salty" db **(95)** n23 t25 f23 b24. Of all the peated whiskies of the world, only Ardbeg can stand shoulder to shoulder with Yoichi when it comes to sheer complexity. Here is an astonishing example of why I rate Yoichi in the best five whiskies in the world. Forget the odd sulphur-tarnished bottling. Get Yoichi in its natural state with perfect balance between oak and malt and it delivers something approaching perfection. And this is just such a bottling. 55%. Nikka.

Yoichi 15 Years Old batch 06I08B db **(91.5)** n22 t23.5 f23 b23. For an early moment or two possibly one of the most salivating whiskies you'll get your kisser around this year. Wonderfully entertaining yet you still suspect that this is another Yoichi reduced in effect somewhat by either caramel and/or sherry. When it hits its stride, though, becomes a really busy whisky that gets tastebuds in a right lather. But I'm being picky as I know that this is one of the world's top five distilleries and am aware as anyone on this planet of its extraordinary capabilities. Great fun; great whisky – could be better still, but so much better than its siblings... 45%

Yoichi 20 Years Old db **(95)** n23 t23 f25 b24. I don't know how much they charge for this stuff but either alone or with mates get some for one hell of an experience. What makes it all the more remarkable is that there is a slight sulphury note on the nose: once you taste the stuff that becomes of little consequence. 52%. Nikka.

Scotch Malt Whisky Society Cask 116.17 Aged 25 Years First fill sherry butt, dist 20 Mar 1987, bott Sep 2012 **(96)** n24.5 t24.5 f23 b24. Not as mouth-puckering as I expected from the nose. The sugars ensure this incredible celebration of all things oak works memorably well. 59.2%. nc ncf sc. 485 bottles.

Scotch Malt Whisky Society 116.18 Aged 18 Years refill butt, dist 2 Feb 94 **(89)** n23 t23 f21 b22. Not one of the truly great Yoichis in its traditional style but a salty, oaky beast of a malt. 64.4%. nc ncf sc. 410 bottles.

◇◇ **Scotch Malt Whisky Society Cask 116.19 Aged 20** Years virgin oak puncheon, dist 2 Feb 94 **(92)** n23 so much bourbon-style honey...the oak influence is majestic; t23.5 fizzing tannins scorch the palate. But those sublime sugars – the manuka honey in particular – kiss everything better; f22.5 bitters very slightly as those tannins take a stranglehold; b23 huh! Just shows what happens when you don't concentrate. Poured the whisky, half noticing the colour. Expected a big blast of sherry (or something adjacent and pretty unpleasant) and got this enormous kick of bourbon. Beautiful; suits the distillery style perfectly. 61.3%. sc.

◇◇ **Scotch Malt Whisky Society Cask 116.20 Aged 26 Years** virgin oak puncheon, dist 7 Nov 87 **(82.5)** n20 t22 f20 b20.5. I'm sure some people will do cartwheels to celebrate this no holds barred malt. For me, simply too old: when you get this degree of eucalyptus on the nose and finish, it has gone way beyond its best before date. Decent sugars briefly on delivery and burnt ones at the death, plus the odd phenolic moment. But more like an over aged rum. 61.6%. sc.

Vatted Malts

All Malt (86) n22 t21 f21 b22. The best example by a mile of an almost unique style of vatted whisky: both malt and "grain" are distilled from entirely malted barley, identical to Kasauli malt whisky in India. Stupendous grace and balance. 40%. Nikka.

All Malt "Pure & Rich" (89) n22 t24 f21 b22. Not unlike some bottlings of Highland Park with its emphasis on honey. If they could tone down the caramel it'd really be up there. 40%. Nikka.

Hokuto Pure Malt Aged 12 Years (86) n20 t22 f22 b22. An oaky threat never materialises: excellent mixing. 40%. Suntory.

Ichiro's Malt Double Distilleries bott 2010 **(86.5)** n22.5 t22 f21 b21. Some imperious barley-rich honey reigns supreme until a bitter wood note bites hard. 46%. Venture Whisky Ltd.

Ichiro's Malt Mizunara Wood Reserve (76) n19 t21 f18 b19. I have my Reservations about the Wood, too... 46%. Venture Whisky Ltd.

Malt Club "Pure & Clear" (83) n21 t22 f20 b20. Another improved vatting, much heavier and older than before with bigger spice. 40%. Nikka.

Mars Maltage Pure Malt 8 Years Old (84) n20 t21 f21 b22. A very level, intense, clean malt with no peaks or troughs, just a steady variance in the degree of sweetness and oak input. Impossible not to have a second glass of it. 43%. Mars.

Nikka Malt 100 The Anniversary Aged 12 Years (73) n18 t19 f18 b18. The depressing and deadly fingerprint of sulphur is all over this. Shame, as the spices excel. 40%

Nikka Pure Malt Aged 21 Years batch 08I18D db **(89)** n23 t22.5 f21.5 b22. By far the best of the set. 43%

Nikka Pure Malt Aged 17 Years batch 08I30B db **(83)** n21 t21 f20 b21. A very similar shape to the 12-years-old, but older - obviously. Certainly the sherry butts have a big say and don't always do great favours to the high quality spirit. 43%

Nikka Pure Malt Aged 12 Years batch 10I24C db (84) n21.5 t21 f20 b21.5. The nose may be molassed, sticky treacle pudding, but it spices up on the palate. The dull buzz on the finish also tells a tale. 40%

Pure Malt Black batch 02C58A (95) n24 t23 f23 b25. Well, if anyone can show me a better-balanced whisky than this you know where to get hold of me. You open a bottle of this at your peril: best to do so in the company of friends. Either way, it will be empty before the night is over. 43%. Nikka.

Pure Malt Black batch 06F54B (92) n24 t24 f21 b23. Not the finish of old, but everything else is present and correct for a cracker! 43%. Nikka.

Pure Malt Red batch 02C30B (86) n21 t21 f22 b22. A light malt that appears heavier than it actually is with an almost imperceptible oiliness. 43%. Nikka.

Pure Malt Red batch 06F54C (84) n21 t22 f20 b21. Oak is the pathfinder here, but the oily vanilla-clad barley is light and mouth-watering. 43%. Nikka.

Pure Malt White batch 02C30C (92) n23 t24 f22 b23. A big peaty number displaying the most subtle of hands. 43%. Nikka.

Pure Malt White batch 06J26 (91) n22 t23 f22 b24. A sweet malt, but one with such deft use of peat and oak that one never really notices. Real class. 43%

Pure Malt White batch 10F46C (90) n23 t23 f22 b22. There is a peculiarly Japanese feel to this delicately peated delight. 43%

Southern Alps Pure Malt (93) n24 t23 f22 b24. This is a bottle I have only to look at to start salivating. Sadly, though, I drink sparingly from it as it is a hard whisky to find, even in Japan. Fresh, clean and totally stunning, the term "pure malt" could not be more apposite. Fabulous whisky: a very personal favourite. 40%. Suntory.

◈ **Suntory Pure Malt Whisky Kiyosato Field Ballet 25th Anniversary** (88) n23.5 gentle: over-ripe plums, green apple and red liquorice; t22.5 the malt surges on delivery for a very sharp introduction; soon calms down with a vague Indian candy sweetness and a more assertive bourbon style; goes tits up as the end approaches; f20 an annoying tang as the balance is compromised; b22 so frustrating: a whisky destined for greatness is side-tracked by some off-kilter casks. 48%

Super Nikka Vatted Pure Malt (76) n20 t19 f19 b18. Decent and chewy but something doesn't quite click with this one. 55.5%. Nikka.

Taketsuru Pure Malt 12 Years Old (80) n19 t22 f19 b20. For its age, heavier than a sumo wrestler. But perhaps a little more agile over the tastebuds. Lovely silkiness impresses, but lots of toffee. 40%. Nikka.

Taketsuru Pure Malt 17 Years Old (89) n21 t22 f23 b23 Not a whisky for the squeamish. This is big stuff – about as big as it gets without peat or rye. No bar shelf or whisky club should be without one. 43%. Nikka.

Taketsuru Pure Malt 21 Years Old (88) n22 t21 f22 b23. A much more civilised and gracious offering than the 17 year old: there is certainly nothing linear about the character development from Taketsuru 12 to 21 inclusive. Serious whisky for the serious whisky drinker. 43%. Nikka.

Zen (84) n19 t22 f22 b21. Sweet, gristy malt; light and clean. 40%. Suntory.

Japanese Single Grain
CHITA

◈ **Scotch Malt Whisky Society Cask G13.1 Aged 4 Years** virgin oak puncheon, dist 31 Oct 10 (83) n22 t22 f19 b20. The first commercial bottling from this excellent grain distillery I have ever seen outside Japan. Sadly, though, hardly representative of many of the outstanding samples I have encountered in the tasting lab over the years, with some poor oak undermining the embracing softness of the grain itself. 58.3%. sc. 622 bottles.

◈ **Suntory Single Grain Chita Distillery** db (92.5) n23.5 one of the typical characteristics of this distillery's nose, indeed its overall character, is its unusual ability to appear soft and yielding yet with a rod of iron at the very same time. It is this dual personality that can be both a blessing from heaven and a curse when blending. But as a single grain it works a treat as the complexity levels are upped immediately, allowing the vaguely bitter-sweet grain and oaks to perform their various tricks; maple syrup also lends a helping hand; t23 just like the nose, there is a bipolar feel to the shape of this grain, the delivery consumed by soft oils, yet a far more rigid note apparent, to which the oak appears to attach. The sugars – or light honey to be more precise – is in line with the silkier oils; f22.5 soft oils persist but the oak turns a little bitter; b23 now that's more like it! Far more down the track of the Chita I have tasted through the years than the SMWS bottling. Then again, this is the brand new official distillery version, so perhaps no surprises there... 43%. Available only in Nagoya Prefecture, Japan.

KAWASAKI

Kawasaki Single Grain sherry butt, dist 1982, bott 2011 db **(95.5) n23.5** clean thick grape offering several layers of depth and intensity. Salty and sharp, too. My god, this is very much alive and kicking...; **t24** classic! Faultless grape arm in arm with rich, fruity fudge. Some spices arrive on impact and slowly spread out with the marauding sugars; **f24** chocolate fudge and garibaldi biscuit...carried far on usual oils for a grain...amazing! **b24** my usual reaction to seeing the words "sherry" and "whisky" when in the context of Japanese whisky, is to feel the heart sinking like the sun. Sulphur is a problem that is no stranger to their whiskies. This, however, is a near perfect sherry butt, clean and invigorating. Grain or malt, it makes no difference: excellent spirit plus excellent cask equals (as often as not) magnificence. 65.5%.

NIKKA

Nikka Coffey Grain Whisky db **(94.5) n24** molten muscovado sugar; **t24.5** soft oils carry the thinned golden syrup aloft. Almost a semi-liqueur, but with that indefinable whiskyness which sets it apart..; **f22.5** the slight bitterness of the cask jolts the serenity of the oily sugars; **b23.5** whisky, from any part of the globe, does not come more soft or silky than this... 45% WB15/401

◇ **Scotch Malt Whisky Society Cask G11.1 Aged 14 Years** re-charred hogshead, dist 1 Dec 99 **(94) n24** a delicious blend of creamy toffee and toasty, bourbon-style liquorice/hickory mix; **t23.5** huge delivery of intense, vanilla-daubed dark sugars – muscovado principally – with even a touch of treacle; **f23** the spices which had begun to form earlier are now in their element; **b23.5** an altogether more rousing experience than the Nikka Coffey Still malt, not least thanks to the big bourbon input and first grade spices. Brilliant! 576%. sc. 190 bottles.

Blends

Black Nikka Aged 8 Years (82) n20 t21 f21 b20. Beautifully bourbony, especially on the nose. Lush, silky and great fun. Love it! 40%. Nikka.

The Blend of Nikka (90) n21 t23 f22 b24. An adorable blend that makes you sit up and take notice of every enormous mouthful. Classy, complex, charismatic and brilliantly balanced. 45%

Evermore (90) n22 t23 f22 b23. Top-grade, well-aged blended whisky with fabulous depth and complexity that never loses its sweet edge despite the oak. 40%. Kirin.

Ginko (78.5) n20.5 t20 f19 b19. Soft – probably too soft as it could do with some shape and attitude to shrug off the caramel. 46%. Number One Drinks Company.

Golden Horse Busyuu Deluxe (93) n22 t24 f23 b24. Whoever blended this has a genuine feel for whisky: a classic in its own right and one of astonishing complexity and textbook balance. 43%. Toa Shuzo. To celebrate the year 2000.

Hibiki (82) n20 t19 f23 b20. The grains here are fresh, forceful and merciless, the malts bouncing off them meekly. Lovely cocoa finale. A blend that brings a tear to the eye. Hard stuff – perfect after a hard day! Love it! 43%. Suntory.

Hibiki Aged 12 Years bott 2011 **(89) n22.5 t22 f22 b22.5.** A sensual whisky full of lightly sugared riches. 43%. Suntory.

Hibiki Aged 17 Years bott 2011 **(84.5) n22 t21 f20.5 b21.** Big oaks and a clever degree of sweetness. But takes the lazy big toffee option. 43%. Suntory.

Hibiki 50.5 Non Chillfiltered 17 Years Old (84) n22 t22 f20 b20. Pleasant enough in its own right. But against what this particular expression was so recently, hugely disappointing. Last year I lamented the extra use of caramel. This year it has gone through the roof, taking with it all the fineness of complexity that made this blend exceptional. Time for the blending lab to start talking to the bottling hall and sort this out. I want one of the great whiskies back...!! 50.5%. Suntory.

Hibiki Aged 21 Years bott 2011 **(96) n24** cherry fruitcake...with more black cherries than cake. Spiced sherry notes embrace the oak with a voluptuous richness; **t24.5** virtually perfect texture: seemingly silk-like but then a massive outbreak of busy oaky vanilla and juicy barley; the creamy mouth feel supports a mix of maple syrup and muscovado sugars; the middle moves towards a walnut oiliness; **f23.5** long, spicy with a gentle date and walnut fade; **b24** a celebration of blended whisky, irrespective of which country it is from. Of its style, it's hard to raise the bar much higher than this. Stunning. 43%. Suntory.

Hibiki Aged 30 Years (88) n21 t22 f22 b23. Still remains a very different animal from most other whiskies you might find: the smoke may have vanished somewhat but the sweet oakiness continues to draw its own unique map. 43%

Hokuto (86) n22 t24 f19 b21. A bemusing blend. At its peak, this is quite superb, cleverly blended whisky. The finish, though, suggests a big caramel input. If the caramel is natural, it should be tempered. If it is added for colouring purposes, then I don't see the point of having the whisky non-chillfiltered in the first place. 50.5%. ncf. Suntory.

Imperial (81) n20 t22 f19 b20. Flinty, hard grain softened by malt and vanilla but toffee dulled. *43%. Suntory.*

Kakubin (92) n23 t23 f22 b24. Absolutely brilliant blend of stunningly refreshing and complex character. One of the most improved brands in the world. *40%. Suntory.*

Kakubin Kuro 43° (89) n22 t23 f22 b22. Big, chewy whisky with ample evidence of old age but such is the intrusion of caramel it's hard to be entirely sure. *43%. Suntory.*

Kakubin New (90) n21 t24 f21 b24. Seriiously divine blending: a refreshing dram of the top order. *40%.*

Kirin Whisky Tarujuku 50° (93) n22.5 t24 f23 b23.5. A blend not afraid to make a statement and does so boldly. A sheer joy. *50%. Kirin Distillery Co Ltd.*

Master's Blend Aged 10 Years (87) n21 t23 f22 b21. Chewy, big and satisfying. *40%.*

New Kakubin Suntory (see *Kakubin New*)

Nikka Master Blend Blended Whisky 12 Years Old 70th Anniversary (94) n24 t23 f24 b23. An awesome blend swimming in top quality sherry. Perhaps a fraction too much sweetness on the arrival, but I am nit-picking. A blend for those who like their whiskies to have something to say. And this one just won't shut up. *58%. Nikka.*

Nikka Whisky Tsuru Aged 17 Years (94) n23 t24 f23 b24. Unmistakingly Tsuru in character, very much in line, profile-wise, with the original bottling and if the caramel was cut this could challenge as a world whisky of the year. *43%*

Robert Brown (91) n22.5 t23 f22.5 b23. Just love these clean but full-flavoured blends: a real touch of quality here. *43%. Kirin Brewery Company Ltd.*

Royal 12 Years Old (91) n23 t23 f22 b23. A splendidly blended whisky with complexity being the main theme. Beautiful stuff that appears recently to have, with the exception of the nose, traded smoke for grape. *43%*

Royal Aged 15 Years (95) n25 t24 f22; b24. Unquestionably one of the great blends of the world that can be improved only by a reduction of toffee input. Sensual blending that every true whisky lover must experience: a kind of Japanese Old Parr 18. *43%*

Shirokaku (79) n19 t21 f20 b19. Some over-zealous toffee puts a cap on complexity. Good spices, though. *43%. Suntory.*

Special Reserve 10 Years Old (94) n23 t24 f23 b24. A beguiling whisky of near faultless complexity. Blending at its peak. *43%. Suntory.*

Special Reserve Aged 12 Years (89) n21 t24 f21 b23. A tactile, voluptuous malt that wraps itself like a sated lover around the tastebuds, though the complexity is compromised very slightly by bigger caramel than the 10-y-o. *40%. Suntory.*

Suntory Old (87) n21 t24 f20 b22. A delicate and comfortable blend that just appears to have over-simplified itself on the finale. Delicious, but can be much better than this. *40%*

Suntory Old Mild and Smooth (84) n19 t22 f21 b22. Chirpy and lively around the palate, the grains soften the crisp malts wonderfully. *40%*

Suntory Old Rich and Mellow (91) n22 t23 f23 b23. A pretty malt-rich blend with the grains offering a fat base. Impressive blending. *43%*

Super Nikka (93) n23 t23 f23 b24. A very, very fine blend which makes no apology whatsoever for the peaty complexity of Yoichi malt. Now, with less caramel, it's pretty classy stuff. However, Nikka being Nikka you might find the occasional bottling that is entirely devoid of peat, more honeyed and lighter in style (21-22-23-23 Total 89 – no less a quality turn, obviously). Either way, an absolutely brilliant day-to-day, anytime, any place dram. One of the true 24-carat, super nova commonplace blends not just in Japan, but in the world. *43%. Nikka.*

Super Nikka Rare Old batch 02I18D **(90.5) n22 t23 f22.5 b23.** Beautiful whisky which just sings a lilting malty refrain. Strange, though, to find it peatless. *43%. Nikka.*

Torys (76) n18 t19 f20 b19. Lots of toffee in the middle and at the end of this one. The grain used is top class and chewy. *37%. Suntory.*

Torys Whisky Square (80) n19 t20 f21 b20. At first glance a very similar blend to Torys, but very close scrutiny reveals slightly more "new loaf" nose and a better, spicier and less toffeed finale. *37%.*

Tsuru (93) n23 t24 f22 b24. Gentle and beautifully structured, genuinely mouthwatering, more-ish and effortlessly noble. If they had the confidence to cut the caramel, this would be even higher up the charts as one of the great blends of the world. And with Japanese whisky becoming far more globally accepted and sought after, now would be a very good time to start. As it is, in my house we pass the ceramic Tsuru bottle as one does the ship's decanter. And it empties very quickly. *43%. Nikka.*

The Whisky (88) n22 t22 f21 b23. A rich, confident and well-balanced dram. *43%. Suntory.*

White (80) n19 t21 f20 b20. Boring nose but explodes on the palate for a fresh, mouth-watering classic blend bite. *40%. Suntory.*

Za (79) n19 t21 f19 b20. Some lively boisterous grain offers a suet-pudding chewiness. A little bitter on the finish. *40%. Suntory.*

European Whisky

The debate about what it means to be European is one that seemingly never ends. By contrast, the discussion on how to define the character of a European whisky is only just beginning.

And as more and more distilleries open throughout mainland Europe, Scandinavia and the British Isles the styles are becoming wider and wider.

Small distillers in mainland Europe, especially those in the Alpine area, share common ground with their US counterparts in often coming into whisky late. Their first love, interest and spirit had been with fruit brandies. It seemed that if something grew in a tree or had a stone when you bit into it, you could be pretty confident that someone in Austria or California was making a clear, eye-watering spirit from it somewhere.

Indeed, when I was writing Jim Murray's Complete Book of Whisky during 1996 and 1997 I travelled to the few mainland Europe distilleries I could find. Even though this was before the days of the internet when research had to be carried out by phone and word of mouth, I visited most – which was few – and missed one or two... which was fewer still.

Today, due mainly to the four solid months it now takes to write the Bible, I can scarcely find the time to go and visit these outposts which stretch from southern Germany to Finland and as far abreast as France to the Czech Republic. It is now not that there is just one or two. But dozens. And I need my good friends Arthur Naegele, Julia Nourney and Birgit Bornemeier to whizz around capturing samples for me just to try and keep up to date.

It is a fact that there is no one style that we can call European, in the way we might be able to identify a Kentucky bourbon or a Scotch single malt. That is simply because of the diversity of stills – and skills – being deployed to make the spirit. And a no less wide range of grains, or blends of grains, and smoking agents, from peat to wood types, to create the mash.

The distillers who have made major financial investments in equipment and staff appear to be the ones who are enjoying the most consistent results. In the Premier League we have the now firmly established Mackmyra in Sweden, Penderyn in Wales and Langatun in Switzerland, all of whom, curiously, use female blenders or distillers. Newly promoted to the highest tier comes St George's in England, and just joining them quality-wise, though not quantity, alas, is their British counterpart Hicks and Healey. In fact, St. George's has established themselves quality-wise in the world's whisky elite. All but the odd one or two of their bottlings have been staggeringly good and their Chapter 6 suite of bottlings had been the best ever not to pick up a major gong in the Whisky Bible's history. Never before have I been confronted with one bottling after another meriting a score of 90 plus. Remarkable, of course, is the youth of the whisky itself. But also the way in which a man fresh to making whisky so perfectly fits the shoes of an old master. The first distiller to set the distillery on the right path was Iain Henderson of Laphroaig fame. He was also, incidentally, the distillery manager who made the malt at Old Pulteney which over 21 years later was to be awarded World Whisky of the Year in the 2012 Whisky Bible. His successor, David Fitt, a former brewer at Greene King, has now proved himself to be unquestionably one of the best distillers in the world and confirmed that with Chapter 14 picking up the Bible's European Whisky of the Year 2015. The fact his spirit has matured into something so technically excellent in so short a time is truly remarkable: Iain Henderson obviously did a very good teaching job. St George's is not just a distillery to watch. It is also, in many respects, an inspiration to would-be major distillers.

Jim Murray's Whisky Bible European Whisky of the Year Winners

2004 Waldviertler Hafer Whisky 2000 (Austria)
2005 Hessicher Whisky (Germany)
2006 Swissky Exklusiv Abfullung (Switzerland)
2007 Mackmyra Preludium 2003 (Sweden)
2008 Mackmyra Privus 2003 (Sweden)
2009 Old Buck 2nd release (Finland)
2010 Santis Malt Highlander (Switzerland)
2011 Mackmyra Brukswhiskt (Sweden)
2012 Mackmyra Moment Urberg (Sweden)
2013 Penderyn Swansea City Portwood (Wales)
2014 Mackmyra Moment Glod (Sweden)
2015 English Whisky Co Chapter 14 (England)
2016 Kornog Chwec'hved 14 BC (France)

AUSTRIA

ACHENSEE'R EDELBRENNEREI FRANZ KOSTENZER Maurach. Working.

Whisky Alpin Grain Whisky Hafer db **(86.5)** n20.5 t23 f21 b22. A glutinous dram, full of thick wheat oils but a surprising lack of spice, though the little which forms works well within the hot cross bun sweetness. 40%

Whisky Alpin Rye & Malt db **(88)** n22 t22 f22 b22. Needs to settle in the glass a little while for the malt to be at its best. But worth the wait. 40%

Whisky Alpin Single Rye Malt db **(81)** n19 t21 f20 b21. Creamy and spicy. Good Demerara sugar thread, but the rye itself struggles to convince. 45%

BRENNEREI ROSSETTI Schwaz. Working.

Rosetti Young & Fine Pure Single Malt bott code L482 db **(85)** n21 t22 f20.5 b21.5. It's young. And fine by me... Clean, thin almost, delicate in its sweetness and salivating, though a slight tang to the finale. Don't expect too much back story. 43.5%

BROGER PRIVATBRENNEREI Klaus. Working.

Broger Burn Out Heavily Peated Malt Getreidebrand bott code: L BO-12 db **(89)** n22.5 t22 f22.5 b22. Now, that really was something very different...Beautifully distilled, though elsewhere technically not brilliant; but a guaranteed quadruple orgasm to the hard core peatophiles out there... 42%.

Broger Distiller's Edition Whisky Madeira Cask bott code: L DE-09 db **(81)** n21 t22 f18 b20 Under-sugared gooseberry tart. Or should that be: under-sugared tart gooseberry? Either way, shame about the slightly furry finish. 58.7%.

Broger Triple Cask Gerstenmalz-Whisky bott code: L TC-09 db **(63)** n14 t17 f16 b16. Just awful on so many levels. But mainly through very poor distillate. 42%.

DACHSTEIN DESTILLERIE Radstadt. Working

Mandlberggut Rock Whisky 5 Years (82) n20 t21.5 f20 b20.5. Rock by name and nature. A massively crisp whisky, as though you are crunching on crystals of sugar and grains of barley. The slight tobacco note means it never quite gets into full song but if owners Bernhard and Doris perhaps slow the stills a tad and cut a little finer, they might have on their hands a rock of ages to come... db 40%.

DESTILLERIE GEORG HIEBL Haag. Working.

George Hiebl Mais Whisky 2004 db **(93)** n23 t23.5 f23 b23.5. More bourbon in character than some American bourbons I know...!! Beautifully matured, brilliantly matured and European whisky of the very highest order, Ye..haahhhh!! 43%

DESTILLERIE KAUSL Mühldorf, Wachau. Working.

Wachauer Whisky "G" Single Barrel Gerste (Barley) bott code L6WG db **(90.5)** n22 t23 f22.5 b23. Absolutely charming and well made malt. 40%

DESTILLERIE ROGNER Rappottenstein. Working.

Rogner Waldviertel Whisky 3/3 db **(86.5)** n20 t22 f22.5 b22. Plane sailing once you get past the tight nose. A beautiful display of crisp sugars and come-back-for more grainy juiciness. Lovable stuff, for all its gliches. 41.7%. ncf.

DESTILLERIE WEIDENAUER Kottes. Working

Waldviertler Classic Haferwhisky bottle code L05 db **(88)** n21 t23.5 f21 b22.5. A busy oat whisky of no little distinction, despite the lightest degree of butyric. Still, they have been making from this grain for a long time... 42%

Waldviertler Dinkelmalz Dinkelwhisky mit 2/3, bottle code L08 db **(83.5)** n20 t22.5 f20 b21. Big, boisterous and, at times, bruising. The spice is out in force, as you might expect. But despite the enormity of the character, the thicker-than-desired cut works against it – on the nose and finish especially. 42%

Waldviertler Dinkelwhisky bottle code L09 db **(94)** n23 lovely wheaty spice, a little earthy but balanced with a stunning, understated, acacia honey and molasses mix t23.5 textbook weight on delivery: the oils slip over the palate and do nothing to obscure the crispness of those sugars, or the brittleness of the spelt grain; f23.5 so long, thanks to those oils. The sugars crumble, while the vanilla adds surprising weight and the correct degree of dryness. But the spices pick up and play gently, underlining the wheaty influence; b24 a beautifully made and matured whisky. So, so subtle... 42%

Waldviertler Hafermalz Haferwhisky mit 2/3 bottle code L09 db **(91)** n22 a hinty whisky: hints citrus, hints of coconut, hints of black pepper...but no hinting at all at the oat, which comes through pretty loud and clear; **t23.5** marvellously intense; the light golden syrup meets a tangerine-tinged, deliciously oiled grain; **f22.5** tangy oak but the concentrated, sugared porridge prevails; **b23** every last drop of flavour successfully extracted. Lovely! 42%

Waldviertler Limited Edition Hafermalz bottle code L08 db **(94) n22** slightly off key, but the voluptuousness of the oils and sugars win through; **t24.5** good grief...!! The nose may have had the odd blemish, but those oils certainly ensure a delivery and follow through to remember. Not sugar if it is the esters or the intrinsic sugars which give this such a continuous still Demerara feel...but there is something distinctly rummy about this. The honey is two-toned in intensity, though it is the light manuka which has the biggest say; **f23.5** long, still estery and enjoys a wonderful lime freshness to the oily oatiness; the late tang is a reminder of the earlier blemish. But it is piffling stuff... **b24** one of a type. Every whisky collector should hunt this down. Superb. 42%

Waldviertler Maiswhisky 100% Maisbrand, bottle code L09 db **(88.5) n21.5 t23 f22 b22.** A busy whisky with reasonable pretentions towards a bourbon style. 42%

Waldviertler Single Malt dunkel Hafer-Whisky bottle code L09 db **(81.5) n20 t22 f19 b20.5.** Massive flavours. But the over generous cut offers a metallic edge. 42%

DESTILLERIE WEUTZ St. Nikolai im Sausal. Working.
Franziska bott code. L070206/02 db The 5% elderflower means this is 100% not whisky. But a fascinating and eye-opening way to create a spirit very much in the young Kentucky rye style, especially in the nose. They certainly can do delicious... For the record, the scoring for enjoyment alone: **(93) n23.5 t23 f23.5 b23.** 48%. Malt refined with 5% elderflower.

LEBE & GENIESSE Lagenrohr. Working
Bodding Lokn cask no. 8, dist 2010, bott 2014 db **(88) n22 t22.5 f21.5 b22.** Tight and toasty. But very young. 42%.

Bodding Lokn Double Cask cask no. 6/11, dist 2010, bott 2014 db **(82) n20 t22 f20 b20.** Pleasant-ish, decently made whisky but way too young for its own good. The nose and finale underscore the serious lack of balance to this. Youthful whisky is acceptable if there is a rhythm to enjoy. Here we have a problem with two different types of oak being flung together yet hardly on speaking terms while at the same time the malt and oak have yet to find any meaningful sync and totter about like Bambi. The single redeeming highlight is the gristy sugars on delivery. But it is always worth remembering that to make the very most of a whisky it invariably needs patience and understanding.

⟫ **Bodding Lokn Double Cask** French oak & oloroso sherry casks, cask no. 6/12, dist 2009, bott 2015 db **(91.5) n23** one very intense whisky: a happy combination of thick fruit, including slightly more subtle greengages, mixed in with some broad oak tones. A slightly wide cut adds a honey-nougat dimension...and extra weight; **t24** good grief! What a delivery!!! Massive sugars – mixing ulmo honey with acacia honey and maple syrup – have a secondary gristy barley effect and light grapey tones....; **f21.5** the feints bite back hard as some bitterness creeps in; **b23** having been knocking on the door, in terms of quality, I do believe they've cracked it! 42%. ncf sc.

⟫ **Bodding Lokn Single Cask** American white oak, cask no. 10, dist 2009, bott 2015 db **(88.5) n22** a tad feinty with plenty of nougat and molasses promised; **t22.5** yep, the feints first to show. But then a delightful mocha-vanilla-barley complexity takes hold; **f22** the outstanding dark sugars, like the minty cocoa, lingers; **b22** now that's better! If I remember correctly, these guys have tended in the past to bottle a little too young. I think this is older distillate. And though not as well made as their cleaner previous bottling, the extra time in the cask has resulted in far greater balance and complexity. 42%. sc.

MICHELEHOF Vorarlberg. Working.
Micheles Single Malt 6 Years Old 100% barley, dist 2008, bott code L8121 db **(78.5) n19 t21 f19 b19.5.** An oily, nutty affair which struggles hard to get over the effect of the wide cut. A few attractive salivating fudgy moments at about the halfway point. 43%

PETER AFFENZELLER Albendorf. Working.
Peter Affenzeller Blend dist 2009, bott code L-1031132 db **(86) n20 t22 f22 b22.** A thinner, though more complex yet clean, version of the tannin-rich single malt bottling. Here, though, the spices strafe the taste buds from the first moment. Curiously satisfying, though. 42%

Peter Affenzeller Grain dist 2009, bott code L-0821021 db **(82.5) n19 t21 f21.5 b21.** Silky soft delivery and mouth feel. Again, the tannins have full control and it is a not unpleasant toasty nuttiness which prevails. 42%

Peter Affenzeller Single Malt dist 2009, bott code L-1031102 db (**81.5**) **n18 t21 f21.5 b21.** Sweet, nutty and all kinds of tannins at play of a singular European style though, intriguingly, sometimes not always easily recognisable as oak. On the downside the malt is lost under the wood while the nose needs a bit of work. 42%

Peter Affenzeller White bott code L-0821011 db (**84.5**) **n21 t21.5 f22 b20.** A pleasant, dry, well-made white spirit with a few decent sugar notes running into cocoa. Not sure how new make like this can be called whisky, though... 42%

PFANNER Vorarlberg. Working.
Pfanner Single Malt dist 2009, bott code L 212 db (**74**) **n19 t20 f16.5 b18.5.** Nutty and some hefty feints late on puts a Pfanner in the works... 43%

REISETBAUER Axberg, Thening. Working.
Reisetbauer Single Malt 7 Years Old Chardonnay and sweet wine cask, bott code LWH 099 db (**85.5**) **n19 t21 f23.5 b22.** A less than impressive nose is followed by a rocky delivery. But the panning out is truly spectacular as harmony is achieved with a rich honey and nougat mix, helped along the way with pecan nuts and figs. The finish is like a top rank trifle and fruitcake mix. A whisky of two halves. 43%

WHISKY-DESTILLERIE J. HAIDER Roggenreith. Working.
Single Malt Selection J.H. bott code L7/02 db (**94**) **n23 t23 f24 b24.** One of their cleanest, most understated bottlings to date. A gem. 46%

Single Malt J.H. Rare Selection bott code L SM 09 SG db (**91**) **n22.5** much of the house nougat-bourbon on show; **t23** thick and multi-layered as usual, the big oils make the most of the manuka honey and liquorice; **f22.5** the still liquorice dominates, even with a vague hint of Fisherman's friend. But now the spices hold the moment...; **b23** as usual, no shrinking violet! 46%

Single Malt J.H. Rare Selection bott code L SM 06 TR db (**94**) **n23** at once subtle and delicate, yet chunky. Much more emphasis on the honey than normal, a little dry diced coconut and a slight hint of treacle; **t24** a sublime delivery with that honey-treacle combination arriving early. But it is the way the malt slowly takes the upper hand – seemingly by tiny degrees at a time – really makes for an exceptional Austrian experience. Near perfect weight with the intensity of the malt; the layering and pace can hardly be bettered; **f23.5** long and boasting spice prickle yet still those honeys and malt radiate, allowing in at last the chalky oaks sign off a very pretty picture; **b23.5** one of the best malts of all time from JH. 46%

Special Single Malt Selection J.H. bott code L15/02 db (**93**) **n22.5 t23 f23.5 b24.** It is obvious that the JH whiskies are coming of age: they are consistently now of a very high standard – and just full of honeyed riches. 46%

◈ **Original Rye Whisky J.H.** bott code L R 08 db (**92.5**) **n23** fantastic weight to this: the rye is no shrinking violet, yet can do nothing to prevent a significant earthy-cocoa backdrop, complete with the heftiest molasses imaginable; **t23.5** for all its brooding intensity on the nose, fast sparkles on the palate as the rye comes up trumps; **f23** duller, with a well balanced oak anchor at play; **b23** a true delight. 41%

Original Rye Whisky Selection bottle code L R 05. db (**91.5**) **n22** a little of the old tobacco style about this, but moves on fast...to rye-soaked nougat; **t23.5** glorious delivery of crick rye dipped in honey; **f23** long as the oils spread; cocoa arrives and deepens; **b23** pure entertainment! 46%

Pure Rye Malt J.H. bott code LPR 07 db (**95.5**) **n24 t24 f23.5 b24.** Clean, unerring and screams "rye" at you. Magnificent. 41%

◈ **Pure Rye Malt** bott code L PR 08 db (**93**) **n22** perhaps a tad too much tobacco in with the grain, alas, but the rye thumps out its presence with gusto; **t24** but no problems on delivery where the rye appears, as expected, in concentrated mode and the richest, most juicy Kentucky style. The intensity of the grain defies both belief and the shortcomings of the wide cut. As usual, the sugars are dark, brooding bordering on manuka-style and entirely in sympathy with the rye; **f23.5** the width of the cut becomes evident as the oils mount. But those honey notes, coupled with the ever-present grain sees the whisky home comfortably; **b23.5** not a rye for the squeamish...even with its faults, something of a masterpiece. 41%

Special Rye Malt Selection Nougat J.H. bott code L SPR 07 SL db (**84.5**) **n20 t22 f21 b21.5.** Big and cumbersome, the nougat effect dulls the rye to a telling degree. No shortage of spices, though. 46%

◈ **Special Rye Malt Nougat** bott code L SPR 08 db (**86.5**) **n20 t23 f21.5 b22.** Massive chocolate at play. But it is the intensity of the rye on delivery which impresses most. Huge feinty nougat on this. For those wishing to reduce the level of it and up the honey, place the tasting glass in a bowl of hot water and allow the feints to burn off. 41%

⬩⬩ **Special Single Malt Selection** bott code L SSM 04 SL db **(82) n18 t22.5 f20.5 b21**. The butyric on the nose rather undoes the good of the nougat and honeycomb also visible. But a much better prospect on the palate, where the wide cut ensures maximum mocha. *46%*

DESTILLERIE WEIDENAUER Kottes. Working.

Waldviertler Hafer-Malz (2007 Gold Medaille label on neck) db **(91) n22 t22.5 f23 b23.5**. One of those whiskies that just gets better the longer it stays on the palate. Also, a master class in achieving near perfection in the degree of sweetness generated. *42%*

BELGIUM
THE BELGIAN OWL

The Belgian Owl Single Malt 'New Make' dist 06/13. db **(93) n23 t24 f23 b23**. Intensely sweet and rather beautifully made with enormous emphasis on concentrated clean, gristy barley. Looks as though they produce better New Make from the Caperdonich stills in Belgium than they could ever manage in Speyside. Strange... *70%*.

The Belgian Owl Single Malt '8 Months' db **(85) n20 t21.5 f23 b20.5**. Typically imbalanced for its age with the first sugary tannins lurching about the malt both blindly and seemingly without a map. Good finish though to this sometimes lush piece. *70%*.

⬩⬩ **The Belgian Owl Single Malt 36 Months** 1st fill bourbon cask, bott code LB036068 db **(89.5) n23** lovely cross between banana and yam on toast – with a little side dish of ulmo honey; **t23.5** the malt arrives in all its gristy glory for a sweet delivery; still plenty of vanilla and banana doing the rounds; **f21** some toasty sugars but an unusual bitterness from the oak for this distillery – in the old Allied cask style; **b22** a beautiful box of Belgian tricks until the unscheduled bitterness arrives. *46%. nc ncf sc.*

⬩⬩ **The Belgian Owl Single Malt 36 Months** ex-Pedro Ximénez cask, bott code LB036069 db **(92.5) n22.5** toasty sugars abound like at a patisserie; the tightness of the sweetness tells you this is PX even before you get to inspect the label...; **t23.5** predictably crisp sugars, though softened by a demur gristiness which surprisingly over-rides the grape; **f23** a big spicy fanfare...; **b23.5** I'm not the greatest fan of PX in whisky, as it so often overwhelms and locks in the character of the distillery itself. But Belgian owl has such a strong personality, it appears more than able to look after itself, thus providing a wonderful two-toned soft-hard-soft-hard malt... *46%. nc ncf sc.*

⬩⬩ **The Belgian Owl Single Malt 40 Months** 1st fill bourbon cask, bott code 4702028 db **(95) n23.5** quite massive: the tannins are there, in all their red liquorice glory. But there is a subtle, dry fruit note, also. The strength melts away into irrelevance, the malts grow substantially as the nose becomes accustomed...; **t23.5** such a soft, beautifully manicured delivery: the sugars range from muscovado to maple, with some decent grist thrown in; **f24** now into overdrive with the vanillas and mocha notes fully relaxed and integrated into the now lightly roasted malts – so complex and beautifully balanced; **b24** how can a whisky just 40 months old have morphed into so many flavours, even given this is from first-fill bourbon? Remains the world's most mind-blowing yet. *74.3%. nc ncf sc..*

The Belgian Owl Single Malt 48 Months 1st fill bourbon cask, bott code. L 260312 db **(86) n21.5 t22 f21.5 b21**. A much thinner bottling than of recent years with the sugars in the ascendancy and the barley devoid of muscle. Attractive and easy, though. *46%. nc ncf.*

The Belgian Owl Single Malt 60 Months cask no. 4276140 db **(94) n23.5 t23 f24 b23.5**. Carries out the dual purpose of giving you the big barley fix of the day...and dissolves any plaque that may have formed around your gums. Breathtaking...in every sense. *76.1%. nc ncf sc.*

The Belgian Owl Single Malt '60 Months' db **(91.5) n22.5 t23 f23 b23**. After being introduced to this distillery's 60 month old at 76.1%abv last year, this is positively a Guardian-reading sop and pacifist by comparison. Gentle and genteel with none of the passion displayed by the previous, unadulterated, version. Something of the Belgian Owl and Pussycat.... *46%. nc ncf.*

The Belgian Owl Single Malt 64 Months 1st fill bourbon cask no. 4275982 db **(90.5) n23 t23.5 f22 b22.5**. Demure and elegant. *50%. nc ncf sc.*

The Belgian Owl Single Malt '64 Months' db **(96) n23.5** ignore the dizzying degree of alcohol: concentrate on the nutty, malty notes and it all makes sense. Quite balmy flaked almonds mixed in with diced green apple and grist...; **t24** and it is the grist first up on delivery, followed by the juice of Williams' Pear. The sugars condense slightly at this point, but most are of an apple origin before the malt really ramps up the intensity; **f24.5** the star turn. Deft oils lengthen the effect f the malt; the sugars are bright yet polite and major on cane juice but still that barley makes its unerring mark...; **b24** what a delicious way to clean your teeth in the morning! Has more class and flair than the Belgian World Cup squad. And that is saying something...*73.7%. nc ncf sc.*

DESTILLERIE RADERMACHER

Lambertus Single Grain Aged 10 Years db **(44)** n12 t12 f10 b10. This is whisky...? Really???!!!!????? Well, that's what it says on the label, and this is a distillery I haven't got round to seeing in action (nor am I now very likely to be invited...). Let's check the label again... Ten years old...blah, blah. Single grain... blah, blah. But, frankly, this tastes like a liqueur rather than a whisky: the fruit flavours do not seem even remotely naturally evolved: synthetic is being kind. But apparently, this is whisky: I have re-checked the label. No mention of additives, so it must be. I am stunned. 40%

FILLIERS DISTILLERY

Goldly's Belgian Double Still Whisky Aged 10 Years db **(88)** n21.5 t23 f21.5 b22. Having actually discovered this whisky before the distillers – I'll explain one day...!! – I know this could be a lot better. The caramel does great damage to the finish in particular, which should dazzle with its complexity. Even so, a lovely, high-class whisky which should be comfortably in the 90s but falls short. 40%

IF GOULDYS

Gouldys 12 Years Old Amontillado Finish First Release bott 2012 db **(89.5)** n23.5 flawless nutty grape with no shortage of must; t22 hugely rich sherry on a background of chocolate mousse; f22 more chocolate – now spiced; b22 a pleasant, gentle experience celebrating a non-sulphur involvement. But the grape influence is just a little too great even for the considerable character of Fillers' grain to show through to advantage. Easy does it, chaps. 43%. ncf nc. WB15/388

Gouldys 12 Years Old Distillers Range cask no. 2600 db **(96)** n24 is it the clarity of the sherry or the punchiness of the grain which grips first? Hard to say. But the refreshing grape does nothing to distract from the crispness of the rye element. The result is stunning...; t24.5 the best sherry-influenced delivery I have tasted so far this year. A gorgeous viscosity to the grape works brilliantly against the firmness of the rye whilst the other grains chime in with confidence. Hard to find a whisky where the sugars, most of them of a Demerara style, work so well with the frothing spice...; f23.5 now much more sedate, though the length defies belief as the grape and rye interweave seemingly into infinity; b24 an essay in complexity. A faultless sherry butt influencing some of the best distillate in Europe: a triumph! 43.7%. ncf nc. WB15/390

Gouldys 12 Years Old Manzilla Finish First Release bott 2012 db **(90)** n23 flawless but heavy duty Manzanilla; t23 superb spices warm the thick, chewy grape. The grains are indistinct but can be detected for a second or two; f23 sweetens and softens, though the spices chatter on; b21 another delightful whisky despite falling into the trap of overwhelming the grain with the grape. Pretty impossible not to love, though. 43%. ncf nc. WB15/389

CZECH REPUBLIC
Single Malt
RUDOLF JELÍNEK DISTILLERY

Gold Cock Single Malt Aged 12 Years "Green Feathers" bott 27/05/09 db **(89.5)** n22 t23.5 f22 b22. From my first ever malt-related trip to the Czech Republic nearly 20 years ago, it was always a pleasure to get hold of my Gold Cock. I was always told it went down a treat. And this is no exception. Not a particularly big whisky. But since when has size counted? 43%

⬥ **Gold Cock Single Malt Whisky 1992 Limited Release Whisky Festival.cz** barrelled Jun 92, bott Apr 15 db **(97)** n23.5 although it doesn't say on the label that this is from Czech oak...the intensity of the sugars, that magnificent mix between golden syrup, ulmo honey and manuka... I'd be pretty amazed if it wasn't; t25 that has to be one of the most beautiful mouthfuls imaginable: golden Czech which, when you get your lips around it, makes your tongue explore its mysterious but inviting depths and then lick every last degree of juicy sweetness from the receptacle, nothing wasted as every last tingle of pleasure is sought and then extracted. A touch salty, and deliciously so, but it is that juicy sweetness, a result of the mature, rampant wood, which form thickening flavour layers, with that oaky hardness rhythmically interweaving with those gushing juices...in, out, in, out...so, so sensual...; f24 really need a lie down after all that. Flickering spices kiss and tease while the echoes of that salt and sugar lingers on the taste buds seemingly forever; b24.5 absolutely one of the great single barrels of the year. And, unquestionably, THE most sensual dram... 61.6%. ncf sc. 198 bottles.

⬥ **Gold Cock Single Malt Whisky Small Batch 1992** barrelled Jun 92, bott May 15 db **(94)** n23 the spices tingle the nose; the slightly creamy sugars ensure depth; t24 a volley of soft creamy sugars and honey (Demerara and ulmo in particular) – exactly like on the nose – bathe and massage the taste buds. And if it seems like Ambrosia, then in a way it is, as there is a milk-rice effect here which perfectly matches the ever-intensifying barley; **f23** just an apologetic degree of oaky bitterness creeps onto the scene, but those deft honey-sugar notes are in quickly to ensure a counter point; those gentle oils drift on forever ...; **b24** just as I was opening this bottle, I spotted a male green woodpecker on the lawn searching for ants, while just three feet above it a male great spotted woodpecker fed contentedly on nuts. And here was me about to taste a whisky derived from an oak which must, at one time or another, offered comfort to a black woodpecker or three; which, like the whisky, is found in the wonderful Czech Republic though not here. So I knew I was in for something different – and rather special – and I wasn't wrong. Because although the oak has maybe spent a season or two too long in the warehouse, the unique alignment of the sugars still ensures a malt of enormous character, quality and personality. *49.2%. ncf. 1,428 bottles.*

STOCK PLZEN - BOZKOV S.R.O.
Hammer Head 1989 db **(88.5)** n22 t22.5 f22 b22. Don't bother looking for complexity: this is one of Europe's maltiest drams...if not the maltiest... *40.7%*

Blends
Gold Cock Aged 3 Years "Red Feathers" bott 22/06/09 **(86)** n22 t21 f21.5 b21.5. Sensual and soft, this is melt-in-the-mouth whisky with a big nod towards the sweet caramels. *40%.*

Granette Premium (82) n21 t22 f19 b20. Lighter than the spark of any girl that you will meet in the Czech Republic. Big toffee thrust. *40%*

Printer's Aged 6 Years (86.5) n21.5 t22.5 f21 b21.5. Blended whisky is something often done rather well in the Czech Republic and this brand has managed to maintain its clean, malty integrity and style. Dangerously quaffable. *40%*

DENMARK
SMALL BATCH DISTILLERS Holstebro. Working
◇ **Peated first-fill 10L French oak casks** db **(78.5)** n21.5 t22 f17 b18. A brave, one might say foolhardy, early bottling from a new distillery. Mixing peat and wine together is not always a winner even for well established distilleries, let alone a new one. Here, they have been caught out when the off-notes from the casks not only becomes apparent but damages the whisky severely, especially towards the furry, off-key finish. That said, the delivery has merits in its intensity. But a price is paid... *54%*

◇ **Very Young Peated second-fill French oak casks** db **(90)** n23 some pretty full-on peat at work here: sharp, almost aggressive phenol only shadow-boxed by the oak; **t23** wine comes to the fore, catching the dryer edges of the peat for a puckering delivery. Intense stuff...; **f21** a slight flaw on the finale as the French oak does its worst. But enough peat around to repair the gouges; **b23** what a brilliant addition to the Scandinavian whisky lexicon! And recovery from their first disappointing attempt of peat and French oak. *62%*

◇ **Young Rye first-fill Hungarian oak casks** db **(74)** n18 t21 f16 b18. Probably the rye-est rye in the history of rye kind. I really must get to this distillery and sample the rye coming off the still: that would be a positive whisky experience the like of which even I have never encountered before. But I would also probably suggest, while there, that they seriously review – and then reboot - their wood policy. *62%*

BRYGHUSET BRAUNSTEIN Køge, Working
◇ **Mikkeller Spirits Black Bourbon Cask (81)** n20 t21 f20 b20. A peculiar whisky with a near apple brandy nose and all pervading fruit throughout. Perhaps been matured in a fruity atmosphere. But doesn't sit right. *43%*

◇ **Mikkeller Spirits Black Oloroso Cask (82)** n21 t22 f19 b20. Again, closer to a fruit brandy than a single malt with apple outscoring the grape on points. The barley is nowhere to be seen. *43%*

◇ **Mikkeller Spirits Black Rum Cask (86.5)** n20 t22.5 f22 b22. The nose is almost identical to their bourbon cask. But the rum influence gives a sugary shield to the malt and keeps some of the fruit at bay. *43%*

STAUNING DISTILLERY Skjern. Working.
Brigantia 3 Years Old bott code L-12/12 db **(79)** n19 t21 f19 b20. Huge malt statement, as is the distillery style. But it appears someone decided to try and extract as much spirit as possible, because the cut seems to be a little too wide for comfort here: the oils are unforgiving. *43%*

Stauning 2nd Edition Traditional bott 2013 db **(85) n20 t21 f22.5 b21.5.** Always interesting to see how a malt develops with time. Compared to a year ago, this has lost a little balance, with the barley just a little too ferocious on the nose and the sugars, though ultimately enjoyable, almost to a liquor-ish degree, are too far removed from the hay-like malt. *55%*

Stauning 2nd Edition Peated dist 2009, bott 2013 db **(94.5) n23 t23.5 f24.5 b24.** If there are awards given for sheer cleverness within peaty malt, then this would win hands down. No matter how many times you taste it, you can never quite decide whether the smoke is simply a charming accompaniment, or actually has its hands on the tiller of the direction of the whisky. Now that is what I call complexity...and a very classy act! *55%*

Stauning 3rd Edition Peated Single Malt dist 2009, bott 2014 db **(94) n23** some serious complexity here: a huge cliff of tannin (surprising for the age) being battered by waves of peat of ever-varying intensity; the hay-malt noticeable on the standard bottling also has room to flourish; **t24** the sugars rise on the palate like the famous mountains of Denmark: just attractive little hills here and there undulating with the even smoke and quite early mocha, which I think last year took longer to evolve; those sugars range from lightly smoked muscovado to, briefly, lightly smoked treacle; **f23.5** a light heather honey strain can be heard as the smoke slowly disperses; **b23.5** such a delightful experience: a peated malt which appears to wish to be inclusive of many other traits. *50%.*

Stauning 3rd Edition Traditional Single Malt dist 2009/2010, bott 2014 db **(87) n22 t22 f21 b22.** A malt on the march. Definitely a notch up from their previous bottling with the grassy malt signature on both nose and delivery standing out starkly against the spices. Still plenty of room for improvement as they progress. *49%*

◈ **Stauning Peated 4th Edition** dist 2011, bott 2014/10 db **(90.5) n22.5** a heavy distillate carries a lighter phenol. Sweet and dry run side by side and even occasionally merge; **t22.5** liquid Demerara sugar blinks first to let in the phenols which refuse to give up their position of power. A little ulmo honey and mocha ensure intensity and complexity; **f23** at first a bitter weakness. But this is overcome by the mind-boggling complexity of the sugar and smoky spice which soon overcomes any tannin negativity; **b22.5** clever harnessing of the sugars and smoke. *53.1%*

◈ **Stauning 5th Edition Peated** dist 2011, bott May 15 db **(93.5) n24** a stunning fanfare of peat: something like a mix between Laphroaig and Caol Ila in style...only with the odd hint of feint; **t23** and with those oils and sugars, a type of Caol Ila delivery and follow through. The vanilla-ulmo honey mix fills the gap before the finish brilliantly; **f23** sweet, oily and yet more soft honey. To be brutally technical, the feints, like the smoke, never quite goes away... but this is truly wonderful stuff; **b23.5** Danish peated whisky in full, confident stride. *51.1%*

◈ **Stauning KAOS** bott 2014/10 db **(89.5) n22.5** a slight feintiness dumbs down the more assured and better structured moments, especially with the light phenols and cranky grains; **t23** fabulously beautiful delivery: sharp as a surgeon's knife and almost as precise, the crispness to the grains ensure a big salivating factor; **f21.5** the feints on the nose return for a bitter, slightly oily finale; **b22.5** to entitle this whisky as Chaos is to do it a great disservice. Complex and challenging, for sure. Chaotic...never. *54.3%*

◈ **Stauning Peated Sherry Cask Finish** dist 2011, bott 2014 db **(74.5) n19 t20.5 f17 b18.** Good, kind, talented people of Stauning Distillery. You took my advice many years ago, hopefully to your advantage. I hope you do so again now: please do NOT use sherry butts for your whisky, especially your peated version. It is far too risky for so little return...indeed, negative impact. *49.3%*

Stauning Peated Single Malt oloroso cask finish, dist 10, bott 13 db **(93) n22.5 t23 f23.5 b24.** Can't say I'm the world's greatest fan of peat and sherry. But the finish on this one really is the stuff of smoky dreams. So impressive. *49.4%*

Stauning Peated Single Malt Pedro Ximenez cask finish, dist 2010, bott 13 db **(85) n21 t22 f21 b21.** Can't say I'm a fan of PX and big peat being thrown together and this does little to alter my view. Simply too much: the tightness of the sugars appears to strangle the life out of any further development. Decent delivery and early shockwaves. But your taste buds feel like they are in a sugary straightjacket. *47.1%*

Stauning Young Rye dist 10/11, bott Jun 13 **(77) n19 t20 f19 b19.** Time to be a little careful, guys. The nougat on the nose means that perhaps a few corners have been cut...and the oils clinging to the finish confirms this. Maybe, after making some earlier excellent make, an eye went off the ball: it is too easy to think that the making of great whisky has been mastered and it is easy. It never is! For rye to achieve its greatest clarity and crispness, the cut has to be precise and never too early. The intensity of the rye goes some way to saving the day. *51.2%*

Stauning Young Rye dist 2010/2012, bott Jun 14 db **(91) n22** oily and full bodied, the fruity charm of the intense rye is almost three dimensional; **t22.5** maybe a bit of a wide cut. But only just: the toasted honeycomb and treacle just add to the ripping rye which offers both soft oils and crisp fruit...gosh! **f24** much cleaner towards the end where the oak and grain really do make the most of each other; **b22.5** if no-one has ever told this distillery they do rye rather well, about time they did. And, better still, they can make it cleaner than this, too... *53.3%*

⬧ **Stauning Young Rye** dist 2012, bott May 15 db **(89) n22** well it's young! And it's rye, for sure! Just a little too much nougat and tobacco has crept into this one; **t22.5** as oily and intense as you would expect from a wide cut involving a massive-flavoured grain; huge honey and spice, too, as the salivation levels keep on rising; **f22.5** dries, though the spices get serious; **b22** big and bruising...but so bloody tasty! *49.5%*

ENGLAND

ADNAMS Saffron Walden. Working.

Adnams Southwold Triple Grain Whisky No 2 American oak, bott 2013 **(87) n22 t22 f21 b22.** For my 999th new whisky for Bible 2015 I wanted, as this book's custom dictates, to choose something a little unusual. And here we have the first-ever Suffolk whisky, made at one of my favourite breweries in the world, Adnams. Not sure what happened to the first bottling but I have the second. And beside me is Percy, my Meyers parrot born in Norfolk not far from the Suffolk border while this cask was maturing. The most remarkable thing to report is the nose. It is, and I really have to find out how, the closest whisky I have ever encountered on nose that matches a decent biryani in its subtle Asian spicy complexity. To taste it is a lot more straightforward: a tad feinty, but those oils conjure up the spices which sit well with the intense sugars. The finish, naturally enough, is a little bitter and foggy from the feints...but with no uncomfortable edges. For now I shall stick to their almost incomparable bitter beer. But I shall be keeping a close eye... *43%. ncf. WB15/407*

COTSWOLDS DISTILLERY Shipton-on-Stour. Working.

⬧ **Cotswolds Distillery New Make** batch no. 08/2015, bott 1 Sept 15 db **(94) n23.5 t24 f23 b23.5.** High quality new make still glistening with a coppery sheen on both nose and taste. And it is on delivery where it really stars, showing a gorgeous weight and great confidence as it maximises the malt. All spices and gristy sugars present and correct. The only thing missing is the usual cocoa dryness present on the finish of most good quality new makes. Maybe hiding behind the new still copper sharpness. *63.5%. ncf.*

⬧ **Cotswolds Distillery 5 Months** batch no. 04/2015, ex-oloroso sherry cask, bott 1 Sept 15 db **(89.5) n21.5 t23.5 f22 b22.5.** The fact that this is, thankfully, a clean sherry butt means we can spot some clues to the future style of this malt. It is clearly small still type, revelling in all its inherent intensity. But we can already see a confirmation of the new make: this a malt which likes to get off to a dramatic start, pitching all the elements of the flavour profile together in the first few moments before letting things unravel. At this age you let the odd jarring moment go, as all maturing spirit lacks a degree of couthness, with a degree of extra roughage from the extra copper. *63.5%. ncf.*

⬧ **Cotswolds Distillery 10 Months** cask no. 32, ex-red wine cask, bott 1 Sept 15 db **(91) n22 t23.5 f22.5 b23.** This one, showing some of the first will-be whisky made at the distillery, has already begun to settle into a flavour rhythm. The body of the spirit is able to hold the powering fresh fruit with ease and allows the malt to interact from an early stage. Some very decent spices abound, though they have to work hard to get through the weightiness of the malt's weight. Again, a little sharpness at the finish: with the stills being brand new, that is entirely expected. Exceptionally promising malt from my neighbours just the other side of Banbury. *63.5%. ncf sc.*

HEALEY'S CORNISH CYDER FARM Penhallow. Working.

Hicks & Healey Cornish Single Malt 2004 Cask #29 (94.5) n24.5 t24 f22.5 b23.5. Fascinatingly, picking up much more apple here than I did at the distillery, mainly because of the ambient aromas around me: a great example why all tasting notes I carry out are in controlled environments. Back in January I headed down to the distillery and after going through their casks suggested this one was, like their very finest apples, exactly ripe for picking. The most noticeable thing was that there, in the still house, I picked up only a fraction of the apple I get here in the controlled environment of my tasting room. The distillery makes, above all else, cider brandy, so the aroma is all pervasive. However, my instincts were probably correct, for the apple (doubtless absorbed from the environment of maturing with apple brandy casks, something like the fruit apparent on the whisky of St George's distillery, California) to be found here only contributes positively rather than detracts, especially on the nose...which I have upgraded from excellent then to near faultless now. As new distilleries go, this rates among the best debut bottlings of the last decade. That is not least because most distillers try and launch on three years to get money back as soon as possible. Here they have more than doubled that time and are reaping the benefit...with interest. A dram, then, to keep your nocturnal cinema going on classic mode: "Last night I dreamt I went to Penhallow again." Hang on: twelve syllables... I feel a book coming on... and a film... *61.3%. sc.*

Hicks & Healey Cornish Whiskey 2004 Cask #32 dist 13 Feb 04, bott Feb 12 db **(96) n24 t24.5 f23.5 b24.** I picked this one up absent-mindedly, nosed...and was carried to Cornwall. I knew what it was without even opening my eyes. Unmistakable. And just so stunningly beautiful... *60.2%. ncf.*

ST. GEORGE'S Rowdham. Working.

The English Whisky Co. Chapter 6 English Single Malt Not Peated ASB casks, cask no. 001, 002, 003, 004, dist May 09, bott Jan 13 db **(95) n23.5 t24 f23.5 b24.** Shows what maturing in truly great casks can do. Any more stylishly English and you'd think it was distilled in Jermyn Street... *46%. nc ncf.*

The English Whisky Co. Chapter 6 English Single Malt Not Peated ASB casks, cask no. 005, 006, 007, 008, dist May 09, bott Feb 13 db **(96) n24 t24 f24 b24.** You taste the Chapter 6 casks 1-4 and think it doesn't get any better...and then...this!!! Truly flawless distillate matured in high quality casks. Not just free of a single off note...free of a hint of a rumour of an off note. Truly sublime whisky showing that youth, when well brought up, can only delight. One of the finest examples of unpeated single malt whisky to have hit the market worldwide in the last three or four years... *46%. nc ncf.*

The English Whisky Co. Chapter 6 English Single Malt Not Peated ASB casks, cask no. 0193, 0194, dist Apr 10, bott Apr 13 db **(95) n23.5 t25 f23 b23.5.** I'm not sure if anything since Supertramp brought out Crime of the Century and Crisis What Crisis? back in the mid 1970s has two, or in this case three, back to back releases been so seamless or faultless. Let me say it and, as an Englishman, say it proudly: this whisky borders genius. *46%. nc ncf.*

The English Whisky Co. Chapter 6 Unpeated cask no. 248, 249, 250, 251, dist Oct 10, bott Nov 13 db **(89.5) n22.5** a light honey thread distracts from the slightly new-makey breeze; **t22** outrageously juicy on delivery, but the malt is febrile and takes time to happily link with the oak; **f23** the slow pulsing of the dry cocoa is sublime though, unusually, this is from the spirit rather than the oak. Just how good the original spirit was becomes clear as the maltiness makes its mark; **b22** a very solid score, though anything under 90 seems like a failure for this particular distillery. A rare occurrence where the youth of the spirit and the influence of the oak have been detached. Still a thing of youthful beauty when all is said and done. *60.2%. WB15/183*

The English Whisky Co. Chapter 7 Rum Cask cask no. 765, 766, dist Oct 09, bott May 14 db **(92) n22.5** confidently crisp rum influence from the kickoff: a light, sugary shell encrusts the beautifully defined barley; **t23** mmmm...!! Such a glorious fanfare of intense barley on delivery, which intensifies even further with a chunky gristiness during the slow progression; **f23.5** quite wonderful finish: the rum remerges somewhat with a light sugary sheen to the charming chalky oak and citrus gristy mix; **b23** an essay in understated deliciousness. A near perfect use of delicate sugar. *46%. nc ncf. 550 bottles. WB15/188*

The English Whisky Co. Chapter 7 Rum Cask cask no. 0765, 0766, dist Oct 09, bott May 14 db **(94) n23 t23.5 f24 b23.5.** Of all the English Whisky bottlings to its sister version (above), this is the closest in style despite the alcohol leap. Everything here, though, is more polished, concentrated and vivid....as you might expect. Quite superb. *59.9%. 96 bottles. WB15/187*

The English Whisky Co. Chapter 7 Rum Finish ASB & rum casks, cask no. 0457, 0458, dist May 09, bott Apr 13 **(91.5) n22 t23.5 f23 b23.** You have to be confident when maturing in rum: this has a propensity to tighten a malt until little but the sugars are heard. This though is 92% proof that St George can slay that particular dragon. *46%. nc ncf.*

⬧ **The English Whisky Co. Chapter 7 Single Malt Rum Cask** cask no. 0459 & 0461, dist May 09, bott Apr 15 db **(91.5) n22.5** the sugars are taught and allow the spices to slowly make their mark; **t24.5** amazing golden syrup notes on delivery and the first few waves, but enlivened with a spicy punctuation. A delivery of your dreams, where the malt also makes an impact, as does the Lubeck marzipan and chocolate; **f22** hardens and draws away from the more complex angles; bitters very slightly; **b22.5** there is quite a profound difference between the delivery and finish. *59.9%. nc ncf.*

The English Whisky Co. Chapter 9 Peated ASB casks, cask no. 064, 065, 066, 103, dist Oct 09, bott Feb 13 db **(92.5) n23.5 t23 f23 b23.** A growling, grumbling, curmudgeonly dram which wants to keep to a separate path from the sugars. *46%. nc ncf.*

The English Whisky Co. Chapter 11 "Heavily Peated" ASB cask no. 645/647/648, dist 08, bott 11 db **(92) n23 t23.5 f22.5 b23.** As the 59.7% version below. Only for wimps. *46%. nc ncf.*

The English Whisky Co. Chapter 11 Heavily Peated ASB casks, cask no. 639, 640, 641 & 642, dist Mar 08, bott Nov 11 db **(91.5) n22.5 t23 f23 b23.** One of the sweetest English whiskies for the last century... 46%. nc ncf.

The English Whisky Co. Chapter 11 Heavily Peated ASB casks, cask no. 0062, 0065, dist Apr 09, bott Jul 12 db **(81) n19 t22 f21 b19.** A rare blemish. This malt is very much less than the sum of its parts as not enough attention was made in balancing out the peats and the sugars. Brief harmony as the sugars and oils hit the palate, but on the nose and for long periods in the mouth this is a free for all: young malts are temperamental. And here the balance has not been found. 46%. nc ncf.

The English Whisky Co. Chapter 11 Heavily Peated ASB casks, cask no. 0104, 0107, dist Nov 09, bott Feb 13 db **(93) n22 t24 f23.5 b23.5.** Superbly made and makes the most of some honey casks. If anything, perhaps too much honey...! 46%. nc ncf.

⬧ **The English Whisky Co. Chapter 12 Single Malt Sherry Cask** cask no. 0872, bott 2012 db **(94.5) n24** gosh, not a nose I encounter that often these days (alas!): roasting sweet chestnut meets moist Melton Hunt cake; Crunchie with the honeycomb in a molten state... and spices, of course. Lots of 'em...; **t24** that velvety meeting of luxurious grape once so common when drinking a Macallan 10 some 30 years ago has returned to my palate: like being in a time warp and sliding into bed with one of your favourite lovers of yesteryear. Oak is fleetingly apparent, with a few tannin-related beats. But they go almost unnoticed as a little manuka honey takes a bow; **f22.5** drier now, showing the sherry's style. Vaguely furry if you look for it and taste for long enough; **b24** an almost flawless sherry butt. Housing just about flawlessly-distilled whisky. The result is something a little special... 60.3%. nc ncf sc.

The English Whisky Co. Chapter 13 Heavily Peated cask no.527, 528, 827, 830, dist 2008, bott 2013 db **(92.5) n23.5** what a tease: the smoke caresses and whispers, though some of its speech is childish: the youth of this whisky is occasionally transparent; just look for that lime on the barley, though! At other times, the conversation is more mature with slightly overcooked raspberry pie out there; **t23.5** that fabulous, slightly buttery feel of cake mix nicked from the mixing bowl, but now with peaty grist sprinkled in; at all times, though, salivating barley refreshes; **f22** just a little bitterness creeps in from the oak. The delicate, citrusy sugars and fingerprints of peat try to counter; **b23.5** take your time with this: like all the best whiskies, this is a moving target never sitting still and with so many elements camouflaged before being spotted. 49%. ncf nc. WB15/397

The English Whisky Co. Chapter 13 St. George's Day Edition db **(91) n22** a telling light furriness tells me to be on the lookout for more fruit characteristics, which are to be found, intriguingly, with a slightly salty tang. More herb garden than fruit, though the delicate molasses heads in the direction of a dry, two-days-on-the-plate Melton Hunt cake....; **t24** the spices rise early on an oily bed which makes for a friendly, though far from docile opening. A mix of malt, red liquorice and hickory forms the van of the attack but deeper fruitier notes rumble, especially the magnificent walnut and dates; **f22** spicy still but the dryness has an unwelcome catch, though a few chocolate fruit and nut notes repairs some of the damage; **b23** the nose suggests sherry butts at work here, as does the slightly furry finale. But this is a superficial wound and the overall composition is rather lovely. 45%. nc ncf. WB15/181

⬧ **The English Whisky Co. Chapter 13 Single Malt St George's Day Edition** 2015 db **(87) n21.5 t22.5 f21 b22.** How odd. Some of the characteristics found on their 2014 St George's day bottling can be found here, too. Except for this latest edition, those flatter notes are flatter still. No shortage of malt, mind. 45%. nc ncf.

The English Whisky Co. Chapter 14 Not Peated cask no. 450, 451, 452, 453, dist Feb 09, bott May 14 db **(96) n24** thick: you need a knife to cut your way through the honey-marmalade mix and wire-cutters to penetrate the barley; **t24.5** the citrus on the nose arrives ahead of the concentrated barley cavalry. Absolutely no need to tell you this is malt whisky: this is the densest malt you will taste this year from any distillery; some cocoa strands arrive relatively early but still cannot distract from the grain: for its age, as near as damn it faultless...; **f23.5** tangy oak gets a word in edgeways; thins at last but that barley still controls with varying intensity. A little salty, oddly enough, and a little Milky Way candy filling sits rather beautifully with the delicate cocoa; **b24** any distiller in the world would give his right hand to lay claim to malt of such exceptionally high quality. 58.8%. 299 bottles. WB15/185

⬧ **The English Whisky Co. Chapter 14 Single Malt (unpeated)** cask no. 205, 181, 182, 183, dist Apr 10, bott May 15 db **(92.5) n23** the oak plays little toffeed patterns upon the malt: soft and belying its age. The vanilla confirms more oak than usually seen from this distillery; **t23.5** a beautiful oily cushion offers a tapestry of intense malt and toffee apple; **f23** vanilla and butterscotch before a little toasted fudge begins to softly clear its throat...; **b23** how can a malt at nearly 60%abv be so silky soft and sexy? A ridiculously gentle and genteel whisky. 58.8%. nc ncf.

The English Whisky Co. Chapter 14 English Single Malt (unpeated) cask no. 582-585, dist 08, bott 13 db **(95) n23.5 t23.5 f24 b24.** This is great whisky in its simplest form – even the complexity, though evident, is untaxing. If you are not an age snob, this, for its gentle elegance, will blow you away. *58.8%. nc ncf.*

The English Whisky Co. Chapter 14 English Single Malt (unpeated) cask no. 582-585, dist May 08, bott Jul 13 db **(93) n23 t23 f23.5 b23.5.** Now there's a thing. Nosed and tasted this and thought: "that's weird! Just about identical to the last one. Gorgeous, but just doesn't quite hit the high notes when singing, or have quite so much bass." Then discovered it was the same whisky, but reduced to 46%. Says it all, really. *46%. nc ncf.*

⬩ **The English Whisky Co. Chapter 15 English Single Malt Heavily Peated** cask no. 041, 042, 043, 043, dist Jun 09, bott Sept 14 db **(94.5) n23.5** much more aggressive than the standard Peated bottling, not so much for the difference in strength, but the slightly more acidic anthracite kick to the peat; **t24** look for faults on the delivery for as long as you like: there aren't any! The oils and phenols are hand in glove, the chewability is off any known scales...; a little ulmo honey mixes with much broader muscovado, then an infusion of bewildering spices which swarm and warm; **f23.5** long; a little timber ensures extra ballast beyond the smoke; **b23.5** if all whiskies were like this, I'd never get this book finished: so easy to go off into another world as you explore the peaty complexity to its character. Just great stuff! *58.4%. nc ncf. 192 bottles.*

The English Whisky Co. Chapter 15 English Single Malt (peated) db **(94.5) n23.5 t24 f23 b24.** If you could take that single flaw out of the equation, you'd have just about perfect whisky for a five-year-old. As it is, you'll just have to make do with bloody magnificent.... And make no mistake: this is no poor man's Islay. It stands up with the world's elite. *58.4%. nc ncf.*

The English Whisky Co. Chapter 15 English Single Malt (peated) cask no. 615-618, dist Apr 08, bott Jul 13 db **(92.5) n23.5 t23.5 f22.5 b23.** A drier, more inert version of the cask strength bottling. Here the peat is a little more dusty, though the gristy sugars do show up better. Simply enjoyable, high class peaty whisky however you look at it. *46%. nc ncf.*

⬩ **The English Whisky Co. Chapter 16 Single Malt Peated, Sherry Cask** cask nos. 693 & 694, dist Nov 07, bott Sept 14 db **(95) n23** the peat, as welcoming as a feathered pillow, snuggles up first, prickly spices by its side. The soft grape sidles up beside the smoke and slowly begins to gently cloak it; **t24.5** oh...my...word...!!! The delivery stops you in your tracks. You sense the youth to this immediately, but that is immaterial. All that matters is the shape-shifting, forming and reforming with the interplay between the lush sherry and the toned, agile peat; beyond this mesmerising scene you might be able to focus also on the dates, sticky molasses and Zambian honey; **f23.5** so the odd furry note is there if you look for it (as I have to do). But the slowly unravelling of the grape must and dry peat soot is far more interesting and entertaining....; **b24** there are few occasions when sherry and peat travel comfortably together, hand-in-hand. But here is one, thanks to the softness (and general cleanness) of the grape and non-bombastic, embracing style of the peat. As gentle giants go, this is benign and enormous... *58.3%. nc ncf.*

The English Whisky Co. Classic (unpeated) db **(88.5) n22 t22 f22.5 b22.** Sweet, young and innocent. *43%. nc ncf.*

⬩ **The English Whisky Co. Classic Single Malt Whisky** db **(88.5) n22** exceptionally young: a glittering array of pre-pubescent citrus notes charm, but don't quite enrapture; **t22.5** wow! Even younger on delivery. But just enough oak notes creep in to prop up the body. What this does show is the exceptionally fine structure of this malt and the high quality of the distillate. More lemons make the barley sparkle; the sugars are light and flirtatious; **f22** remains clean and citrus-breezy, a vague cocoa note – and I am, for once, at a loss to say whether this is from the effect of the young spirit, or the oak; **b22** less St George and more the Lemon Drop Kid... *43%. nc ncf. Distilled by David Fitt.*

The English Whisky Co. Peated db **(93) n23 t23.5 f23 b23.5.** A young whisky which proves, again, that it is the quality of the distillate – especially when peated – which can count over the years. *43%. nc ncf.*

⬩ **The English Whisky Co. Peated Single Malt Whisky** db **(92) n24** young smoky malt rarely comes better than this: weirdly salty for an English whisky, but the charm is in the quiet confidence and evenness of the smoke and the weight diffused by the oils. Never a moment's intensity...yet somehow comes out as pretty hefty phenols; **t23.5** so silky and soft. The light oils form a superb backdrop to the delicate peat and, latterly, the hint of lemon; **f22** shortish finish thanks to the youth of the malt and screams for an oaky backbone; **b22.5** although distilled by Davd Fitt – unquestionably one of the very top new breed whisky-men today – the style would be instantly recognisable by the distillery's first manager Iain Henderson. For this has every hallmark of his previous distillery, Laphroaig, and at times is almost indistinguishable. *43%. nc ncf. Distilled by David Fitt.*

Founders Private Cellar cask no. 0116, dist 12 Sep 07, bott 8 Apr 13 db **(94.5) n24 t23.5 f23 b24.** Yet another bottling from this remarkable distillery which almost defies belief. So clean and proffers the innocence of youth with unsullied beauty. *60.8%. nc ncf sc.*

⇔ **Founders Private Cellar English Single Malt Sassicaia Cask,** cask no. 0792, dist Oct 07, bott Mar 15 db **(93) n23** there's a real flowery feel to this intense grape: a cross between a dessert wine and a walk in a midsummer English garden; **t24** the fruit is high powered, concentrated and sharp. But it is set apart by another slightly intense flavour profile running through it – not unlike the chocolate sauce that adorns ice cream; naturally, spices are busy and all encompassing; **f22.5** maybe a slight tangy buzz, but this is such a busy finish – with no little grape must – you don't really pay much attention; **b23.5** wow! That is some bottling...a malt brimming with flavour and character. Indeed, the flavour profile is nigh on unique worldwide. *61.1%. nc ncf sc. 198 bottles.*

Founders Private Cellar Port Cask, cask no. 0859, dist 20 Jun 07, bott 10 Apr 13 db **(88.5) n22 t23 f21.5 b22.** Technically, this is not A1 spirit at work. However the influence of the Port pipe is so impressive, much, if not all, is forgiven... *59.3% nc ncf sc.*

⇔ **HRH Princess Charlotte of Cambridge** db **(95) n23.5** youthful, but a lot more mature than Princess Charlotte. The barley is proud and unflustered and has taken on just enough positive from the oak to ensure a comfortable balance; **t24** sublime sugars lead from the start. An attractive almost Spey-style gristiness benefits from a sharper citrus edge, so, soon after delivery the salivation factor goes through the roof....; **f23.5** remains clean; perhaps a little bitterness creeping in from the cask. But the grist and vague heather-honey fade ensures it is kept in check with the most attractive and regal of finishes; **b24** to pay tribute to the latest member of the British royal family, I saved this as the 1,028th new and very last whisky for the 2016 Bible. Knowing first-hand her grandfather's taste for fine whisky, I am sure he will, like me, enjoy raising a glass of this most intensely malty bottling, which showcases the distillery in elegant style. *46%*

Stephen Notman Whisky Live Taipei 2013 The English Whisky Co db **(95.5) n24 t24 f23.5 b24.** A ridiculously stunning cask which I selected from St George's to celebrate Stephen Notman's impressive five year stewardship of Whisky Live in Taipei... making this a very English Whisky affair. Bewildering and beguiling for a four-year-old, where the peat is confident yet elegent, the body crisp yet lush and the complexity and balance beyond comprehension for its age. It was a pleasure to help promote not just the best of Bristish, but truly world-class whisky to an appreciative Taiwanese audience. And just shows what magic happens when near perfect spirit meets a near perfect cask. *50.6%*

Whisky Live Taipei 2013 Founders Release B1/416, dist 7/4/09 **(93) n23.5 t23 f23.5 b23.** Beautifully made; excellent sweetness and beautifully smoky. A quietly satisfying malt. *50.6%*

FINLAND
PANIMORAVINTOLA BEER HUNTER'S Pori. Working.
Old Buck cask no. 4, dist Mar 04, bott Apr 10 db **(95) n24 t23 f24 b24.** Just read the tasting notes to the second release because, a dose of what almost seems like corn oil and ancient Demerara rum combined apart, oh - and an extra dose of oak, there is barely any difference. I will never, ever forget how I got this sample: I was giving a tasting in Helsinki a few months back to a horseshoe-shaped audience and a chap who had been sitting to my right and joining in with all the fun introduced himself afterwards as I signed a book for him as non other than Mika Heikkinen, the owner and distiller of this glorious whisky. I had not been told he was going to be there. His actual, touchingly humble words were: "You might be disappointed: you may think it rubbish and give it a low score. It just means I have to do better next time." No, I am not disappointed: I am astonished. No, it isn't rubbish: it is, frankly, one of the great whiskies of the year. And if you can do better next time, then you are almost certainly in line for the Bible's World Whisky of the Year award. *70.6%*

TEERENPELI
Teerenpeli Single Malt Aged 8 Years oak cask db **(86) n21.5 t22 f21 b21.5.** Has moved on a notch or two from the five-year-old. A soft, simplistic experience, dependent on fudgy cream toffee and hazelnut. *43%*

⇔ **Teerenpeli Single Malt Distiller's Choice HOSA 10 Year Old** Black Cask Edition 2nd fill bourbon cask db **(94.5) n24** shadows, hints and whispers of delicate smoke, matched in subtlety by the deftness of the grain and sweetness of the butterscotch sugars; **t24** follows a silky road on the palate, bestowing along the way malty yet vaguely smoky kindnesses and gristy sugars which make a nonsense of the decade in the cask; **f23** long despite being slightly crystalline and crisp. The sugars harden slightly but work handsomely beside the vanilla thread; **b23.5** a distillery renowned for intensity shows it can do subtlety no less impressively *43% 672 bottles.*

⬧ **Teerenpeli Single Malt Distiller's Choice Tallink Silja Edition** Portwood Finish bourbon cask, finished in Port cask db **(93) n23.5** charming clarity with the Port influence more fulsome than just a finish; **t23.5** breathtaking juiciness: the barley is beautifully defined, the sugars no more than a background accompaniment; **f23** gentle grape keeps the oak involvement honest; **b23** typically Teerenpeli in its depth but now with well balanced fruitiness. *43% 1174 bottles.*

Teerenpeli Kaski Single Malt sherry cask db **(90.5) n23 t23.5 f21.5 b22.5.** A pristine sherry butt ensures massive fruit. Impressed. *43%*

FRANCE
Single Malt
DISTILLERIE BERTRAND

Uberach db **(77) n21 t19 f18 b19.** Big, bitter, booming. Gives impression something's happening between smoke and grape... whatever it is, there are no prisoners taken. *42.2%*

DISTILLERIE DES MENHIRS

Eddu Gold db **(93) n22 t23 f24 b24.** Rarely do whiskies turn up in the glass so rich in character to the point of idiosyncrasy. Some purists will recoil from the more assertive elements. I simply rejoice. This is so proud to be different. And exceptionally good, to boot!! *43%*

⬧ **Eddu Grey Rock** db **(87.5) n21.5 t22 f22 b22.** A docile whisky reliant on friendly muscovado sugars which match the vanilla-oak very attractively. *40%*

⬧ **Eddu Grey Rock Brocéliande** db **(86.5) n22 t22.5 f20.5 b21.5.** Dense whisky which enjoys an enjoyable molassed fruitcake theme. A bit thin and wonky towards the finish. *40%*

Eddu Silver db **(81) n20 t22 f19 b20.** A curiosity of a whisky, though not up to the distillery's normal high standards. The base spirit hasn't been cut to advantage, so the feints tend to damage both nose and finish. Some astonishing sugars on deliver, though. *40%.*

Eddu Silver Broceliande db **(92.5) n23** both gentle and busy, the spices pepper but are charming about it; elsewhere there is a tandem between barley and greengage; **t23** wow..! So juicy. A stunning mixture of salivating barley juice and something fruitier, thinned with lime; **f23** heavier now with the spices much more attack-minded. Some caramel tart topped with stewed apple and raisin; **b23.5** pure silk. A beautiful and engaging experience. *40%.*

DISTILLERIE GLANN AR MOR

⬧ **Glann Ar Mor Maris Otter Barley 15** first fill bourbon cask db **(88.5) n21.5** a tad thin, a little feinty...but the barley is crisp and healthy; **t23** huge malt on delivery. For once, the ulmo honey takes a backseat to the barley which positively explodes on the palate, the grist taking its time to add a sweeter dimension. The oak is also firm, as the vanilla testifies; **f22** the traditional cocoa and fudge of slightly over cut malt..; **b22** as an Englishman, so warming to see the French embracing my country's most traditional and home-spun barley... and, certainly on the delivery at least, doing it proud. *46%. Celtic Whisky Compagnie.*

⬧ **Glann Ar Mor Peated Gwech 15** BC db **(93) n23** crisp, nipping barley; firm, fresh oak and a pinch of salt: an embracing, vitalising mix; **t23.5** such clean malt! Oceans of vanilla are circumnavigated by a beautiful, eye-watering, salivating barley and ulmo honey mix; **f23** clean, tapering vanilla and ulmo honey; **b23.5** another very high class malt from these messieurs... *66.2%. Celtic Whisky Compagnie.*

Glann Ar Mor Taol Esa 3ed Gwech 12 first fill bourbon barrel db **(76) n18 t20 f18 b18.** Sweet, oily, feinty. *46%. nc ncf. 674 bottles.*

Glann Ar Mor Taol Esa 4ed Gewch 13 first fill bourbon barrel db **(78) n18 t21 f19 b20.** Looks like the distiller wanted to get as many flavours as he could from the cut. *46%.*

Glann Ar Mor Taol Esa 2l Gwech 13 first fill barrel db **(73) n17 t19.5 f18 b18.5.** I had hoped the feints might have taken a backward step: they haven't. *46%. nc ncf. 955 bottles.*

Glann Ar Mor Taol Esa 1an Gwech 14 first fill bourbon barrel db **(79) n18 t20 f21 b20.** Keeps up its feinty tradition. Ultra malty, though. *46%.*

Kornog 2013 For The Auld Alliance first fill bourbon barrel db **(94.5) n23** salty rock pools; **t24** one of the most eye-wateringly intense deliveries produced by any European mainland distiller this year. The enormity of the barley is immeasurable, then ramped up even further by a big spoon-full of salt; entirely salivating and mind-blowing; **f23.5** calms for the malt now to merely bathe in its own glow; some spices evolve but the usual mocha sweetness (and even a light hint of smoke) sees the malt out, perhaps helped along with gentle manuka honey; **b24** an extraordinary whisky worthy of seeking and enjoying. In a style of its own. And when I say style...I mean style.... Specially tasted on 6th June 2014 to mark the 70th anniversary of the New Alliance... *58.7%.*

Kornog Saint Erwan 2014 first fill bourbon barrel db (**88**) **n23** the usual rather wonderful salty-malty affair from this distillery; **t23** a malt bomb exploding all over the palate; **f20.5** long, spicy, though a tad bitter; **b21.5** a slightly simplistic malt. But entirely charming. *50%.*

◈ **Kornog Saint Erwan 2015** db (**84.5**) **n21 t21.5 f21 b21**. Butter smeared on the delicately smoked malt. Lovely sensations, but doesn't quite fire right. *50%. Celtic Whisky Compagnie.*

◈ **Kornog Saint Ivy 2015** db (**95.5**) **n23.5** despite the oils, sharp, vaguely bourbony with a liquorice lead; **t24** sacre bleu! Formidable...!!! The malt is, in the house style, rounded up and concentrated – guarded by a buttery spiciness. A sub plot of mocha but, beneath it all, the usual suspects of marzipan and ulmo honey. Massive....and increasingly oily! **f24** long, with the rich oils squeezing every last drop of barley from the glass. Vanilla, butterscotch, red and black liquorice and dried ulmo tick every box...; **b24** just love the liquorice theme. And the insane barley concentrate. A great malt looking for a deserving and receptive palate. There's a decent restaurant I have been known to frequent in central London this will do well in... *59.6%. Celtic Whisky Compagnie.*

Kornog Single Malt Saint Ivy 2014 first fill bourbon barrel db (**94**) **n23.5** busy vanilla and ulmo honey. The smoke enters by the back door...and leaves again without anyone really noticing; the light sprinkling of salt on the marzipan is a masterstroke; **t23** beautifully sumptuous malt, thickening almost into a Malteser candy, complete with milky chocolate; the smoke again keeps the very lowest profile imaginable. Despite this light enough for some salivating barley; **f23.5** fabulously complex fade with the understated peat now helping the spices along; lilting mocha signs off; **b24** what an elegant and quite delightful whisky. *58.9%.*

◈ **Kornog Taouarc'h Chwec'hved 14** BC db (**97**) **n24** exceptional: despite the smoke, this is a very light aroma. The phenols are delicate, the citrus fragile. Also, a little nippy and busy, which works perfectly...; **t24** just about faultless: a fabulous match between the peat and the ulmo honey and so light bodied (despite the oils) you can feel every nuance, every play being made; **f24.5** one dreams of finishes like this. A backdrop of Lubeck's finest marzipan, a smattering of cocoa but that honey and smoke does things you can only pray for....; the remainder of this glass (usually poured away) will accompany me to bed tonight...and, for once, there will be no spitting...; **b24.5** delicately distilled, marvellously matured...a triumph of the trade. One of the very best whiskies I have since the 2015 Bible. And confirmation, along with Seizud 14, that this distillery has entered true World Class status. *58.2%..*

Kornog Taouarc'h Kentan db (**94.5**) **n24 t24 f23 b23.5**. Not sure there has been this number of perfectly rhapsodic notes coming out of France since Saint Sans was in his pomp... *57.1%*

Kornog Taourc'h Kentan 13 BC first fill barrel db (**90**) **n22 t22.5 f22 b23.5**. As soft as sun cream being spread over you while basking on a French beach. *46%. nc ncf. 907 bottles.*

Kornog Taouarc'h Kentan 14 BC db (**92**) **n23** soft smoke drifting into a pool of brine; **t22** a sharp delivery, principally because of the slightly chunky distillation; the smoke enters the fray to sooth and settle; struggles a bit at first; **f24** much better now. There is a lovely milky mocha drift to this, aided by impressive Demerara; the smoke is now perfectly poised and elegant; **b23** only the other day I was telling someone about how this distillery's peated malt has a distinctly Islay feel to it. Well, that was before I tasted this: a malt which has very much its own signature and provenance. Incidentally, I tasted this, with all the other Kornog whiskies, on 6th June 2014 to mark the 70th anniversary of the D-Day landings. My late father, after battling Rommel in Africa, was fighting in Italy at the time. So I will use this whisky – combining British influence with the peat, American oak and French water and craftsmanship – to toast all those who showed bravery beyond anything we can possibly imagine. And, in particular, those – on whichever side - who never returned to tell the tale... *46%.*

◈ **Kornog Taouarc'h Seizued 14** BC db (**95**) **n23** wispy smoke: first it's here, then it's not...; strands of peek-a-boo coconut; nipping, fizzing spices...; **t23.5** a ridiculously beautiful delivery: gristy peat, where the sugars dissolve on your tongue like a lozenge. The house ulmo honey style remains as residue, as does the softest smoke imaginable; **f24** long, sophisticated and delicate to the point of being too scared to move...but that smoke just lingers on...; **b24.5** very rare that whiskies just get better and better on the palate. But here is one such case. A whisky of whispers and intrigue. *46%. Celtic Whisky Compagnie.*

◈ **Kornog Taouarh'h Kentan 15** BC db (**94.5**) **n23.5** another busy light peaty number, but now with a citrus hue; **t24** the gristy sugars come out storming! Smoke, citrus, honey (ulmo, what else?), butterscotch...all left in their wake...; **f23** the oak catches up with the grist, the phenols begins to pupate into something more tingling and spicy while a softer Werther's Original candy ups the creaminess; **b24** a gentle giant of a malt: an exercise in restraint and balance. *46%. Celtic Whisky Compagnie.*

❖ **100% Rye** db **(85.5) n21 t23 f20.5 b21.** Massively flavoursome. Aided by a wide cut, the rye at first jolts then quietens as the delicious honey and fudge control the middle. As expected, a bitter finish. *46%. Celtic Whisky Compagnie.*

DISTILLERIE GUILLON
Guillon No. 1 Single Malt de la montagne de Reims db **(87) n22 t21 f22 b22.** Right. I'm impressed. Not exactly faultless, but enough life here really to keep the tastebuds on full alert; By and large well made and truly enjoyable. Well done, Les Chaps! *46%*

DISTILLERIE MEYER
Meyer's Whisky Alsacien Blend Superieur db **(88.5) n22.5 t22.5 f21.5 b22.** Impressively clean, barley-thick and confident: a delight. *40%*

DISTILLERIE WARENGHEM
Armorik db **(91) n23 t22 f23 b23.** I admit it; I blanched, when I first nosed this, so vivid was the memory of the last bottling. This, though ,was the most pleasant of surprises. Fabulous stuff: one of the most improved malts in the world. *40%*

Armorik Double Maturation finished in oloroso casks db **(75) n18.5 t20 f18 b18.5.** Dull and decidedly out of sorts. *46%. ncf.*

Armorik Millésime Matured for 10 Years cask no. 3261 db **(92) n22.5 t23 f23 b23.** Never quite know what you are going to get from these messieurs. Didn't expect this bottle of delights, I must say. The sweetness is a bit OTT at one point, but just copes. *56.1%. sc.*

Armorik Sherry Finish db **(92) n22.5 t23.5 f23 b23.5.** The first sherry finish today which has not had a sulphur problem...and I'm in my eighth working hour...! Bravo guys! If their Classic was a note on sophistication, then this was an essay. *40%*

DOMAINE MAVELA
❖ **P&M Corsican Single Malt Whisky Aged 14 Years** db **(92) n23.5** a kind of strange muscovado-laced tannin with a meaty duck l'orange...unique – and very attractive; **t23** an instant battle between the good sugars and evil oak. Both land telling wounds on the other and it is the molasses which retreat...; **f22.5** pretty bitter and dry as the tannins really squeeze hard, though at least offering some cocoa as compensation; also some oils from a once thick cut begin to accumulate...; **b23** as we are moving back to the earlier days of the distillery, you can pick out the odd technical flaw that appears to have been ironed out later down the line. But always entertaining and intriguing with its series of bold strokes from the chunky oak nose to the bittering finish. *42%*

KAERILIS
Kaerilis Le Grand Dérangement 15 Ans db **(78) n18 t22 f19 b19.** A breakdown of the oils doesn't help reveal the weaknesses from the distillate. A must for fans de nougat. *43%. nc ncf sc.*

Kaerilis l'Aube du Grand Dérangement 15 Ans db **(83.5) n20 t22.5 f20 b21.** Misfires when the revs are up, but purrs for moment on two on delivery as the sugar and barley kicks in to delicious effect. An enigmatic fruitiness enriches. *57%. nc ncf sc.*

WAMBRECHIES DISTILLERY
Wambrechies Single Malt Aged 8 Years db **(83) n20 t21 f21 b21.** There's that aroma again, just like the 3-y-o. Except how it kind of takes me back 30 years to when I hitchhiked across the Sahara. Some of the food I ate with the local families in Morocco and Algeria was among the best I have ever tasted. And here is an aroma I recognize from that time, though I can't say specifically what it is (tomatoes, maybe?). Attractive and unique to whisky, that's for sure. I rather like this malt. There is nothing quite comparable to it. One I need to investigate a whole lot more. *40%*

UNSPECIFIED
❖ **Vicomte Single Malt Whisky Aged 8 Years** Cognac barrels **(86) n22 t22 f21 b21.** Just like so much Cognac, this whisky has a distinctive toffee theme which makes for a rather too easy going malt. Just not enough peaks and troughs to add "interesting" to "enjoyable" in the description of this caramel-laden malt. From the attractive silky texture, I would not be surprised to learn the Cognac barrels in which this whisky laid were hand made by Asterix. *40% (80 proof)*

Blends

P&M Blend Supérieur (82) n21 t21 f20 b20. Bitter and botanical, though no shortage of complexity. 40%. Mavela Distillerie.

P&M Whisky (89) n22 t23 f22 b22. No mistaking this is from a fruit distillery. Still quite North American, though. 40%

Vatted Malts
KAERILIS

Kaerilis Ster Vraz No 9 4 Year Old db **(80) n22 t21 f18 b19.** Plenty of salt and no little citrus. But undone by an oaky bitterness. 45%. nc ncf.

Kaerilis Ster Vraz No 9 4 Year Old db **(87) n21.5 t23.5 f20 b22.** What the hell was that...??? Something different, for sure. At its best, quite stunning. At its worst – at the death – hmmm, not great. Get your bucket and spade out for this one. 61.8%. nc ncf.

GERMANY
BAULAND BRENNEREI ALT ENDERLE ROSENBURG. WORKING.

Alt Enderle Neccarus 8 Years Old Single Malt Whisky db **(90.5) n22** surprisingly salty; **t23** one of Europe's most distinguished deliveries, being both gentle and rounded yet lively. Spicy but with a feel of boiled cherry sweets; **f23** more cough sweet depth, the salt lingers as the oaks arrive; **b22.5** a gently complex, delightful malt. Had it been scotch, I would have thought it was a coastal dram. Odd...! 43%

Alt Enderle Neccarus 12 Years Old Single Malt Whisky db **(94) n23.5** a rich, fruity incarnation; **t23.5** superbly clean malt flushes the palate with myriad lively fruit notes of grape, cherry and plum. The spices are just about perfect in terms of intensity; **f23** long, good vanilla and butterscotch addition, though the fruit and spice carries the load; **b24** technically, among the best malt I have ever encountered from Germany. 43%

Alt Enderle Neccarus 15 Years Old Port Fass Single Malt Whisky db **(92.5) n23** another salty Neccarus: dry grape skin comes over in waves; **t23.5** eye-watering fruit and saline mix; the sugars are subdues and of a fudgy style before mocha begins to soften the moment; **f23** a lovely chocolate and raisin fade; **b23** a chocolate mousse is on the loose. 51%

Alt Enderle Neccarus 15 Years Old Sherry Fass Single Malt Whisky db **(86.5) n21 t22 f21.5 b22.** Clean sherry. But, after the mouth-watering delivery, relatively sweet and simple with just not enough gear changes. Pleasant, if not up to the standard of the other Neccarus. 49%

BRENNEREI DANNENMANN Owen. Working.

Danne's Single Grain Schwäbischer Whisky Vom Bellerhof dist 2006, bott L 0011 db **(85) n21 t22 f21 b21.** A rock hard whisky which crunches its way around the palate giving off flavours as flint might sparks. Eye-watering in places, though the rigid Demerara sugars are a treat. 43%

Danne's Single Grain Schwäbischer Whisky Vom Bellerhof dist 06, cask strength, bott 11 db **(88.5) n22** big oak statement: almost bourbon in its liquorice and hickory firmness; **t22.5** the house crash-bang-wallop delivery can be expected from the 43% abv bottling. Liquorice and hickory coated oils make the Demerara a softer prospect and helps it stick to the palate longer, though the spices have a bit of clout; **f22** thick finale with the accent back on the bourbon: some cocoa teams up with the spiced hickory; **b22** a good example of how reducing a whisky can damage it: compare this to the 43% version and here you see the oils unbroken and softening the flavour procession. 51.1%

Danne's Single Malt Schwäbischer Whisky Vom Bellerhof dist 09, bott code L 0017 db **(81) n19 t21.5 f20 b20.5.** A strange combination of nougat and thinness to the body: the over-widening of the cut usually results in nougat and heavy oils. Never finds a happy rhythm. 43%

Danne's Single Malt Schwäbischer Whisky Vom Bellerhof dist 09, cask strength, bott code L 0017 db **(87) n20 t23 f22 b22.** A huge whisky which kicks a lot harder than its 55% abv. Works a lot better than its sister 43% bottling, making the most of the golden syrup and grist mix, and the spiced cocoa fade. Pretty enjoyable. 54.9%

BRENNEREI FELLER Dietenheim-Regglisweiler, Working

◈ **Augutus Corado Single Grain Whisky Port Cask** db **(83) n21.5 t23 f19 b20.** Unlike their Valerie Amorone cask, where the malt and grape are in perfect harmony, here we have a situation where the fruit influence has bullied the barley into submission. And, sadly, the port pipe appears to have been treated somewhere along the way, thus imparting a dull furriness to the finish in particular. 40%

◈ **Valerie Amarone Single Malt Whisky 4 Years Old** db **(95.5) n23** a thick, indulgent nose, brimming with spice and sherry trifle...; **t24.5** wow...!! What a delivery...what an astonishingly rich mouth feel. The grape is not just clean but absolutely layered with so many stratum of varying intensity and fruit significance that it is almost impossible to count...; **f23.5** long, with continuous spiced strands which almost refuse to fade; **b24.5** I think I'm in love with Valerie. 48%

 Valerie Single Malt Whisky db **(92) n23** orange blossom honey and Turkish delight; malt grist can also be detected, alongside some guttural spices; **t23.5** a real sweetie, living up to the nose's promise. Abounds with diluted honey tones as well as thinned maple syrup and treacle. A little oak- induced toffee makes an entrance. One of the sweetest, yet entirely charming whiskies on the European scene; **f22** a little oily as the vague feints at last reveal themselves. But spices more than compensate; **b23.5** if this was named after someone called Valerie, then she should be thrilled and honoured, as she must be a sweet, well-balanced and beautiful lady... 48%

BRENNEREI FRANK RODER Aalen - Wasseralfingen. Working.
Frank's Suebisch Cask Strength 2008 db **(91) n22 t23 f23 b23.** Frank has really got the hang of how to make the most of his still...a little stunner! And his cleanest yet. 57%

Frank's Suebisch Single Grain 2007 db **(86.5) n21.5 t22 f21.5 b21.5.** Consistent, gristy, mouth-watering fare. Does not try to be spectacular. More dissolving sugars this time. 40%

BRENNEREI HENRICH Kriftel, Hessia. Working.
Gilors Fino Sherry Cask sherry cask, bott code L13032, dist Apr 10, bott May 13 db **(89.5) n21 t22.5 f23 b23.** Bravo! A sherry butt with not a hint of sulphur! 44%. sc. 866 bottles.

Gilors Port Cask sherry, bott code L13033, dist 2010, bott 2013 db **(86) n20 t22 f22.5 b21.5.** Thoroughly enjoyable and full of depth and no little fruit and spice. But the wide cut, apparent in the sherry version, is not tamed in quite the same effortless way. 44%. sc.

BRENNEREI HÖHLER Aarbergen, Kettenbach. Working.
 Whesskey Hessischer Barley-Whisky bott code GW 01-15 db **(84) n19 t22 f21.5 b21.5.** Follows a similar path to the corn whisky, except this has a dried grass/hay edge and never quite reaches those same heights of chocolatey deliciousness. 44%

 Whesskey Hessischer Blend-Whisky bott code BW 01-15 db **(90.5) n23** a wonderful nose, with a Milky Bar nougat and milk chocolate lead and outstanding secondary Demerara sugars; **t22** rich from the off, with sugars linking early with spice to make for a massively busy start; **f23** chewy to the death with a little more nougat now coming in with toffee; the spices ramp up the ante...; **b22.5** a typical Hohler slightly flawed stunner. 44%

 Whesskey Hessischer Corn-Whisky bott code MW 01-15 db **(87.5) n20.5 t23 f22 b22.** Though the nose leaves you in no doubt about the feints at work, the beauty of the chocolate wafer and Nutella is there to be savoured. 44%

 Whesskey Hessischer Rye-Malt-Whisky bott code MW 01-15 db **(84.5) n19 t22 f21.5 b22.** After the usual less than impressive nose, this is an earthy beast which grows on you. Hefty hardly touches it: the chunky sugars aids the clanking rye no end. 44%

 Whesskey Hessischer Single Malt Whisky bott code CA 01-15 db **(81) n18.5 t21 f21 b20.5.** Despite the fact it has all kinds of flavour permutations, it is hard to get beyond the butyric. 44%

 Whesskey Hessischer Whisky au Dinkel bott code DW 01-14 db **(86) n21 t21.5 f22 b21.5.** Brimming with character, the oils ensure the flavours keep building to the sweet end. Gristy at times, then more spicy as the oils accumulate. Plenty of burnt fudge as it progresses. 40%

BRENNEREI MACK, Gütenbach. Working
 Kilpen Single Malt Malt Whisky Single Barrel bott code L14092108 db **(88) n21.5** the vague heaviness of the still is perfectly countered by toffee and dates; **t22.5** gorgeous spice and barley mix. The sugars are half Demerara and half molasses; **f22** more creamy toffee, but beautifully spiced up; **b22** attractively distilled and delightfully matured whisky. 40%

BRENNEREI ZIEGLER Freudenberg, North Württemberg. Working.
 Aureum 1865 5 Year Old db **(87) n21.5 t22 f21.5 b22.** A tad feinty and nutty, but the huge barley makes this entertaining and sweet in all the right places. 43%

 Aureum 1865 2008 Cask Strength db **(84.5) n21 t21.5 f21 b21.** A massive whisky, in no little part due to the very wide cut back in 2008. The usual nougat, hazelnut and cocoa gang up in the thick oils. 53.9%

 Aureum 1865 Château Lafite Rothschild casks, dist 2008, bott 2015 db **(85) n20.5 t23 f20 b21.5.** Tight, hard, grapey, beautifully sweet on delivery but with some furriness. 47%

Aureum 1865 Grave Digger 6 Year Old db (88) n22 salty and oily. Layers of molasses; t22.5 a yielding delivery, soft with fertile malt. Mocha arrives early, a light feint buzz a little later; f22 excellent spice; the mocha notes persist; b22 this grave digger goes deep. *43%*

Aureum 1865 Single Malt 5 Years Old db (86) n20.5 t22.5 f21.5 b21.5. Mocha with plenty of grist and muscovado stirred in. *43%*

Aureum 1865 Vontage Single Malt 2008 db (90.5) n20 t24 f23. Still one enormous barley orgy, though a little bit of chalky butterscotch and cocoa tries to offer a towel of modesty; b23.5 after a less than great start on the nose it truly blows you away with a massive impact. *53.9%*

DESTILLERIE HERMANN MÜHLHÄUSER Working.

Mühlhäuser Oberwalder Single Grain bott code L0612 db (86.5) n22 t22 f21 b21.5. Enjoyable, showing sturdy and at times sophisticated oak and good early sugar structure. The grain is a bit on the shy side, though: may have had a better chance to shine at 46%. *40%*

Mühlhäuser Schwäbischer Whisky aus Korn bott code L1012 db (85) n21 t21 f21.5 b21.5. Clean, crisp, sweet, honeyed: am I the only one who thinks this tastes like distilled Golden Grahams...? *40%*

Mühlhäuser Schwäbischer Whisky aus Korn db (90) n22.5 t23 f22 b22.5. So different! If you are into this, it'll be pastoral perfection. *40%*

EDELBRAENDE-SENFT Salem-Rickenbach. Working.

Senft Bodensee Whisky bott code L-SW39, dist Apr 12, bott Apr 15 db (86) n21.5 t22 f21 b21.5. Now come to expect the feints to be part of the make up! Here, they help generate an attractive toasted nuttiness which, with the slight nougat, toffee and late cocoa, kind of makes an acceptable whisky version of Topic candy...though it has rationed the sugars. *42%. nc.*

Senft Bodensee Whisky dist Dec 2010, bott Dec 2013, bott code L-SW37 db (83.5) n21 t22 f20 b21. Usual feints but really good distribution of sugared almonds. *42%. nc.*

Senft Bodensee Whisky dist Dec 10, bott Jul 14, bott code L-SW38 db (84) n21 t22 f20 b21. Intriguing and attractive mixture of citrus and celery. Some feinty cocoa around. *42%. nc.*

Senft Bodensee Whisky Fabstäke db (87.5) n21 t22.5 f22 b22. Despite the obvious feintiness, strikes out with an impressive boldness. A mysterious smokiness adds lustre to the muscovado sugars and extra weight. *55%. nc.*

FEINDESTILLERIE BÜCHNER Langenbogen. Working

Büchner Single Malt db (89) n22.5 superb malt: clean and alive with gristy sugars. Refreshing and sexy; t22 light oils, but never enough to discourage the barley from showing to full effect; f22.5 those oils confirm the wider cut, but celebrate their extra body with a malty, spicy display of defiance; b22 a wonderfully characterful and enjoyable malt. *43%*

FINCH HIGHLAND WHISKY DISTILLERY Nellingen, Alb-Donau. Working.

Finch Schwäbischer Highland Whisky Barrel Proof bott Jan 15 db (94) n23 intense manuka honey spread over mildly burnt toast: plenty of sugar at work...just most of it lightly incinerated; t24 now that is beautiful in any language; by any standards. A delicate creaminess to the mouth feel helps ensure that lightly fried manuka honey clings to every crevice; there is also a dried dates toffeeness, yet without the whisky being particularly fruity; f23.5 long, with the oils refusing to budge. Continuing waves of manuka break on the toasty, slightly overdone butterscotch tart shore; b23.5 epic! *54%*

Finch Schwäbischer Highland Whisky Single Malt bott Oct 15 db (76.5) n19 t21.5 f17 b19. Too fruity and far too aggressively bitter: I assume a sherry cask is at work here somewhere. What a pity. *42%*

Finch Schwäbischer Highland Whisky XS bott Oct 15 db (86) n22 t22 f20.5 b21.5. A pleasant, even whisky which hardly sweats as it goes through the malty, occasionally sugar-laden motions. Ultra simplistic by Finch standards: a bird which sings only intermittently. *40%*

Finch Schwäbischer Whisky Single Malt Barrel Proof 3/14 db (89) n22.5 t22.5 f22 b22. This distillery has upped its game. Hugely impressive whisky, even if liberties have been taken with the spirit run: you got away with it! Well done, chaps! *54%.*

Finch Schwäbischer Whisky Single Malt Distillers Edition 03/14 db (93) n22.5 a soft mosaic of malt and toffee, enriched by the odd strand of something a little grassy; t23 silky soft delivery, the odd hint of raisin in the creamy fudge; f24 long with the cream bun fade, perhaps with a hint of juicy sherry trifle: delicate and elegant to a fault...and topped with a sublime late spice; b23.5 from inside my tasting room I am looking out onto my quintessential English garden, ancient-walled and rose clad; and the thousand year old church which stands a few tombstones back strikes four bells. The birds continue their frenzy of feeding their young. I am regarding a goldfinch now, its golden wing and red face reflecting the afternoon sun and below it, on the feeders, are greenfinches gorging on the sunflower colonels. Below them, hopping around on the ground are chaffinches, mopping up the fallen seeds. Finches, finches everywhere. Even in my tasting room. And all of them gladdening my heart... *42%*.

HAMMERSCHMIEDE Zorge. Working.

The Alrik Edition 1912 The Early Bird matured in 1st-fill PX hogsheads, finished in fresh 1st-fill PX Butts db **(84) n21 t22 f20 b21.** I have long struggled with PX and peat together. Just find it too much: a bit like having sex while someone is tickling your feet. Certainly this K2 of a malt has its merits, as it is rather wonderfully distilled and the early sugars are a delight. But I have to say the other "s" word is in there also, though under this smoky onslaught, it nearly gets away with it. *52.3%. nc ncf. 1111 bottles.*

The Alrik Edition 1913 Mittsommer matured in three 1st-fill Marsala hogsheads, finished in one 1st-fill PX butt db **(92) n23 t23.5 f22 b23.5.** An enormous, salivating whisky which makes light of the odd defect. Concentrate on the sugar and smoke mix and you will be blown away. *49.7%. nc ncf. 666 bottles.*

The Alrik Edition 1912 Mittwinter 1st-fill PX hogsheads, finished in 1st-fill Château d'Yquem db **(89) n23 t23.5 f20 b22.5.** Nothing too bleak about this Mittwinter... *49.7%. nc ncf.*

The Glen Els Banyul Aged 5 Years Cask Strength cask no. 6/11, dist 26 May 2008, bott 24 Jun 2013, bott code. L1551 db **(92) n23 t23 f22.5 b23.5.** Love the way the sugars are controlled throughout. And a clean wine cask goes a long way... *46.6%. sc.*

The Glen Els Cream Sherry Aged 5 Years Cask Strength cask no. 135, dist 03 Jun 08, bott 04 Mar 14, bott code. L1590 db **(87) n21 t23 f22 b21.** An interesting one, this. As you know, I bang on big time angered by the use of sherry-treated casks in whisky. Here we have a cream sherry cask which appears innocent of any such possible charges against it. It is, to all intents and purposes, clean. Yet on this occasion it disappoints. Like the Malaga bottling it is rounder than a billiard ball and softer than blancmange. But, unlike the Malaga, it doesn't have quite enough personality to entertain. A little bit of a one trick pony, with its toffee-raisin nose, delivery and finish. Enjoyable, but travels over some flat and featureless land. *48.2%.*

The Glen Els Moscatel Aged 5 Years Cask Strength cask no. 146, dist 03 Jun 08, bott 24 Jul 13, bott code. L1552 db **(86) n22.5 t21.5 f21 b21.** A busy little so-and-so. Perfectly enjoyable and clean. But one of those occasions where the fruit and woodsmoke fail to find a common ground, a bit like David Cameron and Angela Merkel at any given moment, meaning there is little room for compromise and plenty for discord. *46%. sc. 251 bottles.*

The Glen Els Rivesaltes Aged 5 Years Cask Strength cask no. 126, dist 26 May 08, bott 22 Apr 13, bott code. L1597 db **(93) n23.5 t23 f23 b23.5.** It is just coming u to two in the afternoon and I have been tasting since 7:30am. And this is the first genuinely enjoyable whisky of the day: thank you Glen Els! *46.6%. sc. 246 bottles.*

The Glen Els Four Seasons 2014 Rich Madiera bott code. L1591 db **(75) n19 t20 f18 b18.** Fruity, for sure. But spoiled by the all too familiar invasion of sulphur. Many Germans, though, will interpret this as "smoke". In this case, no smoke without ire... *45.9%. 264 bottles.*

The Glen Els Four Seasons 2014 Ruby Port bott code. L1589 db **(90) n22 t23 f22 b23.** A miniscule hint of feints on nose and finish but otherwise a malt which really makes the most of the high quality Port influence. *45.9%. 400 bottles.*

The Glen Els Rare & Special Malaga Single Cask Release Aged 6 Years cask no. 83, dist 17 Jan 2008, bott 22 Apr 14, bott code. L1596 db **(94) n24 t23 f23.5 b23.5.** If there was a "Soft As A Baby's Bum" award in this book, this'd probably walk away with it... *46.6%. 348 bottles.*

The Glen Els Rarities 2013 bott code. L1578 db **(88.5) n22 t22 f22.5 b22.** Should be called Varieties: after all, it is the spice of life... *45.9%. nc ncf. 222 bottles.*

The Glen Els Wayfare The Cask Strength bott code. L1587 db **(93) n22.5 t23 f24 b23.5.** Some kind of oily, hallucinogenic, sugar, cocoa and spice concoction which plays is played out at maximum volume. The word "big" hardly does it justice... *57.9%. nc ncf.*

KINZIGBRENNEREI MARTIN BROSAMER Biberach. Working.

◈ **Badischer Whisky Blended** db **(87.5) n21 t22.5 f22 b22.** A little of the distillery's old nougat style shows its ankles, but otherwise, much cleaner with progressive sugars working in tandem with the growing, faintly wide-cut spice. Very pleasant. *42%*

◈ **Biberacher Whisky Single Malt** bott code L:MWJ15 db **(85) n20 t22.5 f21 b21.5.** A forthright, competent and confident delivery maximises every last degree of sugars in the grist for a sumptuous maltfest. The usual over-enthusiastic oils diminish the effect slightly on both nose and finish. *42%*

◈ **Kinzigtäler Whisky Single Malt Smoke** db **(88.5) n21.5** maybe not technically on the money, but the pip-squeakingly dry smokiness also helps introduce a degree of cocoa to the scene; **t22.5** a little fat, as usual, but the sugars now have a third, more phenolic dimension and linger attractively; **f22** a rather lovely mix of chocolate and ginger cake; **b22.5** the phenols have much to say. *42%*

⟐ **Schwarzwälder Whisky Rye** db **(81) n19 t22 f20 b20**. Few aromas are more scary in whisky than over-cut, feinty rye. Here it is in full, spoon-standing oiliness. Which means the flavours can also power through the roof. Not exactly for the purist. *42%*

⟐ **Single Barrel Whisky No. 5 -Select** bott code L:5A14 db **(86) n21.5 t22 f21 b21.5**. An interesting battle between less than technically brilliant spirit and, evidently, some very decent oak. The spirit wins - or loses, if you see what I mean. But the strands of acacia honey and light liquorice are a joy. *40%*

⟐ **Single Barrel Whisky No. 8 -Select** bott code L:8A14 db **(83.5) n19 t21 f22 b21.5**. Fruity nougat. There is a big sherry influence here which makes for an occasionally flat landscape with hills and valleys conspicuous by their absence. But no amount of clean fruit can entirely compensate for the enormity of the nougat. *40%*

KLEINBRENNEREI FITZKE Herbolzheim-Broggingen. Working.

⟐ **Derrina Einkorn-Malz Schwarzwälder Single Malt** bott code L12010 **(83.5) n20.5 t21.5 f20.5 b21**. Where tobacco meet hay lofts. An impressive, even whisky in part with some decent sugar and barley. *43%*

⟐ **Derrina Gerstenmalz Buchenrauch Schwarzwälder Single Malt** bott code L13211 **(88) n21** earthy...complete with vegetables...and bubble gum; **t22.5** neutral at first, then some peculiar phenols and buzzing spices begin to make some interesting little speeches; **f22** long, an expansion of oils; very late on, some gorgeous liquorice and ulmo honey appear as if from nowhere; **b22.5** worth a revisit. On first impression...not happy with it, as the narrative appears incomprehensible and a little ugly. On second...the vague, weird smokiness and spice begins to grow on you. *43%*

⟐ **Derrina Gerstenmalz Torfrauch Stark Schwarzwälder Single Malt** bott code L13111 **(77) n19 t19 f20 b19**. Despite the late injection of maple syrup and mocha, this one fails on many levels. *43%*

⟐ **Derrina Hafer Schwarzwälder Single Grain** bott code L6208 **(94) n24** so many bourbon notes which win the heart: treacle and honeycomb plus the inevitable ulmo honey: magnificent! **t23** a heart-warming blend of what appears to be intense, salivating barley with crisper bourbon tones; fabulous weight and slow spice infusion; **f23.5** outstanding oils and a slow building of chocolate and hazelnut; the busy spice continue to pulse; **b23.5** voluptuously beautiful. *43%*

⟐ **Derrina Karamell-Malz Gerste Schwarzwälder Single Malt** bott code L13411 **(87) n21 t22 f22 b22**. For those who like whisky with their nougat.. Bold, gristy sugars throughout. *43%*

⟐ **Derrina Karamell-Malz Roggen Schwarzwälder Single Malt** bott code L13511 **(83.5) n20 t21 f21.5 b21**. For those who like whisky with their hay bales....Busy spices punctuates the barley sugar. Green doesn't quite over it... *43%*

⟐ **Derrina Karamell-Malz Weizen Schwarzwälder Single Malt** bott code L13311 **(87.5) n21 t22 f22 b22.5**. Toffee nougat with an enjoyable barley and chocolate flourish. Really enjoyable. *43%*

⟐ **Derrina Sorghum-Malz Schwarzwälder Single Malt** bott code L10509 **(88.5) n23.5** I know a lot of Germans settled in Kentucky... The bourbon influence of style is astonishing with honeycomb and liquorice leading the way with a touch of ulmo honey to soften; **t22** light oils and heavy honey. A little feintiness hits the midground; **f21** the earlier rhythm has been lost: goes slightly off course; **b22** a hit and miss malt. But when it scores, it's a bullseye... *43%*

MÄRKISCHEN SPEZIALITÄTEN BRENNEREI Hagen. Working.

⟐ **DeCavo Handcrafted Single Malt** cask no. 9/2044 db **(91) n22** That is one very malty aroma. Clean, too...; **t23**...and no less malty on delivery. Horlicks night drink with grass and maple syrup stirred in; **f23** some light oaky vanillas while the spice is from the work of the stills. But the malt retains its dominance; **b23** a whisky which puts the malt into single malt. *46%. sc.*

⟐ **Edelsthal Moonshiner White Single Malt** db **(88) n19 t23 f23 b23**. Now that is interesting stuff. The nose wins no beauty prizes. But there is no faulting the complexity and richness of the spirit on the palate, nor the astonishing degree of ulmo honey which somehow makes its way into the new make. Beyond the nose, very impressive, indeed. *50%*

⟐ **Tronje Von Hagen Single Malt Höhlenwhisky** cask no. 2, bott 21 Aug 14 db **(94.5) n23** honey roast almonds with Demerara sugar as a side dish...; **t24** brilliant delivery: you expect a brittle crispness to the sugars and they arrive early, but not before the lush, mouth-massaging and intense barley has already made its gristy presence felt: salivating and, as the spices arrive, invigorating...; **f23.5** chocolate honey fade with a little mint sprinkled in. But the spiced barley sugar carries on regardless; **b24** now, just how confident a whisky is that....? 55%. sc.

NORDPFÄLZER EDELOBST & WHISKYDESTILLE Höning. Working.

⬧ **Taranis Pfälzer 3 Years Old Single Malt Whisky** Amarone cask finished, dist Sept 11 db **(86) n21 t22.5 f20.5 b22**. A little feintier and thicker than last bottling. Even so, the quality of the wine cask is exceptional and makes best use of the nougat and toffee on show. 50.5%.

Taranis Pfälzer 4 Years Old Single Malt Whisky Amarone Cask Finished dist Sept 09 db **(88.5) n22 t23.5 f21 b22**. Big and rather beautiful, in its own cumbersome way...especially in its delivery of fruit. 50.80%. 440 bottles.

SAUERLÄNDER EDELBRENNEREI Ruthen-Kallenhardt. Working.

⬧ **Thousand Mountains Mc Raven Single Malt Whisky** cask no. L1003 03.2012 db **(74.5) n16 t21 f18.5 b19**. A massively wide cut means this is a gluepot of a whisky. Best ignore the nose and concentrate on the delivery which has its magnificently sugared moments. But, as is to be expected, an oily, untamed beast. 46.2%

SEVERIN SIMON Alzenau-Michelbach, Aschaffenburg. Working.

⬧ **Simon's Bavarian Pure Pott Still** db **(86) n21 t22 f21 b22**. Always great to renew acquaintances with this idiosyncratic malt. I remember lots of pine last time out. Here the pine is remarkable for its almost lack of interest in this whisky after the nose. Which means this is a better bottling, with the malt – man marked by crisp sugars – having a much louder say than normal. Some soft, creamy toffee and nougat at play. But the spices and barley are most enjoyable. 40%

SLYRS Schliersee-Neuhaus. Working.

Slyrs Bavarian Single Malt Sherry Edition No. 1 finished in Oloroso, lot no. L00354, bott 2013 db **(86) n20 t22 f22 b22**. Anyone out there who loves cream toffee and spice? This malt has your name on it. 46%

Slyrs Bavarian Single Malt Sherry Edition No. 1 finished in Pedro Ximénez, lot no. L02491, bott 2013 db **(88.5) n21 t23 f22 b22.5**. Can't say PX is usually my favourite cask for whisky maturation. But I doff my feathered hat to these clever Bavarians: it has done the trick here! 46%

STEINHAUSER DESTILLERIE Kressbronn, Baden-Württemberg. Working.

Brigantia 3 Years Old bott L-12/12 db **(79) n19 t21 f19 b20** Huge malt statement, as is the distillery style. But it appears someone decided to try and extract as much spirit as possible, because the cut seems to be a little too wide for comfort here: the oils are unforgiving. 43%

WEINGUT MÖSSLEIN Kolitzheim. Working.

⬧ **Mößlein Grain Whisky 5 Years Old** db **(87.5) n21.5 t22.5 f21.5 b22**. It's all about the oak. The tannins are the driving force for both the darker, more brooding phases – of which there are many - and the sugars. Some pleasant minty chocolate to be had if you look carefully enough. 41%

⬧ **Mößlein Single Malt Whisky 5 Years Old** db **(77) n18.5 t20 f19 b19.5**. The early butyric makes it difficult for the malt to re-align to positive effect. 42%

WHISKY DESTILLERIE LIEBL Bad Kötzting. Working.

⬧ **Coillmór Bavarian Single Malt Bordeaux Cask** cask no. 398, dist Oct 09 db **(87) n21.5 t21.5 f22 b22**. A stable bottling allowing the fruit to make the best use of the light nougat to offer a rich, rounded, lightly fruited malt. Well balanced, salivating and a joy to experience. 46%.

⬧ **Coillmór Bavarian Single Malt Port Cask 8 Years Old** cask no. 351, dist 4 May 07 db **(79.5) n21 t20 f19 b19.5**. Even a Port cask has problems seeing off the excesses of the massively heavy nougat. Rough. 46%. 1080 bottles.

⬧ **Coillmór Bavarian Single Malt Alabanach Peat American oak**, cask no. 47, dist 17 Jul 10 db **(81.5) n20 t21 f20 b20.5**. I'll give the peat from this distillery one thing: it really is idiosyncratic. No other smoked whisky is so jarring and a liquid antonym of "rounded." An absolute must for any serious collector or student of peated whisky. 46%. 392 bottles.

⬧ **Coillmór Bavarian Single Malt American Oak** cask nos. 60,214,229,268339, dist May 10 db **(83) n21 t20 f21 b21**. A malt with a huge nougat input. Lots of toffee, but curiously little sweetness. 43%. 1895 bottles.

⬧ **Coillmór Bavarian Single Malt Distillers Edition Peated Oloroso Sherry Cask** cask no. 81, dist 28 Aug 10 db **(80) n20 t21 f19 b20**. When you see peat and oloroso on the same whisky label, it tends to be a bottling you leave until the end of the day's work. If anything can hide sulphur until it is too late, it is peat. Too often have my taste buds been wrecked in this fashion. Well, my palate is still intact. Just. Though it was a close run thing: there is a buzz on the finish which might be the fault of the cask. But so clanking and grinding is the original course peat spirit, it is hard to tell. If you are simply a smoke head, then this really might just be a whisky right down your strasse. *46%. 895 bottles.*

WHISKY-DESTILLERIE ROBERT FLEISCHMANN Eggolsheim. Working.

⬧ **Austrasier Single Cask Grain Whisky** cask no. 2, dist May 08, bott Jun 15 db **(88.5) n22** not dissimilar to a spice-seasoned cake baking; **t23** the softest delivery, then a slow rising of spiced – or is that herbed? – barley; **f21.5** just a little bitter towards the end as the spices and other tannins merge; **b22** few European whiskies come as flavoursome as this. *40%. sc.*

⬧ **Blaue Maus Single Cask Malt Whisky Fassstärke** German oak casks, cask no. 1, dist Jun 98, bott May 15 db **(94) n22.5** whisky...? Pot still rum? A distillate of hay? Cream toffee concentrate...? **t24** though the feints are apparent early on, the oils drag with them a fascinating mix of copper and manuka honey. That is just the start. Next comes that mind-boggling, puzzling and mesmerising display of multi-layered, fizzing, buzzing biting spice...; **f23.5** here comes that toffee again. Though armed to the teeth in spices and ulmo honey; **b24** a sexy, subtle malt which seduces you from the moment the first sweet drop touches your lips... *57.5%. sc.*

⬧ **Blaue Maus Single Cask Malt Whisky Fassstärke** German oak casks, cask no. 2, dist Jun 92, bott Jun 15 db **(92.5) n22** about as salty and coastal as a malt might get...in mainly land-locked Germany; **t24** the lush delivery defies the strength...though the peppery spices don't. The early exchanges are all about honey: on the fourth mouthful, I had counted five different styles at play: manuka and heather lead the way, though. Liquorice and hickory underline the vintage; **f23** dry, with the hickory taking control. A little maple syrup comes to the rescue; but those spices just nip and bite...; **b23.5** an exhausting whisky to taste: so much is happening, it is hard to know which bit to concentrate on... *48.7%. sc.*

⬧ **Blaue Maus Single Cask Malt Whisky** dist Mar 15 db **(89.5) n23 t23 f21 b22.5.** The oils on the tail confirms the hint on the nose that this is a wide-ish cut. But absolutely bursting with delicious malty intent. *78.4%. sc.*

⬧ **Blaue Maus Single Cask Malt Whisky** German oak casks, cask no. 2, dist Apr 07, bott Jun 15 db **(88) n21** usual array of household spices, including ginger; **t22.5** silky despite the low strength with a long cream toffee middle; below deck , the spices burn...; **f22.5** malt and toffee...so, so soft – like a feather run down the spine; **b22** the intensity of fire on the busiest of spice is unique to this distillery. *40%. sc.*

⬧ **Elbe 1 Single Cask Malt Whisky** German oak casks, cask no. 2, dist Jun 06, bott Jun 15 db **(82) n20 t21 f20 b21.** A little too coppery and feinty for its own good. *40%. sc.*

Grüner Hund Single Cask Malt cask no. 2, dist Jun 01 db **(79) n20 t19 f20 b20.** All kinds of German style biscuit spices. But the oil runs too deep. *40%. sc.*

⬧ **Grüner Hund Single Cask Malt Whisky** German oak casks, cask no. 3, dist May 08, bott Jun 15 db **(90) n21** nougat and milk chocolate; **t23** beautiful oils and satisfying toasted honeycomb; **f23** long, lightly spiced with a return of cocoa but now with butterscotch tart; **b23** a satisfying malt full of clever, varying honey tones. *40%. sc.*

⬧ **Mary Read Single Cask Malt Whisky** German oak casks, cask no. 3, dist May 07, bott Jun 15 db **(87) n20 t23 f22 b22.** The feinty, nutty nose never quite finds happiness. But the fizzing, spicy delivery is awash with dark honey. *40%. sc.*

Old Fahr III dist Jul 02 db **(89) n22.5 t22 f22 b22.5.** A complex battle of a dram. *40%*

⬧ **Spinnaker Single Cask Malt Whisky Fassstärke** German oak casks, cask no. 3, dist May 07, bott Jun 15 db **(95) n23.5** all kinds of ginger-spiced tannins and a weird thick cut marmalade citrus note. At times, this appears to be an old pot still Demerara rum. Whatever, you get the feeling you might need seat belts for the delivery...; **t24** bloody hell...! I'm not wrong! Massive doesn't begin to cover it: the spices radiating from the tannins almost blast a hole through your head, from the direction of the roof of your mouth. This is hot: pure oaky spice. But there is a counter, and it is the thick molassed sugars leading the way...; **f23.5** dries enormously thanks to the oak. But some buttery burnt fudge soothes and kisses better; **b24** explosive. And a lesson in balance. *54.2%. sc.*

⬧ **Spinnaker Single Cask Malt Whisky Fassstärke** German oak casks, cask no. 1, dist Jun 88, bott Jun 15 db **(97) n23.5** stewed dates (and yes I have occasionally stewed dates, so I know what I'm talking about!), over-ripe, exploding gooseberries...and a few kilos of timber dipped in treacle....; **t24.5** ridiculously soft, melt-in-the-mouth delivery where the honey tentatively sticks its head out to see if the oaky all clear has sounded. It then emerges as a unique cross between very old, liquorice-infested bourbon and sweet, silky molasses-based Demerara rum that has seen a good 50 years in the barrel. Rather than take the bitter oak route, it stays on this sugary path, but enough hickory is injected from the hard-bitten bourbon-style wood to ensure the sugars don't get carried away and spoil the party; **f24** rather than getting bitter, as anything with this amount of oak influence has a right to do, it instead contents itself with running through a Who's Who of sugar flavours and textures. Manuka and ulmo honeys are the main winners, as might be expected. But a treacle/maple syrup mix helps form a gloss beside the honeycomb waxiness; **b25** when fruit flies pass a few other malts to sup themselves to death in the same glass, you tend to know you are on to a winner. Rule of thumb means they head for the sweetest around: for them to find sugars to die for in a 27-year-old German malt from which you can nearly spit the splinters takes some believing. The intense, but clever, balancing sugars in there really aren't an illusion. Amazing. Truly and so beautifully amazing...! The 700th new whisky tasted for the 2016 Whisky Bible. And if it doesn't win some kind of gong, then this has been one exceptional year!! 42.9%. sc.

◇ **Sylter Watt Single Cask Malt Whisky Aged 7 Years** lot no. 1, dist 2007, bott 15 May 15 **(92.5) n23.5** there we go: that unique arrangement of honey and old leather; **t23.5** soft, chewy, silky and the slow leeching of acacia honey, light liquorice and leather: simply one of the best things you'll ever taste in Germany...though I am always on the lookout for something new...; **f22** slightly more bitter as the feints catch up. But blood orange joins the malt for the finale; **b23.5** quite unmistakable. So delighted the 666th new whisky tasted for the 2016 Bible has turned out to be Devilishly good... 40%. Distilled at Whiskydestillerie Blaue Maus.

Blends

◇ **Kahlgrund Whisky Blend (86.5) n21.5 t22 f21 b22**. A well balanced, impressively weighted whisky full of enjoyable sugars. But definitely from the nougat school of German distilling. 46%

ITALY
PUNI
Puni Alba db **(82) n20 t21 f20.5 b20.5**. Much more feinty, nutty and basic than their first offerings. Very decent body, though. 43%

Puni Opus I db **(89.5) n22.5** a gentle smokiness melts into a malty mass. The sugars are similar to those in lava form on porridge; **t23.5** the first notes are so young its voice hasn't yet broken. But then the incredible intensity of the barley shakes you while a smoky coffee strokes the taste buds; **f22** thins as the vanillas arrive. But keeps its shape...and the light smoke; **b22.5** a really exuberant whisky just choc-a-bloc with character. Bellissimo! 53.72%.

LATVIA
LATVIJAS BALZAMS Riga. Working.
L B Lavijas Belzams db **(83) n20 t22 f20 b21**. Soft and yielding on the palate, this is said to be made from Latvian rye, though of all the world's rye whiskies this really does have to be the softest and least fruity. I'll be astonished if there isn't a fair degree of thinning grain in there, too. 40%

LIECHTENSTEIN
TELSER Triesen. Working.
Telsington V 4 Years Old Pinot Noir Cask db **(88.5) n22 t22.5 f22 b22**. An friendly satisfying malt. The pinot is a bit tight, but the fruit has just enough shine and clarity. 43.5%.

Telsington Moosalp Edition Single Malt Whisky bott 2014 db **(92) n22.5** beautifully constructed: very slight nougat betrays the still while gentle toasted hazelnut and honeycomb balance things well; **t23** a soft silkiness is soon overtaken by a grander, far more robust blast of liquorice, muscovado sugar and treacle – though, cleverly, of limited sweetness. Throughout, the grain ensures a salivating edge while a darker, drier, date and vanilla thread runs confidently through; **f23.5** by far and away the classiest finish from Telser yet: the sugars remain of the right weight an intensity...and somehow last to the very end despite the nudging butterscotch; **b23** benefitting from the use of an excellent cask, a big whisky from a little country. Very distinguished. Just like the Moosalp restaurant. 42%. 50 bottles.

Telsington VI Single Cask Malt, 5 Years Old Pinot Noir cask, Swiss oak db **(94.5) n24** a nose deserving a very long study: the use of Swiss oak imparts an unusual softness to the proceedings, with the tannins willing to caress and filter rather than confront. The spices, fruit, vanilla and even barley all appear to gently drift, though tethered together. This is major sophistication at work...; **t23.5** the barley downs its fruity cape to make the first solo speech on delivery. Soon both fruit and vanilla are back in harness. Just adore the balance between the drier, though never bitter, oak and the proud sugar-gristiness of the barley. The fruit adds the background choir; **f23** long, with a slight tang from the grape but the just-so oils spread the most gentle spices imaginable and late milky mocha; **b24** I wonder if the chap at the top of the hill in that big castle above Vaduz has ever tasted this. For there is something effortlessly regal to this whisky. 43.5%. sc.

Telsington VII 5 Years Old Pinot Noir Finish db **(73.5) n18 t20 f17.5 b18.** A poor wine cask has strangled the life out of this one. A shame, as a few lovely mocha notes can be heard in the distance. Telser VI had to be better than this...where is it? 43.5%. sc.

Teslington Single Cask Malt Black Edition, 5 Years Old Pinot noir cask, French Oak db **(86) n22.5 t22 f20 b21.5.** The trouble, often, with French oak is that its tendency to dominate, even bully, shortens the complexity and ability to experience the full personality of the characters taking part. Sharp, sometimes shrill on the palate, it is certainly big. 43.5%. sc.

Telser Single Cask 100% Rye Malt, 2 Years Old db **(89.5) n22.5** the rye pulses from the glass, heavy, fruity and unmistakable; **t23.5** no other grain on the planet conjours up such intensity of flavour as malted rye – not even peated malt. That is because there is an added intensity from the sugars, usually of a Demerara bent, that amplifies the crisp, sharpness of the grain; a little spiced coffee towards the middle; **f21.5** just drops a degree or two as the heavier oils from the distillate begin to get a grip; **b22** a remarkably memorable first try at malted rye: had the cut been a tad narrower this would have been a very distinguished dram. 42%. sc.

Telsington Single Cask Rye Whisky Aged 3 Years Islay cask finish db **(90) n23** wine must: skins and pips aplenty, softened by the most gentle smoke. The rye itself cannot yet be heard...; **t23**...ah! Now it can. Not so much with the rye itself, though it does penetrate the fruit now and then, but the crispness of the backbone; **f20.5** at last: tangible, juicy rye and light smoke: intriguing and lovely; slight furriness to the finale; **b23.5** rye meets Islay, surely a match made in heaven as my two favourite whisky styles marry. I presume it had been in some kind of wine cask first, though, as there is high fruit dominance. Ticks many a box for me: well distilled, good fruit, firm grain and the most delicate smoke. Just a niggle on the finish, I fear. 42%

LUXEMBOURG
DISTILLERIE DIEDENACKER Niederdonven. Working.

Diedenacker Number One Rye Malt 2008 Aged 5 Years db **(86) n22 t22 f21 b21.** Not quite hitting the heights of their first bottling, but the nut and nougat is balanced well by crystallised treacle. 42%. 450 bottles.

THE NETHERLANDS
ZUIDAM BAARLE Nassau. Working.

◈ **Millstone Barrel Proof Rye 2004 (92.5) n24** think of the most intense rye nose you can either imagine, or have experienced. Then double it...; **t23.5** not just a massive rye surge – seemingly a mix of malted and unmalted due to the change in flavour profile – but a big dollop of acacia honey has been dropped on it to maximise the effect; strangely salty, too...; **f22** the wide cut does a little damage as the oily bitterness creeps in. But the rye and honey still go the distance and find some marzipan as a late companion; **b23** always a bottling I look forward to, as these Dutch guys know how to ramp up the rye. The nose (if you forgive the slightly wide cut!) is textbook and good to see them still flying their flag very high. 58.6%. The Whisky Exchange Exclusive. WB16/001

Millstone Aged 12 Years Sherry Cask dist 26 Feb 99, bott 22 Mar 13 db **(95) n24** superb age on this: almost like opening a bottle of 20-year-old sherry and breathing in the plump spices seeing the world for the first time in decades.... Near perfect on the sweet-dry balance: sublime; **t23.5** fresh, lively grape slowly infiltrated by much heavier and drier tannins. The vanillas really do have a big say and sway; **f23.5** stays dry, with a hint of grape must. Decidedly raisin shortcake biscuit on the finale; **b24** after last year's disappointing sherry bottling, thought I'd need some Dutch courage to tackle this one. But, instead, an excellent cask at work here which ensures an overflow of character. Just underlines the difference between putting a good quality spirit into a less than impressive cask or filling into top quality oak So, so elegant... 46% WB15/399

Millstone 1999 Aged 14 Years sherry cask, cask no. 1355, dist 26 Feb 99, bott 15 Mar 13 **(73) n18.5 t19 f17 b18.5.** Those with a penchant for German spiced biscuits will love this. Personally, I have a problem with those types of spices which can also be tasted in some Indian whiskies. 46%. sc. Distillery Region Netherlands. Milroy's Of Soho.

Zuidam 2007 Dutch Rye virgin American oak barrel, cask no. 449, dist 07, bott 13 (91.5) n24 t23 f22 b22.5. Another impressive bottling from a distillery which proves it certainly knows how to make rye. 46%. sc. Distillery Region Netherlands.

SPAIN

DYC Aged 8 Years (90) n22 t23 f22.5 b22.5. I really am a sucker for clean, cleverly constructed blends like this. Just so enjoyable! 40%

⬧ DYC Selected Blended Whisky (85.5) n21.5 t22 f21 b21. One of the cleanest and perhaps creamiest whiskies in Europe. Some gooseberry, like the malt, occasionally drifts in, ramping up the flavour profile which is anything but taxing. 40%

⬧ DYC Single Malt Whisky Aged 10 Years (91) n22 an aloof, stand-offish nose which reveals its malty and beautifully textured oak only when it gets to know you...; t23 ridiculously clean at first, then a steady build up of malt, like cars at a traffic hold up. Oils slowly form and this introduces the oak, first apologetically...then with an integrated build up of vanillas; throughout there is a gorgeous backdrop of controlled sugars; f23 a little spice begins to warm the cockles. The oak tones are pitch perfect, never too dry or heavy; late vanilla mingles contentedly with the malt; b23 far more complex than it first seems. Like Segovia, where the distillery is based, worth exploring... 40%

SWEDEN

MACKMYRA Gästrikland. Working.

Mackmyra Moment "Glod" (Glow) bott code MM-011 db (96.5) n24.5 t24.5 f23 b24.5. Technically, from a fermentation, distillation and maturation perspective: outstanding. From a blending viewpoint: masterful. Truly idiosyncratic: uniquely Mackmyra! If you are lucky enough to locate one of the remaining 1,088 bottles of this, pay what it takes... 51.2%.

Mackmyra Moment "Jord" bott code MM-004 db (93) n23 t24 f23 b23. Anyone with a fondness for bourbon might just have to get a case of this... hard to believe better casks have been used in maturation anywhere in the world this year. 55.1%

Mackmyra Moment "Källa" bott code MM-010 db (89) n22 t23 f22 b22. A bit pie-in-the-face with the avalanche of syrupy sugar. The vaguest fruitiness, but really a whisky for those looking for deliciously unsubtle power. 53.4%. 1065 bottles.

Mackmyra Moment "Malström" db (96) n24 crisp muscovado sugar but camouflaged by a complex array of malty, vanilla notes of varying hues and perhaps the most subtle spice of the year worldwide. Unusually oak dependent here, though the sweet-dry balance is exceptional; t24.5 salivating barley in almost traditional malt whisky style, but then a more examining series of deft vanilla-honey tones all wrapped as a parcel in an outer skin of heather honey. It is, unusually for a Mackmyra, the intensity of the barley which remains a constant; f23.5 long, still with crisp though controlled sugar abounding, the edge dulled by butterscotch tart. Meanwhile, that malt just keeps on giving... b24 more like "Femalstrom": very gentle and sexy...yet that self-assured power is always there: of its type an unequalled, and dominant malt. World class. 46.4%

Mackmyra Moment "Mareld" (Sea Fire) bott code MM-013 db (95) n23.5 t24 f23.5 b24. Mesmerising. They say not all the wonders have been yet discovered from the sea. Here is one that apparently just has....A malt for people with time on their hands. Anything less than an hour will do you and the whisky a disservice... 52.2%. 1600 bottles.

Mackmyra Midnattssol Single Malt Art No MC-002 db (93.5) n23 t24 f23 b23.5 a happy three-way marriage (how 1970s Swedish!) between malt in the form of breakfast cereal, complete with toasted hazel nuts, oak (displaying a bent towards caramel) and honey, in an ulmo-cum-heather format; t24 pretty fruity and juicy on delivery with an over-ripe plum squash and raspberry jelly mixing it with a more robust saline-topped vanilla and honey; a few nutty, spicy notes arrive late; f23 tangy, with the odd grumble of a tired cask, but repaired by Brazilian coconut biscuit and a vague echo of burnt raisin; the warm spices nibble contentedly; b23.5 fitting that this should be my 750th new whisky for the 2015 Bible: I had scheduled to hit that landmark by midsummer's day, but find myself tasting this just over two weeks later (thanks for nothing, the world's sulphured casks...!). However, this didn't drop into my lab until a few days ago, so it has worked out rather neatly. A silky number, this, with every character met by a calming influence. 46.1%

Mackmyra Midvinter Single Malt Art No MC-001 db (94.5) n23.5 fabulously delicate teasing of nutmeg, the lightest paprika and salted cashews...all with an undercurrent of malt, redcurrant and liquorice...wow! t24 near perfect weight to the delivery with just-so oils filling the mouth and softening things all round: almost ridiculously soft. The spices on the nose buzz, test and tease. Again the malt comes through with clarity despite the hubbub

359

surrounding it. Pretty salty, though the sugars take the strain, offering a slightly caramelled touch to absorb the growing oak; **f23** a little tangy as the oak gets to work; but a more buttery and traditional touch to this now; **b24** how fitting: probably the most Swedish of all the Mackmyra whiskies yet: reminds me of light-challenged days in that country when, at night, you would retreat to a restaurant and finish the evening with an aquavit, spiced to the owner's liking. The seasoning and smoking here takes us very close to that uniquely Swedish style. The sophistication takes the breath away... *46.1%*

Mackmyra Moment "Morgondagg" (Morning Dew) bott code MM-012 db **(93)** n24 t23 f22.5 b23.5. Another masterful Mackmyra experience. Above all, you get the feeling of a heavyweight pulling its punches... *51.1%. 1600 bottles.*

Mackmyra Moment "Rimfrost" db **(95.5)** n24 t24 f23.5 b24. I thought that they had got the name "Rimfrost" from sitting on a Stockholm park bench in the middle of a Swedish winter. Apparently not. *53.2%. 1,492 bottles.*

Mackmyra Reserve Cask ex-sherry cask, cask no. 08-0689, dist 22 Dec 08, bott 28 Aug 12 **(89)** n23 t22 f22 b22.5. The first ever Mackmyra which, on tasting blind, I mistook for an Islay. A very easy mistake to make. *51.7%. Carpets Crawlers Choice.*

◈ **Mackmyra Reserve "Queen of Fucking Everything"** recipe: Rök, Bourbon barrel, Cask no. 32, dist 24/03/2010, bott 04/09/2014 db **(94)** n24 the casual observer may see nothing to excite them here; but wait awhile. Patience and warming in the hand is repaid handsomely as a complex map of interlocking strata comes into focus, the first contours being of a vague smoked bacon variety, perhaps mixed with delicately smoked Swiss cheese. Next, the mildly sweeter vanilla and butterscotch notes – tracing the influence of the oak – begin to surface. Yet the sugars, like the smoke, appear to be kept under a cloak, refusing to display to anyone not patient enough to find them...; **t24** a much more emboldened approach on delivery than the nose ever conveys. The smoke wafts with surprising weight early on and these are reinforced by oaky sugars, juicier and more profound. The smoke takes on several guises, though each relatively deep; the sugars are dark and play their part in the heaviness of the growing mocha personality; **f22.5** a tad too bitter for its own comfort zone. But the late, half-hidden spices remind you a degree of phenols are working in tandem with the sugars until very late on; **b23.5** after over 40 years of tasting whisky – some 25 of them professionally – this is the first time I have ever encountered a brand which includes in its title the word "Everything"... *53.4%*

Mackmyra Special 09: "Vildhallon" (Wild Raspberries) bott Autumn 12, bott code MS.009 db **(89.5)** n22.5 t22 f22.5 b22.5. How interesting. First words to enter my head on nosing this was "meaty, cocoa" and on since checking the Special 08, I see I noted identical attributes. Absolutely no coincidence, that: the hallmark of a blender knowing exactly what she is setting out to achieve. *46.1%*

Mackmyra Special 10: "Kaffegök" bott Spring 13, bott code MS.010 db **(81.5)** n19 t23.5 f19 b20. Mackmyra do this from time to time: throw in a bottling which, I think, misses the target. The problem is the use of a cask or two of spirit which is not distilled with quite the same accuracy as normal. The plus side is that you are unlikely to find any malt this year which kicks off offering such a gorgeous and uninterrupted stream of acacia honey. But those extra oils are ultimately a little too burdensome for greatness. *46.1%*

Mackmyra Svensk Rök bott code MR-001 db **(93)** n23 t23.5 f23 b23.5. A very different Mackmyra in both style and sensory texture. Subtlety is the key and time is the lock. Definitely need a good half hour to unpick this one. *46.1%*

SMÖGEN

◈ **Smögen Primör Svensk Single Malt Whisky** db **(84.5)** n21.5 t22 f20 b21. Not the greatest fan of grape and smoky grist. This has its merits, though, as the fruit is succulent and the decent smoke cowers somewhat in its shadow. That said, the inevitable bitter furriness – hidden for the most part - rears its unwanted head. *63.7%*

◈ **Smögen Svensk Single Malt Whisky Sherry Project 1:1** db **(89.5)** n22.5 suety, sultana-ridden spotted dog pudding; **t22.5** eye-watering salivating from the grape covers over a slight distilling flaw; **f22** bitters very slightly but the spices make their mark; **b22.5** wow! A clean sherry butt! What a difference that makes to a malt. Not as well made as some of their other whiskies, but beautifully matured. *51.8%*

◈ **Smögen Svensk Single Malt Whisky Sherry Project 1:2** db **(94)** n23.5 now that doesn't happen very often. First you get a clean sherry butt. Then high quality smoke. And the two seem meant for each other: love at first flight...; **t23.5** a rare malt where the smoke and grape are not only comfortable bedfellows but actually work in tandem to both ramp up the juiciness and then add a chewy weight by contrast; **f23** the ulmo honey comes in to compensate for the slight suety feel beginning to form on the finish; the smoke is now much quieter; **b24** what a fantastically clever whisky: you want to learn about balance and counter balance? Spend half an hour with this chap. A malt which fully maximises all its positives and papers over the cracks quite brilliantly. *55.7%*

⏩ **Smögen Svensk Single Malt Whisky Single Cask** cask no. 20/2011 db **(93.5) n23.5** young and gristy. Rather beautifully made, if this nose is to be believed... **t24** stunning! Probably the most Islay delivery of any whisky I have ever encountered made away from that beautiful island. The nose has already planted the seeds of Port Ellen (from many years back) in my mind: the melt-in-the-mouth gristiness does nothing to remove me from this weird time and geographic warp I appear to be in; **f22** a tad toastier and spicier now, more in the Laphroaig mould...even complete with bitter cask finish; **b24** don't know whether to sit in shocked silence, or simply applaud. Tasted blind, I would have declared this young malt an Islay whisky. Truly astonishing single malt. *60.9%*

⏩ **Smögen Svensk Single Malt Whisky Single Fresh Sauternes Barrique Cask**, cask no. 7/2011, filled 11 Mar 11, bott 28 Mar 15 db **(95) n23.5** a powering sooty phenol, accompanied by salted celery, of all things; **t24** oooh! That is so good: in a complete turn round from the nose, the wine takes charge, dishing out majestic ulmo honey and spiced grape juice but allowing the phenols to insert a dense weightiness to the proceedings. Now and again the youth of the malt is apparent, but it is an irrelevance; **f23.5** a little oak bitterness seeps in, but no harm is done and the smoke tingles playfully; **b24** truly stunning. Sauternes, unsulphured like this, is unquestionably the most sympathetic of all wine barrels to mix with peat. And if you don't believe me, get your kisser around this gorgeous, naked Swede... *57.3%*

SPIRIT OF HVEN

Hven Dubhe Seven Stars Single Malt No 1 db **(84) n21 t21.5 f20.5 b21.** Very light malt displaying rich fudgy caramels. As simple as it gets, with a slight bitterness at the death. *45%*

Hven Seven Stars Single Malt No. 2 Merak db **(92.5) n23** growling smoke which gathers and intensifies; elsewhere the oak joins the cherry pie to ensure there is no letting up in the weight; **t23.5** a fresh delivery, with dark cherry and juicy barley giving way to both smoke and some tingling spice; **f22.5** dries as the oak holds control; excellent light spice to outline the phenols; **b23.5** a far better bottling than their first effort, this is one which really commands attention. High quality stuff. Well done! *45% WB15/391*

⏩ **Spirit of Hven Sankt Claus** db **(83.5) n22 t21 f20.5 b20.** Pungent, smoky fruit and nut on both nose and delivery. Thick bodied with a building spice, a rich whisky which seems ill-at-ease for, in the babble to say so much, little coherent is spoken at all. *53.2%. sc.*

⏩ **Spirit of Hven Seven Stars Single Malt No. 3 Phecda** db **(86.5) n21.5 t22 f21.5 b21.5.** A youthful, juicy whisky with a pleasing early weight if not depth. Malty, but there are some strange botanical messages being sent, especially those of a juniper bent. *45%*

⏩ **Spirit of Hven Urania** db **(95) n23.5** stunning gooseberry jam meets salty cashew cake; **t24** oh...one of the European deliveries of the year: silky soft and yielding, the clarity and juiciness of the malt is a joy to behold, the dignity of the ulmo honey and salted vanilla something to marvel at; **f23.5** long, charming, beautifully balanced and weighted, with all strands − including the understated spice − having equal shares in the grand finale; **b24** a soft, complex and truly beautiful whisky. *45%*

SWITZERLAND
ANDREAS VON OW DISTILLERY Busingen. Working.

Munot Malt dist Aug 10, bott 19 Sep 13 db **(87.5) n22 t22 f21.5 b22.** Sturdy and steady. The nose appears to offer more as a bourbon than malt and there is plenty of oak to chew on the palate. But the youthfulness is hinted at by firm oils and the light cocoa finish. *46%. sc.*

BRAURERIE LOCHER Appenzell. Working.

Säntis Malt Edition Alpstein No. VIII Aged 7 Years Pinot Noir finish, bott 09 May 14 db **(93) n24** astonishing: we appear to have a mix of bourbon − and every trademark note that possesses − in perfect tandem with fresh, sparkling grape. Yep, there is not a hint of discord or battling for supremacy, despite the massive egos on show; then, to top it all, we have that spiciness peculiar to central Europe including, here, orange and celery...; **t23** sharp flavours, especially the kumquat and orange blossom honey; **f22.5** a little bitteress creeps in, as do a few cocoa notes; **b23** profound whisky, almost three dimensional. Every aspect of it comes at you in the most vivid form imaginable. *48%. 2000 bottles.*

⏩ **Säntis Malt Alpstein Edition No. X Aged 7 Years Merlot Finish**, bott 16 Mar 15 db **(89.5) n22** busy, deep spices with figs and greengages working overtime; **t23.5** a volley of sugars on delivery are met by a salvo of spices; the fruit effect is pretty profound; **f21.5** an annoying bitterness creeps into proceedings, though the spices carry on sizzling; **b22.5** a complex malt that's not without its faults on maturation. But the fun element is far more important. *48%. 2,200 bottles.*

◇ **Säntis Malt Himmelberg Edition** oak beer casks, finished in wine casks db **(88) n22** malt from the spirit? Or malt from the beer barrel, I wonder...Either way it is the mega intense fruit which balances out more comfortably; **t22.5** powering sugars on delivery from a dessert wine type grape with light spices and a vague hop undertone; **f21.5** a few extra hops from the beer barrel appear to blast their way through; **b22** make mine a pint...! *43%*

Snow White Limited Edition No 2. Cherry Finish db **(86) n21 t22 f21.5 b21.5**. Dwarfed by the central European spices. At times tastes like a German, Austrian or Swiss Christmas cake. Add that to the sweetness and we have something a little more like a liqueur. *45%.*

BRENNEREI URS LÜTHY Muhen. Working.

◇ **Herr Lüthy Pure Swiss No. 9** cask no. 502, dist 2011, bott 2014 db **(82.5) n19 t22 f20.5 b21**. For a three year old, shows potential, especially with some many mocha notes already to the fore. But the nose is a bit of a mess and a more precise maltiness would be useful. *43%. sc.*

DESTILLERIE EGNACH Egnach. Silent.

Thursky db **(93) n24 t23.5 f22.5 b23**. Such a beautifully even whisky! I am such a sucker for that clean fruity-spice style. Brilliant! *40%*

DESTILLERIE HAGEN-RÜHLI Hüttwilen. Working.

Hagen's Best Whisky No. 2 lot no. 00403/04-03-08.08 db **(87) n19 t23.5 f22 b22.5**. Much more Swiss, small still style than previous bottling and although the nose isn't quite the most enticing, the delivery and follow through are a delight. Lovely whisky. *42%*

BRENNEREI-ZENTRUM BAUERNHO Zug. Working.

Swissky db **(91) n23 t23 f22 b23**. While retaining a distinct character, this is the cleanest, most refreshing malt yet to come from mainland Europe. Hats off to Edi Bieri for this work of art. Moving stuff. *42%*

Swissky Exklusiv Abfüllung L3365 db **(94) n23 t23 f24 b24**. A supremely distilled whisky with the most subtle oak involvement yet. Year after year this distillery bottles truly great single malt, a benchmark for Europe's growing band of small whisky distillers. *40%*

EDELBRENNEREI BRUNSCHWILER OBERUZWIL. Working

◇ **Brunschwiler B3 Single Malt** db **(86.5) n22.5 t22 f20 b21**. Now, on the nose at least, a fruity fellow. But the bitterness on the finish is out of character with the otherwise charming sugars and even odd touch of ulmo honey. *40%*

ETTER SOEHNE AG Zug. Working.

Johnett Swiss Single Malt 2008 dist May 08, bott Aug 12 db **(84.5) n21.5 t22.5 f20 b20.5** Peaks on delivery with a series of gorgeous rich sugar, semi-gristy notes. Just not enough body, though, to sustain the complexity. *42%*

◇ **Johnett Whisky Swiss Single Malt Single Cask No 43 Pinot Noir** barrel, dist May 10, bott Oct 14 db **(87.5) n22 t23.5 f20.5 b21.5**. As you know, I'm a man who likes a whisky to say what it has to say. However, this could do with a little less aggression when there is so much bitterness on the scene. That said, has some beautiful bourbon-style – or maybe rye - moments, really concentrating on the sugary crispness when it is there to be had. Sort the finish out, and you have a stunning whisky. *57.4%. ncf sc. 290 bottles.*

HUMBEL SPEZIALITÄTENBRENNEREI Stetten. Working.

OURBEER Single Malt Whisky dist 10, bott 23 Jul 14 db **(82) n20 t21.5 f20 b20.5**. A pretty unique aroma and flavour profile, strongly scented with spiced citrus and with a late herbal tang to the standard toffee. *43%*

KOBELT Marbach, St. Gallen. Working.

Glen Rhine Whiskey db **(88) n21 t22.5 f21.5 b22**. Try and pick your way through this one... can't think of another whisky in the world with that kind of fingerprint. *40%. Corn & barley.*

LANGATUN DISTILLERY Langenthal, Kanton Bern. Working.

◇ **Langatun 10 Years Langatun Distillery Single Malt Whisky** Châteuaneuf-du-Pape cask, cask no. 5, dist Mar 08, bott Mar 15 db **(96.5) n23.5** the wine forms the friendliest grape guard of honour to the beautifully married oak and barley. The age is always apparent, yet the depth of the grape gives it a slight polish; t24 a stunningly voluptuous delivery: the first note of two is semi-neutral as the grape juice is almost too soft and yielding to emit any great radiation. But within a few seconds the taste buds are bathed in the promised spices and darker, more intense tones have formed. The spices grow and generate more heat, while the sugars provided are dark, molassed and brooding; the fruit splits between sweeter juice and drier, more complex grape musto; and while all this goes on, the barley slips the cordon and can be detected, a little younger than its ten years; f24.5 so, so long... and so spicy! A little cocoa begins to form, the precursor to a chocolate fruit and nut. With the odd barley sugar note thrown in for good measure. But those spices...my word, those spices!! b24.5 just a few miles from where this distillery, with its ancient walls and in the shadow of a medaeval schloss, now sits is the old town of Langenthal. But it is ancient village of Aarwangen that provides the perfect setting now, with the distillery close to the river from which the community takes its name and where, if you are lucky like me, you might even spot a Hoopoe on its summer visit. And with outstanding cheese made there as well, it is some kind of whisky heaven which the gods have sprinkled a little magic on. 49.12%. nc. 499 bottles.

⚜️ **Langatun Jacob's Dream Single Malt Whisky** pinot noir cask, cask no. 97, dist 23 Mar 09, bott 15 Jun 15 db (92.5) n23.5 despite the grape, it is the youthful malt which can be detected first, the wine mounting soft sultana incursions until it finally takes command...; t24 both malt and grape are neck and neck out of the trap, though the intensity of the fruitcake concentrates the mind ahead of the barley; major Christmas cake/fruitcake influence but the mid-ground celebrates the gentle influence beginning with spice and moving onto a more vanilla-buttery aspect; f22 a little bitterness just becomes slightly entangled; b23 quite astonishing how this malt has the presence to comfortably fit into the shoes of such big wine casks.

Langatun Old Bear Châteauneuf-du-Pape cask, dist Apr 08, bott Jan 12, bott code L1201 db (96) n24 t24 f23.5 b24.5. Whisky for the gods... 64%

Langatun Old Eagle Cask Proof Pure Rye Whisky French oak charred, bott code L0113, dist 08, bott 13 db (92) n21.5 t24 f23 b23.5. To be honest, not quite a perfect distillation here and doesn't hit the unbelievable heights of the bottling last year. But this is infused with so much character that when it gets it right, as on the palate it pretty often does, you are lavishly and sometimes outrageously entertained. 51.7%. nc sc. 200 bottles.

⚜️ **Langatun Old Mustang Bourbon 4 Year Old recipe:** 60% corn, 40% barley malt db (95.5) n23.5 a beautifully busy nose where the malt appears to be lifted onto a plinth by the corn oil. Clean and makes the most of the genteel sugars and intensifying tannins; t24 just brilliant....!! The delivery is couched in corn oil, which ensures the softest possible landing on the palate, but soon makes way for a brilliant array of manuka and ulmo honey as the richer, toastier notes and the more subtle barley notes merge effortlessly; f24 long, with growing spices. Firms up as the darker sugars crystallise, which throws it into a fascinating juxtaposition with the swamp-soft corn; b24 this is Switzerland's answer to bourbon whiskey. Soon there will be a new Canton of Kentucky...yessirree!! Or at least there deserves to be in honour of this great whisky. 62.1%

⚜️ **Langatun Relocation Whisky 7 Year Old** bourbon cask, dist 11 Jan 08, bott 21 Jan 15 db (91.5) n22.5 a gorgeous and intense mix of concentrated barley, oak-drawn caramel and hazelnuts; t23 early sugars plus plenty of oil, but it is the richness of the malt which dominates; f23.5 long, and now those sugars – especially the weightier muscovado ones – begin to move towards ulmo honey and then, inevitably gristy malt; b23 about as intense as an elegant malt can be. A really beautiful barley experience. 49.12%

⚜️ **Langatun Winter Wedding Single Malt Whisky** Châteauneuf-du-Pape, Chardonnay & sherry casks, batch no. L 0614, dist Oct 09, bott Jan 15 db (94.5) n23.5 such weight: amazed my glass isn't cracking under the strain! There is an ashy quality to the grape must; both intricately sweet and dry...great balance and depth; t24 not sure a delivery can be much thicker or weightier than this, yet still have enough about it for you to be able to pick out its individual characteristics. Immense depth, but the fruit seems to sit on top aloof: juicy, grapey and untouched. Beneath, the smokier notes have sunk to the bottom, but there is a layer of barley to ensure a juicy liveliness; f23 a trail of spices that carry on as long as the taste buds are able to detect anything from this malt...and that, despite some late furriness, is for a very long time! b24 oh, and by the way: not only is this a truly great malt, but this has to be the best and most ingenious clasp I have ever seen to open a bottle of whisky! 46%. nc.

RUGENBRAU AG Matten bei Interlaken. Working.

Interlaken Swiss Highland Single Malt "Classic" oloroso sherry butt db (95) n23.5 t24 f23 b24. Hugely impressive. I have long said that the finest whiskies made on mainland Europe are to be found in Switzerland. Game, set and match... 46%

Top Of Europe Swiss Highland Single Malt "Ice Label" bott 2011 (93.5) n23 t24 f23 b23.5. I get a lot of stick for heaping praise on European whisky. OK, there is the odd technical flaw in the distillation – though in some ways it works to its advantage. But how many casks do you find like this in Scotland? For sheer quality of its output, this distillery must rate as high as an Alpine peak... 58.9%. sc.

SANTISBLICK DESTILLERIE

Single Malt Madeira cask, bott code 91 von 300 db (34) n1 t16 f8 b9. This, without question, offers the scariest nose I have ever encountered on a commercially bottled whisky. Appallingly aggressive, I'll make this the last whisky I'll taste today (at least) - for I know I will regret it and my senses will need time to recover. Nosed at a safe distance, if such a thing exists, it appears to have been matured in a petrol barrel, though closer, braver inspection suggests it is peat of some sort at work. The palate gives some lie to this terrifying aroma, as my teeth still seem to be intact. Some burnt fudge running alongside the "smoke" makes the delivery not only bearable but for a few moments quite acceptable. But the finish, by contrast, is dry and after a short while you feel your tongue aflame...and it takes a while to put out the blaze. The Swiss are known as a peaceful people with a history of neutrality. Hardly surprising: with stocks of this stuff at hand, it is unlikely anyone will ever dare invade. 48%

Whisky 3 Years Old bourbon cask, bott code L-130001 db (83.5) n21 t22 f21.5 b19. An odd but attractive whisky where the maltiness has been ramped up to nuclear strength. Best of all, though, is the body and overall mouth feel which is highly satisfying. A peculiar experience, though. 43%

Whisky 3 Years Old sherry cask, bott code 83 von 300 db (59) n13 t18 f12 b15. Probably the weirdest sherry matured whisky I have ever encountered. Words fail me for the nose and finish, the former being unreal and the latter being only too real in its grimness. 43%

WEINGUT CLERC BAMERT Ruteli im Buobental. Working.

Weingut Clerc Bamert Whisky Finest Pure Malt 8 Years Old db (87) n22 t22 f21 b22. Splutters and misfires on the finish, though not as badly as the single engine plane that has just gone, worryingly, overhead. Elsewhere some lovely malt, black cherry and caramel makes for a soft landing. 40%. sc nc.

Vatted Malts
LANGATUN DISTILLERY

The Swiss Malt (95.5) n23 t24 f24 b24.5. Sumptuous and the stuff for late night naval gazing. When Orson Welles, as Harry Lime in the immortal Third Man, made a disparaging summary of all Switzerland's achievements over the centuries as the invention of the cuckoo clock, it was obvious he had never tasted this. A whisky the Swiss distilling nation can be rightly proud of. 50.2%. From 20 Swiss Distillers. 175 miniatures.

WALES
PENDERYN Penderyn. Working.

Penderyn bott code 092909 (93.5) n23 t23.5 f24 b23. Just couldn't have been more Welsh than any potential offSpring of Catherine Zeta Jones by Tom Jones, conceived while "How Green Is My Valley" was on the DVD player and a Shirley Bassey CD playing in the background. And that after downing three pints of Brains bitter after seeing Swansea City play Cardiff City at the Liberty Stadium, before going home to a plate of cawl while watching Wales beating England at rugby live on BBC Cymru. Yes, it is that unmistakably Penderyn; it is that perfectly, wonderfully and uniquely Welsh. 46%. ncf.

Penderyn Bourbon Matured Single Cask cask no. 227B, dist 06 db (89.5) n22 t23 f22 b22.5. Definitely a much bigger Penderyn than you might be used to, and that is only partly because of the cask. 62%. ncf sc.

⋙ Penderyn Celt Peated bott Jul 15 db (82.5) n21 t22 f19.5 b20. Very curious one, this. Much oiler than the norm. But what makes it so unusual for a Penderyn is that, for whatever reason, it is a malt which fails to find its equilibrium. Whether it is the light smoke at fault, it is difficult to say. 41%. ncf.

Penderyn Icons of Wales Dylan Thomas Sherrywood db (91) n21.5 chalky, perhaps a tad too astringent and dry; t24 the delivery is a complete contrast to the aroma: immediately sweet and superbly weighted. Lush without being oily, sultanas abound to magnificent effect; f23 now reverts to something between the nose and delivery: delicate and dry, with vanillas handily placed but the fruit always pushing, probing and allowing in a little ulmo honey at the end; b23 from an unpromising start comes something of a tone poem. 41%. ncf. WB15/402

Penderyn Icon of Wales Red Flag Madeira finish bott Nov 12 db (94) n22.5 t24 f23.5 b24. I thought this was dedicated to Cardiff City, the "red birds" for their promotion to the

Premiership. But apparently not... though this year I was in the boardroom there watching Millwall and celebrating Neil Kinnock's 70th birthday. So maybe the whisky should represent both these landmarks, after all... 41%. ncf.

◇ **Penderyn Legend** bott Feb 15 db **(89.5) n22** enough oil on the nose to offer a sheen to the fruit amid austere oak; **t23** delicate and delightful. A vague layering of ulmo honey creates the sweet backdrop to the house pithy style, though some lemon peel helps, too; **f22** vague fruitcake but bolstered with late but telling spice; **b22.5** you wonder at times if it has the strength to get up the hill. But it surprises. 41%. ncf.

◇ **Penderyn Legend** bott Mar 15 db **(89) n21** dry and fragile; **t21.5** simple sugars with the odd juicy moment to ensure levity; **f23.5** ahhhh...! Now this is worth opening a bottle for. Seriously complex and understated, it is like a very dry chocolate fruit and nut...with the sugars at a minimum; **b23** for the occasional fruit notes which introduce themselves to your taste buds, though only muttering their names, frugality of flavour is the name of the game. But there is enough subtlety and late cocoa to make this enjoyable. Even sophisticated. 41%. ncf.

◇ **Penderyn Legend** bott Apr 15 db **(85) n21 t22.5 f20.5 b21** A little too dull and simplistic by Penderyn's high standards. Pleasant, certainly. But the caramels at the end make for uninspiring whisky. 41%. ncf..

Penderyn Madeira bott May 13 db **(87.5) n23** an unusual sprinkling of spice on the fruit-dappled oak; **t22** some astonishingly delicate oils help ramp up the scant sugars. The oak hits with a dry buzz midway through; **f20.5** a real tang to the grape and citrus; **b22** drier than recent previous bottlings. 46%.

Penderyn Madeira bott Jul 13 db **(95) n23.5** lush, with muscular grape, always rounded and even a touch of muscatel evident; gentle spices warble in the background; **t24** the highly usual delivery style of being both rich and thick on the palate and salivating – all at the same time. The spices are screened slightly by the vanillas-clad oak while gorgeous cocao notes begin to form; **f23.5** the spicies become more confident and are joined by the fruit which has found a second wind; **b24** makes up for the relative limitations of the May 13 bottling. Penderyn at its most irresistible. A real mouth filler....! 46%.

Penderyn Madeira bott Aug 13 db **(91) n22.5** pretty firm barley, encased by a mellow, lazy almost, grape. The prickle is of semi-bourbon variety...; **t22.5** delicate with the fruit at first lethargic but then volumises. Salivating throughout with the spices backing off after a confrontational start; **f23** chewy, though dries at a steady lick. The spices rides again as something akin to a butterscotch tart meets with Madeira trifle...; **b23** about as crisp and sturdy as Penderyn ever gets. 46%.

Penderyn Madeira bott Sept 13 db **(91.5) n22.5** identical to Aug 13 edition!! **t23** ah! Now this is softer bodied but slightly more emboldened than the previous bottling; **f23** later spice and slightly more emphasis on coacoa. But otherwise very similar to Aug 13... **b23** an almost identical set to Aug 13 edition, only the furniture has been moved around a bit. 46%.

Penderyn Madeira bott Oct 13 db **(89) n22** dense with a few extra tannins at play; there is a some black pepper bouncing around with the earthy floral notes; **t23.5** rarely does the Madeira have such an early say: here it is clean and pinging with juicy goodness, with the sugars let on their leash in most un-Penderyn style: a bit like a Jose Mourinho side playing attractive, all out attacking football....; **f21** the flip side is a dull finale with a tanginess hanging onto the remaining spices; **b22.5** perhaps not one of the most complex Penderyn experiences, but certainly one of the fruitiest and, early on, sweetest. 46%.

Penderyn Madeira bott Nov 13 db **(91.5) n22.5** quiet on the fruit front. Certainly a little more oak noise than usual; **t22** dry delivery but a gorgeously rounded mouth feel. Some serious complexity formulates in the mid term...; **t24** now goes into complexity overdrive as the Venzualan cocoa mingles with pithy nut colonels and fruit skins. Rarely has such a dry finsh been so lively and salivating...; **b23** rarely has a Penderyn quite come so much into its own at the death. 46%.

Penderyn Madeira bott Dec 13 db **(88.5) n21.5** some orange pith and tobacco: perhaps a touch too dry and tight; **t22** sumptuous delivery: soft but thinner than the previous month, though spices go on the charge early on; **f23** there is a firm rattle of something not unlike Irish Pot Still here – cuious. Plenty of fruit and nut chocolate – but sexed up with spice, too; **b22** in recent years Penderyn has been working hard to ensure a close proximity from one bottling t the next. Here we have a situation where the Dec version is not just on a different page, but a completely new book. I get the feeling they have tried to correct the lack of fruit in the previous month's incarnation. 46%.

Penderyn Madeira bott Jan 14 db **(95) n23.5** a few molassed sugars tumble around with the ripe plums; **t24** salivating and sensuous, again the sugars and fruit appears locked in arms. Some vanilla, butterscotch and ulmo honey combine to made an important and, frankly, eye-rollingly delicious contribution; **f23.5** dries, as it should, but not enough to undermine the mocha which always seems to appear in this distillery's better moments and the walnut and muscovado fade; b24 a charming little tease of a malt which has got the sugars just right and the change of complexity at a wonderful pace. Standard Penderyn at its very best. 46%.

Penderyn Madeira bott Feb 14 db (87.5) n22 t23.5 f20 b21.5. A strange bottling this, neither fish nor foul. Absent-mindedly you register some tiny degree of smoke on the nose, which then comes into sharper focus on the palate. But it is no more than a hint which works well on thetop-hole, fruit-laden delivery, but falls flat on the disappointingly out of sorts and disjointed finale. 46%.

Penderyn Madeira bott Mar 14 db (92.5) n21.5 dried kumquat and fizzy oak; a little austere; t24 that more like it. Some serious barley at play here – offering the most malt Penderyn for a while; stage right the fruit tries to nudge its way in, but finds its path barred by the drying oak; pretty salivating for a large part of the journey; f23 remains barley-rich. And a little fizzy spice peps u the fruit; b24 a most un-Penderyn-like maltfest. But just love the squabbling between the fruit and oak on the palate. 46%.

Penderyn Madeira bott Apr 14 db (93) n22 usual dry, slightly nipping aroma involving crushed fruit stones and peel; t23.5 usual, fruity, juicy velvet-soft delivery which slowly takes on board a soothing mocha countenance...; f23.5 usual bowing in the presence of vanilla and other drying oaks and spices; b24 the last half dozen or so batches of Penderyn have been, by and large, pretty wonderful. This is business as usual... 46%.

⬦ **Penderyn Madeira** bott Jan 15 db (95) n23 exceptionally fruity and intense so far as Penderyn noses go: the oak offers the usual dry vanilla and the pith is there, too. But the deluge of subtle fruit notes is stirring; t24.5 one of the best Penderyn madeira bottling deliveries of all time: the mix of ulmo honey, over-ripe greengages and complex vanilla and butterscotch is ridiculously beautiful; f23.5 long, thanks to a little extra oil, with the honey and sugar lasting the pace for much longer than usual; b24 standard Penderyn...but on steroids. All its normal attributes are present and correct. But simply magnified several times... 46%. ncf.

⬦ **Penderyn Madeira** bott Feb 15 db (90.5) n22 extra dry thanks to the crushed pips; t23.5 juicy delivery with pear and acacia honey, then wanders off into a sawdusty desert; f22 good sugars linger to balance the oak; b23 a much more recognisably standard, complex but dry version without all the twiddly fruity bits of the previous bottling. 46%. ncf.

⬦ **Penderyn Madeira** bott Mar 15 db (93.5) n23 grapefruit amid the pith and sawdust; t23.5 the sugars show early, then a blend of ulmo and heather honeys allow the malt ample scope to develop; juicy and grassy in the middle-ground; f23 long, with the vanilla – usually dominant at this time – upstaged by the lingering honey and delicate spices; b23.5 a luxurious model, a bit closer in style to the Jan 15 bottling than the Feb 15. Effortlessly sexy stuff... 46%.

Penderyn 41 db (91.5) n22 t23 f24 b22.5. Don't think for one moment it's the reduction of strength that makes this work so well. Rather, it is the outstanding integration of the outlandishly good Madeira casks with the vanilla. At usual strength this would have scored perhaps another couple of points. Oh, the lucky French for whom this was designed... 41%

⬦ **Penderyn Myth** bott Oct 14 db (86.5) n21.5 t22.5 f21 b21.5. Light, at times pretty dry and flits around the palate: perhaps should have been called Penderyn Moth. 41%. ncf.

Penderyn Bourbon Matured Single Cask dist 2000 (96) n24 t24.5 f23.5 b24. Penderyn as rarely seen, even by me. This is as old a Welsh whisky that has been bottled in living memory. And it is one that will live in the memory of this current generation. For I have encountered very few whiskies which revels in a controlled sweetness on so many levels. This is so good, it is frightening. 61.2%

Penderyn Peated bott 2 Nov 12 db (95) n23.5 t24 f23.5 b24. One of the most delicate whiskies you will experience this year. The fact it is smoked makes it even more remarkable. 46%. ncf.

Penderyn Peated bott 3 Feb 13 db (88) n22 t22.5 f21.5 b22. Almost a Laphroaig-style malt, complete with oaky bitterness at the death, too. 46%. ncf.

⬦ **Penderyn Peated** bott 1 Dec 14 db (91) n22 outwardly dry, but a subplot of delicate sugars and phenols intrigue; t23.5 one of the softest and most silky deliveries from Penderyn: a bed of oil allow the honey and lazy smoke to fall onto the palate without any shockwaves; f22.5 long, drying, even with a tangy sharpness. The phenols, half-hearted at their liveliest, allow the spices to take over for the remainder of the flight; b23 a gentle Penderyn with little more than a sprinkling of smoke... 46%. ncf.

Penderyn Portwood bott Mar 13 db (95.5) n24 the kind of heady mix between chunky Demerera sugars, higher, intense bourbon notes and thick, well matured fruitcake which almost makes the head spin. The spices act as little more than standard bearers for the chunky oak which controls itself with aplomb; t24 thick and rich delivery but always light enough for the more delicate elements to filter through. You could swear some malt pings about a bit, but so do does under-sugared redcurrant jam. Stewed under-ripe greengages adds to the mix; f23.5 a little mocha and marzipan is added to the Cadbury Fruit and Nut...; **b24** a mesmerising whisky, changing in the glass every two or three minutes. Not quite to the same breathtaking level as last year's effort, But really does take your palate through its paces. *41%*

Penderyn Portwood bott Oct 13 db (**81.5**) **n**20.5 **t**22 **f**19 **b**20. A Portwood that has hit a bit of a storm. Some very decent plummy moments. But far too many off key ones for a malt of Penderyn's high standards. *41%*

◇ **Penderyn Portwood** Single Cask cask no PT72 db (**96.5**) **n**24.5 is it the peppery spice which arrives first? Maybe. The thick, lush jammy fruit? Possibly. The coconut biscuit? Perhaps...; **t**24.5 a delivery to make the faint of heart swoon. All three dimensions found on the nose appear to gang up and burst through on a wave of thickened fruit juice, yet with what appears to be a faultless weight and pace; the mid ground appears to give way to a stunning French praline narrative; **f**23 that praline continues, now studded with sultanas. Just the very faintest degree of bitterness and vague furriness towards the end, but no worse than overcooked raisin; **b**24.5 the Penderyn Port Wood single cask bottling has now been carved in stone as one of the world's great whiskies; it's unveiling each year one of the stratospheric moments in the world whisky calendar. And yet again, it lives up to its own ridiculously high reputation. If I find a better single cask than this for the 2016 Bible it will be of the proportions of a Cecil B DeMille epic... *59%. ncf sc.*

Penderyn Portwood Swansea City Special db (**96.5**) **n**23.5 **t**24.5 **f**24 **b**24.5. On Saturday 30th April 1966 I was taken by my father to see my very first football game: Millwall versus Swansea Town, as they were then known. On 30th April 2011 I celebrated 45 years of agony and ecstasy (though mainly agony!) with my beloved Millwall with a dinner at The Den as we hosted.... would you believe it? Yep, Swansea! The Swans won that day on their march to deserved promotion to the Premier League and it was my honour to be at Wembley to see them overcome Reading in the Play Off Final to book their place among the elite. I have met their Chairman Huw Jenkins on occasion but not yet had the chance to wish him well in his new rarified environment. I toast you and your grand old club, Huw, with this quite stunning, absolutely world class malt, as Welsh now as laverbread, and look forward to the day when the Lions are back among the Swans...Oh, and in the newly acquired knowledge from a discovery I made while tracing back some of my family history over Christmas 2011 that, as fate would have it, my paternal grandmother's family hail in the 19th century from Neath, on the outskirts of Swansea...; that there is not a jot of Scots in me as Murray's previously believed, but a whole load of Welsh! Perhaps goes to explain why I have so long been such a fan of Penderyn! Or, just maybe, this fabulous whisky does... *59.4%. ncf sc.*

◇ **Penderyn Rich Oak** db (**93**) **n**23 dry, toasty...curiously showing a flavour signal normally broadcast by a German-type still; sandalwood and oak shavings seem to generate the gentle spice; **t**24 decidedly nutty yet enriched by a gorgeous array of sugars, ranging from watered-down maple syrup through to molasses via Demerara; **f**23 dries quickly again and we are back to the vanilla and butterscotch compounds, as well as Brazil nut oil; **b**23 a curious, even unique, line-up of flavours makes for a massively enjoyable and occasionally head-scratching experience. *50%. ncf. 1,113 bottles.*

British Blends

The One British Blended Whisky (**84.5**) **n**22 **t**21.5 **f**20 **b**21. Although it doesn't say so on the bottle, I understand this is made from a blend of malts from England, Ireland, Scotland and Wales. It says "blend" which implies the use of grain, though this is probably not so...another example of the confusion caused by the brainless and arrogant change of terminology from "vatted" to denote a blend of malts insisted upon by the Scotch Whisky Association. Not yet checked, but would have thought that as not scotch, they still would have been entitled to call it a vatting. The mind boggles over what they will do with this whisky if Scotland votes for independence in a few weeks' times. Doubtless the SWA will make some kind of noise... Anyway, back to the action. The label does claim this is a whisky of "intriguing complexity". If true, the term will have to be redefined. The nose, sure enough, does offer just enough smoky and citrus twists and turns to wonder what will happen next. But the delivery on the palate is a disappointment, with any complexity desired submerged under a welter of dull caramels. Just too flat and soft for its own good: back to the drawing board....and possibly without scotch... *40% WB15/406*

MISCELLANEOUS

◇ **Nomad Outland Whisky** (**82**) **n**21 **t**22 **f**20 **b**19. The entire shape of the whisky is lost under the tsunami of the PX casks. So first comes the scary sugars...followed by a very bitter finish with no happy midpoint. All-in-all, I have tasted whisky liqueurs less sweet than this... *41.3% WB16/006*

World Whiskies

I have long said that whisky can be made just about anywhere in the world; that it is not writ large in stone that it is the inalienable right for just Scotland, Ireland, Kentucky and Canada to have it all to themselves. And so, it seems, it is increasingly being proved. Perhaps only sandy deserts and fields of ironstone can prevent its make physically and Islam culturally, though even that has not been a barrier to malt whisky being distilled in both Pakistan and Turkey. While not even the world's highest mountains or jungle can prevent the spread of barley and copper pot.

Outside of North America and Europe, whisky's traditional nesting sites, you can head in any direction and find it being made. South America may be well known for its rum, but in the south of Brazil, an area populated by Italian and German settlers many generations back, malt whisky is thriving. It can now also be found in even more lush and tropical climes with Taiwan and Thailand leading the way.

Japan has long represented Asia with distinction and whisky-making there is in such an advanced state and at a high standard Jim Murray's Whisky Bible has given it its own section - and World Whisky of the Year for 2015!. But while neighbouring South Korea has ended its malt distilling venture, further east, and at a very unlikely altitude, Nepal has forged a small industry to team up, geographically, with fellow malt distillers India and Pakistan. The main malt whisky from this region making inroads in world markets is India's Amrut single malt. Actually, inroads is hardly doing them justice. Full-bloodied trailblazing, more like. So good now is their whisky they were, with their fantastically complex brand, Fusion deservedly awarded Jim Murray's Whisky Bible 2010 Third Finest Whisky in the World. That represented a watershed not just for the distillery, but Indian whisky as a whole and in a broader sense the entire world whisky movement: it proved beyond doubt that excellent distilling and maturation wherever you are on this planet will be recognised and rewarded. Following hard on Amrut's tail is the ever-improving and high-flavoured malt from the Paul John distillery in Goa.

Africa is also represented on the whisky stage. There has long been a tradition of blending Scotch malt with South African grain but now there is single malt there, as well. Two malt distilleries, to be precise, with a second being opened at the Drayman's Brewery in Pretoria.

One relatively new whisky-making region is due immediate further study: Australia. From a distance of 12,000 miles, the waters around Australia's distilleries appear to be muddied. Quality appears to range from the very good to extremely poor. And during the back end of 2004 I managed to discover this first hand when I visited three Tasmanian distilleries and Bakery Hill in Melbourne which perhaps leads the way regarding quality malt whisky made south of the Equator, and had another squint ten years later when I popped over once more. Certainly green shoots are sprouting at the Tasmania Distillery which has now moved its operation away from its Hobart harbour site to an out of town one close to the airport. The first bottlings of that had been so bad that it will take some time and convincing for those who have already tasted it to go back to it again. However, having been to the warehouse – and having tasted samples from every single cask they have on site – I reported in previous Bibles that it was only a matter of time before those first offerings would be little more than distant – though horrific – memories. Well, as predicted, it is now safe to put your head above the parapet. The last cask strength bottling I tasted was a bloody beaut. For Jim Murray's Whisky Bible 2016 I was again flooded with a disarming array of excellent malt whiskies with all the usual suspects chipping in with deliveries far better their cricketing countrymen. As a pretty hard and fast rule now, Limeburners, Sullivan's Cove, Lark Distillery and Timboon came out with staggeringly beautiful bottlings; while Nant has already thrown down the gauntlet with a series of the most massive yet gorgeous malts yet from the Southern Hemisphere. Australia represents some of the highlights of world whisky and the consistency from one year to the next shows, unlike their brief hold of The Ashes, this is not just a passing phase.

The remaining casks of Wilson's malt from New Zealand are disappearing fast, though they are not vanishing without without trace. The NZ Whisky Collection 1988 picked up 96.5 points and Southern Hemisphere Whisky of the Year in the 2015 Bible. Apparently the stills from there are not just making rum in Fiji but whisky as well. We are all aware of the delights of island whisky, but a Pacific Island malt? Which leaves Antarctica as the only continent not making whisky, though what those scientists get up to for months on end no one knows.

ARGENTINA
Blends
Breeders Choice (84) n21 t22 f21 b20. A sweet blend using Scottish malt and, at the helm, an unusually lush Argentinian grain. *40%*

AUSTRALIA
BAKERY HILL DISTILLERY 1999. Operating.
Bakery Hill Peated Malt Cask Strength cask 6512 db **(92.5) n24 t23.5 f23 b24.** Began tasting this first Australian whisky of the year at exactly 11am on Wednesday 10th July. Henry Blofeld, Blowers, is at one end of a BBC microphone, I, Sniffers, exactly 46 miles away as one of his pigeons fly. It is the moment Pattinson bowled a wide for the first ball of the 2013 Ashes series. There is smoke in the air at Trent Bridge, with the Red Arrows having flown past displaying red white & blue. The first Ashes Test I ever saw was also at Trent Bridge, Nottingham, where these present day combatants have set up camp. Roughly about the same time I got the exclusive story about a guy who crashed his bi-plane into the River Trent having flown, illegally, under the bridge next to the historic ground with a girl walking the wing at the time...oh, the days of my comparative youth. A bit like this beaut of a malt. A touch of youth, but wily enough to entertain with aplomb. As I sign off from this first Australian of this edition, England, having decided to bat, have progressed to 16 for no wicket. Oh, that 1981 test at Trent Bridge? England lost, their only defeat in a 3-1 series victory. Bowling for Australia was Dennis Lilley; batting for England Ian Botham. You get the feeling they both would enjoyed a macho malt like this... *60%*

BELGROVE DISTILLERY
◈ **Belgrove Distillery Rye Whisky 100% Rye Aged 3 Years** ex-Overeem French oak Port cask, bott 22 Jun 15 db **(94.5) n23.5** no doubting the grain of choice: bristles with a rigid determination. Perhaps a little nougat in the mix from the cut, but my word...that rye...!!! **t24.5** that is just one fantastic delivery. Perhaps the most concentrated rye arrival I have tasted for a couple of years from any part of the world. Just so sharp, almost three dimensional. On one hand crisp and jagged, as the best rye whiskies should be, but also a more oily, softer, less fruity version underneath; brittle dark sugars at every turn; **f23** takes some time for those light nougaty feints to eat through. Until then, the rye and accompanying sugars – now joined by some biting spices - continue their remarkable show...; **b23.5** what a memorable rye. The grain leads on both nose and delivery in the same way Watson leads with his pads. *61%. ncf.*

HEARTWOOD DISTILLERS
◈ **The Good Convict** Port cask, cask no. HH0543, dist Nov 00, bott Jun 15 db **(96) n24** Australia's earliest settlers were convicts taken to a port. So fitting port should play such an enriching yet soothing part in this big aroma; **t24** a huge delivery led by silky grape; the malt arrives in thick pockets while the oak is marzipan rich; **f24** the most impressive and complex passage: the alcohol has receded, leaving behind a quite stunning layering of both juicy and pithy fruit to balance against the orange blossom honey; **b24** no problems with this cask. Has done its time, and has come away even and rounded. Massively impressive distilling and maturation: just beautiful! *71.3%. sc. 100 bottles.*

◈ **Heartwood The Beagle 3 Tasmania Vatted Malt Whisky** nine Lark & Tasmania Distillery casks, bott May 15 **(95.5) n23.5** think of a ripe, gently spiced sultana. Put it in with 50 others. Multiply by three and then double it. Take away the first sultana. What you are left with is what you have here...; **t24** the delivery is more intense than a community of campers. Massive fruit, spiced and honeyed, gives way to concentrated sherry trifle; **f24** everything plays out like a well rehearsed errr....play. The fruit still has a clean, powering presence, the spices continue to thrill and, finally, the oak chips in with a mix of praline and chocolate fruit and nut; **b24** a more clotted version of Beagle 2. *68.4%. 220 bottles.*

Heartwood 'Convict Redemption' Batch 2 Single Malt Port cask no. HH0611, bott Dec 13, db **(91.5) n23 t23 f22.5 b23.** Scientists have announced today that strong black, sugarless coffee (which I drink every day) is good for destroying plaque and surrounding bacteria. Well, if the coffee didn't do the full job this morning, this must have finished the little blighters off. A not so little beaut! *71.90%. sc.*

◈ **Heartwood Convict Resurrection** American oak Port, cask no. HH0239, dist Mar 00, bott Dec 14 **(82.5) n22.5 t22 f19 b19.** From the crème brûlée nose to the sherry (well, port!) trifle delivery, we know we are in for fruity beast. But, sadly, there is a mildly off-key dullness present which means a balance is never quite achieved. *72%*

◈ **Heartwood Devil in the Detail** bourbon cask, cask no. HH0244, dist Apr 00, bott May 15 db **(95.5) n23.5** rarely do you encounter a malt whisky that is so...malty! Supremely distilled; **t24** a kind of George T Stagg delivery, except it is concentrated malt which is burrowing into your taste buds like a drill might burrow into the earth looking for oil; the sugar seems to be a mixture of grist on steroids and light, buttery tannins in pure, concentrated form; **f24** long, with probably the most complete set of sugars you could ask for. The vanilla and ulmo honey is in near perfect harmony; **b24** probably did the enamel on my teeth few favours, but did my heart good. Magnificent malt! *73.5%. 152 bottles.*

HELLYERS ROAD

Hellyers Road Single Malt Whisky 12 Year Old Original db **(84.5)** n19 t22 f21.5 b22. Forget the nose and get stuck into the massive malt. *46.2%.*

Hellyers Road Single Malt Whisky Henry's Legacy 'The Gorge' db **(83)** n21.5 t21 f20 b20.5. Eye-wateringly sharp in places, its best bits hang on a vaguely smoky, molasses-sweetened coffee note. *46.2%.*

Hellyers Road Single Malt Whisky Original db **(84)** n20.5 t22 f20.5 b21. Bolstered on last year's bottling thanks to a profound malt surge on delivery. Citrus fruity in part, but both nose the tingle at the finish demands more copper. *46.2%.*

Hellyers Road Single Malt Whisky Port Matured db **(88)** n22.5 spiced, juicy fruitcake; t23 superb delivery with the grape ripping home onto the throat with spice, then soothing and kissing better with its salivating freshness; f20.5 a tad off key but the spices are busy and biting; b22 without question the direction this distillery should take. Some wonderful moments. *46.2%.*

◇ **Hellyers Road Single Malt Whisky Port Matured** db **(89.5)** n23 the fruit is meticulously layered, almost prim. This lightness allows the odd off note from the spirit to pass through, but it is hardly noticeable, so complex are the varied grape tones; t23 fabulous. That complexity on the nose is more than matched by the fruit on delivery, offering a delightful juiciness with further hints of honeydew melon and mocha; f21 a few gremlins from the spirit do get through, but still the depth of the mocha and the light layering of muscovado sees it through; b22.5 an absolutely top dog wine cask has done a splendid job on this malt. Impressive. And, what's more, Australia haven't lost a wicket – and even scored 28 runs - in all the time it took me to taste this... *48.9%*

◇ **Hellyers Road Single Malt Whisky Saint Valentine's Peak** db **(85.5)** n22.5 t22 f20 b21. Regular readers of Jim Murray's Whisky Bible know that I traditionally taste the Australian whisky during the First Test of any Ashes series, if one is being played – which seems like every six months in recent years. So it is fitting I tasted St Valentine's on the day of a massacre – the Aussies are currently 128-6 in their second innings, still needing almost 300 more runs to win. This malt has done a lot better than Clarke's motley mob. Still pretty rough towards the finish, the gorgeous fruit effect on the nose works well into the delivery. At least the last embers show some coffee cake attractiveness. Now, I'd better hurry up with the remaining Aussie whiskies before Broad and Co bring the game to an early close on just the 4th day... *60.1%*

LARK DISTILLERY

◇ **The Beagle Tasmanian Vatted Malt Whisky** batch no. 2, bott Aug 14 db **(95)** n23 a beautiful mix of sultana and Dundee cake...with a dollop of treacle for good measure; t24 the enormity of the grape, the alcohol, the spice...it fair takes your breath away: no raisins come more succulent, no spice busier, no oak any more vanilla-bound; f23.5 huge toastiness now: the dryness is profound. But the fruit and sugars from the cake not only offer the perfect balance, but have legs enough to make the finish two or three times the length of most other whiskies..; b24.5 another ridiculously fine whisky from Australia. *68.3%. 160 bottles.*

The Lark Distillery Single Malt Whisky Cask Strength port cask, cask no. 473, bott 2014 db **(94)** n24 a beautifully bright nose: the muscovado sugars are dripping with greengage and black cherry. Not sure the spices could be more effective or disarming; t24 hold tight: the taste buds are under immediate bombardment from rabid spices which have not the slightest intention of taking prisoners; the rich, soft fruit looks on helplessly; thankfully a big dollop of ulmo honey early on helps cushion the blows; f22.5 remains juicy to the end, though it takes a while for the spice to recede. A little blood orange bitterness creeps in; b23.5 and I'd always thought Hobart was a friendly town... *58%.*

The Lark Distillery Single Malt Whisky Distiller's Selection sherry barrel aged, cask no. 475, bott 2014 db **(88.5)** n23 mixed herbs and spices offer up a nose more likely to befound in a delicatessen than a whisky glass. Somewhat busy...; t22 and on delivery turns 180 degrees and offers little or no spice but, rather, a soft toffee-raisin massage. So soft...; f21.5 more toffee-raisin – tangy this time with spice growth; b22 don't go looking for complexity or a quickened pulse. A Steady Eddie dram *46%.*

The Lark Distillery Single Malt Whisky Limited Release sherry cask, bott 2014 db **(86)** n21.5 t23 f20 b21.5. Big fruit and nut ensemble. Not quite Lark's finest ever distillate, mind. *52.1%*

◇ **The Lark Distillery Single Malt Whisky Limited Release** 2nd fill sherry cask, cask no. 689 db **(95)** n23.5 despite its youth, the dominant feature is oak...or fresh tannin to be precise. But there is much else besides to this mind-blowing aroma. The young malt appears in concentrated form, and has to be to cope with the oak. And there is some kind of non-specific fruitiness which lurks in the shadows, as though you are not sure it is your imagination, a trick of the sniff...one second you see it, then you don't....as attractive as it is intriguing; **t23** now there's fruit, as the sugars dissolve slowly on the palate. Not just plum, but also Demerara thickening it out. The grist remains almost pre-pubescently youthful, a little apple-fresh...then comes the manuka honey and cocoa; **f24** a slow unravelling of the myriad complexities, though now butterscotch and ulmo honey lay the softening foundation; **b24** not quite sure how he did it, but my old mate Bill Lark has gone and produced flavour profile not quite like anything else I have found on this planet. The malt and oak, perhaps with still influence, but probably through the youth of the distillate, have forged a nose in particular which needs as much time as you can spare to unravel. What great fun! And probably the best young whisky in the world. 63.3%. 35 bottles.

The Lark Distillery Single Malt Whisky Single Cask Port barrel aged, cask no. 516, bott 2014 db **(90) n23** beautifully rounded and balanced, the spices fit well with the cucumber and sultana; **t23** spices arrive first, then several waves of gentle fruit. The vanilla really has a big say as the oak plays a guiding role; some coconut in syrup thickens and sweetens; **f22** a little late bitterness but the fruit does hang on, though some late oils from the still also grab a foothold. Hence, probably, the bitterness... **b22** an entertaining dram which doesn't always balance out the way it was probably planned but gets there in the end. 43%.

LIMEBURNERS

Limeburners Single Malt Whisky Barrel M23 bott no. 78 db **(90.5) n22.5 t23.5 f22 b22.5.** First time I've tasted anything from this Western Australian mob. Gday fellas! I have to admit, thought it might have been from France at first, as the aroma on nosing blind reminded me of brandy. And not without good reason, it transpires. This no age statement malt spent an unspecified amount of time in American brandy cask before being finished in bourbon casks. Does it work? Yes it does. But now that's torn it lads. You are supposed to start off with a bloody horrible whisky and get better. Now you have gone and made a rod for your own back. Good on you! 61%

Limeburners Single Malt Whisky Peated Barrel M58 ex-bourbon American oak cask db **(89) n22.5 t23.5 f21 b22.** Taken aback when I nosed this: saw the Limeburners tag, but hadn't spotted the style. The smoke gave me a jolt: not seen this from these guys before. Peatburners, more like...and an attractive smoky style the like of which I have never encountered before. 48%. ncf. 133 bottles.

Limeburners Single Malt Whisky Barrel M61 Ex bourbon American oak/ Finished Australian Port Cask, dist 30 Sep 08, Sep 13 db **(94.5) n23.5** the oak positively growls from the glass; as heavy and impenetrable as a tropical jungle. A spiced fruitcake and manuka honey mix plots a safe course through the low-hanging branches; **t24** second innings are usually played out on slightly worn tracks with ever less even bounce. And taking more spin. Well, there is still some nip and fizz to the delivery here, one that gets you on the back foot as you take extra time to cope with the steepling fruit; **f23** an elegant final passage before stumps...oak stumps that is. Remains juicy and full bodied to the end, though; **b24** I really must get out to Perth to see these guys. A very sound and harmonious whisky. I word of contradiction, though. Their back label urges you to add a little water. Don't. Just follow the Murray Method at the front of this Bible...and the whisky's splendour will be fully revealed in good time! 60%. 99 bottles. ncf.

Limeburners Single Malt Whisky M64 Muscat Finish db **(92) n23.5 t23 f22.5 b23.** Macho malt keeps in touch with its feminine side. Tasty and beautifully made. 61%. ncf.

Limeburners Single Malt Whisky Barrel M79 ex-bourbon American oak cask and finished in an old Australian sherry cask db **(93.5) n23 t24 f23 b23.5.** A rare exhibition of a happy marriage between bourbon cask and sherry. 61%. ncf. 113 bottles.

Limeburners Single Malt Whisky Barrel M91 ex-bourbon American oak barrique and finished in an old Australian sherry cask db **(80) n19 t21 f20 b20.** The stale tobacco on the nose and rumbling, off key finish says something about the feints involved. The delicious clarity of the fruit is a tick for the "sherry" cask. 43%. ncf. 355 bottles.

THE NANT DISTILLERY

The Nant 3 Year Old American oak/Port db **(91.5) n22.5 t22 f23 b24.** Beautifully well made whisky. Has the sophistication of a dry martini, but without the olive...yet maintaining the salt. Last year I set out to keep my eyes on these chaps. Not a bad move. 43%

The Nant 3 Years Old Cask Strength American oak bourbon db **(95.5) n23 t24 f24 b24.5** I have really got to get back to Oz to visit these guys. Something majestic is happening here. Whatever it is they are doing, I have to discover first hand...World class. 61.6%

The Nant Distillery 5 Years Old French oak/Port db **(92.5) n23.5 t23.5 f22 b23.5.** Not sure if this is talking French, Portuguese, Oz or a strange dialect incorporating all three. Lovely to listen to, whichever, and makes itself fully understood. 43%

The Nant Distillery 5 Year Old Cask Strength American oak/sherry **(86.5) n21.5 t23 f20.5 b21.5.** A bit of a lollipop of a malt: suck at it and you get plenty of fruity sugar. However, unlike most Nants I have tasted previously, there is a bit of an imbalance between the intense sugar, spices and fuzzy oils from the cut. No faulting the juiciness of the fruit or liveliness of the spice, though. *63%*

The Nant Distillery 5 Year Old Cask Strength French oak/Port **(94) n23.5 t24 f23 b23.5.** If you are looking for a simple, straight up and down dram, you have opened the wrong bottle. This is one very complex offering... *63%*

OLD HOBART DISTILLERY

◇ **Overeem Bourbon Cask Matured Cask Strength** cask no. OHD065 db **(93) n23.5** big vanilla; all kinds of dogged bourbon notes −concentrating on the drier tones at first before the spiced crystallised Demerara starts drifting through, offering a far harder edge; **t23** the sugars are far quicker to arrive than on the nose, chased by creamy mocha then, later, hickory and vanilla; **f22.5** long vanilla, drying and thinning simultaneously; **b23.5** as though someone has exploded a vanilla pod in the centre of an oak tree. Supremely beautiful texture. *60%*

◇ **Overeem Port Cask Matured** cask no. OHD026 db **(94.5) n23.5** a fantastic mix of old pot still Demerara rum, over-ripe greengages and a salty sea breeze. Beautiful..; **t23.5** so complex: a two-toned delivery, seemingly light and ethereal, but as you concentrate on the fruitier notes drifting around, you realise there is a lusher oak-spice-malt combination rumbling far below; **f23.5** the spices continue, but with a fabulous fruit jelly sweetness balancing matters with aplomb. Or do I mean a plum...? **b24** oh! Had only this been at cask strength!!! A joyous experience. *43%*

◇ **Overeem Sherry Cask Matured** cask no. OHD030 db **(90.5) n22** grape must to the fore; a semi hoppy dryness/bitterness is overcome by a toasted fudge sweetness; **t23** clever delivery: a fat barley wine texture seemingly from the malt side of matters, yet equally the fruit powers through, again with a degree of pip and skin in the offing; **f22.5** slightly tart and salty; **b23** for a 43% malt, this has some serious depth and complexity. Impressive stuff. But from this great Down Under distillery, what do you expect....? *43%*

◇ **Overeem Sherry Cask Matured Cask Strength** cask no. OHD032 db **(87.5) n22 t21.5 f22 b22.** No complaints from me about the silky texture of the fruit, or the mouth-watering qualities and spice. But, despite the cocoa finish, all seems just a little too manicured. *60%*

SMALL CONCERN DISTILLERY

◇ **Cadenhead's Authentic Collection Cradle Mountain Aged 18 Years (81) n20 t22 f20 b19.** A nutty monster of a malt. A strange nougat-like note really is packed with hazelnuts. Sadly, the fruit and the grain have yet to find a way to achieve harmony. *52.9%*

Cradle Mountain Pure Tasmanian Malt db **(87) n21 t22 f21 b23.** A knock-out malt from a sadly now lost distillery in Tasmania. Faultlessly clean stuff with lots of new oak character but sufficient body to guarantee complexity. *43%*

SOUTHERN COAST DISTILLERS

Southern Coast Single Malt Batch 001 db **(92.5) n23 t24 f22 b23.5.** "A hint of bushfire in the barley" claims the back label. Well, that one's got me stumped; I pride myself in nosing anything and everything, but that particular aroma has passed me by. Perhaps they mean the heather aroma...? Mind you, I did get pretty close to some scary forest fires near Marseilles nearly 30 years ago, but probably not the same thing... Anyway, back to this fabulous first effort. Wow! Could ask for more in a study of crisp brown sugars and sweet cocoa...; *46%*

Southern Coast Single Malt Batch 002 db **(96) n24 t23.5 f24.5 b24.** Is this the best Australian whisky ever to shamelessly masquerade as Demerara pot still rum? I should think so. Will it ever be beaten? I doubt it. In fact, just how many Demerara rums have I ever tasted of this refinement. One or two, at most. And I have probably tasted more than anyone in the whisky trade living. One of the most astonishing whiskies it has been my honour to taste. Frankly, I am on my knees... *46%*

Southern Coast Single Malt Batch 003 db **(79.5) n18 t19 f23 b19.5.** Third time unlucky. Lots of oils and berserk honey. But too feinty, though this went to some finishing school, believe me...! *46%. ncf.*

Southern Coast Single Malt Batch 004 db **(82.5) n20 t22 f20.5 b20.** An earthy, slightly musty dram with a pleasing essence of honey but struggles to find structure or balance. *46%*

Southern Coast Single Malt Batch 005 db **(83.5) n21.5 t22 f20 b20.** Starts off like a Jack Hobbs or Brian Lara or Alec Stewart taking the Aussie quick bowling apart. There is even an unusual, but mightily attractive, sweetened Vegemite hint to this (not as strange as it sounds, actually). But the middle stump is removed by the hefty finish: the cricketing equivalent of an ungainly, head-up hoick to cow corner.... *46%*

Southern Coast Single Malt Batch 006 db **(95) n24 t24 f23.5 b24.** When I saw these Southern Coast Whiskies before me, my eyes lit up. Here was my journey to Demerara. Much cheaper and less problem-riddled than any trip I normally make to Guyana..and with less chance of coming away with my normal stomach complaint. Batches 4 and 5 let me down. But Batch 6.... even the sun has come out for the first time in three days as I nose this... Georgetown, here I come... 46%

TASMAN DISTILLERY

Great Outback Rare Old Australian Single Malt db **(92) n24 t24 f21 b23.** What can you say? An Australian whisky distillery makes a malt to grace the world's stage. But you can't find it outside of Australia. This will have to be rectified. 40%

TASMANIA DISTILLERY

Sullivan's Cove American Oak Single Cask cask no. HH0014, dist 22 Oct 99, bott 24 Mar 14 db **(90.5) n22** a lively – and lovely – green apple tinge to this while the barley has remained pure and focussed despite 14 passing years in a warm climate; **t23** superb delivery with almost three dimensional clarity to the barley early on. A few juicy, honey-brushed malty notes really do add riches; **f22.5** long, with a distinct lemon meringue tart flourish, especially as the vanilla builds; **b23** clean, ultra malty, high quality whisky in anyone's currency. 47.5%

Sullivan's Cove American Oak Single Cask cask no. HH0015, dist 22 Oct 99, bott 13 May 14 db **(87.5) n21.5 t21.5 f22.5 b22.** Fractionally on the hot side. Barrel HH0014 was more forgiving and softened the burn by allowing the barley to flourish. Here the malt takes longer to get under control, though when it finally does, it makes for a mouth-watering and chewy finale. 47.5%

Sullivan's Cove American Oak Single Cask cask no. HH0016, dist 22 Oct 99, bott 21 May 14 db **(86.5) n20.5 t21.5 f22.5 b22.** From the identical mould as HH15 with the oak not quite able to extract the very best from the distillate. And again, despite the fiery background, the maltiness finally wins through impressively. Degree of copper intensity at work, too. 47.5%

Sullivan's Cove American Oak Single Cask cask no. HH0017, dist 22 Oct 99, bott 21 May 14 db **(86.5) n21.5 t21.5 f22 b21.5.** Another sound, juicy cask though the warmth is again a bit challenging. More comfortable on finish when a little mocha filters through to join the malt. 47.5%

Sullivan's Cove American Oak Single Cask cask no. HH0047, dist 9 Nov 99, bott 30 Apr 14 db **(95.5) n24** hard to imagine a malt whisky being more malt whiskier...the nose celebrates outstanding distilling and classic maturation in a fine cask. The barley is multi-faceted and just about perfectly balanced between barley intensity and the use of deft, still slightly gristy, sugars. The oak chimes in with delicious butterscotch and even a hint of ginger; **t24** few distilleries do weight on delivery better than this one. The intensity of the barley deserves a medal alone, its balance with the gentle vanilla-led oak a bar; **f23.5** long, with a light smattering of cocoa yet the barley still feigns to have a degree of youth...even now; **b24** exemplary malt whisky: absolutely beautiful. 47.5%

Sullivan's Cove American Oak Single Cask cask no. HH0442, dist 22 Aug 99, bott 30 Apr12 db **(85.5) n20 t22 f22.5 b21.** A dodgy cove, one might say. The nose suggests all is not quite right and, despite the big barley blast, balance remains at a premium to this warming dram. Plenty to enjoy, but probably would have been better served stirring up another, duller cask. 47.5%

Sullivan's Cove American Oak Single Cask cask no. HH0460,dist 5 Sep 00, bott 30 Apr 14 db **(92) n23** fabulous mix of ulmo and heather honey really allows the barley to show in a bright light; **t22.5** intense barley from the moment it hits the palate and doesn't cease as the early cocoa arrives; **f23** the spices have been busy from early on but come into their own here. German caramelized biscuit meets Weetabix and malt cereal as the Demerara sugars gain hold; **b23.5** out malts many a Scottish malt distillery. A lovely barrel, complimenting top quality distillate. An assured and wonderfully paced dram of great confidence. 47.5%

Sullivan's Cove Double Cask batch 71, youngest barrel 14 Feb 01, bott 20 Mar 14 db **(89) n22.5** fruit candy; pears and pear drops; **t22** firm, almost aggressive barley aided with the inevitable spice and something not too dissimilar to sherbet; **f22** dries to offer a high cocoa content fruit and nut bar; **b22.5** a satisfying whisky offering penetration on the palate and some decent complexity. 40%

⬦ **Sullivans Cove Double Cask batch DC74**, youngest cask 21 Oct 00, bott 13 May 14 db **(85) n21.5 t23 f19.5 b21.5.** Tasting this while England are recovering from a bright start by the Australians to the first Ashes test. A disappointing finish...and I'm not just talking about in the days play for England. Furry and not remotely right. 40%. 1307 bottles.

⬦ **Sullivans Cove French Oak Cask** cask no. HH386, dist 28 Jul 00, bott 17 Feb 15 db **(94) n23** the tannins are up for a battle. Sharp spices and punchy Demerara sugars offer full support; **t24** now that is quite beautiful. The malt melts early in the proceedings, accompanied by those sugars. But it's the intensity of the mildly belligerent tannins and the way the dovetail with the Demerara and maple syrup which really sing out loud; **f23** a long, oak-laden fade. The vanilla runs into butterscotch while the spices carry just getting hotter...; **b24** a massive whisky which maximises the tannins and sugars yet never faintly goes OTT. Beautiful. 47.5%. 461 bottles.

   Sullivans Cove Winterfeast Special Issue batch no. WF2 db (84.5) n21 t21.5 f21 b21. Almost as dull as Glen McGrath's BBC Test Match Special radio summarising. More of a toffee fest than a Winter's Feast. Shame, because tasting S C whisky is always one of my highlights of the year. 48%

TIMBOON RAILWAY SHED DISTILLERY

   Timboon Single Malt Whisky 2010 dist 05/09/10, bott 03/06/15 db (96) n24 in the words of Twin Peaks: "it is happening...again..." Just one nose of this and you are transported into a different whisky world which makes the hairs stand on the back of your neck. There is nothing else like it: fruit, grapes especially, including pips, skins and most else, in the most marvellously clean yet concentrated form. Scary..; t24 hold on to your bar stools, folks! The fruit is going in! Drier than previous bottlings maybe, but never reaches bitter; the sugars (which pitch up early) wear tin helmets as grape explodes all around. But there is enough tannin, spice, lazy molasses and inevitable cocoa to crank up the complexity and ensure balance..; f24 just more of the same. Forever...; b24 how can any critic fault a whisky this magnificent and mega...? A late night dram...but don't leave it too late to give it the full half hour treatment it deserves. 69%

   Timboon Single Malt Whisky 2015 dist 31/05/15, bott 03/06/15 db (92.5) n23 t24.5 f22 b23. When the label says "oak barrel matured" they may be stretching a point. Or, more likely, having a bit of a laugh. For this has spent precisely one month in the cask, perhaps just about long enough to perceive the most pathetic colouration discernible to the naked eye. That said...what magnificent jazzed up new make this is. Whoever is distilling this stuff knows exactly what the hell they are doing! The nose is rich and a tad earthy (maybe some stainless steel in the still somewhere?) but so, so malty. It is the delivery and immediate follow through which blows you away, though. In every sense. Fabulous gristy sugars peddling as hard as they can to last into the distance. Love it. 70.8%c.

Timboon Single Malt Whisky Bourbon Expression oak barrel, dist 09 Jan 11, bott12 Jul 14 db (87) n22 t21.5 f22 b21.5. A thin chap by Timboon's usually robust standards, but at least the malt has muscles even if the body is lacking. Slightly youthful, too. 40.8%

Timboon Single Malt Whisky Limited Edition Port Expression oak barrel, dist 11 Sep 09, bott 11 Nov 13 db (88.5) n21 t22.5 f22.5 b22.5. The only time I have ever nosed anything like this was when I was crawling around the warehouses of a rum distillery in Guyana checking out some old Demerara. But pretty delicious, once you get used to its alarming idiosyncrasy... 46%

Timboon Single Malt Whisky Port Expression oak barrel, dist 7 Aug 10, bott 20 Jul 14 db (95.5) n23 serious grape and must concentrate: the Port is easy to spot and spices buzz enticingly; t24 serious Timboon-esque delivery of the highest order: massive grape swamping the palate, reinforced by hordes of spice running rampant and taking few prisoners; f24 brilliant, highly intense mocha and Demerara finish which accentuates the treacle at the finale; b24.5 another explosive Timboon experience of majestic quality. 69.9%

TIN SHED DISTILLING COMPANY

   Iniquity Single Malt Port casks Batch 001 db (94) n23 if I say the nose is huge, I am telling only half the story: we have dates, plums, walnuts, raisins...; t23.5 just as silky on the palate as the nose promises: an intense Cadbury's Fruit and Nut feel to this one; f23.5 a predictably long finish, with the spice joining in the rich, fruity fun...; b24 a gorgeous experience and quite a start for this new distillery: they will have to work overtime to keep this standard up. 46%. ncf.

   Iniquity Single Malt Port casks Batch 002 db (87) n21 t23 f21 b22. A sharper, less inclusive bottling than Batch 1. Still profound, silky fruit: a truly lip-smacking start. But a metallic note creeps in later on. 46%. ncf.

   Iniquity Single Malt Port casks Batch 003 rum cask finished db (85) n20 t22.5 f21.5 b21.5. Tin shed loads of personality once you get away from the confused nose. As time allows the glass to settle, the butyric decreases and a degree of South American-style rum begins to make a shout. But it's all a right hubbub and bloody confused. The finish is usually where you get confirmation of all not being quite right with the world and, sure enough, a slightly non-coppery tone emerges. All that said, the delivery is a celebration of all things sugar and entirely enjoyable. Get the feeling, though, that these stills would make better rum than whisky. 46%. ncf.

Vatted Malts

Tasmanian Double Malt Whisky Unpeated (87.5) n22 t22 f21.5 b22. Not a chance of getting bored with this guy. A sweet tooth would be useful. 43%. The Nant Distillery.

BRAZIL
HEUBLEIN DISTILLERY

Durfee Hall Malt Whisky db (81) n18 t22 f20 b21. Superbly made whisky; the intensity of the malt is beautifully layered without ever becoming too sweet. Very light bodied and immaculately clean. Good whisky by any standards. 43%

UNION DISTILLERY

Barrilete db (72) n18 t19 f18 b17. Nothing particularly wrong with it technically; it just lacks vitality. Thin but extremely malt intense. 39.1%

Blends

Cockland Gold Blended Whisky (73) n18 t18 f19 b18. Silky caramel. Traces of malt there, but never quite gets it up. 38%. Fante.

Drury's Special Reserve (86.5) n21.5 t22 f21 b22. Deceptively attractive, melt-in-the-mouth whisky; at times clean, regulation stuff, but further investigation reveals a honeycomb edge which hits its peak in the middle ground when the spices mix in beautifully. One to seek out and savour when in Brazil. 40%. Campari, Brasil.

Gold Cup Special Reserve (84.5) n21 t22.5 f20 b21. Ultra soft, easily drinkable and, at times, highly impressive blend which is hampered by a dustiness bestowed upon it by the nagging caramels on both nose and finish. Some lovely early honey does help lift it, though, and there is also attractive Swiss roll jam towards the finish. Yet never quite gets out of third gear despite the most delicate hint of smoke. 39%. Campari, Brasil.

Gran Par (77) n19.5 t22 f17.5 b18. The delivery is eleven seconds of vaguely malty glory. The remainder is thin and caramelled with no age to live up to the name. And with Par in the title and bagpipes and kilt in the motif, how long before the SWA buys a case of it...? 39%

Green Valley Special Reserve batch 07/01 (70) n16 t19 f17 b18. A softly oiled, gently bitter-sweet blend with a half meaty, half boiled sweet nose. An unusual whisky experience. 38.1%.

Malte Barrilete Blended Whisky batch 001/03 (76) n18 t20 f19 b19. This brand has picked up a distinctive apple-fruitiness in recent years and some extra oak, too. 39.1%

Natu Nobilis (81.5) n22.5 t20 f19 b20. The nose boasts a genuinely clean, Speyside-style malt involvement. But to taste is much more non-committal with the soft grain dominating and the grassy notes restricted the occasional foray over the tastebuds. Pleasant, but don't expect a flavor fest. 39%. Pernod Ricard, Brasil.

Natu Nobilis Celebrity (86) n22.5 t22 f20.5 b21. A classy blend with a decent weight and body, yet never running to fat. Some spice prickle ensures the flavor profile never settles in a neutral zone and the charming, citrus-domiated malt on the nose is immediately found on the juicy delivery. A cut above the standard Natu Nobilis and if the finish could be filled out with extra length and complexity, we'd have an exceptionally impressive blend on our hands. Another blend to seek out whenever in Brazil. 39%. Pernod Ricard, Brasil.

O Monge batch 02/02 (69) n17 t18 f17 b17. Poor nose but it recovers with a malty mouth arrival but the thinness of the grain does few favours. 38.5%. Union Distillery.

Old Eight Special Reserve (85.5) n20 t21 f22.5 b22. Traditionally reviled by many in Brazil, I can assure you that the big bite followed by calming soft grains is exactly what you need after a day's birding in the jungle. 39%. Campari, Brasil.

Pitt's (84) n21 t20 f22 b21. The pits it certainly aint!! A beautifully malted blend where the barley tries to dominate the exceptionally flinty grain whenever possible. Due to be launched later in 2004, this will be the best Brazil has to offer – though some fine tuning can probably improve the nose and middle even further and up the complexity significantly. I hope, when I visit the distillery early in 2005, I will be able to persuade them to offer a single malt: on this evidence it should, like Pitt's, be an enjoyable experience and perfect company for any World Cup finals. 40%. Busnello Distillery.

Wall Street (84) n23 t22 f19 b20. Fabulous nose with a sexy citrus-light smoke double bill. And the arrival on the palate excels, too, with a rich texture and confident delivery of malt, again with the smoke dominating. But falls away rather too rapidly as the grains throw the balance out of kilter and ensures too much bitter oak late on. 38%. Pernod Ricard, Brasil.

BHUTAN

◈ **K5 Premium Spirit Himalayan Whisky** bott 2013 (88) n22 lemon citrus to the fore, making this an even cleaner nose than the GNS directs it to be. The malt does come through though, in a retiring, sweet-gristy manner; t23 just love the delivery: a refreshing bite and nip underlines the citrus and, again, the barley isn't far behind; f21 just a little tangy; b22 absolutely nothing wrong with the Bhutan grain but more judicious cask selection (i.e remove the odd one or two sub-standard Scotch barrels) and this really could be an irresistible little charmer. As a first attempt, really impressive. This whisky is a mix of Scotch malt and grain made in Bhutan. So it was fitting that seeing as parts of that mysterious, land-locked mountainous country rises to some 23,000 feet, I was just slightly above that height when I first learned of the whisky. While on board a flight to Asia I witnessed the brand's manager trying to talk an airline into carrying it. He then assured me I'd love it. Actually, clean that malt up a bit and I really could! 40%

INDIA
AMRUT DISTILLERY

Amrut Fusion batch no. 01, bott Mar 09 db **(97) n24 t24 f24 b25.** One of the most complex and intriguing new whiskies of 2010 that needs about two days and half a bottle to get even close to fathoming. Not exactly a textbook whisky, with a few edges grinding together like tectonic plates. And there is even odd note, like the fruit and a kind of furry, oaky buzz, which I have never seen before. But that is the point of whiskies like this: to be different, to offer a unique slant. But, ultimately, to entertain and delight. And here it ticks all boxes accordingly. To the extent that this has to be one of the great whiskies found anywhere in the world this year. And the fact it is Indian? Irrelevant: from distillation to maturation this is genius whisky, from whichever continent... *50%*

Amrut Fusion batch 10, bott Mar 11 db **(94.5) n24 t24 f22.5 b23.5.** Superb whisky, though to be plotted on a different map to the now legendary Whisky Bible award-winning Batch 1. This is a much more delicate affair: more hints and shadows rather than statements and substance. Still, though, a fabulous malt whisky in Amrut's best style. *50%. nc.*

⬩ **Amrut Greedy Angels 10 Years Old** batch no. 1, bott Sept 14 db **(96.5) n24.5** the oak influence leads the way. But this is a nose of gentle persuasion and whispers; of suggestion and of shadows. This is delicate malt where even the citrus notes are spread across a wide range: with Jaffa oranges and lime, plus a hint of pink grapefruit, too. Even the vanilla offers an echo of ulmo honey...This, unquestionably is one of the great noses of the year...and probably the best nose ever produced on the Indian subcontinent; **t24** you have to laugh: you expect a malt so oaky you are convinced you'll be sucking roots. But not at all. The delivery, just to confound you, kicks off with a salivating mix of barley sugar and orange blossom honey. There is oak enough to ensure the sugars remain in balance and it is this feature of the spiced vanilla which makes the whole thing work; **f23.5** long, with the ulmo honey reappearing to ensure the oak stays in tune, though the busy warming spices appear to already have matters in hand; **b24.5** when I visited my first Indian distillery, some 20 years ago, the last thing I thought I would ever experience would be a native malt reaching double figures in age. All those I tasted showed decline to the point of undrinkability at only half that age. However, cellared warehousing and far more judicial oak selection means that not only is there now an Indian malt whisky reaching double figures in age, it has reached a stage of magnificence on its maturation road. I first tasted this at the distillery itself in the Spring of 2015. But waited until August 2015, making this the second to last whisky sampled for the 2016 Bible, before officially reviewing it under neutral conditions in the UK. What is apparent is that wherever in the world you experience this, you are being royally entertained - bewitched and mesmerised, to be nearer the truth - by one of the most remarkable whiskies of all time. *46%. 284 bottles.*

⬩ **Amrut Greedy Angels 10 Years Old** batch no. 1, bott Sept 14 db **(96) n24 t24 f24 b24.** As above. Except at this strength it is all a little oilier; tighter in its delivery and demeanour, with a bit more shouting where there were once whispers. All the same flavours are present and correct, though they all rush through at a greater pace to get to the finale. Beautiful, salivating...and dazzlingly brilliant. *71%*

Amrut Greedy Angels dist 3 Oct 04, bott 15 Nov 12 db **(96) n25 t24 f23 b24.** So here we have it: an 8-year-old Indian whisky. Matured in a cellar, luckily, but still has the hallmarks often seen on certain Speysiders in their late 30s...a series of Caperdonichs from about five or six years ago spring to mind. Except their noses were never this good: in fact, few noses have ever been better – it is certainly unsurpassed this year...worldwide. A true whisky great of the last decade. *50%*

⬩ **Amrut Naarangi** batch no. 1, bott Dec 14 db **(94) n23** thick, intense sherry...plus. If you think you are detecting a strange, vaguely sharp, blood orange undertone, you might well be...; **t23.5** a no less intense delivery with the grape almost boasting a six pack. But as the sherry effect takes a breather, the vague orangeyness reappears and then vanishes almost as fast as a general fruitcake countenance takes effect; **f24** at last the malt – quite young at times - relaxes and the fruit, a little spent by now, makes way for much softer, less egotistical sugars, muscovado leading the pack. The vanilla has a light ulmo honey tinge while the spices now begin to make a beautifully timed impact; **b23.5** the first sherry I know of worldwide which has had orange peel added to it in the butt to help infuse delicate citrus flavour to the maturing whisky which was to follow. Oddly enough, the whisky is in its element when the fruit levels have receded... *50%. 900 bottles.*

Amrut Peated Port Pipe, cask no. 2713, dist 2 Jun 09, bott 2 Aug 13 **(88.5) n22 t22 f22.5 b22.** So big, it's exhausting... *41%*

Amrut PX Sherry, cask no. 2701, dist 2 Jun 09, bott 2 Aug 13 **(80) n20 t21 f18.5 b20.5.** Big, cloying, fruity but the sugar makes this a little tart. Not the finest finish, either. Just not really my cup of Darjeeling. *43%*

Amrut PX Sherry, cask no. 2702, dist 2 Jun 09, bott 2 Aug 13 **(71) n18 t19 f16 b18.** A poor, sulphury butt gives the fruit no chance to come alive. Dance with the devil...and you get burned... *42%*

Amrut Single Cask peated barley, portpipe, cask no. 2713, dist Jun 09, bott Aug 13 db **(94.5)** n23.5 just adore the gentle assuredness of the peat: firm and thick, yet never aggressive. The grape adds little more than a delicate stratum; t24 works fabulously: the delivery is a near perfect marriage between hefty smoke, juicy barley and no less juicy grape. But such is the cleverness of the amalgamation, none bully the other; f23 softens into a deftly smoked sherry trifle; b24 Amrut showing its ability to a world class player. *59%. sc ncf nc. 346 bottles. Bottled exclusively for Europe. WB15/393*

Amrut Single Cask unpeated barley, bourbon, cask no. 3436, dist Jun 09, bott Aug 13 db **(89.5)** n23 creamy marshmallow; a fresh cappuccino steams away in the background; gristy; t23 fresh delivery: a conflicting battle of newish barley notes and much tangier age-enriched tannins; f21 slight burnt toast; b22.5 for the most part, a beautifully lush, stylish whisky, though the finish was an oversight I fear. *60%. sc ncf nc. 174 bottles.*

Amrut Single Cask unpeated barley, Px-Sherry, cask no. 2699, dist Jun 2009, bott Aug 2013 db **(81.5)** n19 t23 f19 b20.5. Not many distilleries can pull off bottling from PX, which is why I suggest they stay away from it. Either the sweetness of the sherry overwhelms and you end up with a stodgy sticky toffee pudding. Or the sulphur treatment does all kinds of damage. This appears to have elements of both. *62.8%. sc ncf nc. 311 bottles. Bottled exclusively for Europe. WB15/394*

Amrut Two Continents 2nd Edition bott Jun 11 db **(95)** n23.5 t24 f23.5 b24. I didn't expect their 2nd edition of this to get anywhere near the first in quality: it has. Not because of any loss in faith in the distillery – quite the contrary, in fact – but because, if I have learned anything in 20 years reviewing whisky, distillers find it near enough impossible to recreate the sublime. This is a vaguely fruitier effort and all the more fascinating for that. *50%. nc ncf. 892 bottles.*

Amrut 100 Peated Single Malt ex-bourbon/virgin oak barrels db **(92)** n23 t23 f23.5 b22.5. Ironically, though one of the older whiskies to come from this distillery, the nose shows a little bit of youth. A quite different style from Amrut's other peated offerings and it was obviously intended. Further proof that this distillery has grown not only in stature but confidence. And with very good reason. *57.1%. nc ncf.*

JOHN DISTILLERIES

Paul John Brilliance db **(94.5)** n23.5 a complex amalgam of nougat, spotted dog pudding (sans sultanas!) and orange blossom honey with the vanilla spinning tangled webs just beneath. Honey is captured as the bourbon element expands...; a delicate gristiness ushers in a freshness to the custard tart; t24 the mouth feel exudes star quality with the barley generating all kinds of juicy riches and the light Demerara sugars forming an elegant accompaniment. A coppery spine is soon carrying the barley in varied forms while a gorgeous cocoa sub strata heralds in the spices which buzz the taste buds at will; f23.5 beautifully relaxed: a light tingle from the spices pulses contentedly, the vanillas gather in deeper intensity yet the barley and copper stretches to the end; b23.5 yet another astonishing malt from India. *46%*

Paul John Edited db **(96.5)** n24.5 chocolate mint evolves from the delicate peats which sit beautifully with the lesser oaky theme; a comfortable, yet always complex, nose with the smoke soft and relaxed and refusing to bully the juicier barley; t24.5 grassy barley shows first, but then slowly gives way as those most gentle peat notes dissolve onto the palate and begin to build momentum and intensity. Again there is a chocolate mint/mocha theme, as well as a sublime molassed note which injects all the sweetness required; f23.5 long, helped by to-die-for oils, some hints of spice and now some tannins, plus the vanilla. But all is beautifully weighted, patient and poised; Oh, and did I mention the chocolate mint...? b24 a new Indian classic: a sublime malt from the subcontinent. To be more precise: a world classic! Think of Ardmore at its most alluring: one of Scotland's finest and most complex single malts, yet somehow possessing a saltiness and depth more befitting Islay. Then stir in a small degree of ulmo honey and bourbon-style hickory and liquorice. Plus subtle chocolate mint. And there you have it...the smoke drifting around stirring up spicy tales of the east. A world class whisky to be talked about with reverence without doubt... *52.9%*

◈ **Paul John Indian Single Malt Bold** batch no. 01 db **(95.5)** n23.5 the smoke tries to rule the roost, but it is not allowed: a dizzying array of manuka honey, prickly spice and bourbonesque red liquorices make sure of that; t24 melt-in-the-mouth-malt: a silky delivery – what else do you expect from India? – is shaped again by that oak-studded honey. But just as it begins to break up on the palate and lighten, a hefty second wave of spice and then thick, cloudy smoke coat the roof of the mouth, leaving tide marks of dry molasses, peaty soot and a degree of copper in its wake: absolutely delicious....; f23.5 a tad lighter on the finish with the copper really now making an impact. A gorgeous smoked mocha is given a third dimension by the busy, delicate and intricate spices; meanwhile the molasses have time to linger and morph into mocha; b24.5 one of the most weighty and chewable Indian whiskies of all time – yet it is not just about peat. So many elements to this, you expect a bottle to weigh the equivalent of a block of lead. This truly great whisky, so complex and absorbing, needs a good 20 minutes minimum of your time to adequately explore. *46%*

Paul John Single Malt Cask No 161 Non Peated (94) n22.5 t24.5 f23 b24. A malt which has much to say but does so with a quiet intensity. This really is a class act... *57%*

Paul John Single Malt Single Cask No 164 Non Peated (96) n24 t24 f24 b24. It is hardly believable that this is a three year old single malt: the unstinting high humidity of Goa and even higher temperature, perhaps helped along by three months of monsoons, appears to have given this whisky a degree of complexity which, even in Kentucky, it might have taken a dozen years to compile. This is single malt, but one with a hint of paradise...*57%*

Paul John Peated Single Malt db (89) n23 t22 f21.5 b22.5. A delicately peaty guy which gangs up on you slowly. The smoke-infused layering of sugars is the star turn, though. *55.5%*

Paul John Single Malt Cask No 692 Peated db (95.5) n24 t23.5 f24 b24. Hard to believe a whisky apparently so young in years can offer such complexity. But that's Goa for you... *58.5%*

Paul John Single Malt Cask No 777 Peated db (95) n23.5 t24 f23.5 b24. A Paul John which tries to offer as much delicate honey as the peat will allow. Something of rare, understated beauty. And though I often fly 777s, few take off as well as this and here there is no need for a seat belt... *59.7%*

Paul John Single Malt Cask No 780 Peated db (96) n24 t24 f24 b24. Warning. If you are a bit of a dithering, wishy-washy whisky drinker, don't go anywhere near this stuff: this bottling is for serious whisky drinkers only... *573%*

Paul John Single Malt Cask No 784 Peated db (95.5) n23.5 t23.5 f24.5 b24. The understated smoke ensures an elegant yet chewy experience. *59.2%*

Paul John Single Malt Cask No 1444 Non Peated db (95.5) n23.5 soft cereal notes dominate. The oak offers a butterscotch tart sweetness but takes a step back into the wings to allow the malt centre stage; t24 the kind of delivery which stops you in your tracks and makes you purr with delight. A succession of delicate sugar tones is stirred into the lively spice. But all the time, this is paying lip service to the malt, which starts robustly and almost in concentrated biscuit form but then, somehow, intensifies breathtakingly; f24 that intense barley keeps its foot on the throat of the oak, radiating riches far and wide. Spices do slowly gather momentum while the oak offers a hickory alternative; b24 among the most intensely malty Indian whiskies ever to have been bottled. Quite superb. *59.7%*

Paul John Single Malt Cask No 1844 Non Peated db (94.5) n23 oak shapes the majority of the nose, at times reminding you of a 35-year-old Speysider, and, at others, something a lot younger from Kentucky. The sugars play a clever role, just doing enough to ensure a freshness to the malt is maintained; t24 sharp barley contrasts with the attractive bourbon-style oakiness. Lots of liquorice and Demerara-sweetened hickory at play here and enough oil to make for a pleasing chewiness; some delicate ulmo honey supports the fragile sugars; f23.5 much drier now and even a shade spicy. A degree of bitterness has crept in but the deft toasty fudge and maple syrup (seemingly on scorched toast) keeps everything on an even keel; b24 let someone taste this blind, tell them it is three years old...and see their reaction. A big malt showing elegance and good grace throughout. *60.5%*

Paul John Single Malt Cask No 1846 Non Peated db (96) n23.5 a light citrusy breeze sweeps across the oaky plains. The malt, a little brittle and gristy, makes a teasing contribution; t23 superb mouth feel with gentle oils helping the drier oak notes glide across the palate without leaving splinters. The sugars are profound, too, some from an intense malty gristiness. The others have a darker hue; f25 a late scattering of increasingly warming spices works rather beautifully with the toasted oak and malt mix. The manuka honey and Demerara simply cannot be a better combination and now heads, sublimely, down an old Kentuckian path of controlled roastiness; b24.5 a very deep, complex whisky with many hills and canyons to explore. The finish orbits and often touches perfection. A profound malt. *60.8%*

Paul John Single Malt-Classic (Un Peated) db (95) n23.5 an essay in complexity: softly sizzling lightly salted bacon mingles easily with tannins. The barley, offering the vaguest hint of grist, is almost in pastel, so delicate is it, with the deftest touch of citrus and moist syrup cake; t24 much more salivating on delivery than might be expected: the barley shows early and with pride. A bourbony manuka, honey-liquorice mix makes for an attractive spine with toasted honeycomb arriving in the mid ground; f23.5 an elegant finish again with the barley chirping surprisingly brightly on the oak branches. The tannins remain checked and under control with juicy Demerara tones ensuring the softest and friendliest of finishes; b24 further evidence that Indian whisky is on the rise. Just so charming...and irresistible. *55.2%*

Paul John Select Cask Peated (96) n24 a sexy, sultry, sympathetic exhibition of smoke on varying levels...though all of them soft. A tantalising chocolate mint hangs of the embers, which glow both sweet and dry. Peated whisky from outside Islay rarely comes as complex and beautiful as this, or as deliciously gristy; t24 a massive delivery. Massive yet tender and subtle. How does that happen? Again, cocoa quickly fills the middle but there is more than enough molasses to counter. The weight and depth are spot on, as are the spices which get off to a delicate start but soon get into the swing of things; f24 long, fabulously oiled and just-so amounts of gristy sugars clinging to the smoke. As charming and impressionistic as an Indian kitchen fire wafting its smoke over a remote village in the nearby valleys; b24 a peated malt whisky which will make a few people sit up and take even further notice of Indian whisky. World class... 46%

PONDA DISTILLERY

Stillman's Dram Single Malt Whisky Limited Edition bourbon cask no. 11186-90 (94) n23 t23 f24 b24. Well, I thought I had tasted it all with the Amrut cask strength. And then this arrived at my lab...!! I predicted many years back that India would dish out some top grade malt before too long. But I'd be stretching the truth if I said I thought it would ever be this good... 42.8%. McDowell & Co Ltd, India.

Blends

Peter Scot Malt Whisky (84) n20 t21 f22 b21. Enjoyable balance between sweetness and oak and entertainingly enlivened by what appears to be some young, juicy malt. 42.8%.

Rendezvous (95.5) n24 t24 f23.5 b24.5. A new Indian classic. A sublime malt from the subcontinent. 46%

Royal Stag Barrel Select batch 212, bott 17 Feb 12 (75.5) n20.5 t19 f17 b18. Thin and sweet. But should be shot to put it out of its misery. 42.8% Mix of Scotch malt and India grain spirit.

Seagram's Blenders Pride Reserve Collection (77) n19 t20 f19 b19. Way too reliant on the grain and the malt submerged under the caramel. Soft, clean and painfully non-committal. 42.8%. Mix of Scotch malt and India grain spirit.

Signature (81.5) n22.5 t22 f17.5 b19.5. Excellent, rich nose & delivery helped along with a healthy display of peat reek. But more attention has to be paid to the brutally thin finish. 42.8%

NEW ZEALAND
THE NEW ZEALAND WHISKY COMPANY

◈ **The New Zealand Whisky Collection 25 Years Old Single Malt** dist in Dunedin, matured in Oamaru, Ex-Bourbon casks (94.5) n23 attractive apples and intense malt; the most distant peat reek imaginable; t24 the malt strikes early as it fully engulfs the palate: excellent balance as the vanilla begins to merge before those exotic fruits – the proud mark of great age – begin to form and delight. And then, just like on the nose, a mirage of delicate smoke shimmers on the horizon; f23.5 a long, slightly oily finale, full of decent oaky, exotic tones...and still the lightly spiced hint of distant smoke; b24 around the time this was made, some of the malt was very lightly peated. Though it doesn't mention so on the bottle, I strongly suspect that – after 25 years wear and tear in the cask – this is one of them. Seriously charming malt. And historic – and for me, at least, as one of the very few to see it in operation – touchingly memorable. 46%

◈ **The New Zealand Whisky Collection Doublewood 15 Years Old** American oak, finished in French oak ex New Zealand red wine barrels (81.5) n20 t21 f20 b20.5. A curiously thin whisky offering little above the clean fruit. 40%

◈ **The New Zealand Whisky Collection Oamaruvian 16 Years Old** American oak, finished in French oak ex New Zealand red wine barrels, cask no. 328, bott July 15 (87) n21.5 t21.5 f22.5 b21.5. A similar cove to their 58.4% bottling. Actually, I take my hats off to the boys on this one: they started with something pretty ordinary and have turned it through the employment of exceptionally fine casks into a spirit worthy of investigation. Still not a great whisky - in fact far, far closer in personality to a column still rum - but for those who love to see a big clean fruity spirit, then they will enjoy this. The spices are pretty major and the late chocolate liqueur finale is very pleasant. However, the complete lack of body to the spirit base means this can never qualify as a great whisky. Good try, though. 57%

◈ **The New Zealand Whisky Collection Oamaruvian 16 Years Old** American oak, finished in French oak ex New Zealand red wine barrels, cask no. 544, bott July 15 (86.5) n22 t21 f22.5 b21. I think I know what this spirit is. The guys who now own the barrels have done a great job in trying to turn it into something profound and have come pretty close. The problem is that the original grain spirit was distilled to such high strength and so bereft of body and personality, rather than add anything to the mix it is just a case of the alcohol turning up the volume on the absolutely sublime wine casks. However, just adore the chocolate raisin on the finish and worth trying out for that alone. 58.4%

◈ **The New Zealand Whisky Collection South Island Single Malt Aged 23 Years** ex bourbon casks (92) n22.5 a tiring, Puffing Billy of a nose where big, but friendly, tannins more or less obliterate any malt still hanging around. Just moving into the exotic fruit phase...;

t23 beautifully soft and welcoming on the palate. The oak has backed off slightly for a while, allowing the sugars a clear run. Lots of vanilla, hazelnuts and spice...and even a hint of growing salt; **f23** yes, now pretty salty and a little honey seeps into the proceedings; the spices are a last gasp from the cask...; **b23** a slightly stuttering malt, but no off notes and when it does click it does so quite beautifully. *40%*

◈ **The New Zealand Whisky Collection 1987 24 Year Old Single Malt** dist in Dunedin **(84.5) n21.5 t22 f20 b21.** "Not Aged in French Oak" announces the back label, pricking one's curiosity. A bit like the old comedy sketch with a bored pilot (John Cleese, who else?) telling the passengers, out of nowhere, "hello, this is your captain speaking: there is absolutely no cause for alarm....the engines are NOT on fire." That, of course, was in a different, more innocent and enjoyable world than today, pre 9/11. As, indeed, is this whisky...made when there was little interest in World Whisky and the Willowbank Distillery in Dunedin in particular. This may not be the finest bottling from the distillery and, with its fruitiness and bitter finish, unrepresentative of the house style. *43%*

◈ **The New Zealand Whisky Collection 1992 21 Year Old Single Malt (91.5) n22.5** a non-specific fruitiness – halfway between grape and exotic – ensures a very soft aroma; **t23.5** mouth-watering delivery with an exotic fruit and crème brûlée mix I have never quite tasted before from this distillery; the early sugars are tinged with muscovado sugars; **f22.5** creamy textured, but late on, the malt and spices emerge; some late tannins leave you in no doubt of the antiquity; **b23** an odd fruitiness has crept into this one somehow. Delightfully pleasant, but still a bit of a shame to see the complex grain and oak tones, which I know can be quite magnificent from this distillery, somewhat obscured. Probably just down to age. Still a joy, though. *50.7%. sc.*

The New Zealand Whisky Collection Willowbank 1988 25 Years Old cask no. 64, bott 3/13 **(96.5) n24** deft peat forms the most delicate shell imaginable over no less fragile citrus. Soft salt, still a little grist after all these years, background vanilla: almost something akin to a moist lemon drizzle cupcake...with a few atoms of smoke thrown in..; **t24.5** the adroit citrus mingles with the most alluring malt imaginable. The shadow of smoke acts like a siren while the tannins just up their game slightly. Just so well integrated...; **f23.5** long, with a feeble spice buzz. Evidence of the shortage of copper from the cask comes through only at the very death; **b24.5** when I first encountered this whisky it would have been a six-year-old and the Dunedin distillery had a very uncertain future. Question marks hung over the quality of the stock, so they were a bit surprised when I assured them that the vast majority of what they were making was of very decent to high standard. Who then would have thought that some two decades on I would be tasting this as one of the most delicate and sophisticated and complex 25-year-olds imaginable? Only the untidy finish shows the distillery's Achilles: low copper content. On the other hand, it also ensured that it would never be short of character. One of the most poignant and enjoyable whiskies of the year. And memories of the only distillery I ever visited and then took a five minute drive to watch penguins surface from the sea... *55.1%. sc. WB15/396*

THE SOUTHERN DISTILLING CO LTD

The Coaster Single Malt Whiskey batch no. 2356 **(85) n20 t22 f21 b22.** Distinctly small batch and sma' still with the accent very much on honey. Nosed blind I might have mistaken as Blue Mouse whisky from Germany: certainly European in style. Recovers well from the wobble on the nose and rewards further investigation. *40%*

The MacKenzie Blended Malt Whiskey (85) n20 t22 f21 b22. A vaguely spicier, chalkier, mildly less honeyed version of Coaster. Quite banana-laden nose. *40%*

THOMSON WILLOWBANK

Thomson Single Malt 10 Years Old ex-bourbon barrel **(71) n18.5 t19 f16.5 b17.** The sugars are working hard. But have nothing to work with. *40%. Thomson Whisky.*

Thomson Single Malt 18 Years Old (77) n19.5 t20 f18.5 b19. Pleasant, sweet but absolutely no body whatsoever. *46%. sc. Thomson Whisky.*

Thomson Single Malt 21 Years Old (84) n21 t22.5 f20.5 b20. Bit of a bimbo whisky: looks pretty and outwardly attractive but has picked up very little in its 21 years... *46%. sc.*

Thomson Whisky Two Tone European oak & American white oak **(86) n22 t22 f21 b21.** This one had promise. Started full of intent on both nose and delivery, boasting attractive citrus notes. But after a quick rush of clear honey, thins out like the most basic of blends. *40%*

WILSON DISTILLERY

Cadenhead's World Whiskies Lammerlaw Aged 10 Years bourbon, bott 07 **(91.5) n22 t23.5 f23 b23.** Stunning bottlings like this can only leave one mourning the loss of this distillery. *48.9%*

Blends

Kiwi Whisky (37) n2 t12 f11 b12. Strewth! I mean, what can you say? Perhaps the first whisky containing single malt offering virtually no nose at all and the flavour appears to be grain neutral spirit plus lashings of caramel and (so I am told) some Lammerlaw single malt. The word bland has been redefined. As has whisky. *40%.*

Wilson's Superior Blend (89) n22 t23 f21 b23. Apparently has a mixed reception in its native New Zealand but I fail to see why: this is unambiguously outstanding blended whisky. On the nose you expect a mouthwatering mouthful and it delivers with aplomb. Despite this being a lower priced blend it is, intriguingly, a marriage of 60% original bottled 10-y-o Lammerlaw and 40% old Wilson's blend, explaining the high malt apparent. Dangerous and delicious and would be better still at a fuller strength...and with less caramel. *37.5%.*

SOUTH AFRICA
JAMES SEDGWICK DISTILLERY

Three Ships 10 Years Old db **(83) n21 t21 f20 b21.** Seems to have changed character, with more emphasis on sherry and natural toffee. The oak offers a thrusting undercurrent. *43%*

Three Ships Aged 10 Years Single Malt Limited Edition db **(91) n22.5 t22.5 f23 b23.5.** If you are looking for a soft, sophisticated malt whose delicate fingers can sooth your troubled brow, then don't bother with this one. On the other hand, if you are looking for a bit of rough, some entertaining slap and tickle: a slam-bam shag of a whisky - a useful port in a storm - then your boat may just have sailed in... Beware: an evening with this and you'll be secretly coming back for more... *43%*

Bain's Cape Mountain Single Grain Whisky db **(85.5) n21 t22 f21 b21.5.** A lively, attractively structured whisky with more attitude than you might expect. Some lovely nip and bite despite the toffee and surprising degree of soft oils. *43%*

Blends

Drayman's Solera (86) n19 t22 f23 b22. For a change, the label gets it spot on with its description of chocolate orange: it is there in abundance. If they can get this nose sorted they would be on for an all round impressive dram. As it is, luxuriate in the excellent mouthfeel and gentle interplay between malt and oak. Oh and those chocolate oranges... *43%.*

Harrier (78) n20 t20 f19 b19. Not sure what has happened to this one. Has bittered to a significant degree while the smoke has vanished. A strange, almost synthetic, feel to this now. *43%. South African/Scotch Whisky.*

Knights (83) n20.5 t21 f20 b20.5. While the Harrier has crashed, the Knights is now full of promise. Also shows the odd bitter touch but a better all-round richer body not only absorbs the impacts but radiates some malty charm. *43%. South African/Scotch Whisky.*

Knights Aged 3 Years (87) n22 t22 f22 b22. This now appears to be 100% South African whisky if I understand the label correctly: "Distilled Matured and Bottled in South Africa." A vast improvement on when it was Scotch malt and South African grain. Bursting with attitude and vitality. When next in South Africa, this will be my daily dram for sure. Love it. *43%.*

Three Ships Bourbon Cask Finish (90) n22 t23 f22.5 b22.5. A soft, even whisky which enjoys its finest moments on delivery. Clean with a pressing, toasty oakiness to the sweeter malt elements. Always a delight. *43%*

Three Ships Premium Select Aged 5 Years (93) n23 t23.5 f23 b23.5. What a fabulous whisky. The blender has shown a rare degree of craft to make so little smoke do so much. Bravo! *43%. James Sedgwick Distillery.*

Three Ships Select (81) n19 t21 f20 b21. Busy and sweet. But I get the feeling that whatever South African malt may be found in Knights does a better job than its Scotch counterpart here. *43%. James Sedgwick Distillery.*

TAIWAN
KAVALAN DISTILLERY

◇ **Kavalan Distillery Reserve** peaty cask, dist 2007, bott 23 Jan 2015 db **(95) n23.5** the smoke is little more than a tease, a blink and you miss the wisp of phenol; creamy malt with stuttering sugars; **t24.5** much more assured peat on delivery: the smoke maybe delicate but has enough about it meet the barley face to face; toasty tannins steal the scenes in the second and third act but never completely eclipse the crunchy malt; for a few moments the oil let rise to impressive, yet deliciously manageable heights upping the intensity further; **f23** a long trail of spiced tannin: amazingly salivating even to the toasty death; **b24** what a crackerjack cask this malt spent seven worthwhile and highly active and productive years maturing in. Starts so quietly, then becomes pretty loud. *55%.*

◇ **Kavalan Single Malt Amontillado Sherry Cask** cask no. S100623016A db **(97) n24** have you got spare half an hour? If not, don't even think bout opening this bottle: For this is a malt which needs time and temperature; to oxidise and reach the temperature of your pulse. Then, imperceptibly, like an unfurling flower, it opens and reveals its secrets, displaying some of the most deft fruit notes you ill encounter in many a year. The spices nibble, the fruit – clean and dense – sighs rather than shouts its signature, the tannins are latticed so the grape can gain a firm foothold despite its fragility; **t24.5** such a soft delivery on the palate, alternating between a caress and a tender massage. All the times the spices buzz and puncture any forming intensity of the grape; the mid-ground is creamy – mimicking the finest Amotillado wine I have tracked down in the last three decades...; **f24** a slight mashed banana sweetness offers the perfect counter to the drier oak tones. The grape continues to be preoccupied with the spice. Not an off note even on the horizon, the tannins continue in the same faultless vain as the nose and delivery and seemingly never ends...; **b24.5** given the right bottling, Amontillado is probably my favourite sherry style. How many times, though, have I discovered its delicate, complex, understated nature perfectly transferred onto a singe malt? In some 35 years, this must be only the fourth or fifth time, and I doubt any quite displayed such truth to its style, such panache. Forget the unique and intriguing bottle design (though it is hard!). This is a classic whisky on so many levels that it will stay indelibly stamped on both taste buds and memory. What a magnificent whisky experience this is...!!! 56.3%. sc. 744 bottles. Limited edition 2014_1402.

◈ **Kavalan Single Malt Manzanilla Sherry Cask** cask no. S100716002A db **(95.5)** n23 the fruit needs a little coaxing as it grips, limpet-like to a drier, pithy, oak-drenched style; **t24** likewise, the delivery is reserved and then...oh, my word! The shackles are suddenly bust open ad he spices escape en masse. At the same moment the juicy elements of the grape gush forward, as if from nowhere and engulf the palate. Eye-watering and emphatic...; **f24** the palate is coated with the light oils required spread the fruit and spices into the furthermost corners; slows as the oak regains a slightly nervous foothold...; **b24.5** a mouth-watering jape from Kavalan. The nose appears a tad tight and introverted. But as it relaxes on the palate it certainly lets the malt the freedom to take on the grape. Or is it the other way round? A sublime surprise package.... 57.8%. sc. 744 bottles. Limited edition 2014_1402.

◈ **Kavalan Single Malt Pedro Ximénez Sherry Cask** cask no. S100630016A db **(96)** n24 not half this is a PX cask! But one where the fruit is encircled by a crispness of sugars one is more likely to associate with top peso, greatly aged South American column still rum. Curiously those sugars don't always equate to sweetness and it is the spice which really turns the head....towards the glass rather than away from it...; **t24.5** such succulent fruit on delivery: the taste buds are caressed and kissed on delivery....then...: the spices begin as a mere hint but rapidly sweet through the gears until it is a full on pepper attack. Meanwhile the fruit serenely goes about is lightly sweetened business. The result is similar to a boxer being bombarded in the ring by gloves made of silk; **f23.5** reverts to PX type with a vague crispness upping the oak levels alongside the dulling sugars. The tannins are neat and tidy, barely daring to set a foot out of line; a vague kiwi fruit tang is offset by grape; **b24** hard to imagine a malt where the spices play a more telling part. Or where the PX effect comes through so clearly and entirely without the usual minor failings. I rarely mention the bottles used to house a whisky. But this one is gargantuan: a heavyweight leviathan of glass and rounded contours. Somehow the malt inside fits it perfectly.. 56.3%. sc. 407 bottles. Limited edition 2015_1299.

◈ **Kavalan Solist Brandy Cask** cask no. A090620012 db **(95.5)** n23.5 a dual-textured aroma, both crisp and with a secondary softer fruitiness. The harder element leaves no doubt about the cask type; **t24.5** it is that softer character which kicks off proceedings in a fulsome and stylish manner, then that brittle, diamond-hard such plot seers through the second phase somehow intensifying the already profound grape. However, it is the intermingling of the chocolate/mocha subtext which really ensures complexity levels soar to the most rarefied heights; **f23.5** the earlier, even, sugars begin to dissipate and, typically for a brandy cask, a much drier element seeps in. The fade is in line of aloof tannin with a grape must dryness...; **b24** malt matured in brandy and Cognac casks are rare. Outstanding malt matured in these casks is the rarest of the rare... 58.6%. nc ncf sc. 223 bottles.

Kavalan Solist Fino Sherry Cask db cask no. S060814021 **(97)** n24.5 t24 f24 b24.5. It might be argued that the one and only thing that makes this exceptional is the quality of the cask, rather than the actual malt it contains. Well, let me set the record straight in this one. Earlier this week I made a very rare escape from my tasting room and visited the Royal Albert Hall for the 34th Prom of the 2011 season. The highlight of the evening was Camille Saint-Saens Symphony No 3 – "Organ". Now some critics, when they can find time to extract themselves from their own rear ends, dismiss this as a commoners' piece; something to amuse the plebeian. What they appear to not have is neither the wit nor humanity to understand that Saint-Saens sewed into this work a degree of such subtle shade and emotion, especially in the less dramatic second movement, that it can, when treated correctly, affect those capable of normal warmth and feeling. With so many nerve endings tingling and nowhere to go Saint-Saens finally recognised that he required something profound – in this case the organ – to create a backbone. And someone able to use it to maximum effect. And there we had it the other day: the Royal Albert Hall's awe-inspiring organ, and Thomas Trotter to make it come alive: The Solist. And this is what we have here: a perfect fino sherry selected by the maestro Dr Jim Swan. But able to display its full magnificence only because the host spirit is so beautifully composed. Good whisky is, without question, a work of art; great whisky is a tone poem. And here, I beg to insist, is proof. *58.4%. nc ncf sc. 513 bottles.*

Other Brands Available In Taiwan

Eagle Leader Storage Whisky (81.5) n20 t21 f21 b20.5. Attractively smoky with a surprisingly long finish for a whisky which initially appears to lack body. By no means straightforward, but never less than pleasant. *40%*

Golden Hill Single Malt (75) n18 t20 f19 b18. An unwieldy heavyweight. *40%*

Good Deer (in Chinese Characters) *see McAdams Rye Whisky*

McAdams Rye Whisky bott Nov 09 (85.5) n21 t22 f21.5 b21.5. Thoroughly delicious stuff absolutely brimming with juicy, crisp grain notes. The body is lightly oiled and shapely while the finish is sweet and attractive. The odd green apple note, too. *40%. Note: Says it's made in Taiwan, but possesses a maple leaf on the label.*

Sea Pirates (77) n18 t21 f19 b19. More Johnny Depp than Errol Flynn. Attractive smoke, though. *40%*

URUGUAY

Dunbar Anejo 5 Anos (85.5) n20 t22.5 f21.5 b21.5. A clean, mouth-wateringly attractive mix where the grain nips playfully and the Speyside malts are on best salivating behaviour. Decently blended and boasting a fine spice prickle, too. *40%*

Seagram's Blenders Pride (83) n20.5 t22 f20b20.5. The busy, relatively rich delivery contrasts with the theme of the silky grains and caramel. Easy drinking. *40%*

MISCELLANEOUS

House of Westend Blended Whisky (67) n17 t18 f16 b16. No more than OK if you are being generous; some tobacco-dirty notes around. Doesn't mention country of origin anywhere on the label. *40%. Bernkasteler Burghof, Germany.*

Jaburn & Co Pure Grain & Malt Spirit (53) n14 t13 f13 b13. Tastes like neutral grain and caramel to me. Some shop keepers, I hear, are selling it as whisky though this is not claimed on the label. Trust me: it isn't. *37.5%. Jaburn & Co, Denmark.*

Prince of Wales Welsh Whisky (69) n17 t18 f17 b17. Syrupy aroma is compounded by an almost liqueurish body. Thin in true Scotch substance, probably because it claims to be Welsh but is really Scotch with herbs diffused in a process that took place in Wales. Interestingly, my "liqueur" tasting notes were written before I knew exactly what it was I was tasting, thus proving the point and confirming that, with these additives, this really isn't whisky at all. *40%*

Shepherd's Export Finest Blend (46) n5 t16 f12 b13. A dreadful, illdefined grain-spirit nose is softened on the palate by an early mega-sweet kick. The finish is thin and eventually bitter. Feeble stuff. *37.2%. "A superb blend of Imported Scotch Malt whiskies and Distilled N.Z. grain spirit", claims the label which originally gives the strength as 40%, but has been over-written. Also, the grain, I was told, was from the USA. Southern Grain Spirit, NZ.*

The Teeling Whisky Co. Hybrid Malt Whiskey No. 1 Edition (90) n23 t22.5 f22 b22.5. Adorable vibrancy and use of smoke. *44.1%. nc ncf.*

CROSS-COUNTRY VATTED WHISKIES

◈ **Diggers & Ditch Doublemalt Spirit of the Anzacs** (82.5) n21 t21 f20 b20.5. Soft, fruity but never quite gets it together. Always too thin and shapeless. I'll give it a D. *45%. A blend of New Zealand & Australian whisky.*

◈ **Jim Beam Kentucky Dram** (89) n22.5 much more of the rye within the bourbon than the peat in the malt apparent; crisp but with a vaguely weighty sub stratum; t22.5 a curious mouth feel: bourbon but with a chewy oiliness which is not all corn oil; the smoke is lethargic, though the spices appear to offer both peaty and oaky elements; f21.5 wobbles a bit as the peat finally wakes up; ultimately a touch too thin, though; b22.5 there may be some of you reading this who will remember tastings I did 15 or 20 years ago where, for fun and to show balancing effects, I vatted bourbon with smoky Scotch. At last someone has done it commercially. I suspect this is more for the American palate as the peat has been used sparingly. *40% (80 Proof)*

Slàinte

It seems as though you can't have a Bible without a whole lot of begetting. And without all those listed below – a veritable scrumdown of all the world's whisky people – this Jim Murray's Whisky Bible 2016 would never have been begot at all. A huge amount of blood, sweat and tears go into the production of each edition, more than anyone not directly involved could even begin to comprehend. So, as usual, I must thank my amazing team: Vincent Flint-Hill, Billy Jeffrey, Len Davis and David Rankin. Also, special thanks to Julia Nourney and Arthur Naegele for fearlessly contacting the distilleries of Europe on my behalf and extracting their samples. Once again, extra special thanks must be placed on record for the unfailing, glass half full support of Paul and Denise Egerton, Pete and Linda Mayne and David Hartley and Julie Barrie who, collectively them kept me going, and laughing when the weight of whisky and expectation seemed - and was - so daunting. As well as to Mr. and Mrs. Murray of the classic Super Sausage Cafe on the A5 near Towcester whose delicious and occasionally life-saving sausage sandwiches have no equal. As always, a massive hug to Heiko Thieme. And, finally, thanks to those below who have provided assistance and samples for the 2013 Bible onwards. For all those who have assisted in the previous decade, we remain indebted.

Mitch Abate; Ally Alpine; Kevin Atchinson; Duncan Baldwin; Clare Banner; Jan Beckers; Franz Benner; Kirsteen Beeston; Annie Bellis; Barry Bernstein; Stuart Bertra; Menno Bijmolt; Sonat Birknecker Hart; Rich Blair; Hans Bol; Etienne Bouillon; Birgit Bornemeier; Phil Brandon; Stephen Bremner; Stephanie Bridge; James Brown; Sara Browne; Michael Brzozowski; Alexander Buchholz; Ryan Burchett; Amy Burgess; Euan Campbell; Kimla Carsten; Bert Cason; Jim Caudill; Danilo Cembrero; Lisa Chandler; Yuseff Cherney; Julia Christian; Nick Clark; Fredi Clerc; Dr Martin Collis; Jason Craig; David Croll; Danni Cutten; Mike DaRe; Stephen Davies; Alasdair Day; Dick & Marti; Paul Dempsey; Marie-Luise Dietich; Rob Dietrich; Angela D'Orazio; Jean Donnay; Tim Duckett; Camille Duhr-Merges; Mariette Duhr-Merges; Gemma Duncan; Jonas Ebensperger; Ray Edwards; Carsten Ehrlich; Ben Ellefsen; James Espey; Jennifer Eveleigh; Thomas Ewers; Charlotte Falconer; Joanna Fearnside; Hans-Gerhard Fink; David Fitt; Kent Fleischman; Martyn Flynn; Danny Gandert; Patrick Garcia; Dan Garrison; Carole Gibson; John Glaser; John Glass; Emily Glynn; Rodney Goodchild; Jonathon Gordan; Lawrence Graham; Hannah Gregory; Andrew Grey; Rebecca Groom; Jason Grossmiller; Viele Grube; Jasmin Haider; Georgina Hall; Georges Hannimann; Scott E Harris; Alistair Hart; Andrew Hart; Donald Hart; Stuart Harvey; Steve Hawley; Ailsa Hayes; Ross Hendry; Jason Himstedt; Roland Hinterreiter; Bernhard Höning; Emma Hurley; Alex Huskingson; Rachel Showalter Inman; Kai Ivalo; Amelia James; Ulrich Jakob; Michael John; Celine Johns; Robert Joule; Serena Kaye; Colin Keegan; Sara Klingberg; Larry Krass; Armin Krister; Karen Kushner; Ryan Lang; Sebastian Lauinger; Darren Leitch; Christelle Le Lay; Lars Lindberger; Mark T Litter; Steven Ljubicic; Alistair Longwell; Claire Lormier; C. Mark McDavid; John Maclellan; Dennis Malcolm; Tim Marwood; Jennifer Masson; Leanne Matthews; Josh Mayr; Roxane Mazeaude; Stephen R McCarthy; Angela Mcilrath; Catherine McKay; Jonny McMillan; Douglas McIvor; Maggie Miller; Euan Mitchell; Paul Mitchell; Jeroen Moernaut; Henk Mol; Nick Morgan; Maggie Morri; Fabien Mueller; Michael Myers; Arthur Nägele; Andrew Nelstrop; Alex Nicol; Jane Nicol; Jennifer Nicol; Zack Nobinger; Soren Norgaard; Tom O'Connor; Richard Oldfield; Casey Overeem; Ted Pappas; Richard Parker; Sanjay Paul; Percy; Alexandra Piciu; Amy Preske; Rachel Quinn;Sarah Rawlingson; Guy Rehorst; Carrie Revell; Kay Riddoch; Massimo Righi; Nicol von Rijbroek; Patrick Roberts; James Robertson; Anton Rossetti; David Roussier; Ronnie Routledge; Jim Rutledge; Caroline Rylance; Paloma Salmeron Planells; Phil Prichard; Kirsty Saville; John Savage-Onstwedder; Mick & Tammy Secor; Ian Schmidt; Mike Sharples; Rubyna Shekh; Caley Shoemaker; Jamie Siefken; Sam Simmons; Alastair Sinclair; Sukhinder Singh; Barbara Smith; Gigha Smith; Phil Smith; Cat Spencer; Jeremy Stephens; Hawley Steve; Vicky Stevens; Karen Stewart; Katy Stollery; Henning Svoldgaard; Tom Swift; Shoko Takagi; Chip Tate; Marko Tayburn; Marcel Telser; Celine Tetu; Sarah Thacker; Hamish Torrie; Louise Towers; Richard Urquhart; Stuart Urquhart; CJ Van Dijk; Mariah Veis; Aurelien Villefranche; Anna Wilson; Nick White; Robert Whitehead; Stephanie Whitworth; Arthur Winning; Ellie Winters; Stephen Worrall; Kate Wright; Frank Wu; Tom Wyss; Junko Yaguchi; Ruslan Zamoskovny; Rama Zuniga. And, as ever, in warm memory of Mike Smith.